W9-APH-174

TOY CAR

COLLECTOR'S GUIDE

SECOND EDITION

IDENTIFICATION
AND
VALUES
FOR
- **DIECAST**
- **WHITE METAL**
- **OTHER AUTOMOTIVE TOYS & MODELS**

DANA JOHNSON

COLLECTOR BOOKS

A Division of Schroeder Publishing Co., Inc.

On the front cover:
2001 Chevrolet Avalanche, Welly, 1:24
1930 Packard, Signature Models, 1:32
1963 Aston Martin DB5, Chrono, 1:18

On the back cover:
1931 Ford Model A Tudor, Motor City Classics, 1:18
Chaika Limousine, Russian, 1:43
1932 Ford Street Rod, Eagle's Race, 1:43

Cover design: Terri Hunter
Book design: Holly Long

Collector Books
P.O. Box 3009
Paducah, Kentucky 42002-3009

www.collectorbooks.com

Copyright © 2006 by Dana Johnson

All rights reserved. No part of this book may be reproduced,
stored in any retrieval system, or transmitted in any form, or by
any means including but not limited to electronic, mechanical,
photocopying, recording, or otherwise, without the written con-
sent of the author and publisher.

The current values of this book should be used only as a guide. They are not intended to set prices, which can vary from one section of the country to another. Auction prices as well as dealer prices vary and are affected by condition as well as demand. Neither the author nor the publisher assumes any responsibility for any losses that might be incurred as a result of consulting this guide.

Searching for a Publisher?

We are always looking for people knowledgeable within their fields. If you feel that there is a real need for a book on your collectible subject and have a large comprehensive collection, contact Collector Books.

About the Author

Dana Johnson was eight and living in Lansing, Michigan, when he first started collecting toy cars. That was in 1962. His first ones were Matchbox cars. When Hot Wheels blazed on the scene in 1968, he remained unimpressed. At the time, he thought the colors were unrealistic and the wheel wells were too big (... and they had no hoods!).

By the 1970s, he had put his toys aside to pursue other interests — girls. It wasn't until 1985, when he discovered a Hatfield's department store in Madras, Oregon, that stocked a large number of Majorette toys from France, that his interest was rekindled. The store has since gone out of business, but he has amassed a large collection since then, incorporating toy cars, mostly diecast, from all over the world.

Acknowledgments

The list of people to whom I am indebted is growing constantly... and, thanks to the Internet, now it includes collectors from all over the world. Appreciation goes to all whose books, lists, letters, catalogs, and samples have contributed to the completeness of this book. Special thanks to Jeff Bray Jr. of Diecast Miniatures for his exhaustive catalog of 200+ brands of toys and models, to Patrick and Brenda Lacombe of Toys for Collectors for their exquisite yearly updated color catalog; to Joe Altieri, Ivan Fedorkew, Ron Gold, Ron Lohr, and Alger Podewil for their information on Majorettes and other variations; to Bob Blum for his invaluable information on Tomicas, to Dr. Edward Force for his many books on toy cars; to Dr. Michel Sordet of Switzerland, for his comprehensive CD-ROM titled "Jouets Anglais" ("English Toys"), to Boyd Dunson and Alex Antonov for their information on Russian models, to Jerry Rettig for his self-published book "American Wheels", and to Fred Emig for his information on K&R, Western Models, and other brands. Thanks to Dario "Dino" Vidovic for filling in the gaps on Mikansue models. Thanks to Russell Alameda, Dr. Doug Breithaupt, Craig S. Campbell, Bill Cross, John Dean, Harvey Goranson, Tjeng-Bo Lie, Henri C. C. Mueller, Aaron Robinson, Kimmo Sahakangas, Karl Schnelle, Jarek Skonieczny, Robert Speerbrecher, Larry Stitt, Dave Weber, and Brian Willoughby for their various invaluable contributions. Thanks to Dr. Alexander V. Barmasov of St. Petersburg, Russia; Wiebe Buising and Ben Van Roode in The Netherlands; Ian Cousins of New Zealand; Mark Ebery in Australia; Staffan Kjellin and Crister Skoglund in Sweden; Frank Wagner in Germany; and Werner Legrand in Belgium for filling in details on various lesser known brands. Thanks to Jeff Koch for his photos of models otherwise missing from this book, and to many others for providing price lists, variation lists, and mounds of other information used in this book.

Thanks especially to Billy Schroeder, Amy Sullivan, and Gail Ashburn of Collector Books for their continuing enthusiastic support of all my book projects, and to Sharon and Bob Huxford for their book *Schroeder's Guide to Collectible Toys*.

Appreciation also goes to Richard O'Brien for information provided from his *Collecting Toy Cars & Trucks* series of books; Markus R. Karalash for his contributions on the various brands of DeTomaso Pantera models; and Stephen Demosthenes who has provided the most comprehensive list of Porsche models I've ever seen, contributing greatly to models listed in this book.

Special thanks to Claudia Valiquet for encouraging me to collaborate with Collector Books in the first place.

Brand Names

Nearly 1,000 brands and manufacturers of diecast, white metal and related automotive toys and models are listed below, all of which are represented in this book. While some 95 percent of those named below represent diecast toys and models, a few represent brands made of white metal, cast iron, aluminum, plastic, and other materials. Even as this book goes to press, many new brands have been discovered which will have to wait until the next edition for inclusion.

1320 Inc.	ADJ	Alloy Forms, Inc.	Antex	Auburn
A & S	Advanced Products Company	Alterscale	APM	Aurora Cigar Box
A-Line	Agat	AMA	Aguti	Authentic Model Car Series
AAM	AGD	Amar Toy	Aquli	Authenticast
Aardvark	AGM	American Automobile Miniatures	A.R.	AUTOart
A. Barrett & Sons	Agritec	American Classic	AR	Auto Buff
A. B. C. Brianza	Aguti-toys	American Highway Legends	Arbur	Autocraft
A. B. C. Models	AHC	American Limited	Arcade	Autohobby
Abordage	AHI	American National	Armour	Automec
Abraham, L. D.	AHL	American Precision Models (APM)	Arnold	Auto Pilen
A. C. Williams	Albedo	Ampersand	Arnold, Bruce	Auto Replicas
Academy Minicraft	Alezan	AMR – Century	Arpra	Autoreplica
ACB	ALF	AMT Pups	ARS	Aviva
Accucast	ALJ	Andre-Marie Ruf	Art Model	BAM
Ace Implement Company	All-American	Anguplas	Asahi	Bandai
Acme Plastic Toys, Inc.	All American Toy Company	Anker	Ashton	Bandi
Action Performance	Allied	Anso	Athearn	Bandii
Action Products	All-Nu	Anson	Atlas	Bang

3

Banner
Banthrico
Bapro
Barclay
Barlux
Barrett & Sons
Basteltip
Bayshore Repli-Cars
BBR
Bburago
Beanstalk
Beaut
The Beckman Collection
Belgium Trucks
Benbros
Best
Best-Box
Best Model
Best Toys of Kansas
Best Toy Co., Ltd.
Betal
Big River Models
Bijou
Bing
Bison
Bitsi-Toys
Blue Box
Boley
Bonux
Boss
Bossat Dermov
Bourbon
Boutique Auto Moto
Box Model
BP
BradsCars
Brekina Automodelle
Bren L Toys
Breslin
Brianza
Brimtoy
Britains
British Motoring Classics
Brookfield Collectors Guild
Brooklins
Bruce Arnold Models
Brüder Toys / Bruder Spielwaren
Brumm
Bub
Buby
Buccaneer
Buddy L
Budgie
Bugattiana
Burago
Busch/Praliné
Bush
Cam-Cast
Car43
Carette, Georges
Carlo Brianza
Carmania
Carousel 1

Castle Art
C. A. W. Novelty Company
C.B. Car
C.B.G. Mignot
CCC
C.D.
CDC
Century
Chad Valley
Champion
Champion Hardware Company
Champion of the Road
Charbens
Charmerz
Chein
Cherilea
Cherryca Phenix
Chico
Chrono
Ciba
Cigar Box
C.I.J.
Circle N Toys
City
CKO
Classic Collectables
Classic Construction Models
Classic Metal Works
Classy Chassies
Clau-Mar
Cle
Clover
CMA
CMC
Code 3 Collectibles
Cofalu
Cofradis
Collector Case
Collector's Classics
Collectors Mint
Collectoy
Comet – Authenticast
Comet Miniatures
Con-Cor
Condon
Conquest
Conrad
COPy cars
Corgi
Cossack Models
Cougar
Courtland
Cox
CPM
Craftoys
Cragstan
Creative Master
Creative Masters
Crescent Toys
Cristian
Crossway Models
Crown Premiums
C-Scale

Cursor
Custom Miniatures
D&K
Dale Model Company
Dale Jr. / Dale Sr. Models
Dalia
Danbury Mint
Danhausen
Dapper (also see Bandai)
Darda
Dardis Mfg. Inc.
David Deanstyne
Day, John
Days Gone
D.C.M.T.
DDR
Deanstyne, David
Dehanes
Del Prado
Deles
Dent Hardware Company
Deoma Micromodels
Design Studio
Desormeaux
Detail Cars – CDC
DG
DG Productions
Diamond
Diapet
Dibro
Dicascale
Diecast Promotions
Dimension 4
Dinkum
Dinky
Distler
Diti Toys
Dmitriev Workshop
DMP Studios
Doepke
Doll & Company
Doorkey
Dragon Wings
Druge Brothers
Dugu
Duravit
Durham Classics
Dust & Glory
Duvi
Dux
Dyna-Mo
Dyna-Model Products Company
Dynamic
Dyson
Eagle Collectibles/Eagle's
    Race
Ebbro
Edil
Edocar
EFE
Efsi/Holland Oto
E.G.M.
Eidai

E J Enterprises
Eko
Elastolin
Electricar
Elegance
Eligor
Elmont
Elysee
Emek
Empire
Empro
Enchanted
Enchantment Land Coach
    Builders
Enco
Enstone Emergency Models
EPI Sports Collectibles
Epoch
Equipe Gallois
Eria
Erie
E. R. Roach
Ertl
Esci
Esdo
Eska
Espewe
Estetyka
Etzel's Speed Classics
Evrat 87 – LP Creations
Excel
Excite
Exclusive First Editions (EFE)
Exemplers
Exoto
Express Wheels
F&F
Faie
Fairfield Mint
Faller
Faracars
Fastwheel
Feeling 43
Feil
Fidart
Fimcar
Fine Art Models
Fine Model
Finoko
First Choice
First Gear
Fischer, George Heinrich
Fischer, Heinrich
Fischer, Henry
Fisher-Price
F. G. Taylor
Fleer Diecast Collectibles
Fletcher, Barnhardt & White
Fly
Forma
43rd Avenue/Gems 'N'
    Cobwebs
Fournier Enterprises

Framberg, H. L.
France Jouets
Francorchamps
Franklin Mint
Freeway Flyers
Freewheels
Friedag
Frobly
Fun Ho!
Funline
Funmate
Funrise
FYP
G & K
Gabriel
Gad
Gaia
Gaiety
Galanite
Galgo
Galoob
Gama
Gamda /GamdaKoor
Gasquy
Gate
Gateway Global
Gaz
GearBox
Gege
Gemini Jets
Gems 'N' Cobwebs
Generic
Geno
Gescha
Gilco
Gingell
Giodi
Girard
Gloor
Goeso
Golden Classics
Golden Wheel
Goldvarg
Gonio
Goodee
Goody Toys
Göso
Govroski
Gran Toros
Grand Prix
Great American Dreamcar
    /Dust & Glory/Quarter
    Mile
Greppert & Kelch
Grip Zechin
GTS
Guiloy
Guisval
Gulliver
Günthermann
H. L. Framberg
Hallmark
Hartoy

Hasbro
Hasegawa
Hauser
Herpa
Hess Promotional Toys
Hess Toy Company
High Speed
Highway 61 Collectibles
Highway Travelers
Hobbycraft
Holland-Oto
Hongwell
Hornby
Horsman
Hot Wheels
Hot Pursuit
HP Toys
Hubley
Husky
Ichiko
Icibi
Ideal
Igra
IHC
Imperial Diecast
Impy
Imra
Intercar
International Hobby Corp.
Intex
Irwin
Istana
Ites
IXL
Ixo
J43 Kawabatakikaku
J Collection
Jaco
Jada Toys, Inc.
Jane Francis Toys
Ja-Ru
Je Toys
Jemini
JEP
Jet
Jet Wheels
JNG
Joal
Johillco
John Day Models
John Hill & Company
John Smith
Johnny Lightning
Johnny Speed
Jolly Roger
Jordan
Jouef
Jouets de Paris
Joustra
JPS
JRD
JRI

JRL Collectibles
JTE
Juguinsa
Jupiter
Jurgens
K&D Autmobilia
K&M
K&O
K&R Replicas
Kaden
Kado
Kager GmbH
Kansas Toy & Novelty Company
Kawabatakikaku
Kawada
Kay
Kazan
Kellerman
Kelmet
Kembo
Kemlow
Kenna
Kenner
Kenton
Kentoy
Keystone
Kibri
Kidco
Kiddie Car Classics
Kiddietoy
Kiko
Kilgore
Kim Classics
Kimmeria
King K
King of the Road
Kingsbury
King Star
Kingston
Kinsmart
Kintoy
Kirby
Kirk
Kohnstamm, Moses
Kookaburra Models
Kumfy
Kyosho
Lacquer & Leather
Lada
Lansdowne
Lansing Slik-Toys
L D Abraham
Lee Toys
Legends of Racing
Lego
Lehigh Bitsi-Toys
Lehmann
Le Jouet Mecanique
Leksakshust
Le Mans Miniatures
Lemeco
Lenyco

Le Phoenix
Lesney
Les Rouliers
Les Routiers
Liberty Classics
Lincoln
Lincoln Industries
lincoln Internatinoal
Lincoln Toys
Lincoln White Metal Works
Lindberg
Line Mar
Lineol
Lintoy
Lion Car
Lion Models
Lion Toys
Lionel
Lit'l Toy
Litan
Lixin
IJN
Lledo
Loden Aguti
Lomo
Londontoy
Lone Star
Look Smart
Looksmart Models
LP Creations
Lucky Plan
Luso
Luxor
M C Toys
The Ma Collection
Madison Models
Madmax
Mafwo
Magic
Magnason Models
Maisto
Majorette
Malibu International
Mandarin
Mangalick
Manoil
Marklin
Marque
Mars, Inc.
Marsh
Martino Models
Martoys
Marusan
Marushin
Marx
Mascot
Master Models
Masterpieces in Miniature
Master Toy Company
Masudaya
Matchbox
Mark One Collectibles

Mattel
Max Models Mini Auto Toys
Max Models
Maxwell Mini Auto Toys
May Cheong
May Tat
McGregor
Mebetoys
Meboto
Meccano
MegaMovers
Megatoys
Mego
Mercury
Mercury Industries USA
Merit
Merlin
Message Models
Metalcar
Metal Cast Products Company
Metalcraft
Metal Masters
Metal Miniatures
Metosul
Metropolitain
Mettoy
Miber
Microchamps
Micro Machines
Micro Models
Micromodels
Micropet
Microtoys
Midgetoy
Midget Toys
Midwestern Home Products, Inc.
Mid-West Metal Novelty Man-
    ufacturing Company
Mignon
Mignot, C.B.G.
Mikansue
Milano
Milano 43
Milestone Development Cor-
    poration
Milestone Miniatures
Milestone Models
Milestones
Milton
Mimick Toys
Minialuxe
Miniature Auto Emporium
Miniature Pet
Miniature Vehicle Castings Inc.
Miniautotoys
Minic
Minichamps
Minicraft
Minimac
Mini Marque Muky
Mini Metals
Mini Power

Mini Racing
Miniroute
Minix
Mira
Mitrecraft
MK Models
Moboto (or Meboto)
Modelauto/Sun Motor
    Company, Bugattinana,
    Rapitde, Bijou
ModelCast
Model Pet
Model Plan
Model Planning Co. Ltd.
Model Power
Model Products Corpora-
    tion (MPC)
Model Toys
Models of Yesteryear
Moko
Montego
Moose Mountain Toymak-
    ers Limited
Morestone
Moskovich
Motor City Classics
Motor City USA, Design
    Studio & USA Models
Motormax
Motorworks
Mountain Service Interna-
    tional
MPC
MR
MRE
MTC
MTech
Muky
Muscle Machines
MVC
MZKT
Nacoral Intercar
National Motor Museum
    Mint
National Products
National Toys
Neff-Moon
Neuhierl
Nevco
Nevins International, Ltd.
New Clover
New-Ray
New Trax
Nicky Toys
Niedermeier
Nigam
N.J. International
Norev
Norscot
Nostalgic
Novacar
NSG Marketing Corp.

Nutmetg Collectibles
NuToyz
Ny-Lint
NZG
OddzOn
Off 43
OGDI Toys of Yesterday
Old Cars
Old Kingston Product Corporation
Omega
One43
Onyx
Oriental Omnibus Company
Original Omnibus Co.
Orobr
Oto
Oxford diecast Limited
Palitoy
Pan Toys
Papillon Toys
Paradise Garage
Paragon Models & Art
Parker White Metal
Past-Time Hobbies
Pathfinder Models
Paul's Model Art 49
Paya
Peachstate Muscle Car Collectors Club
P.E.M.
Penguin
Penjoy 50
Penny Toys
Pepe
Phat Boyz
Piccolino
Piccolo
Pilen
Pioneer
Piranha
Platypus
Playart
Playing Mantis
Play Power
Playskool
Playtoy
Playtrucks
PM
Pocher
Pocket Cars
Pocketoy
Poclain
Pole Position Collectibles
Polistil
Politoys/Polistil
Poll
PP Models
Praliné
Prämeta
Precision Accucast
Precision Autos
Precision Engineered Models

Precision Miniatures
Pride Lines
Process
Pro Engine
Progetto K
Protar
Provénce Moulåge
PTH Models
Pyro
Q-Models
Qualitoys
Quarter Mile
Quartzo
Quiralu
R&M
R. W.
Race Image Collection
Raceway Replicars
Racing Champions
Racing Collectables Club of America, Inc. (RCCA)
Racing Collectables, Inc. (RCI)
Radar
Radon
R.A.E.
Raf
Ralstoy
Rami
Rapide
Rapitoy
Ra-Ro
Rasant
RBI
RCCA (Racing Collectables Club of America, Inc.)
RCI
Reader's Digest
Real Cars
Real Wheels
Realistic
Realtoy
Record
Redbox
Reen Replica
Rei
Remco
Renaissance
Renwal
Replex
Repli-Cars
Replicars
Replicast
Reuhl Products, Inc.
Revell
Revival
Rex/Rextoys
RHI
Rhino
Richmond
Richmond Toys
Rich Toys
Ricko
Rio

Rivarossi
River Series
Roach Industries
Road Champs
Road Legends
Road Machine
Roadmaster
Roadmates
Road Rovers
Road Runners
Road Tough
Rob Eddie
Roberts
Robin Hood
Roco
Rolux
ROS
Roskopf
Ross
Rosso
Rovex
Rozkvet Mini Models
RS Toys
Ruehl
Ruestes
Rullero
Russ
Russian models
RW
Sablon
Sabra
Safar
Safir
Saico
St. Louis
Sako
Sakura
Salza
Sam Toys
Saratov
Savoye Pewter Toy Company
Scale Models
Scaleworks
Scamold
Schabak
Schuco
Schwung
Schylling
SCM
Scorchers (Hot Wheels)
Scottoys
Septoy
Shackleton
Shinsei Mini Power
Sibur
Sieperwerke
Signature Models
Siku
Silhouette
Silver Pet
Simba
Singfund
Sizzlers

Skoglund & Olson
Sky
Skybirds
Skyline
Slik Toys
SM
Small Wheels and Western Models
Smart Toys
Smer
Smith Family Toys
Smith-Miller
SMTS (Scale Model Technical Services)
Solido
Somerville
South Eastern Finecast
Spa Croft Models
Spark/Spark Model
Spec-Cast
Specialty Diecast
Speed Burners
Speed Classics
Speed Wheels
Speedway Collection
Speedy Power
Speedy Racer
Spiel-Nutz
Spot-On
Stahlberg (or Stallberg)
Starter
Stjerne
Streamlux
Strombecker
Stylish Cars
Summer
Sun Motor Company
Sunnyside
Sunshine Toys
Sun Star
Suntoys
Super Champion
Supercar Collectibles
Superior
SVP
Swan Hill
Tai Cheong Toys
Taiseiya
Takara
Tak-A-Toy
Tamiya
Tantal
Taylor, F.G.
Taylor & Barrett
Taylor Made Trucks
Tbilisi
TD
Team Caliber
Techno Giodi
Technofix
Tekno
TfC
Thimble Drome

Thomas Toys
Timpo Toys
Tin Wizard
Tins' Toys
Tintoys
Tipp & Co.
Tip Top Toy Co.
Toby Toys
Togi
Tomica
Tomy
Tonka
Tonkin
Tootsietoys
Top Gear Trax
Top Marques
Top Model Collection
Topper Toys
Toy Collector Club of America
ToyMark
Toyo Kogyo
Toys of Yesterday
Toys for Collectors
Toy Truck Collector
Trademark Models
Traffic Stoppers
Trax
Tri-Ang
Trident
Troféu
Tron
Trophy Models
True Dimensions
Tucker Box
Tuff Ones
Tuffy
Turner Toys
Turtle Creek Scale Models, Inc.
Uaz
Unique Industries, Inc.
Universal
Universal Hobbies Ltd., Inc.
Uralskiy Sokol
U.S.A. Models
U.S. Model Mint
UT
Vanguard
Vanbo
Vanke
Vaz
Vector
Verem
Victoria
Viking
Vilmer
Vintage Casting
Vitesse
Vivid Imaginations (Tyco Canada)
Voiturette
Volga
Walker Model Service
Walldorf

Wannatoy	Williams, A. C.	Wyandotte	Yorkshire	Zil
Wedico	Wills Finecast	Xonex	Yot	Zinoki
Welly	Winner's Circle	Yat Ming	Zaugg	Ziss
Western Models	Winross	Yatming	Zax	Zowees
Wheeler	Wolverine	Yaxon	Zebra Toys	Zylmex
White Rose Collectibles	World Zechin	Yidalux	Zee Toys/Zylmexx	Zschopau
Wiking	WT	Yoder	Zchopau	

Introduction

The Purpose of this Book

There are just a few books on the market on diecast, white metal, cast iron, pressed steel and tinplate automotive toys and scale models. They cover only the most popular brands such as Corgi, Dinky, Hot Wheels, Hubley, Lledo, Matchbox, Solido, Tootsietoys.... That leaves about 950 other brands that have been essentially ignored — Bburago, Dugu, Joal, Maisto, Majorette, Oto, Pocher, Siku, Tomica, Yat Ming, and Zylmex, just to name a few. The intent of this book therefore is to present the most comprehensive guide to toy cars and scale model vehicles.

The main reasons for producing this book are to provide a comprehensive reference to the lesser known brands, to encourage more people to collect diecast toys, to show collectors how affordable diecast toy collecting can be as a hobby, to demonstrate the value of collecting new models as well as old ones, to showcase current and obsolete models, and to demonstrate to collectors everywhere that they are not alone in their fascination for these diminutive cars and trucks.

Arrangement of this Book

This book is arranged alphabetically by brand name. Whenever applicable, manufacturer model numbers are included, along with description, scale, color, distinguishing marks, and value. The author has attempted to provide a brief profile of each brand represented when any background information is available.

Values

Regardless of the values indicated in this or any price guide, you can often purchase items for far below book value, and I encourage you to seek the lowest price for a particular acquisition. You will most often need to sell for far less than book value as well, especially when you intend to sell an entire collection. So what good are values if not for buying and selling? Stated book values establish a basis for personal evaluation of your collection, for insurance purposes, speculation, auctions and estate sales, and for your own future purchases, because ultimately you or another avid collector may agree to pay full book value for an item if it is considered desirable and worth the asking price. Consider the values indicated in this book to be only a guide.

In order to establish a standard for grading diecast toys, the following is offered as a generally accepted grading system. Note the popular word "mint" has been replaced by the word "new," since it has been argued that "mint condition" indicates something in perfect, unflawed, and untouched condition. "New condition," on the other hand, represents a fairer classification of toys that could show wear even within the sealed package, whether from friction with the package itself or whether from flaws and defects overlooked at the factory. Condition is abbreviated "C" or "c" in most books, with a C10 being the best, and C1 being the worst. All grading systems are arbitrary and somewhat flexible, but are relatively similar for grading most toys. In addition, some collectors base a part of the condition rating on the condition of the package. So here is a guide to help determine the condition of a particular model.

Rule #1: There is no such thing as "mint condition except for..." or "new condition except for....," It is either mint/new, or it isn't. When someone offers something with "a few paint chips, otherwise mint," it is not "otherwise mint," but considerably less than mint, and should be offered that way.

Brands and Models Represented

While this book attempts to represent every known brand and manufacturer of automotive toy and model that fit the book's title, it does not represent every model and variation ever produced by each manufacturer. A separate book could be written for each of the nearly 1,000 brands represented in this book. But the small market for such books would be understandably cost-prohibitive to the consumer as well as the publisher. So, as with most things in life, a compromise is reached by presenting a sampling of each brand of toys produced over nearly a century.

Of course, for every rule, there is an exception. Several brands, such as Tomica, Majorette, and Siku represent a major force in the diecast toy collector market. Many requests have come to me for a book on Tomicas, Majorettes, and selected other brands. So, I have made a special effort to present these brands as comprehensively as possible.

The First Automotive Toys

The earliest commercially produced automotive toys were made of cast iron, tinplate, zinc alloy, or lead. Cast iron models from A. C. Williams, Arcade, and Kenton are the best known. Tootsietoys were the first to offer diecast toys. Tinplate toys were produced mostly in Germany at first, then later in Japan beginning in the late 1950s.

Origin of Diecast Toys

The process of diecasting was first introduced to the world at the Columbian Exposition of 1893, when Charles Dowst observed a new machine known as the Line-O-Type. Mr. Dowst applied the process to the manufacture of various items, eventually producing the first diecast toys in 1910. These toys soon after became known as Tootsie Toys. (Later the name was changed to Tootsietoys.)

The Diecasting Process (and a short spelling lesson)

Diecasting is an injection mold process using a zinc alloy commonly known as "zamak," or less commonly "zamac" (96% zinc, 4% aluminum, trace magnesium) to produce accurately formed metal components. "Mazak" is reportedly a similar alloy that contains slightly more magnesium. The diecast process itself is very inexpensive, but the dies must be made of a very hard metal and are therefore very expensive to produce. But once a die is produced, it can continue to be used for nearly a million castings before showing signs of fatigue. Even then, dies have often been sold to other companies to produce still more models. One example is that Eligor of France has used old Norev dies to produce some of their current models. Another is Muky of Argentina who re-used many old Hot Wheels dies. Many other toy companies have also done this.

The manufacturing of a die for diecasting is very expensive, so production of large numbers of items from one die is necessary to offset the initial cost.

On the matter of spelling, "die cast" is most commonly spelled as two separate words. More recently, it has often been seen on toy packaging and many other places spelled as a single word — "diecast." The Software Toolworks Multimedia Encyclopedia places a hyphen between the two words. While the Die Cast Car Collectors Club separates the two words as well, the Toy Car Collectors Association chooses to use the single word form. In comparison, Asheville DieCast opts for a customized spelling as a company trademark. While all forms are acceptable, the single word form "diecast" is used in this book for standardization.

White Metal

White metal is a lead alloy with a lower melting temperature than zamak, and so it can be cast using less expensive casting techniques. Almost every brand of white metal model is represented in this book. Brands such as Brooklin, Goldvarg, Western, and Durham are just a few examples of models produced using white metal.

The process generally used to produce white metal models includes a mold made of inexpensive vulcanized rubber rather than expensive hard metal dies. The result is that less models can be made before the mold wears out, but more variety is possible due to the inexpensive die. Such models are more expensive than diecast due to their low production numbers. If diecast models were made in such low quantities, the cost would increase dramatically.

Slush Mold/Pot Metal/Lead Toys

Many early metal cast toys used a molten lead process known as "slush mold," but it was eventually replaced by comparatively non-toxic zamak.

Slush mold, or pot metal, toys are similar to white metal models only in that they are made of lead. The process is simply to pour lead into a mold, let it cool, then pour the remaining liquified metal out, leaving a hollow casting. On larger toys, the molten lead was sloshed around to evenly coat the inside of the mold, hence the name "slush mold." While lead alloy white metal models are still produced for the collector market, pot metal toys have been discontinued since the 1930s when lead was discovered to be poison.

Plastic, Resin, Cast Iron, and Other Materials

Although this book is devoted mostly to diecast and white metal toys and models, many plastic, resin, and cast iron toys are also included in this book due to their historical significance or because of their accuracy, scale, detail, or other distinguishing characteristics. Since plastic is now used in addition to metal alloys in most modern diecast toys, the result is a blurring of the line between diecast and non-diecast toys.

A few early toys were even made of flour-base paste. These toys are rare and valuable if found in mint or near-mint condition, because of the tendency for them to crumble or discolor with age and handling.

Safety Factor

Cast iron toys, while popular at the turn of the century, are heavy and would occasionally become destructive weapons when wielded by a rambunctious child bent on rendering them airborne. Beyond that, shipping of cast iron toys was, and still is, expensive due to their weight.

Later, the manufacture of lead alloy toys (pot metal or slush mold) in the 1930s and 1940s, especially toy soldiers, was eventually stopped when was it was discovered that small children were suffering from lead poisoning from putting such things in their mouths.

Safety and lighter weight, therefore, have been major factors in the growth and popularity of diecast toys made of zamak.

Toys Versus Scale Model Miniatures

Many automotive toys demonstrate such precise detail that they can no longer be called toys, but qualify as models. References to models as toys is for simplicity and not for condescension. Whether a toy or a model, they are all represented in this book with apologies to collectors of the latter.

Scale: O, HO, N, S & Z Gauge and Other Scales

The purpose of all this "scale talk" is to acquaint you with the relative size of a model based on its scale, and to expose collectors to the many different sizes of models available on the market.

With the rising popularity of model railroads in the early part of the twentieth century, it was important to establish a standard track size so that various manufacturers could make model railroad cars that fit on each others tracks. O gauge was arbitrarily established as the standard, based on the odd ratio of 7 cm = 1 ft., with rails approximately 1¼" apart. This results in a scale of 1:43 (actually closer to 1:43.5). It seemed a convenient size at the time for most economically producing the electrical systems inside the locomotive that drove the whole system. 1:43 scale automobile models typically measure about 4 to 4½" long. Later, U.S. model makers rounded the 7 centimeters to a quarter inch = 1 ft., making it 1:48 scale.

Later, HO, or "Half O" gauge, representing a ratio of 3.5 cm = 1 ft., was introduced with rails about ⅝" apart. HO translates to roughly 1:87 scale, allowing for a more elaborate layout in less space. Miniature automobiles of this scale are generally about 1½" long and many are made of plastic rather than diecast metal.

The more recent introduction of N gauge model railroads is due to the advance in technology that allowed smaller and smaller electric motors and mechanical parts to be produced, giving rise to what was until recently the smallest gauge railway system produced, with rails just 9 millimeters apart. This scale is so small that few if any diecast car models are made for this scale, opting instead for diminutive plastic models.

Even smaller than N gauge is Z gauge. The fact that electric motors and tracks can be manufactured to fit such a small scale is incredible on its own. Accompanying vehicles are obviously extremely small and almost invariably one piece plastic models, measuring barely a half-inch long.

CONDITION RATING CHART

C10, 100% – New condition with original container

C9, 80-99% – New condition without container

C8, 60-79% – Near new condition, close inspection reveals minor wear

C7, 40-59% – Excellent condition, visible minor wear

C6, 20-39% – Very good condition, visible wear, all parts intact

C5, 10-19% – Good condition, excessive wear, paint chipped, or heavily worn

C4, 4-9% – Fair condition, parts broken or missing

C1 - 3, 2-3% – Poor condition, paint worn off, parts broken or missing

C0, .5-1% – Salvage for parts only

COMMON SCALES USED IN TOY AND MODEL MANUFACTURING

Scale	Equivalent	% of Actual Size	Comments
1:8	1½ inches or 38.1 mm = 1 ft.	12.50%	Used for the most expensive precision models such as Pocher and Bossat Dermov
1:12	1 inch or 25.4 mm = 1 ft.	8.33%	The largest models available from Maisto, Ertl, Solido, and others
1:18	⅔ inch or 16.9 mm = 1 ft.	5.55%	An American standard for diecast models from Bburago, Ertl, Maisto, Motor City Classics, Yat Ming Road Signature, and others
1:24	½ inch or 12.7 mm = 1 ft.	4.17%	L Gauge, the common scale for Franklin and Danbury
1:25	0.48 inches or 12.5 mm = 1 ft.	4%	Most common for plastic model kits and dealer promotional models
1:32	⅜ inch or 9.53 mm = 1 ft.	3.13%	I Gauge
1:42	0.29 inch or 7.5 mm = 1 ft.	2.86%	Popular scale for Spot-On toys
1:43	0.28 inch or 7 mm = 1 ft.	2.30%	O Gauge, actually closer to 1:43.5 scale
1:48	¼ inch or 6.5 mm = 1 ft.	2.08%	Adjusted scale adapted for some US models
1:50	0.24 inch or 6.1 mm = 1 ft.	2.00%	Common scale for construction models
1:55	0.22 inch or 5.5 mm = 1 ft.	1.80%	Most Siku toys are in this scale
1:64	0.19 inch or 4.75 mm = 1 ft.	1.56%	S Gauge, actually closer to 1:64.2; most 3 inch diecast toys are called 1:64 scale but may actually range from 1:56 to 1:100 scale
1:76	0.16 inch or 4 mm = 1 ft.	1.30%	Double O or OO gauge, actually closer to 1:76.2
1:87	0.14 inch or 3.5 mm = 1 ft.	1.15%	Half O or HO Gauge, actually closer to 1:87.1
1:100	0.12 inch or 3.1 mm = 1 ft.	1.00%	Tomica trucks commonly fall into this scale
1:144	⅓₂ inch or 2.1 mm = 1 ft.	0.69%	Racing Champions once issued an assortment of diecast models in this scale
1:152	0.079 inch or 2 mm = 1 ft.	0.66%	Triple O or OOO Gauge, actually closer to 1:152.4
1:160	0.08 inch or 1.9 mm = 1 ft.	0.63%	N Gauge
1:220	0.06 inch or 1.4 mm = 1 ft.	0.45%	Z Gauge
1:250	0.04 inch or 0.3 mm = 1 ft.	0.40%	Larger scale used for airplanes from Herpa, Schabak, and others
1:500	0.02 inch or 0.6 mm = 1 ft.	0.20%	Smaller scale used for airplane models from Herpa, Schabak, and others

Going in the other direction in relation to scale, L gauge has been established for what are referred to as lawn trains, a scale of about 1:24, which for a toy train is quite large.

In addition, double O, or OO, gauge was developed for smaller models of around 1:76 scale with Dinky Dublo models having set the precedent. Why the designation "double O" when size is closer to "HO" remains a mystery to this author, since double O gauge represents 4 mm = 1 ft.

While O scale (1:43) and HO scale (1:87) have been adopted for manufacturers of diecast model vehicles intended for model railroads, other scales were established for diecast models that were popular enough on their own. Siku of Germany established the popular 1:55 scale, in which most of their diecast toys are produced, and which many other manufacturers have adopted.

Manufacturers of heavy equipment miniatures meanwhile lean toward producing 1:50 scale models. Conrad and NZG in particular have concentrated on this scale, although they have produced a few models in other scales.

Another popular scale for miniatures is 1:64, and it is the scale to which Matchbox, Hot Wheels, and others are referred, even though their actual scale varies greatly from one model to the next. In fact, most current diecast miniature cars of the 3" long variety hover around 1:55 to 1:60 scale, while trucks of the same length tend to fall closer to the 1:87 scale down to 1:100 or smaller scale. Ertl is one of few companies that produces a line of specifically 1:64 scale models, particularly farm tractors.

Becoming more popular recently are 1:24 and 1:18 scale models, with a few 1:12 scale models reaching the market as well. Very expensive models, such as Pochers, are even made to 1:8 scale, but their price begins at $500 each for new models of such scale.

Racing Collectibles

Some collectors specialize in racing collectibles. Action Performance, Racing Champions, and Quartzo are primary examples of companies that specialize in producing diecast models specifically for these collectors, but they are hardly the only ones. While an entire book could be written on racing diecast, this book will necessarily present just a survey.

Livery

Livery, as it relates to diecast toys, refers to the various product brands and company logos represented on various toys. Many diecast toys are produced specifically with licensed trademarks, logos, promotions, and advertising on them, such as Coca-Cola, Campbell's, Kodak, and so on. Livery is often the primary attraction for collectors, hence its significance.

Details, Details...

A process many manufacturers use in applying printing to diecast toys is called "tampo" or "tempa." This has been the most common technique of applying logos, trim colors, and accents since the early 1970s. Before that time, decals, labels, and hand-painting were the main methods of applying detail to models. The tampo process is now the prevalent form of applying details, particularly on inexpensive toys. Occasionally, other types of detailing are mentioned in this book to illustrate a variation to the tampo version of a particular model.

A new process just introduced for 2000 is a heat-applied decal that allows for a more efficient and cost-effective application of colors, details, and gradients. The first to use them was Mattel on their Hot Wheels toys.

Customizing and Restoration

Much debate continues between purists — those people who feel that any altering, such as repainting or detailing, of production models renders a model worthless — and hobbyists — those who believe they can make a model better by customizing it. Depending on the original value and condition of a model and the degree of skill involved in making such alterations, a model can in fact be rendered worthless or more valuable. One man, Dan Coviello, a retired New York City policeman now living in

North Carolina, makes a living customizing production model police cars and others to suit whatever state, county, or municipality the buyer wishes to have represented.

Restoring toys is a different matter. Old, rare toys such as Dinky or Tootsietoys are now being restored by skilled artisans to return at least some of their value in lieu of finding such models still in new condition. Resulting value is usually 50 – 60 percent of such a model in original unretouched mint condition.

Second Market

Retail chains such as K-Mart, Shopko, Target, Toys R Us, Wal-Mart, as well as specialty dealers such as EWA, Exoticar, Toys for Collectors, Toys Plus, Asheville DieCast, and others provide the primary sources for many currently available models.

But much of the collector market is supported by what is known as the "second market" consisting of individuals and dealers who buy selected models in smaller quantities, frequently from private individuals or auctions, but often new from retail stores. Because second market dealers sometimes purchase whole collections, they usually try to buy at well below book value. They then resell to individual collectors, whether through hobby shops, collectibles stores, swap meets, mail order price lists, classified ads in popular magazines, or on the Internet.

It is these second market sources that often drive the market of certain models far above current retail prices. Such tactics have received mixed receptions from diehard diecast collectors. Some accept the high price to fill the gaps in their collections. Others complain of artificially inflated price-gouging from people out to make a fast buck. The debate continues.

Auctions are another driving factor in the growing value of diecast toys. Auctioneers such as Bill Bertoia and Noel Barrett who specialize in toy auctions contribute greatly to establishing values for antique and collectible toys. Now Internet auction sites such as eBay provide a huge marketplace for items of every conceivable kind, which drives prices even higher on antiques and collectibles.

The Toy Car Collectors Association

There are many collector clubs devoted to one brand or another of diecast toys, such as Corgi, Ertl, Hot Wheels, and Matchbox, but there is one club that represents a broader appeal, the Toy Car Collectors Association (TCCA). Through its richly illustrated *Toy Car Collector Magazine*, members receive information on new models and old favorites representing many of the manufacturers listed in this book. TCCA membership rates are as indicated below:

1 year – $29.95 to USA, $39.95 to Canada, $49.95 to the rest of the world

2 years – $54.95 to USA, $74.95 to Canada, $94.95 to the rest of the world

3 years – $79.95 to USA, $109.95 to Canada, $139.95 to the rest of the world

To enroll, send check or money order (U.S. funds, please) payable to:
Dana Johnson Enterprises
P O Box 1824
Bend, OR 97709-1824 USA
e-mail: toynutz@earthlink.net
or online at
www.toynutz.com/TCCA.html

1953 Packard, Racing Champions Mint Editions 1:64 scale

1320, Inc.

Mailing Address:
Thirteen-Twenty, Inc.
PO Box 1487
High Point, NC 27261-1487
Shipping Address:
Thirteen-Twenty, Inc.
340 Habersham Road
High Point, NC 27260
Office Hours: 8:00 am – 5:00 pm ET
Toll Free: 888-GET-1320 (888-438-1320)
Phone: 336-882-8585
Fax: 336-882-6284
Website: www.1320inc.com
For general information: info@1320inc.com
For comments/suggestions:
feedback@1320inc.com

1320, Inc. has only been around since 2003, but their popularity has been rising steadily with a growing collector base as news spreads of their exceptional and unique diecast models. Their website at www.1320inc.com states, "1320, Inc. is in the business of providing high-end diecast collectibles to drag racing fans around the globe. We always have the race fan in mind when we develop products, as we are motorsports fans ourselves. All of our product lines are 1:24 scale diecast built-up models which include details such as removeable bodies or cowls, fuel lines, oil lines, cloth seats, belts with photoetched buckles, and soft rubber tires. They are all individually numbered and come with a collector card that includes the history of each piece." Models start around $60 each. Their first issues are already sold out and rising in value. Visit their website to view their most current models or write to them at the address above.

Beebe & Mulligan Dragster $60-75

Don Prudhomme Army Funny Car ...$60-75

A

A & S

A & S of Great Britain was at one time a manufacturer of precision 1:43 scale white metal models.

1958 Ford Thunderbird 2-door hardtop,
#2 ....$450-600
1958 Ford Thunderbird convertible, top down,
#1 ....$450-600
1958 Ford Thunderbird convertible, top down,
with Continental kit, #3 ....$450-600
1958 Oldsmobile Super 98 2-door hardtop,
#2H..$450-600
1958 Oldsmobile Super 98 convertible, top
down, #2-58 ....$450-600

A-Line

Most of A-Line's product line is devoted to freight cars, motors, and parts for HO gauge train sets. Their Fruehauf "Z" Van series features a miniature version of the prototype 40 foot Fruehauf "Z" Van commonly seen on piggyback trains and highways. These Fruehauf semi trailer kits are molded in aluminum and black styrene with separate tires, spoked wheel hubs, mudflaps, doorbars, and other details. Each kit includes two undecorated trailers with complete instructions and a list of correct decals. Kits sell for $15 – 18.

AAM (see American Automobile Miniatures)

Aardvark

Aardvark of St. Paul, Minnesota, now out of business, was a manufacturer of handcrafted resin models.

1969 Chevrolet Camaro Indianapolis 500 Pace Car,
Convertible, top down, #04............$375-425
1961 Maserati Type 61, 1:24 scale,
#241B $375-425

A. Barrett & Sons
(see Barrett & Sons)

A. B. C. Brianza

Mailing Address:
A. B. C. Brianza
C.P.40
21049 Tradate
VA Italy
Showroom:
via Mazzini 23
22070 Locate Varesino
CO Italy

A. B. Carlo Brianza is the founder of the company, hence the "A. B. C." commonly associated with the brand name. It is not clear which A. B. C. Brianza models are diecast and which are plastic or resin. Several brands are actually offered under the Brianza umbrella:

Carlo Brianza models are 1:14 scale masterpieces limited to 1,000 pieces per model.

ABC 1:14 Scale models are high quality plastic (or resin) kits.

Miniland represents 1:18 scale plastic (or resin) kits.

ABC Trucks are beautifully rendered models mostly of vintage racing transporters in 1:43 scale.

ABC Brianza is the primary line, representing some of the world's most unusual cars replicated in 1:43 scale, some are available as kits as well as pre-assembled models.

Autostile is a sub-grouping of A. B. C. offerings.

ABC & AMC is another sub-grouping of A. B. C. offerings.

Carlo Brianza 1:14 Scale

1974 Ferrari 246 GTB Dino.......$1,600-1,800
1974 Ferrari 246 GTS Dino.......$1,600-1,800
Ferrari Dino 246 Coupé $1,600-1,800
Ferrari Dino 246 Spider.............$1,600-1,800
1960 Ferrari 250 SWB $1,600-1,800
1961 Ferrari 250 GT SWB........$1,600-1,800
1962 Ferrari 250 GT SWB California
    Spyder $1,600-1,800
1963 Ferrari 250 GTO Le Mans ..$1,600-1,800
1965 Ferrari 250 LM Le Mans ...$1,900-2,100
Ferrari 250 Le Mans $1,600-1,800
Ferrari 250 Spider California.......$1,600-1,800
1965 Ferrari 275 GTB Short Nose .$1,600-1,800
1967 Ferrari 275 GTB4 ....$1,600-1,800
1967 Ferrari 275 GTB4 Spyder
    N.A.R.T. $1,600-1,800
Ferrari 275 GTS/4 Spider
    N.A.R.T. $1,600-1,800
Ferrari 275 GTB/4 Coupé $1,600-1,800
1984 Ferrari 288 GTO $1,850-2,000
1967 Ferrari 330 P4 "Monza" ...$1,650-1,800
1974 Ferrari 365 GTB4 Daytona .$1,600-1,800
1974 Ferrari 365 GTB4 Daytona
    Spyder $1,600-1,800
1980 Ferrari 365 GT4 BB $1,650-1,800
1984 Ferrari 512 BB $1,650-1,800
Ferrari 365 GTB/4 Daytona
    Spider $1,600-1,800
Ferrari 365 GTB/4 Daytona
    Coupé $1,600-1,800
1967 Ferrari P4 Monza Bandini-
    Amon $1,600-1,800

ABC 1:14 Scale by Carlo Brianza

1972-4 Alfa Romeo GTA Junior
    Ore Jarama $250-400
    Monza.................................$250-400
    Paul Ricard $250-400
1992 Alfa Romeo 155 GTA
    C.I.V.T. $250-400

Nannini $250-400
1989 Lancia Delta 16V $250-400
1991 Lancia Delta Integrale 16V GR.A 1000
Laghi $250-400
1964 Ferrari 250 GT Lusso Tour De
France $250-400
1964 Ferrari 250 GT Lusso Stradale ... $250-400

ABC 1:24 Scale by Carlo Brianza
Ferrari 340 Mexico, kit or built $250-400

ABC 1:43 Scale by Carlo Brianza
1928 Alfa Romeo 1500 Campari Mille Miglia
Winner, #13C $240
1993 Alfa Romeo 155 V6 T.I.D.T.M.
Nannini $250-300
Larini Campione D.T.M. $250-300
Danner $250-300
Francia Team Schubel $250-300
Alfa Romeo 155 GTA C.I.V.T. '92
Nannini $250-300
C.I.V.T. '92 Larini $250-300
1930 Alfa Romeo 1750 Mille
Miglia-Nuvolari/Guidotti, top down,
#16 .... $240
1931 Alfa Romeo 1750 Castagna ... $250-300
1931 Alfa Romeo 1750 GTC Coupé Royal
Touring $250-300
1931 Alfa Romeo 6C 1750 G.S. "Flying Star"
Touring $250-300
1931 Alfa Romeo 6C 1750 G.T.C "Flying Star"
Touring $250-300
1932 Alfa Romeo 6C 1750 GTC Guida Interna
Semirigida $250-300
1934 Alfa Romeo 6C 2300 Pescara
24H $250-300
1934 Alfa Romeo 6C 2300 Touring "Soffio Di
Satana" $250-300
1940 Alfa Romeo 6C 2500 Farina ... $250-300
1940 Alfa Romeo 6C 2500 Touring . $250-300
1947 Alfa Romeo 6C 2500 Michelotti Nino
Farina $250-300
1952 Alfa Romeo 6C 2500 Giardiniera Viotti
"Woody Wagon" $250-300
Alfa Romeo G.P. Tipo 308
v.1 Indianapolis 1940 .... $250-300
v.2 Pintacuda 1º Assoluto Rio De Janeiro
1938 .... $250-300
v.3 500 Miglia Di Indianapolis Louis
Durant $250-300
Alfa Romeo G.P. Tipo 158A
v.1 G.P Livorno 1938 .... $250-300
v.2 Villoresi $250-300
1948 Ferrari 166 All Mille Miglia Winner,
#12 .... $240
1949 Ferrari 166 Mille Miglia, red, #14 .. $240
1963 ATS 2500 GT1958 Ferrari 250 GT
Liliama Di Rethy $250-300
Ferrari 212 Export Giardinetta Vignale .. $250-300
Ferrari 212 Inter Cabriolet "Abbott" $250-300
1952 Ferrari 250 Carrera
Panamericana $250-300
1952 Ferrari 250 Le Mans $250-300
1952 Ferrari 250 S Mille Miglia $250-300

1958 Ferrari 250 GT Liliama Di Rethy .. $250-300
1953 Ferrari 342 America $250-300
1954 Ferrari 375 Mille Miglia $250-300
1959 Ferrari 400 S.A. $250-300
Ferrari 410 Ghia $250-300
1969 Ferrari 275P Berlinetta
Michelotti $250-300
Ferrari Vignale Shooting Brake CH.N.
7963 .... $250-300
1953 Fiat 8V $250-300
1953 Fiat 8V Le Mans Lurani-Mahe ... $250-300
Fiat 8V Zagato $250-300
1953 Fiat 8V Zagato Spider Mille
Miglia $250-300
1953 Fiat 8V Zagato Spider Capelli-
Veronelli $250-300
1954 Fiat 8V Stradale $250-300
1995 Fiat Barchetta
v.1 Arancio (orange?) $250-300
v.2 Gialla (?) $250-300
v.3 Rossa (red?) $250-300
v.4 Azzurra (blue?) $250-300
Lancia Aprilia Aerodinamica $250-300
1993 Lancia Delta Presentazione $250-300
1938 Lancia Astura Cabriolet
Pininfarina $250-300
Maserati Grand Prix Transporter $900
Maserati Grand Prix Transporter with 3 Maserati
250 F cars $1650
1927 Om Superba-Minoja/Morandi, Mille
Miglia Winner, red#15 .... $240
1954 Pontiac Chieftain Custom Catalina, tan,
#22 .... $300
Scuderia Ferrari Transporter $900
Scuderia Ferrari Transporter with 3 Ferrari 801 F1
cars $1650
1936 Scuderia Ferrari Classic Transporter .. $300
1971 Scuderia Ferrari Transporter O.M. 107
Rolfo $700
Scuderia Lancia Support Van Carrera Panamericana $650
1951 Team Alfa Romeo Transporter $300

ABC & AMC 1:43 Scale by Carlo Brianza
Ferrari 348 TS
Massimo Presicci $250-300
Ivan Benaduce $250-300
Ferrari 348 TB
Merzario $250-300
Paolo Rossi $250-300
Gianluca Giraudi $250-300
Benussiglio Mario $250-300

ABC Autostile 1:43 Scale by Carlo Brianza
1926 Alfa Romeo RLSS C.P Avus $250-300
1941 Alfa Romeo 16C Prototype $250-300
Alfa Romeo Disco Volante $250-300
1922 Alfa Romeo RLSS Stradale $250-300
Fiat 509 SM $250-300
1935 Lancia Astura Stradale $250-300
1946 Lancia Astura G.P. Modena $250-300

ABC Indy
Ferrari Indianapolis 1987, 1:43 .... $75-125

ABC Ruby
Bugatti T59 Nuvolari 1934, 1:43 .... $75-125

ABC Trucks by Carlo Brianza
Alfa Romeo Transporto
Auto G.P. Tripoli 1936 .... $250-400
Coppa Vanderbilt Nuvolari 1936 $250-400
Alfa Romeo 500 Transporto Alfa Gran Prix
1950/51 .... $250-400
Alfa Romeo 500 Cassonato 1935 .... $250-400
Alfa Romeo Mille Cassonato $250-400
Autocarro Ceirano 47 CRA Scuderia Ferrari
1929 .... $250-400
Camion Fiat 642 Scuderia Centro Sud . $250-400
Camion Lancia Esatau P Scuderia Lancia
1953 .... $250-400
Camion Thames Trader Scuderia
Maranello $250-400
Fiat 642 NR2 Transporto
Ferrari 1956 .... $250-400
Maserati 1956 .... $250-400
Lancia Eptaiota Torpdeone 1930 Scuderia Fer-
rari $250-400
OM 71-107 "Rolfo" 1971 Transporto
Ferrari $250-400

Miniland by Carlo Brianza
Ferrari 250 GT Lusso, 1:14 .... $1,200-1,400

Speed by Carlo Brianza
Alfa Romeo 166, 1:43 .... $75-125
Fiat Fiorino 1996, 1:43 .... $75-125

A. B. C. Models
A. B. C. Models of Great Britain at one
time manufactured 1:43 scale resin models.

1957 Mercury Turnpike Cruiser convertible, top
down $150-200
1957 Mercury Turnpike Cruiser hardtop ... $150-200

Abraham, L. D. (see L. D. Abraham)

A. C. Williams (cast iron)
It is historically interesting to note that the
popularity of cast iron toys declined during the
decade of 1910–1920, the same time that
diecast toys, which offered lighter-weight more-
detailed alternatives to the heavy iron models,
established their initial dominance in the world
toy market.
Adam Clark Williams purchased the J.
W. Williams Company from his father in
1886, thus beginning one of the more successful toy companies of the era. Mr.
Williams retired from the business in 1919,
but the Ravenna, Ohio, company continued
producing cast iron toys until 1938 when the
company changed direction away from toys.
Few A. C. Williams toys are marked, so most
often the only clues to their heritage are turned
steel hubs and starred axle peens. Most A. C.
Williams toys were so crude as to barely
qualify as "doorstops," according to Ken

Hutchison and Greg Johnson in their out-of-print book The Golden Age of Automotive Toys 1925 – 1941. But A. C. Williams did produce a few exceptional toys. In fact, some are considered the best examples of cast iron toys ever made.

Austin (one of three from car carrier set) ..$150-200
Bus, Fageol Coach, 7¾" $1,000-1,500
Bus, Fageol Double Decker, blue with gold stripes, 7¾" $750-1,000
Car carrier with three Austins, 1920, 12½" $600-800
Chrysler Airflow, 4¾" $125-175
Chrysler Airflow, 6½" $500-650
Coupe, 1936, 3" $150-225
Coupe, 3½" $90-120
Coupe, 4½" $150-225
Coupe, 1928, 6" $200-275
Coupe, 1930s, 7" $900-1,200
Coupe with rumble seat, 1930, 6¾" ...$300-400
Delivery Van, 8" $600-800
Doctor's Coupe with curtains, 5" $350-500
Dodge Woody Pickup, 5" $150-200
Fageol Bus (see Bus, Fageol)
Ford, 1935, 4½" $350-450
Ford Model T Coupe, 6" $200-300
Ford Model T Express Truck, 7¼" $350-500
Ford Opera Coupe, 5" $250-375
Graham Sedan, 5" $120-150
Graham Coupe, 5" $120-150
Laundry Truck, 8" $600-900
Lincoln Touring Car, 7" $300-450
Lincoln Touring Car, 9¼" $700-1,000
Lincoln Touring Coupe, 8¾" $1,000-1,250
Mack Gas Tanker, 3¾" $75-125
Mack Gas Tanker, 5⅛" $150-225
Mack Gas Tanker, 10¼" $275-325
Mack Stake Truck, 3½" 75-125
Mack Stake Truck, 4¼" $200-300
Mack Stake Truck, 5⅛" $175-250
Mack Stake Truck, 8½" $300-450
Packard 900 Light Eight Sedan, 1932, 8" $600-1,000
Packard 900 Light Eight Sedan, 1932, 7" $350-600
Packard 900 Light Eight Stake Truck, 1932, 8" $350-600
Packard Coupe, 4½" $125-150
Packard Roadster, 4½" $125-150
Packard Sedan, 4½" $125-150
Packard Stake Truck, 4½" $125-150
Phaeton with driver and lady passenger, 12" $900-1,200
Plymouth Coupe, 1933, 5¼" $150-175
Plymouth Sedan, 5¼" $150-175
REO Sidemount Sedan, 5" $120-180
Rolls Royce, 3½" $80-100
Stake Truck with Trailer, Coast to Coast Co., 7" $450-600
Stake Truck with Trailer, Coast to Coast cartage Co., 10⅛" $300-400
Streamlined Sedan, 8" $1,000-1,250
Studebaker Coupe, 4¼" $125-150
Studebaker Sedan, two-tone, 4" $175-250
Studebaker Truck, 4½" $125-150
Taxi, 1920s, 5¼" $275-350
Wrecker, 5" $150-200
Wrecker, 6½" $400-525
Wrecker, 7¾" $525-750

Academy Minicraft

The first I'd heard of this company was from a photo sent to me via e-mail of an unusual three-wheel 1935 Morgan Super Sports in 1:16 scale. Since then, I've found an assortment of these offered by Phoenix Model Company of Brooksville, Florida. According to a company representative, these are plastic models sold as kits. Minicraft models encompass the car and airplane assortment, while the Academy brand represents their military models.

Along with an assortment of vintage cars are also armored vehicles, steam locomotives, and airplanes.

1933 Cadillac V-16 Town Car, 1:16, #11208 ....$25-35
Chevrolet Corvette Stingray Mako Shark Show Car, 1:20, #11210 ....$12–16
1902 De Dion Bouton, 1:16, #11206 ..$9–12
1931 Ford Deluxe Roadster, 1:16, #11221 ....$25-35
1931 Ford Model A Delivery Van, 1:16, #11214 ....$25-35
1931 Ford Model A Pickup Truck, 1:16, #11204 ....$35-45
1931 Ford Model A Sedan, 1:1, #11211 6 ....$25-35
1919 Hispano Suiza Alfonso Roadster, 1:16, #11207 ....$20-25
1939 Jaguar SS-100, 1:16, #11216 ...$35-45
1928 Lincoln Dietrich Convertible Sedan, #11217 ....$25-35
1928 Mercedes-Benz SS, 1:16, #11218 ....$60-77
1936 Mercedes-Benz 540K, 1:16, #11219 ....$60-75
1955 Mercedes-Benz 300SL Gullwing, 1:16, #11220 ....$35-45
1948 MG TC Roadster, #11213 ....$25-35
1935 Morgan Super-Sports Three-Wheeler, 1:16, #11212 ....$20-25
Pontiac Bonneville V-8, 1:16, #11222 ..$25-35
1907 Rolls Royce Touring Car, 1:16, #11215 ....$35-45
1961 Rolls Royce Silver Cloud, 1:24, #11209 ....$9–12
Triumph TR-3A, 1:24, #11203 ....$7–9

ACB (also see Le Phoenix)

23 Avenue Carnot
75017 Paris, France
Tel. : 00 33 1 56 68 99 75
Fax : 00 33 1 56 68 99 76

ACB produces 1:10 scale resin models and kits, as well as 1:43 scale metal models and kits under Le Phoenix and Super Le Phoenix brands.

ACB 1:10 Scale Resin Models and Kits

Ferrari 250 TR 1957, limited serial (20 units produced) De Conto, ACB002M,
kit $750-900
built $2,900
Mercedes W 196 1954, ACBK001,
kit $750-900
built $2,000-2,500

Accucast

In the early 1980s, a company called Accucast (or Precision Accucast) was formed by Michael Weston of Massachusetts in order to reproduce some of the Tootsietoy Ford and General Motors toys from the 1920s (and at least one from the 1950s). The venture ended just three or four years later with the death of Mr. Weston. A few Accucast reproductions are reportedly cast from original dies, but most are from new dies made by forming rubber around the originals and using the mold to create a new casting. Accucast reproductions are heavier than the Tootsietoy originals, mostly due to the heavier white metal (lead alloy) used for the castings. The brand is occasionally confused with Authenticast. Value for these reproductions begins at $20 and goes up from there.

1928 Ford Model A Coupe with added "opera windows" $20-35
1950s Chevrolet Panel Truck, 4" $20-35

Ace Implement Company

An e-mail on April 25, 2003, arrived from one Dr. Shatterhand regarding a set of 12 miniature 1930s cars. Prior to his e-mail, I had not heard of Ace Implement Company or their Authentic Model Car Series. The clue to their age is that they are marked "Made in Japan" which identifies them as having been produced no earlier than the 1950s.

They appear to be heavy cast pot metal and somewhat crude, but nevertheless intriguing. Each model is packaged separately in its own clear plastic display box. The 12-car set includes two beige Pierce Arrows and one of every other car.

Ace Implement Company Authentic Model Car Series

Complete Set $150-200
Cord L-29, yellow $12–16
Duesenberg "J," black $12–16
Fiat 520, red $12–16
Ford Model A, dark blue-green $12–16
Franklin 15, blue $12–16
1931 Lincoln V8, red $12–16
Mercedes Benz SSK, gray $12–16

1930 Packard, white $12–16
1931 Pierce Arrow, beige $12–16
1927 Rolls Royce, green $12–16
Stutz Bearcat, beige $12–16

Acme Plastic Toys, Inc.

From 1945 until 1950, Thomas Toys bore the name Acme, the New York City company that marketed Thomas Toys during that period. In 1950, Islyn Thomas purchased Acme from then owner Ben Shapiro, and the Acme name was removed from subsequent Thomas Toys.

Aerocar PT560, "Made In USA Plas-Tex," 7½" $200-225
Airline Limousine, #29, 4½", 1947 ....$30-40
Car carrier, 9" $30-40
Car carrier with two cars $75-85
Convertible Coupe, 4½" $15-20
Coupe and House Trailer, #30, 8½" $25-35
Delivery Truck, #41, 4", 1947 ....$20-30
Dump Truck, #42, 5", 1947 ....$15-20
Esso Gas Truck, #43, 1947 ....$25-35
Jeep with dropping windshield, #17, 1947 ....$25-35
Jeep and Trailer, #19, 8½", 1947 ....$15-20
Limousine and Trailer, #55, 6½" $30-40
Merry-Go-Round Truck, 374, 4½" $25-35
Motorcycle with Rider, #72, 4" $50-60
Motorcycle, chrome plated, #125, 4" $65-75
Police - Fire Chief Radio Car, #67, 4½" ..$25-35
Sedan, #27, 4¾₆", 1947 ....$25-35
Service Motorcycle with rider, #90, 4⅞" ...$30-40
Streamlined Sedan, #77, 4½" $20-30
Streamlined Truck, #18, 5", 1947 ....$20-30
Streamlined Utility Trailer, #48, 2½" $15-20
Texaco Gas Truck, #40, 4", 1947 ....$30-40
Truck and Trailer, #16, 9", 1947 ....$40-50

Action Performance

Action Performance Companies, Inc.
4707 E Baseline Rd.
Phoenix, AZ 85040
Tel: 602–894–0100
Fax: 602–894–6316
1-800-411-8404 Action Racing Collectibles
1-800-952–0708 Racing Collectibles Club of America
602–337–3700 Fan Fueler
602–337–3700 Action's Corporate Office
www.action-performance.com

Action Performance Companies Inc. (ARC) markets and distributes products through a variety of channels, including the 100,000-member Action Racing Collectables Club of America (RCCA), trackside at racing events, mass retail department stores, and a nationwide wholesale network of approximately 5,000 specialty dealers and distributors.

Action Racing Collectables Inc. is the primary retail division, offering a vast array of racing models in various scales.

Besides racing diecast models, Action also produces fulfillment products such as T-shirts, posters, and other racing related promotional items through its group of companies and subsidiaries — Action Racing Collectables Club of America, Action Platinum Series Racing Collectables, Revell Collection, Fan Fueler, and Image Works.

In November 1997, the company announced that it had reached an agreement in principle to purchase the motorsports diecast collectibles business of Revell-Monogram Inc., a unit of Binney & Smith Inc. of Easton, Pennsylvania, for $15 million in cash, and also to form a broad-ranging and long-term strategic alliance with Revell-Monogram. The acquisition includes a 10–year licensing agreement that will provide Action with exclusive use of the trademarked brand names of Revell-Monogram's U.S. motorsports diecast product lines, Revell Racing and Revell Collection, and existing U.S. distribution channels.

Action will exclusively market and distribute Revell-Monogram's plastic model kits into its trackside distribution channel and assist Revell-Monogram in obtaining motorsports merchandise licenses with drivers and racing teams for plastic model products.

Revell-Monogram, the world leader in plastic model kits, was until recently a business unit of Binney & Smith, maker of Crayola and Liquitex brand products and a subsidiary of Hallmark cards Inc. of Kansas City, Missouri. Revell-Monogram has since been purchased (in 2001) by Alpha International, producers of Gearbox Collectibles. Action Performance is the leader in the design, marketing, and distribution of licensed motorsports merchandise. Its products include a broad range of motorsports-related apparel, souvenirs, diecast car replica collectibles, and other memorabilia.

In August 1998, Action Performance also purchased a controlling percentage of Paul's Model Art, at one time a subsidiary of Unique Toys (UT). The purchase includes the acquisition of Minichamps, Danhausen, Lang, and other brands associated with Paul's Model Art. UT, the parent company retained 20 percent control in the company. UT has since been purchased by Gateway Global, and the brand has been incorporated into their AUTOart and Gate assortments.

Action was also producing Winner's Circle cars for Kenner, a division of Hasbro. They have since taken on the Winner's Circle line themselves and now market them through the Action Racing division.

In 2004, Action Performance expanded its empire even further by purchasing Funline, producer of Muscle Machines, and encompassing the sub-series CARtons, Import Tuners, Jesse James West Coast Chppers, Monster Garage, and others.

In summar, Actin now owns ARC (Action Racing Collectibles), Brookfield Collectors Guild, Castaway, Funline Muscle Machines, Minichamps, RCCA (Racing Collectables Club of America), Revell, and Winner's Circle. Since an entire book can be devoted to just racing collectibles, this book provides only a brief list of a few exceptional Action Performance collectibles.

Action Racing 1:64 Scale

2001 UPS Package car, "Official Express Delivery Company of NASCAR," 1:64 Scale, 31,320 produced. $25-40

Alan Kulwicki #7
- Hooters, 20,000 produced $120-145
- AK Racing, 20,000 produced $85-100
- Army, 10,000 produced $95-110

Dale Earnhardt #3
- Winston Cup Champion, 1:64, 1,000 produced $90-115
- Winston Select Silver blister, 1995 Platinum Promotional $250-275
- Goodwrench PitStop blister pack, 1995 Platinum Promotional $80-95
- Goodwrench in black box, 1997 promotional $80-95
- Goodwrench Plus Fan club, 1998 promotional $90-105
- Goodwrench Action Performance blisterpack, 1999 promotional $50-65
- GM Goodwrench Action Performance blisterpack, 2000 promotional $15-20
- Brickyard exclusive, 7560 produced, 2,000 promotional $50-65
- Dale Jarrett #32 White Rain, 1998 promotional $15-20
- Ernie Irvan #28 Havoline, 10,000 produced $70-85

Jeff Gordon #24
- Dupont, 10,000 produced $25-40
- Winston Cup Champion, 1995 Platinum Promotional $70-85
- Brickyard exclusive 7560 produced, 2,000 promotional $25-30

Action Products

Action Products International Inc. is based in Ocala, Florida. They are not connected with Action Performance or its affiliates, but produce essentially generic toys. The example found is a crude 3¼" space shuttle with pull-back motor. Value is not likely to rise on this novelty toy.

In addition, the Action brand has also been associated with Magic and others, with toys marketed through Rite-Aid stores. They are repackaged models from other manufacturers such as Welly, Motormax, Yat Ming, and Sunnyside.

Space Shuttle $1-2

ADJ
ADJ is an obscure brand presumed to be from France, with just one model documented, as listed in *Schroeder's Collectible Toys Antique to Modern*.

Citroën CX Fire Chief Station Wagon $30-40

Advanced Products Company
Cleveland, Ohio, is birthplace to Advanced Products Company, a farm toy producer that emerged after World War II. Best information places the demise of the company in the early 1960s.

Cockshutt 30 Farm Tractor, 1946, non-steerable, 1:16 ....$250-300
  in original box $575-625
Cockshutt 30 Farm Tractor, 1946, steerable, 1:16 ....$250-300
  in original box $575-625
Cockshutt 40 Farm Tractor, late 1950s, 1:16 ....$400-500
  in original box $650-775
Cockshutt 540 Farm Tractor, 1950s, 1:16 ....$250-300
  in original box 300-350
Cockshutt Farm Wagon, red, 1950s, 1:16 ....$100-150,
  in original box $250-300
Co-Op E-3, 1:16, orange, 1950s $275-325
  in original box $450-500
Co-Op Farm Wagon, orange, 1950s $150-175
  in original box $275-325
Ferguson TO-20 Farm Tractor, late 1940s, 1:12 ....$275-325
  in original box $450-500
New Holland Baler, late 1950s, 1:16 ....$375-425
New Holland Baler, late 1950s, 1:32 ....$300-350

Agat (also see Radon)
Agat is a brand of diecast models that has recently emerged from the reformation of the Radon company of Russia. Reportedly, Agat offers a series of GAZ replicas based on the noted Russian brand of cars and trucks.

AGD
Alex Litovskiy reports of the AGD brand from Russia but doesn't provide any details.

AGM
AGM was a British firm, now out of business, that produced precision 1:43 scale model white metal kits and preassembled models.

1947 DeSoto Suburban hearse $150-200
1947 DeSoto Suburban 4-door sedan, #1 ....$150-200
1947 DeSoto Suburban taxi, #2 ....$150-200

Agritec (also see ROS)
According to Bill Molyneaux, diecast collector and dealer, Agritec of Spain is the producer of the ROS brand of construction and farm diecast models.

Carraro 7700 Reversible Tractor, 1:25, #10309 $20-25
Fiat 80-90 Tractor, 1:32, #301 ....$20-25
Fiat 180-90DT Turbo Tractor, 1:18, #10308 ....$30-40
Fiat-Allis Dozer, 1:32, 6", #22 ....$40-50
Fiat-Allis FD14E Bulldozer, 1:32, #22 ....$25-30
Fiat Allis FD14E Bulldozer, yellow, 1:32, #544 ....$35-45
Fiat-Allis FR130 Wheel Loader, 1:32, #21 ....$30-40
Fiat Allis FR130 Wheel Loader, yellow, 1:32, #522 ....$35-45
Fiat Allis FR130.2 Wheel Loader, orange, 1:32, #216 ....$35-45
Fiat-Allis Wheel Loader, 1:32, 9", #21 ...$40-50
Fiat F2100/F130 Tractor, 1:25, #12 ...$20-25
Fiat Hitachi 200 Excavator, yellow, 1:32, #503 ....$35-45
Fiat Hitachi 200.3 Excavator, orange, 1:32, #209 ....$35-45
Fiat Hitachi Bulldozer, Loader, and Excavator, yellow, 1:32, #384 ....$90-120
Fiat Hitachi Bulldozer, Loader, and Excavator, orange, 1:32, #391 ....$90-120
Fiat Hitachi Compactor Loader, orange, 1:32, #612 ....$35-45
Fiat Hitachi CX500 Crane, orange, 1:32, #575 ....$35-45
Fiat-Hitachi Excavator, 1:32, 12", #20....$50-60
Fiat Hitachi FD175 Turbo Bulldozer, orange, 1:32, #223 ....$35-45
Fiat-Hitachi FH200 Backhoe, 1:32, #20 ....$30-40
Fiat-Laverda 3890 Combine, 1:43, #50302 ....$20-25
Ford New Holland Tractor, blue, 1:25, #117 ....$30-40
Hesston 80-90 Tractor, 1:32, #30302 ..$15-20
Hesston 4700 Baler, 1:25, #60114 ....$15-20
Hurlimann H-G170T Tractor, 1:25, #10256 ....$20-25

Hyundai Robex 290 LC Excavator, yellow, 1:32, #568 ....$35-45
Iseki 530 Tractor, 1:32, #202/#30202 .$20-25
Lamborghini 1706 Tractor, #10255 .....$20-25
Landini 783 Crawler, 1:32, #40505 ....$15-20
Massey Ferguson 1014 Tractor, 1:32, #30401 ....$15-20
Massey Ferguson 194F Tractor, #259 ...$20-25
Massey Ferguson 3050/3090 Tractor, 1:32, #30403 ....$15-20
Merlo All-Terrain Forklift, green, 1:32, #490 ....$50-60
Olimpus Backhoe, #802 ....$30-40
Olimpus Turbo Combine, 1:43, #50303 ....$20-25
Pisten Bully Snow Plow, red, 1:32, #285 .$65-85
Same Galaxy 170 Dual Rear Wheel Tractor, 1:25, #10258 ....$20-25
Same Galaxy 170 Tractor, 1:25, #10257 ....$20-25

Aguti Toys (see Loden Aguti)

AHC (also see Auto Pilen)
Many AHC models were made from dies obtained from the defunct Escuderia Pilen company of Spain, producers of 1:43 and 1:64 scale models known as Pilen or Auto Pilen. While based in the Netherlands, many of AHC's models were made in Spain and later China. AHC is also known as a manufacturer of selected Hess Oil collectibles.

AHC 1:43 Scale Models
Ford Escort Van
  metallic medium blue $15-20
  red $15-20
  silver $15-20
  white $15-20
Mercedes-Benz MB100 Van
  "Bundespost," orange and red $25-30
  "Telefonica," green, blue and white ..$25-30
Nissan Maxima
  dark green $15-20
  dark maroon $15-20
  gold and silver $15-20
  white $15-20
Nissan Micra
  black $15-20
  deep red $15-20
  graphite gray $15-20
  green $15-20
  light aqua blue $15-20
  metallic blue $15-20
  red $15-20
  silver $15-20
  metallic light green, "Car of the Year 1993" on pewter plinth $40-50
Nissan Serena Space Cruiser
  blue $15-20
  metallic dark bronze $15-20
  graphite gray $15-20
  red $15-20

Opel Kadett
"Rijkspolitie," white and orange $25-30
Police, navy blue with strobe lights $15-20

Seat Ibiza 3-Door Hatchback
metallic dark blue $15-20
graphite gray $15-20
metallic green $15-20
red $15-20
silver $15-20
white $15-20

Seat Ibiza 4-Door Hatchback, white $15-20

Seat Toledo GT 4-Door, red $15-20

Suzuki Samurai
blue and white $15-20
cream and black $15-20
green and black $15-20
maroon and white $15-20
red and gray $15-20
silver and white $15-20
yellow and black $15-20

Toyota Celica 4x4 Twin Turbo
cream $15-20
graphite gray $15-20

Toyota MR2, silver $15-20

Vauxhall Astra Van
blue $15-20
dark brown on pewter plinth $30-35
"Q8," blue $15-20

Volvo 440
black $15-20
chrome $32
dark maroon $15-20
light blue $15-20
silver $15-20
white $15-20
"Politie," orange stripes $25-30
"Politie," orange and blue stripes $25-30

Volvo 460
black $15-20
graphite gray $15-20
metallic light blue $15-20
red $15-20
silver $15-20
white $15-20
"Taxi," black and yellow $15-20

Volvo 480ES $30-35

Volvo 850
dark blue $15-20
dark green $15-20
red $15-20
GLT "Polis," white and gray $15-20
T5, dark graphite gray $15-20

Ahi

Ahi toys are 1:80 to 1:90 scale diecast toys produced in Japan in the late 1950s and early 1960s. The line offers an assortment of mostly American cars, but also includes some British and other European cars as well as 1:120 scale Dodge military trucks and some antique autos.

Alfa Romeo Giulietta Sprint, 1:90 ....$15-20

Austin A105, 1:90 ....$15-20
Austin Healey, 1:90 ....$15-20
Buick, 1:90 ....$15-20
Cadillac, 1:90 ....$15-20
Chevrolet Impala, 1:90 ....$15-20
Chrysler, 1:90 ....$15-20
Citroën DS 19, 1:90 ....$15-20
Daimler, 1:90 ....$15-20
DeSoto Diplomat, 1:90 ....$15-20
Dodge, 1:90 ....$15-20
Ferrari 375 Coupe, 1:90 ....$25-30
Ferrari 500 Formula 2, 1:90 ....$25-30
Fiat 1800, 1:90 ....$15-20
Ford, 1:90 ....$15-20
Imperial, 1:90 ....$15-20
International Harvester, 1:90 ....$15-20
Jaguar Mk IX, 1:90 ....$15-20
Jaguar XK150 Roadster, 1:90 ....$15-20
Maserati Racer, 1:90 ....$15-20
Mercedes-Benz 220SE, 1:90 ....$15-20
Mercedes-Benz 300SL Roadster, 1:90 ..$15-20
Mercedes-Benz W 25 Racer, 1:90 ....$15-20
Mercedes-Benz W 196 Racer, 1:90 .....$15-20
Mercedes-Benz RW 196 Racer, 1:90 .$15-20
MG TF Roadster, 1:90 ....$15-20
MGA 1600, 1:90 ....$15-20
Midget Racer, 1:90 ....$15-20
Oldsmobile, 1:90 ....$15-20
Opel Kapitän, 1:90 ....$15-20
Plymouth, 1:90 ....$15-20
Pontiac, 1:90 ....$15-20
Porsche 356A, 1:90 ....$15-20
Rambler, 1:90 ....$15-20
Renault Floride, 1:90 ....$15-20
Rolls-Royce Silver Wraith, 1:90 ....$20
Simca Aronde P 60, 1:90 ....$15-20
Volkswagen 1200, 1:90 ....$20
Volvo Amazon 122 S, 1:90 ....$15-20
Volvo PV 544, 1:90 ....$15-20

Ahi Antique Cars

1902 Ali Coold Frankline, 1:80 ....$10-15
1911 Buick, 1:80 ....$10-15
1903 Cadillac, 1:80 ....$10-15
1904 Darracq, 1:80 ....$10-15
1915 Ford Model T, 1:80 ....$10-15
1904 Oldsmobile, 1:80 ....$10-15
1904 Oldsmobile Truck, 1:80 ....$10-15
1903 Rambler, 1:80 ....$10-15
1909 Stanley Steamer, 1:80 ....$10-15
1907 Vauxhall, 1:80 ....$10-15
1914 Stutz Bearcat, 1:80 ....$10-15

Dodge Military Trucks

Dodge Ambulance, 1:120 ....$10-15
Dodge Barrel Truck, 1:120 ....$10-15
Dodge Cement Mixer, 1:120 ....$10-15
Dodge Covered Truck, 1:120 ....$10-15
Dodge Crane Truck, 1:120 ....$10-15
Dodge Lumber Truck, 1:120 ....$10-15
Dodge Missile carrier, 1:120 ....$10-15
Dodge Radar Truck, 1:120 ....$10-15

Dodge Rocket Launcher, 1:120 ....$10-15
Dodge Searchlight Truck, 1:120 ....$10-15
Dodge Tank carrier, 1:120 ....$10-15
Dodge Truck with Machine Gun, 1:120...$10-15

AHL (see American Highway Legends)

Albedo

Albedo-Forkel GmbH
Postfach 1155
D-91556 Heilsbronn, Germany
Phone: +49 (0) 98 72/89 00
fax +49 (0) 98 72/53 86

Collector Ron Gold sent me an Albedo catalog printed in German and featuring a beautiful assortment of 1:87 scale freight trucks. Previously unknown, Albedo models appear to be precision plastic replicas of contemporary semis with an emphasis on spectacular graphics.

Iveco "Jo Vonlanthen," cat #220 012 ....$30-35
Iveco "Magneti Marelli," cat #220 010 ..$30-35
Iveco Semi Freighter "For Motorsport 30 Years of Formula One Power," cat #220 032 ......$25-30
Man Freight Truck with Trailer "Löwenbräu," cat #800 046 ....$20-25
Man Semi Freighter "Polizei Pferdetransporter," cat #800 047 ....$20-25
Mercedes-Benz Actros Semi Freighter "Hansel & Gretel," cat #600 001 ....$35-40
Mercedes-Benz Actros Semi Freighter "D & W," cat #210 001 ....$25-30
Mercedes-Benz Actros Semi Freighter "Müller Drogerie," cat #210 002 ....$25
Mercedes-Benz Freight Truck "ADAC Prüfdienst," cat #200 377 ....$15-20
Mercedes-Benz SK Freight Truck with Trailer "Bitburger," cat #200 376 ....$25-30
Mercedes-Benz SK Semi Freighter "Oro Di Parma," cat #200 375 ....$20-25
Renault AE Benetton "Bitburger," cat #220 001 ....$45-50
Renault AE Benetton "Drive," cat #220 003 ....$45-50
Renault AE Equipment Transporter "elf F1," cat #220 029 ....$20-25
Renault AE Equipment Transporter "Starbird Satellite Services," cat #220 030 ....$20-25
Renault AE Freight Truck with Trailer "König-Pilsener," cat #700 151 ....$20-25
Renault AE Semi Freighter "elf F1," cat #220 028 ....$20-25
Renault AE Semi Freighter "Lösche," cat #700 150 ....$25-30
Renault AE Semi Freighter "Tishlen Deck Dich," cat #600 005 ....$35-40
Renault AE Semi Freighter "Würth," cat #700 152 ....$20-25
Renault AE SZ "F1 Equipment," cat #220 006 .$30-35
Renault Bus with Trailer "Williams Renault F1," cat #220 027 ....$25-3

Renault Premium Semi Freighter "1 FC Kölsch," cat #710 012 ....$20-25

Renault Premium Semi Freighter "Milka-Ostern 1998," cat #710 016 ....$25-30

Renault Premium Semi Freighter "Prince De Bretagne," cat #710 013 ....$20-25

Renault Premium Semi Freighter "Rotkappchen," cat #600 003 ....$35-40

Renault Premium Semi Freighter "Schneewittchen," cat #600 006 ....$35-40

Renault Premium Semi Tank Container "P&O Tankmasters," cat #710 014 ....$20-25

Scania Container Semi "Hyundai," cat #111 126 ....$20-25

Scania Semi Freighter "Jordan," cat #220 033 .$25-30

Volvo FH Freight Truck with Trailer "Wernesgrüner Pils", cat #320 029 ....$25-30

Volvo FH Semi Freighter "Frau Holle," cat #600 002 ....$35-40

Volvo FH Semi Freighter "Frolic," cat #320 033 ....$20-25

Volvo FH Semi Freighter "Milka-Ostern 1998," cat #320 032 ....$25-30

Volvo FH Semi Freighter "SpEdition Vendel," cat #320 029 ....$20-25

Volvo FH Semi Freighter "Wernesgrüner Pils," cat #320 028 ....$25-30

Volvo XL Semi Freighter "750 Jahre Kölner Dom," cat #600 007 ....$25-30

Volvo XL Semi Freighter "Aschenputtel," cat #600 004 ....$35-40

Volvo XL Semi Freighter "Goodyear Racing," cat #220 031 ....$25-30

Volvo XL Semi Freighter "Interblumex," cat #320 026 ....$35-40

Volvo XL Semi Freighter "Ouzo 12," cat #320 027 ....$25-30

Volvo XL Semi Tractor "750 Jahre Kölner Dom," cat #320 031 ....$15-20

Albedo German Democratic Republic (DDR) Banknote Edition

Volvo F12 Freight Truck "20 Mark," cat #600 010 ....$20-25

Volvo F12 Freight Truck "50 Mark," cat #600 011 ....$20-25

Volvo F12 Freight Truck "100 Mark," cat #600 012 ....$20-25

Volvo F88 Freight Truck "5 Mark," cat #600 008 ....$20-25

Volvo F89 Freight Truck "10 Mark," cat #600 009 ....$20-25

Alezan

Alezan of France is a producer of high-qualtiy 1:43 scale resin kits. In addition, Alezan also produced a white metal Pantera in kit form.

Alezan 1:43 Scale Resin Kits

Alfa Romeo Evoluzion, dark red $80-110

1990 Chevrolet Corvette CERV3 Coupe concept car, #167 ....$90-120

1987 Chrysler Lebaron hardtop, #108 .$90-120

1987 Chrysler Lebaron Indianapolis 500 pace car, convertible, top down, #139 ...$90-120

1987 Chrysler Lebaron convertible, top down, #142 ....$90-120

1987 Chrysler Maserati convertible, top down .$90-120

1991 Chrysler 300 concept car, #138 ..$90-120

1986 Dodge Daytona, #55 ....$90-120

1985 Jeep Cherokee, #3 ....$90-120

1986 Pontiac Firebird convertible, Straman Design, top down, #25 ....$90-120

Alezan 1:43 Scale White Metal Kits

DeTomaso Pantera $50-80

ALF

Alex Litovskiy reports of the ALF brand from Ukraine but doesn't provide any details.

ALJ

ALJ is an obscure US company that produced 1:43 scale diecast vehicles in the 1950s.

Late 1950s Ford 2-door Convertible with top down, white and red $12-16

Delahaye 2-Door Roadster, metallic green $12-16

Early 1950s Buick 2-Door Roadster, cream $12-16

Late 1950s Ford 2-Door Convertible with top up, red and gray $12-16

Early 1950s Buick 2-Door Convertible with top up, pink $12-16

All-American

All-American of Los Angeles, California, is known to have produced just one model, in 1949.

All-American Hot-Rod, 9" long $450-500

All American Toy Company

Patrick Russell, president
540 Lancaster SE
Salem OR 97301
503-399-8609 Mon – Fri 9–6 Pacific

Clay Steinke, founder of the All American Toy Company of Salem, Oregon, produced a total of 26,000 1:12 scale cast metal toy trucks from its beginnings in 1948 to 1955. Its assortment of large scale toy trucks, distinctive for their "air horn steering," includes the popular Timber Toter log truck, popular with children whose families worked in the Pacific Northwest logging industry. They originally sold for around $20, considered a high price for toys sold back in the 1950s. Today's values are in the hundreds, even thousands of dollars. Model numbers appeared on the box only, not on the model.

All American Originals

Play-Dozer, 9" long $1,250-1,500

Cattle Liner, 38" long, C-5 ....$1,750-2,000

Cargo Liner, 38" long, CL-8 ....$1,250-1,750

Dyna-Dump, 20" long, early sandcast cab, D-3 ....$1,000-1,500

Dyna-Dump, 20" long, diecast cab, D-3 ....$500-750

Hay-Grain-Feed-Seed with Trailer ..$1,250-1,500

Hay-Grain-Feed-Seed without Trailer ..$750-1,000

Heavy Hauler, 38" long, HH-9 ....$900-1,200

Midget Skagit Log Loader, 18" long, MS $350-500

Play-Loader, 11" long, HD-6 ....$450-600

Scoop-A-Veyor, 16" long, S-1 ....$450-600

Timber Toter, 38" long, early sandcast cab, L-2 ....$1,000-1,500

Timber Toter, 38" long, diecast cab, L-2 ....$500-750

Timber Toter Jr. with Trailer, 20" long, LJ-4 ....$750-1,000

All American New Models

After a false restart in 1990, the All American Toy Company is back in business in its home town of Salem, Oregon, purchased lock, stock, and barrel in 1992 by Patrick Russell, with all the original tooling intact. The company is now reproducing some of those classic models as well as creating new classics. Here are some of the new models. As you will note, current secondary market values are already on the rise.

Founder's Edition Timber Toter, 1992 replica (original retail $595) $1,000-1,250

"Rocky" Galion Dump Truck, 1995 Dyna-Dump replica, maroon cab, silver box, 113 made (original retail $595)................$750-1,000

white cab, blue box ,limited to 112 (original retail $595)...........................$750-1,000

The Heavy Hauler II

double axle "lowboy" trailer (original retail $595) $750-1,000

triple axle "lowboy" trailer (original retail $695) $750-1,000

Motorcycle Hauler, only 100 made (original retail $449) $650-800

Custom Classic Motorcycle for Motorcycle
   Hauler $65-80
1948 Indian Chief, maroon or yellow $75-90

Kenworth Gonzalez-Sanchez Cigar
Hauler ($995 retail).....................$1,000-1,250

Water Toter ($995 retail) $1,000-1,250

Allied

These plastic toys were produced in Corona, New York. For toys that sold for a dime in the 1940s and 1950s, these are remarkably high priced in today's market. Allied toys are easy to identify since they are usually numbered and marked with the brand name logo on the underside or inside of each toy.

Cement Mixer, #197, 4" $30-45
Delivery Service Truck $50-75
Dump Truck, #174, 5½" $35-50
Dump Truck, #191, 4½" $20-25
Emergency Truck, #129, 7" $45-60
Furniture Moving Van with ten pieces of furniture,
   #208, 5½" $45-60
Old Fashioned Car, #218, 4½" $25-40
Racer, #130, 4⅝" $25-40
Stake Truck, 4½ $20-25
Stake Truck with eight farm animals and removable
   racks, #193, 9½" $60-75
Station Wagon, 3½" $15-20
Taxi, 3½" $15-20
Van, 6" $20-25
Wrecker, 4⅜" $25-30
Auto Sales and Station with five
   vehicles $120-150

All-Nu

Crude pot metal slush mold (lead or lead alloy) military toys typify this brand from the 1920-1930s, but the brand also encompasses a few cardboard vehicles. All are marked with "Made in USA" and are often confused with Barclay and other brands.

All-Nu Pot Metal Vehicles
Field Kitchen, 2½" $50-75
Searchlight, 2¾" $50-75
Sound Detector, 2¾" $50-75
Tank, 3" $50-75

All-Nu Cardboard Vehicles
Ambulance, #154 ....$5-10
Cannon, #151 ....$5-10
Jeep, #150 ....$5-10
Tank, #153 ....$5-10
Troop carrier, #155 ....$5-10
Wheeled Anti-Aircraft Gun, #152 ....$5-10

Alloy Forms, Inc.

Alloy Forms models are 1:87 scale kits intended for use with HO gauge train sets. Kits consist of unpainted white metal detail parts. Truck kits also include styrene, brass, and rubber parts.

Alloy Forms Automobiles
1949 Buick Roadmaster $7-10
1953 Buick Skylark Convertible with Continental
   Package $7-10
1959 Cadillac Eldorado Convertible $7-10
1955 Cadillac Fleetwood $7-10
1950 Chevrolet 4-Door Fastback $7-10
1953 Chevrolet Bel-Air $7-10
1955 Chevrolet Bel-Air 2-Door $7-10
1957 Chevrolet Bel-Air Sport Coupe $8-10
1953 Chevrolet Corvette $7-10
1959 Chevrolet El Camino $7-10
1959 Chevrolet Impala Convertible $7-10
1955 Chevrolet Nomad Wagon $7-10
1949 DeSoto 4-Door $7-10
1949 Ford Club Coupe with Engine $8-10
1948 Ford Convertible $8-10
1956 Ford Thunderbird $7-10
1949 Hudson 4-Door $7-10
1949 Mercury 2-Door $7-10
1948 Studebaker Starline $8-10
Plymouth Coupe $8-10
Plymouth Coupe without Engine $8-10

Alloy Forms Trucks
Autocar Block Truck $20-25
1955 Chevrolet 2-Ton Stake Truck $10-15
Ford LTS Block Truck $20-25
1951 Ford Panel Delivery Truck $8-10
1956 Ford Pickup $8-10

1956 Ford Pickup with Camper $10-15
1956 Ford Pickup with Rack $10-15
1954 Mack B-42 Flatbed Truck $18–20
Mack B-42 3-Axle Block Truck $20-25
Mack B-61 2-Axle Refrigerated Box
   Truck $20-25
Mack BQ 3-Axle Box Truck $20-25
Mack BQ 3-Axle Stake Truck $18–20
Mack CJ COE 3-Axle Stake Truck $18–20

Alloy Forms Dump Trucks & Trailers
(Length indicated refers to the original length of the trailer on which the miniature replica is based.)
Autocar with 12' Dump Box $20-25
Autocar with 22' Dump Trailer $25-30
Autocar with Large Dumper $25-30
Autocar Special Dump Truck $35-37
Diamond REO with 7' Dump Bed $20-25
Diamond REO with 11' Dump Bed $20-25
Diamond REO with 22' Dump Trailer $20-25
Ford LNT 2-Axle with 7' Dump Trailer $20-25
Ford LNT 3-Axle with 7' Heil Dump
   Body $20-25
Ford LNT 3-Axle with 30' 3-Axle Dump
   Trailer $35-37
Ford LNT Coal/Gravel with Tandem Axle Dump
   Trailer $25-30
Ford LTS with 12' Heil Dump Bed $20-25
Ford LTS with Dump Body $25-30
Ford LTS with 22' Dump Trailer $25-30
GMC Astro with 22' Dump Trailer $25-30
Mack B-61 Dump Truck $25-30
Mack B-61 2-Axle Dump Truck $20-25
Mack B-61 3-Axle Dump Truck $20-25
Mack B-71 with 30' 3-Axle Dump
   Trailer $35-37
Mack B-71 20' Coal/Gravel with Tandem Axle
   Dump Trailer $25-30
Mack Universal Chassis Dump Truck $20-25
22' 2-Axle Dump Trailer $18–20
30' 3-Axle Dump Trailer $25-30

Alloy Forms Semi-Tractor/Trailers
(Length indicated refers to the original length of the trailer on which the miniature replica is based.)
Autocar Chassis $15-20
Autocar with Log Trailer $20-25
Autocar with 45' "Lowboy" Flatbed Trailer ..$30-35
Diamond REO BBC Refrigerated $20-25
Diamond REO Delivery $20-25
Diamond REO Universal Chassis $15-20
Diamond REO with 40' Flatbed Trailer $20-25
Ford LNT Cab with Universal Chassis $15-20
Ford LNT 2-Axle with Refrigerated Body ...$20-25
Ford LNT 3-Axle $20-25
Ford LTS with Universal Chassis $15-20

GMC Astro 2-Axle $15-20
GMC Astro 2-Axle with 40' "Lowboy" 16-Wheel
   Flatbed Trailer $30-35
GMC Astro 3-Axle with Rectangular Gas
   Tanks $15-20
GMC Astro Short Cab 2-Axle $15-20
GMC Astro Short Cab 3-Axle $15-20
GMC Astro Short Cab with 16' body $20-25
GMC Astro Sleeper $15-20
Mack B-61 Tank 2-Axle $20-25
Mack B-61 Universal Chassis $15-20
Mack B-61 with 16' Body $20-25
Mack B-61 with Logging Trailer $30-35
Mack B-70 with Universal Chassis $15-20
Mack B-71 with Heavy Duty Flatbed
   Trailer $20-25
Mack CF/Pierce $30-35
Mack CF with Universal Chassis $20-25
Mack CF 4-Door $20-25
Mack DM-800 Offset Cab with Universal
   Chassis $15-20
30' Logging Trailer $20-25
37' Depressed Center Flatbed Trailer $20-25
45' 16-Wheel "Lowboy" Trailer $20-25

Alloy Forms Emergency Equipment
Diamond REO Pierce Tanker $25-30
Ford LNT Fire Pumper $25-30
Ford LS Fire Pumper $25-30
Mack B-61 2-Axle Fire Pumper $30-35
Mack B-61 Fire Tanker $20-25
Mack B-61 Open Fire Truck $25-30
Mack CF NYC Fire Pumper $30-35
Pierce Ford LN Pumper $25-30
Pierce Ford LS Pumper $25-30

Alloy Forms Miscellaneous
1947 Clark Fork Lift $5-10

Alterscale
Alterscale Miniature Outboards
Karl E. Beisel
1965 Fountainbrook Ct.
Woodbridge, VA 22192
phone: 703-490-6649
e-mail: K2beisel@comcast.net
websites: www.alterscale.com
www.toyoutboards.com

It seems there is (and apparently has been for over thirty years) a select group of collectors of scale model outboard boat motors. A book has been written about them, and there are a few websites devoted to them. Two manufacturers come to light: K & O brand models apparently manufactured diecast and plastic boat motors from 1952

to 1962. Alterscale is the more recent brand to produce such models. Alterscale now produces several precision 1:8 scale models of Evinrude, Honda, and Johnson outboards. Retail price is around $200 each.

You may consider purchasing *Toy Outboard Motors* by Jack Browning ....$22.95, 150 pages of compiled articles (by Jack Browning) with photos. Available only direct: Jack Browning, 214 16th Street, Roanoke, VA 24017 (phone 540-982-1253). This is the only comprehensive work in existence on this subject. It covers principally the K&O motors (in detail) but touches on many other toy outboards. It includes a list of toy outboard collectors with names and addresses. Jack Browning is one of the world's premier collectors of toy outboards.

AMA
AMA was a brand of 1:43 scale white metal kits made in Great Britain. The company is now out of business.

1935 Auburn Boattail Speedster, top
   down $120-150
1935 Auburn Boattail Speedster, top
   up $120-150
1966 Ford GT Mk IV $120-150

Amar Toy
Amar Toy is a brand of tinplate toy cars produced in Delhi, India. One example of this brand was found representing a prototypical late 1940s American car called "Minister Delux."

Minister Delux (1954 Buick), tinplate, approximately 1:24 scale $45-70

American Automobile Miniatures
American Automobile Miniatures, now out of business, manufactured precision 1:43 scale white metal models.

1960 Chevrolet Impala 2-door
   hardtop $300-450

1937 Cord 812 Phaeton $300-450
1934 Packard Special Model 1106 Sport Coupe
   with rear quarter windows, #01 ..$300-450
1934 Packard Special Model 1106 Sport Coupe
   without rear quarter windows, #02 ..$300-450

American Classic (see Golden Wheel)

American Highway Legends (also see Hartoy)
Hartoy produces a series of 1:64 scale trucks of 1940s and 1950s vintage called American Highway Legends that have become very popular with collectors. Models retail for $10 to $30 each, and sometimes bring higher prices at toy shows and from specialty dealers. The series has now been discontinued in lieu of Hartoy's introduction of a new series of commercial trucks called Precision Engineered Models (PEM). Hartoy is currently located in Lake Worth, Florida.

"Atlas Van Lines," Ford C-Series with 32' Van Trailer,
   L57402 ....$20-25
"Bitter-Sweet," Ford F-5 Straight Chassis,
   H05010 ....$20-25
"Breyer's," Box Truck $18–24
"Coca-Cola," Box Van $18–24
"Coca-Cola," Ford Tractor Trailer $18–24
"Coca-Cola," Mack City Delivery Truck ..$18–24
"Coca-Cola," Mack Stake Truck $18–24
"Eckerd Drug," Ford F-7 with 32' Van Trailer,
   L55403 ....$20-25
"Evinrude," Box Truck $18–24
"Evinrude," Mack BM Straight Chassis,
   L01014 ....$20-25
"Ford Parts," Ford Tractor Trailer $18–24
"Fram Filters," Mack Covered Truck $18–24
"Hershey's," Mack BM 22' Bullnose Truck and
   Trailer, H51100 ....$20-25
"Hershey's Syrup" 32' Tank Trailer,
   H55300 ....$20-25
"Kelly Springfield," GMC Box Truck $18–24
"Maxwell House," Ford F-7 22' Bullnose Truck and
   Trailer, L55103 ....$20-25
"Mobil," GMC Tanker Truck $18–24
"Mr. Goodbar," GMC T-70 Straight Chassis,
   H04050 ....$20-25
"Pennsylvania Railroad," Ford F-7 22' Bullnose
   Truck and Trailer, L55104 ....$20-25
"Pennzoil," Peterbilt Tanker Truck $18–24
"Ray-O-Vac," Mack Stake Truck $18–24
"Reese's," Mack CJ 22' Bullnose Truck and Trailer,
   H52100 ....$20-25
"Royal Oak," Mack CJ Straight Chassis,
   L02042 ....$20-25

"Scott Paper," Mack Tandem Trailer $18–24
"Shell Fuel Oil," Tractor Trailer $18–24
"Timken," Mack Covered Stake Truck $18–24
"Wrigley's," Mack Box Truck $18–24

The Great American Brewery Collection from American Highway Legends

"Dixie Beer," Dixie Brewing Co., Peterbilt 260 Tandem Trailer Truck $30–45

"Hamm's Beer," Pabst Brewing Co., Ford F-7 Freight Truck $30–45

"Jax Beer," Jackson (Pearl) Brewing Co., GMC T-70 Stake Truck $20–25

"Olympia Beer," Olympia (Pabst) Brewing Co., GMC T-70 Covered Truck $20–25

"Pearl Lager Beer," Pearl Brewing Co., Ford F-5 Box Truck $20-25

"Point Special Beer," Stevens Point Beverage Co., Ford F-5 Truck $20-25

American Limited

American Limited models represent precise replica trailer and chassis kits in HO gauge. Collector value is not considered unless model is unassembled and intact in its original box. The exception is when they are assembled and finished so well as to enhance their value rather than decrease it. Models retail for $7-13 each, with component parts available starting at $3.

American National

Pedal cars and pressed steel trucks of exceptional quality were produced during the 1920s and 1930s by American National of Toledo, Ohio. The company was founded by brothers William, Walter, and Harry Diemer around 1894. Since several books are devoted to pedal cars, this book focuses on their trucks, impressive in size, detail, durability, and realism.

American Railway Express Truck, 27" ..$2,000-2,500
Chemical Fire Truck, 28" $3,500-5,000
Circus Truck, 27" $1,500-2,000
Coal Truck $3,000-4,500
Dump Truck, 28" $1,500-2,000
Mack Army Truck, 26½" $1,500-2,000
Moving Van, 28" $1,500-2,000
Open Bed Truck, 29" $2,750-3,750
Richfield Gasoline Truck, 27" $2,400-3,200
Tanker Truck $2,750-3,750

American Precision Models (APM)

American Precision Models
P.O. Box 190
Buffalo, NY 14225 USA
fax: 716-634-7769

e-mail: info@modelbuses
website: www.modelbuses.com

American Precision Models (APM) is a leading manufacturer of injection molded HO scale model buses based on American prototypes. Products are available as undecorated kits, painted and assembled, or custom decorated. APM also handles bus models by Herpa, Wiking, Praline, and Busch.

Flexible
    unassembled, 39013-0 ....$10-12
    blue, 39013-1 ....$15-18
    red, 39013-2 ....$15-18
    green, 39013-3 ....$15-18
    orange, 39013-4 ....$15-18
    maroon, 39013-5 ....$15-18
    Flxible Visicoach
    unpainted kit, AM001 ....$17-20
    preassembled in five colors, AM002 ..$22-25
GM
    North Olmsted, SP-100 ....$25-30
    Cleveland Transit, SP-101 ....$25-30
    Toronto #1960, SP-102 ....$25-30
    Toronto #1963, SP-103 ....$25-30
    NJ Public Service #329, SP-104 ......$25-30
    NJ Public Service #347, SP-105 ......$25-30
GM 4509 Old look coach
    kit, AM007 ....$17-22
    preassembled in four colors, AM007 ...$22-25
GM Transit
    unassembled, 39000-0 ....$12-15
    blue, 39000-1 ....$16-20
    red, 39000-2 ....$16-20
    green, 39000-3 ....$16-20
    orange, 39000-4 ....$16-20
    decal set, 39000-99 ....$3-4
1951 Visicoach American Bus, 1:87 scale
    blue $16-20
    green $16-20
    orange $16-20
    red $16-20

Ampersand

The release of a 1:43 scale model of Arie Luyendyk's 1990 Indy winning Lola T-90 punctuates the 1997 return of Ampersand resin cast kits. Previous issues of Indy racers were marketed a few years earlier.

Lola T-90 Arie Luyendyk, Domino's Pizza, 1990
    Indy 500 winner kit $60-80
    built $95-125

AMR – Century (also see Andre-Marie Ruf)

AMR models are hand-built white metal kits reportedly produced by Andre Marie Ruf, a notable maker of hand-built models from France. The first AMR-produced replica was a Renault R8 Gordini.

AMR Models
Fiat Abarth 1300, limited edition, red ..$375-425
Mercedes-Benz 500 SCL, off white $95-120
Morgan 2+2, white $495-540
Renault Alpine, limited edition, red $250-275
Renault R8 Gordini $600-650

Century models are a less expensive assortment of models from AMR. A considerable assortment of these 1:43 scale white metal models are currently available.

AMR Century Models
1986 Chevrolet Corvette Convertible, top down, #4 ....$75-90
1989 Ferrari 348 GTB, #19 ....$115-130
1966 Ford Mustang, #6 ....$100-120
1966 Ford Mustang Convertible, #16 ....$75-90
1965 Lincoln Continental Convertible, #14 ....$100-120
1948 Lincoln Loewy, #30 ....$100-120
1948 Lincoln Mk 1 Loewy/Derham, #3013 ....$115-130
1989 Mazda MX5 Miata, #22 ....$100-120
1987 Mercedes-Benz 300CE, #8 ....$75-90
1988 Porsche 911 Speedster, #10 ...$100-120
1988 Porsche 911 Speedster Racer, #3010 ....$100-120
Porsche 917/920 #23 Pink Pig, pork cuts labeled in German, #445 ....$90-105
1989 Porsche Carrera 4, #18 ....$100-120
Porsche Turbo Carrera, Martini / LeMans #22, silver, #135 ....$90-105
1949 Volkswagen Beetle Split Window, #3 ..$75-90
1949 Volkswagen Beetle 1200 Convertible, #3014 ....$115-130
1949 Volkswagen Beetle (only 250 made), chrome, #S3002 ....$100-120
1950 Volkswagen Beetle Hebmueller (only 250 made), chrome, #S3003 ....$100-120
1950 Volkswagen Beetle Hebmueller Convertible, #9 ....$75-90
1950 Volkswagen Beetle Hebmueller Convertible, #901/902 ....$100-120
1950 Volkswagen Beetle Krankenwagen, white, #S3001 ....$100-120
1951 Volkswagen Beetle Convertible, #15 ..$75-90
1959 Volkswagen Karmann Ghia Coupe, #12 ....$75-90
1959 Volkswagen Karmann Ghia Coupe, chrome, #3004 ....$115-130

1959 Volkswagen Karmann Ghia Convertible, #13 ....$90-105
1959 Volkswagen Karmann Ghia Convertible, chrome, #3005 ....$115-130
1986 Volvo 480 ES, #5 ....$75-90
1986 Volvo 480 Cabriolet, #24 ....$100-120

AMT Pups (also see Mego Jet Wheels, Jets, and Tuffy)
AMT, originally known as the Aluminum Model Toy Co. when it was founded in 1947, is now known mostly for its plastic model kits. But for a short time around 1967, they produced an inexpensive series of diecast toys called "Pups," 1:64 scale boxed toy cars made in Hong Kong. AMT's Pups were originally intended to compete with Corgi/Husky models and Matchbox in the small-scale diecast market. Their plans were dealt a crushing blow when Hot Wheels arrived in 1968, quickly dominating the US market and wiping out the competition.

Upon realizing that their Pups weren't going to be able to compete, AMT sold the castings to Mego. In turn, Mego reissued them as Mego Jet Wheels, Jets, Tuffy, and Super Speedy, adding more castings to the line before ultimately discontinuing the whole effort by the late 1970s.

AMT Pups
1967 Chevrolet Camaro $45-60
1968 Dodge Charger $45-60
1968 Ford Mustang GT $45-60
1967 Mercury Cougar $45-60

Andre-Marie Ruf (also see AMR)
Sarl Andre-Marie Ruf
B. P. 20 - Route de Violès
84850 - Camaret Sur Aygues, France
Tel: 33 (0) 4 90 37 27 27
Fax: 33 (0) 4 90 37 23 56

Besides models produced under the AMR brand, Andre-Marie Ruf produces 1:43 scale white metal model kits under his own signature brand.

Cadillac Cabriolet DeVille 1967, AMR037K $70-80
Corvette C5R Le Mans 2000, AMR040AK ..$55-65
Ferrari 250 GT 1957
  ch. 0677 1st Place Tour de France 1957, 1st Reims 58, AMR035K $55-65
  ch. 0607 Tour de France 1957, AMR035AK $55-65
Ferrari 250 GTO 1962
  civilian, AMR031AK $55-65
  Tour de France 1964 #175, AMR031BK $55-65

Targa Florio 1962 #86, AMR031CK $55-65
Rallye du Touquet 1965, AMR031DK $55-65
Nürburgring 1965, AMR031EK $55-65
Sebring 1963, AMR031FK $55-65
Targa Florio 1964 #112, AMR031GK $55-65
Ferrari 250 LWB "Interim" Le Mans 1959 #18, 20, AMR025A .$55-65
Tour de France 1959 #164, AMR025B $55-65
Ferrari 290 Mille Miglia 1956 #548 – Eugenio Castellotti, AMR041K $55-65
Ferrari 365 California 1966/67 avec roues "fil" (series limited to 250), AMR003A $55-65
Ferrari 512S LM 1970
  FILIPINETTI #14 & 15, AMR030K $55-65
  SEFAC #s 6, 7 & 8, AMR030AK $55-65
  NART #11, AMR030BK $55-65
  SEFAC #5, AMR030CK $55-65
  FRANCORCHAMPS #12, AMR030DK $55-65
  NART #10, AMR030EK $55-65
  FILIPINETTI #16, AMR030FK $55-65
Ferrari 512S Spa 70 #20, AMR036K ...$55-65
Ferrari Berlinetta Fantuzzi Spyder 1966, AMR038K $55-65
Ferrari Berlinetta Fantuzzi Targa 1965, AMR034K $55-65
Ferrari Pininfarina 1980, AMR042K $55-65

Anguplas
Made in Spain, Anguplas Mini cars are small-scale plastic replicas of popular cars of the 1960s produced in the same era. Mostly produced in 1:86 scale, a few were made to 1:43 scale. They feature a relatively accurate plastic body on a diecast chassis with separate plastic tires on metal hubs. Typical of plastic models, fatigue tends to deform the bodies of the vehicles over the years, making perfect specimens rare. Original price for these models was 25-39 cents each.

Cadillac Fleetwood, #86, 1:86 ....$10-15

Ford Comet, #89, 1:86 ....$10-15

Ford Edsel Convertible, #7, 1:86 ....$10-15

Ford Falcon, #56, 1:86 ....$10-15

Jaguar Mark Nine, #76, 1:86 ....$10-15

Jeep Wagon, #61, 1:86 ....$10-15

Karmann Ghia, #83, 1:86 ....$10-15

Mercedes-Benz Microbus, #51, 1:86 .$10-15

1960 Studebaker Lark, #47, 1:86 ....$10-15

Studebaker Hawk, #92, 1:86 ....$10-15

Volkswagen Beetle, #38, 1:86 ....$10-15

Volvo Sport, #99, 1:86 ....$10-15

Anker

Anker 1:25 scale models are made in Germany.

Alfa Romeo 1300 ....$20-25
Audi 100 ....$20-25
Barkas 153 Van $20-25
Jaguar XJS $20-25
Renault Rodeo Jeep $20-25

Anso (see Anson)

Anson

Anson began their operations from Hong Kong in 1992. Because of the Anson logo with a displaced "N," some collectors have misread the name as "Anso." Ansons are larger scale limited edition diecast models made in China. In 2002, Anson went out of business, and many of their dies were sold to a new company called Signature Models.

Anson, 1:18 scale, except where indicated

2002 BMW, red, #30386 ....$25-40
BMW X5, #30385 ....$25-40
1992 Bugatti EB110, 1:18, #30303
   red $25-40
   blue $25-40
   metallic silver $25-40
1953 Cadillac Eldorado Convertible, white,
   #30371 ....$25-40
1953 Cadillac Eldorado Soft Top, red,
   #30372 ....$25-40
1973 Cadillac Eldorado Convertible, #30387
   red $25-40

bronze $25-40
1973 Cadillac Eldorado Hardtop, black,
   #30357 ....$25-40
1973 Cadillac Eldorado Indy Pace Car,
   #30355 ....$25-40
2002 Cadillac Escalade, #30392 ....$25-40
1946 Cadillac Series 62 Hardtop, 1:18, #30345
   ivory $25-40
   black $25-40
1947 Cadillac Series 62 Convertible, 1:18, #30335
   ivory $25-40
   black $25-40
1998 Cadillac Seville, 1:18, #30337
   black $25-40
   silver $25-40
   dark blue $25-40
1932 Cadillac V16 Sport Phaeton, #30383
   black and silver $25-40
   cream and burgundy $25-40
2000 Chevrolet Silverado Pick Up,
   #30394 ....$25-40
1997 Dodge "Copperhead" Concept Car,
   metallic orange, 1:18, #30333 ....$25-40
Dodge Ram 3500 Dually Pick Up, #30319 ..$25-40
Dodge Ram Dump Truck, #30381 ....$25-40
Dodge Ram Stake Truck, #30382 ....$25-40
Dodge Viper RT/10, #30318
   yellow $25-40

black $25-40
Ferrari 308 GTS, Ferrari, 1:18, #30336
  red $25-40
  yellow $25-40
Ferrari 328 GTS, Ferrari, 1:18, #30308
  red $25-40
  yellow $25-40
Ferrari Dino 246 GT, red or yellow, 1:18, #30301 ....$25-40
Ferrari F550 Maranello, 1:18, #30323
  red $25-40
  yellow $25-40
1963 Ford Thunderbird Hardtop, 1:18, #30344
  Rangoon Red $25-40
  Silver Mink $25-40
1963 Ford Thunderbird Roadster, 1:18, #30334
  Rangoon Red $25-40
  Silver Mink $25-40
2000 GMC Sierra Pick Up, #30391 ....$25-40
1969 Lamborghini Miura, available in several colors, 1:18, #30302 ....$25-40
Lotus Caterham Super 7, 1:18, #30317
  metallic red $25-40
  green $25-40
1968 Mercedes-Benz 280SL Pagoda, #30389 ....$25-40
2000 Mercedes-Benz C-Class, #30390 ...$25-40
Mercedes-Benz CLK, 1:18, #30330
  silver $25-40
  quartz blue $25-40
Mercedes-Benz CLK AMG
  dark blue, #30343 ....$25-40
  Safety Car, #30369 ....$25-40
Mercedes-Benz CLK Convertible, 1:18
  imperial red, #30338 ....$25-40
  silver, #30338 ....$25-40
  silver, #30363 ....$25-40
Mercedes-Benz E-Class Station Wagon, 1:18
  silver, #30328 ....$25-40
  dark blue, #30328 ....$25-40
  Polizei, #30362 ....$25-40
  Service Car, #30370 ....$25-40

1957 Plymouth Fury, cream **$25-40**

Plymouth Prowler
  yellow with top up, 1:18, #30331 ....$25-40
  Hot Rod "Flame" model, #30366 .....$25-40
  Hot Rod "Speed" model, #30367 ....$25-40

1992 Porsche 911 Carrera 2 Targa, 1:18, #30305
  white $25-40
  red $25-40
  purple $25-40
  green $25-40
Porsche 911 Carrera 4 Cabriolet, roof raises and lowers, 1:18, #30306
  silver $25-40
  red $25-40
1992 Porsche 911 Carrera 4 Cabriolet, 1:18, #30309
  red $25-40
  yellow $25-40
  mint green $25-40
  silver $25-40
  dark green $25-40
  black $25-40
Porsche 911 GT1 1996 Version, white with "Mobil" tempo accents, 1:18, #30322 ....$25-40
Porsche 911 GT1 Street Version, 1:18, #30329
  silver $25-40
  white $25-40
Porsche 911 GT2 Rally, 1:18
  Stadler Motorsport, #30325 ....$25-40
  ROHR Motorsport, #30326 ....$25-40
  Team Taisan, #30327 ....$25-40
  Super Cup, #30332 ....$25-40
Porsche 911 GT2 Street Version, 1:18, #30321
  yellow $25-40
  silver $25-40
Porsche 911 Turbo Polizei, 1:18, #30360 ....$25-40
Porsche 911 Twin Turbo, 1:18, #30320
  red $25-40
  black $25-40
Porsche Carrera 4 Cabriolet with top down, 1:14, #30313 ....$95
Porsche GTI 1997 Version, white with "Warsteiner," 1:18, #30339 ....$25-40
Renault Maxi Megane Rally
  "DIAC" France, #30347 ....$25-40
  "GB" UK, #30348 ....$25-40
  "Espagne" Spain, #30349 ....$25-40
  Belgium, #30377 ....$25-40
  Italy, #30379 ....$25-40
Renault Megane Coupe, yellow, #30376 ....$25-40
Renault Megane Cabriolet, #30342
  red $25-40
  yellow $25-40
Renault Spider
  Aeroscreen version, #30346 ....$25-40
  Aeroscreen version, #30388 ....$25-40
  Street version, #30350 ....$25-40

"Kicker" Racing, #30352 ....$25-40
"Cobra" Racing, #30353 ....$25-40
Renault Twingo, 1:18, #30341
  red $25-40
  blue $25-40
  dark green $25-40
Saab 900 Turbo Cabriolet, #30307
  red $25-40
  dark gray $25-40
1957 Studebaker Golden Hawk, metallic gold, #30384 ....$25-40

Anson 1:10 Scale Motorcycles
BMW K1200RS, yellow, 1:10, #80802 ....$25-40
Ducati 916, red, 1:10, #80801 ....$25-40

Anson 1:43 Scale Models
BMW X5, #80808 ....$8-12
2002 Cadillac Escalade, #80809 ....$8-12
2000 Chevrolet Silverado, #80806 ....$8-12
Ford Excursion, #80805 ....$8-12
Ford Expedition, #80804 ....$8-12
Ford F150 Lightning Pick Up, #80801 ......$8-12
Ford F350 Supercab Pick Up, #80802 ....$8-12
2000 GMC Sierra, #80807 ....$8-12
Lincoln Navigator, #80803 ....$8-12

Antex
Only a single model has so far been found to represent this brand.

Porsche 944, 1:43 ....$5

APM (see American Precision Models)

Aquli (See Loden Aguti)

A.R.
A.R. is among the earliest of French manufacturers of miniature vehicles, dating back to the 1920s. A.R. produced toys in a variety of materials, including tinplate, cast iron, lead, and zinc alloy.

Bluebird Record Car, 5" $100-125
Peugeot Andreau Coupe $100-125
Peugeot Andreau Limousine $100-125
Peugeot 301 Mail Truck, 3⅜" $100-125
Renault Paris Bus, 3⅞" $100-125

AR (see Auto Replicas)

Arbur
Among the many more prominent British toy

companies was a comparatively obscure one known as Arbur Products. The roughly 1:43 scale toys, manufactured between 1948 and 1952, were based on Dinky Toys and others.

Dennis Fire Truck, 1:55	$55-65
MG Record Car, 1:43	$45-55
Scammell Tractor Trailer, 1:55	$45-55
Sunbeam 1947 Coupe, 1:43	$45-55
Tractor Trailer Flatbed Truck, 1:55	$45-55
Tractor Trailer Open Bed Truck, 1:55	$45-55
Tractor Trailer Van, 1:55	$45-55

Arcade

The most prominent name in cast iron and zinc alloy toys, Arcade began in 1868 as the Novelty Iron Works in Freeport, Illinois. Arcade reached prominence in 1921 with the introduction of a series of Yellow Cab replicas. The company continued producing toys until the Second World War. Arcade's classic style and detailing creates a bridge between cast iron toys of the day and diecast zinc alloy toys of the future. Here is just a sampling of the over 260 models offered.

A.C.F. Bus, 1927, 11½"	$3,500-4,500
Ambulance, 1932, 7¾"	$750-850
Car carrier with cars, 1931, 24½"	$2,000-3,000
Chevrolet Coupe	$7,000-8,500
Double Decker Bus, 1929, 8½"	$900-1,200
Double Decker Bus, Chicago Motor Coach, 1936, 8¼"	$900-1,200
Ford Coupe, 1923, 6"	$250-375
Ford Coupe, 1924, 6½"	$400-600
Ford Coupe with opening rumble seat, 1934, 6¾," Arcade #1610X	$250-375
Ford Coupe, 1930s, 4¾," Arcade #1190X	$175-250
Ford Fordor Sedan with removable chauffeur, 1924, 6½"	$350-525
Ford Model A Coupe with rumble seat, 1928, 5", Arcade #116X	$350-450
Ford Model A Coupe with rumble seat, 1928, 6¾," Arcade #106	$850-1,300
Ford Model A Coupe, 1928, 4⅛", Arcade #113X	$175-275
Ford Model A Fordor, 1928, 6¾," Arcade #207	$475-675
Ford Model A Tudor, 1928, 6¾," Arcade #108	$750-1,150
Ford Sedan, "Center Door," 1923, 6½"	$450-650
Ford Sedan, 1934, 6⅞", Arcade #1620X	$400-500
Ford Sedan, "Century of Progress," 1934, 6⅞"	$2,000-2,500
Ford Sedan, 1930s, 4¾," Arcade #1200	$300-400
Ford Sedan, "Century of Progress," 1934, 4¾"	$1,000-1,500
Ford Sedan with Trailer, 1937, 12" sedan, 5½" trailer, Arcade #1970	$1,000-1,600
Ford Touring Car, 1923, 6½"	$650-900
Grayhound Cruiser Coach Bus, 1941, 9⅛"	$500-600
Grayhound Cruiser Coach Bus, 1937, 7¾"	$400-500
Red Baby Truck, 1923, 10¾"	$1,250-1,500
Yellow Cab, approx. 7½ to 8", 1936	$8,500-10,000
Yellow Coach Double Decker Bus, 1925, 14"	$4,000-5,000

Armour (also see Detail Cars – C.D.C.)

Armour models are mostly military vehicles made by C.D.C. S.r.l. (Detail Cars), Via F. Lippi No. 19, 20131 Milano, Italy.

CDC Armour Collection 1:72

Flak PZ IV Wirbelwing, #3200	$30-35
Hummer M 1025, European, #3112	$20-25
Hummer M 998, European, #3114	$20-25
LAV 25 European 90MM Gun, #3124	$30-35
Panther Tank, AUSF, #3165	$30-35
PZ KPFW IV Type F1 Tank, #3101	$30-35
PZ KPFW IV Tank, Europe, #3210	$30-35
PZ KPFW IV Tank, Europe, #3211	$30-35
PZ KPFW IV Tank, Europe, #3212	$30-35
PZ KPFW IV Tank, Europe, #3214	$30-35
PZ KPFZ IV, North Africa, #3100	$30-35
PZ KPFZ IV G, North Africa, #3102	$30-35
PZ KPFZ IV G, Europe West, #3103	$30-35
PZ KPFZ IV G, Europe West, #3104	$30-35
Sherman Tank, Europe West, #3130	$30-35
Sherman Tank, North Africa, #3131	$30-35
Sherman Tank, Europe West, #3132	$30-35
Sherman Tank, Europe West, #3133	$30-35
Sherman Tank, Pacific USMC, #3135	$30-35
Sherman Tank, Europe West FR, #3136	$30-35
Sherman Tank, Battle Dress, #3138	$30-35
US 2.5T Tank cargo Truck Europe UK, #3143	$30-35
US Army 2.5T Tanker Truck, #3144	$25-30

Arnold, Bruce (see Bruce Arnold Models)

Arpra

Kits and ready-built models of plastic and metal have been produced under the Arpra brand of Brazil.

Dynapac CA25PD, #29	$24-27
Dynapac CA25D Roller, yellow, #30	$24-27
Mercedes-Benz 0-371 2-Axle Highway Bus, silver, orange and red, #302	$75-90
Mercedes-Benz 1513 Refrigerated cargo Truck, 1:50, #1	$20-24
Mercedes-Benz 1513 Refrigerator Van, blue/white, #2	$24-27
Mercedes-Benz 1513 Van, blue/white, #3	$24-27
Mercedes-Benz 1932 Semi-Cab, white, #39	$24-27
Mercedes-Benz 608, #4	$24-27
Scania Fire Tanker, #304	$65-75
Scania L-111 Semi Gas Truck, orange, 1:50, #310	$65-75
Scania LK-111 Semi-Cab, orange, #11	$24-27
Scania LK-141 Semi-Cab, orange, #9	$24-27
Scania LKS-141 Semi-Tractor with Tandem Axles, 1:50, #8	$20-24
Scania LKS-141 Cab, orange, #10	$24-27
Scania R-142 Semi-Cab, orange, #13	$24-27
Scania T-112 Semi-Cab, orange, #12	$24-27
Scania T-112 Semi Gas Truck, orange, #37	$45-50
Scania T-112 Semi-Cab, green, #136	$24-27
Trailer, Refrigerator, white, #16	$24-27
Trailer, Oil, white, #19	$24-27
Trailer, LP Gas, white, #20	$24-27

ARS

ARS (Alfa Romeo Specialties?) of Italy produces high-quality 1:43 scale versions of Alfa Romeos.

Alfa Romeo 33 Boxer 16V, red, black, #103	$25-30
Alfa Romeo 33 Sedan 1.5L 1E, dark green, #104	$25-30
Alfa Romeo 33 Sedan Permanente, orange, #105	$25-30
Alfa Romeo Spider, top up, red, green, silver, yellow, #101	$25-30

Art Model

Art Model miniatures are licensed 1:43 scale Ferrari models, manufactured in Pesaro, Italy. Art Model vehicles sell for $36 each.

Incidentally, "stradale" is Italian for "street," (as in Fiat Strada,) as compared to "prova," which indicates a racing, proving grounds, or prototype version.

Ferrari 166 MM Coupe Le Mans 1950, yellow, #016 ....$36–40

Ferrari 166 MM Coupe Mille Miglia 1951, red, #010 ....$36–40

Ferrari 166 MM Coupe Prova, red, #001 ....$36–40

Ferrari 166 MM Coupe Stradale, cream, #002 ....$36–40

Ferrari 166 MM Coupe Stradale, black, #003 ....$36–40

Ferrari 166 MM Spyder 12 Ore di Parigi, yellow, #012 ....$36–40

Ferrari 166 MM Spyder Le Mans 1949, red, #011 ....$36–40

Ferrari 166 MM Spyder Mille Miglia 1949, red, #008 ....$36–40

Ferrari 166 MM Spyder Mille Miglia 1950, silver, #017 ....$36–40

Ferrari 166 MM Spyder Prova, red, #005 ....$36–40

Ferrari 166 MM Spyder Stradale, white, #006 ....$36–40

Ferrari 166 MM Spyder Stradale, black, #007 ....$36–40

Ferrari 195 S Coupe Le Mans 1950, blue, #009 ....$36–40

Ferrari 195 S Coupe Mille Miglia 1950, blue, #004 ....$36–40

Ferrari California 250 Spyder 1957, top up $36–40

Ferrari 340 Mexico 1952 ....$36–40

Ferrari 410 S 1955 ....$36–40

Ferrari 500 TRC 1956 Prova, red, #014 ....$36–40

Ferrari 500 TRC Clienti, yellow, #015 ...$36–40

Asahi

Asahi models are made in Japan. Asahi Toy Company first made tinplate toy cars in the late 1940s and early 1950s. It wasn't until 1960 or so that the company produced diecast toys under the "Model Pet" brand. While production reportedly ended in the early 1970s, the 1:43 scale Rolls Royce Camargue has been produced later, as recently as 1980 or so, and is the only recent offering known of the brand.

Asahi Model Pet, diecast

Austin A50 Cambridge, 1:42, #8 .....$150-175

Datsun Bluebird, 1:42, #5 ....$125-150

Datsun Bluebird, 1:42, #17 ....$100-125

Datsun Bluebird, 1:42, #25 ....$75-100

Datsun Bluebird UHT, 1:42, #52 ...$50-65

Datsun Sunny Coupe EX1400, 1:42, #47 ....$50-65

Hillman Minx, 1:42, #9 ....$150-175

Hino Contessa 1300, 1:42, #26 ....$75-100

Hino Contessa 1300 Coupe, 1:42, #29 ....$75-100

Honda 750 Motorcycle, 1:35, #48 ......$30-45

Honda 750 Police Motorcycle, 1:50, #50 ....$30-45

Honda Motorcycle, 1:40, #103 ....$75-90

Honda N360, 1:40, #37 ....$75-100

Honda RC162 Motorcycle, 1:35, #43 ..$30-45

Honda S800 Coupe, 1:42, #35 ......$100-125

Honda S800 Roadster, 1:42, #34 ....$100-125

Isuzu Bellett, 1:42, #18 ....$125-150

Mazda Familia, 1:42, #30 ....$75-100

Mazda R360 Coupe, 1:42, #13 ......$125-150

Mitsubishi Colt 1000, 1:42, #24 ....$75-100

Mitsubishi Galant GTO, 1:, #40 42 .....$50-65

Mitsubishi Galant GTO Rally, 1:42, #58 ....$50-65

Nissan Cedric, 1:42, #10 ....$125-150

Nissan Cedric, 1:42, #33 ....$75-100

Nissan Cedric 2600 GX, 1:42, #54 .....$50-65

Nissan Cedric Taxi, 1:42, #10A $150-175

Nissan Silvia Coupe, 1:42, #32 ....$75-100

Nissan Skyline 2000GT Coupe, 1:35, #45 ....$30-45

Nissan Skyline 2000GT Rally, 1:42, #59 ....$50-65

Prince Gloria, 1:42, #22 ....$100-125

Prince Gloria Taxi, 1:42, #22A $150-175

Prince Skyline Deluxe, 1:42, #6 ....$125-150

Prince Skyline Sports Convertible, 1:42, #15 ....$125-150

Prince Skyline Sports Coupe, 1:42, #16 ....$125-150

Rolls Royce Camargue, yellow, orange or gray, 1:42 ....$20-35

Subaru 360, 1:40, #3 ....$125-150

Suzuki 750GT Motorcycle, 1:35, #44 ...$30-45

Toyota 2000GT Coupe, 1:42, #36 ....$75-100

Toyota Corona, 1:42, #7 ....$100-125

Toyota Corona, 1:42, #27 ....$100-125

Toyota Corona Mk. II 2000G SS, 1:42, #51 ....$50-65

Toyota Crown, 1:42, #12 ....$125-150

Toyota Crown, 1:42, #20 ....$100-125

Toyota Crown, gold plated, 1:42, #1A ...$150-175

Toyota Crown, gold plated, 1:42, #20A $125-150

Toyota Crown Ambulance, white, 1:42, #57 ....$50-65

Toyota Crown Coupe, 1:42, #39 ....$50-65

Toyota Crown Deluxe, 1:43, #1 ....$125-150

Toyota Crown Fire Car, red, 1:42, #56 ...$50-65

Toyota Crown Police, 1:42, #12A $175-200

Toyota Crown Police, black and white, 1:42, #20B $150-175

Toyota Crown Police, black and white, 1:42, #41 ....$50-65

Toyota Crown Station Wagon, 1:42, #11 ....$100-125

Toyota Crown Super, 1:42, #38 ....$50-65

Toyota Crown Taxi, yellow, 1:42, #55 ...$50-65

Toyota Land Cruiser, green, 1:42, #4 ..$150-175

Toyota Land Cruiser, green, 1:42, #23 ....$150-175

Toyota Masterline Ambulance, white, 1:42, #2A $225-250

Toyota Masterline Ambulance, white, 1:42, #21A $150-175

Toyota Masterline Station Wagon, 1:42, #2 ....$125-150

Toyota Masterline Station Wagon, 1:42, #21 ....$100-125

Toyota Publica, 1:42, #14 ....$100-125

Toyota Sports 800, 1:42, #31 ....$75-100

Toyota Sports Coupe, 1:42, #19 ......$100-125

1963 Toyota Toyoace Covered Truck, 1:48, #102 ....$150-175

1963 Toyota Toyoace Truck, 1:48, #101 ....$150-175

Yamaha 650XS Motorcycle, 1:35, #46 ..$30-45

Yamaha Motorcycle with Sidecar, 1:35, #62 ....$30-45

Yamaha Police Motorcycle, 1:35, #61 ...$30-45

Yamaha Police Motorcycle with Sidecar, 1:35, #60 ....$30-45

Asahi Tinplate Models

1950s Pickup, "G.B.C.," yellow, battery operated tinplate, 1:42 ....$30-45

Ashton

Gerhard Klarwasser

Route 1 Scale Models

P O Box 1406

Attleboro Falls MA 02763-0406

Ashton Models of New England are finely-detailed hand-built 1:43 scale fire fighting equipment. The most popular model is the Ahrens-Fox Fire Engine. Gerhard Klarwasser, previously the owner of Toys for Collectors, now produces these models and others under the auspices of Route 1 Scale Models.

Ahrens-Fox Chemical Truck "Bristol" No.3, (1927), #7022A $135-160

Ahrens-Fox Model J "Cincinnati," (1921), #7027 ....$170-195

Ahrens-Fox Piston Pumper "New Orleans" (1921), #7027 ....$110-135

Ahrens-Fox "Cincinnati" K.17 City Service Truck (1923), #7033 ....$195-220

Ahrens-Fox Piston Pumper "Harrisburg" (1921), #7035 ....$110-135

Ahrens-Fox "Vandergrift" NS4 1000 G.P.M. Pumper "Vandergrift" (1925), #7039 ..$95-120

Ahrens-Fox Aerial Ladder Truck "Clifton," #7040 ....$180-205

Ahrens-Fox Ladder Truck "Nashua" (1923), #7046 ....$190-215

Ahrens-Fox H.T. Pumper "F.D.N.Y. 264" (1938), #7051 ....$230-255

Ahrens-Fox Aerial Ladder Truck Buffalo N.Y. (1927), #7060 ....$260-285

Ahrens-Fox KS2 Pumper "Tokyo" (1924), #7062 ....$195-220

Ahrens-Fox PS2 "New South Wales Fire Brigade" Australia (1929), #7063 ....$195-220

FWD Model F50T Pumper "Cedarburg," (1951), #7025 ....$200-225

Mack Pumper Type 95 "Chicago," (1951), #7020A $135-160

Mack Pumper "Centerport" L.I., NY (1953), #7030 ....$170-195

Mack Pumper "Hanover" G.P.M. 750 (1952), #7038 ....$95-120

Mack Type L "F.D.N.Y." Rescue Truck No.1 (1948), #7044 ....$190-215

Mack Fuel Tanker "F.D.N.Y." (1941), #7052 ....$190-215

Mack Pumper L Typ "Bridgeport PA" (1949), #7053 ....$95-120

Mack L Typ 95 Pumper "Chicago" (1954), #7057 ....$95-120

Mack Rescue Truck "Tuxedo Cheverly" (1952), #7058 ....$190-215

Mack with 1956 Rescue Body "Boston Engine No.11" (1947), #7061 ....$195-220

GMC Pumper "Riegelsville, PA" (1961), #7066 ....$195-220

Ashton "Gold Collection"

Ahrens-Fox Aerial Ladder Truck "Newark," #7036G $230-255

Ahrens-Fox Pumper "Newark," #7041G $170-195

Ahrens-Fox HT Pumper "New Worlds Fair" (1938), #7049G $320-345

Ahrens-Fox Pawtucket (1938) No.1, #7055G $320-345

Ahrens-Fox Pawtucket (1938) No.7, #7056G $340-365

FWD Open Cab Truck "Cody," #7034G $175-200

FWD High Pressure Foam Pumper "Chicago" (1949), #7048G $285-310

Mack (1947), #7067G $320-345

Mack Tow Truck "Detroit," #7031G ...$175-200

Mack Quad "Whitehall," #7037G $230-255

Mack 95 1000 GAL.Pumper "Ellensburg" (1949), #7042G $280-305

Mack LT 1000 GAL.Pumper "Glendale" CA (1954), #7043G $285-310

Mack L Type Rescue Truck "Silver Springs" MD (1949), #7045G $285-310

Mack with 1956 Rescue Body "Boston Engine No.14" (1947), #7064G $320-345

Mack with 1956 Rescue Body "Boston Engine No.45" (1947), #7065G $320-345

Fire House display, 2 Fire Trucks + House (carton), #7050G $475-500

Athearn

Athearn is best known for producing high quality HO gauge model railroad cars, locomotives and accessories, but also offers semi tractors, and trailers to accompany model railroads.

Athearn Matching Tractors and Trailers

Bekins	$9-10
Burlington Northern/Northern Pacific	$9-10
Chessie	$9-10
Conrail	$9-10
Hertz	$9-10
Lee Way	$9-10
Penn Central	$9-10
Railway Express Agency	$9-10
Safeway	$9-10
Santa Fe	$9-10
Southern Pacific	$9-10
Time-DC	$9-10
Union Pacific	$9-10
undecorated	$9-10

Athearn Semi Tractors

Kenworth Conventional, with livery

Burlington Northern	$4-5
Conrail	$4-5
Pacific Intermountain Express	$4-5
Santa Fe	$4-5
Southern Pacific	$4-5
Union Pacific	$4-5

Kenworth Conventional, undecorated

black	$4-5
yellow	$4-5
red	$4-5

blue	$4-5
white	$4-5
green	$4-5

White Freightliner Cabover

Bekins	$4-5
Burlington Northern/Northern Pacific	$4-5
Chessie	$4-5
Conrail	$4-5
Hertz	$4-5
Lee Way	$4-5
Penn Central	$4-5
Railway Express Agency	$4-5
Safeway	$4-5
Santa Fe	$4-5
Time-DC	$4-5
Union Pacific	$4-5
undecorated	$4-5

Atlas

Atlas Model Railroads, Inc., offers an assortment of unassembled plastic tractor and trailer kits for HO gauge train layouts The tractor is a Ford LNT 9000 in various colors and a 45 foot Pines trailer in various livery.

Ford LNT 9000 tractor

1. black	$7-9
2. dark blue	$7-9
3. medium blue	$7-9
4. green	$7-9
5. orange	$7-9
6. red	$7-9
7. white	$7-9
8. yellow	$7-9
9. undecorated	$7-9

Pines 45' trailer

1. Beaverville & Southern	$12-14
2. Burlington Motor carriers	$12-14
3. Chicago Central & Pacific	$12-14
4. CSX	$12-14
5. Kankakee	$12-14
6. NS	$12-14
7. Redon	$12-14
8. Vermont Railway	$12-14
9. Xtra Intermodal	$12-14
10. Xtra Lease	$12-14
11. undecorated	$12-14

Auburn

The Auburn Rubber Company of Auburn, Indiana, began producing rubber toy vehicles in 1936. By 1952, rubber toys were being replaced with vinyl toys. The last of the rubber toys were produced in 1956. Auburn moved to Deming, New Mexico, and finally went out of business in 1969.

Auburn Rubber Toys

Ahrens-Fox Fire Engine, 5½" $125-150
Army Motor Scout on Motorcycle $40-60
1940 Oldsmobile Army Staff Car, "US Army" label $35-55
1939 Buick Y Job Experimental Roadster, 9¾" $100-125
1948 Buick Sedanette, 2-door fastback, 7¼" $75-100
1950 Cadillac, 4-door sedan, 7¼" $60-85
1947 Chevrolet Cab Forward Box Truck, 5¾" $35-55
1936 Cord, 4-door coffin-nose sedan, 6" $120-160
1940s Fire Engine, 7¾" $50-75
1935 Ford 2-door slantback sedan, 4" ...$45-65
1935 Ford Coupe, 4" $45-65
Ford Stake Truck, 4¾" $45-65
Futuristic Box Truck, 4⅛" $30-50
Futuristic Box Truck, 5½" $30-50
Futuristic Sedan, rear center fin, late 1940s, 5" $30-50
1938 GMC with articulated trailer, 9" ..$75-100
1938 GMC carry Car Auto Transport, 11½" $75-100
1938 GMC Carry Car Auto Transport, 11¾" $75-100
1937 International Cabover Stake Truck, 3¾" $30-50
1937 International Cabover Stake Truck, 4¼" $30-50
1937 International Cabover Stake Truck, 4⅜" $35-55
1937 International Cabover Stake Truck, "US Army" decal $35-55
1937 International Cabover Stake Truck, Milk Truck, 4¼" $85-110
1937 International Cabover Stake Truck, Ambulance $75-100
1946 Lincoln Convertible, 2-door, 4½" $30-50
1937 Oldsmobile, 4-door sedan, 4½" ...$40-60
1938 Oldsmobile, 4-door sedan, 5¾" ...$50-75
1940 Oldsmobile, 4-door sedan, open fenders, 6" $45-65
1940 Oldsmobile, 4-door sedan, fender skirts, 6" $35-55
1950 Pickup Truck, 4½" $30-50
1939 Plymouth, two-door trunkback sedan, 4¼" $35-55
1940s Pumper with boiler, 7¼" $50-75

Auburn Vinyl Toys

Airport Limousine, 7½" $15-30
Cadillac Convertible, 3½" $10-15
Cadillac Convertible, 5" $20-30
Delivery Truck $15-25

Dump Truck, #352, 10½" $50-75
Fire Truck, #614 ....$15-25
Fire Truck Pumper, #500, 7½" $15-25
Fork Lift with driver, #538, 5" $50-75
Hot Rod, #612, 4¼" $15-25
Jeep $10-15
Station Wagon, #577 ....$20-30
Telephone Truck, #503, 7" $25-35
Utility Truck, #508 ....$20-30

Aurora Cigar Box

Aurora is best known for HO gauge slot cars. Their 1968 Cigar Box line of cars was so named for the clever box in which they were packaged. Each Cigar Box model featured a shiny-colored-chrome plastic body. A diecast metal chassis was held on with two screws so that it could be easily removed and replaced with slot car chassis and motor. The wheels were unimpressive, to say the least, but the cars themselves were fairly realistic for their original retail price, about 50 – 75 cents each. Popularity of these little cars has increased in just the last couple of years. Prices below represent new condition specimens in original box. Out of the box, models are worth about 60 percent of price listed.

AC Cobra, lavender $75-90

Beach Buggy, 6119 ....**$35-50**

BRM Formula 1, #6126 ....$35-50
Buick Riviera $35-50
Chaparral, white, #6114 ....$35-50
Cheetah, yellow $55-70
Chevrolet Camaro, 6115 ....$55-70
Chevrolet Corvette Stingray, #6101 ....$6075
Chevrolet Corvette Stingray Mako Shark, blue, #6103 ....$40-55
Cobra GT $35-50
Cooper Maserati Formula 1, #6123 .....$35-50
Corvette Stingray (see Chevrolet Corvette Stingray)
Cougar (see Mercury Cougar)
Dino Ferrari (see Ferrari Dino)
Ferrari Berlinetta $35-50
Ferrari Dino, yellow, #6111 ....$35-50
Ferrari Formula 1, #6122 ....$35-50

Firebird (see Pontiac Firebird)
Ford GT, metallic lavender/pink, #6105 ..$40-50
Ford J car, yellow, #6104 ....$35-50
Ford Lola Formula 1, #6121 ....$35-50
Ford Lotus Formula 1, #6124 ....$35-50
Ford Mustang Convertible, purple $60-75
Ford Mustang Hardtop $80-95
Ford Thunderbird, #6110
    v.1 yellow $55-70
    v.2 white $55-70
Ford XL-500
    v.1 white, #6107 ....$35-50
    v.2 red, #6207 ....$35-50
Formula 1 BRM, #6126 ....$35-50
Formula 1 Cooper Maserati (see Cooper Maserati Formula 1)
Formula 1 Ferrari (see Ferrari Formula 1)
Formula 1 Honda (see Honda Formula 1)
Formula 1 Lola Ford (see Ford Lola Formula 1)
Formula 1 Lotus Ford (see Ford Lotus Formula 1)
Honda Formula 1, #6125 ....$35-50
Jaguar XKE $35-50
Lola GT $35-50
Mako Shark (see Chevrolet Corvette Stingray Mako Shark)
Mangusta $40-55
Mercury Cougar, #6116 ....$50-65
Mustang Convertible (see Ford Mustang Convertible)
Mustang Hardtop (see Ford Mustang Hardtop)

Oldsmobile Toronado, #6108 ....**$40-55**

Porsche 904, red, #6112 ....$35-50
Thunderbird (see Ford Thunderbird)
Toronado (see Oldsmobile)
Volkswagen $75-90
Willy's Gasser, pink $75-90

Authentic Model Car Series (see Ace Implement Company)

Authenticast (see Comet)

AUTOart (also see Gateway Global, Inc.)

AUTOart is a brand of precision scale diecast models from Gateway Global, the new parent company for UT, as well as new Gate and AUTOart brands. AUTOart models are available in 1:12, 1:18, and 1:43 scale.

AUTOart Signature, 1:12

Mercedes Benz CLK GTR FIA GT 1997 GT1 Champion B. Schneider / A. Wurz / K. Ludwig #11, #12001 ....$50-70

AUTOart Motorcycle, 1:12

Vespa Scooter GS 150, #12501 ....$50-70

AUTOart Contemporary, 1:12

Snowmobile
GT SE 2000, black, #79831 ....$50-70
GT SE 2001, blue, #79832 ....$50-70
MXZ 700 2001, yellow, #79811 ...$50-70
Mach Z 2001, black, #79821 ....$50-70

AUTOart 1:18 Scale

Aston Martin DB-5
green, LH drive, #70023 ....$50-70
green, RH drive, #70024 ....$50-70
metallic red, LH drive, #70025 ....$50-70
metallic red, RH drive, #70026 ....$50-70

silver, James Bond "Goldfinger,"
#70020 ....$50-70

silver, with weapons, James Bond "Goldfinger," #70021 ....$50-70
BMW 2002 Turbo, white, #70501 ......$50-70
BMW Mini Cooper
silver, with sunroof, #74821 ....$50-70
red, without sunroof, #74822 ....$50-70
racing green, without sunroof, #74823 ....$50-70
BMW Z8, James Bond "The World Is Not Enough," #70511 ....$50-70
Callaway C12
1998, silver, #71011 ....$50-70
1998, red, #71012 ....$50-70
1998, yellow, #71013 ....$50-70
"MUKO" car, blue, #71014 ....$50-70
Chaparral 2 "Sport Racer" 1965 #66, #86496 ....$50-70
Chevrolet Corvette 1982 collector edition silver, #71021 ....$50-70
Chevrolet Corvette C5-R
GT2 Rolex 24 Hrs at Daytona R. Fellows / J. Paul Jr. / C. Kniefel car #2, #89906 .....$50-70
GT2 Rolex 24 Hrs at Daytona S. Sharp / A. Pilgrim / J. Heinricy #4, #89907 ....$50-70

ALMS R. Fellows / C. Kniefel / J. Bell #3, #80005 ....$50-70
ALMS A. Pilgrim / K. Collins / F. Freon #4, #80006 ....$50-70
ALMS 2000 Texas Winer R. Fellows / C. Kniefel #3, #80007 ....$50-70
GT2 Class 2001 Rolex 24 Hrs at Daytona R. Fellows / C. Kniefel / J. O'Connell / F. Freon #2, #80106 ....$50-70
2001 Texas 24 at Le Mans Winner A. Pilgrim / K. Collins / F. Freon #64, #80107 .$50-70
Chevrolet Corvette SS 1957, blue, #71051 ....$50-70
Chevrolet Corvette Stingray Experimental 1959

silver, #71000 ....$50-70
red, #71001 ....$50-70
Chevrolet Corvette T-Roof 1978

black $40-60
Chevrolet Corvette Z06 2001
torch red, #71061 ....$50-70
quick silver, #71062 ....$50-70
millenium yellow, #71063 ....$50-70
Chrysler GT Cruiser
silver, #71521 ....$50-70
black, #71522 ....$50-70
Chrysler Panel Cruiser
metallic blue, #71531 ....$50-70
metallic red, #71532 ....$50-70
Dodge Viper GTS-R
1997 Sebring O. Beretta / Ph. Gache #51, #89721 ....$50-70
1997 Sebring T. Archer / J. Bell #52, #89722 ....$50-70
24 Hrs. at Daytona 1997 Sebring O. Beretta / T. Archer / D. Dupuy #94, #89723 ....$50-70
Le Mans 1998 1st Runners Up GT2 Class T. Archer / O. Beretta / P. Lamy #51, #89821 ....$50-70
Le Mans 1998 G. Ayles / J. Hugenholtz / M. Turner #56, #89822 ....$50-70
Le Mans 1998 N. Amorin / G. Gomes / M. Mello-Bryner #55, #89823 ....$50-70

Le Mans 1998 Winner GT2 Class J. Bell / D. Donohue / L. Drudi #53, #89824 ...$50-70
Zakspeed Team #53, #89921 ....$50-70
Petite Le Mans 1999 M. Deuz / O. Beretta / K. Wendlinger #91, #89922 ....$50-70
Winner of Rolex 24 Hrs. at Daytona 2000 O. Beretta / D. Dupuy / K. Wendlinger #91, #80045 ....$50-70
Winner of Le Mans 2000 D. Dupuy / K. Wendlinger / O. Beretta #51, #80047 ....$50-70
Ford Crown Victoria
LAPD Police, #72701 ....$50-70
Des Plaines Police, #72702 ....$50-70
NYPD Police, #72703 ....$50-70
Ford Expedition Himalaya
white, #72781 ....$50-70
Ford Focus WRC
1999 Presentation car, #89910 ......$50-70
1999 C. McRae / N. Grist #7, Rally Monte Carlo, #89911 ....$50-70
Test car, #89912 ....$50-70
1999 C. McRae / N. Grist #7, Rally Portugal, #89913 ....$50-70
1999 C. McRae / N. Grist #7, Rally Safari Kenya Winner, #89914 ....$50-70
2000 C. McRae / N. Grist #5, Rally Monte Carlo, #80012 ....$50-70
2000 C. Sainz / L. Moya #6, Rally Monte Carlo, #80013 ....$50-7
2000 C. McRae / N. Grist #5, Winner of Rally Catalunya, #80014 ....$50-70
2001 C. Sainz / L. Moya #3, Rally Monte Carlo, #80111 ....$50-70
"RS" 2001 F. Delecour / D. Grataloup #17, Rally Monte Carlo, #80112 ......$50-70
Ford Forty Nine
black, #72831 ....$50-70
Ford Mustang Cobra R 2000, Prototype version, #80016 ....$50-70
Ford Mustang Super Stallion
blue, #72710 ....$50-70
Ford Saleen Mustang S351
Coupe, yellow, #72720 ....$50-70
Coupe, white, #72721 ....$50-70
Convertible, metallic red, #72730 ....$50-70
Convertible, yellow, #72731 ....$50-70
Holden Commodore VT Coupe 2000
gold, with certificate #73432 ....$50-70
Honda S 2000
yellow, LH drive, European version, #73201 ....$50-70
black, LH drive, European version, #73202 ....$50-70
white, LH drive, European version, #73203 ....$50-70

silver, LH drive, European version, #73204 ....$50-70
black, LH drive, US version, #73206 .$50-70
white, LH drive, US version, #73207 .$50-70
silver, LH drive, US version, #73208 ..$50-70
yellow, RH drive, Japan version, #73209 ....$50-70
black, RH drive, Japan version, #73210 ....$50-70
white, RH drive, Japan version, #73211 ....$50-70
silver, RH drive, Japan version, #73212 ....$50-70

Jaguar 120C C-Type 1951
green, #73500 ....$50-70
silver, #73501 ....$50-70
bronze, #73502 ....$50-70

Jaguar D Type, short nose
green, #73561 ....$50-70
Jaguar XJ 13, green, #73541 ....$50-70

Jaguar XK SS 1956
blue, #73510 ....$50-70
green, #73511 ....$50-70
cream, #73512 ....$50-70
Jaguar XK-SS 1956, Steve McQueen, green, #73519 ....$50-70

Jeep Grand Cherokee 1999
white, #74011 ....$50-70
black, #74012 ....$50-70
red, #74013 ....$50-70
Jeep Grand Wagoneer 1989, #74001..$50-70

Lamborghini Diablo Coupe VT
titanium silver, #70071 ....$50-70
metallic red, #70072 ....$50-70

Lamborghini Diablo Roadster
red, #70091 ....$50-70
yellow, #70092 ....$50-70
black, #70093 ....$50-70

Lamborghini Diablo SV
black, #70081 ....$50-70
metallic blue, #70082 ....$50-70
yellow, #70083 ....$50-70

Lamborghini Murcielago
metallic yellow, #74511 ....$50-70
metallic orange, #74512 ....$50-70
metallic black, #74513 ....$50-70

Lexus GS 400
black, LH drive, #70041 ....$50-70
silver, LH drive, #70042 ....$50-70

Lexus IS300 1999
yellow, #78701 ....$50-70
blue, #78702 ....$50-70
black, #78703 ....$50-70

Lexus RX 300
silver, LH drive, #70031 ....$50-70
black, LH drive, #70032 ....$50-70

Lincoln Navigator
white, #72761 ....$50-70
black, #72762 ....$50-70

Lotus Esprit Turbo
black, #70061 ....$50-70
Essex blue, #70066 ....$50-70
metallic red, James Bond "For Your Eyes Only," #70060 ....$50-70
white, #70062 ....$50-70

Lotus Esprit Type 79
yellow, #75301 ....$50-70
green, #75302 ....$50-70
James Bond "The Spy Who Loved Me," white, #75300 ....$50-70
James Bond "The Spy Who Loved Me," Submarine, #75306 ....$50-70

Mercedes Benz CL 55 AMG
"F1 limited edition," silver, #70125 ...$50-70

Mercedes Benz CL 500
"Lorinser Verinser," silver, #70121 .....$50-70

Mercedes Benz CL 600
black, #70112 ....$50-70
white, #70113 ....$50-70

Mercedes-Benz CLK GTR
Le Mans 1998 D2 B. Schneider / K. Ludwig / M. Webber #35, #89831 ....$50-70
FIA GT 1998 "Bye Bye" K. Ludwig / R. Zonta #2, #89832 ....$50-70
FIA GT 1998 Champion K. Ludwig / R. Zonta #2, #89833 ....$50-70
FIA GT 1998 Original-Teile Bernd Maylander / Christophe Bouchut #11, #89834 .$50-70
FIA GT 1998 Original-Teile M. Tiemann / J. M. Gounon #12, #89835 ....$50-70

Mitsubishi Lancer Evo VI
blue, #77151 ....$50-70
white, #77152 ....$50-70
silver, #77153 ....$50-70
"Tommi Makinen" edition, red, #77156 ....$50-70
"Tommi Makinen" edition, white, #77157 ....$50-70
"Tommi Makinen" edition, black, #77158 ....$50-70

Mitsubishi Lancer Evo VI WRC
1999 T. Makinen /R. Mannisenmaki #1, Rally New Zealand, #89941 ....$50-70
1999 S. Hayashi / Y. Kataoka #2, Winner of Rally Canberra, #89942 ......$50-70
2000 T. Makinen /R. Mannisenmaki #1, Winner of Rally Monte Carlo, #80041 $50-70
2001 T. Makinen /R. Mannisenmaki #7, Winner of Rally Monte Carlo, #80141 .....$50-70

Mitsubishi Pajero Long Wheel Base 1998
metallic blue, RH drive, #77101 ....$50-70
metallic blue, LH drive, #77103 ....$50-70

metallic red, RH drive, #77102 ....$50-70
metallic red, LH drive, #77104 ....$50-70
white, RH drive, #77105 ....$50-70
white, LH drive, #77106 ....$50-70

Mitsubishi Pajero Short Wheel Base 1998
silver, #77121 ....$50-70
black, #77122 ....$50-70

Mitsubishi Pajero EVO
black, #77131 ....$50-70
red, #77132 ....$50-70
white, #77133 ....$50-70

Nissan Skyline R34 GTR 1999
blue, #77301 ....$50-70
Titanium Silver, #77302 ....$50-70
white, #77303 ....$50-70
Midnight Purple, #77304 ....$50-70

Panoz Esperante GTR-1
Le Mans 1998 E. Bernard / C. Tinseau / J. O'Connell #44, #89851 ....$50-70
Le Mans 1998 D. Brabham / A. Wallace / J. Davies #45, #89852 ....$50-70
FIA GT 1998 E. Bernard / D. Brabham #3, #89853 ....$50-70
FIA GT 1998 D. Brabham / A . Wallace #4, #89854 ....$50-70

Panoz GTR-1 street car
Ocean Extreme, #78201 ....$50-70
gold, #78202 ....$50-70

Panoz Roadster 1998
red, #78211 ....$50-70
silver, #78212 ....$50-70
yellow, #78213 ....$50-70

Porsche 917K
Daytona 24Hr 1970, Redman / Siffert #1, #80031 ....$50-70
Daytona 24 Hr 1970, Kinnunen / Rodriguez #2, #80033 ....$50-70
Kyaiami 1970, Siffert / Ahrens #2, #80035 ....$50-70
Le Mans 1970 Winner, H. Herrmann / R. Attwood #23, #80032 ....$50-70
Le Mans #20, Steve McQueen, #80030 ....$50-70
Sebring Winner 1971, Elford / Larrousse #3, #80034 ....$50-70
Watkins Glen, Larrousse / Van Lennep #35, #80036 ....$50-70

Porsche 996 GT3
red, #77811 ....$50-70
yellow, #77812 ....$50-70
white, #77821 ....$50-70

Porsche 996 Turbo
red, #77831 ....$50-70
silver, #77832 ....$50-70

Range Rover 4.6 HSE
metallic green, LH drive, #70010 .....$50-70

metallic green, RH drive, #70011 .....$50-70
metallic red, LH drive, #70012 ....$50-70
metallic red, RH drive, #70013 ....$50-70
silver, LH drive, #70014 ....$50-70
silver, RH drive, #70015 ....$50-70
metallic black, LH drive, #70016 .....$50-70
metallic black, RH drive, #70017 .....$50-70

Subaru Impreza
22B, metallic blue, #78601 ....$50-70
WRX Type R, yellow, #78611 ....$50-70
WRX Type R, blue, #78612 ....$50-70
WRX 4DRS, white, #78621 ....$50-70
WRX 4DRS, blue, #78622 ....$50-70

Subaru Impreza WRC
1999 R. Burns / R. Reid #5, Rally Monte Carlo, #89992 ....$50-70
1999 R. Burns / R. Reid V-Rally France #5, #89993 ....$50-70
1999 R. Burns / R. Reid #5, Rally Monte Carlo / Night Race, #89994 ....$50-70
Rally German 2000 Team A. Kremer / K. Wicha #4, #80091 ....$50-70
2001 R.Burns / R. Reid #5, Rally of Portugal, #80191 ....$50-70

Toyota Celica GTS 2000
silver, LH drive, #78721 ....$50-70
red, LH drive, #78722 ....$50-70
yellow, LH drive, #78723 ....$50-70
silver, RH drive, #78726 ....$50-70
red, RH drive, #78727 ....$50-70
yellow, RH drive, #78728 ....$50-70

Toyota Corolla WRC
1998 C. Sainz / L. Moya #5, Rally Portugal, #80020 ....$50-70
1998 F. Loix / S. Smeets #9, Rally Portugal, #80021 ....$50-70
1998 C. Sainz / L. Moya #5, Rally Finland, #80022 ....$50-70
1998 D. Auriol / D. Giraudet #6, Rally Great Britain, Australia $50-70
1998 D. Auriol / D. Giraudet #9, Rally Espana, #80025 ....$50-70
1998 C. Sainz / L. Moya #5, Rally Argentina, #80026 ....$50-70
1998 C. Sainz / L. Moya #5, Rally New Zealand, #80027 ....$50-70
1998 Asia - Pacific Rally Champion 1998 Y. Fujimoto / Sircom #16, #80028..$50-70
1998 D. Auriol / D. Giraudet #4, Safari Rally Kenya, #89981 ....$50-70
1998 C. Sainz / L. Moya #3, Safari Rally Kenya, #89982 ....$50-70
2000 S. Prevot / B. Thiry #18, Rally Monte Carlo, #80081 ....$50-70

Toyota Harrier
metallic red, RH drive, #70035 ....$50-70

bronze, RH drive, #70036 ....$50-70

Toyota MR2 Spyder 2000
red, LH drive, #78711 ....$50-70
red, RH drive, #78715 ....$50-70
silver, LH drive, #78712 ....$50-70
silver, RH drive, #78716 ....$50-70
yellow, LH drive, #78713 ....$50-70
yellow, RH drive, #78717 ....$50-70

Toyota Racing Truck
'98 Ivan Stewart #11, #80010 ....$50-70
'97 Ivan Stewart #1, #80011 ....$50-70

Toyota RS200 Altezza 1999
yellow, #78707 ....$50-70
white, #78708 ....$50-70
silver, #78709 ....$50-70

Toyota TS020 LeMans 24TH 1999
M. Brundle / E. Collard / V. Sospiri #1, #89986 ....$50-70
T. Boutsen / R. Kelleners / A. McNish #2, #89987 ....$50-70
U. Katayama / T. Suzuki / K. Tsuchiya #3, #89988 ....$50-70

Toyota V300 Aristo
silver, RH drive, #70045 ....$50-70
black, RH drive, #70046 ....$50-70

Volkswagen New Beetle
reflex yellow, #79731 ....$50-70
vapor blue, #79732 ....$50-70
dune yellow, #79711 ....$50-70
RSI, silver, #79721 ....$50-70

AUTOart 1:43 Scale

Aston Martin DB7
silver, #50201 ....$20-30
red, #50202 ....$20-30
metallic blue, #50203 ....$20-30
metallic green, #50204 ....$20-30

BMW Mini Cooper
silver, #54821 ....$20-30
red, #54822 ....$20-30
racing green, #54823 ....$20-30
blue, #54824 ....$20-30
black, #54825 ....$20-30
yellow, #54826 ....$20-30

Chaparral 2 Sport Racer 1965 #66, #66496 ....$20-30

Chevrolet Corvette Stingray Mako Shark
dark blue, #51061 ....$20-30

Chevrolet Corvette SS 1957
blue, #51051 ....$20-30

Chevrolet Corvette Stingray 1959
silver, #51001 ....$20-30
red, #51002 ....$20-30

Chrysler
GT Cruiser 2001, silver, #51521 ....$20-30
Panel Cruiser 2001, blue, #51531 ..$20-30

PT Cruiser 2001, red, #51511 ....$20-30
Ford Focus WRC 2001, #60111 ....$20-30

Jaguar C-Type
green, #53501 ....$20-30
silver, #53502 ....$20-30
bronze, #53503 ....$20-30

Jaguar D-Type
Long Nose, racing green, #53551 ...$20-30
Short Nose, racing green, #53561 ..$20-30

Jaguar XJ8
blue, #53571 ....$20-30
red, #53572 ....$20-30
gold, #53573 ....$20-30

Jaguar XJR
black, #53601 ....$20-30
white, #53602 ....$20-30
silver, #53603 ....$20-30

Jaguar XK8 Coupe
blue, #53631 ....$20-30
red, #53632 ....$20-30

Jaguar XKR Coupe
green, #53621 ....$20-30
white, #53622 ....$20-30

Jaguar XK SS 1956
blue, #53751 ....$20-30
green, #53752 ....$20-30

Lamborghini Murcielago
metallic yellow, #54511 ....$20-30
metallic orange, #54512 ....$20-30
metallic black, #54513 ....$20-30

Land Rover Discovery V8 1994
green, #54901 ....$20-30
black, #54902 ....$20-30
metallic blue, #54903 ....$20-30

Lotus Esprit Type 79
yellow, #55311 ....$20-30
green, #55312 ....$20-30
red, #55313 ....$20-30

Lotus Esprit V8 1996
red, #55401 ....$20-30
black, #55402 ....$20-30
yellow, #55403 ....$20-30
racing green, #55404 ....$20-30

Lotus Turbo Esprit
pearl white, #55301 ....$20-30
black, #55302 ....$20-30
yellow, #55303 ....$20-30

Mercedes Benz CLK DTM
2000 #1 Bernd Schneider, #60031 .$20-30
2000 #2 Thomas Juger, #60032 ....$20-30
2000 #5 Klaus Ludwig, #60033 .....$20-30
2000 #6 Marcel Fassler, #60034 ...$20-30
2000 #14 Pedro Lamy, #60035 .....$20-30
2000 #15 Darren Turner, #60036 ..$20-30
2000 #18 Marcel Tiemann, #60037 .$20-30
2000 #19 Peter Dumbreck, #60038...$20-30

2000 #24 Pedro Lamy, #60039 .....$20-30
2000 #42 Darren Turner, #60040 ..$20-30
2001 #1 Bernd Schneider, #60131 $20-30
2001 #2 Peter Dumbreck, #60132 .$20-30
2001 #5 Uwe Alzen, #60133 ....$20-30
2001 #6 Marcel Fassler, #60134 ...$20-30
2001 #9 Bernd Maylander, #60135..$20-30
2001 #10 Patrick Huisman, #60136 .$20-30
2001 #14 Thomas Juger, #60137 ..$20-30
2001 #15 Christian Albers, #60138 $20-30
2001 #24 David Saelens, #60139 ..$20-30
2001 #42 Darren Turner, #60140 ..$20-30
Mercedes Benz G-Wagon Short Wheel Base 80s
    – 90s
    blue, #56101 ....$20-30
    purple, #56102 ....$20-30
    red, #56102 ....$20-30
    black, #56103 ....$20-30
    silver, #56104 ....$20-30
    silver, #56111 ....$20-30
    black, #56112 ....$20-30
    metallic red, #56113 ....$20-30
    metallic green, #56114 ......$20-30
    blue, #57101 ....$20-30
Mitsubishi Lancer EVO 6
    white, #57151 ....$20-30
    blue, #57152 ....$20-30
    "Tommi Makinen" edition street car, red,
    #57156 ....$20-30
Mitsubishi Lancer EVO 6 WRC
    1999 #1, #69941 ....$20-30
    1999 #2, #69942 ....$20-30
    2001 Winner of Monte Carlo, T. Makinen, R.
    Mannisenmaki #7, #60141 .....$20-30
Mitsubishi Pajero 1999 Long Wheel Base
    red, #57102 ....$20-30
    white, #57103 ....$20-30
Mitsubishi Pajero 1999 Short Wheel Base
    black, #57111 ....$20-30
    purple, #57112 ....$20-30
    silver, #57113 ....$20-30
Mitsubishi Pajero EVO
    white, #57201 ....$20-30
    black, #57202 ....$20-30
    red, #57203 ....$20-30
Nissan Skyline R34 GTR 1999
    blue, #57301 ....$20-30
    silver, #57302 ....$20-30
    midnight purple, #57303 ...$20-30
Panoz Esperante GTR-1 FIA GT
    1998 #3, #69851 ....$20-30
    1998 #4, #69852 ....$20-30
Range Rover 4.6 HSE
    metallic green, #54801 ......$20-30
    metallic red, #54802 ....$20-30
    metallic silver, #54803 .....$20-30

metallic black, #54804 ....$20-30
Subaru Impreza 22B
    metallic blue, #58601 ....$20-30
Subaru Impreza WRC
    1999 #5, #69991 ....$20-30
    2000 #4, #60091 ....$20-30
    2001 #5, #60191 ....$20-30
Subaru Impreza WRX STI 2001
    silver, #58641 ....$20-30
Subaru Legacy B4 1999
    gold, #58611 ....$20-30
    white, #58612 ....$20-30
    black, #58613 ....$20-30
Subaru Legacy GTB 1999
    gold, #58621 ....$20-30
    white, #58622 ....$20-30
    silver, #58623 ....$20-30
Toyota Corolla WRC
    1999 #4, #69981 ....$20-30
    1999 #3, #69982 ....$20-30
Volkswagen New Beetle
    bright blue, #59731 ....$20-30
    green, #59732 ....$20-30
    yellow, #59733 ....$20-30
    red, #59734 ....$20-30
    dune yellow, #59711 ......$20-30
    RSI, silver, #59721 ....$20-30

Auto Buff

This series of 1:43 scale vintage Ford models were hand built in California by Le Buff Stuff and produced in very small quantities. The series has long since been discontinued and models are now quite scarce. Auto Buff dies were sold to Oakland Models of Michigan in 1982.

Ford Model A Roadster, top down,
    blue/black $125-150
Ford Model A Convertible, top down, medium
    green $125-150
1930 Ford Model A Pickup $125-150
1930 Ford Model A Roadster $125-150
1940 Ford Pickup, red $125-150
1940 Ford Convertible, top down,
    brown $125-150
1940 Ford Convertible, top up, maroon and
    tan $125-150
1948 Ford Coupe, black $125-150
1948 Ford Coupe, red $350-400
1948 Ford Coupe, maroon $125-150
1948 Ford Convertible, top up, black..$125-150
1948 Ford Convertible, top down, dark
    green $125-150
1953 Ford Pickup, black $125-150
1953 Ford "Coke" Panel Van, red $350-400

1953 Ford Stake Truck, white and
    black $125-150

Autocraft (also see Hongwell)

Hongwell is a recent discovery in the ever-expanding world of diecast and plastic toys. Their Autocraft Truck Monster series represents an assortment of trucks in approximately 1:34 scale, all conveniently measuring about 9" long. Only the cab is diecast; the rest is plastic. Features include opening compartments and other working parts. Detail is particularly nice for a toy priced around $15-20. All models are identified as Mercedes-Benz trucks by the prominent trademark three-pointed star on the grille.

Hongwell's Autocraft Road Monster series represents sets that include cars, 4x4s, trailers, and accessories.

Autocraft Road Monster Series

Sedan and Travel Trailer, AC1101 ....$10-15
SUV with 4 Wheel All Terrain Cycle and Trailer,
    AC1105 ....$10-15
SUV with Animal Cage and Animal,
    AC1106 ....$10-15
SUV with Expedition Trailer and Kayaks,
    AC1104 ....$10-15
SUV with Twin Engine Speedboat and Trailer,
    AC1103 ....$10-15
Van and Racing Boat with Trailer,
    AC1102 ....$10-15

Autocraft Truck Monster Series

Auto Salvage Truck, AC2961 ....$15-20
Cement Truck, yellow, AC2921 ....$15-20
Dump Truck, silver cab, blue dumper,
    AC2922 ....$15-20
Fire Engine, red, AC2912
    "Fire Dept. Fire and Rescue Service" ...$15-20
    "Feuerwehr" $15-20
Garbage Truck, yellow, AC2932 ....$15-20
Log Truck with crane and logs, AC2951 ..$15-20
Recycling Truck with bins and crane,
    AC2941 ....$15-20
Skip Truck, yellow with metallic gray skip container, AC2931 ....$15-20
Super Transport Box Truck, blue,
    AC2942 ....$15-20

Autohobby

Autohobby models are limited edition resin hand builts. Resin models are generally sold unfinished with rough, unfinished edges, for hobbyists to finish, assemble, and customize to their liking. Autohobby models on the other hand are preassembled and finished.

1938 Citroën 11B Coca-Cola Van,
#610 ....$60-75

Automec

Toward the end of the 1950s, Automec of England offered 1:55 scale variations of a 1955 Bedford S lorry identical to Dinky Toys #621 except with no brand name, only "Made in England," on the base.

1955 Bedford S Army Covered Truck with Trailer
and Gun $45-60
1955 Bedford S Covered Truck "OXO" ..$45-60
1955 Bedford S Flat Truck $45-60
1955 Bedford S Hopper Bulk Tipper "Highway
Grit Spreader" $45-60
1955 Bedford S Navy Covered Truck $45-60
1955 Bedford S Tipper $45-60

Auto Pilen (also see AHC)

Escuderia Pilen of Spain produced toy cars under the brand names Pilen, Auto Pilen, and Escuderia Pilen. Dr. Craig S. Campbell, assistant professor of geography at Youngstown State University, reports that the predominant scale for these toys is 1:43. Many, but not all, of Pilen's superior line were recastings of French Dinkys, such as the Citroën DS Pallas and the Matra Simca Bagheera. After Pilen's demise in the 1980s, some Pilen dies were used by AHC of the Netherlands. Pilens are comparable to Solido in detail, though their colors are brighter, comparable to SpectraFlame colors on the earliest Hot Wheels.

Auto Pilen 1:43 Scale

Adams Brothers Probe $65-80
Buggi Playero $45-60
Chevrolet Astro I $60-75
Chevrolet Corvette Stingray Split Window,
1967 ....$80-95
Citroën 2 CV $60-75
DeTomaso Mangusta $65-80
Ferrari 512 ....$50-65
Ferrari P5 ....$65-80
Ford Mark II $50-65
Ghibli Maserati $50-65
Javelin $80-95
Mercedes 250 Coupe $60-75
Mercedes Ambulance Sedan $60-75
Mercedes C-111 ....$50-65
Mercedes Taxi $50-65
Mini Cooper $50-65
Modulo Pininfarina $50-65
Monteverdi Hai 450 SS, yellow with black trunk
and hood, #347 ....$50-65

Monza Spider $50-65
Oldsmobile Toronado Police $100-125
Oldsmobile Toronado $105-140
Porsche 917 ....$45-60
Porsche Carrera 6, shocking pink with clear win-
dows, #303 ....$45-60
Renault R-12 S $45-60
Renault R-12 G. C. Trafico $45-60
Seat 124-Sport $50-65
Seat 127 ....$50-65
Seat 600 ....$50-65
Seat 850 Spyder $50-65
Stratos Bertone, #509 ....$45-60
Vauxhall SRV $50-65

Auto Pilen 1:64 Scale

Fiat 131 Wagon, 1:64 ....$15-20
Peugeot 504, 1:64 ....$15-20

Auto Replicas

Great Britain is where Auto Replicas were produced. The now-defunct company, owned by foremost modelmaker Barry Lester, manufactured white metal kits.

1937 Packard Model 1507 Club
Sedan $75-90

Autoreplica

Autoreplica is a brand of 1:43 scale diecast models made in Italy.

1932 Alfa 8C Roadster, top down, red,
#29 ....$60-75
Amilcar Italiana $45-60
1925 Austin Van, "Lucas," dark green,
#101 ....$60-75
1921 Bugatti Brescia Racer, #3, blue,
#4 ....$60-75
1955 Chevrolet Bel Air Convertible, top down,
sea green, #33 ....$40-55
1934 ERA Grand Prix Racer "Romulus," light blue
and yellow, #1 ....$60-75
1950 Fiat Panel Van, #Kit 1 ....$20-30
1936 Morgan 2 Seater, green and black,
#44 ....$60-75
1939 Morgan Plus 4 Tourer, #38 ....$60-75
1937 Packard 12 Roadster, top down, blue,
#16 ....$60-75
1937 Packard Formal Sedan, #24 ....$60-75
1937 Packard Tourer/Town car, #24 ....$60-75
1957 Porsche Speedster, unfinished metal, kit,
#8 ....$60-75
1925-26 Renault Record, #Kit 21 ....$20-30
1954 Sunbeam Alpine Roadster, top down,
#28 ....$60-75

1936-37 Tatra 77-77A, blue, #42 ....$60-75

Aviva (also see Hasbro)

Hasbro has been a powerful force in the toy industry since the 1960s. Toys such as Mr. Machine, the see-through gear-driven walking, animated robot with a top hat, was possibly one of the best known toys of the period, at least if you watched Saturday morning cartoons. The most popular and sustaining line of toys for Hasbro has been G.I. Joe. They have since also purchased Kenner, the brand responsible for Fast 111s and Winners Circle diecast cars.

Collector Steve Reeson notes that one Aviva model he found, imprinted with "AVIVA - 1965 United Feature Syndicate Inc. Made in Japan" is approximately 1:64 scale, and looks very similar to a CAN-AM race car of that era.

"What is so interesting," says Reeson, "is that the wheels have a raised lip on the inside of each wheel very similar to a certain Hot Wheels design. It also has a very springy suspension. Given that the car has 1965 on the bottom, could this design have influenced the design team at Mattel back then?" Good question.

Hasbro has continued through to the present, but it has been overshadowed by the giant called Mattel. In the late 1970s and on, Hasbro has produced Aviva character toys usually sold at Hallmark shops. Predominantly models with Peanuts characters from the comic strip of the same name, Aviva at last word continues to market such items in diecast and plastic. Here is a brief sampling.

Aviva Hasbro Large Diecast

Snoopy drives a red hook and ladder fire truck,
wearing a red helmet, Woodstock sits in the
rear (Aviva #72039/1) $8-12
Snoopy drives a yellow convertible with red and
green accents, Woodstock sits on the back
(Aviva #72039/2) $8-12
Snoopy as the Flying Ace pilots yellow biplane with
red wings, "Snoopy," Woodstock's face is on the
tail of the plane (Aviva #72039/3) $8-12
Lucy Van Pelt Jeep with opening hood, folding
windshield $8-12
Charlie Brown driving a righthand drive red and
white #25 race car $8-12

Aviva/Hasbro Mini Diecast

Snoopy wearing a black tuxedo and top hat, yellow Open car (Aviva #72044-2) $6-8
Snoopy wearing a red hat drives a truck called
"Cat Catcher" (Aviva #72044-5) $6-8

Snoopy as the flying ace drives a red racer (Aviva #720044-6) $6-8

B

BAM (see Boutique Auto Moto, Bruce Arnold Models)

Bandai (also see Dapper)

Bandai is best known for high-quality, accurately scaled lithographed tin battery-operated models from Japan. Values are high for their tinplate models, but also a few diecast models are known to exist of this brand.

BMW 320i, No. 3, orange-red with cross and deer head in a circle, "Fagermeister" on roof and hood $8–12

Bandi

Another one of those obscure brands listed in *Schroeder's Collectible Toys Antique to Modern Price Guide*, possibly a misspelling of Bandii or Bandai. Only one model is listed.

1962 Volkswagen Sedan #742 ....$200-225

Bandii

Although possibly related, Bandii is not the same Japanese company as Bandai, a brand famous for their tin friction and battery-operated toy cars and trucks of great detail and quality.

Bandii is a comparatively obscure company that nevertheless produced an interesting assortment of diecast toys.

Hato Bus, blue/white, 4½" $16-20
Hino Gas Tanker "JAL," 1:87 scale $5-8
Lancia Stratos "Alitalia," 1:87 scale $5-8
Mazda RX7 252i, 1:64 scale $5-8
Mitsubishi Galant, 1:64 scale $5-8
Nissan "JAL" Vacuum car, 1:87 scale $5-8
Nissan "KLM" Vacuum car, 1:87 scale $5-8
Nissan "Nippon" Vacuum car, 1:87 scale ...$5-8
Nissan Ambulance, 1:87 scale $5-8
Porsche 928, blue, 1:43 scale $16-20
Porsche 930, silver, 1:43 scale $16-20
Porsche 935, 1:64 scale $5-8
Tank Lorry "JAL," 1:87 scale $5-8
Tank Lorry "KLM," 1:87 scale $5-8
Tank Lorry "Nippon," 1:87 scale $5-8

Bang

When Box Model of Pesaro, Italy, reorganized in 1991, the result was several new diecast companies, Art Model, Bang, and Best

Model. All Bang models are manufactured to exacting 1:43 scale.

Ferrari 250
  GT Mille Miglia 1957, #415 ....$40-50
  GT Prova 1956-57, red, #405 ....$40-50
  GT Stradale 1956-57, silver, #406 ..$40-50
  GT SWB Prova 1961, red, #7075 ..$35-45
  GT SWB Stradale 1961, silver, #7076 ....$35-45
  GT SWB Stradale 1961, yellow, #7077 ....$35-45
  GT SWB Le Mans 1961, red, #7078 ....$35-45
  GT SWB Le Mans 1961, blue, #7083 ....$30-40
  GT SWB Tour De France 1961, red, #7084 ....$30-40
  GT SWB LeMans 1961, white, #7085 ....$35-45
  GT SWB LeMans 1961, silver, #7086 ....$30-40
  GT Tour De France 1957, red, #1010 ..$40-50
  GTO 3 Ore di Pau, red, #407 ....$40-50
  GTO De Montlhery 1962, red, #7095 ....$35-45
  GTO Laguna Seca 1963, #433 ......$40-50
  GTO Le Mans 1962, red, #464 ......$40-50
  GTO Le Mans 1962, white, #402 ..$40-50
  GTO Prova 1962-63, red, #401 .....$40-50
  GTO Sebring 1962, light blue, #432 ..$40-50
  GTO Spa 1965, yellow, #444 ....$40-50
  GTO Thirty Years, chrome, #1013 ....$35-45
  GTO Tour de France 1964, gray, #458 ....$40-50
  GTO Tourist Trophy 1963, red, 409 ..$40-50
  SWB Coupe Montlhery 1991, silver, #1012 ....$40-50
  SWB Coupe red, #1008 ....$40-50
  SWB Coupe Sport Italia #7, red, #1008 ....$35-45
  SWB Coupe Tour de France 1961, blue, #504 ....$40-50
  Tour de France 3 Ore di Pau 1958 2D #59, blue, #7096 ....$35-45
  Tour de France 1958, gray, #431 ...$40-50
  Tour de France 1958, light blue, #441 ....$40-50
  Tour de France 1959, white, #427 ..$40-50
  Tour de France Gran Prix de Paris 1960, red, #426 ....$40-50
  Tour de France Prova, red, #424 ......$35-45
  Tour de France Stradale, silver, #425 ....$40-50
  Tour de France Mille Miglia 1958, red, #1014 ....$40-50

Ferrari 330 P.4
  Prova, red, #7097 ....$40-50
  1967 24 Ore Le Mans, red, #7098 ....$40-50
Ferrari 348TS
  red, #501 ....$25-30
  white, "Cofradis," #501 ....$35-40
  Stradale TD 1991, red, #8001 ....$35-45
  Stradale TD 1991, yellow, #8002 ...$40-50
  Stradale TD 1991, black, #8003 .....$35-45
Ferrari 348TB
  Challenge #48, red, #8007 ....$35-45
  Challenge Benaduce #8, red, #9308 ....$40-50
  Challenge Cutrera #1, white, #9301 ....$40-50
  Challenge Giudici, white, #9302 .....$40-50
  Challenge Peitra #6, red, #9306 .....$40-50
  Challenge Ragazzi #2, white, #9303 ....$40-50
  Challenge Rossi #5, yellow, #9305 ..$40-50
  Stradale, blue, #8004 ....$40-50
  Stradale, red, #8005 ....$40-50
  Stradale, white, #8006 ....$40-50
Ferrari 456GT
  1993 Prova, red, #8013 ....$45-50
Ford AC Cobra
  289 Le Mans 1963, green, #438 ...$35-45
  Laguna Seca, white, #421 ....$40-50
  Le Mans 1963, #420 ....$40-50
  Sebring 1963, #414 ....$40-50
  Spyder, top up, turquoise, #412 .....$35-45
  Spyder, top up, black and white, #412 ....$35-45
  Spyder, Riverside 1962, #422 ......$35-45
  Spyder Stradale, red, #410 ....$40-50
  Spyder Stradale, black, #411 ....$40-50
  Targa Florio 1964, lavender, #423 ...$35-45
Ford GT40
  Coupe Sport Italia Limited, yellow, #1009 ....$40-50
  Le Mans 1966, white, #453 ....$35-45
  Le Mans 1966, white, #456 ....$40-50
  Le Mans 1968, light blue, #1007 ....$35-45
  Le Mans 1968, "10" blue, #7073 ...$35-45
  Le Mans 1968, "11" blue, #7072 ...$35-45
  Le Mans 1969, "6" blue, #7074 ....$35-45
  Mallory Park 1968, red, #455 ....$35-45
  Stradale 1966, gold, #7071 ....$35-45
Ford Mk II
  Le Mans 1966, blue, #7080 ....$35-45
  Le Mans Stradale 1966, black, #7079 ....$35-45
  Le Mans 1966, black, #7081 ....$35-45
  Le Mans 1966, red, #7082 ....$35-45
  Le Mans 1966, gold, #7092 ....$35-45

Le Mans 1966, yellow, #7093 ....$35-45
Sebring 1966, metallic blue, #7091 ..$35-45
Roadster Sebring 1966, #7094 ....$35-45
Mercedes-Benz 300 SL
  Gullwing 1954, cream, #7087 ....$35-45
  Gullwing 1954, red, #7088 ....$35-45
  Coupe 1955, silver, #7089 ....$40-50
  Coupe 1955, black, #7090 ....$40-50
  Le Mans 1956, "7," silver, #7101 ...$40-50
  Tour de France 1956, "81," red,
    #7100 ....$40-50
  Tour de France 1956, "149," silver,
    #7102 ....$40-50
  Mille Miglia 1989, "224," mint blue,
    #7099 ....$35-45
  Mille Miglia 1989, metallic red,
    #1011 ....$40-50

Banner

Banner was started in the Bronx, New York, in 1944 by Emanual M. Pressner and Bernard Schiller. By 1950, Schiller had already left the company, and its headquarters were moved to Paterson, New Jersey.

Banner produced toys out of various materials including plastic, tin, and stamped steel. The latter was produced from scrap metal left over from the manufacture of cars and appliances.

Banner continued producing toys until 1965 when it went bankrupt. Recovery was short-lived, and the company was sold to Minnesota toy conglomerate Tal-Cap in 1967.

Aerial Ladder Truck, with pressed metal wheels,
  #1143, 20" $200-275
American Express Truck, stamped steel,
  11½" $250-325
American Express Truck, stamped steel,
  11¼" $250-325
American Express Truck, tin, 10" $175-250
Army Ambulance, tin and plastic, 6" $30-45
Army Truck, stamped steel, 12" $60-80
Auto Transport, with wooden wheels, 1940,
  16" $200-275
Buick Sedan, 4½" $15-25
Car Transport, lithographed trailer with two plastic
  cars, 16" $225-300
Circus Train and Tractor, plastic,
  1949 ....$150-225
Clown Van, plastic with tin lithographed windows,
  1950s, 4½" $30-45
Coronation Milk Van $250-325
Cross Country Express Truck, plastic and tin with rubber
  tires, late 1940s - early 1950s, 12" ...$225-300
Fair-Lawn Dairy Truck, pressed metal wheels
Delivery Van, 4¼" $15-25

Dodge 1950, plastic, 4" $15-25
Dump Truck, metal, 4" $15-25
Dump Truck, plastic, 5¼" $15-25
Express Truck, plastic, 7" $35-45
Ford Garbage Truck, plastic, 1954, 4" ...$15-25
Grocery Service Truck, with pressed metal wheels,
  13" $225-300
Grocery Service Truck, with plastic wheels,
  11½" $125-200
Hi-Way Emergency Tow Truck, with tools and two
  spare tires, 1940s, 12" $250-325
International Harvester Metro 1950 Van, plastic,
  4" $15-25
Jewel Tea Van $300-375
Kellogg's Express Truck, pressed metal wheels,
  1940s, 13" $450-600
LaFrance Fire Truck, plastic, 1950, 4" $15-25
Livestock Truck, 5½" $20-30
Livestock Truck, plastic, 7" $35-50
Lumber Truck, with pressed metal wheels, #1140,
  15" $200-275
North American Van Lines Truck and Trailer,
  15" $175-250
Oil Truck, plastic, 4⅜" $15-25
Oldsmobile Station Wagon 1948, plastic,
  4" $25-35
Sedan, plastic, 1950s, 4½" $15-25
Stake Truck, with pressed metal wheels,
  13" $100-150
Stake Truck, plastic, 8" $40-55
Stake Truck, with wooden wheels, 1940s,
  8" $75-125
Stake Truck, 4½" $15-25
Steam Roller, plastic, 4" $20-35
Steam Shovel, plastic, 4" $20-35
Tanker, plastic, 7" $20-35
Toy Truck, with pressed metal wheels,
  13" $175-250
Toy Truck Van, 9" $125-175
Tractor, Wheel Horse, plastic, 3" $20-30
Trailer Steamshovel, plastic, 6¾" $25-40
U. S. Army Truck, plastic and tin, 6" $35-50
U. S. Mail Truck, 11" $55-75
Whelan's Steel Truck $250-325
Wonder Bread Truck, tin lithographed,
  11" $150-200

Banthrico (also see National Products)

Banthrico Inc., "The Coin Bank People," started in Chicago, Illinois, in 1914. The main office moved to Golden Valley, Minnesota, by the 1980s. Whether or where Banthrico still produces models is unknown.

Models are generally antiqued brass-like 1:25 to 1:43 scale pot metal vehicles with a slot in the bottom for coins, often with printing on them for the various banks that gave them away to customers when they opened an account. Besides vehicles, Banthrico produced a huge variety of castings that included heads, buildings and monuments, animals, and other unusual items usually somehow associated with American history and heritage, such as Lindbergh's Spirit of St. Louis, cowboys, Indians, buildings, covered wagons, and more.

Older Banthrico castings were copper or bronze colored, usually with antique patina applied. Newer ones are brass in appearance, with the newest ones in pewter color.

Unlike the bank promos, the dealer promos originally produced by Banthrico under their National Products Division, were painted in the vehicle's authentic colors. The Nash in particular was a dealer promo model.

With the help of avid Banthrico collectors Bob and Robin La Rosa, Larry Stitt, and a book by Steve Butler on dealer promotional models, I am now able to offer this more extensive list with more current values.

Banthrico Car and Truck Banks

Baker 1910 Electric $60-65
Beer Truck 1928 ....$50-65
Buick
  1900 Pillbox Coupe $60-65
  1908 ....$60-65
  1924 ....$50-65
  Skylark 1954 Convertible $60-65
Cadillac
  1908 ....$60-65
  1930 Convertible Roadster $60-65
  1954 Sedan $60-65
Chevrolet
  1915 ....$60-65
  1928 Pickup Truck $60-80
  1951 ....$50-65
  1953 Corvette Coupe $50-60
  1954 4-door Sedan $60-65
  1957 Bel Air 2-door Convertible $90-100
  1963 Corvette Coupe $60-65
Chrysler
  1924 ....$50-55
  Town & Country 1946 ....$60-65
Cord
  Phaeton 1926 ....$55-65
  1936 ....$60-70
Dodge 1914 Touring car $60-70
Duesenberg 1930 ....$60-70
Electric car 1902 ....$60-65
Fire Truck $50-60

Ford

1908, fixed wheels	$55-65
1912 T-Bucket	$50-60
1915 Omnibus	$55-75
1917 Touring car	$50-60
1925 Model T	$50-65
1926 Model T Sedan	$60-65
1927 Model T Sedan, fixed wheels	$75-85
1929 Model A	$60-65
1929 Model A Convertible	$60-65
1934 Coupe	$60-65
1934 Convertible	$60-65
1934 Panel Truck	$55-65
1935 English Taxi Cab	$140-160
1955 Pickup Truck	$70-80
1955 Thunderbird	$70-80
1965 Mustang	$60-65

Horse Drawn Fire Pumper, no horse ... $70-100
Jaguar 1955 ... $50-75
Kaiser 1951 ... $50-65
La Salle 1930 Coupe ... $50-65

Lincoln

1908	$60-75
1912 Coach	$60-65
1927 Brougham	$60-65
1941 Continental	$60-65
1969 Continental	$60-65

Mack Truck 1906 ... $75-90
Mercury 2-door hardtop 1954 ... $60-65
MG Convertible 1953 ... $55-60

Nash

1902 Rambler	$65-70
1949 Airflyte	$55-60

Oldsmobile

1906	$60-65
1923	$50-65

Oldsmobile 88

1953	$75-100
1954	$75-100

Oldsmobile 98 1956 Convertible ... $60-65

Packard

1937 V-12	$50-60
1954 4-door Sedan	$60-65

Pickup 1928 ... $50-65
Pierce Arrow 1917 ... $50-65
Police Wagon 1915 ... $50-65

Pontiac

1926	$65-70
1964	$50-65

Rolls Royce 1937 ... $60-65
Stanley Steamer 1910 ... $75-80

Studebaker

1904	$60-65
1957 Golden Hawk	$70-80

U. S. Mail Truck, recalled by Postmaster General
1919 ... $250-275

Volkswagen Beetle 1977 ... $70-75

Other Banthrico Banks

Buildings, various historical structures ... $95-125
Busts, various heads of historical figures ... $95-125
Cannon ... $75-90
Covered Wagon ... $90-100
Minute Man ... $65-80
Popcorn cart ... $90-100
Robot ... $90-100
Spirit of St. Louis, Lindbergh's solo Trans-Atlantic airplane ... $90-125
Stage Coach ... $55-70
Two-piece Train; engine and coal car ... $300-375

Banthrico Dealer Promos

Buick Roadmaster

1952 4-door	$250-300
1953 4-door	$250-300
1954 2-door hardtop	$350-40
reissue	$100-125
1955 2-door hardtop	$375-425

Buick Super 1956 4-door hardtop ... $375-425
Cadillac 62 1952 4-door ... $175-250

Cadillac Fleetwood 1954 4-door ... $250-325
| reissue | $100-125 |

Cadillac Biarritz 1955 2-door

hardtop	$300-350
reissue	$100-125

Cadillac Biarritz 1956 2-door, hardtop ... $275-350

Chevrolet 210

1953 4-door	$225-275
1954 4-door	$225-275

Chevrolet Bel Air 1955 2-door

hardtop	$200-250
reissue	$100-125

Chevrolet Corvette

1954 Convertible, circa 1973 in red, white, or blue	$100-125

Chevrolet Fleetline

1949 2-door	$325-375
1949 4-door	$325-375
1950 2-door	$225-275
1950 4-door	$250-300

Chevrolet Styleline

1949 2-door	$325-375
1949 4-door	$325-375
1949 Coupe	$350-400
1950 2-door	$225-275
1950 2-door hardtop	$275-325
1950 4-door	$225-275
1950 Coupe	$275-325
1950 Convertible	$225-275

Chrysler New Yorker

1950 4-door	$250-300

1953 2-door hardtop	$350-375
1954 4-door	$400-450
1955 4-door	$325-375
reissue	$100-125
1955 4-door with dealer or color markings	$400-450

Dodge Coronet

1950 4-door	$250-300
1951–52 4-door	$250-300
1953 4-door	$250-300

Dodge Royal 1954 4-door ... $325-375
Ford Custom 1950 4-door ... $175-225

Ford Customline

1953 4-door	$225-275
1956 4-door	$250-300

Ford F-100 1953 Pickup ... $300-350
| reissue | $100-125 |

Ford Fairlane 1955 4-door ... $250-300
| reissue | $100-125 |

Jeep M-715 1967 U. S. Army Stake Truck ... $150-175
Kaiser Manhattan 1953 ... $400-450

Lincoln Cosmopolitan

1953 4-door	$400-450
1954 2-door hardtop	$250-300
reissue	$100-125

Mercury 1951 4-door ... $275-325

Mercury Monterey

1953 4-door	$400-450
1954 2-door hardtop	$275-325
1955 2-door hardtop	$375-425

Nash Rambler

1951–52 2-door hardtop, single color	$325-375
1951–52 2-door hardtop, two-tone	$350-400
1953–54 2-door hardtop, single color	$325-375
1953–54 2-door hardtop, two-tone	$350-400

Oldsmobile 88

1953 4-door	$375-425
1954 2-door hardtop	$250-300
reissue	$100-125

Oldsmobile 98 1955 2-door

hardtop	$450-500

Packard Clipper

1953 4-door	$350-400
reissue	$100-125
1954 4-door, single color	$450-500
1954 4-door, two-tone	$475-525

Plymouth Cranbrook 1953 4-door ... $250-275
Plymouth Belvedere 1955 2-door ... $325-375
Plymouth Savoy 1956 2-door ... $300-350

Pontiac Chieftain 1953 2-door

hardtop	$250-300

Pontiac Starfire 1955 2-door hardtop ...$325-375
Studebaker Commander 1953 2-door hardtop $375-425
Willys 1950 2-door wagon $400-450

Bapro

Bapro was founded in Sweden around 1945 and is known to have produced a pair of Mercedes racing cars 1930s vintage, a Jeep, and a very futuristic "Mooncar."

Jeep, 4", wire windshield frame, wooden wheels $125-150
Mercedes Grand Prix Racer "9," 4¼" ..$175-200
Mercedes Grand Prix Racer, "42," 4⅜" $150-175
Mooncar $200-225

Barclay

From 1924 to 1971, Barclay produced a large assortment of toys from various headquarters in West Hoboken, Union City, and North Bergen, New Jersey, beginning with lead alloy models in the 1930s and 1940s and later changing to zamac (zinc alloy). Most models are fairly common in appearance, but a few represent sleek, streamlined "futuristic" styling that reflects the Art Deco influence of the period. Below is just a sampling of models.

Ambulance, #194, 3½" $40-50
Ambulance, #50, 5" $50-60
Anti-Aircraft Gun Truck, #198, 4" $35-45
Armored Army Truck, #152, 2⅞" $25-35
Army car with two soldiers lying down, gunner on right, driver on left $25-35
Army car with two silver bullhorns, 2½" $40-50
Army Tractor (Minneapolis-Moline), 2¾" ...$25-35
Army Truck with Gun, #151, 2¾" $30-40
Army Truck with Anti-Aircraft Gun, #151, 2½" $25-35
Army Tank Truck, #197, 3⅛" $30-40
Auburn Speedster, #58, ...$30-40
Austin Coupe, 2" $30-40
Auto Transport Set, truck with small trailer, 4½" and 2 cars $60-70
Beer Truck, with barrels $50-60
Bluebird Racer $400-450
Buck Rogers Rocket Ship $900-1200
Bus, "Coast to Coast," "Barclay Toy," two-piece, #405, 2⅞" $75-100
Bus, Futuristic, 3" $25-35
Cannon Car, battery powered light (1935), 3½" $200-250
Chrysler Airflow, 4" $85-110
Chrysler Imperial Coupe, #39 ....$25-35
Convertible with mother and five children, 1920s-1930s $1200
Cord Front Drive Coupe, #40, 3⅝" $35-45
Double Decker Bus, 4" $60-75
1937 Federal Truck $25-40
1940 Anti Aircraft $25-40
Mack Pick Up Truck, 3½" $25-40
Milk & Cream Truck, 3⅝", #377, white rubber tires $60-85
Milk Truck, 3⅝", #377, black rubber tire ..$40-55
Milk Truck shaped like a milk bottle, #567 ....$250-300
Parcel Delivery, #45, 3⅝" $100-150
Renault Tank, #47, 4" $35-45
Searchlight Truck, 4¹⁄₁₆" $150-200
Silver Arrow Race Car, 5½" $35
Station Wagon, 2-piece "Barclay Toy," #404, 2¹⁵⁄₁₆" $60-85
Steam-Roller, 3¼", slush lead with tin roof ..$50-65
Streamline car, #302, 3⅛" $35-45
Taxi, #318, 3¼" $20-30
Wrecker, two-piece diecast, #403, 2⅞" ...$70-85

Barlux

The Italian firm of Barlux started producing diecast toys around 1970 and continued until about 1983. Barlux toys failed to gain popularity in Europe due to their comparatively crude design. They weren't widely distributed and are difficult to find. Values remain low mostly because most collectors have never heard of them.

Brabham-Ford Race Car, 1:66, #73008 .$12-16
BRM Race Car, 1:66, #73003 ....$12-16
Ferrari B2 Race Car, 1:66, #73005 ....$12-16
Fiat 697
- Dump Truck & Loader, 1:43, #762 ...$16-20
- Fire Truck, 1:43, #705 ....$16-20
- Flat Truck & Fork Lift, 1:43, #739 ....$16-20
- Flat Truck & Trailer, 1:43, #747 ....$16-20

Fiat Ambulance, 1:24, #101 ....$30-35
Fiat Carabinieri, 1:24, #102 ....$30-35
Fiat Wrecker, 1:24, #100 ....$30-35
Garbage Truck, 1:43, #73085 ....$16-20
Land Rover and Caravan, 1:43, #73062 ....$16-20
Lotus-Ford 72 V8 Race Car, 1:66, #73002 ....$10-15
Lotus Turbine Race Car, 1:66, #73010 ..$10-15
March-Ford Race Car, 1:66, #73006 ...$10-15
Matra MS-120 V12 Race Car, 1:66, #73001 ....$10-15
McLaren-Ford Race Car, 1:66, #73007..$10-15
MTS-10 Fork Lift, 1:43, #73082 ....$16-20
MTS-20 Shovel Loader, 1:43, #73081 ...$16-20
MTS-20 Snowplow-Sander, 1:43, #73084 ....$16-20
MTS-30 Trencher, 1:43, #73083 ....$16-20
Public Works Vehicle with Snowplow, 1:50, #73810 ....$16-20
Road Roller, 1:43, #73086 ....$16-20
Surtees-Ford Race Car, 1:66, #73009 ...$10-15
Tyrrell-Ford, 1:66, #73004 ....$10-15

Barrett & Sons

In 1945, A. R. Barrett Sr., founder of Taylor & Barrett, along with his two sons Alfred Barrett Jr. and Bert Barrett, started A. Barrett & Sons Ltd. at 9 Sonderberg Road, London, England. At first, they reissued pre-WWII figures, mostly soldiers and some farm and zoo animals. A few years later, children's TV characters were produced for London Toy Co. and doll house furniture for Barton & Co. While the company produced only a couple of vehicles and one airplane, their figures and accessories were popular additions for imaginative play.

Barrett & Sons Vehicles

De Havilland Comet Airplane, #137 ....$55-70
Small Fire Engine, #120 ....$40-50
Small Trolley Bus, #612 ....$40-50

Barrett & Sons Figures

Children Hand-in-Hand, #149 ....$20-25
Firemen Assortment, #135 ....$20-25
Governess Cart Set, #109 ....$40-50
Ladies, #147 ....$20-25
Motorcyclist, #573 ....$20-25
Mounted Policeman, #143 ....$40-50
New Gents, #148 ....$20-25
New Postman, #159 ....$20-25
Traffic Policeman, #142 ....$20-25

Barrett & Sons Accessories

Air and Water, #604 ....$15-20
Fire Escape, #136 ....$40-50
Oil Cabinet, #603 ....$15-20
Petrol Pumps, #130 ....$20-25
Petrol Pumps, #571 ....$15-20
Petrol Pumps, #601 ....$15-20
Safety Island, #607 ....$15-20
Traffic Lights, #615 ....$15-20
Traffic Signal, #141 ....$15-20

Basteltip

Nothing is known about this brand except for one documented model.

Raba Fire Crane, 24" $35-40

Bayshore Repli-Cars

According to information provided by collector Duane Kaufhold, Bayshore Repli-Cars are approximately 1:64 scale models that were made in Holland. He found two examples, a 1919 Ford Model T Crane Truck and a 1919 Ford Model T Pick-Up each in its own blister-pack, with most of 20 other vehicles listed on the back. Original price was 65 cents. Copyright date is 1967 by Bayshore Industries, Inc., New York, NY, a subsidiary of Miner Industries.

BMW 2000 CS, #7	$10-12
Brabham Formula 1 - 3L, #18	$10-12
Citroën ID 19, #10	$10-120
Cooper-Maserati Formula 1 - 3L, #19	$10-12
Ferrari Formula 1 - 3L, #17	$10-12
1919 Ford Model T	
Pickup, #1	$10-12
Crane Truck, #3	$10-12
Delivery Truck, #4	$10-12
Two-Seater, #5	$10-12
Sedan, #6	$10-12
Ford Taunus 17M, #11	$10-12
Jaguar E Type, #13	$10-12
Lotus Formula 1 - 3L, #20	$10-12
Mercedes-Benz	
230 SL, #14	$10-12
250 SE, #16	$10-12
Opel Rekord 1900, #15	$10-12
Porsche, #2	$10-12
Volkswagen 1600 TL, #8	$10-12

BBR

EWA says it best in one of their recent catalogs: "BBR models are outstanding for their superb hand-built quality and detailing. The company was started just over ten years ago in a small town midway between Lake Como and Milan and not far from Monza, in the north of Italy. It quickly achieved world fame for its finely detailed 1:43 scale models with the super paint finish.

"The cars modeled, as befits an Italian company, are mostly race cars and mostly Ferraris, with some Alfa Romeos and Lancias. Other subjects have been covered too, including Porsche, McLaren, Benetton, Williams (and other F1 cars), and Nissan, plus some Lincolns as raced in the Carrera Pan Americana in the early 1950s. Many of the cars modeled are also available as kits."

Alfa Romeo 2900 Berlinetta	
1939 Touring Long	$150-175
8C 1938, maroon, "8"	$195-220
8C 1938, maroon, "19"	$195-220
Alfa Romeo 2500	
SS Villa d'Este 1949 Coupe	$140-165
SS Coupe 1952 Monte Carlo, burgundy	$190-215
6c "Duxia" 1939	$160-185
6c 1950	$160-185
6c 1956 Street, maroon	$185-210
6c 1956 MM Fangio, maroon, "730"	$185-210
Alfa Romeo Villa D'Este	
1949 Coupe, silver	$175-200
1952 Convertible, top down	$155-180
Alfa Romeo 155 V6 DTM 1993	
Nannini	$230-255
Ferrari 125 S 1947 Street, red	$180-205
Ferrari 212	
1950 International Nurburgring, top down, blue	$180-205
1951 Carrera Panamerican "No. 9 Ascari"	$160-185
1952 "Interpininfarina"	$140-165
1952 International Pininfarina Bordeaux, black	$155-180
1951 Carrera Panamerican "No. 3"	$155-180
Ferrari 250	
1954 Europa Street, red	$155-180
1954 Europa "Cabriolet Pininfarina"	$150-175
1954 Europa NY Show, maroon/gray	$195-220
1956 Europa "Boano"	$160-185
1957 GT PR Bernhard, black	$185-210
1959 GTE	$160-185
1959 "Enzo Ferrari"	$160-185
1962 GTO	$160-185
Ferrari 275 1965 GTB	$170-195
Ferrari 288	
1984 GTO	$160-185
1984 GTO 2-door Coupe, red	$180-205
Ferrari 308	
1982 GTB Coupe, red	$180-205
1982 GTB Coupe, silver	$180-205
1982 GTB Coupe, blue	$180-205
1982 GTB Coupe, yellow	$180-205
Ferrari 330	
1965 GT 2+2, available in red, blue, metallic green, or dark gray	$200-225
1967 GTC Liliana Di R, blue	$180-205
1967 P4 LeMans #24	$200-225
Ferrari 348 1993 Cabriolet	$160-185
Ferrari 375	
1954 Am Vign. Turin, yellow	$185-210
1954 MM Pan Am Chinetti, red	$130-155
1955 Am "Giovanni Agnelli"	$160-185
1955 Am Agnl-Torino, green	$180-205

Ferrari 410 1956 SA di Parigi, beige	$175-200
Ferrari 412	
T 1985 2+2, red	$200-225
T 1985 2+2, silver	$200-225
T 1985 2+2, blue	$200-225
T 1985 2+2, metallic green	$200-225
T1 1994 Berger F1 Racer	$220-245
Ferrari 512 1976 BB Coupe, yellow	$185-210
Ferrari 550 1997 Maranello, available in red or yellow	$200-225
Ferrari F40	
1991 Koenig Coupe, red	$175-200
1991 Koenig Coupe, yellow	$175-200
Ferrari F50	
1996 Coupe, red	$200-225
1996 Spyder, red	$200-225
Ferrari Testarossa	
1987 "Giovanni Agnelli" Convertible, silver	$140-165
1987 Straman Convertible, red	$165-190
1988 "Koenig"	$140-165
Porsche 356A 1953	$190-215
Porsche 911 1993 Carrera	$190-215

Bburago (also see Martoys)

Since Bburago (spelled with two B's) entered the diecast miniature market in the mid-1970s as Martoys, their dominance on the US market has risen steadily. Producing precision scale models as well as toys since 1974, Bburago is one of the few diecast collectibles still manufactured in Europe instead of Asia... Milan, Italy, to be specific. The Bburago name was adapted in 1977.

Bburago models mostly replicate Italian sports cars such as Ferrari, Lamborghini, Alfa Romeo, and Bugatti. But also represented are Mercedes-Benz, Jaguar, Porsche, and even a couple of Dodge Vipers and Chevrolet Corvettes, with an ever-expanding assortment. Many models are available both as pre-assembled models and unassembled kits, as listed below.

In addition, Bburago made at least one 1:12 scale model.

Bburago Series

0100 series – Super, 1:24 scale models
0500 series – VIP, 1:24 scale models
1500 series – 1:43 scale trucks, 1974-1980
1500 series – Bijoux, 1:24 scale models
2100 series – 1:14 scale Formula One models, 1976–1981
3000 series – Diamonds, 1:18 scale models
3300 series – Gold Collection, 1:18 scale models
3500 series – DeLuxe, 1:18 scale kits
3700 series – Executive, 1:18 scale kits

4000 series – 1:43 scale models, introduced in 1988

4100 series – Pocket / Street Fire, 1:43 scale models, boxed

4800 series – Pocket, 1:43 scale models, blister packed

4500 series – Portachiavi, 1:87 scale models

5100 series – Kit Super, 1:24 scale kits

5500 series – Kit Bijoux, 1:24 scale kits

6100 series – Grand Prix, 1:24 scale models

7000 series – Kit Diamonds, 1:18 scale kits

Bburago Early 1500 Series

Cement Mixer, #1506 ....$25-30
Covered Dump Truck, #1501 ....$25-30
Crane Truck, #1502 ....$25-30
Dump Truck, #1505 ....$25-30
Fire Crane Truck, #1511 ....$25-30
Fire Ladder Truck, #1509 ....$25-30
Flatbed with Boat, #1512 ....$25-30
Lumber Truck, #1504 ....$25-30
Lumber Truck, #1507 ....$25-30
Milk Tank Truck, #1510 ....$25-30
Quarry Dump Truck, #1503 ....$25-30
Tank Truck, #1508 ....$25-30

Bburago 1:12 Scale

1937 Jaguar SS100, 1:12 scale $125-150

Bburago 1:14 Scale Formula One Models

Brabham BT46 1976, #2103 ....$40-50
Ferrari 312 T2 1976, #2101 ....$50-60
Ferrari 312 T5 1980, #2108 ....$50-60
Lotus 79/JPS MK4 1978, #2105 ....$40-50
Lotus Essex MK3 1981, #2106 ....$40-50
Renault RE20 1980, #2109 ....$40-50
Tyrell 009 1979, #2107 ....$40-50
Tyrell P34/2 1976, #2102 ....$40-50

Bburago 1:18 Scale Models and Kits

Alfa Romeo
  8C 2300 Monza 1931, #3014/3514 ..$25-30
G. P. Mon. 1931, #7014 ....$25-30
2300 Spider 1932, #3008 ....$25-30
2300 Touring 1932, #7008 ....$25-30

BMW M Roadster 1996 ....$25-30

Bugatti EB 110 1991, #3035/3045/
  3055/3735/7035 ....$25-30

Bugatti Type 59 1934
  #3005/3505 ....$25-30
Grand Prix, #7005 ....$25-30
Chevrolet Corvette 1957, #3024/3034/
  3534/3724/7024 ....$25-30
Dodge Viper RT/10 1992, #3025/3065/
  3525/3725/7025 ....$25-30
Ferrari 250
  Testa Rossa 1957, #3007/3507 ....$25-30
  Testa Rossa 1957 Le Mans, #7007...$25-30
  GTO 1962, #3011/3511 ....$25-30
  GTO 1962 Nurburgring, #7011 .....$25-30
Ferrari 348 TB
  1989, #3039/3739/7039 ....$25-30
Evoluzione 1991, #3529 ....$25-30
Evoluzione 1992, #3029 ....$25-30
Ferrari 456 GT 1992, #3036/3746 ....$25-30
Ferrari F40
  1987, #3022/3032/3732/7032 ..$25-30
  1992 Evoluzione, #3042 ....$25-30

Ferrari F50 1995, red $25-30

Ferrari GTO
  1984, #3027/3527/7027 ....$25-30
  1986 Rally, #3057 ....$25-30
Ferrari Testarossa 1984, #3004/3019/
  3519/7019 ....$25-30
Jaguar "E" 1961
  Cabriolet, #3016/3026/3516 ......$25-30
  Cabriolet Tour de France, #7016 .....$25-30
  Coupe, #3018/3038/3718/7018 ..$25-30
Jaguar SS 100 1937
  #3006 ....$25-30
  Targa Florio, #7006 ....$25-30
Lamborghini Countach 1988, #3037/3047/
  3737 ....$25-30
Lamborghini Diablo 1990, #3028/3041/
  3528/3741/7041 ....$25-30
Lancia Aurelia B24 Spider 1955, #3010/
  7010 ....$25-30
Mercedes-Benz 300 SL 1954, #3013/
  3015/3513/7013 ....$25-30
Mercedes-Benz 500 K Roadster 1936, #3020/
  3520/7020 ....$25-30
Mercedes-Benz SSK 1928 #3009/
  3509 ....$25-30
Monte Carlo, #7009 ....$25-30

Mercedes-Benz SSKL 1931 "Caracciola,"
  #3002/3702
    chrome $70-80
    other $25-30
Mille Miglia, #7002 ....$25-30
Porsche 356 B 1961
  Cabriolet, #3031/3051/3731 ......$25-30
  Coupe, #3021/3521/3721/7021 ..$25-30

Bburago 1:22 Scale Models

Rolls-Royce Camargue, cream, 1:22,
  #3001 ....$25-30

Bburago 1:24 Scale Models

Alfa Romeo 75
  Carabinieri, #0189 ....$12-15
  Guardia Di Finanza, #0190 ....$12-15
  Group A, #0119 ....$12-15
  Polizia, #0188 ....$12-15
  #5119 ....$7-10
Alfa Romeo Giulietta Alpilatte, #4110 ....$7-10
BMW 635 CSi, #5173 ....$7-10
Bugatti Atlantic 1936, #0503/1503 ...$12-15
Bugatti EB 110 1991, #0535/1535 ...$12-15
Bugatti 1932 Type 55, #0538 ....$12-15
Chevrolet Corvette 1957
  #1524 ....$12-15
  #5524 ....$7-10
Citroën 15 CV TA 1938
  #1501 ....$12-15
  #5501 ....$7-10
Ferrari 250
  1962 GTO, #0510/#1510 ....$12-15
  1962 GTO, #5510 ....$7-10
  1965 Le Mans, #0506 ....$12-15
  1966 Le Mans "Monza," #1506 .....$12-15
  1966 Le Mans Daytona, #5506 ....$7-10
Ferrari 275 GTB 4 1966, #0511/1511 ..$12-15
Ferrari 308 GTB
  #0148 ....$12-15
  #5148 ....$7-10
Ferrari 348 TB
  1989, #1539 ....$12-15
  1989, #5539 ....$7-10
Evoluzione, #0129 ....$12-15
Monteshell, #5129 ....$7-10
Ferrari 456 GT 1992, #1532/1536 ....$12-15
Ferrari 512 BB, #0133 ....$12-15
Daytona, #5133 ....$7-10
Ferrari F40
  1987, #0532 ....$12-15
  1987, #5540 ....$7-10
  1992 Evoluzione, #0542 ....$12-15
Ferrari GTO
  1984, #0572 ....$12-15
Rally, #0192 ....$12-15

Pioneer, #5172 ....$7-10

Ferrari Testa Rossa 1957
  #1507 ....$12-15
  #5507 ....$7-10

Ferrari Testarossa 1984
  #0104/0504 ....$12-15
  #5504 ....$7-10

Fiat Cinquecento
  #0194 ....$12-15
  Rally, #5194 ....$7-10

Fiat Tipo, #0125 ....$12-15

Ford AC Cobra 427 1965
  #0513 ....$12-15
  #5513 ....$7-10

Jaguar XK 120 1948
  Coupe, #1508 ....$12-15
  Roadster, #1502 ....$12-15
  Roadster, #5502 ....$7-10

Jeep CJ-7 Renegade, #0198 ....$12-15

Kremer Porsche 935 Turbo (see Porsche 935)

Lamborghini Countach
  5000 Quattrovalvole, #0137 ....$12-15
  1988, #0537 ....$12-15
  1988, #5537 ....$7-10

Lamborghini Diablo 1990, #0541 ...$12-15

Lancia Delta S4
  #0115 ....$12-15
  #5115 ....$7-10

Mercedes-Benz 190 E
  #0105 ....$12-15
  #5105 ....$7-10

Mercedes-Benz 300 SL 1954
  #0130 ....$12-15
  #0522 ....$12-15
  #5509 ....$7-10
  #5532 ....$7-10

Mercedes-Benz 500 SEC, #0111 ....$12-15

Mercedes-Benz SSK 1928, #1509 ......$16-20

Peugeot 205
  Safari, #0116 ....$12-15
  Turbo 16, #5106 ....$7-10

Peugeot 405 Raid
  #0131 ....$12-15
  #5131 ....$7-10

Porsche 911 Armel, #5102 ....$7-10

Porsche 911S, metallic blue or metallic silver,
  #0102 ....$12-15

Porsche 924 Turbo
  Group 2, #0199 ....$12-15
  #5199 ....$7-10

Porsche 935 Turbo, Kremer Porsche, #5142 ...$7-10

Porsche 959
  #0121 ....$12-15
  Turbo, metallic gray, #0163 ....$12-15
  1986 Turbo, #0563 ....$12-15
  Raid, #5121 ....$7-10

Range Rover Safari, #0112 ....$12-15

Bburago Grand Prix 1:24 Scale Formula One Racers

Benetton Ford, #6102 ....$7-10

Burago Team, #6109 ....$7-10

Ferrari 64½
  "27," #6101 ....$7-10
  "28," #6128 ....$7-10

Formula 3000, #6121 ....$7-10

Formula USA, #6110 ....$7-10

Grand Prix F.1, #6103 ....$7-10

Indy Team, #6122 ....$7-10

Race Champion, #6104 ....$7-10

Williams FW14, #6108 ....$7-10

Bburago 1:43 Scale Models

Alfa Romeo 33
  #4008/4028 ....$7-10
  Rally, #4124 ....$7-10
  Polizia, #4186 ....$7-10
  Carabinieri, #4187 ....$7-10
  #4193 ....$7-10

Alfa Romeo Giulietta
  Group 2, #4164 ....$7-10
  Polizia, #4176 ....$7-10
  Carabinieri, #4177 ....$7-10

Audi Quattro
  #4003/4023 ....$7-10
  GT Sanyo, #4159 ....$7-10

BMW 535i
  metallic dark champagne red with light gray
    interior, #4158 ....$7-10
  #4178 ....$7-10

BMW M1
  #4007 ....$7-10
  #4027 ....$7-10

GT Cup, white, Valvoline, #4167 ....$7-10

GT Cup, green with "tic tac" Rally accents, gray
  interior, #4167 ....$7-10

Chevrolet Corvette

green, #4124 ....$7-10
  #4152 ....$7-10
  #4192 ....$7-10

Citroën Xantia, #4155/4165 ....$7-10

Dodge Viper GTS Coupe, metallic blue with white racing stripes, #4115 ....$7-10

Dodge Viper RT/10

white, #4130 ....$7-10

metallic blue, #4189 ....$7-10

metallic gray, #4169 ....$7-10
  IMSA, #4105 ....$7-10

BMW M3

DTM, white, Warsteiner, #4197 ....$7-10

black with silver racing stripes, #4105 ..$7-10
red, #4125 ....$7-10
yellow, #4165 ....$7-10

Ferrari 308
#4010/4030 ....$7-10
GTB, #4117 ....$7-10
GTB Rally, red "PIONEER" Rally accents, black interior, light gray steering wheel and Rally lights on nose, #4148 ....$7-10

Ferrari 348 TB
red with cream interior, #4139 ....$7-10
Evoluzione, red with Rally decals, cream interior, #4129 ....$7-10
#4189 ....$7-10

Ferrari 456 GT
red, #4136 ....$7-10
metallic dark blue with pale beige interior, #4146 ....$7-10

Ferrari 512 BB
#4004/4024/4133 ....$7-10
Daytona, #4106 ....$7-10

Ferrari F40
#4108/4128 ....$7-10
Evoluzione, red with Rally accents, silver gray interior, #4168 ....$7-10

Ferrari GTO
Rally, red with Rally logos, white interior, #4107 ....$7-10
yellow with cream interior, #4175 ....$7-10

Ferrari Testarossa
red with white interior, #4104 ....$7-10
yellow with cream interior, #4157 ....$7-10

Fiat Cinquecento / 500

green, #4193 ....$7-10

Rally, metallic gray, #4138 ......$7-10
Fiat Panda
#4005/4025 ....$7-10

Rally, #4113 ....$7-10

Fiat Punto, red, #4144 ....$7-10

Fiat Regata
#4121 ....$7-10
Rally, #4134 ....$7-10
Fiat Ritmo
Totip, #4116 ....$7-10
Abarth, #4168 ....$7-10
Fiat Tipo
Rally, #4134 ....$7-10
#4179 ....$7-10
Fiat Uno
#4119 ....$7-10
Rally, #4120 ....$7-10
Ford Escort Rally 4x4

blue, Michelin, #4173 ....$7-10

white, Gulf, #4119 ....$7-10

Martini, white, #4163 ....$7-10
Ford Focus Rally

red, #4174 ....$7-10
Ford Sierra Group A

Rally, black, Texaco, #4143 ....$7-10

Rally, #4183 ....$7-10
Jeep CJ5 Renegade, #4006/4026/ 4122/4132 ....$7-10
Lamborghini Countach

400S, #4137 ....$7-10

5000, #4127 ....$7-10
Lamborghini Diablo
yellow, #4141 ....$7-10
red with cream interior, #4151 ....$7-10
Lancia Beta
Martini, #4170 ....$7-10
Alitalia, #4172 ....$7-10
Lancia Delta
S4, #4135 ....$7-10
Rally, #4180 ....$7-10
Lancia Stratos
#4001/4021 ....$7-10
VSD, #4108 ....$7-10
Pirelli, #4166 ....$7-10

Land Rover 109 Aziza, red rally, #4131 ..$7-10

Martini, white, #4128 ....$7-10

Land Rover Raid, #4171 .... $7-10

Mazda RX7

#4118 .... $7-10

Group 2, #4174 .... $7-10

MCA Centenaire, metallic silver blue,
#4140 .... $7-10

Mercedes-Benz 190 E, #4102/4149 ... $7-10

Mercedes-Benz 300 SL

#4181 .... $7-10

Convertible, top down, metallic blue, cream
interior, #4109 .... $7-10

Mercedes-Benz 450 SC Mampe,
#4165 .... $7-10

MIG Georgia Centenaire, #4170 ...... $7-10

Peugeot 205

#4002/4022 .... $7-10

GTI, #4125 .... $7-10

Safari, #4116 .... $7-10

Turbo 16, #4123 .... $7-10

Peugeot 405

Raid, #4150 .... $7-10

Safari, #4190 .... $7-10

Porsche 911

#4114 .... $7-10

Carrera 1993, red with light gray interior,
#4185 .... $7-10

Carrera 1997, red, #4178 .... **$7-10**

Carrera Cup, #4195 .... $7-10

Carrera Super Cup, black, #4153 .... **$7-10**

Carrera Super Cup, yellow with Rally accents,
light gray interior, #4153 .... $7-10

Turbo, #4147 .... $7-10

Porsche 924

Turbo, #4103 .... $7-10

Turbo Group 2, #4111 .... $7-10

Porsche 928

Grand Am, #4110 .... $7-10

red with light gray interior, #4191 .... **$7-10**

Porsche 935

#4012/4032 .... $7-10

Vaillant, #4142 .... $7-10

Momo, #4184 .... $7-10

Porsche 959

Rally, #4126 .... $7-10

#4161 .... $7-10

Range Rover

#4011/4031 .... $7-10

T Castrol, #4156 .... $7-10

Renault 9, #4109 .... $7-10

Renault R5 Turbo

#4115 .... $7-10

Monte Carlo, #4160 .... $7-10

Renault R9 Rally, #4112 .... $7-10

Renault Clio

'98, red, #4101 .... $7-10

RT, #4130 .... $7-10

16V, #4160 .... $7-10

Saab 900 Turbo, #4009/4029/
4101 .... $7-10

Shelby Series 1, green **$9–12**

Suzuki Vitara

Raid, #4112 .... $7-10

#4194 .... $7-10

Volkswagen New Beetle

yellow, #4142 .... **$7-10**

metallic blue, #4172 .... **$7-10**

Bburago Portachiavi 1:87 scale

Ferrari Testarossa, #4519 .... $2-4

Ferrari F40, #4532 .... $2-4

Mercedes-Benz 300 SL, #4513 .... $2-4

Porsche 959, #4563 .... $2-4

Bburago Disney Characters, 1:18 Scale

For just one season at Disney World, two 1:18 scale character toy cars were offered for $20-25 each, as reported by collector Robert Birkenes of Tampa, Florida. Each was 10" long and is now considered rare and very valuable.

Goofy, ("Pippo" on package), #8005 .... $75-90

Donald Duck, ("Paperina" on package),
#8006 .... $75-90

Beanstalk

The Beanstalk Group
28 East 28th Street
New York, NY 10016
Tel: (212) 421-6060
Fax: (212) 421-6388
www.beanstalk.com

Beanstalk Group, Inc. is a promotional merchandise management company whose clients include Harley-Davidson, The Coca-Cola Company, The Stanley Works, AT&T, Mary-Kate and Ashley, GE, The Ford Motor Company, Lincoln Navigator, Molson Canadian, and others. Their 1:18 scale diecast models are reportedly produced by Creative Master of China.

silver, BST10027 .... **$30-40**

2003 Aston Martin V12 Vanquish, metallic gray, from James Bond 007 "Die Another Day," BST10011 ....$30-40

2004 Ford F-150 FX4 Pick Up
yellow, BST10025 ....$30-40
black, BST10026 ....$30-40
white, BST10028 ....$30-40
white with mud splatter, BST10028MS ..$30-40
red, BST10029 ....$30-40

Ford GT
yellow with black stripe, BST10020 ..$30-40
white with Navy stripe, BST10021 ....$30-40
red with white stripe, BST10022 ....$30-40

Beaut

"It's A Beaut" was the company slogan for Beaut Manufacturing Company based in northern New Jersey. The company produced just a few simple models from 1946 until 1950. The cars were made of a single casting like Tootsietoys, with large tires. All models are based on a 1942 Chrysler Sedan.

Fire Chief car $20-30
Police car $20-30
Sedan $20-30
Taxi $20-30
Van $20-30

The Beckman Collection

Beckman Jr/Sr High School
1325 9th St. SE
Dyersville IA 52040
319-875-7188.

Beckman Jr./Sr. High School has taken advantage of its location in Dyersville, Iowa, home of the world-renowned Ertl company, to offer an assortment of customized Ertl, Scale Models, and First Gear models for sale as a source of fundraising. As indicated in their ads, all proceeds from the sale of these items go to benefit the educational enrichment of Beckman students. These models are now sold out and rising in value.

Tractor Trailers, 1:64 Scale

Ertl International Harvester with "Chrysler" logos $25-30
Ertl International Harvester COE with "Chrysler" logos $25-30
Ertl GMC with "GMC Motorsports" logos...$25-30
Spec Cast, "Goodyear" $25-30
Spec Cast, "Beckman Collection" $25-30
Ertl, "Cadillac" logos $30-35
Ertl, "Pontiac" logos $30-35

Other Toys

Ertl "Beckman 2nd Edition" 1913 Bank, 1:25 ....$12-16
Ertl "Beckman 3rd Edition" 1950 Bank, 1:25 ....$20-25
Scale Models "Beckman 4th Edition" 1931 Bank, 1:25 ....$20-25
Scale Models "Co-Op" Tanker Bank (Sampler), 1:25 ....$20-25
Scale Models "Co-Op" Tanker Bank (Production), 1:25 ....$20-25
Ertl "Mountain Dew" Delivery Truck, 1:64 ....$12-16
Ertl "Diet Pepsi" Delivery Truck, 1:64 ....$12-16
Ertl "7-Up" Beverage Delivery Truck, 1:64 ....$25-30
First Gear "Dyersville" Grain Truck, 1:34 ...$25-30
First Gear 1951 Ford Dry Goods Van, 1:34 ....$25-30
Ertl International Harvester 90's School Bus Bank, 1:50 ....$30-35
Ertl "University of Notre Dame" 1938 Panel Truck Bank $30-35
Ertl Premier Edition 1955 Ward LaFrance Firetruck Bank, "Dyersville, Iowa" $30-35
Scale Models 1:16 Scale Tractor Series: John Deere A, Allis-Chalmers Series IV, D17 ....$40-50

Belgium Trucks

It is curious that Belgium Trucks has never produced a single truck model, but only one car model in several color variations.

1960 Ford Thunderbird Convertible
green $275-300
yellow $275-300
beige $275-300
pink $275-300
blue $275-300
black $275-300

Benbros

Benbros of Great Britain, originally known as Benson Brothers, was started by Nathan and Jack Benenson. The Benbros name was adopted in 1951. They produced diecast models around the same time as Lesney Products Co. introduced Matchbox toys and were similar in quality. A few models have even been confused with their Matchbox counterparts, especially the Coronation Coach. Some Benbros castings were reissues of Timpo toys produced from 1939 to 1952.

Several series evolved from the Benbros brand including the T.V. Series of 24 models introduced in 1954 with models packaged in little boxes resembling television sets of the period.

By 1957, models were repackaged as Mighty Midgets, and the series continued through 1965. Qualitoys were larger scale items than other Benbros toys. Zebra Toys were introduced in the early 1960s in order to offer models with more working features and more accurate castings for their size. In 1965, Benbros was taken over, and their toy line was discontinued.

AEC Box Van
#23 ....$25-30
Army, #30 ....$30-35
AEC Compressor Lorry, #32 ....$15-20
AEC Crane Lorry, #33 ....$15-20
AEC Dropside Lorry, "Sunderland," 5¼"
#225 ....$150-160
AEC Flat Lorry
Timpo reissue, "Sunderland," 5⅛", #227 ....$150-160
with chains, "Sunderland," 5⅛", #220 ....$175-185
AEC Lorry
with Tilt, #31 ....$15-20
with Tilt, 5¼", #228 ....$150-160
with Tilt, Army, "Sunderland," 5¼", #A106 ....$175-185
with #310 Ruston-Bucyrus 10-RB Crane, "Sunderland" $175-185
with #311 Ruston-Bucyrus 10-RB Excavator, "Sunderland" $175
Armoured car, 3¾," and Field Gun, 4," #A105 ....$45-50
Army Scout car, #12 ....$15-20
Articulated Box Van, Timpo reissue, "Lyons Tea," 5¾" $180-190
Articulated Low Loader, Timpo reissue, 6½," #221 ....$45-50
Articulated Petrol Tanker, Timpo reissue, #224 ....$55-60
Austin Champ, #13 ....$15-20
Bedford
Army Box Van, #30 ....$25-30
Articulated Box Van, #43 ....$25-30
Articulated Crane Truck $15-20
Articulated Flatbed Truck with Chains, #48 ....$25-30
Articulated Lowside Truck, #44 ....$25-30
Articulated Low Loader, #45 ....$25-30
Articulated Petrol Tanker, #46 ....$40-45
Compressor Truck, #32 ....$25-30
Crane Lorry, #33 ....$25-30
Lorry with Tilt, #31 ....$25-30
Milk Float, #39 ....$15-20
Caterpillar
Bulldozer, 4⅜" $55-60
Excavator with driver, 5½" $55-60

Tractor, 3⅞" $55-60
Crawler Bulldozer, #10 ....$15-20
Crawler Tractor with Disc Harrow,
  #17 ....$15-20
Crawler Tractor with Hay Rake, #11 ..$15-20
Crawler Tractor and Trailer, #19 ....$15-20
Centurion Tank, #14 ....$15-20
Chevrolet Nomad Station Wagon (Mighty
  Midget only), #16 ....$15-20
Coronation Coach with 8 horses, 1953 Sou-
  venir of the Coronation of Queen Elizabeth II,
  4½" $150-160
Covered Wagon
  with 4 bullocks, L. Brooks reissue,
    7¼" $125-135
  with 4 horses, 7¼" $125-135
Daimler Ambulance
  #38 ....$30-30
  1:43 ....$75-85
Dennis Fire Engine with Escape Ladder,
  #9 ....$25-30
Dodge Army Radar Truck, 1:50 ....$85-95
ERF Petrol Tanker, #22 ....$25-30
Euclid Dump Truck, copy of Dinky #965,
  5¾" $85-95
Father Christmas Sleigh with 4 reindeer,
  4" $50-60
Ferguson Tractor
  with driver, 2⅞" $50-60
  with Cab and Shovel, 4" $60-70
  2⅞", with Harrow, 4⅜" $75-85
  2⅞", and Log Trailer, 7" $75-85
  2⅞", with Roller Trailer, 4⅜" ...$75-85
Field Gun, #24 ....$10-15
Foden
  8-wheel Flatbed Truck, #20 ......$15-20
  8-wheel Flatbed Truck with Chains,
    #28 ....$25-30
  8-wheel Open Truck, #21 ....$15-20
  Tractor and Log Trailer, #8 .....$25-30
Ford Convertible, American, #40 ....$15-20
Forward Control Box Van, Timpo reissue, "Pick-
  fords Removals" 3⅞" $60-70
Horse Drawn
  Farm cart with farmer, Timpo reissue ...$85-95
  Gypsy Caravan, #5 ....$15-20
  Hay cart, #1 ....$25-30
  Log cart, #2 ....$25-30
  Log Wagon with log, 8¾" $85-95
  Milk cart, #6 ....$25-30
  Water Wagon, Timpo reissue $85-95
Hudson Tourer
  #18 ....$15-20
  Army, #41 ....$25-30
Karrier Bantam "Coca-Cola" Bottle Truck,
  #49 ....$55-60

Land Rover
  "AA," #34 ....$25-30
  Army, #35 ....$25-30
  Army, closed, 4⅜", #A107 ....$75-85
  Army, open, 4⅜", and Field Gun, 4",
    #A101 ....$125-135
  RAC $40-45
  Royal Mail, #36 ....$25-30
  Royal Mail E II R, red, 4⅜", #223 ..$175-180
  AA Road Service, same casting as #A107
    and #223 ....$175-185
Lorry
  with Anti-Aircraft Gun, 4⅜", #A102 ....$45-50
  with Radar Scanner, 4⅜", #A103 .....$45-50
  with Searchlight, 4⅜", #A104 .....$45-50
Motorcycle with Rider, 3¼" $55-60
Motorcycle and Sidecar
  AA, 3¼" $150-160
  Army, #42 ....$40-45
  Military, "AA," #3 ....$30-35
  RAC, #29 ....$40-50
  RAC, 3¼" $150-160
Muir Hill Dumper with driver, 4⅛" $80-90
Petrol Tanker, Timpo reissue, 4⅜", #226 ..$55-60
Rolls-Royce 1906, #27 ....$10-15
Rickshaw with 2 passengers, pulled by Ostrich or
  Zulu, 6" $125-135
Roman Chariot with 2 horses and driver,
  5¼" $125-135
Ruston-Bucyrus 10-RB
  Crane, 1½", #310 ....$125-135
  Excavator, 1½", #311 ....$125-135
Spyker, #25 ....$10-15
Stage Coach with Four Horses, #4 ....$25-30
State Landau with 4 horses, 2 separate footmen,
  4" $50-55
Stephenson's Rocket Locomotive and Coal Tender,
  4⅛" $55-60
Streamlined Express Locomotive (TV Series only),
  #16 ....$25-30
Tanker
  "Esso Motor Oil," 1:45 ....$75-85
  "Petrol Goes a Long Way," 1:45 ...$25-30
Three-Wheeled Electric Milk Trolley, #7 ...$25-30
1904 Vauxhall 5 HP, #26 ....$10-15
Vespa Scooter with Rider, #15 ....$25-30
Wolseley Six-Eighty Police car, #37 ....$15-20

Zebra Toys by Benbros

Austin Mini Van
  AA Patrol Service, #60 ....$250-325
  RAC $250-325
Bedford Cattle Transporter, #20,
  3⅞" $85-100
Daimler Ambulance, #27 & #107,
  4" $130-160

Field Gun, 4" $25-35
Foden Concrete Mixer, #16 & #100,
  2¾" $85-100
Heinkel Bubble car, #34 & #106,
  3⅞" $130-160
Jaguar E Type, #10 & #103, 3½" $145-160
Lansing Bagnall Rapide 2000 Fork Lift Truck,
  3½" $85-100
Routemaster Bus, "Fina Petrol," #30 & #104,
  4⅜" $130-160
Scammell Scarab Articulated Van, "British Rail-
  ways," #36 & #101, 4⅛" $160-200
Triumph Motorcycle
  Police Patrol, 3¼" $50-70
  Rally, 3¼" $50-70
  Army Dispatch, #3, 3¼" $50-70
  Telegraph Boy, #4, 3¼" $50-70
  and Sidecar, RAC, 3¼" $130-160
  and Sidecar, AA, 3¼" $130-160

Best (also see Best-Box, Best Model, Best Toys of Kansas, Best Toy Co., Ltd.)

There are actually four toy manufacturers named Best, all unrelated. One was started in the 1930s in Kansas by John M. Best, Sr., another in just the past decade in Pesaro, Italy, by Marco Grassini. A third company called Best-Box is a brand of miniature vehicles made in Holland. Their resemblance to Efsi toys of Holland is not coincidental since the name Best-Box was changed to Efsi in the 1970s. A fourth toy company named Best is based in Taiwan but is not known to have produced any automotive toys.

Best-Box (also see Efsi/Holland-Oto)

Best-Box toys were made in Holland in the 1960s. Even the crudest of these hard-to-find toys have features that make them distinctive. The Ford Model T's are simple castings, but the plastic spoked wheels and black plastic tires add to their realism. The Porsche 911S features opening doors and represents a fairly accurate representative of the actual car after which the toy is styled. Models produced in the 1970s were issued under the Efsi brand and later Holland-Oto.

BMW 2000 CS, #2507 ....$25-30
Brabham Formula 1, #2518 ....$15-20
BRM Formula 1, #2509 ....$20-25
Citroën ID19 Station Wagon, #2510 ....$20-25
Citroën Dyane, #2521 ....$20-25
Cooper-Maserati Formula 1, #2519 ......$15-20

DAF 600 Saloon, 1:85, #501 ....$25-30
DAF 1400
    Refuse Truck, #502 ....$20-25
    Fire Engine, #503 ....$25-30
DAF Torpedo
    Dump Truck, #504 ....$25-30
    Open Truck, #505 ....$20-25
    Closed Truck, #506 ....$20-25
1966 Ferrari 312 Formula 1, #2517 .....$15-20
1919 Ford Model T
    Breakdown Truck, #2503 ....$20-25
    Delivery Van, #2504 ....$20-25
    Coupe, #2505 ....$20-25
    Sedan, #2506 ....$20-25
    with Advertisement, #2507 ....$20-25
    Pickup, #2501 ....$20-25
    Tanker, #2502 ....$20-25
Ford Taunus 17 M Super, #2511 ....$20-25
Ford Transit Van, #2522 ....$20-25
Honda Formula 1, #2512 ....$20-25
Jaguar E-Type Convertible, #2513 ....$20-25
Lotus Formula 1, #2520 ....$15-20
Mercedes-Benz 220 SE Coupe, #2509 ...$20-25
Mercedes-Benz 230 SL Convertible,
    #2514 ....$20-25
Mercedes-Benz 250 SE Coupe, #2516 ...$20-25
Opel Rekord
    #2512 ....$20-25
    1900, #2515 ....$20-25
Porsche 911S
    green, #2 ....$20-25
    #2502 ....$25-30
Volkswagen 1600 TL, #2508 ....$30-35

Best Model (also see Bang, Art Model / Bang / Best Model / Box Model, Art Model)

Via Toscana, 85
61100 Pesaro, Italy

    Best Models are 1:43 scale precision car replicas produced in Pesaro, Italy, by Marco Grassini. They represent models of Porsches, Alfa Romeos, Jaguars, and Ferraris. While it would seem their product line is extensive, it is actually based on issuing many variations of just a few models.

    Bang, Best Models, Box Models, and Art Models are all produced by the same company in Pesaro, Italy.

Alfa Romeo TZ1
    Clienti, red, #9059 ....$25-30
    Monza 1963, white, #9060 ....$25-30
    Targa Florio 1965, yellow "60,"
      #9061 ....$25-30
    Targa Florio 1965, red "70," #9062 .$25-30

Targa Florio 1964, red "58," #9067 ..$20-25
    Le Mans 1964, blue "40," #9068 ...$20-25
Alfa Romeo TZ2 1965 ....$25-30
Ferrari 250
    GT Lusso 1964 ....$23-30
    LM 1964 Prova, red, #9008 ....$25-30
    LM Nurburgring 1964, red, #9009...$25-30
    LM Le Mans 1965, yellow, #9010 ...$25-30
    LM Le Mans 1965, red, #9025.......$25-30
    LM Le Mans Nurburgring 1965, green "8,"
      #9054 ....$25-30
    LM Monza 1966, white, #9011 ......$25-30
    LM Bridgehampton 1965, silver,
      #9017 ....$25-30
    LM Kyalami 1966, yellow, #9018 ...$25-30
    LM Tour de France 1969, red,
      #9023 ....$25-30
Ferrari 275 GTB/4
    Stradale (Street) Hardtop, red,
      #9001 ....$25-30
    Stradale Hardtop, yellow, #9002 .....$25-30
    Convertible Spyder, top down, yellow,
      #9003R1 ....$25-30
    Convertible Spyder, top down, red,
      #9003G2 ....$25-30
    Convertible Spyder, top up, white,
      #9004 ....$25-30
    Convertible Spyder, top down, black,
      #9005 ....$25-30
    Rally Monte Carlo 1966, hardtop, yellow,
      #9006 ....$25-30
    Targa Florio 1966, hardtop, red,
      #9007 ....$25-30
    Tour de France 1969, silver, 9015 ...$25-30
    Le Mans 1967, red, #9024 ....$25-30
Ferrari 290 MM
    Prova 1957, red, #9063 ....$25-30
    Buenos Aires 1957, red "10,"
      #9064 ....$25-30
    Mille Miglia 1956, red "600,"
      #9069 ....$25-30
    Mille Miglia 1956, red "548,"
      #9070 ....$25-30
Ferrari 330
    GTC 1966 ....$25-30
    P2 Nurburgring 1965, red, #9020 ..$25-30
    P2 Limited Edition, silver plated $45-50
    P2 Limited Edition, gold plated $45-50
Ferrari 365 P2 Le Mans 1965
    "17," red, #9026 ....$25-30
    "18," red, #9021 ....$25-30
Ferrari 750 Monza
    Prova, red #9044 ....$25-30
    Daytona 1955, white, #9055 ....$25-30
    Carrera Panamericana 1954, black "2,"
      #9058 ....$25-30

Goodwood 1955, red, #9045 ....$25-30
Spa 1955, yellow "34," #9046 ....$25-30
Spa 1955, yellow "33," #9049 ....$25-30
Targa Florio 1955, red, #9047 ....$25-30
Tourist Trophy 1955, red, #9048 .....$25-30
MM #254 Alesi 1992 ....$30-35
Limited Edition 1992 silver plated $45-50
Limited Edition 1992 gold plated $45-50
Ferrari 860 Monza
    Prova, red, #9051 ....$25-30
    Sebring 1956, red "17," #9052 .....$25-30
    Mille Miglia 1956, red "556,"
      #9053 ....$25-30
    MM "328" 1992 ....$30-35
Ferrari P2 Prova, red, #9019 ....$25-30
Jaguar E Coupe
    Guida Sinistra, red, #9012R1 ....$25-30
    Guida Sinistra, black, #9012N3 ......$25-30
    Inglese Guida Destra, black,
      #9014V4 ....$25-30
    Inglese Guida Destra, white,
      #9014B5 ....$25-30
    Tourist Trophy 1962, blue, #9016 ...$25-30
    Le Mans 1962, white, #9022 ....$25-30
Jaguar E Spyder
    top down, black, red or silver, #
      9027 ....$25-30
    top down, amaranth or green,
      #9028 ....$25-30
    top up, white with black top, #9029 ...$25-30
    hard top, red, #9030 ....$25-30
    Tourist Trophy 1962, white, #9038 ..$25-30
    Oulton Park 1961, blue, #9036 ......$25-30
    Nurburgring 1963, silver, #9037 .....$25-30
    Brands Hatch 1965, white, #9038 ..$25-30
    1961 ....$25-30
    1962 ....$25-30
    1963 ....$25-30
    1965 ....$25-30
Porsche 908/2 Prova, white, #9040 .....$25-30
Porsche 908/3
    Prova, red, #9033 ....$25-30
    Nurburgring 1970, white $25-30
    Targa Florio 1970, light blue "40,"
      #9034 ....$25-30
    Targa Florio 1970, light blue "36,"
      #9034 ....$25-30
    Targa Florio 1970, light blue "12,"
      #9039 ....$25-30
    1969 ....$25-30
    Targa Florio 1970, white with red "20,"
      #9050 ....$25-30
Porsche 980/2
    Brands Hatch 1969 "54," #9041 ....$25-30
    Brands Hatch 1969 "53," #9042 ....$25-30
    Brands Hatch 1969 "55," #9043 ....$25-30

Watkins Glen 1972, yellow,
#9065 ....$25-30
Zeltweg 1970, white, #9066 ....$25-30

Best Model of Italy – Gold and Silver Series

Ferrari 275 GTB/4 Coupe
silver, #1001 ....$60-65
gold, #2001 ....$75-80
Ferrari 275 GTB/4 Spyder
silver, #1002 ....$60-65
gold, #2002 ....$75-80
Ferrari 330 P2
silver, #1003 ....$60-65
gold, #2003 ....$75-80
Ferrari 750 Monza
silver, #1004 ....$60-65
gold, #2004 ....$75-80

Best Toys of Kansas

It was in the midst of the hard economic times of the 1930s that John M. Best, Sr., started Best Toy & Novelty Factory. His main business as a printer who worked with metal alloys lent itself to a sideline in lead alloy toys. The company started as a family hobby and continued until 1939 when Best was purchased by Ralstoy of Ralston, Kansas. In the meantime, Best maintained a close association with the Kansas Toy Company in John Best's home town of Clifton, Kansas, occasionally swapping dies.

Ralstoy eventually purchased both the Best and Kansas toy companies, so whether these are Best or Ralstoy can sometimes be confusing. Unlike more recent reproductions, Best originals are distinguished by white rubber wheels or embossing of the words "Made in USA." Several models used the metal wheels common to Kansas Toy originals, while others possessed wooden hubs with rubber tires. The familiar oversized white tires made of soft rubber eventually became a standard on Best Toys models.

The original line of Best Toys were an assortment of generic Sedans, Coupes, and Racers typically 3½" to 4" long, along with an Oil Transport measuring 6¾".

Bluebird Racer, #97, record car with driver, large fin, 12 exhaust ports, 4½" $30-35
Coupe, #92, chopped top, heart-shaped grille, possibly a Dodge, 3¾" $30-35
Coupe, #93, streamlined with hood similar to, #91, grid pattern grille, possibly a Cadillac, 3⅝" $30-35

Coupe, #96, same as, #93, 3⅝" $30-35
Coupe, #98 ....$30-35
Coupe, #99, similar to a Pontiac, 4" $30-35
Oil Transport Cab Unit, #101, sleeper cab, slanted grille, similar to an International, 3¼" $25
Oil Transport Trailer, #102, streamlined "GASOLINE," attaches to, #101 Cab Unit, 6¾" $30-35
Racer, #76, 4¼" long $30-35
Racer, #81, 4½" $30-35
Racer, #85, record car with large square fin and driver, 4" $30-35
Sedan, #86, 2-door Fastback, slant grille with grid pattern, possibly a Lincoln, 4" ..$30-35
Sedan, #87, possibly a Brewster $30-35
Sedan, #90, 2-door airflow, hood reaches front bumper with no grille, 3½" $30-35
Sedan, #91, 2-door airflow, high style vee grille, faired front fenders, possibly a Cadillac, 3½" $30-35
Sedan Taxi, #94, 2-door airflow, similar to, #90, 4½" $30-35
Sedan, #95, 2-door, similar to, #94, with 3 headlamps, similar to a Chrysler-Briggs show car, 3½" $30-35
Sedan Police, #95, same as, #94 with "Police Dept." shield on doors, 3½" $30-35
Sedan, #100, similar to a Pontiac, 4" ..$30-35
Sedan, 2-door airflow, similar to a DeSoto, 3⅞" $30-35

Best Toy Co., Ltd.

No.9, Lane 410, Niu Pu Rd.,
Hsinchu, Taiwan, R.O.C.

Not much is known about this company. It is believed not to be in any way connected with any of the other companies and does not produce any toys cars.

Betal

J.H. Glasman Ltd. of London, England, started Betal Works in 1948. Products included diecast toys, tinplate toys, trains and indoor games, with hollow cast toy figures produced in the 1950s.

Austin 16 Saloon, brass wheel hubs, Timpo Toys reissue $50-65
Jowett Javelin Saloon, 1947 without clockwork motor, 1:43 ....$50-65
Jowett Javelin Saloon, 1947 with clockwork motor, 1:43 ....$50-65
Open Fire Engine, 1947, 1:45 ....$45-60
Packard Senior Series, 1942 ....$60-75
Scammell Scarab Articulated Flatbed, 1948, 1:50 ....$50-65

Big River Models (also see Milestone Models)

Big River Models of Sydney, Australia, started producing hand-built models of Australian prototypes circa 1995. Working with Milestone Models, also of Sydney, Big River has released a 1937 Chevrolet Utility (pickup truck), featuring uniquely different styling than its U.S. counterpart. Streamlining is the difference. Holden originally produced this 1937 Australian Chevrolet just prior to the release of the first completely Australian-built FX.

1937 Chevrolet Ute $250-300

Bijou (see Modelauto)

Bing

Beginning in the 1880s, Bing Toy Works of Germany produced tin toys. The company suffered during the 1920s and went bankrupt during the Great Depression. In 1932, Karl Bub of Germany purchased the company.

Double-Decker Bus, 10" $1,800-2,000
Fire Ladder Truck, clockwork motor, composition figures, 13" $4,800-5,200
Fire Pumper, clockwork motor, composition figures, 11" $4,000-4,500
Ford Model T
Coupe circa 1923, black, 6½" $650-725
Doctor's Coupe circa 1924, clockwork motor, black, 6½" $500-750
Roadster circa 1923, black, 6½" ...$650-725
Roadster circa 1924, clockwork motor, red with black and yellow trim, 6½" $1,250-1,500
Sedan circa 1923, black, 6½" $650-725
Sedan circa 1924, clockwork motor, black and cream, 6½" $1,000-1,250
Touring car circa 1923, black, 6½" ..$650-725
Touring car circa 1924, clockwork motor, 6½" $1,000-1,250
Limousine
circa 1908, clockwork motor, maroon with yellow pinstripes, driver, 14" $4,500-5,000
circa 1915, blue and black, clockwork motor, 9½" $1,750-2,000
clockwork motor, driver, 15¼" .$1,500-1,750
Open Two-Seater, 9½" $2,250-2,750
Steam Powered vis-à-vis circa 1902 with driver, 10" $7,500-10,000
Touring car
circa 1920, clockwork motor, red and black with male composition driver, 6" $500-750

circa 1923, clockwork motor, red and black with female composition driver, 6" $500-750
Yellow Taxi circa 1924, clockwork motor, orange and black, 9" $2,000-2,500

Bison

Bison models are made in Germany. No other information is known.

Tatra Dump Truck, 1:43 ....$5-10

Bitsi-Toys (see Lehigh)

Blue Box

Writer/photographer Jeff Koch discovered an unusual Porsche Targa with retractable roof made by an obscure company known only as Blue Box. He paid less than a dollar for it in 1996. Since then, exceptional quality toy soldier sets are all that have been found with this brand name on them.

Porsche Targa with retractable roof, 3" $2-3

Boley (also see High Speed, Sunnyside, Yat Ming)

A seemingly new company, Boley of Los Angeles, California, is a marketing company for essentially generic toys, especially formula racers. Packaged as "Formular Die Cast," three sets of two cars each, upon removal from the package, reveal themselves as High Speed brand toys. Each body style of the six cars is different, not only in color, but in actual casting. Two-car sets sell for $.99 each at popular retail chains. Other Boley toys have been found to be made by Sunnyside and Yatming.

Bonux (also see Cle)

Bonux is a brand of ready-made and kit models marketed by the Cle firm of France in the 1960s. Several models have been produced under this brand. While Cle primarily produced plastic models, their Bonux brand was devoted to diecast miniatures.

Fiat Torpedo 1901 ....$15
Ford 1903 ....$15
Isotta-Fraschini 1902 ....$6
Leyland Double Deck Bus 1920 ....$12
Packard 1912 Town Sedan $15
Peugeot 1898 Brougham $7
Peugeot 203 ....$12
Regal 1914 Sedan $15
Renault 1910 Truck $15
Road Roller $7

Rolls-Royce 1911 Silver Ghost Landau $15
Sizaire-Naudin 1906 Racing car $15

Boss

Little is known of this company, but models are believed to be 1:43 scale white metal.

1970 AMC Javelin, gold $154
1970 Dodge Challenger Trans Am
    hardtop, pink $134
    "Posey #77," green $134

Bossat Dermov

Just when I thought I'd seen the ultimate in diecast in the name of Pocher 1:8 scale models (retail $499 and up), along comes Bossat Dermov! These French masterpieces are outrageously detailed and even more outrageously priced, as you will see from this list of 1:8 scale models listed in the January – March 1995 Exoto, Inc., quarterly publication called *Exoto Tifosi*. Prices listed below are not typographical errors. They are actual prices for new unassembled models in their original boxes. Over 3,000 pieces go into these kits, and even the wire wheels must be strung as part of the assembly. It is estimated to take over three years to fully and properly assemble one of these models. Once properly assembled, the value increases by another $5,000-7,000.

Aston Martin DB4 Zagato
    unassembled................................$26,900
    correctly assembled $32,000-34,000
1929 Bentley "Le Mans"
    unassembled................................$19,900
    correctly assembled $25,000-27,000
BMW 328
    unassembled................................$19,900
    correctly assembled $25,000-27,000
Bugatti Type 13 Brescia
    unassembled................................$5,800
    correctly assembled $11,000-13,000
Bugatti Type 50 Coupe
    unassembled................................$19,900
    correctly assembled $25,000-27,000
Bugatti Type 55
    unassembled................................$16,400
    correctly assembled $22,000-24,000
Bugatti Type 59/50B
    unassembled................................$16,400
    correctly assembled $22,000-24,000
Bugatti Atalante
    unassembled................................$26,900
    correctly assembled $32,000-34,000

Facel Vega III
    unassembled................................$26,900
    correctly assembled $32,000-34,000
Ferrari 512M
    unassembled................................$22,900
    correctly assembled $28,000-30,000
Ferrari Daytona Group IV
    unassembled................................$26,900
    correctly assembled $32,000-34,000
1957 Ferrari 250 TR "Pontoon"
    unassembled................................$9,950
    correctly assembled $15,000-17,000
Mercedes-Benz 540K
    unassembled................................$22,900
    correctly assembled $28,000-30,000

Bourbon

Two models of this obscure French toy manufacturer are known.

Berliet Tanker Semi $30-40
Peugeot D4A Van $25-35

Boutique Auto Moto (BAM)

Aaron Robinson reports that Boutique Auto Moto was a small shop in Paris, France, that at one time produced their own line of white metal models, most notably a line of IMSA Lolas and in particular a "Red Lobster" car from around 1981. Stephen Demosthenes provides a description of one model, a Porsche Carrera 3.0.

Porsche Carrera 3.0, orange, #5 Jagermeister, kit #1 ....$75-95

Box Model (also see Art Model, Bang, Best)

Ferraris dominate the Box Model assortment, made in Italy, all 1:43 scale. Box Model precedes Best Model, Art Model, and Bang, brands that resulted from the reorganization of the company in 1991.

AC Cobra 289 Open
    wire wheels, red, #8410 ....$25-30
    alloy wheels, black, #8411 ....$25-30
Ferrari 250 GT
    silver plated, #101 ....$30-35
    silver plated, #102 ....$30-35
    gold plated, #201 ....$40-45
    gold plated, #202 ....$40-45
    Long, Mille Miglia, #8415 ....$25-30
    1956 Prova Street, red, #8405 ....$25-30
    1956 Prova, silver, #8406 ....$25-30

1957 Pau 3 Hours, red, #8407 ......$25-30
1958 Tour de France, silver, #8431 ..$25-30
1958 Tour de France Shell/Peron,
   #8441 ....$25-30
1959 Tour de France, white,
   #8427 ....$25-30
1960 Tour de France Street, blue,
   #8425 ....$25-30
1960 Tour de France, red, #8426 ...$25-30
1962 Sebring, #8432 ....$25-30
1963 Laguna Seca, #8433 ....$25-30
Ferrari 250 LM
   Street, red, #8434 ....$25-30
1964 Nurburgring Rindt, red,
   #8435 ....$25-30
1965 LeMans Dumay, yellow,
   #8436 ....$25-30
1966 Monza, white with stripe,
   #8437 ....$25-30
Ferrari 275 GTB
   1966 Spyder, top down, red,
   #8418R $25-30
1966 Monte Carlo, #8429 ....$25-30
1966 Spyder, top up, white,
   #8419 ....$25-30
1966 Spyder, wire wheels, black,
   #8428 ....$25-30
Ferrari 275 GTB4
   Targa Florio 1966, red, #8430 ....$25-30
   Tour de France 1969 "142," silver,
   #8442 ....$25-30
Ferrari GTO
   1962 Coupe Street, red, #8401 ......$25-30
   1962 Coupe LeMans '62, light green,
   #8402 ....$25-30
   1963 Coupe TT '63, green,
   #8403 ....$25-30
   1962 Targa Florio O/P, white/brown,
   #8408 ....$25-30
   1963 Coupe TT '63, red, #8409 ....$25-30
Jaguar E Coupe
   1962 black, #8439N $25-30
   1962 left hand drive, red, #8439R ...$25-30
   1962 right hand drive, green and white,
   #8440 ....$25-30
   1962 TT "14," blue, #8443 ....$25-30

BP

The name "BP" was derived from "Brothers Petersen" of Denmark. The short-lived company was founded in 1945 and known to produce only three diecast models.

Ariel Motorcycle and Sidecar, 4¾" $80-110
Ford Coupe, 5" $75-100
Ford Open Truck, 5¾" $75-100

BradsCars

Brighton, England, was home to Bradshaws Model Products, producer of a hard-to-find series of crude one-piece casted toy cars. Produced from around 1952 to 1954 to roughly 1:75 scale, or double O, they were priced higher than the better-made Matchbox toys of the same period, which was likely the reason for their quick demise.

Austin A30 (Austin A7 on base), black, red, or
   green $50-60
Morris 6, black, red, tan, blue, or light
   green $50-60
Riley 1.5, red, black, gray, or green $50-60

Brekina Automodelle

Brekina-Modellspielwaren GmbH
Carl-Benz-Strasse 1
79331 Teningen, Germany
Tel. ++7663 93270
Fax ++7663 4070
www.brekina.de
Brekina Automodelle of Teningen, Germany, offers 1:87 scale (HO gauge) plastic models of exceptional realism, with a heavy emphasis on German cars and trucks. Here is a brief sampling. Some model lists, apparently intended only for the German market, were found written in German, and translation was not available for most of the descriptive text. A few terms, however, have been roughly translated:

   Anhänger – trailer
   Fahrschule – driving school
   Feuerwehr – fire truck
   Lkw – commercial truck
   Politie – Netherlands Police
   Polizie – Germany Police

1955 BMW 311, #27011 ....$10-15
BMW 1600, various colors, #2400 ......$12-16
IFA S 4000-1
   PP-Lkw, sortiert, neue Farbe, #71500 .$10-15
   PP-Lkw "Deutsche Reichsbahn,"
   #71502 ....$10-15
   Lkw mit offenem Plangestell (Kleinserienteil),
   #71511 ....$10-15
   m. Plangestell (Kleinserie) "Handelstransporte,"
   #71512 ....$10-15
   P-Lkw "Wernesgrüner," #71513 ......$10-15
   PP-Lkw with trailer, #71514 ....$10-15
   Koffer "Minol auto kosmetik,"
   #71608 ....$10-15
   Viehaufbau (Handarbeits-Kleinserienteil),
   #71650 ....$10-15

   Viehaufbau (Handarbeits-Kleinserienteil) LPG,
   #71651 ....$10-15
   Fäkalientransporter (Kleinserienteil),
   #71652 ....$10-15
   Behelfs-Omnibus "LPG..." (Handarbeits-
   Kleinserienteil), #71653 ....$10-15
   Stabholz-Möbelkoffer (Handarbeits-
   Kleinserienteil), #71654 ....$10-15
   PP-Lkw m.TSA "Feuerwehrhistorik Ellrich,"
   #71515 ....$10-15
   Feuerwehr SKW 14 "Sebnitz,"
   #71701 ....$10-15
Mercedes Set 3 trucks, WWII, 1945,
   #9031 ....$50-60
Trabant P 50
   1958 Limousine, #27500 ....$10-15
   "Feuerwehr," #27506 ....$10-15
   Sonderausführung, zweifarbig lackiert, TD,
   #27508 ....$10-15
Volkswagen Ambulance
   T2 Hilfsdie, white, #33251 ....$10-15
Volkswagen Beetle
   Standard 1200, 1965, #25000 .....$12-16
   1300, 1966 Sedan, #25060 ....$12-16
   "DRK" Emergency, white, #25090 ....$12-16
   "ADAC" Emergency, #2508 ....$14-18
   Fire, red with white fender, #25100...$12-16
   Polizie, blue, #25101 ....$13-17
   "DB," police, green, #25201 ....$13-17
Volkswagen Fridolin
   Delivery Van, gray or blue, #25900 .$11-15
   "Luthansa," yellow and blue,
   #25902 ....$14-18
Volkswagen Golf I
   Polizei, white and green, #25506 ....$12-16
   GTi, 1974, 2-door, #25505 ....$15-19
Volkswagen Kombi
   T1a Barndoor 2-tone, #31001 ....$12-16
   T1a "NSU-Rennedienst," blue,
   #31002 ....$14-18
   T1a AirPolice, blue, #3121 ....$13-17
   T1b Police, white wtih rack,
   #31601 ....$17-21
   T1b olive with large rack, #31791 ...$14-18
   T1b Luthansa Air, yellow, #3194 ....$13-17
   T2 1979, VWOA (Volkswagen of America)
   edition, #33001 ....$15-19
   T2 Polizei, green, #3306 ....$12-16
   T2 Polizei, white, #3307 ....$12-16
   T2 Polizei, #33080 ....$12-16
   Politie Netherlands, #3309 ....$13-17
   T2 Polizei, white, orange, #3310 .....$13-17
   T2 Mountain Watch with rack, #33130 ..$15-19
   T2 "Luthansa Airliner," #3316 ....$13-17
   T2 Bundeswehr military, #3317 ....$12-16
   T2 Red Cross, camouflage, #33181 .$18–22

T2 DRK Red Cross cream, #33240 ..$13-17
T2 DRK Red Cross, #33250 ....$13-17
Volkswagen Panel
  T1a Barndoor 2-tone, #32000 ....$12-16
  T1a Barndoor 2 styles, #32001 ....$12-16
  T1a "Der Spiegel," white, #32002....$14-18
  T1a "Circus Crone" 1951, #32003 .$13-17
  T1a Commercial "Quick," #3201 ...$14-19
  T1b, blue, US bumpers, #5134 ....$12-16
  T1b "Hawaii Blossoms," #3248 ....$14-18
  T1b US bumpers, coral, #3250 ....$12-16
  T1b "Rosenmehl," blue/yellow,
    #32506 ....$15-19
  T1b Transport, Lufffrachtdiens,
    #32507 ....$16-20
  T1b Red Fire, PLA 250, #3278 ....$13-17
  T2 "Kolsch" beer, #33502 ....$14-18
  T2 1968 Fire Van, #33580 ....$12-16
Volkswagen Pickup
  T2 Polizei, green, #33901 ....$12-16
  T2 Bundesbahn, brown, #33902 .....$12-16
Volkswagen Samba
  T1b 3-window 2-tone, #31801 ....$15-17
Volkswagen Singlecab
  T1 Pickup, #32900 ....$12-16
  T1b Olive Red Cross, #32931 ....$12-16
  T2 1968 Pickup, #33900 ....$12-16
  T2 1968 Red Fire, #33910 ....$12-16
  Pickup "Circus Krone," #33904 ....$13-17
  T2 Military camouflage, #33930 .....$15-19
Volkswagen Squareback
  "Duetsche Auto Club," #26501 ....$13-17
  Polizei, beige, #26510 ....$12-16
  Fire car, red, #26512 ....$ 10-14
Wartburg 311 Limousine
  1956, sortiert, #27012 ....$10-15
  "Fahrschule," #27023 ....$10-15
  "Feuerwehr-Kommandowagen," Seiten-
    blaulicht, #27018 ....$10-15
  "Limousine Service," #27003 ....$10-15
  1000 "de luxe," #27005 ....$10-15
  Taxi, black, #27006 ....$10-15
  "Pneumant-Rallye," #27009 ....$10-15
  "Volkspolizei" (wieder da!), #27010 ...$10-15

Bren L Toys

Bren L Toys were manufactured by Brennel Engineering Co. Ltd., a subsidiary of W. H. Cornelius Ltd. of Great Britain. From 1920 to 1960, Bren L Toys included tin, rubber, and wooden toys. In 1946, the company produced a few diecast cars, simple castings with no interiors, window glazing, or bases.

Bentley Coupe, simplified copy of 1938 Dinky Toys #36B, 1:43 ....$30-45

German Saloon, simplified copy of 1939 Schuco, 1:43 ....$30-45

Breslin

Breslin toys are lead alloy, mostly copies of Barclay and Manoil, manufactured in Toronto, Canada, and are distinguished from the originals by the words "Made in Canada" or "Canada" on them.

Brinks Armored car, 9" $500-650
Brinks Truck Bank, aluminum, 8" $70-95
Motorized Machine Gunner $40-55
Tank $40-55
Truck with Cannon Wagon $40-55

Brianza (see A. B. C. Brianza)

Brimtoy

Brimtoy is one of the best-documented toy car companies of Great Britain, even though they remained essentially unknown in the US.

Below is a chronology of the company from its beginnings in 1914 to its demise in 1981:
1914–1932 British Metal and Toy Manufacturers Ltd.
1923–1932 Brimtoy Ltd.
1919–1932 A. Wells and Co.
1932–1939 Wells-Brimtoy Ltd.
1945–1965 Wells-Brimtoy Distributors
1970–1981 CMT Wells Kele Ltd.
1981 CMT purchased by Casparo Industries Ltd.

The production of a tinplate clockwork train in 1914 heralded the beginning of British Metal and Toy Manufacturers Ltd. in the industrial sector of Riverside Works, Highbury Quadrant, London, England. The first toy car, a tinplate tourer, was introduced in 1919. Just seven years after its start, in 1921, the company filed for bankruptcy due to mismanagement of company funds by its director Mr. Stowe.

In 1923, the company was re-started by a previous director, Mr. Jones, at the same location, producing tin toy cars, boats, trains, a crane, and a tin doll bath. It was in 1923 that the Brimtoy brand first appeared on their toys.

In 1932, Brimtoy was purchased by Wells O' London, a company founded by Alfred W. J. Wells, a rival producer of trains and tinplate cars since 1919. Mr. Wells earned the title of chairman of the British Toy Manufacturers' Association in 1934.

In 1946, Brimtoy developed its own sales division dubbed Wells-Brimtoy Distributors Ltd., at the same time launching its new Pocketoy line of

clockwork models in diecast metal and plastic.

Welsotoys were introduced in 1955 as a new line of plastic toys. With the death of Mr. Wells in 1965, an association was formed with Keith Lowe and a new brand name Kelo Toys was introduced.

Bedford O
  Articulated Pantechnicon "TRANSPORT London-Birmingham-Glasgow," plastic and tinplate, Pocketoy #520 ....$60-75
  Articulated Pantechnicon "LYONS TEA," plastic and tinplate, Pocketoy #520 ......$60-75
  Articulated Pantechnicon "BRIMTOY CIRCUS," plastic and tinplate, Pocketoy #520 ....$60-75
  BP Petrol Lorry, lithographed tinplate ...$55-70
  Long Wheel-base Truck, diecast and tinplate, Pocketoy #510 ....$55-70
  Long Wheel-base Truck, plastic and tinplate, Pocketoy #510 ....$60-75
  Long Wheel-base Covered Van "POCKETOY TRANSPORT," plastic and tinplate, Pocketoy #511 ....$60-75
  Regent Petrol Lorry, lithographed tinplate, #506 ....$60-75
  Removal Milk Van "PRESTA" promotional, lithographed tinplate $90-120
  Removal Van "BENTALLS" promotional, lithographed tinplate $60-75
  Removal Van "POCKETOY," lithographed tinplate, #508 ....$60-75
  Removal Van "WELLS BRIMTOY- ALL ON THE GLOBE," lithographed tinplate, #509 ....$60-75
  Refuse Truck, plastic and tinplate, Pocketoy #527 ....$60-75
  Short Wheel-base Lorry and Trailer, plastic and tinplate, Pocketoy #513 ....$60-75
  Short Wheel-base Breakdown Lorry, diecast and tinplate, Pocketoy #514 ......$55-70
  Short Wheel-base Breakdown Lorry, plastic and tinplate, Pocketoy #514 ......$60-75
  Tipper Truck, plastic and tinplate, Pocketoy #512 ....$60-75
Bedford S
  Articulated Aircraft carrier, plastic and tinplate, Pocketoy #544 ....$60-75
  Articulated Coal Lorry, plastic and tinplate, Welsotoys #545 ....$60-75
  Articulated Milk Tanker "POCKETOY DAIRIES," plastic and tinplate, Welsotoys #546 .....$60-75
  Breakdown Lorry, plastic and tinplate, Welsotoys #514 ....$60-75
  Cement Mixer, plastic and tinplate, Welsotoys $60-75

Circus Lorry, plastic and tinplate, Welsotoys #543 ....$60-75

Esso Petrol Lorry, plastic and tinplate, Welsotoys #903 ....$60-75

Ice Cream Lorry, plastic and tinplate, Welsotoys #902 ....$60-75

Long Wheel-base Covered Van "POCKETOY TRANSPORT," plastic and tinplate, Welsotoys #511 ....$60-75

Mobile Ice Cream Bar, plastic and tinplate, Welsotoys #542 ....$60-75

Open Truck, plastic and tinplate, Welsotoys #512 ....$60-75

Open Truck, plastic and tinplate, Welsotoys #906 ....$60-75

Overhead Repair, plastic and tinplate, Welsotoys #541 ....$60-75

Refuse Lorry refuse type I, plastic and tinplate, Welsotoys #527 ....$60-75

Refuse Lorry refuse type II, plastic and tinplate, Welsotoys #527 ....$60-75

Removal Van "STORX," plastic and tinplate, Welsotoys #900 ....$60-75

Road Cleaning Lorry "CLEANSING Dpt," plastic and tinplate, Welsotoys #540.......$60-75

Side Tip Lorry, plastic and tinplate, Welsotoys #905 ....$60-75

Tipper Lorry, plastic and tinplate, Welsotoys #904 ....$60-75

Van "BRITISH RAILWAYS," plastic and tinplate, Welsotoys #539 ....$60-75

Van "ROYAL MAIL," plastic and tinplate, Welsotoys #538 ....$60-75

Van Ambulance, plastic and tinplate, Pocketoy #537 ....$60-75

Van Pocketoy Snack Bar, plastic and tinplate, Welsotoys #536 ....$60-75

Grocer's Van, plastic and tinplate, Welsotoys #907 ....$60-75

Bedford S II

Sand and Gravel Lorry, plastic and tinplate, Welsotoys #552 ....$60-75

Van Ambulance, plastic and tinplate, Welsotoys #553 ....$60-75

Builder's Lorry "BUILDERS & DECORATORS," plastic and tinplate, Welsotoys #559 ....$60-75

Tanker Esso, plastic and tinplate, Welsotoys #560 ....$60-7

Transport Lorry "SPEEDY TRANSPORT CO," plastic and tinplate, Welsotoys #563 ....$60-75

Tanker "BOROUGH COUNCIL," plastic and tinplate, Welsotoys #583 ....$60-75

Van "HORSE BOX," plastic and tinplate, Welsotoys #583 ....$60-75

Milk Truck "DRINK MORE MILK," plastic and tinplate, Welsotoys #583 ....$60-75

"FIRE TENDER" Truck, plastic and tinplate, Welsotoys #583 ....$60-75

"LIQUID OXYGEN," plastic and tinplate, Welsotoys #583 ....$60-75

"CIDER," plastic and tinplate, Welsotoys #583 ....$60-75

Cement Mixer, plastic and tinplate, Welsotoys #583 ....$60-75

"BBC TELEVISION," plastic and tinplate, Welsotoys #583 ....$60-75

"TELEVISION BROADCASTING," plastic and tinplate, Welsotoys #583 ....$60-75

Breakdown Truck, plastic and tinplate, Welsotoys #583 ....$60-75

Rocket Launcher, plastic, Welsotoys #583 ....$60-75

Buick Coupe
1946, diecast, Pocketoy #505.............$85-100

and Caravan, diecast, Pocketoy #548 ....$125-150

Bulldozer, diecast, Pocketoy #551 ....$60-75

Caterpillar Tractor, diecast, Pocketoy #550 ....$60-75

Ford Consul Saloon 1952, plastic $60-75

Green Line Bus, lithographed tinplate, #507 ....$60-75

Jaguar Mk VII Saloon 1952, plastic $60-75

Lincoln Zephyr saloon 1937 1:38, plastic....$60-75

Long Distance Coach, lithographed tinplate, Pocketoy #518.................$90-120

Morris Minor Saloon 1949
plastic, Pocketoy #519 ....$75-90

and Trailer, plastic, Pocketoy #524....$150-175

Novelty Stop-Go Trolley Bus "(London) TRANSPORT" with music, lithographed tinplate, #516 ...$60-75

Omnibus Double-Decker Bus "(London) TRANSPORT" without music, lithographed tinplate, #517 75-100

Omnibus Small Double-Decker Bus, lithographed tinplate, #503 ....$75-100

Rover 90 Saloon 1954, plastic $60-75

Saloon car, lithographed metal, Welsotoys #908 ....$40-55

Steam Roller, lithographed tinplate, #501 ....$60-75

Sunbeam Talbot 2-Liter Saloon 1946
with clockwork motor, diecast, #502.....$75-90

without motor, diecast, #502.............$60-75

Trailer Caravan, #547.................$60-75

Tractor, #549 ....$60-75

Vauxhall 10 Coupe 1947, diecast..........$60-75

Vauxhall 14 Saloon 1946, diecast, #504 ....$60-75

Vauxhall Velox Saloon 1952, plastic........$60-75

Britains

William B. Britain introduced a line of hollow-cast toy soldiers in 1893 from his plant in Lambton Road, Hornsey, London, England. In 1987, Britains Ltd. became part of the Dobson Industries Group and the name was changed to Britains Petite. Britains Petite Ltd. was purchased in 1998 by the Ertl Company of Dyersville, Iowa, which was purchased by Racing Champions on April 15, 1999, forming Racing Champions / Ertl. In 2003, Racing Champions / Ertl was renamed RC2.

Armored Car
#274.................$75-90

#1321 ....$400-450

Army Ambulance #1512, wounded man and stretcher, doors open, 6"..............$200-250

Army Lorry
caterpillar type, #1333 ....$250-300

4-wheel type, #1334.................$200-250

with driver, #1335 ....$225-275

Army Staff Car with officer and driver, #1448
smooth white tires, black fenders $350-400

white tires, khaki colored body and fenders $350-400

rubber tires, 1948–1950 version, rectangular windshield $300-350

lead tires, 1951–1957, gray colored ..$325-375

black plastic tires, 1958–1959 .....$275-325

Army Tender
caterpillar type, covered, #1433 ...$175-200

10-wheel covered, #1432 ....$175-200

Balloon Barrage Unit with lorry, winch, and balloon, #1757 ....$1,500-1,750

BMW 600CC Motorcycle, black and chrome, #9694 ....$95-110

Bren Gun carrier #876 ....$75-90

Corporation Motor Ambulance with driver, wounded patient and stretcher, #1514 ....$800-1,000

Covered Lorry with gun and drivers, #1462.................$425-475

Dispatch Rider
#200.................$40-65

#1791 ....$175-225

Drag Racing Motorcycle with rider, blue ...$50-65

Greeves 250CC Scrambler Motorcycle, #9692 ....$65-80

Harley-Davidson, rider with guitar on back, #9689 ....$115-140

Heavy-Duty Lorry
with driver, searchlight, battery, and lamp, #1642 ....$700-800

underslung, #1641.................$500-600

underslung with driver, #1643 ....$1,000-1,250

Howitzer 4.5," #1725 ....$30-45

Mobile Searchlight #1718 ....$60-75

Mobile Unit, 2-Pounder, #1717.............$60-75

Motorcycle Machine Gun #199 ....$100-125

Police Car with two officers, #1413 ....$750-825

Range Rover Discovery, 1:32, 1996 ....$20-35
Regular Limber #1726 ....$25-40
Speed Record Car "The Bluebird,"
    #1400 ....$350-400
Tank #1203 ....$200-225

British Motoring Classics

British Motoring Classics are high-quality 1:32 scale slot cars of British rally and racing classics from the 1950s, 1960s, and 1970s, in various colors and liveries.

Austin 1100 Mk I, bmc1110, Road car
    kit $75-95
    preassembled $160-175
Built "Driving School" car
    kit $75-95
    preassembled $160-175
Austin A30 2-door saloon (1950s), bmc700
    kit $75-95
    preassembled $160-175
Austin A35 (larger rear window), bmc735
    kit $75-95
    preassembled $160-175
Austin A40 Farina Mark I (1960s), bmc1400
    kit $75-95
    preassembled $160-175
Austin Westminster (1950s), bmc900
    kit $75-95
    preassembled $160-175
E.R.A. Mini Turbo (1980s turbocharged Mini with body kit), bmc1290
    kit $75-95
    preassembled $160-175
M.G. 1100/1300 4-door saloon (1960s), bmc1100
    kit $75-95
    preassembled $160-175
M.G. Magnette ZB (1950s), bmc800
    kit $75-95
    preassembled $160-175
M.G.A. roadster (open), bmc1600
    kit $75-95
    preassembled $160-175
M.G.A. Fixed Head Coupe, bmc1601
    kit $75-95
    preassembled $160-175
M.G.B. Roadster Mk I (open), bmc1800
    kit $75-95
    preassembled $160-175
M.G.B. Historic Racer, bmc180
    kit $75-95
    preassembled $160-175
M.G.C. roadster + half tonneau, bmc1830
    kit $75-95
    preassembled $160-175

M.G.C.GT Sebring Racer, bmc1831
    kit $75-95
    preassembled $160-175
Morris 1100 Mk I Saloon, bmc1120, small production runs
    Road Car kit $75-95
    Built Police or Driving School Car, preassembled $160-175
Morris Mini Clubman 1275 GT, bmc1275
    kit $75-95
    preassembled $160-175
Morris Mini Broadspeed 2+2 GT (fastback coupe), bmc1280
    kit $75-95
    preassembled $160-175
Riley 1.5, bmc1510
    kit $75-95
    preassembled $160-175
Riley Elf Mk III, bmc1200
    kit $75-95
    preassembled $160-175
Triumph Herald Coupe, bmc2050
    kit $75-95
    preassembled $160-175
Triumph Herald Driving School, bmc2052
    kit $75-95
    preassembled $160-175
Triumph Herald Police car, bmc2051
    kit $75-95
    preassembled $160-175
Triumph Spitfire Historic Racer, bmc2060
    kit $75-95
    preassembled $160-175
Triumph TR2 sports (open), bmc2102
    kit $75-95
    preassembled $160-175
Triumph TR3 sports (open), bmc2103
    kit $75-95
    preassembled $160-175
Triumph TR4 sports (open), bmc2104
    kit $75-95
    preassembled $160-175
Triumph TR6 sports
    (a) open convertible
    (b) closed convertible, bmc2106
    kit $75-95
    preassembled $160-175
Triumph TR6 Group 44 racer, bmc2144
    kit $75-95
    preassembled $160-175
Wolseley 1500, bmc1500
    kit $75-95
    preassembled $160-175
Wolseley Hornet Mk I, bmc1210
    kit $75-95
    preassembled $160-175

Wolseley Hornet Mk I "Crayford" convertible, bmc1257
    kit $75-95
    preassembled $160-175

Brookfield Collectors Guild

Brookfield Collectors Guild, Inc.
16312 West Glendale Drive
New Berlin, Wisconsin 53151-9917 USA

Brookfield Collectors Guild has been producing plastic scale promo models and diecast replicas since 1992. Most of their diecast models are coin banks, usually with a slot hidden in a trunk, under the chassis, or some other discreet location.

Meanwhile, back in 1980, even before Brookfield had a name, company president Kenneth Dahlke established a reputation for excellence when he produced lavish models of the 1908 Model T for the Henry Ford Museum in Dearborn, Michigan. Around the same time, his company released a replica of Louis Chevrolet's first car for the company that bears his name. These two early models were clad in silver plate and fitted with diamond headlights and ruby taillights, and manufactured in a very limited edition.

Since then, an assortment of diecast banks have been produced. The first ones, Chevrolet Suburbans, had the coin slot in the top. Later versions put the slot on the bottom so as not to ruin the integrity of the model.

Presented below is a complete Brookfield product history, including production year, description, quantity produced (issue price), and current value. The reason some models list no price is that they were offered as incentive bonuses for dealers purchasing a certain quantity of the regular production models.

Brookfield Collectors Guild is now owned by Action Performance as of the summer of 1999.

Early Brookfield Models

1908 Model T Ford, issued in 1980, produced for the Henry Ford Museum (no pricing information available) - Author's best guess at current value $10,000-25,000
First Chevrolet, issued in 1980 as a commemorative for corporate executives of General Motors. (no pricing information available) - Author's best guess at current value $900-1,500

The Brookfield Collection

The April 1997 issue of *Brookfield Forecast*, published by Brookfield Collectors Guild, has provided the following comprehensive list of Brookfield issues.

* These models have a hidden coin slot in chassis.

** These models have a hidden coin slot in trunk.

Brookfield Collectors Guild Diecast Coin Banks

Chevrolet Dually*
- 1995 Brickyard 400 Pace Truck, #636....$40-55

Chevrolet Dually* & Trailer
- 1994 Dale Earnhardt Combination, #528 .$150
- 1994 Dale Earnhardt Combo, silver, #632.......$20-35
- 1994 Brickyard 400, #561 ....$75-90
- 1994 Brickyard 400, yellow, #565 ...$90-105
- 1995 Racing Thunder, #670 ....$75-90
- 1995 Indy 500 Hauler, #638 ....$65-80
- 1995 Indy 500, silver special $120

Chevrolet Express Van
- 1996 Brickyard 400 #672BF...........$45-60
- White, #672W $40-55
- Adriatic Blue, #672B $40-55

Chevrolet Suburban*
- 1992 Dale Earnhardt #3.....................$125
- 1993 Indy 500 Suburban Bank, #525.......$40-55
- 1993 Indy 500 Emergency Truck, #532.......$25-40
- 1993 Jeff Gordon Rookie of the Year ...$40-55
- 1994 Brickyard 400, #563 ....$35-50
- 1994 Brickyard 400, white box, pre-production, #563A.......$20-35
- 1994 Brickyard 400, yellow truck, #564.......$20-35
- 1994 Chevrolet Racing Thunder $45-60
- 1995 #3 Goodwrench, white truck, #572.......$40-55
- 1995 John Force $45-60
- 1995 Dale Earnhardt, 7 Time Champion, #577 ....$105-125
- 1995 Dale Earnhardt, silver, #577S.....$90-105
- 1995 Teal Chevrolet Suburban, #517 ..$45-60
- 1995 Indy 500, #646 ....$35-50
- 1995 Brickyard 400, #644 ....$40-55

Chevrolet Tahoe*
- Truck of the Year, #717 ....$40-55

Chrysler Concorde**
- 1993 CharGold, #506 ....$55-70
- 1994 Green, #537 ....$50-65
- 1995 Red, #649 ....$50-65
- 1995 Rosewood, #649R $75-90
- 1996 Spruce, #680 ....$35-50

Chrysler LHS**
- 1994 CharGold, #519 ....$55-70

- 1995 Spruce Pearl, #651 ....$50-65
- 1995 Rosewood, #651R $75-90
- 1996 Drama Gold, #682.............$50-65

Chrysler New Yorker**
- 1994 Black, #515 ....$55-70
- 1995 Wild Berry, #650 ....$55-70
- 1995 Rosewood, #650R $75-90

Chrysler Sebring Convertible**
- Red, #767R.......$35-50
- Green, #767N $35-50
- Gold, #767G $35-50

Dodge Intrepid**
- 1993 Cherry, #508 ....$55-70
- 1994 Ram Blue, #538 ....$45-60
- 1995 Black, #642.......$50-65
- 1995 Rosewood, #642R $75-90
- 1996 Candy Apple Red, #679 ....$50-65

Dodge Viper
- GTS Coupe, blue with white stripe, #726 ....$100-115
- RT/10 Convertible, Red, #504 .....$100-115

GMC and Chevrolet Suburban* 2-packs
- 1995 7&7 Twin Pack, Petty/Earnhardt, #633.......$75-90
- 1995 7&7 Twin Pack, reverse colors, #656 ....$125-140

GMC Dually* & Trailer
- 1995 #42 Kyle Petty Mello Yello, #599.......$65-80
- 1995 #42 Kyle Petty, silver, #601 ..$20-350
- 1995 7&7 Portrait: Earnhardt/Petty, #635.......$65-80
- 1995 7&7 Portrait, reverse colors $85-100
- 1995 #30 M. Waltrip Pennzoil, #616.......$60-75
- 1995 #30 M.Waltrip, silver, #618 .....$175

GMC Suburban*
- 1994 Don Prudhomme.......$40-55
- 1995 #30 Pennzoil, M. Waltrip, #617 ..$35-50
- 1995 #30 Pennzoil Brickyard 400....$20-35
- 1995 #30 Pennzoil, silver $275
- 1995 #42 Mello Yello, Kyle Petty, #600.......$35-50
- 1995 #42 Mello Yellow, Thanks Fans, #605.......$35-50
- 1995 #42 Mello Yello, silver, #602....$90-105
- 1995 Teal GMC Suburban, #518....$45-60
- 1995 7&7 Split Petty/Earnhardt, #643...$40-55
- 1995 7&7 Split, reverse colors, #643R.......$80-95

Jeep Grand Cherokee*
- 1993 Black, #539B.......$25
- 1994 Red, #539R $30
- 1994 White, #539W.......$30
- 1994 Orchid, #539LD $55
- 1995 Camp Jeep, #539C $25

- 1995 Orvis, #539G.......$25
Oldsmobile Bravada, #758 ....$40-55
Plymouth Minivan*
- 1993 gold wheels, #540 ....$30
- 1994 silver wheels (4 mil.), #540.......$30
- 1995 red graphics, #540RE $55

Brookfield Collectors Guild Winston Cup Diecast Racing Collectibles, 1:25 Scale

Chevrolet Crew Cab Pickup
- Jeff Gordon/DuPont, #579C.......$75-90
- Bobby Labonte/Interstate #584C.......$70-85
- Terry Labonte/Kellogg's #589C $75-90
- Sterling Marlin/Kodak #594C $70-85
- Ken Schrader/Budweiser #607C $75-90
- Darrell Waltrip/Parts America #611C ...$70-85
- Earnhardt Chevrolet Racing Thunder #670.......$75-90
- Dale Earnhardt Victory #701 ....$40-55
- Dale Earnhardt Show Car & Trailer #708.......$70-85

Chevrolet Crew Cab Pickup, Trailer & Race Car
- Jeff Gordon/DuPont Trackside #764 ..$75-90
- Budweiser Trackside #765.......$75-90
- Terry Labonte Kellogg's Trackside #766.......$75-90
- Dale Earnhardt Trackside #763 ....$75-90

Chevrolet Express Van
- Ken Schrader/Budweiser #755.......$40-55
- Terry Labonte/Kellogg's #756.......$40-55
- Jeff Gordon/DuPont #757 ....$40-55
- Dale Earnhardt/#3 Goodwrench #761.......$80-110

Chevrolet Pace Truck
- Brickyard 400 ....$40-55

Chevrolet Suburban
- Jeff Gordon/DuPont #580C $40-55
- Bobby Labonte/Interstate #585C.......$40-55
- Terry Labonte/Kellogg's #590C $40-55
- Sterling Marlin/Kodak #595C $40-55
- Ken Schrader/Budweiser #607C $40-55
- Darrell Waltrip/Parts America #612C, #636.......$40-55
- Brickyard 400 #644.......$40-55
- Indy 500 Trackside #646.......$40-55
- Dale Earnhardt Victory #700 ....$80-110
- Earnhardt AC Delco #790 ....$80-110

Chevrolet Tahoe
- Dale Earnhardt/Goodwrench, #575 ..$80-110
- Ricky Craven/Budweiser #752 ....$40-55
- Terry Labonte/Kellogg's #753.......$40-55
- Jeff Gordon/DuPont #754 ....$40-55
- Dale Earnhardt Olympic Trackside #723.......$80-110

GMC Suburban
- Kyle Petty #600.......$40-55

Johnny Benson, Jr./Pennzoil #776......$40-55
GMC Transporter, Johnny Benson, Jr./Pennzoil
#777 ....$70-85

Brookfield Collectors Guild Diecast Sets
Dale Earnhardt Stars & Stripes, 3 car set,
   #722 ....$135-150
Dale EarNhardt Olympic Combination Set,
   #724 ....$120-135
Earnhardt AC Delco Replica (GM Dealer),
   #744 ....$150-175
Earnhardt AC Delco/Goodwrench Twinpack,
   #784 ....$95-110
Earnhardt AC Delco Trackside Combo Set,
   #785 ....$100-115
Earnhardt AC Delco Replica (Distributor),
   #788 ....$120-150
AC Delco Distribution Version, #789 ...$100-115
1995 Jeff Gordon Brickyard 400 Twin Pack:
   Monte Carlo Pace car & Lumina Race car,
   #573 ....$60-75
1995 Earnhardt Racer & Custom Monte Carlo,
   #662 ....$50-65
1995 Earnhardt Racer & Silver Monte Carlo,
   #662S $90-105

Brookfield Collectors Guild Plastic Promotional Models, 1:25 Scale
Chevrolet Monte Carlo
   1994 Brickyard 400, tan interior,
      #558 ....$30-45
   1994 Brickyard 400, black interior,
      #558A $60-75
   1994 Brickyard 400, T. George,
      #566 ....$35-50
   1995 Black, #661B $25-40
   1995 Red, #661R $30-45
   1995 Silver, #661S $60-75
   1996 Earnhardt Street, #640 ....$25-40
   Adriatic Blue, #736B $25-40
   Purple Pearl Metallic, #736P $25-40
Chrysler Cirrus
   1995 Medium Fern, #552 ....$20-35
   1995 Rosewood, #552R $60-75
   Black, #742 ....$25-40
Dodge/Plymouth Neon
   Sedan, 1994 Emerald Green,
      #568 ....$20-35
   Sedan, 1994 Nitro Green, #542 .....$25-40
   Celebrity Challenge Racer, Yellow,
      #718 ....$30-45
   Celebrity Challenge Racer, Black,
      #696 ....$25-40
   Light Iris, #695 ....$25-40
   Coupe, Magenta, #678 ....$25-40
   Expresso Coupe, Lapis, #693 ....$25-40

SCCA Club Racer, Black, #669 ....$25-40
Sedan 1994 Emerald Green, #544 ..$20-35
Sedan 1994 Nitro Green, #567 ......$25-40
Sedan 1994 White Racer, #534 ......$20-35
Sedan 1995 Special Black, #545 ....$60-75
Sedan 1996 White, #694 ....$30-45
Dodge Stratus
   1995 Light Fern, #551 ....$25-40
   1995 Rosewood, #551R $150
   Candy Apple Red, #743 ....$25-40
Oldsmobile Aurora
   Dark Teal Metallic, #648T $30-45
   White, #648W $25-40
   Champagne, #648C $30-45
   Garnet Red, #648R $30-45
   Silver Teal, #648S $60-75
   Indy Racing League Pace car,
      #648P $30-45

Brookfield Collectors Guild 1:32 Scale Chevrolet Corvette Series, 1992
Chevrolet Corvette
   1953 Convertible, white...................$35-50
   1954 Convertible, black..................$35-50
   1955 Convertible, red.....................$35-50
   1956 Convertible, black and silver.....$35-50
   1957, green and beige $35-50
   1958, turquoise and white...............$35-50
   1959, snowcrest white $35-50
   1960, Roman red and ermine $35-50
   1961, Fawn beige $35-50
   1962, Roman red $35-50
   1963, Daytona blue $35-50
   1964, Riverside red $35-50
   1965, Nassau blue $35-50
   1966, Rally red $35-50
   1967, G.W. green $35-50
   1968, Silverstone $35-50
   1969, Monza Red $35-50
   1970, Ontario orange $35-50
   1971, yellow $35-50
   1972, Elkhart green $35-50
   1973, medium blue $35-50
   1974, medium red $35-50
   1975, silver $35-50
   1976, classic white...........................$35-50
   1977, black $35-50
   1978, silver on silver $35-50
   1979, light beige $35-50
   1980, dark brown $35-50
   1981, red $35-50
   1982, silver beige $35-50
   1984, bright red $35-50
   1985, gold metallic $35-50
   1986, yellow $35-50
   1987, medium blue metallic $35-50

1988, metallic dark red $35-50
1989, metallic gray $35-50
1990, metallic turquoise $35-50
1991, metallic quasar blue $35-50
1992, bright red...............................$35-50

Brooklins
Brooklin Models Ltd.
Pinesway Industrial Estate
Ivo Peters Road
Bath, Avon
BA2 3QS England
E-mail: brooklin_models@talk21.com
Website: www.brooklinmodels.co.uk/

Brooklin, Lansdowne & Robeddie are all brands of Brooklin Models Limited of Brooklin, Ontario, Canada. Started in 1974 by John Hall in his basement, the company has since become the world's leading manufacturer of hand-built 1:43 scale collectible model automobiles. Brooklins are now manufactured in a 10,000 square foot factory in Bath, England.

While their replication of 1950s and 1960s vintage US cars makes them popular with collectors, Brooklins sometimes lack the fine detailing of comparable models, opting instead for heavy, solid construction and exacting scale. Some enthusiasts prefer to add chrome foil for finish trim, applying thin metallic film in a fashion similar to gold leaf. This preference leads back to the argument of the purist versus the hobbyist, as mentioned in the introduction to this book.

Brooklins focus on American (US) cars. Lansdowne models are replicas of British cars. The series was introduced in 1993 to present a completely new line of models for collectors.

Robeddie models meanwhile concentrate on Swedish vehicles, Volvos mostly, with a 1969 Saab 99 thrown in for variety.

The Brooklin Collection
In recent years, secondary market values have dropped somewhat for Brooklins because of increasing competition from other companies producing the same or similar models of equal or better quality for considerably lower price. While many models have been reissued in numerous color schemes, the 1948 Tucker Torpedo provides an example of the many variations issued of each Brooklin model.
1953 Airstream Wanderer Travel Trailer, British
   issue #54 ....$55-70

1948 Buick Roadmaster, British issue #45 .$75-90
1949 Buick Roadmaster Coupe, British issue #10 ....$65-150
1953 Buick Skylark, British issue #20 ..$250-275
1940 Cadillac V16, British issue #14 ..$100-225
1957 Cadillac Eldorado Brougham, British issue #27 ....$125-150
1947 Cadillac Series 62 Convertible, British issue #74 ....$55-70
1948 Cadillac Series 62 Sedanet, British issue #40A $55-70
1948 Chevrolet Aero Sedan, British issue #50 ....$55-70
1947 Chevrolet Aero Sedan Police, British issue #50A $55-70
1954 Chevrolet Bel Air Sport Coupe, British issue #68 ....$55-70
1955 Chevrolet Cameo Pick-Up Truck, British issue #53 ....$55-70
1963 Chevrolet Corvette, British issue #21 ....$55-300
1937 Chevrolet Coupe, Canadian issue #4 ....$125-275
1937 Chevrolet Coupe, British issue #4 ..$95-115
1959 Chevrolet El Camino, British issue #46 ....$55-70
1958 Chevrolet Impala Sport Coupe, British issue #48 ....$55-70
1960 Chevrolet Impala Convertible, British issue #61 ....$55-70
1961 Chevrolet Impala, British issue #44 ....$55-70
1955 Chevrolet Nomad, British issue #26 ....$175-225
1959 Chrysler 300E, British issue #41A $55-70
1934 Chrysler Airflow, Canadian issue #7 ....$95-115
1934 Chrysler Airflow, British issue #7 ...$55-100
1955 Chrysler C300, British issue #19A .$50-75
1961 Chrysler Imperial, British issue #67 ..$45-60
1951 Chrysler Imperial Convertible, British issue #79 ....$55-70
1941 Chrysler New Yorker Convertible, British issue #85 ....$55-70
1940 Chrysler Newport 4-door, Canadian issue #8 ....$95-115
1940 Chrysler Newport, British issue #8 ....$85-100
1941 Chrysler Newport Indy Pace car, Canadian issue #8A..................................$250-275
1941 Chrysler Newport Indy Pace car, British issue #8A..................................$50-200
1955 Classic American Speedboat and Trailer, British issue #71 ....$55-70
1959 DeSoto Adventurer, British issue #82 ....$55-70

1935 Dodge Pickup, British issue #16 ...$65-250
1954 Dodge Royal 500 Convertible, British issue #30 ....$55-70
1935 Dodge Van, British issue #16 ......$50-300
1949 Dodge Wayfarer, British issue #70 ....$55-70
1958 Edsel Citation, British issue #22A .$55-125
1960 Edsel Ranger Convertible, British issue #75 ....$55-70
1940 Ford Delivery Van, Canadian issue #9 ....$300-450
1940 Ford Delivery Van, British issue #9 ....$65-350
1952 Ford F1 Ambulance, British issue #42 ....$70-95
1948 Ford F-1 Pick Up, British issue #76 ..$55-70
1956 Ford Fairlane Victoria, British issue #23 ....$55-90
1963 Ford Falcon Sprint, British issue #58 ....$55-70
1956 Ford Mainline Police, British issue #23A $55-70
1930 Ford Model A 2-door Coupe, Canadian issue #5 ....$135-150
1930 Ford Model A 2-door Coupe, British issue #5 ....$80-120
1930 Ford Model A 2-door Sedan, recalled due to "bad casting," Canadian issue #5 (highly speculative)..................................$250-300
1968 Ford Shelby Mustang, British issue #24 ....$125-150
1957 Ford Skyliner, top down, British issue #35A $55-70
1960 Ford Sunliner, British issue #37 ....$55-70
1957 Ford Thunderbird Convertible, British issue #13 ....$85-175
1959 Ford Thunderbird, British issue #64 ....$40-60
1965 Ford Thunderbird Convertible, British issue #47 ....$55-70
1947 Ford V-8 Station Wagon, British issue #83 ....$55-70
1930 Ford Victoria 2-door, Canadian issue #3 ....$95-115
1930 Ford Victoria 2-door, British issue #3 ....$85-150
1951 Ford Victoria Hardtop, British issue #51 ....$55-70
1939 Graham "Sharknose," British issue #38 ....$55-70
1931 Hudson Greater 8 Boattail, British issue #12 ....$65-150
1952 Hudson Hornet, British issue #36 ....$55-70
1954 Hudson Italia, British issue #49 ......$75-90
1941 Hupmobile Skylark, British issue #52 ....$55-70

1953 Kaiser Manhattan, British issue #29A................................$55-225

1934 Lasalle Coupe, British issue #84 .....$55-70
1956 Lincoln Continental Mark II, British issue #11 ....$65-150
1960 Lincoln Continental Convertible, British issue #57 ....$55-70

1949 Lincoln Cosmopolitan, #94 ....$65-80

1959 Mercury Commuter Wagon, British issue #77 ....$75-90
1950 Mercury Convertible, British issue #15 ....$55-150
1946 Mercury Sportsman Convertible Coupe, British issue #69 ....$55-70
1957 Mercury Turnpike Cruiser, British issue #28 ....$55-200
1954 Nash Ambassador, British issue #34 ....$55-70
1949 Oldsmobile 98 Coupe, British issue #73 ....$55-70
1953 Oldsmobile Fiesta, British issue #39 ....$55-70
1951 Packard Mayfair, British issue #55A $55-70
1956 Packard Patrician, British issue #66 ....$55-75
1932 Packard Standard 8, Canadian issue #6 ....$210-240
1932 Packard Standard 8, British issue #6 ....$85-150
1948 Packard Station Sedan, British issue #43A $55-70
1941 Packard Super Clipper, British issue #18A $65-300
1938 Phantom Corsair, British issue #33 ..$55-70
1936 Pierce Arrow 1601, British issue #81 ....$55-70
1933 Pierce Arrow Silver Arrow, Canadian issue #1 ....$250-400

1933 Pierce Arrow Silver Arrow, British issue #1 ....$85-150

1937 Pierce Arrow Travel Trailer, British issue #80 ....$55-70

1956 Plymouth Fury, British issue #63 ......$55-70

1953 Pontiac Van, British issue #31 ....$55-70

1958 Pontiac Bonneville Convertible, British issue #25 ....$55-200

1957 Rambler Rebel, British issue #59.....$55-70

1958 Shasta Airflyte Travel Trailer, British issue #72 ....$55-70

1936 Stout Scarab, British issue #78.....$75-125

1950 Studebaker Starlight, British issue #17 ....$50-100

1953 Studebaker Champion Starliner, British issue #32A $55-70

1935 Studebaker Commander, pale yellow, #93 ....$65-80

1948 Tucker Torpedo

medium blue with gray interior, Canadian issue #14 ....$125-150

dark blue with gray interior, Canadian issue #14.................................$125-150

very dark blue with gray interior, Canadian issue #14 ....$125-150

black with beige interior, Canadian issue #14 ....$125-150

black with light gray interior, Canadian issue #14.................................$125-150

maroon, Canadian issue #2 ....$200-225

metallic medium blue, Canadian issue #2 ....$125-150

metallic dark blue with gray interior, Canadian issue #2 ....$125-150

metallic light maroon, no gas cap, British issue #2 ....$95-110

metallic light maroon, with gas cap, British issue #2 ....$95-110

metallic maroon, British issue #2.......$95-110

metallic dark maroon, with gas cap, British issue #2 ....$95-110

metallic gold with tan interior, British issue #2A.................................$55-70

metallic dark gold with tan interior, British issue #2A.................................$55-70

metallic maroon with tan interior, 500 m. Tucker Club, British issue #2A........$125-150

metallic silver with tan interior, Harrah's, British issue #2A.................................$125-140

metallic light brown with gray interior, Harrah's, British issue #2A.............$125-140

metallic gold with beige interior, Harrah's, British issue #2A $125-140

metallic Lazer red, Paramount Pictures, British issue #2A.................................$95-115

metallic Stratus silver, Paramount Pictures, British issue #2A.................................$95-115

metallic turquoise, Paramount Pictures, British issue #2A.................................$95-115

green, prototype $250-400

Sierra beige, prototype $250-400

black, prototype.............................$250-400

Signa amber, prototype $250-400

champagne, prototype $250-400

zircon blue, prototype $450-600

Jaguar coral, prototype $250-400

white, prototype.............................$250-400

light blue, Tucker Club 2nd issue $95-115

1947 Wesley Slumbercoach Travel Trailer, British issue #65 ....$45-60

Lansdowne Models

1955 Austin A30 Countryman, #18........$45-65

1958 Austin A105 Westminster, #12 .....$45-65

1958 Austin Healey Sprite Mk I, #1 ....$45-65

1953 Austin Somerset, #9 ....$45-65

1956 Ford Squire Estate, #20 ....$50-75

1954 Ford Zephyr Zodiac, #7 ....$45-65

1956 Hillman Minx, #10 ....$45-65

1963 Hillman Super Minx Convertible, #13 ....$45-65

1961 Humber Super Snipe Series III, #16..$45-65

1950 Lea Francis Estate car, #21 ....$55-70

1956 MG Magnette 2A, #3 ....$45-65

1962 Morris Mini Van Mk I, #4 ....$45-65

1957 Rover 90 P4, #5 ....$45-65

1965 Rover P5 Mk II, #15.....................$45-65

1963 Singer Gazelle Series III, #14........$45-65

1963 Sunbeam Alpine, #11 ....$45-65

1954 Triumph Renown, #8 ....$45-65

1968 Triumph Vitesse, #19 ....$45-65

1957 Vauxhall Cresta, #2 ....$45-65

1956 Willerby Vogue Caravan, #17......$45-65

1961 Wolseley 6-110, #6.....................$45-65

Rob Eddie Models

1969 Saab 99, red, #3...........................$45-65

1935 Volvo PV 36 carioca, #12............$45-65

1937 Volvo TR 704, #14......................$45-65

1946-50 Volvo PV60, maroon, #5.........$45-65

1950 Volvo PV831 Disponent, blue, #4....$45-65

1953 Volvo PV445 Duett Station Wagon, red and gray, #7 ....$45-65

1953 Volvo PV445 Van, Scandinavian Airlines System, red and blue, #8 ....$45-65

1956 Volvo P1900 Sports, #13.............$45-65

1957 Volvo PV120 Amazon 4-door, blue and gray two-tone, #9 ....$45-65

1964 Volvo PV544, yellow, #6 ....$45-65

1969 Volvo P1800S, red, #1 ....$45-65

1969 Volvo PV 221 Amazon Station Wagon, #10 ....$45-65

1972 Volvo 1800 ES, #11 ....$45-65

1973 Volvo 144GL, white, #2...............$45-65

1973 Volvo 145 Express, #15A $45-65

1973 Volvo 145 Station Wagon, #15 ...$45-65

Bruce Arnold Models

465 Ridge Road
Novato, CA 94947
phone: (415) 892-9588
fax: (415) 898-8213
email: info@brucearnoldmodels.com

This distinctive collection from Bruce Arnold of Novato, California, is comprised of 1:43 scale hand-built white metal models made in Europe.

1953 Cadillac 60 Special, #BAM2 ...$175-225

1960 Cadillac Fleetwood 75 limousine, fall 2001, made in Great Britain $175-225

1953 Cadillac Eldorado "Aretha" custom, pearlescent hot pink, 2000 Celebrity Series CS1 ....$175-225

1958 Packard Hawk, Frobley model, made in France, detailed by Bruce Arnold ...$175-225

Brüder Toys / Bruder Spielwaren

Brüder Toys America
279 E Redondo Beach Blvd
Gardena, CA 90248
tel. toll free 877-450-5152
tel 310-352-4665
fax 310-352-4733
www.brudertoysamerica.com

Brüder Toys (Spielwaren) of Germany are high quality injected plastic toys with lots of functioning parts for high play value. Founded in 1926, Brüder Toys is one of the largest family owned and operated manufacturers of high quality toys. Located in the small town of Burgfarnbach in Southern Germany, the family business currently employs over 350 local townspeople and operates a 368,000 square feet factory. Going into its ninth decade, Brüder Toys continues its commitment to remain one of the most reliable specialty toy manufacturers in Europe. Prices of Brüder toys are considerably higher than your average plastic toy trucks, but then these are not your average plastic toy trucks.

Brüder toy trucks range from garbage trucks, cement mixers, and tow trucks, to tractors, combine harvesters, snow plows, and fire engines. Brüder toys are divided into several categories:

Baby Toys. age 0–2
Roadmax Series, age 2–4
Standard Series, age 3–7
Pro Series, age 3–7
Top Pro Series, age 3–10
Brüder Ships, age 3–7
Farm Toys, age 3 and up
Top Pro Series, age 3–10
Professional Series, age 3 and up
Brüder Mini - HO gauge (1:87 scale) cars

The list below represents only a scant sampling of the hundreds of toys the company has produced over the years.

BMW 730, Brüder Mini 1:87 scale...........$2-4

Case 5150 Tractor, Professional Series
#02275 ....$21-26
Case Tractor with Front Loader, Professional Series
#02276 ....$25-30

**Caterpillar Bulldozer, Professional Series
#02422..$32-36**

Citroën 2CV, Brüder Mini 1:87 scale $2-4

Citroën CX, Brüder Mini 1:87 scale $2-4

Covered Dump Truck, 1½"............................$1
Crane Truck, Roadmax Series #20010....$40-45

Dozer, 1½"...$1

Dump Truck, Roadmax Series #20000 ....$34-39
Fiat Road Loader, Professional Series
#02425 ....$24-29
Fiat Tractor with Front Loader, Professional Series
#02291 ....$24-29
Forklift, Professional Series #02510 ....$22-27

**Garbage Truck, Roadmax Series
#20002.......................................$43-48**

Jalopy, 1½"...$1

Land Rover Vacation Car, 1:32...............$32-37
Liebherr Power Shovel, Professional Series
#02476 ....$24-29

Mercedes-Benz 300 G-Wagon (Gelandewagen), Brüder Mini 1:87 scale $2-4

Mercedes-Benz 450 SL, Brüder Mini 1:87 scale $2-4

Mercedes-Benz Transporter with working crane, Professional Series.................$50-75

Mercedes-Benz Unimog Snow Plow, Professional
Series #02522 ....$31-36

Mercedes-Benz Unimog with Crane Lift, Professional Series #02574 ....$30-35

Off Road Vehicle (Jeep), Professional Series #02540 ....$14-19

Old Car, 1½" $1

Porsche 911 Coupe, 1:25 ....$11-14

Porsche 924, Brüder Mini 1:87 scale......$2-4

**Power Shovel, Roadmax Series
#20050** $30-35

Race Car, 1½" $1

Road Roller, Professional Series #02423 ..$29-34

Silo Truck, Professional Series #02468 .....$43-48

Tractor, Professional Series #02275 ....$21-26

Tractor with Front Loader and Backhoe, Roadmax Series #20105 ....$35-39

Tractor with Front Loader, Roadmax Series #20102 ....$29-34

Tractor with Dumping Trailer, Roadmax Series #20115 ....$44-49

Truck with Backhoe, Roadmax Series
#20005 ....$39-44

Volkswagen Golf, 1:43 ....$6-8

Volkswagen Golf LS, Brüder Mini 1:87 scale $2-4

Volkswagen Van, Brüder Mini 1:87 scale $2-4

Wheel Loader, Professional Series #02420 ....$30-35

Wheeled Excavator, Professional Series #02421 ....$29-34

Brumm

Brumm SNC
Mr. Rio Tattarletti
via Bizzarone 3
22070 Oltrona San Mamette
Como - Nord Italy
E-mail: brumm@brumm.it
Website: www.brumm.it

Brumista was the name given towards the end of the nineteenth century to the hackney-coach drivers of Milan, those grandfathers of today's taxi drivers... and it is from this word, el Brumm, that the trademark BRUMM, miniature styling for collectors of models scale 1:43, was derived.

The Brumm Company of Oltrona S. Mamette, a small village near Como, Italy, was the creation of three friends who began production in 1972 of models of period horse-drawn carriages, with and without horses in the Brumm and Historical series.

Then in 1976, they expanded to include steam-powered vehicles, Old Fire, and the first motor cars in the now famous Revival series, of which the three-wheeler Morgan was the first.

Today the company manufacturers some 250 different models, all faithfully reproduced in

1:43 scale. The car models produced by Brumm have been mainly dedicated to those of a more historical nature, the exception being one or two contemporary racing cars.

From 1986 onwards, the company has also produced a yearly series of limited edition models of 5,000 pieces each, all now eagerly sought after. Likewise, in 1987, production ceased on the first 10 models in the Revival series which immediately became coveted collectors items. Brumm will continue its policy of bringing to the collectors releases of interesting and well made models, all of which may take pride and place in any collection the world over.

Products List
Brumm Revival – classic cars
Brumm Limited Edition – limited edition cars
Brumm out of production – Revival model variants
Brumm – classic carriages
Brumm Historical – classic carriages with horses
Brumm Old Fire – steam powered fire engines

Brumm Revival
Alfa Corsa 1911, R026 ....$24-30

Alfa Romeo 8C 2900 B
    1938 R139 ....$24-30
    1938, R140 ....$24-30
    Mille Miglia 1938, R141 ....$24-30

Alfa Romeo 33 SC12
    500 Km Monza 1977, Vittorio Branbilla, R282 ....$24-30
    Pergusa, Coppa Florio 1977, Arturo Merzario, R283 ....$24-30

Alfa Romeo 33 TT12
    Prototype 1974, R237 ....$24-30
    1000 Km Monza 1975, R238 ....$24-30
    1000 Km Monza 1975, R239 ....$24-30
    1000 Km Spa 1975, R240 ....$24-30
    1000 Km Spa 1975, R241 ....$24-30

Alfa Romeo 158
    1950, R036 ....$24-30
    1951, S021, Fangio World Champion F1, Limited Edition 1993 ....$35-45

Alfa Romeo 159
    1952, R043 ....$24-30
    Grand Prix Spain 1951, Farina, R36, 1992 out of production $40-50

Alfa Romeo 1900
    R089 ....$24-30
    Carrera Mexico 1954, R145, 1989 out of production..................................$50-65
    Mille Miglia 1954, R090, 1989 out of production $50-65
    Polizia, R091 ....$24-30

Alfa Romeo 2300
    1931, R077 ....$24-30

Allestimento Speciale 1931, R77, 1989 out
of production $50-65
Mille Miglia 1932, R078 ....$24-30
two tone 1931, R138 ....$24-30
Grand Prix Bremgarten, S010, Limited Edition
1988 ....$35-45
Auto Union 12 Cylinder
1936, R038.....................................$24-30
Ruote Gemellate 1936, R110 ....$24-30
Auto Union Rekordwagen
1935, R107.....................................$24-30
Carenata 1937, R108 ....$24-30
Auto Union Type D 1938, R109 ....$24-30
Bedelia sport
open, 1913, R005.........................$24-30
closed, 1913, R006 ....$24-30
Bentley 1930
open, R099 ....$24-30
closed, R100 ....$24-30
Bentley Compressore 1932, R114 ....$24-30
Bentley Speed Six

Barnato 1928, R184...............................$24-30

Blue-Train Match 1928, R185 ....$24-30
Le Mans 1930, Birkin-Chaasagne, R114,
1994 out of production $40-50
Benz Blitzen
1909, R019.....................................$24-30
1911, R073.....................................$24-30
Berlino-Avus 1911, S011, Limited Edition
1988 ....$35-45
Indy 1911, R081 ....$24-30
Bugatti 57S
1936 Blue, R087 ....$24-30
1936 Black, R088 ....$24-30
8 Cylinder 3900cc 1936, R169 ......$24-30
closed, 1936, R170........................$24-30
Tourist Trophy 1935, S012, Limited Edition
1988...$35-45
Bugatti Brescia
Great Britain, 1921, R039 ....$24-30
France, 1921, R040........................$24-30
1921, R082......................................$24-30
Bugatti Type 59
1933, R041.....................................$24-30
1933, R174.....................................$24-30
Grand Prix Italy 1931, R173, 1994 out of
production...................................$40-50

Biposto 1933, R042.......................$24-30
Ruote Gemellate 1933, R173 ....$24-30
Cooper T51 Grand Prix
Monaco 1959, Jack Brabham, R278..$24-30
Italy 1959, Stirling Moss, R279 ....$24-30
Gran Bretagna 1959 Jack Brabham, S051,
Limited Edition 1998 ....$45
Cooper T53 Grand Prix
Gran Bretagna 1960, Bruce McLaren,
R299 ....$24-30
Gran Bretagna 1960, Jack Brabham,
R300 ....$24-30
Darmont sport
open, 1929, R003........................$24-30
closed, 1929, R004 ....$24-30
Darracq V8 1905, R115................$24-30
Ferrari 125
Mille Miglia 1947, R182 ....$24-30
Circuito Di Pescara 1947, R183 ....$24-30
Circuito di Parma 1947, Franco Cortese,
R264 ....$24-30
Ferrari 125S
Circuito Di Piacenza 1947, R183, 1993 out
of production $40-50
Ferrari 126 C2 Grand Prix
Italy 1982, Patrick Tambay, R287 .....$24-30
Italy 1982, Mario Andretti, R288.......$24-30
San Marino 1982, Gilles Villaneuve,
R267 ....$24-30
San Marino 1982, Didier Pironi,
R268 ....$24-30
Long Beach 1982, Gilles Villeneuve,
R272 ....$24-30
Long Beach 1982, Didier Pironi,
R273 ....$24-30
Ferrari 126 C4
Alboreto Agosto 1984, R142 ....$24-30
Arnoux Gennaio 1984, R143...........$24-30
Ferrari 156
1961, R123....................................$24-30
Baghetti Grand Prix France 1961,
R222 ....$24-30
F1 Grand Prix Siracusa 1961, 1° classified
Baghetti, Limited Edition for La Mini Miniera,
Cuneo, Italy, 1000 units, S96/06....$75-90
Grand Prix Austria 1964, Lorenzo Bandini,
R289 ....$24-30
Grand Prix Belgium 1961, S009, Limited Edi-
tion 1988 ....$35-45
Grand Prix Monza 1961, R124........$24-30
Ferrari 158 Grand Prix
Italy 1965, Nino Vaccarella, R296....$24-30
Italy 1964, John Surtees, R290 ....$24-30
Mexico 1964, John Surtees, R291 .....$24-30
Mexico 1964, Lorenzo Bandini, Limited Edi-
tion 3000 units, R291b..................$32

Ferrari 312 F1
Jacky Ickx 1968, R171....................$24-30
Chris Amon 1968, R172...................$24-30
Grand Prix Italy 1967, Chris Amon,
R255 ....$24-30
Grand Prix Italy 1969, Pedro Rodriguez,
R256 ....$24-30
Ferrari 312 PB
1971 Prototype, R257 ....$24-30
1000 Km Buenos Aires 1971, Ignazio Giunti,
R258 ....$24-30
1000 Km Monza 1971, Ickx - Regazzoni,
R259 ....$24-30
6 Hours at Daytona 1972, Ickx - Andretti,
R260 ....$24-30
1000 Km Monza 1972, Ickx - Andretti,
R261 ....$24-30
Ferrari 312 F1
Prova Modena 1969, with raised wings,
Chris Amon, R294 ....$24-30
Prova Modena 1969, with small rear spoiler,
Chris Amon, R295 ....$24-30
Grand Prix Spagna 1969, Chris Amon,
R301 ....$24-30
Grand Prix Francia 1969, Chris Amon,
R302 ....$24-30
Grand Prix Monte Carlo 1969, Chris Amon,
R303 ....$24-30
Grand Prix USA 1968, Chris Amon, R171,
1992 out of production $40-50
Ferrari 330
Piper-Atwood 1966, S013, Limited Edition
1989.......................................$35-45
P3 1° 1000 Km Spa 1966,
R157.......................................$24-30
P3 Coupe 1967 Daytona, S028, Limited Edi-
tion 1994 ....$35-45
P3 Spyder Le Mans 1966, R158.......$24-30
P3 Targa Florio 1966, S036, Limited Edition
1995 ....$35-45
P3 Targa Florio 1966, Bandini-Vaccarella,
50a, S036, Limited Edition 1995 .....$45
P4 1° 1000 Km Monza 1967,
R159.......................................$24-30
P4 Coupe 1967 Daytona, S027, Limited Edi-
tion 1994 ....$35-45
P4 Coupe 1967 Le Mans, S029, Limited Edi-
tion 1994 ....$35-45
P4 Coupe 1967 Le Mans, S030, Limited Edi-
tion 1994 ....$35-45
P4 Coupe 1967 Le Mans, S031.......$35-45
P4 Francorchamps 1967, S015, Limited Edi-
tion 1989 ....$35-45
P4 Le Mans Filipinetti 1967, R161 .....$24-30
P4 NART 1967, S014, Limited Edition
1989.......................................$35-45

P4 Scuderia Maranello, S016, Limited Edition 1989 ....$35-45

P4 Spyder 1967 Daytona, S026, Limited Edition 1994 ....$35-45

P4 Spyder Le Mans 1967, R160 ....$24-30

P4 Targa Florio 1967, S037, Limited Edition 1995 ....$35-45

P4 Targa Florio 1967, Vaccarella-Scafiotti, 51a, S037, Limited Edition 1995 ..$45-55

Ferrari 357 1951

First Ferrari victory in F.1, Silverstone, 1951 with Gonzales, Limited Edition for Replicars, The Netherlands, 600 units, S96/03 ....$125-150

Ferrari 375

F1 1951, R125 ....$24-30

Grand Prix Monza 1951, R191 ....$24-30

Indianapolis 1952, R126 ....$24-30

Indianapolis 1952, R168 ....$24-30

Thin Wall Special 1951, R192 ....$24-30

Ferrari 500 F2

SC. Epadon 1953, R167 ....$24-30

1952, R035 ....$24-30

1952, R044 ....$24-30

Ferrari 512

Grand Prix Germany 1964 John Surtees, S052, Limited Edition 1998 ....$45

Grand Prix Italy 1965, Lorenzo Bandini, R297 ....$24-30

Grand Prix Italy 1965, John Surtees, R298 ....$24-30

BB LM 1980, prodotta per il 20° anno di attività della ditta, S072/92, Limited Edition 1992 ....$35-45

BB LM Prototype 1980, R210 ....$24-30

BB LM Le Mans Sc. Rosso 1980, R211 ..$24-30

BB LM SC. Emka 1980, R212 ....$24-30

BB LM Le Mans Ch. Pozzi 1980, R213 .$24-30

BB LM Le Mans 1980, R214 ....$24-30

M 1000 Km Austria 1970, R228 ......$24-30

M Daytona 1971, R229 ....$24-30

M Le Mans 1971, R230 ....$24-30

M Le Mans 1971 N.A.R.T. Team, S043, Limited Edition 1998 ....$45

M Le Mans 1971 Ecurie Francochamps, S044, Limited Edition 1998 ....$45

M Le Mans 1971 Scuderia Filipinetti, S045, Limited Edition 1998 ....$45

M Le Mans 1971 Escuderia Montjuich, S046, Limited Edition 1998 ....$45

M Le Mans 1971 Gelo Racing Team, S047, Limited Edition 1998 ....$45

M Prototype 1970, R227 ....$24-30

M Watkins Glen 1971, R231 ....$24-30

S Buenos Aires 1970, R203 ....$24-30

S Daytona 1970, R200 ....$24-30

S SC. Francorchamps 1970, R201....$24-30

S Spa 1970, R202 ....$24-30

Ferrari 801 1957, R122 ....$24-30

Ferrari 815

Circuito Di Pescara, S003, Limited Edition 1986...................................$35-45

Mille Miglia 1940, R067, 1989 out of production $50-65

Sport 1940, R066 ....$24-30

Ferrari D50

1956, S024, Fangio World Champion F1 Limited Edition 1993 ....$35-45

Grand Prix Germania 1956 Juan Manuel Fangio, S049, Limited Edition 1998 ......$45

Grand Prix Italy - Monza 1956, R76, 1989 out of production $50-65

Ferrari D246

Grand Prix Belgio 1948, S008, Limited Edition 1987 ....$35-45

1958, R068 ....$24-30

Grand Prix Italy 1958, R069 ....$24-30

Ferrari-Lancia D 50 1956, R076 ....$24-30

Ferrari Squalo

1953, R196 ....$24-30

Grand Prix Italy 1953, R197 ....$24-30

Ferrari Testa Rossa, R094 ....$24-30

Le Mans 1957, R093 ....$24-30

Governors Trophy Race 1960, R156, 1993 out of production $40-50

Mexico, R155 ....$24-30

P. Rodriguez, R156 ....$24-30

Ferrari TR59

1959 Targa Florio, S035, Limited Edition 1995 ....$35-45

Targa Florio 1959, Behra-Brooks, 43a, S035, Limited Edition 1995 ....$45

Fiat 75 HP course 1904, R009 ....$24-30

Fiat 110 HP course 1905, R010 ....$24-30

Fiat 1100 508c Versione Gasogeno 1937, R33, 1989 out of production $50-65

Fiat 500 I Series

1936, open, R021 ....$24-30

closed, R022 ....$24-30

Methane, R023 ....$24-30

Vigili Del Fuoco, R024 ....$24-30

Fiat 500A

1936, Roman Holiday, Limited Edition for Replicars, The Netherlands, 600 units, Fiat 500A Campari, R054 ....$24-30

Isobella, R056 ....$24-30

Mille Miglia 1937, R047, 1989 out of production $50-65

Minivan, R050 ....$24-30

Ramazotti, R052 ....$24-30

Stato Del Vaticano 1936, R022, 1989 out of production $50-65

Targa Florio 1948, R021, 1993 out of production $40-50

Fiat 500B

Gilette, R079 ....$24-30

Minivan, Expo Model Fossano 4-12/5/1996, Limited Edition for La Mini Miniera, Cuneo, Italy, 1000 units, S96/07 ....$75-90

Minivan PT 1946-49, R045 ....$24-30

Minivan Stipel, R046 ....$24-30

Van Vigili Del Fuoco 1946/49, R246 .$24-30

Fiat 500C

1949-55, open, R012 ....$24-30

1949-55, closed, R013 ....$24-30

Belvedere, open, R028 ....$24-30

Belvedere, closed, R029 ....$24-30

Belvedere, Commissari Di Gara, 38a Targa Florio 1954, S032, Limited Edition 1995 ......$45

Commissari Di Gara 1954 Targa Florio, S032, Limited Edition 1995 ....$35-45

Giardinetta, open, R048 ....$24-30

Giardinetta, closed, R049 ....$24-30

Mille Miglia 1937, R013, 1993 out of production $40-50

Minivan, R051 ....$24-30

Minivan Marmitte Abarth 1956, R266 .....$24-30

Ramazotti, R053 ....$24-30

Campari, R055 ....$24-30

Isobella, R057 ....$24-30

Vigili Del Fuoco, R080 ....$24-30

Fiat 600

1a series 1955, 1996 Toy Fair car, Milan Toy Fair, 1,000 units for the Italian market, S96/01 ....$75-90

1st series 1955, 1996 Toy Fair car, Nuremberg Toy Fair, 100 numbered units, S96/02 ....$500-750

1960, Ramazzotti, R285 ....$24-30

Derivazione Abarth 750 1956, R265 ....$24-30

Hard Top 1955, R247 ....$24-30

Multipla 1956, Limited Edition for Federico Motta Editore, Milan, Italy, advertisement vehicle, 1000 units, S96/05 ......$75-90

Multipla 1956, R250 ....$24-30

Multipla 1956 Taxi de Milano, R251 ....$24-30

Multipla 1960, Ramazzotti, R286 ......$24-30

Multipla carabinieri 1956, R309 ....$24-30

Multipla D, R333 ....**$24-30**

Multipla Encyclopedia Motta 1956,
R310 ....$24-30
Soft Top Closed 1955, R249..........$24-30
Soft Top Open 1955, R248 ....$24-30
Street Police 1960, R308 ....$24-30

Fiat 1100
monotone 1937-39, R030 ....$24-30
two-tone 1937-39, R031 ....$24-30
Methane, R032 ....$24-30
508 C, Gasogeno, R033
1937-39 ....$24-30
508 C, Armed Forces, R034
1937-39 ....$24-30
508 C, Taxi 1937-39, R062 ....$24-30
508 C, Vigili Del Fuoco, R063 ....$24-30
508 C, Spyder 1937-39, R083 ....$24-30
508 C, Closed 1937-1939, R084 ...$24-30
508 C, Colonial, R085 ....$24-30
508 C, Diplomatic Corps, R086 ......$24-30
E.I.A.R. 1948, R242 ....$24-30
Van Campari 1952, R245 ....$24-30

Fiat 1100B
1948-49, R064 ....$24-30

Fiat 1100E
Taxi 1949-53, R215 ....$24-30
Van 1947-48, R177 ....$24-30
Van, 1950, Rammazzotti, R284 ......$24-30
Van Vigili Fuoco 1947-48, R178 ......$24-30
Van Croce Rossa 1947-48, R179 ....$24-30
Van Croce Rossa Militare, R180 ......$24-30
Vigili Fuoco, R181 ....$24-30
1949-53, R065 ....$24-30
Van, Van, Olio carli 1946, R311 .....$24-30

Fiat 1400B
Street Police 1956, R307 ....$24-30
1956-58, R165 ....$24-30
Taxi 1956-58, R216 ....$24-30
two-tone 1956-58, R166 ....$24-30

Fiat Abarth 750
Mille Miglia 1955, Domenico Ogna,
R304 ....$24-30
500 Km Nurburgring 1962, R305 ....$24-30

Fiat Abarth 850
TC Pieve Santo Stefano 1962, Piero Falorni,
R306 ....$24-30

Fiat F1 Corsa, S002, Limited Edition
1986 ....$35-45
Fiat F2 1907, R016 ....$24-30
Fiat Mefistofele 1923, R014...............$24-30
Fiat S61 1903, R017 ....$24-30
Fiat S74 course 1911, R011 ....$24-30

Ford 999
1902, R015 ....$24-30
Record 1905, R025 ....$24-30

Jaguar D Type
1955, R1294..............................$24-30

Le Mans Cunningham 1954, R130 ...$24-30
Mille Miglia 1957, R146 ....$24-30
1° Le Mans 1955, R147 ....$24-30
Prototype 1954, R148 ....$24-30
1° Le Mans SC. Ecosse, R149
1956 ....$24-30
Le Mans Biposto, R150 1956 ....$24-30
SC. Belga 1956, R151 ....$24-30
Silverston SC. Ecosse 1956, R152 ....$24-30
Record 1960, R154 ....$24-30

Jaguar XK120
1948, S007, Limited Edition 1987....$35-45
Coupe 1948, R105 ....$24-30
Coupe Rally Alpi 1953, R163 ....$24-30
Linas-Montlhlery, R106 ....$24-30
Roadster, open, 1948, R101 ....$24-30
Roadster, closed, 1948, R102 ....$24-30
Roadster Mille Miglia, R103 ....$24-30
Roadster Le Mans, R104 ....$24-30
Roadster Rally Alpi 1953, R164 ......$24-30
Silverstone 1951, Stirling Moss, R101, 1994
out of production $40-50

Lancia Aprilia
1936-48, R058 ....$24-30
Gasogeno 1939-44, R060 ....$24-30
Methane 1939-48, R059 ....$24-30
Mille Miglia 1947, R061 ....$24-30
Prima Series 1958, R58, 1992 out of produc-
tion $40-50

Lancia Aurelia B20
1951, R095 ....$24-30
Carrera Mexic, R097o $24-30
Le Mans 1951, R162 ....$24-30
Le Mans 1952, Bonetto-Anselmi, R162, 1994
out of production $40-50
Mille Miglia, R096 ....$24-30

Lancia B24
Allestimento Speciale 1955, R131, 1992 out
of production $40-50
open, 1955, R131........................$24-30
closed, 1955, R132 ....$24-30
America, open, 1956, R133 ....$24-30
America, closed, 1956, R134 ....$24-30
Mille Miglia 1955, R186 ....$24-30

Lancia D24
1954 Targa Florio, S033, Limited Edition
1995 ....$35-45
Ascari Mille Miglia 1954, R204........$24-30
Commissari Di Gara, 38a Targa Florio 1954,
S033, Limited Edition 1995 ....$45
Fangio Carrera Mexico 1953, R205...$24-30
Taruffi Targa Florio 1954, R209 ......$24-30

Lancia Ferrari D50
Monte Carlo 1956, R127 ....$24-30
Belgio 1956, R128 ....$24-30
Locomobile 'Old 16' 1906, R020 ....$24-30

Maserati 8 Cylinder
1939, R075 ....$24-30
Indianapolis 1940, R111 ....$24-30
Grand Prix Tripoli 1938, R112.........$24-30

Maserati 250
12 Cylinder Prova 1957, R223 ....$24-30
F 1957, R092 ....$24-30
F 1957, S025, Fangio World Champion F1
Limited Edition 1993 ....$35-45
F Grand Prix Argentina 1957 Juan Manuel
Fangio, S050, Limited Edition 1998 .$45
F Iniezione 1957, R137 ....$24-30
F Muso Corto Monte Carlo 1957,
R135 ....$24-30
F Muso Corto 1957, R136 ....$24-30

Mercedes-Benz 196C
Grand Prix Francia 1954, J. M. Fangio,
R280 ....$24-30
Grand Prix Francia 1954, Karl Kling,
R280b $24-30
Grand Prix Francia 1954, Hans Herrmann,
R280c....................................$24-30
Monza 1955, Stirling Moss, R281 ....$24-30

Mercedes-Benz 300SLR
1° Piero Taruffi, 38a Targa Florio 1954,
S034, Limited Edition 1995 ....$45
Coupe 1955, R187 ....$24-30
Le Mans 1955, Levegh-Fich, R188, 1994 out
of production $40-50
Mille Miglia 1955, R190 ....$24-30
Targa Florio 1955, R189 ....$24-30
Targa Florio 1955, S034, Limited Edition
1995 ....$35-45

Mercedes-Benz W125
1937, R070................................$24-30
1938, R071................................$24-30

Mercedes-Benz W154
1939, R037................................$24-30
Grand Prix Tripoli 1953, S. Lang, R37, 1992
out of production $40-50
Indianapolis 1947, R175 ....$24-30

Mercedes-Benz W196
1954-60, R072 ....$24-30

1954, S006, Limited Edition 1987 ....$35-45

1954, S022, Fangio World Champion F1
Limited Edition 1993 ....$35-45
1955, S023, Fangio World Champion F1
Limited Edition 1993 ....$35-45

1954, S048, Grand Prix Germania Juan Manuel Fangio, Limited Edition 1998 ....$45-55

Morgan MX-4 Super Sport Barrelback
1935, 1980 USA Coast to Coast 7500 units, LE-4 ....$28
closed 1935, R293 ....$24-30
open 1935, R292 ....$24-30

Morgan Sport
open, 1923, R001 ....$24-30
closed, 1923, R002 ....$24-30

Napier 6 1905, R116 ....$24-30

Porsche 356
Carrera Mexico 1952, R206...........$24-30
Carrera Mexico 1952, S019, Limited Edition 1990 ....$35-45

Coupe 1952, R119 ....$24-30

Coupe Mille Miglia 1952, R120 ......$24-30
Coupe Targa Florio 1952, R144.......$24-30
Coupe Tetto Open 1952, R121........$24-30
Coupe Carrera 1952, R208 ....$24-30
Mille Miglia 1952, R120, 1989 out of production $50-65
Polizia Tedesca 1952, R198A..........$24-30
Polizia Olandese 1952, R198B $24-30
Polizia Portugal 1952, R198C $24-30
Polizia Switzerland 1952, R198D.....$24-30
Rally Delle Alpi 1952, S017, Limited Edition 1990..................................$35-45
Rally Monte Carlo 1952, S020, Limited Edition 1990 ....$35-45
Speedster 1952, R117 ....$24-30
Speedster 1952, R117S $24-30
Speedster James Dean 1954, R117, 1993 out of production $40-50
Speedster, closed, 1952, R118 ....$24-30
Spyder Mille Miglia 1952, R207 ......$24-30
Targa Florio 1952, S018, Limited Edition 1990 ....$35-45
C Coupe 1963/65, R226 ....$24-30

C Spyder 1963/65, R224 ....$24-30
C Spyder closed 1963/65, R225 ....$24-30

Porsche 365
Circuito Avus, S001, Limited Edition 1986 ....$35-45
Rally Delle Alpi, S004, Limited Edition 1986..................................$35-45

Porsche 550
Coupe Le Mans 1956, R193 ....$24-30
Spyder Le Mans 1955, R194 ....$24-30
Spyder Mille Miglia 1954, R195 ......$24-30
RS 1000 Km Nurburgring 1956, R236 ....$24-30
RS America, R234 ....$24-30
RS Carrera Mexico 1954, Salvador Lopez - Chavez, R274 ....$24-30
RS Carrera Mexico 1954, Fletcher Aviation, Pasadena CA, Hans Herrmann, R275 ....$24-30
RS Carrera Mexico 1954, Jaroslav Juan, R276 ....$24-30
RS Carrera Mexico 1954, Fernando Segura - Herbert Linge, R277 ....$24-30
RS Carrera Mexico 1953, R235 ....$24-30
RS Street 1954, R232 ....$24-30
RS Street two-tone 1954, R233 ....$24-30
RS Le Mans 1955, Olivier - Jeser, R263 ..$24-30

Porsche 917
Le Mans Martini Racing 1971, R220...$24-30
Le Mans Porsche-Salzburg, R218 ....$24-30
Monza Wyer/Gulf 1970, R219......$24-30
Monza Wyer/Gulf 1971, R221.......$24-30
Prototype 1970, R217 ....$24-30
K 6 Hours at Daytona 1970, Scuderia Wyer-Gulf, Siffert - Redman, R269 ....$24-30
K 6 Hours at Watkins Glen 1970, Scuderia Martini Racing, Larousse-Van Lennep, R271...$24-30
K 1000 Km Austria 1970, Scuderia Salzburg, Ahrens - Marko, R253 ....$24-30
K 1000 Km Monza 1971, Scuderia Martini Racing, Elford - Larrousse, R252 ...$24-30
K Le Mans 1970, Scuderia Piper, Piper - Van Lennep, R254 ....$24-30
K Kyalami 1970, Scuderia Martini Racing, Siffert - Ahrens, R270 ....$24-30

Renault, Parigi-Madrid, 1903, R027........$24-30
Renault Grand Prix 3B 1906, R018 ....$24-30

Sanford Sport
open, 1922, R007 ....$24-30
closed, 1922, R008 ....$24-30

Simca 5
1956, R176...............................$24-30
Military D-Day 1944, R243 ....$24-30
Minivan 1936, R244......................$24-30

Simca Hult Le Mans 1938, Camerano - Loveau, R262 ....$24-30

Talbot Lago F1
1948, R074.............................$24-30
Belgio 1951, R113 ....$24-30

Vanwall
1957, R098 ....$24-30
F1 1958, S005, Limited Edition 1987.................................$35-45
F1 Grand Prix Belgium 1957, R199 ..$24-30

Brumm Classic Carriages

Landaulet, B01 ....$65-75
Landaulet, Open, B02 ....$65-75
Coupe, B03 ....$65-75
Coupe Dormeuse, B04 ....$65-75
Landau, B05 ....$65-75
Landau, Open, B06 ....$65-75
Spyder, B07 ....$65-75
Spyder, Open, B08 ....$65-75
Phaeton, B09 ....$65-75
Dog cart, B11 ....$65-75
Vis-A-Vis, B12 ....$65-75
Vis-A-Vis, Open, B13 ....$65-75
Milord, B14 ....$65-75
Milord, Open, B15 ....$65-75
Coupe A Huit Ressorts, B16............$65-75
Mail-Coach, B17 ....$65-75
Duc A Huit Ressorts, B18 ....$65-75
"Brumm" De Milan, B19 ....$65-75
Berlina Papale Da Viaggio, B20 ......$65-75
Cab, B21 ....$65-75
Dress Chariot, B22 ....$65-75
"Post - Cais," B23 ....$65-75
Royal Mail-Coach, B24 ....$65-75
Tilbury, B25 ....$65-75
Carrozza Napoleonica, B26.............$65-75

Brumm Historical

Cavallo Con Finimenti Ed Attacchi, H00...$65-75
Pariglia Eques. Con Finimenti Ed Attacchi, H01 ....$65-75
Doppia Pariglia Con Finimenti Ed Attacchi, H02 ....$65-75
"Brumm" De Milan Con Cavallo, H03 .....$65-75
"Berlina Da Viaggio" Pio X, H04 ....$65-75
"Duc A Huit Ressorts" of Napoleon III, H05 ....$65-75
"Mail Coach" Vettura Da Posta Inglese, H06 ....$65-75
"Cab" Dell'attrice Rejane, H07 ....$65-75
"Coupe Dormeuse" of Paolina Bonaparte, H08 ....$65-75
"Phaeton" of Emile Loubet, H09...........$65-75
"Vis-A-Vis Gran Gala" Nuzial, H10 e ...$65-75
"Dog car" of Guglielmo II of German, H11 y...................................$65-75
"Botticella De Roma," H12 ....$65-75

"Dress Chariot" of Count of Caledonia,
H13 ....$65-75
"Milord" of Eugenia Montijo, H14 ....$65-75
"Spyder" of Geroge San, H15 d $65-75
"Poste Chaise" Vettura Da Noleggio Inglese,
H16 ....$65-75
Landau Bavarese, H17 ....$65-75
Royal Mail-Coach, H18 ....$65-75
Tilbury, H19 ....$65-75
Portantina Spagnolesca, H20 ....$65-75
Carrozza Napoleonica Da Campo,
H21 ....$65-75

Brumm Old Fire Steam Powered Vehicles
Fardier Par "Cugnot" 1769, X01 ....$65-75
Carro Di Newton 1680, X02 ....$65-75
Diligenza Di Gurney 1825, X03 ....$65-75
Carro Di Trevithick 180, X04 3 ....$65-75
Carro Di Bordino 1854, X05 ....$65-75
Turbina Di Verbiest 168, X06 1 ....$65-75
Vettura Di Pecquer 1828, X07 ....$65-75
Anfibio Di Evans 1801, X08 ....$65-75

Brumm Champions, famous drivers ready to put behind the wheel of your favorite Brumm racecar
Gilles Villeneuve for Ferrari 126C2 1982,
R267/272, CH01 ....$10-15
Didier Pironi for Ferrari 126C2 1982,
R268/273, CH02 ....$10-15
Patrick Tambay for Ferrari 126C2 1982, R287,
CH03 ....$10-15
Mario Andretti for Ferrari 126C2 1982, R288,
CH04 ....$10-15
Clay Regazzoni for Ferrari 312PB 1971,
R259/261, CH05 ....$10-15
Jacky Ickx for Ferrari 312PB 1971, R259/261,
CH06 ....$10-15
Mario Andretti for Ferrari 312PB 1972, R260,
CH07 ....$10-15
Ignazio Giunti for Ferrari 312PB 1971, R258,
CH08 ....$10-15

Bub

Karl Bub of Germany dominated the tin toy car market in Europe for the first half of the twentieth century. He purchased Carette Toy Company of Germany in 1917 from Georges Carette who retreated to France at the beginning of World War I, and took over Bing Toy Works of Germany in 1932.

Coupe with rumble seat, clockwork
motor $750-1,250
Limousine circa 1915, red and black, clockwork motor,
opening doors, hand brake, 14" .$2,500-3,000

Limousine with front crank clockwork motor, green
and black, 9½" $1,500-1,750
Limousine with driver, wind-up, 11" ...$1,750-2250
Limousine, wind-up, 8" $750-1,000
Mercedes Limousine circa 1928, green and
black, opening doors, folding windshield,
headlamps, toolboxes, clockwork motor,
13½" $2,250-2,500
Roadster with driver circa 1908, 9" ..$2,250-2,500
Sedan with high headlights, 1919, wind-up,
14" $2,400-2,600
Tourer, two-seater, wind-up, 9½" $2,250-2,500

Buby (also see Collector's Classics)

Haroldo Nicolás "Buby" Malher is the son of German immigrants. His father moved to Argentina in 1922, his future mother a year later. They married in 1928. "Buby" was born in 1931. His father nicknamed him Buby, and the name has stuck ever since. Mr. "Buby" Malher made his first model in 1955 at the age of 24. His first factory was in Ranelagh, Argentina.

Reasonably priced but hard to find, Buby toys are nice models for the price. A few models are from old Solido dies, but most are original. Later models were issued as Collector's Classics to avoid a blatant connection with the Buby name when the company suffered through a few public relations issues. The last Collector's Classics models were produced in 1995. Mr. Malher has talked of restarting his business sometime in 2004, but no news of such a restart has so far surfaced.

Buick Century
Ambulance, white, 1:43, #1000 ......$10-15
Army Ambulance, green, 1:43,
#1000A $10-15
Station Wagon, blue and white, 1:43,
#1001 ....$10-15
Chevrolet C60
"Esso," 1:64, #2020 ....$5-10
Fire Pumper, 1:64, #2030 ....$5-10
Chevrolet Camaro
1967, 1:43, #1046 ....$45-60
Rally 1967, 1:43, #1047 ....$45-60
Chevrolet Chevrolet Nova
1:64, #8 ....$5-10
1:64, #1081 ....$5-10
Rally 1968, 1:43, #1033 ....$45-60
Carrera, 1:64, #24 ....$5-10
Chevrolet Semi
Refrigerator Truck, 1:64, #2040 ....$5-10
Cattle Truck, 1:64, #2050 ....$5-10
Chevron, 1:43, #1012 ....$45-60
Citroën 3CV
1:64, #6 ....$5-10

1:64, #1060 ....$5-10
Carrera, 1:64, #22 ....$5-10
Citroën Ami 6, 1:64, #9 ....$5-10
Fiat 125
1:43, #1028 ....$25-35
Carrera, 1:43, #1029 ....$25-35
Fiat 128
1:43, #1036 ....$20-25
1:64, #12 ....$5-10
Rally, 1:43, #1037 ....$20-25
Rally, 1:64, #25 ....$5-10
Fiat 600
1:64, #3 ....$5-10
Carrera, 1:64, #19 ....$5-10
Fiat 619 N1
Carga General Tandem Trailer Truck, 1:64,
#15 ....$10-15
Fiat 697 N
Truck with three tanks, 1:64, #16 ......$10-15
Crane Truck, 1:64, #17 ....$10-15
Fiat 700 S Tractor, 1:43, #1038 ....$25-35
Fiat 1500 Rally, 1:64, #20 ....$5-10
Fiat Cement Mixer, 1:64, #2060 ....$5-10
Ford Bronco
1:64, #1220 ....$5-10
"NASA," 1:64, #1224 ....$5-10
Wagon, 1:64, #1227 ....$5-10
with roll bar, 1:64, #1221 ....$5-10
4x4 "Old Iron," 1:64, #3050 ....$5-10
4x4 "Outlaw," 1:64, #3060 ....$5-10
Ford F100
Army Pickup, green, 1:43, #1004A $60
Covered Pickup, blue and black, or green and
black, 1:4, #1004B3 ....$60-75
Pickup, red, 1:43, #1004 ....$60
Tow Truck, 1:64, #1190 ....$5-10
Ford Fairlane 500
blue and white, 1:43, #1002 ....$10-15
Rally, red, 1:43, #1002A $10-15
Policia, blue and white, 1:43, #1003 ...$10-15
Ford Falcon
1:43, #1020 ....$45-60
1:64, #2 ....$5-10
Carrera, 1:43, #1021 ....$45-60
Carrera, 1:64, #18 ....$5-10
Police, 1:64, #1 ....$5-10
Taxi, 1:43, #1045 ....$45-60
Ford Mustang
"Dukes of Hazzard," 1:64, #1051 ......$5-10
Ford Mustang II
1:64, #1050 ....$5-10
Cobra, 1:64, #1052 ....$5-10
Ford Sierra
1:64, #1070 ....$5-10
XR4, 1:64, #1250 ....$5-10
XR4 "Bardahl," 1:64, #1251 ....$5-10

Ford Van
"Coca Cola," 1:64, #1231 ....$5-10
"Las Lenas," 1:64, #1234 ....$5-10
"Marlboro," 1:64, #1230 ....$5-10
"Peugeot," 1:64, #1235 ....$5-10
4x4 "Thunder," 1:64, #3010 ....$5-10
4x4 "Cracker," 1:64, #3020 ....$5-10

Ika Torino
1:43, #1022 ....$45-60
1:64, #7 ....$5-10
Carrera, 1:64, #23 ....$5-10
Police, 1:43, #1043 ....$45-60
Rally, 1:43, #1023 ....$45-60

Jeep CJ5
1:64, #1270 ....$5-10
4x4 "Mad Mex," 1:64, #3030 ....$5-10
4x4 "Vagabond," 1:64, #3040 ....$5-10

Maserati Bora
1:64, #1090 ....$5-10
Rally, 1:64, #1091 ....$5-10

Maserati Indy
1:64, #30 ....$5-10
1:64, #1030 ....$5-10
Rally, 1:64, #31 ....$5-10

McLaren Ford
1:64, #11 ....$5-10

Mercedes Benz 1112
Dump Truck, 1:43, #1019 ....$25-35
Dump Truck, 1:64, #10 ....$10-15
Open cargo Truck, 1:43, #1018 ......$25-35

Mercedes-Benz 350SL
1:64, #1040 ....$5-10
Rally, 1:64, #1041 ....$5-10

Opel Kapitän 1964 Ambulance, 1:64,
#1180 ....$5-10

Peugeot 404
1:64, #5 ....$5-10
Carrera, 1:64, #21 ....$5-10
Taxi, 1:64, #28 ....$5-10

Peugeot 504
1:43, #1030 ....$25-35
1:64, #13 ....$5-10
1:64, #1030 ....$5-10
Carrera, 1:43, #1031 ....$25-35
Fire Chief, 1:43, #1051 ....$25-35
Fire Chief, 1:64, #29 ....$5-10
Rally, 1:64, #26 ....$5-10

Pontiac Racing Custom, 1:43, #1041 .....$45-60

Renault 6
1:43, #1034 ....$45-60
Multipurpose version, 1:43, #1035 ...$45-60

Renault 12
1:64, #14 ....$5-10
1:64, #1140 ....$5-10
Polizia, 1:64, #1142 ....$5-10
Rally, 1:64, #27 ....$5-10

Rally, 1:64, #1141 ....$5-10
Station Wagon, 1:64, #1170 ....$5-10
Station Wagon "Rescue," 1:64, #1171 ...$5-10

Renault 18
1:64, #1160 ....$5-10
Polizia, 1:64, #1161 ....$5-10
"Marlboro," 1:64, #1162 ....$5-10

Renault Fuego
1:64, #1240 ....$5-10
"Cazalis," 1:64, #1241 ....$5-10

Renault Kombi
1:64, #1260 ....$5-10
"Aerolineas," 1:64, #1261 ....$5-10
Ambulance, 1:64, #1262 ....$5-10
"Lufthansa," 1:64, #1265 ....$5-10
School Bus, 1:64, #1263 ....$5-10
"World Tour," 1:64, #1264 ....$5-10

Volkswagen Buggy, 1:64, #1212 ....$5-10
Volkswagen Facel (Fox), 1:64, #1120 ......$5-10

Buccaneer

Until collector Steve Mason provided photos of a toy 1937 Packard with the brand name "Buccaneer" stamped into the base, I had never heard of Buccaneer brand. Latest information indicates that Buccaneer is actually a mid- to late-1970s pirate of early Tootsietoys and Dinky Toys, hence the name "Buccaneer" (another name for "Pirate"). What distinguishes Buccaneer from the original is the weight. Buccaneer models are white metal and are therefore considerably heavier than their zinc alloy counterparts.

According to Martin Van de Logt of the Netherlands, Buccaneer models started out as "easy" white metal kits costing around £5 (about $8 US) and that they were never meant to fool collectors.

Armstrong Siddeley 30HP 1934, #15 .....$20-25
Armstrong Siddeley Typhoon, #28 ....$20-25
Bedford Van 1938
"Use Kodak Film," #40 ....$20-25
"Wakefield's Castrol Motor Oil" $20-25
Bentley 3.5 11934 Coupe, #14 ....$20-25
Bentley 1937, #8 ....$20-25
Buick Limousine 1937, #23 ....$20-25
Caravan 1934, #31 ....$20-25
Chrysler 1939 ....$20-25
Chrysler Airflow 1934, #2 ....$20-25
Chrysler Royal Limousine 1937, #20 ......$20-25
Daimler Limousine 1934, #7 ....$20-25
Graham Saloon, #17 ....$20-25
Ford Van 1935
"Bisto," #37 ....$20-25
"Dunlop Tyres," #38 ....$20-25
1935 "Hovis for Tea," #36 ....$20-25

1935 "Virol for your Child," #39 ....$20-25
Frazer Nash 1939, #26 ....$20-25
Humber Vogue 1933 Saloon, #11 ....$20-25
Jaguar SS100
#16 ....$20-25
1939, #27 ....$20-25
La Salle 1935 Sedan, #9 ....$20-25
Lincoln Zephyr 1937 Coupe, #5 ....$20-25
MG EX 135 Record Car, #25 ....$20-25
MG TF 1953, #3 ....$20-25
Morris Van 1934
"Carter Patterson," #33 ....$20-25
"Crawford's Biscuits," #35 ....$20-25
"Meccano Engineering," #32 ....$20-25
"Pickford's," #34 ....$20-25
Oldsmobile Super Six 1937, #22 ....$20-25
Packard Super 8 1937 Limousine, #21 ...$20-25
Rolls Royce Phantom
1934 Coupe, #4 ....$20-25
Town Sedan, #10 ....$20-25
Rolls Royce Thunderbolt 1938 Record Car
Rover 14HP 1934 Streamline Saloon, #12 ..$20-25
Salmson 1933 4-Seater, #18 ....$20-25
Salmson 1937, #2 ....$20-25
Studebaker State Commander 1937,
#19 ....$20-25
Vauxhall Limousine 1935, #6 ....$20-25

Buddy L (also see Imperial Diecast)

Buddy L toys were first manufactured in 1921 by the Moline Pressed Steel Company of Moline, Illinois, which got its start manufacturing car and truck parts in 1913. They are named after the owner Fred Lundahl's son Buddy Lundahl. The first Buddy "L" toys were especially made for his son and built to support a man's weight. Soon, the fathers of Buddy's playmates started asking for them. So began the manufacture of Buddy "L" toys. The heavier toy trucks gave way to lighter models in the early 1930s. The company has been variously known as the Buddy "L" Corp. and Buddy "L" Toy Co. It wasn't until later that the quotation marks were removed from around the "L." Recently, the brand name has been resurrected and new models issued. One in particular, through the licensing of Buddy L by Imperial Toy Corporation of Hong Kong, is a large scale pressed steel Hummer H2 in various colors issued at the beginning of 2004. Buddy L is now owned by Alpha International, also the parent company of the recently acquired GearBox Collectibles.

While many pressed steel toy trucks were produced throughout the long history of Buddy L, only a few passenger vehicles were made. In

2004, Imperial Diecast of Hong Kong produced a series of diecast Ford and Chevrolet models packaged as Buddy L toys. See them listed in the Imperial Diecast section.

Flivver Coupe, 1920s, 11", #210B $375-425
Flivver Roadster, 1920s, 11", 210A....$575-625
Greyhound Bus, 16".....................$1,000-1,250
Hot Rod with Motorcycles on Trailer, 17" ...$475-525
Hummer H2, Imperial Toy Corp, 2004 ....$35-55
Motor Coach, #208 ....$5,250-5,750
Scarab, #711, 1930s, red...............$125-175

Budgie (also see Morestone)

Like Corgi, Dinky, Impy, and many other diecast toys of the 1950s and 1960s, Budgies are a product of Great Britain. While Corgi is named after the Welsh Corgi, a popular dog in Wales, Budgie is named after a budgerigar (parakeet), another popular pet for many Brits, as well as for bird lovers around the world.

Budgie was originally owned by Morris and Stone (Morestone), who introduced the first castings as Esso promotional models before changing their name to Budgie. The brand was later purchased by Guitermans.

Budgie toys were popular in England and the US in the 1960s, but were eclipsed by Corgi, Dinky, and especially Matchbox, eventually going out of business.

Latest news indicates dies and castings have been purchased by a new company in England called Autocraft which is reproducing Budgie models in small quantities.

0-6-0 Tank Locomotive "British Railways," 1:76, #224 ....$35-50
AEC Merryweather Fire Escape, 1:72, #254 ....$35-50
AEC Routemaster Bus
  "Shop Linker," 1:60, #704 ....$35-50
  "25 Faithful Years," 1:60, #705........$35-50
  "Watford FA Cup Final," 1:60, #706.......$35-50
  "Esso Uniflow," with windows, 1:60, #236.........$35-50
  "Esso Golden," 1:60, #236 ....$35-50
  "Go Esso, Buy Esso, Drive Esso," 1:60, #236.........$35-50
  "Uniflo SAE W50 Motor Oil," 1:60, #236.........$35-50
  "Sheraton-Heathrow Hotel," 1:60, #236........$35-50
AEC Routemaster Double-Decker Bus "Esso Uniflow," without windows, 1:60, #236...........$35-50
AEC Super Fueller Tanker, 1:65, #280....$35-50

Albion Overhead Maintenance Vehicle, 1:50, #316 ....$35-50
Alvis Salamander Crash Tender, #298.....$35-50
Austin Articulated Container Truck "British Railways'," 1:76, #252 ....$35-50
Austin Breakdown Truck, 1:43, #244......$35-50
Austin FX4 Taxi
  1958, 1:43, #101 ....$35-50
  1958, 1:43, #703 ....$35-50
  25th Anniversary, #101 ....$50-65
Aveling-Barford Road Roller, 1:36, #701 ....$35-50
Bedford Ice Cream Van, 1:43, #290......$35-50
Bedford Long Wheelbase Tipper Truck "Ham River Grit," 1:72, #276...........$35-50
Bedford Super Tipmaster, #312 ....$35-50
Bedford TK
  Glass Transporter, 1:72, #304..........$35-50
  Horse Box, 1:72, #294 ....$35-50
Blue Line Sightseeing Coach "Washington D.C.," 1:60, #296 ....$55-70
Commer Cabin Service Lift Truck "BOAC," 1:50, #302 ....$35-50
Commer Douglas Prospector Duomatic Tipper, 1:50, #324 ....$35-50
Daimler Ambulance 1949, 1:43, #258....$35-50
Euclid Dumper, 1:65, #242 ....$35-50
Euclid Mammoth Articulated Dumper, 1:60, #318 ....$35-50
Euclid Scraper, 1:65, #282 ....$35-50
Fiat Tractor
  with Dozer Blade, 1:50, #314 ....$35-50
  with Shovel, 1:50, #306 ....$35-50
Ford Thames Trader Refuse Truck, 1:60, #274 ....$35-50
Foden Aircraft Refuelling Tanker, 1:65, #256 ....$35-50
Foden Dumper, 1:72, #226 ....$35-50
Horse Drawn Covered Wagon with 4 horses, 1:50, #404 ....$45-60
Horse Drawn Hansom Cab, #100 ....$35-50
International Articulated Refrigerator Truck, 1:76, #202 ....$35-50
International Low Loader with Caterpillar Tractor, 1:76, #234 ....$35-50
International Tank Transporter with tank, 1:76, #222 ....$35-50
Karrier Bantam Bottle Truck, 1:36, #228 ..$35-50
Land Rover
  AA, 1:40, #268 ....$35-50
  RAC, 1:40, #278 ....$35-50
Lewin Sweepmaster Road Sweeper, 1:50, #300 ....$35-50
Leyland Articulated Petrol Tanker, 1:72, #270 ....$35-50
Leyland Bulk Flour Tanker, 1:72, #288 ....$35-50

Leyland Bulk Milk Tanker, 1:72, #292.....$35-50
Leyland Cement Mixer, 1:72, #310........$35-50
Leyland Hippo
  "Coal and Coke" Truck, 1:76, #206...$35-50
  Cattle Transporter, 1:76, #220 ....$35-50
Motorcycle and Sidecar
  "Express Delivery," 1:36, #266........$35-50
  with rider, AA, 1:36, #452 ....$35-50
  with rider, RAC, 1:36, #454 ....$35-50
Motorcycle
  Dispatch Rider, 1:36, #456..............$35-50
  G.P.O. Messenger, 1:36, #456.......$35-50
  Police Patrol, 1:36, #456.................$35-50
  T. T. Rider, 1:36, #456....................$35-50
  with rider, 1:36, #456.....................$35-50
Motorway Express Coach "Midland Red," 1:60, #296 ....$35-50
Personnel carrier
  RAF, 1:50, #208 ....$35-50
Personnel carrier, US Army, 1:50, #210..$35-50
British Army, 1:50, #212 ....$35-50
Racing Motorcycle
  1:36, #262 ....$35-50
  Combination, 1:36, #264 ....$35-50
Renault Truck, 1:72, #216 ....$35-50
Rolls Royce Silver Cloud Saloon, 1959, 1:45, #102 ....$35-50
Ruston-Bucyrus 10-RB Excavator, 1:65, #260 ....$35-50
Scammell Highwayman Gas Transporter, 1:72, #326 ....$35-50
Scammell Routeman Pneumajector Transporter, 1:72, #322 ....$35-50
Scammell Scarab Articulated Van
  "British Railways," 1:50, #238, #238........$35-50
  "Railfreight," 1:50 ....$35-50
  "LMS," 1:50, #702 ....$35-50
  "GWR," 1:50, #702 ....$35-50
  "Royal Navy," 1:50, #702.............$35-50
Scammell Scarab Articulated Wagon with Tilt, 1:50, #240 ....$35-50
Seddon AA Mobile Traffic Unit Control, 1:76, #218 ....$35-50
Seddon Articulated Timber Transporter, 1:76, #230 ....$35-50
Seddon Low Loader with Cable Drums, 1:76, #232 ....$35-50
Seddon Pit Aligator Low Loader, 1:76, #308 ....$35-50
Stage Coach
  Small, with 4 horses, 1:50, #410......$45-60
  Large, with 4 horses, 1:50, #434......$50-65
Supercar of Gerry Anderson 1960 TV Show, 1:43, #272 ....$35-50
Thornycroft Mobile Crane, 1:76, #214 ...$35-50

Triumph Motorcycle and Sidecar with rider
AA, 1:36, #452 ....$35-50
RAC, 1:36, #454 ....$35-50
Triumph Motorcycle with rider, 1:36,
#456 ....$35-50

Volkswagon Microbus, #12 ....$30-45

Volkswagen Pick-Up, "Express Delivery,"
1958, 1:43, #204 ....$35-50
Wagon Train Set, 1:50, #430..............$50-65
Wagon Train Covered Wagon
with 2 horses, 1:50,
#432 ....$45-60
Wolseley Six-Eighty Police car
black, 1:43, #246 ....$35-50
light blue, 1:43, #246 ....$35-50

Bugattiana (see Modelauto)

Burago (see Bburago)

Busch/Präline

Busch GmbH & Co. KG
Heidelberger Straße 26
D-68519 Viernheim/Germany
Telefon: 0 62 04 - 60 07 10
Telefax: 0 62 04 - 60 07 19
Email: info@busch-model.com
Website: www.busch-model.com

Busch models are precise 1:87 scale (HO gauge) plastic models made in Germany, exquisitely detailed, and neatly packaged in a clear plastic display box.

Bentley Convertible Coupe, top down $7-9

Borgward Isabella Coupe....................$12-15
1950 Buick Sedan Limousine...................$9-11

1954 Cadillac Ambulance, cream with chrome plastic trim, #3452 ....$8-10

1952 Cadillac Coupe DeVille, 2-door
hardtop $10-12
1959 Cadillac Eldorado, 2-door
pink $9-11
white, "Just Married" $10-12
1970 Cadillac Station Wagon Deluxe.......$9-11
1952 Cadillac Yellow Cab, yellow ambulance
body..$10-12
1957 Chevrolet Bel Air
Coupe......................................$10-12
Convertible, top down $10-12
1995 Chevrolet Caprice
4-door Sedan..............................$10-12
Classic $8-10
Yellow Cab................................$8-10
1956 Chevrolet Corvette Convertible,
blue $9-11
Citroën AX
2-door hardtop with sunroof $6-8
France Telecom $7-9
French Post Office $7-9
Citroën DS19
plain $11-13
two-tone $11-13
4-door sedan..............................$11-13
Rallye Monte Carlo, blue..................$11-13
Taxi, black $11-13
Dodge Monaco 4-door sedan, yellow with
blue roof $10-12
Ferrari GTO
red :....................................$7-9
Racing, blue $10-12
Ford Crown Victoria Sedan, red.........$11-13
Ford Escort
2-door convertible, top down $9-11
4-door hardtop............................$6-8
Croatia Police 4-door hardtop $9-11
Municipal Vehicle,orange with red and white
safety stripes $8-10
Sport Edition 4-door hardtop $9-11
1964 Ford Mustang Convertible
top down $11-13
top up $11-13
Ford Probe 24V 2-door Hardtop $9-11
1956 Ford Thunderbird Convertible, top
down $10-12
Mercedes-Benz 170
S Convertible LX, top down $7-9

V Convertible, top down.......................$7-9
V 4-door Sedan $7-9
Mercedes-Benz 220 SE 4-door Hardtop with
closed sunroof...........................$8-10
1960s Mercedes-Benz 300 Limousine
Kennedy's Berlin Visit, with figures.......$23-25
Deluxe $11-13
Pope, with figures.........................$23-25
Queen Elizabeth, with figures............$23-25
Mercedes-Benz A-Klasse
Classic, red...............................$8-10
Motorsport, silver.........................$14-16
Mercedes-Benz M-Klasse ML 320 ....$10-12
Jurassic Park: Lost World $19-21
1928 Mercedes-Benz SSK 2-seat Roadster, top
down.....................................$19-21
1931 Mercedes-Benz SSK Mille Miglia ...$19-21
1955 Messerschmitt Kabinenroller KR 200 Bau-
jahr.......................................$7-9
MG Midget TC Convertible $9-11
Morgan Plus 8 Convertible
top up $8-10
top down $9-11
Rallye Race car, top up $10-12
Le Mans, top up...........................$10-12
1965 NSU TT
2-door Hardtop............................$8-10
Rallye $11-13
1938 Opel Olympia
2-door Hardtop............................$8-10
Convertible, top down $7-9
1973 Pontiac Trans Am
plain......................................$7-9
golden eagle on hood $8-10
Renault R5 ....$6-8
Rolls Royce Convertible, top up $11-13
Rolls Royce Silver Cloud III.....................$11-13
Smart, red and black $9-11
Volkswagen Beetle
1951 Export Model with chrome $8-10
1952 2-door with open sunroof $6-8
1953 with oval windows, whitewall tires and
chrome $8-10
"1 Million," gold $9-11
"Crazy cars"...............................$9-11
"Lufthansa" blue and yellow $8-10
Convertible, top down, 2-tone yellow and
black....................................$10-12
Convertible, top up........................$9-11
German Post $7-9
Volkswagen Karmann-Ghia 1600
Coupe.....................................$9-11
Volkswagen Passat 1985 Station
Wagon.....................................$8-10
Volkswagen MHD Emergency Doctor.......$11-13
Volvo 544 2-door Hardtop....................$9-11

Bush

Bush was a producer of diecast promotional models during the 1950s. Not much is known about them, and no model list is available.

C

Cam-Cast

Cam-Cast of Edgerton, Ohio, produced just a few toy trucks in the 1950s. They appear to be one fairly thick, crude lump of metal with details painted on or applied with decals. They carry a high value for such simple toys, mostly due to rarity.

Oil Tanker
"Gulf" $40-75
"Marathon Oil" $40-75
"Sunoco" $40-75
Van
"Evan Motor Freight" $40-75
"North American Van Lines" $40-75
"Pillsbury's Best" $40-75
"Western Auto" $40-75

Car43

Car43 is an obscure Swiss manufacturer of 1:43 scale models most likely resin cast.

AC Cobra 427, Edition 28112.............$10-15
Alfa Romeo 156, Edition 28110 ....$10-15
Audi A4, Edition 28105 ....$10-15
BMW 507, Edition 28103....................$10-15
BMW M1, Edition 28108....................$10-15
Citroën 2CV, Edition 28107 ....$10-15
Fiat 500, Edition 28101......................$10-15
Ford Capri, Edition 28109..................$10-15
Mini Cooper, Edition 28100................$10-15
Morgan Plus 4, Edition 28106............$10-15
Porsche 911 Carrera 4, Edition 28102 ...$10-15
Porsche 930, Edition 28104.................$10-15
Volkswagen New Beetle, Edition 28111 ......$10

Carette, Georges

From 1886 until 1917, Georges Carette produced what have become the rarest and most desirable German tinplate toys ever made. Their fine workmanship and quality of materials set them apart from all the others. Born in France, Carette moved to Nuremburg, Germany, in 1886 and remained there until World War I when he fled back to France, and Karl Bub took over his factory.

Landaulet Limousine $5,000-7,000
Limousine, circa 1911, 9"............$1,250-1,750
Limousine, 15½"....................$10,000-12,500

Limousine with chauffeur, circa 1920,
   12½" $2,750-3,250
Limousine with driver, luggage rack, high headlamps, 15" $5,750-6,250
Limousine with clockwork motor, 1
   6" $4,750-5,250
Limousine with opening doors, roof rack, circa
   1911, 12¼" $3,750-4,250
Open car, carette/Bub, clockwork motor, tinplate
   driver, red and black, forward and reverse
   gear, circa 1911, 6½" $1,750-2,250
Open Phaeton with driver, circa 1906,
   12" $5,000-5,500
Open Tourer, 4-seater with two bisque figures,
   12½" $15,000-17,500
Phaeton 4-seater with two figures,
   9" $3,000-3,500

Carlo Brianza (see A.B.C. Brianza)

Carmania

Carmania of France offers an assortment of 1:64 and 1:43 scale models.

Carmania 1:64 Scale

Chevrolet Camaro
   1976 Z28, pink, #10......................$5-10
   1980 Z28, purple, #43...................$5-10
   1981, yellow, #11..........................$5-10
Chevrolet Corvette
   Convertible, silver, #12 ....$5-10
   Coupe, maroon, #13.......................$5-10
Ferrari 308 1974
   Coupe, blue, #14...........................$5-10
   Coupe, maroon, #15.......................$5-10
   Roadster, red, #16..........................$5-10
Ferrari 365 GT, yellow or pink, #17.........$5-10
Ferrari Testarossa, red, #18 ....$5-10
Ford Thunderbird 1989 Rally, orange,
   #19..$5-10
Ford F250 4WD Pickup, white, #21 ....$5-10
Honda CRX Coupe, red, #22...................$5-10
Lamborghini Countach, blue, #23 ....$5-10
Mercedes 307 Van, yellow/white, #26 ....$5-10
Morgan Plus 4 Roadster, green, #27 ....$5-10
Nissan Mid 4 Coupe, black, #28..............$5-10
Pontiac GTO 1969 Hardtop, #32............$5-10
Pontiac Firebird
   1976 T-Top, #34 ....$5-10
   1981 Convertible, #33.....................$5-10
Porsche 928
   blue, #36 ....$5-10
   "Pennzoil," #37 ....$5-10
Suzuki Samurai, #39 ....$5-10
Toyota Extended Cab Pickup, #40 ....$5-10
Vauxhall 1920, #42 ....$5-10

Volkswagen Beetle Baja Bug, yellow, #44 .$5-10

Carmania 1:43 Scale

Schnauzer Team P7 "Esso," white, #100 .$15-20

Carousel 1

Mason Distributing Company
2203 Patterson Ave.
Roanoke VA 24016
toll-free 1-800-777-3977
www.carousel1.com

Carousel 1 models first appeared on the market around August 1999. Historic racing sports cars and Indianapolis 500 racers are the focus of this brand of highly detailed precision 1:18 scale models. Some of the details that set this brand apart from others are clear-faced gauges, full chassis detail, diecast engines, detailed cockpits, positionable front wheels, imprinted markings and hinged hoods. Among the marques represented are Porsche, Lotus, Penske Racing, Watson Roadster, Kurtis Kraft Roadster, Coyote Racers, and Carousel 1's Hobby Horse line of 1:43 scale models.

Jim Clark 1965 Indy 500 Winner, Lotus
   38 ....$100-125
Mark Donohue #66 1973 "Sunoco" ...$100-125
A. J. Foyt #1 "Bowes" 1961 Indy 500
   Winner $50-75
A. J. Foyt 1967 Indy 500 Winner $85-110
Dan Gurney #36 Belgium Winner AAR
   Eagle...$90-115
Dan Gurney #36 1967 Weslake V-12 ..$90-115
Parnelli Jones #98, white and blue........$85-110
Rutherford "Gatorade," McLaren NR $70-95
Bob Swelkert #6, pale pink and white....$85-110
Bill Vukovich Jr., "Sugaripe" AAR Eagle $55-80
Rodger Ward #3, white and red $85-110

Castle Art (see Gaiety)

C. A. W. Novelty Company

C.A.W. Novelty Company was started in 1925 in Kansas by Charles A. Wood. His fine examples of "slushmold" (lead alloy) toys were not fully appreciated by collectors until as late as 1990 when one collector named Chic Gast described a group of unidentified toys as "orphans." The toys were also marketed by the name of Mid-West Metal Novelty Manufacturing Company in 1929.

World War II brought lead casting to a halt in 1940 and C.A.W. went with it. The last employee of the company, Rod Hemphill, and newfound partner Howard Clevenger purchased the company assets and started C&H Manufacturing Company.

C.A.W. toys originally sold for 10 cents to a dollar.

Air Drive Coach, #25, 3⅞"	$30-40
DeSoto Sedan, #32, 3⅞"	$30-40
Dump Truck, 3⅛"	$30-40
Fuel Tanker, 3¾"	$30-40
Marvel Racer, #31, 3⅜"	$30-40
New Design Racer, #38, 3⅜"	$30-40
Overland Bus, 3¾"	$30-40
Sport Roadster, 3½"	$30-40
Streamline Coupe, #30, 3"	$30-40
Tank Truck, 3⁵⁄₁₆"	$30-40
Transparent Windshield Racer, #39, 3"	$30-40
Wonder Special, #33, 3⅜"	$30-40

C.B.Car

From Milan, Italy, Esci produced a series of 1:24 scale cars called "Real Cars" under the "C.B.Car" brand.

Porsche 959, opening doors and engine compartment, wheels steer, #105	$16-20

C.B.G. Mignot (see Mignot, C.B.G.)

CCC

Collector Bill Cross reports that these are resin models, hand made in France. The range now includes "unusual" European cars like Ford Vedettes, Peugeot 203, and the tiny Rovin Microcar.

1936 Ford Roadster	$125
1955 Ford Crown Victoria	$125
Ford Vedette	$130
Delahaye Fire T-140	$135
1958 Mercedes Benz 220 S	$130
Peugeot 203	$130
Rovin Microcar	$130

C.D.

One of the most obscure French toy companies, C.D. produced a small assortment of cast toy vehicles in the 1920s.

Bugatti Sports car	$90-115
Chenard & Walcker	
Ambulance	$90-115
Limousine	$90-115
"Ricard" Van	$90-115
Wrecker, 3⅜"	$90-115
Delage Limousine	$90-115
Delahaye	
Ambulance	$90-115
Fire Truck	$90-115
Limousine	$90-115
Torpedo	$90-115
Van	$90-115
Ford Model T	$90-115
Hotchkiss Limousine	$90-115
Latil	
Farm Truck	$90-115
Van, 3¾"	$90-115
MG Record Car	$90-115
Panhard Tractor	$90-115
Peugeot Sans Soupape	$90-115
Renault 40CV	
Sedan	$90-115
Coupe	$90-115
Limousine	$90-115
Torpedo	$90-115
Ambulance	$90-115
Truck	$90-115
Renault Vivaquatre Coupe	$90-115
Rosengart Super Traction	
Fastback	$90-115
Roadster	$90-115

CDC (see Detail cars)

Century (see AMR)

Chad Valley

Anthony Bunn Johnson founded Chad Valley in 1823, although the name was not applied until 1919 even though manufacturing was moved to Harborne, England, near the Chad River in 1897. Before producing toy cars, the company specialized in games, books, and teddy bears.

Chad Valley eventually purchased several other toy companies including Peacock Ltd., AS Cartwright Ltd., Barronia Metal, Winfeld, Acme, and others. From the 1930s through the 1950s, Chad Valley was one of the U.K.'s largest producers of tinplate cars and trains, third only to Wells-Brimtoy and Mettoy.

In 1949, Chad Valley was commissioned by the Rootes Group, manufacturers of Hillman, Humber, Sunbeam, and Commer vehicles, to manufacture promotional models for them. From that agreement, Wee-Kin diecast clockwork toys were produced from 1949 to 1954 and sold in Rootes dealerships and in toy stores.

Other diecast vehicles were produced in various sizes until 1954. In 1972, Chad Valley merged with Barclay Toy Group Ltd., was acquired by Palitoy of Great Britain in 1978, and finally sold to Woolworth's in 1989.

Chad Valley Wee-Kin Series

Bulldozer, #243	$45-60
Commer	
Avenger 1949 Coach, #240, 1:60	$45-60
Breakdown Lorry, #229, 1:50	$45-60
Cable Layer, #228, 1:50	$45-60
Fire Engine, #231, 1:50	$45-60
Flat Truck, #226, 1:50	$45-60
Low Loader Articulated Truck, #242, 1:45	$45-60
Milk Float, #230, 1:50	$45-60
Milk Tanker, #233, 1:50	$45-60
Open Lorry, #225, 1:50	$45-60
Refuse Truck, #239, 1:50	$45-60
Tanker "Petrol," #234-1 1:50	$45-60
Tanker "Regent," #234-2, 1:50	$45-60
Timber Wagon, #227, 1:50	$45-60
Tower Repair Wagon, #232, 1:50	$45-60
Farm Trailer, #244, 1:36	$45-60
Fordson Tractor 1949, #503, 1:36	$45-60
Guy	
"Chad Valley" Van, #501, 1:50	$45-60
Double Decker Bus 1949, #224, 1:60	$45-60
"Guy Motors" Van, #502, 1:50	$45-60
"Lyons Ice Cream" Truck, #504, 1:50	$45-60
Hart Manure Spreader, #245, 1:36	$45-60
Hay Rake, #509, 1:36	$45-60
Hillman Minx saloon 1949, #236, 1:43	$60-75
Humber	
Hawk 1949, #507, 1:43	$60-75
Super Snipe Saloon 1949, #237, 1:43	$60-75
Karrier Public Health Vehicle, #241	$45-60
Massey Fergusson 1949 Tractor, #235, 1:36	$45-60
Rolls Royce Razor Edge	
1949 Saloon, #220, 1:43	$60-75
Traffic Control car with loudspeaker, #221, 1:43	$60-75
Police car, #222, 1:43	$60-75
Stacatruc, #247, 1:36	$45-60
Sunbeam	
Record Car, #223, 1:43	$45-60
Talbot 80/90 saloon 1949, #238, 1:43	$45-60

Chad Valley Midget Series with Clockwork Motor, 1:86 Scale

Ambulance, #554	$45-60
Post Office Van, #553	$45-60
Saloon, #550	$45-60
Single Decker Coach, #551	$45-60
Van, #552	$45-60

Champion

Champion is a brand of 1:66 scale Formula 1 racers made in France in the 1970s. Their 1:43 scale models were marketed as Super Champions.

Champion 1:66 Scale

Ferrari F1
  maroon, car #26, J. Ickx, 1:66..........$10-15
  maroon, car #10, C. Amon, 1:66.....$10-15
Honda F1
  white, car #16, John Surtees, 1:66 ....$10-15
  white, car #14, John Surtees, 1:66 ....$10-15
Matra F1
  blue, car #7, Beltoise, 1:66 ....$10-15

blue, car #15, Pescarolo, 1:66 ....$10-15

McLaren F1
  yellow, car #1, 1:66 ....$10-15
  yellow, car #2, D. Hulme, 1:66 ....$10-15
Lotus Ford F1
  maroon, car #9, Hill, 1:66 ....$10-15
  maroon, car #10, 1:66 ....$10-15
Porsche 917
  Monza, gulf blue, car #7, Rodriguez & Oliver, 1:66 ....$10-15
  Nurburgring, Yellow, car #3, Atwood & Muller, 1:66 ....$10-15
  Spa, white, martini, car #22, Van Lennep & Mario, 1:66 ....$10-15
  Le Mans, red, car #23, Larrousse & Kaunsen, 1:66........................$10-15

Super Champion 1:43 Scale

Porsche 917 #19, 1:43 ....$25-40
Lola T70 Mk. 3B, 1:43 ....$25-40

Champion Hardware Company

The Champion Hardware Company was in business from 1883 to 1954, and produced cast iron toys from 1930 through 1936 from Geneva, Ohio.

Airflow, 4¾".....................................$500-600
Delivery Truck, #536, 1930s, 8" $300-400
Gas and Motor Oil Truck, 8" $550-650
Mack Dump Truck, 7" $250-350
Mack Express Truck, 7½" $200-250

Mack Stake Truck, 4½", circa 1930.....$150-200
Mack Stake Truck, 7½" $600-800
Mack Wrecker, 9" $650-850
Panel Delivery, 7¾" $1,500-2,000
Plymouth-style Coupe with opening rumble seat, 7½" $600-800
Race car with two riders, 5½" $300-400
Race car, 9" $275-350
Reo-style Coupe, 7½" $750-1,000
Sedan, 5¼" $175-250
Stake Truck, 8" $500-600
Wrecker, 4" $175-250
Wrecker, 7½" $500-600
Wrecker, C-Cab, 8¼".................$2,000-2,500
Wrecker, 9" $450-550

Champion of the Road (also see Universal)

This obscure brand represents the American marketing division of Universal Toys of Hong Kong. Collector value is essentially nonexistent for these relatively unremarkable toys.

Charbens

Charbens were begun in Andover Yard, Hornsey Road, London, England, by Charles and Benjamin Reid in 1920. Charles previously worked for the Britains company and learned much about diecasting while employed there. From 1928 to 1929, Charbens provided models for Taylor & Barrett. The company continued until 1966.

While pre-war horse-drawn models were produced as Charbens, slush mold (lead alloy) copies of Tootsietoy Mack trucks were produced as "Mimic Toys." Post-WWII Charbens are comparatively more crude than their pre-WWII counterparts.

In 1951, Saalheimer and Company, under the brand name Salco, marketed Disney vehicles such as a Mickey Mouse fire engine.

In 1960, Charbens reproduced veteran and vintage vehicles in 1:86 scale diecast, dubbed "Old Crocks." The designation "OC" was replaced by "M" for military models.

Charbens Pre-WWII (1920–1942) Lead Slush-Mold Vehicles

Ambulance Van, 1935, 1:43................$45-60
Armoured car
  1928, 1:48 ....$45-60
  1935, 1:45 ....$45-60
Bluebird 1936 Record Car, 1:50...........$65-80
Cape cart with Horse, 1:45 ....$75-90
Coal cart with man and horse, 1:45........$75-90
Coster cart and Donkey, 1:40 ....$75-90
Farm Wagon, four-wheel, 1:36 ....$75-90
Goat cart with girl, 1:45 ....$65-80

Governess cart with donkey, 1:45..........$45-60
Gypsy Caravan
  with man, woman with baby, fire and clothes line, 1:45..............................$90-110
  and Horse, 1:45 ....$65-80
Llama cart, 1:45 ....$45-60
London Midland Scottish Railway Wagon, 1:36 ....$50-65
Milk cart, 4-wheel
  "United Dairies," 1:36 ....$45-60
  "Express Dairy," 1:36 ....$45-60
Milk Float with "Pure Milk" label, 1:36 .....$45-60
Organ Grinder with monkey and donkey, 1:45 ....$45-60
Pedestrian Electric Vehicle, "Dairy Milk," 1:43 ....$100-120
Pedestrian Electric Vehicle, "Hovis," 1:43 ...$100-120
Police Van, 1935, 1:43 ....$45-60
Racer
  Small, 1930, Mimic Toy, 1:43 ....$45-60
  Large, 1930, Mimic Toy, 1:41 ....$45-60
Road Tanker, 1935, 1:43 ....$45-60
Saloon, 1935 ....$45-60
Tree Wagon, 1:36 ....$45-60

Charbens Post-WWII (1945–1966) Diecast Vehicles

Alfa Romeo Alfetta Gran Prix, 1950, 1:48, #32 ....$100-125
Armoured car, 1955, 1:36, #26 ....$50-65
Commer Low Loader with cable drums, 1948, 1:55, #31 ....$75-90
Cooper Bristol F1, 1952, 1:48, #33 ...$100-125
Coster Cart and Donkey, 1:40 ....$65-80
Delivery Van, "Hovis Bread," 1:36 ....$40-50
Farm Tractor with Harvester, 1:43, #19 ....$80-100
Farm Mower, 1:43, #18 ....$80-100
Farm Tractor
  Small, 1950, 1:45 ....$60-75
  Large, 1950, 1:43 ....$65-80
  and Three Trailers, #17 ....$75-85
  1:43 ....$30-45
Farm Wagon, four-wheel, 1:36 ....$40-55
Ferrari Gran Prix, 1952, 1:48, #34....$100-125
ennis Fire Engine, 1950, 1:50, #15 .....$80-100
Jowett Javelin Saloon, 1946, 1:43 ......$100-125
Light Van, 1948
  1:45 ....$45-60
  "Carter Paterson," 1:45 ....$45-60
  "Police," 1:45 ....$45-60
  "Royal Mail," 1:45 ....$45-60
Maudsley Horse Transport Box, 1950, 1:50, #36 ....$80-100
Milk Float, post-war, 1:36 ....$35-40
Mobile Coffee Wagon with attendant and horse, pre-war, 1:45 ....$60-75

Mobile Crane, #20......................$45-60
Morris Estate car, 1947, 1:43............$80-100
Morris Z Van, 1947
   "Carter Paterson," 1:43, #12............$65-80
   "Post Office Telephones," 1:43, #14 ...$75-90
   "Esso," 1:43 ....$75-90
   "Police," 1:43, #13 ....$75-90
   "Royal Mail," 1:43, #10 ....$75-90
   Ambulance, 1:43, #11 ....$75-90
   Morris Z Open Fire Engine with five firemen,
      1947, 1:43 ....$80-100
Motor Coach, #9 ....$80-100
Muir Hill Dumper, #21 ....$60-75
Road Tanker, 1948, 1:55 ....$75-90
Rocket Gun on Truck and Trailer, 1:55,
   #37 ....$75-90
Scammell Scarab Mechanical Horse
   "GWR," 1948, 1:45 ....$65-80
   "LNER," 1948, 1:45.....................$65-80
Steam Roller, #28 ....$45-60
Streamline Coach, 1948, 1:60 ....$45-60
Tipping Truck, #8 ....$50-65
Tipping Wagon, 1948, 1:55 ....$45-60
Tree Wagon, 1:36 ....$35-50
Tumbril cart, 1:36 ....$45-60

Charbens "Mimic" Series Mack Truck (Tootsietoy copies, lead, 1:60 scale)

1928 Mack
   Cattle Truck $30-35
   Dump Truck $30-35
   Gun Truck $30-35
   Searchlight Truck $30-35

Charbens Road Repair, Traffic, and Road Sign Sets, Lead, Pre-War

"30 MPH" Sign $10-15
"No Road" Sign...........................$10-15
Beacon...................................$10-15
Bus Stop.................................$10-15
Gas Pump.................................$10-15
Lamp Island $10-15
Lamp Post................................$10-15
Man with Pick............................$10-15
Man Shoveling $10-15
Man Standing with Shovel.................$10-15
Man with Drill...........................$10-15
Motorcycle Policeman, 1:45...............$10-15
Night Watchman with hut, nightstick, and
   bench $20-25
Police Motorcycle and Sidecar, 1:45......$35-40
Policeman Directing Traffic $15-20
Postman $10-15
Telephone Box............................$25-30
Traffic Signal, Single $10-15
Traffic Signal, Two Way..................$10-15

Tram Stop $10-15
Trestle and Poles $10-15

Charbens Old Crock Series, 1:86 Scale, 1960

1909 Albion Pickup, OC16.................$25-40
Armored car, M35.........................$25-40
Articulated Breakdown Truck, OC27........$25-40
1904 Autocar, two wheels in front, one in back,
   OC23 ....$25-40
Bedford Horse Transport, M19.............$30-45
1904 Bus, OC23...........................$25-40
1900 Daimler, OC22.......................$25-40
1894 Darracq Genevieve, red, orange, or blue,
   OC1 ....$25-40
1906 De Dion Bouton, OC6.................$25-40
Fire Engine, OC26........................$30-45
1907 Ford Model T Coupe, cast in 2 halves,
   OC4 ....$25-40
1907 Ford Model T Coupe, single casting,
   OC4 ....$25-40
1870 Grenville Steam carriage, OC24 .....$25-40
1910 Lanchester, OC20....................$25-40
1911 Mercedes-Benz, OC18 ....$25-40
1913 Mercer Runabout, OC28...............$25-40
Mobile Searchlight, M30 ....$25-40
Mobile Twin Bofor Gun, M31 ....$25-40
Mobile Radar, M32 ....$25-40
Mobile Field Gun, M33 ....$25-40
Mobile Rocket Gun, M34 ....$25-40
1922 Morris Cowley Roadster, OC21 ....$25-40
1905 Napier Record Car, OC25 ....$25-40
1914 "Old Bill" Double Decker Bus, OC3
   cast in two halves....................$25-40
   single cast with separate upper
     deck seats.........................$35-50
1905 Packard Runabout, OC12 ....$25-40
1908 Packard Runabout, light green,
   OC11 ....$25-40
1898 Panhard, blue, light green & silver, or
   brown & silver, OC7...................$25-40
Rocket Tender, OC15......................$25-40
1906 Rolls-Royce Silver Ghost, silver,
   OC8 ....$25-40
1912 Rover Roadster, OC17 ....$30-45
1904 Spyker, yellow and black, OC2 ......$25-40
1903 Standard 6 HP, OC9..................$20-35
Stephenson's Rocket Locomotive, OC14.....$25-40
1900 Straker Steam Lorry, OC13 ....$25-40
1905 Vauxhall Hansom Cab, OC12......$25-40
1907 Vauxhall, green, OC5................$25-40
1902 Wolseley, turquoise, OC10 ....$25-40

Charmerz (also see Playart, Majorette)

Charmerz are repackaged Playart and Majorette toys marketed by New York distributor Charles Merzbach. Identification as Charmerz is only possible if they are still in their original packages. Otherwise the cars themselves carry only the original maker's name and bear no mention of the Charmerz brand. Value is comparable to the same model in its own branded package.

Chein

Julius Chein (pronounced "Chain") started producing lithographed tin toys in Harrison, New Jersey, in 1903. The company continued there until 1979, then moved to Burlington, New Jersey, where it reportedly still functions today.

Airflow, wind-up with garage $550-650
Grayhound Bus, wind-up, 9"...............$350-450
Limousine, wind-up, 1930s, 7"...........$500-600
Peanuts Bus, "Happiness Is An Annual Outing,"
   1970s $150-225
Racer #3, wind-up, 1920s, 6½".........$300-325
Racer #52, wind-up, 6½" $225-300
Roadster, circa 1925, 8½" $550-650
Sedan, wind-up, 6 windows, 8½"......$600-700
Taxi, wind-up, 1920s, 7"................$400-500
Touring car, 7".........................$450-550
Woodie Sedan, wind-up $250-325
Woodie Station Wagon, wind-up.......$150-225

Cherilea

W. Cherrington and J. Leaver, two ex-employees of Johillco, created Cherilea in 1946 in Bumley, England, and started producing a variety of diecast zinc alloy road signs in roughly 1:43 scale. In 1950, Cherilea purchased Fylde Manufacturing Toys, a manufacturer of lead figures, and the factory was moved to Blackpool, England. In 1955, plastic replaced metal. They are easily identifiable by "Cherilea England" embossed on the back. Value for metal Cherilea road signs is $6-12 each. Plastic versions are $4-8 each.

Cherryca Phenix

Taiseiya of Japan originally marketed these exceptional 1:43 scale diecast models, some with battery-operated lights, under the "Micropet" brand in the early 1960s. Taiseiya was later purchased by Yonezawa, known for Diapet diecast models.

Buick Electra
   #6 ....$275-300
   #FL-1 ....$275-300
Cadillac 62 Special, #20.................$300-325

Chevrolet
  #21 ....$125-150
    Impala, #5 ....$275-300
Citroën DS 19 Convertible, #19 ....$325-350
Daihatsu Berlina/Compagno, #41 .....$200-225
Datsun
  #4 ....$100-125
  1200 Pickup, #13 ....$250-275
  1200 Station Wagon, #12 ....$250-275
Bluebird, #22 ....$425-450
Bluebird, #32 ....$225-250
Bluebird Rally, #46 ....$250-275
    Fairlady Roadster, #16 ....$275-300
1901 Decauville Vis-a-Vis, #0T5 ....$75-100
1901 Delahaye Vis-a-Vis, #0T6 ....$75-100
Dodge Polara, #10 ....$225-250
Ford Falcon
  #7 ....$275-300
  #FL-2 ....$275-300
Ford Thunderbird, #15 ....$275-300
Fordson Major Tractor and Trailer,
  #001 ....$225-250
Hino Contessa
  #1 ....$250-275
  #34 ....$225-250
Honda S 600 Roadster, #38 ....$225-250
Isuzu Bellet
  #30 ....$250-275
  2000 De Luxe, #14 ....$275-300
  GT, #50 ....$250-275
Jaguar Type E Roadster, #23 ....$250-275
Lincoln Continental, #17 ....$325-350
Mazda Luce, #44 ....$225-250
Mercedes-Benz
  220 SE, #18 ....$275-300
  300 SL Hardtop, #11 ....$275-300
  300 SL Roadster, #3 ....$275-300
  300 SL Roadster, #29 ....$275-300
Mitsubishi
  Colt 1000 #33 ....$225-250
  Colt 1000 Rally, #45 ....$250-275
  Debonair, #42 ....$200-225
Nissan
  Cedric, #25 ....$250-275
  Cedric Police car, #43 ....$250-275
  Cedric Station Wagon, #2 ....$250-275
  Cedric Taxi, #35 ....$275-300
  Prince Gloria, #24 ....$250-275
  Prince Gloria Rally, #48 ....$250-275
  Prince Skyline 1500, #31 ....$250-275
  Prince Skyline Rally, #47 ....$250-275
  Prince Sprint Coupe, #39 ....$225-250
Peugeot
  1892, #0T1 ....$75-100
  1896, #0T2 ....$75
  1898 Victoria, #0T3 ....$75-100

  1899 Victoria, #0T4 ....$75-100
Toyota/Toyopet
  Corona, #28 ....$250-275
  Corona Coupe, #40 ....$225-250
  Crown, #26 ....$250-275
  Crown Police car, #36 ....$275-300
  Crown Station Wagon, #27 ....$250-275
  Crown Taxi, #37 ....$275-300
Volkswagen
  1200, #8 ....$275-300
  Karmann Ghia Roadster, #9 ....$325-350

Chico (see Tekno)

Chrono (also see ModelCast)

Chrono - A Model Collection Co. Ltd.
Room 3105, Diamond Square
Shun Tak Centre
168-200 Connaught Road
Central Hong Kong, China
fax +852-2785-3901

    The specialty of this Hong Kong-based company just now gaining more prominence is 1:18 scale diecast models.

1963 Aston Martin DB5

green ,1998, #791001, H1001 ....$25-35
  dark red, 1998, #791002 ....$25-35
  metallic light blue, 1998, #791003 ..$25-35
  silver, James Bond, 1998, #791080 ....$25-35
1968 Fiat 24 Spider
  red, 1998, #791090 ....$25-35
  yellow, 1998, #791091 ....$25-35
  black, 1998, #791092 ....$25-35
  white, Hardtop, Abarth, 1998,
    #791100 ....$25-35
  red, Hardtop, Abarth, 1998,
    #791101 ....$25-35
  metallic blue, Pininfarina, 1998,
    #791110 ....$25-35
  metallic green, Pininfarina, 1998,
    #791111 ....$25-35
1998 Lotus Elise
  Spider, yellow, 1998, #791020 .....$25-35
  Spider, blue, 1998, #791021 ....$25-35
  Spider, black, 1998, #791022 ....$25-35
  Hardtop, red, 1998, #791030 ....$25-35
  Hardtop, green, 1998, #791031 .....$25-35

  Hardtop, silver, 1998, #791032 ......$25-35
Nissan Primera STW-CUP
  Asch, 1998 ....$25-35
  Massen, 1998 ....$25-35
Opel Vectra STW-CUP
  Alzen, 1998 ....$25-35
  Thiim, 1998 ....$25-35
1953 Porsche 550 RS
  silver, 1998, #791060 ....$25-35
  blue, 1998, #791061 ....$25-35
  red, 1998, #791062 ....$25-35
  silver, Nr. 40, 1998, #791070 ....$25-35
  silver, James Dean, 1998,
    #791080 ....$25-35
1969 Triumph Spitfire MK IV
  Cabrio, white, 1998, #791040 ......$25-35
  Cabrio, green, 1998, #791041 .....$25-35
  Cabrio, black, 1998, #791042 ......$25-35
  Hardtop, red, 1998, #791050 ....$25-35
  Hardtop, blue, 1998, #791051 ......$25-35
  Hardtop, yellow, 1998, #791052 ....$25-35

Ciba

    Mercedes-Benz cars in 1:43 scale appear to be the only models issued by Ciba.

Mercedes-Benz 300E
  blue $10-15
  green $10-15
  red $10-15
  yellow $10-15

Cigar Box (see Aurora Cigar Box)

C.I.J.

    Compagnie Industrielle du Jouet, better known as C.I.J. of France, first produced 1:43 scale models in 1933 out of plaster and flour. Other materials used in producing models included tinplate, lead cast and, from 1938 to 1964, diecast. The firm of J.R.D. was purchased in 1963, and a few C.I.J. models were reissued unchanged as J.R.D. models and vice versa. Here is an assortment of known models. Introduction year and current value follow the description.

Berliet GLR 19
  Tank Truck, #3/23, 1959 ....$75-90
  "Shell" Tanker, #3/24, 1959 ....$75-90
  Berliet Semi-Trailer Truck, #3/77,
    1965 ....$110-125
  Berliet Weitz Mobile Crane, #3/84,
    1964-65 ....$90-105
  Caravan Trailer, #3/27, 1959 ....$55-70
  Cattle Trailer, #3/28, 1962 ....$55-70

Chrysler Windsor Sedan, #3/15,
   1956 ....$140-155
Citroën AMI 6, #3/6, 1964 ....$55-70
Citroën ID19
   Ambulance, #3/41, 1964 ....$85-100
   Estate car, #3/4, 1958-59 ....$85-100
Citroën 11CV, #3/11, 1964-65 ....$55-70
   (reissued as J.R.D. #112)
Citroën 1200KG
   Van, #3/89, 1965................$90-105
   Police Van, #3/89, 1964-65.........$90-105
   Citroën 2CV Mail Van, #3/76,
   1965.....................$80-95
   Crane Truck, #3/81, 1956 ....$90-105
   De Rovin Open Two-Seater, #3/1,
   1954..........................$85-100
   Facel Vega Facellia, #3/3, 1958-60 .$90-105
   Fire Engine, #3/30, 1959...........$110-125
   Mercedes-Benz 220 Sedan, #3/12,
   1959.......................$55-70
Panhard "BP" Tank Truck, #3/20, 1951 .$60-75
   Panhard Dyna 130, #3/47, 1950 ...$70-85
   54, #3/54, 1955.........................$70-85
   Junior, #3/5, 1954.....................$85-100
Peugeot 403
   Break, #3/46, 1955 ....$60-75
   Ambulance, #3/46, 1962 ....$75-90
Police car, #3/46, 1960 ....$55-70
Peugeot 404 Sedan, #3/13, 1965 ....$55-70
   (reissued as J.R.D. #151)
Plymouth Belvedere Sedan, #3/16,
   1957 ....$140-155
Renault 1000KG
   Van, #3/60, 1955.....................$55-70
   Astra Van, #3/60, 1957...............$90-105
   Boucherie Van, #3/60, 1960.......$90-105
   Mail Van, #3/60, 1957 ....$90-105
   Belgian Mail Van, #3/60, 1957 ..$125-140
   "Shell" Van, #3/60, 1956..........$90-105
   Van and Trailer, #3/60, 1957 .....$115-130
   Ambulance, #3/61, 1955 ....$110-125
   Army Ambulance, #3/61, 1959 ..$110-125
   Bus, #3/62, 1955 ....$90-105
   Police Van, #3/63, 1955 ....$80-95
Renault 2.5 Ton
   Bottle Truck, #3/94, 1963............$95-105
   Fire Engine, #3/95, 1963...........$120-135
   Gun Truck, #3/99, 1964...........$100-115
   Radar Truck, #3/98, 1964...........$100-115
Renault 300KG
   Van, #3/67, 1957 ....$55-70
   Mail Van, #3/68, 1957 ....$70-85
Renault 4CV
   #3/48, 1950 ....$70-85
   Police car, #3/49, 1950.................$70-85
Renault 7-Ton Covered Truck, #3/25, 1953 ..$40-55

Renault Alpine Coupe, #3/50, 1958-59 ...$55-70
Renault Atomic Pile Transporter, #3/75,
   1957 ....$180-195
Renault Bus, #3/40, 1954 ....$80-95
Renault Colorale
   Ambulance, #3/55, 1956 ....$80-95
   #3/44, 1953 ....$55-70
Renault Covered Trailer, #3/26, 1953 ...$40-55
Renault Domane
   Break, #3/53, 1958 ....$60-75
   Ambulance, #3/53, 1960 ....$75-90
Renault Dauphine
   #3/56, 1956 ....$60-75
   Taxi, #3/56, 1958.....................$60-75
   Police, #3/57, 1958 ....$60-75
Renault Dauphinoise
   Break, #3/66, 1956-57 ....$55-70
   Police car, #3/69, 1955 ....$80-95
Renault Dump Truck, #3/80, 1955 ....$80-95
Renault E-30
   Farm Tractor, #3/33, 1959.........$110-125
   Tractor and Trailer, #3/34, 1959 .$165-180
Renault Estafette
   Bus, #3/92, 1961 ....$70-85
   Van, #3/90, 1963.....................$75-90
   Police Bus, #3/93, 1962 ....$75-90
   Police Van, #3/91, 1963 ....$75-90
Renault Etoile Filante Record Car, #3/2,
   1957 ....$90-105
Renault Excavator, #3/88, 1964-65 ......$75-90
Renault Floride, #3/58, 1960................$55-70
Renault Fregate
   #3/51, 1951 ....$60-75
   Grand Pavois, #3/52, 1958 ....$60-75
Renault Police Pickup and Trailer, #3/65,
   1962 ....$100-115
Renault Prairie
   #3/42, 1953 ....$55-70
   Taxi, #3/45, 1955 ....$55-70
Renault Savane, #3/43, 1953 ....$55-70
Renault Searchlight Truck and Trailer, #3/96,
   1963 ....$100-115
Renault Semi Truck - Trailer, #3/70,
   1955 ....$80-95
Renault Semi Tank Truck - Trailer, #3/72,
   1958 ....$100-115
Renault Semi Log Truck - Trailer, #3/73,
   1956 ....$80-95
Renault "Shell" Tank Truck, #3/21, 1952 ..$60-75
Renault Tractor and Sling cart Trailer, #3/39,
   1959 ....$160-175
Renault Tractor and Trailer, #3/38,
   1959 ....$160-175
Renault Wrecker, #3/83, 1964 ....$90-105
Sailboat on Trailer, #3/76, 1964 ....$55-70
Saviem Bottle Truck, #3/79, 1965.....$100-115

Saviem Missile Launcher, #3/97,
   1964 ....$100-115
Seed Trailer, #3/32, 1959 ....$55-70
Shovel Truck, #3/82, 1958 ....$90-105
Simca 1000
   Coupe Bertone, #3/9, 1964 ....$55-70
   Sedan, #3/7, 1962-63 ....$55-70
   Police car, #3/8, 1963 ....$55-70
Sling cart Trailer, #3/36, 1959 ....$60-75
Sugar Beet Trailer, #3/31, 1959 ....$60-75
Tipping Farm Trailer, #3/37, 1959 ....$60-75
Unic Cab and Trailer with railroad car,
   #3/78 ....$140-155
Volkswagen, #3/10, 1954..................$65-80
Water Tank Trailer, #3/35, 1959.........$55-70

Circle N Toys

Similar in appearance to Tootsietoys, Circle N Toys is a previously unknown company until collector Jarek Skonieczny discovered a toy Jeep with the name and logo on the underside in September 1999. More research is needed.

Jeep, 3"..$2-6

City (see Vitesse)

CKO (also see Kellerman)

The trademark logo on the bottom of CKO models is all that identifies these models. The C forms an arc around the K with the O to the right. These tinplate models are made in Germany and are quite rare for their vintage, having been produced sometime between the mid-1960s and mid-1970s. Prior to the application of the CKO brand, the company offered models under the Kellerman brand.

Ferrari Formula 1, red $125-150
Mercedes-Benz SL 350, metallic light
   blue, #440 ....$125-150
Mercedes-Benz Taxi, cream................$125-150
Porsche 911, #432, metallic gold tinplate,
   1:40 ....$125-150
Volkswagen Pickup, blue $145-170
Volkswagen Beetle, #425, yellow $45-70

Classic Collectables
9 Springvale Park
Northland Road
Londonderry, Northern Ireland BT48 0NY
phone: 011442871267000 (BST)
e-mail: info@ccsales.net
website: www.ccsales.net

In October 2004, Classic Collectables announced the release of a 1:50 scale 1933

Commer Holland Coachcraft truck, hand built by Brooklin Models of Bath, England, and offered exclusively by mail order. Two liveries of only 400 each were scheduled to be produced for $174 US plus shipping and handling.

Commer Holland Coachcraft Truck,
1:50 ....$200-250

Classic Construction Models

Classic Construction Models
6590 SW Fallbrook Place
Beaverton OR 97008
phone 503-626-6395
fax 503-646-1996
website: www.ccmodels.com

These impressive precision scale construction vehicles from Classic Construction Models are made of brass in Beaverton, Oregon. The series represents models issued in limited edition of 1,000 each.

Classic Construction Models 1:87 Scale
Caterpillar 325 L $30-40
Caterpillar D8R $30-40

Classic Construction Models 1:48 Scale
American Hoist & Derrick Model 518 Self-Slewing
Steam Derrick..............................$595-620
Dresser TD-40B Crawler Tractor with Cargo
Winch or 3 Shank Ripper $140-175
Link Belt HC-268 Truck Crane.......$1,195-1,275

Classic Construction Models 1:48 Scale Excavator Attachments
Esco Rock Breaker $30-60
Hendrix Compaction Wheel $30-60
Kent Vibrating Plate Compactor $30-60

Classic Construction Models Classic Collectibles
1911 Marmon Wasp, detailed pressed steel
replica of the first car to win the Indianapolis
500 ....$500-525

Classic Construction Models Country Classics
1929 Kenworth Lumber Truck Bank, #1 ...$40-65
1929 Kenworth Log Truck Bank, #2 ....$40-65

Classic Metal Works

6465 Monroe Street
Suite 204
Sylvania OH 43560-1302
Phone: 419-885-1448
Fax: 419-882-1253

Website: www.classicmetalworks.com

Incorporated in 1997, Classic Metal Works, Inc. products are distinguished by their quality and detail. According to the monthly trade magazine The Toy Book (December 1998, page 10), Classic Metal Works models are hand-assembled vehicles with more than 50 parts, including spark plug wiring, a separate engine, opening doors and hood, and steerable wheel, packaged in full-color corrugate window packages. Each vehicle comes with its own collector's stackable display case. Prices listed are suggested retail.

Classic Metal Works Blueprint Series – 1:24 Scale, limited edition of 15,000 numbered pieces
1970 Chevrolet Chevelle SS454, introduced in
1998, #10101 ....$30-35
1967 Chevrolet Corvette L-71 Roadster, introduced in 1998, #10102.................$30-35
1949 Mercury Deluxe Coupe, introduced in
1998, #10103..............................$30-35
1971 Plymouth 426 Hemi 'Cuda, introduced in
1998, #10104..............................$30-35

Classic Metal Works Police Interceptor Series 1 – 1:24 Scale 1999 Ford Crown Victorias, limited edition of 25,000 numbered pieces
State Pursuit Cars
1999 Ford Crown Victoria
California Highway Patrol, introduced in
1999, #20101 ....$35-40
Florida Highway Patrol, introduced in 2000,
#20109 ....$35-40
Illinois State Police, introduced in 1999,
#20103 ....$35-40
Michigan State Police, introduced in 2000,
#20108 ....$35-40
New York State Police, introduced in 2000,
#20105 ....$35-40
Ohio Highway Patrol, introduced in 1999,
#20102 ....$35-40
Texas Highway Patrol, introduced in 2000,
#20107 ....$35-40
Wisconsin State Police, introduced in 2000,
#20104 ....$35-40
Municipal Pursuit Cars
1999 Ford Crown Victoria
Chicago City Patrol, introduced in 2000,
#25102 ....$35-40
Cleveland City Police, introduced in 2000,
#25105 ....$35-40
Dallas City Police, introduced in 2000,
#25104 ....$35-40

Denver Patrol, introduced in 2000,
#25103 ....$35-40
Los Angeles Police, introduced in 2000,
#25106 ....$35-40
New York City Patrol, introduced in 2000,
#25101 ....$35-40

Other Classic Metal Works 1:24 Scale 1999 Ford Crown Victoria Models
New York City Taxicab, introduced in 2000,
#50101 ....$35-40

Classic Metal Works Mini Metals – precision 1:87 scale models with diecast body and chassis, real rubber tires, opening hoods, detailed engines, and factory official paint colors, introduced in 2000
1955 Chevrolet Bel Air, #30106 ....$8-12
1970 Chevrolet Chevelle, #30108 ....$8-12
1961 Chevrolet Impala, #30103 ....$8-12
1948 Ford Convertible, #30102.............$8-12
1950 Ford Pickup, #30104....................$8-12

1951 Ford Stake Truck $8-12
1953 Ford Victoria Convertible, #30101 ..$8-12
1948 Ford Woody, #30107 ....$8-12

Metro Delivery Truck $8-12
1941 Plymouth Coupe, #30105.............$8-12

Classy Chassies (see MegaMovers)

Clau-Mar

One of the many obscure brands currently available is a series of 1:43 scale Clau-Mar models from Argentina, all variations of a particular bus with various liveries.

Camello 3-Deck Bus
silver, "Chevalier" $15-20
white, "El Condor" $15-20

white, "Expreso Rojas" $1-205
white, "Expreso Singer" $15-20
silver, "International" $15-20
white, "La Estrella" $15-20
white, "Rio Del Plata" $15-20
white, "Siera Cordoba" $15-20

Cle (also see Bonux)

Clément Gaget founded the Cle firm of France in 1958 and began manufacturing plastic toy vintage cars. The company also produced a series of diecast models under the Bonux brand.

Bentley 1927 Tourer, #217, 1:48 ....$5-10
Bentley 1929 Le Mans, #220, 1:48 ....$5-10
Berliet
    Box Van, 1:90 ....$4-6
    Dump Truck, 1:90 ....$4-6
    Flat Truck, 1:90 ....$4-6
    Flat Truck with Box, 1:90 ....$4-6
    Flat Truck with Bottles, 1:90 ....$4-6
BRM Race car, 1:40 ....$6-12
Chapparal Mark III, 1:40 ....$6-12
Citroën 1923 B2 Ambulance, #214, 1:48 ..$5-10
Citroën 2CV
    1:48, 1958.................................$5-10
    1:64, 1958.................................$4-6
    Van, 1:48, 1958.........................$5-10
    Van, 1:64, 1958.........................$4-6
Citroën 11CV, 1:48, 1958, #2 ....$5-10
Citroën 15-Six
    1:48, 1958.................................$5-10
    1:64, 1958.................................$4-6
Citroën 1200 KG Van $5-10
Citroën Ami 6, 1:48, #25 ....$5-10
Citroën DS19, 1958 ....$4-6
De Dion-Bouton 1900
    Doctor's Coupe, #207, 1:48 ....$5-10
    Vis-A-Vis, #206, 1:48.....................$5-10
Delahaye 1901, #208, 1:48 ....$5-10
Ferguson Race Car, 1:40 ....$6-12
Ferrari 330 P2, 1:40 ....$6-12
Ferrari Race Car, 1:40 ....$6-12
Fiat 600, 1:48, #20 ....$5-10
Ford GT Mark II, 1:40 ....$6-12
Gauthier-Wehrle 1897, #204, 1:48 ....$5-10
Georges Richard 1902 Tonneau, #209,
    1:48...$5-10
Hispano-Suiza 1922 Torpedo, #213,
    1:48...$5-10
Isotta-Fraschini 1926 Town Sedan, #216,
    1:48...$5-10
Lion-Peugeot 1908, #212, 1:48 ....$5-10
Lotus Race car, 1:40 ....$6-12
Matra-BRM 620, 1:40 ....$6-12

McLaren-Elva Mark 2, 1:40 ....$6-12
Mercedes-Benz SS 1928
    #218, 1:48 ....$5-10
    Tourer, #224, 1:48 ....$5-10
Packard 1930
    Sport Phaeton, #221, 1:48 ....$5-10
    Roadster, #222, 1:48....................$5-10
Panhard Dyna
    1:48, 1958, #16 ....$5-10
    1:64, 1958.................................$4-6
    Convertible, 1:64, 1958 ....$4-6
    Convertible, 1:48 ....$5-10
Panhard-Levassor 1926 Limousine, #215,
    1:48...$5-10
Peugeot 1895 with roof, #202, 1:48 ....$5-10
Peugeot 1895 Vis-A-Vis, #203, 1:48 ....$5-10
Peugeot 1905 5CV, #210, 1:48 ....$5-10
Peugeot 203
    1:48, 1958, #1 ....$5-10
    1:64, 1958.................................$4-6
Peugeot 403
    1:64, 1958.................................$4-6
    4-door sedan, 1:48, 1958, #3 ....$5-10
    Break (station wagon), 1:48, #21 ....$5-10
    Convertible, 1:64, 1958 ....$4-6
Peugeot 404
    1:48, #24 ....$5-10
    Convertible, 1:48 ....$5-10
    Coupe, 1:48 ....$5-10
Porsche 1960 Race Car, 1:40 ....$6-12
Porsche Carrera 6, 1:40 ....$6-12
Renault 1900 Coupe, #205, 1:48 ....$5-10
Renault Caravelle
    Convertible, 1:48, #13 ....$5-10
    Coupe, 1:48, #12 ....$5-10
Renault Dauphine
    1:48, 1958, #11 ....$5-10
Renault Floride
    Convertible, 1:48, 1960 ....$5-10
    Convertible, 1:64, 1960 ....$4-6
    Grand Pavois, 1:48, 1958...............$5-10
    Hardtop, 1:48, 1960.....................$5-10
Renault R4L, 1:48, #26 ....$5-10
Rolls-Royce 1931 Phantom 2, #223, 1:48 ..$5-10
Scotte 1892 Steamer, #201, 1:48 ....$5-10
Simca 1000, 1:48, #27 ....$5-10
Simca 1300, 1:48 ....$5-10
Simca Oceane, 1:64, 1960 ....$4-6
Simca P60
    1:48, 1960, #6 ....$5-10
    1:64, 1960.................................$4-6
    Grand Large, 1:48, 1960 ....$5-10
    Grand Large, 1:64, 1960 ....$4-6
Simca Plein Ciel, 1:64, 1960................$4-6
Sizaire-Naudin 1906 Racing Car, #211,
    1:48...$5-10

Unic Flat Truck
    with box, 1:90 ....$4-6
    with bottles, 1:90 ....$4-6

Clover (also see New Clover)

Clover models are manufactured in Korea, China, and other Asian manufacturing centers.

Bobcat X225 Skid Loader, 1:25 ....$35-45
Bobcat 743B Skid Loader, 1:19 ....$25-35
Bobcat 753 Skid Loader, 1:50 ....$10-15
Bobcat 753 Skid Loader, 1:25 ....$25-35
Bobcat 7753 Skid Loader, 1:25 ....$25-35
1959-1962 Melroe (Bobcat) M-200 Loader,
    1:25 (replica of 1st machine built by Melroe
    Company)....................................$18-25
Semi Flatbed with three Bobcat 753 Skid Loaders,
    1:50 ....$55
Kiamaster Ambulance, 1:43 ....$18-25
Kiamaster Kombi, 1:43 ....$18-25
Pontiac Firebird Coupe, 1:59.................$5-10

CMA (also see Creative Masters)

CMA is reputed to make a number of top-quality 1:24 scale diecast vehicles. They are more expensive than the Mints - Franklin and Danbury – in the $600 to $2,000 range. Marshall Buck is the reported owner of the company. Attention to exact detail is apparently what sets CMA models apart from the rest. No listing available as of this writing, but EWA lists "CMA" as an abbreviation for "Creative Masters."

CMC

CMC of Germany is one of the more recent arrivals on the diecast scale model scene. Their precision scale models are offered by just a few dealers. The price is already rising on these exceptionally fine models.

Exoticar and Toys for Collectors both offer a 1:24 scale model of The Black Prince. Created and built from a 1930 Mercedes SSK chassis as a one-of-a-kind sports car by Count Trossi, The Black Prince survived sixty years and many different owners. Now owned by Ralph Lauren, it won the Concours d'Elegance at Pebble Beach.

The 1:24 scale model offers amazing detail that includes a beautiful black lacquer finish, photo etched metal wire wheels, brakes, grille, and exhaust, hand-painted engine detail with exposed metal exhaust headers, complete with leather bonnet strap and photo etched metal buckle. The interior is leather and fully carpeted with accurately detailed gauges and steering wheel, and an opening trunk with spare tire.

In addition, TfC offers another 1:24 scale CMC model of a 1936 Mercedes-Benz 500 K Spezialroadster of which only 25 of the real car were ever made. Only five of the original cars remain, but the miniature model is just as beautiful. Hand assembled from over 200 parts, it has exquisite engine and chassis detail and real leather seats. The red body is offset with 30 chrome moldings and chrome wire wheels with whitewall tires.

Besides the remarkable models so far mentioned, CMC also provides an assortment of 1:43 scale Jie Fang trucks for the Chinese market and highly detailed 1:12 scale BMW motorcycle models with real leather seats.

Benz Patent Motorwagen 1886, 1:10
   scale...$175-225
BMW R 1100 RS Motorcycle, 1:12 scale
   silver...$50-75
   green $50-75
   white...$50-75
   red $50-75
Jie Fang Truck, 1:43 scale hand built in China for Chinese market
   fire tanker, red with "Beijing" on tank,
      1:43 ....$60-70
   tanker truck, blue with white tank,
      1:43 ....$60-70
   high lift truck, yellow, 1:43 ....$60-70
   military missile launcher truck, green,
      1:43 ....$60-70
   military troop carrier truck, green, 1:43 ..$60-70
   open cargo truck, blue-gray, 1:43 ......$60-70
Mercedes-Benz 300SL-S $130-145
Mercedes-Benz 450SL, 1:24
   red $130-145
   silver $130-145
Mercedes-Benz 500 K Spezialroadster in red or blue, 1:24 scale $145-160
Mercedes-Benz 540 K Cabriolet B 1936
   red and black, 1:24 scale $145-160
   blue and silver, 1:24 scale...........$145-160
Mercedes-Benz SSK Trossi "Schwarzer Prinz" (Black Prince), 1:24 scale $135-150
Mercedes-Benz W 196 Silberpfeil (Monoposto) 1954, 1:18 scale.......................$150-175
Porsche 550 Spyder 1954/55, 1:24
   scale..$135-150

Code 3 Collectibles (also see Funrise)

6115 Variel Avenue
818-598-2298
Woodland Hills CA 91367-3727
Worldwide website: www.code3.net

Code 3 Collectibles of Woodland Hills, California, was a short-lived diecast division of Funrise, maker of electronic toy cars and trucks. The first model to appear on the market, in the summer of 1997, was a 1:64 scale Seagrave fire engine. It is beautifully packaged in an elegant clear display package and sold for around $20. Here is a brief sampling of their ever-growing line.

Ford Crown Victoria Police, 1:24, 1998
   California Highway Patrol, February
      1998......................................$25-30
   Georgia State Patrol, February 1998 ..$25-30
   Florida, February 1998.....................$25-30
   Massachusetts, April 1998...............$25-30
   Nevada, April 1998 ....$25-30
   Buffalo, NY, April 1998 ....$25-30
   New York State Police, June 1998 .....$25-30
GMC Suburban, 1:64, 1998
   Boston, January 1998 ....$20-25
   New York, March 1998 ....$20-25
   Los Angeles, May 1998 ....$20-25
   Baltimore EMS, June 1998 ....$20-25
Saulsbury Heavy Rescue Trucks, 1:64, 1998

FDNY Rescue $20-25

Seagrave Fire Engine, 1:64, 1997
   City of Los Angeles, April 1997, 25,000
      issued, sold out $25-30
   Houston Fire Department, July 1997, 25,000
      issued, sold out $25-30
   Philadelphia Fire Department, September
      1997, 25,000 issued, sold out ...$25-30
   Fire Department of New York, November
      1997, 25,000 issued, sold out ...$25-30
   Honolulu Fire Department, November 1997,
      15,000 issued $25-30
   Louisville Fire Department, November 1997,
      15,000 issued $25-30
   Denver Fire Department, February
      1998...$20-25
Seagrave Tractor Drawn Aerial, 1:64, 1998
   Washington D.C., January 1998 ....$35-40
   Honolulu, April 1998 ....$35-40
   Baltimore, June 1998 ....$35-40

Cofalu

In the 1960s, Cofalu of France produced a small assortment of plastic models in 1:40 scale.

Go-Kart, 1962 ....$15-20
Peugeot 203 with bicycles, 1960 ....$15-20
Peugeot 404 with bicycles, 1962 ....$15-20

Cofradis

Two Cofradis models have been found in 1:43 scale, both determined to be modified Solido models.

Shelter Euro Missile, #100......................$25-30
Mack "Danone" Van, #117 ....$25-30

Collector Case

Most unpainted models such as Collector Case resemble pewter, but are likely made of cast aluminum or the more common "zamak,"the zinc alloy common to diecast models. If these didn't cost so much, I would think the intent would be for the collector to paint them. But I would be very hesitant to alter a model that costs $60 to $80. Unless expertly done, it would likely render the model worthless. Diehard hobbyists, however, would likely consider it a challenge to do a good job of customizing.

Collector Case models are available in unpainted base metal, except where noted.

Collector Case 1:43 Scale

1936 Auburn Speedster, #625 ....$45-60
1953 Austin Healy 3000 RDS, top down,
   #621 ....$60-75
1956 Chevrolet Corvette, red, #701.......$45-60
1961 Chevrolet Corvette Stingray Racer,
   #631 ....$60-75
1963 Chevrolet Corvette Coupe, #602...$60-75
1974 Chevrolet Corvette
   Convertible, top down, #604............$60-75
   Corvette T-Top, #606 ....$50-65
1986 Chevrolet Corvette
   Coupe, #619 ....$45-60
   Convertible, top down, #620............$45-60
1933 Duesenberg SJ, #629...................$45-60
1932 Ford Coupe, #624 ....$45-60
1936 Ford
   Convertible 4-door, top down, #608 ..$45-60
   Roadster, #615 ....$60-75
   Phaeton 4-door, top up, black & tan,
      #607......................................$45-60
1948 Ford Convertible 2-door, top down,
   #614 ....$60-75
1956 Ford Thunderbird
   Convertible, top down, #628................$60
   Thunderbird Coupe, #616 ....$45-60
1966 Ford Mustang GT Coupe, #617 ....$60
1937 Mercedes-Benz 540 K, #612 ....$45-60
1948 MG TC, #618 ....$50-65

1957 Porsche 356 Speedster, top down,
   #633 ....$60
Porsche 928, #622 ....$45-60
Shelby Cobra 427, #609 ....$60

Collector Case 1:72 Scale Airplanes
Douglas DC-3, #905 ....$60-75
F4F Wildcat, #903 ....$60-75
F4U-1 Corsair, #901 ....$60-75
F15 "Desert Storm," #907...................$60-75
P-40 Warhawk, #904 ....$60-75
P-51 Mustang, #902 ....$60-75

Collector Case 1:76 Scale
A series of Chevrolet Corvette Coupes and Convertibles from 1963 to 1982 were produced which retailed for $18 each, with the exception of a 1964 Corvette on a pewter-like base for $30.

Collector's Classics (also see Buby)

Collector Classics are 1:43 scale models of American cars from the 1940s, 1950s, and 1960s, produced in Argentina by Haroldo "Buby" Malher up until 1995. They are later issues of Buby models renamed to avoid a blatant connection with the Buby name amidst some public relations problems. See more company history in the section of this book devoted to Buby toys.

1955 Chevrolet Bel Air
   Hard Top......................................$55-65
   Convertible, top down $55-65
1969 Chevrolet Camaro RS Convertible, top
   down...$55-65
1956 De Soto Adventurer
   white & gold $55-65
   black & gold $55-65
1956 De Soto Fireflite
   Hard Top......................................$55-65
   Convertible, top up $55-65
   Convertible, top down $55-65
1956 De Soto Indy Pace Car $55-65
1953 Ford Sunliner
   Convertible, top up $55-65
   Convertible, top down $55-65
   Hard Top......................................$55-65
1953 Ford Indy Pace Car, limited $55-65
1946 Lincoln Continental
   Convertible, top up $55-65
   Convertible, top down $55-65
   Indy PaceCar $55-65
1954 Mercury Monterey
   Convertible, top up..........................$55-65
   Convertible, top down $55-65

1954 Mercury Sun Valley Coupe............$55-65
1956 Packard Caribbean
   Convertible, top up..........................$55-65
   Convertible, top down $55-65
   Hard Top......................................$55-65
1964 Studebaker Avanti Sports Coupe, #21 .$55-65

Collectors Mint

These are pewter models in 1:43 scale made by Richardi Auto Models of New Jersey. No model list is known.

Collectoy

Collectoy of Japan produces diecast toys, some with friction drive, in a wide range of styles. Inaccuracy of scale is mostly due to over-sized wheels on some of the models. As with many Japanese brands, the Collectoy brand was discovered by Bob Speerbrecher in a Japanese language book on diecast cars issued in 1998. Included in the assortment are several vintage American and European cars. The friction toys, at least one circa 1958 Ford Station Wagon, has mention of Line Mar Toys on the box. Vintage of cars would indicate the toys to be produced in the 1960s, but may be much newer.

DeSoto $20-35
Ford Edsel $20-35
Jaguar XK-150 ....$20-35
Mercedes 300SL Convertible..................$20-35
Mercedes 300SL Gullwing $20-35
Porsche 356.....................................$20-35
Triumph TR-3 ....$20-35

Comet – Authenticast

Comet – Authenticast (not to be confused with Accucast or Comet Miniatures) started in Queens, New York, as "Comet Metal Products" by the Slonim family around 1940. Starting with toy soldiers, Comet switched to producing 1:108 scale identification models of military vehicles for the government on the verge of World War II. They continued selling them as toys after the war until the early 1960s.

Reissues have recently been produced by Quality Castings of Alexandria, Virginia, using the original molds. Original models are currently valued at $25-50. Reissues are worth around $10-20.

Daimler Armored Car, #5008 original $25-50
   reissue.......................................$10-20

Comet – Authenticast WWII Japanese Vehicles

Amphibian Tankette, #5051 original $25-50
   Quality reissue...............................$10-20
Heavy Medium Tank, #5057 original.....$25-50
   Quality reissue...............................$10-20
Light Tank, #5056 original $25-50
   Quality reissue...............................$10-20
Medium Tank, #5053 original $25-50
   Quality reissue...............................$10-20
Medium Tank, #5054 original $25-50
   Quality reissue...............................$10-20
Tankette, #5052 original $25-50
   Quality reissue...............................$10-20
Tankette, #5055 original $25-50
   Quality reissue...............................$10-20

Comet – Authenticast WWI German Vehicles
8-Wheeled Armored Car, #5108,
   original..$25-50
   Quality reissue...............................$10-20
Half-Track, #5112 original $25-50
   Quality reissue...............................$10-20
Panther, #5110 original......................$25-50
   Quality reissue...............................$10-20
Panzerjager, #5102 original $25-50
   Quality reissue...............................$10-20
Pz35T, #5109 original........................$25-50
   Quality reissue...............................$10-20
PzKw III, #5100 original.....................$25-50
   Quality reissue...............................$10-20
PzKw I, #5101 original $25-50
   Quality reissue...............................$10-20
PzKw IV G, #5103 original....................$25-50
   Quality reissue...............................$10-20
PzKw IV F, #5104 original $25-50
   Quality reissue...............................$10-20
PzKw II, #5105 original $24
   Quality reissue...............................$10-20
PzKw III, #5106 original $25-50
   Quality reissue...............................$10-20
Tiger, #5107 original..........................$25-50
   Quality reissue...............................$10-20
Sturmgeschutz, #5111 original $25-50
   Quality reissue...............................$10-20

Comet – Authenticast WWI U.S. Vehicles
6x6 Truck, #5181 original $25-50
   Quality reissue...............................$10-20
75mm Gun on Half Track, #5150
   original..$25-50
   Quality reissue...............................$10-20
76mm Sherman Tank, #5169, original.........$25
   Quality reissue...............................$10-20
Airborne Tank, #5170 original $25-50
   Quality reissue...............................$10-20
Atomic Cannon, #5189 original............$25-50

Quality reissue.................................$10-20
Command car, #5182 original $25-50
   Quality reissue.................................$10-20
DUKW, #5173 original $25-50
   Quality reissue.................................$10-20
General Chaffee Tank, #5166 original....$25-50
   Quality reissue.................................$10-20
General Pershing Tank, #5156 original....$25-50
   Quality reissue.................................$10-20
General Scott, #5157 original...............$25-50
   Quality reissue.................................$10-20
General Patton, #5179 original $25-50
   Quality reissue.................................$10-20
General Stuart, #5158 original $25-50
   Quality reissue.................................$10-20
Greyhound Armored car, #5153 original...$25-50
   Quality reissue.................................$10-20
Half-track, #5154 original $25-50
   Quality reissue.................................$10-20
Hawk Missile Transporter, Launcher, Mobile Radar
   and crew, #5193 original.................$25-50
   Quality reissue.................................$10-20
Heavy Tank M6, #5151 original $25-50
   Quality reissue.................................$10-20
Hellcat, #5155 original $25-50
   Quality reissue.................................$10-20
Honest John Launcher and crew, #5194
   original...$25-50
   Quality reissue.................................$10-20
Jeep, #5160 original $25-50
   Quality reissue.................................$10-20
King Kong, #5164 original $25-50
   Quality reissue.................................$10-20
LVT Amphibian, #5176 original $25-50
   Quality reissue.................................$10-20
LVTAA Amphibian Tank, #5175 original ..$25-50
   Quality reissue.................................$10-20
M3 Medium Tank, #5192 original $25-50
   Quality reissue.................................$10-20
M32 Tank Recovery, #5174 original $25-50
   Quality reissue.................................$10-20
M42 Duster Twin 40mm AA, #5196
   original...$25-50
   Quality reissue.................................$10-20
M48 Tank, #5187 original $25-50
   Quality reissue.................................$10-20
M67 Tank, #5186 original $25-50
   Quality reissue.................................$10-20
M103 Heavy Tank, #5188 original........$25-50
   Quality reissue.................................$10-20
Medium Tank, #5178 original...............$25-50
   Quality reissue.................................$10-20
Nike-Ajax Launcher and crew, #5195
   original...$25-50
   Quality reissue.................................$10-20
Ontos Self Propelled Rocket Launcher, #5197

original...$25-50
   Quality reissue.................................$10-20
Priest, #5156 original..........................$25-50
   Quality reissue.................................$10-20
Quack, #5163 original $25-50
   Quality reissue.................................$10-20
Scout Car, #5162 original.....................$25-50
   Quality reissue.................................$10-20
Self Propelled 155mm Howitzer, #5191
   original...$25-50
   Quality reissue.................................$10-20
Sherman Tank, #5152 original...................$25
   Quality reissue.................................$10-20
Slugger Tank, #5168 original.................$25-50
   Quality reissue.................................$10-20
Slugger II Tank, #5167 original $25-50
   Quality reissue.................................$10-20
Staghound Armored Car, #5171 original.$25-50
   Quality reissue.................................$10-20
T98 S.P. 105mm Gun, #5190 original ...$25-50
   Quality reissue.................................$10-20
Trailer, #5184 original $25-50
   Quality reissue.................................$10-20
Troop Carrier, #5183 original $25-50
   Quality reissue.................................$10-20
Twin 50 Armored car, #5172 original.....$25-50
   Quality reissue.................................$10-20
Utility Tank, #5177 original $25-50
   Quality reissue.................................$10-20
Walker Bulldog, #5180 original $25-50
   Quality reissue.................................$10-20
Weapons Carrier, #5185 original $25-50
   Quality reissue.................................$10-20
Weasel, #5161 original $25-50
   Quality reissue.................................$10-20
Wolverine, #5159 original $25-50
   Quality reissue.................................$10-20

Comet – Authenticast WWI Russian Vehicles

Josef Stalin Tank, #5202 original.............$25-50
   Quality reissue.................................$10-20
Josef Stalin III Tank, #5207 original.........$25-50
   Quality reissue.................................$10-20
KV-1 Heavy Tank, #5200 original...........$25-50
   Quality reissue.................................$10-20
KV-2 Heavy Tank, #5201 original...........$25-50
   Quality reissue.................................$10-20
ST2 Armored Carrier, #5205 original......$25-50
   Quality reissue.................................$10-20
T34 Medium Tank, #5203 original $25-50
   Quality reissue.................................$10-20
T34/85 Medium Tank, #5206 original...$25-50
   Quality reissue.................................$10-20
T70 Light Tank, #5204 original $25-50
   Quality reissue.................................$10-20

Quality Castings New Issues of German Vehicles

105 Howitzer, #4065 ....$10-20
2 cm FLAF on or off trailer, #4027..........$10-20
2 cm Quad FLAF and trailer, #4062 ....$10-20
222 Armored Car, #4052 ....$10-20
234/I Armored Car, #4055.................$10-20
250/I Half-track, #4046 ....$10-20
250/7 Mortar Half-track, #4068 ....$10-20
3.7 FLAK on traile, #4063 r $10-20
3.7 PAK, #4031 ....$10-20
5 cm PAK, #4051 ....$10-20
7/2 Half-track with 3.7 FLAK, #4061 .....$10-20
7.5 INF Gun, #4035...........................$10-20
7.5 PAK, #4018 ....$10-20
88 Flak on or off bogie wheels, #4026 ...$10-20
88 PAK, #4064 ....$10-20
BMW Cycle, #4037............................$10-20
Brumbar, #4054 ....$10-20
Elefant, #4067 ....$10-20
Ferdinand, #4066 ....$10-20
Hetzer, #4044 ....$10-20
Hummell, #4049 ....$10-20
Kubelwagen, #4036 ....$10-20
Marder III, #4045 ....$10-20
Opel Blitz, #4023 ....$10-20
Pz38t, #4041 ....$10-20
Tiger II with Porsche Turret, #4058..........$10-20
Wespe, #4017 ....$10-20
Wirblewing FLAK, #4042 ....$10-20

Comet Miniatures (also see Simba)

Comet Miniatures is an English company that has reportedly produced a pair of replicas, under the "Mini Metal" brand, of the Seaview and Flying Sub from the popular 1970s TV series *Voyage to the Bottom of the Sea.* The models, according to R. C. Johnston of White Rock, British Columbia, were produced in 1988. The "Mini Metalls" brand is also used by Simba, a company that offers 1998 Volkswagen New Beetle models in various colors and styles, as reported by collector Tjeng-Bo Lie of Plano, Texas. (See Simba.)

Voyage to the Bottom of the Sea Flying Sub,
   MM-03, 1988 ....$20-35
Voyage to the Bottom of the Sea Seaview Sub-
   marine, MM-07, 1988 ....$20-35

Con-Cor

Con-Cor vehicles are 1:87 scale pre-painted plastic models that feature full-color lettering on sides and ends. All vehicles are pre-assembled. Included in the series are semis with trailers, separate semi trailers, rail containers, cars, and buses, all designed for use with HO gauge railroad layouts.

Con-Cor Semi with Trailer

Double Freighter
    Riteway $11-16
    Transcon $11-16
Freight Truck
    Atchison, Topeka & Santa Fe $8-10
    Brillion $8-10
    Chiquita $9-12
    Evergreen...$8-10
    Hi-Way Dispatch $8-10
    Rollins $8-10
    Pacific Fruit Express $8-10
    Pepsi $8-10
    US Mail $9-12
Log Truck
    Miller Truck..$8-10
Moving Van
    Mayflower $12-15
Open Back Truck
    Palumbo $8-10
    Registered Texas Longhorns...................$8-10
Tanker
    Safety Kleen $10-12
    Texaco $10-12
    Texas Oil $8-10
    Union $8-10

Con-Cor "America 500 Years" Semi with Trailer, Special Edition

Columbus...$17-22
Monuments...$17-22
New York Skyline......................................$17-22
Space..$17-22
US Capital $17-22
Wild West $17-22

Con-Cor Bluebird School Buses

Camp Woebegon $11-15
County #4 ....$11-15
Good Shepherd...$11-15
Helping Hand Temporary Labor $11-15
Maintenance-of-Way $11-15
Unified School Dist. #2 ....$11-15
US Army $11-15
Washington HS $11-15

Con-Cor Autos & Others

'57 Chevrolet..$8-10
'69 Mustang...$8-10
Ferrari Testarossa $8-10
Fire Chief 4x4 ....$3-4
Ford Mustang $8-10
Lamborghini...$8-10

Mercedes-Benz 300E $3-5

Condon

Four models are known to have been produced by this British diecast toy company. No other information is known.

Double-Decker Bus, 1:60 ....$45-60
1948 Muir Hill Dumper, 1:43 ....$45-60
1948 Muir Hill Dumper with Crane,
    1:43 ....$45-60
Tractor $45-60

Conquest

Conquest models are exquisite 1:43 scale cars hand built in England.

1957 Buick Roadmaster 75 Riviera 4-door hard
    top, #7 ....$195-220
1956 Buick Special convertible, top down,
    #15 ....$195-220
1955 Buick Super hard top, three-tone,
    #3 ....$205-230
1955 Buick Super convertible, top down,
    #11 ....$195-220
1955 Buick Super convertible, top up,
    #11a $195-220
1955 Buick Super convertible, top down, continental kit, #11D $275-300
1947 Cadillac Fleetwood 75, #30 ....$275-300
1958 Cadillac Fleetwood, #18 ....$230-255
1960 Cadillac Fleetwood Sixty Special 4-door
    hard top, #12.....................................$195-220
1962 Cadillac Series 62 convertible, heather and
    maize, #32 ....$270
1960 Chevrolet Impala convertible, top down,
    #2 ....$185-210
1960 Chevrolet Impala convertible, top up,
    #2a $185-210
1963 Ford Country Squire Station Wagon,
    #9 ....$195-220
1963 Ford Galaxie 500 XL convertible, top
    down, #4 ....$185-210
1963 Ford Galaxie 500 XL hard top, limited,
    #4a $205-230
1957 Ford Thunderbird hard top, #16..$185-210
1957 Imperial Crown Southhampton 4-door hard
    top, #6 ....$195-220
1950 Lincoln Cosmopolitan 4-door Sedan,
    #10 ....$195-220
1954 Oldsmobile 98 Holiday hard top,
    #5p $195-220
1954 Oldsmobile Starfire 98 convertible, top
    down, two-tone, #1 ....$185-210
1954 Oldsmobile Starfire 98 convertible, top
    down, one-tone, #1a......................$165-190

1955 Oldsmobile 98 Holiday 4-door hard top,
    #19 ....$235-260
1960 Plymouth Fury, #20 ....$205-230
1956 Plymouth Savoy 4-door Sedan,
    #13 ....$175-200
1954 Pontiac Star Chief convertible, top down,
    #8 ....$195-220
1954 Pontiac Star Chief Custom Catalina hard
    top, #17 ....$185-210
1948 Pontiac Torpedo Eight Deluxe convertible,
    top down, #14 ....$185-210
1948 Pontiac Torpedo Eight Deluxe convertible,
    top up, #14a $185-210

Conrad (also see Gescha)

Conrad of Germany is a brand name applied in the 1970s to a line of heavy equipment models originally introduced under the Gescha brand in the 1960s. Conrad models are currently available. Gescha models meanwhile are no longer made, so they are increasingly rare and highly valued.

American LaFrance Fire Truck, 1:43
    #1019..$55-70
    #1023..$70-85
    #1024..$90-105
Atlas 1304 Wheel Excavator/Clam, 1:50,
    #2904..$50-65
Atlas 1704
    Track Backhoe, 1:50, #2903 ....$45-60
    Track Excavator, 1:50, #2902..........$55-70
Atlas Wheel Backhoe with Blade, 1:50,
    #2901 ....$55-70
Audi 100, 1:43, #1022 ....$10-15
Audi 80 Coupe, 1:43, #1012 ....$10-15
Audi Quattro Coupe, 1:43, #1020 ......$15-25
Bedford Semi Flatbed, 1:50, #3330.......$70-85
Bomag BW120 AD-2 Roller, 1:50,
    #2711 ....$35-55
Bomag BW213 D Roller, 1:50, #2710 ...$45-60
BPR Cadillon GT2210 Truck Crane, 1:87,
    #2013 ....$75-90
Case 1085B Wheel Backhoe, 1:35,
    #2964 ....$55-70
Case 125B Track Backhoe, 1:35,
    #2965 ....$55-70
Case 1280 Track Excavator, 1:35,
    #2962 ....$70-85
Case 1845C Uniloader, 1:50, #5401...$40-50
Case 2188 Track Excavator, 1:50,
    #2894 ....$55-65
Case 580 D Construction King Loader/Backhoe,
    1:35, Silver Anniversary 1957-1982,
    #1282 ....$90-120
Case 580 D Tractor Loader, 1:35, #2931....$70-85

Case 580 E Tractor Loader, 1:35,
#2933 ....$80-95

Case 580 G Tractor Loader, 1:35,
#2932 ....$80-95

Case 580 K Tractor Loader, 1:50,
#2935 ....$55-70

Case 580 Super K with serial number, gold,
1:35, #2934 ....$85-100

Case 586E Forklift, 1:35, #2993 ....$65-80

Case 590X Tractor Backhoe Load, 1:35,
#2936 ....$70-85

Case 621 Wheel Loader with attachments, 1:35,
#2426 ....$55-70

Case 760 Trencher, 1:35, #2966 ....$55-70

Case DH4B Trencher, 1:32, #2963 ....$70-85

Case Drott 50 Track Backhoe, 1:35,
#2960 ....$70-85

Case Drott 980B Track Backhoe, 1:35,
#2961 ....$70-85

Case Vibromax 1102 Roller, 1:35,
#2703 ....$55-70

Case Vibromax 854K Roller, 1:35, #2704...$45-60

Case W102 Roller, #2705 ....$30-45,

Case-Poclain 1088 Maxi Backhoe, 1:50,
#2892 ....$45-55

Case-Poclain 81P Excavator, 1:50,
#2893 ....$50-60

Caterpillar 60 Diesel 1931, limited numbered edition, 1:25, #2873 ....$70-85

Caterpillar 936 Wheel Loader, 1:50,
#2886 ....$40-70

Caterpillar 950
Loader, 1:25, #2840 ....$90-105
Loader-Ripper, 1:50, #2841 ....$65-75

Caterpillar CS653 Roller, 1:50, #2889 ..$40-55

Caterpillar D10 Dozer-Ripper, 1:50,
#2850 ....$65-75

Caterpillar D11 Dozer, 1:50, #2854 ...$95-105

Caterpillar D11N Dozer-Ripper, 1:50,
#2852 ....$65-75

Caterpillar D400 Dump Truck, 1:50,
#2862 ....$55-70

Caterpillar D6H Bulldozer, 1:50, #2851 ...$65-75

Caterpillar Forklift, 1:25, #2980 ....$30-40

Caterpillar PS500 Compactor, #2741 ...$45-65

Clark 720 Crane Truck, 1:50, #2073 ...$85-95

Clark ECA Forklift, 1:25, #2971 ....$40-50

Clark Forklift, 1:25, #2972 ....$25-35

Clark H500 Forklift, 1:25, #2970 ....$40-50

Condecta Mobile Crane, 1:87, #2000 ..$85-95

Demag AC155 Truck Crane, 1:50,
#2086 ....$75-90

Demag AC435 Superlift Crane, 1:50,
#2081 ....$105-120

Demag H135S Hydraulic Shovel, 1:50,
#2772 ....$105-115

Demag SC40DS-2 Compressor, 1:24,
#5406 ....$40-55

Dennis 1910 Fire Truck, 1:43, #1025 ....$50-65

Dresser 210M 55 Ton Mining Dump Truck, 1:50,
#2722 ....$65-80

Dresser 830E 200 Ton Dumper, 1:50,
#2721 ....$105-120

Dresser Track Excavator, 1:50, #2819 ....$40-50

Dresser Wheel Excavator, 1:50, #2818..$35-45

Dresser Wheel Loader, 1:50, #2420 ......$65-75

E-1 Hush
80' Ladder Fire Truck, 1:50, #5506 ....$80-95
95' Ladder Fire Truck, 1:50, #5505 ....$80-95
Pumper Fire Truck, 1:50, #5510 ....$80-95

E-1 Titan III, 1:50, #5507 ....$70-85

Elgin Pelican Street Sweeper, 1:50,
#5066 ....$65-80

Ericsson Radar, 1:50, #3085 ....$35-50

Falcon Fire Truck, 1:50, #5512 ....$70-85

Faun Mobile Crane, 1:50, #2084 ....$85-100

Fenwick T20 Forklift, 1:25, #2983 ....$30-45

Fiat-Allis Dozer-Ripper, 1:50, #2910 ....$65-80

Freightliner Conventional
"Air Products," 1:50, #3819...........$90-105
"Talbert," 1:50, #3812..................$70-85
Dump Trailer, 1:50, #3826...........$65-80

Freightliner T/T Container, 1:50,
#3520 ....$90-105

Freightliner Truck with Box Trailer, 1:50,
#3820 ....$55-70

Freightliner with "Air Products" Trailer, 1:50,
#3519 ....$55-70

Fuchs Excavator with Magnet Lift, 1:50,
#2842 ....$55-70

Furukawa 345 Wheel Loader, 1:50,
#2421 ....$65-75

Furukawa 625E Track Backhoe, 1:50,
#2819 ....$50-60

Furukawa W625E Wheel Backhoe, 1:50,
#2817, #2818..........................$50-60

GHH LF12 Wheel Loader, 1:50, #2430...$65-70

Gottwald Hydraulic Crane, 1:50, #2074 ...$85-95

Graf & Stift 1917 Fire Truck, 1:43, #1018...$55-70

Grove AMZ66 Manlift, 1:50, #2502 .....$35-65

Hanomag 15F Wheel Loader, 1:50,
#2427 ....$35-45

Hanomag 70E Wheel Loader, 1:50,
#2425 ....$55-70

Hanomag CL310 Compactor/Bucket,
#2428 ....$65-70

Hanomag Dozer, 1:50, #2853 ....$45-55

Hanomag Wheel Loader, 1:50 ....$40-50

Huffermeister Roll-Off, 1:50, #4178 ....$70-85

Iveco 4-Axle Dump, 1:50, #3274 ....$65-80

Iveco Euro
Cargo Truck, 1:50, #4236 ....$45-60

Trekker Dump Truck, 1:50, #4840.....$40-55
Truck, 1:50, #4898 ....$45-55

Iveco Eurostar with Tank Trailer, 1:50,
#4961 ....$70-85

Iveco Eurotech Truck, 1:50, #4298.........$55-70

Iveco Stetter 4-Axle Mixer, 1:50, #3264....$70-85

Iveco Transporter, 1:50, #4220 ....$35-50

Jungheinrich ECE Forklift, 1:25, #2984 ...$30-45

Jungheinrich EJC 12.5 Forklift, 1:25,
#2997 ....$45-60

Jungheinrich Forklift, 1:25
#2994.................................$55-70
#2995.................................$55-70

Kalmar Forklift 40' Container, 1:50,
#2999 ....$90-105

Kalmar LMV 22 Forklift, 1:50, #2991 .....$65-80

Kassbohrer Pisten Bully Snow, 1:43,
#5201 ....$90-105

Krupp 250 GMT Crane, 1:50, #2077 ...$85-95

Krupp 70 GMT Crane, 1:50, #2080 ...$95-110

Krupp 80T Crane Truck, 1:50, #2070 ....$85-95

Lansing Forklift, 1:25, #2996 ....$40-55

Lattice Tower Extensions
for 2011 Potain Tower Crane, 1:87,
#9997 ....$15-20
for 2012 Zeppelin ZBK100 Tower Crane,
1:50 1:87, #9998 ....$15-20
for 2013 BPR Cadillon GT2210 Tower
Crane, 1:87, #9999 ....$15-20

Liebherr 1090 Crane, 1:50, #2085.....$95-110

Liebherr 112 HC-K Tower Crane, 1:87,
#2022 ....$100-110

Liebherr 1160 Truck Crane, #2082 ....$105-120

Liebherr 21K Tower Crane, 1:50, #2021 ...$70-85

Liebherr 28K Mobile Tower Crane, 1:50,
#2023 ....$85-95

Liebherr 531 Wheel Loader, 1:50,
#2887 ....$55-70

Liebherr 722 Dozer, 1:50, #2803 ....$50-60

Liebherr 731 Dozer-Ripper, 1:50, #2801 ..$55-65

Liebherr 912 Excavator, 1:50, #2822 ....$55-70

Liebherr 921 Excavator, 1:50, #2821 ....$55-70

Liebherr 922 Hydraulic Excavator, 1:50,
#2825 ....$65-75

Liebherr 932 Track Scrap Hand, 1:50,
#2835 ....$65-75

Liebherr 952 Excavator, 1:50, #2826 ....$55-70

Liebherr 954 Backhoe, 1:50, #2834......$65-75

Liebherr 984 Backhoe, 1:50, #2828...$85-100

Liebherr 984 Shovel, 1:50, #2827 ......$85-100

Liebherr 991 Backhoe, 1:50, #2823 ....$55-70

Liebherr 991 Excavator, 1:50, #2824 ....$55-70

Liebherr A310 Wheel Backhoe, 1:50,
#2833 ....$55-70

Liebherr A912 Lit. Wheel Clam, 1:50,
#2830 ....$55-70

Liebherr A932 Scrap Grapple Excavator, 1:50, #2832 ....$65-75

Liebherr Boom Extensions, 1:50, #9996 ..$15-20

Liebherr Crane Truck, 1:50, #2072 ....$85-95

Liebherr HC120 Tower Crane, 1:87, #2020 ....$65-80

Liebherr HS881 Hydraulic Cable Excavator, 1:50, #2831 ....$105-120

Liebherr HS882 Track Lat Crane, 1:50, #2831 ....$115-130

Liebherr L507 Wheel Loader, 1:50, #2883 ....$40-70

Liebherr L522 Wheel Loader, 1:50, #2882 ..$40-55

Liebherr LT 1060 Crane, 1:50, #2079 ....$95-110

Liebherr LTF1030 Crane, 1:50, #3088 ...$90-105

Liebherr LTM 1030 Crane, 1:50, #2076 ....$85-95

Liebherr LTM1025 Truck Crane, 1:50, #2083 ....$65-80

Liebherr R912 Track Hoe, 1:50, #2829 .....$55-70

Liebherr RL422 Pipe Layer, 1:50, #2804 ..$55-70

Liebherr Track Loader, 1:50, #2802 ....$55-70

Linde E25 Forklift, 1:25, #2985 ....$55-70

Linde Lift Truck, 1:25, #2983 ....$20-35

Linde R14 Forklift, 1:25, #2981 ....$55-70

Linde R16 Forklift, 1:25, #2982 ....$50-65

Losenhausen Vibromax Roller, 1:35, #2702 ....$55-70

Mack Airport Plow and Sweeper, 1:50, #3669 ....$105-120

Mack Dump Truck, 1:50, #3640 ....$55-70

Mack Refuse Truck, 1:50, #3641 ....$50-65

Magirus 1950 Low Side Dump Truck, 1:43 ....$40-50

Magirus 4-Axle Dump, 1:50, #3274 ......$35-50

Magirus Liebherr Mixer, 1:50, #3245 .....$45-60

Magirus Stetter 1958 Old Timer Concrete Mixer, 1:43, #1033 ....$50-60

Man 1920 Gas Tanker "Messer Griesham," 1:43, #1035 ....$40-55

Man 1921 Old Timer Fire Engine, 1:43, #1027 ....$55-65

Man 4-Axle Mixer "Liebherr," 1:50, #4165 ....$55-70

Man 4-Axle Roll-Off, 1:50, #4167 ....$55-70

Man Atlas 130.1 Crane Truck, 1:50, #4199 ....$55-70

Man Drain Cleaner, 1:50, #4179 ....$50-65

Man F2000
    Liebherr 904 Mixer, 1:50, #6165 .....$55-70
    Semi Container Truck, 1:50, #6107 ..$80-95

Man Haller Suction Truck, 1:50, #4166 ...$70-85

Man KVB "Messer Griesheim" Gas Van, 1:50, #1032 ....$35-45

Man Luxury Coach Bus, 1:50, #5423 .....$70-85

Man Schmitz Heavy Haulage Trailer, 1:50, #4111 ....$90-105

Man Semi
    Concrete Mix Stetter, 1:50, #4150 ...$70-85
    Linde TVTS30 Tanker, 1:50, #4127 ..$70-85

Man Small Truck, 1:43, #3037 ....$15-25

Man Type L2000 Truck, 1:50, #6036 .....$40-55

MAN-Wolff Tower Crane, 1:08, #20307 ....$85-95

Massey Ferguson 50B Loader, 1:35, #2951 ....$70-85

Massey Ferguson 50D Loader, 1:35, #2952 ....$70-85

Massey Ferguson 60HX Loader/Backhoe, 1:35, #2954 ....$90-105

Mercedes Farm Tractor, 1:43, #5016 .....$25-35

Mercedes Semi Bulker L Hoist, 1:50, #3015 ....$80-95

Mercedes Van Type 208, 1:50, #1608 ....$30-45

Mercedes-Benz "Messer Griesheim" Bulk Gas Semi, 1:50, #3523 ....$70-85

Mercedes-Benz 100/130/150 Bus, 1:50, #1605 ....$55-70

Mercedes-Benz 1300 Tractor, 1:50, #3043 ....$55-70

Mercedes-Benz 170 Van, 1:50, #1606 ....$30-45

Mercedes-Benz 1955 Racing Transporter, 1:43, #1034 ....$45-55

Mercedes-Benz 200 TD-300 TD Wagon, 1:35, #1503 ....$30-45

Mercedes-Benz 200-280 T Wagon, 1:35
    #1001/#1502 ....$15-25
    #1607 ....$30-45

Mercedes-Benz 207 D
    Bus, 1:50, #1602 ....$15-25
    Van, 1:50, #1603 ....$15-25

Mercedes-Benz 230 C-280 CE
    1:35, #1000 ....$15-25
    #1501 ....$15-25
    1:35, #1601 ....$15-25

Mercedes-Benz 280-450
    1:35, #1076 ....$15-25
    Sedan, 1:35, #1002 ....$15-25

Mercedes-Benz 300 CE Coupe, 1:35, #1504 ....$30-45

Mercedes-Benz 507 D Van, 1:43, #1620 ...$15-25

Mercedes-Benz 800 Tractor, 1:43, #5017 ....$15-25

Mercedes-Benz Articulated Bus, 1:50, #5422 ....$98

Mercedes-Benz Cement Mixer, 1:50
    #3044 ....$90-105
    #3045 ....$90-105

Mercedes-Benz Container
    Semi, 1:50, #3020 ....$90-105
    Truck, 1:50, #3048 ....$90-105

Mercedes-Benz Covered Semi, 1:50, #3030 ....$90-105

Mercedes-Benz Covered Truck, 1:50, #3032 ....$90-105

Mercedes-Benz Covered Truck & Trailer, 1:50, #3031 ....$90-105

Mercedes-Benz Dump Truck, 1:50, #3040 ....$90-105

Mercedes-Benz Faun Drain Cleaner Vacuum, 1:50, #3079 ....$65-80

Mercedes-Benz Gas Cylinder Semi
    "Air Products," 1:50, #3019 ....$90-105
    "Messer Griesheim," 1:50, #3024 ..$90-105

Mercedes-Benz Gas Tanker Semi, #3023, ...$90-105

Mercedes-Benz Highway Bus, 1:50, #5421 ....$55-70

Mercedes-Benz Liquid Truck, 1:43, #1035, #1036 ....$35-45

Mercedes-Benz Low Loader Semi, 1:50
    #3010 ....$90-105
    #3025 ....$90-105

Mercedes-Benz Messer Griesheim Acetylene Cutter, 1:50, #5404 ....$95-110

Mercedes-Benz Mixer "Blank Betonova," 1:50, #3064 ....$70-85

Mercedes-Benz Open Semi, 1:50
    #3030 ....$90-105
    #3046 ....$90-105

Mercedes-Benz Pipe carrier, 1:50, #3021 ....$90-105

Mercedes-Benz Putzmeister
    52/5 5-Axle Concrete Pump, 1:50, #3086 ....$90-105
    Mixer/Pumper, 1:50, #3052 ....$90-105

Mercedes-Benz Refrigerator Truck, 1:50, #3038 ....$90-105

Mercedes-Benz Schorling P17 Snow Sweeper, 1:50, #3069 ....$95-110

Mercedes-Benz Schwing 32XL Pump, 1:50, #3093 ....$80-95

Mercedes-Benz Semi
    Suction Unit, 1:50, #3060 ....$90-105
    Tanker "Linde," 1:50, #3027 ....$70-85
    Trailer Truck, 1:50, #3029 ....$90-105

Mercedes-Benz Silo Transporter, 1:50, #4196 ....$70-85

Mercedes-Benz Single car Transporter, 1:50, #3054 ....$90-105

Mercedes-Benz Spitzer Silo Semi, 1:50, #3014 ....$90-105

Mercedes-Benz Suction Vehicle Vacuum TA, 1:50, #3066 ....$55-70

Mercedes-Benz Tank Truck, 1:50, #3053 ..$90-105

Mercedes-Benz Tanker Semi, 1:50, #3022 ....$90-105

Mercedes-Benz Titan Truck Tractor, 1:50, #3009 ....$90-105

Mercedes-Benz Truck & Trailer, 1:50
 #3012 ....$90-105
 "BayWa," 1:50, #3011 ....$90-105
 "MobelspEdition" or "Pfenning" logo, 1:50,
 #3016 ....$90-105
 "Spedition Lueg," 1:50, #3013 ......$90-105
Mercedes-Benz Van, 1:50, #1604 ....$15-25
Mercedes-Faun Garbage Truck, 1:50,
 #3049 ....$90-105
Mercedes-Haller Garbage Truck, 1:50,
 #3039 ....$90-105
Mercedes-Hegla Glass Truck, 1:50,
 #3034 ....$90-105
Mercedes-Kuka Garbage Truck, 1:50,
 #3033 ....$90-105
Mercedes-Leach Garbage Truck, 1:05,
 #30410 ....$90-105
Mercedes-Liebherr Cement Mixer, 1:50,
 #3050 ....$90-105
Mercedes-Meiller Dump Truck, 1:50,
 #3026 ....$90-105
Mercedes-Schorling Sweeper, 1:50,
 #3042 ....$90-105
Multicar Utility, 1:50, #5068 ....$40-55
O&K L55 Wheel Loader, 1:50, #2422 ....$55-70
O&K RH120C Shovel, 1:50, #2771 ..$120-130
OAF Fire Truck, 1:43, #1018 ....$50-65
P & H Omega Crane, 1:50, #2075 ....$85-95
P & H T-1300 Crane Truck, 1:50,
 #2071 ....$85-95
Peiner Container Lift, 1:87, #2110 ....$70-85
Peiner Tower Crane, 1:87, #2010 ....$85-95
Potain GMR Crane, 1:50, #2014 ....$75-90
Potain Truck Crane, 1:87, #2011 ....$75-90
Putzmeister 3-Axle Concrete Pump, 1:50,
 #3095 ....$70-85
Putzmeister Cement Pump, 1:50,
 #2040 ....$100-115
Putzmeister Concrete Mixer Trailer, 1:35,
 #5405 ....$55-70
Putzmeister Worm Pump, 1:50, #5402 ..$35-50
Rosenbauer Fox Fire Pump, 1:50, #5403 ....$35-50
Scheid PV 60 Roller, 1:50, #2920 ....$70-85
Schorling Street Sweeper, 1:50, #3047 ....$90-105
Sennebogen 526 Excavator, 1:50,
 #2814 ....$55-70
Sennebogen Backhoe, 1:50
 #2812 ....$55-70
 with Blade, #2817 ....$55-70
Sennebogen Mobile Crane, 1:50,
 #2810 ....$55-70
Steyer Farm Tractor, 1:43, #5018 ....$20-30
Steyer/Stetter 4-Axle Mixer, 1:50, #3464 ..$70-85
Tamrock Tunnel Drill, #2501 ....$50-65
Terex 72/71 Wheel Loader, 1:43, #2410 ...$85-95
Terex Articulated Dump Truck, #2762 ......$50-60

Terex TS-14B Scraper, 1:04, #24113 ....$85-95
Voest-Alpine Road Roller, 1:35, #2701 ...$55-70
Volkswagen Kombi, 1:43
 #1016 ....$20-30
 with Glass Rack, #1017 ....$20-30
Volkswagen Passat GLS, 1:43, #1010 ....$15-25
Volkswagen Passat Variant, 1:43,
 #1011 ....$15-25
Volkswagen Polo C, 1:43, #1014 ....$10-15
Volkswagen Polo Coupe, 1:43, #1021 ..$15-25
Volkswagen Santana GL, 1:43, #1015 ..$15-25
Volkswagen Scirocco GLI, 1:43,
 #1013 ....$55-70
Volvo 1928 Flat Truck, 1:43, #1026 ......$55-70
Volvo 1928 Old Timer Fire Engine, 1:43,
 #1030 ....$45-65
Volvo 1947 LV153 Stake Truck, 1:43,
 #1028 ....$45-55
Volvo 1949 LV293 C2LF Stake Truck, 1:43,
 #1029 ....$45-65
Volvo Double Trailer Truck, 1:50, #4327 ...$55-70
Volvo Euro Trotter, 1:50, #4372 ....$55-70
Volvo F12
 Air Crash Tender, 1:50, #4392 ....$70-85
 Semi Bulk carrier, 1:50, #4315 ....$70-95
Volvo F16 Logging Truck/Trailer, 1:50,
 #4317 ....$70-95
Volvo FH12 with Refrigerator Trailer, 1:50,
 #4608 ....$85-100
Volvo FH16 with 4-Axle Trailer, 1:50,
 #4609 ....$90-105
Volvo FL10 3X Concrete Mixer, 1:50,
 #4564 ....$65-80
Volvo FL6 Container Tailgate Lift, 1:50,
 #4589 ....$65-80
Volvo Low Sideboard Truck, 1:50, #3776 ...$45-65
Volvo NL10 Water Truck, 1:50,
 #3777 ....$70-85
Volvo NL12
 Atlas Gondola Truck, 1:50, #3755 ...$70-85
 Concrete Mixer, 1:50, #3744 ....$70-85
 Conventional Dump Truck, 1:50,
 #3775 ....$70-85
 Semi with Refrigerator Trailer, 1:50,
 #3928 ....$90-105
Volvo Schwing KVM52 Concrete Pump, 1:50,
 #4594 ....$115-130
Volvo Semi With Talbert Lowboy, 1:50,
 #3912 ....$70-85
Volvo Titan L395 Flatbed Truck, 1:43,
 #1037 ....$45-60
White 1902 Old Timer Pie Wagon, 1:43,
 #1031 ....$30-40
Wirth Rotary Drill Truck, 1:50, #2078 ...$95-110
Yale Forklift, 1:25
 #2990 ....$65-80

#2992 ....$65-80
#2998 ....$45-60
Zeppelin ZBK 100 Truck Crane, 1:87,
 #2012 ....$75-90
Zeppelin ZM15 Wheel Excavator, 1:50,
 #2817 ....$40-60
Zeppelin ZR28 ABI Pile Driver Excavator, 1:50,
 #2815 ....$75-90

COPy cars

Jeff Mantyak reports that COPy cars are similar to Road Champs police cars (likely customized off Road Champs chassis), but are produced by a Canadian model company. The models are Chevrolet Caprices representing an assortment of Canadian police vehicles, with opening doors and trunks, and pullback motor. Order from
Coppers Collectibles,
2514-23 Avenue South
Lethbridge, Alberta T1K 1K9 Canada,
phone: 403-329-8378
fax: 403-329-4055,
email: coppers@telusplanet.net

Chevrolet Caprice
 Ontario Provincial Police $15-20
 Peel Regional Police $15-20

Corgi (also see Original Omnibus Co., Oriental Omnibus Co., Race Image Collection, Husky, Detail Cars)

The Corgi legacy is a rich one, beginning in 1934 with parent company Mettoy of Swansea, South Wales. In 1956 Mettoy merged with Playcraft Ltd. to form Mettoy Playcraft Ltd. In 1993, Mattel bought the Corgi brand and attempted for a short time to maintain the tradition of producing Corgi quality collectible toys. Shortly afterward, employees of the British manufacturing center reportedly bought back the Corgi Collectibles line. Corgi has since been purchased (as of July 1999) by Zindart, an American-owned company based in Hong Kong. Visit Corgi's new Corgi Shop Website at www.corgi-shop.co.uk/

Several books have been written about Corgis, and the multitude of models produced certainly could fill a book or more. So instead we present a survey of the models produced over the years, along with current collector values.

Popular Corgi models such as the Beatles' Yellow Submarine are now being reproduced to give new collectors a second chance at getting the good ones at a reasonable price.

A Survey of Corgi Models Through the Years

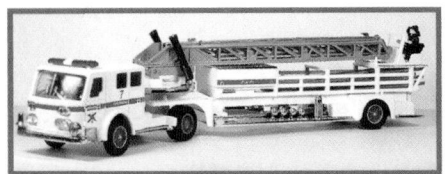

American LaFrance Ladder Truck, white, #97387 ....$50-65

Aston Martin DB4, #309, 1962-1965 ....$50-65

Aston Martin DB5 (see James Bond)

The Avengers Gift Set #40, 1966-1969, Includes John Steed & Emma Peal figures, #318 Emma's Lotus Elan, #9001 John Steed's Bentley $250-300

The Avengers 1927 Bentley with John Steed figure, #9001, 1964-1969 ....$125-150

The Avengers 1927 Bentley with John Steed figure, 1998 reissue $40-60

Batmobile, #267, 1966 ....$450-500

Batboat, #107, 1967 ....$350-375

Batmobile and Batboat, Gift Set #3, 1967-1981 ....$850-900

The Beatles Yellow Submarine, #803, 1969-1970 ....$600-750

The Beatles Yellow Submarine, 1997 reissue ..$55-70

1954 Bentley R Type, #815.................$20-30

Cadillac Superior Ambulance, #437, 1962-1968 ....$65-80

Chevrolet Camaro SS 350, #338, 1968-1970 ....$80-100

1939 Chevrolet Sedan, Memphis Fire Dept., 2003 ....$10-15

Chipperfield's Circus Karrier Booking Office Truck, #426, 1962-1964.....................$125-150

Chipperfield's Circus Chevrolet Booking Office Truck, #426, 1978-1981 ....$45-60

Chipperfield's Circus Cage Wagon, #1123, 1961-1968 ....$75-90

Chipperfield's Circus Crane Truck, #1121, 1960-1968 ....$90-110

Chipperfield's Circus Crane Truck, #1144, 1969-1972 ....$100-125

Chipperfield's Circus Giraffe Truck, #503, 1964-1971 ....$90-110

Chipperfield's Circus Horse Van, #1130, 1962-1972 ....$100-125

Chipperfield's Circus Land Rover and Elephant Cage, Gift Set #19, 1962-1969 ...$125-150

Chipperfield's Circus Parade Vehicle, #487, 1969-1979 ....$75-90

Chipperfield's Circus Performing Poodles Truck and Ring, #487, 1967-1979 ....$75-90

Chipperfield's Circus Transporter, #1139, 1968-1972 ....$100-125

Chitty Chitty Bang Bang car, #266, 1968-1972 ....$450-600

Chitty Chitty Bang Bang car, 1992 reissue ...$175-225

Citroën Ski Team car with skier, #475, 1964-1967 ....$45-60

Ecurie Ecosse Racing Transporter, #1126, 1961-1965 ....$90-120

Ford Holmes Wrecker, #1142, 1967-1974 ....$100-125

Ford Express Semi-Trailer Truck, #1137, 1965-1970 ....$80-110

1957 Ford Thunderbird, #810, 1983 .....$50-65

Garbage Truck, #1116, 1979 ....$30-40

Green Hornet's Black Beauty, #268, 1967-1972 ....$425-450

Jaguar XJ12C, #286, 1974-1979..........$25-40

Jaguar XJS Motul, #318, 1983 ....$20-30

James Bond Aston Martin DB5
1st issue #261 metallic gold, 1965-1968 ....$125-175
2nd issue #270 metallic silver with red tire rippers, 1968 ....$90-120
3rd issue #271 metallic silver with Whizzwheels, 1978 ....$45-65
4th issue with spoked wheels, 1997 reissue ..$40

James Bond Citroën 2CV
#272, 1981-1982 ....$50-65
1997 reissue $40

James Bond Lotus Esprit
#269, 1977 ....$60-75
1997 reissue $40

James Bond Mercedes Saloon, from "Octopussy," 2003 ....$12-16

James Bond Moon Buggy
1972 ....$600
1997 reissue $40

James Bond Toyota 2000 GT
1967 ....$625
1997 reissue $40

Lincoln Continental Stretch Limousine with lighted TV in back seat, #262, 1967-1969 ....$100-125

Man from U.N.C.L.E. Blue Oldsmobile, #497, 1966 ....$450

Mazda B1600 Pickup, #493, 1975-1978 ....$25-40

1956 Mercedes-Benz 300S Convertible
Top Down, #806, 1983 ....$35-50
Top Up, #805, 1983 ....$35-50

MGB GT, #327, 1967-1968 ....$60-75

MGC GT, #345, 1969 ....$60-75

The Monkees Monkeemobile, #277, 1968 ....$525

The Muppets Kermit's car, #2030 ....$30-45

The Muppets Fozzie Bear's Truck, #2031 ....$30-45

The Muppets Miss Piggy's Sports Car, #2032 ....$30-45

The Muppets Animal's Percussionmobile, #2033 ....$30-45

Plymouth Sports Suburban Station Wagon
#219, 1959-1963 ....$100-125
#445, 1963-1965 ....$75-90

Mail car, #443, 1963-1966 ....$65-80

1953 Pontiac Chieftain Deluxe 8 Van, Newark Fire Department, 2003 ....$10-15

Popeye's Paddle Wagon, #802, 1969 .....$650

Rolls-Royce Corniche, #279, 1979 ....$30-40

The Saint's Volvo P1800, #258, 1965 ....$225-275

Studebaker Golden Hawk, #211, 1958-1965 ....$65-80

Thornycroft Bus

yellow and red, Charlie Chaplin's Production "A Woman of Paris," #858..$25-35

red and white, National Motor Museum, #858 ....$25-35

Tour de France Citroën, #510, 1970-1972 ....$65-80

Tour de France Commer TV Camera Van, #479, 1967-1972 ....$60-75

Tour de France Renault, Gift Set #13 includes bicyclist and car with movie camera, 1968-1972.$65-80

Corgi Truckers

In the early 1980s, Corgi issued a series of 1:64 scale contemporary trucks marketed as Corgi Truckers that have since been incorporated into Mattel's Corgi Auto-City line. New models as of 1997 are called Hot Wheels Haulers.

Ford Cargo Truck
"Pepsi" $5-7
"Kraft Dairylea Cheese Spread" $5-7
Ford Dump Truck $5-7
Ford "Duckham's" Tanker $5-7
Kenworth "7UP" $5-7
M.A.N. "Raleigh" Truck $5-7
M.A.N. Dump Truck $5-7
M.A.N. "BP" Tanker $5-7

Corgi Greyhound Buses

Greyhound's "Dog and Target" design was first used to demonstrate solidarity with Great Britain during the attack on London by the Germans in 1939. Below are listed several variations of one bus style. All of these models were currently available as of this writing.

Greyhound Coach
"Philadelphia" $35-50
"New York Central RR" $30-45
"Pennsylvania RR" $30-45
"Trailways," teardrop design $30-45
"Trailways," pinstripe design $30-45
"Champlain," with billboard $30-45
"Los Angeles" $35-50
"New York" Public Service Coach.....$35-50
"WACS" $30-45

"WAVES" $30-45
New York / Albany / Montreal Coach with billboard $30-45

Corgi Mack Fire Trucks
Mack Pumper, "Chicago," 1994 ....$25-30
Mack "B" Pumper, "Paxtonia," 1995 ......$35-40

Corgi Race Image Collectibles

From Corgi's website: "The Corgi brand has been the hallmark of high-quality diecast models for over 40 years and, as a result, has worldwide following for both old and new production. All products are designed in Britain to the highest standards and traditions which guarantee the authenticity of every model.

"Corgi now brings this considerable experience to the US racing collectibles market and offers the following features on exciting models at an affordable price:

"Super detailed 1:64 scale semi's, strictly limited editions, numbered certificates of authenticity, chromed stack and wheels, diecast cabs, chrome mirrors, soft tires, twin wheels, Ford Aeromax and Kenworth T800 cabs." The Race Image brand is now associated with Lucky Plan. Corgi Race Image models are now out of production.

Corgi Race Image Transporter & Car, 1:64 Scale
The Family Channel Racing Team $15-20
Kellogg's Corn Flakes Racing $15-20
Kodak Racing $15-20
La Victoria / Winnebago with rail dragster $20-25
Maxwell House / Bobby Labonte $15-20
Mopar Xpress / Tommy Johnson Jr. Top Fuel with rail dragster $20-25
Quaker State / Brett Bodine $15-20
Slick 50 / Ricky Smith $15-20
Slick 50 / Western Auto $15-20
Slick 50 / Winston Drag Racing $15-20
Syntec with rail dragster $20-25
Texaco Havoline / Davey Allison $15-20
Valvoline / Mark Martin $15-20
Winn Dixie Racing $15-20
La Victoria / Mike Dunn $40-45
Pennzoil / Eddie Hill $40-45
Castrol Syntec / Pat Austin $40-45
Valvoline / Joe Amato $40-45
Western Auto / Al Hofmann $40-45
Mooneyes / Kenji Okszaki $40-45
Kendall / Chuck Etchells $40-45

Corgi Race Image Cars Only, 1:64 Scale
John Force, 2 car set............................$45-50

Don Prudhomme / Skoal Bandit.............$45-50
NHRA 40th U.S. Nationals Drags $45-50

Corgi Rockets
#906 Jensen Interceptor, 1:64...............$15-20

Husky Models

Corgi produced a series of small, inexpensive models in the 1960s called Husky, later changed to Corgi Jrs. Here are just a few examples of Husky models. Typically, current values are around $15-20 each, with a few notable exceptions as listed below.

Batmobile, Husky Extra, 1966 ....$350-400
Bedford TK 7-Ton Skip Truck, #27 ....$25-30
Chitty Chitty Bang Bang, 1967 ....$400-450
James Bond Silver Aston Martin, 1966 .$400-450
Jeep, #5, with #19 Boat and Trailer $30-45
Man from U.N.C.L.E., 1966 ....$375-425
Monkeemobile, 1967 ....$400-450

Corgi Jrs.

Corgi Jrs., successors to the Husky line, are still being produced today. Current models are available for about $2-4 each. Here is a sampling of current and past models. While the high prices on a few models may seem extremely high, they are nevertheless what at least one dealer is asking for these apparently hard-to-find items. When Mattel purchased Corgi, Corgi Jrs. became Corgi Auto-City models.

Batmobile, 1967 ....$325-375
Batboat, 1967 ....$325-375
BMW...$3-5
BP Van $3-5
Buick Regal Police $3-5
Chitty Chitty Bang Bang, 1968 ....$275-325
Corvette...$3-5
Garbage Truck $3-5
Helicopter $3-5
Ironside Police Van, 1970 ....$325-375
Jaguar Racer $3-5
James Bond Silver Aston Martin, 1966 .$400-450
Mercedes-Benz Ambulance $3-5
Mercedes Convertible $3-5
Mercedes Taxi $3-5
Military Jeep $3-5
Monkeemobile, 1968 ....$275-325
Popeye's Paddle Wagon, 1971 ....$275-325
Porsche Targa.......................................$3-5
Shell Tanker $3-5
Stagecoach..$12-16
Stern Wheeler $12-16
Team Racing Van $3-5

Tipping Lorry.................................$3-5

Kiko Toys from Corgi

Kiko is the Mexican division of Corgi Jrs. Here is a small sampling of models from this series.

Austin Metro, #55, white.........................$4-6
Caravan, #61, red $4-6
Caravan Fire, #806, red $4-6
Caravan Police, #821.............................$4-6
Chevrolet Van "Monica"...........................$4-6
Renault 4 Van, #M5, red $4-6
Rover 3500 Fire Chief, #805......................$4-6
Scania Van "Cascao"..............................$4-6
Simca 1308, #M9..................................$4-6
Volkswagen Golf, #51, red........................$4-6
Volkswagen Golf Fire Chief, #809, red $4-6
Volkswagen Van "Correios," #M6.............$4-6

Corgi 1:18 Scale

With the rise in popularity of 1:18 scale models, this is Corgi's first entry into this genre.

1996 MGF Convertible, green, introduced in 1996, #95102 ....$40-50

Cossack Models

Alex Litovskiy reports of the Cossack Models brand from Ukraine but doesn't provide any details.

Cougar (see Solido)

Courtland

Camden, New Jersey, was home to Courtland Manufacturing Company, makers of a large assortment of tin lithographed toy cars and trucks. Remaining in Camden from 1944 to 1953, the name was changed to Courtland Toy Company and headquarters were moved to Philadelphia, Pennsylvania, in 1953. Meanwhile, the Korean War created a demand for tin and other metals, and around the same time counterfeit Courtlands were showing up around the country which were inferior to the originals but came with a lifetime warranty that the real Courtland Toy Company was forced to honor, which put them in a real financial bind. At the same time, the move to Philadelphia was badly timed as the popularity of tin lithographed toys was waning swiftly with the introduction of plastic and diecast toys. The company didn't have the resources to change with the changing market and went out of business the same year.

Cox

Roy Cox produced an assortment of gas-powered toy cars, some of them designed to be tethered to a pole by a string to drive in a large circle, hence the name "tether car." Other models had wind-up motors, one had a propeller on the rear, and a couple others were designed as non-powered "pushers." While later Cox models are of only moderate value on the collector market, earlier Thimble Drome racers are considered much more valuable. Another company, Ohlsson & Rice, made similar models.

Roy Cox Thimble Drome

No. 2 Special pusher racer, 8"..........$200-300
No. 25 Racer....................................$300-400
No. 28 Special with motor $450-600
No. 81 ....$300-500
Champion Racer................................$400-600
Prop Rod $100-150
Pusher Racer...................................$300-400
Racer with engine $400-600
Special, wind-up..............................$600-800

Cox Gas Powered Cars

Adam 12 Squad Car.......................$150-200
Army Jeep.....................................$125-175
Corvette, 1966, 8"..........................$150-200
Dune Buggy $50-75
Ford GT-40....................................$175-250
Funny car, plastic, 12" $15-20
Matador..$100-150
Vega Funny Car..............................$60-90
Volkswagen $60-90

CPM

1:43 scale models made in England comprise this series of vehicles.

Austin Healey 100-6 Roadster $40-45
1939 Buick 4-door Sedan $40-45
Daimler SP250 Roadster $40-45
Guy "Eveready" Van $125
Jensen 541 Coupe..............................$40-45
Morris 1000 4-door Sedan, gray..........$40-45
Morris 1000 Convertible, white $40-45
1939 Studebaker Commander 2-door Sedan, navy blue..........................$40-45
Sunbeam Alpine Roadster, red/white/green.$40-45
Sunbeam Tiger Roadster.......................$40-45
Triumph Spitfire Roadster, red $40-45

Craftoys

Omaha, Nebraska, was the home of Craftoys, an assortment of slush mold (lead alloy) toys similar to the early Best, Ralstoy, and

Kansas Toy models. A short-lived company, it lasted just a few years before World War II set in and the lead was needed for the war.

Cement Mixer, #78, 3¾" $16-20
Fire Truck, #101, 4½" $30-40
Fordson Tractor, #17, 2½" $16-20
Freight Train, #3600, 16½", includes:
   Locomotive 0-6-4 "KT&N RR," 4½".....$12-16
   Railroad cars, 3¾" ....$12-16 each
   Caboose, 2¾".................................$12-16
Miller FWD Indy Racer, #81, 4½" $20-25
Oil Truck, #104, 3¾".............................$30-40
Racer, #100, 4¼".................................$30-40
Speed Car, #103, 4¼"..........................$30-40
Station Wagon, #105, 3¾".....................$30-40
Streamlined 2-door Sedan, #92, 4".......$30-40
Tanker, #102, 6¾"................................$30-40

Cragstan (also see Gamda Koor, Sabra)

Cragstan is best known for battery operated robots, of which Cragstan's Mr. Atomic is most highly valued. In the late 1960s to early 1970s, Cragstan dabbled in diecast and produced some noteworthy 1:43 scale models made in Israel. Around the rest of the world, these models were sold as Gamda Koor or Sabra models, but in the U.S., they were sold under the Cragstan "Detroit Seniors" brand.

Cragstan Detroit Seniors

1966 Buick Riviera
   various colors, #8108.....................$30-45
   Israeli Presidential car, #8108/1......$35-50
Cadillac De Ville Convertible, #8123.....$35-50
Cadillac Eldorado
   various colors, #8110.....................$35-50
   Israeli Presidential car, #8110/1......$35-50
   Sheriff's car, dark blue, #8110/2 .....$35-50
Chevrolet Camaro SS, various colors, #8120 ....$35-50
1966 Chevrolet Chevelle Station Wagon
   various colors, #8100.....................$35-50
   Police, #8100/1 ....$35-50
   United Nations, #8100/2 ....$35-50
   Israeli Military, #8100/3 ....$35-50
   Israeli Post Service, #8100/4 ....$35-50
   Sabra Diving Club, #8100/5 ....$35-50
Ambulance, white with red cross, #8101..$35-50
Ambulance Israeli Magen David, cream with star, Hebrew text, #8101/1 ....$35-50
Ambulance Israeli Military Ambulance, beige with white label, #8101/2....................$35-50
Fire Chief, red "Fire Chief," #8102...$35-50
Israeli Fire Service, #8102/1..........$35-50

1967 Chevrolet Corvair Monza Coupe,
    #8113 ....$30-45
1968 Chevrolet Corvette Stingray
    various colors, #8105 ....$30-45
    stock car, #8105/1 ....$35-50
1966 Chevrolet Impala
    various colors, #8103 ....$30-45
    Fire Chief, red, #8103/1 ....$30-45
    Israeli Police, blue, #8103/2 ....$30-45
    Police, dark blue, #8115 ....$35-50
    Israeli Police, red, #8115/1 ....$35-50
    Taxi, yellow, #8116 ....$35-50
    Israeli Taxi, #8116/1 ....$35-50
Chevrolet Pickup
    various colors, #8122 ....$35-50
    Israeli Police, #8122/1 ....$35-50
    Israeli Military, #8122/2 ....$35-50
    Coastguard with boat, #8122/3 .....$35-50
    Wrecker, Israeli Police Breakdown truck,
    #8122/4 ....$35-50
    Wrecker, Breakdown Truck, #8122/5 ..$35-50
    Wrecker, Israeli Military Breakdown Truck,
    #8122/6 ....$35-50
Chrysler Imperial Convertible, various colors,
    #8111 ....$35-50
1966 Dodge Charger
    various colors, #8112 ....$35-50
    United Nations, white, #8112/1 .....$35-50
    Flower Power, #8112/2 ....$35-50
    Israeli Police, #8112/3 ....$35-50
Ford GT, #8104 ....$35-50
Ford Mustang
    various colors, #8106 ....$35-50
    psychedelic colors, #8106/1 ....$35-50
Ford Thunderbird
    various colors, #8118 ....$35-50
Ford Torino, various colors, #8121 ....$35-50
Oldsmobile Toronado
    various colors, #8109 ....$35-50
    Israeli Police, red, #8109/1 ....$35-50
1965 Plymouth Barracuda
    various colors, #8114 ....$30-45
    Israeli Military, white, #8114/1 ....$35-50
Pontiac Firebird, various colors,
    #8119 ....$35-50
1967 Pontiac GTO
    various colors, #8107 ....$30-45
    Israeli Tourist Bureau, cream with red label,
    Hebrew text, #8107/1 ....$35-50
Volkswagen Beetle
    various colors, #8117 ....$35-50
    Hippie, with Flower Power decoration,
    #8117/1 ....$35-50
    Polizei, green and gray, #8117/2 ...$35-50
    Deutsches Bundes Post, yellow,
    #8117/3 ....$35-50

PTT (Swiss), yellow, #8117/4 ....$35-50
Airport "Follow Me," #8117/5 ....$35-50

Creative Master (also see Creative Masters)

Creative Master International, Inc.
Guangdong Province
People's Republic of China
CEO: Carl Ka Wing Tong (as of 10/21/98)
    You won't see this brand on anything the company makes. They contract their work to other companies whose name goes on the model.
    Creative Master International, Inc., founded in 1986 by carl Tong and Leo Kwok, is a Hong Kong-based company with manufacturing facilities in Guangdong Province of the People's Republic of China, according to a 1998 company prospectus. Creative Master manufactures premium collectible car replicas in the $20–220 price range sold by such companies as Danbury Mint, Hallmark, Mattel, and Action Performance.
    The company was recently awarded the prestigious Hong Kong Productivity Council Industry Award in the Productivity Category.

Creative Masters (also see CMA, Creative Master)

    In December 1995, Revell, now a subsidiary of Alpha International along with Gear-Box, introduced a 1:20 scale "Creative Masters" diecast replica of the original 1989 Dodge Viper RT/10 Roadster. Revell is so serious about faithfully reproducing this model in miniature that a miniature price sheet is included on the model on the windshield. The connection between Revell and Creative Master is somewhat complex, but in a nutshell, Revell obtained permission to use the name (with the "s" added to make the name plural) for US marketing of their products. It wasn't long before the two companies had a "falling out," the result of which is still unclear.

Shelby Cobra, red, 1:20 ....$125-150
1989 Dodge Viper RT/10 Roadster,
    1:20 ....$175-190
Shelby Mustang GT350, "incorrect" black engine,
    #8820 ....$200-250
Shelby Mustang GT350, "correct" blue engine,
    #8820 ....$175-190

Crescent Toys (also see D.C.M.T.)

    The Crescent Toy Company was born in a 30 square foot backyard workshop in London, England, in 1922. Through the 1920s and

1930s, Henry Eagles and Arthur Schneider manufactured lead alloy toy soldiers, cowboys, kitchen sets, and other items.
    After World War II, Crescent resumed making their toys, adding "DCMT" into the casting, evidence of their marketing of toys from the firm of Die Casting Machine Tools Ltd.
    The DCMT mark was removed from models made in 1948 and later. DCMT meanwhile went on to make Lone Star models. Crescent continued making toys until 1981.

Artillery Gun, #155 ....$30-45
Aston Martin DB3S Racing car, #1291 ..$80-105
B.R.M. Mk II Racing car, #1285 ....$100-125
British Tank, #696 ....$50-65
Bulldozer, #1822 ....$30-45
Cannon, operable, #235 ....$75-100
1970s Cement Mixer, #1360 ....$15-20
Connaught A Series Racing Car,
    #1287 ....$100-125
1970s Container Truck, #1350 ....$30-40
Cooper Bristol Racing Car, #1288 ....$100-125
1970s Covered Truck, #1361 ....$10-15
Ferrari 625 Racing Car, #1286 ....$100-125
1940s Fire Engine with Extending Ladder,
    #1221 ....$60-75
1940s Flat Truck, #424 ....$20-30
1970s Girder Truck, #1352 ....$30-40
Gordini 2.5 Litre Racing Car, #1289 .$100-125
Hayloader, #1815 ....$20-30
Horse Drawn Timber Wagon, #1813 .$130-145
Howitzer, unpainted, with spring and plunger,
    #695 ....$15-20
1940s Jaguar, #800 ....$40-50
1940s Jaguar Police Car, #804 ....$35-45
Jaguar D-Type Racing Car, #1292 ......$85-100
Large Farm Wagon, #1819 ....$35-45
1940s LaSalle Sedan, #425 ....$40-50
Maserati 25OF Racing Car, #1290 ..$100-125
Mercedes-Benz W196 Racing Car,
    #1284 ....$100-125
Military Set, includes two 696 British Tanks, 698 Scout
    car, 699 Russian Tank, #650 ....$225-275
Mobile Crane, #1269 ....$65-75
Mobile Space Rocket, #1268 ....$110-135
1940s Nash Roadster, #422 ....$45-60
1940s Petrol Tanker, #423 ....$20-30
1970s Petrol Tanker, #1351 ....$30-40
1970s Platform Truck, #1353 ....$30-40
PloughTrailer, #1814 ....$20-30
1940s Race Car, #223 ....$45-60
1970s Recovery Vehicle, #1363 ....$15-20
Roller Harrow, #1816 ....$15-20
Scammell Scarab and Low Loader Trailer,
    #1274 ....$110-135

Scammell Scarab and Oil Tanker, Shell or Esso, #1276 ....$150-200
Scammell Scarab Articulated Truck, #1272 ....$110-135
Scammell Scarab Set, #2705 ....$350-400
Scout Car, #698 ....$40-50
Set 1, includes #s 1284-1289, #6300 .$600-700
Set 2, includes #s 1285-1290, #6300 .$600-700
1970s Super Karner, #1364 ....$10-15
Timber Trailer, #1817 ....$15-20
1970s Tipper Truck, #1362 ....$15-20
Tipping Farm Wagon, #1818 ....$15-20
Vanwall Racing Car, #1293 ....$15-200
Western Stage Coach, #2700 ....$100-125

Cristian

The Cristian brand represents inexpensive 1:43 scale models made in Argentina.

DAF Car Transporter $4-8
1960 Fiat Car Transporter.........................$4-8
Fiat 1500 Ramco Coupe $4-8
Ika Torino Coupe $4-8
1960 Mercedes-Benz 220 ....$4-8
Renault Dauphine $4-8

Crossway Models

Crossway Models
2 Salem St.
Gosberton, Spalding, Lincs
PE11 4NQ England
phone/fax 011-44-1775-841-171

Every Crossway Model is hand finished and exquisitely detailed. Meanwhile, Jemini models, a white metal model car manufacturer in England, at one time produced some unusual British car models. Now Jemini has merged with Crossway Models of England. Issues are limited from 10 to 500 of each model.

Austin A70
   Saloon, black, 25 produced,
      #CMM1 ....$90-120
   black, #JSE008.............................$90-120
Austin 1100 Mk. 3, Bermuda blue and white, Metropolitan Police, #JSE009 ....$90-120
Austin/Morris 11/1300,
   #CK 01(£60 UK) $90
Austin 1100 MK2, flame red, 25 produced, #CMM2 ....$90-120
Austin 1300 GT, flame red, #JMR006 .$90-120
MG 1300 GT MK2, #JMR 007
   Bermuda blue..............................$90-120
   snowberry white $90-120
MG TD, red with wire wheels, 25 produced, #CMM3 ....$90-120

MGB, black, #JSE007 ....$90-120
Morris 100 Traveler, green and red, 100 produced, #JSE 003 ....$90-120
Riley RMA Saloon, 600 produced
   black $90-120
   dark red $90-120
Rover 75 Saloon, #CM 01
   black $90-120
   Connaught green..........................$90-120
   ivory $90-120
Standard Vanguard
   Estate, black, 50 produced, #JSE 002 ....$100-125
   Van, black, 100 produced, #JSE 002 .$90-120
Sunbeam Rapier, velvet/sage green, #CP10 ....$90-120
Sunbeam Tiger, white, Metropolitan Police, #JSE004
   open...$90-120
   closed $90-120
Triumph Dolomite Sprint, 600 produced
   carmine $90-120
   pageant blue $90-120
   vermilion $90-120
Wolseley Six, black, #JMR002............$90-120
Wolseley 1300 MK2, #JMR003
   teal $90-120
   harvest gold $90-120
   green mallard..............................$90-120
   black tulip $90-120

Crown Premiums

Crown Premiums
3310 East Woodview Avenue
Oak Creek WI 53154 USA
website: www.crownpremiums.com
email: info@crownpremiums.com

Crown Premiums entered the diecast bank replica industry in 1981 designing promotional items for Harley-Davidson, Snap-On Tools, Lennox, CITGO, Conoco, Tropicana, and other notable companies. In 1996, Crown Premiums introduced the first pedal car bank replica. Each issue is limited to 5,000 units. Below is a small sampling of models.

1:6 Scale Pedal Car Bank Replica Banks
1941 Garton Fire Engine.................$120-130
1948 BMC CT Convertible $120-130
1947 BMC Racer $120-130
1948 BMC Stake Truck $120-130
1947 BMC car Racer.....................$120-130

1:12 Scale Die Cast Petite Pedal Car Banks
1941 Garton Fire Engine.....................$60-70

1948 BMC CT Convertible $60-70
1947 BMC Racer $60-70
1948 BMC Stake Truck.......................$60-70
1947 BMC Car Racer.........................$60-70

C-Scale

C-Scale models are 1:43 scale white metal kits made in Great Britain. No model list is available.

Cursor

Although the Cursor line consists mainly of plastic models, these models from Germany are practically indistinguishable from diecast models in their precision, scale, and appearance. Newer Cursor models are diecast as well.

Cursor models represent a variety of German and other European cars and trucks, including the first Daimler and Benz cars produced in 1886.

Benz 1886 First Three-Wheel car, 1:43, #1 ....$15-20
Benz Blitzen 1911 Racer, silver, 1:43, #8 ..$20-25
Büssing 1904 Bus, 1:35, #14 ....$20-25
Daimler 1896 Fire, red, 1:43, #2 ....$20-25
Daimler 1897 Taxi, blue, 1:43, #3 ......$20-25
Double Decker Bus, 1:35, #982 ....$35-40
Fendt LB Farm Tractor, green, 1:43, #678 ..$20-25
Fendt LS Farm Tractor, green, 1:43, #677 ..$20-25
Graft & Stift Kaiser Wagon, 1:40, #189..$45-60
Hanomag Wheel Loader, #569............$30-35
Holder Culitrac Farm Tractor, 1:35, #880 .$25-30
Holder Farm Tractor, 1:35, #484 ....$25-30
Iveco Dump Truck, 1:50, #280 ....$25-30
Kaessbörer Setra S8 Bus, 1:60, #986 ...$45-60
Magirus Oil Truck, #780 ....$20-25
Man 1903 Truck, #982T $35-45
Man Truck, 1:35, #12932..................$30-35
Man Wood Transporter, 1:35, #12935.$30-35
Matador Van Pickup, blue, #266..........$70-75
Mercedes-Benz 190E, 1:35, #1182.....$20-25
Mercedes-Benz 300E, #1084 ....$20-25
Mercedes-Benz 500
   with closed sunroof, 1:43, #2911....$30-35
   with open sunroof, 1:43, #2912 .....$30-35
Mercedes-Benz L408D, silver, 1:43, #1300 ....$20-25
Mercedes-Benz Unimog, 1:50, #100 ....$20-25
Panther
   6x6 Fire Truck, #311................$120-135
   8x8 Fire Truck, #312.................$125-140
Volkswagen Bus, light gray, 1:43 ......$120-135

Custom Miniatures

One limited edition model is available from this brand, of which only 500 were made.

1957 Chevrolet Bel Air 2-door Hardtop, 5-spoke mag wheels, 1:43, maroon, white, and silver...$120-140

D

D & K

Alex Litovskiy reports of the D & K brand from the Ukraine but doesn't provide any details.

Dale Model Company

According to collector Jarek Skonieczny, Frank Dale originally worked for H. L. Framberg, manufacturer of cast metal World War II identification models used by the military to assist in recognizing military vehicles from a distance. Frank Dale left the Chicago-based company to form his own firm called Dale Model Company and continue producing military toys. More information is needed on both the Dale Model Company and H. L. Framberg. Original ID models were sold without a package. Later souvenir models were sold in boxes, most notably from F.A.O. Schwarz.

Dale Military Identification Models

Duck Amphibious $40-50
Half Track $40-50
Jeep, M715 1960s $40-50
Jeep, MB $70-85
Stuart M5 Tank $40-50
T-17 Armored Car................................$40-50

Dale Jr. / Dale Sr. Models (also see Revell)

In January 1999, Bryan Roy Hawthorne, bryanroy@mail.utexas.edu, listed the following Dale Jr. items, plus a few Sr. items, for sale on rec.toys.cars newsgroup. These are completely unrelated to Dale Model Company however, referring instead to race car driver Dale Earnhardt Sr. and his son Dale Earnhardt Jr.

Mr. Hawthorne wrote that these are "rare, hard-to-find 1997 Revell Collection Wrangler cars, which come in an acrylic case with a certificate of proof out of 5,004 produced... These were the first Dale Jr. cars besides his RCCA Mom n Pop's cars in 1994."

Dale Jr. Sets

1:43 scale 1997 Wrangler Revell
    Collection....................................$90-120
1:24 scale 1997 Wrangler Revell
    Collection....................................$200-250
1:18 scale 1997 Wrangler Revell
    Collection....................................$175-225

Dale Sr. Models

ARC/RCCA
    1:64 1994 HO Lumina $25-50
ARC
    1:24 1996 Olympic Goodwrench
        Box $75-100
    1:24 1997 GW Plus $50-75
    1:24 1997 GW Plus Black Window
        Bank $50-75
    1:64 1997 GW Plus $10-20
    1:64 1997 AC Delco Japan $10-20
    1:24 1998 GW Plus $50-75
    1:64 1998 GW Plus $10-20

Dalia (also see Tekno, Solido)

Dalia of Spain was begun in the 1920s. By World War II, Dalia had produced a number of diecast toys. By the late 1950s, Dalia produced a series of 1:38 scale Vespa and Lambretta scooters. Around the same time, the company became the licensed distributor for Solido in Spain. About a decade later, Dalia established a working relationship with Tekno of Denmark to produce a group of 1:43 scale models made in Spain. While the original box says "Dalia-Tekno," the models only say Tekno on the base.

Dalia 1:43 Scale

Go-kart, red and blue, #26 ....$90-120
Lambretta A Scooter
    Army, with Sidecar, olive, #21 ....$75-90
    Army, olive, #20 ....$75-90
    with Sidecar, "Coca-Cola," white and orange,
        #38 ....$75-90
    with Sidecar, orange and black, #12 .$75-90
    with Sidecar, silver, #6 ....$75-90
    "Coca-Cola," white and orange, #37.$75-90
    blue and orange, #2........................$75-90
    orange and black, #11 ....$75-90
Lambretta B Scooter
    with Sidecar, orange and black, #7 ..$75-90
    gray and pink, #3 ....$75-90
Lambretta Motor Tricycle
    Army, olive, #27 ....$75-90
    "Butano," orange, #8 ....$75-90
    "Coca-Cola," white and orange, #33 ..$75-90
    Milk Delivery, white and beige, #15 .$75-90
    Water Delivery, silver and beige, #17 .$75-90
    Wine Delivery, light blue and beige,
        #16 ....$75-90
    with Buckets, orange and beige, #13 .$75-90
    with Cases, white and beige, #30 ....$75-90
    with Drums, orange and beige, #14 .$75-90
    beige and green, #4 ....$75-90
    Red Cross, gray and white, #36 ....$75-90

Lambretta Scooter
    with Sidecar, "Butano," orange, #42 ..$75-90
    "Butano," orange, #41 ....$75-90
Vespa S Scooter
    with Sidecar, Army olive, #23 ....$75-90
    Army olive, #22 ....$75-90
    with Sidecar, green and yellow, #19 ..$75-90
    white and green, #18 ....$75-90
Vespa Scooter
    "Policia" with sidecar, black, #25 .....$75-90
    "Policia," black, #24........................$75-90
    "Telegrafos," beige, #28 ....$75-90
    Rally, blue, #34 ....$75-90
    Red Cross, white and gray, #9.........$75-90
    with Sidecar "Mop," yellow and beige,
        #40............................$75-90
    with Sidecar Red Cross, white and gray,
        #10............................$75-90
    with Sidecar, "Iberia," silver, #32 .....$75-90
    with Sidecar, "Telegrafos," beige,
        #29............................$75-90
    with Sidecar, light blue, #5 ....$75-90
    with Sidecar, Rally, blue, #35 ....$75-90
    "Iberia," silver, #31 ....$75-90
    "Mop," yellow and beige, #39........$75-90
    green, #1 ....$75-90

Dalia 1:66 Scale Cars

Chaparral 2F, #503 ....$30-45
De Tomaso Mangusta, #505 ....$30-45
Ford GT Le Mans, #502 ....$30-45
Porsche Carrera 6, #501 ....$30-45
Renault Alpine, #506 ....$30-45
Seat 850 Coupe, #504..........................$30-45

Dalia-Solido Models, 1:43 Scale

Alfa Romeo 2600 Coupe
    "Iberia" silver, #64 ....$120
    Bertone, cream, dark red, blue, green, or silver, #23 ....$90-120
Alfa Romeo Carabo Bertone, orange,
    #65 ....$75-90
Alfa Romeo Giulia TZ, blue or orange, #44 ...$90
Alfa Romeo Giulietta Roadster, red, orange, light blue, or green, #16.......................$75-90
Alpine F3, dark green, #39 ....$75
Alpine Renault, yellow, #66 ....$75-90
Aston Martin DB4, blue, yellow, red, silver, copper, #18................................$90-120
Aston Martin DB 5 Vantage
    "The Saint," white, #26-2 ....$175
    white, cream, blue, green, or copper,
        #26-1 ....$90-120
B.R.M. F.1, yellow or metallic green, #38.$75-90
BMW 2000 CS, white, #48 ....$65
Buggy Bertone, metallic green, #73 ....$50-75

Chaparral 2F, blue and red, blue and black, or white and red, #51 ....$60
Chaparral Z D, red, #47 ....$50-75
Citroën Ami 6 S.W.
    "Butano," orange, #52 ....$150-175
    "Falck," white, #52 ....$150-175
    Ambulance, white, #52 ....$150-175
    blue, green, #52......................$75-90
    white and green, or white and blue, #19 ....$90-120
Cooper 1500 F.Z (tan, white and blue, or yellow and white, #6 ....$90-120
De Tomaso Mangusta, tan, #50 ....$60
Ferrari 156 F.1, light blue or red, #20 ..$90-120
Ferrari 2.5 L, red, #32 ....$90-120
Ferrari 250 GT 2+2, red, green, or yellow, #17 ....$125-150
Ferrari 330 P3, light blue, #43 ....$90-120
Ferrari 365 GTB4, red, #72 ....$75-90
Ferrari Testa Rossa (red, white, cream), #4 ....$150-175
Fiat 2300 S Ghia Convertible
    "Autopistas," orange, #30 ....$150
    green, red, blue, or white, #30 ......$90-120
Fiat Abarth
    1000, orange, silver, or tan, #21 ...$90-120
    Record, orange, red, or white, #13 ..$90-120
Ford GT 40 Le Mans, yellow and blue, #42 ..$70
Ford Mustang
    "Policia," black, #58 ....$125-150
    Rally, red, #57 ....$75-90
    Taxi Barcelona, black and yellow, #59 ....$125-150
    Taxi Madrid, black and red, #60 .$125-150
    red, white, metallic light blue, #37 ..$90-120
Ford Thunderbird
    Taxi, black and yellow, #55 ....$125-150
    "Policia," black, #56 ....$150-175
    red, blue, tan, metallic green, #31 ..$90-120
Harvey Indianapolis, dark green or yellow, #34 ....$75-90
Jaguar D Le Mans, red, green, or blue, #1 ....$90-120
Lancia Flaminia Coupe Pinin Farina, red, silver, blue, or green, #12.....................$90-120
Lola Climax V8 F.1, tan and red, #40........$70
Lola T70 MK 3B, red, #68 ....$50-75
Lotus F1, yellow or black, #11 ....$75-90
Maserati 250F, red, yellow, or green, #2 ....$90-120
Maserati 3.5 L Mistral
    Rally, yellow and black, #67...........$75-90
    "NASA," orange, #36-1 ....$150-175
    beige, #36-1 ....$75-90
    copper, #36-1 ....$75-90
    metallic blue, #36-1 ....$90-120

yellow, #36-1 ....$75-90
Matra 650, blue, #70 ....$65
Mclaren M8 B Can Am, orange, #69 ....$65
Mercedes-Benz 190SL Roadster, copper, silver, or white, #10.....................$90-120
Mercedes-Benz 220 SE Coupe
    "Autopistas," orange, #22 ....$150
    "Falck," white, #22 ....$150-175
    "Policia," black, #22 ....$150-175
    "PTT," white, #22 ....$150-175
    blue or red, #22 ....$90-120
    Red Cross, white, #22 ....$150-175
NSU Prinz, red, blue, green, or orange and black, #28 ....$75-90
Oldsmobile Toronado
    Rally, orange, #61 ....$75-90
    orange or green, #45 ....$65
Opel GT 1900, metallic blue, metallic green, #54 ....$75-90
Panhard 24 BT
    "Urgencias," white, #46 ....$125-150
    silver, #46 ....$60
Panhard DB Le Mans, blue, silver or white, #25 ....$75-90
Porsche 550/1500 RS (red and black, yellow and black, or silver and green, #5 ....$125-150
Porsche 914/6, yellow, #71 ....$60
Porsche Carrera 6, yellow and red, #41 .$75-90
Porsche F2, #7
    silver and red $125-150
    yellow and black $125-150
    orange and silver $125-150
Porsche GT Le Mans, green, blue, silver, #29 ....$125-150
Renault Floride Convertible, copper, red, or blue, #9 ....$90-120
Seat 1400-C
    Taxi, Barcelona, black and yellow, #14 ....$150-175
    "Iberia," silver, #27 ....$150
    black and green, black and silver, red, or green and yellow, #8 ....$150-175
    Taxi, Madrid, black and red, #15 .$150-175
    "Policia," black, #24 ....$150-175
Seat 1500
    "Policia," black, #33 ....$150-175
    Taxi Barcelona, black and yellow, #33 ....$150-175
    Taxi Madrid, black and red, #33 .$150-175
    white, green, or metallic blue, #33 .$125-150
Simca 1100
    Red Cross, white, #62 ....$150-175
    Taxi, black and yellow, #63 ....$125-150
    yellow, #49 ....$75-90
Simca Oceare Convertible, green or metallic blue, #35 ....$90-120

Vanwall Racing car, light blue or green, #3 ....$90-120

Dalia-Tekno 1:43 Scale
Ford D 800
    Stake Truck, #915 ....$50-75
    Truck, #914 ....$50-75
Ford Mustang
    Convertible, #834 ....$50-75
    Hardtop, #833 ....$50-75
Ford Taunus Van
    "Autopistas," orange, #415........$250-300
    "Butano," #415 ....$250-300
    "Iberia," black, #415 ....$250-300
    "Mop Projectos," yellow and tan, #415 ....$250-300
    "Policia," black, #415 ....$250-300
    "Tekno," #415 ....$250-300
    "Telegrafos," #415 ....$250-300
    Ambulance (white), #415 ....$250-300
Lincoln Continental, #829 ....$65
M.G. 1100, #832 ....$50-75
Mercedes-Benz 230SL
    Hardtop, #928 ....$50-75
    Roadster, #929 ....$50-75
Monza GT
    Coupe, #930............................$50-75
    Roadster, #931 ....$50-75
Oldsmobile Toronado, #933 ....$50-75

Danbury Mint
47 Richards Avenue
Norwalk CT 06857

Between Danbury Mint and Franklin Mint, some of the most popular and collectible precision models have been produced. Jay Olins, editor of the monthly *Precision Die Cast Car Collectors Club* newsletter, is perhaps the most avid collector of both. Every three months, he publishes a complete up-to-date list of models produced by each company. Collectors are very critical of authenticity and detail, so they often write to the manufacturer and to Mr. Olins regarding any discrepancies discovered. Olins apparently has the inside track with both companies, and he relays all such comments to the manufacturer. All Danbury Mint models are currently available.

Aston Martin DB7, James Bond $140-150
1920s Borden's Milk Truck, white with black trim, 1:24 ....$140-145
1930s Borden's Milk Truck, white with black trim, 1:24 ....$140-145
1955 Borden's Delivery Truck, white with yellow top, 1:24...............................$140-145

1938 Budweiser Delivery Truck, 1:24 ..$155-160

1955 Budweiser Delivery Truck, 1:24 ..$155-160

1953 Buick Skylark Convertible, blue with blue-gray interior, 1:24 ....$115-120

1953 Buick Skylark Convertible, burgundy, 1:24 ....$115-120

1932 Cadillac V-16 Sport Phaeton, green, 1:24 ....$115-120

1953 Cadillac Eldorado Convertible, pearl white with red interior, white hardtop, 1:16 ....$200-210

1959 Cadillac Series 62 Convertible, red with red interior, 1:24 ....$115-120

1932 Cadillac V-16 Sport Phaeton, green with beige interior, 1:24 ....$115-120

1920s Campbell's Soup Delivery Truck, red, 1:24 ....$125-130

1931 Campbell's Soup Delivery Truck, red, 1:24 ....$125-130

1940s Campbell's Soup Delivery Truck, red, 1:24 ....$125-130

1950s Campbell's Soup Delivery Truck, red, 1:24 ....$125-130

1931 Chevrolet Roadster Pickup, turquoise blue with black bed, 1:24 ....$115-120

1941 Chevrolet Pickup, blue with black fenders, 1:24 ....$115-120

1941 Chevrolet Special DeLuxe, beige, Convertible top down, 1:24 ....$115-120

1953 Chevrolet 3100 Pickup, green, 1:24 ....$115-120

1953 Chevrolet Wrecker, red, 1:24 ..$140-145

1955 Chevrolet Bel Air, burnt orange and white, 1:24 ....$115-120

1955 Chevrolet Bel Air, red and white, 1:18 ....$200-210

1955 Chevrolet Nomad, blue and white, 1:24 ....$115-120

1955 Chevrolet Nomad, turquoise with white roof, 1:24 ....$115-120

1955 Chevrolet Nomad Street Machine, red, 1:24 ....$115-120

1957 Chevrolet Bel Air Convertible, teal blue, 1:24 ....$115-120

1957 Chevrolet Cameo carrier Pickup, red with white bed, 1:24 ....$115-120

1957 Chevrolet Bel Air Convertible, blue with light and dark blue interior, 1:24.........$115-120

1958 Chevrolet Apache Pickup, bright blue, 1:24 ....$115-120

1958 Chevrolet Impala Convertible, turquoise with blue interior, 1:24 ....$115-120

1962 Chevrolet Corvette Convertible, red, 1:24 ....$115-120

1966 Chevrolet C-10 Pickup, dark blue with white roof, 1:24 ....$120-125

1968 Chevrolet Chevelle SS-396, red, 1:24 ....$115-120

1968 Chevrolet El Camino SS-396, black $120-130

1969 Chevrolet SS/RS Camaro Convertible, blue with white interior, 1:24 ....$115-120

1969 Chevrolet SS/RS Camaro Convertible, white with orange stripes, 1:24 ....$115-120

1972 Chevrolet Cheyenne, red and white, 1:24 ....$125-130

1942 Chrysler Town & Country Station Wagon, black and wood, 1:24 ....$115-120

1948 Chrysler Town & Country Convertible, maroon and wood with maroon interior, 1:24 ....$115-120

1957 Chrysler 300C, cream, 1998, 1:24 ....$115-120

1927 Coca-Cola Delivery Truck, yellow and black, 1:24, 1995 ....$150-160

1928 Coca-Cola Delivery Truck, yellow and black, 1:24 ....$150-160

1931 Coca-Cola Delivery Truck, yellow and black, 1:24 ....$150-160

1938 Coca-Cola Delivery Truck, red, 1:24 ....$150-160

1929 Cord L-29 Special Coupe, turquoise blue with tan top, 1:18 ....$200-210

1950s Divco Borden's Milk Truck, white, yellow, gray with red trim..............$140-145

1929 Dodge Pickup, black with yellow stripe, 1:24 ....$115-120

1957 Dodge Sweptside, red and white two-tone, 1:24 ....$115-120

1935 Duesenberg SSJ Speedster, gray-red with beige interior, 1:24 ....$115-120

1958 Edsel Bermuda Station Wagon (see Ford Edsel)

1958 Ferrari 250 Testa Rossa, red with red interior, 1:24 ....$115-120

1920s Ford Model T Paddy Wagon, black, 1:24 ....$115-120

1925 Ford Model T Coupe, black, 1:24 ....$115-120

1925 Ford Model T Pickup, black with wood bed, 1:24 ....$115-120

1927 Ford Coca Cola Delivery Truck, yellow and black, 1:24 ....$130-140

1931 Ford Borden's Delivery Truck, red.$135-145

1931 Ford Campbell's Soup Delivery Truck, red...$125-135

1931 Ford Model A Deluxe Roadster, black-brown, 1:24 ....$115-120

1931 Ford Model A Deluxe Roadster, light brown, 1:24 ....$115-120

1931 Ford U.S. Mail Truck, dark green.$130-140

1936 Ford Deluxe Cabriolet, dark blue, 1:24 ....$115-120

1938 Ford Pickup, dark blue, 1:24 ...$115-120

1940 Ford Deluxe Coupe, red with beige interior, 1:24 ....$115-120

1940 Ford Hot Rod, black with yellow flames, 1:24 ....$115-120

1942 Ford Pickup, dark green, 1:24 .$115-120

1952 Ford F-1 Pickup, dark green, 1:24 ....$115-120

1955 Ford Fairlane Crown Victoria, two-tone cream and black, 1:24..............$115-120

1956 Ford F-100 Pickup, red, 1:24 ..$115-120

1956 Ford Sunliner Convertible, two-tone red and white, 1:24 ....$115-120

1956 Ford Thunderbird, red with red and white interior, 1:24 ....$115-120

1956 Ford Thunderbird, white, 1:24 .$115-120

1958 Ford Edsel Bermuda Station Wagon, orange and off-white with wood paneling, 1:24 ....$115-120

1962 Ford Thunderbird Sports Roadster, cream with red interior, 1:24 ....$115-120

1966 Ford Mustang Convertible, cream/blue-cream, 1:24 ....$115-120

1966 Ford Mustang Hardtop, maroon with black roof, 1:24 ....$115-120

1938 GMC car carrier, dark blue, 1:24.$145-150

1938 GMC Coca-Cola Delivery Truck, red...$130-140

1953 Good Humor Truck, white, 1:24 .$135-140

1940s Heinz Delivery Truck, white with red fenders, 1:24 ....$125-130

1934 Hispano Suiza J-12, blue, 1:24 .$115-120

1938 Indian Four Motorcycle, 1:10...$125-130

1948 Indian Chief, 1:10 ....$125-130

1949 Jaguar XK120, sand with red interior, 1:24 ....$115-120

1949 Jaguar XK120, metallic silver with red interior, 1:24 ....$115-120

1926 Mack AC Rotary Pumper Fire Engine, 1992, 1:32 ....$180-190

1931 Mercedes-Benz SSKL, white with black interior, 1:24 ....$115-120

1949 Mercury Club Coupe, black with beige interior, 1:24 ....$115-120

1949 Mercury Fire Chief's car, red, 1:24 ....$115-120

1949 Mercury Police Cruiser, black with white
   doors, 1:24 ....$115-120
1950 Mercury Custom, plum/magenta,
   1:24 ....$115-120
1920s Morton's Salt Delivery Truck,
   1:24 ....$125-130
1930s Morton's Salt Delivery Truck,
   1:24 ....$125-130
1940s Morton's Salt Delivery Truck,
   1:24 ....$125-130
1950s Morton's Salt Delivery Truck,
   1:24 ....$125-130
1955 Oldsmobile Super 88, red and white two-
   tone, 1:24 ....$115-120
1934 Packard V12 LeBaron Speedster, red and
   black, 1:24 ....$115-120
1933 Pierce Silver Arrow, silver, 1:24 ..$115-120
Plymouth Prowler, purple, top up, 1:24.$115-120
1965 Pontiac GTO, lavender, 1:24 ..$115-120
1969 Pontiac GTO "The Judge," carousel red,
   1:24 ....$115-120
1938 Rolls Royce Phantom III, maroon and black,
   1:24 ....$115-120
1937 Studebaker Pickup, red, 1:24 ..$115-120
1957 Studebaker Golden Hawk, gold,
   1:24 ....$100-110
1927 Stutz Black Hawk Speedster, black,
   1:24 ....$115-120
1927 Stutz Black Hawk, Custom Series, black
   and red, 1:24 ....$115-120
1956 Texaco Pickup Truck, red, 1:24.$130-135
1925 U.S. Mail Truck, 1:24 ....$135-140
1931 U.S. Mail Truck, 1:24 ....$135-140
1935 U.S. Mail Truck, 1:24 ....$135-140

Danbury Mint Pewter Models
1932 Alfa Romeo Sedan.....................$80-110
1936 Alvis Speed 25 ....$80-110
1935 Auburn 851 Speedster $80-110
1953 Austin-Healey 100 ....$80-110
1930 Bentley Barnato $80-110
1927 Bugatti Royale $80-110
1909 Cadillac "30" Tourer $80-110
1913 Cadillac Roadster $80-110
1932 Chevrolet Phaeton.....................$80-110
1932 Chevrolet Sport Roadster............$80-110
1932 Chrysler LeBaron.......................$80-110
1929 Cord L29 ....$80-110
1937 Cord 812 ....$80-110
1931 Daimler Double-Six....................$80-110
1932 Delage Cabriolet.......................$80-110
1938 Delahaye $80-110
1934 Duesenberg SJ..........................$80-110
1926 Fiat..$80-110
1909 Ford Model T.............................$80-110
1912 Hispano Suiza $80-110

1926 Isotta Fraschini..........................$80-110
1906 Itala Targa Florio $80-110
1936 Jaguar SS/100.........................$80-110
1937 Lagonda Rapide........................$80-110
1929 Lancia Dilambda $80-110
1927 Lincoln Sportster.......................$80-110
1928 Lincoln Convertible....................$80-110
1941 Lincoln Continental....................$80-110
1939 Mercedes-Benz 540K..............$80-110
1913 Mercer 35J...............................$80-110
1948 MG TC $80-110
1912 Packard $80-110
1930 Packard Convertible..................$80-110
1937 Packard Coupe.........................$80-110
1933 Pierce Silver Arrow....................$80-110
1905 Rolls Royce 10 HP $80-110
1907 Rolls Royce Silver Ghost $80-110
1909 Rolls Royce Silver Ghost $80-110
1911 Rolls Royce Silver Ghost 40/50 HP Limousine $80-110
1913 Rolls Royce Alpine Eagle............$80-110
1923 Rolls Royce Springfield Silver Ghost..$80-110
1936 Rolls Royce Park Ward $80-110
1939 Rolls Royce Silver Wraith $80-110
1954 Rolls Royce Silver Dawn III..........$80-110
1968 Rolls Royce Phantom VI $80-110
1912 Simplex....................................$80-110
1909 Stanley Steamer $80-110
1914 Stutz Bearcat............................$80-110
1931 Stutz Bearcat............................$80-110
1907 Thomas Flyer $80-110
1924 Vauxhall $80-110
1934 Viosin 17CV $80-110

Danhausen (also see Paul's Model Art)
Danhausen Modelcar
Postfach 485
5100 Aachen, Germany
   Danhausen models and kits come from Aachen, Germany, near the border of Belgium and the Netherlands. Besides the proprietary Danhausen line, Danhausen also offered models from Pocher, ABC Brianza, and some Russian-made diecast items. Like many current models produced in Europe, obtaining them in the U.S. is nearly impossible.

Ferrari BB Spyder, red, 1:43 ....$60-75
1931 Mercedes SSK L, 1:43 kit...........$20-30
Porsche 917/930, Sunoco, unfinished white
   metal, 1:43 kit $20-30

Dapper (also see Bandai)
   Dapper is a division of Bandai of Japan. One diecast model, produced in the 1980s, is known of this brand.

Hato Bus, 4½", 1980, #203...............$20-25

Darda
   Darda Toys of Germany are mostly plastic-body cars with a distinction. They are the fastest pullpack action toy cars ever made. A powerful high-tech spring-driven motor helps Dardas fly around loops and curves at a scale speed of 500–600 scale miles per hour! A huge assortment of Darda models is available, along with a large assortment of track sets.

Corvette by Darda..............................$7-10
Porsche by Darda...............................$7-10
Sonic Shifter by Darda $8-11
State Police car by Darda.....................$7-10
Stop N Go Camaro by Darda.................$7-10
Stop N Go Mercedes Police car by Darda.$7-10
Stop N Go Nissan 300 ZX by Darda.......$7-10
Stop N Go BMW 850i by Darda $7-10
Turbo Racer by Darda..........................$7-10
Ultra Porsche Boxter by Darda..............$8-11
Ultra Speed Camaro Z-28 by Darda......$8-11
Ultra Speed Corvette by Darda $8-11
Ultra Speed Lamborghini Diablo by Darda.$8-11
Ultra Speed Mercedes SLK by Darda........$8-11
Ultra Speed Mustang by Darda.............$8-11
Ultra Speed Panther by Darda..............$8-11
Ultra Speed Stop N Go Jaguar by Darda ..$8-11
Ultra Speed Stop N Go Porsche by Darda ..$8-11
Volkswagen Beetle by Darda $7-10
Yellow Canon Ultra Speed Formula 1 by
   Darda..$8-11

Dardis Mfg. Inc.
   At first glance, the Dardis GMC dump truck resembles a Hubley, except that it is larger, about nine inches long, and embossed underneath with "Dardis Mfg. Inc., Racine, Wis." For about six years in the 1950s, from around 1953 to 1957 or '58, Dardis was the product of parent company Richards Tool & Mold Company of Racine, Wisconsin. By 1959, Dardis was out of production, coincidentally the same year that Carter Tru-Scale added diecast GMC trucks to its product line.

   Twelve years later, in 1971, a set of diecast trucks appeared again from Tru-Scale, four models measuring over six inches each. Included were a dump truck, log truck, stake truck, and wrecker. Since Tru-Scale produced International trucks almost exclusively, it is unlikely that they created these models, but instead produced them from someone else's dies. Although unmarked, their conspicuous similarities to Dardis castings point toward Dardis molds.

Dardis GMC Dump Truck, 9"..............$45-60
unmarked GMC Dump Truck, 6¼"..........$15-25
unmarked GMC Log Truck, 6¼"............$15-25
unmarked GMC Stake Truck, 6¼"..........$15-25
unmarked GMC Wrecker, 6¼"..............$15-25

David Deanstyne

This United States brand is known for one hollow cast metal bus.

GM 3702 Coach, Adirondack Transit Lines,
8½"...$200-225

Day, John (see John Day Models)

Days Gone (see Lledo)

D.C.M.T. (also see Crescent, Impy, Lincoln, Lone Star, River Series, Roadmaster)

Die Casting Machine Tools Ltd. of Great Britain started producing toys as a sideline in the 1940s in north London in order to demonstrate the potential of their equipment. While most of their toys were produced under the Crescent brand, a few were simply marked "D.C.M.T." Some had friction motors in them.

The Crescent Toy Company originated from England in 1922. Through the 1920s and 1930s, Henry Eagles and Arthur Schneider manufactured lead alloy toy soldiers, cowboys, kitchen sets, and other items.

After World War II, Crescent resumed making their toys, adding "DCMT" into the casting, evidence of their marketing of toys from the firm of Die Casting Machine Tools Ltd. Crescent became the marketing firm for these models as well as their own Crescent brand.

One brand of which there is some dispute is a series of toys issued under the "River" brand. Neither the model or the box had any mention of Lone Star, Crescent, or D.C.M.T., and the castings were inferior to the other lines produced, which led to metal fatigue with which D.C.M.T. models were not so plagued. Regardless of such controversy of whether D.C.M.T. produced them or not, the author lists them below.

The D.C.M.T. mark was removed from models made in 1948 and later. D.C.M.T. meanwhile went on to make Lone Star models. Crescent continued making toys until 1981. Here are a few models made under the D.C.M.T. mark, followed by the "River" series. Lincoln Industries of Auckland, New Zealand, reportedly produced remakes from old D.C.M.T. tooling.

D.C.M.T. Models

Low Loader Tractor Trailer..............$45-60
Military Truck..............................$45-60
Tanker Truck...............................$45-60
Timber Truck with real "log"............$60-75

River Models

Austin A40 Somerset.....................$60-75
Buick Roadmaster.........................$75-90
Daimler Conquest........................$60-75
Ford Prefect..............................$60-75
Standard Vanguard Saloon...............$60-75
Standard Vanguard Station Wagon.......$60-75

DDR

As it turns out, DDR toys are wooden toys made in East Germany (DDR = Deutsche Demokratische Republik) prior to reunification. The toys are similar to Brio but with more accuracy, according to collector Brian Willoughby.

1950 Deutz Dump Truck...................$5-10
1950 Deutz Fire Ladder..................$5-10
1950 Deutz Lumber Truck.................$5-10
1950 Deutz-Fahr Farm Tractor...........$5-10
1980 Zetor Tractor.......................$5-10
1985 IFA Semi Fish Van..................$5-10
1985 IFA Van "Fernverkehr"..............$3-8
Deutz Fire Trailer.......................$5-10

Deanstyne, David (see David Deanstyne)

Dehanes

Dehanes brand models are 1:55 scale models, mostly of freight trucks, with a few exceptions.

1946 Chevrolet "Western Pacific".....$150-175
1939 Chrysler Airflow, #001...........$150-175
Ford C600
    "Johnny Walker," #104.............$65-75
    "UPS," #105.......................$65-75
International Conventional "PIE," #915.$140-155
Mack B "Heinz 57," #101................$65-75
Mack B80 Dump Truck, #205.............$65-75
Mack "Coca Cola" Van, #956............$65-75
Mack COE "Johnny Walker," #106........$65-75
1955 Mack H63T "Hennis," #914.........$145
Mack L Oil Truck "Hooker," #801.......$65-75
Mack Semi "Navajo," #957..............$110-125
1955 White Semi "Wise".................$110-125
White 3000
    "Threemor," #103..................$65-75
    "Mason Dixon," #103...............$65-75
    Semi "Mason Dixon," #916..........$130-145

Del Prado

Model Auto Review issue #138 and #139 reveal that The Edizioni del Prado Car Collection of Italy consists of seventy 1:43 scale diecast models produced in China. Many models are apparently copies of models from The Dinky Collection from Matchbox, Vitesse, and Solido. A complete model list has not been found.

Alfa Romeo 156..........................$35-50
1976 Alpine A110, French blue...........$35-50
Aston Martin DB5, metallic gray.........$35-50
Audi A4.................................$35-50
1970 BMC Mini Cooper, red with white
    roof.............................$35-50
BMW 507, cream.........................$35-50
BMW 850i................................$35-50
Bugatti T41 Royale......................$35-50
Cadillac Eldorado.......................$35-50
1963 Chevrolet Corvette Stingray, metallic light
    blue.............................$35-50
1964 Citroën DS19, black with white
    roof.............................$35-50
Dodge Viper.............................$35-50
Facel Vega HK 500.......................$35-50
Ferrari 512 Testarossa..................$35-50
1965 Fiat 500F, light blue (wrong color, the same
    as Vitesse model)................$35-50
1967 Ford Mustang Fastback, red (copied
    from The Dinky Collection by Match-
    box).............................$35-50
Hispano Suiza H6B.......................$35-50
Honda Civic.............................$35-50
1961 Jaguar E Type Spyder, dark green..$35-50
Jaguar XJ 220...........................$35-50
Jeep Grand Cherokee.....................$35-50
1966 Lamborghini Miura, yellow..........$35-50
Lancia Delta Integrale..................$35-50
Maserati Bora...........................$35-50
Mercedes-Benz 300 SL Gullwing, metallic
    gray.............................$35-50
Mercury Coupe...........................$35-50
MGB.....................................$35-50
Morgan Plus 4...........................$35-50
Oldsmobile Toronado.....................$35-50
Opel Calibra............................$35-50
1989 Porsche 911 Carrera Cabriolet,
    black............................$35-50
Rolls-Royce Silver Cloud................$35-50
Saab 900S...............................$35-50
Toyota Celica GT4.......................$35-50
Triumph TR3.............................$35-50
Vauxhall Viva...........................$35-50
Volkswagen 1300, white (copy of Jouef
    model)...........................$35-50

Deles

Discovered in a drug store recently is an assortment of inexpensive toy cars in roughly 1:43 scale with the name Deles on the bottom and made in China. A couple of late model Mercedes-Benz Coupes, a Porsche 356 Convertible, and a few other models sold for $1.25 each. Typically, models have very lightweight bodies, plastic chassis, and rubber tires on crude wheel hubs.

Mercedes-Benz Coupe $1-3
Porsche 356, pale blue............................$1-3

Dent Hardware Company

Since 1895, Dent Hardware Company operated out of Fullerton, Pennsylvania. Dent toys are historically significant for their contribution to the toy market of the early twentieth century. Their first cast iron vehicles emerged in 1898. In the 1920s, Dent attempted to market aluminum toys, but they failed to catch buyers' attention and were quickly phased out. Even though the company survived until 1973, toy production ceased during the Great Depression of the 1930s. Very few, if any, of Dent's toys were marked. Experts recognize them because of extensive experience in buying, selling, and trading. Richard O'Brien's book *Collecting Toy Cars and Trucks* provides a list of known Dent automotive models. If identifiable as Dent cast iron models, values start at $110 and can be over $10,000 for the rarest models.

Mack American Oil Co. Tanker,
    10½".....................................$1,500-1800
Mack American Oil Co. Tanker,
    15".....................................$2,500-3,000
Bus, 6¼"...................................$700-800
Coast to Coast Bus, 7½"...................$250-300
Coast to Coast Bus, 15"............$1,500-1,800
Coupe, 5"..................................$250-300
Mack Junior Supply Company, New York –
    Philadelphia, 16"............$10,000-12,500
Public Service Bus, 13½"............$4,500-6,000

Deoma Micromodels (or Microtoys of Italy)

A series of military models were sold under the Deoma Micromodels name during the late 1950s and early 1960s. Some models are crude copies of Dinky models of that era.

Austin 1-Ton Truck
    Covered Truck, 1¾", #6...................$15-20
    Covered Truck, 1¾", #23.................$15-20
    Open Truck, 1¾", #3.....................$15-20
Bedford Truck
    Covered Truck, 2¼", #5...................$15-20
    Open Truck, 2¼", #4.....................$15-20
Combat Car, 2", #8 ....$15-20
Daimler Armored Car, 1⅝", #2 ....$15-20
General Patton Tank, 2⅜", #7 ....$15-20
High Speed Tractor, 2¼", #10..............$15-20
Jeep, 1⅝", #9.............................$15-20
T-34 Tank, 2½", #1........................$15-20
Tank Transporter, 2¾", #14 ....$15-20
Three-Axle Truck
    Civilian Truck, 2⅜", #12 ....$15-20
    Covered Truck, 2⅜", #15 ....$15-20
    Open Truck, 2⅜", #11 ....$15-20
"Long Tom" 155mm Cannon, 3¾",
    #16.....................................$15-20

Design Studio (see Motor City USA, Design Studio & USA Models)

Desormeaux

Two 1:43 scale lead alloy vehicles are known to have been produced by Desormeaux of France. Description, production year, and value are indicated below.

1923 Citroën 5CV, 1957...............$125-150
1910 Le Zebre, 1958 ....$125-150

Detail Cars – CDC (Corgi Detail Cars, also see Armour)

Collector Bill Cross reports that these are mass produced in China, often looking as if they come from the same source as Minichamps. They are marketed by CDC in Italy and by Corgi in Great Britain. Armour is a division of CDC that produces military models.

1958 Alfa Romeo Giulietta
    Monoposto Mille Miglia, red, #206 .$25-30
    Spyder Hardtop, red, #203............$25-30
    Spyder Hardtop, white, #204.........$25-30
    Spyder Soft Top, gray, #205 ....$25-30
    Spyder, blue, #202...................$25-30
    Spyder, red, #200 ....$25-30
    Spyder, white, #201 ....$25-30
1952 BMW 502
    Convertible, cream, #246 ....$25-30
    Convertible, top down, blue, #242...$25-30
    Convertible, top down, red, #244....$25-30
    Convertible, top up, silver, #243 ......$25-30
    Coupe, black, #240 ....$25-30
    Coupe, red, #241 ....$25-30
    Coupe, two-tone gray, #245 ....$25-30
1959 BMW 503
    Convertible, red, #253 ....$25-30
    Coupe, black, #252 ....$25-30
    Coupe, red, #250 ....$25-30
    Coupe, silver, #251 ....$25-30
1993 Chevrolet Corvette ZR1
    Convertible, top down, green, #214.$25-30
    Convertible, top down, red, #211 ....$25-30
    Convertible, top up, yellow, #212 ....$25-30
    Coupe 40th Anniversary, red, #215 .$25-30
    Coupe, white, #210....................$25-30
    metallic blue, #213 ....$25-30
1993 Ferrari 456GT
    metallic blue, #190 ....$25-30
    metallic red, #191 ....$25-30
    red, #193.............................$25-30
1993 Ferrari 512 TR
    Coupe, red, #140 ....$25-30
    top down, yellow, #142 ....$25-30
    top up, yellow, #144....................$25-30
1994 Ferrari F355 Berlinetta
    Convertible, blue, #295 ....$25-30
    Convertible, yellow, #294 ....$25-30
    Coupe, blue, #292 ....$25-30
    Coupe, red, #290 ....$25-30
    Coupe, yellow, #291 ....$25-30
    Spyder, red, #293 ....$25-30
    TS, top up, gray, #296 ....$25-30
1987 Ferrari F-40
    LeMans, red, #151 ....$25-30
    Monte Shell, multicolor, #154 ....$25-30
    Totip, multicolor, #155 ....$25-30
    Italian Racing Club, red, #153.........$25-30
    red, #150.............................$25-30
1964 Fiat 600 D, white, #311 ....$25-30
1973 Ford Capri 2600 GT, metallic red with
    black roof, #305 ....$25-30
1994 Ford Mustang GT
    Convertible, bright blue, #285 ....$25-30
    Coupe, yellow, #281 ....$25-30
    blue, #282............................$25-30
    red, #280.............................$25-30
    Indy Pace car, red, #287 ....$25-30
1993 Jaguar XJ220
    Coupe, green, #171 ....$25-30
    Coupe, silver, #170 ....$25-30
    GT LeMans, #172 ....$25-30
    GT Martini, #174 ....$25-30
1992 Jaguar XJS
    Convertible, top down, blue, #131...$25-30
    Convertible, top up, silver, #132 ......$25-30
    Coupe, red, #133 ....$25-30
Lamborghini Diablo
    1990 Roadster, blue, #113 ....$25-30
    1990, yellow, #110 ....$25-30
    1992 Roadster, yellow, #112 ....$25-30

1993 Coupe, black, #114 ....$25-30
1994 S, red, #111 ....$25-30
1994 Mercedes-Benz 320 SL
    Convertible, metallic silver, #230 ......$25-30
    Convertible, red, #231 ....$25-30
    Coupe, blue, #234 ....$25-30
    Coupe, gray, #235 ....$25-30
    Coupe, metallic blue, #233 ....$25-30
1991 Nissan 300 ZX
    Convertible, red, #163 ....$25-30
    Monza, multicolor, #165 ....$25-30
    Soft Top, blue, #162 ....$25-30
    Convertible, red, #161 ....$25-30
    Coupe, black, #160 ....$25-30
    Coupe, silver, #164 ....$25-30
1959 Porsche 356A
    Convertible, silver, #229 ....$25-30
    Convertible, top down, metallic yellow,
        #225 ....$25-30
    Convertible, top down, silver, #223 ..$25-30
    Convertible, top up, blue, #224 ......$25-30
    Convertible, top up, red, #222
    Coupe Carrera Panamerica #153, silver,
        #228 ....$25-30
    Coupe Carrera Panamerica #200, white,
        #227 ....$25-30
    Coupe Mille Miglia, silver, #226 ......$25-30
    Coupe, red, #220 ....$25-30
    Coupe, silver, #221 ....$25-30
1994 Volkswagen Concept 1
    Convertible, green, #265 ....$25-30
    Convertible, red, #264 ....$25-30
    Convertible, silver, #266 ....$25-30

Convertible, yellow, #263 ......$25-30
    green, #262 ....$25-30
    red, #261 ....$25-30
    yellow, #260 ....$25-30
Volkswagen Golf Cabriolet
    red, #273 ....$25-30
    silver, #274 ....$25-30
    yellow, #275 ....$25-30
Silverstone, multicolor, #277 ....$25-30
    red, #270 ....$25-30
    silver, #271 ....$25-30
    white, #272 ....$25-30

DG

DG stands for Dave Gilbert, the producer of white metal hand built models and kits from Great Britain. Two series, one regular and one "Dinky style," were produced, although numbers may be intermingled. DG was started in 1973. The DG Dinky series represents models Dinky could have made in the 1930s and 1940s but didn't. Thanks to Harv and Kay Goranson for updates and information.

Collector and dealer Noel Glucksman adds that "DG Models continue to this day by Dave Gilbert under his company name of AUTOCRAFT – Hand Made White Metal Models, 101 Enville Road, Kinver, West Midlands, England. Phone/Fax 011-44-1384-873-239 (from USA).

"He has been making an exquisite line of motorcycles with hand-painted riders for about three years or so," adds Glucksman. "A firm in the USA that sells them is MOTO Mini, McKinney, Texas."

1930 Bentley Speed 6, #4 ....$35-45
1936 Cord, #5 ....$35-45
1944 Dodge 4x4 Army Ambulance, #2 .$35-45
1938 MG Tickford (kit) $50-60
MG Y Saloon (kit) $50-60
1934 Morris "Chivers," #3 ....$35-45
1921 Murphy Duesenberg (kit) $50-60

DG Productions

DG Productions, Inc.
760 Florida Central Parkway
Suite 212
Longwood FL 32750
Customer Service 407-331-1195

DG Productions is a Florida-based manufacturer of a high-quality plastic 1997 GM Topkick model coin banks with working lights and extensive details. D.G. Productions has plans on a series of these trucks. Some have shortened wheel bases, some with different markings, etc., according to wiseg@msdlouky.org in May 1998.

1997 GM Topkick Delivery Truck "Schwan's Ice Cream and Fine Foods," production limit 5,000 ....$50-65

Diamond

Russell Alameda provides the following information on this otherwise unknown brand.

1964 Shelby Cobra 427 SC, white, 1:18, limited edition of 2,100 ....$75

Diapet

Diapet is a popular Japanese brand of quality diecast vehicles produced by Yonezawa Toys.

Acura NSX, 1:40 ....$20-25
Airport Bus, B32 ....$20-25
Bus, 3-Axle Double-Decker, 4½", 11 ....$30-35
Bus "Hishi Nippon," 231 ....$20-25
Cordia XG1600 Turbo, G13 ....$20-25
Corvette, G76 ....$60-75
Datsun 280Z, G3, G116 ....$20-25
Datsun 280Z Police, P53 ....$20-25
Datsun F2 Coupe, G15 ....$20-25
Datsun Leopard 4-door Sedan, G2 ....$20-25
Datsun Mail Van, 271 ....$20-25
Datsun Silvia 200SX, G39/G125 ....$20-25
Datsun Tow Truck, 272 ....$20-25
1930 Duesenberg, G124, 1:27 ....$34
DP2 Backhoe, K23 ....$20-25
DP2 Backhoe/Loader, K24 ....$20-25
Fuso Bus, B36 ....$20-25
Fuso Truck Crane, K30 ....$20-25
Hato Bus, B40 ....$25-30
Hato Double Decker Bus, B47, 1:75 ......$25-30
Honda Acura NSX, SV26, 1:40 ....$25-30
Honda Beat, SV33, 1:35 ....$20-25
Honda Prelude, SV34, 1:40 ....$20-25
Honda Prelude 2.0 SI, G55, 1:40 ....$20-25
Ihi 1600 Clamshell Bucket Crane, K21,
    1:40 ....$34
Ihi IS-110 Power Shovel, K3, 1:50 ....$20-25
Ihi IS-110 Clamshell (Bucket), K5, 1:50 ...$20-25
Ihi IS-110 Track Backhoe, K4, 1:50 ....$20-25
Ihi IS-220 Track Backhoe, K17, 1:40 ....$34
Infiniti Q45, SV18, 1:40 ....$25-30
Isuzu "Shell," 107 ....$20-25
Isuzu Shovel, K53 ....$20-25
Isuzu Mixer, 109 ....$20-25
Isuzu Semi TV, B47 ....$20-25
Jr. Highway Bus, B5, 1:60 ....$25-30
Kawasaki 88 ZII Wheel Loader, K31,
    1:28 ....$30-35
Komatsu D20QF Track Loader, K31,
    1:28 ....$20-25
Kubota Tractor, 1:23 ....$20-25
Lexus Coupe, SV22 ....$30-35
Lincoln Continental Mk IV, 01427 ....$30-35
Mack car carrier, T54, 1:40 ....$37
Mazda Cosmo 2-door Hardtop, 1:40 ....$20-25
Mazda Miata MX 5, SV14, 1:40 ....$20-25
Mazda RX7, SV35, 1:40 ....$25-30
Mazda RX7 Police, P57 ....$20-25
Mercedes-Benz 230S 4-door Sedan, 167 .$25-30
Mercedes-Benz 560SEL, G8, 1:40 ....$25-30
Mini Cooper 1000, SV3 ....$25-30
Mitsubishi Crawler Crane, K39, 1:60 ....$20-25
Mitsubishi GTO, SV27, 1:40 ....$20-25
Mitsubishi MS280 Track Backhoe, K42,
    1:60 ....$20-25
Mitsubishi School Bus, B35 ....$20-25

Mitsubishi Starion 2000 GSR Coupe, silver,
    G17 ....$35-40
Neoplan Skyliner Bus, B41, 1:60 ....$30-35
Nissan Ambulance, P13, 1:35 ....$20-25
Nissan Cedric Ambulance, 283 ....$20-25
Nissan Cedric Police, P64 ....$20-25
Nissan Cedric Taxi, P65 ....$20-25
Nissan Cedric Ultima Station Taxi, P29 ...$35-40
Nissan Cherry Camper, T8 ....$20-25
Nissan Kombi "1008," T4 ....$20-25
Nissan Kombi Police, P3 ....$20-25
Nissan Fairlady 300 ZX, red, SV15 ......$25-30
Nissan Infiniti, SV18, 1:40 ....$25-30
Nissan Prairie, G22 ....$20-25
Nissan S&B 30 Mini Backhoe, K16,
    1:26 ....$30-35
Nissan Safari, T1 ....$20-25
Nissan Silvia Coupe, G37 ....$20-25
Nissan Skyline Police car, P43, 1:30 .....$20-25
Nissan Taxi, P16/P65, 1:40 ....$20-25
1980 Pontiac Firebird, G67 ....$20-25
Porsche 911S, red with black interior, 248,
    1:40 ....$20-25
Porsche Turbo, metallic brown/silver, blue win-
    dows, black interior, G-47, 1:40 .....$20-25
Porsche 911S, metallic gold, #0158,
    1:43 ....$20-25
Rolls-Royce Silver Shadow, G71, 1:40 ...$25-30
Sakai Roller, K8 ....$20-25
Sakai TS150 Tire Roller, K12, 1:40 ......$20-25
School Bus, B4 ....$20-25
Seibu Tour Bus, B1, 1:75 ....$20-25
Sightseeing Bus, B39 ....$20-25
Subaru Leon 2-door Hardtop, G128 ......$20-25
Subaru Mail Van, 462 ....$20-25
Sumitomo-FMC LS3400 Track H, K37,
    1:42 ....$35-40
Suzuki Fronte Police, 296 ....$20-25
Toyota 2000GT, 162 ....$20-25
Toyota carib (Tercel) 4x4 Wagon, G23 .$20-25
Toyota carib (Tercel) Radio car, P5 ......$20-25
Toyota Celica 2800 GT/G5 ....$20-25
Toyota Corolla 1500SR 3-Door Sedan,
    G21 ....$20-25
Toyota Corolla Levin Coupe, G29 ....$20-25
Toyota Crown Police, 613/P62 ....$20-25
Toyota Crown Taxi, P63 ....$20-25
Toyota Fire Chief's car, P17, 1:40 ....$20-25
Toyota Hiace Ambulance, P43/P55,
    1:36 ....$15-20
Toyota Hiace Camper, T6 ....$20-25
Toyota Jobsun 7 Skid Loader, K11, 1:22 .$25-30
Toyota Landcruiser FJ-60, T-100, 1:30 ....$30-35
Toyota Landcruiser Army, T2, 1:30 ....$20-25
Toyota Lexus SC, SV22, 1:40 ....$25-30
Toyota Mini School Bus, B37 ....$20-25

Toyota Pickup 4x4, T3 ....$20-25
Toyota Police Van, P42 ....$20-25
Toyota Previa Van, T-70, 1:40 ....$25-30
Toyota Soarer (Lexus) Coupe, G1/G27 .$20-25
Toyota Supra 3.0GT Turbo, G50, 1:40 .$20-25
Volkswagen 1300 Beetle, 165 ....$20-25
Volkswagen 1600TL, 157 ....$20-25
Yamaha Snowmobile, 287 ....$20-25

Dibro

Dibro, 8/10 Lily Road, Liverpool, England, manufactured crude friction-motor tinplate replicas of several Dinky Toys during the 1950s and 1960s. Dibro specialized in small metal clockwork toys and toy watches.

Austin A40 Devon 1948 (copy of Dinky Toys
    40D) $30-45
Hudson Commodore sedan 1948 (copy of Dinky
    Toys 139B) $30-45
Jaguar XK120 coupé 1952 (copy of Dinky Toys
    157) $30-45
Chrysler Airflow sedan 1934 (copy of Dinky Toys
    30A) $30-45

Dicascale

Dicascale of Japan is reported to have produced a number of diecast cars, but only one has been documented.

Nippon Kotsu Coach, 1:100, #212 ....$9-12

Diecast Promotions

Trademark Models / Highway 61 Collectibles
P.O. Box 882
10478 St. Joseph Drive
Dubuque IA 52004-0882
Toll Free: 877-874-5467
Direct: 563-583-0636
http://12.26.242.144/trucks.cfm

Diecast Promotions offers 1:64 scale trucks and motor coaches produced by F.F. Ertl III, Inc. Trademark Models represents the company's line of agricultural and construction vehicles, and Highway 61 offers an assortment of model cars.

Dimension 4 (also Specialty Diecast, Lucky Plan, Speedway Collection, Mark One) (also see Hot Pursuit)

Dimension 4
c/o Specialty Diecast Company
370 Miller Road
Medford, NJ
800-432-1933

First discovered in January 1998, the Speedway Collection is a series of 1:43 scale diecast NASCAR models manufactured by Lucky Plan Industries, produced by Specialty Diecast Company, distributed by Dimension 4 of Bell California and packaged in a clear plastic display box with the name "Mark One Collectibles" on top. Confused? I am. It would appear to be a marketing collaboration to offer yet another line of racing collectibles to an apparently starved market. In fact, there appears to be a glut of new diecast racing collectibles flooding the market in recent months, from Kenner's Winner's Circle collection to numerous Racing Champions' permutations and Mattel's Hot Wheels Pro Racing series, not to mention Racing Collectibles Club of America, Action Racing, and others.

The distinction, if indeed there is any, is that the Speedway Collection is the first high-quality low-priced series offered in mass-market retail stores such as Wal-Mart. Models sell for about $5 each. Listed below is just one of those models. Most recent models from Lucky Plan are being sold under the Race Image brand, which also happens to be a brand produced by Corgi. Dimension 4 purchased Hot Pursuit Collectibles in 1997 shortly after Hot Pursuit was started, then went out of business in December 1999.

Pontiac Grand Prix, Bobby Labonte "#18," "Interstate Batteries," #97018 ....$9-12

Dinkum

It was previously assumed that Dinkum toys of Australia were given their name to capitalize on the similar-sounding Dinky brand name of England. But as collector Bill Cross reports, Dinkum is Australian vernacular which, roughly translated, means "good," or "true," as in "fair dinkum, mate!"

Ford Falcon GT, red & black $95-110
1969 Ford Mustang Boss, red, 1:43 ......$65-80
1985 Holden Commodore, white, 1:43 .$35-45
Holden FJ Panel Van, dark blue $85-100

Dinky

Excellent collector reference books have already been written on these great little gems from Great Britain, as indicated in this book's bibliography section. So, instead of trying to duplicate those works, this book will present a short history and highlight only a few of the numerous models produced.

Dinky Toys started out in 1933 as Modelled Miniatures, produced and marketed under the Frank Hornby name, the original manufacturer. Hornby also produced electric trains, and the first models produced were intended as accessories to these train sets.

Simultaneously in Liverpool, England, and Bobigny, France, the British and French Dinky Toys were put into production in 1934. French-made Dinky Toys, particularly the post-war models, are more highly valued in the U.S., and perhaps Europe, because the French models focused on American cars of the era, and serve as accurate models of the era.

The advent of Hot Wheels by Mattel in 1968 posed a major threat to companies such as Dinky Toys, contributing to the close of the French facility in 1972, although Pilen of Spain continued to produce some French Dinky models later in the 1970s, while Solido of France attempted a similar feat in 1981.

The British firm, meanwhile, attempted to stay in business by farming out production of some models to Polistil of Italy and to Universal of Hong Kong. Universal eventually purchased the rights, and incorporated the brand into the Matchbox line, which Universal had purchased in 1982.

Several other firms staked a claim on the Dinky brand from time to time, including Tri-Ang of England in 1963, Mercury of Italy, Mercury Industries based in the US and Canada, Gibbs of Ohio, Best Box/Efsi of the Netherlands, and most notably Meccano of England.

The Dinky brand vanished with the purchase of Matchbox in 1992 by Tyco. All that is now left of Dinky models are there frequent appearance as Matchbox Collectibles out of Beaverton, Oregon, a division of Tyco that markets models through mail-order advertising in such publications as *Parade*, and in specialty magazines such as *Collecting Toys*, *Diecast Digest*, and others.

For a more complete detail of the complete line, Dr. Edward Force's book on Dinky Toys is available in bookstores or by special order.

Modelled Miniatures – The First Dinky Toys, 1933

Delivery Van	$300-350
Farm Tractor	$200-250
Motor Truck	$175-225
Sports Coupe	$250-300
Sports Roadster	$350-400

A Survey of Dinky Toys Through the Years

Austin A105, 1958	$20
Berliet Dump Truck, 1961	$125
Bristol Canadian Pacific Airline, 1959	$95
Brockway Pontoon Bridgelayer Truck, #884, 1961–1970	$1250
Buick Riviera, 1965–1967	$90-120
Buick Roadmaster, 1954	$225-240

Cadillac Superior Ambulance, 1974 .$75-90

Corvair Monza, 1965	$90-110
Ford GT, 1966	$50-65
Hudson Hornet, 1958	$150-175
Jaguar XK120, 1954	$125-140
Johnson Street Sweeper, 1977	$45-55
Lady Penelope's Fab 1 Limousine (from "Thunderbirds" TV Series), #100, 1966–1976	$125-150
Maserati 2000, 1958	$90-105
Meccano Delivery Van, 1934	$250
Mercury Seaplane, 1939	$100
Oldsmobile 88, 1965	$90-105
Packard Super 8, 1939	$250-275
Plymouth Belvedere, 1957	$150-165
Pontiac Police car, 1971	$75-90
Rambler Classic, #006, 1965–1967	$90-105

Rambler Cross Country, 1961 ....$95-110

Riley Saloon, 1947	$85-100
Rolls-Royce Silver Wraith, 1959	$90-105
Rover 3500 Police, 1979	$50-65

Speed of the Wind, 1936, #23 ....$120-135

Star Trek Klingon Battle Cruiser, large, #357, 1980	$550-600
Star Trek Klingon Battle Cruiser, small, 804, 1980	$100-125
Star Trek U.S.S. Enterprise, large, #358, 1976–1980	$600-700
Star Trek U.S.S. Enterprise, small, #803, 1980	$100-125
Studebaker Commander, 1949	$425-450
Studebaker Golden Hawk, 1958	$150-175
Talbot Lago, 1953	$75-90

Viceroy 37 Bus, 1972, #296 ....$25-40

Mini-Dinky

Aston Martin DB6, #17	$15-20
Buick Riviera, #27	$15-20
Cadillac, #20	$15-20
Caterpillar Grader, #99	$15-20
Chevrolet II, #14	$15-20
Corvette Stingray, #12	$15-20
Euclid R40, #97	$15-20
Ferrari 250 LM, #13	$15-20
Ferrari F1 Racing car, #28	$15-20
Ferrari Superfast, #24	$15-20
Fiat 2300 Station Wagon, #21	$15-20
Ford Corsair, #10	$15-20
Ford GT, #29	$15-20
Ford Mustang, #16	$15-20
Ford Zephyr 6, #25	$15-20
International Bulldozer, #94	$15-20
International Skid Shovel, #95	$15-20
Jaguar E-Type, #11	$15-20
Jaguar Mark 10, #33	$15-20
Mercedes-Benz 230 SL, #18	$15-20
Mercedes-Benz 250SE, #26	$15-20
MGB Sports car, #19	$15-20
Michigan Scraper Earth Mover, #98	$15-20

NSU Rho	$45-60
Oldsmobile Toronado, #22	$15-20
Payloader Shovel, #96	$15-20
Rolls Royce Silver Shadow, #15	$15-20
Rover 2000, #23	$15-20
Vauxhall Cresta, #32	$15-20
Volkswagen 1600 TL, #31	$15-20
Volvo 1800S, #30	$15-20

Distler

Distler was a German manufacturer that began producing clockwork, wind-up, and later battery-operated, tin lithographed automobiles in the early 1900s and continued well after WWII. Models marked "Made in Western Germany" were sold just after the war.

BMW Wanderer, wind-up...............$450-550
Coupe with driver, clockwork
    motor $1,250-1,500
Eccentric Saloon car, wind-up, driver's head pops
    through roof, 8".....................$1,000-1,250
Electro Magic 7500 Porsche Cabriolet, lime
    green with red seats, "Made in Western Ger-
    many" circa 1950, battery
    operated $750-1,000
Ford Convertible, multiple speed transmission,
    10"......................................$400-500
Ford Roadster, multiple speed transmission,
    10"......................................$400-500
Jaguar Roadster, multiple speed transmission,
    10"......................................$550-700
Limousine with chauffeur, battery operated head-
    lights, clockwork motor, 12"...$1,750-2,250
Limousine, extended front bumper, rear luggage
    compartment, 15½" $1,450-1,600
Mercedes Convertible Coupe, multiple speed
    transmission, 10"...................$400-500
Mercedes Roadster, multiple speed transmission,
    10"......................................$400-500
Packard Convertible, 1950s $400-500
Saloon, 10" $400-500
Uncle Wiggly car $3,750-4,250

Diti Toys

Rafi Ilivitzky reports, "Diti toys were manufactured in Israel in the 1970s, and Vectis UK has several pictures of them in their archive. I don't know much about them, and that is the reason for asking, "If you do find more info, please let me know."

Dmitriev Workshop

Alex Litovskiy reports of the Dmitriev Workshop brand from Russia but doesn't provide any details.

DMP Studios

DMP is a Canadian company that specializes in custom hand-built or "studio" models and factory-approved conversions of Brooklins.

1961 Chevrolet Impala Convertible, (converted
    Brooklin Impala Sports Coupe), Honduras
    maroon..$125

Doepke

At the end of World War II, The Charles Wm. Doepke Mfg. Co., Inc. of Rossmoyne, Ohio, began manufacturing large, durable toys called Doepke (pronounced DEP-key) "Model Toys." Production continued until 1959. Doepke toys are sturdy large scale cast metal and pressed steel toys with heavy rubber tires.

Adams Diesel Road Grader, 26" long,
    #2006..................................$350-500
American LaFrance Aerial Ladder Fire Truck, 23"
    long, #2014.........................$500-650
American LaFrance Aerial Ladder Truck, 28" long,
    #2008..................................$650-800
American LaFrance Pumper Fire Truck, 18" long,
    #2010..................................$500-650
Barber-Greene High Capacity Bucket Loader, 13"
    high, #2001 ....$500-650
Barber-Greene Mobile High-Capacity Bucket
    Loader, 22" long, #2013 ....$500-650
Caterpillar D6 Tractor and Bulldozer, 15" long,
    #2012..................................$600-750
Clark Airport Tractor and Baggage Trailers,
    #2015..................................$500-650
Euclid Earth Hauler Truck, 27" long,
    #2009..................................$450-600
Heiliner Earth Scraper, 29" long,
    #2011 ....$450-600
Jaeger Concrete Mixer, 15" long,
    #2002..................................$600-750
Jaguar, 1955, #2018 ....$850-1,000
MG, 1954 15" long, #2017...........$750-900
Searchlight Truck, 1955, #2023.$1,250-1,500
Unit Mobile Crane, 11½", #2007......$450-600
Wooldridge Heavy Duty Earth Hauler, 25" long,
    #2000..................................$600-750

Doll & Company

An obscure brand of unknown origin, Doll & Company produced at least two steam-powered toy vehicles, now extremely rare and valuable.

Open Touring car, live steam motor, hand-painted
    tin, four opening doors, 19"...$3,750-4,250
Open Bed Truck, live steam motor, chain driven,
    19".................................$6,250-6,750

Doorkey

Doorkey models are mostly 1:43 scale diecast made in various worldwide factories for the Holland-based company. Note that besides being marketed under the Doorkey brand, they are also produced for AHC of Holland. The list includes description, scale, origin, model number, and current value.

BMW 325i 1994, 1:43, China, DO401..$9-12
BMW 507 Sports, 1:43, China, DO155.$20-30
BMW 2000 Saloon, 1:43, China,
    DO154 ....$20-30
DAF MB230 Bus Lila Pause (300 made), 1:43,
    made in Spain for AHC, refinished in Holland,
    D200LP $60-70
DAF den Oudsten Bus Politie (300 made), 1:43
    made in Spain for AHC, refinished in Holland,
    D200DP $60-70
Ford Escort Van 1993 various colors, Spain,
    DO110.......................................$25-35
Lexus SC 400 1994, 1:43, China, DO403.$9-12
Mercedes-Benz 500SEL 1994, 1:43, China,
    DO402 ....$9-12
Mercedes-Benz 100 Van
    plain colors 1:50, Spain, DO101T...$25-35
    Spanish Telephones 1:50, Spain,
        DO101T $25-35
    Spanish Post 1:50, Spain, DO101C..$25-35
Nissan Maxima
    Spain, DO115 ....$25-35
    with spoiler, Spain, DO114 ....$25-35
Nissan Serena "People carrier," Spain,
    DO116..$25-35
Nissan Micra
    3-door right hand drive, Spain, DO117.$25-35
    3-door left hand drive, Spain, DO117 .$25-35
    5-door right hand drive, Spain, DO118.$25-35
    5-door left hand drive, Spain, DO118 .$25-35
Opel Kadett Combo Van, left hand drive, Spain,
    DO106 ....$25-35
SEAT Ibiza Hatchback, Spain, DO125...$25-35
SEAT Toledo various colors, Spain, DO126.$25-35
Suzuki Samurai 4 x 4, Spain, DO104 ....$25-35
Toyota Celica, 1:43, China, DO150.....$20-30
Toyota Landcruiser, 1:43, China, DO151 .$20-30
Toyota MR-2, 1:43, China, DO152 ......$20-30
Toyota Supra, 1:43, China, DO153 .....$20-30
Vauxhall Astramax Van
    left hand drive, Q8 Lubricants, Spain,
        DO108Q $30-40
    right hand drive, Spain, DO108Q....$25-35
Volvo 440
    GL 1994 restyle, Spain, DO130......$25-35
    Turbo 1994 restyle, Spain, DO131 ..$25-35
    Politie (Dutch police), 1:43 made in Spain for
        AHC, refinished in Holland,
        D130DP $45-55
Volvo 460 Saloon 1996, Spain, DO1xx .$25-35
Volvo 480 Turbo 1994 restyle, Spain,
    DO133 ....$25-35
Volvo 850
    GLT (10 colors), Spain, DO135 ....$25-35
    Estate car 1996, Spain, DO136......$25-35
    T-5 (10 colors) stock, Spain, DO139.$25-35

GLT Polis (Swedish police), 1:43 made in Spain for AHC, refinished in Holland, D135SP.................................$35-45

GLT Douane (Customs), 1:43 made in Spain for AHC, refinished in Holland, D135D..................................$35-45

Volvo 850 GLT Politie (Dutch police), 1:43 made in Spain for AHC, refinished in Holland, D135DP.................................$35-45

Volvo B10M Bus Maastricht (300 made), 1:43 made in Spain for AHC, refinished in Holland, D200SM................................$60-70

Dragon Wings
Dragon Models
B1-10/F., 603-609 Castle Peak Rd.
Kong Nam Industrial Building
Tsuen Wan, N. T., Hong Kong
phone: (852) 2493-0215
fax: (852) 2411-0587
e-mail: info@dragon-models.com
website: www.dragon-models.com

Dragon Wings are 1:400 scale precision diecast airliner miniatures of exceptional quality from Dragon Models of Hong Kong.

Druge Brothers
Druge Brothers Manufacturing Company of Oakland, California, produced a couple of scale model lumber yard "straddle buggies" designed for hauling lumber. The company produced just a few models around 1948, original price $9.75. Models appear to be in 1:50 scale.

Cari-Car Lumber carrier, yellow..........$200-250
Hyster Lumber carrier, yellow $225-275

Dugu
One of the premier miniature model companies of Italy was known as Dugu, a company that produced some beautiful models in 1:43 to 1:50 scale. The company started in 1963 by marketing Miniautotoys and Museo models. They represented real cars from the Automotive Museum of Torino, Italy.

Miniautotoys are high quality 1:43 scale models similar to Rio, while Museo models are 1:50 scale simplified, less expensive models. A third series called Sispla was also produced in 1974.

Dugu Miniautotoys, 1:43
1896 Bernardi 3.5HP
   top up, 1967, #9 ....$50-65
   top down, 1966, #10....................$50-65

1936 Cord Phaeton
   top up, 1968, #18 ....$180-200
   top down, 1968, #20..............$180-200
1931 Duesenberg SJ Town car
   1967, #13 ....$140-165
   1968, #19 ....$135-150

1899 Fiat 3.5HP
   top down, 1966, #11 ....$45-60
   top up, 1966, #12 ....$45-60
1907 Fiat Grand Prix, 1964, #4 ....$55-70
1911 Fiat 4
   Closed Tourer, 1962, #1 ....$50-65
   Open Tourer, 1963, #3.................$50-65
1911 Fiat S-76 Record Car, 1971, #24 .$80-95
1925 Fiat 509
   2-door Sedan, 1967, #14 ....$50-65
   Open Tourer, 1967, #15 ....$50-65
1934 Fiat Balilla Coppa D'Oro, 1968,
   #17 ....$55-70
Fiat-Eldridge Grand Prix, 1975, #23 .....$80-95
1907 Itala Palombella, 1966, #6 ....$50-65
1909 Itala 35/45HP Limousine, 1968,
   #16 ....$50-65
1912 Itala 25/35HP
   Closed Tourer, 1965, #7 ....$50-65
   Open Tourer, 1965, #8.................$50-65
1925 Lancia Lambda
   Sedan, 1962, #2 ....$50-65
   Torpedo, 1964, #5 ....$50-65
1934 Rolls-Royce Silver Ghost
   top up, 1969, #21 ....$120-145
   top down, 1969, #22................$120-145

Dugu Museo, 1:50
1923 Ansaldo 4C Open Tourer, 1970,
   #M12.......................................$40-50
1893 Benz Victoria, 1964, #M1 ....$40-50
1899 Benz Estate car, 1964, #M3 ....$40-50
1908 Brixia Zust Phaeton, 1967, #M9 ..$40-50
1948 Cisitalia 202 Coupe, 1968, #M10.$55-65
1902 Darracq Tourer, 1964, #M4 ....$40-50
1903 De Dion-Bouton Populaire, 1964,
   #M5 ....$40-50
1936 Fiat 500A
   Coupe, 1966, #M8......................$60-70
   Convertible Coupe, 1969, #M13....$60-70
1923 Fiat 519S Tourer, 1971, #M14 ..$40-50
1914 Lancia Theta, 1968, #M11........$40-50
1908 Legnano 6/8HP Spider
   top up, 1965, #M6 ....$40-50
   top down, 1965, #M7..................$60-70
1894 Peugeot Vis-a-Vis, 1964, #M2 .....$40-50

Dugu Sispla, 1:43, 1974
Fiat 56 550HP Farm Tractor, #2 ....$260-280

Fiat 697N Dump Truck, #3.................$90-105
Fiat 90NC Dump Truck, #4a $90-105
Fiat Tank Truck, #5............................$90-105
OM Dump Truck, #4b.........................$90-105
Same Centauro Farm Tractor, #1 ....$260-280

Duravit
Duravit models are made in Argentina.

Mercedes Semi Oil Truck, 23"..............$20-25

Durham Classics
A small assortment of Durham Classics of Canada is currently available. These American classic cars are exquisitely replicated in white metal and represent some of the best-detailed and most accurate 1:43 scale models on the market.

1941 Chevrolet
   Convertible, top down, #10A $95-115
   Coupe, blue, #5 ....$95-99
   Coupe "Michigan State Police," #5D .$95-115
   Coupe "Idaho State Police," #5E $95-115
   Panel Delivery Van, #12................$95-115
   Panel Delivery Van "Labatts," #12B.$95-115
   Suburban "Niagara Tours," #17 ..$105-125
1934 Chrysler Airflow
   Two-door 30th Anniversary, #1F...$115-135
   "California Highway Patrol," #1G .$115-135
1939 Ford Panel Delivery
   "Sacramento Bee," #3S $115-135
   "The Sacramento Bee," #13A........$95-115
1941 Ford Coupe, #15A $95-115
1951 Ford Monarch 2-door Coupe,
   #14A.......................................$95-115
1953 Ford
   Pick-Up, blue, #2........................$95-115
   Pick-Up, red with "Wurlitzer" juke box,
   #2H $115-135
   Telephone Repair Truck "General," #6A.$105-125
1954 Ford Panel Wagon
   "Canadian Colonial Airways," #7 ..$95-115
   "Prairie Airways," #7A $95-115
1938 Lincoln Zephyr
   Coupe, black, #4........................$95-115
   Convertible, top down, #9............$95-115
   Convertible, top up, #9D............$95-115

Dust & Glory (see Great American Dreamcar)

Duvi
Albert Sattler of Melbourne, Australia, wrote via e-mail, "I have recently acquired an exquisite 1:43 scale Renault Dauphine from DUVI. I can

only tell you what's on the box: 'Vente Interdite Aux Moins De 14 Ans.' Does that help at all?" Unfortunately it doesn't, since it appears to be French for "Not intended for children under 14 years." Mr. Sattler didn't mention what price he paid, so an educated guess is all I can provide.

Renault Dauphine, 1:43 ....$45-60

Dux

Dux of Germany at one time produced a series of large-scale diecast models, the exact scale of which is unknown.

Mercedes-Benz 300 Sedan....................$40-65
Mercedes-Benz 300 Streamliner Racer....$50-75
Mercedes-Benz W196 Gullwing $40-65
Porsche 356 ....$40-65
Studebaker...$40-65
Veritas Comet $60-85
Volkswagen $40-65

Dyna-Mo (see Dyna-Model Products Company)

Dyna-Model Products Company

1:87 scale Dyna-Mo brand models are manufactured on Long Island, New York, specifically for use with HO gauge railroad layouts. They feature cast metal bodies with separate tires and wheels. (Some assembly required.) Models are available pre-painted or unpainted.

Airport Platform Tractor & Two Baggage Wagons
    painted $8-10
    unpainted $6-8
Buick 1908 painted $7-9
    unpainted $4-6
Caterpillar Bulldozer painted.................$10-12
    unpainted $6-8
Caterpillar Crawler painted $8-10
    unpainted $5-7
Coal Conveyor painted...........................$6-8
    unpainted $4-6
Ford Pickup Truck 1947 painted................$7-9
    unpainted $4-6
Fork Lift (2-pack) painted $10-12
    unpainted $6-8
Maxwell 1911 painted..............................$7-9
    unpainted $4-6
Packard Twin Six 1916 painted..................$7-9
    unpainted $4-6
Stanley Steamer 1909 painted $7-9
    unpainted $4-6
Stutz Bearcat 1914 painted.......................$7-9
    unpainted $4-6

Dynamic (also see Sunnyside)

A recent find revealed a toy car in a blister-pack labeled Dynamic. The package's resemblance to a Majorette blisterpack was obviously more than coincidental. It is an obvious attempt to copy Majorette's packaging and capitalize on Majorette's popularity. In addition, only the packaging says "Dynamic." Inside, the model itself is found to be made by Sunnyside.

Dyson

J. B. Dyson & Sons of Birmingham, England, produced various toys and games from 1932 until 1939, but are known to produce only three lead cast (slush mold) toy cars, clearly marked "Dyson" and "British Made."

1931 SS Swallow Wolseley Hornet Two-Seater
    Roadster, 1:43 ....$50-65
1931 Jaguar SS 1 Coupe, 1:43 ....$50-65
1932 MG Magic Midget Record Car, 1:43 .$50-65

E

Eagle Collectibles / Eagle's Race

Eagle's Race and Eagle Collectibles are brands of Universal Hobbies of Hong Kong, introduced in 1998 after the purchase of Jouef of France in 1996.

Alfa Romeo Spyder
    Hardtop, red, 1:18, #3302 ....$30-32
    Hardtop, silver, 1:18, #3306 ....$30-32
    black, 1:18, #3304......................$30-32
    metallic green, 1:18, #3308 ....$30-32
    red, 1:18, #3301 ....$30-32
    white, Limited Edition, 1:18, #3307 .$35-37
    yellow, 1:18, #3305 ....$30-32
1941 Chevrolet
    Convertible Hot Rod, 1:18, #4355 ..$30-32
    Convertible beige, 1:18, #4350 .....$30-32
    Convertible black, 1:18, #4352 ......$30-32
    Convertible red, 1:18, #4351 ....$30-32
    Deluxe Soft Top, 1:18, #4353 ....$30-32
    Deluxe Soft Top, 1:18, #4354 ....$30-32
1963 Chevrolet Corvette Grand Sport
    #2 Sebring, 1:43, #2001 ....$18-20
    #3 Sebring, 1:43, #2002 ....$18-20
    #67 Road America, 1:43, #2006 ...$18-20

#80 Nassau, 1:43, #2003 ....$18-20

    Roadster #7, 1:43, #2007 ....$18-20
    Roadster #10 1:43, #2005 ....$18-20
    Roadster #12, 1:43, #2004 ....$18-20
1969 Dodge Charger Daytona
    #22, 1:43, #1403.....................$18-20
    #6, 1:43, #1405 ....$18-20
    #71, 1:43, #1401 ....$18-20
    #99, 1:43, #1404 ....$18-20
    Chrysler Race, 1:43, #1402 ....$18-20
    Street, white, 1:43, #1408 ....$18-20

Street, black, 1:43, #1410...................$18-20

    Street, blue, 1:43, #1409.............$18-20
    Street, dark blue, 1:43, #1407.......$18-20
    Street, red, 1:43, #1406 ....$18-20
Dodge Prowler
    Convertible 1999, black, 1:43,
        #3644 ....$18-20
    Convertible 1999, purple, 1:43,
        #3640 ....$18-20
    Convertible 1999, red, 1:43, #3646.$18-20
    Convertible 1999, yellow, 1:43,
        #3642 ....$18-20
    Convertible "PPG," 1:43, #3648.....$18-20
    Soft Top 1999, black, 1:43, #3645 .$18-20
    Soft Top 1999, purple, 1:43, #3641.$18-20
    Soft Top 1999, red, 1:43, #3647...$18-20
    Soft Top 1999, yellow, 1:43, #3643.$18-20
Dodge Ram 2500 V10
    amethyst, 1:43, #3655 ....$18-20
    black, 1:43, #3651......................$18-20
    chestnut, 1:43, #3656 ....$18-20
    gray and silver, 1:43, #3652.........$18-20
    green and silver, 1:43, #3653 ....$18-20
    red and silver, 1:43, #3654 ....$18-20
Dodge Viper
    ACR Record, 1:43, #3667 ....$18-20
    GT2 Champion, Limited Edition, 1:43,
        #3665 ....$20-22
    GTS 1996, blue and white, 1:43,
        #3601 ....$18-20
    GTS 1998, red and white, 1:43, #3628 .$18-20
    GTS 1998, silver and blue, 1:43,
        #3630 ....$18-20
    GTS 1999, black and silver, 1:43,
        #3631 ....$18-20
    GTS PPG Pace car, 1:43, #3666....$18-20

GTS-4 #53 Le Mans, 1:43, #3660 .. $18-20
GTS-R #48 Le Mans, 1:43, #3607 ... $18-20
GTS-R #49 Le Mans, 1:43, #3604 ... $18-20
GTS-R #5, white and blue, 1:43,
    #3603 .... $18-20
GTS-R #50 Le Mans, 1:43, #3608 ... $18-20
GTS-R #51 GT2 Champion, 1:43,
    #3662 .... $18-20
GTS-R #51 Le Mans, 1:43, #3605 ... $18-20
GTS-R #51 Le Mans, 1:43, #3661 ... $18-20
GTS-R #52 GT2 Champion, 1:43,
    #3616 .... $18-20
GTS-R #53 GT2 2nd, 1:43, #3663 .. $18-20
GTS-R #61 Le Mans, 1:43, #3617 ... $18-20
GTS-R #62 Le Mans, 1:43, #3614 ... $18-20
GTS-R #63 Le Mans, 1:43, #3615 ... $18-20
GTS-R #64 Le Mans, 1:43, #3612 ... $18-20
GTS-R #98 Daytona, 1:43, #3606 ... $18-20
GTS-R Taisan 1997, 1:43, #3618 .... $18-20
GTS-R TAISAN 1998, 1:43, #3664 ... $18-20
GTS-R, black, 1:43, #3611 .... $18-20
RT/10 #40 Le Mans, 1:43, #3609 ... $18-20
RT/10 #41 Le Mans, 1:43, #3610 ... $18-20
RT/10 1996, blue and white, 1:43,
    #3624 .... $18-20
RT/10 1996, silver and blue, 1:43,
    #3627 .... $18-20
RT/10 1996, white and blue, 1:43,
    #3620 .... $18-20
RT/10 Soft Top, black, 1:43, #3621 ... $18-20

1932 Ford
Coupe "EAT MY DUST," 1:43, #1212 .. $18-20
Coupe "SHARK," 1:43, #1208 .... $18-20
Coupe, black and blue, 1:43, #1209 .. $18-20
Coupe, blue and red, 1:43, #1211 .. $18-20
Coupe, purple and pink, 1:43, #1207 .. $18-20
Coupe, red, 1:43, #1210 .... $18-20
Roadster, black, 1:43, #1202 .... $18-20

Roadster, black with yellow flames, 1:43, #1206 .... **$18-20**

Roadster, light blue, 1:43, #1203 ..... $18-20
Roadster, red and yellow, 1:43, #1204 ... $18-20
Roadster, white and purple, 1:43,
    #1205 .... $18-20
Roadster, yellow, 1:43, #1201 .... $18-20

1940 Ford
Coupe, black, 1:18, #3801 .... $30-32
Coupe, burgundy, 1:18, #3810 .... $30-32

Coupe, cream, 1:18, #3808 .... $30-32
Coupe, dark metallic, blue, 1:18,
    #3803 .... $30-32
Coupe, gray, 1:18, #3811 .... $30-32
Coupe, red, 1:18, #3802 .... $30-32
Deluxe Coupe, black, 1:18, #3801 ...... $22
Deluxe Coupe, red, 1:18, #3802 .... $22
Deluxe Coupe, white, 1:18, #3808 ...... $22
Deluxe Hot Rod, black with yellow flames,
    1:18, #3806 .... $22
Deluxe Hot Rod, blue with pink flames, 1:18,
    #3805 .... $22
Deluxe Hot Rod, red with yellow flames, 1:18,
    #3804 .... $22
Deluxe Hot Rod, yellow with red flames 1:18,
    #3807 .... $22
Hot Rod green and yellow, 1:18,
    #3814 .... $30-32
Hot Rod, black and yellow, 1:18,
    #3806 .... $30-32
Hot Rod, blue and pink, 1:18,
    #3805 .... $30-32
Hot Rod, purple and red, 1:18,
    #3812 .... $30-32
Hot Rod, red and yellow, 1:18,
    #3804 .... $30-32
Hot Rod, yellow and red, 1:18,
    #3807 .... $30-32

Ford GT40
#1, blue, 2nd 24 Hrs. Le Mans 1966, 1:18,
    #3039 .... $20
#1 Le Mans 1966, 1:18, #3039 ..... $30-32
#2, black, 1st 24 Hrs Le Mans 1966, 1:18,
    #3019 .... $20
#2 Le Mans 1966, 1:18, #3019 ..... $30-32
#5, gold, 3RD 24 H Le Mans 1966 1:18,
    #3040 .... $20
#5 Le Mans 1966, 1:18, #3040 ..... $30-32
#6 Le Mans 1969, 1:18, #3008 ..... $30-32
#22 Sebring 1969, 1:43, #1138 .... $18-20

#98 Daytona Winner 1966, 1:43, #1120 ..$18-20

Mk II #3 Le Mans, 1:18, #3168 .... $30-32
Mk II #57 Le Mans, 1:43, #1139 .... $18-20
Mk II #6 Le Mans, 1:18, #3171 .... $30-32
Mk II #68 Le Mans, 1:18, #3172 .... $30-32
Mk II #8 Le Mans, 1:18, #3164 .... $30-32
Street, green and black, 1:18, #3174 .. $30-32
Street, silver, 1:18, #3173 .... $30-32

Ford Model T
Dreyer's, 1:18, #4305 .... $30-32
Ford Service, 1:18, #4306 .... $30-32
Police, 1:18, #4304 .... $30-32
Touring, black, 1:18, #4301 .... $30-32
Touring, dark blue, 1:18, #4303 ...... $30-32
Touring, red, 1:18, #4302 .... $30-32

1965 Ford Mustang Fastback
red with blue stripes, 1:18, #3159 .... $21
yellow, 1:18, #3178 .... $30-32
dark green, 1:18, #3169 .... $30-32
light blue, 1:18, #3170 .... $30-32

1965 Ford Mustang GT350
Hertz white & gold, 1:18, #3154 .... $20
Shelby, white & dark blue, 1:18, #3101 .. $20
blue and white, 1:18, #3128 .... $30-32
red and white, 1:18, #3116 .... $30-32
white and blue, 1:18, #3101 .... $30-32

1966 Ford Mustang
GT350, black and red, 1:18, #3167 ... $30-32
GT350, blue and dark blue, 1:18,
    #3152 .... $30-32
GT350, green and yellow, 1:18,
    #3153 .... $30-32
GT350, pink and white, 1:18,
    #3166 .... $30-32
GT350, red and blue, 1:18, #3159 ... $30-32
Hertz, black and gold, 1:18, #3118 ... $30-32
Hertz, green and gold, 1:18, #3175 ... $30-32
Hertz, red and gold, 1:18, #3124 .... $30-32
Hertz, white and gold, 1:18, #3154 ... $30-32

1994 Ford Mustang
Convertible, black, 1:18, #3131 ...... $30-32
Convertible, metallic blue, 1:18,
    #3176 .... $30-32
Convertible, orange and black, 1:18,
    #3138 .... $30-32
Coupe, black and gold, 1:18,
    #3135 .... $30-32
Coupe, silver, 1:18, #3177 .... $30-32
Coupe, blue, 1:18, #3158 .... $30-32
Coupe, blue and white, 1:18,
    #3155 .... $30-32
Coupe, red and gold, 1:18, #3157 .. $30-32
Coupe, white and blue, 1:18,
    #3156 .... $30-32

Ford Mustang Mach III
black, 1:43, #1049 .... $18-20
red, 1:43, #1005 .... $18-20
yellow, 1:43, #1050 .... $18-20

Land Rover
Hardtop AA Rescue, 1:18, #4401 .... $30-32
Hardtop, beige and brown, 1:18,
    #4402 .... $30-32
Pickup, black, 1:18, #4406 .... $30-32
Pickup, red and white, 1:18, #4405 ... $30-32

Soft Top Medic, 1:18, #4404 ....$30-32
Soft Top, bright green, 1:18, #4403 ...$30-32

Land Rover Freelander
　closed, light gold, 1:43, #1506 ....$18-20
　closed, light green, 1:43, #1504 .....$18-20
　closed, light purple, 1:43, #1505 ...$18-20
　open silver, 1:43, #1503 ....$18-20
　open, black, 1:43, #1501 ....$18-20
　open, red, 1:43, #1502 ....$18-20

1949 Mercury
　Coupe, black, 1:43, #1550 ....$18-20
　Coupe, red, 1:43, #1551 ....$18-20
　Custom, black and yellow, 1:43,
　　#1556......................................$18-20
　Custom, purple and yellow, 1:43,
　　#1554......................................$18-20
　Custom, red and yellow, 1:43,
　　#1557......................................$18-20
　Custom, silver and green, 1:43,
　　#1555......................................$18-20
　Fire Chief, red, 1:43, #1553 ...$18-20
　Police, black and white, 1:43,
　　#1552......................................$18-20

MGB
　#202 Targa Florio 1968, 1:43,
　　#1140......................................$18-20
　#47 Marathon 1966, 1:43, #1092 ..$18-20
　GT "JUBILEE," Limited Edition, 1:43,
　　#1155......................................$20-22
　GT East Sussex Police, 1:43, #1150...$18-20
　GT, Limited Edition, 1:43, #1154 .....$20-22
　GT, purple, 1:43, #1152 ....$18-20
　GT, red, 1:43, #1151 ....$18-20
　GT, white, 1:43, #1153..................$18-20
　Mk II Convertible, Limited Edition, bright green,
　　1:43, #1021 ....$18-20
　Mk II Convertible, Limited Edition, light blue,
　　1:43, #1020 ....$18-20
　Mk II Convertible, Limited Edition, light blue,
　　1:43, #1060 ....$18-20
　Mk II Police, black, 1:43, #1063 .....$18-20
　Mk II Police, white, 1:43, #1064 .....$18-20
　Mk II Soft Top, orange, 1:43, #1059 ..$18-20
　Mk II Soft Top, yellow, 1:43, #1062 ...$18-20
　Mk II, black and silver, Limited Edition, 1:43,
　　#1065......................................$20-22
　Mk II, bronze and gold, Limited Edition, 1:43,
　　#1066......................................$20-22

MGF 1.8L
　Convertible, bright green, 1:43,
　　#1071......................................$18-20
　Convertible, orange, 1:43, #1073...$18-20
　Convertible, purple, 1:43, #1072 .....$18-20
　Convertible, red, 1:43, #1070 ....$18-20
　Soft Top, blue, 1:43, #1075 ....$18-20
　Soft Top, burgundy, 1:43, #1076 .....$18-20

Soft Top, light gray, 1:43, #1074 .....$18-20

Porsche
　1971 AFRICA SAFARI, Limited Edition, 1:43,
　　#1603......................................$25-27
　1973 AFRICA SAFARI, Limited Edition, 1:43,
　　#1601......................................$25-27
　1974 AFRICA SAFARI, Limited Edition, 1:43,
　　#1602......................................$25-27

1973 Porsche Carrera
　black and red, 1:18, #3204 ....$30-32
　blue, 1:18, #3207 ....$30-32
　green and black, 1:18, #3206........$30-32
　light blue, 1:18, #3211 ....$30-32
　orange, 1:18, #3214 ....$30-32
　orange and black, 1:18, #3215.......$30-32
　red, 1:18, #3205 ....$30-32
　silver, 1:18, #3210 ....$30-32
　white and red, 1:18, #3201 ....$30-32
　yellow and green, 1:18, #3203 ....$30-32

Porsche 911 2.4L
　green, 1:43, #1018 ....$18-20
　red, 1:43, #1019 ....$18-20
　yellow, 1:43, #1096 ....$18-20
　#48 Le Mans, 1:18, #3209 ....$30-32
　#80 Le Mans, 1:18, #3208 ....$30-32
　silver, 1:43, #1130 ....$18-20
　Tour De France, 1:18, #3212 ....$30-32

Porsche 911S
　#15 Monte Carlo, 1:43, #1041 .....$18-20
　#80 Le Mans, 1:43, #1044 ....$18-20

Porsche 917K
　#2 Daytona 1970, 1:18, #3904 .....$30-32
　#2 Kyalami, 1:18, #3908 ....$30-32
　#2 Monza 1971, 1:18, #3903.......$30-32
　#22, Le Mans 1971, 1:18, #3901 ..$30-32
　#3 Daytona 1970, 1:18, #3907 .....$30-32
　#3 Sebring 1971, 1:18, #3905 ......$30-32
　#57, Le Mans 1971, 1:18, #3906..$30-32

Porsche 917L #23, Le Mans 1970, 1:18,
　　#3902 ....$30-32

Porsche 956 #19 IMOLA 1984,
　　1:18, #4707 ....$30-32

Porsche 956L
　#1 ROTHMANS, 1:18, #4701 ....$30-32
　#2 ROTHMANS, 1:18, #4702 ....$30-32
　#21 KREMER, 1:18, #4703 ....$30-32
　#7 NEWMAN 1984, 1:18, #4704...$30-32
　#7 NEWMAN 1985, 1:18, #4705...$30-32
　#8 Sport America, 1:18, #4706 .....$30-32

Porsche Carrera
　"GALLIA," 1:43, #1131 ....$18-20
　RSR #14, 1:43, #1136 ....$18-20
　RSR #53, 1:43, #1135 ....$18-20
　RSR #65, 1:43, #1134 ....$18-20
　RSR #66, 1:43, #1132 ....$18-20
　RSR #69, 1:43, #1133 ....$18-20

RSR Start, 1:43, #1137 ....$18-20
blue and black, 1:43, #1094 ....$18-20
white and blue, 1:43, #1090 ....$18-20

Renault
　#598 Tour Italy, 1:43, #1706........$18-20
　#7 Tour De Corse, 1:43, #1704 .....$18-20
　Corte Ingles, 1:43, #1707 ....$18-20
　Corte Ingles, 1:43, #1801 ....$18-20
　Sport Trophy, 1:43, #1802 ....$18-20
　Tour De France, 1:43, #1705 ....$18-20
　Turbo #9 Monte Carlo, 1:43, #1703 ..$18-20

Renault 5 Turbo
　blue, 1:43, #1702 ....$18-20
　red, 1:43, #1701 ....$18-20

1999 Renault Sport Trophy, 1:43
　#1803 ....$18-20
　#1804 ....$18-20
　#1805 ....$18-20

Shinoda Boss Mustang
　Convertible, black, Limited Edition, 1:18,
　　#3147......................................$35-37
　Convertible, blue, Limited Edition, 1:18,
　　#3144......................................$35-37
　Convertible, red, Limited Edition, 1:18,
　　#3146......................................$35-37
　Coupe, black, Limited Edition, 1:18,
　　#3143......................................$35-37
　Coupe, yellow, Limited Edition, 1:18,
　　#3130......................................$35-37

Triumph TR2
　#28 Le Mans, 1:43, #1088 ....$18-20
　#29 Le Mans, 1:43, #1098 ....$18-20
　#68 Le Mans, 1:43, #1099 ....$18-20
　Convertible, black, 1:43, #1087 .....$18-20
　Convertible, pearl white, 1:43,
　　#1086......................................$18-20

Triumph TR3
　Convertible, light blue, 1:43, #1084 ..$18-20
　Convertible, light yellow, 1:43,
　　#1083......................................$18-20
　Hardtop, beige, 1:43, #1093..........$18-20
　Soft Top, green, 1:43, #1095 ....$18-20
　Tour De Corse, 1:43, #1085 ....$18-20

Triumph TR3A
　#25 Le Mans, 1:43, #1081 ....$18-20
　#26 Le Mans, 1:43, #1082 ....$18-20
　#27 Le Mans, 1:43, #1089 ....$18-20
　Convertible, Limited Edition, bright green,
　　1:43, #1007 ....$18-20
　Convertible, Limited Edition, red, 1:43,
　　#1006......................................$18-20
　Hardtop, blue and white, 1:43, #1128 ..$18-20
　Hardtop, Limited Edition, black, 1:43,
　　#1008......................................$18-20
　Hardtop, Limited Edition, silver, 1:43,
　　#1009......................................$18-20

Rochester NY Fire, 1:43, #1097.......$18-20

Volkswagen Beetle

"BIG," green, Limited Edition, 1:43,
#1105...................................$20-22

"CITY," red, Limited Edition, 1:43,
#1104...................................$20-22

"FIRE BRIGADE," 1:43, #1109 ....$18-20

"FLOWER POWER," 1:43, #1124 ...$18-20

"FLOWER POWER," 1:43, #1125 ...$18-20

"JEANS," yellow, 1:43, #1103.........$18-20

"JEANS," yellow, Limited Edition, 1:43,
#1106...................................$20-22

"POLIZEI," 1:43, #1108 ....$18-20

"ROAD PATROL," 1:43, #1110.......$18-20

Convertible, light yellow, 1:43,
#1115...................................$18-20

Convertible, black, 1:43, #1025 ......$18-20

Convertible, red, 1:43, #1024 ....$18-20

Soft Top gold, 1:43, #1107.............$18-20

Soft Top, light blue, 1:43, #1027.....$18-20

Soft Top, silver, 1:43, #1114 ....$18-20

apple green, 1:43, #1112 ....$18-20

orange, 1:43, #1111 ....$18-20

yellow and black, Limited Edition, 1:43,
#1101...................................$20-22

Ebbro

c/o Great Eagle Trading Co.
Unit 5, 5/F, Favor Industrial Centre,
2-6 Kin Hong St.,
Kwai Chung, N.T.
Hong Kong
Danny Ngan, sales manager
www.ebbro.com

First seen in *Model Auto Review* (June 1999), Ebbro is a brand of mostly 1:43 scale diecast models made in Japan and exported exclusively by Great Eagle Trading Company of Hong Kong. Their product list is extensive and includes models new and old from Daihatsu, Dome, Honda / Acura, Nissan / Prince / Infiniti, Toyota / Lexus, Isuzu, Mazda, Porsche, and Subaru. You can find a current listing at www.ebbro.com. Listed below is just a brief sampling, mostly of their Honda / Acura models.

Honda / Acura Integra Type-R

Race 2002 M-Line, #43421, 1:43 ...$30-40

endurance race #1 Shin Tokyo-Castrol,
#43510, 1:43 ....$30-40

endurance race #100 Shin Tokyo-Castrol,
#43511, 1:43 ....$30-40

(98-Spec), white, #43118, 1:43....$35-45

(98-Spec), yellow, #43119, 1:43.....$30-40

(98-Spec) metallic gun gray, #43120,
1:43...................................$30-40

(98-Spec), red, #43169, 1:43 ....$30-40

2001 (DC5), white, #43221, 1:43..$30-40

2001 (DC5) black, #43222, 1:43 ...$30-40

2001 (DC5) blue, #43223, 1:43.....$30-40

Honda / Acura MDX, 2003

black, #43457, 1:43......................$30-40

sage, #43458, 1:43.......................$30-40

silver, #43462, 1:43......................$30-40

Honda / Acura New NSX Type-R, 2002

white, #43328, 1:43.....................$30-40

2002, yellow, #43353, 1:43..........$35-45

2002, red, #43354, 1:43 ....$35-45

Honda / Acura New NSX Type-S, 2001

monza red pearl, #43325, 1:43 ......$30-40

metallic lime green, #43326, 1:43 ...$30-40

2001, black, #43327, 1:43...........$30-40

Honda / Acura NSX Type-S, 2001 (Facelift)

red with black roof, 1:24......................$24-30

Honda / Acura NSX

Type-R Tokyo Motor Show 2001 Prototype,
#43390, 1:43 ....$30-40

2001 Facelift, silver, #24013, 1:24...$65-80

Targa, yellow, #43034, 1:43 ....$30-40

Targa metallic blue, #43035, 1:43 ...$30-40

Type-S 2001 Facelift, red, #24014,
1:24...................................$65-80

JGTC 2000 Takata, #43127, 1:43 ..$35-45

JGTC 2000 Castrol, #43128, 1:43 ..$35-45

JGTC 2000 Raybrig, #43129, 1:43 ..$35-45

JGTC 2001 Loctite, #43201, 1:43 ..$35-45

JGTC 2001 Takata, #43202, 1:43 ..$30-40

JGTC 2001 Raybrig, #43203, 1:43 ...$30-40

JGTC 2002 Mobil 1, #43283, 1:43 ..$30-40

JGTC 2002 Test car, #43329, 1:43 ...$35-45

JGTC 2002 MUGEN, #43330, 1:43...$35-45

JGTC 2002 Takata, #43331, 1:43 ..$35-45

JGTC Late 2002 Raybrig, #43332,
1:43.......................................$30-40

JGTC Late 2002 Mugen, #43355,
1:43.......................................$35-45

JGTC Late 2002 Takata, #43356,
1:43.......................................$35-45

JGTC 2003 Takata, #43459, 1:43....$30-40

JGTC 2003 Mugen, #43460, 1:43...$30-40

JGTC 2003 Raybrig, #43461, 1:43 ..$30-40

Suzuka 1000Km 2002 Regain, #43357,
1:43.......................................$30-40

Honda Accord / Acura TSX Sedan RHD, 2003

white pearl, #43280, 1:43..............$30-40

graphite pearl, #43281, 1:43..........$30-40

black pearl, #43282, 1:43..............$30-40

metallic silver, #43426, 1:43..........$30-40

blue metallic, #43427, 1:43 ....$30-40

metallic mist green, #43428, 1:43 ....$30-40

Honda Accord Euro R / Acura TSX, 2003

red, #43439, 1:43........................$30-40

blue, #43440, 1:43 ....$30-40

pearl white, #43441, 1:43 ....$30-40

Honda Accord Tourer, 2003

white pearl, #43402, 1:43..............$30-40

desert pearl, #43403, 1:43.............$30-40

blue pearl, #43404, 1:43 ....$30-40

graphite pearl, #43429, 1:43..........$30-40

ruby red pearl, #43430, 1:43 ....$30-40

black pearl, #43431, 1:43..............$30-40

green pearl, #43432, 1:43..............$30-40

silver metallic, #43433, 1:43...........$30-40

Honda Civic 1200 Hi-Deluxe

white, #43121, 1:43......................$35-45

red, #43122, 1:43........................$35-45

green, #43123, 1:43.....................$35-45

red, #43296, 1:43........................$35-45

white, #43297, 1:43......................$35-45

red, #43442, 1:43........................$30-40

orange, #43443, 1:43 ....$30-40

green, #43444, 1:43.....................$30-40

Honda Element, right hand drive, 2003

silver, #43473, 1:43......................$30-40

green, #43474, 1:43.....................$30-40

black, #43475, 1:43......................$30-40

beige, #43476, 1:43.....................$30-40

orange, #43489, 1:43 ....$30-40

Honda FCX Fuel Cell Concept, 2003, #43451,
1:43.......................................$30-40

Honda Fit / City ARIA 1.5, 2003

beige, #43434, 1:43.....................$30-40

taffeta white, #43435, 1:43............$30-40

eternal blue, #43436, 1:43 ....$30-40

ice blue, #43437, 1:43..................$30-40

satin silver, #43438, 1:43 ....$30-40

Honda Fit / Jazz, 2001

silver, #43217, 1:43......................$30-40

black, #43218, 1:43......................$30-40

red pearl, #43219, 1:43 ....$30-40

light yellow, #43220, 1:43.............$30-40

pearl white, #43225, 1:43 ....$30-40

white, #43226, 1:43......................$30-40

mint pearl, #43227, 1:43 ....$35-45

metallic blue, #43228, 1:43 ....$30-40

Honda Fit / Jazz, 1.5T

titanium silver, #43412, 1:43 ....$30-40

royal blue, #43413, 1:43.................$30-40

Honda Insight
 red, #43133, 1:43.........................$30-40
 metallic yellow, #43134, 1:43.........$30-40
 metallic blue, #43135, 1:43.............$30-40

Honda Inspire / Accord, 2003 V6
 metro silver, #43477, 1:43..............$30-40
 pearl white, #43478, 1:43...............$30-40
 satin silver, #43479, 1:43...............$30-40
 nighthawk black pearl, #43480,
  1:43......................................$30-40
 eternal blue, #43481, 1:43..............$30-40
 graphite gray, #43482, 1:43...........$30-40

Honda Life, 2003
 green, #43522, 1:43......................$30-40
 ivory, #43523, 1:43........................$30-40
 brown, #43524, 1:43.....................$30-40
 storm silver, #43525, 1:43.............$30-40

Honda Mobilio, 2002
 white, #43303, 1:43......................$30-40
 light blue, #43304, 1:43................$30-40
 light brown, #43305, 1:43.............$30-40

Honda Mobilio SPIKE, 2002
 pearl white, #43277, 1:43...............$30-40
 blue, #43278, 1:43.......................$30-40
 red, #43279, 1:43........................$30-40
 silver, #43423, 1:43.......................$30-40
 black, #43424, 1:43.......................$30-40
 green, #43425, 1:43......................$30-40

Honda Mugen Fit / Jazz
 pearl white, #43350, 1:43...............$30-40
 red, #43351, 1:43........................$30-40
 silver, #43351, 1:43.......................$30-40
 blue, #43422, 1:43 ....$35-45

Honda Mugen Integra Type-R (DC2-98)
 white, #43309, 1:43......................$30-40
 black, #43310, 1:43.......................$30-40

Honda Mugen S2000, 2001
 silver, #43323, 1:43.......................$30-40
 white, #43324, 1:43......................$30-40
 silver, #43287, 1:43.......................$30-40
 black, #43288, 1:43.......................$30-40

Honda N360 Canvas Top, yellow, #43190,
 1:43 ....$30-40
Honda N360S, blue, #43189, 1:43.....$35-45
Honda N600, green, #43188, 1:43.....$35-45
Honda New Odyssey, 2003
 purple, #43526, 1:43.....................$30-40
 pearl white, #43527, 1:43...............$30-40
 meteor silver, #43528, 1:43 ....$30-40

Honda New Odyssey Absolute, 2003
 white pearl, #43554, 1:43..............$30-40
 Milano red, #43555, 1:43...............$30-40
 black, #43556, 1:43.......................$30-40

Honda Odyssey Absolute, 2002
 silver, #43268, 1:43.......................$30-40

red, #43269, 1:43.................$30-40
white, #43270, 1:43.................$30-40
Honda RA271 F-1 West German Gran Prix,
 1:20, #22004, 1:24 ....$65-80
Honda RA273 F-1 1966 #18 Italian Gran Prix,
 1:20, #22002, 1:24 ....$65-80
Honda RA300 F-1 1967 John Surtees #14,
 1:20, #22001, 1:24 ....$65-80
Honda RA301 F-1 1968 Surtees #5
 Mexico Gran Prix, 1:20, #22003,
 1:24 ....$65-80
Honda S600 Coupe
 white, #43445, 1:43.....................$30-40
 red, #43446, 1:43........................$30-40
Honda S600 Road Star
 red, #43060, 1:43........................$30-40
 harbor blue, #43061, 1:43.............$30-40
Honda S800
 white, #43397, 1:43.....................$30-40
 yellow, #43398, 1:43.....................$30-40
 red, #43399, 1:43........................$30-40
Honda S2000
 white, #24001, 1:24.....................$65-80
 silver, #24002, 1:24.......................$65-80
 white, #43039, 1:43.....................$30-40
 metallic black, #43043, 1:43 ....$30-40
 left hand drive, silver, #43041L,
  1:43......................................$30-40
 left hand drive, red, #43042L, 1:43 ....$30-40
Honda Step Van
 white, #43130, 1:43......................$35-45
 light blue, #43131, 1:43................$30-40
 pale yellow, #43132, 1:43.............$30-40
Honda Step Wagon SPADA, 2003
 pearl white, #43507, 1:43...............$30-40
 metallic red, #43508, 1:43..............$30-40
 metallic black, #43509, 1:43 ....$30-40
Honda Stream iS, 2001
 red, #43162, 1:43........................$30-40
 blue, #43163, 1:43 ....$30-40
 gold, #43164, 1:43.......................$30-40
Honda THAT'S, 2002
 black, #43320, 1:43.......................$30-40
 ice blue, #43321, 1:43...................$30-40
 silver, #43322, 1:43.......................$30-40
1967 Nissan Bluebird 510 SSS Coupe, 1:43

pale yellow, #43543 ....$18-20

Nissan Prince R380 II

1983 Speed Trial Version, #43553.......$18-20

Porsche 911 Carrera RS, 1973
 white, #24010, 1:24......................$65-80
 yellow, #24011, 1:24 ....$65-80
Nissan Fairlady 240ZG
 white, #24019, 1:24......................$65-80
 brown, #24020, 1:24
Nissan Fairlady Z-L, 1969
 white, #24007, 1:24......................$65-80
 red, #24008, 1:24.........................$65-80

Subaru 360, 1:43, pale blue w/ white roof ...$18-20

Subaru Young 360, 1:43, cream with black roof $18-20

1983 Toyota Corolla Levin AE86

white, #43271, 1:43..............$18-20

red, #43272, 1:43..............$18-20

black, 43273, 1:43..............$18-20

Toyota 2000GT, 1967
   white, #24003, 1:24...............$75-90
   red, #24004, 1:24...............$75-90
   silver, #24005, 1:24...............$75-90
   gold, #24006, 1:24...............$75-90

Edil

Edil Toys of Italy are detailed 1:43 scale models produced from 1965 to 1970. Models reproduced afterwards in Turkey by Meboto still hold the Edil brand name but are comparably inferior castings with crude finishes that give them away as later models.

Alfa Romeo Giulia GT
   1965, #1.........................$50-75
   Police car, 1966, #5 ....$50-75
   TI, 1966, #4 ....$50-75
Ferrari 275 GTB, 1967, #9...............$50-75
Fiat 850, 1966, #2...............$50-75

Fiat 1500 Sedan, 1966, #6...............$50-75
Fiat 124 Sedan, 1967, #7...............$50-75
Fiat 850 Coupe, 1967, #8...............$50-75
Iso Grifo, 1968, #12...............$50-75
Lamborghini Bertone Marzal, 1968, #13...............$50-75
Lamborghini Miura, 1968, #10...............$50-75
Lancia Flavia Coupe, 1966, #3...............$50-75
Mercedes-Benz 250SE, #11...............$50-75

Edocar (also see Zee Toys / Zylmex)

Edocar is a trademark of the Netherlands-based company of Fred Beheer BV or Edor BV. Edor is evidently a reseller of various brands within the "Benelux," the tax union of Belgium, the Netherlands, and Luxembourg, later known as the Common Market.

A set of Coca-Cola race cars from Edocar were determined to be castings from Action Racing Collectibles, according to David Weber of Warrington, Pennsylvania. He indicates that these were unauthorized alterations of the latter suspected to be illegally obtained from the Action Racing Collectibles factory in China.

A 1988 Edocar catalog provided by collector Werner LeGrand of Brecht, Belgium, features models issued in the US as M C Toys Mini Racers (later reissued as Maisto Turbo Treads), Yat Mings currently offered as Ja-Ru Real Wheels. Also included in the catalog are models that are recognizable as Lledo models of England.

Prices are for models in original Edocar package, otherwise models are not identifiable as Edocars but only as their original brand. Brand name in parentheses indicates manufacturer.

4x4 Pickup, Coca-Cola, CC-5 (M C Toys)....$4-6
AEC Autobus, EA-5 (Lledo)...............$10-12
Ambulance, EM-39 (Yat Ming)...............$3-5
Audi Quattro, EM-1 (M C Toys)...............$3-5
Bedford Van, Coca-Cola, CC-6 (Yat Ming)...$4-6
BMW M1, EM-46 (M C Toys)...............$3-5
Buick Le Sabre, EM-14 (M C Toys)...............$3-5
Cadillac Seville, EM-34 (Yat Ming)...............$3-5
Chevrolet Blazer, Coca-Cola, CC-3 (M C Toys)...............$4-6
Chevrolet Blazer, EM-16 (Yat Ming)...............$3-5
Chevrolet Corvette, Coca-Cola, CC-7...............$6-8
Chevrolet Corvette, EM-3 (Yat Ming)...............$4-6
Chevrolet Corvette 1957, EM-17 (Yat Ming)...$5-7
Chevrolet Corvette 1986 Convertible, EM-11 (M C Toys)...............$3-5
Chevrolet Van, Coca-Cola, CC-2 (Yat Ming)...$4-6
Chevrolet Van, EA-8 (Lledo)...............$10-12

Citroën 2CV, EM-2 (M C Toys)...............$3-5
Datsun, EM-20 (Yat Ming)...............$3-5
Delivery Truck, Coca-Cola, CC-4 (Yat Ming)...$4-6
Dennis Fire Engine, EA-2 (Lledo)...............$10-12
Dennis Van, EA-4 (Lledo)...............$10-12
Dodge Sheriff, EM-41 (Yat Ming)...............$5-7
Extending Ladder Fire Engine, EM-24 (Yat Ming)...............$4-6
Ferrari 308 GTB, EM-48 (M C Toys)...............$3-5
Ferrari Testarossa, EM-31 (M C Toys)...............$3-5
Ford Escort, EM-4 (M C Toys)...............$3-5
Ford Granada, EM-8 (M C Toys)...............$3-5
Ford Lorry, EM-9 (Yat Ming)...............$4-6
Ford Lorry Trailer, EM-10 (Yat Ming)...............$6-8
Ford Model T Petrol Tanker, EA-1 (Lledo)...$10-12
Ford Mustang, EM-38 (Yat Ming)...............$3-5
Ford Sierra XR4i, EM-49 (M C Toys)...............$3-5
Ford Station Wagon, EM-29 (Yat Ming)...............$6-8
Ford Taxi, EA-3 (Lledo)...............$10-12
Formula 1, white with red accents, "Valvoline," EM-51 (M C Toys)...............$3-5
Formula 1, black with white, blue, and red accents, EM-52 (M C Toys)...............$3-5
Jaguar XJ6, EM-28 (M C Toys)...............$3-5
Jeep, 4 x 4 Hardtop, EM-12 (Yat Ming)...............$4-6
Jeep, 4 x 4 Open Jeep, EM-45 (Yat Ming)...$3-5
Jeep, 4 x 4 Open Military Jeep, EM-23 (Yat Ming)...............$3-5
Lancia Rally, EM-7 (M C Toys)...............$4-6
Mazda RX-7, EM-32 (Yat Ming)...............$4-6
Mercedes-Benz 500 SEC, EM-36 (M C Toys)...$3-5
Mercedes-Benz 500 SL, #13 (Zee Toy)...............$2-4
Mercedes-Benz 500 SLC, EM-13 (M C Toys)...$3-5
Mercedes-Benz 560, EM-21 (M C Toys)...............$3-5
Mercedes-Benz Van, EM-25 (M C Toys)...............$3-5
Military Lorry, EM-43 (Yat Ming)...............$4-6
Mobile Crane, EM-22 (Yat Ming)...............$5-7
Nissan 300 ZX, EM-15 (M C Toys)...............$3-5
Packard Ambulance, EA-6 (Lledo)...............$10-12
Peugeot 205 GTI, EM-47 (M C Toys)...............$3-5
Peugeot 309, EM-27 (M C Toys)...............$3-5
Pontiac Firebird 1986, Coca-Cola, CC-8...............$6-8
Porsche, Coca-Cola, CC-1...............$6-8
Porsche 928, EM-26 (M C Toys)...............$3-5
Porsche 956, EM-44 (M C Toys)...............$3-5
Porsche 959, EM-37 (M C Toys)...............$3-5
Porsche Turbo, EM-40 (M C Toys)...............$3-5
Renault 25 Turbo, EM-19 (M C Toys)...............$3-5
Rolls Royce, EM-5 (M C Toys)...............$4-6
Rolls Royce Phantom II, EA-7 (Lledo)...............$10-12
Suzuki SJ413QJX Sidekick, EM-42 (M C Toys)...$3-5
Tipper Truck, EM-30 (Yat Ming)...............$3-5
Tow Truck, EM-33 (Yat Ming)...............$5-7
Toyota MR-2, EM-35 (M C Toys)...............$3-5
Volkswagen Golf GTi, EM-6 (M C Toys)...............$3-5
Volkswagen Scirocco, EM-50 (Yat Ming)...............$4-6

Volvo 760 GLE, EM-18 (M C Toys) $3-5

EFE (see Exclusive First Editions)

Efsi / Holland-Oto (also see Best-Box)

Efsi toys are well made but crude toys from Holland. They are durable, authentic replicas representing mostly European vehicles that sell for about $4 each. Each of the dozen or so Efsi models manufactured is available in many different variations and liveries. What they lack in accuracy they make up in charm. Older models were produced under the Best-Box brand. In April 2000, collector Jan Scholten reported that Efsi now goes by the name of Holland-Oto, although the Efsi brand continues in Germany.

BMW 2000 CS
 #4070..$15-20
 Rally, #4071 ....$15-20
Brabham Formula 1, #2040 ....$10-15
BRM Formula I, #2010 ....$10-15
Citroën ID 19
 #4090..$15-20
 Ambulance, #4091 ....$15-20
Citroën Dyane 6, #4100......................$15-20
Commer
 Ambulance, #3021 ....$15-20
 Army Ambulance, #3024 ....$15-20
 Fire Van, #3023 ....$15-20
 Service Van, #3022 ....$15-20
 U.S.A. Army Van, #3021 ....$15-20
 Van, #3020 ....$15-20
Ferrari Formula I, #2030 ....$15-20
1919 Ford Model T
 Ambulance, #1070 ....$10-15
 Crane Truck, #1030 ....$10-15
 Fire Van, #1100 ....$10-15
 Sedan, #1060................................$10-15
 Tanker, #1020...............................$10-15
 Truck, #1010 ....$10-15
 Two Seater, #1050 ....$10-15
 Van, #1040 ....$10-15
Ford Taunus
 17 M, #4010 ....$15-20
 Stock car, #4011 ....$15-20
Ford Transit
 Van, #4110 ....$15-20
 Ambulance, #4111 ....$15-20
 Police Van, #4112 ....$15-20
Honda Formula I, #2020 ....$10-15
Jaguar E Type, #4030...........................$15-20
Lotus 49 C Formula I, #2060 ....$10-15
Mclaren Formula I, #2050 ....$10-15

Mercedes-Benz
 Army Dump Truck, #3051 ....$10-15
 Army Truck, #3042.........................$10-15
 Covered Truck, #3040......................$10-15
 Dump Truck, #3050 ....$10-15
 Fire Engine, #3080 ....$10-15
 Open Truck, #3030 ....$10-15
 Red Cross Truck, #3041 ....$10-15
 Tanker "ARAL," #3092 ....$15-20
 Tanker, Army, #3093 ....$15-20
 Tanker "ELF," #3091 ....$15-20
 Tanker "SHELL," #3090 ....$15-20
Mercedes-Benz 250 SE Coupe
 #4060..$15-20
 Rally, #4061 ....$15-20
Mercedes-Benz 280SL, #4040 ....$15-20
Opel Rekord 1900, #4050 ....$15-20
Porsche 911 S
 #4020..$15-20
 Dutch Police car, #4021 ....$15-20
 Rally, #4022 ....$15-20
Trailer
 Army Trailer, #3062 ....$10-15
 Red Cross Trailer, #3061 ....$10-15
 Trailer, #3060 ....$10-15
Volkswagen 1600 TL, #4080 ....$20-25

E.G.M.

E.G.M. toys were manufactured in Italy in 1959.

Alfa Romeo Giulietta Spyder, 1:43......$200-250
 (if ever actually produced)
Dean Van Lines Special, 1:43 ....$150-200
Tarf Speed Record Car, 1:43 ....$150-200

EiDAI (also see Grip Zechin)

EiDAI Corporation
2.8.7. Higashiogu, Arakawaku
Tokyo, Japan

Made in Japan, EiDAI scale models are occasionally sold under the Model Power brand. Many EiDAI models replicate those sold under the Grip Zechin, Madmax, and World Zechin brands, all produced by EiDAI.

Airport Bus, 1:100 ....$15-20
Boom Truck, 1:87 ....$12-16
DeTomaso Pantera GT-35, 1:28 (Technica series)..$25-30
Ladder Truck, 1:87 ....$12-16
March 761B "Rothmans" #10 Ian, 1:43 ...$20-25

E J Enterprises (also see Sunnyside)

15736 E. Valley Blvd.
City of Industry, CA 91744 USA

Recently discovered are larger scale pull-back action diecast toys in a black box with colorful graphics and the name E J Enterprises. The models looked familiar, so I removed them from the box and looked at the base. They're made by Sunnyside of Hong Kong.

Eko

Schroeder's Collectible Toys lists two Eko diecast models from Spain.

Eko Die-Cast Models

1911 Daimler Convertible, silver, #6010...$10-15
Hispano Suiza Alphonso XIII Convertible, red & cream, #6005.................................$15-20

Eko Ho Gauge Plastic Models

Eko 1:87 scale models are appropriately-colored molded plastic, imported from Spain, with painted details, available from Walthers. While not diecast metal, Eko models are exquisite additions to any HO gauge collection or train layout.

Alco Double Decker Bus $3-5
Alfa Romeo Giulietta Sprint.........................$3-5
BMW
 501 ....$3-5
 Coupe $3-5
Borgward Isabella $3-5
Chausson Motor Bus $3-5
Chevrolet El Camino $3-5
Citroën
 2CV $3-5
 AMI $3-5
 Break $3-5
 DS 19 ....$3-5
Commer
 Beer Barrel $3-5
 Dump Truck $3-5
 Soda Truck $3-5
DAF
 Coupe $3-5
 Daffodil...$3-5
DeSoto Diplomat $3-5
Dodge Dart $3-5
Fiat
 124 ....$3-5
 600 Multipla $3-5
 850 ....$3-5
 1500 ....$3-5
 1800 Station Wagon.............................$3-5
 Seat 124 ....$3-5
Ford
 Anglia $3-5
 Comet $3-5

Consul $3-5
Falcon $3-5
FK Kombi Ambulance $3-5
Thunderbird $3-5
Zephyr $3-5
Ford Truck
　Flat Bed Truck $3-5
　Flat Bed Truck with Canvas Top $3-5
　Gas Oil Tank Truck $3-5
　Thames Flat Bed Truck $3-5
Jaguar
　D $3-5
　E Coupe $3-5
　Mark Nine $3-5
　Racer $3-5
Jeep...$3-5
Karrier
　Garbage Truck $3-5
　Gas Bottle $3-5
Land Rover, Open Top $3-5
Leyland Double Decker Bus $3-5
Magirus
　Flat Bed $3-5
　Flat Bed with Canvas Top $3-5
　Tank Truck $3-5
Mercedes-Benz 190SL
　Convertible..$3-5
　Coupe $3-5
Mercedes-Benz
　220 ....$3-5
　300 ....$3-5
　Racer $3-5
MG 1600 ....$3-5
Morris Mini $3-5
Opel Rekord $3-5
Panel Truck Fourgon $3-5
Pegaso
　Auto Transport with 5 autos................$8-10
　CAMPSA Oil Truck..............................$3-5
　Cement Delivery Truck.........................$3-5
　Delivery Truck....................................$3-5
　Motor Bus $3-5
　Semi Tank Truck $4-6
　Tank...$3-5
Renault
　4-L $3-5
　4/4 ....$3-5
　Dauphine $3-5
　R-8 ....$3-5
Rover 3/L $3-5
Saab 96 ....$3-5
Sava
　Butano Delivery Truck $3-5
　Garbage Truck $3-5
Seat
　600 Coupe $3-5

1400 Panel Truck................................$3-5
1400 Sedan $3-5
1400C Sedan $3-5
Skoda Coupe $3-5
Soft Drink Truck
　"Eko Cola" $3-5
　"Piper Cola" $3-5
Studebaker
　Avanti $3-5
　Hawk $3-5
T245 Army Tanker/Dozer $3-5
Thames
　Beer Delivery Truck $3-5
　Flatbed Truck $3-5
　Soda Delivery Truck $3-5
Titan Semi Lo-Boy with cargo Tank...............$5-7
Volkswagen
　Beetle $3-5
　Beetle Convertible $3-5
　Karmann Ghia $3-5
Volvo Sport $3-5

Elastolin

The Rivalry between Elastolin and Lineol remained fierce in a limited market for military toys. Brothers Otto and Max Hausser formed the O&M Hausser firm in 1904 in Ludwigsberg, Germany, and assigned the trade name Elastolin to their line of detailed military toys. While Lineol made sturdy roughly 1:25 scale tin-plate military vehicles for their 7½ centimeter composition soldiers, Elastolin toys are somewhat more delicate and fragile, but in the same scale.

Ambulance, #738, camouflaged, with rubber
　tires $2,900-3,100
Anti-Aircraft Truck
　#0/740 ....$2,300-2,500
　camouflaged, #1/740 ....$2,650-2,850
Command car, with luggage,
　#733/12 ....$3,900-4,100
Communications car, #733/10...$3,900-4,100
Communications Truck, light gray,
　#745 ....$4,800-5,200
Flakwagen (Gun Truck)
　camouflaged, with British troops,
　　#739N $2,650-2,850
　army green $2,100-2,300
Heavy Truck with Kitchen Wagon, troops,
　#794 ....$4,150-4,350
Kubelauto (Staff car), #1/733
　metal wheels $600-800
　rubber wheels...............................$550-750
Kubelwagen (Staff car), WWII,
　#733/2 ....$800-1000
Panzer Spahwagen
　#744 ....$13,000-15,000

#1744 ....$2,900-3,100
Prime Mover
　"Chrysler" front, with US troops, post-WWII,
　　#731 ....$2,100-2,300
　camouflaged, #730N $2,400-2,600
　large, #731 ....$15,000-17,000
　six-wheel, with canopy,
　　#730/10.....................$2,900-3,100
　with US troops, post-WWII,
　　#730 ....$1,400-1,600
Searchlight car
　with Luftwaffe troops, #734.....$2,300-2,500
　with British troops, #743........$1,100-1,300
　Searchlight Truck, camouflaged, with Luftwaffe
　　troops $2,800-3,200
　Tank, camouflaged $2,100-2,300
Zugsmachine (Troop Transport),
　#734 ....$3,500-3,700
Zugswagen (Troop Transport),
　#1/734 ....$2,900-3,100

Electricar (see Old Kingston Product Corporation)

Elegance

Fabulous 1:43 scale model Cadillacs are offered under the Elegance brand. The 1951 Cadillac Pullman in particular (Elegance #117) was produced in 1986 and modeled after the car owned by King Ibn Saud of Saudi Arabia. Coachwork on the original car was done by Hess and Eisenhardt.

Cadillac
　1951 Pullman 6-door limousine, midnight
　　blue, mirrored passenger windows,
　　#117 ....$450-500
　1975 86 El Clasico....................$475-525
　1976 Fleetwood $400-450
　1976 Silverhawk 6-door limousine...$525-575

Eligor

Eligor France
Paul and Anne-Marie Vullierme, owners
605n Zi La Plaine
01580 Izernore, France
Tel: 4-74-76-56-56
e-mail: eligor@wanadoo.fr

Eligor USA
John Vullierme
Eligor, Inc.
630 Bradford Lane
Earlysville, VA 22936
phone: 434-973-7638
fax: 434-975-6080

e-mail: eligorusa@eligor.com
website: www.eligor.com

Eligor represents a series of popular vintage 1:43 and a few 1:25 scale models, mostly diecast but a few resin models as well, originally manufactured by Jacques Greilsamer in Martignat, France, starting in 1976. Eligor models are available from finer hobby shops and mail-order houses. The company used many of Norev's original toolings. In 1986, Greilsamer sold the brand to Louis Surber, who had been producing Eligor models for Greilsamer. In 1996, Eligor was acquired by Paul and Anne-Marie Vullierme. In 1998, Eligor relocated to a newly designed facility in Izernore, France. Eligor currently offers over 300 models and variations of vintage and modern cars selling for around $25 each, and nearly 300 modern and vintage semi-tractor/trailers and commercial trucks for $89 suggested retail price.

Eligor models have been sold by several other small firms, such as Frobly, after being modified and customized.

1965 Austin Mini
850, green with black roof, #1110, 1:43.................$25-30
Parisienne, black with rattan doors, #1113, 1:43.................$25-30
Police, white, #1112, 1:43.............$25-30
1967 Bentley T Sedan, #1048, 1:43.....$25-30
1975 Bentley Sedan, metallic brown, #100092, 1:43.................$25-30
1967 BMW 2000
Sedan, gray, #100505, 1:43.........$25-30
Fire Chief, red, #1118, 1:43..........$25-30
Fire Chief, red, #100408, 1:43......$25-30
Polizei RFA, green and white, #1116, 1:43.................$25-30
Polizei RFA, green and white, #100406, 1:43.................$25-30
Rallye, white, #1117, 1:43.............$25-30
Rallye, white, #100407, 1:43.........$25-30
Taxi, black, #1115, 1:43.............$25-30
Taxi, black, #100405, 1:43...........$25-30
Tilux Sedan, blue, #1114, 1:43.......$25-30
1927 Bugatti 35 B
Course, #1025, 1:43 ....$25-30
Course, blue, #100044, 1:43........$25-30
Sport, #1045, 1:43.................$25-30
Sport, red, #100089, 1:43.........$25-30
1962 Chevrolet Corvair Monza
green, #1136, 1:43.................$30
beige, #100510, 1:43.................$25-30

blue, 100511, 1:43....................................$25-30

red, #100512, 1:43.................$25-30
Police USA, black and white, #100274, 1:43.................$25-30
Fire Dept. Los Angeles, red and white, #100275, 1:43 ....$25-30
1958 Chrysler New Yorker Convertible
top down, baby blue #1100, 1:43...$25-30
top down, pink, #100509, 1:43 .....$25-30
Citroën 3 CV
Fire Dept. Paris, #100394, 1:43 ......$25-30
Michelin, #100396, 1:43 ....$25-30
Camionette, gray, #100518, 1:43...$25-30
Citroën 5 CV
1925 Torpedo, top down, #1017, 1:43.................$25-30
1925 Torpedo, top down, #100032, 1:43.................$25-30
1925 Torpedo, top up, #1037, 1:43.................$25-30
1926 Camionette, "Bally," #1057, 1:43.................$25-30
1926 Camionette, "Michelin," #1054, 1:43.................$25-30
1926 Pompiers (Fire Van), #1056, 1:43.................$25-30
1926 Pompiers (Fire Van), #100117, 1:43.................$25-30
Citroën 5 HP 1925
Covered, yellow with black trim, #100073, 1:43.................$25-30
Camionette, "Michelin," #100113, 1:43.................$25-30
Camionette, Postes, #100090, 1:43...$25-30
Fire Department, #100115, 1:43.....$25-30

1938 Citroën 15CV Traction Avant, 1:43 ...$30-35
Citroën 500 KG 1934
yellow, #100014, 1:43 ....$25-30
"Caran D'Ache," #1015, 1:43........$25-30
"Lion Noir," #1026, 1:43 ....$25-30
"Phillips," #100097, 1:43 ....$25-30
"PTT," #100005, 1:43 ....$25-30

Ambulance, #1021, 1:43.............$25-30
Ambulance, #100040, 1:43 ....$25-30
Juragruyere, #100012, 1:43 ....$25-30
Nicolas, #100022, 1:43 ....$25-30
Postes, green, #100004, 1:43........$25-30
Service Des Sapeurs Pompiers (Fire Pumper) with ladder and hoses, #100039, 1:43.................$25-30
Saint Raphael, #100038, 1:43 ....$25-30
Start Pilote, red, #100016, 1:43......$25-30
Citroën AMI 6
Fire Department, 1:43 #100450, 1:43..$25-30
Sedan, blue, #100521, 1:43 ....$25-30
Sedan, two-tone green, #100525, 1:43.................$25-30
Break, brown, #100526, 1:43 ....$25-30
Citroën Berlingo
green, #100646, 1:43 ....$25-30
Fire Department, #100658, 1:43......$25-30
Reseau Citroën, #100659, 1:43 ......$25-30
Poste, #100677, 1:43.................$25-30
Multispace, blue, #100704, 1:43 ....$25-30
Citroën C 15
Fire Department, #100379, 1:43......$25-30
Poste, yellow, #100381, 1:43 ....$25-30
white, #100542, 1:43 ....$25-30
1967 Citroën DS 21
black, #100531, 1:43.................$25-30
Administration, #100227, 1:43 ......$25-30
Sedan, bronze, #1119, 1:43 ....$25-30
Etat-Major Des Pompiers, black, #1126, 1:43.................$25-30
Fire Department Lyon, #100231, 1:43.................$25-30
Fire Chief, red, #1122, 1:43 ....$25-30
Gendarmerie, blue, #1123, 1:43 ....$25-30
Gendarmerie, #100232, 1:43 ....$25-30
Ministerielle, #1120, 1:43 ....$25-30
Police Parisienne, black and white, #1121, 1:43.................$25-30
Police of Paris, #100228, 1:43 ......$25-30
"Rallye Du Maroc," #100700, 1:43...$25-30
"Rallye Monte Carlo," light blue, #1124, 1:43.................$25-30
Taxi Parisienne, #1125, 1:43..........$25-30
Citroën Fire, 1:25 ....$55-65
Citroën H Van
gray, #100338, 1:43 ....$25-30
Fire Dept. PTT "Bureau Mobile," #100363, 1:43.................$25-30
Fire Dept. Lyon with ladder, #100355, 1:43.................$25-30
Gendarmerie, #100352, 1:43 ....$25-30
"Kodak," #100435, 1:43 ....$25-30
Citroën Rosalie
1933 Sedan, #1005, 1:43 ....$25-30

1933 Sedan, yellow with black fenders, #100513, 1:43 ....$25-30
1933 Fire Dept., #100009, 1:43 ....$25-30
1933 Taxi, red and black, #100069, 1:43 ....$25-30
1934 Taxi, #1035, 1:43 ....$25-30
1934 60th Anniversary, black, #100007, 1:43 ....$25-30
1934 Pompiers (Fire Truck), #1020, 1:43 ..$25-30
Citroën SM Gendarmerie, #100444, 1:43 ....$25-30
Citroën T.A.V.
    1938 Sedan 11 BL, #1031A, 1:43 ...$25-30
    1947 Sedan 11 BL, #1031B, 1:43 ...$25-30
    1948 Sedan Pompiers (Fire Chief), #1033, 1:43 ....$25-30
    1938 Cabriolet, top down, #1001, 1:43 ....$25-30
    1938 Cabriolet, top up, #1002, 1:43 ....$25-30
    1939 Taxi, #1053, 1:43 ....$25-30
1938 Citroën Traction 11 BL Covered Cab, #100002, 1:43 ....$25-30
DAF XF 95
    Super Space "gefco," #111416, 1:43 ....$85-95
    DHOLLANDIA, #111424, 1:43 ....$85-95
Dekra Euro Truck, #110981, 1:43 .....$115-130
1934 Delage D8 Cabriolet
    top down, #1038, 1:43 ....$25-30
    top up, #1039, 1:43 ....$25-30
    #100074, 1:43 ....$25-30
1962 Ferrari GTO, 1:43 ....$25-30
1932 Ford
    Roadster Fire Chief, 1:43 ....$25-30
    Roadster, baby blue, 1:43 ....$25-30
    Roadster Police, 1:43 ....$25-30
    Sedan, green, 1:43 ....$25-30
    Sedan Police, 1:43 ....$25-30
    V-8 Sedan "Tudor," maroon, #1205, 1:43 ....$30-35
    V-8 Limousine "Fordor," green, #1204, 1:43 ....$30-35
    V-8 Roadster, top up, yellow, #1201, 1:43 ....$30-35
    V-8 Roadster, top down, maroon, #1200, 1:43 ....$30-35
    Van Police, 1:43 ....$25-30
1965 Ford Cortina
    Sedan, red, #1102, 1:43 ....$25-30
    Police, blue, #1104, 1:43 ....$25-30
    Autoroute G.B., #1105, 1:43 ....$25-30
    Rallye, white, #1103, 1:43 ....$25-30
Ford V-8
    1933 Covered Pickup, "Boots The Chemist Express Delivery," #1068, 1:43 ..$25-30

1933 Covered Pickup, "Guinness," #1066, 1:43 ....$25-30
1933 Covered Pickup, "Texaco Motor Oil," #1069, 1:43 ....$25-30
1933 Pickup, "Texaco," 1:43 ....$35
1933 Pickup, "Goodrich," 1:43 ....$25-30
1933 Pickup, black, #1080, 1:43 ....$25-30
1933 Pickup, green with wooden cargo box, #1059, 1:43 ....$30
1934 Ambulance, #1081, 1:43 ......$25-30
1934 Fire Truck, "Trenton," #1082, 1:43 ....$25-30
1934 Fire Truck, "Washington," #1084, 1:43 ....$25-30
1934 Panel Van, "Ford Service," #1070, 1:43 ....$25-30
1934 Panel Van, "Air Show," 1:43 ...$25-30
1934 Panel Van, "Castrol," #1072, 1:43 ....$25-30
1934 Panel Van, "Cobham's," #1079, 1:43 ....$25-30
1934 Panel Van, "Crosse & Blackwell," #1073, 1:43 ....$25-30
1934 Panel Van, "Firestone," 1:43 ....$25-30
1934 Panel Van, "Guinness," #1076, 1:43 ....$25-30
1934 Panel Van, "Lindt," #1071, 1:43 ..$25-30
1934 Panel Van, "Longines," #1075, 1:43 ....$25-30
1934 Panel Van, "Lyons Tea," #1074, 1:43 ....$25-30
1934 Panel Van, yellow "Mobiloil," #1077, 1:43 ....$25-30
1934 Panel Van, "RCA His Master's Voice," #1092, 1:43 ....$25-30
1934 Panel Van, "Stephens," #1078, 1:43 ....$25-30
1934 Pickup, covered, green and white "Carlsberg Beer," #1085, 1:43 ..$25-30
1934 Pickup, open, green and white "Carlsberg Beer," #1086, 1:43 ....$25-30
1934 Tanker, blue and white "Milkmaid," #1088, 1:43 ....$25-30
1934 Tanker, yellow "Mobiloil," #1090, 1:43 ....$25-30
1934 Tanker, red "Trenton No. 8 Fire Dept.," #1091, 1:43 ....$25-30
1934 Wrecker, yellow and green, #1087, 1:43 ....$25-30
1934 Wrecker, red "Fire Dept.," #1087P, 1:43 ....$25-30
1934 Ford Sedan, green, 1:43 ....$25-30
Iveco Eurotech
    MP 2x4 "Ferrari 1995," #110948, 1:43 ....$85-95
    "Martini Racing," #110970, 1:43 .....$85-95

Iveco Eurostar, "Iveco," 11126, 1:43 ......$85-95
1960 Jaguar 3.4 L
    Sedan, red, #1127, 1:43 ....$25-30
    "Tour De France," #1128, 1:43 ....$25-30
    Police Autoroute G.B., white, #1129, 1:43 ....$25-30
    Police G.B., dark blue, #1130, 1:43 ..$25-30
1960 Jaguar Mk 1, 1:43 ....$25-30
1960 Jaguar E-Type, 1:43 ....$25-30
1964 Jaguar E-Type Roadster, top down, red, #1152, 1:43 ....$25-30
Kenworth W 900
    "DHL," 110936, 1:43 ....$85-95
    Timber Truck, 111559, 1:43 ....$75-85

Kenworth T2000, CLR, 1:64, #200012...$75-85
1958 Lancia Aurelia B 20 Coupe, 1:43 scale gray bronze, #1143, 1:43 ....$25-30
    "Mille Miglia," black, #1144, 1:43...$25-30
1963 Lancia Flaminia Sedan, blue, #1132, 1:43 ....$25-30
1959 Lotus Elite, 1:43 ....$25-30
Man 19.422 "Total," 110953, 1:43 .....$85-95
Man F 2000 King of the Mountain, #111221, 1:43 ....$85-95
Mercedes-Benz Actros
    Mory N.L., #111100, 1:43 ....$85-95
    Deflecteur Ferlay, #111384, 1:43...$85-95
1948 Mercedes-Benz, "Berlin 2000," #110932, 1:43 ....$85-95
Mercedes-Benz
    1929 Nurburg Limousine, #1043, 1:43 ....$25-30
    1931 Taxi D'Hotel "Kaiserhof," #1044, 1:43 ....$30
1965 Mini Cooper "Rally Monte Carlo" #1111, 1:43 ....$25-30
    #100215, 1:43 ....$25-30
Mini 850 Parisienne, #100218, 1:43 ....$25-30
1925 Opel Laubfrosch
    Camionette, "Kaffee Hag," #1060, 1:43 ....$25-30
    Camionette, "Ovomaltine," #1064, 1:43 ..$25-30
    Fire Truck, #1095, 1:43 ....$25-30
    Torpedo, top down, #1093, 1:43 ....$25-30
    Torpedo, top up, #1094, 1:43 ....$25-30
1937 Panhard Dynamic
    Sedan, #1006, 1:43 ....$30-35
    Sedan, gray and black, #100010, 1:43 ....$25-30
    Taxi, #1006T, 1:43 ....$30-35

Taxi, red and black, 100011, 1:43........$30-35

1963 Panhard PL 17 Break
 Poste, yellow, #100220, 1:43 ....$25-30
 green, #100580, 1:43 ....$25-30
1931 Peugeot 201
 Sedan, #1016, 1:43 ....$25-30
 gray, #100582, 1:43 ....$25-30
 Fire Department, #100030, 1:43......$25-30
1954 Peugeot 203
 Sedan, blue, #100587, 1:43 ....$25-30
 Fire Dept. Loiret, #100309, 1:43......$25-30
 Taxi G7, red and black, #100397,
  1:43..$25-30
Peugeot 204 Break
 green, #100597, 1:43 ....$25-30
 Fire Dept., #100438, 1:43.............$25-30
 Gendarmerie, #100439, 1:43.........$25-30
1965 Peugeot 403
 Sedan, blue, #1145, 1:43...............$25-30
 Sedan, beige, #100591, 1:43 ....$25-30
 Break Fire Dept. Lyon, #100430,
  1:43..$25-30
 Taxi G7, black with red roof, #1146,
  1:43..$25-30
 Taxi G7, black with red roof, #100428,
  1:43..$25-30
Peugeot 404
 1954 Coupe, red, #1101, 1:43......$25-30
 1954 Coupe, white, #100595, 1:43 ...$25-30
 1964 Break, beige, #1137, 1:43 ....$25-30
 1964 Break, black, #100601, 1:43..$25-30
 1964 Break Ambulance, white, #1141,
  1:43..$25-30
 1964 Break Fire Dept. Soultz, #100261,
  1:43..$25-30
 1964 Break Gendarmerie, blue, #1139,
  1:43..$25-30
 1964 Break Gendarmerie, #100259,
  1:43..$25-30
 1964 Break Police, black, #1138,1:43...$25-30
 1964 Break Police Municipale, #100258,
  1:43..$25-30
 1964 Break Poste, yellow, #100256,
  1:43..$25-30
 1964 Break Secours Pompiers, red, #1140,
  1:43..$25-30
 1964 Break Taxi, black, #1142, 1:43...$25-30
 1964 Pickup Fire Dept. Lyon, #100286,
  1:43..$25-30

Peugeot Partner
 blue, #100667, 1:43 ....$25-30
 Fire Dept., #100699, 1:43.............$25-30
1968 Porsche 911 Targa
 metallic blue, #1147, 1:43 ....$25-30
 Rallye, white with rally markings, #1148,
  1:43..$25-30
Porsche 917 24 Hrs. Du Mans, No. 12,
 #100312, 1:43.................................$25-30
Renault 1000 KG
 Camionette, #100486, 1:43 ....$32
 Fire Dept. 4x4, #100632, 1:43...........$35
1954 Renault 4 CV
 green, #100610, 1:43 ....$25-30
 Sedan, tan, #1106, 1:43.................$25-30
 Fire Chief, red, #1109, 1:43.............$25-30
 Police, black, #1108, 1:43...............$25-30
 "Renault Service," #100421, 1:43....$25-30
 "Tour De France," #1107, 1:43........$25-30
Renault 5
 green, #100616, 1:43 ....$25-30
 Fire Department Marseille, #100462,
  1:43..$25-30
Renault AE
 500 "A.F.T. - I.F.T.I.M.," #110766,
  1:43..$85-95
 430 Restyle Bils Deroo, #111372,
  1:43..$85-95
Renault B 120
 Fire Dept., #110028, 1:43..............$25-35
 Reanimation, #110045, 1:43 ....$25-35
 Fire Dept. Izernore, #110439, 1:43..$25-35

Renault Car Iliade Bus, #130042, 1:43..$85-95

Renault G 340 TI Citerne Dentressangle N.L.,
 #111049, 1:43.................................$85-95
1938 Renault Juvaquatre
 Sedan, #1014, 1:43 ....$30
 Sedan, yellow, #100608, 1:43 ....$25-30
 Camionette Tolee, blue, #100643,
  1:43..$25-30
 Fire Dept. with boat and trailer, #100703,
  1:43..$25-30
 Pompiers (Fire Chief), #1014P, 1:43 ...$25-30
1928 Renault KZ
 Coupe Chauffeur, #1041, 1:43 ....$25-30
 Pompiers (Fire Truck), #1048, 1:43....$25-30
 Fire Department with ladder, #100702,
  1:43..$25-30

Taxi, #1042, 1:43...........................$25-30
1927 Renault NN Torpedo, covered, blue
 and black, #100076, 1:43.............$25-30
Renault Premium
 Norbert Directionel, #110569, 1:43 .$85-95
 Norbert Auto-Porte, #110570, 1:43.$85-95
 Lamberet, #110749, 1:43...............$85-95
 Distribution Poste, #111246, 1:43 ....$65
 Porteur Danzas, #111412, 1:43 ....$65
 Renault R 312 Bus, "S.T.V.U.,"
  #130046, 1:43..............................$85-95
Renault R 350 "Auto Ecole Alain,"
 #110063, 1:43................................$85-95
Rolls Royce
 1928 Limousine 20/25, #1030, 1:43...$30
 1929 Taxi D'Hotel "Carlton," #1051,
  1:43...$30

**1930 Limousine de Ville Noir, black with
yellow wicker, #1055, 1:43.........................$30**

1975 Silver Shadow, #100091, 1:43 ....$25-30

1976 Silver Shadow Sedan, #1047, 1:43 ..$30
Scania Series 3 TRPS Jarlaud, #110997,
 1:43 ....$85-95
Scania Series 4
 Peugeot Sport F1 97, #111125,
  1:43..$85-95
 Toit Bas Pivoin, #111237, 1:43 ....$85-95

Sapeurs Pompier, #111947, 1:43 ....$85-95

Scania Topline Boreal Services, #111395,
 1:43 ....$85-95
Simca Break
 1500, burgundy, #100620, 1:43....$25-30

Marly, yellow, #100617, 1:43 ....$25-30
Marly Ambulance Fire Dept., #100412,
    1:43 ....$25-30
1930 Talbot Pacific
    Limousine, #1036, 1:43 ....$25-30
    Limousine, #100070, 1:43 ....$25-30
    Hotel Taxi, "Hotel De France," #1052,
      1:43 ....$25-30
    Hotel Taxi, brown and red, #100109,
      1:43 ....$25-30
1968 Triumph
    TR5 Cabriolet, top down, dark green,
      #1133, 1:43 ....$25-30
    TR5 Cabriolet, top up, red, #1134,
      1:43 ....$25-30
    TR6 "Coupe Des Alpes, blue, #1135,
      1:43 ....$25-30
Volvo FH
    "KLM cargo," #111003, 1:43 ....$85-95
    Peugeot Sport 1998, #111371,
      1:43 ....$85-95

Elmont (also see Timpo Toys)

    Elmont of Great Britain represents a short-lived series of Timpo Toys plastic trucks with friction motors, produced in the mid-1950s. These toys failed in the market because they were not as appealing or realistic as similar toys made by Wells-Brimtoy or Tri-Ang Minic. What identifies Elmont as having been produced by Timpo Toys is the milk tanker marked "Timpo – Tanker."

AEC Tower Truck, "Danger Overhead Repair" ..$30-45
Fire Engine $30-45
Foden
    Cable Layer Truck $30-45
    Cask Truck $30-45
    Coal Truck $30-45
    Road Tanker, " Esso" $30-45
    Road Milk Tanker, "Timpo - Tanker" $30-45
    Sand Truck $30-45
    Truck with Case "Atom-Load" $30-45
    Truck with Bricks...............................$30-45
    Van "Elmont Toys" $30-45
Ford
    Articulated Flat Truck, "Elmont Road
      Haulage" $30-45
    Breakdown Truck, "Elmont Breakdown" ..$30-45
    Dumper, "Elmont Sand - Ballast" $30-45
    Tank...$30-45

Elysee

    More information is needed on this brand likely made in France. Only one model is known.

1940 Dodge Coupe, 1:43 ....$55-75

Emek

Emek-Muovi Oy
Kapulametsäntie 9
09430 Saukkola, Finland
Tel.: + 358-(0)19-371 500
Fax: + 358-(0)19-371 502
e-mail: emek@pp.kolumbus.fi

    Emek represents plastic collectible quality 1:25 scale models made in Saukkola, Finland. Below is just a short sampling.

Lännen excavator, #6070 ....$15-20
Scania T-Cabin
    dumper, #1014 ....$15-20
    tipper with tipper trailer, #2045 ....$25-30
Volvo FL10
    dumper, #1018 ....$15-20
    tipper, #2095 ....$15-20

Empire (see Zaugg)

Empro

    Empro toys were manufactured in England in the late 1940s. Just one model is known, a 1948 Allard Roadster derived from a Robin Hood casting. The difference is that the Empro version has a hole in the front to accomodate a wind-up motor powered by a rubber band. Approximate scale is 1:38–1:40.

Empro 1948 Allard Roadster $45-60

Enchanted (see Enchantment Land Coach Builders)

Enchantment Land Coach Builders

    Specializing in 1:43 scale limousines and hearses, these custom hand-built cars are created both on and off major model manufacturers' chassies. The home base for the company is believed to be in New Mexico (Land of Enchantment). The fact that Enchanted and Enchantment Land Coach Builders list the same Packard models indicates the two companies are one.

Buick
    1947 Flexible Landau Hearse, black,
      B5 ....$135-150
    1947 Flexible Limousine Hearse, black,
      B6 ....$135-150
    1947 Flexible Limousine Ambulance, white,
      B7 ....$135-150
    1953, top down, Z20 ....$115-130
    1949 Riviera, Z10 ....$135-150

Cadillac
    1931 Indy 500 Pace car, white,
      C10 ....$135-150
    1947 Meteor Hearse Limousine, black,
      C12 ....$135-150
    1947 Series 75 Ambulance, white,
      C13 ....$135-150
    1947 Series 75 Limousine, black,
      C14 ....$135-150
    1966 Superior Hearse, black,
      C16 ....$135-150
    1978 Seville, C4 ....$95-110
Chevrolet
    1957 Nomad Wagon, C11........$105-120
    1957 Nomad, W23 ....$105-120
Chrysler
    1947 Durham Continental Hardtop,
      C1 ....$105-120
    1947 Town & Country Coupe, C2 ..$95-110
    1947 Windsor Convertible, C3 ......$95-110
    1947 Stretch Limousine, maroon,
      C6 ....$115-130
    1947 Hearse, maroon, C7 ....$115-130
    1947 Flower car, maroon, C8......$115-130
    1955 Convertible, Z19 ....$115-130
DeSoto
    1947 Convertible, D1 ....$95-110
Dodge
    1940 Station Wagon, tan, D2......$115-130
Ford
    1935 Siebert Hearse Limousine, gray,
      F3 ....$125-140
    1935 Siebert Ambulance, white, F4 ..$135-150
    1948 Convertible, W22 ....$79
    1951 Victoria Hardtop, F2 ....$95-110
    1956 Convertible, Z23 ....$135-150
    1958 Edsel Convertible, Z22........$115-130
    1960 Thunderbird 2-door Hardtop, T1 ..$95-110
    1965 Thunderbird Convertible, top down,
      T2 ....$95-110
    1982 Mustang Notchback Coupe,
      M5 ....$95-110
    1986 Mustang Convertible, top down,
      M4 ....$95-110
    1988 Mustang GT Convertible, M2 ..$95-110
Graham
    1940 Hollywood Sedan, maroon,
      G1 ....$135-150
Kaiser
    1951 Henry J Sedan, K2...............$95-110
    1953 Manhattan, K3....................$85-100
    1953 Manhattan, K5....................$85-100
    1954 Darrin Roadster, top down, yellow,
      K1 ....$115-130
LaSalle
    1938 Carved Panel Hearse, black, L4 ..$149

1938 Limousine Hearse, black, L5 ....$149
1938 Limousine Ambulance, white,
  L6 ....$149

Lincoln
  1941 Mark 1 2-door Hardtop,
    L1 ....$115-130
  1956 Mark 2 Convertible, Z11 ....$135-150

Meteor
  1950 Convertible, W21 ....$95-110

Packard
  1937 4-door Taxi, P14 ....$105-120
  1937 12-Passenger Coach Bus,
    P15 ....$115-130
  1937 Art-Carved Flower car, black,
    P21 ....$115-130
  1937 Art-Carved Hearse, black,
    P20 ....$115-130
  1937 Club Coupe, P6 ....$85-100
  1937 Club Sedan, P16 ....$95-110
  1937 Continental Sedan, P4 ....$79
  1937 Coupe Fire Service, P17 .....$125-140
  1937 Coupe Police Service, P19 ....$95-110
  1937 Dual Cowl Phaeton, P1 ....$85-100
  1937 Hollywood Darrin Convertible,
    P11 ....$95-110
  1937 Landaulet, P5 ....$85-100
  1937 Panel Delivery, P9 ....$85-100
  1937 Pickup, P7 ....$85-100
  1937 Pickup Fire Service, P18 ......$125-140
  1937 Station Wagon, beige, P3.....$95-110
  1937 Stretch Limousine, black, P8 ...$115-130
  1937 Town Car, P2 ....$95-110
  1937 Van Fire Service, P23.........$125-140
  1937 Van Funeral Service, black,
    P24 ....$115-130
  1937 Van Police Service, P22 ......$125-140
  1937 Victoria, P10.............................$79
  1937 Victoria, top down, P13 ....$85-100

Pontiac
  1968 Convertible, P1 ....$95-110

Willys
  1937 Coupe, W1 ....$95-110

Enco

In late March 1999, collector Peter Max Polshek inquired about the Enco Model Company of England, of which I had not previously known. He reports one model, a Jensen Interceptor FF in 1:43 scale. EWA's Internet search engine (http://ewa1.commodels) has no models listed, but does include Enco in their abbreviation chart (www.ewacars.comtx/wabbrev) as "ENC." More information is needed.

Jensen Interceptor FF, 1:43 ....$45-60

Enstone Emergency Models

Enstone Emergency Models are British hand-built white metal models and kits in 1:48 scale.

Daimler DC27 Ambulance, 1:48 ....$75-90

EPI Sports Collectibles

EPI Group Limited
250 Pequot Ave.
Southport CT 06490
phone: 203-255-1112

Chris Reynolds is president of EPI Group. The EPI Sports Collectibles division is known to have produced at least one very accurate Shell oil tanker in approximately 1:43 scale. As with most diecast models in recent years, EPI models are manufactured in China.

1995 Shell Oil Company's Diecast Collectible Tanker Truck, short tanker truck with tandem tanker, yellow and chrome, 1:43, 10,000 produced $25-30

Epoch (also see MTech)

MTech models are produced by Epoch, Ltd., of Japan. More information can be found under the section on MTech.

Equipe Gallois

Although Bryan Garfield-Jones of Great Britain produced a number of white metal kits under the Equipe Gallois brand, but only one model has been documented.

1949 Buick Roadmaster, #6 ....$60-90

Eria

Eria of France produced 1:46 scale models between 1957 and 1961.

Citroën ID19
  Ambulance, 1961, #38 ....$25-30
  Break, 1961, #39 ....$25-30
Jaguar D Type, 1960, #36 ....$25-30
Panhard PL17, 1960, #34 ....$25-30
Peugeot 403, 1957, #31 ....$25-30
Peugeot 404, 1961, #37 ....$25-30
Renault Dauphine, 1958, #32 ....$25-30
Renault Estafette Van, 1960, #35 ....$30-35
Simca P60 Aronde, 1959, #33 ....$25-30

Erie

Parker White Metal Company of Erie, Pennsylvania, was the source for Erie toys manufactured beginning around 1935. The founder was F. W. Ziesenheim in 1935. All Erie models are white metal, some unpainted, with wooden wheels. The company continued until the early 1960s although toy production ceased in 1941 at the start of World War II.

Cabover Truck, 1937, 3¼" $35-50
Champion Coal Truck, 1935, 5" $80-105
Ford Ice Truck, 1935, 5" $75-90
Ford Pickup Truck, 1935, 5" $65-80
Ford Tow Truck, 5" $75-90
Futuristic Coupe, 1939, no chassis, 4¼" ...$50-65
Futuristic Sedan, 1939, 4¼" $65-80
Lincoln Zephyr Sedan, 1936
  5½" $90-120
  3½" $65-80
Packard 1936 Roadster
  6" $90-120
  3½" $65-80
Tow Truck, 1939, 4¼" $65-80

E. R. Roach (see Roach Industries)

Ertl

Fred J. Ertl Sr. started The Ertl Company in 1945 from his Dubuque, Iowa, home. He applied the diecasting techniques he had learned in his homeland Germany to manufacture licensed farm toys from John Deere's and International Harvester's original blueprints. Soon after, he moved operations to Dyersville, Iowa, where the company remains today. From diecast farm toys, Ertl has expanded to the manufacture of pressed steel and diecast toy trucks, diecast scale model cars, and an assortment of other toys. Their large assortment of diecast vehicle banks has been extremely popular for decades.

On February 1, 1999, Racing Champions announced it would purchase the Ertl Company. The arrangement was completed by April 15, 1999.

Ertl's immense product line represents thousands of models, all designed after real vehicles. As you might guess, an entire book is needed to present the broad range of models produced. Ertl collectors are an elite group, many of whom only collect special issue limited edition models. Others specialize in just Ertl tractors or Ertl banks.

Several collectors clubs exist for Ertl models. While the official Ertl Collectors Club no longer exists, Ertl still published *The Replica* newsletter. *The Replica* is a full-color publication featuring product previews from their farm toy and collectibles lines. It is a bi-monthly magazine that also includes subscriber exclusives, feature articles related to the industry, as well as a classified ad/show listing section. Circulation is around 30,000 worldwide and current subscription rates are U.S. $12.00 for 1 year (6 issues); outside the U.S. $16.00 for 1 year (6 issues). The address for subscriptions is Ertl A/R Replica Subscriptions, P.O. Box 500, Dyersville, IA 52040.

Ertl previously was a subsidiary of Kidde, Inc., makers of fire extinguishers, smoke detectors, and a broad range of other products. Other brands such as Spec-Cast, Liberty Classics, First Gear, and a few others have sprung up in Iowa, inspired by Ertl's success. Spec-Cast, in fact, is a direct offspring of the Ertl Company.

While Ertls were originally made in Iowa, most are now manufactured in China, Korea, or other Asian manufacturing centers. A confusing numbering system on the package is rarely reflected on the model, so an alphabetical listing is therefore presented by description, followed by model number, scale, introduction year, where made, and current value. Many models are reissued year after year, so information is often incomplete. Here is just a sampling.

Ertl 1:18 Scale American Muscle Collection

1935 Auburn 851 Boattail Speedster
  red $35-40
  black................$35-40
  cream................$45-55
1970 Buick GSX, yellow/red/black $30-40
1971 Buick GSX, black/gold.............$30-40
1969 Chevrolet Camaro SS 396, orange and
  white $30-40
1969 Chevrolet Camaro Z-28, red and
  white $30-40
1996 Chevrolet Camaro Z-28 Convertible,
  green or red................$25-35
1970 Chevrolet Chevelle SS 454 LS6
  metallic blue with white accents $30-40
  yellow with black accents $30-40
1967 Chevrolet Corvette L-71 Roadster,
  Sunfire yellow................$40-50
1963 Chevrolet Corvette Stingray,
  dark blue $30-40
1964 Chevrolet Impala SS, black $25-35
1994 Chevrolet Lumina
  Western Auto, D. Waltrip.........$30-40
  Goodwrench, Earnhardt............$30-40
  Interstate, Jarrett $30-40
  #24 Dupont, Jeff Gordon $75-85
1995 Chevrolet Monte Carlo Goodwrench
  #3, Dale Earnhardt $75-85

1969 Dodge Superbee

metallic blue................$30-40

metallic gold................$30-40

pale yellow................$30-40

1970 Dodge Challenger
  T/A $30-40
  R/T $30-40
1978 Dodge Li'l Red Truck $30-40
1978 Dodge Warlock pickup truck $30-40
1995 Dodge Ram Truck, red or black......$25-35
Ferrari 275 GTB4, red................$30-35
1940 Ford Deluxe Coupe, maroon $25-35
1956 Ford Sunliner

two-tone coral pink and black............$30-40

cream and pumpkin orange................$30-40

1996 Ford F-150 Pickup, red or green......$25-35

1970 Ford Mustang Boss 302, yellow with
  black accents $30-40
1970 Ford Mustang Boss 429, Grabber
  green................$40-50
1995 Ford Smokin' Joes #23, Jimmy
  Spencer................$75-85
1992 Ford Thunderbird
  #1 Baby Ruth, Jeff Gordon $75-85
  Budweiser, Elliott $30-40
  Valvoline, Martin $30-40
1959 Ford Starliner, powder blue $30-40

**Land Rover Freelander, black, Ertl
Britains................$35-45**

1949 Mercury Coupe, black $30-40

**1969 Oldsmobile 4-4-2, metallic
gold................$30-40**

1970 Plymouth AAR 'Cuda, lime green $30-40
1969 Plymouth GTX $30-40
1969 Plymouth Hemi Roadrunner
  yellow $30-40
  limited edition Scorch Red................$30-40
1990 Pontiac Grand Prix
  STP, R. Petty................$30-40
  Miller Genuine Draft #27, Rusty
    Wallace $75-85
  Pennzoil, M. Waltrip $30-40
  Miller Genuine Draft #2, Rusty
    Wallace $75-85
  Mello Yello, K. Petty................$30-40

1969 Pontiac GTO "The Judge"
v.1 metallic light blue $30-40
v.2 green/yellow/white $30-40
1996 Pontiac TransAm Coupe, metallic red or
burgundy $25-35
Shelby Cobra 427 S/C, red/white $30-40

Ertl 1:43 Scale American Muscle
Class of 1970 Set....................................$30-40
1970 Olds 442, metallic gold $10-12
1970 Chevrolet Nova SS396, deep
green $10-12
1970 Ford Torino Cobra, bright
orange-red $10-12
Class of 1967 Set....................................$30-40
1967 Camaro SS396, metallic teal blue ...$10-12
1967 Pontiac Firebird, black $10-12
1967 Ford Mustang Shelby GT350, red ...$10-12

Ertl Air & Space
Army Helicopter...$3-5
Coast Guard Helicopter, #1509, AIR &
SPACE series..............................$3-5
Space Shuttle with Booster Rockets & Launch
Pad, #1515, 1:500, Hong Kong $5-7

Ertl Farm Machines 1:64
Allis-Chalmers 8070 Tractor, #1703-1819,
China...$6-8
Case 2594 Tractor, #1704, 1986, Korea ...$6-8
Ford TW-20 Tractor with Cab, #1703-1621,
China...$6-8
Ford TW-35 Tractor with Cab, #1703-832,
Korea $6-8
International Harvester 5088 Tractor with
Cab, #1703-1797, Korea...................$6-8
John Deere Tractor with Cab, #1703-1619,
Hong Kong $6-8
Massey-Ferguson 2775 Tractor, #1703-1622,
China...$6-8
Anhydrous Ammonia Tank, #1589-1550,
Hong Kong $3-5
International Harvester Farm Wagon, #1589-
1755, Korea $3-5
International Harvester Mixer Mill,
#1589-1551, Korea $3-5
International Harvester Round Baler,
#1589-1758, Korea $3-5
New Holland Forage Wagon, #1589AO,
1986, Korea $3-5
John Deere Forage Wagon.........................$3-5
International COE Grain Hauler, #1518-1238,
China $8-10

Ertl John Deere Tractor Collection
Seven-piece set in original box $45-60

1892 Froelich......................................$6-8
1914 Waterloo Boy $6-8
1923 John Deere Model D $6-8
1939 John Deere Model A Row Crop..........$6-8
1952 John Deere Model 60 ....$6-8
1958 John Deere 730 Row Crop $6-8
1960 John Deere 4010 Row Crop $6-8

Ertl Mighty Movers 1:64
Case 1845C Uni-Loader........................$8-10
Caterpillar Road Grader, #1848, China $8-10
International Excavator 640, #1854 ....$8-10
International Hauler 350 Dump Truck, #1852,
China $8-10
International Scraper 412B, #1855 Earth Mover,
China $8-10
International TD20 Series E Crawler, #1851,
China $8-10
International Wheel Loader 560, #1850,
China $8-10

Ertl Vintage Vehicles, 1:43 scale, introduced in 1985

1912 Buick, #5, #2516 ....$16-20

1952 Cadillac Coupe DeVille Model 62 4-door,
#12, #2541 ....$16-20
1959 Checker Cab, #16, #2587 ....$16-20
1930 Chevrolet ½-Ton Delivery Truck, #7,
#2518 ....$16-20
1930 Chevrolet Stake Truck, #3,
#2503 ....$16-20
1957 Chevrolet Bel Air 2-door Hardtop, #11,
#2540 ....$16-20
1960 Chevrolet Corvette, #14, #2588...$16-20

**1913 Ford Model T Van "Ta-Pat-Co,"
#2, #2502...$16-20**

1923 Ford Fordor, #8, #2519 ....$16-20

1932 Ford Panel Truck "Perfection Stoves,"
#4, #2504 ....$16-20
1932 Ford Roadster, #1, #2501 ....$16-20
1940 Ford Woody Station Wagon, #6,
#2517 ....$16-20
1957 Ford Thunderbird, #17, #2802.....$16-20
1930 Packard Boattail Speedster, #10,
#2542 ....$16-20

Ertl Vintage Farm Vehicles, 1:43 Scale
Allis-Chalmers C with Roto-Bailer, F-9,
#4298 ....$16-20
Allis-Chalmers D-21, F-13 ....$16-20
Case 500 Diesel, F-1, #2510 ....$16-20
Case 600, F-11 ....$16-20
Case "L," F-12, #2554.........................$16-20
English Fordson, F-6, #2526 (dark blue or
gray)...$16-20
Ford 8N with Loader, F-3, #2512 ....$16-20
Ford 961, F-5 ....$16-20
Ford 981, F-15 ....$16-20
International Harvester Farmall 300, F-4,
#2513 ....$16-20
International Harvester Farmall 350 Wide Front,
F-10, #2244 ....$16-20
1934 John Deere Model A, F-14, #5598...$16-20
1936 Massey-Harris Challenger, F-2,
#2511 ....$16-20
Massey-Harris Model 44, F-8, #2528 .....$16-20
McCormick-Deering Farmall, F-7, #2527 ...$16-20

Ertl Batman, The Movie Collectibles
Batmobile
1:64 ....$5-10
1:43 ....$15-20
Joker Van, 1:43 ....$12-15

Ertl Batman, The Animated Series Collectibles, 1:64
Batmobile...$6-8
Bruce Wayne's car $6-8
Police Helicopter....................................$6-8

Ertl Dick Tracy Movie Replicas 1989, 1:64
Dick Tracy's 1936 Ford, #2679 ....$6-8

Dick Tracy's 1936 Ford Fordor Police car,
#2676 ....$6-8
Itchy and Flattop's 1939 Chevrolet,
1990, #2677 ....$6-8
Tess's 1937 Plymouth, 1990, #2678.........$6-8

Ertl Dukes of Hazzard
TV Series Replicas 1:64
Dukes' Dixie Challenger $15-20
Cooder's Pickup Truck $10-15
Hazzard County Sheriff's car...................$10-15
Boss Hogg's Cadillac $10-15

Ertl The Cannonball Run Movie Replicas
1:64
Ferrari Dino 246 GT $8-10

Ertl Made in America Series
Corvette, Made In USA $1-3
Charger, Made In USA $1-3
Fiero, Made In USA $1-3
Firebird, Made In USA $1-3

Other Ertl Models
1950 Chevrolet 3100 Pickup Stake Truck,
1:24 ....$15-20
1951 Chevrolet, 1:64 ....$6-8
1955 Chevrolet Bel Air with garage box,
1:24 scale $15-18
Chevrolet Stepside Pickup "Bell System,"
1:64 ....$15-20
1931 Hawkeye Flatbed, 1:43 ....$15-20
Horse-Drawn Van "Telephones 5¢ Per Day"
and "New Nickel Service" $60-75
Land Rover, 1:64 ....$3-5
Lamb Chops Train, 1994 ....$5-7
Mack 1926 Bull Dog "Let Your Fingers Do The
Walking" Yellow Pages delivery truck ..$60-75
Pontiac GTO, 1:43 ....$8-10

**Rolls Royce Silver Shadow, metallic blue,
Ertl European Classics, 1:64 scale $5-8**

Ertl NASA Commemoratives
"Columbia" Command Module-Apollo 11 ...$10-12
"Eagle" Lunar Module-Apollo 11 ....$10-12
"Friendship 7" Mercury Capsule $10-12
Lunar Rover-Apollo 15 ....$10-12

Esci (see C.B.Car)

Esdo
Dominique Esparcieux is the founder of Esdo of France which offers a series of 1:43 scale models. One representative model is known.

Oldsmobile Omega Sedan, gold $65-75

Eska
What little is known about this brand is that Eska Company Inc. was based in Dubuque, Iowa, and produced at least one diecast promotional bank, a 1961–1971 International Scout Metro Mite Convertible.

1961–1971 International Scout Metro Mite, top
down...$100-150

Espewe
Espewe of Germany makes these models of various scales, some or all are plastic.

1911 Horch 4-door car, 1:43................$18-24
1913 Audi Convertible, top down, 1:43 ...$18-24
Ifa Truck, 1:120 ....$5-7
Stake Truck with load, blue plastic, 1:87.......$5-7

Estetyka
Estetyka is a manufacturer from Poland that produces an assortment of 1:43 scale models of mostly Italian vehicles.

1926 Bugatti 35 Roadster, #1 ....$8-10
Ferrari Dino, #6 ....$11-15
Ferrari P4, #5 ....$11-15
Fiat 126 2-door Sedan, #7 ....$8-10
1926 Isotta Fraschini, #2 ....$8-10
Polonez 4-door Sedan, #8 ....$8-10
Ursus C385 Tractor, #9 ....$18-24
1904 Wanderer Roadster, #4..................$8-10

Etzel's Speed Classics
Recently discovered on eBay are these 1:25 scale resin model kits in a plain box with black and white graphics imprinted on a label affixed to the box.

Kuzma Offy, 1954, 1956, 1957 National
Champion, 8 bids, starting $80, winning
bid..$122
Stutz Blackhawk, Frank Lockhart's 1928 Land
Speed Record, 1 bid, starting $40,
winning bid......................................$80

Evrat 87 - LP Creations
Evrat 87
Yves Evrat

Apis Technology
10 Avenue du Quebec
BP 537
Courtaboeuf Cedex 91946 France
phone: 011-33-169-86-12-09
fax: 011-33-169-29-03-18
Evrat 87 produces very high quality resin model kits of high performance street and race cars with etched metal detail. Recently Evrat has also produced 1:43 scale racing models.

Alpine A110, 1:87, 1600S..................$20-30
Tour de l'Aisne $20-30
Gendarmerie $20-30
Maclaren Mercedes MP4/13 1st
Australian Grand Prix 1998, 1:43...$80-100
Williams Renault FW15, 1:87
A. Prost 1993 ....$20-30
Hill 1993 ....$20-30
Hill 1994 ....$20-30
A. Senna 1994 ....$20-30

Excel (also see Goodee)
Only one example of this New Jersey diecast company has been documented.

1950 Jeep CJ2, 5"................................$20-25

Excite (also see Sunnyside)
Excite / Magic
1270 Champion Circle
Carrollton, TX 75006 USA
Excite offers an assortment of 1:32 scale stretch limos with an uncanny resemblance to Majorette 3045-series limousines. The copy is so blatant that the box even indicates the same number 3045 on the back. While the Excite models are the same length as the Majorettes, about 9 inches long, they are wider than the Majorettes, giving them more accurate proportions.

Upon removal from the package however, the base of the Excite model bears the unmistakable "Flying S" logo that identifies it as a Sunnyside model. So it appears that Excite simply repackages Sunnysides with their own name on the box. Similarly, E.J. Enterprises also has repackaged Sunnyside models as their own.

Another diecast toy assortment that goes by the Magic brand curiously bears the same address on the back of their package as Excite models. Closer inspection, particularly of the Chevrolet Caprice fire department command car, reveals them to be Welly toys. Apparently this practice of repackaging and re-branding diecast toys is not as uncommon as we might think.

Exclusive First Editions (EFE)

Bill Cross reports that Exclusive First Editions are 1:76 scale diecast models, in tune with the scale of British "00" gauge model trains. They now produce a very extensive range of vintage and modern British buses and trucks. The brand was started in 1989 in Milton Keyes, England. Models are produced in Asia.

Exclusive First Edition Automobiles

Austin-Healey Sprite
#701 ....$10-12
#703 ....$10-12
MGB
#501 ....$10-12
#503 ....$10-12
Triumph Roadster
#401 ....$10-12
#403 ....$10-12
Triumph Vitesse
#601 ....$10-12
#603 ....$10-12

Exclusive First Edition Commercial Service Vehicles

AEC Mammoth Major 6 Wheel Dropside
"Fenland," #10301 ....$12-15
"Cyril Ridgeon & Son," #10302........$12-15
"J. D. Lown," #10303 ....$12-15
AEC Mammoth Major 6-Wheel Flatbed
"Furlong Bros.," #10701 ....$12-15
"Blue Circle," #10702 ....$12-15
"Wimpey," #10703..........................$12-15
"Wimpey," #10703R $12-15
AEC Mammoth Major 6-Wheel Tanker
"Haygates," #10901 ....$12-15
"Lord Rayleighs Farms," #10902 ....$12-15
"LPG Transport," #10903 ....$12-15
"Welch's," #10908 ....$12-15
AEC Mammoth Major 8-Wheel Dropside
"British Steel," #10801 ....$12-15
"Whitbread," #10802 ....$12-15
"Marley," #10803 ....$12-15
"Macready's," #10804 ....$12-15
AEC Mammoth Major 8 Wheel Flatbed
"Bath & Portland," #10401 ....$12-15
"London Brick," #10402 ....$12-15
AEC Mammoth Major 8-Wheel Tanker
"Century Oils," #10601 ....$12-15
"J. & H. Bunn," #10602 ....$12-15
"Mobilgas," #10604........................$12-15
"Regent," #10605..........................$12-15
AEC Mammoth Major 8-Wheel Tipper
"Wimpey," #12001 ....$12-15
"Tarmac," #12002..........................$12-15
AEC Mammoth Major Box Van

"London Carriers," #10501 ....$12-15
"Startrite," #10502 ....$12-15
"BRS," #10503 ....$12-15
"PEK," #10504 ....$12-15
"Oxydol," #10505 ....$12-15
"Croft," #11001 ....$12-15
"Pickfords," #11002 ....$12-15
"Lacons," #11005 ....$12-15
"Rose's," #11106 ....$12-15
AEC Routemaster London Transport,
#15623 ....$12-15
AEC RT Bradford Bus, #10114............$12-15
AEC RT Dundee Bus
"Courier," #10113 ....$12-15
AEC RT Greenline Bus
"Buxted," #10102 ....$12-15
AEC RT London Country Bus
"Birds Eye," #10103 ....$12-15
AEC RT London Transport Bus
"Duracell," #10101 ....$12-15
"Schweppes," #10104 ....$12-15
"Dulux," #10107 ....$12-15
"Bird's Custard," #10109 ....$12-15
"Barclays," #10111 ....$12-15
"Vernons," #10112 ....$12-15
AEC RT Open Top Bus, #10201
"Beachy Head" $12-15
"Colemans" $12-15
"Caronation" $12-15
"Typhoo Tea" $12-15
Atkinson 6-Wheel Box Van
"Wells," #12501 ....$12-15
Atkinson 6-Wheel Dropside
"McNicholas," #12601 ....$12-15
Atkinson 8-Wheel Box Van
"Fyffes," #12901 ....$12-15
Atkinson 8-Wheel Flatbed
"McPhees," #12801 ....$12-15
Atkinson 8-Wheel Tanker
"Charringtons," #12701 ....$12-15
Atkinson 8 Wheel Tipper
"St. Albans," #13301 ....$12-15
Atkinson Car Transporter
#13001 ....$12-15
"Swift's," #13002 ....$12-15
"Midlands," #13303 ....$12-15
B.E.T. Halifax, #24310 ....$12-15
Bristol LS Wilts & Dorset, #16312DL........$12-15
Bristol VR Open Top Southern National,
#18501 ....$12-15
Daimler CVG6 West Bromwich, #19808 ..$12-15
Deluxe Road Transport Set, #99903........$25-30
Fisherman's Friend 3-Piece Gift Set, #19006 ..$25-30
Harrington Cavalier Coach
#11901....................................$12-15
#12101....................................$12-15

"East Yorkshire," #12102 ....$12-15
"Grey Green," #11903 ....$12-15
"Hebble," #12103 ....$12-15
Harrington Grenadier Coach
#12201....................................$12-15
"Premier Travel," #12202 ....$12-15
#12301....................................$12-15
"Grey Cars," #12302 ....$12-15
Leeds Horsefield Tramcar
"CWS/Tizer," #13402 ....$12-15
"Jacob's," #13403 ....$12-15
Manchester MCW Atlantean Devon General,
#24702 ....$15-20
Rank Hovis 3-Piece Gift Set, #19902...$25-30
RTL Double Decker Bus
"Lockey's," #11104 ....$12-15
"Brylcreem," #11105 ....$12-15
RTL 3-Piece Gift Set, #19003 ....$25-30
Tate & Lyle 3-Piece Gift Set, #19901.......$25-30
Taylor Woodrow Gift Set, #19904........$25-30

Exem (also see Progetto K)

This unusual brand from Portugal offers an assortment of 1:43 scale Austin Healey Sprites in diecast resin.

Austin-Healey "Bugeye" Sprite, 1:43
Red, Open Top, #7004 ....$30-40
British Racing Green, Open Top, #7005 ...$30-40
Black, Top Up, #7006 ....$30-40

Exemplers

No information is available except for documentation of a single model produced under this brand name.

DeTomaso Pantera, silver, 1:45..............$16-24

Exoto

Exoto Inc. offers a broad assortment of precision scale models in their Exoto Tifosi catalog. Exoto Models represent highly detailed precision models, mostly in 1:18 scale, mostly of race cars.

For 1998, Exoto expands their offerings with a new series called ThunderTrac, a line of 1:18 scale models showcased by variations of the popular AM General High Mobility Multi-purpose Wheeled Vehicle, abbreviated HMMWV and better known as the Humvee or Hummer.

AC Cobra Daytona Coupe
1964 Gurney/Bondurant LeMans Class
Winner #5, Viking blue $130
1965 Sutcliffe and Harper #59, red $130
Chevrolet Corvette Grand Sport 1963
metallic blue.......................................$110

Grand Prix Tyrell 003
    1971 Jackie Stewart #2 ....$110
    Francois Cevert #9 ....$110
Lotus Ford 49
    1967 Jim Clark #5 ....$110
Lotus Ford 49B
    1968 G. Hill #9 ....$130
    1968 G. Hill #10 ....$130
    1968 M. Andretti #12 ....$130
    1968 Siffert #22 ....$130

Exoto ThunderTrac Series

Humvee
    civilian soft top, 1:18 ....$80
    civilian wagon, 1:18 ....$80
    Desert Storm, 1:18...............................$80
    military command car, 1:18 ....$80

Express Wheels (see Suntoys)

F

F&F

Starting in 1954 and continuing until 1967, Fiedler and Fiedler of Dayton, Ohio, produced inexpensive cereal premiums for Post cereals under the auspices of F & F Mold and Die Works. The three inch long cars are one-piece plastic with no interior, base, or window glazing. A preponderance of Fords is evident in the assortment. Values are remarkably high for these inexpensively produced toys.

1950 Ford 4-door Sedan $30-45
1951 Ford 4-door Sedan $30-45
1954 Ford Crestline Hardtop..................$15-25
1954 Ford Crestline 4-door Sedan $15-25
1954 Ford Crestline Sunliner....................$15-25
1954 Ford Customline Ranchwagon........$15-25
1954 Ford Customline 2-door Sedan.......$15-25
1955 Ford Customline 2-door Sedan.......$15-25
1955 Ford Fairlane Crown Victoria $15-25
1955 Ford Fairlane Sunliner $15-25
1955 Ford Thunderbird Convertible $15-25
1957 Ford 4-door Hardtop Sedan $15-25
1957 Ford Ambulance $15-25
1957 Ford Convertible $15-25
1957 Ford Fire Chief car $15-25
1957 Ford Highway Patrol....................$15-25
1959 Ford Thunderbird Convertible $15-25
1959 Ford Thunderbird Hardtop $15-25
1961 Ford Thunderbird Convertible $15-25
1961 Ford Thunderbird Hardtop $15-25
1961 Ford Thunderbird Roadster,
    single seat $15-25
1966 Ford Mustang Convertible $15-25

1966 Ford Mustang Fastback.................$15-25
1966 Ford Mustang Hardtop $15-25
Ford Tractor / Fruehauf Trailer Enclosed $15-25
Ford Tractor / Fruehauf Trailer Trailer
    Flatbed..$15-25
Ford Tractor / Fruehauf Trailer Trailer
    Lowboy $15-25
Ford Tractor / Fruehauf Trailer Trailer Moving
    Van $15-25
Ford Tractor / Fruehauf Trailer Trailer Oil
    Tanker $15-25
Greyhound Bus $15-25
Greyhound Scenicruiser Double-Decker
    Bus $15-25
1954 Mercury Monterrey 4-door Sedan...$15-25
1954 Mercury Monterrey 2-door Sedan...$15-25
1954 Mercury XM-800 Show car...........$15-25
1967 Mercury Cougar Hardtop..............$15-25
1969 Mercury 2-door Hardtop $15-25
1969 Mercury 4-door Sedan...................$15-25
1969 Mercury Cougar Hardtop..............$15-25
1969 Mercury Cyclone Fastback $15-25
1960 Plymouth Convertible $15-25
1960 Plymouth Hardtop Coupe $15-25
1960 Plymouth Station Wagon...............$15-25

Faie

It is unknown who is the US distributor for Faie models of Hong Kong. It is common for such "generic" models to be widely sold in drugstores and supermarkets, among other places. You'll likely notice that once removed from the package, these models have no identifying marks. Note the misspelling of McLaren on the package back ("Mc Larem"). Such mistakes indicate they were produced and marketed for the English-speaking market by non-English-speaking manufacturers, a common trait of cheaply made Asian knockoffs, whether of diecast toys or other products.

Ferrari 412 M...$1-2
Fox Bat FW 1 ....$1-2
Heskith B 52 ....$1-2
Lotus TPS76, yellow with Goodyear #9 ....$1-2
McLaren M32, red with Dunlop/Goodyear F1
    #2 ....$1-2
Porsche Audi $1-2
Porsche Turbo 936 ....$1-2
Simca Matra 670 ....$1-2
Tiager Jawg 18, orange with Agip/Lucas #4...$1-2

Fairfield Mint (also see National Motor Museum Mint)

The Fairfield Mint / National Motor Museum Mint
1004 Hope Street
Box 4185

Stamford, CT 06907-0185 or
20 Academy Street
Norwalk, CT 06852-7100
toll free: 1-800-964-8908

Fairfield Mint of Norwalk, Connecticut, entered the diecast model market around 1995. The company has contracted with several companies to produce models for them, including Solido, Yat Ming, Ertl, Motor City Classics, and others. The difference is in color variations issued exclusively under the Fairfield Mint brand name.

The first in the series of 1:12 scale models is a white '58 Chevrolet Corvette produced for Fairfield by Solido of France, now a division of Majorette. It retailed for $94 in 1995.

Other models include a 1959 Chevrolet Impala Convertible in 1:18 scale and a 1955 Ford Fairlane Crown Victoria in 1:18 scale, both produced for Fairfield by Yat Ming. Variations of these models are also packaged as Road Legends. They sell for $20–35 each.

Also available is a 1953 Chevrolet Pickup in 1:18 scale that appears to be one produced by Mira of Spain.

The Fairfield Mint catalog is extensive. To order their latest issue, write or call via the contact information above.

1958 Chevrolet Corvette, 1:12, white with
    silver side scoops $75-95
1959 Chevrolet Impala Convertible, 1:12,
    top down, metallic cornflower blue with
    white interior $35-50
1955 Ford Crown Victoria, 1:12, bright pink
    and white $35-50
1953 Chevrolet Pickup, 1:12, red $35-50

Faller

Among a large number of plastic models, Faller of Germany has produced several beautifully rendered 1:18 scale diecast Mercedes-Benz models.

Mercedes-Benz 220 SE
    Cabriolet, top down, white, #4310 ...$40-45
    Cabriolet, top down, burgundy, #4311 ..$40-45
    Cabriolet, top up, limited edition, #4312 ..$45-50
    Coupe, blue or white, #4315 ....$40-45
Mercedes-Benz 220 S, 1956
    black or gray, #4321 ....$40-45
    Taxi, #4322 ....$45-50
    two-tone, open sun roof, #4325 ....$40-45
    two-tone, closed roof, #4326............$40-45

Faller also offers smaller diecast vehicles. Here is a small sampling.

Citroën DS-21 ....$15-20
Porsche 904 GT $15-20
Volkswagen Polizei $15-20

Other Faller models are 1:87 scale motorized plastic vehicles designed to travel on special roadways as part of an HO gauge railroad layout.

Faracars

Faracars is a brand of 1:43 scale diecast race car made in France for a Chicago company. They produced only one car, a Parnelli Jones Indy 500 STP Turbine car similar to a Hot Wheels Shelby Turbine. Nicely detailed, it was one of two models planned. The second car, reportedly a Novi Special, was planned but something went wrong and it never happened. Thanks to Greg Ford for the information.

Indy 500 STP Turbine car, 1:43 ....$25-35

Fastwheel (see Yat Ming)

Feeling 43

Feeling 43 of France offers super-detailed diecast model kits and preassembled models in 1:43 scale.

Feeling 43 Kits

Ferrari 250 Le Mans
   n°26 Le Mans 1965 Short Nose ...$275-290
   1er Le Mans 1965 new $275-290
Ferrari 250 P, 1st Le Mans 1963
   superkit $275-290
Ferrari 250 TR 1957 ....$275-300
Ferrari 330 P4
   Coupe kit.................................$300-315
   Spyder kit $300-315
Ferrari 375
   0488 AM King Leopold 1954......$275-290
   Carrera Panamericana 1954
      superkit.................................$235-250
   Mille Miglia 1954 superkit...........$235-250
   plus winner Le Mans 1954 superkit...$235-250
Ferrari 512M Sunoco $300-315
Maserati A8GCS Tour de France 1963 super
   kit..$235-250

Feeling 43 Built Models

Ferrari 250P 1st Le Mans 1963 super-
   detailed model.....................$1,400-1,550
Ferrari 330 P4
   Coupe monte built $2,450-2,600
   Spyder monte built $2,450-2,600

Ferrari 375
   Mille Miglia 1954 superdetailed
      model $1,200-1,350
   Carrera Panamericana 1954 super-
      detailed model $1,200-1,350
   plus winner Le Mans 1954 super-
      detailed model $1,200-1,350
Maserati A8GCS Tour de France 1963
   superdetailed model $1,200-1,350
Riva Ariston 1965 Boat.....................$600-750

Feeling 43 Transkits – enhancement kits of made from other manufacturers' models or kits

Ferrari 290 Mille Miglia, AMR base:....$105-120
Ferrari 550 Le Mans 2002, 5 versions transkit
   for BBR kit NEW..............................$85-95
Jaguar Type D 1955-57, SMTS base, all
   opening features..........................$130-145

Feil

Richard Feil, a German-American goldsmith, has produced mostly pewter replicas in 1:43 scale.

1934 Auto Union Racer, 1:43...............$45-55

Fidart

Any clue to the background of this brand would be greatly appreciated. This short list of models is the only information known.

Lola GT Coupe, 1:64, #2 ....$3-4
Super Turbo, 1:64, #3...............................$3-4
Volkswagen Dune Buggy, 1:64, #1 ....$3-4

Fimcar

Fimcar models are from Australia. Only a few other notable brands hail from there, Fun Ho!, Top Gear Trax, Micro Models, and probably one or two others. Where Fimcar fits into the picture, I don't know. But based on the $35 retail price tag, they must be fairly nice representations of the real thing.

1948 Holden Pickup, light blue, 1:43 .....$35-45
1953 Holden Pickup, 1:43...................$35-45

Fine Art Models

Fine Art Models
Post Office Box 225
Birmingham, Michigan 48012, USA
telephone: 248-288-5155
fax: 248-288-4412
e-mail: info@fineartmodels.com
website: www.fineartmodels.com

No one tells the story of Fine Art Models better than Gary Kohs, President, as extracted

from their website at www.fineartmodels.com:

"Fine Art Models produces museum-quality limited-edition scale models that many feel are the finest available in the world today. These are the products of a small Royal Oak, Michigan, company formed in 1990 with the singular goal of being the best in the world at what we do. Our focus is producing the finest models available at a price that represents a value and providing customer service without equal. We have no dealers, only one price, and our models can be found in museums and private collections around the world.

"We focus on transportation models including trains, planes, ships, and automobiles. Our models are not limited to American subjects, as Fine Art Models has a presence in the European market with specific models. In as many situations as possible, we personally deliver our models. The scale of our models corresponds to accepted museum standards and, in every case, it is a scale that allows us to replicate the subject without compromise to detail.

"Our models contain no plastic and, in most cases, are made of brass, nickel silver, or stainless steel. The wood on the models is real wood, and the glass in the windows is real scale glass. You will never find a compromise in the design or construction of our models.

"Our ship models have no equal. Period! We feel we have elevated the art of ship model building in many ways, including high-definition resin hulls that reproduce every detail of a real hull, laser-cut and etched wood decks with every detail of a real wood deck and photo-etched brass superstructures that provide every detail of the real ship's superstructure. To understand the level of this detail, you only have to look at our ship models including the USS *Arizona*, USS *Missouri*, *Bismarck*, *Edmund Fitzgerald*, PT Boat and many more. And now we have introduced the first model ever of RMS *Titanic* built in cooperation with the original builders of *Titanic*, Harland & Wolff. This has already been called the model of the century.

"Our train models are 1:32 scale 'Gauge 1' — the original gauge for all trains going back to the late 1800s. We have produced several train models that have sold out and continue to appreciate in value in the secondary market. Our present locomotive, the New York Central J-3a Hudson, is considered the finest train model ever produced, with our patented sound system replicating every sound of the original locomotive. Models on the drawing board include the Union Pacific Big Boy, Pennsylvania

11 Decapod, Pennsylvania B6sb Switcher, Norfolk & Western Class A and the German Bay S3/6. The sign of a great model is that one's eye is not drawn to any one feature on the model while viewing it, yet one can study the model for hours and continually find something new. This describes our models in every respect.

"Our automobile models are built around the Bugatti marque. Rather than try to be everything to everyone, we chose what we consider to be the finest automobile ever built from all points of view. We will make our name in automobile models by building Bugatti. Our Bugatti models are 1:8 scale and are made entirely of hand-fabricated brass — there is no plastic anywhere. The bodies are formed over wooden bucks as were the real Bugattis seventy years ago. We don't feel there are finer automobile models anywhere at any price.

"Having risen to the top in these respective areas, we focused on airplanes, perhaps the greatest challenge of all. These are all-metal airplanes with working control surfaces, operating controls, and virtually every detail found on the real airplane whether one can see it or not. Our 1:15 scale FG-1D Corsair may be the most difficult airplane model of all, and we chose it to be our first for this reason. It is all-metal with fabric-covered outer wings, wood ailerons, fabric-covered tail surfaces, folding wings with working controls, and every other detail found in the original airplane. Following the Corsair, we will do the P-51D Mustang, P-38 Lightning, Spitfire Mark I and many more.

"As a company, we will never become larger than we are today and we will never increase the size of our limited editions regardless of demand. With few exceptions, that maximum number is 139 pieces, the edition size of our very first model.

"Fine Art Models has a 100-plus-page catalog detailing the more than one hundred different model editions we have built over these years, and we publish a quarterly newsletter that keeps everyone informed of our new releases we invite you to contact us for additional information. One of our many customers best described our models as truly fine art that has a tendency to elevate everything around them. Please give us a call any time."

Fine Art Models 1:8 Scale Automobiles

1909-1921 Bugatti Type 13 Brescia, black or red, 1996, 14 built, sold out $8,500-10,000
1924-1926 Bugatti Type 35A, 1999, 50 built.............................$8,500-10,000
1924-1925 Bugatti Type 35B, 1999, 50 built.............................$8,500-10,000

1926 Bugatti Type 37, 1999, 50 built.............................$8,500-10,000
1927-1931 Bugatti Type 37A, 1999, 50 built.............................$8,500-10,000
1927-30 Bugatti Type 43, 1999, 50 built.............................$9,500-11,000
1931-32 Bugatti Type 50/59, 1999, 50 built $10,000-12,500
1931-34 Bugatti Type 51, 1999, 50 built.............................$9,000-10,500
1931-35 Bugatti Type 55, 1999, quantity not provided.....................$10,000-12,500
1938 Bugatti Type 57C, 1998, 50 built $16,000-17,500
1904 Mercedes Simplex, white with red or black interior, 1994, 50 built, sold out $16,500-18,000
1913 Mercer J Raceabout, yellow or blue, 1994, 25 built, sold out...............$16,500-18,000

Fine Model

Collector Robert Speerbrecher reports that these models are likely 1:43 scale and represent mid-1960s to early 1970s Japanese cars. Four models are shown in a Japanese language book. They appear to be a Datsun 240Z, Datsun 240Z Police, and two versions of an unidentified two-door sedan.

A phone number, 03 (3806) 1219, is shown in the book as a contact for the company, and values are shown as 9,000 Japanese yen each, which converts to around $65–66 US.

Datsun Fairlady 240Z, red......................$60-75
Police, black and white with roof light and spotlight.............................$60-75
Two-door Japanese Sedan
    pale blue $60-75
    metallic light blue............................$60-75

Finoko

644083 Glinki street, 4 - 41, Omsk, Russia
contact: Fisyn Alexsander Olegovich

Finoko buses are made-to-order 1:43 scale bus models produced by Finoko workshop, Omsk, Russia. Material is tin-lead castings, with windows of "organic glass" inside, and bottom equipment is available. Quality is good, quantity is limited, prices are moderate, according to Andrey U. Pogorely of Russia.

LAZ 695E $60-75
LAZ 695M...$60-75
LAZ 695N $60-75
LAZ 699R $70-85
LAZ 697M...$60-75

LAZ 697E $60-75
LAZ 697R $60-75
LIAZ 677 ....$75-90
LIAZ 5256 ....$85-100
LIAZ 52565 ....$85-100
PAZ 652 ....$55-70
PAZ 672 ....$55-70
PAZ 3201 ....$55-70
PAZ 3205 ....$55-70
PAZ 32051 ....$55-70
ZIS 154 ....$60-75
ZIS 155 ....$60-75
ZIL 158 ....$60-75
ZIY 9V $85-100

First Choice

Since about 1987, First Choice has produced plastic toys with electronic lights and sounds. In 1997, the Canadian company produced their first diecast vehicle, a Seagrave Fire Pumper in two current Windsor, Ontario, liveries. A limited production of 1,000 of the first color and 2,500 of the second will assure a high resale value for collectors and dealers.

Seagrave Fire Pumper, 1,000 produced ..$30-45
Seagrave Fire Pumper, 2,500 produced ..$25-35

First Gear

First Gear models are 1:34 scale trucks made of heavy diecast metal that are often customized to the buyer's requirements. Various clubs and companies contract First Gear to produce a limited edition model or series of models that feature their company logo or advertising (known as "livery.") Just a few base models are used, but the variations are numerous.

First Gear Toy Collector Club of America 1994 Remington Arms Company Commemorative Series

'51 Ford Truck
    "Dove," 2nd in the series, #10-1098......$45-50
    "Pheasant," 3rd in the series, #10-1139....$45-50
    "Quail," 4th in the series, #10-1094 ......$45-50
    "Turkey," 6th in the series, #10-1133......$45-50
'52 GMC Truck
    "Goose," 5th in the series, #10-1134.....$45-50
    "Mallard," 1st in the series, #10-1082 ....$45-50

Other First Gear Models

1949 Chevrolet Truck
    "Genuine Chevrolet".........................$30-40
    "Mercy Hospital" Ambulance.............$30-40
    "Pepsi Big Shot"...............................$40-50
    "Rock Solid Chevrolet" $30-40

1951 Ford Truck
- "GlasUrit Autolack System" Box Van....$45-55
- "1995 Hershey" Stake Bed $45-55
- "Auto Value" Box Van $60-70
- "Barq's Root Beer".........................$40-50
- "Navajo" Box Van $35-45
- "Red Star" Box Van $50-60
- "Royal Crown Cola" Beverage Truck ..$40-50

1952 GMC Truck
- "Burlington" Box Van.......................$35-45
- "Carstar" Wrecker..........................$40-50
- Chicago Fire Wrecker $100-110
- "Falstaff Beer" $40-50
- "FDNY Oxygen" Stake Bed $40-50
- "Harley Custom Chrome" $50
- "McLean Trucking" $100-110
- Montgomery County Wrecker...........$45-55
- "Morton Salt" Stake Bed..................$35-45
- "O'Doul's Oasis Beer" $35-45
- Philadelphia Rescue $50-60
- "Railway Express" Stake Truck $40-50
- "Stroh's Beer" $40-50
- U. S. Mail Stake Truck $40-50
- "Whitney Volunteer" Tanker $40-50

1953 Ford C600 Truck
- "Roadway" Box Van.........................$35-45

1957 International Harvester Truck
- "AAA of Sacramento" Wrecker $45-55
- "Atlas Van Lines" $70-80
- Boston Engine #54 Fire Truck............$70-80
- "Campbell Soup" Box Van $40-50
- "Dart Towing of the Bronx" $40-50
- "Esso" Tanker...............................$35-45
- "FDNY Garage" Tow Truck $45-55
- "Gulf Oil Refinery" Fire Truck $40-50
- "Gulf Oil" Wrecker $50-60
- "Hershey Chocolate" Van.................$55-65
- "Mobil Oil Refinery" Fire Truck............$45-55
- "Paul Arpin" Double Freighter Moving Van $50-60
- Philadelphia Tow Truck $60-70
- "Shell" Aviation Tanker $35-45
- "SOCAL" Tanker $45-55
- "Tow Times" Wrecker $60-70
- US Army Wrecker $45-55
- "Von Der Ahe" Double Freighter Moving Van $50-60
- Zephyr Lubes" Box Van $30-40

1960 Mack Truck
- "Adley Express" $90-100
- "Campbell Soup"............................$70-80
- "Columbian" Moving Van $80-90
- "Eagle Snacks" $55-65
- "Eastern Express"...........................$55-65
- "Great Northern" $90-100
- "Hershey Anniversary"....................$65-75

- "Humble Oil" $90-100
- "Mack Trucks" $140-150
- "New York Central" $55-65
- "Pepsi Cola" $90-100
- "Red Star" $130-140
- "Smith & Wesson" $90-100
- "St. Johnsbury" $60-70

First Gear 1:54 Scale Series, 1997

- Freightliner FLD 120 conventional tractor with 48-foot trailer $65-75
- Fuel Tanker $65-75
- International 4900 Series trucks $65-75
- Refrigerated Box Truck $65-75
- Stake Truck $65-75

Fischer, Georg Heinrich

It would appear by a little research that Georg Heinrich Fischer is the full proper name of Henry Fischer, the founder of the early twentieth century company known to produce lithographed tinplate toys.

Hi-Way Henry, 10" $1,250-1,400

Fischer, Heinrich (see Fischer, Georg Heinrich)

Fischer, Henry (see Fischer, Georg Heinrich)

Fisher-Price

Most of what Fisher-Price has produced is preschool toys, and along with so many other companies, they've also marketed diecast and plastic diecast toys. Fisher-Price is now a brand owned by Mattel, along with Tyco, Matchbox, and other brands, as well as their own original Hot Wheels. Below is a list of the Sesame Street toys produced under the Fisher-Price brand.

Previously, Hasbro had the license to produce Sesame Street preschool toys. For 1998, Mattel has issued twelve diecast and plastic models under the Tyco Preschool / Matchbox brand. Models are made in China, distributed by Mattel Australia Pty., Ltd., and sold (in the US) in sets of three for $5.99 or individually for $1.97 each. 1999 models are packaged under the Fisher-Price brand, but on the base is printed either "Matchbox" or "Tyco."

- Baby Bear's Buggy, lime green with orange roll bar and base, blue wheels $2-3
- Bert's Tow Truck, lime green with blue boom, orange base, yellow wheels $2-3
- Big Bird's Buggy, lime green with blue roll bar, orange base, yellow wheels $2-3

- Big Bird's Fire Engine, red and white with yellow wheels.....................................$2-3
- Big Bird's Mail Truck, red cab, white container, blue base and wheels.........................$2-3
- Cookie Monster's Airplane, white with yellow trim and propeller, red base, blue wheels $2-3
- Cookie Monster's School Bus, yellow with blue base, red wheels..............................$2-3
- Elmo's Cement Mixer, blue and red with yellow base, silver barrel, red wheels.............$2-3
- Elmo's Dump Truck........................$2-3
- Elmo's Locomotive, blue with red smokestack and wheels, yellow trim $2-3
- Elmo's Taxi, yellow with red base, blue wheels...$2-3
- Ernie's Cement Mixer, yellow with red barrel and wheels..............................$2-3
- Ernie's Dump Truck........................$2-3
- Ernie's Police car............................$2-3
- Fozzie Bear's Dump Truck, blue with red dumper, yellow base, red wheels $2-3
- Fozzie Bear's Police car, white with black doors, orange base, blue wheels $2-3
- Grover's Helicopter, red and yellow with blue skids, silver propeller and tailfin $2-3
- Oscar the Grouch's Garbage Truck, silver with orange container, yellow base, lime green wheels...$2-3
- Telly's Front Loader, yellow with lime green scoop and wheels $2-3
- Zoe's Convertible, red with yellow base, blue wheels...$2-3

F. G. Taylor (see Taylor, F. G.)

Fleer Die-Cast Collectibles (see White Rose Collectibles)

Fletcher, Barnhardt & White

Fletcher, Barnhardt & White is not so much a brand as an advertising and marketing firm. The offerings listed below are collectible premiums sold only at Shell gas stations. Thanks to collector Dave Lehrer who reports that he discovered a generic Porsche 959 Shell Promo produced in China, similarly crude in quality and construction to Summer models. Says Mr. Lehrer, "It even sports wheels similar to some I have seen on Summer models. However, inside the baggie was a card that said that defective merchandise could be exchanged by writing FBW, 327-B W. Tremont, Charlotte, NC 28203. FBW=Fletcher, Barnhardt & White? Probably."

Lehrer continues, "A quick web search turned up a listing for this company in North Carolina... as an advertising/specialties firm. I would be interested in hearing anything regarding the source of these models and if there are any more to be had."

Chevrolet Monte Carlo Stock car, #18 Dale Jarrett, Interstate Batteries, approx. 1:43, black painted metal chassis..........................$8-10
Ford Mustang Stock car #3 Tommy Archer, Shellzone, approx. 1:43, black plastic chassis $8-10
Honda Indy car
    #10 Motorola, approx. 1:50, black painted metal chassis $8-10
    #4 Rahal-Hogan Racing, approx. 1:50, black painted metal chassis.............$8-10
Porsche 959.......................................$8-10

Fly

Fly is the brand name of exceptional slot cars believed to be from Italy. For an online search, type the phrase "Fly slot car" in the search engine to find sources and model listings.

Forma (also see Yaxon)

An assortment of 1:43 scale models were marketed by this Italian firm under the Forma name which became Yaxon of Italy after 1977.

Fiat 130 Semi-Trailer Truck, #300 ....$30-35
Fiat 170 Truck
    Overhead Service Truck, #301.........$30-35
    Garbage Truck, #302......................$30-35
    Lumber Semi-Trailer Truck, #303........$30-35
    Open Semi-Trailer Truck, #304 ....$30-35
    Covered Semi-Trailer Truck, #305 ......$30-35
    Container Semi-Trailer Truck, #306.....$30-35
Mercedes-Benz 2232 Truck
    Truck and Trailer, #311 ....$30-35
    Container Truck, #317 ....$30-35
Farm Tractor
    Same 130 Farm Trailer, #385 ....$30-35
    Lamborghini Farm Tractor, #386 ....$30-35
    Fiat 780 Farm Tractor, #355.............$30-35
    Fiat 880 Farm Tractor, #356.............$30-35
Farm Trailer
    2-Wheel Open, #370 ....$30-35
    4-Wheel Open, #381 ....$30-35
    Hay Loader Trailer, #382 ....$30-35
    Manure Spreader, #371 ....$30-35
    Tank Trailer, #372 ....$30-35

43rd Avenue / Gems 'N' Cobwebs

43rd Avenue is an eclectic British brand of hand-built white metal replicas of US cars. In addition, 43rd Avenue's assortment of English replicas called Gems & Cobwebs features a 1997 release of a 1938 prototype Jaguar SS-100 Coupe in 1:43 scale which was show-

cased in an article in the February 1997 issue of *Mobilia* magazine. The fact that this model even exists celebrates the rarity of the real car which was never put into production.

43rd Avenue

1959 Cadillac Flattop 4-door Sedan,
    1:43................................$100-125
1968 Ford Torino 2-door Convertible,
    1:43.................................$100-125
1951 Studebaker
    Business Coupe 2-door, 1:43........$100-125
    Coupe 2-door, 1:43 ....$100-125

43rd Avenue Gems 'n Cobwebs

Alvis TF21
    open $95-120
    Saloon $95-120
Austin A60
    Pickup $95-120
    Van $95-120
Ford Zephyr Convertible $95-120
Humber Super Snipe.............................$95-120
Jaguar
    420 G................................$95-120
    Mark II $95-120
    Mark IX $95-120
    Mark IX Hearse $95-120
    MX $95-120
    S Type Saloon $95-120
    S Type Police.......................$95-12
    1938 SS-100 Prototype Coupe.....$110-135
    V12 E Type hardtop.......................$95-120
    V12 E Type Convertible $95-120
    XJ6 ....$95-12
    1994 XJR $95-120
    XK150S Coupe $95-120
    XK150S Roadster........................$95-120
Riley Pathfinder
    Police $95-120
    Saloon $95-120

Fournier Enterprises

13326 West Star Drive
Shelby Township, Michigan 48315
phone: 586-323-9160
toll free: 800-501-3722
fax: 586-323-9161
website: www.fournierenterprises.com

Fournier Enterprises was founded in 1991, but the story of founder Ron Fournier and his career in metal fabrication goes back over 40 years. The Fournier Enterprises website provides his in-depth story:

"His career began with Holman and Moody in 1964, and since that time racing

greats such as Roger Penske, A.J. Foyt, Kar Kraft, and Bob Sharp Racing have all utilized Ron's unique skills to transform metal into various components for their championship-winning race cars. General Motors, Ford, and Chrysler have also contracted for his fabrication and training services. In the mid-seventies, Ron founded Race Craft, which soon developed a reputation as one of the finest metal fabrication shops in the country. Ron and his wife Susan have written two books now considered essential references in the automotive metal work field: *Metal Fabricator's Handbook* and *Sheet Metal Handbook*. In 1984 *Metal Fabricator's Handbook* received a Moto Award, the highest achievement in automotive journalism.

"In 1991, Ron and his family founded Fournier Enterprises, a custom metal fabrication company with a variety of business divisions including full-size custom built vehicles, Metal Fabrication Workshops, instructional videos, tool design, and development as well as a line of hand fabricated vintage racing models. Ron is honored to have two of his models, "The Fuel Injection Special" and "The John Zink Special" on display at the Indianapolis Speedway Hall of Fame Museum next to the original classics. Recent projects include a 1938 Bugatti body build, a one-off aluminum bodied roadster and a full schedule of workshops, and industry show appearances. Through the years Ron has worked diligently to promote the craft of metal work and has placed an emphasis on education and training so that the art to which he has dedicated his life's work will continue to thrive for many years to come."

While restoring real cars is his full-time business, Fournier has produced a few hand-built 1:8 scale models of Kurtis Indy Roadsters. These all-metal models represent momentous times in Indianapolis history and feature hand-fabricated aluminum bodies, leather seats, and treaded rubber tires. Models measure approximately 21 inches long and are limited editions of 500 each.

Kurtis Kraft Trio Brass Special, Johnnie Parsons,
    1:8 scale, 500 produced ...$10,000-20,000
Kurtis Kraft Fuel Injection Special, Bill Vukovich,
    1:8 scale, 500 produced ...$10,000-20,000

Framberg, H. L. (also see Dale Model Company)

H. L. Framberg manufactured World War II identification models for use during the war in identifying military vehicles from a distance. More research is needed on this Chicago-based company. After W.W.II, Frank Dale left the firm to form his own Dale Model Company and continue making cast metal military toys based on those made by H. L. Framberg. Nothing more is known about either company except that values on H. L. Framberg models are reportedly around $100 each. The Dale counterparts are valued around $70 each.

France Jouets

Marseilles, France, was the home of France Jouets, founded in 1959. When production was discontinued in 1969, the dies were sold to Safir, also of France. Just six basic chassis provided the basis for a variety of models.

France Jouets 100 Series – Berliet Gak Trucks

Bucket Truck, 1965, #116	$70-85
Cement Mixer, 1962, #107	$70-85
Covered Truck, 1962, #103	$70-85
Crane Truck, 1964, #108	$70-85
Crane Truck, 1964, #114	$70-85
Dump Truck, 1962, #104	$70-85
Farm Truck, 1964, #111	$70-85
Garbage Truck, 1964, #109	$70-85
Glass Truck, 1964, #113	$70-85
Grocery Truck, 1962, #105	$70-85
Lumber Truck, 1962, #102	$70-85
Overhead Service Truck, 1964, #110	$70-85
Pipe Truck, 1964, #112	$70-85
Street Sweeper, 1962, #106	$70-85
Tank Truck, 1962, #101	$70-85
Tow Truck, 1964/65, #115	$70-85

France Jouets 200 Series – Pacific Heavy Truck

Atomic Cannon, not mounted on a truck, 1967, #207	$120-145
Atomic Cannon Truck, 1966/67, #206	$120-145
Atomic Cannon Truck, 1967, #208	$120-145
Cement Truck, 1966, #205	$120-145
Crane Truck, 1967, #201	$120-145
Pipe carrier Truck, 1959, #202	$120-145
Rocket Launcher Truck, 1959, #203	$120-145
Transformer Carrier, 1965, #204	$120-145

France Jouets 300 Series – GMC Truck

Ambulance Truck, 1959, #301	$70-85
Anti-Aircraft Gun Truck, 1959, #303	$70-85
Covered Truck, 1961, #302	$70-85
Crane Truck, 1961	$70-85
Dump Truck, 1961	$70-85
Dump Truck and Trailer, 1961	$70-85
Dump Truck with Shovel, 1961, #306	$70-85
Fire Truck, 1961	$70-85
Lance-Rocket Truck, 1959, #304	$70-85
Lumber Truck, 1959	$70-85
Quarry Dump Truck, 1961	$70-85
Radar Truck, 1959	$70-85
Road Repair Truck, 1961	$70-85
Rocket carrier Truck, 1965, #305	$70-85
Searchlight Truck, 1959	$70-85
Street Sweeper, 1961	$70-85
Tank Truck, 1961	$70-85
Troop Carrier, 1959	$70-85

France Jouets 400 Series – Dodge Truck

Ambulance Truck, 1966, #409	$70-85
Anti-Aircraft Truck, 1960, #404	$70-85
Army Troop Carrier, 1964, #402	$70-85
Covered Army Truck, 1960, #403	$70-85
Fire Truck, 1966, #407	$70-85
Lance-Rocket Truck, 1966, #408	$70-85
Open Army Truck, 1960, #401	$70-85
Radar Truck, 1960, #405	$70-85
Searchlight Truck, 1960, #406	$70-85

France Jouets 500/600 Series – Jeep

Anti-Aircraft Gun Trailer, 1960	$60-75
Anti-Tank Gun without Jeep, 1961, #605	$60-75
Army Jeep with Anti-Aircraft Guns, 1961, #503	$60-75
Army Jeep with Lance-Rockets, 1961, #504	$60-75
Army Jeep with Searchlight, 1961, #506	$60-75
Army Radar Jeep, 1961, #505	$60-75
Covered Army Jeep, 1964, #502	$60-75
Fire Jeep, 1961, #507	$60-75
Jeep and Anti-Tank Gun, 1961, #601	$60-75
Jeep and Generator Trailer, 1961, #602	$60-75
Jeep and Open Trailer, 1961, #603	$60-75
Lance-Rocket Trailer, 1960	$60-75
Open Army Jeep, 1961, #501	$60-75
Police Jeep, 1965, #508	$60-75
Radar Trailer, 1960	$60-75
Searchlight Trailer, 1960	$60-75

France Jouets 700 Series – Berliet Stradair Truck

Coca-Cola Truck, 1967, #708	$70-85
Dump Truck, 1967, #701	$70-85
Garbage Truck, 1967, #707	$70-85
Glass Truck, 1967, #704	$70-85
Grocery Truck, 1967, #702	$70-85
Street Sweeper, 1967, #706	$70-85
Tow Truck, 1967, #703	$70-85

Francorchamps

These are 1:43 scale plastic race cars presumed to have been sold in the 1950s exclusively at Spa-Francorchamps, the Formula One Grand Prix race course in Spa, Belgium.

Maserati 2890cc, 3⅜"	$12-16
Mercedes W196, 3½"	$12-16
Porsche Spyder, 3⅜"	$12-16

Franklin Mint

Between Danbury Mint and Franklin Mint, some of the most popular and collectible precision models have been produced. Jay Olins, editor of Precision Die Cast Car Collectors Club newsletter, is perhaps the most avid collector of both. Every three months, he publishes a complete up-to-date list of models produced by each company. Collectors are very critical of authenticity and detail, so they often write to the manufacturer and to Mr. Olins regarding any discrepancies discovered. Olins apparently has the inside track with both companies, and he relays all such comments to the manufacturer.

In the past couple of years, Franklin Mint has suffered some financial difficulties. Various reports claim Franklin Mint is now out of business, but news from Jay Olins indicates new variations are still being produced in limited quantities. Apparently the company has scaled back its production but hasn't discontinuted it completely.

Franklin Mint 1:6 Scale
Corvette

1957 283HP Engine	$125-140

Franklin Mint 1:8 Scale
Benz

1886 Patent Motorwagen	$125-140

Franklin Mint 1:10 Scale
Indian

1942 442 Motorcycle	$120-140

Harley-Davidson

1957 XL Sportster Motorcycle	$120-140
1985 Heritage Softail Classic Motorcycle	$120-140

Franklin Mint 1:16 Scale
Bugatti

1931 Royale Coupe De Ville	$115-135

Ford

1913 Model T	$115-135
1930 Model A	$115-135

Rolls Royce

1905 10HP	$115-135

Stanley Steamer

1911 62 Runabout	$115-135

Franklin Mint 1:24 Scale

Alvis
1938 Speedster 4.3 Litre, green and silver with beige interior $85-125

Auburn
1935 851 Speedster, white with red interior $85-125

Buick
1949 Skylark Convertible, pale yellow with red interior $85-125
1949 Riviera, light blue and gray with gray interior $85-125

Bugatti
1930 Royale Coupe Napoleon 2, black and blue $85-125
1936 Atalante Type 57 SC, red and black with beige interior $85-125

Cadillac
1910 Thirty Roadster, black and beige ..$85-125
1932 V-16, blue 2-tone, brown with canvas top...$85-125
1953 Eldorado, white/red $85-125
1957 Eldorado Brougham, black and stainless steel with blue and white interior $85-125
1959 Eldorado Biarritz, light blue with white interior $85-125

Chevrolet Bel Air
1955 Bel Air Convertible, gypsy red and white with red and white interior $85-125
1955 Bel Air Fire Chief #12, red with red and white interior $85-125
1955 Bel Air Hardtop, red and white with red and white interior...............$85-125
1955 Bel Air Hardtop, blue and white with blue and white interior $85-125
1955 Bel Air Police Chief #67, black and white.......................................$85-125
1956 Bel Air Convertible, green and white with green and white interior......$85-125
1957 Bel Air Convertible, black with red and silver interior, issued March 1995 ..$85-125
1957 Bel Air Convertible, red with red and silver interior $85-125
1957 Bel Air Hardtop, red and white with red interior $85-125
1957 Bel Air Hot Rod, black with flames, black interior..............................$85-125

Chevrolet Corvette
1953 Corvette, cream and red........$85-125
1955 Corvette, metallic blue with beige interior..............................$85-125
1956 Corvette, turquoise and white with white interior...........................$85-125
1957 Corvette, red and white $85-125
1957 Corvette, fuel Injected, black and silver with red interior $85-125

1959 Corvette, red with red interior, issued March 1995 ....$85-125
1963 Corvette Sting Ray, black and blue with black interior $85-125
1967 Corvette Sting Ray, black and blue with black interior $85-125
1967 Corvette L-88 Sting Ray, blue with blue interior $85-125
1978 Corvette Silver Anniversary Edition, silver with silver interior $85-125
1986 Corvette, yellow with black interior $85-125
1986 Corvette, white with white and black interior $85-125

Chevrolet Impala
1960 Impala white with white interior.....$85-125
1960 Impala red $85-125

Christie
1912 Front Drive Steamer Fire Engine $85-125

Chrysler 1948 Town & Country Convertible, dark green and wood with red and beige interior $85-125

Cord
1937 812 Phaeton Coupe, light yellow with black interior...........................$85-125

Duesenberg
1930 J Derham Tourist maroon and beige with gray interior $85-125
1930 J Derham Tourist, Gary Cooper, silver and black with black interior $85-125
1933 J Victoria, Greta Garbo, blue and black with blue interior $85-125
1933 Twenty Grand SJ, silver and beige with green interior $85-125
1935 Model J550 Convertible, maroon with white interior...........................$85-125

Edsel Citation (see Ford Edsel)

Ferrari
1989 F40, red with red interior $85-125

Ford
1913 Model T, black.....................$85-125
1932 Deuce Coupe, black with beige interior $95-105
1949 "Woody" Wagon, maroon and beige $85-125
1955 Fairlane Crown Victoria, pink and white with pink and white interior ..$85-125
1956 Thunderbird, turquoise with turquoise interior $85-125
1957 Fairlane 500 Skyliner, white and red with white and red interior $85-125
1958 Edsel Citation, pink with pink interior $85-125

Hispano Suiza
1924 Tulipwood Speedster, wood and copper.......................................$85-125
1925 Kellner H6B, maroon/white $85-125

Jaguar
1938 SS-100, cream/brown $85-125
1961 XKE, gray/beige $85-125

Lamborghini
1985 Countach 5000S, red/beige $85-125
1985 Fraternal Order of Police, black with white interior............................$85-125

Lincoln
1941 Continental Mark I, maroon with red interior $85-125

Maybach
1939 Zeppelin, black/gray...........$85-125

Mercedes Simplex
1904, white/brown $85-125

Mercedes-Benz
1935 500K Roadster, red and beige with red and black interior................$85-125
770K Pullman Limousine, red-black ...$85-125
1954 Gullwing 300SL, silver with plaid interior $85-125
1954 Gullwing 300SL, red with plaid interior $85-125
1926 Model K, midnight blue with burgundy and paisley interior $85-125
1954 W196 Racer, silver with red interior $85-125
1957 300 SC Roadster, burgundy with tan and black interior $85-125

MG
1948 TC Roadster, red/beige $85-125

Nash
1956 Metropolitan, aqua-white/aqua/white.....................................$85-125

Oldsmobile
1977 Petty NASCAR, blue-red "43" $85-125

Packard
1912 I-48 Victoria, white with black top.......................................$85-125

Plymouth
1970 Superbird Petty NASCAR, blue "43" $85-125

Porsche 1988 911 Carrera Targa
red with black interior $85-125
black.......................................$85-125

Rolls Royce
1907 Silver Ghost, silver with green seats $85-125
1911 Tourer, white with tan top.......$85-125
1925 Silver Ghost Tourer, silver-black/black.......................................$85-125
1929 Phantom I Cabriolet De Ville, black-blue/black..............................$85-125
1992 Corniche IV, white/beige $85-125
1992 Corniche IV, blue/tan $85-125

Stanley Steamer
1911 62 Runabout, red with black top .$85-125

119

Stutz
  1915 Bearcat, yellow $85-125
  1928 Black Hawk, red/black $85-125
Tucker Torpedo
1948, light blue/gray $85-125
Volkswagen
  1962 Microbus, salmon & cream/
    cream $85-125
  1967 Cabriolet, red/black $85-125
  1967 Beetle, yellow/white $85-125
  1967 Beetle, white $95-105

Franklin Mint 1:32 Scale
Ahrens-Fox
  1922 R-K-4 Pumper Fire Engine $65-75
American LaFrance
  1954 Fire Engine $65-75
Peterbilt Truck
  1988 Model 739 - Cab & Trailer $65-75

Franklin Mint 1:43 Scale
Bugatti
  1931 Royale Sedan DeVoyage $50-65
Buick
  1953 Skylark $50-65
  1963 Riviera $50-65
Cadillac
  1930 V-16 .... $50-65
  1959 Eldorado $50-65
  1963 Eldorado $50-65
Chevrolet Bel Air
  1955 Bel Air $50-65
  1957 Bel Air Convertible $50-65
Chevrolet Corvette
  1953 Corvette $50-65
  1957 Corvette $50-65
  1958 Corvette $30-40
  1963 Corvette Sting Ray $50-65
Chevrolet
  1956 Nomad $50-65
  1960 Corvair $50-65
  1967 Camaro $50-65
Chrysler
  1950 Town & Country $50-65
Cord
  1931 L-29 .... $50-65
DeSoto
  1952 .... $50-65
Duesenberg
  1929 J $50-65
Dodge
  1968 Charger $50-65
Edsel (see Ford)
Ford
  1950 Station Wagon $50-65
  1955 Crown Victoria $50-65

  1956 Thunderbird $50-65
  1958 Edsel Citation $50-65
  1958 Thunderbird $50-65
  1959 Skyliner $50-65
  1962 Thunderbird $50-65
  1964? Mustang $50-65
Hispano Suiza
  1928 H6B $50-65
Hudson
  1951 Hornet $50-65
Isotta Fraschini
  1928 .... $50-65
Jaguar
  1946 Mark IV $50-65
Lincoln
  1927 Sport Touring $50-65
  1956 Continental Mark II $50-65
  1961 Continental $50-65
Mercedes-Benz
  1939 770K Grosser Cabriolet $50-65
Mercury
  1951 Monterey $50-65
Nash
  1950 .... $50-65
Oldsmobile
  1956 Starfire $50-65
Packard
  1934 .... $50-65
  1955 .... $50-65
  1953 Caribbean $50-65
Pierce
  1933 Silver Arrow $50-65
Plymouth
  1957 Fury $50-65
Pontiac
  1964 LeMans GTO $50-65
Rambler
  1963 Classic 660 .... $50-65
Rolls Royce
  1922 Silver Ghost $50-65
Studebaker
  1953 Starliner $50-65
  1963 Avanti $50-65

Freeway Flyers (see Playart)

Freewheels

Details regarding this brand are nearly nonexistent. Only one model is known.

Mercedes-Benz 190E, silver $10-15

Friedag

William Freidag (pronounced "Friday") started producing cast iron toys at the Freidag Manufacturing Company and Foundry in Freeport,

Illinois, in 1920. Production continued until 1932. Lack of distinguishing marks make these difficult to identify.

Auto with Chauffeur, 1920s $600-800
Bus, 6¾" $350-475
Coupe, 5¾" 1924 .... $450-600
Double Decker Bus, 9¼" $1,750-2,250
Flatbed Truck, 10" $900-1,200
Panel Delivery Truck, 7½" $2,750-3,250
Pickup Truck, 7½" $900-1,200
Racer with driver and passenger, 6½" ... $900-1,200
Roadster, 9¼", 1922 .... $900-1,200
Taxi, 7," 1920s $800-1,000
Taxi with black driver $1,250-1,500
Yellow Cab, 5" $1,000-1,250

Frobly

According to collector Bill Cross, "Frobly models are hand-built resin/white metal models made in France. The proprietor has recently discontinued the range — he is associated with a French collector's model shop, the name of which escapes me at present. The first model in the Frobly range was an incredibly ugly Packard Hawk." There seems to be an association with another French company Eligor, at least with some castings.

Citroën
  DS19 4-door Sedan $70-85
  DS19 Convertible $70-85
  ID19 4-door Sedan $70-85
Ford
  1932 Convertible Roadster, top up,
    Frobly Eligor $80-95
  1932 Convertible Roadster, top down,
    Eligor $80-95
  1961 Econoline Van $75-90
  1961 Econoline Pickup $75-90
Mercury
  1951 Convertible $85-100
Packard Hawk $100-115

Fun Ho! (also see Streamlux)

Fun Ho! castings were first produced in 1939 by H. J. Underwood of Underwood Engineering Company of New Zealand. The first ten Fun Ho! models (always with an exclamation point) consisted of lead hollow-cast vehicles hand poured into molds and sold in association with lead soldiers, farm and other animals, trees, fences, and similar items. The fact that they were hand poured resulted in inconsistencies in thickness of the castings.

Ian Cousins of New Zealand reports that the models are not called Fun Ho! because they approximate HO scale but because the manufacturer wanted a name that conjured up the concept of toys that were a lot of fun... the name therefore arose in a similar way to the wagoner's or military call "Forward Ho!"

The original series of Fun Ho! midgets were produced starting in 1940 using the Streamlux dies from Australia — many of these early Fun Ho! models still have the Streamlux markings on the base plate making it sometimes difficult to establish whether the model was made in New Zealand or Australia. From 1952 on, plastic wheels replaced the crude rubber ones.

After 1945, health regulations fairly well ended the use of lead in the alloys, but production of the large aluminum cast toys continued into the 1970s. Accuracy varied from one model to the next.

A zinc alloy diecast range of toys was introduced in 1962 in a promotional arrangement with Mobil oil and marketed as Fun Ho! Mobil Midgets. This new range featured chromed and coppered finishes in the beginning, but later gave way to more conventional paint finishes. Production of the original line ended in 1982. For a short time afterwards, Asian imported toys, including Zee Toys, were marketed as "Distributed by Fun Ho!" but lacked the distinctiveness of the originals.

In 1964, Underwood Engineering acquired the dies from the Streamlux range of Australian toys and applied the Fun Ho! Midgets brand name to them along with some upgrades to the castings.

The Fun Ho! National Toy Museum is open to the public and is located in Taranaki, New Zealand.

Fun Ho! Original Castings

Armored Jeep, 2⅜", 1977-1982, #59.....$30-35
Army
  Ambulance, 2¼", 1977-1982, #62...$30-35
  Bulldozer, 2⅜", 1977-1982, #64......$30-35
  Dump Truck, 2⅞", 1977-1982, #68..$30-35
  Each Scraper, 3⅝", 1977-1982, #69..$30-35
  Front End Loader, 2¹⁵⁄₁₆", 1977-1982, #72.......................................$30-35
  Grader, 4⅛", 1978-1982, #66 ....$40-45
  Jeep, 2⅜", 1977-1982, #63 ....$30-35
  Road Roller, 2¾", 1977-1982, #65...$30-35
  Tanker, 3¾", 1977-1982, #71 ....$30-35
  Tractor Shovel, 2-7/8," 1977-1982, #70.......................................$30-35
  Transporter, 3½", 1977-1982, #67 ...$30-35
Austin
  1100, 1¾", 1966-1972, #32..........$40-45
  Articulated Truck, 3" with trailer, 1966-1972, #18.......................................$75-80
  Mini, 1⅜", 1965-1972, #17 ....$50-55
  Open Back Truck, 2", 1964-1972, #3..$55-60
  Petrol Tanker, 2", 1964-1972, #4.....$55-60
  Tip Truck, 2", 1964-1972, #8 ....$70-75
Aveling Road Roller, 2¾", 1967-1982, #37...$40-45
Bedford
  Articulated Milk Tanker, 3⅝", 1967-1982, #40.......................................$40-45
  Articulated Tanker, 3⅝", 1966-1982, #27.......................................$40-45
  Articulated Truck, 3⁹⁄₁₆", 1966-1982, #22.......................................$60-70
  Truck, 2⅜", 1966-1982, #29 ....$40-45
Breakdown Truck, 2⅜", 1971-1982, #53 ..$30-35
Car Trailer
  1½", 1966-1982, #30 ....$40-45
  1⅝", 1967-1978, #38 ....$20-25
Caterpillar
  Bulldozer, 2¹¹⁄₁₆", 1969-1982, #46 ...$30-35
  D8 Tractor, 2", 1969-1982, #42......$30-35
  Front End Loader, 2¹⁵⁄₁₆", 1969-1982, #44.......................................$30-35
Chevrolet Bel Air, 2¹¹⁄₁₆", 1966-1982, #24 ....$45-45
Commer Coach, 2⅛", 1964-1972, #7
  British Overseas Airways Corporation (BOAC) Bus $55-60
  Australian National Airways (ANA) Coach.....................................$55-60
Farm Trailer, 2⅛", 1967-1982, #39........$20-25
Fire Engine, 2⅜", 1966-1982, #21.........$40-45
Ford
  Cortina Estate car, 1⅞", 1966-1972, #14.......................................$50-55
  Falcon Sedan, 2⅛", 1965-1972, #10.......................................$50-55
  Thames Freight Van, 2", 1966-1979, #20.......................................$40-45
  Thames Freighter Pickup (Ute), 2", 1966-1982, #26 ....$40-45
  Zephyr Mk 4, 2½", 1969-1977, #41...$30-35
Ford D Truck
  6-Wheel Truck, 3½", 1970-1982, #48.......................................$30-35
  Dump Truck, 2¾", 1970-1982, #50 ..$30-35
  Low Loader, 3½", 1970-1982, #51...$30-35
  Sand Dumper, 3¾", 1970-1982, #49...$30-35
Fordson Super Major Tractor, 1¾", 1965-1982, #16 ....$50-55
Forklift Truck, 2⅜", 1970-1982, #47 ....$30-35
Front End Loader, 2¹³⁄₁₆", 1972-1982, #54 ....$30-35
Hillman Imp, 1½", 1966-1972, #15 ....$50-55
Holden
  FE (EK) Special Sedan, (marked as EK but is actually an FE), 2⅛", 1964-1972, #2..$55-60
  HR Sedan, 2⅜", 1967-1982, #34 ....$40-45
  HR Ambulance Panel Van, 2¼", 1967-1982, #35.......................................$40-45
  HR Panel Van, 2¼", 1978-1982, #61...$30-35
  HR Police Panel Van, 2¼", 1967-1982, #36.......................................$40-45
  HR Ute, 2⅜", 1971-1982, #57.........$30-35
Jaguar
  E-Type, 2⅛", 1969-1982, #43 ....$30-35
  Mark 10, 2½", 1966-1982, #23......$40-45
Jeep, 2⅜", 1976-1982, #58..................$30-35
Land Rover, 1¹³⁄₁₆", 1966-1978, #19.......$40-45
Landliner Bus, 3⅝", 1971-1982, #56......$30-35
Massey-Ferguson 35 Tractor, copper finish, chromed wheels, towbar, 1⅝", 1964-1970, #1...$55-60
Mercedes-Benz
  230, 2½", 1969-1982, #45 ....$30-35
  W196 Racer, 2", 1964-1972, #6....$55-60
MGB Sports car, 1⅞",1966-1970, #25..$40-45
Morris
  850 Mini-Minor, 1⅜", 1965-1972, #11..$50-55
  1100, 1¾", 1965-1972, #13..........$50-55
  J2 Pickup, 2⅛", 1966-1971, #28......$40-45
Oliver Tractor, 1941, #81 ....$75-80
Racing car, 1941, #76.........................$75-80
Road Grader, 4," 1978-1982, #60.......$45-50
Rolls Royce Phantom V, 1⅝", 1967-1982, #33 ....$40-45
Sand Dump Trailer, 3¼", 1970-1982, #52..$30-35
Tractor Scraper, 3⅝", 1971-1982, #55...$30-35
Vauxhall Velox, 2⅛", 1965-1972, #12 ...$50-55
Volkswagen
  Combi Bus, 2⅛", 1964-1982, #5 .....$55-60
  Sedan, 1⅝", 1964-1972, #9...........$55-60
White Heavy Duty Tip Truck, 2¼", #31 ....$40-45

Fun Ho! King Size

International
  Army Dump Truck, 1978-1982, K-4...$50-55
  Army Supply Truck, 1978-1982, K-3 ..$50-55
  Articulated Truck, 5½", 1973-1982, K-1...$50-55
Dump Truck, 1976-1982, K-2 ....$50-55

Fun Ho! Recasts from Message Models

Car Trailer, approximately 1,500 produced, 1996-present, #38 ....$12-15
Chevrolet Bel Air, approximately 500 produced, 1996-present, #24 ....$15-20
Farm Trailer, approximately 5,000 produced, 1996-present, #39 ....$10-12
Fire Engine, approximately 1,200 produced, 1996-present, #21 ....$15-20

Ford Thames Ute, approximately 2,500
produced, 1991-present, #26 ....$15-20
Fordson Tractor, approximately 400
produced, 1996-present, #16 ....$18-24
Fork Lift, approximately 3,000 produced,
1996-present, #47 ....$15-20
Holden HR
Ambulance Panel Van, approximately 1,000
produced, 1996-present, #35 .....$15-20
Panel Van, approximately 300
produced, 1996-present, #61 .....$25-28
Police Panel Van, approximately 1,000
produced, 1996-present, #36 .....$15-20
Sedan, approximately 2,500
produced, 1996-present, #34 .....$15-20
Ute, approximately 1,500 produced,
1996-present, #57 ....$15-20
Jaguar
E-Type, approximately 1,400 produced,
1996-present, #43 ....$15-20
Mark 10 Saloon, approximately 400
produced, 1991-present, #23 .....$15-20
Land Rover, approximately 600 produced,
1996-present, #19 ....$15-20
Mercedes-Benz 230, approximately 700
produced, 1996-present, #45 ....$18-24
Rolls Royce Phantom V, approximately 4,500
produced, 1996-present, #33 ....$15-20
Volkswagen Combi Bus, approximately 1,000
produced, 1996-present, #5 ....$15-20

Funline (see Muscle Machines)

Funmate

Funmate toys were packaged in laundry detergent in the 1970s, according to collector John Dean. One model is of a Volkswagen Beetle in shiny metallic copper tinted chrome. More recently, collector Jonathan Hardin reported finding two 1972 Ford models shrink wrapped to five bars of Zest soap. Value is likely to remain relatively low on these fairly generic toys.

1972 Ford Maverick $6-8
1972 Ford Mustang Mach 1 ....$6-8
Volkswagen Beetle...................................$6-8

Funrise (also see Code 3 Collectibles)

While Funrise is mostly known for plastic toys with electronic sirens, sound effects, and lights, the company has produced a few diecast toys as well, according to Loraine Price whose son has a collection of them. Here are some models she has listed.

Airport Fire Truck...............................$8-10

Ambulance..$8-10
Chevrolet Police Car $8-10
Chevrolet Tahoe.......................................$8-10
Fire Engine $8-10
Fire Rescue Truck $8-10
Ford Explorer $8-10
Ford Ranger Police Truck $8-10
Metro Tow Truck $8-10
Rescue Helicopter $8-10
Van Ambulance..$8-10

FYP

Harvey Goranson reports that Yves Pebernet produced the FYP range of resin models from 1986 until 1995.

Rolls Royce Phantom V Landaulet,
white & black.............................$425-475
Rolls Royce Silver Wraith "Gulbenkian,"
dark green.................................$350-400

G

G & K (see Greppert & Kelch)

Gabriel

For a short time after Gabriel took over Hubley, the company reissued Hubley diecast model kits under the Gabriel name.

1929 Ford Model A Station Wagon
unassembled in sealed box $45-60
assembled or partly assembled with
original box...............................$25-30

Gad (see Great American Dreamcar)

Gaia

Model Power, Inc., has repackaged Gaia brand American LaFrance fire trucks as models for 1:87 (HO scale) railroad sets. Other models from Model Power are made by Playart, another manufacturer famous for repackaging their models under a different brand.

American LaFrance
Fire Pumper, 1:87 ....$13-17
Ladder Truck, 1:87 ....$15-19
Snorkel Truck, 1:87 ....$15-19

Gaiety

Gaiety Toys is a brand established in the 1930s by Castle Art, a silverworks shop on Goodman Street in Birmingham, England. The only known models are an exceptionally well-done prototypical roadster in three scales and a

Morgan Three Wheeler. Every model is marked with both Gaiety Toy and Castle Art.

Roadster, 1930
1:32...$55-70
1:38...$50-65
1:43...$45-60
Morgan Three-Wheeler, 1930, 1:32 ......$60-75

Galanite

Sweden is the source for Galanite toys, soft plastic cars in roughly 1:48 scale (4" long).

Bedford Wrecker $12-16
Farm Tractor $12-16
Mercedes...$12-16
Morris Mini.......................................$12-16
Scania Truck.....................................$12-16
Saab..$12-16
Volkswagen $12-16
Volvo...$12-16
Volvo Truck.......................................$12-16

Galgo

An interesting assortment of these inexpensive models manufactured in Argentina are available in 1:43 and 1:64 scale.

Galgo 1:64 Scale
Dodge Challenger "A-Team," white & red $3-5
Fiat
Dump Truck $3-5
Snorkel Fire Truck..........................$3-5
Semi "BJ Bear" $3-5
Lancia Stratos $3-5
Scania Oil Tanker
"Aeronafta" $3-5
"Agip" $3-5
"Esso" $3-5
"Shell" $3-5
Scania Semi
"Camel Cigarettes" $3-5
"Cazalis" $3-5
"Coca Cola" $5-7
"Fargo" $3-5
"Frigor" $3-5
"Lee" $3-5

Galgo 1:43 Scale
BMW 3.5 "1st National," #1 ....$14-16
Cametal Luxury Bus, #2.......................$14-16
Dodge Dart 2-door Hardtop Rally, orange,
#45...$8-10
Ford Falcon 4-door Sedan Rally, #44........$8-10
Mercedes School Bus, #26 ....$14-16
Peugeot 505 4-door Sedan, #27...........$14-16

Porsche 935
  "Canon," #29 ....$14-16
  "Rothmans," #30 ....$14-16
  "Jagermist," #31 ....$14-16
Renault 18
  4-door Sedan, #33 ....$14-16
  Fire Chief, #34 ....$14-16
Renault Alpine "Elf," #32 ....$14-16
Scania Semi
  "A-Team," #38 ....$8-10
  "Adidas," #35. ....$8-10
  "Cheese," #37 ....$8-10
  "Coca Cola," #39 ....$8-10
  "Paint," #40 ....$8-10
  "Volkswagen Parts," #43 ....$8-10
  "Wine," #42 ....$8-10
  Van, #36 ....$8-10
Volkswagen Van "Bagley," #46 ....$8-10

Galoob (see Micro Machines)

Gama

Gama models were manufactured in Furth, Bavaria, by the Georg Adam Mangold company. Begun in 1882, Gama started producing diecast models in 1959. Gama models have been issued under the Schuco brand starting in 1994. Gama models remain some of the most distinctive models of our time.

Aerial Ladder with pump $250-300
Audi 80, 1:43, #1173 ....$15-20
BMW 325i, 1:24, #2103 ....$40-45
BMW 325i Coupe, 1:43, #1021 ....$15-20
BMW 525i Touring Wagon, 1:43, #1011 ..$15-20
BMW 600, 1959, #907 ....$45-50
BMW Isetta, 1:43, #1150 ....$35-40
BMW M3, 1:24, #2105 ....$40-45
Cadillac $700-900
Crane with clam bucket.....................$225-275
Demag Excavator, 1969, #925.1 ....$50-55
Faun Cement Truck, 1962, #919 ....$50-55
Ford Mondeo, 1:43, #1020 ....$15-20
Ford Taunus 17M, 1959, #901 ....$45-50
Henschel Wrecker, 1969, #31 ....$20-25
Mercedes-Benz 1921 SSK Sportwagen, 1:21 ..$45-60
Mercedes-Benz 300CE, 1:43, #1168....$15-20
Messerschmitt Tiger/Kabinenroller
  red, closed, 1:43, #1007 ....$20-25
  yellow, open, 1:43, #1008 ....$20-25
  silver, closed, 1:43, #1009 ....$25-30
  black, open, 1:43, #1010...............$20-25
NSU Ro-80, 1:63, 1968, #5 ....$20-25
Opel Astra Cabriolet, 1:43, #1026.......$15-20
Opel Astra GSi, 1:43, #1013 ....$30-35
Opel Corsa, 1:43, #1005 ....$15-20

Opel Frontera, 1:43, #1003 ....$15-20
Opel Kadett, 1:43, 1979, #890 ....$30-35
Opel Rekord, 1:43, 1978, #893 ....$30-35
Opel Senator, 1:43, #1133 ....$15-20
Porsche 911
  metallic green with tan interior, license #FU-GA555, 1:42, #973 ....:.............$30-35
  green with black hood, 1:42, #973 ..$30-35
  Police, white with black hood, 1:43, #973.4 ....$30-35
  Police, white and green with blue light on roof, 1:43, #973.6 ....$30-35
  Rallye, green with black hood, black and white check stripe, "2," 1:43, #973.5 ...$30-35
Porsche 911R, metallic dark green with tan interior, checker stripe, "10," 1:42, #973 ......$30-35
Porsche 914
  silver, 1:43, #982.0 ....$30-35
  Police, white with green hood and top, 1:43, #982.1 ....$30-35
Porsche 917, blue, #5, 1:42, #960.5....$30-35
Porsche 924, silver with black interior, 1:43, #892 ....$25-30
Porsche Carrera 6
  1:63, 1968, #1 ....$20-25
  bronze, #2, 1:39, #960.1 ....$25-30
Tractor and Trailer, 17" $150-200
Volkswagen 1302, 1:63, 1969, #13 ....$20-25

GAMA for AHC of Holland – 1:43 Diecast in Germany, refinished in Holland.
Opel Kadett
  boot, Rijkspolitie (Dutch police), GA001R ...$25-30
  hatch, Marechausee (Dutch customs police), GA001R $25-30

Gamda / GamdaKoor (also see Crescent Toys, D.C.M.T., Impy, Lone Star, Sabra, Cragstan)

An Internet bulletin board posting on America OnLine was from a collector seeking Gamda diecast cars and trucks made in Israel in the early to mid 1960s, alternately known as Gamda Sabra, Gamda Koor, and a small line of US cars produced under the Cragstan Detroit Seniors brand.

Collector Bill Cross reports, "There was an article in a recent issue of *Model Collector* on this range. If memory serves, the range had its beginnings in the Lone Star products of the D.C.M.T. company in Great Britain. There were few models in the range and were, I think, mostly post-WW2 British vehicles." If my latest research is any indication, it seems a lot of brands originated from D.C.M.T., including Crescent and Lone Star. Some Gamda models

are in fact enhanced versions of D.C.M.T. models, with windows added and better paint jobs applied. Reissues of Dinky toys also made it into the Gamda line-up. In addition, the brand name Gamda-Sabra can be found on the bases of several models. Cragstan is yet another associated brand.

Collector Rafi Ilivitzky adds that Gamda and GamdaKoor are different ranges of products from different periods both manufactured by the same company, but Gamda was the original line (early 60s) and GamdaKoor came into light after a joint venture with Cragstan and was manufactured at the mid-end 60s early 70s.

Gamda Models
25-Pounder Gun, tan $30-35
Armored car, tan $50-55
Articulated Truck
  Flat Truck, blue and red.....................$75-80
  Tanker, "DELEK" $100-105
  Tanker, "PAZ" $100-105
  Tanker, "SONOL" $100-105
  Tanker, "TNUVA" $100-105
  Tanker, UN, white $100-105
  Timber Truck, blue and red $75-80
Bedford "Driving School" Truck $90-95
Centurion Tank
  1:45, tan $60-65
  1:90, tan $45-50
  1:120, tan.................................$30-35
Covered Truck
  "AMCOR" $60-65
  Dairy Truck, "TNUVA," blue and cream ..$75-80
  Mail Truck $75-80
Daimler Conquest Saloon, gray...........$100-105
Dump Truck $50-55
Ford Prefect, cream or green $65-70
Leyland Bus
  "Egged," blue and gray, plain wheels $150-165
  "Egged" blue and gray, chrome wheels $90-120
  "El Al," green and blue, plain wheels $135-150
Massey Ferguson Tractor, red.................$60-65
Military Truck
  Covered Truck, tan $75-80
  Open Truck, tan $50-55
Mobile Canteen Truck...........................$75-80
Quicklime Spreader $30-35
Roadmaster Coupe, white and red $80-85
Tank Transporter, tan $85-90
Tipping Truck $65-70
Truck $65-70
Truck with Gas Cylinders $75-80

Vanguard
Ambulance, white $90-95
Military Ambulance, tan $75-90
Willys
Jeep, white or red...........................$45-50
Jeep, UN, white..............................$55-60
Military Ambulance, tan $60-65
Military Jeep, tan $45-50
Military Police Jeep, green $45-50
Station Wagon Ambulance, white ..$100-105
Station Wagon Army Van, tan.......$100-105
Station Wagon Police Van, green ..$100-105
Station Wagon Van, orange $100-105

Gasquy (also see Septoy)

Belgium is the source for these quality toys, first produced around 1947 under the Septoy brand and later under Gasquy. The company only lasted a few years before going out of business in the early 1950s. While Septoy models are single castings with axle posts, similar to Tootsietoys in America, Gasquy models have sheet metal bases and are more realistic.

Army Bus, green..............................$150-175
Buick Coupe, green, blue, or red........$125-150
Buick Coupe with clockwork motor, red ..$175-200
Bus, red, yellow, green, or gray $150-175
Chevrolet Sedan, red, blue, or gray $300-325
FN Breakdown Truck, gray, or green ...$100-125
FN Covered Military Truck, green........$100-125
FN Military Breakdown Truck, green $100-125
FN Open Truck, green, red, or gray $100-125
FN Stake Truck, red or green $100-125
FN Tanker, green, red, gray and green,
gray and red, gray and yellow......$100-125
Ford Tudor, blue, gray, red, or green ...$325-350
Maserati Race car, green, red, or cream ...$75-100
Mercury Ambulance, white, cream, and
red $150-175
Mercury Army Ambulance, green $125-150
Mercury Mail Van, yellow $200-225
Mercury Van, red $150-175
Mercury Van with clockwork motor, red...$150-175
Plymouth Sedan, red, brown, green,
gray, or chrome-plated $125-150
Plymouth Staff car, green $200-225
Renault 4CV, light gray-brown.............$275-325
Studebaker Champion, blue, brown,
gray, or green $400-450
Tatra, blue, red, brown, green, or gray ..$400-450
Willys Army Jeep, green....................$125-150
Willys Jeep, red $125-150
Willys Jeep Station Wagon, red and
yellow...$300-325
Willys Red Cross Jeep, white $100-125

Gate (also see Gateway Global)

It was around May 1999 that Gateway Global, a new company, introduced their Gate line of low-end 1:18 scale diecast models, starting with several color variations each of the Mazda Miata and Volkswagen New Beetle.

Mazda MX-5 Miata
red, #01011 ....$15-25
blue, #01013................................$15-25
silver, #01015...............................$15-25
emerald green, #01017 ....$15-25
Peugeot 406 Coupe
red, #01021 ....$15-25
yellow, #01022.............................$15-25
metallic blue, #01023 ....$15-25
silver, #01024..............................$15-25
Porsche 996 Coupe
red, #01041 ....$15-25
silver, #01042..............................$15-25
black, #01043 ....$15-25
yellow, #01044.............................$15-25
red, #01051 ....$15-25
silver, #01052..............................$15-25
black, #01053 ....$15-25
yellow, #01054.............................$15-25
Volkswagen 1998 New Beetle Coupe
light blue, #01031 ....$15-25

green, #01032.................................$15-25
black, #01033 ....$15-25
dark blue, #01034..........................$15-25
white, #01035...............................$15-25
yellow, #01036.............................$15-25
red, #01037 ....$15-25
silver, #01038..............................$15-25

Gateway Global, Inc.

(Includes AUTOart, Gate, and UT models)
Gateway Global of Europe GmbH
Postfach 485
D-52005
Aachen, Germany

Gateway Global Limited
3/F, 8 Yip Cheong Street
On Lok Tsuen, Fanling
New Territories, Hong Kong

Gateway Global USA, Inc.
10485 NW 28th St
Miami, FL 33172-2152 USA

Gateway AUTOart Canada
9620 Ignace Local L,
Brossard, Quebec,
Canada J4Y 2R4

Gateway Global is the new (1999) parent company to UT models, and the new AUTOart and Gate brands. See their listings under their separate brand name headings.

Gaz (see Volga)

Gearbox

Gearbox
4515 20th Avenue SW
Cedar Rapids, IA 52404
phone: 319-390-1405
fax: 319-390-1413

Gearbox is a recent entry into the diecast market that an eclectic assortment of diecast models, as the product list below illustrates. Binney & Smith is the parent company.

Gearbox 12" 1920s Wayne Gas Pump Mechanical Coin Banks

Amoco Regular $40-50
Amoco Silver $40-50
Amoco Ultimate.................................$40-50
British Petroleum $40-50
Ford Benzol $40-50
Gulf $40-50
International Harvester $40-50
John Deere $40-50
John Deere, 24 karat gold plated $120-150
Mobilgas $40-50
Pennzoil $40-50
Phillips 66 ....$40-50
Shell $40-50
Skelly $40-50
Skelly Aromax $40-50
Texaco Fire Chief $40-50
Texaco Fire Chief, 24 karat gold plated...$120-150
Texaco Sky Chief, red..........................$40-50
Texaco Sky Chief, yellow $40-50
Union 76 ....$40-50

Gearbox 1950s Tokheim Gas Pump Coin Banks

John Deere, available from John Deere dealers
only $35-45
Mobil Regular $30-40
Mobil Special $30-40
Phillips 66 ....$30-40

Phillips 66 Flite Fuel................................$30-40
Shell...$30-40
Skelly Powermax.....................................$30-40
Skelly Premium..$30-40
Super Shell...$30-40
Texaco Fire Chief, red.............................$30-40
Texaco Fire Chief, red and white.............$30-40
Texaco Sky Chief, red with Texaco Star
    globe..$30-40
Texaco Sky Chief, red with Sky Chief Wing
    globe..$30-40
Texaco Sky Chief, silver with Sky Chief Wing
    globe..$30-40

Gearbox 8" 1920s Wayne Gas Pumps
Amoco Regular..$15-20
Amoco Silver..$15-20
Amoco Ultimate.......................................$15-20
British Petroleum......................................$15-20
Ford Benzol...$15-20
Gilmore..$15-20
Gulf..$15-20
John Deere...$15-20
Magnolia...$15-20
Mobil Regular..$15-20
Mobil Special...$15-20
Pennzoil...$15-20
Phillips 66..$15-20
Shell...$15-20
Skelly...$15-20
Skelly Aromax..$15-20
Socony...$18-24
Texaco Fire Chief.....................................$15-20
Texaco Sky Chief, red...............................$15-20
Texaco Sky Chief, silver............................$15-20
Wadhams...$18-24
White Eagle..$18-24
White Star...$18-24

Gearbox Die Cast Vehicle Coin Banks
1912 Ford Delivery car
    Campbell's...$20-25
    Hershey...$20-25
    Pepsi-Cola...$20-25
    Pepsi-Cola Keystone Cops.................$20-25
    Red Crown..$20-25
    Shell..$20-25
1912 Ford Oil Tanker
    Ford Benzol......................................$25-30
    Red Crown..$25-30
    Skelly..$25-30

Gearbox Die Cast Aircraft Coin Banks
1932 Stearman Biplane
    Pepsi-Cola Keystone Cops.................$40-50
    Pepsi-Cola Sterling Silver.............$125-150

RCA Victor...$40-50
1938 Grumman Goose
    Campbell's Soup...............................$45-55
    Gearbox..$45-55
    Gulf...$45-55
    Shell..$45-55
    U. S. Coast Guard.............................$45-55
    U. S. Navy...$45-55
Stinson Detroiter
    Shell..$45-55
    Gulf...$45-55
    Mobilgas...$45-55
    Pennzoil..$45-55
    Lone Star...$45-55
Stinson Reliant
    Royal Navy..$45-55
    Gulf...$45-55
    U. S. Army Air Corps........................$45-55
    U. S. Army Air Force.........................$45-55
    U. S. Coast Guard.............................$45-55
Waco Biplane
    Amoco Regular.................................$45-55
    Amoco Silver.....................................$45-55
    Amoco Ultimate................................$45-55

Gearbox Precision Vehicles
1912 Ford Model T Delivery Van
    Campbell's Soup.............................$150-175
1913 Ford Model T Delivery Van
    brown, Texaco................................$150-175
    black, Texaco.................................$150-175
1953 Ford F-100
    Pick-Up, Texaco Fire Chief.............$150-175
    Delivery Van, Texaco Fire Chief.....$175-200
1965 Ford Mustang
    Hardtop, 1:18................................$150-175
    Convertible, 1:18...........................$150-175
1940 Ford Coupe
    Hardtop, 1:18................................$150-175
    Convertible, 1:18...........................$150-175
1958 Chevrolet Bel Air
    Hardtop, 1:18................................$150-175
    Convertible, 1:18...........................$150-175
1963 Chevrolet Impala SS
    Hardtop, 1:18................................$150-175
    Convertible, 1:18...........................$150-175
1950 Buick Roadmaster
    Hardtop, 1:18................................$150-175
    Convertible, 1:18...........................$150-175

Gearbox Precision Aircraft
1917 Sopwith Pup Biplane
    British Military....................................$75-90
    German Military.................................$75-90
    Military, blue......................................$75-90
    U. S. Army...$75-90

U. S. Military..$75-90
1918 AIRCO DH4 Biplane
    British Military....................................$75-90
    U. S. Air Mail....................................$75-90
    U. S. Navy...$75-90
Grumman Wildcat F4F-3...........................$75-90
Grumman Tigercat F7F-3...........................$75-90
Vought Corsair XF4U................................$75-90

Gearbox Mailbox Banks
Express Mail, white..................................$25-30
Priority Mail, red......................................$25-30
U. S. Mail, dull green...............................$25-30
Zippy Zip Code, blue...............................$25-30

Gearbox Texaco 4" Pedal cars
    Four different models comprise this assortment, each in three different liveries and three different colors, packed sixteen red versions, sixteen black, and four green to each carton, making the green ones the least plentiful and therefore the most highly valued on the collector market.

1940 Ford Coupe
    Texaco Fire Chief, red......................$12-16
    Texaco Fire Chief, black....................$12-16
    Texaco Fire Chief, green...................$16-20
    Texaco Sky Chief, red.......................$12-16
    Texaco Sky Chief, black....................$12-16
    Texaco Sky Chief, green....................$16-20
    Texaco Star, red................................$12-16
    Texaco Star, black.............................$12-16
    Texaco Star, green............................$16-20
1955 Chevrolet Bel Air
    Texaco Fire Chief, red......................$12-16
    Texaco Fire Chief, black....................$12-16
    Texaco Fire Chief, green...................$16-20
    Texaco Sky Chief, red.......................$12-16
    Texaco Sky Chief, black....................$12-16
    Texaco Sky Chief, green....................$16-20
    Texaco Star, red................................$12-16
    Texaco Star, black.............................$12-16
    Texaco Star, green............................$16-20
1956 Ford T-Bird
    Texaco Fire Chief, red......................$12-16
    Texaco Fire Chief, black....................$12-16
    Texaco Fire Chief, green...................$16-20
    Texaco Sky Chief, red.......................$12-16
    Texaco Sky Chief, black....................$12-16
    Texaco Sky Chief, green....................$16-20
    Texaco Star, red................................$12-16
    Texaco Star, black.............................$12-16
    Texaco Star, green............................$16-20
1957 Chevrolet Bel Air
    Texaco Fire Chief, red......................$12-16
    Texaco Fire Chief, black....................$12-16

Texaco Fire Chief, green $16-20
Texaco Sky Chief, red $12-16
Texaco Sky Chief, black.....................$12-16
Texaco Sky Chief, green $16-20
Texaco Star, red $12-16
Texaco Star, black $12-16
Texaco Star, green $16-20

Gearbox Texaco 9" Pedal Car Coin Banks
Sold in 12 packs of 11 black and 1 green versions.
1940 Ford Coupe
   Texaco Fire Chief, black...................$40-50
   Texaco Fire Chief, green $65-80
   Texaco Sky Chief, black....................$40-50
   Texaco Sky Chief, green $65-80
   Texaco Star, black $40-50
   Texaco Star, green $65-80
1955 Chevrolet Bel Air
   Texaco Fire Chief, green $65-80
   Texaco Fire Chief, black...................$40-50
   Texaco Sky Chief, green $65-80
   Texaco Sky Chief, black....................$40-50
   Texaco Star, green $65-80
   Texaco Star, black $40-50
1956 Ford T-Bird
   Texaco Fire Chief, black...................$40-50
   Texaco Fire Chief, green $65-80
   Texaco Sky Chief, black....................$40-50
   Texaco Sky Chief, green $65-80
   Texaco Star, black $40-50
   Texaco Star, green $65-80
1957 Chevrolet Bel Air
   Texaco Fire Chief, black...................$40-50
   Texaco Fire Chief, green $65-80
   Texaco Sky Chief, black....................$40-50
   Texaco Sky Chief, green $65-80
   Texaco Star, black $40-50
   Texaco Star, green $65-80

Gearbox 4" Factory Color Pedal Cars
1955 Chevrolet Bel Air two-tone
   blue and black..................................$15-20
   green and beige................................$15-20
   green and black................................$15-20
   plum and beige $15-20
   red and white...................................$15-20
   turquoise and white $15-20
1957 Chevrolet Bel Air
   black..$15-20
   blue $15-20
   green $15-20
   red $15-20
   turquoise $15-20
1956 Ford T-Bird
   black..$15-20
   blue $15-20

coral $15-20
red $15-20

buckskin tan.......................................**$15-20**
   white..$15-20
   yellow $15-20

Gearbox 9" Factory Color Pedal Car Coin Banks
1940 Ford Coupe
   plum $40-50
   gray $40-50
   black..$40-50
   dune beige $40-50
   white..$40-50
   red $40-50
1955 Chevrolet Bel Air two-tone
   black and blue..................................$40-50
   black and green $40-50
   green and beige...............................$40-50
   plum and beige $40-50
   red and white...................................$40-50
   turquoise and white $40-50
1956 Ford T-Bird
   black..$40-50
   blue $40-50
   coral $40-50
   red $40-50
   tan $40-50
   white..$40-50
   yellow $40-50
1957 Chevrolet Bel Air
   black..$40-50
   blue $40-50
   green $40-50
   red $40-50
   turquoise $40-50

Other Gearbox Products
Gearbox 5" Wayne Gas Pump...............$15-20
Gearbox 4" Stearman Bi-Plane $15-20
   1:48 Scale 1912 Tanker...................$25-30
   1:48 Scale 1912 Delivery Truck........$25-30

Gege
Plastic bodies and diecast chassis typify these 1:20 and 1:43 scale Gege toys from France. Just a few 1:43 scale models exist, all produced in 1956.

Citroën DS19 ....$70-80
Ford Vendome $70-80
Ford Vedette $70-80
Peugeot 203 ....$70-80
Peugeot 403 ....$70-80
Renault Fregate Amiral......................$70-80
Simca Aronde $70-80
Simca Versailles $70-80

Gemini Jets
GeminiJets Incorporated / Airliners Distributing Inc.
6414 Windy Street
Las Vegas, Nevada 89119 USA
phone: 702-614-0900
fax: 702-914-8036
e-mail: feedback@geminijets.com
website: www.geminijets.com

Precision diecast commercial jet models are produced under the Gemini Jets brand of Las Vegas, Nevada.

Gems 'N' Cobwebs (see 43rd Avenue)

Generic
So-called "generic" diecast toys are those that, while the package in which they were originally sold may be marked with one brand or another, the model itself is basically unmarked, other than "made in Hong Kong" or "made in China." A few, such as Zee Toys and M C Toys, may have just a logo and perhaps a model number on the base. Often, these generic models are unlicensed copies, or "knockoffs," of established brands such as Matchbox or Tomica, matching size and sometimes even markings.

Brands such as Imperial Diecast, Rhino, Sunnyside (usually designated only with an "SS" number), and MegaMovers are only identified by the package they come in. Once removed from the package, they become unbranded generic toys, some nicely produced, others made cheaply.

Listed below and pictured is a sampling of generic models with no markings to indicate brand or manufacturer. Because it is difficult to determine brand or manufacturer, their value is not due to rise, but some are especially good copies of name brand models.

1930 Bugatti T50, red and black, pull-back action, 1:43 ....**$4-5**

1958 Chevrolet Impala, red, 1:24 ....$15-20

Ferrari 308, gray, 3", based on Yat Ming casting..$1-2

Jaguar E-Type, green with thin yellow stripes, 3", based on Yat Ming casting....$1-2

Japanese tin car, 6" $12-16

Geno

G. Nören of Göteborg, Sweden, introduced the Geno brand in 1958. One diecast model is known to exist, marketed under both the Geno and Lenyco brand names.

Volvo PV544, 3¾".............................$250-300

Gescha (also see Conrad)

Since 1923, Gescha has manufactured a variety of toys, but they didn't start producing diecast models until the 1960s. In the 1970s, the line of Gescha diecast toys was renamed Conrad, while the Gescha name continued with its mechanical tinplate and other toys.

Because the Gescha name is not included on diecast models produced after 1977, it becomes easier to recognize these earlier models, now considered quite valuable.

Fiat-Allis 41-B Dozer..........................$100-125
Caterpillar 769B Quarry Truck $75-90

Gilco

Gilco produced a wide range of diecast road signs during the 1950s from their factory in Birmingham, England. The company reproduced some thirty different British signs in boxed sets of 10 different signs each. Sets in original boxes are valued at $75-125 each.

Gilco Road Signs with Circle on Top

End of 15 MPH Limit.............................$6-9
Halt at a Major Road Ahead.....................$6-9
Keep Left One Way Only.........................$6-9
No Entry..$6-9
No Left Turn $6-9
No Right Turn $6-9
Slow Major Road Ahead..........................$6-9
Speed Limit 15 MPH.............................$6-9
Turn Left One Way Only.........................$6-9

Road Signs with Triangle on Top

Ahead Road Junction.............................$6-9
Bend..$6-9
Cross Roads $6-9
Crossing No Gates...............................$6-9
Hospital $6-9
Hump Bridge $6-9
Left Road Junction $6-9
Level Crossing $6-9
Low Bridge $6-9
Narrow Bridge...................................$6-9
Parking...$6-9
Right Road Junction $6-9
Road Narrows $6-9
Roundabout $6-9
School $6-9
Steep Hill......................................$6-9

Other Road Signs

Belisha Beacon $6-9
Bus Stop..$6-9
Derestriction $6-9
Telegraph Pole $6-9
Two Sided Traffic Lights $6-9

Gingell

Gingell Diecasting Manufacturing Ltd. produces a line of inexpensive generic diecast toys manufactured in China and packaged in 25-car sets for $5. As with typical budget toys, they are cheaply produced, lack much detail, and are lightweight metal with plain plastic chassis. Value of these will not likely rise, and identification of individual models is difficult or impossible, which also detracts from any future collector value. Gingell toys are best considered as a novelty rather than a serious addition to a collection.

Giodi (also Techno Giodi)

Giodi is a relatively obscure Italian manufacturer of mostly Fiat models. Below is a list of models and current values. The company produced models until they went bankrupt in 1993. The company offered finished models as well as kits.

Ferrari Daytona
  Coupe black, 1:18, #1 ....$30-35
  Coupe, red, 1:18, #74011 ....$30-35
  Coupe yellow, 1:18, #1 ....$30-35
  Spyder red, 1:18, #3 ....$30-35
  Spyder, black, 1:18, #74002 ....$30-35
  Spyder, yellow black top, 1:18, #74003 ....$30-35
Fiat "Jumbo" Farm Tractor, yellow and black, 1:28, #73030............................$15-20
Fiat 4WD Tractor with Snowplow, orange, 1:43, #73084 ....$15-20
Fiat Crane Truck, 1:35, #73109 ....$15-20
Fiat Dump Truck with Tractor, yellow and black and red, 1:35, #73076.................$15-20
Fiat Farm Tractor and Loader, 1:28, #73038 ....$15-20
Fiat Farm Tractor and Backhoe, 1:28, #73039 ....$15-20
Fiat Flatbed Truck
  with Load, orange and black and silver, 1:35, #73073 ....$15-20
  with Trailer & 2 Loads, orange and black and silver, 1:35, #73074.........$20-25
Fiat Jeep
  "Algiers-Cape Town," orange and white, 1:25, #73053 ....$15-20
  "Ambulance," white, 1:25, #73092 ..$15-20
  "Grand Canyon," blue and white, 1:25, #73051 ....$15-20
  "Police," blue and white, 1:25, #73056 ....$15-20
  "Safari," tan, brown, camouflage, 1:2, #730645 ....$15-20
  "SOS" Road Service Tow, orange and yellow, 1:25, #73091 ....$15-20
  and Camper "Expedition," orange and white, 1:25, #73062 ....$15-20
  and Camper "Grand Canyon," blue and white, 1:25, #73093...............$15-20
Fiat MTS-10 Forklift with Pallet, yellow and silver and orange, 1:43, #73082 ....$15-20

Fiat MTS-40 Road Roller, orange and black, 1:43, #73085..............................$15-20
Fiat Snorkel Fire Engine, 1:35, #73070...$20-25
Fiat Turbo DT 180-90 Farm Tractor, brown and white and black, 1:28, #73035.......$15-20
Kenworth
    Cement Truck, orange, 1:35, #73106 ..$15-20
    Conventional Semi-Cab & Load, 1:35, #73077 ....$15-20
    Flatbed Semi with F. Dump, red and black and yellow, 1:35, #73107........$15-20
    Semi Milk Truck, orange and blue and gray, 1:35, #73104 ....$20-25
1968 Mercedes-Benz 280SL, silver cabriolet, 1:18, #99999 ....$30-35

Girard

C. G. Wood founded Girard Model Works in 1906 in Girard, Pennsylvania, and continued until 1980. Soon after, his son Frank joined the firm as partner. They began making mechanical toys 1918. By 1920, they were being marketed under the name "Wood's Mechanical Toys." Sometime between the 1920s and the 1930s, the company changed ownership and the name "Girard" was adopted. When the depression hit in the early 1930s, the company laid off its only salesman, Louis Marx, who was causing delays with Girard's customers while trying to build his own plant. Luckily for Marx, his customers were more familiar with him than they were with the Girard firm, so Marx eventually took over the company.

The primary product offered by Girard was pressed tin vehicles.

Army Truck with cloth canopy, 1940s ..$250-325
Auto Transport, early 1930s $500-575
Bus with driver, wind-up, 14" $325-400
Coupe, 6"..$40-65
Coupe, battery-operated, with working headlights, 14" $650-725
Fire Chief car, 15" $350-425
Fire Chief Siren Coupe, win-up, 14"....$575-650
Fire Truck, 1920s, 12" $90-120
Gasoline Tanker, late 1930s $175-250
Ladder Truck, 1930s, 7" $300-375
Pierce-Arrow Coupe, green, orange and ivory, wind-up, early 1930s, 14" $450-525
Pump Truck, battery-operated, with working headlights, 10".........................$200-250
Race car, with pull rod, 1920s $225-300
Race car, wind-up, 8" $475-625
Roadster, with working lights, 14½" $375-450

Side Dump, 11½"..............................$250-325
Stake Truck, with working headlights, 10" $250-325
Tank Truck, 11½"..............................$150-225
Touring Bus, early 1920s, 12"...........$250-325
Wrecker with mechanical boom, 1930s, 10" $500-625

Gloor

The improbable and otherwise unknown Gloor brand is represented by one model.

1960 Chevrolet Stepvan "UPS," 1:43 .....$35-40

Goeso (see Göso)

Golden Classics (see Golden Wheel)

Golden Wheel (also see Ja-Ru)

Golden Wheel (U.S.A.) Inc.
200 Fifth Avenue, Suite 618
New York, NY 10010 USA
website: www.goldenwheeldiecast.com

Golden Wheel toys represent inexpensive miniature replica cars and trucks made by Golden Wheel Die Casting of China.

Golden Classics Ford Model T gift banks from the same company are so similar to Ertl banks that they can be easily mistaken for them at first glance. Closer inspection shows a few differences, most notably a plastic roof secured to the windshield by a crudely melted post, and the distinctive phrase "Coins Bank" in script on each model. These models are such a blatant attempt to capitalize on the popularity of Pepsi-Cola collectibles and coin banks that they even say gift bank on the box, and the tanker even declares "Collectable Models" right on the tank.

Still, considering the $12 price tag, they are comparably nice models to the more expensive $20–35 Ertl versions, and they do make attractive, affordable gifts.

Other models in the ever-expanding Golden Wheels catalog represent a diversity of diecast toys and replicas, many of them promotional models intended to advertise various products. Their website illustrates a huge catalog of models. Here is a small sampling.

The latest find from Golden Wheel is an assortment of 3" models packaged as "American Classic" and labeled "Classic Auto Pageant, Scale 1:64" but are marked only with "Made in China" on the base of the

model. Nine models have been found so far, but specific car models are not marked on the package or the model, in order to avoid licensing fees. For that reason, the specific descriptions of the cars listed are for reference only.

Golden Wheel Models

Ferrari, 3", various colors..............................$2-4
Ford Model T
    Delivery Van, white with blue roof and fenders "Drink Pepsi-Cola" $12-15
    Tanker, white with red roof and fenders, "Pepsi-Cola" $12-15
    Tanker, "Mountain Dew" $12-15
Mercedes-Benz, 3," various colors $2-4

Pedal Power Car and Trailer, about 7"...$8-10

Pedal Power Police Car, about 4" $6-8
Tractor Trailer
    1:87, "Pepsi" $4-5
    1:87, "Mountain Dew" $4-5
    1:64, "Pepsi" $9-12
    1:64, "Mountain Dew" $9-12
Golden Wheel American Classic / Classic Auto Pageant, 1:64 scale
Chevrolet Bel Air, turquoise.........................$2-3
Chevrolet Camaro, yellow $2-3
Chevrolet Corvette Sting Ray Split Window, metallic silver...................................$2-3
Chevrolet Corvette Sting Ray Mako Shark, black $2-3
Ford Mustang Convertible, red $2-3
Ford Mustang Fastback, green.....................$2-3
Ford Mustang Fastback, white $2-3
Ford Thunderbird, sky blue with white roof $2-3
Pontiac Convertible, dark blue $2-3

Goldvarg

The Goldvarg Collection
Sergio & Mariana Goldvarg
2428 Deer Creek Rd
Weston, FL 33327 USA
e-mail: goldvarg@MYACC.net
tel: 954-217-1066

The Goldvarg Collection is a series of 1:43 scale American cars of the 1940s, 1950s, and 1960s. The white metal assortment was first produced by Mariana and Sergio Goldvarg of Buenos Aires, Argentina, in 1989. As of January 1, 2000, after being out of production for nearly three years, The Goldvarg Collection models are again being produced in cooperation with SMTS (Scale Model Technical Services) of England.

Cadillac 1949 Series 62 4-door Sedan,
GC15 ....$85-100
Chevrolet
    1946 Stylemaster 4-door, GC2 ....$85-100
    1954 Bel Air 4-door Sedan, GC8 ...$85-100
Chrysler 1951 Crown Imperial Limousine
    LWB, blue, GC3 ....$85-100
Ford 1946 Deluxe Sedan, GC16 ....$85-100
Henry J
    1951 Kaiser 2-door Sedan, dark gray,
    GC12 ....$85-100
    1951 Standard, GC12-B $85-100
Lincoln 1956 Premiere Hardtop Coupe,
    GC4 ....$85-100
Mercury
    1956 Montclair Coupe, GC7 ....$85-100
    1959 Park Lane 2-door Hardtop,
    GC11 ....$85-100
Nash 1952 Golden Airflyte
    Ambassador Sedan Pininfarina, GC9 ..$85-100
    GC18 ....$85-100
Oldsmobile
    1957 Starfire 98 hardtop, blue, GC1 ..$85-100
    1957 Starfire 98 Fire Chief, GC1-F ..$85-100
    1958 Sedan, GC14 ....$85-100
Packard 1950 Woody Station Wagon,
    green, GC6 ....$85-100
Plymouth
    1949 Commercial Utility Station
    Wagon, GC13 ....$85-100
    1960 Fury, GC17 ....$85-100
Pontiac
    1955 Star Chief Convertible, red, GC5 ..$85-100
    1959 Bonneville 2-door Hardtop,
    GC10.............................$85-100

Gonio

These 1:24 scale tinplate military models from Czechoslovakia are made to the highest degree of authenticity. Though they do not exactly fit the definition of "diecast," they represent an important contribution to the area of highly collectible authentic scale models. Examples below are provided by Toys for Collectors and Diecast Miniatures. Features include steerable wheels and other working parts.

Dodge WC-51
    with foldable side guards, #1007 ...$100-115
    Powerwagon Weapons carrier,
    #08657, USA, olive drab $85-100
Dodge WC-52A
    Arctic white $150-165
    olive drab $130-145
Jeep Kommando with trailer and supplies,
    #1010 ....$125-140
M3A1 Halftrack Armored Personnel
    carrier, #1011 ....$190-205
M3 Halftrack, olive drab $160-175
M3T Tunis Halftrack.......................$180-195
Volkswagen T-82 Porsche Kubelwagen
    Ambulance East, #1002, top down ...$55-70
    #086XX, sand......................$80-95
    #1001, top down, Africa Corps, sand ..$50-65
    #1001L, top up, camouflage, limited
    edition $65-80
    East, #1004, top down....................$50-65
Volkswagen 166 Porsche Schwimmwagen
    (Amphibious Vehicle) # 08655,
    olive drab................................$100-115
    West, #1006 ....$100-155
White 160AX Powered M-3 Halftrack, #08661,
    USA, olive drab $125-140
Willys Jeep, foldable windshield, #1008,
    opening hood $75-90

Goodee

Goodee toys are very similar to Tootsietoys in that they are generally zinc alloy single-cast bodies with no chassis or windows. Goodee diecast vehicles were manufactured by Excel Products Company of Brunswick, New Jersey, in the 1950s. 6-inch and 3-inch models were produced, some of the larger models with wind-up motors. Below is a list of known models with corresponding current values.

Goodee 6" Models
American LaFrance Fire Pumper $25-30
Box Truck $20-25
DeSoto 1954 Station Wagon.................$25-30
Ford 1953 Police Cruiser $25-30
Ford 1955 Fuel Truck............................$25-30
GMC 1953 Pickup Truck.......................$25-30

Military Jeep $25-30

Goodee 3" Models
American LaFrance Fire Pumper $15-20
Cadillac 1953 Convertible....................$15-20
DeSoto 1954 Station Wagon.................$15-20
Ford 1953 Police, 2-door Sedan $25-30
Ford 1954 C600 Oil Truck $25-30
Ford 1955 Fuel Truck............................$15-20
GMC 1953 Pickup Truck.......................$15-20
Land Speed Racer $15-20
Lincoln 1953 Capri Hardtop $15-20
Military Jeep $15-20
Moving Van $15-20
Step Van $15-20
Studebaker 1953 Coupe $20-25

Goody Toys

This obscure British company is known to have produced a couple of diecast Vauxhall Saloons around 1937.

1937 Vauxhall Saloon
    4-window, 1:43 ....$45-60
    6-window, 1:43 ....$45-60

Göso

Beginning in the late 1940s and continuing through the early 1960s, Göso of Nuremburg, West Germany, produced an assortment of tinplate toys.

Tanker Truck, yellow with red cab, 12⅝",
    #411 ....$95-115
Post Office Truck, yellow, 12⅝" flywheel
    drive, #412 ....$175-195
US Military Jeep, 4¾", 1949...............$115-135
Volkswagen Van, 1:20, early 1960s ..$165-185

Govroski (also see Russian models)

Quality diecast toys from Russia, Govroski is represented in *Schroeder's Collectible Toys* by just one model.

Volga Sedan, metallic blue $35-40

Gran Toros (also see Hot Wheels, Mebetoys, Johnny Lightning)

When Mattel purchased Mebetoys of Italy around 1970, they applied the Hot Wheels name to several 1:43 scale models and dubbed them Gran Toros. The Gran Toros name was later acquired by Playing Mantis who currently issues their own small line of 1:43 scale diecast cars dubbed Gran Toros by Johnny Lightning.

Grand Prix

Grand Prix models are from Great Britain and produced by Brian Harvey, available in 1:43 scale white metal kits.

Austin Seven Twin Cam (kit) $18-24
1983 Ferrari "Martini" (kit) $18-24
Ford Escort "Castrol" (kit) $18-24
Lotus Elan Roadster (built).........................$45-60

Great American Dreamcar / Dust & Glory / Quarter Mile

Great American Dreamcars, occasionally also known as Great American Dream Machines or simply "GAD," are 1:43 scale white metal models marketed by Phil Alderman's Autofare of New Jersey. He also offers Dust & Glory, a line of vintage American racers, and Quarter Mile dragster replicas. Original models are casts of SMTS, MCM, and possibly a few others.

1956 Buick Centurion 2-door Show Car, red and white, #12 ....$180-190
1939 Buick Y Job Show Car, black, #3 ..$180-190
1939 Buick Y Job–EXC 4 Minicar, gray, #3MC.................................$180-190
1954 Cadillac El Camino 2-door Coupe, silver, #7 ....$180-190
1954 Cadillac La Espada Show Car, yellow, #5 ....$180-190
1965 Chevrolet Corvette Mako Shark II, dark blue, #6.................................$180-190
1954 Chevrolet Corvette Nomad, blue, #2 ....$180-190
1952 Chrysler C-200 Convertible Show Car, black and green, #14.................$180-190
1951 Chrysler K-310 Show Car, two-tone blue, #8 ....$180-190
Don Garlits Swamp Rat 1 Dragster, #1M..$180-190
1955 Lincoln Futura Show car, green, #4 ....$180-190
1903 Packard Gray Wolf $200-210
1956 Packard Predictor Show car, pearl white, #9 ....$180-190

Greppert & Kelch

Brandenburg, Germany, is the home of Greppert & Kelch, manufacturers of tinplate clockwork toys of the early twentieth century.

"Ruck-Ruck" 3-wheel car with driver.$1,200-1,500
Tricycle ("Drierad"), 1920 ....$1,200-1,500

Grip Zechin (also see EIDAI)

Grip Zechin
EiDAI Corporation

2.8.7. Higashiogu, Arakawaku
Tokyo, Japan

Grip Zechin is a hard-to-find brand of unusual toys made in Japan by Eidai. Recently, Jeff Kopis of Clallam Bay, Washington, reports a few models found in 1977 in a Seattle, Washington, Bon Marche department store, where he recalls that the store had a complete line of Grip Zechin models. Unfortunately, he only purchased three at the time, all Caterpillar models. Nevertheless, his additional information is invaluable.

Most Grip Zechin models were also sold under the Madmax Grip and World Zechin brands, according to Roy Ferguson of Manchester, Iowa. He reports that the models were available in all three names but some were only available in one name. The models were available in the early 1970s, and from price stickers on the box, Ferguson concludes that they may have been a little pricey for the time, and that this may have led to their demise. Some of the dies were reused by Tomica, and a larger model, a four-axle crane in 1:75 scale, showed up in the Diapet line.

Aichi
Basket Truck, World Zechin #25........$30-40
Crane Auger E-600, 1:62, Grip Zechin #9 ....$30-35
Skymaster AS-C2, 1:62, Grip Zechin #40 ....$30-40
Airport Bus, World Zechin #28 ....$30-40
Ambulance, Grip Zechin #43 ....$30-40
Bullet Train, Grip Zechin #35 ....$30-40
DeTomaso Pantera GT-35, Eidai/Grip Technica series, 1:28 ....$45-60
Carferry "Sunflower," 1:1600, Grip Zechin #22 ....$50-65
Caterpillar
14E Snowplow Motor Grader, Grip Zechin #23.................................$30-35
620 Wheel Loader, blue, World Zechin #20.................................$30-40
621 Motorscraper, 1:111, Grip Zechin #36.................................$30-40
769 B Dump Truck, 1:98, Grip Zechin #1 ....$30-40
769 Quarry Truck, Madmax Grip #1 ...$30-40
920 Wheel Loader, 1:76, Grip Zechin #7 ....$30-35
920 Snowplow Wheel Loader, 1:76, Grip Zechin #11 ....$30-35
D5 Bulldozer, 1:56, Grip Zechin #5 ..$25-30
D5 Dozer, Madmax Grip #2 ....$30-40
D5 Rakedozer, 1:56, Grip Zechin #8 ..$25-30
D5 Rotary Rake, red, World Zechin #24 ....$30-40

D5 Snowplow Bulldozer, 1:56, Grip Zechin #4 ....$25-30
Motor Grader, 1:96, Grip Zechin #19 ....$25-35
Fuso
Mixer car, 1:70, Grip Zechin #13.....$25-30
Sewage Truck, 1:70, Grip Zechin #15 ....$25-30
Vacuum car, 1:70, Grip Zechin #27 ....$25-30
Hino
3-Axle Ladder Truck, 1:100, red, World Zechin #4 ....$30-40
Fire Engine, 1:100, Grip Zechin #12 ..$30-35
Semi Tanker, "Shell," 1:100, Grip Zechin #38 ....$30-40
Semi Tanker "Shell," 1:100, Madmax Grip #12 ....$30-40
Snorkel car, 1:100, Grip Zechin #18 ...$30-40
Suction Truck, 1:100, World Zechin #21 ....$30-40
Suction Truck, 1:100, Madmax Grip #20 ....$30-40
TC30 Snorkel Fire Engine, 1:100, Grip Zechin #16.................................$25-30
Tractor with Trailer, 1:100, World Zechin #16 ....$30-40
Hitachi
Earth Auger, 1:70, Grip Zechin #28 ..$35-40
UH 03 D Shovel, 1:70, Grip Zechin #21 ....$30-35
UH 03 D Crumshell, 1:70, Grip Zechin #25 ....$30-35
Wheel Crumshell, 1:70, Grip Zechin #26 ....$30-35
Wheel Shovel, 1:70, Grip Zechin #29 ....$35-40
Hovercraft MV PP-5, 1:210, Grip Zechin #10 ....$40-45
Isuzu
Bulk Powder Transport, 1:100, Grip Zechin #39 ....$25-30
Bulldozer carrier, 1:100, Grip Zechin #34 ....$35-45
Cargo Trailer, 1:100, Grip Zechin #44 ....$35-45
Lift Truck, 1:62, Grip Zechin #20.......$25-30
Racing carrier with racing car, 1:100, Grip Zechin #17.................................$35-40
Jeep
J 52 1:42, Grip Zechin #31 ....$25-35
J 52 Army with gun, 1:42, Grip Zechin #33.................................$30-35
with roll bar, red, World Zechin #26...$30-40
Kato Oil Pressure Crane, 1:140, Grip Zechin #14 ....$40-50

Nakamichi Truck Backhoe, 1:62, Grip Zechin
#3 ....$30-40

P & H Machinery Crane, 1:100, Grip Zechin
#24 ....$35-40

Police Accident Investigation Truck, Grip Zechin
#42 ....$30-40

Prinoth Snow Groomer with Snowmobile, 1:70,
Grip Zechin #6 ....$35-45

Road Sweeper, 1:85, Grip Zechin #37...$30-40

Sakai Vibration Roller SV-100, 1:60
Grip Zechin #2 ....$35-45
red, World Zechin #2 ....$35-45

School Bus, yellow, Madmax Grip #26 ...$30-40

Scissor Lift Airport Truck, Madmax Grip #8...$30-40

Semi with Container "Japan National Rail," Grip
Zechin #45 ....$30-40

Yamaha Policeman Side car, 1:43, Grip Zechin
#47 ....$45-50

GTS (See Le Mans Miniatures)

Guiloy

Guiloy is a brand of models made in Spain. They are best known for their great miniature renditions of motorcycles. But they also produced a truck series called Mini Camiones and an assortment of car models.

Guiloy Motorcycles

Blue American Custom, Guiloy Superbike, 1:6...$50

BMC Ecureuil motocross bike, 1:10,
GY3163.................................$45-60

BMW
R-80 motocross bike, 1:10, GY3118 ..$45-60
R100RT street bike, 1:10, GY3147 ...$45-60
R1000RS street bike, 1:18, GY2896 ..$16-20

Classic American Iron, Guiloy Superbike, 1:6 ..$50

Custom Cherokee, Guiloy Superbike, 1:6 .....$50

Custom Angel, Guiloy Superbike, 1:6 ....$50

Harley Davidson
Custom Classic, 1:10, GY3801........$50-65
Custom Classic, 1:18, GY2815........$18-24
Custom Sport, 1:18, GY2872 ....$18-24

Honda
"Campsa," 1:18, GY2803 ....$16-20
"Castrol," 1:10, GY3166 ....$45-60
"Repsol," 1:18, GY2802 ....$16-20
Racing Motorcycle, 1:10, GY3106...$45-60

1948 Indian Chief, 1:10 Scale

GY17227 ....$30-45
Anniversary Edition, burgundy or yellow,
G15 ....$50-65

Kawasaki "Metzeler," 1:18, GY2804 .....$16-20

Suzuki
"Pepsi," 1:10, GY3187 ....$45-60

"Pepsi" Racer, 1:18, GY2807 ....$16-20

Yamaha
"Garriga" racer, 1:10, GY3146 ....$45-60
Custom New York, Guiloy Superbike,
1:6 ....$60-75
1:6, GY6244 ....$100-120
1:6, GY6247 ....$100-120

Guiloy 1:18 Scale Models

Aston Martin DB-7 1995
wine, G1 ....$30-40
black, G1 ....$30-40
black, #67007 ....$35-45
black, #67517 ....$35-45
blue, G1 ....$35-40
dark green, #67537 ....$35-45
green, G1 ....$30-40
violet, #67550.........................$35-45

BMW 327 1937
Coupe, Top Line #68560.................$70-85

Cabriolet, Top Line #68565..............$70-85

Chrysler Atlantic, Top Line #68570 ....$70-85

Ferrari 250 GTO 1964
yellow, #67526 ....$3-50-45
red, #67525 ....$3-50-45
metallic red, #67502 ....$3-50-45
green, #67540 ....$3-50-45

Ferrari Mythos
red, #67511 ....$3-50-45
blue, #67512 ....$3-50-45
yellow, #67524 ....$3-50-45
metallic silver, #67538 ....$3-50-45

McLaren F-1, 1993, red, blue, silver, or metallic
burgundy, G2 ....$3-55-40

Mercedes C-111
1969, metallic orange or silver, G16 ..$3-55-40
gold color, #67501 ....$3-50-45
green, #67520 ....$3-50-45
metallic silver, #67521 ....$3-50-45

Prototype LM
orange, #67510 ....$3-50-45
red, #67530 ....$3-50-45
yellow, #67539 ....$3-50-45
metallic silver, #67558 ....$3-50-45

Guiloy 1:24 Scale

Aston Martin DB7 Coupe, #64544.........$12-16

1937 BMW 327 Coupe, red and black...$40-55

Ferrari F-40
metallic silver, #64508 ....$12-16
light blue, #64514 ....$12-16
red, #64519 ....$12-16
yellow, #64521 ....$12-16

Ferrari Testarossa
red, #64515 ....$12-16
yellow, #64517 ....$12-16
metallic silver, #64532 ....$12-16

Lamborghini Countach 5000, red,
#64516...$12-16

Mercedes-Benz 500 SL
Cabriolet, green, #64540 ....$12-16
Cabriolet, violet, #64518 ....$12-16
Coupe, #64501 ....$12-16
Coupe, red metallic, #64531 ....$12-16

Mercedes-Benz 500 SEC, blue, #64535...$12-16

Mercedes-Benz C-111, 1969, gold color,
#64549 ....$12-16

Porche 911 Carrera 4 Targa
red, #64505 ....$12-16
white, #64542 ....$12-16

Porche 959 Turbo
blue, #64527 ....$12-16
red, #64569 ....$12-16

Guiloy 1:25 Scale Models

Mercedes-Benz 350SL Coupe, #50 ....$25-30

Porsche 911
Coupe, #51 ....$25-30
Rally, "Rothmans," white, blue, red, and
green, #524 ....$25-30
Rally, Martini," yellow, #525 ....$25-30

Guiloy 1:64 Scale Models

Fiat Ritmo 4-door Sedan, #2 ....$3-5

Fiat (Seat) 131 wagon, #7 ....$3-5

Ford Fiesta 2-door Sedan, #5 ....$3-5

Ford Torino, 1976, #8 ....$3-5

Land Rover Range Rover wagon, #1 ....$3-5

Peugeot 504 4-door Sedan, #6 ....$3-5

Renault 4 Van, #4 ....$3-5

Talbot 150 4-door Sedan, #3..................$3-5

Guiloy Mini Camiones, circa 1970s

Guiloy Mini Camiones are a series of trucks in 1:66 scale, all based on the same truck tractor with various backs or trailers attached to create a variety of models. Based on photocopied catalogs from Dr. Craig Campbell, assistant professor of geography at Youngstown State University, I was able to translate the Spanish descriptions of most models by the pictures. Some however remain a mystery, such as #50 "Bomber." The Spanish descriptions are in italics. The 50-66 series represents the same truck with different backs. The 1000 series represents the same truck with various trailers attached.

Guiloy 1:66 Scale Trucks

Crane Truck, Gria, #51 ....$10-15
Container Truck, Contenedor Mudanzas,
    #59 ....$10-15
Covered Lorry, Toldo, #57 ....$10-15
Dumper, #56 ....$10-15
Flatbed Truck with I-Beams, Vigas, #64 ....$10-15
Ladder Fire Truck, Bomber, #50 ....$10-15
Log Truck, Troncos, #66 ....$10-15
Missile Launcher, Misil, #53 ....$10-15
Military Anti-Aircraft Gun Truck,
    Ametralladora, #54 ....$10-15
Military Cannon Truck, Cateon, #55........$10-15
Military Container Truck, Contenedor Militar,
    #61 ....$10-15
Military Covered Lorry, Toldo Militar, #58 ..$10-15
Military Open Lorry, Cajón Militar, #62 ....$10-15
Open Lorry, Cajón Normal, #63 ....$10-15
Pipe Truck, Tubos, #65 ....$10-15
Refrigerated Container Truck, Contenedor
    Frigorifico, #60 ....$10-15
Texaco Tanker, Gasolina, #52 ....$10-15

Guiloy 1:66 Scale Tractor/Trailers

Covered Lorry, Toldo, #1001.................$15-20
Crane Truck...$15-20
Gasoline Tanker, Campsa, #1000 ....$15-20
Gasoline Tanker, Elf, #1018 ....$15-20
Gasoline Tanker, Esso $15-20
Military Glider Transporter with glider, Planeador
    Militar, #1009 ....$15-20
Military Tank Transporter with two armored tanks,
    Tanques Militar, #1008 ....$25-30
Open Lorry, Cajón, #1004 ....$15-20
Pipe Truck, Tubos, #1005 ....$15-20
Pressurized Tanker, Amoniaco, #1014 ....$15-20
Pressurized Tanker, Cemento, #1013 .....$15-20

Guisval

Guisval of Spain offers an assortment of vehicles in an unusual variety of scales that include 1:30, 1:37, 1:43, 1:66, and 1:80. Some are said to be direct knockoffs of Matchbox Models of Yesteryear, such as the Mercedes-Benz 540K. Guisval started in 1967 and survives to this day.

Adler, 1907
    #501 ....$25-30
    Tow car, #505 ....$25-30
Alfa Romeo Osi Scarabeo, 1:66, #44 ....$15-20
Audi Quattro
    Ambulance, 1:64, #99 ....$3-5

Coupe, #447 ....$15-20
BMW Deportivo, 1:37, #129 ....$15-20
Bugatti T50 Coupe, #752 ....$15-20
Cadillac 1931 Roadster, 1:64, #97 ....$3-5
Caravan
    Ambulance, 1:64, #98 ....$3-5
    Ski, #523 ....$15-20
Case Bulldozer, 1:80, #47 ....$15-20
Chaparral, 1:66, #1 ....$15-20
Chevrolet Astro, 1:37, #101 ....$15-20
Chevrolet Camaro, 1:37
    1979, #108 ....$15-20
    Rally Safari, #116 ....$15-20
Chevrolet Corvair Monza, 1:66
    #25 ....$15-20
    chrome plated, #43 ....$15-20
Chevrolet Van, 1:37
    "Moto Club," #128 ....$15-20
    "Paris Dakar," #139 ....$15-20
    "Polar," #529 ....$15-20
    Fire Van, #516....................................$15-20
Citroën 2CV, 1:37
    Sedan, #102 ....$15-20
    Sahara Travesta, #105 ....$15-20
Citroën BX, 1:37
    4-door Sedan, #403............................$15-20
    "Autoveri," #441 ....$15-20
    "Shell," #444 ....$15-20
Citroën SM, 1:37
    Ambulance, white, #104 ....$20-25
    Tour De France, #106 ....$15-20
Daffy Duck Plane, 1:43, #2 ....$25-30
Datsun Pickup with Cage, 1:64, #707 ....$3-5
Dune Buggy, 1:66, #21 ....$15-20
Ferrari 330 P2, 1:66, #8 ....$15-20
Ferrari Can-Am, 1:37, #102 ....$15-20
Ferrari Dino Pininfarina, 1:66, #39.........$15-20
Ferrari P4, 1:66, #18 ....$15-20
Ferrari Testarossa, 1:30, #918 ....$15-20
Fiat 100, 1:37
    Policia, #119 ....$15-20
    Taxi, #125 ....$15-20
Fiat 130 Coupe, 1:37, #110 ....$15-20
Fiat Ritmo/Strada 4-door Sedan, 1:64, #803....$3-5
Fiat Zero Roadster
    top down, #506 ....$25-30
    top up, #502 ....$25-30
Ford 4000 Tractor, 1:66, #46 ....$15-20
Ford Capri, 1:37
    #103..$15-20
    Policia, #109 ....$15-20
    Rally, #107 ....$15-20
    Ski Club, #105 ....$15-20
Ford Escort "Goodyear, 1:37, #446" $15-20
Ford Lotus, 1:66
    40, #5 ....$15-20

Ski, #467 ....$25-30
STP, #33 ....$15-20
V8 Racer, #36 ....$15-20
Ford Mustang, 1971, 1:66
    #35 ....$15-20
    Circus, #37 ....$15-20
Ford Sierra
    4-door Sedan, #402 ....$15-20
    "Esso," #406 ....$15-20
    "Esso," #442 ....$15-20
    "Gitnes," #449 ....$15-20
    "NASA," #462 ....$25-30
    Police, #457 ....$25-30
Go Bug, 1:66
    #23 ....$15-20
    Fire, #24 ....$15-20
Goofy Train, 1:43, #1 ....$25-30
Hatra, 1:80
    Cement Truck, #50 ....$15-20
    Dumper, #49 ....$15-20
    Shovel, #42 ....$15-20
Helicopter, 1:37
    Military Helicopter, #140.....................$15-20
    Red Cross Helicopter, #137 ....$15-20
    Rescue Helicopter, #135 ....$15-20
Hispano Suiza Convertible, 1926, 1:64
    top down, #95 ....$3-5
    top up, #96 ....$3-5
Horse Box, 1:80, #20 ....$15-20
Hot Rod, 1:66, #15 ....$15-20
Isotta Fraschini 8A
    1924 Town Car, #503 ....$25-30
    1924 Convertible, #504 ....$25-30
Jeep, 1:37
    Military Jeep with gun, #126 ....$15-20
    Policia, #120 ....$15-20
    Renegade, #127 ....$15-20
    with Ladder, #124 ....$15-20
Kenworth Fire Ladder, 1:64, #72 ....$3-5
Lamborghini Marzal, 1:66, #41 ....$15-20
Lancia 037
    "Marlboro," #331 ....$15-20
    "Mobil," #332 ....$15-20
    "Bridgestone," #333 ....$15-20
Land Rover, 1:66
    Circus, #19 ....$15-20
    with missile, #14 ....$15-20
Lincoln 1928 4-door Sedan, #755 ....$15-20
Lotus 49B Racer, 1:66, #38....................$15-20
Lotus 63/2, 1:66, #34 ....$15-20
Magirus Truck, 1:37
    Cement Truck, #131 ....$15-20
    Covered Transporter, #136.................$15-20
    Troop Carrier, #139 ....$15-20
Mercedes-Benz 350 SL, 1:37
    Rally, #115 ....$15-20

Club Regatta, #113 ....$15-20

Mercedes-Benz 406 Van, 1:37

#117 ....$15-20

Ambulance Van, #134 ....$15-20

Policia Van, #132 ....$15-20

Radio Van, #117 ....$15-20

Red Cross Van, #138 ....$15-20

Mercedes-Benz 540K, #754 ....$15-20

Mercedes-Benz Truck

Animal Transporter, #454 ....$40-45

Bottle Truck, #452 ....$40-45

Covered Truck, #450 ....$40-45

Crane Truck, #451 ....$40-45

Log carrier, #453 ....$40-45

Mercedes-Benz Unimog

Fire, #922 ....$15-20

Safari, #923 ....$15-20

MG 1100, 1:66, #26 ....$15-20

Mini Cooper, 1:66, #16 ....$15-20

Morris 1100, 1:66, #28 ....$15-20

Morris Mini with skis, 1:66, #13 ....$15-20

Nissan Jeep

Fire Jeep, #905 ....$15-20

Tow Truck, #901 ....$15-20

with Plow, #903 ....$15-20

Panther Bertone, 1:66, #45 ....$15-20

Peterbilt Semi Cow Transporter, 1:64, #665 ...$3-5

Peugeot 505

"Esso," #453 ....$40-45

4-door Sedan, #404 ....$15-20

Ambulance, #463 ....$25-30

Plymouth Horizon 4-door Sedan, 1:64, #805 ...$3-5

Porsche 917, 1:66, #40 ....$15-20

Porsche 959, 1:30, #917 ....$25-30

Porsche Carrera, 1:37, #107 ....$15-20

Porsche with Skis, 1:37, #122 ....$15-20

Refuse Truck, 1:80, #17 ....$15-20

Renault 5 2-door Sedan, 1:64, #802 ....$3-5

Renault 9 "Road Services," #461 ....$25-30

Renault 12 TS Familian, 1:37, #101 ....$15-20

Renault 16, 1:66, #31 ....$15-20

Renault 17, 1:37

Coupe, #115 ....$15-20

Coupe, #144 ....$15-20

Safari Rally, #112 ....$15-20

Renault Espace

Police, #906 ....$15-20

School Bus, #904 ....$15-20

Renault R12 TS Policia, 1:37, #109 ....$15-20

Scammell Truck, 1:50

Articulated, with 2 cars, #152 ....$15-20

Articulated, with 2 racers, #156 ....$15-20

Articulated, with 2 tractors, #151 ....$15-20

Articulated, with 2 trucks, #153 ....$15-20

Articulated, with 2 trucks, #157 ....$15-20

Breakdown Truck, #171 ....$20-25

Cement Truck, #175 ....$20-25

Dump Truck, #174 ....$20-25

Fire Engine, #172 ....$20-25

Stake Truck, #173 ....$20-25

Seat 124, 1:66

#27 ....$15-20

Policia, #29 ....$15-20

Seat 850 Coupe, 1:66

#30 ....$15-20

Rally, #32 ....$15-20

Taylor Crane, 1:80, #48 ....$15-20

Toyota Celica

"Esso," #337 ....$15-20

"Avis," #338 ....$15-20

"Avis," #339 ....$15-20

Volvo Truck, 1:37

Elevator Truck, #130 ....$15-20

Ladder Truck, #114 ....$15-20

Military Gun Truck, #119 ....$15-20

Military Rescue Truck, #118 ....$15-20

Wrecker, #111 ....$15-20

Street Maintenance Truck with signs,

#123 ....$15-20

Gulliver

Four models were produced by Gulliver of France, three in the late 1930s, one in 1950.

Berliet Bus, 6", 1930s $130-150

Berliet Covered Truck, 5¼", 1930s $90-110

Renault Celtaquatre, 4", 1930s $130-150

Renault 4CV, 1950 ....$145-165

Günthermann

The Günthermann toy company was in existence decades before the advent of the automobile and the quality tin lithographed toy cars that Günthermann produced to mimic them. Even after the death of its founder S. G. Günthermann, the company continued to thrive well into the first half of the twentieth century. When Adolf Weigel, the company's manager, married Günthermann's widow, he had his initials added to the S. G. logo. After Weigel's death in 1919, the company changed its logo back to the original one. Siemens purchased the company in 1965.

Auto Candy Container $1,250-1,500

Captain Campbell's Blue Bird Racer, clockwork

motor, 20" $2,000-2,500

Clown car, clockwork motor, 6" $2,000-2,500

Double Decker Bus, electric headlights, early

1930s, 12" $750-1,000

Fire Ladder Truck with 4 firemen and ladder,

16" $3,750-4,500

Fire Pumper, wind-up, late 1800s,

7¾" $3,750-4,250

Fire Pumper with 2 firemen, clockwork motor, circa

1898, 8¼" $3,500-4,000

Fire Pumper with 3 composition firemen,

8¼" $3,750-4,250

Georgian Window Limousine with driver,

clockwork motor, circa 1908 ...$2,250-2,750

Gordon Bennett Coupe, 5¾" $2,750-3,250

Hansom-style car $1,500-2,000

Horseless carriage with driver, clockwork motor,

7" $2,250-2,750

Limousine with painted driver, clockwork motor,

opening doors, circa 1920 ....$2,250-2,750

Limousine / Touring car with removable roof,

clockwork motor, 10¼" $1,750-2,250

Open Phaeton with driver, wind-up,

7" $1,250-1,750

Open Two-Seater car with driver in top hat,

circa 1899, 7" $2,250-2,750

Paris to Berlin Race car $2,250-2,750

Kaye Don's Sunbeam Silver Bullet Racer,

22" $1,750-2,250

Taxi with driver, convertible back, clockwork

motor, circa 1912, 10½" $2,500-3,000

Vis-a-Vis with driver, wind-up, 5" $1,750-2,250

Vis-a-Vis with driver, wind-up, 10¼" ...$2,750-3,250

H

H. L. Framberg (see Framberg, H. L.)

Hallmark (also see Kiddie Car Classics)

Hallmark has produced numerous promotional and novelty items for their stationery stores. Among the offerings are a few whimsical diecast toys called Road Rovers, not much more than a heavy lump of zamak, in simplified shapes for toddlers or as novelties. On the other hand, their recent offerings of miniature pedal cars are just short of spectacular. See a list of them under the Kiddie Car Collectibles heading. Value is based on a March 1999 eBay auction of #2 Banana Bus in mint condition with original box that sold for $15. Note that the assortment is labeled Series I. What Series II is and if it was ever issued is not known.

Hallmark Series I Road Rovers – Diecast Metal, Hand Painted

Banana Bus, #2 ....$5-8

in original box $12-15

Blue Blob, #4 ....$5-8

in original box $12-15

Chocolate Mouse, #1 ....$5-8

in original box $12-15

Firey Fred, #10 ....$5-8

   in original box $12-15

Flash, The Garbage Eater, #12 ....$5-8

   in original box $12-15

Fudge Drudge, #11 ....$5-8

   in original box $12-15

Fuzz Mobile, #3 ....$5-8

   in original box $12-15

Little Dumpy, #5 ....$5-8

   in original box $12-15

Merry Mover, #7 ....$5-8

   in original box $12-15

Purple Squash, #8 ....$5-8

   in original box $12-15

Red Rover, #6 ....$5-8

   in original box $12-15

Scuttle Bug, #9 ....$5-8

   in original box $12-15

Hartoy (also see American Highway Legends, Precision Engineered Models)

1967 10th Avenue North

Lake Worth, Florida 33461

phone: 561-586-5556

fax: 561-586-5558

toll free: 1-800-245-1264

e-mail: hartoyinc@aol.com

website: www.hartoy.com

Back in 1999, Hartoy was based in Lake Worth, Florida. The company has since gone out of business. In its day though, Hartoy produced its own American Highway Legends series of 1:64 sclae trucks in various liveries, as well as modified models from Lledo and others to produce various promotional models through a licensing agreement with numerous companies.

An assortment of Coca-Cola vehicles and Chevron gas station promotionals are some of the better-known Lledo models from Hartoy.

American Highway Legends was at one time the most prominent series from Hartoy, and is dealt with in its own section of this book (see American Highway Legends).

Preceision Engineered Models (PEM) was the next generation of promotional trucks from Hartoy (see Precision Engineered Models).

Lledo and Days Gone models marketed by Hartoy are likewise listed with the rest of the Lledo models in this book (see Lledo).

Hasbro (also see Aviva, Kenner, Playskool)

Hasbro has been a powerful force in the toy industry since the 1960s. Toys such as Mr.

Machine, the see-through gear-driven walking, animated robot with a top hat, was possibly one of the best known toys of the period, at least if you watched Saturday morning cartoons. But Hasbro's solid claim to fame is G. I. Joe action figures and accessories, a perennial favorite for some 30 years.

Hasbro has continued through to the present, but it has been overshadowed by the giant called Mattel. In fact, Mattel failed in an attempt to purchase Hasbro in 1995.

G. I. Joe aside, Hasbro's product line at one time included a line of Aviva character toys usually sold at Hallmark shops. Predominantly Peanuts characters from the comic strip of the same name, Aviva at last word continues to market such items in diecast and plastic. See Aviva for a sampling of a few of the diecast items issued.

Hasbro has also issued Kenner Winner's Circle NASCAR models (produced by Action Performance and later marketed under the Action Performance brand) and Playskool diecast vehicles featuring Barney the Purple Dinosaur and friends. Go to the respective brands for a product listing.

Hasegawa

If not for the fact that they produced a few exquisite 1:24 scale plastic model kits, Hasegawa would receive no mention at all in this book. Their new Volkswagen Samba 23-Window Minibus is a worthy addition to any toy car collection.

Volkswagen 23-Window Minibus, plastic

   kit $30-35

Hauser

Hauser was one of many late nineteenth century–early twentieth century German manufacturers of tinplate wind-up and clockwork toys, although Hauser is one of the more obscure brands.

Horse Drawn Beer Wagon, clockwork

   tinplate, circa 1890s $750-1,150

Herpa

Herpa Miniaturmodelle GmbH

LeonrodstraBe 46/47

D-90599

Dietenhofen, Germany

Website: www.herpa.de/

Among the wide assortment of models available under the Herpa brand name is a series of 1:87 scale cars and trucks with plastic bodies. The accuracy and detail of these diminutive vehi-

cles is remarkable for their size. In the larger 1:43 scale, Herpa produces an assortment of diecast models that are especially nice, although they feature no working parts such as opening doors, hood, or trunk.

Herpa 1:43 Scale Diecast Models

BMW 740i

   arctic white.............................$18-21

   bright red $18-21

   metallic blue $18-21

   Oxford green $18-21

Ferrari 288 GTO

   red $18-21

   yellow $18-21

Ferrari 348tb

   black.......................................$45-50

   metallic blue $45-50

   red $45-50

   red $45-50

   yellow $45-50

Ferrari 348ts

   metallic green $45-50

Ferrari F40

   black...$45

   red $45-50

   yellow $45-50

Ferrari Testarossa

   red $45-50

   Convertible, red $45-50

   Coupe, yellow.........................$45-50

   Spyder, yellow.........................$45-50

   Spyder, silver..........................$45-50

Mercedes-Benz 600

   AMG $40-45

   SEL $40-45

Mercedes-Benz E320 Sedan

   metallic blue $18-21

   metallic gray...........................$18-21

   red $18-21

   black.......................................$18-21

   blue $18-21

   Convertible, blue $18-21

   Convertible, white $18-21

Mercedes-Benz 320

   Convertible...............................$20-25

   Coupe.....................................$20-25

   Sedan $20-25

   Wagon $20-25

Mercedes-Benz 600 SEL

   green $18-21

   gray $18-21

   purple $18-21

   red $18-21

Volkswagen Polo

   4-door $20-25

2-door $20-25

Herpa Jr. 1:66 Scale Models
BMW 325i

    blue $5-8

    green....................................$5-8

    red $5-8

    yellow $5-8

BMW 528 Fire Chief car (plastic), red $5

Herpa HO Gauge (1:87 Scale) Plastic Models
AC Cobra $9-12

Alfa Romeo 155 DTM

    Street version $9-12

    Racing version $12-15

Audi 90 Quattro Coupe $12-15

Audi V8, metallic finish $9-12

Audi STW 4-door Sedan 1997 ....$12-15

BMW AC Schnitzer $9-12

BMW 325 Convertible, top down $9-12

BMW 325 Convertible, top up $9-12

BMW 325 Hardtop 4-door Sedan...........$9-12

BMW 325 Hardtop 2-door Coupe $9-12

BMW 3-Series 1998 ....$9-12

BMW 525i Touring Wagon $8-11

BMW 528i Touring Wagon

    without roof rack....................$9-12

    with roof rack........................$9-12

BMW 5-Series Sedan $9-12

BMW 535i

    Notarzt.............................$7-10

    Sedan Alpina, metallic $20-24

    Sedan, metallic $9-12

BMW 740i Sedan $9-12

BMW 850I Coupe $9-12

BMW M3 Schnitzer $9-12

BMW 1602 ....$9-12

BMW GTR Coupe

    with spoiler........................$12-15

    metallic $10-13

BMW M Coupe $9-12

BMW Z1 Convertible Coupe $7-10

BMW Z3 Roadster........................$10-13

BMW Z3 Coupe $9-12

Buick Grand National $9-12

Ford Mustang 1969 Fastback $9-12

Ford Thunderbird 1989 ....$9-12

Chevrolet Bel Air 1957 ....$9-12

Chevrolet Camaro 1985 ....$9-12

Chevrolet Corvette

    1963 Sting Ray $9-12

    ZR1 ....$9-12

Citroën 2CV

    "Charleston" $7-10

Citroën Evasion Minivan......................$12-15

Ferrari 288 GTO

    yellow $20-24

    red $30-35

Ferrari 348tb $12-15

Ferrari 348ts $12-15

Ferrari 512, yellow $12-15

Ferrari F40

    red $12-15

    yellow $12-15

Ferrari F50 ....$20-25

Ferrari Testarossa

    red $12-15

    black $12-15

Fiat 124 Spyder $9-12

Fiat Cinquecento Hardtop Coupe $7-9

Fiat Ulysses Minivan $9-12

Ford Galaxy Minivan $9-12

Jaguar XJ12 ....$8-11

Jaguar E-Type $9-12

Jeep Grand Cherokee $8-11

Lamborghini Diablo.......................$12-15

Mazda 323F $9-12

Mazda MX5 Miata $9-12

Mazda Xedos 9 Sedan $9-12

Mercedes-Benz 300CE $8-11

Mercedes-Benz 300TE Station Wagon $8-11

Mercedes-Benz A Class $10-13

Mercedes-Benz AMG C180 ....$12-15

Mercedes-Benz C180T Station Wagon ...$10-13

Mercedes-Benz C220 Sedan $9-12

Mercedes-Benz CLK $10-13

Mercedes-Benz E280 ....$10-13

Mercedes-Benz E320

    Convertible..........................$9-12

    Sedan $20-23

    T Station Wagon, enhanced trim and

      interior $20-30

    T Station Wagon, standard $10-13

    Coupe $9-12

Mercedes-Benz 500SL Coupe $12-15

Mercedes-Benz S600 Sedan $9-12

Mercedes-Benz SLK Roadster..............$12-15

Mercedes-Benz Vito OHL Express Van $12-15

Mini Cooper

    hardtop $9-12

    folding top open $9-12

    Mayfair Hardtop Coupe $9-12

Opel Calibra $12-15

Opel Corsa 4-door $7-10

Opel Corsa GLS Coupe $7-10

Opel Kadett..............................$7-10

Opel Omega

    Caravan MV6 Wagon $9-12

    GL Sedan $9-12

    GT Sedan $10-13

    Taxi $12-15

Opel Vectra................................$9-12

Peugeot 806 Minivan $9-12

Porsche 356B Convertible $9-12

Porsche 911, 1966 ....$9-12

Porsche 928 ....$7-10

Porsche 959 ....$12-15

Porsche 996 ....$11-14

Porsche Boxster $12-15

Porsche Carrera S4 ....$12-15

Porsche Turbo Coupe $7-10

Renault Clio 16V

    Coupe $8-11

    Sedan $10-13

    Williams $21-25

Renault Laguna Sedan $9-12

Renault Twingo $7-10

Seat Alhambra

    red $29-33

    all other colors $10-13

Seat Cordoba.............................$9-12

Triumph TR3 ....$9-12

Volkswagen Beetle, 1969 ....$9-12

Volkswagen Corrado Coupe $8-11

Volkswagen Golf Tour Fahrschule (Driving

    School) $11-14

Volkswagen Passat $9-12

Volkswagen Polo $11-14

Volkswagen Sharan $10-13

Volkswagen T4

    California Coach Pop-Up Camper......$15-18

    Minivan $8-11

    Trabant 601S $7-10

Hess Promotional Toys (also see Taylor Made Trucks)

While Hess trucks are plastic, they represent a large portion of the scale model truck collector market, and are mentioned here due to their popularity. Hess trucks are issued by the Hess Oil Company.

Hess trucks are manufactured for the Hess Oil Company by Taylor Made Trucks under the auspices of Toy Truck Collector of Englewood, New Jersey.

Hess Promotional Toys–[original selling prices in brackets]

1964–B-Model Mack Tanker Truck, made in Hong Kong (Same tanker was used by Service, Wilco, Gant, Billups, Etna & Travelers) [$1.39] $1,900-2,050

1965–same as 1964

1966–"Hess Voyager" Tanker Ship, made in the U.S.A. by Marx Toys [$1.89]..$2,300-2,450

1967–Split Window Tanker Truck with "Red Velvet" base on box, no rivets on battery switch, made in the U.S.A. [$2.89] ...$2,400-2,550

1968–same as 1967 except no velvet box was used, no rivets on battery switch, made in Hong Kong [$1.49] $675-825

1969–same as 1968

1969–Split Window Tanker "Amerada Hess," Made in Hong Kong, rare, not sold to public.$2,500-2,750

1970–Red Pumper Fire Truck, made in Hong Kong by Marx Toys [$1.69] $700-775

1971–same as 1970 except box was labeled "Season's Greetings" [$1.69] ..$3,000-3,250

1972–Split Window Tanker Truck–Same as 1968 except has "rivets" on battery switch [$1.79] $375-400

1973–no promotion offered

1974–same as 1972 [$1.89] $375-400

1975–Semi Box Truck, 3 oil drums, no Hess labels on drums, 1pc. cab on tractor, made in both U.S.A. & Hong Kong [$1.99] $400-425

1976–same as 1975 except oil drums have Hess labels & tractor cab is made in 2 pieces [$2.29] $400-425

1977–Semi Tanker Truck, large rear label 1.5" x 1", made in Hong Kong [$2.39] ...$175-200

1978–same as 1977 except–small rear label 1" x ⅞" [$2.49] $185-210

1979–no promotion offered

1980–GMC Training Van, dated 1978 sold but sold in 1980, Made in Hong Kong [$3.29] ..$400-450

1981–no promotion offered

1982–'33 Chevrolet "Home Delivery" Tanker Truck, box marked "First Hess Truck", not a bank, made in Hong Kong [$4.69] ..$95-120

1983–same as 1982 (reissued), not a bank, made in Hong Kong [$5.29] $95-120

1984–similiar to 1977-78 Semi Tanker Truck except made into a bank, made in Hong Kong [$4.99] $95-120

1985–'33 Chevrolet "Home Delivery" Tanker bank, distributed in the north $125-150

1985–reissued 1984 Tanker, distributed in the south $95-120

1986–White Semi Box Truck with 3 Hess labeled oil drums, made in both Hong Kong & China [$5.49] $100-125

1987–same as 1986 [$5.99] $75-90

1988–White "Toy Truck & Racer," made in both Hong Kong & China [$6] $70-85

1989–White Aerial Ladder Fire Truck with dual siren sounds, made in China [$8.99] ...$65-80

1990–White Semi Tanker Truck, back up and air horn sounds, made in China [$9.99] $45-55

1991–same as 1988 except different style race car, larger truck cab, made in China [$10.99] $35-45

1992–White "18 Wheeler" Box Truck with racer, made in China [$11.99] $40-50

1993–Hess Patrol car, white and green, sirens & lights, larger scale toy [$11.99] $30-40

1993–Hess Premium Diesel Tanker given as a gift to Hess bulk diesel dealers, reissue of the 1990 semi tanker with new graphics, special box wrapped in green paper, and special gift card from the Hess company, not sold to public $1,000-1,250

1994–same as 1993, not sold to public $1,000-1,250

1994–Hess Rescue Truck, white and green with red ladder, larger scale toy [$14.99] .$25-30

1995–Hess Toy Truck & Helicopter, white, green, flatbed semi with detachable helicopter [$15.99] $20-25

1996–Hess Heavy Rescue Ladder Truck, white, green [$15.99] $45-55

1997–Hess Semi-Tractor and Trailer, trailer has window on left side revealing two cars (included) [$15.99] $50-60

1998–Hess Race Car Transporter, window in driver's side reveals race car (included) [$15.99] .$50-60

1999–Hess Shuttlecraft Transporter [$19.99] ..$60-75

2000 Hess Hook and Ladder Fire Truck [$18.99] $35-40

Hess Toy Company

Matthieu Hess founded the Hess Toy Company of Germany in 1825. The JLH trademark was adopted when his son Johann Leonard Hess inherited the business after Matthieu Hess's death in 1886. Hess first introduced the Hessmobile around 1918, a toy car with a flywheel drive operated by a hand crank and clutch mechanism. The crank was turned to give the flywheel momentum, then the hood-mounted clutch was released to engage the power to the rear axle to drive the vehicle.

Hessmobile

Open Phaeton with driver, 8½", circa 1918 ....$1,500-2,000

Racer with driver and hand crank, 8" $750-1,000

Limousine

with clockwork drive, green and red, 9" $900-1200

with flywheel drive, green and black, circa 1920, 7½" $750-1,000

with flywheel drive, blue and black, circa 1920, 9" $1,250-1,500

Open Two-Seater

tin lithographed, 8" $1,500-2,000

10½" $1,750-2,250

Racer

tin lithographed, two seater, clockwork drive, 8¾" $1,500-2,000

with driver, 5" $1,500-2,000

Speedster with driver, flywheel drive, 8" $650-900

High Speed (also see Reader's Digest)

Whether High Speed brand toys can be considered diecast is debatable. These inexpensive generic toys are mostly plastic. On the samples found, only the truck cab and upper chassis are diecast. Nevertheless, they possess the charm of a well-designed toy, while lacking the identity of a scale model.

While suggested retail of $2.49 seems high to me, the $.99 paid at Toy Liquidators makes them reasonably priced. Values will not likely rise on such toys in the near future, let's say the next twenty years, but they are "cute" additions to a well-rounded toy car collection. High Speed has since begun producing better, more realistic models.

More recently, some particularly realistic toy cars measuring about 3" long have been issued as promotional items through *Reader's Digest*. No list is available for specific models, but a 1955 Chevrolet Bel Air is one of the items in the series.

1948 Task Master Fire Truck for Reader's Digest $5-8

1955 Chevrolet Bel Air $12-15

Box Truck $1-3

Cement Truck $1-3

Dump Truck $1-3

Utility Truck $1-3

Highway 61 Collectibles

Trademark Models / Diecast Promotions
P.O. Box 882
10478 St. Joseph Drive
Dubuque, IA 52004-0882
toll free: 877-874-5467
direct: 563-583-0636
http://12.26.242.144/vehicles.cfm

Highway 61 Collectibles are produced by F.F. Ertl III, Inc., grandson of Fred Ertl Sr., founder of the Ertl Company of Dyersville, Iowa. Highway 61 models are highly detailed precision diecast metal replicas with subject matter ranging from the high-powered Arnie Beswick 1966 Pontiac GTO Drag Car, to the thrifty but stylish 1951 Studebaker Champion. Trademark Models represents the company's line of agricultural and construction vehicles, while Diecast Promotions offers an assortment of model trucks.

Arnie Beswick 1966 Pontiac GTO Drag car, 1:18, #50024 ....$70-80

1941 Chevrolet Flatbed, 1:16
    Green, #50060 ....$80-90
    Red, #50061 ....$80-90
    Orange, #50062 ....$80-90
    Brewster Green, #50065 ....$80-90
    Boatswain Blue, #50066 ....$80-90
1966 Hairy Hurst Oldsmobile Cutlass Drag Car,
    1:18, #50089 ....$70-80
1967 Plymouth GTX
    with Magnum 440, Black, #50029...$50-60
    with Magnum 440, Bright Blue,
        #50051 ....$50-60
    with Hemi 426, Yellow, #50050 ......$50-60
1951 Studebaker Champion V8 Commander, 1:18
    Sahara Sand, #50114 ....$50-60

Black Cherry, #50115............................$50-60
    Maui Blue, #50116 ....$50-60

Highway Travelers

Highway Travelers
P O Box 187
Oakdale, NY 11769-0187
    Highway Travelers of Oakdale, New York, are white-metal models of exceptional quality.

Cadillac Allante
    1987-93 Convertible, #105C $155-170
    1987-93 Hardtop, #105H $155-170
    1992 Indianapolis 500 Pace Car,
        #105P $170-185
Frazer Manhattan
    1951 Convertible, #103C $220-235
    1951 Softtop, #103S $220-235
Plymouth Fury
    1961 Convertible, #104C $190-205
    1961 Hardtop, #104H $220-235
    1961 Softtop, #104S $190-105
Studebaker Lark
    1962 Convertible Indianapolis 500 Pace
        Car, #102P $170-185
    1962 Daytona with sunroof,
        #102S $160-175

Hobbycraft

1-1 Jimbo-Cho
Chiyoda-ku
Tokyo, Japan
    Until April 2002, I had not heard of this company. It was then that Larry Abbs wrote via e-mail about a gas powered model midget racing car he thinks was purchased by his uncle during the Korean War. So the car dates back to the early 1950s. Value remains a mystery, so an educated guess has been assigned.

Midgetee Summit, gas model racing car with
    Fuji 0.19 engine $250-350

Holland-Oto (see Efsi/Holland-Oto)

Hongwell (see Autocraft)

Hornby Series (also see Dinky Toys, Meccano)

    Frank Hornby (1863–1936) is the forefather of the British toy car industry. His first invention was in 1901 and described as "Mechanics Made Easy," a line of various construction sets In 1907, the Meccano brand was applied to these sets, with the name Meccano Ltd. applied to the company in the following year. Meccano was the earliest brand name applied to Erector sets.

    The now-famous Binns Road factory was established in Liverpool, England, in 1914. In 1916, *Meccano Magazine* was launched. Hornby Trains were introduced in "O" gauge. The establishment of the Meccano factory in France in 1921.

    The first Meccano car construction kits with clockwork motors were introduced in 1930, followed by airplane and speed boat construction kits, Elektron electric sets, Kemex chemistry sets, and Dolly Varden doll houses in 1932.

    In 1933, Modelled Miniatures, otherwise known as the Hornby Series, were introduced as O gauge toy cars designed to accompany the Hornby trains. The name was changed to Dinky Toys in April 1934.

    After the 1936 death of Frank Hornby, the Hornby Dublo series was introduced in 1938. Meccano continued until 1964 when the company was purchased by the Lines Brothers (Tri-Ang).

    The list below represents the two-year timespan between 1933 and 1934 when the Hornby Series was issued. After that time, the series was renamed Dinky Toys.

Army Tank, 1:48, 1933 ....$500-650
Delivery Van, 1:48, 1933 ....$1,500-1,750
Farm Tractor, 1:48, 1933 ....$550-700
Motor Truck, 1:48, 1933 ....$450-500
Sports car, 1:48, 1933 ....$650-800
Sports Coupé, 1:48, 1933 ....$600-750

Horsman

    Fiero fanatic Ray Paulk first contacted me in March 1999 regarding this brand. "Horsman King of the Road World Class Series" is the complete name on the box of these approx. 1:32 scale models. On the end of the box is printed.
© 1988 Horsman
Division of Gata Box Ltd.
New York NY 10010
Made in Macao.

    Paulk says, "This particular box shows NO. 07900. The sample model is a rather heavy diecast metal white 1988 Corvette with opening doors and hood. The interior is all black plastic but nicely detailed and under the hood is a chrome engine insert. The back of the box pictures the Corvette in red along with a silver BMW and a black Pontiac Fiero notchback."

    The original price sticker still remains on the box. This model was originally sold at Farm + Fleet for $4.49. Paulk recently won it in an eBay auction for a winning bid of $10.51. As an avid collector of Fiero toys and memorabilia, Paulk wants to find the Fiero model pictured on the back.

BMW, metallic silver $5-10
Pontiac Fiero, black...............................$5-10
Chevrolet Corvette 1988, red $5-10

Hot Wheels

    The author of this book purposely makes no attempt to present the full Hot Wheels line in this book since there are several other books devoted to Hot Wheels already in print. Nevertheless, there are a few interesting observations worth mentioning:

    Since 1968, Mattel's Hot Wheels line has maintained a solid lock on the US diecast toy car market. While many other toy manufacturers, even Matchbox, suffered the humiliation of lost market share, near bankruptcy, and repeated buyout, Hot Wheels toys have remained market-stable. Prototypes and production models alike from Hot Wheels' first few years are commanding high prices, as are new special issues and even some regular issues. Much speculation — and some would say overspeculation — and debate ensues over the value of new regular production issues.

    One such prototype is a 1969 issue #6274 Beach Bomb, a Volkswagen van with two surfboards projecting out the back window. While the production model with side panels added to the cast to hold the surfboards is fairly common and priced at $40 to $80, only some

14–20 specimens of the prototype are believed to exist. The value of this rare Hot Wheels model has exceeded $4,000.

A second prototype, a hybrid Beach Bomb with the sides of the base extended outward to accomodate the eventually redesigned side-mount surfboard ports, but with surfboards sticking out the back, was found to be the only one of its kind. It sold at auction for $70,000.

In late 1996, Mattel made the announcement that the company was working on purchasing Tyco Toys, the current owner of Matchbox, Dinky, and several other toy brands. By mid-1997, the sale was complete.

A few years earlier, Mattel purchased the Corgi brand and incorporated many of the Corgi Jrs. into the Hot Wheels line. Eventually, though, the original employees of Corgi in Swansea, South Wales, bought back the larger scale Corgi Collectibles series from Mattel. Will the same thing happen to Matchbox? Will some Hot Wheels take on the look of Matchbox models? Or will the Matchbox series be kept distinct from the Hot Wheels offerings?

Since the merger, Matchbox toys have reportedly already been seen in Hot Wheels five-packs, and retail advertising has had Matchbox five-packs shown with the Hot Wheels logo on them. In addition, Hot Wheels models have shown up in Matchbox sets.

To do justice to the entire line of toys, it would take an entire book. Collector Books has published a two-volume reference titled *Hot Wheels: The Ultimate Redline Guide* (ISBNs 1-57432-441-1 & 1-57432-325-3). Volume 1 offers a guide to the core line of Hot Wheels from 1968 to 1973. Volume 2 covers Chop Cycles, Earthshakers, Farbs, Hot Birds, Hot Shots, Hot Line, Revvers, RRRumblers, Sizzlers, Small Shots, and Zowees.

Since the two books represent over 550 pages by themselves, it would be an enormous task to make such a listing fit between the covers of this book. So, due to space constraints, I refer you to the previously mentioned books.

Hot Pursuit

There seems to be no shortage of new diecast companies. Hot Pursuit Collectibles is (or at least was) one of those. Based in Cherry Hill, New Jersey, Hot Pursuit Collectibles offered an assortment of 1:24 scale coin banks through various specialty outlets. The models, an assortment of 1978 Dodge Monaco and 1968 Plymouth Fury police cars introduced in 1997, are similar to the 1:43 scale Chevrolet Caprice

police cars first introduced by Road Champs a few years ago, except that opening the trunk reveals a hidden coin slot. Why a bank? It immediately appeals to more collectors — those that collect diecast models and those that collect diecast banks, as well as those that collect model police cruisers.

The cross-cultural approach didn't work though, and Hot Pursuit went out of business in 1997, the same year they started, and existing inventory was purchased by Dimension 4, now also out of business.

New York Police Department	$25-30
California Highway Patrol	$25-30
Michigan State Police	$25-30
Oklahoma Highway Patrol	$25-30
Ohio State Highway Patrol	$25-30
Arkansas State Trooper	$25-30
New York City Taxi	$25-30
New Jersey	$25-30
Virginia	$25-30
Florida	$25-30
Alabama	$25-30
Georgia	$25-30
New York	$25-30
Maryland Police (2 car set)	$55-65
Chicago Fire Department	$25-30
New York Fire Department	$25-30
San Francisco Fire Department	$25-30
Philadelphia Fire Department	$25-30

HP Toys

HP Toys were made in Denmark sometime in the mid-1980s.

1984 Leyland Farm Tractor, 1:25	$25-30

Hubley

Hubley toys were made in Lancaster, Pennsylvania, and remain some of the most popular and collectible toys on the collector market. The first Hubley toys were cast iron. The company that made them has been traced back to 1892. By 1940, lighter diecast zinc alloy replaced heavy cast iron, thus cutting the cost of worldwide shipping. Plastic toys make up a significant portion of the Hubley line. Richard O'Brien's book *Collecting Toy Cars and Trucks* provides a detailed history of Hubley toys.

Besides the assembled toys, Hubley also produced diecast model kits in the 1960s. These kits, unassembled and still in the original box, are gaining renewed popularity with collectors.

Gabriel purchased Hubley in the 1960s and for a short time reissued a few Hubley diecast metal kits under the Gabriel name.

In the mid-1980s, Hubley was purchased by Ertl, and a few more Hubley toys and kits have been reissued by them.

A good example is the classic Hubley school bus. The original Hubley version featured clear plastic labels and no windows. The earlier Ertl version is windowless while a later version issued by Ertl has dark tinted plastic windows. The Hubley version is priced around $45–55. The two Ertl versions retailed for around $15.

A Survey of Hubley Toys

Airflow car, 5¼"	$80-95
Bell Telephone Truck with telephone pole trailer, 24"	$180-195
Jaguar, 7½"	$185-190
Motorcyde Delivery Van with Driver, "Say It With Flowers," cast iron (extremely rare)	$40,000-42,500
Packard Sedan, 1939-1940, 5½"	$70-85
Packard Dietrich, 1:22	$70-85
Panama Digger, 3½"	$575-625
Panama Digger, 9½"	$1,600-1,700

Hubley Kiddietoys

A popular series of Hubley toys were marketed as Kiddietoys. Here is a sampling.

Dump Truck, #476	$140-165
Dump Truck, #510	$250-265
MG TD Sport car, #485, 9"	$190-205
Racer, #457, 6½"	$55-70
Sedan, #452, 7"	$30-35
Taxi, #5	$25-30
Tractor	$45-60
1946 Ford Stake Truck, #461	$170-195

Hubley Model Kits, 1:20 Scale

1932 Chevrolet Roadster, #4862-400	$75-90
Duesenberg SJ, #4864	$60-75
Duesenberg Model SJ Town car, #4868	$80-110
Ford Model A Pickup, #4855	$65-80
1930 Packard Roadster, #4860	$75-90

Hubley Real Toys (U.S.A.) / Real Types (Canada), 1:60 Scale

A few toys representing U.S. cars were issued around 1958 to 1960 in 1:60 scale. They were marketed in the U.S. as Real Toys, and in Canada as Real Types, a series of cars of approximately 3" – 3½" long.

Buick, #RT 90, light blue	$55-70
Chevrolet Corvair, #RT340, turquoise	$55-70
Chevrolet Corvette RT 80, red	$45-70
Ford Country Squire, #RT250, two-tone cream and brown	$55-70

Ford Fairlane, #RT 20, mint green............$55-70

Ford Falcon, light blue.........................$55-70
GMC Firebird III, #RT 350, red...............$60-75
Studebaker Hawk, #RT 50, red...............$65-80

Husky (also see Corgi)

Husky toys were the first series of smaller toys produced by Corgi. Later the line would be renamed Corgi Juniors. Husky toys were light-weight and inexpensive, but highly accurate ren-derings of common European vehicles of the mid-1960s, considering their original price of 39 to 49 cents each. For a sample listing of Husky models, go to the Corgi section of this book.

I

Ichiko

Ichiko Corporation
5F., Excel Bldg., No. 4-1-3-Chome
Komatugawa, Edogawa-Ku,
Tokyo, Japan
phone: 81-3-3682-6121
fax: 81-3-3682-6126

Only one example from Ichiko Collection Tin Toys of Japan is known and documented here. It was one of several such models found at a liq-uidator store in 1999 for $10. While most of the others suffered damage to the models inside (mostly flattened roofs), this one only suffered damage to the poorly constructed box.

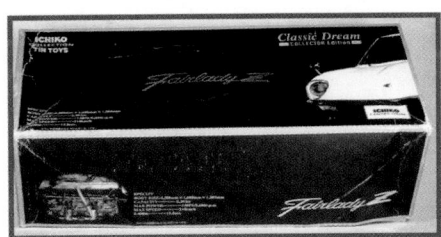

Datsun Fairlady Z, maroon, tin friction, Classic Dream Collector Edition 1 of 3,000, produced April 27, 1998 ....$20-30

Icibi

Icibi is a brand of 1:25 scale models of undetermined quality made in Greece.

Deutz Fire Engine, 1:25, #5020................$7-9
Deutz Fire Ladder Truck, 1:25, #270..........$7-9
McLaren CanAm, 1:25, #900 ....$7-9
Porsche 911 Police, 1:25, #1431 ....$7-9

Ideal

The Ideal Toy Company, also known as Ideal Novelty & Toy Company, existed from 1903 to 1978 when it was purchased by CBS Toys. The company, based in Long Island, New York, was distinguished as the first toy manufac-turer to mass produce teddy bears, inspired by the legend of Theodore Roosevelt sparing the life of a young bear while on a hunting trip.

Ideal has produced an extensive number of toys of all kinds. An entire book could be written on the subject, and it surprises me that no such book exists. In the realm of toy cars, Ideal has made many, mostly all-plastic dime store toys.

In the 1960s, Ideal was at its peak with the introduction of Mr. Machine, thanks to massive television advertising during Saturday morning cartoons. It was a windup plastic robot with all the internal gears visible through its clear shell.

Army Ambulance, 5"..............................$35-50
Cadillac 4-door sedan, 1948, 4"..........$40-55
Corvette...$130-160
Sedan, 5" $20-30
Sedan with opening doors, 9¼".............$40-55

Igra

Igra models are quality 1:38, 1:43, and 1:87 scale plastic models made in Czechoslo-vakia, now known as the Czech Republic.

Avia Box Van, Velkopopovicky Kozel Beer,
    1:87, #757 ....$9-12
Bugatti T35 (Matchbox Models of
    Yesteryear copy), #IG465 ....$6-8
1906 Laurin/Klement, #6 ....$15-18
Liaz Articulated Box Truck, Gambrinus Beer
    Pilsen, 1:87, #755............................$9-12
Liaz Box Truck, Velkopopovicky Kozel Beer,
    1:87, #756 ....$9-12
1907 Praga Charon, #7 ....$15-18
Skoda 120 LS Saloon car, #IG463.............$6-8
1924 Tatra Sedan, #1 ....$15-18
1924 Tatra Phaeton, #2 ....$15-18
Tatra T613 Saloon car, #IG464.............$6-8
1906 Velox car, #9 ....$15-18
Zetor Crystal Tractor, #12.....................$15-18

Zetor Tractor/Loader, #13 ....$15-18
Zetor Manure Spreader, #14.................$15-18

IHC (see International Hobby Corp.)

Imperial Diecast

Imperial Toy Corp.
2060 East 7th St.
Los Angeles, CA 90021 USA
phone: 213-489-2100

Imperial Toy Corporation has its US headquar-ters in Los Angeles, California. Other international headquarters include Imperial Toy Canada Ltd, in Mississauga, Ontario, and its Great Britain distribu-tor Titan Toys International Ltd. The distinction of these models may lie mostly in their colorful pack-ages and regal logo. The actual models are made better than most generics, and sell for comparably more. Featured are pull-back action motorcycles with tiny "training wheels" to propel them, nicely made commercial jets, a series of helicopters that are also equipped with pull-back action, and vari-ous other somewhat attractive toys.

Mixed in with the generic offerings from Imper-ial are the distinctive models issued under the Impe-rial Toys Freeway Flyers brand. The bases are the dead giveaway that these were produced by Pla-yart. What distinguishes them as Imperial Toys is the package. Out of the package, they are unidentifiable as anything but Playarts. What is curious is that they are more valuable as Playarts in Imperial packaging than they are as Imperial toys.

More recently, Imperial has taken on the Buddy L license and is issuing 1:64 scale diecast models and a few larger pressed steel Hummer H2 models under the Buddy L brand.

In the case of Buddy L issues, the model is only identifiable as such if in the original pack-age. On the other hand, Playart models are almost as valuable out of the Imperial Freeway Flyers package as in it.

Alfa Carabo Bertone, Freeway Flyers
    #706-13, Playart casting.................$10-12
Alfa Romeo P33, Freeway Flyers #706-12,
    Playart casting $10-12
AMC
    AMX "390," Freeway Flyers #706-10,
        Playart casting $10-12
    Javelin SST, Freeway Flyers #706-07,
        Playart casting $10-12
Austin Mini Cooper S Mk II, Freeway Flyers
    #706-57, Playart casting.................$10-12
Batmobile, Freeway Flyers #706-00, Playart
    casting $30-45

BMW 2002, Freeway Flyers #706-35,
 Playart casting $10-12
Cadillac Eldorado, Freeway Flyers #706-15,
 Playart casting $10-12
Cement Mixer, Freeway Flyers #706-26,
 Playart casting $10-12

**Chevrolet 3100 Pickup, green, Imperial
Mighty Machines Mighty Classics, 2003...$1-2**

Chevrolet Astro-1, Freeway Flyers #706-21,
 Playart casting $10-12
Chevrolet Camaro

**orange, Imperial Mighty Machines Mighty
Classics 5-pk, 2003 ....$1-2**

 SS, Freeway Flyers #706-09, Playart
 casting...$10-12
Chevrolet Corvette

**Convertible, medium blue, Imperial Mighty
Machines Mighty Classics, 2003 ....$1-2**

 Stingray, Freeway Flyers #706-36,
 Playart casting $10-12
 Stingray Mako Shark, Freeway Flyers
 #706-06, Playart casting $15-20

**Chevrolet Impala, red, Imperial Mighty
Machines, 2003.....................................$1-2**

Datsun 240Z, Freeway Flyers #706-37,
 Playart casting $10-12

DeTomaso Mangusta 5000 Ghia, Freeway
 Flyers #706-05, Playart casting $10-12
Dump Truck, Freeway Flyers #706-28,
 Playart casting $10-12
Fiat 124 Sport, Freeway Flyers #706-58,
 Playart casting $10-12
Fiat Dino, Freeway Flyers #706-34, Playart
 casting...$10-12
Fire Chief, Freeway Flyers #706-18, Playart
 casting...$10-12
Fire Truck, Freeway Flyers #706-30, Playart
 casting...$10-12
Ford Capri 1600 GT, Freeway Flyers
 #706-50, Playart casting..................$10-12
Ford Convertible Coupe, 1953, red

Buddy L, 2003 ....$2-3

Imperial Mighty Machines, 2003.............$1-2

Ford Cortina GXL, Freeway Flyers #706-55,
 Playart casting $10-12
Ford Fairlane, 1959, black

Buddy L, 2003 ....$2-3

Imperial Mighty Machines, 2003.............$1-2

**Ford Hot Rod Convertible, Imperial Mighty
Machines 2-pk, 2003..............................$1-2**

Ford Hot Rod Hardtop

**black with orange flames, Imperial Mighty
Machines 2-pk, 2003..............................$1-2**

**yellow with black fenders, Imperial Mighty
Machines 2-pk, 2003..............................$1-2**

Ford Mustang

**Fastback, green, Imperial Mighty Machines,
2003 ....$1-2**

**Fastback, red, Imperial Mighty Machines,
2003 ....$1-2**

Freeway Flyers #706-20, Playart casting ..$10-12
 Hardtop, Freeway Flyers #706-16,
 Playart casting $10-12
Ford Pickup, 1950s

red, Buddy L, 2003.................................$2-3

purple with yellow flames, Imperial Mighty
Machines, 2003...$1-2

Ford Sunliner Convertible, yellow and black two-tone

Buddy L, 2003 ....$2-3

Imperial Mighty Machines, 2003............$1-2

Ford Thunderbird, Freeway Flyers #706-03,
Playart casting $10-12
Ford Woody Wagon, 1940s, blue with light yel-
low trim, "wood" paneling

Buddy L, 2003 ....$2-3

Imperial Mighty Machines, 2003............$2-3

Gasoline Truck, Freeway Flyers #706-31,
Playart casting $10-12
Honda 2GS / Civic, Freeway Flyers
#706-52, Playart casting $10-12
Honda N360, Freeway Flyers #706-39,
Playart casting $10-12
Honda S800, Freeway Flyers #706-40,
Playart casting $10-12

Isuzu 117 Coupe, Freeway Flyers #706-45,
Playart casting $10-12
Jaguar 'E' Type 2+2, Freeway Flyers #706-23,
Playart casting $10-12
Jensen FF, Freeway Flyers #706-11, Playart cast-
ing...$10-12
Lamborghini Miura, Freeway Flyers, #706-08,
Playart casting $10-12
Man From U.N.C.L.E. Thrushbuster car, Freeway
Flyers #706-19, Playart casting $15-20
Maserati Marzal, Freeway Flyers #706-25,
Playart casting $10-12
Mercedes-Benz 350 SL, Freeway Flyers
#706-54, Playart casting...................$10-12
Mercedes-Benz C111, Freeway Flyers
#706-14, Playart casting...................$10-12
Mitsubishi Galant GTO MR Hi-pup Coupe, Free-
way Flyers #706-56, Playart casting ..$10-12
Nissan Sunny 1200 Coupe GX, Freeway Flyers
#706-47, Playart casting...................$10-12
Opel GT, Freeway Flyers #706-04, Playart
casting $10-12
Pickup Truck, Freeway Flyers #706-27, Playart
casting $10-12
Plymouth Barracuda, Freeway Flyers #706-01,
Playart casting $10-12
Police car, Freeway Flyers #706-32, Playart
casting $10-12
Porsche Carrera 910, Freeway Flyers #706-02,
Playart casting $10-12
Porsche Targa 911S, Freeway Flyers, #706-44,
Playart casting $10-12
Rolls Royce, Freeway Flyers #706-33, Playart
casting $10-12
Rover 2000 TC, Freeway Flyers #706-51,
Playart casting $10-12
Toyota 2000 GT
Freeway Flyers #706-22, Playart casting...$10-12
Convertible, Freeway Flyers #706-17,
Playart casting $10-12
Toyota Celica 1600 GT, Freeway Flyers #706-
42, Playart casting $10-12
Toyota Corona Mark II 1900 Hardtop SL, Free-
way Flyers #706-41, Playart casting ..$10-12
Toyota Corolla Sprinter SL, Freeway Flyers
#706-46, Playart casting...................$10-12
Toyota Crown Hardtop SL, Freeway Flyers
#706-43, Playart casting...................$10-12
Volkswagen Beetle, Freeway Flyers #706-24,
Playart casting $10-12
Volkswagen Porsche 914, Freeway Flyers
#706-38, Playart casting...................$10-12
Wrecker Truck, Freeway Flyers #706-29, Playart
casting $10-12
Yamaha Super Discmatic Rotary Coupe, Freeway
Flyers #706-4, Playart casting............$10-12

Impy (see Lone Star, also Crescent, D.C.M.T.)

A British company called Lone Star produced a series of toys known as Impy toys. But
the actual name on the base is "Lone Star Road-
Master Impy Super Cars." No wonder everyone
called them Impy. For more on Impy models,
see Lone Star.

Imra (or IMRA)

Originating in southern California, these
white metal models are prepainted kits, according to Harvey Goranson. As nearly as Goranson can recall, several Imra molds have ended
up as Precision Miniatures kits.

1975 Indy 500 Winner Jorgenson #48,
1:40 ....$275-300
Eagle Dan Gurney/Bobby Unser, 2-tone
blue, 1:40 ....$275-300

InterCar (see Autopilen)

International Hobby Corp. (IHC)

IHC, otherwise known as International
Hobby Corp., caters to the HO gauge hobby
market in providing various plastic model vehicles, buildings, and accessories in 1:87 scale.
Quality varies from model to model but is generally good considering the very reasonable price.
Below is a sampling of vehicles offered.

Cement Mixer, #916................................$3-5
Harvester, #903 ....$3-5
Livestock Transporter, #918......................$3-5
School Bus, 1940s Style, 911 ....$3-5

Intex (see Zee Toys)

Irwin

Beginning with celluloid baby rattles and
pinwheels, Irwin Cohn started the Irwin Company in 1922. Toy cars and trucks produced by
Irwin were made of an assortment of materials.
In 1973, Irwin was purchased by Miner Industries. Recent models have been sold under the
Joal brand by Irwin and listed separately in this
book under Joal heading as well as below.

Army Bus, plastic $45-50
Barney Rubble Car, plastic, circa
mid-1960s $30-35
Buick Convertible, plastic, 1948, 5".........$15-20
Chevrolet Panel Delivery, plastic, 6".........$15-20
Chevrolet Pickup Truck, plastic, 1952, 5¼"...$15-20
Dream Car Convertible, metal, 16"......$350-400

Ford Sunliner, plastic friction, 9" $75-95
Ice Cream Truck, plastic $80-100
Ives Horseless carriage Runabout, plastic,
6½" $4,000-4,500
Ives Steamer, cast iron, 19½"...........$800-1,000
Jaguar Roadster, plastic, 6" $55-70
Packard Sedan, plastic friction, 1952, 9" ...$30-35
Pontiac Hardtop Coupe, plastic friction, 1952,
6" $20-25
"Skipper" Convertible, plastic, 1962....$250-300
Steeraway Wonder car, plastic..........$160-185

Joal Classics Collection by Irwin (see Joal)

Istana

This company, based in Spain, has produced a few distinctive diecast toys identifiable by the Istana brand embossed on the base.

Istana Ambulance, pull-back action, 1:64 ...$3-5

Ites

Ites is an obscure brand from Czechoslovakia of which more information would be greatly appreciated.

Mirage Racer, 1:32 ....$18-24

IXL

IXL made a few crude tinplate models in Birmingham, England, for a short time from 1951 to 1952.

Sunbeam Talbot Saloon 1951, 1:43.......$30-40
Vauxhall Velox Saloon 1952, 1:43.........$30-40

Ixo

Premium & Collectibles Trading Company Limited
Shenzhen, Hong Kong, China
fax: +853-837716
e-mail: sales@ixomodels.com
web: www.ixomodels.com

Ixo Models (more properly, "ixo-MODELS," according to the website) are made in China by Sonic International (Toys) Limited. Their factory is located nearby Shenzhen, 60kms north of Hong Kong.

In June 2001, Ixo reportedly purchased castings from the bankrupt Vitesse Group of Portugal and incorporated them into the Ixo assortment. Counter to that claim, Vitesse has since been associated with Chrono of China. However, it may be that Chrono is also affiliated with Ixo.

The Ixo product line consists of the following series:

Classic Le Mans & GT Cars (LMC, GTC)
Modern Le Mans & GT Cars (LMM, GTM)
Le Mans Winners (LM)
Classic Rally Cars (RAC)
Modern Rally Cars (RAM)
Classic Roadcars (CLC)
Modern Roadcars (MOC)
Classic Racing Bikes (CLB)
Modern Racing Bikes (RAB)
Modern Street Bikes (STB)

Ixo Models 1:43 Scale Cars

Alfa Romeo 8C
#9 P. Etancelin–L. Chinetti Winner Le Mans
1934, LM1934 ....$15-30
#16 Lord Howe–H. Birkin Winner Le Mans
1931, LM1931 ....$15-30
Alpine Renault 1800S
J–C. Andruet Winner Monte Carlo Rally
1973, RAC013 ....$15-30
Alpine Renault A442
#2 D. Pironi–J. P. Jaussaud Winner Le Mans
1978, LM1978 ....$15-30
#7 P. Tambay–J. P. Jaussaud Le Mans 1977,
LMC042 ....$15-30
#8 P. Depailler–J. Laffite Le Mans 1977,
LMC043 ....$15-30
#9 J–P. Jabouille–D. Bell Le Mans 1977,
LMC044 ....$15-30
#19 J–P. Jabouille–P. Tambay Le Mans
1976, LMC041 ....$15-30
Aston Martin DBR1
Stirling Moss–J. Fairman #4 Le Mans 1959,
LMC048 ....$15-30
M. Trintignant–P. Frere #5 2nd Le Mans
1959, LMC049 ....$15-30
R. Salvadori–C. Shelby #6 winner Le Mans
1959, LM1959 ....$15-30
Aston Martin Vanquish
Silver, MOC018 ....$15-30
British Racing Green, MOC022 ....$15-30
Audi R8
#1 Audi Sport F. Biela–T. Kristansen–E. Pirro
Winner Le Mans 2001, LMM001...$15-30
#1 F. Biela–T. Kristensen–E. Pirro Winner Le
Mans 2002, LMM046 ....$15-30
#1 F. Biela–T. Kristensen–E. Pirro Winner Le
Mans 2001, LM2001 ....$15-30

#1 F. Biela–T. Kristensen–E. Pirro Winner Le
Mans 2002, LM2002 ....$15-30
#2 Audi Sport L. Aiello–R. Capello–C.
Pescatori 2nd Le Mans 2001,
LMM002 ....$15-30
#2 R. Capello–J. Herbert–C. Pescatori 2nd Le
Mans 2002, LMM047 ....$15-30
#3 "Champion Racing" J. Herbert–R. Kelleners–D. Theys Le Mans 2001,
LMM003 ....$15-30
#3 M. Krumm–P. Peter–M. Werner 3rd Le
Mans 2002, LMM048 ....$15-30
#4 "Gulf" S. Johansson–T. Coronel–P.
Lemarie Le Mans 2001, LMM004 ..$15-30
#5 "Team Goh" S. Ara–Y. Dalmas–H. Katoh
7th Le Mans 2002, LMM036 .....$15-30
#5 Audi Sport Japan, LMM049 ....$15-30
#6 Audi Champion, LMM050 ....$15-30
#7 Audi Sport UK, LMM051 ....$15-30
"Crocodile" R. Capello–A. McNish Winner
Adelaide 2000, GTM001 ....$15-30
Austin FX4 London Taxi
Black 1985, CLC022 ....$15-30
"Yellow Pages" 1990, CLC026 ....$15-30
Austin Seven 1922
Dark Red and Black, CLC014 ....$15-30
Bentley 3 Liter Convertible 1924
Dark Green, CLC016 ....$15-30
Bentley Experimental Speed 8
#7 M. Brundle–S. Ortelli–G. Smith Le Mans
2001, LMM029 ....$15-30
#8 A. Wallace–B. Leitzinger–E. Van de Poele
3rd Le Mans 2001, LMM030 .....$15-30
Bentley Speed Six
#1 W. Barnato–H. Birkin Winner Le Mans
1929, LM1929 ....$15-30
#1 W. Barnato–H. Birkin Winner Le Mans
1929, LMC020.......................$15-30
#4 W. Barnato–G. Kidston Winner Le
Mans 1930, LM1930 ....$15-30
Bentley Sport 3. 0 Liter
#8 J. Duff–F. C. Clement Winner Le
Mans 1924, LMC012..............$15-30
BMW M3GTR V8
"Ready To Race" White, MOC013 ....$15-30
#6 "Yokoyama" H. Stuck–B. Said–B. Auberlin
Alms 2001, GTM005 ....$15-30
#43 "BMW Motorsports" D. Muller–J.
Muller Winner GT3R Alms 2001,
GTM006...............................$15-30
BMW V12LMR
#15 P. Martini–Y. Dalmas–J. Winkelhock
Winner Le Mans 1999, LM1999 ...$15-30
Bugatti 57C
#1 J–P. Wimille–P. Veyron Winner Le Mans
1939, LM1939 ....$15-30

#1 J–P. Wimille–P. Veyron Winner Le Mans 1939, LMC024......................\$15-30

Bugatti 57G

#1 R. Labric–P. Veyron Le Mans 1937, LMC040......................\$15-30

#2 J–P. Wimille–R. Benoist Winner Le Mans 1937, LM1937 ....\$15-30

Bugatti T35B 1935

Blue, CLC029......................\$15-30

Checker

New York Yellow Cab 1985, CLC020 ..\$15-30

Citroën Saxo

Kit Car G. Hotz Swiss Rally Champion 2001, RAM057......................\$15-30

P. Bugalski–J. P. Chiaroni Rallye Monte Carlo 2001, RAM047......................\$15-30

Super 1600 #65 "Race Club" D. Sola Winner S1600 Catalunya 2002, RAM062......................\$15-30

Super 1600 "Augier" A. Pellerey Rallye Monte Carlo 2001, RAM048.....\$15-30

Super 1600 "Multyrama" A. Dallavilla Rallye Monte Carlo 2002, RAM060.....\$15-30

Super 1600 "Ready-to-Race" red, MOC025......................\$15-30

Super 1600 S. Loeb Tour De Corse 2001 (S1600 World Champion), RAM056.............\$15-30

Citroën Xsara

Kit Car S. Loeb–D. Elena French Rally Champion 2001, RAM032........\$15-30

T4 J. Puras Catalunya Rally 2001, RAM007......................\$15-30

T4 P. Bugalski Catalunya Rally 2001, RAM006......................\$15-30

WRC C. McRae–D. Ringer 2nd Rallye Monte Carlo 2003, RAM107.....\$15-30

WRC C. Sainz–M. Marti 3rd Rallye Monte Carlo 2003, RAM108...............\$15-30

WRC C. Sainz–M. Marti Winner Turkey Rally 2003, RAM113 ....\$15-30

WRC J. Puras–M. Marti Winner Tour De Corse 2001, RAM040 ....\$15-30

WRC S. Loeb–D. Elena Monte Carlo 2002, RAM074......................\$15-30

WRC S. Loeb–D. Elena Winner Deutschland Rally 2002, RAM090 ....\$15-30

WRC S. Loeb–D. Elena Winner Rallye Monte Carlo 2003, RAM100..............\$15-30

Citroën ZX Rallye Raid

P. Lartigue–M. Perrin Winner Paris–Dakar 1996, RAC019 ....\$15-30

Dodge Viper GTS-R

#7 "Chereau" M. Duez–C. Bouchut–J. P. Belloc Winner 24 Hour Spa 2001, GTM004 ....\$15-30

#50 "Chereau" C. Bouchut–P. Gueslard–V. Vosse Le Mans 2002, LMM039...\$15-30

#51 "Chereau" J–L. Chereau–J. C. Lagniez–C. Rosenblad Le Mans 2002, LMM040 ....\$15-30

#52 "Oreca Playstation" J–P. Belloc–J. Cochet–B. Treluyer Le Mans 2002, LMM034......................\$15-30

#53 "Carsport" M. Hezemans–A. Kumpen–G. Matteuzzi Le Mans 2002, LMM035......................\$15-30

#55 Team Belmondo (Red/Blue) V. Vosse–V. Ickx–C. Rosenblad Le Mans 2001, LMM005......................\$15-30

#56 Team Belmondo (Yellow/Blue) J. C. Lagniez–G. DeGalzin–A. Kumpen Le Mans 2001, LMM006 ....\$15-30

#57 Equipe De France D. Terrien–J. Cochet–J. Ph. Dayraut Le Mans 2001, LMM007......................\$15-30

#58 Chereau G. Bouchut–J. P. Belloc–T. Monteiro Le Mans 2001, LMM008 .....\$15-30

#91 O. Beretta–D. Dupuy–K. Wendlinger Winner Daytona 24 Hours 2000, GTM003 ....\$15-30

"Larbre" C. Bouchut–P. Goueslard–S. Zacchia Le Mans 2003, LMM053 ....\$15-30

"Zakspeed" Zakowski–Lamy–Lechner Winner Nurburgring 24 hours 2002 GTM011 ....\$15-30

Ferrari 250LM

#21 M. Gregory–J. Rindt Winner Le Mans 1965, LM1965 ....\$15-30

Ferrari 250TR

#14 O. Gendebien–P. Hill Winner Le Mans 1958, LM1958 ....\$15-30

Fiat 131 Abarth

W. Rohrl–C. Geistdorfer Winner Rallye Monte Carlo 1980, RAC018 .....\$15-30

Fiat 600 Multipla 1958, Light Blue, CLC036 ..\$15-30

Fiat Punto

Kit Car, A. Navarra Winner Rally Del Molise 2000, RAM017 ....\$15-30

S1600, #53, "Kayak" G. Basso Rallye Monte Carlo 2002, RAM058.....\$15-30

S1600, #73, "Andorra" A. Llovera Rallye Monte Carlo 2002, RAM059.....\$15-30

Super 1600, "Daniel Jean Richard" A. Dallavilla Catalunya 2001, RAM026..........\$15-30

Super 1600, "Framesi" G. Basso Rallye Catalunya 2001, RAM018 ....\$15-30

Super 1600, "Omv" R. Stohl Rallye Catalunya 2001, RAM027 ....\$15-30

Ford Escort RS 1800

#2 "red & white" B. Waldegaard 2nd Monte Carlo 1979, RAC012 ....\$15-30

#5 "Ford white & blue" H. Mikkola 5th Monte Carlo Rally 1979, RAC009 ....\$15-30

"Eaton's Yale" H. Mikkola Winner Rac Rally 1979, RAC004 ....\$15-30

"Rothmans" B. Waldegaard Winner Acropolis Rally 1979, RAC008 ...\$15-30

"Rothmans" Vatanen–Richards Winner Acropolis Rally 1981, RAC001 ...\$15-30

Ford Escort RS Cosworth

F. Delecour–D. Grateloup Winner Monte Carlo 1994, RAC022 ....\$15-30

Ford Focus WRC

"ERG" P. Andreucci–Giusti Italian Rally Champion 2001, RAM033 ....\$15-30

"Ford Germany" Kremer–Wicha Monte Carlo 2002, RAM073 ....\$15-30

"Ford RS" M. Martin Acropolis Rally 2002, RAM089......................\$15-30

"In Memoria 11. 09. 2001" F. Delecour New Zealand Rally 2001, RAM034...\$15-30

"Martini Racing" C. McRae Winner Acropolis 2001, RAM019 ....\$15-30

"Martini Racing" C. McRae Winner Argentina 2001, RAM009 ....\$15-30

"Martini Racing" C. McRae Winner Cyprus 2001, RAM016 ....\$15-30

"Martini Racing" C. McRae–N. Grist winner Acropolis Rally 2002, RAM086 ..\$15-30

"Martini Racing" C. McRae–N. Grist winner Safari Rally 2002, RAM087 ....\$15-30

C. McRae–N. Grist Monte Carlo 2002, RAM077......................\$15-30

C. Sainz–L. Moya Safari Rally 2001, RAM050......................\$15-30

C. Sainz–L. Moya Winner Argentina Rally 2002, RAM081 ....\$15-30

Ford Fordor Sedan 1947

Dark Blue, CLC035 ....\$15-30

Ford GT40

#9 "Gulf" P. Rodriguez–L. Bianchi Winner Le Mans 1968, LMC025..........\$15-30

#10 "Gulf" P. Hawkins–D. Hobbs Le Mans 1968, LMC026......................\$15-30

#11 "Gulf" J. Oliver–B. Muir Le Mans 1968, LMC027......................\$15-30

"Gulf" #9 P. Rodriguez–L. Bianchi Winner Le Mans 1968, LM1968 ....\$15-30

Ford Mk IV

B. McLaren–M. Andretti Winner 12 Hours Sebring 1967 Yellow, GTM007 ...$15-30

Presentation Car (white with blue strips) 1967, GTM009 ....$15-30

#1 Gurney–Foyt (Red) Winner Le Mans 1967, LM1967 ....$15-30

#1 Gurnwy–Foyt (Red) Winner Le Mans 1967, LMC004 ....$15-30

#2 B. McLaren–M. Donohue (Yellow) 2nd Le Mans 1967, LMC009 ....$15-30

#3 M. Andertti–L. Bianchi (Gold) Le Mans 1967, LMC010 ....$15-30

#4 L. Ruby–D. Hulme (Dark Blue) Le Mans 1967, LMC011 ....$15-30

Ford Model T

"Runabout" 2-seater 1925 Opened Black, CLC012 ....$15-30

"Runabout" 2-seater 1925 Closed Blue & Black, CLC013 ....$15-30

"Touring" Open Roof 1909 Carmine Red, CLC001 ....$15-30

"Touring" Closed Roof 1909 Brewster Green, CLC002 ....$15-30

Gulf Mirage

#11 Derek Bell–Jacky Ickx Winner Le Mans 1975, LM1975 ....$15-30

Hyundai Accent WRC

EVO2 A. McRae Rallye Portugal 2001, RAM022 ....$15-30

EVO2 K. Eriksson Rallye De Portugal 2001, RAM023 ....$15-30

F. Loix–S. Smets Monte Carlo 2002, RAM075 ....$15-30

F. Loix–S. Smets Rallye Monte Carlo 2003, RAM104 ....$15-30

Jaguar D-Type

#3 Bueb–Flockhart Winner Le Mans 1957, LMC001 ....$15-30

#55 M. Hawthron–H. Bueb Winner Le Mans 1955, LM1955 ....$15-30

"Cunningham" P. Walters–B. Spear Le Mans 1955, LMC029 ....$15-30

"Ecurie Francorchamps" J. Claes–J. Swaters 3rd Le Mans 1955, LMC037 .....$15-30

Jaguar XC120-C

#20 C. Laurent–De Tornaco Le Mans 1953, LMC005 ....$15-30

Jaguar XJR9

#1 "Silk Cut" Brundle–Nielsen Le Mans 1988, LMC006 ....$15-30

#2 "Silk Cut" Lammers–Dumfries–Wallace Winner Le Mans 1988, LMC002 ..$15-30

#2 "Silk Cut" Lammers–Dumfries–Wallace Winner Le Mans 1988, LM1988 ....$15-30

#22 "Silk Cut" Daly–Cogan–Perkins 4th Le Mans 1988, LMC007 ....$15-30

Jaguar XJR12

#1 M. Brundle–A. Ferte–D. Leslie Le Mans 1990, LMC015 ....$15-30

#2 J. Lammers–A. Wallace–F. Konrad 2nd Le Mans 1990, LMC016 ....$15-30

#3 "Silk Cut" Brundle–Nielsen–Cobb Winner Le Mans 1990, LMC008 ....$15-30

#3 M. Brundle–J. Nielsen–P. Cobb Winner Le Mans 1990, LM1990 ....$15-30

#4 D. Jones–M. Ferte–E. Salazar Le Mans 1990, LMC017 ....$15-30

Jeepney Taxi

Manila 1990 Blue and Silver, CLC037 ..$15-30

Lamborghini Countach

500S Pace Car, Monaco Grand Prix 1982, White, CLC018 ....$15-30

5000S 1984, Black, CLC017 ....$15-30

5000QV, Quattrovalvole 1988, CLC024 ....$15-30

LP400S, White with blue interior, CLC005 ....$15-30

LP500S, 1985 Red witn tan interior, CLC006 ....$15-30

LP500S, "Walter Wolf" 1978 Dark Metal Blue, CLC025 ....$15-30

Lancia Delta

4WD "Martini Racing," B. Saby Winner Monte Carlo Rally 1988, RAC015 ....$15-30

HF Integrale "6" Martini Roadcar, White, CLC028 ....$15-30

HF Integrale Evoluzione 1992, Monza Red, CLC015 ....$15-30

Lancia Fulvia

Coupe 1. 6HF 1968 Red, CLC019 ..$15-30

HF1600, S. Munari–M. Manucci Winner Monte Carlo Rallye 1972, RAC005 ....$15-30

Lancia Stratos

"Alitalia," S. Munari Winner Monte Carlo Rallye 1976, RAC011 ....$15-30

Lincoln Limousine Continental 1967

Black, CLC033 ....$15-30

Maserati Coupe Cambiocorsa

2002 Rosso Mondiale Red, MOC027 ..$15-30

2002 Azzuro Argentina Metal Blue, MOC028 ....$15-30

Maserati Spyder Cambiocorsa

2002 Giallo Gran Turismo, MOC029...$15-30

2002 Nero Carbono, MOC030 ....$15-30

2003 Closed Convertible, Silver with Red Interior, MOC035 ....$15-30

Maserati Trofeo

"Presentation Version" 2003, GTM014 ..$15-30

#28 E. Smurra, GTM016 ....$15-30

2003, GTM015 ....$15-30

Matra MS670B

#7 H. Pescarolo–G. Larrousse Winner Le Mans 1974, LMC013 ....$15-30

#7 H. Pescarolo–G. Larrousse Winner Le Mans 1974, LM1974 ....$15-30

#8 J.-P. Jaussaud–J. Dolhem–B. WolleckLe Mans 1974, LMC014 ....$15-30

#9 J.-P. Jabouille–F. Migault 3rd Le Mans 1974, LMC019 ....$15-30

Mazda 787B

#18 "Mazdasport" Kennedy–Johansson–Sala Le Mans 1991, LMC028 ....$15-30

#55 "Renown" Weidler–Herbert–Gachot Winner Le Mans 1991, LMC023 ....$15-30

#55 "Renown" Weidler–Herbert–Gachot Winner Le Mans 1991, LM1991 .....$15-30

Megane Schlesser "Gauloises"

J. L. Schlesser–H. Magne 1st Paris–Dakar 2000, RAM020 ....$15-30

J. M. Servia–J. M. Lurquin 4th Paris–Dakar 2000, RAM021 ....$15-30

J. L. Schlesser Winner Paris–Dakar 1999, RAM063 ....$15-30

Mercedes-Benz 240D Limousine 1974, CLC034 ....$15-30

Mercedes-Benz M-Klasse 2003

Dark Silver, MOC034 ....$15-30

MG Metro 6R4

"33 Export" Rallye Des Garrigues 86 D. Auriol Champion de France, RAC002 ...$15-30

"Belga" M. Duez, RAC016 ....$15-30

"Mobil" M. Wilson–N. Harris Rally 1985, RAC007 ....$15-30

"Rothmans" J. McRae–M. Grindrod Rac Rally 1986, RAC006 ....$15-30

Mini 2000

Black, MOC003 ....$15-30

Red, MOC004 ....$15-30

Mini Cooper S 2002

Silver, MOC010 ....$15-30

Metallic Blue, MOC011 ....$15-30

Mitsubishi Carisma WRC

F. Loix Sanremo Rally 2001, RAM055...$15-30

Mitsubishi Lancer

Evo. VI "Cordoba" G. Pozzo–D. Stillo World Champion Gr. N 2001, RAM045 ..$15-30

Evo. VI T. Makinen Winner Portugal Rally 2001, RAM005 ....$15-30

Evo. VI T. Makinen Winner Safari Rally 2001, RAM029 ....$15-30

Evo. VI. 5 T. Makinen–R. Mannisenmaki Winner Monte Carlo 2001, RAM003.......$15-30

Evo. VI. 5 Roadcar White, MOC005 ..$15-30

Evo. VII 2001 Red, MOC008 ....$15-30

Evo. VII 2001 White, MOC009 ....$15-30

Evo. VII Ralliart, MOC016 ....$15-30

Evo. VIII White, MOC024 ....$15-30

Evo. VIII Yellow, MOC033 ....$15-30

WRC A. McRae–D. Senior Tour De
   Corse 2002, RAM079 ....$15-30

WRC F. Delecour–D. Grateloup Monte
   Carlo 2002, RAM071 ....$15-30

WRC T. Makinen Sanremo Rally 2001,
   RAM054 ....$15-30

Mitsubishi Pajero

"Argos" J. P. Fontenay–G. Picard Paris–
   Dakar 2002, RAM067 ....$15-30

"Metabo Playstation" J. Klienschmidt–A. Schultz
   Paris–Dakar 2002, RAM066 ....$15-30

"Mitsubishi Oil" Masuoka Winner Paris–
   Dakar 2002, RAM068.............$15-30

Di–D "Telefonica" M. Prieto Paris–
   Dakar 2001, RAM015.............$15-30

Panoz LMP

#22 J. Policand–M. Duez–P. McCarthy Leader
   Le Mans 2002, LMM037.........$15-30

EVO #11 D. Brabham–J. Magnussen–B.
   Herta Le Mans 2002, LMM041 $15-30

EVO #12 G. Jeannette–D. Donohue–B. Auberlen
   Le Mans 2002, LMM042 ....$15-30

Peugeot 203 1955, light gray, CLC040 ...$15-30

Peugeot 205 Turbo 16, Winner 1985,
   RAC017 ....$15-30

Peugeot 206 WRC

"A–Online" R. Sperrer Winner A1–Ring Rally
   2001, RAM012.....................$15-30

"Belgium" B. Thiry Rallye Monte Carlo 2002,
   RAM082.............................$15-30

"Clarion" G. Panizzi–H. Panizzi Turkey Rally
   2003, RAM110....................$15-30

"Danzas" S. Lindholm Finland Rally Champion 2001, RAM038 ....$15-30

"Fortuna" L. Monzon Rallye Catalunya
   2001, RAM028....................$15-30

"Havoline" Papadimitriou Rallye De Portugal
   2001, RAM014.....................$15-30

"Michelin" Valentino Rossi Great Britain Rally
   2002, RAM093....................$15-30

"Red" R. Burns–R. Reid Rallye Monte Carlo
   2003, RAM101....................$15-30

"Silver Team" A. Lopes Portugal Rally
   Champion 2002, RAM065 ......$15-30

"Silver Team" A. Lopes Rallye De Portugal
   2001, RAM013.....................$15-30

"Total" (blue) H. Rovanpera–Pietilainen Monte
   Carlo Rally 2002, RAM070......$15-30

D. Auriol Winner Catalunya 2001,
   RAM008 ....$15-30

G. Panizzi Winner Tour De Corse 2002,
   RAM083 ....$15-30

G. Panizzi Winner Catalunya 2002,
   RAM084 ....$15-30

G. Panizzi Winner Sanremo Rally 2002,
   RAM091 ....$15-30

H. Panizzi Winner Sanremo 2001
   RAM039 ....$15-30

H. Rovahpera Winner Swedish Rally 2001,
   RAM004 ....$15-30

H. Rovahpera Safari Rally 2001,
   RAM051 ....$15-30

M. Gronholm–T. Rautianen Winner Cyprus
   Rally 2002, RAM085 ....$15-30

M. Gronholm–T. Rautianen Winner Finland
   Rally 2002, RAM088 ....$15-30

M. Gronholm–T. Rautiainen Winner New
   Zealand Rally 2002, RAM092 ..$15-30

M. Gronholm–T. Rautianen Winner Australia
   Rally 2002 special set, RAM095 ..$15-30

M. Gronholm–T. Rautiainen Winner Swedish
   Rally 2003, RAM106 ....$15-30

M. Gronholm Winner Australia Rally 2001,
   RAM046 ....$15-30

M. Gronholm Winner Finland Rally 2001,
   RAM036 ....$15-30

M. Gronholm Winner Great Britain Rally
   2001, RAM052 ....$15-30

M. Gronholm Winner New Zealand,
   RAM114 ....$15-30

M. Gronholm Winner Swedish Rally 2002,
   RAM078 ....$15-30

R. Burns–R. Reid Monte Carlo 2002,
   RAM069 ....$15-30

Renato Travaglia Italy Rally Champion 2002,
   RAM097 ....$15-30

Peugeot 405

A. Vatanen–B. Berglund Winner Paris–Dakar
   1989, RAC027 ....$15-30

J. Ickx–C. Tarin 2nd Paris–Dakar 1989,
   RAC030.............................$15-30

Peugoet 905

#1 D. Warwick–Y. Dalmas–M. Blundell Win-
   ner Le Mans 1992, LM1992.......$15-30

#2 M. Baldi–P. Alliot–J. P. Jabouille 3rd Le
   Mans 1992, LMC038..............$15-30

#31 K. Wendlinger–E. Van De Poele–A. Ferte Le
   Mans 1992, LMC039..............$15-30

Range Rover

3. 5 2-door 1970, Sahara Dust, CLC003....$15-30

3.5 2-door 1970, Lincoln Green,
   CLC004.............................$15-30

3.5 4-door 1982, Sierra Silver,
   CLC010.............................$15-30

4-door, M. Miele–V. Total Winner Camel Trophy
   Madagascar 1987, CLC011........$15-30

Vogue 1980, CLC038 ....$15-30

Renault 4CV

#46 J. Sandt–H. Coatalen Le Mans 1950
   (Category Winner), LMC047 ......$15-30

#57 C. Hardy–M. Roger Le Mans 1949,
   LMC046 ....$15-30

1947 Ivory, CLC023 ....$15-30

"PIE" Police de Paris, CLC043 ....$15-30

Renault 5

Gr. 2 "Calberson" J. Ragnotti 2nd Monte
   Carlo Rally 1978, RAC010 ....$15-30

Gr. 2 Saby MC79, RAC025............$15-30

Maxi Turbo "33 Export" D. Auriol Tour De
   Corse 1985, RAC003 ....$15-30

Turbo 1 1982 Metallic Red, CLC009 ..$15-30

Renault 8 Gordini

1300 Blue, CLC027 ....$15-30

J.-L. Therier–M. Callewaert Rallye Monte
   Carlo 1969, RAC020 ....$15-30

Rondeau M379

#55 "Merlin Place" J. Rondeau–J. Haran Le
   Mans 1979, LMC021 ....$15-30

Rondeau M379B

#8 "L'Automobile" P. Streiff–J. L. Schlesser–J. Haran
   2nd Le Mans 1981, LMC050........$15-30

#15 "ITT–Le Point" H. Pescarolo–J. Ragnotti Le
   Mans 1980, LMC022...............$15-30

#16 "ITT–Le Point" J–P. Jaussaud–J. Rondeau
   Winner Le Mans 1980, LMC018 ..$15-30

Rondeau M379C

#7 "OTIS" F. Migault–G. Spice 3rd Le
   Mans 1981, LMC051 ....$15-30

Saleen S7R

2001 #60 "Konrad–BASF" T. Borcheller–O. Gavin–F.
   Konrad Le Mans 2001, LMM031 ......$15-30

2001 #61 "Brun" T. Sailer–W. Brun–C. Slat-
   ter Le Mans 2001, LMM032 ......$15-30

2001 #62 "Cranium" I. McKellar–B. Lambert–J.
   Mowlem Le Mans 2001, LMM033 ..$15-30

2002 #66 "Konrad" F. Konrad–T. Borcheller–T.
   Seiler Le Mans 2002, LMM043 .....$15-30

2002 #67 "Konrad" W. Brun–C. Slater Le
   Mans 2002, LMM044 ....$15-30

2002 #68 "Cin–Vodaphone" C.
   Pickering–M. Ramos–P. Chaves Le Mans
   2002, LMM045 ....$15-30

2003 #64 "Transvu" T. Erdos–P. Chaves–M.
   Newton Le Mans 2003, LMM054 ..$15-30

2003 #66 "H&R" F. Konrad–T. Seiler–W.
   Brun Le Mans 2003, LMM055 ...$15-30

Metallic Orange, MOC020 ....$15-30
Silver, MOC021 ....$15-30
Saviem SG2 Assistance Van
Rallye Monte Carlo 1973, RAC014 ..$15-30
Seat Cordoba WRC
"Seat Deutschland" M. Kahle–
Schneppenheim 2000, RAM031...$15-30
E3 "Repsol" M. Blasquez Rallye De Portugal
2001, RAM010 ....$15-30
E3 "Telefonica" S. Canellas Rallye De
Catalunya 2001, RAM011 ....$15-30
Seat Ibiza Tdi 2002
Yellow, MOC032 ....$15-30
Skoda Octavia
RS WRC, "Allianz" A. Schwarz Rallye Monte
Carlo 2001, RAM024.............$15-30
RS WRC, "Allianz" B. Thiry Rallye Monte
Carlo 2001, RAM025..............$15-30
WRC, "FWU" U. Forkert–F. Winklhofer
ADAC Rally 2001, RAM030......$15-30
WRC, "Total" B. Thiry Winner Condroz
Rally 2001, RAM042 ....$15-30
WRC, A. Schwarz Safari Rally 2001,
RAM053 ....$15-30
WRC, D. Auriol–D. Giraudet Rallye Monte
Carlo 2003, RAM105.............$15-30
WRC, K. Eriksson–M. K. Thorner Monte
Carlo 2002, RAM076.............$15-30
Subaru Impreza
2. 0 WRX 2000 Lhd Metallic Blue,
MOC001 ....$15-30
2. 0 WRX 2000 Rhd Silver,
MOC002 ....$15-30
STI Metallic Blue, MOC014..............$15-30
STI Metallic Blue, MOC026..............$15-30
STI 2003 Metallic Blue, MOC031 ....$15-30
WRC "Infineon" A. Mortl–S. Eichroner Tour
De Corse 2001, RAM041 ....$15-30
WRC B. Rousselot French Rally Champion,
RAM098 ....$15-30
WRC M. Martin–M. Park Rallye Monte
Carlo 2001, RAM002...............$15-30
WRC P. Solberg–P. Mills Rallye Monte
Carlo 2002, RAM080...............$15-30
WRC P. Solberg–P. Mills Winner Great
Britain Rally 2002, RAM096.......$15-30
WRC R. Burns–A. Reid World Champion
2001 (Special Set), RAM044 .....$15-30
WRC R. Burns–R. Reid Rallye Monte Carlo
2001, RAM001 ....$15-30
WRC R. Burns–R. Reid Safari Rally 2001,
RAM049 ....$15-30
WRC R. Burns Winner New Zealand Rally
2001, RAM037 ....$15-30
WRC T. Makkinen–K. Lindstrom Winner
Monte Carlo 2002, RAM072.....$15-30

WRC T. Makkinen–K. Lindstrom Rallye Monte
Carlo 2003, RAM103...............$15-30
Tatra 603 1961
Black, CLC030 ....$15-30
Toyota Celica
D. Auriol–B. Occelli Winner Rallye Monte
Carlo 1993, RAC029 ....$15-30
Toyota Corolla WRC
"Elf–Vergokan" P. Tsjoen Belgian Rally
Champion Winner 2001, RAM035 .$15-30
"Pepsi" H. Lundgaard–J. Canker Rally El Corte
Ingles 2001, RAM043...............$15-30
A. Kremer European Rally Champion 2001,
RAM061 ....$15-30
Toyota TS010
"Casio" M. Sekiya–P–H. Raphanel–F. K.
Acheson #33 2nd Le Mans 1992,
LMC031 ....$15-30
"Tom's" G. Lees–G. Brabham–U. Katayama
#7 Le Mans 1992, LMC032......$15-30
"Zent" J. Lammers–A. Wallace–T. Fabi #8 Le
Mans 1992+M189, LMC033 ...$15-30
#36 "Nippo Denso" Sekiya–Suzuki–Irvine
4th Le Mans 1993, LMC054......$15-30
#37 "Nippo Denso" Raphanel–Acheson–
Wallace Le Mans 1993, LMC055 ..$15-30
#38 "Nippo Denso" Lees–Lammers–Fangio
Le Mans 1993, LMC056 ....$15-30
Tuk Tuk Bangkok Taxi, CLC041 ....$15-30
Volga M21 1955
Light Blue, CLC032 ....$15-30
Volkswagen Beetle
2. 0 "Cow Special," MOC006 ....$15-30
2. 0 "Wasp Special," MOC007 ...$15-30
Mexico, Bright Yellow, CLC021 .....$15-30
RSI 2000, Silver, MOC012 ....$15-30
Volkswagen New Beetle
"53," MOC015 ....$15-30
Cup, Patrick Michels Winner 2001,
GTM008 ....$15-30
Cup, "HP" F. Heitmeier 2002, GTM010...$15-30
Speed, Light Metal Blue 2002,
MOC023 ....$15-30

Ixo 1:24 Scale Motorcycles

Aprilia RS3 Regis Laconi Moto Grand Prix
2002, RAB051 ....$15-30
Aprilia RSV Mille R Yellow, STB009 ....$15-30
Bimota SB8R, STB021 ....$15-30
BMW R1100S Boxer Cup Replica,
STB025 ....$15-30
BMW R1150GS Adventure, Silver,
STB016 ....$15-30
Buell Firebolt XB9R, STB020 ....$15-30
Derbi 125 "Derbi Racing" Youichi UI 2001,
RAB023 ....$15-30

Ducati 900 Monster Red, STB018...........$15-30
Ducati 996R T. Bayliss Winner Superbike
Championship 2001, RAB025 ....$15-30
Ducati 998R
"Infostrada" T. Bayliss Superbike 2002,
RAB046 ....$15-30
"LandM" B. Bostrom Superbike 2002,
RAB048 ....$15-30
Pierfrancesco Chili Superbike 2002,
RAB050 ....$15-30
Ducati 999S, STB010
Honda CBR 900RR Red, STB015 ....$15-30
Honda NS500 Freddie Spencer World
Champion 500cc 1983, CLB008 ....$15-30
Honda NSR250 Luca Cadalora World
Champion 250cc 1991, CLB009 ....$15-30
Honda NSR500
"Bridgestone" J. V. D. Goorbergh Moto
Grand Prix 2002, RAB045.........$15-30
"Nastro Azzuro YPF" V. Rossi 2001,
RAB011 ....$15-30
"Nastro Azzuro YPF" V. Rossi Italian Grand
Prix 2001 (Special Decoration),
RAB019 ....$15-30
"Pramac" T. Harada Moto Grand Prix 2002,
RAB032 ....$15-30
"Team Repsol YPF" A. Criville 2001,
RAB013 ....$15-30
"Team Repsol YPF" T. Ukawa 2001,
RAB014 ....$15-30
"West" A. Barros Moto Grand Prix 2002,
RAB028 ....$15-30
"West" L. Capirossi Moto Grand Prix 2002,
RAB029 ....$15-30
"West Team Pons" A. Barros 2001,
RAB007 ....$15-30
'West Team Pons' L. Capirossi 2001,
RAB008 ....$15-30
#3 R. Mamola 1984, CLB011 ....$15-30
Michael Doohan World Champion 1998,
CLB002 ....$15-30
Wayne Gardner World Champion 1987,
CLB004 ....$15-30
Honda RC45 John Kocinsky Superbike World
Champion 1997, CLB010..............$15-30
Honda RC51 1000 Silver and Black (US version),
STB006 ....$15-30
Honda RC211V
"Fortuna Gresini" D. Katoh Moto Grand Prix
2002, RAB031 ....$15-30
"Honda HRC" S. Itoh Moto Grand Prix 2002,
RAB030 ....$15-30
"Repsol" V. Rossi Moto Grand Prix 2002,
RAB026 ....$15-30
"Repsol" T. Ukawa Moto Grand Prix 2002,
RAB027 ....$15-30

"Team Honda Repsol" V. Rossi Moto Grand
Prix 2003, RAB055 ....$15-30
"Team Honda Repsol" N. Hayden Moto
Grand Prix 2003, RAB056........$15-30
"Team Pramac Pons" T. Ujawa Moto Grand
Prix 2003, RAB058 ....$15-30
"Telefonica" D. Kato Moto Grand Prix 2003,
RAB060 ....$15-30

Honda RS125
"Gilera Team" M. Poggiali World Champion
125 2001, RAB021 ....$15-30
"Telefonica Movistar" T. Elias 2001,
RAB022 ....$15-30
Loris Capirossi World Champion 125cc
1991, CLB007 ....$15-30

Honda VTR
1000 SP1, Red and Silver 2001,
STB005..................................$15-30
1000 SP2, White, STB007 ....$15-30
SP1 "Elf" Carpentier–Costes–Gimbert Winner
24H. Le Mans 2000, RAB012 ..$15-30
SP1 "Team Honda" V. Rossi–C. Edwards
Winner Suzuka 8 hours 2001,
RAB047 ....$15-30
SP2 "Castrol" C. Edwards Superbike Cham-
pion 2002, RAB043 ....$15-30
SP2 "US FLAG" C. Edwards Superbike 2002
(Laguna Seca), RAB044.............$15-30

Kawasaki ZX-12R Dark Silver, STB008.....$15-30
Kawasaki ZXR-R
Garry McCoy Moto Grand Prix 2003,
RAB071 ....$15-30
Andrew Pitt Moto Grand Prix 2003,
RAB072 ....$15-30

KTM LC8
Fabrizio Meoni Winner Dakar 2002,
RAB052 ....$15-30
#1 "Gauloises" F. Meoni 3rd DAKAR 2003,
RAB054 ....$15-30

MV Agusta
500 3–Cylinder Giacomo Agostini World
Champion 1967, CLB006 ....$15-30
750 F4S Red and Silver, STB013 ......$15-30

Suzuki GS1400F, STB022....................$15-30
Suzuki GSX-R
600, Yellow, STB001 ....$15-30
750, Red, STB002 ....$15-30
1000, Blue, STB003 ....$15-30
1000, 2003, Blue and White,
STB017..................................$15-30
1300 Hayabusa, Metallic Gold,
STB014..................................$15-30
C. Guyot–S. Scarnato–N. Dussauge Winner
Le Mans 2001, RAB024 ....$15-30
J-M. Bayle–N. Dussauge–S. Gimbert Winner
Le Mans 2002, RAB053 ....$15-30

Suzuki RGB500
Marco Lucchinelli World Champion 500cc
1981, CLB013 ....$15-30
Suzuki RGV500
"Telefonica Movistar" K. Roberts Jr. 2001,
RAB015 ....$15-30
"Telefonica Movistar" S. Gibernau 2001,
RAB016 ....$15-30
Kevin Schwantz World Champion 1993,
CLB003 ....$15-30
Suzuki Xreo
"Telefonica Movistar" K. Roberts Jr. Moto
Grand Prix 2002, RAB041 ....$15-30
"Telefonica Movistar" S. Gibernau Moto
Grand Prix 2002, RAB042........$15-30
Suzuki TL 1000R Blue, STB012 ....$15-30
Triumph 955i, STB019 ....$15-30
Yamaha RD05 Phil Read World Champion
250cc 1968, CLB014 ....$15-30
Yamaha R7 750, Red 1999, STB004 ....$15-30
Yamaha TZ250L Christian Sarron World
Champion 1984, CLB005 ....$15-30
Yamaha XJR1300, STB023 ....$15-30
Yamaha YZF
R1 Red and Black, STB011 ....$15-30
R7 "Yamaha Motor France" J. M. Deletang
2000, RAB001 ....$15-30
Yamaha YZR250
"Chesterfield" O. Jacque World Champion
250 2000, RAB020 ....$15-30
Yamaha YZR500
"Antena 3 D'Antin" N. Abe, RAB005 ..$15-30
"Antena 3 D'Antin" J. L. cardoso,
RAB006 ....$15-30
"Antena 3" N. Abe Moto Grand Prix 2002,
RAB037 ....$15-30
"Antena 3" P. Riba Moto Grand Prix 2002,
RAB038 ....$15-30
"Marlboro" M. Biaggi 2001,
RAB017 ....$15-30
"Marlboro" C. Checa 2001,
RAB018 ....$15-30
"Red Bull Wcm" G. McCoy 2001,
RAB009 ....$15-30
"Red Bull Wcm" N. Haga 2001,
RAB010 ....$15-30
"Tech 3 Gauloises" O. Jacque 2001,
RAB003 ....$15-30
"Tech 3 Gauloises" S. Nakano 2001,
RAB004 ....$15-30
"Tech 3 Gauloises" O. Jacque Moto Grand
Prix 2002, RAB035 ....$15-30
"Tech 3 Gauloises" S. Nakano Moto Grand
Prix 2002, RAB036 ....$15-30
Wayne Rainey World Champion 1993,
CLB001 ....$15-30

Kenny Roberts World Champion 500cc
1979, CLB012 ....$15-30
Yamaha YZR–M1
"Marlboro Team" M. Biaggi Moto Grand Prix
2002, RAB033..........................$15-30
"Marlboro Team" C. Checa Moto Grand Prix
2002, RAB034..........................$15-30

J

J43 Kawabatakikaku (see Kawa-batakikaku)

J Collection (also see Kyosho)

J-Collection Models
Kyosho Corporation
Atsugi Operation Center
153 Funako Atsugi
Kanagawa 243
Japan
Tel: 0462-2294462
Fax: 0462-2299252
e-mail: diecast@kyosho.co.jp
www.jcollection-models.com

The J-Collection series from Kyosho features exclusively 1:43 scale diecast collectible models of Japanese cars. Kyosho works in cooperation with the Japanese car industry to offer 1:43 scale car models of the newest cars launched in the market from brands such as Mazda, Toyota, Lexus, or Nissan.

The scale models sold in the Japanese markets feature only Japanese specifications (RHD only). For models sold outside Japan, Kyosho offers European/USA versions when available.

J Collection Japan Market Models
Mazda Atenza, Pearl White,
JC17029W $20-30
Mazda MPV L V6 2500 4WD, Red,
JC120027R $20-30
Mazda MPV Sport V6 2500, White,
JC12012W $20-30
Mazda MPV Sport, Silver, JC120032S ...$20-30
Mazda MPV, White, JC12043W $20-30
Mazda MX-5 Open Roadster RS1800, Red,
JC04004R $20-30
Mazda MX 5 Roadster NR-A, White,
JC04035W $20-30
Mazda Roadster, Black, JC04056K $20-30
Mazda Roadster, Green, JC04053G......$20-30
Mazda Roadster VS1800 DOHC, Grace Green
Mica, JC04018G $20-30
Mitsubishi Grandis, Metallic Green,
JC21046G $20-30

J Collection

Mitsubishi Grandis, Pearl White,
  JC21058W $20-30
Nissan Cedric 300LV, White,
  JC02002W $20-30
Nissan Cima 450 VIP, Black,
  JC08024BL $20-30
Nissan Cima 450XV, Champagne Silver,
  JC08008S $20-30
Nissan Cube SX, Air Blue, JC20039B $20-30
Nissan Cube, Orange, JC20060P $20-30
Nissan Cube, Pearl White,
  JC20046PW $20-30
Nissan El Grand 2002, White Pearl,
  JC16025W $20-30
Nissan El Grand, Champagne Silver,
  JC16052S $20-30
Nissan El Grand, Silver, JC16044K $20-30
Nissan Gloria GT300 Ultima Z, Dark Blue Mica,
  JC02015B $20-30
Nissan March, Active Red, JC18059R $20-30
Nissan March, Brilliant Blue,
  JC18033B $20-30
Nissan March, Paprika Orange,
  JC18033P $20-30
Nissan Primera 2.0C, Diamond Silver,
  JC09026S $20-30
Nissan Primera 20L, Silica Brass,
  JC09009G $20-30
Nissan Skyline Coupe, Diamond Silver,
  JC21040S $20-30
Nissan Skyline Coupe, Pearl White,
  JC21061W $20-30
Nissan Skyline Coupe, Silver,
  JC21045S $20-30
Nissan Stagea 250 RS, Black,
  JC15054K $20-30
Nissan Stagea 300 RX, Diamond Silver,
  JC15021S $20-30
Nissan Stagea 300 RX, White Pearl,
  JC15038W $20-30
Nissan X-Trail, Black, JC19047BL $20-30
Nissan X-Trail GT, Titanium Silver,
  JC19037S $20-30
Nissan Z Coupe Version S, Sunset Orange,
  JC13023P $20-30
Nissan Z Coupe, Blue, JC13049B $20-30
Nissan Z Fairlady Coupe, Diamond Silver,
  JC13013S $20-30
Nissan Z Roadster Cabriolet, Silver,
  JC13048S $20-30
Subaru Legacy 2.0 GT Station Wagon, White,
  JC24051W $20-30
Subaru Legacy Sedan, Black,
  JC23050K $20-30
Toyota Aristo V300 Vertex Edition, Black,
  JC03003K $20-30

Toyota Aristo V300 Vertex Edition, White Pearl
  Crystal Shine, JC03020W $20-30
Toyota Celsior, Black, JC05041K...........$20-30
Toyota Celsior, Dark Blue Mica,
  JC05005B $20-30
Toyota Celsior, Silver, JC05057S...........$20-30
Toyota Celsior, White Pearl Crystal Shine,
  JC05017W $20-30
Toyota Corolla Allex G-Edition, Metal Blue,
  JC07022G $20-30
Toyota Corolla Runx X150 G-Edition, Super Red,
  JC07007S $20-30
Toyota Crown Athlete V, Two-Tone White,
  JC10028 ....$20-30
Toyota Crown Royal Saloon G, White,
  JC10010W $20-30
Toyota Estima Aeras, Champagne Metallic,
  JC01001G $20-30
Toyota Estima Aeras, Silver,
  JC01042S $20-30
Toyota Estima Aeras, White Pearl Mica,
  JC01016W $20-30
Toyota Mk II 2.5 Grande D, Silver,
  JC11011W $20-30
Toyota Mk II 2.5 Grande IR-V, White,
  JC11030W $20-30
Toyota RAV4 5-doors JXl, Silver Metallic,
  JC06006R $20-30
Toyota RAV4 5-doors JX, Blue,
  JC06019B $20-30
Toyota Soarer 430 SCV, Open, White,
  JC14014W $20-30
Toyota Soarer, Blackish Red Mica,
  JC12040R $20-30
Toyota Soarer, Closed with Metal Top, Blue,
  JC14055B $20-30

J Collection Export Market Models
Infiniti G35, Caribbean Blue, JC037 ....$20-30
Infiniti G35 Sedan, Ivory Pearl, JC050 .....$20-30
Infiniti Q45, Black, JC024 ....$20-30
Lexus GS300, Black, JC003 ....$20-30
Lexus GS430, Platinum Metallic, JC020 ..$20-30
Lexus LS430, Cashmere Gold, JC017 .....$20-30
Lexus LS430, Navy Blue, JC005 ....$20-30
Lexus SC430 Closed Convertible, Silver,
  JC031 ....$20-30
Lexus SC430 Open Convertible, Blackish Red
  Mica, JC014 ....$20-30
Mazda 6 2002 5-door, Metallic Red,
  JC029 ....$20-30
Mazda MPV, Metal Green, JC012 ....$20-30
Mazda MPV, Red, March 2004,
  JC027 ....$20-30
Mazda MX-5 Open Convertible, Dark
  Green, JC018 ....$20-30

Mazda MX-5 Open Roadster, Classic
  Red, JC004 ....$20-30
Mazda MX-5 Roadster NR-A (racing
  version), JC032 ....$20-30
Mazda MX-5 Roadster NR-A (racing
  version), White, JC033 ....$20-30
Mitsubishi Grandis MPV, White Pearl,
  JC038 ....$20-30
Nissan 350 Z Coupe, Silver, JC013 ....$20-30
Nissan 350 Z Coupe European Version,
  Blue, JC034 ....$20-30
Nissan 350Z Roadster Cabriolet, Orange,
  JC039 ....$20-30
Nissan Cedric, White, JC002 ....$20-30
Nissan Cedric Taxi Tokyo, JC047 ....$20-30
Nissan Cima 450XV, Black, JC008 ....$20-30
Nissan Cube, Air Blue, JC035 ....$20-30
Nissan El Grand 2002, Champagne
  Metallic, JC025 ....$20-30
Nissan Gloria, Silver, JC015 ....$20-30
Nissan Micra 2002, Metallic Orange,
  JC030 ....$20-30
Nissan Navara Pick Up, Aruba Blue and
  Blade Silver (2-tone), JC042 ....$20-30
Nissan Navara Pick Up, Paris-Dakar
  2003–A. Vatanen, JC045 ....$20-30
Nissan Navara Pick Up, Paris-Dakar
  2003–D. Housieaux, JC046 ....$20-30
Nissan Navara Pick Up, Paris-Dakar
  2003–G. de Villiers, JC043 ....$20-30
Nissan Primera 2.0C, Metal Blue, JC026 ..$20-30
Nissan Primera 20L, Silver, JC009.........$20-30
Nissan Skyline 350GT, Silver, JC036 ......$20-30
Nissan Skyline V35 Sedan Red Garnet Fire
  March 2004, JC049......................$20-30
Nissan Stagea Station Wagon, Silver,
  JC021 ....$20-30
Nissan X-Trail 4WD, Red, JC023 ....$20-30
Nissan X-Trail 4WD, Silver, JC044 ....$20-30
Subaru Legacy 3.5GT Sedan, Red,
  JC040 ....$20-30
Subaru Legacy 3.5GT Station Wagon,
  Blue Mica, JC041 ....$20-30
Toyota Corolla 5-door, Red, JC007 ....$20-30
Toyota Corolla 5-door, Metal Blue,
  JC022 ....$20-30
Toyota Crown Athlete V, Silver, JC028 .....$20-30
Toyota Crown Japanese Police, JC048 ....$20-30
Toyota Crown Royal Saloon G, 2-Tone
  White, JC010................................$20-30
Toyota Mk II 2.5 Grande G, Silver, JC011 ..$20-30
Toyota Previa Sparkling, Beige Metallic,
  JC001 ....$20-30
Toyota Previa White, Pearl, JC016 ....$20-30
Toyota RAV4 5-doors, Antalya Metal Silver,
  JC006 ....$20-30

Toyota RAV4 5-doors, Atlantis Metal Blue, JC019 ....$20-30

Jaco

Listed below is a small assortment of these 1:43 scale models of construction equipment of which little else is known.

Shovel, #531 ....$11-14
Compactor, #532 ....$11-14
Bulldozer, #534 ....$11-14
Loader, #535 ....$11-14
Road Roller, #544 ....$11-14
Dozer/Ripper, #733 ....$11-14
Compactor/Loader, #933 ....$11-14

Jada Toys, Inc.

Jada Toys, Inc.
2531 S. Alameda St.
Los Angeles, CA 90058
tel: 323-234-8100
fax: 323-234-8111
website: www.jadatoys.com

Jada Co., Ltd.
Houston Centre, Suite 509
63 Mody Road, Tsimshatsui East
Kowloon, Hong Kong
tel: 011.852.2156.1968
fax: 011.852.2156.9399

Jada sums it best from their own website at www.jadatoys.com: "Jada is rocking the planet with a stunning new generation of uniquely American diecast automotive collectibles. Inspired by the coolest, baddest automotive trends on the street and off, each vehicle is designed with the same passion for authenticity, exquisite detail, and quality workmanship that drives discriminating collectors wild."

The first issues from Jada, the Showroom Floor series, were unfettered, strictly assembly line stock models. Since introducing first the outrageous Dub City and Street Low models, then the Road Rats and others, Jada has never looked back.

Dub City is a licensed series of cars, pickups, and SUVs equipped with replicas of the monster automotive sound systems straight out of the pages of *Dub Magazine*.

Street Low focuses on dazzling custom lowriders, while Road Rats are flat-finish pin-striped custom cars.

Homierollerz are produced in cooperation with Homies, the 1:24 scale caricature figures that typify the street-wise youth of East L. A.

Jada Street Low, 1:24

1947 Cadillac 62 Convertible, 1:24 ......$10-15
1947 Cadillac 62 ST, 1:24 ....$10-15
1953 Cadillac 62 Convertible, 1:24 ......$10-15
1953 Cadillac 62 ST, 1:24 ....$10-15
1959 Cadillac El Dorado Convertible, 1:24 ....$10-15
1959 Cadillac El Dorado HT, 1:24 ....$10-15
1959 Cadillac El Dorado ST, 1:24 ....$10-15
1939 Chevrolet Delivery, 1:24 ....$10-15
1947 Chevrolet Fleetline, 1:24 ....$10-15
1951 Chevrolet 3100 Pick Up, 1:24 ......$10-15
1953 Chevrolet Bel Air Convertible, 1:24..$10-15
1953 Chevrolet Bel Air HT, 1:24 ....$10-15
1953 Chevrolet Pick Up, 1:24 ....$10-15
1953 Chevrolet Tow Truck, 1:24 ....$10-15
1957 Chevrolet Suburban, 1:24 ....$10-15
1959 Chevrolet El Camino, 1:24 ....$10-15
1960 Chevrolet Impala Convertible, 1:24 ..$10-15
1960 Chevrolet Impala Hardtop, 1:24....$10-15
1961 Chevrolet Impala Convertible, 1:24 .$10-15

1961 Chevrolet Impala Hardtop, bright orange, 1:24..$10-15

1964 Chevrolet Impala Wagon, 1:24 ....$10-15
1967 Chevrolet Impala HT, 1:24 ....$10-15
1972 Chevrolet Cheyenne Pick Up, 1:24...$10-15

2000 Chevrolet Suburban, metallic red, 1:24 ....$10-15

Jada Street Low, 1:64

1947 Chevrolet Fleetline, 1:64 ....$4-6
1953 Chevrolet Bel Air, 1:64 ....$4-6

1953 Chevrolet Pick Up, 1:64..................$4-6

1957 Chevrolet Suburban, 1:64 ....$4-6
1959 Chevrolet El Camino, 1:64 ....$4-6

1960 Chevrolet Impala Coupe, 1:64 ....$4-6
1970 Chevrolet Monte Carlo, 1:64 ....$4-6
2001 Chevrolet Astro Van, 1:64 ....$4-6

Jada Homierollerz, 1:24

1947 Cadillac Series 62 Hardtop with character figures, 1:24 ....$15-20
1947 Chevrolet Aerosedan Fleetline with character figures, 1:24 ....$15-20

Jada Dub City, 1:24

2002 Cadillac Escalade, 1:24..............$4-6
2000 Chevrolet S-10, 1:24 ....$4-6
2000 Chevrolet Suburban, 1:24 ....$4-6
2001 Chevrolet Astro Van, 1:24 ....$4-6
2001 Chevrolet Avalanche, 1:24 ....$4-6

Jada Dub City, 1:64

2002 Cadillac Escalade, 1:64..............$4-6
2000 Chevrolet S-10, 1:64 ....$4-6
2000 Chevrolet Silverado, 1:64 ....$4-6
2000 Chevrolet Suburban, 1:64 ....$4-6

2001 Chevrolet Astro Van, 1:64.............$4-6

2001 Chevrolet Avalanche, 1:64 ....$4-6

Jada Showroom Floor, 1:24

1947 Cadillac Series 62 Softtop, 52520, 1:24..$9-12
1947 Cadillac Series 62 Hardtop, 53530, 1:24..$9-12
1953 Cadillac Series 62 Convertible, 53560, 1:24...$9-12
1953 Cadillac Series 62 Convertible, 53590, 1:24 1947 ....$9-12
1953 Cadillac Series 62 Hardtop, 53570, 1:24..$9-12
1953 Cadillac Series 62 Softtop, 53550, 1:24..$9-12
1959 Cadillac Eldorado Convertible, 53280, 1:24 ....$9-12
1959 Cadillac Eldorado Hardtop, 53270, 1:24..$9-12
1959 Cadillac Eldorado Softtop, 53320, 1:24 1959 ....$9-12
2002 Cadillac Escalade, 53630, 1:24 ....$9-12
1939 Chevrolet Delivery Sedan, 53360, 1:24..$9-12
1947 Chevrolet Aerosedan Fleetline, 53210, 1:24 ....$9-12

1953 Chevrolet Tow Truck, 53100, 1:24 ...$9-12

1953 Chevrolet 3100 Pickup, 53110, 1:24 ....$9-12

1953 Chevrolet Stake Truck, 53120, 1:24 ...$9-12

1953 Chevrolet Flatbed Truck, 53130, 1:24 ....$9-12

1960 Chevrolet Impala Hardtop, 53150, 1:24 ....$9-12

1960 Chevrolet Impala Convertible, 53160, 1:24 ....$9-12

1964 Chevrolet Impala Station Wagon, 53200, 1:24 ....$9-12

2001 Chevrolet Astro Van, 53190, 1:24 ..$9-12

1951 Chevrolet 3100 Pickup, 53220, 1:24 ....$9-12

1953 Chevrolet Bel Air Hardtop, 53230, 1:24 ....$9-12

1953 Chevrolet Bel Air Convertible, 53250, 1:24 ....$9-12

1957 Chevrolet Suburban, 53260, 1:24 ..$9-12

1960 Chevrolet Impala Hardtop, white, 1:24 ....$9-12

1960 Chevrolet Impala Convertible, white, 1:24 ....$9-12

1961 Chevrolet Impala Hardtop, 53290, 1:24 ....$9-12

1961 Chevrolet Impala Convertible, 53300, 1:24 ....$9-12

1967 Chevrolet Impala, 53310, 1:24 ......$9-12

1970 Chevrolet El Camino, 53350, 1:24 1959 ....$9-12

1972 Chevrolet Cheyenne Pickup, 53580, 1:24 ....$9-12

2002 Chevrolet Avalanche, 53330, 1:24 2001 ....$9-12

Chevrolet S-10 Pickup, 53170, 1:24 ....$9-12

Chevrolet Suburban, 53180, 1:24 ....$9-12

Jada Road Rats 1:24

1953 Cadillac Series 62, 1:24 ....$10-15

1959 Cadillac Deville, 1:24 ....$10-15

1939 Chevrolet Sedan Delivery, 1:24 .....$10-15

1956 Chevrolet Bel Air, 1:24 ....$10-15

1961 Chevrolet Impala, 1:24 ....$10-15

1951 Lincoln Mercury, 1:24 ....$10-15

Jada Road Rats 1:64

1947 Cadillac 62, 1:64 ....$4-6

1953 Cadillac Series 62, 1:64 ....$4-6

1959 Cadillac El Dorado, 1:64 ....$4-6

1962 Cadillac Series 62, 1:64 ....$4-6

1939 Chevrolet Delivery, 1:64 ....$4-6

1947 Chevrolet Fleetline, 1:64 ....$4-6

1953 Chevrolet 3100 Pick Up, 1:64 ....$4-6

1953 Chevrolet Bel Air, 1:64 ....$4-6

1957 Chevrolet Suburban, 1:64 ....$4-6

1959 Chevrolet El Camino, 1:64 ....$4-6

1960 Chevrolet Impala, 1:64 ....$4-6

Chrysler PT Cruiser, 1:64 ....$4-6

1932 Ford, 1:64 ....$4-6

1940 Ford, 1:64 ....$4-6

1951 Mercury, 1:64 ....$4-6

Jada Import Racer! 1:24

Lexus GS430, Copper, 1:24 ....$10-15

Lexus GS430, Silver, 1:24 ....$10-15

Lexus IS300, Black, 1:24 ....$10-15

Lexus IS300, Yellow, 1:24 ....$10-15

Mazda RX-7, Black, 1:24 ....$10-15

Mazda RX-7, Candy Blue, 1:24 ....$10-15

Mitsubishi Lancer Evo VI C, .Purple, 1:24 ..$10-15

Mitsubishi Lancer Evo VI, White, 1:24 ......$10-15

Subaru Impreza WRX STi, Silver, 1:24 .....$10-15

Subaru Impreza WRX STi, White, 1:24 ....$10-15

Toyota Celica, Blue, 1:24 ....$10-15

Toyota Celica, Red, 1:24 ....$10-15

Toyota MR-2 Spyder, Copper, 1:24 ....$10-15

Toyota MR-2 Spyder, Ch. Yellow, 1:24 ..$10-15

Toyota Supra, Orange and Black, 1:24 ..$10-15

Toyota Supra, Silver, 1:24 ....$10-15

Jada Import Racer! 1:18

Mitsubishi Eclipse, C. Purple, 1:18 ....$20-25

Mitsubishi Lancer Evo VIII, Silver, 1:18 ....$20-25

Mitsubishi Lancer Evo VIII, White, 1:18 ....$20-25

Nissan 350Z, Copper, 1:18 ....$20-25

Nissan 350Z, Red, 1:18 ....$20-25

Subaru Impreza WRX STi, C. Purple, 1:18 ..$20-25

Toyota Celica, Black, 1:18 ....$20-25

Toyota Celica, Yellow, 1:18 ....$20-25

Toyota MR-2 Spyder, Metallic Blue, 1:18 ..$20-25

Toyota MR-2 Spyder Metallic Red, 1:18 ...$20-25

Toyota Supra, C. Blue and Silver, 1:18 ....$20-25

Toyota Supra, C. Red, 1:18 ....$20-25

Toyota Supra, D. Blue, 1:18 ....$20-25

Jada Import Racer! Show Glow Neon Series, 1:18

Mitsubishi Eclipse, Black, 1:18 ....$20-25

Toyota Celica, Metallic Red, 1:18 ....$20-25

Jada Import Racer! 1:64

Lexus GS 430, Green, 1:64 ....$4-6

Lexus GS 430, White, 1:64 ....$4-6

Lexus IS 300, Black, 1:64 ....$4-6

Lexus IS 300, Yellow, 1:64 ....$4-6

Mitsubishi Eclipse, Bronze, 1:64 ....$4-6

Mitsubishi Eclipse, Orange, 1:64 ....$4-6

Toyota MR-2 Spyder, Red, 1:64 ....$4-6

Toyota MR-2 Spyder, Yellow, 1:64 ....$4-6

Toyota Celica, Blue, 1:64 ....$4-6

Toyota Celica, Red, 1:64 ....$4-6

Toyota Supra, Orange, 1:64 ....$4-6

Toyota Supra, Silver, 1:64 ....$4-6

Lexus GS 430, Black, 1:64 ....$4-6

Lexus GS 430, Silver, 1:64 ....$4-6

Lexus IS 300, Copper, 1:64 ....$4-6

Lexus IS 300, Red, 1:64 ....$4-6

Mitsubishi Eclipse, Purple, 1:64 ....$4-6

Mitsubishi Eclipse, White, 1:64 ....$4-6

Toyota MR-2 Spyder, Orange, 1:64 ....$4-6

Toyota MR-2 Spyder, Silver, 1:64 ....$4-6

Toyota Celica, Silver, 1:64 ....$4-6

Toyota Celica, Yellow, 1:64 ....$4-6

Toyota Supra, Blue, 1:64 ....$4-6

Toyota Supra, Green, 1:64 ....$4-6

Mazda RX-7, Blue and Silver, 1:64 ....$4-6

Mazda RX-7, Red, 1:64 ....$4-6

Mazda RX-8, Blue, 1:64 ....$4-6

Mazda RX-8, Green, 1:64 ....$4-6

Mitsubishi Eclipse, Ch. Yellow, 1:64 ....$4-6

Mitsubishi Eclipse, Orange/Purple, 1:64 .....$4-6

Mitsubishi Evo-8, White, 1:64.....................$4-6
Mitsubishi Evo-8, Yellow, 1:64....................$4-6
Nissan Z, Charcoal and Copper, 1:64........$4-6
Nissan Z, Silver, 1:64................................$4-6
Toyota Supra, Red and Gold, 1:64 ....$4-6
Toyota Supra, Purple, 1:64........................$4-6

Jada Thunder Crusher 1:64
1953 Chevrolet 3100 Pick Up, 1:64..........$4-6
2000 Chevrolet Silverado, 1:64..................$4-6
2000 Chevrolet Suburban, 1:64..................$4-6
2000 Chevrolet S-10, 1:64 ....$4-6

Jada Thunder Crusher 1:32
1953 Chevrolet 3100 Pick Up, 1:32..........$6-8
1953 Chevrolet Tow Truck, 1:32................$6-8
2000 Chevrolet Silverado, 1:32..................$6-8
2000 Chevrolet Suburban, 1:32..................$6-8
2000 Chevrolet S-10, 1:32 ....$6-8

NYPD 1:24
NYPD Suburban, 1:24 ....$10-15
NYPD Astro Van, 1:24 ....$10-15
NYPD Tow Truck, 1:24 ....$10-15

Hot Rigz 1:32
Kenworth T200 Tractor, 1:32 ....$9-12
Peterbilt 379 Tractor, 1:32 ....$9-12
Freightliner 120 Tractor, 1:32...................$9-12
Peterbilt 387 Tractor, 1:32 ....$9-12
Peterbilt 379 Hauler, 1:32 ....$9-12
Kenworth T2000 Hauler, 1:32 ....$9-12
Freightliner Hauler, 1:32...........................$9-12
Pennzoil Hauler, 1:32...............................$9-12
Purex Hauler, 1:32...................................$9-12
Valvoline Hauler, 1:32..............................$9-12
Union 76 Double Oil Tanker, 1:32............$9-12
Shell Double Oil Tanker, 1:32...................$9-12
Firestone Hauler, 1:32..............................$9-12
All American Flag Hauler, 1:32.................$9-12
Peterbilt 387 Leopard Hauler, 1:32 ....$9-12
Kenworth Hot Rod Hauler, 1:32 ....$9-12
Peterbilt Tow Truck, 1:32 ....$9-12
Tow Truck with Peterbilt 379, 1:32 ....$9-12
Tow Truck with Kenworth T2000, 1:32......$9-12
Tow Truck with Freightliner 120, 1:32........$9-12

Jane Francis Toys
Jane Francis started making toys in 1942, during World War II. Her first toys were stuffed handmade Gingham Dogs, Calico Cats, and Jumbo the Elephant toys for a Pittsburgh hospital gift shop. When Gimbel's department store requested 12 dozen stuffed toys, Jane Francis Toys was begun.

Her husband joined the operation towards the end of the war to introduce a line of crude diecast cars and trucks, among other items. In 1945, ther first models reached the market. By 1949, the last diecast toys were produced, But the Francis' daughter Jane Francis Vanyo continued her father's business, the A. W. Francis Company, in producing diecast lawn and garden accessories. As of 1993, the company was still in operation from its headquarters in Somerset, Pennsylvania.

This author found one Jane Francis toy buried in some backyard with only a vestige of its original beige paint left on it but with no rust or corrosion, and with axles and wheels missing. It has since been repainted red. On the underside of this single-cast toy is clearly marked "Jane Francis." Value in this condition is only a $1 to $4 at best, but in near mint original condition, wheels, axles, and paint intact, it would be worth around $20. Below is a list of the models produced from 1945 to 1949, with length and associated current collector values.

Gulf Box Truck with tin cargo cover, 5" $45-60
Pickup Truck, 5".......................................$25-40
Pickup Truck, 5".......................................$25-40
Pickup Truck, 6½".....................................$45-60
Sedan, futuristic, 6½".................................$35-50
Sedan, futuristic with wind-up motor..........$45-60
Tow Truck, 5"...$35-50

Ja-Ru (also see Golden Wheel)
Jacksonville, Florida, is home base for Ja-Ru toys made in China. Several lines of toys appear to exist under the Ja-Ru brand. Golden Wheels are inexpensive toy cars and trucks made by Golden Wheel Die Casting of China for Ja-Ru. Golden Classics Ford Model T gift banks are so similar to Ertl banks that they can be easily mistaken for them at first glance. But closer inspection shows a few qualitative differences, most notably a plastic roof secured to the windshield by a crudely melted post, and the distinctive phrase "Coins Bank" in script on each model. These models are such a blatant attempt to capitalize on the popularity of Pepsi-Cola collectibles and Ertl coin banks that they even say gift bank on the box. The Model T tanker truck even declares "Collectable Models" right on the tank. Talk about obvious!

Still, considering the $12 price tag, they are comparably nice models to the more expensive $20–35 Ertl versions, and they do make attractive, affordable gifts.

Ja-Ru has also recently produced some fairly attractive "Matchbox" size models called Real Wheels. Among the assortment are some fairly nice models of military vehicles labeled "Fighting Army" and some notable toy cars sold under the Collectors moniker. Removed from the brightly colored package, the models are rendered generic, with no markings on them to distinguish them from other such generic toys, except for some models which feature a number on the base and the words "Made In China."

Lately, many Ja-Ru Real Wheels have turned out to be repackaged Yat Ming and Zylmex models.

Ja-Ru Golden Wheels
Ford Model T Delivery Van, white with blue
    roof and fenders "Drink Pepsi-Cola" $12-15
Ford Model T Tanker, white with red roof
    and fenders, "Pepsi-Cola" $12-15
Ford Model T Tanker, "Mountain Dew" $12-15
Tractor Trailer, 1:87, "Pepsi" $4-5
Tractor Trailer, 1:87, "Mountain Dew"..........$4-5
Tractor Trailer, 1:64, "Pepsi" $9-12
Tractor Trailer, 1:64, "Mountain Dew".......$9-12
Diet Pepsi Tanker, white with red and
    blue accents, opaque silver-gray windows
    and base, 2½" $1-2
Pepsi Nissan Pathfinder, white with red and
    blue accents, opaque silver-gray
    windows, Rally lights and base, 2¼" $1-2

Ja-Ru Real Wheels
Army Jeep, No. 1608, army green with tan and
    dark green camouflage markings, 2¾".....$1-2
Audi Quattro, white with two-tone blue accents,
    "35" $1-2
BMW, metallic gray to magenta with Rally
    markings, #1029 ....$1-2
Cadillac Seville, metallic blue with gold, silver
    and black stripe accents on sides $1-2
F1 Racer, green, #1312 ....$1-2
F1 Racer, white, #1308 ....$1-2
F1 Racer, pale orange, #1311 ....$1-2

Mercedes-Benz Coupe, yellow, 1:64 .....$1-2

Military Covered Truck, #1362, army green with
    tan and dark green camouflage $1-2
Military Helicopter, army green with tan and dark
    green camouflage $1-2
Military Tank, #1102, army green with tan and
    dark green camouflage........................$1-2

Toyota Supra, white with red accents, "36," "yat-ming no.1036" on base $1-2

Je Toys

Like so many inexpensive toys, Je Toys is a manufacturer of an assortment of generic toys that includes cars, motorcycles, airplanes, racers, etcetera. Quality and scale are not issues with these miniatures. They are strictly low budget toys built for play and throw away. As collectibles, they are an oddity. In terms of collector value, they are worthless. Once removed from the vaguely identifiable packaging, they are rendered anonymous.

Regardless of that fact, Je Toys have produced a "cute" set of miniature antique vehicles in roughly 1:43 scale called Classic Cars that sell for about $2 apiece.

Jemini (see Crossways Models)

Jemini models are white models made in England. Most recently, Jemini merged with Crossways Models of England. See Crossways for a list of current and recent models.

JEP (see Jouets de Paris)

Jet

Best information indicates that Jet toys were produced by Jet Mechanics of Argentina. The list below might be confused with Jet Wheels by Mego.

Buick Riviera $12-16
Camaro, metallic blue-green, 1:64 ....$9-13
Dodge Charger $9-13
1976 Ford Taunus, 1:64 ....$9-13
Lamborghini Countach, red.....................$12-16
Mercury Cougar $10-14
Mustang II $12-16

Jet Wheels (see Mego)

Jet Wheels are a series of diecast cars produced by Mego. Other Mego series include Speed Burners.

JNG

From an otherwise unknown brand comes a replica DeTomaso Pantera in 1:45 scale.

DeTomaso Pantera, lime green, 1:45.......$20-30

Joal

Joal Juguetes y Herrajes
JOAL, S.A.
Avda. de la industria, 12 Apdo.

47 03440 IBI (Alicante) Spain
tel: (96) 555 08 01 or 555 08 02
fax: (96) 555 07 65
website: www.joal.es/

Since 1949, Juguetes Joal S.A., primarily manufacturers of 1:50 and 1:32 scale diecast construction models, has been based in Spain. Recently, Irwin Toy Limited of Toronto, Canada, established a short-lived marketing agreement whereupon they issued a set of six vintage sports cars dubbed the Joal Classics Collection. The models are detailed, accurate, and realistic, with opening doors, hoods, and trunks. Models possess an ephemeral charm that is not often reproduced these days. Joal models are currently manufactured in Macau and marketed in the U.S. by

Intermarket-Carmania
Skylake Industrial Park
19591 NE 10th Ave., Bay E
North Miami Beach, FL 33179 USA
phone: 305-651-8887
fax: 305-651-7131

Joal Classics Collection by Irwin

Ferrari 250 LeMans, red, #50114 ....$8-10
Jaguar E-Type Cabriolet, British racing green
        with beige interior, #50100................$8-10
Lamborghini Miura 6 P-400 Deslizante,
        yellow, #50125.............................$8-10
Mercedes-Benz 300SL Cabriolet, black with
        red interior, #50107......................$8-10
Mercedes-Benz 230SL, white with black roof,
        red interior, #50109......................$8-10
Porsche Carrera 6 Deslizante, white with
        blue doors and hood, #50111 ....$8-10

Joal Cars, Trucks, Heavy Equipment ad Other Models

Adams Probe 16, #118 ....$25-30
Agusta Helicopter, 220mm, #182 ....$15-20
Akerman
        EC620ME Digger, 250mm, 1:50,
        #180.....................................$25-30
        EW200 Wheel Backloader/Excavator,
        1:50, #232 ....$16-20
        H-7C Digger, 160mm, 1:50, #160 ..$16-20
        H-7C with Hydraulic Hammer, 160mm,
        1:50, #249 ....$16-20
        H-25D Excavator, 210mm, 1:50,
        #172.....................................$22-28
        Telescopic Crane, 205mm, 1:50,
        #236.....................................$18-24
Albion Cement Mixer, 1:43, #202 ....$15-20
Alfa Romeo Giulia
        55, #112................................$25-30

TZ1 Canguro, #105 ....$25-30
Aveling Dump Truck, 1:4, #2003 ....$15-20
BT
        Forklifts and Pallet Lift, 1:25, #187 .....$25-30
        RT1350SE Forklift, #188 ....$16-20
Bulldozer, #210 ....$25-30
Carmix Mixer, 161mm, 1:50, #171 ......$16-20
Caterpillar
        12-G Leveller/Road Grader, 168,
        1:50, #217 ....$18-24
        225 Hydraulic Excavator, 216mm,
        1:43, #216 ....$18-24
        375 Excavator, 1:50, #189.............$25-30
        518 Grapple Skidder, 193mm, 1:43,
        #226.....................................$16-20
        591 Pipelayer, 105mm, 1:50, #224 ...$22-28
        631 Tilt Tractor, 173mm, 1:70,
        #222.....................................$16-20
        631-D Wheel Tractor Scraper, 204mm,
        1:70, #219 ....$18-24
        773 Truck, 133mm, 1:70, #223......$15-20
        825-B Compactor, 147mm, 1:43,
        #218.....................................$16-20
        918F Wheel Loader, 265mm, 1:25,
        #177.....................................$30-35
        920 Wheel Loader, 123mm, 1:50,
        #214.....................................$16-20
        935 Traxcavator, #213 ....$25-30
        955/L Track-Type Loader, 100mm,
        1:50, #213 ....$18-24
        "V" Snow Plough with Spreader,
        175mm, 1:43, #229 ....$16-20
        CB-534 Compactor with Cab, 99mm,
        1:50, #244 ....$15-20
        CB-534 Compactor, 99mm, 1:50,
        #248.....................................$15-20
        Challenger 65 Tractor, 122mm, 1:5,
        #2330....................................$16-20
        Challenger 65 with Disc Harrow, 9⅛", 1:50,
        #253.....................................$22-28
        D5C Tractor, 79mm, 1:50, #174 .....$15-20
        D-10 Chain Tractor, 150mm, 1:70,
        #220.....................................$18-24
        Digging Crane, 10¼", 1:43,
        #225.....................................$20-25
        IT18F Loader, 280mm, 1:25, #184.......$32
        IT18F Tool carrier, 1:25, #387 ....$39
        V80F Lift Truck, 113mm, 1:25,
        #215.....................................$16-20
Chaparral 2F, #113 ....$25-30
Chevrolet Monza, #108 ....$25-30
Chrysler 150, #128 ....$25-30
        with Ferrari Formula I and Trailer,
        #155.....................................$25-30
Citroën CX Pallas
        #127.....................................$25-30

and Trailer, #152 ....$25-30

Citroën SM

#126..$25-30

with Ford Fiesta and Trailer, #153......$25-30

Ebro 6100 Tractor

117mm, 1:38, #250.........................$16-20

and Trailer with Hay Bails, 255mm, 1:38, #251...$25-30

with Sprayer, 10¼", 1:50, #252 ......$15-20

Euclid

R-32 Dump Truck, 160mm, 1:50, #228...$16-20

R-858 Dump Truck, 205mm, 1:50, #242...$25-30

Farm

Trailer, #204...................................$12-16

Pulverisator, #205............................$12-16

Fiat (Seat) 132 4-door Sedan, 1:43, #123...$16-20

Fire Engine, 215mm, 1:50, #173 ....$25-30

Ferrari

250 Le Mans, #114.........................$25-30

512S, 1:43, #119...............................$35

612 Can-Am, #116.........................$25-30

Ford Fiesta, #129...........................$25-30

Heavy Duty Transporter

with #182 Agusta Helicopter, 14½", #326..$25-30

with #216 Caterpillar 225 Hydraulic Excavator, 14½", #320 ....$30-35

with #220 Caterpillar D-10 Chain Tractor, 14½", #321............................$30-35

with #225 Caterpillar Digging Crane, 14½", #323.................................$30-35

with #227 Volvo BM L-160 Wheel Loader, 14½", #324................................$30-35

with #229 Caterpillar "V" Snow Plough with Spreader, 14½", #322..................$30-35

with #237 Volvo BM L-160 High Lift, 14½", #325...$30-35

International Transport, 350mm, 1:50, #176...$16-20

Iso Rivolta Coupe, 1:43, #115...............$25-30

Jaguar E Type Roadster, 1:43, #100......$30-35

JCB

435 Track-Type Loader, 211mm, 1:35, #243...$19

4CX Centermount Backhoe Loader, 345mm, 1:35, #185 ....$30-35

4CX Sitemaster Backhoe Loader, 345mm, 1:35, #175 ....$28

525-58 Telescopic Loader, 210mm, 1:35, #245 ....$16-20

525-58 with Pallet Fork, 210mm, 1:35, #166 ....$16-20

712 Dump Truck, 72mm, 1:35, #246 ..$16-20

---

801 Mini Backhoe Excavator, 146mm, 1:35, #162 ....$16-20

930 Tough Terrain Forklift, 146mm, 1:35, #161 ....$16-20

Komatsu PC400

EX, 1:32, #186 ....$60-65

LC Excavator, 425mm, 1:32, #183.......$48

Lamborghini Miura Coupe, 1:43, #125 ..$16-20

Leyland Dumper

#200..$25-30

"Construccion," #200 ....$25-30

Massey Ferguson

Skat 516 Load, 1:32, #192............$16-20

Tractor, #203 ....$25-30

Tractor with Mechanical Shovel, #206..$25-30

McLaren M80, #122 ....$25-30

Mercedes-Benz

230SL Hardtop, #109 ....$25-30

230SL Roadster, #110.....................$25-30

230SL and Trailer, #151 ....$25-30

300SL, #107..................................$25-30

350SL Coupe, 1:43, #124 ....$16-20

C-III, #117.....................................$25-30

Michigan L-320 Wheel Loader, 217, 1:50, #239 ....$19

New Holland TX-34 Combine Harvester

8⅞", 1:42, #240 ....$22-28

with Maice (Corn) Head, 10", 1:42, #247 ....$22-28

Pegaso

Articulated Truck, #212 ....$25-30

Multibucket, #211 ....$25-30

Tanker, "BUTANO," #208 ....$25-30

Tanker, "CAMPSA," #209.............$25-30

Truck with Boat Motor, #207.............$25-30

Porsche

917K, #121 ....$25-30

Carrera 6, #111 ....$25-30

PPM

530 ATT Crane, 1:50, #168 ....$40

Superstacker, 1:50, #169 ....$34

Renault

R8, #102 ....$25-30

R10, #104 ....$25-30

Seat

124, #106 ....$25-30

850 Coupe, #103 ....$25-30

Simca 1000, #101............................$25-30

Steam Roller, 114mm, 1:50, #221........$12-16

Taylor Crane Truck

#201..$25-30

"Autopistas," #201..........................$25-30

Twin Mill, #120 ....$25-30

Valmet

4-Wheel Tractor, 140mm, 1:35, #178...$15-20

8-Wheel Tractor, 140mm, 1:35, #179...$16-20

Pulling Tractor, 1:35, #191 ....$16-20

Tractor with Grapple Skidder Trailer, 14½", 1:35, #254 ....$30-35

Volvo

A-35 Cement Mixer, 245mm, 1:5, #1670 ....$19

A-35 Grapple Stacker, 10¼· 1:50, #170...$22-28

BM 6300 Excavator Loader, 210mm, 1:50, #230 ....$22-28

BM A-25 Articulated Dump Truck, 195mm, 1:50, #231.............................$16-20

BM A-35 Articulated Dumper, 216mm, 1:50, #238.............................$18-24

BM L-160 High Lift, 212mm, 1:50, #237..$19

BM L-160 Wheel Loader, 160mm, 1:50, #227 ....$16-20

Coach, 240mm, 1:50, #149...........$18-24

L-70 Skidder, 160mm, 1:50, #235...$16-20

L-70 Wheel Loader, 148mm, 1:50, #234...$16-20

L-70 with Handing Arm, 215mm, 1:50, #165...$16-20

L-70 with Pallet Fork, 170mm, 1:50, #163...$16-20

L-70 with Snow Blade, 173mm, 1:50, #164...$16-20

L-70C Wheel Loader, 1:50, #181 ....$16-20

L-160 Compactor, 160mm, 1:50, #241...$16-20

Wrecker and Ford Fiesta, #154 ....$25-30

Johillco

From 1898 until 1960, John Hill & Company of London, England, produced lead figures. During the 1930s, the company also produced a few toy vehicles that included cars, trucks, land speed record cars, motorcycles, carts, military trucks, and garage and road accessories such as gas pumps and street signs.

Johillco toy cars were the first to use separate rubber tires, although the later models were produced with metal wheels. Three main groups of toy vehicles were produced by the company: copies or reissues of Pre-WWII Tootsietoy castings, realistic land speed record cars, and various other models.

Johillco was most successful during the 1930s with over 400 employees. In 1946, Johillco was purchased by Alec Standing of Burnley, England.

Production of toy vehicles ceased after WWII, and they replaced their lead cast figures with plastic ones.

Johillco Tootsietoy Copies / Reissues

1920 American Farm Tractor, 1:50	$20-30
1918 Ford Model T, 1:50	$20-30
1920 Ford Model T Pickup, 1:50	$20-30
1930 Ford Model A Coupe, 1:60	$20-30
1930 Ford Model A Van, 1:60	$20-30
1920 6-Window Saloon, 1:50	$20-30
1920 Mack AC Truck with searchlight, 1:65	$20-30
1920 Mack AC Coal Truck, 1:65	$20-30
1920 Mack AC Stake Truck, 1:65	$20-30
1920 Mack AC with Gun, 1:65	$20-30
1920 Mack AC with Live Shells, 1:65	$20-30
1920 Mack AC with War Balloon, 1:65	$20-30

Johillco Land Speed Record Cars

Bluebird II Napier Lyon engine, 246.09 mph, February 1931, Malcolm Campbell, 1:50 ....$35-45

Irving Napier Golden Arrow, 231.446 mph, March 1929, driven by Henry Segrave, 1:65 ....$35-45

MG Magic Midget 1932, George Eyston, Class H (Flying Scud), 1:43 ....$35-45

Speed of the Wind Rolls Royce Kestrel engine 1935, George Eyston, Class A, 1:50 ..$35-45

Sunbeam Silver Bullet, unofficial 186.046 mph, March 1930, Kaye Don, 1:50 ....$35-45

Other Johillco Models

Bulldozer, 1:70	$20-30
Cannon Truck, 1:50	$20-30
Double-Decker Bus 1930, 1:70	$20-30
Double-Decker Tram 1925, 1:70	$20-30
Farm Tractor, 1:50	$20-30
Fire Engine with ladder and 5 firemen, 1:50	$20-30
Gun, 1:50	$20-30
Police Motorcycle and sidecar, 1:36	$20-30
Police Motorcycle, 1:36	$20-30
Renault Tank, 1:45	$20-30
Small Van, 1:87	$20-30
Small Van Ambulance, 1:87	$20-30
Small Open Coach 1920, 1:100	$20-30

John Day Models (also see Precision Autos)

John Day of Great Britain produced models of cars he hadn't seen produced by any other manufacturer during the late 1970s. As reported by Bob Shapton, the Shelby has no markings and is very heavy for its size. Evaluation is difficult, so the values below are educated guesses.

Parnelli #215 1975 Formula One Racer driven by Mario Andretti, 1:43 ....$250-500

Shelby Cobra, 1:43, blue $250-500

John Hill & Company (see Johillco)

John Smith (see Smith Family Toys)

Johnny Lightning (also see Topper Toys)

Johnny Lightning
Playing Mantis / Thomas Lowe Ventures, Inc.
Tom Lowe, President and Founder
Billing Address:
P O Box 388
Mishawaka, IN 46546
Shipping Address:
3618 Grape Rd.
Mishawaka, IN 46545
phone: 219-256-0300
toll-free: 1-800-626-8478 (1-800-MANTIS-8)
fax: 219-252-0500 general business
fax: 219-256-2657 sales/orders
e-mail: PlayingM@aol.com
website: www.johnnylightning.com

Johnny Lightning cars were originally produced from 1969 to 1971 by Topper Toys, owned by Henry Orenstein, but charges of business fraud forced Orenstein out of business.

Twenty-three years later, Thomas E. Lowe, a businessman who remembers as a kid the toy cars that beat Hot Wheels on their own track, purchased the Johnny Lightnings license to reproduce several of the original designs in a commemorative series under the new company name of Playing Mantis. The series has proven itself so popular with collectors that ten color variations, limited to 10,000 each, have been issued during 1994, and indicated as series A through J.

In 1995, Playing Mantis made a major departure from its original direction by creating all-new models called Muscle Machines, relying on the popularity of the brand name and the passion for American muscle cars. Each model/color variation is produced in limited quantities of 20,000 or less.

Johnny Lightnings really took off in 1996, with many new issues. Dragsters USA feature popular funny cars from the 1970s, 1980s, and 1990s. Indy race cars and pace cars consist of a two-pack of one Indy winning race car and the corresponding pace car for that year. Wacky Winners are the brainchild of Tom Daniel, noted automotive designer with a flair for the bizarre.

Aside from all the regular production models, several promotional models were issued as well. By special order, private individuals, groups, and dealers had various models reproduced with special markings to designate them as promotionals for their business or organization. All are listed below following a chronology of the original Topper line.

This book only provides a partial listing of all the models and variations issued by Playing Mantis. By the year 2000, there were so many different series being issued that they would consume a book. So a new book, *Tomart's Price Guide to Johnny Lightning Vehicles,* has been compiled which lists every model issued through 2001. Offered below is a list of Topper Johnny Lightnings and the first Playing Mantis Johnny Lightning Commemorative reproductions from 1994. The rest of the Johnny Lightning line consumes another whole book.

Topper Johnny Lightning Models, 1969 to 1971

The first price listed is for mint condition out of package; the second price is for model in original package. Primary description is the one imprinted on the base of the model. Description in parentheses is the name printed on the package.

A. J. Foyt Indy Special, 1970 ....$50-250
Al Unser Indy Special, 1970 ....$175-500
Baja, 1970 ....$125-400
Big Rig, 1971 Customs $125-300
Bubble, 1970 Jet Power cars $100-150
Bug Bomb, 1970 ....$75-225
Condor, 1970 ....$200-1,250
Custom Camaro, prototype $2,000-3,000
Custom Charger, prototype $2,000-3,000
Custom Continental, prototype $2,000-3,000
Custom Dragster (Super Twin Engine Dragster), 1969
  mirror finish with dome, 1969 ....$300-1,000
  standard finish with dome, 1969 ...$150-250
  standard finish with no dome, 1970 ...$75-150
Custom El Camino (Custom El Camino Surfer), 1969
  mirror finish, doors open $500-1,500
  standard finish, doors open $200-600
  standard finish, doors don't open $300-900
Custom Eldorado (Custom Cadillac Eldorado), 1969
  mirror finish, doors open $400-1,200
  standard finish, doors open $200-400
  standard finish, doors don't open ..$750-1,750
Custom Ferrari (Custom Ferrari Berlinetta), 1969
  mirror finish, doors open $500-1,000
  standard finish, doors open $250-500
  standard finish, doors don't open $75-150
Custom '32 Ford (Custom '32 Ford Hot Rod), 1969 mirror finish, doors open .$1,000-1,500
  standard finish, doors open $75-175
  standard finish, doors don't open $60-120
Custom G.T.O. (Custom Pontiac G.T.O.), 1969 mirror finish (none known to exist) $1,000-1,500
  standard finish $75-200

Custom Mako Shark, 1969
  mirror finish, doors open.............$500-1,600
  standard finish, doors open $200-600
  standard finish, doors don't open ..$400-1,250
Custom Mustang, prototype.........$2,000-3,000
Custom Spoiler, 1970 ....$50-100
Custom T-Bird (Custom Thunderbird), 1969
  mirror finish, doors open.............$400-1,600
  standard finish, doors open $200-600
  standard finish, doors don't open ..$400-1,250
Custom Toronado (Custom Olds Toronado), 1969
  mirror finish, doors open.............$500-1,800
  mirror finish, doors open, exhaust pipes
    on base...............................$400-1,400
  standard finish, doors open $200-1,200
  standard finish, doors open, exhaust pipes
    on base...............................$600-2,000
  standard finish, doors don't open ..$500-1,500
  standard finish, doors don't open,
    exhaust pipes on base $300-1,250
Custom Turbine (Turbine Special X-2000), 1969
  mirror finish, painted interior $500-1,250
  mirror finish, unpainted interior $250-750
  standard finish, painted interior $100-250
  standard finish, unpainted interior $75-150
Custom XKE (Custom Jaguar XKE), 1969
  mirror finish, doors open.............$500-1,200
  mirror finish, doors don't open $600-1,250
  standard finish, doors open $200-750
  standard finish, doors don't open $50-150
Double Trouble, 1970 ....$125-1,500
Flame Out, 1970 ....$75-250
Flying Needle, 1970 Jet Power..........$150-250
Frantic Ferrari, 1970.........................$75-125
Glasser, 1970 Jet Power $125-200
Hairy Hauler, 1971 Customs.............$175-350
Jumpin Jag, 1970 ....$50-150
Leapin Limo, 1970.............................$75-400
Mad Maverick, 1970 ....$75-300
Monster, 1970 Jet Power $50-150
Movin Van, 1970...............................$50-150
Nucleon, 1970 ....$50-200
Parnelli Jones Indy Special, 1970 ....$50-250
Pipe Dream, 1971 Customs $125-300
Sand Stormer, 1970
  black roof $100-200

roof same color as body...................$50-150

Screamer, 1970 Jet Power $50-150
Sling Shot, 1970 ....$75-200
Smuggler, 1970 ....$50-100
Stiletto, 1970 ....$50-200
TNT, 1970 ....$75-200

Triple Threat, 1970 ....$50-200

Twin Blaster, 1971 Customs $125-300
Vicious Vette, 1970.............................$75-200
Vulture, 1970 ....$175-500
The Wasp, 1970 ....$125-400
Wedge, 1970 Jet Power $125-250
Whistler, 1970...................................$125-250
Wild Winner, 1971 Custom cars $125-300

Playing Mantis Johnny Lightning Commemoratives, 1994

Each model has been produced in ten different color variations and designated Series A through J. Polished metalflake colors include Cherry Red, Emerald Green, Slate Blue, Light Purple, and Chocolate, while high-gloss enamel colors are Black, Yellow, Turquoise, and Hot Pink. Aside from the regular issues listed below, exclusive sets were issued by FAO Schwarz in red, gold, silver, or blue chrome colors and by Toys "R" Us in silver and gold.

Bug Bomb, #105, 1994
  all colors, except those listed below.........$4-9
  hot pink $9-12
  pearl white metalflake ("A Bonus" /
    "White Lightning") $24-32
  pearl white metalflake with Johnny Lightning logo,
    1994 NPS on roof, promotional.......$9-15
  red-orange (Target/Shopko).................$9-12
  sky blue (Target/Shopko)....................$9-12
  slate blue...$4-9
  unpainted Q-Car...............................$15-25
Custom Continental, #109, 1995
  all colors, except those listed below.........$3-6
  champagne (Target/Shopko).................$4-7
  pearl white metalflake ("A Bonus" /
    "White Lightning") $12-16
  pearl white metalflake with Johnny Lightning logo,
    1994 NPS on roof, promotional.......$9-15
  unpainted.......................................$12-16

Custom El Camino, #101, 1994
  all colors except those listed below.........$3-6
  champagne (Target / Shopko)..............$4-7
  pearl white metalflake ("A Bonus" /
    "White Lightning") $12-16
  pearl white metalflake with Johnny
    Lightning logo, 1994 NPS on roof,
    promotional..............................$9-15
  unpainted..12-16
Custom GTO, #102, 1994
  all colors except those listed below..........$3-6
  pearl white metalflake ("A Bonus" /
    "White Lightning") $12-16
  pearl white metalflake with Johnny Lightning logo,
    1994 NPS on roof, promotional $9-15
  unpainted..$12-16
Custom Mako Shark, #114, 1995
  all colors, except those listed below.........$3-6
  champagne (Target/Shopko).................$4-7
  pearl white metalflake ("A Bonus" /
    "White Lightning") $12-16
  pearl white metalflake with Johnny Lightning logo,
    1994 NPS on roof, promotional.......$9-15
  unpainted..$12-16
Custom Mustang, #112, 1995
  all colors, except those listed below.........$3-6
  champagne (Target/Shopko).................$4-7
  pearl white metalflake ("A Bonus" /
    "White Lightning") $12-16
  pearl white metalflake with Johnny Lightning logo,
    1994 NPS on roof, promotional.......$9-15
  unpainted..$12-16
Custom Spoiler, #113, 1995
  all colors, except those listed below.........$3-6
  champagne (Target/Shopko).................$4-7
  pearl white metalflake ("A Bonus" /
    "White Lightning") $12-16
  pearl white metalflake with Johnny Lightning logo,
    1994 NPS on roof, promotional.......$9-15
  unpainted..$12-16
Custom Thunderbird, #111, 1995
  all colors, except those listed below.........$3-6
  champagne (Target/Shopko).................$4-7
  pearl white metalflake ("A Bonus" /
    "White Lightning") $12-16
  pearl white metalflake with Johnny Lightning logo,
    1994 NPS on roof, promotional.......$9-15
  unpainted..$12-16
Custom Toronado, #110, 1995
  all colors, except those listed below.........$3-6
  champagne (Target/Shopko).................$4-7
  pearl white metalflake ("A Bonus" /
    "White Lightning") $12-16
  pearl white metalflake with Johnny Lightning logo,
    1994 NPS on roof, promotional.......$9-15
  unpainted..$12-16

Custom Turbine, #115, 1995
  all colors, except those listed below........$3-6
  champagne (Target/Shopko)................$4-7
  pearl white metalflake ("A Bonus" /
    "White Lightning") $12-16
  pearl white metalflake with Johnny Lightning logo,
    1994 NPS on roof, promotional......$9-15
  unpainted........................$12-16
Custom XKE, #103, 1994
  all colors except those listed below........$3-5
  pearl white metalflake ("A Bonus" /
    "White Lightning") $9-12
  unpainted........................$12-16
Movin' Van, #106, 1994
  all colors except those listed below........$3-6
  pearl white metalflake ("A Bonus" /
    "White Lightning") $9-12
  unpainted........................$12-16
Nucleon, #117, 1995
  all colors, except those listed below........$3-6
  champagne (Target/Shopko)................$4-7
  pearl white metalflake ("A Bonus" /
    "White Lightning") $12-16
  pearl white metalflake with Johnny Lightning logo,
    1994 NPS on roof, promotional......$9-15
  unpainted........................$12-16
'32 Roadster, #104, 1994
  all colors except those listed below........$3-5
  pearl white metalflake ("A Bonus" /
    "White Lightning") $9-12
  pearl white metalflake with Johnny
    Lightning logo, 1994 NPS on roof,
    promotional $9-15
  unpainted........................$12-16
T.N.T., #118, 1995
  all colors, except those listed below........$3-6
  champagne (Target/Shopko)................$4-7
  pearl white metalflake ("A Bonus" /
    "White Lightning") $12-16
  pearl white metalflake with Johnny Lightning logo,
    1994 NPS on roof, promotional......$9-15
  unpainted........................$12-16
Triple Threat, #116, 1995
  all colors, except those listed below........$3-6
  champagne (Target/Shopko)................$4-7
  pearl white metalflake ("A Bonus" /
    "White Lightning") $12-16
  pearl white metalflake with Johnny Lightning logo,
    1994 NPS on roof, promotional......$9-15
  unpainted........................$12-16
Vicious Vette, #107, 1994
  all colors except those listed below........$3-5
  pearl white metalflake ("A Bonus" /
    "White Lightning") $9-12
  unpainted........................$12-16
The Wasp, #108, 1994

all colors except those listed below.........$2-4
pearl white metalflake ("A Bonus" /
  "White Lightning")....................$4-7
unpainted........................$12-16

Assorted Johnny Lightning Models
Abrams M1A1 military tank $4-6

Acura Integra Type R, Import Heat $4-6

AMC Hornet, red, from James Bond
movie "Octopussy" $4-6

1958 Austin Healey Sprite, American
Graffiti................................$5-7

Batmobile, 1950s Comic Book
diecast model kit....................$12-16
Batmobile, 1960s Comic Book diecast model
  kit $12-16

1971 Buick Riviera, Super 70s................$4-6
1959 Cadillac Eldorado Convertible, Classic
  Gold................................$4-6
1955 Chevrolet Bel Air Convertible $4-6

1968 Chevrolet Camaro, Classic Gold...$4-6

1969 Chevrolet Camaro, Peterson Cover
  Cars $4-6

1954 Chevrolet Corvette, Culture Cars..$4-6
1962 Chevrolet Corvette
  red with whitewall tires, Peterson Cover
    Cars................................$4-6

red with blackwall tires, silver trim,
Super Chevrolet................................$4-6

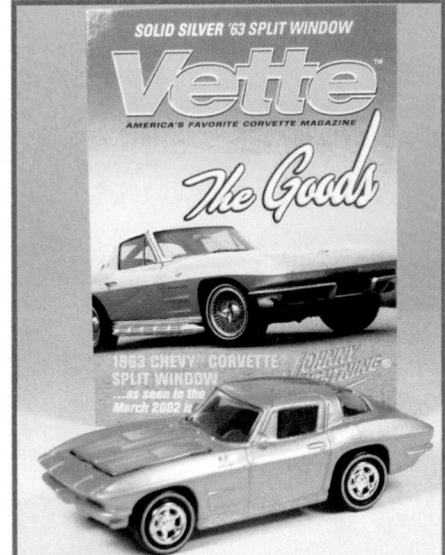

1963 Chevrolet Corvette, Peterson Cover
Cars................................$4-6

1994 Chevrolet Corvette, Corvette
50th Anniversary................................$4-6

1958 Chevrolet Impala, Motor Trend $5-7

1971 Chevrolet Monte Carlo, Super 70s.....$4-6

1955 Chevrolet Nomad, Thunder
Wagons $4-6

1956 Chevrolet Nomad, Peterson
Cover Cars...$4-6

1957 Chevrolet Nomad, Thunder
Wagons $4-6

Chrysler 300, Marilyn Monroe "There's
No Business Like Show Business" $7-9

Chrysler PT Cruiser, Billboards
Coca-Cola $4-6

1959 Desoto Police, American Heroes....$5-7

1966 Dodge Charger, Muscle Cars USA.....$5-7

1969 Dodge Charger Daytona.................$6-8

1966 Dodge Hemi Charger, Muscle
Cars USA $5-7

Dodge Viper GTS, Americana
Coca-Cola Boxed Set...............................$7-9

Tow-Nado 2000 Ford F-350, Rebel Rods.....$4-6

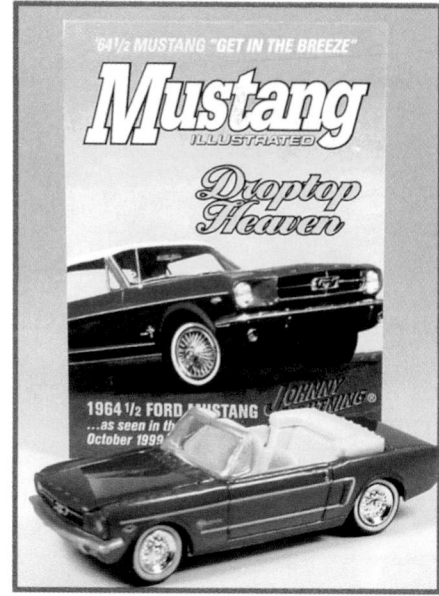

1964? Ford Mustang Convertible,
Peterson Cover Cars $4-6

1971 Ford Mustang Mach 1, Peterson Cover
Cars $4-6

1973 Ford Mustang Convertible $4-6

Ford Mustang Fastback, Americana
Coca-Cola Boxed Set...............................$7-9

1955 Ford Panel Delivery, Custom Woodys and Panels $4-6

1940 Ford Sedan Delivery, Surf Rods $4-6

1956 Ford Thunderbird Roadster, Thunderbird series $4-6

1958 Ford Thunderbird Hardtop, Thunderbird series $4-6

1959 Ford Thunderbird Hardtop, Thunderbird series $4-6

1961 Ford Thunderbird Convertible, Thunderbird series $4-6

1967 Ford Thunderbird Hardtop, Thunderbird series $4-6

1968 Ford Thunderbird Hardtop, Thunderbird series $4-6

Ford Torino, metallic green, red striped tires $4-6

Hispano Suiza, brown and tan, from James Bond movie "Moonraker" $4-6

2003 Hummer H2, red, Classic Gold Collection...$4-6

Jeep CJ5, Classic Gold $4-6

1955 Lincoln Futura..................................$6-8

1949 Custom Mercury, American Graffiti....$5-7

1951 Mercury Convertible, top up, Ragtops...$4-6

Mini Cooper S, 1:58 scale

British Racing Green, white roof $4-6

metallic gun-metal gray, white roof $4-6

2004 Mitsubishi Lancer Evolution, Lightning Strike 2004 New Cars $4-6

Nash Metropolitan $4-6

1977 Oldsmobile Cutlass Supreme, Super 70s $4-6

1962 Plymouth Belvedere, Muscle Cars USA $5-7

1971 Plymouth Duster, Super 70s $4-6

1970 Plymouth Hemi Cuda, Street Freaks..$4-6

1997 Plymouth Prowler with collectible tin $5-7

Plymouth Savoye, Marilyn Monroe "Bus Stop" $6-8

1971 Pontiac Grand Prix, Super 70s.......$4-6

1967 Pontiac GTO $6-8

1961 Pontiac Ventura, Muscle Cars USA....$5-7

Rumblur, Thunder Wagons $4-6

Scooby Doo Mystery Machine, 1:18 scale $25-40

Shut Out, Tom Daniel's Fearless Funny Cars $4-6

1948 Tucker Torpedo.............................$4-6

1966 Volkswagen Beetle, Volkswagen series $4-6

Volkswagen Beetle, Americana Coca-Cola Boxed Set $7-9

Volkswagen Beetle, Herbie, The Love Bug, 1:18 scale $25-40

Volkswagen Microbus, Billboards Coca-Cola $4-6

Volkswagen Samba Bus, Classic Gold Bob Novak's.....................................$5-7

1974 Volkswagen Thing, Classic Gold...$4-6

1966 Volkswagen Type 2 Pickup,
Volkswagen series $4-6

Wildkat Custom Pickup, Retro Rods $4-6

1953 Willys, Willys Gassers II..................$4-6

Johnny Speed

Prior to the 1969 introduction of Johnny Lightnings, Topper Toys produced a large scale remote control car that resembles a Jaguar.

Johnny Speed remote control car, circa
1967 ....$125-250

Jolly Roger

Jolly Roger diecast toys were made in Wales from 1946 to 1948. The line consists of a few modified Gasquy-Septoy castings.

Maserati-styled Grand Prix Race car, 1947...$35-50

Plymouth 1939 Sedan $55-70
Caravan $40-55

Jordan

Jordan Highway Miniatures are high quality detailed 1:87 scale model kits of exceptional quality.

Ahrens Fox 1927 Fire Pumper $7-9
American LaFrance 1924 Fire Pumper........$8-10
Essex 1926 2-door Hardtop $5-7
Ford
   1911 Model T Delivery Truck $6-8
   1913 Model T Fire Pumper $5-7
   1914 Model T Touring car $7-9
   1920 Model T Sedan $6-8
   1925 Mail Truck..........................$5-7
   1925 Panel Truck.........................$5-7
   1925 Roadster/Pickup $5-7
   1928 Model A Pickup......................$7-9
   1928 Model A Sedan......................$7-9
   1929 Model A "Woody" Station Wagon ...$5-7
   1929 Model AA One-Ton Railway
      Express Agency...........................$6-8
   1929 Model AA Tank Truck with
      period oil and gas cans $7-9
   1934 21-Passenger Bus.......................$7-9
   1940 Standard V-8 Sedan $6-8
Mack 1923
   "Bulldog" Dump Truck......................$7-9
   "Bulldog" Hi-Lift Coal Dump Truck $7-9
   "Bulldog" Stake Truck.....................$7-9
   "Bulldog" Tank Truck......................$7-9
   Aerial Ladder Truck $8-10
Oldsmobile 1904 Railroad Inspection
   car and Curved Dash Auto...................$6-8
Packard 1922 Stake Truck.........................$7-9

Jouef

Until its bankruptcy in 1996, the head office for Jouef was in Champagnole, France, with US distribution based in Mequon, Wisconsin.

Plastic models were once the predominant Jouef product, but most recently the company produced an exceptional assortment of diecast models in 1:18, 1:24, and 1:43 scale. Dubbed Jouef Evolution, named after their flagship model Ferrari GTO Evoluzione, the models represented are high quality replicas for a reasonable price.

Castings and licenses for Jouef were purchased in 1998 by Universal Hobbies of Hong Kong and are now issued, along with many new castings, as Eagle's Race and Eagle Collectibles.

Jouef 1:18 Scale

Alfa Romeo Spyder, #3301 ....$40-50
   hard top, #3302 ....$40-50
   soft top, #3303 ....$40-50
   open top, #3304..........................$4050
Ferrari 250 GT SWB, 1961
   red, #3022 ....$40-50
   yellow, #3023..........................$40-50
   Le Mans 1961, #3012.....................$40-50
Ferrari 250 GTO, 1964, #3002 ....$40-50
   #27 Le Mans 1964, #3016 ....$40-50
Ferrari 330 P4, #3029 ....$40-50
   Coupe #24 Le Mans 1967, #3030....$40-50
   Coupe Targa Florio 1976, #3031 ....$40-50
   Coupe B, #21 Le Mans 1967, #3017...$40-50
   Spyder, #3005 ....$40-50
Ferrari 412 P
   #23 Le Mans 1967 (Limited Edition),
      #3018..............................$50-60
   #25 "N.A.R.T." Le Mans 1967, #3024..$40-50
Ferrari GTO Evoluzione, #3001 ....$40-50
Ford GT 40
   #6 Le Mans Winner, 1969, #3008 .....$40-50
   Mk II #21 Le Mans Winner 1966,
      #3019...............................$40-50
   Mk II Street Version, #3021 ....$40-50
Ford Mustang 350 GT 1965, #3101.....$40-50
Ford Mustang Cobra
   Convertible 1994 Indy Pace car, red,
      #3108............................$45-55
   Coupe, 1994, #3119, Rio red........$45-55
   Coupe, 1994, #3119, white $45-55
   Coupe, 1994, #3119, black $45-55
Ford Mustang GT 1994
   Convertible, red, #3110 ....$45-55
   Convertible, teal, #3110 ....$45-55
   Convertible, yellow, #3110 ....$45-55
   Coupe, red, #3111 ....$45-55
   Coupe, teal, #3111 ....$45-55
   Coupe, yellow, #3111 ....$45-55
Nissan 300 ZX
   red, #3501 ....$40-50
   gray, #3503 ....$40-50
   yellow, #3504..........................$40-50
Porsche 911 1973
   RS 2.7 L, white and red, #3201........$40-50
   RS 2.7 L, yellow and black, #3203 ...$40-50
   RS 2.7 L, black and red, #3204........$40-50
   S 2.4, red, #3205 ....$40-50
   Honda Acura NSX, gray, #3502 ....$40-50

Jouef 1:24 Scale

Ferrari 250 GTO
   1964, #3003 ....$15-20
   #25 Le Mans 1964, #3028 ....$20-25
Ferrari 330 P 4 Spyder, #3027.............$20-25

Ford GT 40, #3007 ....$15-20

Jouef 1:43 Scale
Ferrari 250
    GT SWB, 1961, #3011 ....$12-16
    GTO 1964, #3004.....................$12-16
Ferrari 330 P4
    #3009.....................................$12-16
    #2 Le Mans Winner 1966, #3025...$12-16
Ferrari GTO Evoluzione, #3000 ....$12-16
Ford GT 40, #3006 ....$12-16
Mk II, #2 Le Mans Winner 1966,
    #3026......................................$12-16
Porsche 911 RS 2.7 L 73, #3027 ....$12-16

Jouets de Paris (JEP)
The Societe Industrielle de Ferblanterie was founded in 1899. In 1928, the name Jouets de Paris was adopted, then later changed to Jouets en Paris (abbreviated J.E.P.), until 1965 when the company went out of business. A variety of models and materials make up this eclectic collection of toys from France, with a predominance of tinplate models.

Autobus, "Madeline-Bastille," 10¼" circa
    1928 ....$2,000-2,250
Citroën DS19, 1:43, 1958 plastic body,
    diecast chassis $150-225
Delage Limousine, 13½" circa 1929 ...$2,000-2,250
Panhard Dyna, 1:43, plastic body, diecast
    chassis, 1958.......................$150-225
Peugeot, 1:43, plastic body, diecast
    chassis, 1958.......................$150-225
Renault Dauphine, 1:43, plastic body,
    diecast chassis, 1958 ....$150-225
Renault Town car 40HP President of the Republic,
    tinplate, 1:11 scale, 17".....$6,000-10,000
Simca Versailles, 1:43, plastic body, diecast
    chassis, 1958.......................$150-225

Joustra
The resemblance of Joustra diecast models of France to early Gama trucks indicates that Joustra may have manufactured these models under license from Gama, since most Joustra toys are tin windups.

Meiller Dump Truck, 4⅜".....................$40-45
Meiller Excavator Truck, 6¼"..................$40-45

JPS
BP 25
58130–Guerigny, France
tel: 33 (0) 3 86 37 36 74
fax: 33 (0) 3 86 37 00

JPS models are 1:43 scale prepainted resin kits made in France.

ACR Le Mans 1980, JPS065..................$40-50
ALD C289
    Le Mans 1989, JPS140............$45-55
    Le Mans 1990, JPS054............$40-50
    Le Mans 1994, JPS095............$45-55
Alpa Le Mans 1994, JPS096 ....$40-50
Alpine A110
    Championnat Course de Côte 1977,
        JPS025.............................$40-50
    Ronde Cévenome 1975, JPS011 ......$40-50
    Rallye des 1000 pistes 1976
        Andruet, JPS122 ....$40-50
    Rallye du Maroc 1974, JPS041........$40-50
    Rallye du Bandama Pescarolo, JPS086..$40-50
    Rallycross 1977 Bruno Saby, JPS132....$45-55
Alpine A310
    Le Mans 1978, JPS108............$45-55
    V6 1st Var 1976, JPS137.................$40-50
    V6 GR5 "Carlberson," JPS165 .....$45-55
    V6 GR5 Tour de France 1976, JPS170..$40-50
Alpine A610
    JPS048 ....$40-50
    "Magy cours," JPS049.....................$40-50
    1993, JPS111 ....$45-55
    Le Mans 1994, JPS071............$40-50
Alpine GTA Production 1986, JPS012 .....$40-50
Austin Healey "Frogeyes," JPS037 ....$40-50
Barquette Hommel
    JPS116....................................$45-55
    record du monde 100,000 km,
        JPS142 ....$45-55
Berliet Stradair Transporter Matra Gitanes,
    JPS226.................................$80-100
Berlinette Echappement, JPS073 ....$40-50
BMW 2002 Le Mans 1975, JPS184......$45-55
Bugatti 251
    JPS080....................................$40-50
    3-Car Set, JPS081 ....$105-120
Bugatti 332
    Grand Prix de Tours 1923, JPS050....$40-50
    "Juneck" with figures, JPS084 ....$40-50
Chevrolet Styleline
    1952 Convertible, JPS179................$40-50
    1952 Fastback Coupe, JPS196.........$40-50
    1952 Sedan, JPS167 ....$40-50
    Bel Air Coupe, JPS221 ....$40-50
Chevron B8 LM 1969, JPS192..............$45-55
Chevron B12 Repco Le Mans 1968,
    JPS216..................................$45-55
Chevron B16 Le Mans 1970
    JPS082....................................$40-50
    3-Car Set, JPS083 ....$100-120
Citroën U55 "Chamboursy," JPS075 ....$75-90

Citroën ZX Kit car
    Rallycross 1996 Caty Caly, JPS121 ...$40-50
    Spain Winner 1997, JPS134............$40-50
Courage C52 "Pescarolo Sports" Le Mans
    2000, JPS219......................$45-55
Daewoo Promotech
    Andros #12, JPS152.................$45-55
    Andros 1999 #11, JPS182 ....$45-55
    Andros 1999 #19/45, JPS181 ....$45-55
Debora
    Le Mans 1994, JPS076....................$40-50
    Le Mans 1995, JPS105..............$45-55
    Le Mans 1996 or 4 Hours of Le Mans
        1996, JPS127 ....$45-55
    Le Mans 2000, JPS224..............$45-55
    LMP296 Le Mans 1998, JPS171......$45-55
Facel Vega Excellence, JPS191 ....$45-55
Helem V6 RJ Racing Essais
    Le Mans 1997 #36, JPS144 ....$45-55
    Le Mans 1997 #37, JPS145 ....$45-55
Hotchkiss 686GS
    Coach 1939, JPS042....................$40-50
    Coupe 1939, JPS057....................$40-50
Inaltera Le Mans 1976 #1 or 2, JPS233 ..$45-55
Jeep Cherokee
    "Limited" Pompiers Meurthe et Moselle,
        JPS061 ....$45-55
    Chief 2-door, JPS059 ....$40-50
JIDE 1600 Renault Cévennes 1971,
    JPS203.................................$45-55
Joest 1st Le Mans 1997, JPS138............$45-55
Jules 6 roues Paris Dakar 1984, JPS008...$40-50
Leyland Matra camion utilisé par l'équipe
    Matra Sports, JPS193 ....$110-130
Leyland Transporter Ligier Gitanes,
    JPS214 ....$110-130
Leyland Transporter Matra Gitanes,
    JPS227 ....$110-130
Lola T212 Le Mans 1971#50 "Camel–
    Philips," JPS231 ....$45-55
Lola T292 1st Gr6 Le Mans 1976,
    JPS228 ....$45-55
Lola T298
    Le Mans 1979 #20, JPS212 ....$45-55
    Le Mans 1980 #27, 1981 #31-33,
        JPS198.............................$45-55
    Le Mans 1981 #31, JPS199 ....$45-55
March 75S LM 75, JPS211 ....$45-55
Matra 530
    "Sonia Delauney," JPS036 ....$40-50
    LX, JPS027 ....$40-50
    SX, JPS056 ....$40-50
Matra 630
    Le Mans 1967 #29/30, JPS180......$45-55
    Le Mans 1968 Pescarolo–Servoz–
        Gavin, JPS172 ....$45-55

Matra 660 Le Mans 1971, JPS229 ....$45-55
Mazda Kudzu Le Mans 1995, JPS097 ....$40-50
Mercedes-Benz SLK
   "Carlsson" 1998, JPS169 ....$45-55
   "Carlsson" 24 Hours at Nurburgring
      2000, JPS218 ....$45-55
   "Carlsson" Presentation, JPS187 ....$45-55
Moynet Simca XS Le Mans 1969, JPS225 ...$45-55
Nissan Micra 3-Door
   "Lagoon ou Cypia," JPS149 ....$40-50
   Andros 1998 24 Hours of Chamonix,
      JPS157 ....$45-55
   Andros 2000 #4 Collard Malcher,
      JPS206 ....$45-55
   Andros 2000 #7 Richelmi Balas,
      JPS209 ....$45-55
   phase 2, Andros, JPS186.................$45-55
   phase 2, JPS190 ....$40-50
Nissan Terrano 2 Chassis court, JPS078 ...$40-50
NSU 1000 C, JPS174 ....$40-50
NSU 1300 Groupe 2 J P Schwartz,
   JPS100 ....$40
NSU Pick-Up, JPS168 ....$40-50
NSU Silhouette GR5, JPS045 ....$40-50
NSU Spider Wankel, JPS158 ....$45-55
Opel Astra "Silhouette" Champion 2000,
   JPS223 ....$45-55
Panhard DB "Le Mans" Cabriolet, JPS200 ..$45-55
Panhard Riffard
   Le Mans 1953 #50 or 61, JPS079 ...$40-50
   Le Mans 1954 #58 or 59, JPS128 ...$45-55
   Le Mans 1954 #60, JPS135 ....$40-50
Peugeot 104 ZS Gr.2 Tour de Corse
   1977, JPS201 ....$45-55
Peugeot 201C
   Convertible, JPS094 ....$40-50
   Coupe, JPS094 ....$40-50
Peugeot 205 GTI Gr.N Var 1987
   (Delecour), JPS235.......................$45-55
Peugeot 306
   16S, 24 Hours of Spa "Laffite–
      Witmeur," JPS161 ....$45-55
   16S, JPS162................................$40-50
   16S, "Magny-cours," JPS163 ....$40-50
   16S, "Gendarmerie," JPS164............$40-50
   GR. N Tour de Corse 1999,
      JPS197 ....$45-55
Peugeot 406 Coupe 100,000 kms,
   JPS205 ....$45-55
Peugeot 607 HDI Raid endurance 500,000
   Km, JPS232 ....$45-55
Peugeot d'Angel Paris Dakar 1986,
   JPS017 ....$40-50
Peugeot J7 Matra, JPS215.......................$65
Porsche 908/03 Le Mans 1976 "Egon
   Evertz," JPS185 ....$45-55

Porsche 924 Le Mans 1980 #2-3-4,
   JPS202 ....$45-55
Porsche 934
   Le Mans 1976 #54 "Meznaries,"
      JPS230....................................$45-55
   Le Mans 1976 #57 "Gelo,"
      JPS159....................................$45-55
   Le Mans 1978 "Urcun," JPS155 ....$45-55
   Le Mans 1978 #68 "Jagermeister,"
      JPS141....................................$45-55
   Le Mans 1980 #80, JPS220 ....$45-55
   kit non peint pour décalcs BAM, Solido
      etc., JPS150...............................$35-45
Renault 2CV Proto, JPS018 ....$40-50
Renault 4CV Proto, JPS035 ....$40-50
Renault 5
   Alpine GR 2 Monte Carlo 1978 #12 or
      19, JPS124 ....$40
   Alpine GR2 Monte Carlo 1980
      Saby, JPS166..............................$40-50
   Alpine Turbo Groupe 2 Didier Auriol,
      JPS089....................................$40-50
   Didier Auriol (2-Car Kit Set and
      figures), JPS090 ....$70
   Turbo, JPS034 ....$40-50
   Turbo 1, JPS091 ....$40-50
   Turbo GR B Monte Carlo 1983
      Ragnotti, JPS147.........................$45-55
   Turbo GR B Monte Carlo 1983
      Ragnotti, JPS148.........................$45-55
   Turbo GR B Tour de Corse 1986
      Manzagol, JPS156 ....$45-55
   Turbo Rallye de Lorraine Didier Auriol,
      JPS088....................................$40-50
Renault Spider
   Legeay Sport Essais Le Mans 1996 #31
      red, JPS117 ....$45-55
   Legeay Sport Essais Le Mans 1996 #32
      blue, JPS118 ....$45-55
   RJ Racing Warm Up Le Mans 1996,
      JPS126....................................$45-55
   RJ Racing 4 Hours of Le Mans 1996,
      JPS129....................................$45-55
Renault Clio 16S GR N Tour de Corse
   1995 McOudry, JPS112 ....$45-55
Renault Dauphine Queron Cévennes
   1971, JPS154 ....$45-55
Renault Espace
   "Magy cours," JPS046...................$40-50
   "Pompiers du Loir et Cher," JPS051.....$45-55
   "Renault F1," "Transport Motors,"
      JPS021....................................$45-55
   Ambulance Pompiers Meurthe et
      Moselle, JPS062 ....$45-55
   Phase 2, JPS022 ....$40-50
Renault F1 Motor Home, JPS020.........$110-130

Renault Mégane
   Andros 1999 Ragnotti, JPS177..........$45-55
   Andros 2000 #12 Fina, JPS208........$45-55
   Andros 2000 #33 Pierrot Gourmant,
      JPS207....................................$45-55
Renault Clio Trophy Andros 2000 L.
   Fouquet, JPS210.........................$45-55
Renault Primaquatre "Saprar" 1939
   Convertible, JPS131 ....$45-55
   Roadster, JPS130 ....$45-55
Renault Twingo V6
   Andros 1998, JPS160.....................$45-55
   Andros 1999 (phase 2), JPS178........$45-55
Rondeau M482 Le Mans 1983
   "Concessionnaires Ford," JPS234......$45-55
Salmson 2300S Charbonneaux, JPS047 ...$40-50
Simca 1000 5-door Station Wagon
   "Gendarmerie," JPS189 ....$40-50
Simca 1100 5-Door Station Wagon,
   JPS188 ....$40-50
Spice
   Le Mans 1991 #45 "Financial
      Times," JPS136.........................$45-55
   Le Mans 1993 #24, JPS055 ....$40-50
   Le Mans 1991 #39, JPS143 ....$45-55
Spice C2
   Le Mans 1990 #102, JPS023 ....$40-50
   Le Mans 1990 #116, JPS024 ....$40-50
Talbot Coupe 2.5 Liter 1955, JPS107 .....$45-55
TOJ SC206 BMW Le Mans 1979,
   JPS217 ....$45-55
Triumph 1800 Roadster 1949 (maquette
   C.P.C.), JPS236............................$45-55
Vespa 400, JPS074 ....$35-45
WM P78 Le Mans 1978, JPS103 ....$40
WM P176 Le Mans, JPS195.................$45-55

JRD

From 1935 to 1962, J. R. D. produced toys from Montreuil, France. Beginning in 1958, J.R.D. started marketing diecast models. Prior to that time, they were made of plaster and flour. When J.R.D. failed in 1962, C.I.J., also of France, purchased the dies and packaging, and marketed them as their own, sometimes by placing a simple label over the previous brand name on the package.

Citroën 2CV
   EDF Van, 1:45, 1958, #108 ....$80-105
   Fire Van, 1:45, 1958, #109..........$90-115
   Sedan, 1:45, 1958, #110...........$80-105
   Van, 1:45, 1958, #111.................$75-90
   Road Service Van, 1:45, 1958,
      #117....................................$90-115
   "Air France" Van, 1:45, 1958, #118...$90-115

Citroën 11CV Sedan, 1:45, 1958,
#112 ....$90-115
Citroën 1200 KG
Police Van, 1:45, 1962, #106 ......$80-105
Red Cross Van, 1:45, 1958, #107...$90-115
Van "Esso," 1:45, 1958, #113...........$100
Citroën Ami 6, 1:45, 1962, #154.........$75-90
Citroën DS19
Cabriolet, 1:45, 1962, #152 ....$75-90
Sedan, 1:45, 1958, #116............$80-105
Citroën P55
Covered Truck, 1:45, 1958, #114...$75-90
Army Truck & Trailer, 1:45, 1958,
#115......................................$90-115
Berliet Bottle Truck, 1:45, 1962, #134 ..$160-185
Berliet Fire Truck, 1:45, 1961, #133....$175-200
Berliet Garbage Truck, 1:45, 1960,
#131......................................$145-160
Berliet Semi-Trailer
"Kronenbourg," 1:45, 1958, #120.......$175-200
Tanker "Total," 1:45, 1958, #121...$160-175
"Antargaz," 1:45, 1961, #132 ...$160-185
Berliet Weitz Crane Truck, 1:45, 1959,
#125 ....$145-160
Fruehauf Truck Trailer, 1:45, 1959,
#129 ....$120-145
Mercedes-Benz 220S Sedan, 1:45,
1962, #153 ....$75-90
Peugeot 404 Sedan, 1:45, 1962, #151...$75-90
Simca 1000 Sedan, 1:45, 1962, #155...$75-90
Unic Cab, Trailer & Railroad car, 1:45,
1958, #123 ....$200-225
Unic Izoard Circus Train, 1:45, 1958,
#124 ....$200-225
Unic Liquid Transporter, 1:45, 1960,
#130 ....$145-160
Unic Tank Truck
"Antar," 1:45, 1958, #122.........$145-160
Milk, 1:45, 1959, #128..............$160-185
Unic Van
"Hafa," 1:45, 1959, #126.........$175-200
"Transports Internationaux," 1:45,
1959, #127 ....$175-200

J.R.D. 1980s Reissues from C.I.J.

Citroën DS19
#111, previously #116.....................$25-30
Convertible, #112, previously #152....$25-30
Citroën 2CV
Sedan, #211, previously #110.........$25-30
Fire Van, #221, previously #109.......$25-30
Van, #223, previously #111 ....$25-30
Citroën 11CV Sedan, #401, previously
#112 ....$25-30
Citroën HY Van, #301, previously #113...$25-30

JRI (see Road Champs)

JRL Collectibles

JRL Toys
23158 Bernhardt St
Hayward, CA 94545 USA

JRL has offered just a few precision detailed diecast models. The specimen I acquired as an example is a 1:18 scale Dodge Ram 3500 "Dually" Pick Up that has opening doors, hood, and tailgate, functional steering, fully detailed engine, drive train, and exhaust system, and Goodyear Wrangler AT blackwall tires. The model is copyright dated 1995; the box is copyrighted 1997. The price marked from a local collectibles dealer was $40, but I purchased it for 25 percent off during an after-Christmas sale. EWA listed the same model in black and red, and a 1:12 scale Viper in red or black. At last check, JRL is out of business.

Dodge Ram 3500 1995 "Dually" Pickup
black and red, 1:18, #01 ....$45-60
white, 1:18 #01 ....$45-60
Dodge Viper RT/10
black, 1:12, #7120B..................$150-175
red, 1:12, #7120R.....................$150-175

JTE

A single model has been identified from JTE. Harvey Goranson reports that John Day also produced an Inaltera among the hundreds of other early crude white metal kits. There may be a connection.

Inaltera Team 1978, blue, 1:43 ....$25-50

Juguinsa

Juguinsa of Venezuela produced a small but eclectic assortment of 1:43 scale models.

AMC Javelin 343 Coupe, 1:43...............$20-25
Fiat 124 Coupe, 1:43 ....$20-25
Monteverdi Coupe, 1:43 ....$20-25

Jupiter

Jupiter is a brand of 1:43 scale white metal models from Belgium. When the brand was introduced and whether they are still in business is not known. What is known is that they produced a 1960 Plymouth Valiant and a T-Bird in the early 1990s. Dick Brown, who reported these model via e-mail (DICKATL@aol.com) in March 2000, says they are an offshoot of a firm called Gaston that makes truck models. They are quite expensive even by 1:43 scale white metal standards.

1960 Plymouth Valiant, circa 1993 ....$200-250
1960 Ford Thunderbird, circa 1993
convertible, top up $200-250
convertible, top down.................$200-250
hardtop with sunroof....................$200-250
2-seat roadster............................$200-250

Jurgens

Jurgens models are hand-built 1:43 scale models reportedly made in Germany.

1937 Packard Wagon..........................$65-80
1940 Dodge Wagon $65-80
1948 Chrysler Town & Country
Convertible $65-80
1950 Buick Wagon..............................$65-80

K

K&D Automobilia

Toys for Collectors of Watertown, New York, offers eleven K&D models. Their website at www.tfcusa.com reports that these are hand-built 1:43 scale white metal models by Milestone Miniatures, commissioned by K&D Automobilia and produced in England in small numbers by expert Old World craftsmen.

1951 Chrysler Saratoga Club Coupe, 1:43,
pea green with black roof, "32" on
doors $165-175
red with "7" on doors $165-175
1952 Chrysler Windsor Deluxe Coupe, 1:43,
two-tone green..........................$165-175
1968 Ford Torino Convertible, 1:43,
metallic gold $120-120
1966 Mercury Comet Convertible, 1:43,
metallic light blue $120-130
metallic bronze $120-130
1947 Nash Pace Car, 1:43, cream with
black roof..................................$160-170
1948 Nash, 1:43, two-tone $140-150
1965 Plymouth Fury Pace Car, 1:43,
white..$150-160
1939/40 Studebaker Van, 1:43, yellow,
"Studebaker Authorize Service"......$130-140
1940 Studebaker Champion Deluxe, 1:43,
brown with tan roof $130-140

K&M

K&M Planning Co., Ltd., of Japan is known to have issued just one model, a 1979 Dome-O RL LeMans entry, according to Harvey Goranson, who attended LeMans in 1981 and witnessed a single such car sponsored by Amada. ("The team had cool samurai shirts!")

1979 Hayashi Dome-O Exotic car, white
with orange and black stickers, sponsored
by Roland, 1:43.............................$38-45

K&O

From 1952 to 1962, K & O was the premiere manufacturer of toy boat motors in both metal and plastic. A list of models produced can be found on Alterscale's website at www.alterscale.comkolist.html and in a book titled *Toy Outboard Motors* by Jack Browning, $22.95, 150 pages of compiled articles (by Jack Browning) with photos. Available only from the author: Jack Browning, 214 16th Street, Roanoke, VA 24017 (phone: 540-982-1253). Comment: This is the only comprehensive work in existence on this subject. It covers principally the K&O motors (in detail) but touches on many other toy outboards. It includes a list of toy outboard collectors with names and addresses. Jack Browning is one of the world's premier collectors of toy outboards. Values are otherwise unknown.

K&R Replicas

www.kandrreplicas.co.uk

K&R represents 1:43 and 1:24 scale white metal kits and hand-built models, mostly of British sports cars. Harvey Goranson reports that they have been around since the late 1970s to early 1980s, and have at one time been connected with Abingdon Classics, as referenced by the "ACE" model number designation.

K&R Replicas 1:24 models

Austin Healey 3000
  Mk 2, late form wind-up windows,
    KAR2426, 1:24, kit price...........$90-95
  built price single color $225-240
  built price two-tone body $245-260
  Mk 3, kit builds either the Phase I or
    Phase II, KAR2424, 1:24,
    kit price $120-145
  built price single color $250-300
  built price with two-tone body $350-400
Daimler Sovereign, KAR2428, 1:24,
    kit $120-140
  built $275-300
Ford Escort
  Mk 2 RS2000 1975-77, KR90, 1:24,
    kit $30-35
    built..$70-80
  Mk 2 RS2000 1978-80, KR91, 1:24,
    kit $30-35
    built..$70-80
  Mk 2 RS1800, KR92, 1:24, kit........$30-35

built..............................$70-80
Mk 2 Mexico, KR93, 1:24, kit $30-35
  built..$70-80
Mk 2 1300 Sport, KR98, 1:24, kit....$30-35
  built..$70-80
Mk 2 1600 Sport, KR99, 1:24, kit....$30-35
  built..$70-80
Mk 2 Harrier, KR100, 1:24, kit $30-35
  built..$70-80
Mk 2 RS2000 XPAC/Zakspeed Road
  Car, KR131, 1:24, kit....................$30-35
  built..$75-80
Mk 2 Flat Fronted XPAC/Zakspeed Road
  Car, KR132, 1:24, kit....................$30-35
  built..$75-80
Mk 2 RS2000 Merseyside Police,
  KRES2, 1:24, kit.........................$30-35
  built..$80-85
Mk 2 Nottingham Police Panda Car,
  KRES4, 1:24, kit.........................$30-35
  built..$80-85
Mk 2 Heathrow Police Panda Car,
  KRES5, 1:24, kit.........................$30-35
  built..$80-85
Mk 2 Metropolitan Police Panda
  Car, JYH605N, KRES6, 1:24,
  kit $30-35
  built..$80-85
Mk 2 Metropolitan Police Panda
  Car, UYX797S, KRES7, 1:24,
  kit $30-35
  built..$80-85
Mk 2 Metropolitan Police Panda
  Car, CYW536W, KRES8, 1:24,
  kit $30-35
  built..$80-85
Mk 2 British Airways Rally car, KRRL39, 1:24,
  kit $30-35
  built..$80-85
Mk 2 Eaton Yale Rally car, KRRL40, 1:24,
  kit $30-35
  built..$80-85
Mk 2 Haynes Rally car, KRRL41, 1:24,
  kit $30-35
  built..$80-85
Mk 2 Allied Polymer Li-Lo 1978 Mintex
  Rally, KRRL42, 1:24, kit $30-35
  built..$80-85
Mk 2 Allied Polymer Cow Gum 1978
  Manx Rally, KRRL43, 1:24, kit $30-35
  built..$80-85
Mk 2 Cossack 1976 RAC Rally,
  KRRL44, 1:24, kit.......................$30-35
  built..$80-85
Mk 2 Allied Polymer 1975 RAC
  Rally, KRRL45, 1:24, kit $30-35

built..............................$80-85
Mk 2 Allied Polymer Gandy 1976 Texaco
  Tour of Britain, KRRL46, 1:24, kit ...$30-35
  built..$80-85
Mk 2 Daily Express 1977 RAC Rally,
  KRRL47, 1:24, kit.........................$30-35
  built..$80-85
Mk 2 Andrews Heat For Hire 1979
  RAC Rally, KRRL54, 1:24, kit.......$30-35
  built..$80-85
Mk 2 Rothmans 1980 Mintex Rally 1ST
  Vatanen, KRRL38, 1:24, kit $30-35
  built..$85-90
Mk 2 Rothmans 1980 Acropolis Rally
  Vatanen or Mikkola, KRRL55, 1:24,
  kit $30-35
  built..$85-90
Mk 2 Rothmans 1980 RAC Rally
  Vatanenor, KRRL56, 1:24, kit $30-35
  built..$85-90
Mk 2 Rothmans 1981 RAC
  Rally Vatanen/Airikkola/Wilson,
  KRRL57, 1:24, kit.........................$30-35
  built..$85-90
Mk 2 Rothmans 1981 Acropolis Rally
  Vatanen or Wilson, KRRL58, 1:24,
  kit $30-35
  built..$85-90
Mk 2 Rothmans 1981 Swedish Rally
  Vatanen or Airikkola, KRRL59, 1:24,
  kit $30-35
  built..$85-90
Mk 3 XR3, KR115, 1:24, kit $30-35
  built..$70-80
Mk 3 XR3i, KR116, 1:24, kit $30-35
  built..$70-80
Mk 4 RS Turbo Series 2, KR128, 1:24,
  kit $30-35
  built..$70-80
RS 1600i, KR114, 1:24, kit.............$30-35
  built..$70-80
RS Turbo Series 1, KR113, 1:24,
  kit $30-35
  built..$70-80
Ford P100 Pickup, KRCV13, 1:24,
  kit $30-35
  built..$70-80
Ford Sierra
  RS Cosworth 3-Door, KR144, 1:24,
  kit $30-35
  built..$70-80
  RS 500, KR129, 1:24, kit $30-35
  built..$70-80
  Sapphire RS Cosworth, KR121, 1:24,
  kit $30-35
  built..$70-80

Sapphire Cosworth, KR122, 1:24, kit...$30-35
   built..................................$70-80
Sapphire Northumbria Police, KRES9, 1:24,
   kit $30-35
   built..$80-85
Sapphire Q8 RAC Rally 1990 Wilson,
   KRRL64, 1:24, kit............$30-35
   built..$80-85
Sapphire Texaco Havoline Manx Rally
   1990 Brooks, KRRL65, 1:24,
   kit $30-35
   built..$80-85
Sapphire Q8 1000 Lakes Rally 1990
   Airikkola or Wilson, KRRL71, 1:24,
   kit $30-35
   built..$80-85

Ford V8 Pilot
   Saloon, KR17, 1:24, kit...................$25-30
   built..$70-80
   Woodie, KR18, 1:24, kit $30-35
   built..$70-80
   Police car, KRES1, 1:24, kit $30-35
   built..$70-80

Jaguar C-Type
   1951 Le Mans Winner, KAR2401, 1:24,
   kit $90-95
   built $200-225
   1951 Le Mans Winner, KRRL29, 1:43,
   kit $25-30
   built..$70-80
   1952 Seneca Cup Winner–John Fitch,
   KAR2412, 1:24, kit..................$90-95
   built $200-225
   1952 Seneca Cup Winner, KRRL68, 1:43,
   kit $25-30
   built..$70-80
   1953 Le Mans Belgian Team car, KAR2410,
   1:24, kit...................................$90-95
   built $200-225
   1953 Le Mans Winner, KAR2405, 1:24,
   kit $90-95
   built $200-225
   1953 Le Mans Winner, KRRL30, 1:43,
   kit $25-30
   built..$70-80
   1954 Ecurie Ecosse Spanish Grand Prix
   Team, LFS672, one nose stripe, 1:24,
   KAR2407, 1:24, kit..................$90-95
   built $200-225
   1954 Ecurie Ecosse Spanish Grand Prix
   Team, LFS671, two nose stripes, 1:24,
   KAR2408, 1:24, kit..................$90-95
   built $200-225
   1954 Ecurie Ecosse Spanish Grand Prix
   Team, LSF420, three nose stripes, 1:24,
   KAR2409, 1:24, kit..................$90-95

   built $200-225
1954 Le Mans Belgian Team car,
   KAR2411, 1:24, kit..................$90-95
   built $200-225
1954 Rheims Winner, KAR2425, 1:24,
   kit $90-95
   built $200-225
1954 Spanish Grand Prix Ecurie Ecosse
   Team LFS 672 one nose stripe, KRRL31,
   1:43, kit $25-30
   built..$70-80
1954 Spanish Grand Prix Ecurie Ecosse Team
   LFS671 two nose stripes, KRRL32, 1:43,
   kit $25-30
   built..$70-80
1954 Spanish Grand Prix Ecurie Ecosse
   Team LSF420 three nose stripes,
   KRRL33, 1:43, kit......................$25-30
   built..$70-80
1953 Belgian Team car Le Mans, KRRL69,
   1:43, kit $25-30
   built..$70-80
1954 Belgian Team Le Mans, KRRL70,
   kit $25-30
   built..$70-80

Jaguar D-Type
   1955 Le Mans Winner, KAR2402, 1:24,
   kit $90-95
   built $200-225
   1955 Le Mans Briggs Cunningham car
   (NO. 9), KAR2413, 1:24, kit $90-95
   built $200-225
   1956 LM Winner, KAR2406, 1:24,
   kit $90-95
   built $200-225
   1956 Reims Winner, KAR2429, 1:24,
   kit $90-95
   built $200-225
   1957 LM Winner, KAR2403, 1:24,
   kit $90-95
   built $200-225
replica Lynx '57 SAL' 1987 Record Breaker
   (50 MILES, 100KM, 200KM, 1 HOUR,
   200 MILES) Limited Edition of 150 built
   only, mounted on plinth, KAR2416,
   1:24 ....$325-350
Jaguar Mk 2 Saloon, KAR2420, 1:24,
   kit...$110-125
   built $250-275
Jaguar XJ6 Series 3, KAR2427, 1:24,
   kit...$120-140
   built $275-300
Jaguar XJ13, KAR2417, 1:24, kit........$110-125
   built $250-275
Jaguar XK120
   Road car, KAR2418, 1:24, kit......$110-125

   built $250-275
   Montlhery car, KAR2419, 1:24,
   kit...$110-125
   built $250-275
   Road car gold plated, Limited Edition of 25
   built only, KAR2421, 1:24 .....$300-325
Triumph 2.5 Mk 2 PI
   KR123, 1:24, kit $30-35
   built..$70-80
   Estate, KR140, 1:24, kit $30-35
   built..$70-80
Triumph 2000
   Mk 2, KR119, 1:24, kit....................$30-35
   built..$70-80
   Mk 2 Estate, KR137, 1:24, kit..........$30-35
   built..$70-80
   TC, KR124, 1:24, kit.......................$30-35
   built..$70-80
   TC Estate, KR138, 1:24, kit $30-35
   built..$70-80
Triumph 2500
   S, KR125, 1:24, kit........................$30-35
   built..$70-80
   S Estate, KR141, 1:24, kit................$30-35
   built..$70-80
   TC KR120, 1:24, kit.......................$30-35
   built..$70-80
   TC Estate, KR139, 1:24, kit $30-35
   built..$70-80
Triumph Dolomite
   1300 KR80, 1:24, kit......................$30-35
   built..$70-80
   1500 KR81, 1:24, kit......................$30-35
   built..$70-80
   1500 HL, KR82, 1:24, kit $30-35
   built..$70-80
   1850 HL, KR66, 1:24, kit $30-35
   built..$70-80
   Sprint, KR65, 1:24, kit.....................$30-35
   built..$70-80
Triumph GT6
   Mk 1, 1:24, KR142, 1:24, kit..........$25-30
   built..$70-80
   Mk 2, 1:24, KR63, 1:24, kit $25-30
   built..$70-80
   Mk 3, 1:24, KR31, 1:24, kit $25-30
   built..$70-80
Triumph Herald
   12/50 Sunroof, open, KR75, 1:24,
   kit $25-30
   built..$70-80
   12/50 Sunroof, closed, KR76, 1:24,
   kit $25-30
   built..$70-80
   13/60 Convertible, top down, KR61, 1:24,
   kit $25-30

built............................$65-75

13/60 Saloon, KR62, 1:24, kit........$25-30
built............................$70-80

13/60 Sunroof, open, KR77, 1:24,
kit $25-30
built............................$70-80

13/60 closed, KR78, 1:24, kit........$25-30
built............................$70-80

1200 Convertible, top down, 1961 to
Mid-1963, KR83, 1:24,
kit $25-30
built............................$65-75

1200 Convertible, top down, Mid-1963
onward, KR72, 1:24, kit $25-30
built............................$65-75

1200 Convertible, top up, Mid-1963
onward, KR72H, 1:24, kit........$25-30
built............................$70-80

1200 Coupe, KR74, 1:24, kit $25-30
built............................$70-80

1200 Saloon 1961 to Mid-1963, KR84,
1:24, kit $25-30
built............................$70-80

1200 Saloon Mid-1963 onward, KR73,
1:24, kit $25-30
built............................$70-80

Triumph Spitfire

1500 Convertible, top down, KR27, 1:24,
kit $25-30
built............................$65-75

1500 Convertible, top up, KR27H, 1:24,
kit $25-30
built............................$70-80

1500 Hardtop, KR27HT, 1:24, kit $25-30
built............................$70-80

1500 US version Convertible, top down,
KR29, 1:24, kit $25-30
built............................$65-75

1500 US version Convertible, top up,
KR29H, 1:24, kit....................$25-30
built............................$70-80

1500 US version Hardtop, KR29HT, 1:24,
kit $25-30
built............................$70-80

Mk 1 Convertible, top down, KR55, 1:24,
kit $25-30
built............................$65-75

Mk 2 Convertible, top down, KR56, 1:24,
kit $25-30
built............................$65-75

Mk 3 Convertible, top down, KR57, 1:24,
kit $25-30
built............................$65-75

Mk 4Convertible, top down, KR28, 1:24,
kit $25-30
built............................$65-75

Mk 4Convertible, top up, KR28H, 1:24,
kit $25-30
built............................$70-80

Mk 4Hardtop, KR28HT, 1:24, kit $25-30
built............................$70-80

Triumph Stag

Mk 1 Convertible, top down, KR45, 1:24,
kit $25-30
built............................$70-80

Mk 1 Convertible, top up, KR45H, 1:24,
kit $30-35
built............................$70-80

Mk 1 Hardtop, KR45HT, 1:24, kit $30-35
built............................$70-80

Mk 2 Convertible, top down, KR46, 1:24,
kit $25-30
built............................$70-80

Mk 2 Convertible, top up, KR46H, 1:24,
kit $30-35
built............................$70-80

Mk 2 Hardtop, KR46HT, 1:24, kit $30-35
built............................$70-80

Triumph TR2

Convertible top down, KR4, 1:24,
kit $25-30
built............................$65-75

Convertible, top up, KR4H, 1:24, kit ...$30-35
built............................$70-80

Hardtop, KR4HT, 1:24, kit............$30-35
built............................$70-80

High Speed car, KRRL36, 1:24, kit $25-30
built............................$65-75

Triumph TR3

Convertible, top down, KR5, 1:24,
kit $25-30
built............................$65-75

Convertible, top up, KR5H, 1:24,
kit $30-35
built............................$70-80

Hardtop, KR5HT, 1:24, kit............$30-35
built............................$70-80

Triumph TR3A, 1:24,

Convertible, top down, KR6, 1:24,
kit $25-30
built............................$65-75

Convertible, top up, KR6H, 1:24,
kit $30-35
built............................$70-80

Hardtop, KR6HT, 1:24, kit............$30-35
built............................$70-80

Triumph TR4, 1:24,

Convertible, top down, KR7, 1:24,
kit $25-30
built............................$65-75

Surrey Top, KR7ST, 1:24, kit $25-30
built............................$70-80

Triumph TR4A, 1:24,

Convertible, top down, KR8, 1:24,
kit $25-30
built............................$65-75

Surrey Top, KR8ST, 1:24, kit $25-30
built............................$70-80

Triumph TR5, 1:24,

Convertible, top down, KR9, 1:24,
kit $25-30
built............................$65-75

Surrey Top, KR9ST, 1:24, kit $25-30
built............................$70-80

Triumph TR6

European version Convertible, top
down, KR13, 1:24, kit $25-30
built............................$65-75

European version Convertible, top up,
KR13H, 1:24, kit................$25-30
built............................$70-80

European version Hardtop, KR13HT, 1:24,
kit $25-30
built............................$70-80

US version Convertible, top down, KR14,
1:24, kit $25-30
built............................$65-75

US version Convertible, top up, KR14H,
1:24, kit $25-30
built............................$70-80

US version Hardtop, KR14HT, 1:24,
kit $25-30
built............................$70-80

Triumph TR7

FHC, KR85, 1:24, kit....................$30-35
built............................$70-80

DHC, Convertible, top down, KR87, 1:24,
kit $30-35
built............................$70-80

Triumph TR8

DHC, KR117, kit $30-35
built............................$70-80

FHC, KR118, kit $30-35
built............................$70-80

Triumph TR250

Convertible, top down, KR130, 1:24,
kit $25-30
built............................$65-75

Surrey Top, KR130ST, 1:24, kit........$25-30
built............................$70-80

Triumph Vitesse

Mk 1 Convertible, top down, KR105, 1:24,
kit $25-30
built............................$65-75

Mk 1 Saloon, KR106, 1:24, kit........$25-30
built............................$70-80

Mk 2 Convertible, top down, KR58, 1:24,
kit $25-30

built.............................$65-75

Mk 2 Convertible, top up, KR58H, 1:24,
   kit.............................$25-30
   built.............................$70-80
Mk 2 Saloon, 1:24, KR60, 1:24, kit...$25-30
   built.............................$70-80

K&R Replicas 1:43 Scale Models

Austin Healey 100/4 BN1
   Convertible, top down, KR41, 1:43,
      kit.............................$25-30
      built.............................$65-75
   Convertible, top up, KR41, 1:43, kit....$25-30
      built.............................$70-80
   24 carat gold plated Limited Edition of 50
      built only, with individual certificate,
      1:43, KR64.............................$75-85

Austin Healey 100/4 BN2
   Convertible, top down, KR42, 1:43,
      kit.............................$25-30
      built.............................$65-75
   Convertible, top up, KR42H, 1:43,
      kit.............................$25-30
      built.............................$70-80

Austin Healey 100/6 2-seater
   Convertible, top down, KR32, 1:43,
      kit.............................$25-30
      built.............................$65-75
   Convertible, top up, KR32H, 1:43,
      kit.............................$25-30
      built.............................$70-80
   Hardtop, KR32HT, 1:43, kit.............$25-30
      built.............................$70-80
   Ear's Court Show Car 1958 "Goldie"
      limited Edition of 250, KR33, 1:43
      built only.............................$80-90

Austin Healey 100/6 4-seater
   Convertible, top down, KR16, 1:43,
      kit.............................$25-30
      built.............................$65-75
   Convertible, top up, KR16H, 1:43,
      kit.............................$25-30
      built.............................$70-80
   Hardtop, KR16HT, 1:43, kit.............$25-30
      built.............................$70-80

Austin Healey 100M
   Convertible, top down, KR43, 1:43,
      kit.............................$25-30
      built.............................$65-75

Austin Healey 100S
   Convertible, top down, KR44, 1:43,
      kit.............................$25-30
      built.............................$70-80
   Mille Miglia 1955 (Healey), KRRL61, 1:43,
      kit.............................$30-35
      built.............................$70-80

Sebring 1955 (Moss), KRRL62, 1:43,
   kit.............................$30-35
   built.............................$70-80
Nassau Trophy 1955 (Moss), KRRL63, 1:43,
   kit.............................$30-35
   built.............................$70-80

Austin Healey 3000
   Mk 2 Luxembourg Rally Car 1997
      Historic Grand Prix of Europe
      (Brandy), KRRL48, 1:43, kit.........$30-35
      built.............................$70-80
   Rally Car Regular. NO. 2754DK, KRRL34,
      kit.............................$25-30
      built.............................$75-80
   Rally Car Himalayan Rally car, KRRL35,
      kit.............................$30-35
      built.............................$70-80
   Works Car Le Mans 1962 DD300, KRRL37,
      kit.............................$25-30
      built.............................$70-80

Austin Healey 3000
   Works Rally Car 2754DK, KRRL34, 1:43,
      kit.............................$30-40
      built.............................$75-85
   Rally Car–Himalayan Rally, KRRL35, 1:43,
      kit.............................$30-35
      built.............................$70-80
   Works Car Le Mans 1962 DD300, KRRL37,
      1:43, kit.............................$25-30
      built.............................$70-80
   Mk 1 Convertible, top down, KR20, 1:43,
      kit.............................$25-30
      built.............................$65-75
   Mk 1 Hardtop, KR20HT, 1:43, kit.....$25-30
      built.............................$70-80
   Mk 1 2-seater, Convertible, top down,
      KR97, 1:43, kit.............................$25-30
      built.............................$65-75
   Mk 1 2-seater, Hardtop, KR97HT, 1:43,
      kit.............................$25-30
      built.............................$70-80
   Mk 2 Luxembourg Rally Car 1997,
      KRRL48, 1:43, kit.............................$30-35
      built.............................$70-80
   Mk 2 Convertible, top down, KR21, 1:43,
      kit.............................$25-30
      built.............................$65-75
   Mk 2 Convertible, top up, KR21H, 1:43,
      kit.............................$25-30
      built.............................$70-80
   Mk 2 flat screen 2-seater, Convertible,
      top down, KR102, 1:43, kit........$25-30
      built.............................$65-75
   Mk 2 flat screen 2-seater, Convertible, top up,
      KR102H, 1:43, kit.............................$25-30
      built.............................$70-80

Mk 2 flat screen 2-seater,
   Hardtop, KR102HT, 1:43, kit......$25-30
   built.............................$70-80
Mk 2 flat screen 4-seater, Convertible,
   top down, KR104, kit.............$25-30
   built.............................$65-75
Mk 2 flat screen 4-seater, Convertible,
   top up, KR104H, kit.............$25-30
   built.............................$70-80
Mk 2 flat screen 4-seater,
   Hardtop, KR104HT, kit.............$25-30
   built.............................$70-80
Mk 2A Convertible, top down, KR26,
   1:43, kit.............................$25-30
   built.............................$70-80
Mk 3 Convertible, top down, KR1, 1:43,
   kit.............................$25-30
   built.............................$65-75
Mk 3 Convertible, top up, KR1H, 1:43,
   kit.............................$25-30
   built.............................$70-80
Mk 3 Hardtop, KR1HT, 1:43, kit.......$25-30
   built.............................$70-80
Mk 3 European Healey Meeting
   Luxembourg 1999 Limited Edition
   model, KR110, 1:43.............$75-80
Mk 3 Phase I, Convertible, top down,
   KR103, 1:43, kit.............$25-30
   built.............................$65-75
Mk 3 Phase I, Convertible, top up,
   KR103H, 1:43, kit.............$25-30
   built.............................$70-80

Austin Healey Sprite
   Mk 1 9-Stud (Frogeye) Convertible, top
      down, KR12A, 1:43, kit.............$25-30
      built.............................$65-75
   Mk 1 9-Stud (Frogeye) Convertible,
      top up, KR12AH, 1:43, kit..........$25-30
      built.............................$70-85
   Mk 1 2-Stud (Frogeye) Convertible,
      top down, KR12B, 1:43, kit........$25-30
      built.............................$65-75
   Mk 1 2-Stud (Frogeye) Convertible,
      top up, KR12BH, 1:43, kit..........$25-30
      built.............................$70-85
   Mk 1 2-stud (Frogeye) Hardtop,
      KR12BHT, 1:43, kit.............$25-30
      built.............................$70-85
   Mk 2 1961/62, Convertible, top
      down, KR36, 1:43, kit.............$25-30
      built.............................$65-75
   Mk 2 1962/64, Convertible, top
      down, KR37, 1:43, kit.............$25-30
      built.............................$65-75
   Mk 3 1964/66, Convertible, top
      down, KR38, 1:43, kit.............$25-30

built $65-75

Mk 4 1966/69, Convertible, top
   down, KR39, 1:43, kit $25-30
   built $65-75
Mk 4 1969/71, Convertible, top
   down, KR40, 1:43, kit $25-30
   built $65-75

BRM P25
   KRRL15, 1:43, kit..................$25-30
   built $65-75
   Dutch Grand Prix Winner Jo Bonnier,
   KRRL49, 1:43, kit.................$25-30
   built $65-75

Connaught A-Type
   British Grand Prix 1952, KRRL22, 1:43,
    kit $25-30
    built $65-75
   International Trophy 1952, KRRL23, 1:43,
    kit $25-30
    built $65-75

Cooper Bristol Mk 2
   KRRL14, 1:43, kit..................$25-30
   built $65-75
   Belgian Grand Prix 1952 Hawthorn,
   KRRL52, 1:43, kit...................$25-30
   built $65-75
   British Grand Prix 1953 Wharton,
   KRRL25, 1:43, kit...................$25-30
   built $65-75
   Lavant Cup 1952 Hawthorn, KRRL53, 1:43,
    kit $25-30
    built $65-75
   Cooper Monaco 61M, KRRL2, 1:43, kit...$25-30
   built $65-75

Ferrari 246 Dino
   Behra / Brooks 1959, KRRL9, 1:43, kit ..$25-30
   built $70-80
   US Grand Prix Sebring 1959 Phil Hill,
   KRRL26, 1:43, kit...................$25-30
   built $70-80
   Ferrari 375 1951 Gonzalez Silverstone,
   KRRL5, 1:43, kit....................$25-30,
   built $70-80

Ferrari 500
   1952/53 Ascari British Grand Prix, KRRL3,
    1:43, kit $30-35
    built $70-80
   1952 Rosier Italian Grand Prix, KRRL50,
    1:43, kit $25-30
    built $70-80
   1953 Swaters Winner Avus Ring, KRRL3,
    1:43, kit $25-30
    built $70-80

Ferrari 553 Squalo
   International Trophy 1954 Gonzalez,
   KRRL20, 1:43, kit...................$25-30

built $70-80

French Grand Prix 1954 Gonzalez,
   KRRL19, 1:43, kit....................$25-30
   built $70-80
Spanish Grand Prix 1954 Hawthorn,
   KRRL16, 1:43, kit...................$25-30
   built $70-80

Ferrari 625
   1954 Gonzalez British Grand Prix,
   KRRL4, 1:43, kit....................$25-30
   built $70-80
   Daily Express Trophy 1954 Parnell,
   KRRL18, 1:43, kit...................$25-30
   built $70-80

Ferrari 625A
   1953 Argentina Grand Prix Gonzalez,
   KRRL17, 1:43, kit...................$25-30
   built $70-80
   1955 Trintingnant Monte Carlo, KRRL6,
    1:43, kit $25-30
    built $70-80
   Ferrari Tasman Dino Hoare NZ Grand
    Prix 1961, KRRL8, 1:43, kit........$25-30
    built $70-80
Ferrari Thinwall Special Vandervell, KRRL7,
   1:43, kit............................$25-30
   built $70-80
Ford King Cobra, KRRL1, 1:43, kit..........$25-30
   built $65-75

Jaguar C-Type
   1951 Le Mans Winner, KRRL29, 1:43,
    kit $25-30
    built $70-80
   1952 Seneca Cup Winner, KRRL68, 1:43,
    kit $25-30
    built $70-80
   1953 Belgian Team car Le Mans,
   KRRL69, 1:43, kit...................$25-30
   built $70-80
   1953 Le Mans Winner, KRRL30, 1:43,
    kit $25-30
    built $70-80
   1954 Belgian Team Le Mans, KRRL70,
    1:43, kit $25-30
    built $70-80
   1954 Spanish Grand Prix Ecurie Ecosse
    Team LFS 672 one nose stripe,
    KRRL31, 1:43, kit...................$25-30
    built $70-80
   1954 Spanish Grand Prix Ecurie Ecosse
    Team LFS671 two nose stripes,
    KRRL32, kit $25-30
    built $70-80
   1954 Spanish Grand Prix Ecurie Ecosse
    Team LSF420 three nose stripes,
    KRRL33, kit $25-30

built $70-80

Lola T70 MK3B
   Nurburgring 1969, KRRL10, 1:43,
    kit $25-30
    built $70-80
   Le Mans 1969, KRRL11, 1:43, kit $25-30
    built $70-80
   Monza 1969, KRRL12, 1:43, kit.......$25-30
    built $70-80
   Daytona/Sebring 1969, KRRL13, 1:43,
    kit $25-30
    built $70-80

MG 1925 Old No. 1
   ACE11, 1:43, kit....................$25-30
   built $65-75
   Land's End Trial–Kimber, KRRL60, 1:43,
    kit $30-35
    built $75-85

MG EX 135 Humbug
   ACE5, 1:43, kit.....................$25-30
   built $70-75
   Brooklands 500 Mile International Trophy
    1935, KRRL21, 1:43, kit.........$25-30
    built $65-75

MG J2
   Swept Wings, ACE52, 1:43, kit $25-30
   built $75-85
   Cycle Wings, ACE53, 1:43, kit........$25-30
   built $75-85

MG M-Type Midget
   Convertible, top down, ACE33, 1:43,
    kit $25-30
    built $65-75
   Midget Police car with driver and
    passenger, Convertible, top down,
    KRES3, 1:43, kit $30-35
    built $70-80

MG Magnette
   MK III, ACE 54, 1:43, kit $30-35
   built $70-80
   MK IV, ACE 55, 1:43, kit...............$30-35
   built $70-80

MG Midget
   1500, Convertible, top down, ACE29,
    1:43, kit $25-30
    built $65-75
   Mk 1 1961/62, Convertible, top
    down, ACE23, 1:43, kit $25-30
    built $65-75
   Mk 1 1962/64, Convertible, top down,
    ACE24, 1:43, kit $25-30
    built $65-75
   Mk 2 1964/66, Convertible, top
    down, ACE25, 1:43,
    kit $25-30
    built $65-75

Mk 3 1966/69, Convertible, top
down, ACE26, 1:43, kit $25-30
built.................................$65-75

Mk 3 1969/71, Convertible, top
down, ACE27, 1:43, kit $25-30
built.................................$65-75

Mk 3 1972/74, Convertible, top
down, ACE28, 1:43, kit $25-30
built.................................$65-75

MG PA Midget 2-seater

Convertible, top down, ACE56, 1:43,
kit $25-30
built.................................$65-75

Convertible, top up, ACE56H, 1:43,
kit $25-30
built.................................$70-80

ACE58, 1:43, kit $30-35
built.................................$70-80

MG PB Midget 2-Seater

Convertible, top down, ACE57, 1:43,
kit $25-30
built.................................$65-75

Convertible, top up, ACE57H, 1:43,
kit $25-30
built.................................$70-80

Airline, ACE59, 1:43, kit.............$30-35
built.................................$70-80

MG TA

Midget 1948/49, Convertible, top
down, ACE45, 1:43, kit $25-30
built.................................$65-75

Tickford Convertible, top down,
ACE47, 1:43, kit $25-30
built.................................$65-75

Tickford Convertible, top up, ACE47H,
1:43, kit $25-30
built.................................$70-80

MG TB

Midget Convertible, top down, ACE46,
1:43, kit $25-30
built.................................$65-75

Midget Coupe De Ville, ACE47CDV,
1:43, kit $25-30
built.................................$70-80

Tickford, Convertible, top down,
ACE48, 1:43, kit $25-30
built.................................$65-75

Convertible, top up, ACE48H, 1:43,
kit $25-30
built.................................$70-80

Coupe De Ville, ACE48CDV, 1:43,
kit $25-30
built.................................$70-80

MG TC Midget

1948/49, Convertible, top down,
ACE40, 1:43, kit $25-30

built.................................$65-75

1948/49, Convertible, top up,
ACE40H, 1:43, kit $25-30
built.................................$70-80

1945/7, Convertible, top down,
ACE41, 1:43, kit $25-30
built.................................$65-75

1945/7, Convertible, top up,
ACE41H, 1:43, kit $25-30
built.................................$70-80

Kent Police car Regular JKR411,
KRES12, 1:43, kit $25-30
built.................................$65-75

MG TD

Dundrod Tourist Trophy 1950 Lund/Phillips/
Jacobs, KRRL66, 1:43, kit $30-35
built.................................$70-80

Silverstone InternationalTrophy 1950 Lund/
Phillips / Jacobs, KRRL67, 1:43,
kit $30-35
built.................................$70-80

Midget 2-wiper windscreen, Convertible,
top down, ACE30, 1:43, kit.......$25-30
built.................................$65-75

Midget 2-wiper windscreen, Convertible,
top up, ACE30H, 1:43, kit.........$25-30
built.................................$70-80

Midget 2-wiper windscreen,
Newcastle Police, Convertible, top
down, KRES10, 1:43, kit............$25-30
built.................................$65-75

Midget 3-wiper windscreen, Convertible,
top down, ACE31, 1:43, kit.......$25-30
built.................................$65-75

Midget 3-wiper windscreen, Convertible,
top up, ACE31H, 1:43, kit.........$25-30
built.................................$70-80

MG TF Midget

Convertible, top down, ACE49, 1:43,
kit $25-30
built.................................$65-75

Convertible, top up, ACE49H, 1:43,
kit $25-30
built.................................$70-80

MGA 1500

Roadster Convertible, top down,
ACE7A, 1:43, kit $25-30
built.................................$65-75

Roadster Convertible, top up, ACE7AH,
1:43, kit $25-30
built.................................$70-80

Roadster Hardtop, ACE7AHT, 1:43,
kit $25-30
built.................................$70-80

Roadster Twin Cam 1958, Convertible,
top down, ACE7B, 1:43, kit.......$25-30

built.................................$65-75

Roadster Twin Cam 1958, Convertible,
top up, ACE7BH, 1:43, kit $25-30
built.................................$70-80

Roadster Twin Cam 1958,
Hardtop, ACE7BHT, 1:43, kit $25-30
built.................................$70-80

Coupe, ACE34, 1:43, kit.................$25-30
built.................................$70-80

MGA 1600

Mk 1 Roadster Convertible, top
down, ACE8A, 1:43, kit $25-30
built.................................$65-75

Mk 1 Roadster Convertible, top up,
ACE8AH, 1:43, kit....................$25-30
built.................................$70-80

Mk 1 Roadster Hardtop, ACE8AHT,
1:43, kit $25-30
built.................................$70-80

Mk 1 Coupe, ACE36, 1:43, kit $25-30
built.................................$70-80

Mk 2 Roadster Convertible, top down,
ACE9, 1:43, kit $25-30
built.................................$65-75

Mk 2 Roadster Convertible, top up,
ACE9H, 1:43, kit......................$25-30
built.................................$70-80

Mk 2 Roadster Hardtop, ACE9HT, 1:43,
kit $25-30
built.................................$70-80

Mk 2 Roadster De Luxe Convertible,
top down, ACE10, 1:43, kit......$25-30
built.................................$65-75

Mk 2 Roadster De Luxe Convertible, top
up, ACE10H, 1:43, kit $25-30
built.................................$70-80

Mk 2 Roadster De Luxe Hardtop,
ACE10HT, 1:43, kit...................$25-30
built.................................$70-80

Mk 2 Coupe, ACE38, 1:43, kit $25-30
built.................................$70-80

Mk 2 De Luxe Coupe, ACE39, 1:43,
kit $25-30
built.................................$70-80

MGA Twin Cam

1958 Coupe, ACE35, 1:43, kit $25-30
built.................................$70-80

1960 Roadster Convertible, ACE8B,
top down, 1:43, kit....................$25-30
built.................................$65-75

1960 Roadster Convertible, top up,
ACE8BH, 1:43, kit....................$25-30
built.................................$70-80

1960 Roadster Hardtop, ACE8BHT,
1:43, kit $25-30
built.................................$70-80

1960 Coupe, ACE37, 1:43, kit $25-30
    built......................................$70-80

MGB

Mk 1 Convertible Roadster, top down, ACE1,
    1:43, kit $25-30
    built......................................$65-75

Mk 1 Convertible Roadster, top up, ACE1H,
    1:43, kit $25-30
    built......................................$70-80

Mk 1 Hardtop Roadster, ACE1H, 1:43,
    kit $25-30
    built......................................$70-80

Mk 1 Hardtop Roadster Devon Police Car
    Duo 383C, KRES11, 1:43, kit $25-30
    built......................................$70-80

Mk 2 Convertible Roadster, top down,
    ACE2, 1:43, kit $25-30
    built......................................$65-75

Mk 3 Convertible Roadster, top down,
    ACE3, 1:43, kit $25-30
    built......................................$65-75

MGB GT

Jubilee model, ACE19, 1:43, kit........$30-35
    built......................................$70-80

LE model, ACE20, 1:43, kit $30-35
    built......................................$70-80

rubber bumper, ACE17, 1:43, kit $30-35
    built......................................$70-80

V8 chrome bumper, ACE16, 1:43,kit ...$30-35
    built......................................$70-80

V8 rubber bumper, ACE18, 1:43, kit...$30-35
    built......................................$70-80

Mk 1 ACE12, 1:43, kit...................$30-35
    built......................................$70-80

Mk 2 ACE13, 1:43, kit...................$30-35
    built......................................$70-80

Mk 3 recessed grille, ACE14, 1:43, kit...$30-35
    built......................................$70-80

Mk 3 honeycomb grille, ACE15, 1:43, kit..$30-35
    built......................................$70-80

MGB LE

Convertible Roadster, rubber bumper,
    top down, ACE4, 1:43, kit $25-30
    built......................................$65-75

Convertible Roadster, top down,
    ACE32, 1:43, kit $25-30
    built......................................$70-80

Convertible Roadster, top up, ACE32H,
    1:43, kit $30-35
    built......................................$70-80

MGB Roadster US version

1971/74, Convertible, top down, ACE42,
    1:43, kit $25-30
    built......................................$65-75

1974, Convertible, top down, ACE43,
    1:43, kit $25-30

built......................................$65-75

LE model, Convertible, top down,
    ACE44, 1:43, kit $25-30
    built......................................$70-80

rubber bumper, Convertible, top
    down, ACE50, 1:43, kit $25-30
    built......................................$65-75

Costello version, Convertible, top down,
    ACE 51, 1:43, kit $25-30
    built......................................$65-75

MGC

GT, ACE22, 1:43, kit $30-35
    built......................................$70-80

Roadster, Convertible, top down,
    ACE6, 1:43, kit $25-30
    built......................................$65-75

Morris 1000 Van–Abingdon Spares
    Limited Edition of 100 built, KRCV12,
    1:43..................................$70-80

K-Line

K-Line Electric Trains, Inc., Chapel Hill, North Carolina, is primarily known for their HO gauge (1:87 scale) electric trains, K-Line also produces a series of HO gauge semi tractor/trailers in various liveries, intended as accessories for their train sets.

Diet Coke Tractor Trailer with railroad flat car,
    K-666703TT...........................$30-40

Father's Day Bank, K-820301 ....$30-40

Ferrara Nougat Candy Tractor Trailer,
    K-813301TT...........................$30-40

Happy Birthday Gift Bank, K-826101......$30-40

Hershey's "Take a Bite," K-811201TT......$30-40

Hershey's "The Great American Chocolate Bar,"
    K-811202TT...........................$30-40

Hershey's "Life is Sweet!," K-811203TT....$30-40

Hershey's "First Love," K-811204TT $30-40

K-Line Electric Trains Vintage Delivery Truck
    Bank, K-8201 ....$30-40

K-Line Oil Company Vintage Tanker,
    K-82601 ....$30-40

Ringling Bros. and Barnum & Bailey Circus
    Tractor Trailer, K-665603TT $30-40

Special Addition Vintage Truck Bank (Boy),
    K-820202..............................$30-40

Special Addition Vintage Truck Bank (Girl),
    K-820801..............................$30-40

Valentine's Gift Bank, K-820302 ....$30-40

Kaden

KADEN s.r.o. Novy Hrádek
Rokolská 126
549 22 Novy Hrádek, Czech Republic
tel.: 491 478 215
fax: 491 478 283

tel./fax: 494 665 512, 494 665 141, or 494 665 141
e-mail: kaden@kaden.cz
www.kaden.cz

Kaden Ltd. produces diecast replicas in 1:24, 1:43 and 1:87 scales. Besides scale models, Kaden, based in Novy Hrádek, Czech Republic, also manufactures water meters and satellite dish supports and stands.

Kaden 1:24 Scale Models

Dodge WC-51, 1:24

Army Truck, Army green, no canopy,
    K607 ....$20-35

Wrecker, blue, K611 ....$20-35

Tunis, K624 ....$20-35

Dodge WC-52, 1:24

Arctic, white, K609 ....$20-35

Covered Army Truck, Army green, K608 ..$20-35

Feuerwehr (Fire Department), red,
    K610 ....$20-35

Krankwagen (Wrecker), red, K612 ....$20-35

Halftrack M3, 1:24

K623 ....$20-35

A1 with armaments, K626 ....$20-35

Ardeny, K625 ....$20-35

Personnel, K627 ....$20-35

US ¼-Ton Trailer, K628 ....$20-35

Volkswagen 82 Kübelwagen, 1:24

Tropic, K615 ....$20-35

Afrikakorps, K613 ....$20-35

Ambulance, K614 ....$20-35

East, K616 ....$20-35

Luftwaffe, K620 ....$20-35

Volkswagen 166 Schwimmwagen

East, K617 ....$20-35

West, K618 ....$20-35

Officer, K619...............:..............$20-35

Willys Jeep, 1:24

Ambulance, K622 ....$20-35

Commando, K602 ....$20-35

Commando Invasion, with ¼-Ton Trailer
    and Equipment, K604 ....$20-35

Feuerwehr (Fire Department), red,
    K606 ....$20-35

Military Police, K 603 ....$20-35

U. S. Mail, K605 ....$20-35

US Army with ¼-Ton Trailer, 1:24,
    K621 ....$20-35

Kaden 1:43 Scale Models

Skoda Fabia, 1:43

gold, K0567................................$15-25

red, K0567 ....$15-25

Skoda Fabia Wagon, 1:43, K0567

metallic blue $15-25

white $15-25
black $15-25
Skoda Octavia, 1:43
Sedan, white, K0556 .... $15-25
Sedan, black, K0556 .... $15-25
Sedan, red, K0556 .... $15-25
Sedan, metallic green, K0556 .... $15-25
Sedan, metallic silver-blue, K0556 .... $15-25
Wagon, red, K0558 .... $15-25
Wagon, black, K0558 .... $15-25
Wagon, metallic silver blue, K0558 .... $15-25
Wagon, metallic green, K0558 .... $15-25
Police Sedan, K0564 .... $15-25
Police Wagon, K0565 .... $15-25
Sedan Mobile Service, K0560 .... $15-25
Wagon Mobile Service, K0562 .... $15-25
Sport, K0100 .... $15-25
Skoda Superb, 1:43
silver $15-25
red $15-25
blue $15-25
Police, white $15-25
Police, black $15-25
Tatra 613 Mini, 1:43, K0447 .... $15-25
Tatra 815, 1:43
Auto Salvage, K0508 .... $15-25
Auto Transporter, K0500 .... $15-25
CAS 32, K0488 .... $15-25
Dump Truck, K0499 .... $15-25
Grand Tourist Caravan, K0486 .... $15-25
Paris-Dakar Rally Support Vehicle, K0480 .... $15-25
Paris-Kapske Mesto Rally Support Vehicle, K0501 .... $15-25
Paris-Peking 4x4 Rally Support Vehicle, K0514 .... $15-25
Paris-Peking 6x6 Rally Support Vehicle, K0514 .... $15-25
Racing Team, K0543 .... $15-25
Safari, K0495 .... $15-25

Kaden 1:87 Scale Models

Skoda Fabia, 1:87, K0573 .... $10-20
Coupe, silver $10-20
Coupe, green $10-20
Coupe, yellow $10-20
Wagon, metallic burgundy $10-20
Wagon, blue $10-20
Wagon, green $10-20
Skoda Superb Sedan, 1:87
blue $10-20
silver $10-20
black $10-20
white $10-20
red $10-20
Police $10-20

Kado

Kado of Japan offers 1:43 scale diecast models (not to be confused with Kato, also of Japan).

F-1 Racer $40-45
Hayashi Dome-O Exotic car $40-45
1957 Opel Rekord (tin) $40-45
Porsche 930 Coupe $40-45
Porsche 356 Speedster, silver with brown seats, chrome bumper $40-45
Porsche 356 Speedster, blue with brown seats, chrome bumper $40-45
Porsche 356 Speedster, red, with brown seats, chrome bumper $40-45
Porsche 930 Turbo, metallic green with black interior,wipers, mirror $40-45
Porsche 930 Turbo, metallic gold with black interior, wipers, mirror $40-45

Kager GmbH

13 Borsigstrasse
Heusenstamm 63150 Germany
phone: 49-6104-2098
fax: 49-6104-5943

Whether Kager is still in business is unknown. What is known is that the German company licensed Chrono of China to produce a 1:18 scale Lotus Elise for them. According to the Sands Mechanical Museum website at www.sandsmuseum.com, the model is of mediocre quality and was produced in several other colors besides the Norfolk Mustard listed below.

Lotus Elise 1997, Norfolk Mustard, 1:18, Kager / Chrono H1020 .... $25-35

Kansas Toy & Novelty Company

Kansas Toy & Novelty Company started in 1923 when Arthur Haynes, an auto mechanic, began making toys out of his Clifton, Kansas, shed. The association between Kansas Toy, Ralstoy, and others based in the Midwest in the 1930s and 1940s is that they swapped dies with each other to establish a partnership. This makes discerning one brand from another very difficult since models were usually not marked.

Army Tank, #74, 2¼" $50-65
Austin Bantam Sedanette, #58, 2¼" $35-50
Bearcat Racer
#26, 4" $75-90
#33, 3" $50-65
Buick Roadster
with rumble seat, #54, 2⅜" $20-35
with no trunk, #54, 2¼" $35-50
Case Steam Tractor, #25, 3" $70-85
Chevrolet Sedan
2⅞" $30-45
2¼" $40-55
Chrysler Convertible Coupe
#8, rear mount spare, 3⅛" $40-55
#8, no rear mount spare, 3⅛" $60-75
5" $75-90
Chrysler Roadster
#14, 3⅛" $35-50
no number, 3⅛" $50-65
Convertible Coupe
2⅞" $60-75
#35, 2¼" $50-65
Coupe, 3⅛" $60-75
Dump Truck, #42, 3½" $70-85
Fageol Overland Bus
#9, 3½" $75-90
no number, 3½" $60-75
Farm
Dirt Scraper, #65, 3⅝" $50-65
Dirt Tumble, #64, 4" $40-55
Disc Harrow, #62, 4" $70-85
Planter, #61, 4" $70-85
Plough, #63, 4" $60-75
Tractor, #17, 2⅞" $50-65
Tractor, no number, 2⅝" $60-75
Fire Engine, #70, 2¼" $75-90
Ford
Pickup Truck, #51, 2¾" $50-65
Stake Truck Semi & Trailer, #55, 4" $65-80
Fordson Farm Tractor, #57, 1¾" $25-40
Golden Arrow Record Car Racer, #46, 2⅞" $25-40
Indy Racer, #10, 3⅛" $50-65
John Deere Model D Large Farm Tractor, no number, 4⅞" $75-90
Large Lady Racer with driver, 6" $60-75
Midget Racer
with no driver, 3" $40-55
with driver, 3" $80-95
#31, 2⅛" $20-35
#67, 1½" $90-105
Pickwick COE
1928 Nite Coach Tour Bus, #49, 2⅜" $60-75
Tour Bus, #59, 3⅜" $50-65
Racer, 1" $35-50
Railroad
Box car, #38, 3¼" $40-55
Caboose, #40, "KT&N RR," 2¾" $60-75
Livestock car, #41, "KT&N RR" $60-75
Locomotive Tender, #36, 4⅜" $15-20
Pullman car, #37, 3½" $40-55
Tank car, #39, "KT&N RR," 3⅛" $60-75
Sedan
Limousine, 3⅜" $60-75
#60, 3½" $45-60

Separator-Thresher

#27, 3"..............................$70-85

#72, 2"..............................$50-65

Steam

Road Roller, #43, 3¼"........$20-35

Tractor, #71, 2½"...............$20-35

Three-Wheel Coupe, #66, 3½" $60-75

Truck, #20, 3⅛".................$30-45

Warehouse Tractor, #48, 3"..................$35-50

Kawabatakikaku (or J43 Kawabatakikaku)

As reported by Robert Speerbrecher (see Silver Pet), this Japanese brand is represented by mid-1960s Japanese sports cars in 1:43 scale. Such an unusual name begs for more research, but no information is found on the Internet or anywhere else.

Datsun Fairlady 200P $60-70

Honda S600..............................$60-70

Kawada

www.kawadamodel.co.jp (Japanese)

www.kawadamodel.co.jp/e/index.html (English)

Kawada of Japan produces radio-controlled model kits.

Kay

Kay was best known in Great Britain for manufacturing electrical, chemistry, and tool sets, as well as lead miniatures. The company also served as the packaging company for Taylor & Barrett and Charbens. The Kay brand was part of the Kempner family, located in Carlisle Road, London, England. At one time, Kay also produced a range of 1:70 scale prototypical diecast toy cars with clockwork motors. Only the Austin Devon is recognizable as a replica of a real car.

Ambulance..............................$35-45

Austin A40 Devon $45-55

Bus $35-45

Coupe..............................$35-45

Double Decker Bus $35-45

Fire Pumper..............................$35-45

Taxi..............................$35-45

Truck $35-45

Van $35-45

Kazan

Only since the fall of the Iron Curtain have we in the USA discovered such a goldmine of diecast toys from the former Soviet Union. Kazan models are named after the town in which they were produced. Started in 1979, Kazan's main focus was on the many variations

of the Kamaz truck introduced in 1978. The following list offers the various versions of this workhorse truck.

Kazan 1978 Kamaz Truck, 1:43

4x2 Dropside Truck

#5325..............................$24-28

with tilt "Sovtransavto," #5325..........$25-35

Dropside Truck

#5320..............................$25-35

"1945-1985," #5320..............$25-35

"1917-1987," #5320..............$25-35

with tilt, #5320..............$25-35

with tilt "Lada Spares," #5320..........$25-35

Dump Truck

#55105..............................$25-35

#5511..............................$25-35

"Mocctpon," #5511..............$25-35

"Moscow 1980," #5511..............$25-35

Long Wheelbase Truck

#53212..............................$25-35

with tilt, #53212..............$25-35

with tilt "Sovtransavto," #53212........$25-35

Military Truck 6x6, #43105..................$25-35

Tanker "Moloko," #53212..............$25-35

Tractor Unit

#5410..............................$12-16

and Trailer, #5410..............$25-35

Trailer and Tilt, #5410..............$30-40

Kellerman (see CKO)

Kellerman of Germany is synonymous with CKO. Whenever listings are found on eBay, particularly eBay Germany (www.ebay.co.de), Kellerman is always referenced in tandem with CKO.

Kelmet

Kelmet of Chicago, Illinois, produced large, heavy pressed steel toys starting in 1925. Typical weight of these durable toy trucks was around ten pounds. Trumodel and Big Boy are associated brands.

Big Boy Steam Shovel........................$500-800

Trumodel Derrick with power hoist and tip

bucket........................$2,000-2,500

White

Aerial Ladder Truck, 30".........$1,500-2,000

Army Truck, 1929, 25"....$1,750-2,250

Chemical Truck $1,750-2,250

Coal Pocket Loader $2,750-3,250

Crane Truck........................$5,750-6,250

Dump Truck, #501, 25".........$2,500-3,000

Fire Truck with Ladder............$2,750-3,250

Sand Loader........................$2,000-2,500

Scissor Dump Truck, 25".........$1,200-1,500

Tank Truck, 27"....................$4,500-5,000

Kembo

Lovell Bros. & Jardine of 60 Priory Road, Southpark, Reigate, Surrey, England, formed the Kembo trademark in 1948, specializing in zinc alloy and aluminum diecasting.

Excavator..............................$45-60

1947 Jowett Javelin

Saloon..............................$45-60

Saloon with motor $45-60

Police car with loudspeaker $45-60

Police car with loudspeaker and motor ...$45-60

Scammell

Articulated Truck.....................$45-60

Articulated Flat Truck $45-60

Breakdown Truck $45-60

Kemlow

Kemlow Diecasting Products Ltd. was founded in North London, England, by Kempster and Lowe. The box is typical of 1950s diecast from Great Britain. The distinction is that it is marked "A Wardie Product," likely indicating its distributor B. J. Ward Ltd. "Master Model," "Sentrybox" and "Wee World Series" are other monikers applied to the model's box. Recognizing such models out of their respective boxes is a bit more difficult. Here is a list of known models.

Kemlow produced models for Automec, and possibly Kembo. Their own 1950s Master Models line specialized in accessories and garage equipment for model railroads.

Kemlow Models

Armored car

1:60..............................$50-60

with Field Gun, 1:60......................$75-90

Articulated Lumber Truck, 1:50 ....$50-60

Bedford S Military Covered Truck

1:50..............................$50-60

with Munition Trailer and Field Gun,

1:50........................$100-120

Caravan, 1:43 ....$50-60

Field Gun, 1:60..............................$25-30

Flat Truck, 1:50..............................$50-60

Ford Zephyr Mark I, 1:43 ....$100-120

Munition Trailer, 1:50..........................$25-30

Removal Van "Pickford's," 1:60..........$100-120

Thornycroft Mighty Antar

1:43..............................$75-90

1:60..............................$50-60

Tractor and Farm Cart $50-60

Ford Zephyr 1953 Saloon

1:43..............................$50-60

Caravan, 1:43 ....$100-120
Thornycroft Mighty Antar, 1:60..............$50-65

Kemlow Master Models
Esso Garage $20-30
Esso Petrol Pumps $20-30
Esso Oil Cabinets $20-30

Kenna
6, Edwards Close, Byfield, Daventry
Northants NN11 6XP Great Britain
phone/fax: 01327 260835
e-mail: petekenna@freenetname.co.uk
http://kennamodels.tripod.com/Default.htm

Besides the beautiful handcrafted white metal 1:43 scale models from Great Britain that Pete Kenna makes, his company also produces models and masters for Spa Croft Models.

Kenna 1:43 Scale White Metal Models
Allard K2
    black...$120-130
    white...$120-130
    yellow $120-130
    dark red $120-130
Austin A40 Convertible
    pale green $155-170
    pale yellow $155-170
    red $155-170
Austin A40 Devon
    peacock blue $155-170
Austin A40 Devon Countryman $140-155
Austin A40 Dorset
    white...$155-170
Austin A70 Hereford
    brown $155-170
    maroon and silver $155-170
Austin A70 Hereford Convertible
    top down, powder blue $140-150
    top up, fawn $140-150
Austin A70 Hereford Countryman
    white...$155-170
    maroon $155-170
Daimler DE36 Straight Eight
    silver and red $140-155
    black and red............................$140-155
Ford Woody Wagon 1939.............$120-135
Lotus II...$110-125
Lotus Hexagon Estate car.................$135-150
MG 18/80, yellow and black two-seat
    roadster, 1:43, KE015AF.............$110-125
MG TF
    black...$115-130
    white...$115-130
    red $115-130
    British racing green.....................$115-130

Standard Ambulance $135-150
Standard Vanguard
    Pick Up $135-150
    Racing Car Transporter $140-155
Triumph Herald 12/50 Saloon..........$140-155
Wolseley Nine $135-150

Kenna 1:43 Scale Pedal Cars
J40 (based on the Austin A40 Devon)
    blue $45-60
    red $45-60
    white...$45-60
Joy 1 (based on the Austin 8)
    red $45-60
    silver...$45-60
    white...$45-60
Pathfinder Special Racing Car
    beige $45-60
    red $45-60

Kenner
Kenner, now owned by Hasbro (who also now owns Tonka and several other venerable toy brands), is well known for its huge assortment of toys. It's Girder & Panel and Bridge & Turnpike construction sets were extremely popular in the 1960s and 1970s. Hasbro in turn is sustained by the perennial popularity of its G. I. Joe action figures.

Most familiar of the Kenner diecast line is Kenner Fast 111's, produced around 1980 and styled after the wildest Hot Wheels and Johnny Lightnings. But their popularity (and speed) could never compete much with either. Still, Kenner Fast 111's are slowly and steadily gaining popularity as a collectible and can still be purchased very cheaply, around $2 apiece or less.

Kenner has recently produced a five-car set of 1:64 scale vehicles based on the movie *Batman Forever* which is slowly rising in value. The set is currently worth about $8 – 10.

Currently, the Kenner brand mostly encompasses Star Wars figures and playsets. In March of 1996, Mattel failed in an attempt to buy out Hasbro, securing the integrity of the Kenner brand as well.

Beginning in 1997, Kenner offered a line called Winner's Circle. 1997 Stock Car Series Winner's Circle cars are 1:64 scale cars with a trading card depicting the driver. Also produced are a couple of rail dragsters and funny cars. By 2003, the Winner's Circle line, originally produced for Kenner by Action Performance, was taken over by Action Performance.

Kenner Fast 111's
Chevrolet Monza "Fun 'E'" Car....................$5-7
    1980 Corvette Stingray $5-7
    1980 Firebird.......................................$5-7
Gravel Grinder Jeep, white with yellow stars,
    blue stripes..$5-7
Master Blaster
    red with white, black, yellow tampo,
        yellow "2" on hood $5-7
    white with blue, black, red tampo, red "2"
        on hood...$5-7
1980 Mustang Cobra $5-7
NA 217 ....$5-7
Pipe Dreamer, red with blue and black stripes ..$5-7
Rallye Champ, white with red, blue, purple
    flames, "Rallye" on spoiler $5-7

Shark Car with fins, #1027 ....$5-7

Sporty Shifter, orange with blue, white, black
    race tampos.......................................$5-7
Street Boss, black with rebel flag $5-7

T R Terrific, blue with yellow and green stripes, yellow "8" on hood.....................$5-7

Trans Am...$5-7

Turbo Turret $5-7

Twin Tank Turbo..................................$5-7

Kenner Winner's Circle, 1:64 Scale

Bobby Labonte #18 Interstate, 1997 ....$5-10
Dale Earnhardt #3
    Goodwrench, 1997 ....$45-60
    Silver 2nd release, 1997 ....$25-30
    '96 Goodwrench, 1997 ....$30-35
    Wheaties (Wheaties uniform on card),
        10,107 produced, 1997.......$145-160
Jeff Gordon #24
    DuPont, 1997 ....$5-10
    '96 DuPont, 1997 ....$5-10
Mike Skinner #31, '96 Lowe's, 1997........$5-10
Ward Burton #22, Caterpillar, 1999 ....$5-10

Kenton (also see Kingsbury)

Kenton Hardware Company of Kenton, Ohio, produced cast iron toys, banks, and an assortment of household hardware from 1890 to 1952. Sales sagged by 1931, so a partnership was formed between Kenton and Kingsbury. An entire 184-page book (*Kenton Cast Iron Toys*, Schiffer Publishing, ISBN 0887409806) has been devoted to Kenton toys. Below is a small sample listing of their oldest transportation toys from the late 1800s to the 1920s.

Auto Bus, #516, 6½" circa 1920 ....$1,250-1,750
Auto Circus Calliope, 1924 ....$1,250-1,750
Auto Dump Truck, 6½" $400-550
Buckboard, mechanical, #650, 1902,
    9" $2,750-3,250
Coal Truck, 10⅜" early 1930s $500-750
Clown Chariot with clown driver and camel,
    circa 1900, 10" $700-900
Empire State Express Train with Locomotive, Coal
    car, 1 short and 1 long Passenger Coach,
    circa 1900, 82" $2,000-2,500
English Trap, one horse carriage with driver and lady
    passenger, circa 1900,14½" $3,000-3,500
Fire Patrol
    two horses with driver and four other firemen,
        P310, pre-1900s $1,750-2,250
    three horses with driver and four other firemen,
        P325, pre-1900s $2,250-2,750

two smaller horses with driver and four other
    firemen, P510, pre-1900s...$1,500-2,000
Hansom
    mechanical, #610, 1902,
        6½".................................$2,750-3,250
    non-mechanical, #615, 1902,
        6½".................................$2,750-3,250
Hansom Cab, one horse and driver, 1902,
    8"...$500-750
Happy's Police Patrol, mechanical, two horses,
    driver and policeman, 1905,
        17½"...............................$4,750-5,250
Hose cart, two horses and driver, circa 1900,
    17".................................$1,750-2,250
Katzenjammer Toy, single-axle cart pulled by
    donkey, driver, 1905, 12"
    passenger spanking a child $2,750-3,250
    passenger spanking a child, second passenger
        standing, 1905, 12"........$2,750-3,250
Lift Dump Truck, 6½" circa 1930....$1,000-1,500
Locomotive, mechanical, #630, 1902,
    7½" $1750-2250
Log Wagon, two horses and black driver,
    1901, 16" 1,000-1,500
Lumber Truck with two planks, 1930,
    11¾".................................$1,750-2,250
Overland Circus Hippopotamus Cage
    Truck, 1924, 8" $1,150-1,650
Ox Team and Log Wagon with two oxen
    and black driver, 1900, 17½"...$2,250-2,750
Rabbit cart, rabbit-drawn with rabbit driver,
    nickel plated, 1903, 4⅞" $350-500
Red Cross Ambulance, with one horse, gong
    and driver, 1902, 16"...........$3,250-3,750
Seeing New York 899, 10½" 1905 ...$4,250-4,750
Side-Wheeler Steamboat, mechanical,
    #601, 1902, 7½"..................$3,250-3,750
Sight Seeing Auto 899, 10½"
    1905 ....$3,250-3,750
Spider Phaeton, one horse with driver,
    1901, 13½" $2,550-3,250
Sulky, one horse with driver, silver painted with
    red wheels, 8," circa 1900 ....$300-450
Surrey
    mechanical, #620, 1902, 7"...$3,250-3,750
    non-mechanical, #625, 1902,
        7".................................$3,250-3,750
Water Tower Truck, 1916, 24"....$2,250-2,750

Kentoy

Kentoy is a relatively obscure brand of toys made in Hong Kong. Their brand name has been seen on plastic toy trucks issued as Tonka trucks in the 1990s and on a few import tuners from Boley. No model list is available as of this writing.

Keystone

Boston, Massachusetts, was home to Keystone from around 1922 until 1958. Chester Rimmer and Arthur Jackson started the company in Malden, Massachusetts, first under the name of Jacrim, then shortly thereafter established a facility at 288 "A" Street, Boston. Keystone produced movie projectors, pressed wood forts and garages, wooden boats, and sturdy steel trucks.

Aerial Ladder Truck, #79, 30½".....$1,250-1,750
American Railway Express Truck, #43,
    26" $2,250-2,750
Bus, 7¼" plastic, circa 1955 ....$75-90
Cabover Dump Truck, 25".................$350-500
Chemical Pump Fire Engine, #57,
    27½"..................................$1,250-1,750
Circus Cage Truck, "World's Greatest Circus,"
    circa 1930s, 26"..................$3,000-4,500
Coast to Coast Bus, wind-up, #84,
    31"..................................$2,500-3,000
Divco Dairy Delivery Truck, "Pure Milk," #D-402,
    circa 1950 ....$300-400
Dugan Brothers Truck, #41, 26½".....$1,000-1,250
Dump Truck, #41, 26½"...............$1,000-1,250
Dump Truck, "Keystone" on door, electric lights,
    1937, 23" $500-750
Fire Truck, #49, 27½".......................$450-600
Fire Truck, #52, 27½" $1,250-1,750
Hydraulic Dump Truck, #62, 26" $500-750
Military Ambulance, #73, 27" $1,500-2,000
Police Van, 1920s $500-750
Sedan, circa 1950, 4½" plastic, hood opens,
    gas tank fills and drains....................$45-60
U. S. Army Truck with canvas canopy, #48,
    26" $650-900
U. S. Mail Truck, #45, 26" $1,500-2,000
Water Tower, #59 ....$2,750-3,250

Kibri

Walthers devotes several pages to their extensive assortment of 1:87 scale plastic Kibri model kits, exceptional in detail and accuracy, most of them currently available. Kibri of Germany at one time produced at least one diecast model, the Auto Union racer listed below.

Atlas Tracked Shovel, 1:87.....................$35-40
Atlas Model 1064 Wheeled Shovel,
    1:87 ....$30-35
Auto-Union Streamlined Racing car, diecast,
    4⅛"..$50-55
Demag DF120P Road Surfacer, 1:87......$35-40
Hamm Road Roller, 1:87 ....$20-20

Hamm Rubber-Tired Compactor, 1:87 .....$35-40
Komatsu Heavy-Duty Model R992, 1:87
Hydraulic Tracked Shovel..................$65-75
Tracked Shovel $65-75
Liebherr Hy-Rail Shovel
1:87 ....$30-35
with blade, 1:87 ....$30-35
Liebherr Modern
Tracked Shovel, 1:87........................$30-35
Wheeled Shovel, 1:87......................$30-35
O&K Grader, 1:87...............................$30-35
Road/Land Grader, 1:87 ....$30-35

Kidco

When Kidco of Illinois started is unknown. But somewhere around 1985, Kidco was purchased by Universal while Universal still owned the Matchbox brand. The Burnin' Key cars and Lock-Ups assortments were originally a Kidco product that was incorporated into the Matchbox lineup for a short time in the 1980s. At last word, Burnin' Key cars were owned by Maisto.

Firebird Trans Am V8, Hong Kong, 1981 .....$2-3
'57 Corvette, white with red stripes, hood opens, 1977 ....$2-3

Kiddie Car Classics

Hallmark offers these exquisite miniature replicas of vintage pedal toys made of heavy diecast metal and great paint jobs. They are working models with pedals that turn the wheels and functional steering.

1935 American Airflow Coaster, Limited Edition of 29,500 made, 5" long $45-60
1964½ Ford Mustang, 7" long................$55-70
1940 Garton Aero Flite Wagon, Limited Edition of 24,500 made, 7" long $50-65
1959 Garton Deluxe Kidillac, issued 3/95, retired 1:97, 7½" long............$55-70
1961 Garton Casey Jones Locomotive, issued 3/95, retired 1:97, 6½" long ..$55-70
1950 Garton Delivery Cycle, 6¾" long.....$40-55
1956 Garton Dragnet Police car, Limited Edition of 24,500 made, 6¼" long.....$50-65
1956 Garton Hot Rod Racer, 5½" long $55-70
1956 Garton Kidillac, issued 7/94, retired 12/94, 7⅜" long..................$50-65
1956 Garton Mark V, Limited Edition of 24,500 made, 6¼" long $45-60
1963 Garton Speedster, 5" long.............$40-55
1966 Garton Super-Honda, 6¼" long $45-60
1964 Garton Tin Lizzie, 5¾" long $50-65
1941 Keystone Locomotive, 5" long.........$45-60
1939 Mobo Horse, 3⅞" long $45-60
Late 1940s Mobo Sulky, Limited Edition of 29,500 made, 7" long.................$50-65
1941 Murray Airplane, Limited Edition of 14,500, issued 10/92, retired 10/93, 7¼" long $50-65
1958 Murray Atomic Missile, Limited Edition of 24,500 made, 7¾" long...............$55-70
1968 Murray Boat Jolly Roger, Limited Edition of 19,500 made, issued 3/93, retired 2/96, 6⅛" long $50-65
1955 Murray Champion, Limited Edition of 14,500, issued 10/92, retired 10/93, 6⅛" long $60-75
1961 Murray Circus car, Limited Edition of 24,500 made, 7" long.................$50-65
1953 Murray Dump Truck, yellow, Limited Edition of 14,500, issued 10/92, retired 10/93, 7½" long...................$50-65
1955 Murray Dump Truck, orange/black, Limited Edition of 19,500, issued 3/94, retired 3/96, 7½" $50-65
1955 Murray Fire Chief, Limited Edition, issued 9/93, retired 1:96, 6⅛" long ..$45-60
1955 Murray Fire Truck, red, Limited Edition of 14,500 made, issued 10/24, retired 10/93, 7" long.....................$50-65
1955 Murray Fire Truck, red/white, Limited Edition of 19,500 made, issued 3/94, retired 1:96, 7" long $50-65
1958 Murray Police Cycle, Limited Edition of 29,500 made, 5½" long...............$55-70
1948 Murray Pontiac, 5⅞" long $50-65
1955 Murray Ranch Wagon, Limited Edition of 19,500 made, issued 1:94, retired 2/96, 6⅛" long $50-65
1955 Murray Red Champion, Limited Edition of 19,500 made, issued 3/94, retired 3/96, 6⅛" long $45-60
1955 Murray Royal Deluxe, Limited Edition of 29,500 made, 6¼" long...............$55-70
1961 Murray Speedway Pac car, Limited Edition of 24,500 made, 6⅛" long.....$45-60
1962 Murray Super Deluxe Fire Truck, 7½" long...$55-70
1961 Murray Super Deluxe Tractor with Trailer, 7¼" long tractor, 4¼" long trailer...$55-70
1950 Murray Torpedo, issued 3/95, retired 1:96, 6¼" long $50-65
1955 Murray Tractor and Trailer, Limited Edition of 14,500, issued 10/92, retired 12/93, 11⅛" long $55-70
1935 Sky King Velocipede, 5" long $45-60
1937 Steelcraft Airflow by Murray, Luxury Edition, 24,500 made, 6⅞" long $55-70
1935 Steelcraft Airplane by Murray, Limited Edition of 29,500 made, 7¾" long.....$50-65
1937 Steelcraft Auburn, Luxury Edition, 24,500 made, issued 7/95, retired 4/96, 8½" long $65-80
1935 Steelcraft by Murray, Luxury Edition, 24,500 made, 7¼" long $65-80
1939 Steelcraft Lincoln Zephyr by Murray, Limited Edition of 24,500, 6¾" long ...$50-65
1941 Steelcraft Spitfire Airplane by Murray, Limited Edition, 19,500, issued 3/94, retired 1:96, 7¼" $50-65
1937 Steelcraft Streamline Scooter by Murray, 6¼" long..$35-50
1935 Steelcraft Streamline Velocipede by Murrary, 4½" long.................................$45-60

Kiddietoy (see Hubley)

Kiko (see Corgi)

Kilgore

Westerville, Ohio, was home to Kilgore, a company that produced some of the most elegant toys of the 1930s. These cast iron cars were accurate representations of vehicles of the period, comparable to the best diecast of any era. Graham models were the specialty for these high quality miniature marvels.

Arctic Ice Cream Truck
8" $1,250-1,500
9" $800-1,050
with three interchangeable bodies, 6⅜" $1,250-1,500
Bus, plastic, 1937, 4"............................$30-45
Double Decker Bus, circa 1930, 6"..$750-1,000
1932 Graham Blue Streak
Coupe, 4" $175-350
Coupe, 6½"..........................$2,200-2,500
Roadster, 4" $175-350
Roadster, 6½".........................$2,200-2,500
Sedan, 4"..................................$175-350
Sedan, 6½" $2,200-2,500
Graham Stake Truck, 4" $100-150
Graham Wrecker, 4".........................$100-150
Graham Dump Truck, 4" $100-150
Pierce Arrow-styled car
Coupe, 4" $100-150
Coupe, 5" $125-175
Roadster, 4" $100-150
Roadster, 5" $125-175
Sedan, 4"..................................$100-150
Stutz Roadster........................$2,250-2,750
Taxi, plastic, 4", 1937......................$35-50
Toy Town Delivery Truck, 6⅛" $400-500

Kim Classics

From England come these new 1:43 scale white metal models from Kim Classics, a division of Western Models.

1972 Buick Electra 225 Sedan	$230-255
Cadillac Limousine "Maloney," #2	$200-225
1960 Chrysler Saratoga, #7	$130-155
GMC Sierra Police Suburban, #3Z	$150-175
1992 Jaguar XJ6 Sedan, #6	$115-140

Kimmeria (Techno-Exclusive)

Alex Litovskiy of Russia reports of the Kimmeria brand from Ukraine but doesn't provide any details. Luckily, Alex Antonov from Virginia provides a list of 1:43 scale Kimmeria Techno-Exclusive models he offered for sale (in May 2004) through Scale 43 Illustrated Models Online at www.scale43.com.

AC-8 MAZ-200 Fuel	$100-110
ATZ-4.0 ZIL-130 Airfield Fuel Tanker	$90-100
BTR-40 Open Top	$60-70
BTR-40B	$60-70
GAZ-72 Pobeda 4x4 Soviet Army	$40-50
K-104 Autocrane on YaAZ-210 chassis	$190-205
KRAZ 250 and Doll-German Dump-Semi	$130-140
KRAZ-219 cargo	$90-100
KRAZ-260	$90-100
MAZ-200	$70-80
MAZ-200G	$80-90
MAZ-502	$100-110
MAZ-504 Air Control Army	$110-120
MAZ-504 and MAZ-8522 Semi-Trailer	$130-140
Opel-Kadett 1938	$40-50
Parm ZIS-5 Mobile Workshop	$90-100
TZ-22 Airfield Fueller on KRAZ-250	$110-120
TZ-22 Airfield Fueller on YaAZ-210	$110-120
YaAZ-210 cargo	$90-100

King K (also see Xonex)

Since 1987, King K has been the business of Ed and Ken Kovach from Frankfort, Illinois, producing some of the most exquisite miniature cars, buses, and flivvers ever made. So when Ken Kovach made his first resin-cast miniature pedal car in 1990, a 1955 Champion, he started the newest trend in collectible toys. His replicas average about 12 inches long (1:3 scale), bigger than average for such models. (Compare to Kiddie Car Classics at approximately 6 inches.) Limited production runs of 10, 50, or 100 make these rare and highly collectible.

Newer models are also produced in a much smaller 1:18 scale. Xonex has since reproduced King K's models in diecast, and in larger production runs of 10,000 for around $60–80 each. Xonex has since gone out of business.

King K
c/o Ken Kovach
8300 W. Sauk Trail
Frankfort, IL 60423
phone: 815-469-5937

1955 Champion pedal car, 1:3 scale, 1990 original price $165	$300-450
1940 Silver Pursuit Plane pedal car, 1991 original price $300	$350-500

King of the Road (see Horsman)

Kingsbury

The Kingsbury company dates back to 1886 in Keene, New Hampshire. Around 1910, Harry Kingsbury purchased the Wilkins Toys Company. After World War I, he changed the Wilkins brand name to Kingsbury to produce toys usually made of pressed steel with wind-up motors. While the firm remains in business, toy production apparently ceased after 1942. Values range from $400 to $2,500. In 1931, Kenton formed a partnership with Kingsbury to bolster sagging sales of its cast iron toys and products.

Aerial Ladder Truck	
wind-up, 1920s, 33"	$2,750-3,250
wind-up, fireman goes up and down ladder, 25," 1941	$550-700
wind-up, 1920s, 9"	$450-600
Airflow	
rubber tires, circa 1934, 14"	$550-700
clockwork motor, 14"	$550-700
Army Truck, circa 1941	$225-300
Bluebird Racer	$1,750-2,250
Brougham Sedan, wind-up, 13"	$1,350-1,650
Coupe	
#74200	$1,250-1,500
#244	$1,750-2,250
#344, 13½"	$900-1,150
#444, electric lights, 13½"	$1,000-1,250
rumble seat, electric light, circa 1930, 12½"	$550-700
wind-up, 11"	$1,500-2,000
DeSoto, wind-up, circa 1938, 14½"	$500-650
Divco	
Borden's Van	$650-800
Grocery Van	$550-700
Ford Sedan and House Trailer, 1937, 23"	$650-800
Golden Arrow Racer, wind-up, 20"	$750-1,000
Greyhound Bus, wind-up, 18"	$850-1,100
Lincoln Zephyr and Travel Trailer, circa 1936, 22½"	$600-750
Phaeton, rubber tires, 1900, 9½"	$1,350-1,600
Pure Milk Truck	$225-275
Roadster	
#242/433, electric headlights, clockwork motor, 13"	$650-900
11"	$600-750
Sunbeam Racer, clockwork motor, 19"	$850-1,100
Transit Truck, 1930s, 19"	$300-450
Yellow Cab, 1934	$600-750

King Star

King Star toys of Korea, while lightweight and low priced, are relatively accurate scale models. Here is a small sampling of models produced.

Fuso Van	$5-7
Fuso Cement Truck	$5-7

Mercedes-Benz 450 SLC 5.0, 1:50	$5-7
Mercedes-Benz 450 SLC Police Car	$5-7
Pontiac Firebird	$5-7

Porsche 930 Turbo, 1:60	$5-7

Kingston (see Old Kingston Product Corporation)

Kinsmart (see Kintoy)

Kintoy

Kintoy diecasting Manufactory Ltd. of China is known to produce several color variations of a 1:43 scale BMW Isetta with pull-back action for around $6 each. Other models include several color variations of a Volkswagen New Beetle, 5" long with pull-back action, recently found for just $2 each. Identification of these models requires referencing the package, as most Kintoy and Kinsmart toys have no identifying marks other than "Made In China" on the base, rendering them generic. Both Kintoy and

Kinsmart toys are sold in bulk display packs and have no individual packaging.

Kintoys

BMW Isetta, 1:43 ....$4-6
Humvee Power Climber, 2¾", pull-back motor
    blue $2-4
    metallic red..$2-4
    black $2-4
    yellow..$2-4
    red $2-4
    white $2-4
    metallic green $2-4
Volkswagen New Beetle, 5" $2-4

Kinsmart

Chevrolet Caprice Taxi, with pull-back motor, 1:43..$6-8

1957 Chevrolet Corvette, with pull-back motor, 1:64

white with red $2-4

black with red $2-4
    red with white $2-4
1955 Chevrolet Stepside, 1:64, with pull-back motor
    red $2-4
    metallic red..$2-4
    yellow..$2-4
    cream..$2-4
    black $2-4
    metallic blue..$2-4
    metallic green $2-4
1950 Chevrolet Suburban, with pull-back motor, 1:36...$5-7

Dodge Viper GTSR, opening doors, pull-back motor, 1:36
    black with silver racing stripes................$5-7

metallic blue with white racing stripes ..$5-7
    metallic silver with blue racing stripes $5-7
    red with silver racing stripes...................$5-7
    white with blue racing stripes..................$5-7
    yellow with black racing stripes $5-7
1949 Ford Woody Wagon, 1:82 with pull-back motor
    black $2-4
    beige $2-4
    burgundy $2-4
1999 Lincoln Town Car Stretch Limousine, opening front and back doors, sunroof and hood, 1:38
    silver with black landau roof $6-8

Love Limousine, white with pink ribbon...$8-10
New Mini Cooper, 1:28
    black with white roof.............................$5-7
    dark blue with white roof $5-7
    dark red with white roof.........................$5-7
    metallic dark green with white roof..........$5-7
    metallic silver with black roof $5-7
    yellow with white roof $5-7
Nissan Fairlady 350Z, 1:34
    metallic blue $5-7
    metallic light copper..............................$5-7
    metallic silver...$5-7
    red $5-7
    white $5-7
Toyota Celica Rally, opening doors, pull-back motor, 1:34

black with yellow, blue and red rally trim...$5-7

metallic blue with red, black and silver rally trim...$5-7

red with silver, black and purple trim.....$5-7

yellow with silver, black and purple rally trim...$5-7

Kirby

    An HO gauge Atlas Backhoe is the only known model by Kirby.

Atlas 2004LC Track Backhoe, 1:87 ....$25-30

Kirk

    The Kirk brand of Denmark is hard to find, since most of the models they marketed were first produced by other companies. The connection is somewhat confusing, but Tekno and H. Lange are two Danish companies whose products ended up in the Kirk product line. Even though Kirk produced models since 1960, it wasn't until 1969 that the company actually put the Kirk name on the base. Here is a list of 1:43 scale Kirk models.

Chevrolet Monza
    GT $60-75
    Spyder $45-60
Ford D 800
    Brewery Truck $65-80
    Covered Truck $45-60
    Lumber Truck...$45-60
    Tipper Truck..$45-60

Jaguar E Type $65-80
Mercedes-Benz 0302 Bus $60-75
  "PTT" $75-90
Mercedes-Benz 280 SL $65-80
  Police $45-60
Oldsmobile Toronado $65-80
Porsche 911 S $45-60
Saab 99 ....$65-80
Toyota 2000 GT $60-75

Kohnstam, Moses (see Moko)

Kookaburra Models

c/o Weico Models
PO Box 283, Reservoir
Victoria, Australia.
phone/fax international: 061 3 9462 2560
e-mail: weicomodels@bigpond.com
www.users.bigpond.com/weicomodels
  Kookaburra Models is the brand name of 1:43 scale white metal replicas from Weico Models of Victoria, Australia, also makers of Wizard OO (Double O) gauge models.

Holden EK
  1962 Station Sedan, #005 ....$125-150
  Taxi, RSL Cabs, Sydney, #001,
    100 made...........................$175-225
  Morris Major......................$125-150

Kumfy

  Kumfy is the brand name of an obscure British toy company that existed from 1948 to 1950 of which just one model, and no company history, is known.

1946 Leyland Double-Decker Bus, approx.
  1:60 ....$75-90

Kyosho (also see J Collection)

Kyosho Corporation
Atsugi Operation Center
153 Funako, Atsugi
Kanagawa 243-0034, Japan
  These fine quality diecast precision scale models from Japan are part of a line of toys that include radio-controlled cars, boats, and planes, and detailed plastic model kits.
  In addition, Kyosho has recently added 1:43 scale models to their offerings, dubbed the Museum Collection.

Kyosho 1:18 Scale Models

Acura (see Honda)
Austin Countryman, blue, #0300 ....$50-60

Datsun Fairlady 240Z-G, maroon $50-60

Ferrari 512 BB
  yellow, limited edition, #0201 ....$100
  black, limited edition, #0202 ....$100
  silver limited edition, #0203 ....$100
  red, #08171R $50-60
  yellow, #08171Y $50-60
Honda Acura 1991 NSX, #7001
  red $90-100
  silver with black roof $90-100

**Honda Acura 1991 NSX-R, white,
#7001R $50-60**

Lancia Stratos
  Rally, #0171 ....$50-60
  HF Rally "Alitalia," #08132A $50-60
  HF Rally, red, #08131R $50-60
  HF Rally, yellow, #08131Y $50-60
Lotus Caterham Super 7, British racing green,
  red, blue, or yellow, #7015 ....$50-60
Lotus Europa Special
  white, #0190 ....$50-60
  black, #0191 ....$50-60
  green, #0192 ....$50-60
  black, #08151K $50-60
  green, #08151G $50-60
  white, #08151W $50-60
Mazda Miata MX5
  LHD, yellow, #0400 ....$50-60
  LHD, light blue, #0401 ....$50-60
  top down, Superman blue, #7011 .....$40-50
Mazda RX7
  red, #7009 ....$90-100
  silver, #7009 ....$90-100
  black, #7010 ....$90-100
  yellow, #7010.............................$90-100
Mercedes-Benz 300 SL Gullwing, silver,
  #7005 ....$90-100
MGB Mk 1 1966
  green, #7017 ....$50-60
  red, #7017 ....$50-60
  white, #7017 ....$50-60

Mini Cooper 1275S, green, red, white, or
  British flag, #7008 ....$80-90
Morgan 4/4 Series-II
  green, #08111G $50-60
  white, #08111W $50-60
  blue, #08111B $50-60
  red, #08111R $50-60
Morris Traveler, green, #0301 ....$50-60
Nissan 300ZX
  yellow, #0500 ....$50-60
  1992 Twin Turbo, red or metallic
    blue, #7002 ....$50-60
  T-Top, red, #7003 ....$90-100
Nissan Skyline GTR 1993
  Unisea, #7002J $50-60
  multicolor, #7002J $50-60
Porsche 356A/1600
  red, #7007 ....$80-90
  silver, #7007 ....$80-90
Shelby Cobra 427 S/C
  Racing, silver, #08041S $50-60
  red, #0600 ....$50-60
  red with white stripe, #7006RW........$50-60
  green, #7006G $50-60
  blue, #7006Z $50-60
Toyota Supra with wing
  red, #7013 ....$90-100
  red, #7014 ....$90-100
  black, #7014 ....$90-100
  silver, #7014 ....$90-100

Kyosho 1:43 Scale Museum Collection

Shelby AC Cobra 427 S/C
  red, #03011R $25-30
  silver, #03011S $25-30
Nissan Skyline 2000 GTR
  silver, #03021S $25-30
  white, #03021W $25-30
Racing, white with blue and red accents,
  #03022B $25-30
Toyota 2000 GT
  Hardtop red, #03031R....................$25-30
  Hardtop Trial Car, yellow, #03032Y...$25-30
  Convertible, white, #03033W.........$25-30
Caterham Super Seven, green,
  #03151G $25-30
Jaguar E-Type Roadster-Green, #1601 .....$30-35

L

Lacquer & Leather (or Lack & Ledder)

  This German brand reportedly offered an unauthorized enhanced custom version of Maisto's Mercedes-Benz Concept car in 1:18 scale.

Mercedes-Benz Concept car, custom leather
interior, enhanced exterior finish $45-60

Lada

Lada, also known as Vaz, is a brand of
diecast models from Russia. Quality is exceptional for the price, and models are 1:43 scale
except where noted.

AWA, 1:66, #1116.................................$5-7
NIVA Standard, #2121 ....$12-14
Saloon
   Rally car, #2101 ....$8-10
   Standard, #2101 ....$8-10
   Standard, #2105 ....$9-11
   Standard, #2107 ....$9-11
   Standard with luggage rack, #2101 ....$8-10
   Standard with luggage rack, #2105 ....$9-11
   Standard with luggage rack, #2107 ..$12-14
   Traffic Police, #2101 ....$8-10
   Training car, #2101 ....$8-10
   Traffic Police, #2105 ....$12-14
Estate
   Standard, #2102 ....$8-10
   Rally Support car, #2102 ....$8-10
   Standard with luggage rack, #2102 ....$8-10
   with symbols, #2102 ....$8-10
   Fire Chief, #2102.............................$8-10
   Traffic Police, 5-door with beacon,
     #2109....................................$12-14

Lansdowne (see Brooklins)

Lansing Slik-Toys (see Slik Toys)

L. D. Abraham

Vintage toy car collector Staffan Kjellin of
Sweden reports that L. D. Abraham models
were made in London, England, in the late
1940s. The model Kjellin provided as an
example has a clockwork motor and was
seen advertised in a January 1948 magazine.

Vauxhall 10..$35-45

Lee Toys

A recent offer on the Internet revealed a
vintage set of diecast farm toys by a company
called Lee Toys. The set includes a tractor and
five other farm implements vacuum sealed in
an attractive display box. The set sold on eBay
for $20.

Farm Set, with tractor and five toy farm
   implements.....................................$15-25

Legends of Racing

Legends of Racing are 1:43 scale resin
models made in China for the Huntersville,
North Carolina, company. Each car is packaged in a clear display box with a card that
provides a few paragraphs of details on the
model inside.

1974 Chevrolet Malibu, "Buddy Baker" ...$10-20
1955 Chrysler 300.............................$10-20
1969 Dodge Daytona, "Jim Vandiver" $10-20
1965 Ford Galaxie 500
   "#41," "Curtis Turner," "Harvest Ford," white
     and red, 1:43, issued 1992 ......$10-20
   "Ned Jarrett" $10-20
   "Fred Lorenzen" $10-20
1952 Hudson Hornet, "Flock" $10-20
1969 Mercury Cyclone
   (independent driver) $10-20
   "Woods Brothers" $10-20
1960 Pontiac Bonneville $10-20
   "Fireball Roberts" $10-20

Lego

This Danish firm founded in 1932 is now
world-famous for its popular construction sets.
Lego started producing plastic toys in 1947. For
a short time beginning in 1955, Lego offered
the 600 series of realistic HO gauge (1:87
scale) plastic vehicles to go along with their play
sets. Those were followed by a larger 900
series semi-tractor with tanker trailer. Other trailers and loads were sold separately.

Lego 600 Series
Bedford
   Dump Truck, #660............................$35-50
   Ladder Truck, #655 ....$45-60
   Tanker, "Esso," #650 ....$40-55
   Transport Van $30-45
   Wreck Truck, #656 ....$40-55
Citroën DS19, #603.............................$45-60
Farm Tractor $45-60
Fiat
   1500, #604 ....$35-50
   1800, #605 ....$35-50
Ford Taunus
   17M, #663 ....$30-45
   #668..$30-45
Jaguar E Type, #606............................$25-40
Mercedes-Benz
   190SL, #666....................................$35-50
   220S, #664......................................$35-50
   Ladder Truck, #655 ....$45-60
   Moving Van, #651 ....$30-45
   Moving Van and Trailer, #652 ....$40-55

Open Truck, #653.................................$25-40
Open Truck and Trailer, #654...........$35-50
Semi-Trailer, #657................................$35-50
Semi Tanker-Trailer................................$35-50
Tanker, "Esso," #650 ....$40-55
Tanker, "Shell," #649 ....$40-55
Morris 1100, #601 ....$25-40
Motorcycle and Bike, #670 ....$45-60
Opel Rekord, #662 ....$30-45
Tanker Semi
   "Esso" $40-55
   "Shell" $40-55
Volkswagen
   Kombi, #607 ....$40-55
   Kombi Bus..$40-55
   Van, #658 ....$40-55
   Pickup, #659 ....$40-55
   #661..$45-60
   Karmann Ghia, #665 ....$35-50
   1500, #667 ....$35-50

Lego 900 Series
Semi Tractor, Chevrolet-style with Tanker-Trailer,
   large, "BP," #913 ....$175-200
Semi-Trailer
   Coal Trailer, #904P $40-55
   Freight Trailer, #901P $40-55
   Gasoline Tank Trailer, #903P $40-55
   Gravel Trailer, #905P $40-55
   Livestock Trailer, #907P $40-55
   Open Truck Trailer, #902P................$40-55
Load
   Coal, #904 ....$40-55
   Freight, #901 ....$40-55
   Gas, #903 ....$40-55
   Gasoline Tank, #908 ....$40-55
   Gravel, #905 ....$40-55
   Livestock, #907 ....$40-55
   Milk, #902 ....$40-55

Lehigh Bitsi-Toys

Around the year 1950, a company called
Lehigh produced a small assortment of heavy
1:64 scale diecast toys known as Bitsi-Toys.
Here are the only two known models.

1949 Chevrolet Coupe, 2½" $20-25
1948 Reo Tractor/Trailer, 5½" $30-35

Lehmann

Ernst Paul Lehmann started the Lehmann
toy company in Germany in 1881. The
founder's initials "EPL" served as the trademark on these colorful tin lithographed
mechanical wind-up toys. Even after
Lehmann's death in 1934, the company con-

tinued thanks to his cousin Johannes Richter. In 1951, Richter opened a new factory in Nuremburg, then and now Germany's toy manufacturing center and home to the yearly world-renowned Nuremburg Toy Show. At last report, Lehmann is still in the toy-making business.

Aha Delivery Van, 1920s, 5½" $1,000-1,250
Autobus, "Lehmann's Autobus 590"
    red $1,750-2,250
    brown.......................................$2,250-2,750
Baker and Chimney Sweep, 5¼"...$5,750-6,250
Berolina Car $3,250-3,750
Deutsche Reichspost, postal truck with driver, 1927 ....$2,000-2,500
Galop Racer #1, with garage $1,500-1,750
Gnom Series
    Sedan #807, circa 1935, 4½" $450-550
    Racing Car, #808, circa 1935, 4½".$400-550
Ito Sedan, 1920s, 6½" $1,000-1,250
Lana Auto $2,500-3,000
Li La Car, 5½" $2,250-2,750
Lo Lo Car, with driver...................$1,000-1250
Lu Lu Delivery Truck, 7¼" $3,750-4250
Mensa Delivery Van, #688, red and blue three-wheeler, circa 1912,
    5¼" $2,750-3,250
Mixtum Comic Car, 1920s, 5½" $550-650
Motor Coach, 1920s, 5½" $550-650
Naughty Boy...............................$1,500-1,750
Oho, c. 1903 ....$700-900
Onkel...$750-1,000
Panne Touring Car, 6½" $1,000-1,250
Peter Clown Car $1,800-2,300
Royal Mail Van, with driver, 6¾"....$1,800-2,300
Sedan, 5½".................................$450-600
Terra $1,500-1,750
Tut-Tut, driver with horn, 6¾" $1,500-1,750
Uhu Amphibious Car $2,000-2,500
Velleda, clockwork open sedan with
    chauffeur $1,750-2,250

Le Jouet Mecanique

Dating from around 1955, just one reference to Le Jouet Mecanique (literally, "the mechanical toy") has been found, a diecast model with clockwork motor.

Panhard Dyna, 1:45 ....$60-75

Leksakshust

From somewhere in Eastern Europe or Russia comes this obscure brand.

Greyhound Bus, 1:43............................$25-30

Le Mans Miniatures

Mike Burt of Ridgefield, Washington, relayed this information from the manufacturer of Le Mans Miniatures of Foulletourte, France. Figurines and dioramas are the main offerings from Le Mans Miniatures. An assortment of 1:43 scale models from their GTS Collection is also available.

Le Mans Miniatures

Driver running at start of Le Mans,
    1:24, FLM124001 ....$10-15
French Fireman of the 80s and 90s,
    1:24, FLM124005 ....$10-15
1994 Dauer Porsche Le Mans Winner
    diorama $50-65
1996 Joest Porsche WSC Le Mans
    diorama, 12 figurines, race car and
    accessories..................................$45-60
1968 Ford GT 40 Le Mans, 1:24,
    124019 ....$35-50

Le Mans Miniatures GTS Collection

Peugeot 406 Coupe
    metallic gray, #02.0 ....$25-30
    metallic blue, #02.1 ....$25-30
    yellow, #02.2 ....$25-30
    metallic green, #02.3.......................$25-30
    metallic red, #02.4 ....$25-30
    Cosmos gray, #02.5 ....$25-30
    Riviera blue, #02.6 ....$25-30
    metallic green, #02.7.......................$25-30
    metallic red, #02.8 ....$25-30
Renault 12 Gordini
    blue, #04.0 ....$25-30
    orange, #04.1 ....$25-30
    yellow, #04.2 ....$25-30
Renault Alpine A 310 Pack GT
    marine blue, #05.0 ....$25-30
    white, #05.1 ....$25-30
    red, #05.2 ....$25-30
Renault R8 GT Turbo 1985
    pearly white, GTS, #01.0.................$25-30
    red, #01.1 ....$25-30
    white, #01.2 ....$25-30
    black, #01.3 ....$25-30
    blue, #01.4 ....$25-30
    silver, #01.5 ....$25-30
Simca 1000 Rallye 2 1973
    green, #03.0................................$25-30
    Tacoma white, #03.1 ....$25-30
    red, #03.2 ....$25-30

Lemeco

From 1950 to 1954, Lemeco of Stockholm, Sweden, produced a series of diecast models loosely based on Dinky Toys of that period.

Austin Devon, ML71 ....$175-200
Field Kitchen Trailer $75-90
Ford 1950 Sedan, ML58 ....$175-200
Ford Tanker, "Shell" $125-150
Frazer Nash-BMW Convertible, ML44 ....$150-175
Mack Tank Truck, "Shell," ML32 ....$125-150
Open Trailer, ML90............................$65-80
Road Roller, ML67 ....$125-150
Willys Jeep, ML47............................$75-90

Lenyco (see Geno)

Le Phoenix (also see ACB)

Super Le Phoenix models have been described as the finest quality 1:43 scale hand-built models from France that feature leather interior, full photo-etched metal and trim, detailed cockpit, limited between 100 and 200 piece production run of only 10 units per item available. Le Phoenix is the lower priced version. Both are brands of ACB of France.

Super Le Phoenix

Ferrari Dino 206 1966 Le Mans 2-car set in
    elegant presentation case with metal
    Dino emblem, limited to 120
    pieces $1,300-1,350
Ferrari 250 GTO 1964 Le Mans #26 ...$600-650
Ferrari 250 TR 1959/1960 Le Mans
    #11 ....$600-650
Ferrari 275 NART Spyder
    red $600-650
    yellow $600-650
    metallic gray $600-650
Ferrari 365 GTB/4 Daytona 1972 Le Mans
    #39 ....$600-650
Ferrari 500SF 1966, metallic blue or
    maroon $600-650

Le Phoenix

Ferrari Daytona Gr. IV LeMans 1974 NART,
    1:43 scale metal $80-100

Lesney (see Matchbox)

Les Rouliers

The obscure French toy company Les Rouliers is known to produce only one model.

Renault Etoile Filante, 1:43, 1961 ....$50-65

Les Routiers

A diminutive series of 1:90 scale diecast vehicles were produced in 1959 under the French firm name Les Routiers.

Berliet Dump Truck, #3 ....$50-60
Bus, #13 ....$50-60
Caterpillar Dumping Tractor, #6 ....$50-60
Caterpillar Quarry Bucket, #9 ....$50-60
Caterpillar Road Grader, #8 ....$50-60
Citroën Wrecker, #4 ....$50-60
Citroën Dump Truck, #5 ....$50-60
Mobile Crane, #14 ....$50-60
Panhard Tank Truck, #1 ....$50-60
Renault Byrrh Tank Truck, #11 ....$50-60
Renault Etoile Filante, #12 ....$50-60
Richier Road Roller, #7 ....$50-60
Tractomotive Excavator, #10 ....$50-60
Unic Semi Trailer, #2 ....$50-60

Liberty Classics (also see Spec-Cast)

Liberty Classics are made in Libertyville, Illinois, and distributed by Spec-Cast of Iowa. Below is just a small sampling of their broad range of models.

1937 Chevrolet Pickup, red, #12516 .....$20-25
1929 Ford Tanker
    "Amalie Motor Oil," #2005 ....$26-31
    "Fina Petroleum," #2004 ....$15-20
1932 Ford Model A Roadster
    "A&W," #1553 ....$27-32
    "Fina," #1547 ....$16-21
Travel REA "Goodyear Racing #1," #326 ...$24-29
White New Idea Crate Pickup, #1026 ...$18-23

Lincoln (see Lincoln Industries, Lincoln International, Lincoln Toys, Lincoln White Metal Works)

Several companies around the world used the name Lincoln, including Lincoln Industries of Auckland, New Zealand; Lincoln International of Hong Kong; Lincoln Toys of Windsor, Ontario; and Lincoln White Metal Works of Lincoln, Nebraska. Read more about them below.

Lincoln Industries

During the 1950s, Lincoln Industries of Auckland, New Zealand, produced a line of models thought to be made from D.C.M.T. castings.

Austin A Somerset, 1:43 ....$50-65
Buick Roadmaster, 1:43 ....$75-90
Bus, 1:87 ....$20-30
Dumper, 1:87 ....$20-30
Fire Engine, 1:87 ....$25-35
Ford Prefect, 1:43 ....$75-90
Jaguar XK120, 1:87 ....$25-35

Land Rover, 1:87 ....$40-55
Massey Ferguson Tractor $20-30
Pickup Truck, 1:87 ....$25-35
Racing car, 1:87 ....$20-30
Tanker, 1:87 ....$25-35
Van, 1:87 ....$20-30
Wrecker, 1:87 ....$20-30

Lincoln International

This Hong Kong-based company produced some stylish trucks and tractors of late 1950s to early 1960s vintage. Their Major series offers durable and attractive diecast toys measuring around 8 inches long. Lincoln International also produced some fairly plain tinplate toys.

Dump Truck, red cab, silver painted grille,
    black chassis, yellow dumper $60-75
Front End Loader Tractor, red with yellow
    loader and wheel hubs, black engine
    with silver accents $60-75
Timber Truck, red cab, silver painted grille,
    yellow bed, black chassis, scored
    wooden block simulates load of lumber ..$60-75

Lincoln Toys

Lincoln Toys of Windsor, Ontario, Canada, produced several pressed steel toys, typified by streamlined prototypical styling.

Auto Transport
    24" $350-400
    "Lincoln Transport," early 1950s,
        24" $325-375
Cement Truck, 13" $150-200
Coca Cola Truck, 16" $750-1,000
Crane Truck $350-400
Dump Truck
    7" $150-200
    "Department of Highways," 19" $200-250
    "Hi Dump," 20" $175-225
    "Phil Wood," 7" $125-150
    "Phil Wood," 12" $150-200
    "Phil Wood," 17" $200-250
    "Sand Truck," 14" $175-225
Express Truck, "Highway Express," 17" ...$400-500
Heinz Pickle Truck $550-650
Ice Truck, 1949 ....$425-475
Ladder Truck, 1950s
    15" $250-300
    17" $275-325
Moving Van
    "Allied Van Lines," 23" $350-400
    "Lincoln Van Lines" $425-475
Shovel, 16" $250-300
Telephone Service Truck $275-325

Tow Truck
    with two spare tires, 17" $375-425
    rounded fenders, 13" $200-250
    "Dunlop Wrecker," 13" $225-275
    "Dunlop Wrecker," 10" $250-300

Lincoln White Metal Works

From 1931 to 1940, Lincoln White Metal Works sold pot metal toys to Woolworth, Kress, Kresge, Schwartz Paper Co., and many other markets. Identifying these models becomes difficult as not all of them are specifically marked with the Lincoln name.

Bluebird Record Car
    with V-8 engine, 4" $75-90
    with V-8 engine, 6" $120-145
    with V-12 engine, 4⅜" $110-135
Chrysler Airflow Sedan, 3¾" $75-100
Fire Engine, Graham-like grille, "Made in
    USA," 3½" $60-75
Ford V-8 Sedan $125-150
Miller FWD Special Indy Racer, 5⅛" $60-75
Oldsmobile Coupe, 4" $60-75
Pierce-Arrow Silver Arrow Sedan, 3½" $60-75
Streamlined Railcar, 4½" $85-100
Tanker Truck, COE, "Made in USA,"
    3¾" $60-75
Wrecker car, Graham-like grille, "Made in
    USA," 3½" $60-75

Lindberg

Lindberg is best known for plastic kits of airplanes. In the mid 1960s to early 1970s, they produced a small assortment of fairly realistic 1:64 scale plastic kits with diecast chassis called Mini-Lindy. Thanks to Steve Mellon for the complete list. Values are for unassembled kits in their original packaging.

Austin Healey 3000, No. 18 ....$12-15
Bobtail "T," No. 29 ....$12-15
Buick Riviera $12-15
Cement Mixer, No. 14 ....$12-15
Chevrolet 1968 Corvette, No. 17 ....$12-15
Chevrolet Camaro SS, No. 9 ....$12-15
Chevrolet Corvette Stingray, yellow with
    black stripes, No. 3 ....$12-15
Chevrolet Van, No. 8 ....$12-15
Dump Truck, No. 11 ....$12-15
Dune Buggy, No. 27 ....$12-15
Fire Engine, No. 10 ....$12-15
Ford '67 Mustang Fastback with black
    interior, No. 5 ....$12-15
Ford Camper, No. 22 ....$12-15

Ford GT, No. 30 ....$12-15
Ford Pick-Up, 30s vintage, green with black
    bed interior and brown chassis, No. 2$12-15
Highway Bus, "Greyhound," No. 12........$12-15
Jaguar D Type, No. 28 ....$12-15
Jaguar XK-E, red with twin white racing stripes
    and brown interior, No. 4.................$12-15
Jeepster, No. 6 ....$12-15
Mail Truck, No. 13 ....$12-15
Mercedes-Benz SSK, No. 20.................$12-15
MG TD Sports car, blue with brown top,
    No. 15 ....$12-15
Oldsmobile Vista-Cruiser, No. 31 ....$12-15
1930 Packard, No. 21 ....$12-15
Pontiac Firebird, No. 25 ....$12-15
Porsche Carrera
    white with blue stripes, red interior and chrome
    engine, No. 1 ....$12-15

yellow $12-15
Porsche Targa, No. 26 ....$12-15
School Bus, No. 23 ....$12-15
Stake Truck, No. 32 ....$12-15
Tow Truck, No. 16 ....$12-15
Tractor Trailer, No. 24 ....$12-15
Volkswagen, No. 19 ....$12-15
Volkswagen Camper Van, No. 7 ....$12-15

Line Mar (also see Collectoy, Marx)

Line Mar (also spelled "Linemar") of Japan produced the Collectoy series of diecast friction toys representing American cars and trucks. In addition, Line Mar offered tinplate lithographed wind-up and friction toys, many of them quite whimsical, in the late 1940s and through the 1950s. Line Mar is associated with Marx, which is hinted at in the name. Lu Mar is another Marx affiliation.

1907 Touring car, tinplate lithographed
    friction toy, orange with black
    fenders, elaborate trim $45-60
Mr. Hounddog's Campus Express, with plastic dri-
    ver, tinplate lithographed friction toy, rear
    wheels wobble, crank in front makes ratchet-
    ing sound, graffiti: BALCONY SEATS 10
    CENTS XTRA - BLONDES ONLY - CAPACITY
    5 GALS - LOOKA ME red with black trim
    stripe, roof and fenders $45-60
Old Jalopy, with plastic driver, tinplate lithographed
    friction toy, graffiti red-orange.........$45-60
    orange $45-60

Universal Riggers Crane Truck, red truck, yellow
    crane $45-60

Lineol

Oscar Weiderholz founded Lineol in Brandenburg, Germany, in 1906. Military tinplate toys were the mainstay for the company, produced roughly 1:25 scale tinplate military vehicles to accompany their 7½ centimeter composition soldiers.

Ambulance, #1041 ....$3,800-4,200
Armored car, #1215 ....$3,400-3,600
Bridge Truck, #1218 ....$6,400-6,600
Command Staff car
    army green, #1211 ....$1,200-1,400
    camouflage, #1211 ....$1,400-1,600
Communications car, #1205/5 ...$5,800-6,200
Panzer Tank, #1280 ....$1,900-2,100
Searchlight Truck, #1010 ....$3,400-3,600
Six-Wheel Prime Mover, gray,
    #1225/6...........................$2,800-3,200
Staff car, with luggage rack,
    #1206/5...........................$5,800-6,200
Tank, WWI style..............................$400-600
Troop Transport, no canopy, WWI style,
    #1011 ....$3,400-3,600

Lintoy

Until I received in the mail a diecast 1:64 scale Mercedes-Benz C-111 made by Lintoy, I had forgotten ever having heard of them. The model measures 3" and is metallic red with flat black painted metal base, black plastic interior, made in Hong Kong, and the rear engine compartment opens. As it turns out, Lintoys are made by Bachmann, the German model maker and producer of electric trains and sets, in the early to mid 1970s. The toy cars resemble a Playart, Tomica, or Matchbox of that period. Excellent detail and fair wheels punctuate this little model. Several others were listed with the letter of inquiry included with the model. Thanks to Helen Shaffer for the information and the model.

Lintoy 3" cars
    BMW Turbo, orange $9-12
    Fiat Abarth, avocado $9-12
    Ford Mk IV, white $9-12

Mercedes-Benz C-111, metallic red, 1:64 ....$9-12

Mercedes-Benz 350SL......................$9-12
Porsche 911, yellow..........................$9-12

Lion Car (see Lion Toys)

Lion Models

Lion Models are 1:87 scale diecast kits from Germany, according to Werner Legrand of Belgium. He comments that, to the best of his knowledge, Gunther Frieherr (Baron) von Dobeneck founded the company that is reportedly still in business.

AC Cobra Shelby 427 1965, #35 ....$16-24
Austin Healey Sprite 1958-61, #25 ....$16-24
Autobianchi Bianchina Transformabile 1957-62,
    #70 ....$16-24
Borgward Isabella Coupe 1957-61, #69...$16-24
Bugatti Type 41 Royale
    Cabriolet 1931, #33.....................$16-24
    Fiacre Coupe 1928, #48................$16-24
Bugatti Type 55
    Coupe 1932-35, #30 ....$16-24
    Roadster 1932-35, #65 ....$16-24
Ferrari 250 GT
    Berlinetta SWB 1959-62, #66.........$16-24
    Spyder 1961-63, #47 ....$16-24
Ferrari 365 GTB-4 Daytona
    Coupe 1969-73, #64 ....$16-24
    Spyder 1969-73, #54 ....$16-24
Fiat 500
    A Topolino 1936-48, #3 ....$16-24
    Giardiniera Familiare 1961, #11 ......$16-24
    Luxus 1961, #4............................$16-24
Fiat Panda 1000 CL 1986, #43 ....$16-24
Ford Fiesta 1989-96, #41 ....$16-24
Ford Taurus
    Cabriolet 1951, #53......................$16-24
    Special G-73 A 1950-51, #20........$16-24
Ghia Fiat 500 Jolly, #68 ....$16-24
Glas Goggomobil
    Cabrio Prototype, #15 ....$16-24
    Coupe 1964-69, #7 ....$16-24
    S35 Coupe Prototype 1959, #8 ....$16-24
Honda Beat 1991-95, #62 ....$16-24
Isdera
    Imperator 108i 1984-91, #28 ....$16-24
    Spyder 033i 1982, #29.................$16-24
Jaguar Mk 2 1959-67, #50 ....$16-24
Jaguar XK 150 Roadster 1957-60
    #34..$16-24
    #38..$16-24
Lloyd LC 300 Coupe 1952, #14 ....$16-24
Lloyd LP 300 1950-51, #12................$16-24
Lloyd LS 300 Kombi 1952, #26............$16-24
Lotus Super Seven 1961-66, #32 ....$16-24

Marcos Mantula 3500 V8 1985-93,
#42 ....$16-24
Mazda 121 1990-96, #57 ....$16-24
Mazda MX-5 Miata 1989, #45............$16-24
MG Midget Mk III 1966-69, #52 ....$16-24
Mini 1000 Mk III, #40 ....$16-24
Mini Broadspeed GT Coupe 1966-68,
#61 ....$16-24
Mini Cabrio 1990, #55 ....$16-24
Mini Clubman
    Estate 1969-80, #59 ....$16-24
    Saloon 1969-80, #56 ....$16-24
Mini Morris
    Minivan 1960, #58 ....$16-24
    Traveler 1960-69, #60 ....$16-24
Mini Pick-Up 1961, #51 ....$16-24
Nissan Figaro 1991, #67 ....$16-24
NSU Fiat 500
    C 1952-55, #17 ....$16-24
    Spyder-Sport Weinsberg 1939,
    #18 ....$16-24
    Weinsberg Coupe 1960-63, #10 ....$16-24
Peugeot 205
    1983, #19 ....$16-24
    Turbo 16 1985, #27 ....$16-24
Riley Elf Mk III 1966-69, #46 ....$16-24
Rometsch Beeskow Cabrio 1951-54,
#39 ....$16-24
Studebaker President Speedster 1955,
37 ....$16-24
Stutz Royale 1979-88, #36 ....$16-24
Triumph TR 3 1955-57, #63 ....$16-24
Tucker Torpedo 1948, #49 ....$16-24
Veritas Saturn Coupe 1950, #21............$16-24
Veritas Comet Roadster 1950, #22........$16-24
Volkswagen Polo 1981-90, #44 ....$16-24
Volkswagen Porsche 914 1969-74, #13 ..$16-24

Lion Toys

Lion Toys of Holland were originally sold as Lion car, a brand of simple diecast models from the Netherlands. The company was founded as Lion Rail by A. van Leeuwen in the mid-1940s. Production of diecast toys started in 1956. Some models are refinished in the UK. Since 1995, the brand has been ressurected under new management, the new name and a new approach to scale and accuracy. Current models are detailed accurate replicas of European freighter semi-trucks in 1:50 scale. Thanks to Jan Scholten for the updates.

Commer Walkthru
    "Amusements: Fairground," 1:43,
    #LN003...................................$40-45
    "BRS Parcels," 1:43, #LN005 ....$40-45

    "Marples Construction," 1:43,
    #LN004.................................$40-45
    "Rutland Fire Brigade," 1:43,
    #LN002.................................$25-30
Commer Van
    #28 ....$100-125
    "Technische Unie," #49 ....$125-150
    "Van Gend & Loos," #54 ....$50-75
    Mail Van, #55 ....$50-75
Covered Trailer, #25 ....$35-50
DAF 33 Van
    #33 ....$100-125
    #39 ....$75-100
    "Remia," #39 ....$150-175
    "Groenpol," #39 ....$150-175
DAF 44
    "GVB Amsterdam" or "Marathon,"
    #44................................$250-300
    #40...................................$125-150
    "Camel DAF Racing Team," #40...$150-175
    "Lyons International," #40 ....$150-175
Coupe
    Sedan, #44 ....$100-125
    Station Wagon, #41 ....$75-100
DAF 46 Sedan, #46 ....$100-125
DAF 55 Coupe with DAF emblem,
#40 ....$150-175
DAF 66 SL Coupe, #40 ....$75-100
DAF 600, 1958, #29 ....$150-200
DAF 750 Pickup
    #31 ....$125-150
    with hood, #46.....................$100-125
    with tilt, #31 ....$125-150
DAF 1300
    Breakdown Lorry, #26.............$100-125
    Chassis and Cabin, #20 ....$125-175
    Flatbed Truck, #21 ....$100-125
    Truck, #22..........................$100-125
DAF 1400
    Army Truck with tilt, #23 ....$125-150
    Breakdown Lorry, #26..............$100-125
    Semi-Trailer, #35 ....$75-100
    Semi-Trailer Army, olive, #35...........$75-100
    Truck with logo, #22 ....$150-175
    Truck with tilt, #23 ....$125-150
DAF 2000/2200
    Bulk Carrier, #47.....................$50-75
    Covered Truck, #43 ....$50-75
    Military Covered Truck, olive, #43 .....$50-75
    Tipping Truck, #56....................$50-75
    Truck & Trailer, #48 ....$50-75
DAF 2300
    Articulated Van Placketts, 1:50,
    #LN001 ....$30-35
    Covered Truck, #68 ....$50-75
    Military Covered Truck, olive, #68...$100-125

DAF 2600
    Eurotrailer, #36 ....$50-75
    Tank Trailer, #37 ....$100-125
    Car Carrier, #50 ....$100-125
    Container Trailer, #57 ....$75-100
DAF 2800
    6-Wheel Tanker, #67.................$50-75
    6-Wheel Covered Truck, #66............$25-50
    6-Wheel Truck and Trailer, #64.........$50-75
    Car Transporter, #60 ....$75-100
    Container Trailer, #61 ....$50-75
    Covered Truck, #58 ....$50-75
    Dump Truck, 1:43.....................$25-30
    Eurotrailer, #59 ....$50-75
    Tank Trailer, #62 ....$50-75
    Truck and Trailer, #63 ....$50-75
DAF Daffodil
    750, 1963, #30 ....$150-200
    gold-plated, #30 ....$300-350
DAF Pony
    Semi, #42 ....$100-125
    Truck, #45 ....$100-125
DAF SE 200 Bus, #38......................$75-100
DAF Torpedo
    Truck, #32 ....$100-125
    Semi-Trailer, #34 ....$100-125
DAF Truck and Trailer, #70...............$50-75
DKW Sonderklasse 316, #13 ....$250-300
Flatbed Trailer, #24 ....$15-25
Opel Rekord, #12 ....$225-275
Open Trailer with tilt, #25.................$15-25
Renault 4 CV, #11 ....$250-300
Renault Dauphine, #14 ....$150-200
Renault Goelette Van, #27 ....$225-275
Volkswagen 1200, #10.................$250-300

Lionel

Lionel has set the standard for electric toy trains for most of this century. Now they produce a number of vehicles for use with train sets, specifically HO gauge semi trucks and trailers with various liveries. These are recently introduced models that are still available from hobby shops and specialty dealers for $65 to $80 each.

In addition, an assortment of Lionel plastic 1955 Ford Custom 2-door Sedans is also offered in blue, red, white, or yellow for $15 each.

Lionel is also the producer of Revolvers, reversible cars that convert from one car to another when flipped over. A growing interest in these unusual toys has sparked several Hong Kong-based companies to produce knockoff versions, including Ja-Ru Real Wheels and Imperial Diecast.

You can also find many Lionel licensed diecast models from Liberty Classics and other companies.

Lit'l Toy (Mercury Industries U.S.A.)

In March 1999, collector Bruce Mibeck of Illinois reported of an unusual toy among his collection of Matchbox, Budgie, Husky, Lone Star, Penny, and other toys. It has the designation "Lit'l Toy by Mercury Inds. U.S.A." on the base. This is the first and only reference to this brand I've seen. Value is highly speculative since I've never seen the particular model and have found no other reference to the brand.

International Dozer No. 101 .... $15-40

Litan

Litan is one of the emerging model manufactures to originate from Russia. Their line of models includes Samara and Lada vehicles and Belarus tractors. No details are known about the models as to scale, color, or markings.

Belarus Tractor $12-24
Lada $12-24
Samara $12-24

Lixin

Lixin models are made in China, and little else is known about them.

Beijing
    Fire Ladder Truck (tin), 9" $20-25
    Double Decker Bus (tin), 9" $20-25
BMW 507 Convertible
    top down, 1:25 .... $20-25
    top up, 1:25 .... $20-25
Buick Super 1950
    Convertible, top down (tin), 1:25 .... $20-25
    Coupe (tin), 1:25 .... $20-25
Cadillac 1950
    2-door Hardtop, 1:25 .... $20-25
    Convertible, top down, 1:25 .... $20-25
Chevrolet Corvette
    1955 Convertible, top up (tin), 1:25 .. $20-25
    1955 Convertible, top down (tin), 1:25 .. $20-25
    1957 Convertible, top down, 1:25 ... $20-25
    1957 Convertible, top up, 1:25 .... $20-25
Dong Feng 1932 4-door Sedan (tin),
    1:25 .... $20-25
Douglas DC3 Overseas Airplane, 9" $20-25
Harley Davidson 1950 with Sidecar, 1:25 .. $20-25
Jaguar E-Type
    2+2 Coupe, 1:25 .... $20-25
    Convertible, top down, 1:25 .... $20-25
Jeep CJ2 1950 Army, 1:32 .... $20-25
Mercedes-Benz
    300SL Gullwing Coupe, 1:25 .... $20-25

450 4-door Sedan, 1:25 .... $20-25
Toyota Crown 1960 Ambulance (tin), 1:25 .. $20-25
Ford Thunderbird 1961 2-door Hardtop,
    1:25 .... $20-25
Volkswagen
    1970 Bus, 1:43 .... $20-25
    Karmann Ghia Coupe, 1:25 .... $20-25

LJN (also see Hallmark)

LJN has produced a number of inexpensive diecast toys that are essentially generic and of generally low quality. An exception is a line of whimsical toys made for Hallmark in the 1970s known as Road Rovers. See Hallmark for list and values.

Lledo

When Lesney sold the Matchbox line of diecast toys to Universal Holding Company of Hong Kong in 1982, John W. "Jack" Odell left the firm, of which he was a partner for many years, to form Lledo (Odell spelled backwards). Lledo models are also known as Days Gone and designated as DG.

Every one of the hundreds of Lledo models produced for the first six years are variations of approximately 30 base models. Color and markings are what differentiate each model. Here is a list of the basic models, from which the numerous variations have arisen through the years. the value of each model depends on the number of each variation produced from year to year. Most regular production models sell for $7 to $10 each.

Limited edition models vary considerably, depending on availability and quantity produced. Dr. Force's book *Lledo Toys* serves as an excellent source for variations and values.

The latest addition to the Lledo product line is the Vanguard series. These 1950s and 1960s British vehicles are strongly reminiscent of the kinds of toys issued by Corgi and Dinky some 30 years ago.

In 1999, Lledo filed for bankruptcy and went into receivership. By November 1999, Lledo was purchased by the same newly formed Zindart of Hong Kong, the same company that only a month earlier had purchased the Corgi brand.

Each of the models listed below was produced in numerous versions with various colors and markings. An entire book could be written and, in fact, has been by Dr. Edward Force (Schiffer Books ISBN 076430013X).

Lledo Days Gone Models

AEC
    Double Decker Bus, DG15, 1985 ..... $10-15

Regent 1932 Open Top Bus, DG68,
    after 1987 .... $10-15
Renown 1931 Double Decker Bus,
    DG49, after 1987 .... $10-15
Albion Single Decker Coach, DG10,
    1984 .... $10-15
Austin 1933 Taxi, DG47, after 1987 ..... $10-15
Bedford 30cwt
    1950 Truck, DG59, after 1987 .... $10-15
    1950 Delivery Van, DG63, after
    1987 .... $10-15
Bentley 1930 4½ Litre
    DG46, after 1987 .... $10-15
    "Blower," SL46, dark green, SL46000 .... $10-15
    "Blower," SL46, blue, SL46001 .... $10-15
    "Blower," SL46, red, SL46002 .... $10-15
    "Blower," SL46, gray, SL46004 .... $10-15
Bentley 'S' Series
    DG92, after 1987 .... $10-15
    SL92, maroon and silver, SL92000 .... $10-15
Brewer's Dray, DG31, after 1987 .... $10-15
Bristol LD6G Lodekka 1957 Bus, DG75,
    after 1987 .... $10-15
Chevrolet 1934 Bottle Truck, DG26, 1987

Schweppe's $10-15

Chevrolet 1938 Pickup, DG36, after
    1987 .... $10-15
Chevrolet 1939, DG48, after 1987 .... $10-15
Chevrolet 1939 Pickup Truck, DG30, after
    1987 .... $10-15
Chevrolet Van, DG21, 1986

Dr. Pepper $10-15

Delivery Van, DG3, 1983 .... $10-15

Dennis 1926 Delivery Van, DG66, after
1987 ....$10-15
Dennis F8 1955 Fire Engine, DG60, after
1987 ....$10-15
Dodge 1939 Airflow, DG78, after 1987...$10-15

**Dodge 1942 Army Ambulance, DG29,
after 1987** $10-15

Fire Engine
DG5, 1983...$10-15
DG12, 1984 ....$10-15
Foden 1930 Steam Wagon, DG91, after
1987 ....$10-15
Ford
1935 3-Ton Articulated Truck, DG67,
after 1987 ....$10-15
1935 Tanker, DG62, after 1987 ......$10-15
1939 Fire Engine, DG79, after
1987 ....$10-15
1939 Tanker, DG57, after 1987 ......$10-15
Woody Wagon, DG7, 1984 ....$10-15
Ford Model A 1930 Coupe, DG82, after
1987 ....$10-15
Ford Model A 1930 Stake Truck, DG20, 1986

British Oxygen, tank load.....................$10-15

Goodrich, tire load $10-15

Ford Model A 1934 Van, DG13, 1984

Godfrey Davis Ford..............................$10-15

Heinz Cream of Tomato Soup $10-15

Ford Model A Touring car, top down, DG9, 1984

Police...$10-15

Ford Model A Touring car, top up, DG14, 1985

Taxi $10-15

Ford Model T 1920 Coupe, DG33, after
1987 ....$10-15

**Ford Model T 1920 Sedan, Singer Sewing
Machine Company**...............................$10-15
Ford Model T 1920 Tanker

Pennzoil, DG8, 1984...............................$10-15

Ford Model T 1920 Van
DG6, 1983...$10-15
Kodak Film, DG8, 1983.........................$10-15
GMC 1966 Tanker, DG90, after 1987..$10-15

**Greyhound Scenicruiser Bus, DG23,
1987** $18-24

Heavy Goods Van, DG16, 1985

Kiwi Polishes..............................$10-15

Lledo

Horse Drawn Brewer's Dray, DG102000

McMullen Original $10-15

William Younger & Co. $10-15

Horse Drawn Milk Float, DG2, 1983 ......$10-15
Horse Drawn Tram, DG1, 1983.............$10-15
Horse Drawn Van, Large, DG11, 1984 ..$10-15
Karrier E6 1928 Trolley Bus, DG41, after
    1987 ....$10-15
Long Distance Coach, DG17, 1985 ....$10-15
Mack 1934 Canvas Back Truck, DG28,
    1987 ....$10-15
Mack 1934 Tanker Truck, DG42, after
    1987 ....$10-15

Mack Breakdown Truck, DG27, 1987 ...$10-15

M.A.N. 1951 Van, DG87, after 1987...$10-15
Morris
    1926 Bullnose Van, DG50, after
        1987..$10-15
    1931 Van, DG43, after 1987.........$10-15
    1935 Truck, DG52, after 1987 ....$10-15
    1950 Van, DG58, after 1987..........$10-15
    1959 LD 150 Van, DG71, after
        1987..$10-15
    1960 Traveller, DG65, after 1987 ....$10-15
Omnibus, DG4, 1983 ....$10-15

Packard Town Van, DG18, 19, 22, 24, 25

FTD Florist, butter cream and black ..$10-15

Pontiac 1953 Van, DG61, after 1987 ....$10-15
Renault 1912 Van, DG85, after 1987 ....$10-15
Rolls-Royce 1907 40/50 hp Ghost, SL32
    silver, SL32000 ....$10-15
    red with silver cowl, SL32002 ....$10-15
Rolls-Royce 1926 20 hp Landaulet, SL53
    mushroom and maroon, SL53000......$10-15
    cream and brown, SL53002 ....$10-15
Rolls-Royce 1929 Phantom II "D" Back, SL54
    white and brown, SL54000 ....$10-15
    yellow and black, SL54001 ....$10-15
    two-tone green, SL54005 ....$10-15
Rolls-Royce 1959 Silver Cloud, SL89
    metallic gray and silver, SL89000 ......$10-15
    black, SL89001 ....$10-15
Rolls Royce Phantom II, DG19, 1985 .....$10-15
Rolls Royce Playboy Convertible Coupe, DG24,
    1987 ....$10-15

**Rolls Royce Silver Ghost Tourer, DG25,
1987 ....$10-15**

Scammell 1937
    6-Wheeler, DG44, after 1987..........$10-15
    Tanker, DG77, after 1987 ....$10-15
    Tanker, DG80, after 1987 ....$10-15
Sentinel DG4 1931 Steam Wagon, DG88,
    after 1987 ....$10-15
Volkswagen
    1955 Camper, DG86, after 1987....$10-15
    1955 Transporter Van, DG73, after
        1987 ....$10-15

Lledo Vanguard Models
Austin
    A3, VA235 ....$30-35
    A40 Van, dark green, Ransome's Lawn-
        mowers, VA3000.....................$20-25

Bedford "S" Type
    Tanker, Regent, VA7000 ....$25-30
    Tanker, Shell-BP, VA7001 ....$25-30
    Van, Heinz 57 Varietie, VA8000s $25-30
Commer Boxback, VA28 ....$30-35
Ford Anglia
    white and maroon, .VA1002 ....$20-25
    Van, pale blue, Hotpoint, VA4002.....$20-25
Ford Thames Trader
    Tanker, North Eastern Gas,
        VA9000.....................................$25-30
    Van, Martini, VA6000................$25-30
Hillman Imp, VA26 ....$30-35
Jaguar E Type $20-25
Karrier Boxback, VA24 ....$30-35
Mini Cooper, VA25 ....$30-35

Morris Minor Traveller, VA10005 ....$20-25

Regal Reliant, VA22.............................$30-35

Rover P4, VA19005.............................$20-25

Triumph Herald
    red, VA5000 ....$20-25
    yellow, VA5002 ....$20-25

cream, VA5008.....................................$20-25

Volkswagen Cabriolet
    red, VA2000 ....$20-25
    light blue, VA2001 ....$20-25
Volkswagen Beetle, VA12000
    beige $20-25

baby blue $20-25

Lledo Land Speed Legends
Bluebird, LP5267 ....$20-25
Railton Mobil Special, LP5269 ....$20-25
Sonic 1, LP5270 ....$20-25
Thrust 2, LP5268 ....$20-25
Thrust SSC, LP4903 ....$40-45

Loden Aguti
Loden Aguti, also known as Aguti Toys, are roughly 1:64 scale models made in Argentina. At least two models are pirated copies of Matchbox toys, #75 Alfa Carabo and #33 Datsun 126X. By Aguti's own model numbers, it would appear that there were at least nine models in the series, but so far only five have been documented.

Alfa Carabo $3-5
Datsun 126X, #9 ....$3-5
Dodge Charger Show car $3-5
Renault 12 Sedan.......................$3-5
Renault 12 Taxi.......................$3-5

Lomo
ZIS and GAZ models dominate the product line of this Russian manufacturer of 1:43 diecast models, but no model list has been found.

Londontoy
From 1945 to 1950, Londontoy diecast toys were produced in London, Ontario, and in the US by the Leslie Henry Company. The difference can be found in the absence or presence of the words "Made In Canada." Tires are usually white rubber or wood. Bodies are similar to Tootsietoys, with no chassis or base and no interior. Thanks goes to Paul Voorhis for providing additional details, including model numbers and correct length.

Mr. Voorhis writes, "All the 6" Chevrolets that I have seen have a wind-up motor geared to the front axle. All were painted white with "POLICE" decals on doors and trunk. Does M stand for motorized or mechanical as in early Corgi toys? Was there a version of this without the motor, a plain #54? There are also black rubber wheels, and on the 6" Chevrolets they appear with large, shiny axle ends to

simulate hubcaps. Some Londontoys have white wheels made of what appears to be thick cardboard."

Canadian Greyhound Bus, #33, 5".........$40-55
Chevrolet Master Deluxe Coupe 1941
  #14, 4"........................$25-40
  #54M, 6".......................$30-45
City Bus
  4" $30-45
  6" $30-45
Ford
  1939 Deluxe Six-Window Sedan, #31,
    5".......................$40-55
  1940 Standard Six-Window Sedan, #31,
    5".......................$40-55
  1941 Fire Truck, 6"...........................$30-45
  1941 Open Cab Firetruck, #16, 4"...$25-40
  1941 Panel Delivery, #32, 5" $40-55
  1941 Pickup Truck, #12, 4"..............$25-40
  1941 Pickup Truck, 6" $30-45
GMC Cabover 1941
  Beverage Truck, #15, 4"..................$25-35
  Beverage Truck, #41, 5," marked "ARMY
    SERVICE TRUCK" underneath.......$30-45
  Oil Tanker, #13, plain, 4"................$30-45
  Oil Tanker, #13, Imperial Esso, 4"......$30-45
  Oil Tanker, #13, 6".........................$30-40
  Oil Tanker, #53................................$40-55
  Hawker Hurricane Airplane, #11, 4"..$40-55
Large Truck
  Car Transporter..............................$90-115
  Dump Truck....................................$90-115
  Lumber Truck $90-115
  Moving Van with tin body $90-115
  Stake Truck....................................$90-115
  Tractor and Van Trailer....................$90-115
  Steam Switch Locomotive, possibly #1,
    3"...$50-65
  Thunderbolt Racer, 6"......................$40-55

Lone Star (also see Crescent, D.C.M.T., Impy, Roadmaster)
While Lone Star of Great Britain has produced many toys, perhaps the most popular models were those better known as Impy toys. The complete name for one series of toys is Lone Star Road-Master Impy Super Cars, so it is no wonder that they are better known as Impy toys. "Roadmaster" was spelled with a hyphen in 1956 (Road-Master), and later without the hyphen beginning in 1962.

The Lone Star brand was originated in 1951 by Die Casting Machine Tools Ltd., otherwise known as D.C.M.T. Besides toy cars, Lone Star specialized in cap pistols and cowboy out-

fits, hence the reference. The Road-Master line of toy cars debuted in 1956. A second offering, combining the hyphenated words into "Roadmaster," was released in 1962.

Flyers
In response to the introduction of Hot Wheels in 1968, Lone Star issued newer models dubbed Road-Master Flyers Super Cars. They lacked the rhinestone headlights and the "Impy" name of the earlier models.

Numeric Designations
1956 issued models had no model number designation, while those issued in 1962 were given numbers in the 1400 range. Later Impy Roadmaster models were given just a two-digit designation.

Tuf-Tots
In 1969 was introduced Lone Star Tuf-Tots series, 1:118 scale trucks and 1:86 scale cars all of comparatively crude castings. Around the same time as Tuf-Tots (1969), Lone Star also introduced Roadmaster Majors, 1:43 scale trucks of simple castings.

D.C.M.T.
D.C.M.T. was founded in 1940 by engineers Sidney Ambridge and Aubrey Mills. Besides producing products under the Lone Star brand, D.C.M.T. also manufactured diecasting machinery for Lesney (the original company that produced Matchbox toys) and Kemlows. The first toys manufactured by D.C.M.T. were marketed by Crescent of England. D.C.M.T. and Lone Star went out of business in 1983.

Lone Star Chronology
1940 – D.C.M.T. manufacturing firm founded
1951 – Lone Star brand introduced
1956 – Road-Master series begun
1960 – D.C.M.T. strikes a deal with Tootsietoys to produce Classic Series of 1:50 scale American cars
1962 – Roadmaster name adopted, new models added to the line
1966 – Impy Roadmaster name adopted, more new models offered
1968 – Flyers introduced with new wheels and axles to compete with Hot Wheels, Impy trucks renamed Lone Star Commercials
1969 – Tuf-Tots, Roadmaster Majors introduced
1976 – Flyers, Commercials discontinued, cheaper series of new Impy toys introduced
1983 – Lone Star and parent company D.C.M.T. go out of business

Lone Star Model Listing A to Z, including Road-Master, Roadmaster, Flyers, and Commercials

Alfa Romeo Giulia Spyder
Roadmaster #23 ....$30-40
Flyers #23 ....$15-25
Austin Western Mobile Crane, #33 ....$25-35
Builder's Supply Truck, Commercials,#41 ...$15-25
Cadillac 62 Sedan, #1472, 1962 ......$65-80
Cadillac Coupe de Ville, white & blue....$95-120
Cadillac Eldorado, Flyers #40 ....$25-30
Case International Harvester 946 Farm.
Tractor.......................................$18-25
Chevrolet Corvair 1962
#1470, coral............................$65-80
#1470, white...........................$90-110
Fire car, #1479 ....$45-60
Feuerwehr, #1479 ....$55-70
Staff car, #1480 ....$45-60
Chevrolet Corvett, 1964, teal $25-30
Flyers #38 ....$20-30
Gran Turismo Coupe, Roadmaster #11 ..$30-45
Gran Turismo Coupe, Flyers #11 ....$20-35
Chevrolet El Camino, #1474, 1962 ....$60-75
Chrysler Imperial
Flyers #12 ....$25-40
Roadmaster #12, metallic blue..........$60-75
Citroën DS 19, #1482, 1962 ....$55-70
Daimler 1904, 1956 ....$35-50
Daimler Conquest Roadster, 1956, 1:40...$65-80
Darracq Genevieve (1904), 1956.........$35-50
Dodge Dart Phoenix 1962
metallic blue, #1475 ....$95-120
Police, #1477.................................$45-60
Polizei, #1477 ....$60-75
Euclid 82-80 Crawler Tractor, #34..........$20-35
Fiat 2300 S Coupe
Roadmaster #21 ....$25-35
Flyers #21 ....$15-25
Foden COE Tilt Cab 8-Wheel Dump Truck,
Roadmaster #24, 1962 ....$20-35
Foden Half-Cab
High-Side Lorry, Commercials #47 .....$20-30
Hopper Lorry, Commercials #48 ....$20-30
Tipper, Commercials #49 ....$20-30
Tipper, Commercials #42 ....$15-25
Foden Truck
"Express Freight," Commercials #29 ...$25-35
"Express Freight," Roadmaster #29 .....$25-35
"Lucas Batteries," Commercials #29....$15-25
"Lucas Batteries," Roadmaster #29 .....$25-35
Fuel Tanker, "Mobil," Commercials
#26, 1968 ....$20-30
Fuel Tanker, "Mobil," Roadmaster #26,
1962 ....$25-40
Tipper, Commercials #24, 1968.......$18-25
Ford 7610 Farm Tractor $18-25

Ford Corsair
Fire Chief Car, #32 ....$25-35
Flyers, #18 ....$20-30
Roadmaster, #18 ....$25-35
Ford Zodiac Estate Car
Flyers #14 ....$20-35
Police car, Flyers #16 ....$20-35
Police car, Roadmaster #16 ....$30-45
Roadmaster #14 ....$30-45
Ford Model T (1912), 1956 ....$45-60
Ford Mustang Fastback, Flyers #39 ....$25-30
Ford Sunliner Convertible, #1473, 1962,
pale blue...............................$115-140
Ford Taunus 12M
Flyers #27 ....$20-30
Roadmaster #27 ....$25-40
Ford Thunderbird, 1:40.......................$65-80
Ford Transit Breakdown Truck
Commercials #31, 1968 ....$15-25
Roadmaster #31, 1962 ....$25-35
Ford Zodiak Estate $35-40
Garage, lock-up, #402 ....$20-35
Garage Ramp, #401 ....$30-45
International Harvester 946 Farm Tractor with
shovel, #25 ....$20-30
Jaguar Mk. 10
Roadmaster #10 ....$35-40
Flyers #10 ....$25-30
Leyland Lorry
Drop-Side, Commercials #46 ....$20-30
High-Side, Commercials #47 ....$20-30
Hopper, Commercials #48 ....$20-30
Locomotive $25-30
London Taxi, 1:50.............................$25-30
Lotus Europa, Flyers #36 ....$20-30
Marine Transport Truck with plastic boat,
Commercials #44 ....$20-30
Maserati Mistral, Flyers #9.....................$20-30
Massey Ferguson 3070 Tractor................$18-25
Mercedes-Benz 220SE, #17 ....$25-35
Police car, Flyers #16M $20-30
Police car, Roadmaster #16M $25-35
Merryweather Turntable Fire Engine,
Commercials #30 ....$30-40
MG TF, 1:35, 1956 ....$65-80
Military Jeep, olive drab $65-75
Morris Bullnose (1912), 1956 ....$35-50
Peugeot 404
Flyers #28 ....$15-25
Roadmasters #28 ....$20-30
Pumps and Sign, "Mobil," #404 ....$20-35
Rambler 1962
Ambulance, #1478 ....$45-60
Army Ambulance, #1481 ....$45-60
Army Station Wagon, #1471 ....$50-65
Station Wagon, #1471 ....$45-60

Rolls-Royce 1962 Silver Cloud, #1476....$55-70
Convertible, Flyers #22.....................$15-25
Convertible, Roadmaster #22 ....$25-35
Routemaster Double Decker Bus $18-25
Toyota 2000 GT, Flyers #13................$20-30
Vauxhall Firenza Coupe, Flyers #7.........$25-30
Volkswagen Microbus
Ambulance, Flyers #20 ....$25-40
Ambulance, Roadmaster #20 ....$25-40
Flyers #15 ....$25-35
Roadmaster #15 ....$40-55
Volvo P1800S
Roadmaster #19 ....$25-35
Flyers #19 ....$20-30

Tuf-Tots Series, 1969
Big L Dump Truck, #607 ....$7-9
Caravan, #625 ....$15-18
Cement Mixer Truck, #615 ....$7-10
Circus Cage Truck, #626......................$7-10

Citroën Coupe, #619, 1:66....................$12-15
Citroën DS Sports, #602.......................$12-15
City Refuse Truck, #614 ....$7-10
Dodge Dart
Coupe, #621 ....$12-15
Sport, #604............................$12-15
Earth Mover, #627 ....$7-10
Esso Tanker, #601 ....$15-20
Express Freight Truck, #611 ....$7-10
Fire Engine, #624 ....$7-10
Herts Farms Jeep and Trailer, #608 ....$12-15
Horse Box, #617 ....$12-15
L.S. Construction Tipper Truck, #610..........$7-10
London Bus, #623 ....$12-15
M Autos Truck with Petrol Pumps, #609....$12-15
Mercedes
Coupe, #622 ....$15-18
Sport, #605............................$12-15
Milk Delivery Truck, #616 ....$12-15
Speedboat and Trailer, #613 ....$12-15
Stingray
Coupe, #620 ....$15-18
Sports, #603 ....$12-15
Tow Truck, #606 ....$12-15
Waste Disposal Truck, #618 ....$7-10

New Impy Series, 1976
Articulated Transporter with pipes and water
tank, #184..................................$12-15

Boat Transporter, #188 ....$15-18
Breakdown Truck with Lotus Europa, #186 ...$15-18
Bulk carrier and Trailer, #191 ....$12-15
Cadillac, #72 ....$12-15
Cadillac with speedboat on trailer, #185 ...$15-18
Cement Mixer and Trailer, #192............$12-15
Corvette GT Rally, #76 ....$12-15
Corvette Stingray Fastback, #74............$12-15
Crane Truck, #181 ....$10-12
Esso Fuel Tanker, #182 ....$10-12
Ford Mustang, #79 ....$15-18
Jaguar, #77 ....$15-18
   with cabin cruiser on trailer, #185 .....$15-18
Lotus Europa, #80 ....$12-15
Low Loader with Tuf-Tots car, #183.........2-15
Maserati Mistral, #78 ....$15-18
Mercedes-Benz, #82 ....$10-12
Petrol Tanker and Trailer, #190 ....$15-18
Range Rover, #71 ....$12-15
   Police car, #75 ....$10-12
   with speedboat on trailer, #185........$15-18
Six-Wheel Truck
   Bulk carrier, #51 ....$10-12
   Cement Mixer, #54 ....$10-12
   Crane Truck, #52 ....$10-12
   Express Freight Truck, #55 ....$10-12
   Low Sided Truck, #56 ....$10-12
   Marine Transporter, #53 ....$10-12
   Petrol Tanker, #61 ....$10-12
   Sand Truck, #58 ....$10-12
   Timber Truck, #60 ....$10-12
   Tipper, #50 ....$10-12
   Water Pipe Truck, #59 ....$10-12
   Water Tank Truck, #57 ....$10-12
Timber Truck, #189 ....$10-12
Toyota Coupe, #73 ....$12-15
Volvo 264 Coupe, #81.......................$12-15

Look Smart (see Looksmart Models)

Looksmart Models

Casella Postale 17
21047 Saronno (VA) Italy
e-mail: info@looksmartmodels.com
website: www.looksmartmodels.com

   Looksmart creates limited edition handmade 1:43 scale models of 500–1,000 each in resin, photogravure, white metal, and turned parts.

Alfa Romeo 1750 '68 ....$100-125
Alfa Romeo 2000 '71 ....$100-125
Alfa Romeo 33/2 Prototipo Speciale
   1969 ....$100-125
Alfa Romeo 8C Salone di Francoforte
   2003 ....$100-125

Alfa Romeo Alfetta 158 F1 ....$100-125
Alfa Romeo BAT 5 Salone di Torino
   1953 ....$100-125
Alfa Romeo BAT 7 1954 ....$100-125
Alfa Romeo BAT 9 1955 ....$100-125
Alfa Romeo Discovolante 1900 C52
   Coupé '52 ....$100-125
   Spider '52 ....$100-125
Alfa Romeo Giulia
   1600 Super 1971 "Polizia" 1971 ..$100-125

Cabrio 1600 GTC '64.........................$100-125

   Carabinieri – 1° Version $100-125
   Coupé 1600 Sprint GT $100-125
   Coupé 1600 Sprint GTA.............$100-125
   Coupé 1750 GT Veloce '69 ....$100-125
   Coupé 2000 GT Veloce $100-125
   Coupé GT 1300 Junior '66 ....$100-125
   Coupé GTA 1300 Junior '68 ....$100-125
   Super T1 1° Version Carabinieri.....$100-125
Alfa Romeo Giulietta
   1300 SS $100-125
   1600 SS $100-125

Alfa Romeo Montreal $100-125

Alfa Romeo Super 1971 ....$100-125
Audi Le Mmans Quattro $100-125
Audi Nuvolari Quattro.......................$100-125
Bugatti Chiron Study 1999.................$100-125
Bugatti T52S Atlantic 1936 ....$100-125
Bugatti Veyron Study 2003 ....$100-125
Bugatti 57SC Atlantic ch57, #374 1936,
   Winner Pebble Beach 2003 ....$100-125
Ferrari "Scocca Matta" 1987 ....$100-125
Ferrari 166 Inter 1949 ....$100-125
Ferrari 206 Berlinetta GT Telaio
   00106 ....$100-125
Ferrari 208
   GTB Turbo 1982 ....$100-125
   GTS Turbo 1982 ....$100-125
Ferrari 250
   GT Boano 1957 ....$100-125
   GT Speciale California $100-125

GT Speciale Sud Africa $100-125
P5 Pininfarina 1968 ....$100-125
Ferrari 275 P Coupé "Michelotti" 1968....$100-125
Ferrari 288 GTO Evoluzione $100-125
Ferrari 3 GTZ 1971 ....$100-125
Ferrari 308
   GT Rainbow "Bertone" 1976 ....$100-125
   GTB "speciale" by Pininfarina
     (Millechiodi) 1977 ....$100-125
   GTB 1975 ....$100-125
   GTS 1977 ....$100-125
Ferrari 330 Coupé "Zagato" 1974 .....$100-125
Ferrari 360 GTC $100-125
Ferrari 365
   GT/4 2+2 1967 ....$100-125
   GT/4 "Croisette" SW S/N 18255 by
     Felber $100-125
   P Berlinetta "Pininfarina" 1966.......$100-125
   P Berlinetta "Pininfarina" G. Agnelli
     1967 ....$100-125
   P Berlinetta 1966........................$100-125
   P Berlinetta 1966 "G. Agnelli" 1966..$100-125
Ferrari 400
   Superamerica 1959 ....$100-125
   Superamerica 1963 ....$100-125
   I 1980 ....$100-125
Ferrari 410 Super America 0721 SA...$100-125
Ferrari 412
   2+2 1985 ....$100-125
   2+2 Spider 1985 ....$100-125
   I Cabriolet Pavesi 1985 ....$100-125
Ferrari 512 TR $100-125
Ferrari 612 Scaglietti 2003 ....$100-125
Ferrari Cabriolet "Scaglietti" Prototype
   1986 ....$100-125
Ferrari Dino GT Berlinetta 1966 ....$100-125
Ferrari F512M $100-125
Ferrari La Rossa by Pininfarina $100-125
Ferrari Mondial
   8.8 32, 24 hr Spa Francochamps ..$100-125
   8T Soft Top $100-125
   T Cabrio....................................$100-125
   T Coupé....................................$100-125
Ferrari PPG Pace Car 1987 ....$100-125
Ferrari Prototipo
   "Pinin" 1980.............................$100-125
   512 S 1969 ....$100-125
Ferrari Rossa Salone Di Torino 2000,
   red $100-125
Ferrari Testarossa
   1° serie 1984 ....$100-125
   Cabriolet 1985 ....$100-125
   Spider "G. Agnelli" 1987 ....$100-125
Lamborghini 291 F1 ....$100-125
Lamborghini 350
   GT $100-125

GT Spider.....................$100-125

GTV..........................$100-125

GTZ Zagato 1965 ....$100-125
Lamborghini 400 GT
  2+2.............................$100-125
  Flying Star II 1966 ....$100-125
Lamborghini Athlon 1980 ....$100-125
Lamborghini Bravo 1974 ....$100-125
Lamborghini Cala 1995 ....$100-125
Lamborghini Countach Evoluzione ,1985 ..$100-125
Lamborghini Espada 400 GT $100-125
  Open Roof.........................$100-125
Lamborghini Gallardo $100-125
Lamborghini Islero 1968 ....$100-125
Lamborghini Jalpa,1981 ....$100-125
  Spider 1987......................$100-125
  Targa.................................$100-125
Lamborghini Jaramas
  Sport 1972 ....$100-125
  GT 2+2 1970......................$100-125
  GT 2+2 1972......................$100-125
Lamborghini Marzal, 1967 ....$100-125
  Jarama Sport $100-125
Lamborghini Monza 400 1966..........$100-125
Lamborghini P140 (1987–1993)........$100-125
Lamborghini Portofino 1987 ....$100-125
Lamborghini Raptor 1996 ....$100-125
Lamborghini R-GT Race Version $100-125
Lamborghini Urraco
  200.....................................$100-125
  250.....................................$100-125
  300.....................................$100-125
  300 Bob Wallace......................$100-125
  3000 Silhouette 1976 ....$100-125
Pagani Zonda $100-125
Porsche 928
  1977....................................$100-125
  S GTS 1979 ....$100-125

LP Creations (see Evrat 87)

Lucky Plan Industries, Ltd. (see Dimension 4)

Luso

These are diecast and plastic models made in Portugal in the early to mid 1980s. Harvey

Goranson reports that they made a nice racing version of the BMW 320 in Liechtenstein livery as raced at LeMans.

BMW 320 ....$35-40
Citroën GS Pallas "Michelin," yellow.......$35-40
Porsche 935, Martini racing, car #4, blue 7,
  red stripes, #M8, 1:43 ....$35-40

Luxor

Holland, The Netherlands, is home to Luxor, a brand known to produce at least one plastic toy car around 1945.

Armstrong-Siddeley Coupe, red with pale gray
  plastic wheels, 5".............................$40-55

M

M C Toys (see Maisto)

The Ma Collection
Michel Sordet
MA Collection
17 ch. de la Bergeronnette
CH-1228
Plan-Les-Ouates, Switzerland
fax: 00 41 22 731 66 75
e-mail: sordetmaco@bluewin.ch
website: www.macosordet.com

A brochure from Sinclair's Mini-Auto describes the 1:43 scale 1946 "Rita Hayworth" Delahaye 135M as "the sensuously-bodied Convertible that Prince Ali Khan gave to Hollywood star Rita Hayworth. Custom coachwork by Figoni Falaschi, this fabulous 1:43 scale miniature is by the famous Ma Collection of Switzerland." Only 150 copies of this model have been made promising high resale value. Other 1:43 scale Ma models are made in France.

Also produced for the Ma Collection were some resin hand-built models in the mid-1970s.

Bugatti 57
  Milord 1937, yellow and black.....$350-400
  1939, yellow and black..............$350-400
  1939, green and black...............$350-400
Bugatti 101 Antem 1953, red and black ..$350-400
Delahaye V12 Roadster 1938, red $350-400
Delahaye 135M
  "Rita Hayworth" 1946..................$350-400
  Guillore 1949, blue $350-400
Hispano Suiza K6 1945 ....$350-400
Talbot Lago T26 GS 1948
  blue $350-400
  white...................................$350-400

black.............................$350-400

Madison Models
Madison Models are 1:43 scale white metal models made in Great Britain.

1952 Buick Super
  Two-door Hardtop $175-200
  Convertible $175-200
1957 Chrysler New Yorker
  Hardtop, two-tone blue $175-200

Madmax (see Grip Zechin)

Mafwo
This obscure British diecast company is known to have produced just two models in roughly 1:43 scale, simple zinc alloy castings with metal wheels.

Alvis 4-Seater Tourer $45-60
Grand Prix Racing car.........................$45-60

Magic (also see Excite)
Magic / Excite
1270 Champion Circle
Carrollton, TX 75006 USA

A diecast toy assortment that goes by the Magic brand curiously bears the same address on the back of their package as Excite models. Closer inspection, particularly of the Chevrolet Caprice fire department command car, reveals it to be made by Welly. Apparently this practice of repackaging and re-branding diecast toys is not as uncommon as we might think.

Magnuson Models
Magnuson models, manufactured by Wm. K. Walthers, Inc., are one piece resin-cast unpainted miniature kits in 1:87 scale (HO gauge). Cast metal wheels are included in these easy-to-build kits, and some models feature separate metal bumpers. They are apparently no longer produced since they aren't listed in the 1999 Walther's catalog.

1939 Sedan Delivery, #439-911 ....$5-7
1940 Panel Truck, #439-928 ....$5-7
1940 Traveler 4-Door Sedan, #439-920.....$5-7
1941 Convertible with top up, #439-913....$5-7
1941 Pickup Truck, #439-919 ....$5-7
1948 Coupe, #439-910 ....$5-7
1948 Diamond T Coal Truck, #439-932...$8-10
1953 Flatbed Truck, #439-935................$8-10
1953 Hardtop, #439-912 ....$5-7
1953 Tank Truck, #439-921 ....$8-10

1954 Panel Truck, #439-922 .... $5-7
1956 Hardtop, #439-946 .... $8-10
1956 Semi Tractor, #439-924 .... $5-7
1956 Delivery Truck, #439-926 .... $5-7
1957 LP Gas Delivery Truck, #439-934 .... $8-10
1959 Checker Marathon Taxi, #439-914 ... $5-7
1964 Step Van, #439-931 .... $5-7
Crew Cab Pickup Truck, #439-933 .... $8-10
Divco Milk Truck, #439-917 .... $5-7
Heavy Duty Coal Truck, #439-936 ...... $8-10
Model "R" Semi Tractor, #439-929 .... $5-7
Oil Truck, #439-930 .... $5-7
Railway Express Agency Delivery Truck,
    #439-923 .... $8-10

Maisto

Maisto International, Inc., based in Fontana, California, is the US division of Master Toy Co. Ltd. of Thailand, with May Cheong Toy Products Factory Ltd. of Kowloon as the Hong Kong subsidiary. The company also encompasses May Tat, the budget toy division. Previously marketed in the US under the brand name of M C Toys, Maisto has become a dominant force in the precision scale model market as well as the diecast toy industry. Previously, their smallest toys, comparable to Matchbox toys and Hot Wheels in size and price, were called M C Toys Mini Racers. Since unifying the product line to the Maisto brand in 1994, these approximately 1:64 scale toys have been renamed Maisto Turbo Treads, and have been produced with new color variations and packaging.

Meanwhile, Maisto has made a huge impact in the larger scale model industry, starting with their Trophy series models of approximately 1:43 scale that sell for $4 or less, and crowning the product line with 1:12 scale diecast masterpieces that retail for over $100 each. Every Maisto model shows exquisite attention to detail that establishes the company as a strong competitor to the big name brands. In fact, Maisto has become one of the big name brands.

As is the case with many brands, M C Toys, Intex Recreation, and Zee Toys were all related in one way or another. The intermixing of models and castings blurred the lines that demarcated one company's product from the others'. Maisto's willingness to market their wares under retailers' proprietary brands is a major factor in their success. K-Mart sells them as MegaMovers. Wal-Mart offers them as Road & Track models, commemorating the fiftieth anniversary of the magazine of the same name.

In 1998, to commemorate Tonka's fiftieth anniversary, Maisto began a series of 3¼" long miniature versions of classic Tonka vehicles that sell for $1.99 each. Models are listed at the end of this section. Larger renditions in diecast are also available for around $5 each.

Also in 1998, Maisto introduced a series of farm implements in approximately 1:64 scale dubbed Countryside Farm & Field. These are an obvious attempt to capitalize on the popularity of Ertl's similar 1:64 scale offerings and cut into their market with similar models and sets competitively priced.

Maisto 1:10 Scale Motorcycles
BMW R1100R, 1995, #31601
    red $30-35
    blue $30-35
Honda Shadow VT1100C2, 1995, #31602
    turquoise $30-35
    red $30-35
Indian Chief Roadmaster, #31604
    red and white $30-35
    yellow $30-35
    light blue $30-35
Moto Guzzi California 1100, 1995, #31603
    yellow $30-35
    red $30-35

Maisto 1:18 Scale Motorcycles
BMW R1100R $5-6
BMW R1100RS $5-6
Honda NR $5-6
Honda Valkyrie $5-6
Honda VT1100C2 .... $5-6
Indian Chief $5-6
Indian Four $5-6
Kawasaki KLX250SR $5-6
Kawasaki Ninja ZX-9R $5-6
Malaguti Phantom F-12 .... $5-6
Moto Guzzi V10 Centauro $5-6
Yamaha FZ600R $5-6
Yamaha TT250R $5-6
Yamaha V-Max $5-6
Yamaha XV1000 Virago $5-6

Maisto 1:12 Scale
Jaguar XJ220 1992
    green, #33201 .... $110-135
    metallic dark blue, #33201 .... $110-135
    red, #33201 .... $110-135
    silver, #33201 .... $110-135
    turquoise, #33201 .... $110-135
    white, #33201 .... $110-135
    yellow, #33201 .... $110-135
    yellow with XJ220 graphics on sides,
        #33203 .... $110-135
Cadillac Eldorado Biarritz Convertible, 1959,
    #33202

pink $110-135
red $110-135
white $110-135

Maisto 1:18 Scale
Alfa Romeo Spider, #31831
    red $15-20
    black $15-20
Alpine Renault 1600S, 1971
    blue with Rally markings, #35850 ...... $18-24
    metallic blue, #31850 .... $15-20
BMW 325i 1993
    Convertible, black, #31812 .... $15-20
    Convertible, red, #31812 .... $15-20
    Convertible, silver, #31812 .... $15-20
    black, #31816 .... $15-20
    blue, #31816 .... $15-20
    red, #31816 .... $15-20
    white, #31816 .... $15-20
BMW 502 Convertible, 1955
    dark blue, #31817 .... $15-20

cream, #31817 .... **$15-20**
    blue and white, #35817 .... $15-20
    custom airbrushed graphics, #30817 ... $25-30
BMW 850i, 1990, #31805
    metallic red $15-20
    teal $15-20
    blue $15-20
    black $15-20
Bugatti EB110, 1992, #31808
    red $15-20
    blue $15-20
Cadillac Eldorado Biarritz, 1959, #31813
    pink $15-20

red **$15-20**
    white $15-20
Chevrolet Fleetmaster "Woody," 1948,
    #31854, 1998
    brown $15-20
    burgundy $15-20
    gray $30-35

Citroën 2CV, 1952
closed top, gray, #31834...............$15-20
closed top, cream, #31834.............$15-20
open top, gray, #31835..................$15-20
open top, cream, #31835.............$15-20
Citroën 15CV, 1952
6-Cylinder, black, #31837...............$15-20
6-Cylinder, gray, #31837...............$15-20
black, #31821................................$15-20
burgundy, #31821.........................$15-20
burgundy and black, #35821.........$15-20
gray, #31821.................................$15-20
Taxi, red and black, #35821T........$18-24
yellow with Rally markings,
#35821.................................$15-20
Corvette Convertible, 1998, #31846
red..$15-20
white..$15-20
Corvette Coupe, 1996, #31840
red...$15-20
green...$15-20
Corvette Indy Pace car, 1995, #31827
burgundy and white......................$15-20
Corvette LT-4 Convertible, 1996, #31830
magenta.......................................$15-20
blue...$15-20
silver...$15-20
Corvette ZR-1, 1992, #31809
burgundy......................................$15-20
red..$15-20
white..$15-20
Dodge Caravan, 1996, #31913
burgundy.....................................$15-20
green...$15-20
Dodge Concept Vehicle (Copperhead),
#31851.....................................$15-20
Dodge Viper GTS Coupe, 1996
blue with white stripes, #31832.......$15-20
Indy Pace car, blue with white stripes,
#31828.................................$15-20
Dodge Viper GTS-R, #31845, white with
blue stripes................................$15-20
Ferrari 348ts, 1990, #31804
red..$15-20
yellow..$15-20
Ferrari F50 1995
Coupe, yellow, #31822F...............$15-20
Coupe, silver, #31822F..................$15-20
Coupe, red, #31822F.....................$15-20
Barchetta, yellow, #31823.............$15-20
Barchetta, red, #31823..................$15-20
Ferrari F550 Maranello, #31839
red..$15-20
yellow..$15-20
Ford F-150 Pickup, #31921
burgundy......................................$15-20

silver..$15-20
blue...$15-20
Ford GT-90 Concept car, 1994, #31827/9
white...$15-20
black..$15-20
Ford Mustang Mach III, 1994, #31815
red..$15-20
dark blue.....................................$15-20
white...$15-20

Hummer Civilian Wagon, red............$18-24

Jaguar Mark II, 1959, #31833
green...$15-20
cream..$15-20
Jaguar XJ220, 1992, #31807
metallic dark blue.........................$15-20
silver...$15-20
Jaguar XK8, #31836
green...$15-20
blue...$15-20

Jaguar S, silver....................................$20-25

Lamborghini Diablo SV, #31844,
white..$15-20
Lamborghini Jota, #31829L, 1996
metallic purple.............................$15-20
blue...$20-25
Lamborghini Diablo
1990, red, #31803......................$15-20
1990, yellow, #31803..................$15-20
SE, metallic purple, #31819...........$15-20
SE, green, #31819.......................$15-20
McLaren F1, 1992, #31810
gray...$15-20
metallic gold................................$15-20
silver...$15-20
Mercedes-Benz 190SL Convertible, 1955,
#31824

red..$15-20
white...$15-20

Mercedes-Benz 280SE, 1966, #31811
burgundy......................................$15-20
white..$15-20
Convertible, #30811, custom
airbrushed..............................$25-30
Mercedes-Benz 300S, 1955
burgundy, #31806.......................$15-20

metallic green, #31806.......................$15-20
black, #31806...............................$15-20
white, #31806...............................$15-20
Convertible, custom airbrushed,
#30806..................................$25-30
Mercedes-Benz 500 SL 1989/1990, #31801
aqua..$15-20
lilac...$15-20
silver...$15-20
cranberry.....................................$15-20
black..$15-20

Mercedes-Benz 1997 A Class, blue..$18-24

Mercedes-Benz A Class Formula 1, #35841
metallic silver with red and black accent
trim.......................................$18-24
Mercedes-Benz A140, #31841
red..$15-20
black..$15-20
Mercedes-Benz SLK, #31838
silver...$15-20
yellow..$30-40

Mercedes-Benz SLK 230 Cabriolet, #31842
  red $15-20
  white...$15-20
Porsche 550A Spyder, #31843, silver $15-20
Porsche 911 Carrera, 1994, #31818
  red $15-20
  blue $15-20
  yellow $15-20
Porsche 911 Speedster 1989, #31802
  red $15-20
  yellow $15-20
  white...$15-20
Porsche Boxster, #31814
  black..$15-20
  silver..$15-20
Porsche No. 1 Type 356 Roadster 1948,
  #31853, 1998.............................$18-24
Smart, with interchangeable body panels,
  #31852

yellow/red, 1998 ....$18-24
  white, 1998 ....$18-24
  black, 1998 ....$18-24
Snowmobile with pullback motor.................$6-8
Volkswagen Beetle, 1951

Cabriolet, red $20-25

Convertible, baby blue, #31826 ....$15-20
Convertible, dark green and yellow,
  #35826 ....$15-20
Convertible, pink, #31826 ....$15-20
Coupe, light blue and white, #35820 .....$15-20
Coupe, pink with flowers, #35820 ....$15-20
Export Sedan, gray, #31820 ....$15-20

Export Sedan, black, #31820 ....$15-20

Export Sedan, green, #31820 ....$15-20

Maisto 1:24 Scale (except where noted)
Bugatti EB110, blue or red, #31908 ......$10-12
Chevrolet Camaro Z28, 1996, 1:25, #31924
  white...$10-12
  teal $10-12
Chevrolet Corvette, 1997
  red, #31940 ....$10-12
  white, #31940 ....$10-12

Chevrolet Impala Taxi.........................$10-12

Chrysler Plymouth Voyager, 1:26
  white, #31928 ....$10-12
  blue, #31928...............................$10-12
Dodge Caravan / Chrysler Voyager, 1996, 1:26
  maroon, #31913 ....$10-12
  green, #31913 ....$10-12
Dodge Ram Pickup, 1995
  black, 1:26, #31912....................$10-12
  Indy Pace Truck, 1995, blue with white stripes,
    1:26, #319121.......................$15-18

red, 1:26, #31912 ....$10-12
  Supersport SS/T, black with white stripes,
    1:26, #31930 ....$10-12
Dodge Viper GTS Coupe, 1995, blue with white
  stripes, #B0600 ....$10-12
Dodge Viper RT/10
  1995, Pace car, red, #319151........$15-18
  1995, yellow or green, #31915.......$10-12
  1996, white with blue stripes, #31914 ..$10-12
  1997, blue, #31932 ....$10-12
Ferrari 348ts
  red, #31904 ....$10-12
  yellow, #31904............................$10-12
Ferrari 550 Maranello
  red, #31939 ....$10-12
  silver, #31939 ....$10-12
Ferrari F50
  Convertible, red, #31922 ....$10-12
  Convertible, silver, #31922 ....$10-12
  Coupe, 1995, red, #31951 ....$10-12
  Coupe, 1995, yellow, #31951........$10-12
  Hardtop, yellow, #31923 ....$10-12
  Hardtop, red, #31923 ....$10-12
Ferrari F355
  Cabriolet, black, #31927 ....$10-12
  Cabriolet, white, #31927 ....$10-12
  Coupe, 1996, red, #31925 ....$10-12
  Coupe, 1996, yellow, #31925........$10-12
Ford Explorer
  1992, burgundy, with "Eddie Bauer" on
    doors, #31906 ....$10-12
  1992, burgundy, without "Eddie Bauer" on
    doors, #31906..........................$10-12
  1992, dark blue, with "Eddie Bauer" on
    doors, #31906..........................$10-12
  1992, dark blue, without "Eddie Bauer" on
    doors, #31906..........................$10-12
  1992, green, with "Eddie Bauer" on doors,
    #31906 ....$10-12
  1992, green, without "Eddie Bauer" on
    doors, #31906..........................$10-12
  1992, metallic teal, with "Eddie Bauer" on
    doors, #31906..........................$10-12
  1992, metallic teal, without "Eddie Bauer" on
    doors, #31906..........................$10-12
  1992, white, with "Eddie Bauer" on doors,
    #31906 ....$10-12
  1992, white, without "Eddie Bauer" on
    doors, #31906..........................$10-12
  1995, black, #31909.....................$10-12
  1995, green, #31909 ....$10-12
Ford F-150
  black, 1993, with ATV in back & driver,
    1:25, #31911 ....$10-12
  black, 1993, without ATV in back & driver,
    1:25, #31911 ....$10-12

Flareside, 1997, silver or dark blue, 1:26, #31921 ....$10-12

Indy Pace Truck, 1996, red, #31916...$15-18

metallic teal, 1993, with ATV in back & driver, 1:25, #31911.................$10-12

metallic teal, 1993, without ATV in back & driver, 1:25, #31911 ....$10-12

red, 1993, with ATV in back & driver, 1:25, #31911 ....$10-12

red, 1993, without ATV in back & driver, 1:25, #31911 ....$10-12

Ford F-350 Super Duty Pickup, 1999
silver with flatbed, 1:27, #31937......$10-12
red with stake bed, 1:27, #31937....$10-12

Ford Mustang, 1994
GT, red, #31905 ....$10-12
goldenrod, #31905 ....$10-12
green, #31905 ....$10-12
dark blue, #31905 ....$10-12
Pace Car, red, #31917 ....$15-18

Jaguar XJ220
metallic dark blue, #31907 ....$10-12
silver, #31907 ....$10-12

Jaguar XK8, #31936 ....$10-12

Lamborghini Diablo
red, #31903 ....$10-12
SE, 1994/1995, metallic magenta, #31919 ....$10-12
SE, 1994/1995, metallic green, #31919 ....$10-12
yellow, #31903 ....$10-12

Lamborghini Jota
purple, #31929 ....$10-12
blue, #31929 ....$10-12

McLaren F1, red or silver, #31910 ....$10-12

Mercedes-Benz 500SL
burgundy, #31901.......................$10-12
light blue, #31901 ....$10-12
metallic dark gray, #31901 ....$10-12

Mercedes-Benz M-Class ML320
silver, #31947 ....$10-12
black, #31947 ....$10-12

Mercedes-Benz SLK 230 Cabriolet
red, #31942 ....$10-12
yellow, #31942 ....$10-12

Plymouth Prowler, purple, #31931 ....$10-12

Porsche 911 Speedster
blue, #31902 ....$10-12
red, #31902 ....$10-12
white, #31902 ....$10-12

Porsche Boxster, red or silver, #31933.....$10-12

Maisto Trophy/Special Edition, 5" Models

Aston Martin DB7, 1:40, metallic purple.......$3-4
Aston Martin Virage, metallic green $3-4
BMW Z1 Cabriolet, metallic silver $3-4

BMW 325i Cabriolet, 1:37, white $3-4
BMW 850i, metallic red $3-4
Bugatti EB110, blue.............................$3-4

1957 Chevrolet Corvette, 1:39
black with white trim $3-4
silver with red trim $3-4

1963 Chevrolet Corvette Stingray, 1:38, metallic silver $3-4

Chevrolet Corvette ZR-1 1:38
white $3-4
yellow.......................................$3-4

Dodge Viper RT/10, 1:39, red...................$3-4
Ferrari 288 GTO, 1:36, red.....................$3-4
Ferrari 348ts, 1:38, yellow $3-4
Ferrari 456GT, 1:39, red $3-4
Ferrari F40, 1:39, red $3-4
Ferrari F50, 1:39, red $3-4
Ferrari Testarossa, 1:39, red $3-4
Jaguar E Cabriolet, British racing green $3-4
Jaguar XJ220, 1:40, metallic dark blue........$3-4

Jaguar XJS V12 Cabriolet, 1:40
blue $3-4
metallic silver.............................$3-4
red $3-4

Lamborghini Diablo, 1:40, yellow..............$3-4
Lotus Elan, 1:36, metallic blue $3-4
Lotus Esprit, 1:38, metallic silver $3-4

Mercedes-Benz 500SL
black $3-4
metallic blue $3-4
metallic teal $3-4

MG RV8, 1:37, metallic green..................$3-4

Porsche 911
Carrera, 1:38, yellow $3-4
Speedster Cabriolet, 1:38, red $3-4
Speedster Cabriolet, 1:38, silver $3-4
Turbo Flat Nose Cabriolet, white $3-4

Porsche 959, 1:36, silver......................$3-4

Maisto Power Racers, 4" models with pullback motors–suggested retail $2.99

A pullback motor distinguishes these models from their non-motorized Trophy counterparts. Many Trophy models are duplicated in this series. Here is just a sampling.

Acura RSX Type S, 1:36............................$3-4

Aston Martin DB7, purple $3-4

Dodge Ram Quad Cab, 1:43.............$3-4

Hummer H2 4-door Pickup, 1:46 ....$3-4

Hummer H2 4-door Wagon, 1:46.............$3-4

Hummer H2 SUV, white, 1:46 ....$3-4

Jaguar XJ220, silver.................................$3-4

Jeep Liberty, 1:43 ....$3-4

Lotus Esprit Turbo, silver $3-4

Mini Cooper S, 1:36 ....$3-4

Renault Clio V6 Sport, 1:39 ....$3-4

Maisto Mini Transporters, 1:87 scale semi
    tractor-trailers suggested retail price.......$2.99
Semi Boat Transporter, #M64 ....$3-4
Semi car Transporter, #M63 ....$3-4
Semi Fire Engine #M59 ....$3-4
Semi Freighter "North American," #M61 ......$3-4
Semi Freighter "Trans America Express,"
    #M61 ....$3-4
Semi Police Helicopter Transporter, #M62 ....$3-4
Semi Rescue Helicopter Transporter, #M57 ...$3-4
Semi Racing Boat Transporter, #M58 ....$3-4
Semi Tanker "Shell," #M60 ....$3-4

Maisto 3" Toys: Turbo Treads, M C Toys Mini
Racers, Tonka, Special Edition, Wal-Mart kid connection, Walgreen's Speed Wheels

    These toys match Matchbox regular series
models in size and accuracy of scale. In fact,
before they were Maistos, collectors quipped that
"M C" stood for "Matchbox Copy." (It actually
stands for "May Cheong.") While most models
have no moving parts, such as opening doors,
their quality is remarkable for their usual price of
$1 each or less. These are also issued as Maisto
Fantasy series, in Wal-Mart stores under the Kid
Connection brand, at Walgreen's as Speed
Wheels, and at various stores as Tonka toys.

    While most models are currently available,
their quality and rising popularity should make
them more valuable as collectible toys over the
years. The fact that the value has already risen
from $1 to $2 for these models attest to their
popularity and quality, although the value will
likely not soon rise above that figure. In addition, they can often still be purchased for 50
cents each, and occasionally for less.

Ambulance Truck $1-2

ATV $1-2

Audi Quattro, #8447 ....$1-2

BMW 750il, #8742 ....$1-2

BMW 850i, #9005 ....$1-2

BMW M1, #8448 ....$1-2

2001 Buick Bengal Concept $1-2
Buick LeSabre Stock Car, #8618 ....$1-2

2001 Cadillac Vizon Concept $1-2

2002 Cadillac Cien Concept $1-2

Caterpillar Quarry Dump Truck $1-2

Chevrolet 3500 Van $1-2

Chevrolet Borrego Concept $1-2
Chevrolet Corvette ZR-1, 1997, #8617 ....$1-2

Chevrolet SSR, 2000 ....$1-2

Chevrolet Trailblazer, Speed Wheels Series
    XI $2-3
Chrysler Concept Vehicle (Dodge "Copperhead"),
    1998 ....$2-3
Citroën 2CV, #8732 ....$1-2

City Taxi $1-2

Commando Hum-Vee, yellow......................$1-2

Dirt Bike $1-2

Dodge Concept Vehicle $1-2
Dodge Viper GTS....................................$1-2

Dodge Viper RT/10.............................$1-2

Ferrari 250 GTO, #8736....................$1-2

Ferrari 308 GTB, #8445 ....$1-2
Ferrari 348ts, #9101 ....$1-2

Ferrari 365 GTB, #9004 ....$1-2

Ferrari F40, #9001 ....$1-2

Ferrari Testarossa, red

M C Toys Mini Racers pkg, #9010..........$2-3

Maisto Turbo Treads pkg $1-2
Fire Ladder Truck......................................$1-2
Fire Truck

safety green, "Ontario International Airport," Tonka series..............................$1-2

Ford Econovan, #9008 ....$1-2
Ford Escort 1.6i, #8449 ....$1-2

Ford Explorer $1-2
Ford Granada 2.8 GL, #8451 ....$1-2
Ford Interceptor

black and white, "Internet Highway Patrol," Tonka series................................$1-2

Ford Pick-Up 4x4, #8739 ....$1-2

Ford Sierra XR4Ti, #8441...............$1-2

Ford Street Kar $1-2

Formula 1 Racer
    #8733 ....$1-2
    #8734 ....$1-2
Garbage Truck..$1-2

2001 GMC Terracross Concept..............$1-2

Haywood Police..................................$1-2

2001 Hummer H2 SUT.........................$1-2

2003 Hummer H2 SUV $1-2

Hummer H2 ....$1-2

Jaguar XJ220 ....$1-2

Jaguar XJ-S V-12, #8613 ....$1-2

Jeepster $1-2

Jumbo Crane, styled after Matchbox Taylor Jumbo Crane

bright orange, "Red's Crane Service," Tonka series...$2-3

Lamborghini Countach, #8735...............$1-2

Lamborghini Diablo, #9006 ....$1-2

Lamborghini Murcielago............................$1-2

Lincoln Continental Mark VII.........................$1-2
Mazda RX-7, #8738..................................$1-2

Mercedes-Benz 260 SL, #8615................$1-2

Mercedes-Benz 500 SL

#9011 ....$1-2
  #8452..$1-2
Mercedes-Benz CLK-GTR $1-2
Mercedes-Benz ML-320 ....$1-2
Mercedes-Benz Van, #8450 ....$1-2
Mighty Tonka Backhoe, #21 ....$2-3
Mighty Tonka Crane, #16..........................$2-3
Mighty Tonka Quarry Truck, yellow dumper
  with black cab, grill and chassis, #1
unnumbered blisterpack, 1998...................$4-5
  numbered blisterpack, 1999.................$2-3
Mighty Tonka Road Grader, yellow with
  black and white accents, #2
unnumbered blisterpack, 1998...................$4-5
  numbered blisterpack, 1999.................$2-3
Motorcycle $1-2
Mustang Mach III.....................................$1-2
Nissan MID-4, #8737 ....$1-2
Nissan 4x4 Dirt Truck...............................$1-2
Nissan 300ZX, #8620...............................$1-2

Peugeot 205 GTI, #8611 ....$1-2

Peugeot 309, #8614...................................$1-2
Peugeot 405 Turbo 16, #8741 ....$1-2

Pontiac Firebird, #8443..............................$1-2

Pontiac Rev Concept.............................$1-2

Porsche 356A, #9003 ....$1-2

Porsche 911 Speedster, #9012.................$1-2
Porsche 956, #8442 ....$1-2

Porsche 959, #9009................................$1-2

Porsche Turbo 911, #8444 ....$1-2

Renault 25V6 Turbo, #8612......................$1-2

Suzuki SJ413Q Samurai, #8622 ....$1-2
Tank Truck

**Grande, Your Milk Marketers... And A
Whole Lot More**......................................$1-2

Tonka Auto Club Tow, #30 ....$2-3
Tonka Baja Bug, #15 ....$2-3
Tonka Big Mike, #51 ....$12-16
Tonka Bulldozer, modern, green with
    silver-gray plow, #23 ....$2-3
Tonka Bulldozer, styled after larger pressed
    steel version from the 1950s

orange, "State Hi-Way Dept." $2-3

Tonka Cable Vision Bucket, #32 ....$2-3
Tonka Camp Tonkawa Bus, khaki, #18........$2-3
Tonka Cement Mixer, #9.............................$2-3
Tonka Chevrolet Caprice Sheriff, #20 ....$2-3
Tonka Chevrolet Silverado, black, #11 ....$2-3
Tonka City Recycler, #38 ....$2-3
Tonka Classic 1949 Dump Truck, red with
    green dumper, #4
    unnumbered blisterpack, 1998 ....$4-5
    numbered blisterpack, 1999 ....$2-3
Tonka Classic 1956 Pickup Truck, dark blue,
    #3, unnumbered blisterpack, 1998........$4-5
    numbered blisterpack, 1999 ....$2-3
Tonka Coast Guard Helicopter, MH-60K
    Night Hawk, red, #10 ....$2-3
Tonka Daimler Tour Bus, #50 ....$2-3
Tonka Dodge Dakota, #33...........................$2-3
Tonka Dog Recovery Van, silver, #12...........$2-3
Tonka Fertilizer Van, #37............................$2-3
Tonka Fire Engine, #35 ....$2-3
Tonka Fire Support, #46..............................$2-3
Tonka Ford Explorer, #47 ....$2-3
Tonka Ford Grand Prix Trailblazer, #25 ....$2-3
Tonka Ford Pickup, #41 ....$2-3
Tonka Forest Ranger, #49............................$2-3
Tonka Front End Loader, #14 ....$2-3
Tonka Front End Shovel, #5 ....$2-3
Tonka Hummer Commando Hum-V, #26......$2-3
Tonka LAX Crash Tender Command Truck, #6...$2-3
Tonka Locksmith Van, #36 ....$2-3
Tonka M-923 A1 Big Foot Storm Truck, "El
    Nino Storm Relief," #8...........................$2-3
Tonka Mercedes-Benz ML 320 SUV, #13 ....$2-3
Tonka Mountain Dew Delivery, #48.............$2-3
Tonka MT Towing, purple with black ramp,
    gray plastic side trim, #17......................$2-3
Tonka News Copter, #44 ....$2-3
Tonka Ocean Gear Ford Econovan, green
    with wave graphics, "Ocean Gear," #24 ...$2-3

Tonka Party Supply Truck, white with red
    interior, "Party Supplies 555-PRTY," #22 ...$2-3
Tonka Pipe Truck, #42 ....$2-3
Tonka Police Launch, #34...........................$2-3
Tonka Police Ranger, #28 ....$2-3
Tonka Power Shovel

**safety green and black, "Tonka Mighty
768," 3"**...$2-3

Tonka Prerunner Toyota SR5 4x4 Pick Up, yellow
    with black, white and silver accents, #19 ...$2-3
Tonka Quarry Dump, #40 ....$2-3
Tonka Road Roller

orange, "Tonka Highway Department," 3"....$2-3

Tonka Rescue 4 Ambulance, red, "Emergency
    Response Vehicle," #7 ....$2-3
Tonka Rumblin' Dump, metallic burgundy with gray
    dumper, "Rumblin' Dump Co.," #27.......$2-3
Tonka Sportsman Camper, #29 ....$2-3
Tonka Super Duty, #45 ....$2-3
Tonka Tanker, #39 ....$2-3
Tonka Tractor, #31 ....$2-3
Tonka Traffic Equipment Truck, #43.............$2-3
1949 Tonka Utility Hauler, styled after the
    larger 1949 pressed steel version

**orange with bright green utility box, "Tonka
Toys"**..$2-3

1953 Tonka Wrecker, styled after the larger 1953 pressed steel version

blue with red boom, "Tonka Toys Tow Service" $2-3

Toyota MR-2, #8619	$1-2
Toyota SR5, #8621	$1-2
Trabant, #9002	$1-2
Volkswagen 1300 Beetle, #8731	$1-2
Volkswagen Dune Racer, #8740	$1-2
Volkswagen Eurovan	$1-2
Volkswagen Golf GTi, #8446	$1-2

Volkswagen Golf GTi, red, kid connection $1-2

Volkswagen New Beetle, 3" $1-2
Volkswagen NR-1060, #9007 ....$1-2
Volvo 760 GLE, metallic gray, 3"

M C Toys Mini Racers #8616 ....$2-3

Maisto Turbo Treads $1-2

Maisto 3" Fantasy Vehicles

This bizarre assortment of models appears to be available exclusively at Wal-Mart under their kid connection brand.

Ghostlee $1-2

Hoop de Coupe $1-2

Kraniator $1-2

Mach Schnell $1-2

Mozkeeto $1-2

Octa-blitzer $1-2

Puff Adder $1-2

Skooter $1-2

Snarlly $1-2

Sprint Booster...$1-2

Maisto Dirt Mover Sets

Set 1, includes wheel loader with excavator, crane with ripper, and wheel loader with pile driver, #224200........................$30-35

Set 2, includes snow plow with ripper, wheel loader with ripper, and fork lift with log loader, #224300........................$30-35

Maisto Airline Series – Commercial Airliners, 4" – 5" long, in attractive window box

Swissair $4
British Airways..$4
Japan Air Lines $4
Lufthansa $4
Alitalia $4
Air France $4
United..$4
Cathay Pacific $4

Maisto 2-Wheelers – 1:18 Scale Motorcycles, highly detailed, working suspension

Honda NR, red, silver and black $3-4
Kawasaki KLX250SR Dirt Bike, lime green with bright yellow, pink & purple accents $3-4
Kawasaki Ninja ZX-9R, red and silver...........$3-4
Suzuki GSX750 Police Motorcycle, white and chrome $3-4
Yamaha XV1000 Virago Chopper, metallic red and chrome $3-4

Maisto Countryside Farm & Field Trucks and Trailers (Assortment #15091)

Ford F350 Super Duty
    Cattle carrier...................................$5-7
    Horse Transport..................................$5-7
    Tractor Trailer $5-7

Maisto Countryside Farm & Field Implements (Assortment #15093)

Bale Throw Wagon $3-5
Ford Tractor
    Harvester...$3-5
    Mulcher with Front End Loader................$3-5
Hay Rake $3-5
Hydra-Push Spreader..................................$3-5
Mower Conditioner $3-5

Mulch Tiller $3-5
Rectangular Baler......................................$3-5
Rotary Cutter $3-5
Round Baler $3-5
Row Crop Planter $3-5
Sprayer $3-5
Wing Disc $3-5

Maisto Countryside Farm & Field Workin' Trucks (Assortment #15094)

AG Service Sprayer Truck $5-7
Dairy Transport Truck $5-7
Delivery Truck with Tractor $5-7
Dealership Implement Truck $5-7
Farm Feed Delivery Truck $5-7

Maisto Countryside Farm & Field Tractors (Assortment #15095)

Ford Tractor
    blue $4-6
    blue with cab....................................$4-6
    blue with front end loader $4-6
    green..$4-6
    green with cab..................................$4-6
    green with front end loader $4-6
    red $4-6
    red with cab......................................$4-6
    red with front end loader $4-6
    yellow..$4-6
    yellow with cab................................$4-6
    yellow with front end loader $4-6

Majorette

Majorette History and Heritage

Some of the world's most popular, or at least most prolific, diecast toy cars and trucks come from the French company known as Majorette F, founded in 1961 as Rail-Route by Emile Veron, one-time candidate for Premier of France. His brother Joseph M. Veron founded Norev ("Veron" spelled backwards) in 1946 and started producing 1:43 scale diecast cars in 1953.

Rail-Route and Early Majorettes

Rail-Route started producing plastic toy trains in 1961 and followed them with toy cars and trucks in 1965. During the early years, availability of Majorettes was very limited. Rail-Route originally was represented by 15 models, numbered from 1 to 15. By 1967, the number had reached 25.

Add 100 to the model number of 1965, and you arrive at the 100-Series model numbers for 1966. 1 became 101, 2 became 102, and so on.

The line was changed again in 1967 when the 200-Series was introduced. By then, the brand name was changed from Rail-Route to

Majorette SA, even though many models still carried the Rail-Route name. At the same time, the 300-Series was introduced combining 200-Series cars with various trailers.

Globe Toys – The German 100 Series

What was originally thought to be an anomaly turns out to be a reissue series. Majorette #222 Skip Truck is the first of these to be discovered by Dana Johnson, found at a toy show and out of its original package, leaving it a mystery as to its origin. All he knew is that it was a Majorette casting that didn't say "Majorette" on it. Upon closer comparison with the Majorette versions, it is revealed that the "Majorette" name on the base is blocked out by a raised section with the number "114" imprinted on it. The remnants of the last "E" are barely visible at one end of the blocked portion of the base.

Several such Majorette castings were altered around 1980 to be issued as generic models for the German toy market. The blister-pack says "Globe Toys" and "Hergestellt in Frankreich" (Made in France), but no mention is made of the Majorette name on the package....and like the Skip Truck, the name is also blanked out on the bases of all these models, and the usual 200 numbers are replaced with 100 numbers. They have been most commonly spotted at toy swapmeets in Germany in the eighties and early nineties.

The list is likely incomplete. It is estimated that there may be as many as 24 different models in this range, often with lesser detail than their Majorette-branded counterparts.

TC Toys

Collector Mark Foster reports: I have two Majorette cars still in their packages, packed as "TC TOYS." The blister card is yellow, red, and blue. A white and blue checkered flag comes out of the "O" in "TOYS." The back of the card says "Hours of fun with TC TOYS." "Distributed by Thomas Cork SM Ltd. Nottingham NG7 2PW." There is no mention of Majorette except on the cars themselves. They are made in France. The cars are the #213 Chevrolet Impala Taxi and the #266 Land Rover.

North American Market Expansion

In 1982, Majorettes became more readily available to the US with the establishment of Majorette USA, with headquarters in Miami, Florida.

It was not the best of times to try expanding the diecast toy line to the US, as the 1980s saw the downfall, merger, or sellout of many popular toy companies such as Matchbox, Corgi, Dinky and Solido. Nevertheless, Majorette inadvertently created a small but devoted following of collectors in the US and Canada.

Solido Acquired

Solido of France, meanwhile, was almost one of the casualties of the era. This venerable brand of toys had existed independently since 1930. But as with other toy companies, Solido suffered financially too, eventually being purchased by Majorette in 1980. Fortunately the Solido line survives, as does Majorette.

Bankruptcy and Recovery

In 1990, bankrupt Majorette was purchased by Ideal Loisirs, pronounced ee-dee-ALL LEE-zhurs, a French toy conglomerate. In turn, Playmates toy company of Hong Kong purchased a 37.5 percent interest in Ideal Loisirs in mid-1992.

Playmates made its mark in the toy industry with its popular licensed line of Teenage Mutant Ninja Turtles action figures. Since then, the company has been held together by the powerful force and extraordinary popularity of its Star Trek, Next Generation, and Deep Space Nine action figures, models, and play sets.

Novacars of Portugal Acquired

About the same time, a Portuguese brand of small, accurate-scale, mostly plastic toy vehicles called Novacars was assimilated into the Majorette line, becoming the new Majorette Novacars 100 Series. A listing of these models can be found separately under the Novacar listing.

Belgian Novacar Models

Doug Breithaupt reports: This story gets more interesting. I purchased these ex-Majorette models in Belgium in 1990. They were in rather generic green packages, and they do use the Novacar – Portugal name. I think that Novacar was at that time reproducing Majorette models that were out of production. This would be before Novacar was purchased by Majorette. On the base of these models it says the model name, scale, and "Made in France," with the Majorette name blanked out. The model numbers are restamped on a raised plate over the old numbers. I bought all the cars they had but no trucks except the Renault 4L.

Survival of the Species

A recent change in the business occurred when TA Triumph-Adler of Nuremberg, Germany, took a controlling share in the Ideal Loisirs Group. Triumph-Adler Toy Division is known for

the Zapf brand of dolls, Tronico radio-controlled cars, Cartronic car racing tracks, Europlay summer toys, and Kidtech children's computers.

The result of this merger/buyout is that Majorette now belongs to one of the largest toy conglomerates in Europe, and one of the leading toy manufacturers in the world.

As this book is published, the availability of Majorettes in the US and Canada has dropped to an all-time low, with promises from SharAl of Minnesota, the new importer/wholesaler for 2000, of restoring the American market availability of Majorettes.

Mira, Norev, Verem Join the Majorette Empire

Mira of Spain has been known for producing exceptional 1:18 scale models. In September 2000, unconfirmed reports indicate that Mira has been purchased by Majorette/Slido. New models have been issued under the Mira/Solido brand.

Norev, the company started by Emile's brother Joseph is now owned by Ideal-Loisirs, the same parent company that owns Majorette. Verem is another acquisition. See respective models listed in their own sections of this book.

Renumbering Complicates Issues

There are three distinct series issued as the 100-Series. The earliest is the 1966 Rail-Route series. Around 1980 came Globe Toys of Germany. Then ten years later came the Novacar series, the result of Majorette's purchase of the Portuguese line of toy cars around 1990.

P. Colson has written about the beginnings of the Majorette brand in the French magazine *argus de la miniature*, issue 120. Ron Gold provided us with a copy of the article, and Ron Lohr was able to decipher a few things from the article. Apparently, a French company known as Rail-Route started a line of diecast toy vehicles in 1965 dubbed Majorettes. As previously mentioned, earlier models were produced as far back as 1961 but were not widely distributed, nor did they apparently carry any distinguishing marks that would make them identifiable as Majorettes.

The "Rail-Route" name appears on the base of models issued in 1965. Even as the 1966 models were being released, the "Rail-Route" name was being replaced by "Majorette SA" on packages. Even so, the "Rail-Route" name and series apparently continued through

1967.

The numbering system was simple in 1965. Models were issued consecutive numbers starting with 1 and eventually reaching 25. In 1966 the numbering system was changed to a 100-Series by simply doing the mathematical addition of 100 to each of the 1965 models. 1 became 101, 2 became 102, and so on. In 1967, the 200-Series was introduced, first with simple variations of models already issued under the previous series.

Around 1970, the whole numbering system was revised again, reassigning 200-Series numbers to single models, 300-Series numbers to semi-trucks, buses, and cars with trailers. The 600-Series was introduced around 1975 specifically for 1:87 scale semi-trucks.

Majorette Sub-Series

Several sub-series have been marketed, which are included in the variations below. One of those is Kool Kromes, models in various colors of chrome. Another is Road Eaters, models with advertising for food and candy on them. A third sub-series is Smelly Speeders, "Not Stinky–Just For Kids," models each with distinctive scents and appropriate trademark names. These models are repeated in their own section for easier cross-reference.

In 1995, another sub-series was introduced called Supers, models that steer. Since they have been assigned new numbers that don't coincide with the regular 200 series, they have been listed following the 200 Series.

Variations in this edition have been organized and grouped according to similarities. Because of this, variation numbers on newly discovered variations have pushed older variations farther down the list. As of this edition, future variations will be added to the end of each list. The result may make it more confusing to find different variations of similar models, but it is necessary to establish a standard variation number so that this book may become the standard in referencing Majorettes. I hope this will help more than hinder fellow collectors in identifying their Majorette toys.

2000 and Beyond

Majorette's 2000 dealer catalog for the first time displayed models with no assigned model numbers, adding to the confusion even more, particularly with new models never previously assigned a number. It becomes nearly impossible to list those new models with any degree of order until one actually acquires the model and finds a model number imprinted on the base.

While Majorette has offered larger, more accurate models geared toward collectors, they have as yet not acknowledged that their regular offerings of toy cars and trucks are anything more than cheap toys. At least a few collectors in the US and Canada heartily disagree with the company, as this book illustrates. Nevertheless, it is unlikely that Majorette company officials will ever acknowledge their toys as collectibes, despite a growing number of Majorette collectors in the US and Canada. Since 2002, Majorettes have completely disappeared from the US market except for a few specialty stores and Internet sources who carry older stock.

Majorette Wheel Variations

Over 30 distinctive wheel types have been documented so far on Majorette 200-Series models. Below is a key to the abbreviations used to identify them. Unless otherwise noted, spokes, circles, and rings are raised chrome portions of a wheel.

3kk – inner and outer rings with three inner "knobs" or "bumps" alternating with three outer "knobs" or "bumps"

3spb – 3 broad spokes that taper from center to outside, enclosed by a ring

3spn – 3 slightly narrower spokes that taper from center to outside, enclosed by a ring

4c – "4 leaf clover" in contoured circle

5d – 5 dashes, arcs between an inner and outer circle

5pw – 5-pointed pinwheel

5sp – 5 broad spokes that widen from center to outer ring

6sp – 6 spokes in a circle

6spk – 6 spokes in a circle with "knobs" or "bumps" on inside of circle between each spoke

8h – 8 holes within a broad chrome circle

8hr – variation of 8h in red chrome, other colors also produced

8sp – 8 spokes in a circle, or 4 pairs of V-pattern spokes

8p – 8 pin; 4 pairs of parallel pins projecting from a circle, found on 300-series trailers

atv–solid rubber tire used on 6-wheel all-terrain vehicle

bw1 – single piece black plastic wheel used on many Majorettes from the 1960s

bw2 – single piece black wheel with separate black hubcap, usually a front wheel on a Bernard truck

bw3 – one-piece black wheel, usually a rear wheel assembly on a Bernard truck; hub extends out further than the side of the tire and has 8 lug nuts molded in; the axle is visible in the center of the wheel

bw4 – dual wheels, but together as one piece; axle doesn't show, so the outside wheel is attached to the inside wheel after the inside wheel is attached to the axle; hub has 8 lug nuts, and a molded cap over the axle

ct* – construction tire, a variety of tires found on construction vehicles

ct3c – "3 leaf clover" in a circle

ct4sp – 4 spokes in a circle

ctb – single piece black wheel with four unchromed spokes

ctsc – square inside of a circle, commonly used as front wheels on current farm tractor models

ft* – farm tire, a variety of styles found on farm tractors

ft1 – single piece plastic wheel

ft2 – tire separate from colored plastic wheel hub

ft3 – solid black plastic wheel with coarse treads, found on the earliest farm tractors

ft4 – similar to ft2 but with larger, more detailed plastic hub and thinner tire

rt – racing tire with separate hub used on 1960s Majorette F1 racers

rw – wide racing wheel with chrome circle, usually projects out well beyond wheel well

spiral – chrome spiral wheel, found on some dune buggies

thc – single piece tire with chrome hubcap

Majorette Variations and Values

Understanding Model Designation and Variation Numbers

The upper case letter after the model number indicates the major casting variation. The lower case letter after it indicates minor casting changes. Model descriptions printed in italics indicate the French model designation. Within the variations listings, italics offer the name of the subseries in which the variation is found.

Understanding Values in this Book

Values stated in this book are for a model in new condition. If a second value follows the first, it generally represents a higher value for a model in its original package.

Rail-Route 1-25 Series and Earlier Issues

Beginning in 1961, a limited number of fairly generic models were issued by the company that would eventually come to be known as Majorette. The name Rail-Route

was applied to these models in 1965. These early models comprise the first series of 25 models produced between 1961 and 1966.

1-A BRM F1, has a driver, numbers 11 thru 19 on a small round sticker, grille has 10 bars, 1:55, 1961 – 1962

white.................................$15-18
blue $15-18
green $15-18
turquoise $15-18
orange $15-18
red $15-18
number 29 on a small round sticker, silver...................................$15-18
numbers 1 thru 5 on a larger round sticker, large or small numbers, grille has 8 bars, metallic burgundy, 1966 ....$15-18
numbers 1 thru 5 on a larger round sticker, large or small numbers, grille has 8 bars, metallic green $15-18
numbers 1 thru 5 on a larger round sticker, large or small numbers, grille has 8 bars, metallic blue $15-18
numbers 1 thru 5 on a larger round sticker, large or small numbers, grille has 8 bars, metallic dark blue $15-18
numbers 1 thru 5 on a larger round sticker, large or small numbers, grille has 8 bars, on a keychain...........................$15-18

2-A Porsche F1, has a driver, numbers 21 thru 28 on a small round sticker, grille with small checkered pattern, 1:55, 1962

white.................................$15-18
blue $15-18
green $15-18
turquoise $15-18
orange $15-18
red $15-18
number 29 on a small sticker, silver.....$15-18
numbers 1 thru 5 on a larger round sticker, large or small numbers, grille with large checkered pattern, metallic burgundy, 1966......................................$15-18
numbers 1 thru 5 on a larger round sticker, large or small numbers, grille with large checkered pattern, metallic green $15-18
numbers 1 thru 5 on a larger round sticker, large or small numbers, grille with large checkered pattern, metallic blue....$15-18
numbers 1 thru 5 on a larger round sticker, large or small numbers, grille with large checkered pattern, metallic dark blue.................................$15-18

numbers 1 thru 5 on a larger round sticker, large or small numbers, grille with large checkered pattern, on a keychain..........$15-18

3-A Citroën H Vending Truck *Etalmobil*, clear plastic opening side panels, 1:100, 1965
"AU BON PATE" on silver or translucent background, light turquoise, 1965...$15-18
"AU BON PATE" on silver or translucent background, red, 1965..............$15-18
"AU PETIT POUCET," blue, 1965 ......$15-18
no markings, various colors, 1966–67....$15-18
"FRUITS DE PROVENCE," various colors, 1967–68........................$15-18

4-Aa Bernard Fire Ladder Truck *Grand Eschelle Pompiers*, with driver, opening plastic doors, base doesn't have "1/100," red base only under cab, silver painted bumper, metal ladder, 1:100, 1965 – 1968, red, "Ville de MEGEVE" cast on doors, red plastic ladder base held on by visible rivet, red plastic base under cab only, "Rail Route" on base, unpainted metal ladder, bw1 and bw4 ....$15-18
red, red interior $15-18

4-Ab Bernard Fire Ladder Truck *Grand Eschelle Pompiers*, same as 4-A except base has "1/100," 1965, red..............$15-18

4-Ac Bernard Fire Ladder Truck *Grand Eschelle Pompiers*, same as 4-B except doors are part of casting and have "VILLE de MEGEVE" cast into them, 1966, red.....................$15-18

5-Aa Bernard Dump Truck *Benne Carriere*, with driver, opening plastic doors, base has "1/100," base only under cab, silver painted bumper, tilting dump, 1:100, 1965
red $15-18
green $15-18
pale blue $15-18
orange $15-18

5-Ab Bernard Dump Truck *Benne Carriere*, same as 5-A except with cast doors, 1966
red $15-18
green $15-18
pale blue $15-18
orange $15-18

6-Aa Bernard Open Truck, with driver, opening plastic doors, red base only under cab, silver painted bumper, tailgate plastic, 1:100,1965
blue $15-18
pale blue $15-18
turquoise $15-18
red $15-18
dark red..........................$15-18
orange-red $15-18

6-Ab Bernard Open Truck, with driver, doors part of casting and have "PEINTURES GALIACOLOR LYON" cast into them, red base only

under cab, silver painted bumper, tailgate plastic, 1:100, 1966
blue $15-18
pale blue $15-18
turquoise $15-18
red $15-18
dark red..........................$15-18
orange-red $15-18

6-Ba Bernard Flat Truck with Chains, with driver, opening plastic doors, red base only under cab, silver painted bumper, 1:100, 1965
blue $15-18
turquoise $15-18

6-Bb Bernard Flat Truck, with driver, doors part of casting and have "PEINTURES GALIACOLOR LYON" cast into them, red base only under cab, silver painted bumper, 1:100, 1966
blue $15-18
turquoise $15-18

7-Aa Hotchkiss Jeep towing one-axle Dump cart, with driver, plastic windscreen, 1:65, 1965
yellow $15-18
bright red $15-18
orange-red $15-18
brick red $15-18
green $15-18
pale blue $15-18
blue-green $15-18

7-Ab Hotchkiss Jeep towing one-axle Dump cart, with driver, metal windscreen, 1:65, 1966
yellow $15-18
bright red $15-18
orange-red $15-18
brick red $15-18
green $15-18
pale blue $15-18
blue-green $15-18

7-Ba Hotchkiss Jeep with Reel on back, with driver, plastic windscreen, 1:65, 1965
yellow $15-18
bright red $15-18
orange-red $15-18
brick red $15-18
green $15-18
pale blue $15-18
blue-green $15-18

7-Bb Hotchkiss Jeep with Reel on back, with driver, metal windscreen, 1:65, 1966
yellow $15-18
bright red $15-18
orange-red $15-18
brick red $15-18
green $15-18
pale blue $15-18
blue-green $15-18

8-Aa Bernard Snow Plow, with driver, opening

plastic doors, base only under cab, low open dump on back, 1:100, 1965
pale blue $15-18
turquoise $15-18

8-Ab Bernard Snow Plow, with driver, doors part of casting and have "VILLE de MEGEVE" cast into them, base only under cab, low open dump on back, 1:100, 1966
pale blue $15-18
turquoise $15-18

9-Aa Ferrari 250 LeMans, with driver, numbers 1 thru 5, 1:55, 1965
metallic burgundy $15-18
metallic green $15-18

9-Ab Ferrari 250 LeMans, with driver, numbers 1 thru 5, 1:55, 1966
silver.............................$15-18

10-Aa Ferrari F1 Grand Prix car, with driver, numbers 1 thru 5, 1:55, 1965
metallic burgundy $15-18
metallic green $15-18
metallic gray-blue $15-18

10-Ab Ferrari F1, with driver, numbers 1 thru 5, 1:55, 1966, silver $15-18

10-Ac Ferrari F1, same as 10-A, on a keychain $15-18

11-Aa Jeep towing one-axle Cattle Cart, with driver and horse, plastic windscreen, 1:65, 1965
yellow $15-18
bright red $15-18
orange-red $15-18
brick red $15-18
green $15-18
pale blue $15-18
blue-green $15-18

11-Ab Jeep towing one-axle Cattle Cart, with driver and horse, metal windscreen, 1:65, 1966
yellow $15-18
bright red $15-18
orange-red $15-18
brick red $15-18
green $15-18
pale blue $15-18
blue-green $15-18

12-Aa Bernard Circus Truck, with driver and 3 lions, opening plastic doors, base only under cab, silver painted bumper, cage on back, 1:100, 1965
pale blue with red interior $15-18
turquoise $15-18

12-Ab Bernard Circus Truck, with driver and 3 animals, doors part of casting and have "PEINTURES GALIACOLOR LYON" cast into them, base only under cab, silver painted bumper, cage on back, 1:100, 1966
pale blue with red interior $15-18

turquoise with red interior..................$15-18

13-Aa Citroën DS21, license number "7217 GH 13," orange hubs, gray tires, 2 single headlights, "Rail-Route" on base and box, 1:65, 1965
metallic burgundy............................$15-18
metallic green.................................$15-18
metallic blue..................................$15-18
metallic pale blue...........................$15-18
metallic royal blue..........................$15-18
metallic red..................................$15-18
metallic gray-blue, "Auto Ecole," 1966...$15-18

13-Ab Citroën DS21, license number "7217 GH 13," gray hubs, black tires, 2 single headlights, "Majorette No 13" on base, "Rail-Route" on box, 1:65, 1966
metallic dark red............................$15-18
metallic lime.................................$15-18
blue..$15-18

14-A Citroën DS 21, 13-A with Boat Trailer, boat is orange and turquoise, 1:65, 1965
orange wheels with gray tires, 1966 – 1967...............................$18-21
gray wheels with black tires, 1966 – 1967...............................$15-18

15-A Citroën DS 21, 13-A with Sterkeman Lovely House Trailer, 1:65, 1965
white trailer with red interior, green base................................$20-25

16-A Peugeot 404 Station Wagon, opening doors, hood, hatch, 1:65, 1967 – 1968
metallic slate blue..........................$25-30

16-B Peugeot 404 Saloon 1:65, 1967 – 1968, no details known......$25-30

17-A Renault R16 and Alpine F3 Racer on Trailer, 1:65, 1967 – 1968
various colors.................................$20-25

18-A Bernard Refuse Truck *Benne Ordures*, 1:100, 11967 – 1968
various colors with a gray container, gray interior....................................$25-30

19-A Bernard Farm Truck *Fourragere*, stake body, 1967 – 1968
various colors, gray interior..............$25-30

20-A Bernard Log Truck *Fardier*, twigs held by chains, 1967 – 1968
various colors, gray interior..............$25-30

21-A Renault R16 Sedan, opening hood and doors, tow hook
orange wheels, gray tires, 1:65, 1967...$25-30
gray wheels, black tires, 1:65, 1968...$25-30

22-A Bernard Low Loader *Surbaisse*, 12 trailer wheels, ramp, equipment, 1:100, 1968

various colors, gray interior..............$25-30

23-A Renault R16 Sedan, 17-A and Glider Trailer *Planeur*, 1968, various colors, orange and white glider.........................$25-30

24-A Bernard Gondola Semi Trailer, 2 color trailer, 1:100, 1968, orange and gray two-tone paint, gray interior...........................$25-30

25-A Peugeot 404, 16-A and Horse Trailer, 1:65, 1968, various colors, tan trailer...$25-30

Rail-Route 100 Series, 1966

101-A BRM Formula 1 Racer, reissue of 1-A
unchromed....................................$15-18
chromed.......................................$15-18

102-A Porsche Formula 1 Racer, reissue of 2-A
unchromed....................................$15-18
chromed.......................................$15-18

107-A Hotchkiss Jeep towing one-axle Dump cart, with driver, metal windscreen, 1:65, reissue of 7-A
yellow...$15-18
bright red.....................................$15-18
orange-red....................................$15-18
brick red......................................$15-18
green..$15-18
pale blue......................................$15-18
blue-green....................................$15-18

107-B Hotchkiss Jeep with Cable carrier, reissue of 7-B
yellow...$15-18
bright red.....................................$15-18
orange-red....................................$15-18
brick red......................................$15-18
green..$15-18
pale blue......................................$15-18
blue-green....................................$15-18

109-A Ferrari 250 LeMans, 1967 reissue of 9-A
unchromed....................................$15-18
chromed.......................................$15-18

110-A Ferrari Formula 1 Racer, 1966 reissue of 10-A
unchromed....................................$15-18
chromed.......................................$15-18

113-A Citroën DS21, hood and trunk lid open, separate tires on chrome hubs, clear windows, 1966 reissue of 13-A
green with light yellow interior............$15-18
green with tan interior......................$15-18
gray with orange interior...................$15-18
blue with orange interior...................$15-18
blue with white interior.....................$15-18
pale blue with white interior...............$15-18

116-A Peugeot 404 Station Wagon Ambulance *Break*, beacon on top, "MAJORETTE" on

unpainted base, box has "RAIL ROUTE," 1:65, white...........................$15-18
metallic red, orange interior, clear windshield, wheels: gray hub and black tire...$15-18
red, clear windshield, wheels: gray hub and black tire.............................$15-18
light blue, clear windshield, wheels: gray hub and black tire......................$15-18
metallic green, white interior, clear windshield, wheels: gray hub and black tire......................................$15-18

116-B Peugeot 404 Saloon variations unknown...........................$30-35

117-A Peugeot 404 Station Wagon metallic slate blue...........................$25-30

Globe Toys, Issued in Germany circa 1980

Globe Toys are generic versions of familiar Majorettes with base altered to obscure brand name and original model number.

101 = 209-A Camper, blue pickup truck, amber windows, white camper shell, 4 headlights, 3spb...$5-7
103 = 230-B Renault 4L, yellow, black accents, "RENAULT," 3kk............................$5-7
105 = 220-A Volvo 245 DL......................$5-7
106 = 221-B Citroën GS Camargue...........$5-7
108 = 213-B Mercedes 350 SL................$5-7
112 = 265-A Citroën CX.........................$5-7

114 = 222-A Magirus Skip Truck *Multi Benne*, **orange with red skip, 3kk.................$5-7**

115 = 257-A Renault 5..........................$5-7
116 = 231-A Citroën Dyane Safari............$5-7
117 = 251-A Ford Capri.........................$5-7
123 = 248-A Dune Buggy.......................$5-7

Novacars: The New Majorette 100 Series

Novacar models, previously from Minia Porto Jogos E Brinquedos Lda. of Paredes, Portugal, were originally packaged in either a display blister card or a hook blisterpack. The list below combines the original models along with new Majorette variations. Models were most commonly marketed in a four-car blisterpack set for $1.99. Many of these models have been converted from plastic to diecast metal and incorporated into the 200-Series for 1997 and later. For a complete listing, go to the Novacars section of this book.

Majorette 200 Series

201-A St. Tropez Travel Trailer, 1:68
yellow with blue decals $5-7
white with water and beach tampos........$4-6
white Caravan with guitar tampo on one
    side and trumpet on the other side,
    "music pop"....................................$5-7
201-B Citroën GS, "201" on unpainted
metal base unless otherwise noted,
1972 – 1973
    yellow, cream interior, clear windows, "201"
      not on base, thc5 ....$4-6
    light blue, cream interior, clear windows,
      thc5 ....$4-6
    orange, cream interior, amber windows,
      thc5 ....$4-6
    light green, cream interior, clear windows,
      thc5 ....$4-6
    metallic green, cream interior, clear windows,
      thc5 ....$4-6
    pink, cream interior, clear windows, thc5 ...$4-6
    metallic red, cream interior, clear windows,
      thc5 ....$4-6
    flourescent red, cream interior, clear windows,
      thc5 ....$4-6
    red, white interior, amber windows, thc5 ...$4-6
201-C Citroën Visa Chrono, rear hatch opens,
1:52 white, blue interior, clear windows, red
and blue accents, "CHRONO," 6sp $4-6
    white, blue interior, clear windows, red and
      blue accents, "4 ROUES MOTRICES,"
      6sp $4-6
    white, blue interior, clear windows, red and blue
      accents, "4 ROUES MOTRICES," 8h ...$4-6

yellow, blue interior, clear windows, red and black accents, "4 ROUES MOTRICES," 8h $4-6

    white, blue interior, clear windows, blue
      "1789 – 1989 Bicentennaire" on roof,
      8h..$4-6
201-D Ford Model A Van, 1:60, 1992
    metallic red, black fenders, gold trim, cream
      canopy, "TEA SHOP," "MADE IN PORTU-

GAL" on base, 5d........................$4-6
navy blue with gold trim, black fenders, cream
    canopy, "TEA SHOP," "Made in France"
    on base, 5d................................$4-6
orange, black fenders, "Willy Wonka runts,"
    Road Eaters, "Made in France," 6sp $3-5

red, black fenders, "Campbell's Teddy Bears," Road Eaters, "Made in France," 5d $3-5

    blue, "Cadbury Dairy Milk"....................$6-8
    blue, "Cadbury Buttons" $6-8
    blue, "Orange Company," plastic upper half of
      van body is white, "Made in Thailand" ..$3-5
    blue-green, black fenders, "Toys Shop,"
      white canopy, "Made in Thailand,"
      5d, 1999 ....$3-5
    white, black fenders, "Wilton House"
      "Salisbury," 5d............................$4-6
    white, red fenders, blue cap with "Pepsi Cola,"
      old-time policeman, "It's worth a dime"
      graphics on roof, 5d......................$3-5
201-E Fiat Coupe, 1:58, steerable wheels,
"Made in Thailand,"
    yellow, black lower body, tan interior, clear
      windows, 8h $4-6
    silver, black lower body, red interior, clear win-
      dows, black and blue tampos, 8h $4-6
    blue, yellow interior, rally graphics, "5,"
      5pw, 2000 ....$2-4
202-A Volkswagen 113, Rail-Route, 1967 ...$8-10
202-B Volkswagen 1302 Beetle *Coccinelle*,
trunk opens, 1:60, 1972-74, compare
to 202-E, 203-D
    red with yellow lightning bolt on trunk,
      3kk $8-10
    pink, with yellow lightning bolt on trunk,
      3kk $8-10
    white, white interior, thc........................$8-10
    yellow, black hood, white interior, 3kk ..$8-10
    yellow, white interior, 3spb..................$8-10
202-C Triumph TR7, 1:53, 1982 – 1987
    red with blue and white accents, "TR7," "35,"
      yellow interior, rw........................$2-4
    red with blue and white accents, "TR7," "35,"
      yellow interior, 6sp......................$2-4
    red with blue and silver accents, "TR7," "35,"

    yellow interior, rw........................$2-4
    red, no markings, yellow interior, rw........$2-4
    red, no markings, yellow interior, 6spk.....$4-6
    orange, red and white accents, "TR7," "35,"
      yellow interior, rw........................$2-4
    orange, red and white accents, "TR7," "35,"
      red interior, rw............................$2-4
202-D Peugeot 405 T16, 1:60, 1990
    white, red interior, clear windows, blue,
      black, red and yellow tampos,
      "Pioneer," "204," blue bumpers,
      "Made in France," 6sp $3-5
    yellow, white interior, clear windows, blue,
      red and white tampos, "Racing Service,"
      "203," black bumpers, "Made in
      France," 6sp..............................$3-5

yellow, red interior, clear windows, blue, red, and white tampos, "Racing Service," "203," yellow bumpers, "Made in France," 6sp..$3-5

    yellow, red interior, clear windows, blue, red,
      and white tampos, "Racing Service,"
      "203," yellow bumpers, same as 3 but
      "Service" on sides is larger, "Made in
      Thailand," 6sp............................$3-5
    orange chrome, cream interior, clear windows,
      light pink tampo on sides, "11," gray
      bumpers, "Made in France," orange
      chrome 6sp................................$3-5
    orange chrome, cream interior, clear windows,
      no tampo, gray bumpers, "Made in
      France," orange chrome 6sp.............$3-5
    dark blue chrome, cream interior, clear win-
      dows, yellow tampo on sides, "11," gray
      bumpers, "Made in France," light blue
      chrome 6sp................................$3-5
    dark blue chrome, cream interior, clear win-
      dows, yellow tampo on sides, "11," gray
      bumpers, "Made in France," dark blue
      chrome 6sp................................$3-5
    light blue chrome, white interior, clear win-
      dows, white tampo on sides, "11," black
      bumpers, "Made in Thailand," dark blue
      chrome 6sp................................$3-5
    red, red interior, clear windows, no tampo,
      yellow bumpers, "Made in
      Thailand," 6sp............................$3-5

202-E Volkswagen 1302 Beetle *Coccinelle*, trunk
doesn't open, 1:60
silver, blue windows, "CIBIE" stickers on doors,
"54" on roof, 3kk, 1980 ....$10-13

**blue, clear windows, 3spb, part of 311
set $3-5**

red, white interior, 3spb $10-13
silver, blue windows, blue and white Volkswagen labels on doors, 3spb...........$10-13
same as 1., 3spb, 1980 ....$10-13
multicolored blown paint in green, blue, red,
yellow, and black, "CIBIE" stickers on
doors, "54" on roof, yellow windows,
3spb, 1979.............................$20-25
yellow, white interior, clear windows,
3kk $4-6
yellow, white interior, clear windows,
3spb $4-6
orange, white interior, amber windows,
3kk $4-6
red, white interior, 3kk $10-13
203-A Warehouse Vehicle *Etalmobil*, 1:50,
1967 reissue of 3-A $15-18
203-B Fiat 127, doors open, dog on back seat
looking out left rear window, 1:55
hot pink, 3kk, part of 323 set..............$8-10
blue $6-8
metallic blue $6-8
red with white interior, 3spb...............$8-10
red with white interior, thc1 ....$8-10
lime green with white interior, thc1 ....$8-10
lime green with white interior, 3spb.......$8-10
lime green with white interior, 3kk.........$8-10
metallic yellow-green...........................$6-8
yellow with white interior, thc1 ....$9-12
orange with white interior, 5sp $8-10
203-C Police Motorcycle
blue with black rider, white saddle bags, chrome
engine and exhaust pipes $30-35
bright blue with dark blue rider, white saddle
bags, chrome engine and exhaust
pipes....................................$30-35
203-D Volkswagen 1302 Beetle *Coccinelle*, trunk
doesn't open, compare to 202-B
lime green, 3kk $3-5
blue, 3kk...................................$3-5
light blue, 3kk $4-6

orange with blue and white accents, 3kk,
blue tires $5-7
purple, 3kk, "Cadbury Dairy Milk Buttons" on
doors.....................................$6-8
yellow, no markings, 3kk.......................$4-6
yellow with red random design, like two M's
back to back, 3kk $4-6
light blue, white interior, with same red
random design as 6., 3kk, 1999 .....$3-5
green with same type of random design as
6. but in white, 3kk, 2000 ....$3-5
203-E 1996 Ford Mustang GT Coupe
yellow with red interior, black bumpers $2-4
black, red interior, clear windows, red and
white accents, "17," "Gambler,"
"Super Cams" on hood, 8h $2-4
204-A Bernard Ladder Truck *Grand Eschelle
Pompiers*, with driver, doors part of casting
but have nothing cast into them, plastic base
covers up "Rail Route" on chassis, box has
"Rail-Route" on it, 1:100, 1967 – 1972
red, gray interior, red plastic ladder base,
gray plastic base with incorporated gas
tanks extends under entire truck, chrome
plastic ladder, bw1 and bw2 ......$10-12
red, "Grand Echelle" on ladder base, "Ville
de MEGEVE" cast on doors, red base
under cab, bw3 and bw4 ....$10-12
red, silver ladder, no markings..............$8-10
204-B Fire Rescue, 4 headlights, ladder on roof,
1:80, 1973 – 1978
red, no tampos, 3kk $6-8
red, no tampos, 5sp $6-8
red, "fire brigade" tampo with coat of arms
on doors, 3kk $6-8
red, "fire brigade" tampo with coat of arms
on doors, 3spb $6-8
red, "fire brigade" tampo with coat of arms
on doors, 5sp $6-8
olive drab, star on hood, 3kk $6-8
olive drab, no accents, 3spb, part of 343-A
set.......................................$6-8
204-C Bank Security Armored Truck, with rear
door that slides up to open, 1:57, 1980 –
1988, reissued as 231-C, 1999
yellow with green "Bank Security" label ...$3-5
yellow, black interior, grille guard and back
door, red, white and blue "Bank
Security" labels, "Made in France,"
5d $3-5
yellow, black interior, grille guard and back
door, red, white and blue "Bank
Security" tampos, "Made in France,"
5d $3-5
white, black interior, grille guard and back
door, red and blue accents, "Bank

Security," shield has red background,
"8694" on hood and under side doors,
"Made in France," 5d $3-5
white, black interior, grille guard and back
door, clear windows, red and blue
accents, "Bank Security," shield has
white background, "8694" on hood only,
"Made in France," 5d...................$3-5
silver, black interior, grille guard and back
door, "Made in France," 5d $5-7

**yellow, black interior and grille guard,
amber windows, white and blue "Post"
labels, 5d...............................$5-7**

blue, black interior and grille guard, no tampos, "Made in France," 5d............$6-8
blue, yellow interior, grille guard, black rear
door, white "Bank Security," "7003," red
circle with dollar sign, "Made in Thailand,"
5d, 1999 ....$6-8
blue, yellow interior, grille guard, black rear
door, white "Bank Security," "7003," red
circle with dollar sign, "Made in Thailand," 5dbl, blue tires, 1999 ....$6-8
yellow, black interior and grille guard, "L"
shaped green label with "Bank Security"
on a white shield and 3 black diagonal
stripes on sides of truck, no accents on
hood, "Made in France," 5d $3-5
yellow, black interior and grille guard, amber
windows, yellow, red and black decal on
hood, "Bank Security" and two crossed
skeleton keys, "Made in France," 5d...$3-5
plain yellow truck, four security workers, a
black dog, guns, gold bricks and
wagons, and stickers in red, white, blue
and yellow. The yellow part is in the
shape of a lock. The stickers are in 4
languages. "Bank Security," "Geld-trans-
port," "Furgone Blindato," and "Transport
de Fonds," on a #786 8x11 inch
card....................................$10-13
204-D Ferrari 456 GT, 1994
red.......................................$3-5
204-E Ferrari F50 Coupe, 1996
red with black interior...........................$3-5
205-Aa Bernard Dump Truck *Benne Carriere*,
with driver, doors part of casting but have

nothing cast into them, plastic base covers up "Rail Route" on chassis, box has "Rail-Route" on it, tilting dump, 1:100, 1967 – 1968

red $15-18

green $15-18

pale blue $15-18

orange $15-18

blue with silver dump, bw1 ....$8-10

red with red dump, bw1 ....$8-10

205-Ab Bernard Dump Truck *Benne Carriere*, 3 axles, bumper is part of plastic base, 1969 – 1973

red with metallic red dump, gray base and bumper, gray interior, bw1 and bw2......................................$8-10

205-Ac Bernard Dump Truck *Benne Carriere*, 3 axles, bumper is part of cab casting, 1974 – 1975

blue with metal silver dump with hole drilled in front, gray base, bw5 ....$8-10

205-Ba Saab Scania Dump Truck, roof light cast in cab, no cab guard, box dumper has tailgate, 1976 – 1980

yellow with red dumper, 3kk $6-8

silver with red dumper, 3kk $6-8

orange, "58" sticker on hood, orange dumper, 3kk $6-8

red, yellow dumper, clear windshield, white interior and base, 3kk $6-8

red, orange dumper, clear windshield, black interior and base, 3kk $6-8

olive drab, brown dump, gray interior, star on hood, 3kk...............................$20-25

1977 ....$6-8

205-Bb Saab Scania Dump Truck, roof light cast in cab, cab guard on open back contoured dumper, 1981 – 1982

yellow with red dumper, 3kk $6-8

silver with red dumper, 3kk $6-8

orange with orange dumper, "58" sticker on hood, 3kk $6-8

red with yellow dumper, 3kk $6-8

red with orange dumper, 3kk $6-8

red with silver dumper, "SERVICE" sticker with yellow and black diagonal bars, yellow tailgate, 3kk $8-10

205-C Renault Super Cinq GT Turbo, 1:51, "C RENAULT 1985" on base, 1987 – 1991

black with light gray interior and trim, clear windows, red and yellow graphics, "NRJ," "Made in France," 6sp, 1988.........$2-4

blue with pink interior and bumpers, "Made in France," 6sp, 1989 version $2-4

red with white interior and bumpers, "Racing Team" on hood, white "VH" accents, "45," "Made in France" deleted from base, 6sp $2-4

metallic aqua with gray interior and bumpers, clear windows, red and yellow "NRJ" accent, "Made in France," 6sp $2-4

metallic silver with gray interior and bumpers, clear windows, black, yellow and white rally accents, "19," "MONTE CARLO," "Vive le Sport," "Made in France" deleted, 6sp..$2-4

red, orange-red interior and bumpers, yellow "TURBO" on sides and back window, 6spk...$2-4

205-D Jaguar XJ6 Police, 1994, also see 293-B

white with red interior, clear windows, red and yellow side stripe, "Police" on hood and trunk

4c $3-5

8h $3-5

black square with white "POLICE" on roof, 8h $3-5

205-E 1996 Ford Mustang GT Convertible

red with black interior, "OFFICIAL PACE CAR," 8h $3-5

black with tan interior, 8h $3-5

205-F Peugeot 206, 1999

yellow, 8h $3-5

blue, black interior, clear windshield, black stripe, 8h.......................................$3-5

silver-gray, clear windshield, black stripe black interior, 5pw............................$3-5

6sp $3-5

206-A Bernard Flat Truck with Racks, 1:100, 1967 ....$12-15

206-B Bernard Flat Truck with Scraper, 1:100, 1967 ....$12-15

206-C Peugeot 404 Ambulance *Break*

white, white interior, clear windshield, red cross, clear roof light, wheels: gray hub and black tires..............$12-15

206-D Citroën Ambulance, with blue flags on front fenders, car may be white or cream color, 1973

white with red cross decal on hood only, white tailgate, 3spb....................$8-10

same as 1., 3kk $8-10

cream with red cross and curved "AMBU-LANCE" decal on side doors, amber windows, cream tailgate

5sp $8-10

3spb $8-10

3kk $8-10

white, straight "AMBULANCE" decal, red cross on side doors, roof and hood, blue windows

3spb $10-13

3kk $10-13

white, red cross and curved "AMBULANCE" decal on side doors, cream interior, blue windows, white tailgate, 3spb $8-10

white, red cross and straight "AMBULANCE" decal on side doors, blue windows, blue tailgate, 3spb $8-10

white, small red cross on hood, blue windows, blue tailgate, 3spb

blue cross and straight blue "Ambulance" tampo on doors, ...$8-10

red cross and straight "Ambulance" decal on side doors......................$8-10

red cross on roof $8-10

white, no "AMBULANCE" decal, red cross on side doors, roof and hood, blue windows, white tailgate, 3spb, 1980 catalog ..$8-10

white, amber windows, red cross on roof only, white interior, white tailgate, 3kk.....$8-10

206-E Pontiac Fiero, 1986 – 1991

white, blue lower body, red interior, amber windows, "Made in France," rw

black "3" and "FIERO" on hood, black "turbo" on roof, red accents, ...$3-5

no tampos.....................................$3-5

orange, black lower body, white interior, yellow windshield, "42," white and black accents, "Made in France," rw.........$3-5

yellow, red interior, rw $3-5

yellow, blue lower body, yellow windshield, "3," "Turbo," "Made in France," rw, red stripes across body,

including rear trunk, red interior, ...$3-5

none on rear trunk, red interior $3-5

none on rear trunk, white interior........$3-5

red, black lower body, "42," yellow windshield, "Made in France," rw

white interior, white side stripe $3-5

red interior, red side stripe, ...$3-5

blue, white lower body, red interior, red side stripe, "42," yellow windshield, "Made in France," rw $3-5

206-F Renault Twingo Minivan, 1995

blue, red interior, clear windows, dark gray fenders, 4c $3-5

baby blue, red interior, clear windows, dark gray fenders, 4c............................$3-5

light green, red interior, clear windows, dark gray fenders, 4c............................$3-5 yellow, red interior, clear windows, dark gray fenders, 4c $3-5

neon green body, red interior, strange side and roof graphics, 4c, 2000 ....$3-5

207-A Jaguar XKE 2+2 V12, engine can be same color as body of the car, unpainted metal, or painted silver; all have decal of a jaguar on hood, hood opens, 1:60, 1972 – 1978

dark metallic blue, 3spb $8-10

light metallic blue, white interior, 3spb ...$8-10

bright red, 3spb $8-10

dark metallic red, 3spb $8-10

dark metallic red, thc1 ....$8-10

salmon pink, 5sp $8-10

light metallic blue, 5sp $8-10

dark metallic blue, white interior, 3kk.....$8-10

dark metallic red, ivory interior, amber windscreen, jaguar decal on hood, 3kk ...$8-10

207-B Pop Rock Festival Motorcycle, includes motorcyclist carrying a guitar, 1980 – 1983

red with yellow rider, black saddle bags, brown guitar, 1980 catalog........$20-25

red with white rider, black saddle bags, brown guitar...........................$20-25

yellow motorcycle casting, part of 3066-B $20-25

207-C Extending Ladder Fire Truck *Pompier*, 1:100, 1986

red with no lettering, white ladder $4-6

red with gold lettering, "F.D.S.F.," wheat laurel insignia, white ladder, 4c...............$3-5

red with gold lettering, "F.D.N.Y.," four petal insignia, medium gray ladder, 4c.............$3-5

darker red with gold lettering, "F.D.N.Y.," four petal insignia, dark gray ladder, 4c...$3-5

white, yellow interior, dark gray ladder, red/yellow "Fire Rescue" graphics, 4c, 2000 ....$2-4

207-D Renault Clio, 1:53

metal flake blue with white interior and bumpers, "5" $3-5

metal flake teal with gray interior, white "Clio" script on sides, Supers steerable........$3-5

208-A Bernard Snow Plow, with driver, doors part of casting but have nothing cast into them, plastic base covers up "Rail Route" on chassis, box has "Rail-Route" on it, low open dump on back, 1:100, 1967

pale blue, bw3 and bw1 ....$15-18

turquoise, bw3 and bw1 ....$15-18

light green with metal unpainted plow, bw3 and bw1 ....$15-18

208-B Chrysler 180, 4-door, front doors open, 1:60, 1972–1977

bright green, white interior, blue windshield, thc $10-13

metallic red, white interior, amber windshield, 3kk $10-13

orange, white interior, amber windshield, 5sp $10-13

orange, white interior, clear windshield, 3spb $10-13

orange, white interior, clear windshield, 3kk $10-13

blue, white interior, thc $10-13

gold $10-13

metallic red, white interior, amber windshield, 3spb $10-13

metallic green, white interior, amber windshield, 3spb $10-13

208-C Farm Tractor, 1:65, 1980

light blue, black engine and fenders, cultivator, ft2 yellow rear hubs, 1999 ....$3-5

blue, yellow engine and fenders, no cultivator, ft2 ....$2-4

green, black fenders, cultivator, ft2 ....$2-4

green, yellow fenders, no cultivator, ft2 ....$2-4

green, yellow fenders, cultivator, ft2......$2-4

green, green fenders, no cultivator, ft2 ....$2-4

green, black engine and fenders, yellow rear hubs, no cultivator, ft2 ....$2-4

green, black engine and fenders, chrome hubs, no cultivator, ft2 ....$2-4

red, black fenders, cultivator, ft2, black wheels...............................$2-4

yellow, green fenders, no cultivator, ft2 ....$2-4

yellow, green fenders, exhaust and engine, brown cultivator, black ft2 ....$2-4

blue, yellow engine and fenders, cultivator, ft2 ....$2-4

red, yellow engine and fenders, cultivator, ft1 ....$2-4

209-A Pickup Camper, 1973–1980

orange pickup truck with white camper shell, 3spb $12-15

red pickup truck with white camper shell, 3spb $12-15

yellow pickup, amber windows, white camper, 2 single headlights, 3kk.............$12-15

blue pickup truck, amber windows, white camper shell, 4 headlights, 3spb, German issue, "Majorette" deleted from base, reissued as Globe Toys #101.

209-B Porsche 911 Turbo, doors open, 1:57, 1982

black with red and white "911" tampos, white interior, rw.............................$3-5

bright blue chrome with white interior, bright blue chrome rw, *Kool Kromes*.......$3-5

bronze chrome with white interior, bronze chrome rw, *Kool Kromes* $3-5

copper chrome with white interior, copper chrome rw, *Kool Kromes* $3-5

fluorescent orange with white interior and tampos, "SWANSON KIDS FUN FEAST," *Road Eaters*, rw.............................$3-5

red with gold lettering, "F.D.N.Y.," four petal insignia, white interior and base, rw ...$3-5

red with gold lettering, "F.D.N.Y.," four petal insignia, black interior and base $3-5

red with gold lettering, "F.D.N.Y.," four petal insignia, white interior, red base $3-5

red with black and silver tampos, "16," "Porsche," "turbo," rw $3-5

red with "CAMPBELL'S DINOSAUR VEGETABLE SOUP," *Road Eaters*, rw $3-5

white with "22" on doors and hood, orange and black rally tampos, rw, 1999 ....$3-5

yellow with yellow base, red interior, orange and blue tampos, 6sp $6-8

yellow with red base, blue interior, "CHOCOLATE WAVE," *Smelly Speeders,* **light brown tires, chrome rw** $3-5

yellow with orange and green tampos, "16" and "turbo" on hood, red interior, rw..........................$3-5

pink with white interior, "HIT PARADE," blue and silver tampos, red base, rw.......................$3-5

white with orange base, black interior, clear windows, orange and black rally accents, "22" on doors and hood, "CHAMPION" on hood and roof, chrome rw 1999 ....$2-4

yellow with orange and blue accents, "16" and "turbo" on hood, red interior, rw..........................$2-4

yellow with orange and blue accents, "16" and "turbo" on hood, red interior, 6sp..........................$2-4

fluorescent orange, rw, in "Girls" package with a mini-bag key ring..................................$4-6

209-C Ferrari 456 GT

black with tan interior, "33," red and white tampos $3-5

209-D Porsche 996, doors open, 1999

yellow with red interior, black plastic base, 5pw.................................$3-5

silver, black interior, Porsche logo on hood, 5pw, 2000 ....$2-4

blue front/silver rear body, yellow interior, racing graphics, "65," 5pw, 2000 Speed Wheeler....................$2-4

210-A Volkswagen K70, doors open, 1:60, 1974 – 1976

yellow, thc...........................$8-10

red, white interior, amber windows, 5sp..............................$8-10

bright red-orange..............................$8-10

blue, white interior, amber windows, 5sp..............................$8-10

metallic blue, white interior, amber windows, 3kk..............................$8-10

metallic red, white interior, 3spb $8-10

metallic blue-green, 3spb....................$8-10

light blue, 3spb..............................$8-10

orange, yellow interior, clear windows, 3kk $8-10

red, white interior, amber windows, 3kk $8-10

light green, thc $8-10

pink, white interior, 3kk $8-10

210-B Volkswagen Golf, rear hatch opens, 1:60, 1979 – 1985

red, yellow interior, amber windows, yellow "GOLF" tampo on sides, 3spb $4-6

red, yellow interior, amber windows, silver "GOLF" tampo on sides, 3spb $4-6

metallic lime green, white interior, no graphics, 3spb $5-7

blue, red interior, no graphics, 3spb........$3-5

silver, orange interior, green windows, black "GOLF" tampo on sides, 3spb $4-6

black, red interior, red "GOLF" tampo on sides, 3spb $4-6

black, white interior, red "GOLF" tampo on sides, 3spb $4-6

210-C Peugeot 205 CTi/GTi Cabriolet, unpainted metal base, clear windshield, 1:53, compare to 281-A

white with red interior, black "Cti" on sides, '"Made in France"' deleted from base, 6sp..............................$2-4

white with red interior, no markings, 6sp $2-4

white with red & white interior, black "Cti" on sides, 6sp $2-4

white with white interior, black "Cti" on sides, 6sp $2-4

white with black interior, red "Cti" on sides, 6sp $2-4

white with silver-gray & black interior, red "Cti" on sides, 6sp..............................$2-4

white with red interior, "jacadi," *promo,* 6sp $5-7

pink with white interior, "Aerobics," *Girls,* 6sp $3-5

pink, color changes with temperature, red interior, black "Cti" on sides, 6sp..........$2-4

silver with pink interior, blue & orange spots, 6sp..............................$2-4

silver with pink interior, blue & orange spots, blue 6sp..............................$2-4

metallic blue with white interior, yellow "Cti" on sides, 6sp..............................$2-4

metallic blue with white interior, red "Cti" on hood and sides, "Made in France," 6sp..............................$2-4

metallic blue with white interior, "Tennis," 6sp..............................$3-5

metallic blue with red interior, "Aerobics," 6sp..............................$4-6

blue with silver interior, "Made in Thailand," 4c..............................$2-4

pale green with red interior, black "Cti" on sides, "Made in France," 6sp..............................$2-4

210-D Peugeot 205 CTi/GTi Hardtop, 1:53, see 281-A, compare to 210-C

211-A Hotchkiss Jeep with Cattle Trailer, reissue of 11-A..........................$16-20

211-Ba Wheel Loader *Tracto-Pelle,* steering wheel cast into interior, cast cab, 1972 – 1978

orange with unpainted silver bucket, cast steering wheel, silver plastic base and engine $8-10

orange with unpainted silver bucket, plastic steering wheel, silver plastic base and engine $8-10

pale yellow with yellow bucket, gray plastic base and engine, plastic steering wheel.........................$8-10

211-Bb Wheel Loader *Tracto-Pelle,* plastic steering wheel separate from casting

orange-yellow with painted silver bucket, plastic steering wheel, silver plastic base and engine................................$8-10

pale yellow with yellow bucket, gray plastic base and engine, plastic steering wheel $8-10

olive drab with star on front..............$20-25

211-C Tractor with Snow Plow, var. of 211-B, 263-A

red with silver metal snow plow, metallic gray interior and engine, ct4s with black rims................................$10-13

red with red metal snow plow, yellow interior and engine, ct4s with black rims................................$10-13

211-D Road Grader Shovel $4-6

211-E Ferrari GTO, 1:56, 1987 – 1994

red with black interior, Ferrari logo on hood, "Made in France," rw....................$2-4

red with black interior, white lower body, gold "23" on doors, "Made in France" removed, rw................................$2-4

red with gold "23" on doors, rw............$2-4

red with black interior, sticker of a movie frame on hood with a blonde girl wearing sunglasses, "Made in France," rw, part of *Girls* series 2200, 1989................$4-6

211-F Ferrari Testarossa, 1997 diecast adaptation of Novacar 104
red, 8h, 1999 Catalog $3-5
yellow, black interior, 8h $3-5

211-G Ford Mondeo

silver, light brown interior, Supers steerable, 8h................................$3-5

silver, tan interior, 8h..........................$3-5

blue, white tampos, "15," 8h................$3-5

212-A Bernard Circus Truck, 1:100, 1967 ....$16-20

212-B Wrecker / Service Truck, produced with dual or single headlights, same casting as 204-B
white with blue roof light $6-8

red with unpainted metal boom, yellow roof light, 3kk................................$6-8

orange with "Service" stickers on doors, unpainted metal boom, dual headlights, 3kk................................$10-13

orange with "Service" stickers on doors, yellow boom, 3kk $10-13

white with blue roof light, black boom, red hook, "Mondial Assistance" on sides, dark red accents, single headlights, 3kk................................$6-8

same as 5 with natural metal boom........$6-8

white with red diagonal accents with black "SOS" on doors, natural metal boom, 3spb, 1980 catalog $6-8

orange with "Service" stickers on doors, yellow boom, 5sp......................$10-13

red with amber windows and lights, yellow boom, no accents, 5sp $6-8

olive drab with star on hood, 3kk $8-10

olive drab with number on door, 3spb ...$8-10

212-C Ford Escort XR3, rear hatch opens, 1:52, 1983 – 1988
black, red interior, amber windows, red and white accents, "XR3i" on doors and hood, Ford logo on hood, rw....................$2-4

yellow, red interior, red and black accents, "XR3" on sides and hood, gold Ford logo on hood......................$2-4

red, yellow interior, with black, yellow and orange accents, "XR3" on sides, 6sp...$2-4

black, red interior, gold accents, "XR3" on sides only, white Ford logo on hood..........$2-4

metallic red, red interior, "Team FdF," "972," black and white tampos, rw..............$2-4

red, yellow interior, "Team FdF," "972," orange, black and yellow tampos, 6sp $2-4

red, yellow interior, amber windows, "Team FdF," "972," orange, black and yellow tampos, "Made in France," rw $2-4

silver, red interior, amber windows, green and red tampos, 'XR3i' on doors and hood, red Ford logo on hood, "Made in France," rw................................$2-4

red, yellow interior, with black, yellow and orange accents, "XR3" on sides, 6spk...$2-4

212-D Pontiac Firebird, hood opens, 1995
blue with racing tampos, bright pink interior, 4c, 1999 ....$2-4

blue with red interior, red and white rally accents, "3," 8h................................$2-4

blue with red interior, red and white rally accents, "3," 5pw................................$2-4

green front, black rear body with white interior, racing graphics, "34," 2000 *Speed Wheeler*, 5pw................................$2-4

yellow with red interior, no markings, 8h ...$2-4

yellow with black and red racing graphics, "23," 8h................................$2-4

213-A Citroën DS19, 1967
blue with red interior $12-15

213-B Citroën DS21, headlights covered, base has number 13, unpainted metal base, clear windshield, 1969 – 1971
Base type 1: "Made in France" at front, scale at rear
Base type 2: "Made in France" at left, scale at right
metallic blue with orange interior, wheels: gray hub and black tires w/tread, base 1 ....$10-13

metallic blue with light blue interior, wheels: gray hub and black tires w/tread, base 1 ....$10-13

metallic red with light blue interior, wheels: gray hub and black tires w/tread, base 1 ....$10-13

silver-gray with light blue interior, wheels: gray hub and black tires w/tread, base 1 ....$10-13

metallic green with light blue interior, wheels: gray hub and ridged black tires, base 1 ....$10-13

blue with light tan interior, thc15, base 2........................$10-13

yellow-green with light tan interior, thc 15, base 2........................$10-13

metallic red with light tan interior, thc15, base 2........................$10-13

213-C Mercedes-Benz 350SL Convertible, trunk opens, 1:60

silver with light green interior, red-orange stripes, 3spb................................$4-6

silver with yellow interior, yellow windshield, yellow accents, "Team 8" on hood, 3kk $6-8

silver with yellow interior, yellow windshield, yellow accents, "Team 8" on hood, 3spb $6-8

white with yellow windshield, no markings,
5sp $6-8

white with red interior, 3spb...............$6-8

white with red interior, 3kk $6-8

yellow with black interior, yellow windshield,
3spb $6-8

yellow with red interior, yellow windshield,
5sp $6-8

213-D Mercedes-Benz 450 SL
no details known $10-12

213-E Mercedes-Benz Stake Truck, with hay bales, 1:100, also 254-A

brown stake bed with yellow bales, black interior and front grille and base, clear windows, "254" and "213" on base, 3spb ...$6-8

brown stake bed with yellow bales, black interior and front grille and base, clear windows, "254" and "213" on base, 3kk.........$6-8

213-F Chevrolet Impala Taxi, 1:69, also 219-A, compare to 240-B, 1987 – 1992, reissued in 2000, model number unknown

black front and rear with yellow doors and roof, blue interior, amber windows, "444-4444," "Yellow Cab," "870" on hood and trunk, 8h $3-5

black front and rear with yellow doors and roof, blue interior, amber windows, "444-4444," "Yellow Cab," "870" on hood and trunk, "870" on front fender, rectangular tampo on rear fender, 8h $3-5

black front and rear with yellow doors and roof, blue interior, amber windows, "444-4444" and "Yellow Cab" on doors, 8h.........$3-5

yellow with black interior, clear windows, black accents, "444-4444," "YELLOW CAB" on hood with "444," "870" on hood, trunk and front fenders, 8h $3-5

yellow with blue interior, amber windows, "444-4444," "Yellow Cab," 8h.................$3-5

213-G F1 Racer, 1995

yellow, rw $3-5

purple, rw $3-5

orange, blue front wing, black rear wing, black and white accents, "2" on front, "ENERGY" on side pods, checkered flag behind cockpit, rw $3-5

red, rw $3-5

blue with no markings, white wing and interior, red base and front wing, rw.............$3-5

blue with yellow and red tampos, white wing and interior, red base and front wing, "19," "FAT," "Performance," rw........$3-5

blue with gold and red tampos, white wing and interior, red base and front wing, "19," "FAT," "Performance," rw........$3-5

blue, red base, white interior, no accents, white wing, rw..................................$3-5

213-H Roadster, designed after a Dodge Viper
metal flake blue with black interior, white and black stripes....................................$3-5

red with black interior, silver wheels.........$3-5

214-A Citroën DS 21, same as 213 with Boat Trailer boat is turquoise and white, box has "RailRoute" on it, 1:65, 1966 ....$15-18

214-B Saviem Modular Site Office Truck
yellow with brown office module $8-10

metallic blue with cream office module...$8-10

214-C Saviem Container Truck, 1:100, 1976 – 1984

white cab and container, clear windows, black base, red/white/blue label, larger "PEPSI," square corners on color, 3kk.............$6-8

white cab, blue container, "ADIDAS" logo, 3kk $5-7

white cab and container, clear windows, black base, "chambourcy," "YOGHOURTS DESSERTS FROMAGES FRAIS," label, 3kk........................$8-10

red cab, clear windows, gray base, white container, "MAJORETTE" on driver's side, "CONTAINER" on passenger side, tampo, 3kk..................................$8-10

red cab, clear windows, gray base, white container, "MAJORETTE" on driver's side, "CONTAINER" on passenger side, tampo, 3kk/ 3spb $8-10

orange cab, clear windows, gray base, white container, "MAJORETTE" on driver's side, "CONTAINER" on passenger side, tampo, 3kk/ 5sp $9-12

white cab and container, clear windows, black base, "BRESSE BLEU FROMAGERIES," label, 3kk...............$10-13

white cab, white container, clear windows, black base, "BRESSE BLEU FRO-

MAGERIES," label, 3spb/3kk..$10-13

dark blue cab and container, clear windows, black base, "ALDI," tampo, "MAJORETTE" not cast on base, *promotional*, 3kk $10-13

metallic blue cab, clear windows, black base, white container, "TRANSPORT REZE," tampo, "MAJORETTE" not cast on base, *promotional*, 3kk $10-13

metallic blue cab, clear windows, black base, white container, "T.I.J. FAUCHER," tampo, "MAJORETTE" not cast on base, promotional, 3kk................................$10-13

red cab clear windows, black base, red container, made for the Danish toystore "BR-LEGETOJ," "Velkommen i BR" and "BR LEGETOJ," BR Toys, label, 3kk $10-13

white cab and container, clear windows, black base, red/white/blue label, smaller "PEPSI," round corners on color, 3kk $6-8

white cab and container, clear windows, black base, red and black "READING PAINT SERVICES," tampo, English *promotional*, 3kk $10-13

white cab and container, clear windows, black base, red/white/blue label, larger "PEPSI," square corners on color, 3spb $6-8

white cab and container, clear windows, blue/yellow/red label with picture of freighter and container truck, 3spb $6-8

white cab, clear windows, white container, "CGM," "TRANSPORT EXPRESS," 3kk..$9-12

red cab, clear windows, black base, white container, "BRESSE BLEU FROMAGERIES," label, 3kk...............$10-13

white cab, clear windows, gray base, white container, "chambourcy," "YOGHOURTS DESSERTS FROMAGES FRAIS," label, 3kk $8-10

white cab and container, clear windows, black base, "MAJORETTE" on driver's side, "CONTAINER" on passenger side, tampo, 3spn.............................$8-10

214-D 20 Panel Truck
no details known $10-13
214-E Nissan 300ZX Turbo T-Roof, doors open, headlights raise and retract, 1:62, 1988
blue with red interior, amber windows, gold "300ZX" tampo on hood, 8h $3-5
metallic blue with red interior, gold "300ZX" tampo on hood, white headlights, "Made in Thailand," 8h $3-5
orange with red interior, no accents, yellow headlights, "Made in Thailand," 8h ..$3-5
orange with red interior, no accents, red headlights, "Made in Thailand," 8h $3-5

red with white interior, "17 Racing Team" on white panel on hood, white headlights, "Made in France," 8h $3-5

red with white interior, "17 Racing Team" on white panel on hood, white headlights, "Made in Thailand," 4c $3-5
red with bright green interior, black and white accents, "17 Racing Team" on white panel on hood, white headlights, 8h.......................................$3-5
red with bright green interior, clear windows, yellow and white accents on hood and roof, white headlights, "Made in Thailand," 8h $3-5
white with black, red and blue "Mobil 1" accents, 8h $3-5
white with red interior, amber windows, red "300ZX" tampos, white headlights, "Made in France," 8h.....................$3-5
yellow with red interior, blue and white accents, white headlights, "Made in Thailand," 8h $3-5
yellow with red interior, red and black accents, "17" on hood, yellow headlights, "Made in Thailand," 8h $3-5
yellow with red interior, yellow headlights, "Made in Thailand," 8h $3-5
214-F 6x6 Pumper, 1999
red, "Sapeurs Pompiers," gray rotating nozzles on roof, ctsc $3-5
red, "Fire Dept" in white on sides, gray rotating nozzles on roof, red baseplate, "Made in Thailand," ctsc $3-5
215-A Citroën DS 21, same as 213 with Sterkeman Lovely House Trailer

trailer is white, "Majorette No 15" on base, box has "Rail-Route" on it, 1:65, 1966.......................................$15-18
215-B Unimog with Fork Lift, 1:82, 1976 – 1982, reissued in late 1990s

white with blue canopy, "AIR FRANCE" label, yellow forks, blue windshield, 8sp............$6-8

white with blue canopy, "AIR FRANCE" label, red forks, blue windshield, 8sp $6-8
red, green canopy, yellow forklift, 8sp ...$15-18
orange, blue windshield and light, yellow forks, from 1999 Construction Set, 5d........$3-5
215-C Chevrolet Grand Prix Corvette, doors open, also 268-B, 1:57, 1984
black with gold and black tampos $3-5
black with clear windows, white and gold tampos, light green interior, rw $3-5
black with silver and gold tampos $4-6
black upper, white lower body, yellow windshield, red interior, red and white tampos, red "3" on roof and hood, rw $3-5
black with red and white tampos, "43, tsp, GOODYEAR"................................$3-5
black with "ZR1" on doors, yellow interior, "Corvette" on hood, rw $3-5
black with yellow windshield, silver and gold tampos, "61 Turbo" on roof and hood, rw ..$3-5
blue with red and white tampos, "43, tsp, GOODYEAR," rw $3-5
blue with gold and black tampos, red interior, rw...$4-6
cream with red and black tampos, "500 Miles" on hood, yellow windshield, Color Pack $3-5
orange, "15," blue and white tampos, rw ..$3-5
orange, "15," blue and white tampos, orange rw $3-5
red with black and gold tampos, "500 MILES".......................................$3-5
red with black and gold tampos, "ZR1," black interior, amber windows, rw $3-5
red with white and blue rally tampos, green interior, "4" on hood, rw $3-5
red with white, blue and yellow racing tampos, "4" on doors and roof..............$3-5

red with silver and gold tampos $3-5
red with pink and gold tampos, "500 MILES"...............................$3-5

red with "ZR1" on doors, "CORVETTE" and logo on hood, black interior, rw.............$3-5

red with "ZR1" on doors, "CORVETTE" and logo on hood, red interior $3-5
red with rally tampos, yellow/white/blue on doors and roof, "4 Roadlifter Speed" on hood, yellow interior, rw.................$3-5
red, silver tampos, "19 Turbo" on hood, rw....$3-5
pearl with red and black tampos, "500 MILES, 6," rw $3-5
white with "2000" on hood, "18"...........$4-6
yellow with red and black tampos, "500 MILES, 6," rw $3-5
216-A Peugeot 404 Police, unpainted metal base, 1969 – 1971
dark blue, tan interior, clear windshield, no markings, clear roof light, wheels: gray hub, black tires $10-13
dark blue, tan interior, clear windshield, "Police," clear roof light, wheels: gray hub, black tires $10-13
green, tan interior, clear windshield, "Police," clear roof light, wheels: gray hub, black tires $10-13
216-B 1970 Plymouth Fury Police, 1973 – 1980
black, star and "2" on hood, emblem on sides, clear windows, 3spb $15-18
metallic dark blue, star and "2" on hood, emblem on sides, clear windows, 3spb $15-18
metallic blue, star and "9" on hood, emblem on sides, clear windows, 3spb $15-18
metallic blue, emblem on hood, white "POLICE" side tampos, blue windows, 3spb $15-18
metallic blue, white interior, star and "6" on hood, 3kk $30-35
metallic blue, clear windows, ivory interior, amber roof lights, star and "5" on hood, "POLICE" and shield on sides, 5sp $15-18
yellow, police markings, 3kk.............$15-18
216-C Toyota Lite Ace Van Wagon, 1:52, 1983 – 1992

black, red interior, amber windows, gold "eagle" tampos on sides and roof, "Made in France," 6sp $3-5

blue, white interior, clear windows, no accents, "Made in France," 6sp $3-5

metallic teal blue, white interior, clear windows, yellow and orange accents, pouncing cougar profile on sides, cougar outlined in black, "Made in Thailand," 6sp $3-5

metallic blue, white interior, clear windows, silver and orange accents, pouncing cougar profile on sides, "Made in France" removed, 6sp.....................$3-5

silver, red interior, amber windshield, red accents, "eagle," "Made in France," 6sp............$3-5

mustard yellow, red interior, amber windows, bluebird accent on sides, "Made in France," 6sp.......................$3-5

mustard yellow, red interior, amber windows, bluebird accent on sides, "Made in France," 6spk $3-5

white, red interior, amber windows, red "eagle" tampos on sides and roof, "Made in France," 6sp $3-5

white, red interior, clear windows, red, blue and yellow children's drawings, "Made in Thailand," 6sp.................$3-5

blue, pink interior, clear windows, no accents, "Made in France," 6sp $3-5

blue, white interior, clear windows, "First Sport," "Turbo" accents, "Made in France," 6sp..........................$3-5

blue, pink interior, clear windows, no accents, "Made in France," 6sp $3-5

metallic blue, red interior, clear windows, "First Sport," "Turbo" accents, "Made in France," 6sp...............................$3-5

white, red interior, amber windows, "Made in France," 6sp, found in Majokit 7501 – may have optional red, white and blue label "Hotel Restaurant" on sides.......$4-6

216-D Mercedes A Class, 1999

red with black interior, 4c $3-5

blue with black interior, 4c...................$3-5

blue with black interior, 8h...................$3-5

217-A Peugeot 404 Station Wagon with Alpine F3 car on trailer, beacon on top,

"MAJORETTE" on base, box has "RAIL_ROUTE," 1:65; Alpine F3 has orange rims, and can be metallic blue, green and yellow, green and gray, or red and yellow

green; Alpine F3 has orange rims, metallic blue $15-18

turquoise; Alpine F3: orange rims, metallic blue $15-18

metallic burgundy; Alpine F3: orange rims, metallic blue $15-18

217-B BMW Turbo, gullwing plastic doors open

silver, black doors, yellow interior, "LIEGE SOFIA LIEGE," 3spb....................$8-10

blue, black doors, white interior, clear windows, white "BMW," "TURBO," "56" tampos, 3spb $8-10

white, blue doors, blue interior, clear windows, dark and light blue tampos, "BMW Turbo" on hood, 3spb $8-10

silver, black doors, white interior, "LIEGE SOFIA LIEGE" label on hood, 3spb $8-10

silver, black doors, white interior, "LIEGE SOFIA LIEGE" label on hood, red and yellow "24" label on back, 3spb ...$8-10

mint green, black doors, white interior, 3spb..$8-10

silver, black doors, pale yellow interior, green windows, "LIEGE SOFIA LIEGE" label on hood, 3spb $8-10

metallic green, ivory interior, clear windows, 3spb $8-10

217-C Ford Thunderbird Turbo, hood opens, unpainted metal baseplate with trailer hitch, 1:67, 1986 – 1995

red, black interior, side trim and bumpers, clear windows, "Made in France," 8h..$2-4

metallic red, black interior, side trim and bumpers, clear windows, "Made in France," 8h. $2-4

yellow, black interior, side trim and bumpers, clear windows, "Made in France," 8h..$2-4

metallic blue, black interior, side trim and bumpers, clear windows, "Made in France," 8h. $2-4

metallic blue, black interior, side trim and bumpers, clear windows, "Made in France" removed from baseplate, 8h. $2-4

metallic blue, yellow interior, side trim and bumpers, clear windows, "Made in France" removed from baseplate, 8h. $2-4

metallic blue, red interior, side trim and bumpers, clear windows, "Made in France" removed from baseplate, 8h. $2-4

metallic blue, red interior, side trim and bumpers, clear windows, "Thunderbird" on sides and "3" on hood and roof in red and dull gold, "Made in France," 8h......................$2-4

metallic blue, red interior, side trim and bumpers, clear windows, "Thunderbird" on sides and "3" on hood and roof in red and yellow, "Made in Thailand," 8h. $2-4

metallic blue, red interior, side trim and bumpers, clear windows, "Thunderbird" on sides and "3" on hood and roof in red and yellow, "Made in Thailand," green 8h..$2-4

metallic blue, pink interior, side trim and bumpers, clear windows, "Thunderbird" on sides and "3" on hood and roof in red and yellow, "Made in Thailand," green 8h..$2-4

yellow, black interior, side trim and bumpers, clear windows "Gambler" in red and black on sides, hood and trunklid. "4" in blue and black on hood and roof, "Made in Thailand," 8h $3-5

black, pink interior, side trim and bumpers, clear windows "Gambler" in gold and red on sides, hood and trunklid. "4" in blue and black on hood and roof, "Made in Thailand," 8h................................$2-4

white, dark brown interior, side trim and bumpers, clear windows brown, red, black, yellow, blue and green tampos showing a dancing coconut on hood, coconut branch with "Cool Coconut" on doors and "Smelly Speeders, Not Stinky Just For Kids" on trunklid, white 8h...............$2-4

yellow, light brown interior, side trim and bumpers, clear windows "Gambler" in red and black on sides, hood and trunklid, "4" in blue and black on hood and roof, "Made in Thailand," 8h $2-4

217-Da Chevrolet Extended Cab Pickup, Novacar 116, plastic body, "Novacar" removed from baseplate, "Majorette" added, "MADE IN PORTUGAL" on base

translucent chartreuse with chrome sparkles embedded in body, red interior, clear windows, 8h $2-4

translucent red with chrome sparkles embedded in body, white interior, clear windows, 8h $2-4

translucent purple with chrome sparkles embedded in body, white interior, clear windows, 8h $2-4

translucent chartreuse, no sparkles, white interior, clear windows, 8h.....................$2-4

transparent blue, no sparkles, red interior, clear windows, 8h $2-4

clear body, no sparkles, orange interior, clear windows, 8h $2-4

217-Db Chevrolet Extended Cab Pickup, 1997 diecast version of Novacar 116

black, red interior, amber windows, no markings, "Made in Thailand," 8h $2-4

black, red interior, amber windows, "Sheriff," "911" markings in white, shield on hood, "Made in Thailand" $2-4

black, red interior, amber windows, "Sheriff" in white, shield on hood, "Made in Thailand" $2-4

white, red interior, amber windows, red, blue and yellow accents, "RACING," "CHAMPION" livery, yellow "90" outlined in blue, "Made in Thailand," 8h, 1999, window in roof $2-4

white, red interior, amber windows, red, blue and yellow accents, "RACING," "CHAMPION" livery, yellow "90" outlined in blue, "Made in Thailand," 8h, 1999, window in roof $2-4

217-E Stock car

white, yellow interior, red and black tampos, "71".......................$2-4

blue, black interior, red and white tampos, "28".......................$2-4

black, yellow interior, white roll cage, steerable wheels, "Supers" on baseplate, "Made in Thailand," 6sp.................$2-4

black, yellow interior, white roll cage, gold and red tampos, "2," "BOLIDS," "Made in Thailand," 6sp............................$2-4

red, yellow interior, gray roll cage, yellow and black tampo showing arrows with "3," "SPORT," "BOLIDS" and "STAR," steerable front wheels, "Made in Thailand," 6sp....$2-4

218-A Bernard Garbage Truck, with driver, doors part of casting and have "VILLE de MEGEVE" cast into them, plastic base covers up "Rail Route" on chassis, back of garbage truck tips, 1:100, 1967

metallic green cab, metallic gray plastic refuse tipper, bw1 ....$12-15

yellow cab, metallic gray plastic refuse tipper, bw1..$12-15

blue cab, metallic gray plastic refuse tipper, bw1..$12-15

red cab, metallic gray plastic refuse tipper, bw1..$12-15

green cab, metallic gray plastic refuse tipper, bw1..$12-15

orange cab, gray plastic refuse tipper, gray interior, bw3 front, bw1 ....$12-15

red cab, dark gray plastic refuse tipper, gray interior, bw3 front, bw1 ....$12-15

218-B Mercedes-Benz Sanitation Truck, 1:100

green with metallic gray container, amber windshield, "VILLE DE PARIS" label, 3kk....$4-6

green with metallic gray container, amber windshield, "VILLE DE PARIS" label, 3spb.........................$4-6

green cab, gray container, hippo on sticker, 3kk $2-4

orange cab, metallic gray container, "VILLE DE PARIS" label, 3kk.........................$4-6

orange cab, gray container, "VILLE DE PARIS" label, 3kk.....................................$6-8

orange cab, gray container, amber windshield, no sticker, no raised area for sticker, 3kk .$3-5

orange cab, clear windows, metallic gray container, red "VILLE DE PARIS" label, 3spb $4-6

218-C Peugeot 405 Mi 16, opening doors 1:62, 1989

red, black bumper trim and interior, black pinstrip on sides, "Mi16 on rear doors, 8h..$2-4

red, white bumper trim and interior, white "Mi16" tampo on lower sides, 8h $2-4

blue, white bumper trim and interior, 8h...$2-4

white, red interior, clear windows, 8h, none

white, red bumper trim and interior, red "Peugeot" on sides, 8h.........................$2-4

white, pink bumper trim and interior, clear windows, red "Peugeot," 8h.................$2-4

white, pink bumper trim and interior, multicolored "Mi16" on doors and hood, 8h...........$2-4

white, black interior, clear windows, "TandN," "Abex," 8h, *promo* $9-12

metallic blue, white bumper trim and interior, gold "Style" on roof, "mi16" on lower sides, 8h.........................$2-4

metallic blue, white interior, clear windows, gold "Mi16," 8h...........................$2-4

218-D Peugeot 406 Mi 16, sunroof or light bar, 1:60, 1997

metallic blue, black plastic base, dark gray interior, clear windows, black stripe, "Esso" on baseplate, 8h $2-4

white, black base and bumpers, gray interior, blue and red accents, "POLICE," red roof light, "Esso" removed from baseplate, "Majorette" added, 8h....................$2-4

metallic blue, black plastic base, dark gray interior, clear windows, black stripe, 5pw...$2-4

red, dark red plastic base, dark gray interior, clear windows, black stripe, 8h........$2-4

metallic light blue, black plastic base, dark gray interior, clear windows, black stripe, 8h.........................$2-4

maroon, black plastic base, dark gray interior, clear windows, 8h $2-4

orange, dark blue plastic base, white interior, clear windows, "8," "Bolids'" 8h $2-4

white, black plastic base, dark blue interior, clear windows, "POLICE," red roof light, 8h.........................$2-4

white, black plastic base, dark blue interior, clear windows, "POLICE," red roof light, 5pw.........................$2-4

219-A Bernard Cattle Carrier Stake Truck *Fourragére*, bumper part of base, back gate swings down, 1:100, 1967 – 1971

blue, gray interior, clear plastic windows, brown plastic stake, bw3 front, bw1 rear $8-10

orange, gray interior, clear plastic windows, brown plastic stake, bw3 front, bw1 rear...$8-10

219-B Bernard Stake Truck, removable stake, bumper part of cab, 1972 – 1973

no example available $8-10

219-C Matra Simca Bagheera, 1:55, 1974 – 1982

blue, white interior, clear windshield and rear window, "62" on roof, "RALLYE" on doors, 3spb $5-7

blue, white interior, clear windshield and rear window, "K Way Groupe Sportif" on hood in black and dark blue, 3spb..................$5-7

blue, white interior, clear windshield and rear window, "Bagheera" on doors, 3spb...$5-7

white, red interior, clear windshield, amber rear
window, black and red decals, 3spb $5-7
yellow, white interior, amber windshield and
rear window, 5sp $5-7
yellow, white interior, amber windshield and
rear window, 3spb $5-7
orange, white interior, blue windshield and
rear window, black "bagheera" tampo
on doors, 3spb $5-7
yellow, white interior, clear windshield,
amber rear window, 3spb $5-7
blue, "7" and "PARIS" on doors, 3spb $5-7
219-D Honda Accord, doors open, 1:59,
1984 – 1988

**metallic mint green, red interior, amber
windows, white accents, 6sp $3-5**

metallic green, red interior, amber
windows, white accents, "Made in
France," 6sp $3-5
yellow, red interior, amber windows, blue
accents, 6sp $3-5
yellow, red interior, clear windows, blue
accents, "Made in France," 6sp $3-5
yellow chrome, *Kool Kromes* $3-5
metallic pink, yellow interior, light amber
windows, yellow tampo, "Made in
France," 6sp $3-5
red, black interior, clear windows, white and
silver tampo, "Accord," "Made in France"
removed from baseplate. "Made in
Thailand," 6sp $3-5
219-E Chevrolet Impala Taxi, see 213-F,
compare to 240-B
219-E Lamborghini Diablo, 1:58, 1992
black, white interior, clear windows, "CRY
BABY" candy logo, Road Eaters,
"Made in France," rw $3-5
red with logo on hood, rw $2-4
white, black interior, clear windows, "PEPSI"
logo, Road Eaters, "Made in France,"
rw $4-6
yellow, black interior, clear windows, "Willy
Wonka Everlasting Gobstopper," Road
Eaters, "Made in France," rw $4-6
yellow with no markings $2-4
yellow, black interior, clear windows, small
black logo on hood, "Made in France,"
rw $2-4

**yellow, black interior, clear windows, large
black logo on hood, "Made in Thailand,"
yellow chrome rw $2-4**

fluorescent yellow, black interior, clear windows, large black logo on hood, "Made
in Thailand," yellow chrome rw $2-4
red chrome, black interior, clear windows,
Kool Kromes, "Made in France," red
chrome rw $3-5
yellow chrome, black interior, clear windows,
Kool Kromes, "Made in France," yellow
chrome rw $3-5
219-G Porsche Boxster–This car looks like it was in
the *Supers* line, but it has never been found
packaged as such. Numbers 219/220 and
also 269 on baseplate. "Made in Thailand"
metal flake teal with red interior, clear headlights, Porsche shield on hood $3-5
yellow, white interior, clear windscreen, blue
accents, red "8," rw $3-5
red with blue tampos, black interior, 6sp,
2000 Catalog $3-5
metallic purple, white interior, clear windscreen, rw $3-5
silver, red interior, clear windshield, black,
yellow and red Porsche logo on front,
steerable wheels, 6sp $3-5
220-A Volvo 245 DL Station Wagon, opening
rear hatch, with or without trailer hitch, 1:60,
1976 – 1983
red, white interior, clear windows, trailer hitch,
3spb $6-8
red, white interior, amber windows, trailer
hitch, 3spb $6-8
red, white interior, amber windows, trailer
hitch, 3kk $6-8
red body, yellow interior, trailer hitch, 3spb ..$6-8
green, white interior, clear windows, trailer
hitch, 3spb $6-8
green, white interior, clear windows, trailer
hitch, 3kk $6-8
green, white interior, clear windows, trailer
hitch, yellow and red labels on hood and
sides trailer hitch, 3kk $6-8
brown, pale yellow interior, clear windows,
yellow "Touring Club de France" decals,
trailer hitch, 3kk $6-8
gold/brown, white interior, no trailer hitch,
3spb $6-8

white, red interior, clear windows, yellow and
black "Tour De France" decals, "OFFI-
CIALS" on sides, trailer hitch, 3spb $6-8
metallic brown, ivory interior, blue windows,
5sp $6-8
220-B Mustang SVO, 1:59, 1986 – 1995
metallic periwinkle, 6sp $4-6
metallic periwinkle blue, black interior and
bumpers, "Made in France," rw $4-6
metallic periwinkle blue, black interior and bumpers,
red and white accents, "44" on hood and
doors, "Made in France," rw $4-6
metallic turquoise, black interior and bumpers,
"Made in France," rw $4-6
white, black interior and bumpers, red stripes
over top of car and down sides, rw ..$2-4

**white, red interior and bumpers, black and
red "Mustang 1" accents, "Made in France"
removed from baseplate. "Made in Thailand," 6sp $3-5**

white, red interior and bumpers, black and
red "Mustang 1" accents, "Made in
France" removed from baseplate,
"Made in Thailand," rw $3-5
white with bright blue front half, black interior
and bumpers, red and black diagonal
stripes on sides, "5" on hood and roof,
"Made in France" removed from baseplate, "Made in Thailand," rw $3-5
white with blue front half, black interior and
bumpers, red and black diagonal stripes
on sides, "5" on hood and roof, "Made
in France" removed from baseplate,
"Made in Thailand," rw $3-5
white with green front half, black interior and
bumpers, red and black diagonal stripes
on sides, "5" on hood and roof, rw, in 5
pack $5-7
white with metallic blue front half, red
diagonal stripes on sides, rw $3-5
red with horse and "MUSTANG" on sides,
6sp $2-4
red, black interior and bumpers, horse and "MUS-
TANG" on sides, "Made in France" removed
from baseplate, "Made in Thailand," rw ..$2-4
red, blue interior and bumpers, horse and
"MUSTANG" on sides, "Made in
France" removed from baseplate, "Made
in Thailand," rw $2-4

red, silver and black accents, "44" on hood and doors, "Made in France" removed from baseplate, "Made in Thailand," rw......$2-4

220-C Honda Acura NSX, 1997 Majorette adaptation of Novacar 117

plastic body, red, black interior, clear windows, 8h $4-6

metal body, red, 8h.............................$3-5

metal body, yellow with racing graphics, checkered flag, "2," "BandL," 8h......$3-5

metal body, yellow, red interior, "2," rallye tampos, 8h...$3-5

light blue front/dark blue rear body, red interior, racing graphics, "26," 5pw, 2000 Speed Wheeler $3-5

metal body, yellow with racing graphics, checkered flag, "2," "BandL," 5pw...........$3-5

221-A Renault R16, 1969 – 1972

red, white interior $10-13

red, red interior, unpainted hubs $10-13

221-B Citroën GS *Bertone Camargue*

white with unpainted base, green interior, clear windshield, "Holiday Inn" shield on hood, 3spb $5-7

white with unpainted base, green interior, clear windshield, "Holiday Inn" globe on hood, 3spb $5-7

metallic blue with unpainted base, blue interior, clear windshield, Union Jack on hood, "MacKeen Junior," 3spb..................$5-7

metallic blue with unpainted base, blue interior, clear windshield, Union Jack on hood "MacKeen Junior," 3kk $5-7

metallic blue with unpainted base, light green interior, clear wndshield, Union Jack on hood "MacKeen Junior," 3spb $5-7

metallic blue with no markings $6-8

blue with unpainted base, white interior, clear windshield, white "RACING, 3spb....$5-7

blue with unpainted base, white interior, clear windshield, white "RACING," 3kk $5-7

blue with unpainted base, green interior, clear windshield, white "RACING," 3kk $5-7

blue with unpainted base, no markings $5-7

red with unpainted base, white interior, amber windshield, white "RACING," #106 on base, German issue, 3spb.................$5-7

red with unpainted base, white interior, light amber windshield, "MacKeen Junior," 3spb $5-7

red with unpainted base, white interior, light amber windshield, 3spb $5-7

red with unpainted base, white interior, light amber windshield, 3kk $5-7

red with yellow base, black interior, light amber windshield, 3spb.................$5-7

red with orange base, black interior, light amber windshield, 3spb.................$5-7

metallic maroon with light yellow base, black interior, light amber windshield, 3spb $5-7

metallic maroon with light yellow base, black interior, light amber windshield, 3kk $5-7

metallic maroon with light yellow base, black interior, light amber windshield, 5sp $5-7

metallic green with yellow base, black interior, amber windshield, 3spb......$5-7

221-C Audi Quattro, 1:58, 1984 – 1988

white, multicolor "Monte Carlo" Rally markings $3-5

blue, black and gold accents $3-5

white, black interior, clear windows, no markings, "Made in France," rw.......$3-5

white, black interior, clear windows, red and black tampos,"AUDI SPORT," "12," "Made in France," rw......................$3-5

white, black interior, clear windows, red and black tampos,"AUDI SPORT," "12," "Made in France," 6sp $3-5

white, black interior, clear windows, red and black stripe tampos,"Audi" on hood, "Made in France" removed from base, 6sp $3-5

white, black interior, clear windows, red and black stripe tampos,"Audi" on hood, two yellow stripes down sides, "3" on doors, rw $3-5

221-D Renault X54 *Safrane*, 1:63, 1992. These were originally thought to be two distinct models, but there is no mention of a Renault X54 in the catalogs. The 1992 catalog simply has a blank picture with "Renault" underneath.

blue with black interior, 6sp $2-4

metallic blue, black interior, 6sp..............$2-4

white, red interior, red rallye markings, "8 RALLYE," 8h...$2-4

white, red interior, red rallye markings, "8 RALLYE," 6sp $2-4

222-A Scania Skip Truck *Multi Benne*, reissued as Globe Toys 114-A, 1:100, 1976 – 1982, reissued as Globe Toys 114-A

orange with green skip, gray base, no labels, 3kk, 1976–1978 ....$8-10

orange with blue skip, yellow and black "SERVICE" label, "8" on hood in yellow circle, black base, 3kk, 1980........$8-10

orange with blue skip, yellow and black "SERVICE" label, no label on hood, black base, 3kk $8-10

orange with blue skip, yellow and black "SERVICE" label on skip, no number on hood, black base, 3spb................$8-10

orange with blue skip, yellow and black "SERVICE" label on skip, no number on hood, black base, 3kk $8-10

red with yellow skip, red and black "SERVICE" label, black base, 3kk....................$6-8

red with yellowish-orange skip, black interior, black base, no labels, 3kk...............$6-8

222-B Renault 25 V6, front doors open, 1:63, 1987 – 1991

metallic burgundy, gray interior, clear windows, "Made in France," 8h $2-4

metallic pale green, gray interior, clear windows, "Made in France," 8h $2-4

metallic blue, orange and yellow flames, 6sp $2-4

metallic dark gray, gray interior, clear windows, "Made in France," 8h $2-4

metallic deep blue, gray interior, clear windows, "Made in France" deleted from base, 8h $2-4

metallic silver, gray interior and
bumpers, "Made in France" deleted
from base, 8h $2-4

metallic burgundy, black interior, clear
windows, "Made in France,"
8h $2-4

metallic dark gray, black interior, clear windows, "Made in France," 8h $2-4

223-A Mobile Office, 1976 – 1979
orange with white office module on
back $8-10

223-Ba Crazy car 4x4, low chassis, also see
267-B, 1981 – 1982
lime green, black interior, rw $6-8
metallic gold, black interior, rw $6-8

223-Bb Crazy car 4x4 / Desert Raider 4x4, high
chassis, also see 267-B, 1981 – 1982,
"Made in France"
gray-blue, orange interior, ct4sp.......$4-6
blue, yellow interior, orange/yellow/red
labels on hood and roof, ct4sp $4-6
black with red interior, yellow and red accents,
"desert raider" on hood, ct4sp...........$3-5
blue, yellow interior, "Crazy car" multicolored
tampo on hood and roof, ct4sp........$4-6

223-C '57 Chevrolet Hot Rod, 1991
white, chrome interior, clear windows,
"CHEE-TOS CHESTER CHEETAH" logo,
"Made in France," 6sp, *Road Eaters* .$3-5
white, chrome interior, clear windows,
"PETER PAN CREAMY" logo, "Made
in France," 6sp, *Road Eaters* $3-5
copper chrome, chrome interior, clear
windows, white "Hot Engine" and
pinstripes on sides, "Made in France,"
6sp copper chrome, *Kool Kromes* ...$3-5
copper chrome, chrome interior, clear windows, white "Hot Engine" and pinstripes on sides, "Made in France,"
8h yellow chrome front wheels, 6sp
copper chrome rear wheels, *Kool
Kromes* $10-13
copper chrome, chrome interior, clear windows,
no tampos, "Made in France," 6sp copper
chrome wheels, *Kool Kromes*.........$10-13
yellow chrome, chrome interior, clear windows, white "Hot Engine" and pinstripes
on sides, "Made in Thailand," 6sp yellow
chrome, *Kool Kromes* $3-5
blue chrome, chrome interior, clear windows, yellow "Hot Engine" and pinstripes on sides,
"Made in France," 6sp blue chrome, *Kool
Kromes* $3-5
red, chrome interior, clear windows, orange
and yellow flame accents, "Made in
France," 6sp...................................$2-4

**red, chrome interior, clear windows,
orange and yellow flame accents, "Made in
France," 6sp blue chrome** $2-4

baby blue, chrome interior, clear windows, magenta and white accents "FIFTIES," 6sp $2-4
baby blue, chrome interior, clear windows,
red and white accents "FIFTIES," "Made
in Thailand," 6sp...............................$2-4
baby blue, chrome interior, clear windows,
red and white accents "FIFTIES," "Made in
Thailand," 6sp pink tires $2-4
metallic teal blue, chrome interior, clear windows, red and yellow flames on sides, roof
and trunk, "Made in Thailand," 6sp....$2-4
metallic teal blue, chrome interior, clear windows, red and yellow flames on sides
only, "Made in Thailand," 6sp $2-4
pale yellow, chrome interior, clear windows,
mauve and white accents, "Made in
Thailand," 6sp $3-5
pink, chrome interior, clear windows, blue
and white accents, "FIFTIES," "Made in
Thailand," 6sp $3-5
red, chrome interior, clear windows, light
orange and black flames, "Made in
Thailand," 6sp $2-4
red, white "Coca Cola" tampo, "Made in
Thailand," 6sp; issued by Coke and
Walmart for their "Radio Grill" restaurant at
Walmart. It has the "Radio Grill" logo on the
roof. It was a Walmart exclusive.............$3-5

224-A Unimog Snow Plow, 1:82, also 259 in
1992, 1976 – 1980
green, amber windows, orange canopy, yellow
windshield, unpainted metal plow, 8sp ...$6-8
green, black interior, baseplate and grill, dark red
windows, no canopy, unpainted metal plow,
"Made in France," 5d, 1992................$6-8

**orange, blue windows, orange canopy,
three white trees on sides, unpainted metal
plow, 8sp**...$6-8

red, white interior, red and yellow label: "Fire
Service," red canopy, "T3" on blue sunroof, blue windshield, 8sp $6-8
224-B Fourgon (Van) Motor Home, 1:67,
1982 – 1986
beige, white interior, blue windows, pale yellow rear
door, green, yellow and red label of landscape
scene on sides, "Made in France," 3spn ...$8-10
beige, blue windows, pale yellow rear door, no
labels, "Made in France," 3spn $8-10

**white, white interior, blue windows, brown
rear door, green, yellow and red label of
landscape scene on sides, "Made in
France," 3spn**.............................$8-10

white, white interior, clear windows, brown
rear door, green, yellow and red label of
landscape scene on sides, "Made in
France," 4c $8-10
224-C Fourgon (Van) Ice Cream Truck *Glacier*,
see 259-C
224-D Jeep Cherokee Limited, with surfboards on
roof, compare to 285-B, 1:60, 1990
black with gold accents, "Limited" on doors,
orange surfboards, charcoal interior,
"Made in France" deleted, 5d $2-4

**black with gold accents, "Limited" on
doors, hot pink surfboards, charcoal interi-
or, 5d**..$2-4

black with gold accents, "Limited" on doors,
red surfboards, 5d..........................$2-4
black with gold accents, "Limited" on doors,
yellow surfboards, "Made in France" deleted, "4x4" on base, 5d....................$2-4
black with blue and white waves, orange surfboards, translucent pink interior, 5d...$2-4
dark blue with yellow fenders, orange surfboards, 5d....................................$2-4

dark blue with yellow fenders, red surfboards, "Surf" on sides, 5dbl dark blue tires, 5-pack $2-4

metallic green with tan lower body, tan interior, clear windows, red surfboards, gold "Surf" on doors and hood, 5d 1998.............$2-4

metallic blue with yellow lower body, "Surf," fish graphics, 5d 1999 ....$2-4

metallic green with tan lower body, tan interior, clear windows, dark red surfboards, gold "Surf" on doors only, 5d $2-4

224-E Jeep Cherokee Sheriff, see 285-B

225-A Safari Truck, 1:80, brush bar on front, same casting as 242-A, 1973 – 1980

yellow, brown plastic canopy, paint streaks off hood, black brush bar, 3kk..........$10-13

orange, brown plastic canopy, paint streaks off hood, black brush bar, 3kk..........$10-13

black with green, brown, and white paint streaks off hood and down sides, 3kk, dark green canopy, black brush bar $10-13

white with black zebra stripes, green canopy with "AFRICAN SAFARI" label, red tires on roof, black brush bar, green tinted windows, 3spb.............$8-10

white with black zebra stripes, green canopy with "AFRICAN SAFARI" label, red tires on roof, black brush bar, green tinted windows, 3kk.............$8-10

orange, olive drab canopy, paint streaks off hood, black brush bar, 3spb $10-13

green (very little), mostly pink and yellow over entire truck, pale amber windshield, olive drab canopy, black brush bar, 3spb.........$8-10

green, black, yellow, and orange over entire truck, pale amber windshield, olive drab canopy, black brush bar, 5sp $8-10

light green, mostly orange-pink and yellow on hood, pale amber windshield, olive drab canopy, black brush bar, 5sp $8-10

orange, paint streaks off hood, olive drab canopy, black brush bar, 5sp $10-13

225-B Citroën BX 4TC, 1987 – 1989, unpainted metal base, clear windshield

white, black interior, "15," "Total," "MICHE-LIN" on hood, opening doors, rw ...$8-10

white, black interior, "15," "Total," stripes, opening doors, rw.............$8-10

white, black interior, "15," "Total," stripes, doors cast shut, rw.............$8-10

225-C Renault 19 Convertible, 1993

metallic silver.............$3-5

metallic blue, red interior, 6sp.............$3-5

white, red interior, "RENAULT" on doors and hood, 6sp $3-5

white, red interior, "Vive la Sport" on doors and hood, 6sp $3-5

226-A Repco F1 Racer, with driver, 1:55, 1969 – 1973

metallic green with white "5" tampo on nose, rt.............$10-13

metallic red with "8" decal on nose, rt ...$10-13

metallic red/burgundy with white "5" surrounded by a design on front $10-13

metallic red, "7" in roundel with a trident decal above it $10-13

metallic green, "3" and "Bosch" decals clear plastic windshield, silver rear mounted engine and black exhaust, white plastic driver, with red cap, rt.............$10-13

metallic purple, "3" and "Shell" decals, clear plastic windshield, silver rear mounted engine and black exhaust, white plastic driver, with red cap, rt.............$10-13

metallic purple, "5" surrounded by a design on front $10-13

metallic green, "7" in roundel with a trident decal above it $10-13

226-B Volkswagen Panel Van (Fourgon Volkswagen Tole), white rear hatch opens 1:66, 1974 – 1980, some early models didn't have a ridge around the beltline.

orange, white interior, yellow windows, no center belt line, 3spb $10-13

orange, white interior, yellow windows, white "SIEMENS, EEN KLASSE APART," 3spb $10-13

orange, white interior, yellow windows, black "SERVICE" on red/white striped rectangle, 3spb $10-13

orange, white interior, blue red and white tampos, "SERVICE AUTOROUTE," blue windows, 3spb $10-13

orange, white interior, blue red and white tampos, "SERVICE AUTOROUTE," blue windows, 3kk.............$10-13

orange, white interior, blue red and white tampos, "SERVICE AUTOROUTE," yellow windows, 3spb $10-13

orange, white interior, blue red and white tampos, "SERVICE AUTOROUTE," yellow windows, 3kk.............$10-13

red, "Café Hag," white accents, white interior, 5sp.............$10-13

red, "Café Hag," white accents, white interior, 3kk.............$10-13

red, "Café Hag," white accents, white interior, 3spb.............$10-13

pink, white interior, 3spb.............$10-13

white, blue Volkswagen symbol and "VAG" on sides, 3kk.............$10-13

olive drab, blue on white "US ARMY" and a star, yellow windows, white interior, olive rear hatch, no center belt line, 3spb $10-13

olive drab, blue on white "US ARMY" and a star, yellow windows, white interior, white rear hatch, no center belt line, 3spb.......$10-13

olive drab, blue on white "US ARMY" and a star, clear windows, white interior, olive rear hatch, no center belt line, 3kk.......$10-13

olive drab, no tampos, white interior, olive rear hatch, no center belt line, 3spb $10-13

red, belt line ridge, no tampos, #244 base, wheel type unknown.............$10-13

white, amber windshield, white label with red "la boule OBUT" on sides, 3kk.....$10-13

226-C Road Roller, 1982

yellow with black roller and interior, "1" and "Made in France" on base, metal axle on roller, ct3c.............$2-4

yellow with black roller and interior, "1" on base, "Made in France" deleted from base, metal axle on roller, ct3c.........$2-4

yellow with black roller and interior, "2" on base, "Made in France" deleted from base, metal axle on roller, ct3c.........$2-4

yellow with black roller and interior, "2" on base, "Made in France" deleted from base, black plastic rivet holding roller, ct3c $2-4

227-A Lotus F1 Racer, with driver, no stabilizer fins on nose, 1969 – 1972

metallic orange-copper with black tampos, "2" $10-13
metallic dark blue with white tampos, "2" ..$10-13
metallic green with white tampos, "2" ...$10-13
metallic red with black tampos, "2" $10-13
metallic brown with black tampos, "2" ..$10-13
metallic gold with black tampos, "2" ...$10-13

227-B Lotus F1 Racer, with driver, stabilizer fins on nose, 1973 – 1974
metallic blue with "BP" and "3" decals on nose $10-13
metallic copper with "3" decal on nose...$10-13

227-C Magirus Cement Mixer *Beton*–The rear wheels have gears on them to turn the drum, hence the special 5sp wheels on the rear axle similar to the 237-B Maharajah with the rotating umbrella. 1:100, 1977 – 1982
red cab, orange body, mixer with blue front, yellow back, 3spb with 5sp rearmost wheels $8-10
red cab, orange body, yellow and pale orange mixer, 3spb $8-10
red cab, orange body, blue mixer with yellow and black stripe around mixer, 3spb with 5sp rearmost wheels $6-8
red cab, orange body, mixer with yellow front, blue back, 3spb with 5sp rearmost wheels..$8-10
red cab, orange body, mixer with green front, yellow back, 3spb with 5sp rearmost wheels, from 4060 Heavy Duty Construction Set $8-10

227-D Ford Mustang GT Convertible, hood opens, 1:59, 1988 – 1994
yellow, black interior, dark gray engine and bumpers, clear windows, "OFFICIAL PACE CAR" in black on sides, "Made in France," 6sp.....................................$2-4
flourescent yellow, black interior, light gray engine and bumpers, clear windows," OFFICIAL PACE CAR " in black on sides, "Made in France," 6sp $2-4
yellow, black interior, "MUSTANG GT" in black on sides, "Made in France" removed from baseplate, 6sp...........$2-4

yellow, black interior, "MUSTANG GT" in black on sides, "Made in France" removed from baseplate, "Made in Thailand," 8h $2-4
black, orange interior, orange, white, red, yellow, and blue tampo, "Dunkin' Orange" on sides and "Smelly Speeder, Not Stinky Just For Kids" on trunklid, "Made in France" removed from baseplate, orange rw ...$2-4

metallic aqua, orange interior, black, red, white tampo on sides, showing stripe and scribbles, "Made in France" removed from baseplate, orange rw......................$2-4

same as 6., 6sp..................................$2-4
blue, orange interior, white and orange tampo," TURBO" on hood, "Made in France" removed from baseplate, "Made in Thailand," 6sp............................$2-4
purple, orange interior, white and orange tampo, " TURBO" on hood, "Made in France" removed from baseplate, "Made in Thailand," 6sp............................$2-4

227-E Ford Ka, 1998
metallic purple, proposed but not found ...$3-5
metallic silver, proposed but not found $3-5
metallic teal, proposed but not found $3-5

228-A BRM F1 Racer, 1:65, 1969 – 1973
red, "8" on front, rt............................$10-13
green, white "8" and accents on front, rt...$10-13
copper, white "3" and accents on front, rt...$10-13
green, white "3" and accents on front, rt....$10-13
purple, white "8" and accents on front, rt ...$10-13

228-B Chevrolet Blazer Wrecker *Depanneuse*, compare to 228-D, 291-A, 1:62, 1983 blue, yellow interior, amber windows, silver label on hood, "Express 24/24," ct4sp $2-4

blue, yellow interior, amber windows, yellow, red, and white tampos "Express 24/24" on hood, ct4sp $2-4

fluorescent orange, blue, white and black tampos "Express 24/24" on hood on white background, ct4sp $2-4
fluorescent orange, black interior, amber windows, black and white "24 HR SERVICE" on hood and doors, "623-2900," "Made in France," ct4sp $2-4
fluorescent orange, black interior, amber windows, black and white checkerboard pattern on sides "SERVICE," ct4sp $2-4
silver, yellow interior, amber windows, yellow, red and black tampos, "auto assistance" on hood, "Made in France," ct4sp ...$2-4
silver, yellow interior, amber windows, no markings, ct4sp................................$4-6
red, yellow interior, amber windows, blue, white, and black accents "auto assistance" on hood, "Made in France," ct4sp ...$2-4
red with black and white accents "EMERGENCY ROAD SERVICE," ct4sp......$2-4
red, no markings, ct4sp, blue "24/24 quick TOWING" stickers are from MajoKit set $3-5
white, red interior, clear windows, blue lettering, red accents, "EMERGENCY ROAD SERVICE," "Made in Thailand," ct4sp $2-4
silver, blue and yellow tampos, "4/4 TOWING" on hood, ct4sp $2-4
fluorescent orange, black interior, amber windows, blue, white, and black tampos "Express 24/24" on hood, "Made in France," ct4sp $2-4
red, Crazy Monster decal on sides, flames on hood, ct4sp.................................$2-4
fluorescent orange, black on blue "Auto Assistance" tampo on doors, ct4sp $2-4
fluorescent orange, black interior, amber windows, silver and black tampos, flames on hood, "crazy monster," "Made in France," ct4sp...$2-4
white, red interior, amber windows, blue lettering, red accents, "EMERGENCY ROAD SERVICE," "Made in Thailand," ct4sp........$2-4

228-C Chevrolet Blazer Pickup 4x4, see 291-A
228-D Saviem Crane Truck *Grue*, with extending crane, Crane Truck, 3 axles, 1977
orange with green and black crane, yellow hook, 3 axles, amber windshield, black plastic base, 3spb........................$8-10
red with yellow and black crane, yellow hook, blue windshield, black plastic base, 3spb..............................$8-10
orange with yellow and black crane, yellow hook, amber windshield, black plastic base, 3spb $8-10

229-A Ferrari F1 Racer, 1969 – 1974
    metallic purple with checkered stripe ...$10-13
    dark red metallic, checkered stripe, "4" ..$10-13
229-B Datsun 260Z, 1:60, 1977 – 1984
    black, white interior, no markings, 3sp....$5-7
    metallic light green, no tampos, 3kk $5-7
    metallic turquoise, no tampos, 3sp $5-7
    red, white interior, 3spb $4-6
    white, red "SOS" decals on doors, green symbol on hood, 3spb $4-6
    yellow, red tampos on hood, 3kk $3-5
    yellow with red, black and yellow tampos ..$3-5
    blue, white interior, no tampos, 3kk........$3-5
    blue, white interior, amber windows, no tampos, 3spb $3-5
    yellow, white interior, no tampos, 3spb ...$3-5
    yellow, white interior, no tampos, 3kk......$3-5
    white, white interior, amber windows, no tampos, 3spb $3-5
    metallic blue, white interior, 3spb, no tampos..$3-5
    silver, yellow interior, 5sp....................$3-5
    yellow, white interior. dark red/blue tampos on the hood and sides, 3spb $3-5
    light olive, white interior, 3kk, part of 363-B ...$3-5
229-C BMW 325i, front doors open, 1:56, 1987
    white, black interior, clear windshield, red and blue accents on sides, blue "325" on sides, "Made in France," 6sp...........$3-5
    white, black interior, clear windshield, red, blue and black accents on sides, blue "325" on sides, "Made in France," 6sp $3-5

silver, black interior, clear windshield, red and black accents, same tampo pattern as 2, 6sp $3-5

    white, black interior, clear windshield, diagonal red, blue and black accents, "Made in France," 6sp..................................$3-5
    white, black interior, clear windshield, red "PROFI" on sides, 6sp, *promotional* model....$12-16
229-D Aston Martin DB7, doors open, 1994

metallic blue, no markings, black interior, 6sp $3-5

metallic blue, rally graphics,"ZOOM," "17," 6sp, 1999................................$2-4
230-A Peugeot 204C Roadster / Cabriolet, unpainted metal base, clear windshield, opening doors, 1969 – 1973
    red, black interior, wheels: gray hubs, black tires, gb $6-8
    red, black interior, thc5 ....$6-8
    metallic red, thc5 ....$6-8
    metallic red, black interior, wheels: gray hubs, black tires $6-8
    metallic orange, black interior, wheels: gray hubs, black tires $6-8
    metallic orange, black interior, thc5.........$6-8
    medium blue, black interior, wheels: gray hubs, black tires $6-8
    metallic blue, black interior, wheels: gray hubs, black tires................................$6-8

metallic bright blue, cream interior, thc, part of 314-C $10-13

    metallic green, black interior, wheels: gray hubs, black tires $6-8
    turquoise, black interior, wheels: gray hubs, black tires, part of 331-A.................$6-8
    light yellow, black interior, thc5 ....$6-8
    dark yellow, black interior, thc5 ....$6-8
230-B Renault 4L Delivery Van, 1:55, 1975 – 1981
    red with yellow coat of arms on hood and doors, 2 axes and helmet on rear panels, fire brigade, clear windows, 3spb $4-6
    red with yellow coat of arms on hood and doors, 2 axes and helmet on rear panels, fire brigade, clear windows, 5sp $4-6
    blue with white telephone dial logo, black interior, clear windows, 3spb.................$4-6
    blue with white telephone dial logo, black interior, clear windows, 3kk...................$4-6
    yellow, "service RENAULT," clear windows, 3spb $4-6
    yellow, "service RENAULT," clear windows, 3kk $4-6
    yellow, black tampo of telephone with receiver off hook on sides, tampos on doors, 5sp $4-6
230-C Volvo 760 GLE, 1:61, 1987 – 1991
    silver, red interior, red and black accents, black "VOLVO" and "760 GLE," "Made in France," 3kk..............................$3-5

silver, red interior, clear windows, red and black accents, black "VOLVO" and "760 GLE," "Made in France," 3spn.........$3-5
silver, red interior, clear windows, red and black diagonal markings across doors, "Made in France," 8h....................$3-5
silver, red interior, red diagonal markings across doors, red "VOLVO" and "760 GLE," "Made in France," 8h...........$3-5
metallic periwinkle blue, white interior, clear windows, red and black accents, no diagonal markings, black "VOLVO," 3spn $3-5
metallic dark green, red interior, no markings, "Made in France," 8h $3-5
metallic green, red interior, no markings, 8h $3-5
metallic teal blue, black interior, no markings, "Made in Thailand," 8h $3-5
metallic teal blue, no markings, white interior, 8h $3-5
light green, red interior, red and black accents, diagonal markings across doors, 8h $3-5
metallic green, red interior, silver stripe, black "VOLVO" and "760 GLE," "Made in France" removed, 8h $3-5
metallic blue, no markings, black interior," "Made in France" removed, 8h........$3-5
silver, red interior, clear windows, *French oil company promotional*, red "ANTAR" on hood and doors, "Made in France," 8h $3-5
230-D Ford Transit Custom Tow Truck, see 295-A
230-E Toyota RAV4, 1999
    metallic green with silver lower body, tan interior, 5st..$3-5
231-A Citroën Dyane Raid, 1976 – 1983
    white with red, red interior and brush bar, "3" on sides, unchromed 3spb wheels ..$8-10
    metallic brown, black interior and brush bar, 3spb $8-10
    light green, white interior, black brush bar, cream sunroof, red 3spb $3-5
    gold, white interior, gray roof, black brush bar, roll bar and spare tire, 3spb $8-10
    red, white interior, gray roof, black roll cage and grill, "31" on hood, rally accents, red 3spb $4-6
    red, white interior, gray roof, black roll cage and grill, 3spb $4-6
    white with red, red interior and brush bar, red 3spb $8-10
231-B Mercedes-Benz 190E 2.3-16, 1:59, 1986 – 1995
    metallic green, red interior, clear windows, 8h $3-5
    metallic green, yellow interior, clear windows, "Made in France," 3spn.................$3-5

metallic green, yellow interior, clear windows, 8h.................$3-5

metallic pewter gray, red interior, clear windows, "Made in France," 8h..........$3-5
metallic bronze-gray, yellow interior, clear windows, 8h.................$3-5
metallic silver, red interior, clear windows, "Made in France," 8h.................$3-5
white, black interior, blue and orange rally tampos, "13," 8h.................$2-4
white, red interior, blue and orange rally tampos, "13," "Made in France" removed from baseplate, 8h.................$2-4
231-C Bank Security, 1999 reissue, see 204-C
232-A Porsche LeMans Racer, 1:65, 1969 – 1978
metallic red, "5" on front, 5sp.............$9-12

yellow, 3spb $9-12

red, "3" on front, "elf" on back fender, 3kk.................$9-12
red, "5" on front, yellow "BOSCH" tampo on top of rear fender, chrome interior, unique black wheels.................$10-13
232-B Ferrari 312 T2 F1, 1977 – 1983
red, blue driver, white plastic cockpit, "1" on the front, yellow and white decals.....$4-6
232-C Formula 1 Brabham, 1:53, 1986 – 1989
blue and white, white base, "parmalat," "2," black wing, "Santal" on front wings and nose, "F1 BRABHAM" on base, "Made in France," rw $2-4
black and light gray, "parmalat".............$2-4
dark blue and white, white base, "parmalat," "2," black wing, "Santal" on front wings and nose, "F1 BRABHAM" deleted from base, "Made in France," rw $2-4
232-D Dune Buggy, 1:55, 1992, compare to 248-A
hot pink, white roof, black seats, black baseplate, "FUN BUGGY," chrome engine and headlights, rw.................$4-6
hot pink, white roof, yellow seats, yellow baseplate, "ICE CREAM," chrome engine and headlights, "Made in France," rw $3-5

pink with white roof, "Buggy," "3" on roof, chrome engine and headlights, rw $4-6

red, white roof, rally tampos on roof, chrome engine and headlights, rw.........$4-6

red, yellow roof, green baseplate, green seats, blue engine and headlights, "Made in Thailand," rw 1999 ....$4-6
red, white roof, "Buggy," "3" on roof, chrome engine and headlights, "Made in Thailand," rw.................$4-6
red, white roof, yellow seats, "ICE CREAM" on roof, chrome engine and headlights, "Made in Thailand," rw.................$4-6
blue, white roof, black seats, black baseplate, "ICE CREAM" on roof, chrome engine and headlights, "Made in Thailand," rw.....$4-6
blue, white roof, yellow seats, yellow baseplate, "ICE CREAM" on roof, chrome engine and headlights, "Made in Thailand," rwblc, blue chrome $4-6
232-E Mercedes CLK+ GTR, 1999
silver, red interior, "M2" and racing graphics, 6sp.................$3-5
yellow front/black rear body, red interior, racing graphics, "21," 6sp, 2000 Speed Wheeler.................$2-4
white front, red rear, green interior, racing accents, "5," "CR," 6sp, 2000
233-A Panther Bertone Course Racer, 1:65, 1969 – 1976
orange with yellow base, gray spoiler, "3" decal on front, 3kk.................$10-13

orange with yellow base, gray spoiler, "4" decal on front, 3kk.................$10-13

lime green with yellow base, gray spoiler, thc1.................$10-13

metallic blue with yellow base.............$10-13
red with light blue base.................$10-13
233-B Mercedes Public Works Truck *Trax Publics*, 1:70, 1978 – 1981—This casting remained in the 300 series as #321 until 1986.
orange, blue canopy, amber windows, cream tow bar, 3kk.................$5-7

orange, blue canopy, light blue windows, white tow bar, 3kk.................$5-7

orange, blue canopy, clear windows, white tow bar, 3kk.................$5-7
orange, yellow canopy with "works" stickers, blue windows, white tow bar, 3kk, part of #321 set.................$5-7
orange, white canopy with "works" stickers, amber windows, blue "1" on roof, white tow bar, 3kk.................$5-7
metallic light blue, white canopy with road works signs on sides, light blue windows, 3kk, part of #321 set.................$4-6
green, white canopy, dark blue windshield, extra blue light on top of canopy, 3spb.........$6-8
233-C Renault Express Van, 1:53, 1988

orange, black interior, clear windows, "europcar rentacar," black rear doors, 6sp.................$5-7

white, black interior, clear windows, "europcar rentacar," white rear doors, 6sp.......$5-7
red, black interior, clear windows, "AVIS," white rear doors, 6sp.................$4-6
red, black interior, clear windows, "AVIS," red rear doors, 6sp.................$4-6
red, "AVIS," yellow rear doors, 6sp.......$8-10
blue, "SATELLITE SERVICE," yellow rear doors, 6sp.................$3-5
yellow, "La Poste" on doors, 6sp.............$5-7

orange, black interior, clear windows, "europcar rentacar," orange rear doors, 6sp $5-7

red, black interior, clear windows, red rear doors, white Chinese script for "Mail," this model was packaged with a stick of "Kabaya" brand chewing gum around 1995, probably in Japan, 6sp $4-6

red, black interior, clear windows, no markings, red rear doors, 6sp $4-6

234-A Locomotive, three axles, black $18

234-B Simca 1100 TI, rear hatch opens, 1:60, 1975 – 1980, "Made in France"

dark blue, white "Police" tampos $4-6

black, white "Police" tampos, 3kk, unpainted metal trailer, white police boat, from 300-Series $4-6

blue, white interior, yellow windshield, red and yellow flame accents, 3spb.............$4-6

metallic green, white interior, amber windshield, clear lock over trailer hitch, smaller rear license plate, 3spb $4-6

metallic blue, white interior, amber windshield, 3kk $4-6

red, white interior, 3spb $4-6

metallic blue, white interior, amber windshield, large rear license plate, 3spb $4-6

metallic green, white interior, Clear windows, yellow and red decal on sides "Club Louis," yellow, white and black decal on hood "Port Louis," 3spb or 3kk, 1980 ....$4-6

metallic green, white interior, amber windshield, 3kk..........................$4-6

234-C Ford *Fourgon* (Van) no side windows, 1:53, 1982, compare to 234-D, 234-E, 250-B, 279-A

white, red interior, amber windshield, red, green and white "Fruits" label, red rear doors, "Made in France," 6spk $2-4

white, red interior, amber windshield, red, green and white "Fruits" label, red rear doors, "Made in France," 6sp..........$2-4

white, red interior, amber windshield, red, green and white "Fruits" tampo, white rear doors, 6sp $2-4

white, amber windows, red fenders, red rear door, blue, red and black tampo, "Hawaiian Surfer," "Made in France," 6sp...................$3-5

yellow, red interior, amber windows, yellow red and black "racing team" label, 6sp.....$2-4

yellow, red interior, amber windows, red trim, black, white, green and red tampos, "ELEPHANT RESERVE," "MADE IN PORTUGAL," 6sp, part of 344 Elephant Cage Transporter $2-4

yellow, red interior, amber windows, red trim, "MAGIC CIRCUS" sticker, "Made in France," 6sp...$3-5

white, red interior, amber windows yellow, red, and black "racing team" label, red rear doors, 6sp...........................$2-4

white, blue fenders, "BASEBALL" $2-4

white, blue fenders, clear windows, blue fenders, blue rear doors, black, yellow, pink, green, and blue tampos on sides, "SKATE BOARD," "Made in France" removed from base, 6sp $2-4

red, white interior, white trim and rear doors, "Coca-Cola," sun, "Made in Thailand," 6sp 1995.......................................$4-6

blue, "Cadbury Dairy Milk Buttons" $6-8

red, red interior, clear windows, red trim and rear doors, "Avis," no side doors or window, "Made in Thailand," 6sp, 1998.........$2-4

blue, "Cadbury's Dairy Milk," blue rear doors ..$5-7

yellow, "Cadbury"s Mini Eggs," purple accents $5-7

yellow, "Magic Circus," red rear doors, yellow windshield.....................................$2-4

red, red interior, clear windows, "Surf" graphics and scene same as 248 VW, "Made in Thailand," 6sp red tires, 1999......$2-4

white, red interior, red grille/fenders/rear doors, "Canon," "Made in France," 6spk, 1982 ....$3-5

234-D Ford *Fourgon* (Van), porthole side windows, compare to 234-C and E, 250-B, 279-A

red, red interior, grille and lower side trim, white "Avis" tampo, red rear doors, "Made in Thailand," 6sp, 1998 ......$2-4

yellow, blue interior, grille and lower side trim, blue windows, yellow rear doors, red and white flame tampo on sides, baseplate: "ECH.1/65 MAJORETTE U.S. VAN"; "No 250" and "Made in France" removed $2-4

234-E Ford *Fourgon* (Van), rectangular side windows, compare to 234-C and D, 250-B, 279-A

white with red base, red "Canon" tampos ..$4-6

234-F Ford Police *Fourgon* (Van), see 279-A

235-A BMW 2800CS Coupe

no details available $16-20

235-B Motorboat and Trailer

no details available $10-13

235-C BMW 3.0 CSI, 1:60, 1973 – 1977

yellow, white interior, amber windows, 5sp ...$4-6

metallic bluish green $4-6

metallic yellowish green $4-6

metallic red, white interior, amber windows, 3kk $4-6

orange, white interior, amber windows, 5sp

metallic green, white interior, light amber windows, 3spb $4-6

red, white interior, light amber windows, 3spb $4-6

copper, white interior, amber windows, 3spb

red, white interior, amber windows, 5sp ..$4-6

235-D Citroën Acadiane Service Van, 1:60, 1980 – 1985, "Made in France"

yellow, white interior, clear windows, white rear doors, white envelope insignia on sides, 3spb $4-6

yellow, white interior, white rear doors, white envelope insignia on sides, 3kk ...$4-6

yellow, white interior, white rear doors, "Charbonnier" in red on sides, 3kk............$4-6

yellow, white interior, light amber windows, white rear doors, 3spb $4-6

blue, white interior, light amber windows, white rear doors, 3spb $4-6

blue, white interior, light amber windows, white rear doors, 3kk $4-6

235-E Volkswagen Golf GTI 16S, 1:56, 1988 – 1992

yellow, black interior, clear windows, dark blue and white accents, "Made in France," 6sp $2-4

yellow, black interior, clear windows, light blue and white accents, tampo on hood slightly larger than 1, "Made in France," 8h...$2-4

flourescent green, black interior, clear windows, dark blue and white accents, "Made in France" removed from baseplate, 6sp $2-4

lime green, black interior, clear windows, "Made in France," 6sp $2-4

lime green, black interior, clear windows, "Made in France," 8h $2-4

green, black interior, clear windows, "Made in Thailand," 8h..................$2-4

green, "4," "Champions," "Racing" tampos, copper and white accents, "Made in Thailand," 6sp..................$2-4

green, black interior, clear windows, dark blue and white accents, "Made in France" removed from baseplate, 6sp..........$2-4

red, black interior, clear windows, "Made in France," 6sp..................$2-4

235-F Sport Proto Racer, 1997

white, yellow, and black accents, yellow strip over top, "66," "RACING TEAM," "Star," 6sp $2-4

white, no tampos, 6sp $2-4

236-A Sterckeman Lovely 400 Travel Trailer; 1:65, see 259-B

236-B Bernard Truck with Chalet, 1973 – 1974
no details available $12-15

236-C Saviem Truck with Chalet, 1975 – 1978 ....$12-15
red, brown chalet, 3kk $9-12

236-D Jeep Cherokee 4x4, tailgate opens, 1:64, 1980–present—Early versions featured a dog in the back, double side window trim and ribbed roof. Later versions eliminated the dog. Most recent versions feature simplified side window casting and no roof ribs.

black, white interior, "CHEE-TOS CHESTER CHEETAH," no dog, plain roof, "Made in France," "4x4 Cherokee" removed from base, ct4sp, Road Eaters..................$3-5

blue, white interior, "Franco American SpaghettiOs/TeddyOs," "Made in France," ct4sp, Road Eaters..................$3-5

fluorescent green, black interior and tailgate, clear windows, red and white flames, no dog, plain roof, ct4sp..................$2-4

fluorescent orange, blue and white flame accents, ribbed roof, ct4sp..................$2-4

fluorescent orange, "Big Chief," red and black accents, ribbed roof, black tailgate, ct4sp..$2-4

green, white interior, amber windows, ribbed roof, dog in back, "Made in France," 5d......$2-4

light brown, "BIG CHIEF," dog in back, ribbed roof $3-5

metallic brown, "BIG CHIEF," dog in back, ribbed roof $5-7

red, black "MAD BULL" accents, ribbed roof, ct4sp..................$4-6

red, gold and black "MAD BULL" accents, ribbed roof, black interior, "Made in France," ct4sp..................$4-6

red, white, and black, orange and blue rally accents, dog in back $3-5

red, white, and black, orange and blue rally accents, no dog in back..................$2-4

white, brown interior, blue, red, yellow, and black tampo showing a polar bear on skis "Coca-Cola" polar bear, "Made in Thailand," ct4sp $10-13

white, brown interior, black irregular shaped spots all over, "Made in Thailand," ct4sp..................$2-4

yellow, amber windows, red and black accents, Indian head on hood, dog in back, ribbed roof, "Made in France," ct4sp..................$3-5

yellow, brown interior, "ROCKIN' BANANA," plain roof, Smelly Speeders, "Made in France," ct4spy, yellow tires..................$3-5

yellow, brown interior, western motif, "INDIAN" and Indian with head-dress on roof, tomahawk on hood, cactuses on sides, "Made in France" deleted from baseplate, "Made in France," ct4sp $2-4

yellow, brown interior, green, red, black, and white accents, "Safari" on sides and hood, animal tracks, "Made in France" removed from baseplate, "Made in Thailand," ct4sp $2-4

yellow, black irregular shaped spots all over, "Made in France" removed from baseplate, "Made in Thailand," ct4sp......$2-4

yellow, black interior and back door, clear windows, "Made in France" deleted from base, ct4sp $2-4

fluorescent yellow, black interior and tailgate, clear windows, red and black "Mad Bull" tampo on hood and sides, plain roof, "Made in France," ct4sp $2-4

red, black interior and tailgate, clear windows, black and gold "Mad Bull" tampo on hood and sides, plain roof, "Made in France," ct4sp $2-4

fluorescent lime green, black interior and tailgate, clear windows, red and white flames, no dog, plain roof, ct4sp......$2-4

yellow, red interior, clear windows, black tailgate, red and black tampo showing an Indian face, "big chief," dog in back, "Made in France," ct4sp $3-5

green, white interior, amber windows, ribbed roof, green tailgate, dog in back, "Made in France," 6spk..................$3-5

metallic brown, white interior, amber windows, ribbed roof, white tailgate, dog in back, "Made in France," 5d..................$3-5

237-A Mercedes-Benz 280SE, 1969 – 1972
pink, amber windows, white interior, thc...$10-13

237-B Maharajah, 1975 – 1978, modified Citroën Dyane with rotating umbrella and elevated chair with steps, 5sp wheels on back axle drive cogs that turn umbrella as car rolls across a hard surface

yellow, white interior, white umbrella with orange and yellow accents, 3sp front, 5sp rear ..$8-10

green, white interior, white umbrella with red and green accents, 3kk front, 5sp rear $8-10

metallic blue, white interior, other details unknown $8-10

red, white interior, white umbrella with green accents, 5sp front and rear $8-10

237-C Lamborghini Countach, 1:56, 1980 – 1995
red with black spoiler, white interior, black and yellow stripe accents, "Made in France," rw..$2-4

red with black spoiler, black interior, black and yellow stripe accents, "Made in France," rw..$2-4

red with black spoiler, black interior, black and yellow stripe accents, "NIGRIN" and "36" on front, "BD" on roof, "ARVOR" on top of rear fenders, "Made in France," rw...$2-4

red with red spoiler, white interior, no markings, "Made in France," rw ....$2-4 red with red spoiler, white interior, white "COUNTACH" accents, "TM" after "LAMBORGHINI" on base, "Made in France," rw $2-4

red with red spoiler, white interior white "COUNTACH" accents, "TM" removed from base, "Made in France," rw $2-4

red, black interior, yellow spoiler, black and white checkered accents, white "78" on sides, yellow "78"s in front of spoiler, "TM" after "LAMBORGHINI" on base, "Made in France" deleted from base, rw..$2-4

red, black interior, "Lamborghini" on yellow spoiler, black and white checkered accents, yellow "78" on sides, "TM" after "LAMBORGHINI" on base, "Made in France" deleted from base, rw $3-5

metallic light blue, amber windows, white interior, "countach" on sides, "Made in France," rw $2-4

red, white interior, clear windows, no spoiler, "countach" on sides, rw...................$2-4

black, white interior, red and yellow flame tampos on hood and roof, "TM" removed from base, "Made in France," rw $2-4

purple, white interior, white spoiler, "Made in France," rw, *Color Changer* $3-5

red, black interior, yellow spoiler, black tampo of bull on front, "Made in France," "Made in Thailand," rw red chrome.............$2-4

237-D Audi TT, 1999

metallic gold, 5st...................................$2-4

metallic silver, gray interior, 5st, 2000.....$2-4

red, gray interior, racing graphics, "29," 5st, 2000 *Speed Wheelers* $2-4

red, black interior, 5st, 2000 ....$2-4

white, gray interior, black, red and blue racing graphics, "51," 5st.........................$2-4

238-A Peugeot 604, unpainted base, hood opens, 1977 – 1982, also 236-C

black, white interior, light amber windshield, 3kk $5-7

black, white interior, clear windshield, 3spb ..$5-7

black, white interior, light amber windshield, 3spb...$5-7

metallic steel blue, white interior, light amber windshield, 3spb $5-7

metallic steel blue, white interior, light amber windshield, 3kk...............................$5-7

metallic steel blue, white interior, light amber windshield, 3kk, white stripes on sides.........$5-7

metallic medium blue, white interior, light amber windshield, 3spb, white stripes on sides...$5-7

metallic medium blue, white interior, light amber windshield, 3kk, white stripes on sides...$5-7

metallic medium blue, white interior, light amber windshield, 3kk....................$5-7

metallic red, white interior, light amber windshield, 5sp $5-7

metallic red, white interior, light amber windshield, 3spb $5-7

metallic red, white interior, light amber windshield, 3kk $5-7

gold, white interior, clear windshield, 3spb $5-7

gold, yellow interior, light amber windshield, 3spb $5-7

gold, yellow interior, light amber windshield, 3kk $5-7

metallic brown, white interior, 3spb.........$5-7

metallic light green, white interior, light amber windshield, 5sp $5-7

metallic light green, white interior, light amber windshield, 3spb..............................$5-7

metallic dark green, white interior, light amber windshield, 3spb..............................$5-7

238-B Formula 1 Racer, 1:55, 1986

green, black interior, red base, red and white accents, "Benetton," black wing, "8," "Made in France," may have tow bar attached to front, rw $6-8

green, black base, red spoiler and interior, white, blue and orange accents, "HOT WINNER," "62" red wing, "Made in France" deleted from base, "MADE IN PORTUGAL," rw.............................$4-6

green, red, and white accents, "62," red wing, rw $2-4

light blue, black interior, red base, black "Rallye" on yellow accents, blue "41" on red accent, black wing, "Made in France" deleted from base, rw $2-4

silver, red base, red, blue, and green accents, "RACING","2," black wing, rw........$2-4

yellow, red base, red, blue, and green accents, "2," "RACING," black wing, "Made in France" deleted from base, rw $2-4

yellow, red base, red and black accents, "WARNING," "3," "STAR," "Made in France" deleted from base, "MADE IN PORTUGAL," rw...........................$4-6

yellow, blue accents, "Shell" logo on back, "tsp" on front, "Tictel","12," black wing, "Made in France," rw $2-4

yellow, blue panel on side, small "A little jump out of the country" and large "SUPER PHARM"...... AGAIN" written in Hebrew on panel, black wing, Israeli, rw, 2000 ....$5-7

yellow, red base, black wing, blue, red and green accents, "RACING" on sides, blue "2" on green background on nose, rw, part of 3098 set $4-6

silver, red base, black wing, red Shell logo, "12," "Tictal," "tsp," 3 black stripes on sides, "2" on nose, rw, part of 3098 set $4-6

white, blue accents, blue wing, "2" on front, "ELF" on sides, rw...........................$4-6

238-C Dodge Concept Car "Copperhead," 1999

metallic gold, 1999 Catalog $3-5

dark metallic yellow, black interior, 5st, 2000 ....$2-4

black, red interior, racing graphics, "56," 5st, 2000 *Speed Wheelers* $2-4

metallic yellow-gold, tan interior, 5st, 2000 ....$2-4

239-A Peugeot 504, with opening doors, hood and trunk, unpainted metal base, clear windows, 1969 – 1972

medium blue, tan interior, bw2 ....$12-15

metallic red, tan interior, bw2.............$12-15
metallic green, tan interior, bw2.........$12-15
metallic light blue, light green interior,
    thc5...$12-15
light yellow, tan interior, bw2.............$12-15
orange, white interior, thc5...........$12-15
orange-red, white interior, thc5..........$12-15
lilac, white interior, thc5 ....$12-15
239-B Matra Simca 670, 1975 – 1979

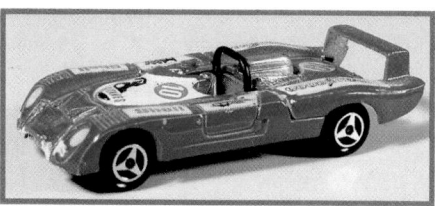

metallic blue, "10, Goodyear, Shell".......$5-7
metallic dark blue, "10, Goodyear,
    Shell"......................................$5-7
239-C Fiat Ritmo / Strada, 1981 – 1986
yellow, black interior, clear windows, black
    accents, "ABARTH 2000" on sides,
    3spb...$4-6
red, black interior, clear windows, black
    accents, "ABARTH 2000," 3spb......$4-6
red, black interior, clear windows, no mark-
    ings, 3spb..................................$5-7
metallic orange/pink, black interior, clear win-
    dows, black accents, "ABARTH 2000,"
    3spb...$4-6
orange, black interior, clear windows,
    3spb...$4-6
239-D Audi 90, doors open, 1:60, 1989, also 2
59-E, black, white interior, light blue windows,
    yellow and white tampo, "11" and "Bolids,"
    "Made in France," 8h $3-5

**yellow, black interior, light blue windows,
black tampo, "Audi 90" and emblem on
doors, "Made in France," 8h.................$3-5**
239-E Chevrolet Blazer 4x4, 1995, also 249-D
GMC Jimmy, 1996
red with "Racing Team 3"...................$2-4
red with no markings.........................$2-4
red, black interior, clear windows, black lower
    body, grille and bumpers, "GMC" on
    grille, ct4sp..............................$2-4
red, black interior, clear windows, black lower
    body, grille and bumpers, "GMC" on
    grille, orange, blue interior, clear windows,

blue lower body, grille and bumpers,
    "GMC" on grille, blue and white rally
    graphics, "ROCO," "10," ct4sp........$2-4
orange, blue interior, clear windows, blue
    lower body, grille and bumpers, "GMC"
    on grille, ct4sp $2-4
yellow and black tampos, "Magnum Roller"
    and "3," ct4sp.............................$2-4
yellow "Pinder Circus" $5-7
yellow, black interior, clear windows, black
    lower body, grille and bumpers, "GMC"
    on grille, ct4sp...........................$2-4
metallic blue, gray interior, clear windows,
    gray lower body, Chevrolet emblem on
    grill, ct4sp $2-4

**black, metallic gray interior and lower body,
clear windows, ct4sp...............................$2-4**

240-A Simca 1308, 1:60, rear hatch opens,
    1977 – 1982
metallic bright blue, gray interior, 3spb $6-8
metallic bright blue, gray interior, 3kk $6-8
burnt orange, "Chrysler Simca" and Chrysler
    logo on sides, 3spb.....................$8-10
burnt orange, "Chrysler Simca" and Chrysler
    logo on sides, 3kk.......................$8-10
orange, gray interior, turquoise windows,
    black "Europe 1" on sides, "E 1 Europe
    1" on hood, 3spb.........................$8-10
metallic dark silver $6-8
metallic light silver with "Chrysler Simca"
    and Chrysler logo on sides, gray interi-
    or, 3kk $6-8
metallic light silver with "Chrysler Simca" and
    Chrysler logo on sides, gray interior,
    3spb..$8-10
light bronze, gray interior, amber windows,
    3spb..$10-13
light bronze, gray interior, amber windows,
    5sp...$10-13
dark green, pale yellow interior, amber
    windows, yellow and brown "Federa-
    tion Equestre Francais" decal on
    hood, 3kk..................................$10-13
240-B Chevrolet Impala Police car, 1:69, 1986,
    compare to 213-F, 219-A

white, blue interior and windshield, black
    accents, "POLICE," "N 31" on rear
    fenders and roof, "Made in France,"
    8h...$3-5
white, blue interior and windshield, black
    accents, "POLICE," "N 31" on rear fend-
    ers, "Made in France" deleted from base,
    8h...$3-5

**black and white, blue interior and wind-
shield, gold accents, "HIGHWAY PATROL,"
"N 31" on trunk, gold stars on hood and
doors, "Made in France" deleted from base,
8h...$3-5**
black with white doors, blue interior and
    windshield, "POLICE," "N 31" on
    trunk and rear fenders, "SERVICE"
    shield on front doors and hood,
    "Made in France" deleted from base,
    8h $3-5
light blue, white roof, blue interior, blue win-
    dows and roof lights, white accents,
    "911" on trunk, "POLICE" on hood and
    sides, 8h, 1999 ....$2-4
black, "Police" shields, wide gold stripes from
    front to back over car, 8h $4-6
light blue, white roof, blue interior, blue win-
    dows and roof lights, white accents,
    "911" on trunk, "POLICE" on hood and
    sides, 5pw, 2000...........................$2-4
Minnesota State Police.....................$12-15
Illinois State Police $12-15
240-C Chevrolet Impala Taxi, see 213-F
241-A DAF 2600 Canvas Top Truck, 1:100,
    1969 – 1975
green with silver platform sides and orange
    canopy, "Services Rapide Lempereur and
    Cuparc," bw1 ....$7-9
green with gray platform sides and orange
    canopy, "Services Rapide Lempereur and
    Cuparc," bw1 ....$7-9
blue with green platform sides and gray
    canopy, "Services Rapide Lempereur and
    Cuparc," bw1 ....$7-9
orange with gray platform sides and orange
    canopy, no markings, bw1.............$7-9
red with green platform sides and gray
    canopy, "Services Rapide Lempereur and
    Cuparc," bw1 ....$7-9

yellow with orange platform, bw1, bw2.............$7-9

241-B Saviem Canvas Top Truck, 1976 – 1982

orange with red canopy, "JOE CIRCUS," found loose without documentation that the model was released with this cab color and canopy combination.................$4-6

blue with white canopy, "SERNAM" towards front of truck, green accents towards rear, black base and interior, 3kk front, 3spb rear...............$3-5

blue with white canopy, "SERNAM" towards front of truck, green accents towards rear, black base and interior, 3kk front and rear...............$3-5

blue with white canopy, "SERNAM" towards rear of truck, green accents towards front, black base and interior, 3kk front and rear...............$3-5

blue, yellow canopy, "SAVIEM SERVICE," black base and interior, 3kk.............$5-7

red with cream canopy, "Majorette Metal," 3kk...............$4-6

green with cream canopy, "Majorette Metal," gray base and interior...............$4-6

blue, yellow canopy, "MICHELIN," 3kk...$5-7

blue with yellow canopy "MICHELIN," 3spb, black base and interior...............$5-7

blue with yellow canopy "MICHELIN," 3kk, black base and interior...............$5-7

red with yellow canopy "JOE CIRCUS," 3spb, black base and interior...............$5-7

red with yellow canopy, "SAVIEM," front wheels 3kk, rear wheels 3spb, gray base and interior...............$5-7

green with white canopy, "SERNAM" towards front of truck, green accents towards rear, 3kk, gray base and interior...............$5-7

white with white canopy, "SERNAM" towards front of truck, green accents towards rear, 3spb, black base and interior...........$5-7

red with orange canopy, "Siemens," 3kk, black base and interior...................$5-7

blue with blue canopy, "adidas," 3kk, black base and interior...............$5-7

red with orange canopy, "SERVICES RAPIDES LEMPEREUR and DUPARC," 3kk; gray base and interior...............$5-7

green cab with cream canopy, "MAJORETTE metal," 3kk, gray base and interior, green trailer with cream canopy, "MAJORETTE metal," 3spb...............$5-7

blue cab with yellow canopy, "SAVIEM," 3kk, black base and interior, blue trailer with yellow canopy, "SAVIEM," 3kk........$5-7

blue cab with yellow canopy, "MICHELIN,"

3spb black base and interior, blue trailer with yellow canopy, "MICHELIN," 3spb...............$5-7

military brown cab with olive brown canopy, 3kk, gray base and interior, military brown trailer with olive brown canopy, 3spb...........$5-7

red cab with cream canopy, "MAJORETTE metal," 3kk, gray base and interior, red trailer with cream canopy "MAJORETTE metal," 3spb...............$5-7

red cab with cream canopy, "MAJORETTE metal," 3kk front wheels, 5sp rear wheels, gray base and interior, red trailer with cream canopy, "MAJORETTE metal," 3spb...............$5-7

white cab with blue canopy, "adidas," 3kk, black base and interior, white trailer with blue canopy, "adidas," 3spb...............$5-7

white cab with blue canopy, "adidas," 3kk, black base and interior, white trailer with dark blue canopy, "adidas," 3kk......$5-7

red cab with cream canopy, orange "DICKSON CONSTANT COPERTONE SINTETICO," red "SYNTHETIC TARPAULINS," 3kk, gray base and interior red trailer with cream canopy, orange "DICKSON CONSTANT COPERTONE SINTETICO," red "SYNTHETIC TARPAULINS," 3kk.......$5-7

green cab with cream canopy, orange "DICKSON CONSTANT COPERTONE SINTETICO," red "SYNTHETIC TARPAULINS," 3kk front wheels, 5sp rear wheels, gray base and interior, green trailer with cream canopy, orange "DICKSON CONSTANT COPERTONE SINTETICO," red "SYNTHETIC TARPAULINS," 3spb...........$5-7

green cab with cream canopy, orange "DICKSON CONSTANT COPERTONE SINTETICO," red "SYNTHETIC TARPAULINS," 3kk, gray base and interior, green trailer with cream canopy, orange "DICKSON CONSTANT COPERTONE SINTETICO," red "SYNTHETIC TARPAULINS," 3kk .$5-7

green cab with cream canopy, green "DICKSON CONSTANT BACHES SYNTHETIQUES," blue "BESCHICHTETE PLANEN," 3kk front wheels, 5sp rear wheels, gray base and interior, green trailer with cream canopy, green "DICKSON CONSTANT BACHES SYNTHETIQUES," blue "BESCHICHTETE PLANEN," 3kk........$5-7

red cab with cream canopy, green "DICKSON CONSTANT BACHES SYNTHETIQUES," blue "BESCHICHTETE PLANEN," 3kk, gray base and interior, red trailer with cream canopy, green

"DICKSON CONSTANT BACHES SYNTHETIQUES," blue "BESCHICHTETE PLANEN," 3kk...............$5-7

green cab with cream canopy, clear windows, green "DICKSON CONSTANT BACHES SYNTHETIQUES," blue "DICKSON CONSTANT BESCHICHTETE PLANEN," gray base and interior, 3kk ...$5-7

blue with yellow canopy "JOE CIRCUS," gray base and interior, 3kk, found loose without documentation that the model was released with this cab color and canopy combination $5-7

white cab with blue canopy, "adidas," 3spb, black base and interior...............$5-7

241-C Ford Covered Truck, long narrow side windows on cab, 1:100, 1984, also see 366-B

green body, yellow canopy, "super cargo" label, 3kk...............$3-5

green body, yellow canopy, "super cargo" label, 4c...............$3-5

red body, yellow canopy, "super cargo" label, 3spb...............$3-5

red body, white canopy, "super cargo" label, part of 366-B, 3spb...............$3-5

white body, metallic gray canopy, "majorette" tampo, 3kk...............$3-5

white body, white canopy, "majorette" tampo, 3kk...............$3-5

white body, yellow canopy, no tampo or label, 3spb...............$3-5

white body, blue canopy, brown "majorette" label, 4c...............$3-5

white body, blue canopy, red "majorette" label, part of 366-B, 4c...............$3-5

241-D Ford Covered Truck, no narrow side windows on cab, 1:100, see 366-C

white body, blue canopy, "MOVING STUDIO" tampo, black base and interior, 4c......$2-4

white body, "ELF Competition" label, black base and interior, 4c...............$2-4

red with white cargo cover, "Coca-Cola," 4c, 1995 catalog...............$3-5

blue "Cadbury Roses Chocolates" label, black base and interior, 4c...............$6-8

white body, blue canopy, "DELIVERY" tampo, black base and interior, 4c...............$2-4 white body, white canopy, "ALCATEL," "Your 2HGZ Movers," 4c $3-5

241-E Ford Tanker, base may be numbered 241, but tanker is issued as 245; see 245-C, 245-D

242-A Snow Top Truck, with or without plow, 1972–1977

orange with plow, orange canopy, amber windshield, "SERVICE" stickers on doors, blue label on hood, single headlights, 3spb $6-8

orange, no plow, 3sp, orange canopy, yellow windshield, "SERVICE" stickers on doors, blue label on hood, single headlights, 3kk $5-7

yellow with paint streaks, olive drab canopy, black brush bar, no plow, 3spb, part of 343-A set $5-7

yellow with paint streaks, olive drab canopy, black brush bar, no plow, 3kk, part of 343-A set $5-7

orange with plow, orange canopy, amber windshield, label on hood, 5sp $6-8

242-B Power Shovel *Pelle Mechanique / Pelleteuse*, 1:100

red body, yellow base, yellow shovel $3-5

yellow body, black base and shovel $3-5

243-A DAF Covered Trailer
no details available $12-15

243-B Shadow DN5 F1 Racer, 1:50, 1977–1984

black, white "20," white base, yellow tampo with red stars in front of cockpit, "Valvoline" on rear wing, yellow driver, rw.......$6-8

white, two red stripes on left side of cowling, two black stripes on right side of cowling, British flags on front wings, yellow driver, may have tow bar attached to front, rw.....................$4-6

dark blue, white base, white "20," yellow and red tampo in front of cockpit, US flag on front wings, yellow driver, rw............$4-6

dark blue, white base, yellow, red, and white accents, yellow tampo with red stars in front of cockpit, "Valvoline" and "SHADOW DN5" on rear wing, "16" on front, yellow and white tampos on front wings, yellow driver, rw $6-8

243-C Ford Transit Van, right side door slides open, 1:60, 1988, compare to 295-A

blue with silver and gold tampos, blue interior and bumpers, "CITY BUS," 6sp........$4-6

metallic pale green with blue interior and bumpers, 6sp $3-5

metallic pale green with hot pink interior and bumpers, 6sp $3-5

metallic pale green with red interior and bumpers, 6sp $4-6

pearl white with hot pink interior and bumpers, tropical tampos, 6sp $3-5

red with blue and white tampos, white interior and bumpers, 6sp $3-5

red with blue and white tampos, red interior and bumpers, 6sp $3-5

red with yellow interior and bumpers, blue "City Bus" tampo in script, "210291" on sides, 6sp $3-5

red with blue and white tampos, yellow interior and bumpers, 6sp $3-5

white with blue and red tampos, blue interior and bumpers, "CITY BUS," yellow windshield, 6sp $4-6

white with black interior and bumpers, "CITY BUS," 6sp.....................$3-5

white with red and blue diagonal stripes, 6sp $3-5

white with red, metallic blue and green tampos, pink interior and bumpers, 6sp ..$3-5

white with red interior and bumpers, "LE MANS SPORT SERVICE Assistance," 6sp $3-5

white with pink interior and bumpers, pink, green, orange and blue "Splish Splash" tampos, 6sp $3-5

white ambulance with orange stripes, red lights on top, door doesn't open, *Sonic Flashers*, 6sp.....................$5-7

yellow "School Bus" with red interior and

bumpers, 6sp $3-5

244-A Volkswagen Emergency Van *Kombi*, 1:66, 1973–1980, has side windows, roof light, white ambulance interior and rear hatch. Rear hatch may be metal or plastic.

metallic blue, long white stripe on side with large black "POLICE," blue windows, clear light, 3spb $8-10

metallic blue, long white stripe on side with large black "POLICE," blue windows, clear light, side windows screened, 3spb $8-10

metallic blue, long white stripe on side with large black "POLICE," blue windows, clear light, side windows screened, 3kk $8-10

metallic blue, white rectangle on side with blue "POLICE," white interior, blue windows and light, 3spb $8-10

metallic blue, black "POLICE" on white background, blue windows and light, 3spb $8-10

metallic blue, black "POLICE" on white background, amber windows, red painted over yellow light, 3spb.....................$8-10

white, "AMBULANCE" and red crosses label on sides and roof, yellow windows and light, 3spb, 1976–78 ....$6-8

white with red cross on doors, "AMBULANCE" tampo, blue windows and light, thc $6-8

white with red cross on doors, "AMBULANCE" tampo, blue windows and light, ambulance interior, 3spb.....................$6-8

white with red cross on doors, "AMBULANCE" tampo, blue windows and light, ambulance interior, regular interior, 3spb $6-8

white with red cross on doors, "AMBULANCE" tampo, yellow windows and light, 3spb.....................$6-8

white, blue "CROIX ROUGE FRANCAISE" and small red cross, red cross on roof, yellow windows and light, 3spb, 1976–78? $6-8

red, "Fire Brigade," yellow light, yellow windows, 3kk, 1976–78 ....$20-25

red, "Fire Brigade," yellow light, yellow windows, metal rear door, wheels probably 3spb $20-25

red, white interior, no markings, clear light, 2 gray figures in van, 3spb.............$20-25

olive drab, yellow windows and light, olive rear hatch, 3spb, 1978.............$20-25

olive drab, red on white crosses on sides and roof, yellow windows and light, olive rear hatch, 5sp $20-25

olive drab, red on white crosses on sides and roof, yellow windows and light, olive rear hatch, 3kk..................$20-25

olive drab, white interior, red on white crosses on sides and roof, clear windows and light, white rear hatch, 3spb........$20-25

white, "POLIZEI" on green stripe, yellow windows and light, 3spb?, 1979 .....$20-25

white, "AMBULANCE" and red crosses label on sides and roof, yellow windows and light, metal rear hatch, wheel type unknown, 1974-75. ....$20-25

metallic blue, no tampos, yellow windows and light, 3 seat interior, wheels unknown, 1973.....................$20-25

white, red cross on roof and small red cross on side door, "Croix-Rouge Francaise," white interior, yellow windows and light, 5sp

white, red cross on roof and small red cross on side door, "Croix-Rouge Francaise," white interior, yellow windows and light, 3spb

metallic blue, white rectangle on side with blue "POLICE," white interior, blue windows and light, windows screened, 3spb $8-10

metallic blue, long white stripe on side with large black "POLICE," amber windows, amber light, 3spb.......................$8-10

244-B Jeep 4x4, modified, raised chassis, with or without plastic roof, no roll bar, 1:54, 1983-1987, reissued 1992, compare to 268-A, 290-A

black, yellow interior, yellow roof, yellow jerry can, eagle logo on hood, "Made in France," ct4sp $3-5

metallic light green, black roof, red interior, black/green/light blue accents, "RENEGADE," red jerry can, "Made in France," ct4sp.................................$2-4

red, black roof and interior, black/red/blue/light blue accents, "RENEGADE," red jerry can, "4x4 Jeep" on base, "Made in France," ct4sp $3-5

metallic copper, white roof, white interior, yellow and brown "golden eagle" decal on hood, "JEEP" on baseplate, 5d.........$3-5

black, brown roof, tampo on hood, ct4sp...................................$3-5

metallic green, yellow roof, red interior, red, yellow and orange decal on hood, "JEEP CJ" on base, 5d, part of set 318......$3-5

black, yellow interior, yellow eagle tampo on the hood, no roof, ct4sp..................$2-4

red, black roof and interior, black/red/blue/light blue accents, "RENEGADE," black jerry can, "JEEP CJ" on base, "Made in France" deleted from base, ct4sp $2-4

black, red interior and rollbar, no roof, yellow, orange and red label on hood, "Made in France," ct4sp $3-5

244-C BMW Z3 Coupe, 1999

metallic blue, 4kk $4-6

metallic blue, red interior, 6sp..............$3-5

metallic blue, tan interior, 6sp, 2000 ......$3-5

yellow front/blue rear body, black interior, racing graphics, 6sp, 2000 *Speed Wheelers* ...$3-5

245-A DAF 2600 Tanker, 1:100, 1969-1974

red cab, yellow plastic tank, "SHELL" on sides and back of tank, bw $10-13

red cab; white plastic tank, "Esso," bw....$10-13

green cab; white plastic tank, "BP," bw.....................................$10-13

245-B Saviem Tanker, 1:100, 1975-1982

red cab, clear windows, gray base, yellow tank, "Shell," tampo, 3kk/5sp..........$6-8

red cab, clear windows, black base, yellow tank, "Shell," tampo, 3kk $6-8

red-orange cab, clear windows, black base, yellow tank, "Shell," tampo, 3kk/5sp .$6-8

red cab, clear windows, black base, white tank, "Shell," tampo, 3kk $8-10

blue cab, clear windows, gray base, yellow tank, "Shell," tampo, 3kk $7-9

red cab, clear windows, black base, white tank, "Esso" in blue oval, flame in diamond towards rear of tank, tampo, 3kk $18

red cab, clear windows, black base, white tank, "Esso" in red oval, flame in diamond towards rear of tank, tampo, 3kk $8-10

red cab, clear windows, black base, white tank, "Esso" in red oval, 3spb $8-10

red cab, clear windows, gray base, white tank, "Esso" in red oval, 3kk $8-10

red-orange cab, clear windows, black base, white tank, "EWING OIL CO.," decal, 3kk $20-25

red cab, clear windows, black base, white tank, "TEXACO" with black and red stripes, decal, 3spb/3kk $8-10

red cab, clear windows, black base, "TEXACO" with black and white stripes, decal, 3kk $10-13

dark blue cab, clear windows, black base, white tank, "TEXACO" with black and red stripes, decal, 3kk $12-15

blue cab, clear windows, black base, white tank, "ARAL," tampo, 3kk $12-15

blue cab, clear windows, black base, white tank, "ARAL," tampo, 3spb $12-15

green cab, clear windows, black base, white tank, "AVIA," tampo, 3kk $15-18

dark blue cab, clear windows black base, cream tank, "Gulf," decal, 3kk.....$10-13

dark blue cab, clear windows. black base, white tank, "Gulf," decal, 3kk $10-13

dark blue cab, clear windows, black base, white tank, "Gulf," decal, 3spb $10-13

olive drab cab, clear windows, greenish gray base, khaki tank, "US ARMY" with star on sides and cab roof, decal, 3kk.....$15-18

red cab, clear windows, black base, white tank, "miki HOUSE," tampo, *promotional*, 3kk $15-18

red cab, clear windows, black base, white tank, "TEXACO" with black and white stripes, decal, 3kk/ 3spb............$10-13

red cab, clear windows, gray base, white tank, "Esso" in red oval, flame in diamond towards front of tank, tampo, 3kk/3spb.............................$8-10

red cab, clear windows, gray base, white tank, "Esso" in red oval, flame in diamond towards rear of tank, tampo, 3kk/5sp..............................$8-10

red cab, clear windows, black base, white tank, "Esso" in red oval, flame in diamond towards front of tank, tampo, 3kk....$8-10

245-C Ford Tanker *Citerne*, long narrow side windows on cab, see 327-A, 1984-1991

"Shell," Ivory cab and bed, white tank, black grille and front base, silver-gray interior and rear base, 4c $4-6

"Shell," yellow cab and bed, white tank, black grille, interior, and base, 4c $4-6

"Shell," yellow cab and bed, white tank, black grille, interior, red base, 4c..............$4-6

"Shell," yellow cab and bed, white tank, black grille, interior, black front half of base, red back half of base, 4c.......................$4-6

"Milky the good milk," pale blue cab and bed, amber windows, white tank, black grille and front base, dark gray interior and rear base, 3spn, part of 327-A..............$4-6

"Milky the good milk," pale blue cab and bed, clear windows, white tank, black grille and front base, silver-gray interior and rear base, 3spn, part of 327-A...............$4-6

"Milky the good milk," pale blue cab and bed, clear windows, white tank, black grille and front base, silver-gray interior and rear base, 4c, part of 327-A.................$4-6

"Milky the good milk," pale blue cab and bed, clear windows, white tank, black grille, base and interior, 4c, part of 327-A $4-6

245-D Ford Tanker, no narrow side windows on cab, 1992

"Cadbury's caramel," yellow cab, bed, and tank, black grille, base, and interior, 4c.....................................$6-8

"Cadbury's creme eggs," red cab, yellow bed, blue tank, black grille, base, and interior, 4c.....................................$6-8

Cartoon cow, milk, and grass, pale blue cab and bed, white tank, black grille, base and interior, 4c $4-6

"PETROL COMPANY," yellow cab and bed, white tank, black grille, base, and interior, 4c.....................................$4-6

"Shell," yellow cab and bed, white tank, black grille, base, and interior, 4c $4-6

Star "20420653,"sand cab, bed, and tank, black grille, base, and interior, 4c.....$5-7

"Cadbury's DAIRY MILK," purple cab, bed, and tank, black grille, base, and interior, 4c.....................................$6-8

"Esso," white cab, bed, and tank, black grille, base, and interior, 4c $4-6

"GT Gas Tanker," orange cab and bed, gray tank, black grille, base, and interior, 4c $4-6

"PAZ" written in Hebrew in a yellow triangle with black border, yellow cab, white tank, Israeli, 4c, 2000, PAZ is largest Fuel Company in Israel $8-10

245-E Ford Transit Wrecker

yellow with red interior, "BCR Enterprises" in red.....................................$3-5

red with white interior, "24," "Emergency Road Service"................................$3-5

246-A DAF 2600 Bucket Truck, 1:100, 1971–1974

red with yellow bucket and crane base, red arm on crane, bw1 ....$15-18

246-B Range Rover Rescue Unit, with open rear section, 1:60, 1979–1987

red, white interior and ladder, blue windshield, blue riders in back, 5d, part of 376-A $4-6

red, white interior and ladder, clear windshield, blue riders in back, 8sp, part of 376-A $4-6

red, white interior and ladder, blue windshield, blue riders in back, 5d, part of 376-A $4-6

red, white interior and ladder, blue windshield, no riders in back, "Rescue Team" label on hood, 8sp.....................................$4-6

red, white interior and ladder, clear windshield, no riders in back, "Rescue Team" label on hood, 8sp.........................$4-6

246-C Range Rover Rescue Unit, with closed rear section, 1:60, 1988

red with black interior, clear windows, gray ladder, gold "DISTRICT 3 FIRE DEPT," 5d ..$3-5

red with black interior, clear windows, dark gray ladder, gold "DISTRICT 3 FIRE DEPT.," 5d $3-5

red with black interior, clear windows, white ladder, gold "DISTRICT 3 FIRE DEPT.," 5d $3-5

red with black interior, clear windows, dark gray ladder, gold "DISTRICT 3 FIRE DEPT.," 5st, 2000.........................$2-4

red with black interior, clear windows, dark gray ladder, gold "RESCUE UNIT," 8sp.....$2-4

red with black interior, blue windows, white ladder, gold "RESCUE UNIT," 5d............$2-4

red with white interior, clear windows, white ladder, blue shield, 5d $3-5

white with blue lights and windshield, red/yellow "Engine No. 3 Fire Rescue" graphics, 5st, 2000 ....$4-6

247-A DAF 2600 Crane Truck, 1:100, 1971–1975

yellow, black crane, gray plastic base, bw1 ....$12-15

metallic light green, black crane, gray plastic base, bw1 ....$12-15

247-B Porsche 924, 1:60, 1978-1985

green, amber windows, white "Porsche" tampos, 3spb $6-8

green, amber windows, white "Porsche" tampos, 3kk.....................................$6-8

green, red interior, clear windows, white "Porsche" tampos, 3spb $6-8

pale green, amber windows, white "Porsche" tampos, 3kk $6-8

red, red interior, amber windows, silver "Porsche" tampos, 3spb $6-8

red, red interior, amber windows, no tampos, 3kk.....................................$4-6

silver, red interior, amber windshield, black "Porsche" tampos, 3spb $4-6

silver, amber windshield, black "Porsche" tampos, 3kk.....................................$5-7

metallic blue, red interior, clear windows, orange "Porsche" tampos, 3spb $4-6

metallic blue, red interior, clear windows, orange "Porsche" tampos, 3kk $4-6

247-C Refuse Truck Benne Ordures, 1:100, 1988, compare to 218-A, 218-B

green body, gray container, no markings, 4c.....................................$5-7

green body, clear windows, orange container, no markings, "Made in France," 4c $4-6

lime green body, clear windows, orange container, green, white and gray hippo label on sides, "Made in France," 4c.....................................$3-5

lime green body, tan container, tampo of 3 hippos on sides, 4c $2-4

red body, yellow container, "CITY of NEW YORK".......................................$2-4

white body, orange container with 3 hippos on sides $2-4

red body, clear windows, fluorescent yellow container, black tampo of 3 hippos on sides, "Made in France" deleted from base, 4c.....................................$2-4

yellow body, black interior, clear windows, white deflector on roof, green container, black "Clean World" tampo, "Made in France" deleted from base, 4c 1998...............................$2-4

green body, clear windows, yellow container, tampo cartoon of dancing trashcans on sides, "Made in France" deleted from base, 4c...............................$2-4

green body, gray container, single hippo on sides, yellow windshield, 3kk...........$2-4 green body, clear windows, gray container, green, white and gray hippo label on sides, "Made in France," 4c $3-5

lime green body, clear windows, orange container, black hippo tampo on sides, "Made in France," 4c $3-5

lime green body, clear windows, gray container, green, white and gray hippo label on sides, "Made in France," 4c..$3-5

248-A Dune Buggy, 1971–1981, random flower and lightning decals on roof, Jaguar on nose, 1:55, compare to 232-C

red, black roof, spiral $8-10

lime green, white roof, spiral $8-10

lime green, black roof, spiral $8-10

metallic blue, white roof, 8sp $6-8

black, red interior, yellow 8sp wheels, yellow top, "37" on top, yellow 8sp wheels................$6-8

yellow, white roof, 8sp.........................$6-8

248-B Pontiac Firebird Trans Am, hood opens, compare to 258-C, also 293-A, 1:62, 1982

black, red interior, amber windows, brown/red and gold firebird insignia on hood, "TRANS AM" on doors, "Made in France," rw.........................$2-4

black, yellow interior, amber windows, reddish brown and gold firebird insignia on hood, "TRANS AM" on doors, "Made in France," rw $2-4

black, red interior, amber windows, reddish brown and gold firebird insignia on hood, "TRANS AM" on doors, "Made in France," 3spn...................$2-4

black, red interior, clear windows, no markings, "Made in France," 3spn $4-6

black, red interior, clear windows, red markings, "Made in France," 3spn $4-6

green, yellow interior, amber windshield, silver accents, "19 Turbo" on hood, "Made in France," rw $2-4

metallic blue, red interior, amber windows, brown/red and gold insignia on hood, "TRANS AM" on doors, rw..............$2-4

metallic blue, red interior, amber windows, black and gold insignia on hood, "TRANS AM" on doors, rw..............$2-4

pink...$2-4

red, amber windows, black and white racing tampos, "8," "TURBO RACING," rw .$2-4

red with gold firebird insignia on hood $2-4

red, black interior, light amber windows, silver and black firebird insignia on hood, "TRANS AM" on doors, "Made in France"..$2-4

red, black interior, dark amber windows, silver and black firebird insignia on hood, "TRANS AM" on doors, "Made in France" $2-4

red, amber windshield, "Pringles," *promotional*, rw..................................$2-4

red, yellow interior, amber windshield, silver accents, "19 Turbo" on hood, "Made in France," rw $2-4

red, yellow interior, amber windshield, silver accents, "FIREBIRD" on doors, "Made in France" deleted from base, rw $2-4

248-C Volkswagen Van *Combi*, derived from Novacar #113

red plastic body, "Surf" tampos $3-5

249-A Ski-Doo Nordic Snowmobile *Moto-Neige*, with tread, compare to 259-H, 284-B, also see 352-A

red, amber window, silver skis and handlebars, possible "BP" label on cowl $16-20

yellow, silver skis and handlebars $16-20

orange, orange skis, silver handlebars...$16-20

gold, black seat, amber window, chrome handlebars and skis, Esso tiger on side, roundel with "4" on front $16-20

249-B Mercedes-Benz 450 SE, front doors open, 1:60, 1979–1985

metallic gold, red interior, clear windows, 3psb $3-5

metallic lime green, red interior, amber windows, 3spb $3-5

metallic silver, yellow interior, clear windows, 3spb...$2-4

metallic olive green, red interior, amber windows, 3spb..............................$3-5

metallic olive green, red interior, clear windows, 3spb..............................$3-5

249-C Toyota Celica 2.0 GT, doors open, 1:58, 1988–1993

red, yellow interior, opaque windows, white "CELICA" accent on sides, headlights open and retract, "Made in France," 8h......$3-5

red, yellow interior, clear windows, white "CELICA" accent on sides, headlights open and retract, 8h......................$3-5

red, yellow interior, opaque windows, no tampos, headlights open and retract, 8h...$3-5

white, red interior, light blue windows, red and green rally accents, "STAR," headlights cast closed, "Made in Thailand," 8h........$2-4

white, red interior, opaque windows, red and black accents, black "2" on doors, hood and roof, "TOYOTA" on hood, headlights open and retract, "Made in France," 8h........$2-4

red, red interior, opaque windows, white and yellow accents, "2" on doors, headlights open and retract, "Made in France," 8h........$3-5

249-D GMC Jimmy, 1996, see 239E Chevrolet Blazer

250-A Citroën Maserati SM, 1971–1978

Base type 1: no fog lamps, narrow rear axle cover, no number

Base type 2: fog lamps, narrow rear axle cover, no number

Base type 3: fog lamps, narrow rear axle cover, number 250

Base type 4: fog lamps, wide rear axle cover, number 250

Base type 5: fog lamps, wide rear axle cover, no number

dark blue, light tan interior, clear windows, 5sp, base 1 ....$8-10

dark green, light tan interior, clear windows, 5sp, base1 ....$8-10

light tan, light tan interior, clear windows, 5sp, base 1 ....$8-10

blue, light tan interior, clear windows, thc5, base 1 ....$8-10

orange, white interior, clear windows, "2," 2 stripes front to back, thc5, base 1....$8-10

pale yellow, white interior, clear windows, thc5, "3," "D," base 2 ....$8-10 pale yellow, cream interior, clear windows, thc5, "4," stripes across hood, base 2 ....$8-10

light lime, white interior, clear windows, thc5, "3," stripes across hood, base 2 ....$8-10

light green, white interior, clear windows, thc5, "5," stripes across hood, base 2 ......$8-10

yellow, white interior, clear windows, thc5, "4," stripes across hood, base 2 ....$8-10

yellow, white interior, clear windows, thc5, "8," stripes across hood, base 2 ....$8-10

light blue, white interior, clear windows, thc5, "8," stripes across hood, base 2 ....$8-10

red, white interior, amber windows, thc5, base 3 ....$8-10

light blue, white interior, clear windows, thc5, base 3 ....$8-10

bronze, white interior, clear windows, thc5, base 3 ....$8-10

yellow, white interior, clear windows, thc5, base 3 ....$8-10

orange, white interior, amber windows, 3spb front, 3kk rear, base 4 ....$8-10

bronze, white interior, amber windows, 3spb front, 3kk rear, base 4 ....$8-10

bronze, white interior, amber windows, 3kk, base 4 ....$8-10

light yellow, cream interior, clear windows, 3spb, base 4 ....$8-10

metallic green, white interior, amber windows, 3spb, base 5 ....$8-10

metallic green, white interior, amber windows, 3kk, base 5 ....$8-10

red, white interior, amber windows, 3kk front, 3spb rear, base 5 ....$8-10

bronze, white interior, amber windows, 3spb front, 3kk rear, base 5 ....$8-10

metallic turquoise, white interior, amber windows, 3spb front, 3kk rear, base 5 ...$8-10

metallic turquoise, white interior, amber windows, 3kk, base 5 ....$8-10

blue, white interior, amber windows, 3kk, base 5 ....$8-10

lime green, white interior, amber windows, 3kk, base 5 ....$8-10

blue, white interior, 3spb.................$10-13

250-B Ford US Van, with large rectangular window and two smaller ones on left side, circular window on right side, exhaust pipe on driver's side, 1:65, compare to 234-C, 234-D, 234-E, 279-A

black, white interior, light amber windows, white rear doors, black, yellow, orange, and red label on sides showing fire, white grille and lower side trim, baseplate: "ECH.1/65 No 250 MAJORETTE U.S. VAN "Made in France," 6sp $5-7

black, white interior, light amber windows, white rear doors, black, yellow, orange and red label on sides showing fire, white grille and lower side trim, baseplate: "ECH.1/65 No 250 MAJORETTE U.S. VAN Made in France," 6spk $5-7

yellow with blue fenders and grille, red and white flame design on sides..................$6-8

250-C Mercedes-Benz 300TE Station Wagon, hatch opens, 1:63, 1990

blue with charcoal gray interior and bumpers, clear windows, no markings, chrome dashboard and grille, "Made in France," 6sp $3-5

blue with light blue interior and bumpers, white accents, "Assistance," "Mercedes" logo on hood, 6sp $3-5

light gray/blue, charcoal gray interior and bumpers, clear windows, no tampos, "Made in France," 6sp $3-5

metallic aqua with dark gray interior and bumpers, clear windows, Mercedes logo tampo on hood, chrome dashboard and grille, "Made in Thailand," 6sp $3-5

metallic aqua with white interior and bumpers, clear windows, Mercedes logo tampo on hood, chrome dashboard and grille, "Made in Thailand," 6sp.................$3-5

metallic blue with blue interior and bumpers, white accents, "ASSISTANCE," gray dashboard and grille, "Made in Thailand," 6sp.....$3-5

metallic blue with white interior and bumpers, no tampos, 6sp.........................$3-5

pale green with charcoal interior, blue accents, "Sport Assistance," bicycle tampo on hood, light gray dashboard and grille, "Made in Thailand," 6sp.................$3-5

white with charcoal gray interior and bumpers, blue and white "Mercedes-Benz SERVICE," "Made in France," 6sp $3-5

white ambulance, red Japanese script on side and red accents, on Japanese card, 6sp.....$8-10

251-A Ford Capri, 1978–1983

blue with white roof, white interior, amber windows, dark blue, light blue, and white hood stripes, 3spb.........................$6-8

blue with red roof, white interior, amber windows, 3spb, part of 372-E $6-8

orange with black roof, black stripes on the sides, 3spb $6-8

orange with white roof, cream interior, green windows, black tampo, "5" on door, 3spb ..$6-8

orange with white roof, cream interior, clear windows, black tampo, "5" on door, 3spb $6-8

red with white roof, white interior, green windows, 3spb.............................$7-9

251-B Ford Bronco 4x4, 1:56, produced in 1987 with sunroof, in 1988 without sunroof

black with silver tampos and gold stars on sides, no sunroof, red interior, ct4sp ..$3-5

black with diagonal silver and gold tampos, no sunroof, ct4sp $3-5

black with diagonal silver and gold tampos, with sunroof, ct4sp $3-5

blue, red interior, clear windows, black, white and red rally accents, "467," "PIONEER," "TELEFUNKEN," sunroof $3-5

blue, red interior, clear windows, black, white and red rally accents, "467," "PIONEER," "TELEFUNKEN," no sunroof, ct4sp $2-4

mustard yellow, no markings, ct4sp.........$4-6

white, red interior, clear windows, diagonal blue and red tampos, sunroof, ct4sp..................$2-4

251-C Service Boom Truck / Utility Truck, 1:100, 1998, Compare to 283-A, also 283-B 1993

dark blue, blue windows, white boom and bucket, white "PHONE" tampo on doors, 4c..................$2-4

yellow, black boom and bucket, no accents, 4c..................$2-4

yellow, blue windows, orange boom and bucket, black "PHONE" tampo on doors, 4c..................$2-4

252-A Magirus Dump Truck, box dumper has tailgate, no cab guard, 1978–1980, compare to 205-D

yellow with red dumper, gray interior, black tailgate, 1978..................$9-12

red with red dumper, "SERVICE" sticker with red and black diagonal bars, "22" on hood, yellow tailgate, 3kk, 1979–1980..................$8-10

252-B Dune Buggy Surfer JP4, with surfboard, 1:47, 1983-1987

blue with pink plastic trim, yellow roll cage, 3spb..................$4-6

blue with pink plastic trim, yellow **roll cage, 6sp** $4-6

red with white plastic trim, black roll cage, blue surfboard, 3spb..................$4-6

red with white plastic trim, black roll cage, blue surfboard, 6sp..................$4-6

blue with pink plastic trim, yellow roll cage, blue surfboard, 6spk..................$4-6

252-C Honda Prelude 4WD, doors open, 1:58, 1990

red, black interior, amber windows, black and silver accents, "Prelude" on doors, silver Honda logo on hood, "Made in France," 6sp $3-5

252-D Morgan convertible, top off, 1999, compare to 261-A

cherry red, white interior, blue windshield, 5d..................$2-4

metallic teal, white interior, blue windshield, Majorette website, rw..................$2-4

metallic blue, white interior, blue windshield, Majorette website, rw..................$2-4

metallic red, white interior, blue windshield, Majorette website, rw..................$2-4

253-A Ford 5000 Farm Tractor, 1:55, 1971–1978

blue with white fenders, white wheel hubs..................$8-10

red with white fenders, black wheel hubs ..$6-8

red with white fenders, white wheel hubs..................$8-10

253-B Oldsmobile Omega, 1:75, 1981–1986

metallic blue, white interior, light amber windows, 3spn..................$6-8

metallic blue, white interior, amber windows, 4c..................$6-8

white, red interior, amber windows, black and red accents, "Firestone 23 SEIKO," 3spn..................$6-8

white, red interior, amber windows, black and red accents, "Firestone 23 SEIKO," 8h..................$6-8

white, red interior, amber windows, 3spn, found in some Majokits..................$8-10

silver, red interior, amber windows, black and red "ZZ" stripes on sides, 3spn.........$6-8

silver, white interior, amber windows, black and red "ZZ" stripes on sides, 3spn..................$6-8

253-C Cadillac Allante, 1:59, 1989–1994

dark gray body, red interior, blue windshield, "Made in France," 8h..................$2-4

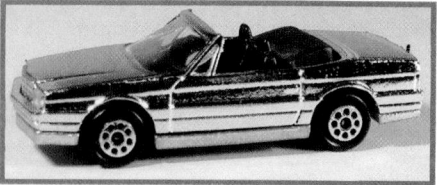

chrome light yellow, black interior, clear windshield, Kool Kromes, "Made in France," light yellow chrome 8h $2-4

chrome dark yellow, white interior, blue windshield, Kool Kromes, "Made in Thailand," dark yellow chrome 8h.........$2-4

chrome light green, black interior, clear windshield, Kool Kromes, "Made in France," yellow chrome 8h..................$2-4

chrome dark green, white interior, light blue windshield, Kool Kromes, "Made in Thailand," green chrome 8h..................$2-4

light blue, Kool Kromes..................$2-4

fluorescent lime green, white interior, blue windshield, "Franco American SpaghettiOs," Road Eaters, "Made in France," 8h..$3-5

green, white interior, blue windshield, red/white/blue/pink accents, "FUN" on trunk, "Made in France," 8h..................$2-4

hot pink, white interior, blue windshield, blue/orange/green/yellow accents, "FUN" on trunk, "Made in France," 8h..................$2-4

hot pink, white interior, light blue windshield, no markings, "Made in France," 8h ..$2-4

red, white interior, clear windshield, no markings, "Made in Thailand," 8h $3-5

green, red interior, clear windshield, no markings, "Made in Thailand," 8h $3-5

254-A Mercedes-Benz Stake Truck with Hay Load, 1:100, see 213-E

254-B Mercedes Cattle Truck, 1:100, 1978–1986, compare to 213-E

yellow with light brown box, gray door, clear windows, 1 black, 1 cream steer, 254/213 on base, 3kk..................$6-8

light yellow with dark brown box and gray door, 1 black, 1 white steer, 254 on base, 3spb..................$4-6

light yellow with dark brown box and gray door, 1 black, 1 white steer, 254 on base, 3kk front, 3spb rear..................$4-6

254-C Citroën XM, hood opens, 1:61, 1991
metallic light green, green interior, clear windows, "Made in France," 8h $3-5

metal flake silver, black interior, clear windows, "Made in France," 8h $3-5

metal flake silver, black interior, clear windows, 6sp $3-5
metal flake silver, black interior, clear windows, "Made in Thailand," 4c $3-5
metal flake silver, black interior, clear windows, "CIC/Banque CIAL," 8h, promo $5-7
pale gray, black interior, clear windows, 8h, promo $5-7
black, black interior, clear windows, 8h, promo $5-7
white, black interior, clear windows, "SOS" in red with blue medical shield on hood and sides, "Made in Thailand," 8h $3-5
white, black interior, clear windows, "Made in Thailand," 8h..............................$3-5
white, 4c $3-5
255-A Hanomag Bulldozer, 1:70
red with silver blade and base, green plastic cab $6-8
red with silver blade with red and white sticker, silver base, green plastic cab $6-8

red with yellow blade and base, yellow plastic cab, gray interior.........................$6-8

yellow with silver blade and base $6-8
yellow with yellow blade and base.........$6-8
255-B Renault R5 Turbo, no cast protruding rally lights above grille, 1:53, 1981–1984
red, yellow interior and lower body, amber windows, "TURBO," 6spk $4-6
red, yellow interior and lower body, amber windows, yellow "TURBO" on sides, 6sp $4-6

red, red interior and lower body, yellow "TURBO" on sides, 6spk.................$4-6
white, yellow interior and lower body, yellow windshield, "TURBO," 6spk $4-6
255-C Renault Maxi 5 Turbo, cast protruding rally lights above grille, 1:53, 1985, revised casting. Rear license plate lights, licence plate recess and keyhole are no longer detailed. An extra set of racing lights are added between the headlights.
blue, red interior and lower body, amber windows, red and white rally accents, "PHILIPS," "elf," "3," "MAXI 5 TURBO" on baseplate, "Made in France," rw......$3-5
255-D Ambulance Truck, 1:60, 1991
white with blue windows, orange and blue accents, blue "NYC EMS AMBULANCE," "222" on doors, dark gray baseplate, "Made in France," 4c $2-4
white with light blue windows, orange and blue accents, blue "NYC EMS AMBULANCE," "222" on doors, black baseplate, "Made in Thailand," 8h $2-4
white with light blue windows, red and blue accents, blue "NYC EMS AMBULANCE," "222" on doors, black baseplate, "Made in Thailand," 8h $2-4

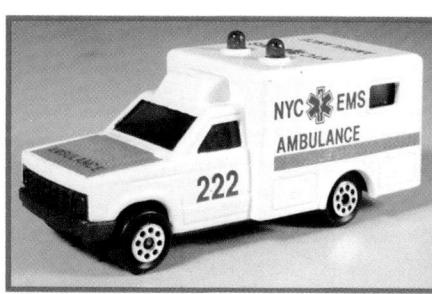

white with opaque windows, orange and blue accents, blue "NYC EMS AMBULANCE," "222" on doors, dark gray baseplate, *Sonic Flashers,* **8h $3-5**
256-A Amphibie ATF/ATV All Terrain Vehicle, 6-wheel amphibious one-man all-terrain vehicle 1:35, 1971–1974

green with white interior and base, black plastic gear, decal of eyes on front....$12-15

orange-red with yellow interior and base, decal of eyes on front $12-15
orange-red with white interior, decal of eyes on front $12-15
turquoise with white interior, decal of leaping leopard on front, white baseplate, headlights painted red $12-15
256-B BMW 733, 1:60, 1979–1986, front doors open, 1979 without sunroof outline on roof, 1980 with sunroof outline
burgundy, light brown interior, amber windows, yellow "FEDERATION EQUESTRE FRANCAISE" and "Ligue Rhone Alpes" on hood, sunroof, 3kk $5-7
burgundy, light brown interior, amber windows, yellow "FEDERATION EQUESTRE FRANCAISE" and "Ligue Rhone Alpes" on hood, sunroof, 3spb..................$5-7

burgundy, light brown interior, amber windows, yellow "FEDERATION EQUESTRE FRANCAISE" and "Ligue Rhone Alpes" on hood, no sunroof, 3spb $5-7

silver, white interior, sunroof, no accents, 5sp $5-7
silver, white interior, sunroof, no accents, 3spb $5-7
silver, white interior, sunroof, no accents, 3kk $5-7
metallic light green, cream interior, green tinted windows, no accents, sunroof, 3kk ...$5-7
metallic light green, cream interior, green tinted windows, no accents, sunroof, 3spb ..$5-7
metallic light green, cream interior, green tinted windows, no accents, sunroof, BMW logo decal on hood.......................$5-7
white, amber windows, green/orange/yellow horse and horseshoe label on hood, light brown interior, no sunroof, 3spb.......$5-7
white, amber windows, green/orange/yellow horse and horseshoe label on hood, light brown interior, sunroof, 3kk, 1985 and 1986 catalog...............................$5-7
yellow, white interior, blue windshield, sunroof..$5-7
gold, from "Dallas" TV series, 3kk $15-18
256-C Mack Tow Truck, 1:100, 1990, also 297-B, compare to 297-A

red, gray plastic deck and base, clear windshield, black boom, chrome grille and stacks, silver metal hook, 6sp 1996 ....$2-4

red, gray plastic deck and base, opaque windshield, black boom, chrome grille and stacks, silver metal hook, 6sp $2-4

257-A Renault 5 LeCar, with antenna and rear view mirrors, 1:55, 1974–1981, compare to 280-A

metallic silver, red interior, clear windows, red tampos, "A5" on sides, chrome mirrors, 3spb $8-10

metallic silver, red interior, clear windows, red tampos, "A5" on sides, black mirrors, 3spb $8-10

metallic silver, red interior, clear windows, red tampos, "A5" on sides, black mirrors, 3kk $8-10

metallic silver, red interior, clear windows, "A5" on sides, black mirrors, 3kk $8-10

pale yellow with chrome mirrors, 3kk.....$8-10

red with white "RTL" on blue and yellow tampos, black mirrors, "RTL" leaning left on sides only, white interior, 3kk $8-10

red with white "RTL" on blue and yellow tampos, chrome mirrors, "RTL" on hood and leaning right on sides, 3spb..........$8-10

metallic red with white interior, no tampos, 3kk $8-10

pink, white interior, amber windows, chrome mirrors, 5sp $8-10

pale yellow with chrome mirrors, 3spb ..$8-10

yellow, white interior, amber windows, chrome mirrors, 5sp $8-10

blue, white interior, amber windows, chrome mirrors, 5sp $8-10

257-B Mazda RX7 Daytona, doors open, 1:56, 1986–1990

blue, red interior, clear windows, silver "21," black "MAZDA," "Made in France", rw $2-4

orange, blue interior, clear windows, light and dark blue accents, "RX7," blue interior, rw...................................$3-5

orange, blue interior, clear windows, light and dark blue accents, "RX7," blue interior, 6sp..................................$4-6

orange, blue interior, clear windows, silver "21," black "MAZDA," rw $3-5

orange, blue interior, clear windows, black and silver "RX7," rw.....................$4-6

orange, blue interior, clear windows, blue and white tampo, "RX7," "Made in France," 6spk $4-6

white, black and red accents, "23".........$2-4

white, red interior, clear windows, red, blue and black accents, "Mobil 1" on sides and hood, "Made in France," rw $2-4

black, red interior, clear windows, silver "21," gold "MAZDA," "Made in France," rw...$2-4

257-C BMW 325i, doors open, 1:56, 1993

metallic dark olive green, gray interior and bumpers, 8h $2-4

burgundy $2-4

metal flake teal, blue interior, 8h $2-4

metallic blue, gray interior and bumpers, 8h...$2-4

white, green doors with "Polizei," dark gray interior, 8h, 1999 Rescue Force 3-pack...................................$2-4

white, green doors and hood with "Polizei," dark gray interior, clear windows, 5pw, 2000 ....$3-5

white, red interior and bumpers, clear windows, red and blue rally accents on hood, roof and sides, "STAR," "3," 8h........$2-4

white, red interior and bumpers, clear windows, red and blue rally accents on hood, roof and sides, "STAR," "3," 5pw $2-4

white, red interior and bumpers, clear windows, red and blue rally accents on hood and roof only, "STAR," "3," 8h........$2-4

metallic aqua, gray interior and bumpers, clear windows, 8h $2-4

metallic dark green, gray interior and bumpers, clear windows, 8h $2-4

258-A Dune Buggy, with awning-like rectangular roof, 1972–1975

yellow, cream interior, amber windshield, white awning, yellow flower design on roof with red outline, green leaf, spiral wheels.....................................$10-13

yellow, cream interior, amber windshield, white awning, dark blue pansy design on roof, spiral wheels $10-13

red, cream interior, amber windshield, white awning, red and yellow flower design on roof, spiral wheels $10-13

red, cream interior, amber windshield, white awning, dark blue pansy design on roof, spiral wheels $10-13

258-B Mercedes-Benz Fire Engine *Pompier Aeroport,* 1:70, 1979–1985

red, white rear bed, "No. 4 Fire and Rescue" on yellow with orange sticker, blue windshield, gray water cannon, 3spb $6-8

red, white rear bed, no sticker, blue windshield, black water cannon, 3spb $6-8

red, white rear bed, no sticker, blue windshield, black water cannon, 3kk $6-8

red, white rear bed, no sticker, blue windshield, gray water cannon, 3spb $6-8

258-C Pro Stocker Firebird with oversized engine, 1:62, 1989, compare to 248-B, 293-A

white, amber windows, red and blue stars and stripes, red "Number One" on roof, "Made in France," 6sp $3-5

white, amber windows red and blue stars and stripes, red "Number One" on roof, "Made in France" deleted from base, 6sp...$3-5

yellow, amber windows, red and black tampo, "8," "Made in France" removed from baseplate, "Made in Thailand," 6sp...$3-5

fluorescent yellow, amber windows, red and black tampo, "8," "Made in France" removed from baseplate, "Made in Thailand," 6sp....................................$3-5

259-A Unimog Snow Plow, 1:82, see 224-A

259-B Sterckeman Lovely 400 Travel Trailer, 1:65, 1969, also see 236-A

gold and white two-tone, yellow windows, bw1..$12-15

gold and white two-tone, yellow windows, 5sp...$12-15

white, 3spb......................................$12-15

259-C Fourgon (Van) Ice Cream Van *Glacier,* 1982–1989, reissued 1996, compare to 224-C red, yellow interior, clear windows, yellow awning, graphic on roof, 3spn.........$5-7

red, yellow interior, pale blue windows, yellow awning............................$5-7

red, pink windows, yellow awning, off-white interior, ice cream cone on side, 4c ..$5-7

red, clear windows, yellow awning and interior, graphic on roof, 8h $5-7

metallic red, yellow interior, pale blue windows, yellow awning, 8h $5-7

fluorescent pink, yellow interior, blue windows, brown, yellow, green, and white tampo showing an animal with a triple scoop ice cream cone, yellow awning, no tampo, "Made in France," 8h $5-7

metallic pink, cream interior, pink windows, yellow awning with green tampo, "Made in France," 3spn....................$5-7

metallic pink, cream interior, pink windows, yellow awning, "Made in France," 4c. $5-7

yellow with blue windows, white awning with no graphics, cream interior, 3spn......$6-8

yellow, red awning, red "PINDER" on roof, clown faces on doors, red and white tampos, 4c..........................$5-7

yellow with pink windows, white awning, no graphics, cream interior, "Made in France," 3spn.......................$6-8

green, yellow interior, yellow awning, 8h ..$5-7

turquoise, yellow interior, clear windows, red awning, yellow stars and "Ice Cream" on roof, "Made in Thailand," 4c, 1999 ....$2-4

turquoise, yellow interior, clear windows, red awning, yellow stars and "Ice Cream" on roof, "Made in Thailand," 4c, 1999 ....$2-4

white, yellow interior, clear windows, orange awning, black, brown, red, and yellow pictures of cones on roof, "Made in Thailand," 4c, 1998 ....$2-4

259-E Motor Home *Fourgon* (Van), see 224-B

259-F Audi 90, 1:60, see 239-D

259-G British Bus, 1:125, also 286-A

red, amber windows, white interior, light blue, red, and white stickers, large black "Visit London" across entire label, "Made in France," 3spb.........................$4-6

red, pale yellow interior, amber windows, "Sealink Ferries," no "286" on base, "Made in France," 3kk....................$6-8

red, amber windows, white interior, clear windows, dark blue, red and white stickers, large black "Visit London," no "286" on base, "259" added to base, "Made in Thailand," 3kk $4-6

red, pale yellow interior, amber windows, "British Airways," "286" on base, "Made in France," 3kk $6-8

259-G Snowmobile Moto-Neige, same casting as 249-A but without tread, also 284-B

white with amber windshield, silver skis and handlebars, red and blue tampos, "92" $6-8

white with amber windshield, red skis and handlebars, "Olympic Racing," "6" on front $6-8

white with amber windshield, dark brown-gray skis and handlebars, "Olympic Racing" $6-8

white with amber windshield, gray skis and handlebars, black plastic base, red and blue accents, "92" $6-8

white with amber windshield, black skis and handlebars, black plastic base, red and blue accents, "92" $6-8

red with amber windshield, dark gray skis and handlebars, blue and white tampos, "92" $5-7

red with amber windshield, white skis and handlebars, white snowflakes, 1999.....$3-5

260-A Renault 17 TS, 1973–1978

orange, white interior, amber windows, decals on the sides with logos: driver's side has "Mobil, Firestone, BOSCH, BP, WYNN'S, Esso, KLG"; passenger side has "Castrol, Norma, Marchal, Elf, Cibie, Goodyear, Shell, Ferodo," 3kk $9-12

orange, white interior, amber windows, no tampos, 3kk $6-8

blue, amber windows, decals on the sides with logos: driver's side has "Elf, Sev Marchal, Cibie, Tudor, Shell, Dunlop, Firestone"; passenger side has "Castrol, Norma, Marchal, Elf, Cibie, Goodyear, Shell, Ferodo," 3kk $9-12

orange, white interior, amber windows, no tampos, 3spb $6-8

metallic lime body, white interior, amber windows, decals on the sides with logos: driver's side has "Castrol, Norma, Marchal, Elf, Cibie, Goodyear, Shell, Ferodo"; passenger side has "Elf, Sev Marchal, Cibie, Tudor, Shell, Dunlop, Firestone," "Made in France," 3spb..............................$9-12

orange body, white interior, amber windows, decals on the sides with logos: driver's side has "Castrol, Norma, Marchal, Elf, Cibie, Goodyear, Shell, Ferodo"; passenger side has "Esso, Radiomatic Auto Radio, Martini, BP, Dunlop, Champion, Shell," "Made in France," 3spb......$9-12

red, white interior, light amber windows, 3spb $6-8

red, white interior, light amber windows, rally accents, 3spb $6-8

260-B Explorateur 4x4, 1:59, 1983–1986 reissued 1995–Based on a Volvo P2304, this all-terrain, four-wheel-drive vehicle was used by the Swedish Armed Forces and the United Nations in the 1970s.

gold with cream canopy with green design, brown interior, ct4sp $5-7

metallic aqua-blue, white interior, amber windows, white canopy with blue, red, black, yellow, and green tampo, "Tunis" and "Dakar" in red, "483" in black, "Pacific" in yellow,"vsd" in red, yellow, and green, "Made in France," ct4sp $5-7

metallic aqua-blue, white interior, amber windows, white canopy with blue, red, black tampo, "Tunis" and "Dakar" in red, "483" in black, "Pacific" and "vsd" removed from tampo, "Made in France," ct4sp........$5-7

metallic blue, light brown interior, amber windows, white canopy, red, black and blue tampo, "Off Road," "340," "Paris-Dakar," and "RB," ct4sp $5-7

metallic blue, light brown interior, amber windows, white canopy, red, black, and blue tampo, "Off Road," "340," "Paris-Dakar" and "RB," "No 260," and "Made in France" deleted from baseplate, "No 261" added, "Made in Thailand," ct3c $5-7

260-C Mercedes-Benz 500SL Roadster, 1:58, 1991, opening hood

red, gray lower body, dark gray interior, clear windscreen, black steering wheel and engine, blue, black, purple and white tampo, "Nerds," "Made in France," 6sp $3-5

metallic red, burgundy lower body, brown interior, clear windscreen, black steering wheel and engine, "Made in France," 8h.....................$3-5

metallic red, dark gray interior, clear windscreen, black steering wheel and engine, "Made in France," 6sp $3-5

metallic red, burgundy interior, clear windscreen, black steering wheel and engine, "Made in France," 6sp red chrome...$3-5

metallic red, burgundy interior, clear windscreen, black steering wheel and engine, white tampo on hood and trunklid, "Made in France," 6sp $3-5

red chrome, gray lower body, white interior, clear windscreen, black steering wheel and engine, "Made in France," 6sp red chrome $3-5

fluorescent pink, white interior, clear windscreen, black steering wheel and engine, black, green, yellow, and blue tampo, "Strawberry Speedster" on doors, "Smelly Speeders, Not Stinky Just For Kids" on trunklid, "Made in France," 6sp red tires..........$3-5

dark green chrome, dark gray interior, clear windscreen, black steering wheel and engine, "Made in France," 6sp green chrome $3-5

light green chrome, gray lower body, light gray interior, clear windscreen, light gray steering wheel and engine, "Made in France," 6sp green chrome.............$3-5

light silver, white interior, clear windscreen, black steering wheel and engine, "Made in Thailand," 6sp.....................$3-5

light metallic tan, light brown interior, clear windscreen, black steering wheel and engine, "Made in France," 6sp.................$3-5

silver, gray lower body, dark gray interior, clear windscreen, black steering wheel and engine, "Made in France," 6sp red chrome $3-5

silver, gray lower body, dark gray interior, clear windscreen, black steering wheel and engine, "Made in France," 6sp $3-5

silver, gray lower body, dark gray interior, clear windscreen, black steering wheel and engine, "Made in France," 6sp blue chrome $3-5

silver, gray interior, distinctly lighter than above models, clear windshield, black steering wheel and engine, "Made in France," 6sp.....................$3-5

silver, gray lower body, maroon interior, clear windscreen, black steering wheel and engine, 6sp $3-5

black, gray lower body, dark gray interior, clear windscreen, black steering wheel and engine, "Made in Thailand," 6sp.......$3-5

maroon, gray lower body, dark gray interior, clear windscreen, black steering wheel and engine, "Made in Thailand," 6sp $3-5

261-A Morgan Convertible, top on, 1:50, 1979–1992, compare to 252-C

dark red with cream roof and interior, yellow windshield, 8sp $3-5

dark red with cream roof and interior, amber windshield, 8sp $3-5

red with white interior, cream top $3-5

cherry red with black top, gray interior, clear windshield, 8sp $3-5

lavender with white interior and roof, blue windshield, Color Pack, 5sp $3-5

dark purple, cream roof and interior, light amber windshield, 5d.....................$3-5

blue chrome, white interior, clear windshield, *Kool Kromes / Top Chromes*, 5d blue hubs $3-5

dark blue, cream roof and interior, light amber windshield, 5d.....................$3-5

metallic blue with white roof and interior, amber windshield, 5d.....................$3-5

green chrome with white interior, clear windshield, *Kool Kromes*, 5d green hubs $3-5

dark green with cream roof and interior, amber windshield, 8sp $3-5

dark green with white roof and interior, amber windshield, 8sp $3-5

dark green with white roof and interior, clear windshield, 8sp $3-5

dark green with brown roof and interior, clear windshield, 8sp $3-5

dark green with brown roof and interior, amber windshield, 8sp...................$3-5

pale green with white interior and roof, COLOR PACK, 5sp $3-5

metallic green with cream roof and interior, amber windshield, 5d.....................$3-5

metallic mint green with white roof and interior, light blue windshield, 5d $3-5

261-B Explorer, 1995, see 260-B

262-A Airport Minibus, 1:87, 1979

white, red "TWA" tampos, cream interior, clear windows, 5 light brown passengers, 3spb.....................$6-8

white, red "TWA" tampos, cream interior, clear windows, 4 light brown passengers, 3spb.....................$6-8

white, red "TWA" tampos, white interior, clear windows, 3kk.....................$6-8

white, red "TWA" tampos, white interior, green tinted windows, 5 passengers, 3spb.....................$6-8

white, red "TWA" tampos, white interior, green tinted windows, 4 passengers, 3kk.....................$6-8

white, red "TWA" tampos, white interior, green tinted windows, 5 dark brown passengers, 3kk.....................$6-8

white, blue "AIR FRANCE" tampo, red and blue accent, blue interior, clear windshield, 4 passengers, 4c $6-8

white, blue "AIR FRANCE" tampo, red and blue accent, blue interior, blue windshield, 4c.....................$6-8

white, blue "AIR FRANCE" tampo, red and blue accent, cream interior, clear windshield, 4 blue passengers, 4c..........$6-8

white lower, red upper, "JAPAN AIR LINES" tampos, white interior, clear windows, 5 passengers, 3kk $4-6

white lower, red upper, "JAPAN AIR LINES" tampos, white interior, slight green tint to windows, 3spb.....................$4-6

white lower and upper, blue interior, red and black abstract design on sides, blue windows, 4 brown passengers, 4c.........$2-4

white lower and upper, blue interior, red and black abstract design on sides, blue windows, 5 brown passengers, 4c........$2-4

white, Israeli Bus, "EGGED" written in Hebrew on both sides and top – looks like red circle with a zigzag through it, 4c........$2-4

white lower, red upper, "AIRPORT" and plane in blue, white interior, 4 passengers, slight blue tint to windows, 4c $2-4

white, blue "AIRPORT" tampos, red broad and red and blue narrow stripe, blue interior, 5 brown passengers, slight blue tint to windows, 4c $2-4

red, "Coca-Cola," sun holding Coke bottle, white interior, clear windows, 4 pink passengers, 4c $5-7

red, "Coca-Cola," sun holding Coke bottle, white interior, clear windows, 5 pink passengers, 4c $5-7

green lower, white roof, "Alitalia" in black and red with red stripe, pale yellow interior, brown driver and 5 passengers, clear windows, 3spb, 1979 ....$2-4

green lower, white upper, soccer graphics, blue interior, blue windows, 4 passengers, 4c $2-4

green lower, white upper, brown interior, blue passengers, 4c $2-4

green lower, white upper, white interior, clear windows, 4 passengers, 4c...........$2-4

green lower, white upper, blue interior, blue windows, 4 brown passengers, 4c...$2-4

263-A Front End Loader, 1:87, 1981, variation of 211-D

orange, orange bucket, gray engine and stack, "Made in France" on base, ct3c ..$2-4

orange, orange bucket, light gray engine and stack, "Made in France" on base, ct3cb...........................$2-4

yellow, light gray engine and stack, "Made in France" on base, ct4sp $2-4

yellow, dark gray engine and stack, "Made in France" removed from base, ct4sp....$2-4

yellow, light gray engine and stack, "Made in France" removed from base, ct4sp....$2-4

light blue with dark gray engine and stack, ct3c $3-5

264-A Alpine A310 Special Team Unit, 1979–1985

dark blue, light blue tinted windows, white interior, smaller white/blue "POLICE" tampo inside door lines, 3spb.................$8-10

white, blue windshield, blue interior, red "SOS" on sides, 3spb.................$8-10

white, blue windows, red/white/blue "POLICE" label, 3spb $8-10

darker blue than 1, blue tinted windows, white interior, larger red/white/blue "POLICE" label extending outside of door lines, 3spb $8-10

white, blue windshield, blue interior, red "SOS DOCTOR" on sides, 3spb.............$8-10

dark blue, white interior, white "POLICE" tampo inside door lines, blue "POLICE" on white tampo on hood, 3spb $8-10

264-B Custom Ford Transit Van Pickup

red with white bumper and interior, "RACING SERVICE" $4-6

264-C Volkswagen Golf, 1:56, 1993

red, black interior, clear windows, "Made in France," 8h $4-6

silver, black interior, clear windows, "Made in France," 4c $2-4

teal, black interior, clear windows, "Made in Thailand," 8h....................$2-4

blue, 8h, yellow interior, green bumpers ..$2-4

blue, 8h, black interior $2-4

blue, black interior, rally tampos, "12" on hood and roof, "Sport," "MAX," "Motor," "STAR," "RALLYE," "Made in Thailand," 8h......$2-4

blue, green base and bumpers, yellow interior, clear windows, "25," "RACING," rally tampos, "STAINLESS" on hood, "Made in Thailand," 8h...................$2-4

teal, yellow interior, clear windows, "Made in Thailand," 8h...................$4-6

264-D Volkswagen Golf IV, 1:56, 1999

metallic light green with white interior, 8h, seen only on Majorette website, not found in stores $3-5

silver, black interior, clear windows, "Made in France," 8h............................$2-4

red with gray interior, yellow, white, and black rally tampos, "71," 8h $2-4

red with black interior, yellow, white, and black rally tampos, "71," 8h...........$2-4

black with gray interior, blue and red rally tampos, "5," 6sp $2-4

265-A Citroën CX, 1:60, doors open unless otherwise noted, 1979–1984

metallic light gold-brown, white interior, amber windows, 3spb..........................$2-4

silver-gray, white interior, amber windows, 3spb $2-4

silver-gray, red interior, clear windows, doors don't open, 112 on base, 3spb, German issue $4-6

dark maroon, cream interior, amber windows, 3spb $2-4

dark maroon, cream interior, amber windows, 3spb front, 3kk, back....................$2-4

265-B Container Truck, with air deflector on cab roof, 3 axles, 1:100, 1987—Unless otherwise indicated, all models have a white air deflector and a black grille, base, and interior.

"Yoplait" label, lime green body, white container, 4c $3-5

"WEST LINES" label, red body, white container, 4c $3-5

"RESTAURANT PIZZA DEL ARTE" label, red body, white container, 4c $3-5

"DIET PEPSI," white body, white container, Road Eaters, 4c $4-6

"PETER PAN," white body, white container, Road Eaters, 4c $3-5

"PETER PAN," red body, white container, Road Eaters, 4c $3-5

"Swanson Kids Growlin' Grilled Cheese Fun Feast Barnie Bear," flourescent orange body, white container, Road Eaters, 4c..$3-5

"ROQUEFORT SOCIETE," white body, white container, 4c $3-5

"Total," white body, white container, 4c ..$4-6

"Cadbury's Roses Chocolates," blue body, blue container, red grille, base, and interior, 4c $6-8

"Cadbury's Dairy Milk," blue body, blue container, 4c $6-8

"FUTURA MOTORS PTY. LTD.," white body, white container, *Australian promotional issue*, 4c $15-18

Dancing clowns graphics, blue body, white container, 4c, 1998.................$2-4

No design, lime green body, white container, 4c..$4-6

"Clairgel," white body, white container, 4c $8-10

"Leon's," "CANADA'S ONLY FURNITURE SUPERSTORES," yellow body, yellow container, premium – no package, 4c $12-15

No design, white body, white container, 4c, 1999 ....$2-4

No design, blue body, white container, 4c...$2-4

"Coca Cola," ice cube design, red body, red container with "Coca-Cola" tampo in white on sides, tampo on roof shows ice cubes opening a can, 4c $6-8

"Coca Cola," ice cube design, red body, white container, 4c.....................$6-8

"Coca Cola," soccer ball, red body, turquoise container, 4c ...$4-6

"Yoplait," white body, white container, 4c ...$4-6

"Wild Cherry PEPSI," blue body, red container, red grille, base, and interior, 4c...$6-8 eyes and green bars; blue body, red air deflector, yellow container, red grille, base, and interior, green wheels, 4c $12-15

"CIRCUS," red body, yellow air deflector, yellow container, 4c $3-5

"PINDER," red body, yellow air deflector, yellow container, 4c $6-8

"ULTRAMAR DIAMOND SHAMROCK" White body, white container, premium – no package, 4c $12-15

"3rd S.A. and VIC. Coca Cola SWAP MEET," white body, white container, *Australian promotional* issue, 4c, 1994........$15-18

"A. CHIPIER," white body, white container, *promotional*, 4c $10-13

"Abex," red body, white container, *promotional*, 4c $10-13

"afpa," red body, white container, *promotional*, 4c $10-13

"FRANCE LOCATION," white body, white container, *promotional*, 4c..........$10-13

"Frandem," red body, white container, *promotional*, 4c $10-13

"FRV," green body, white container, *promotional*, 4c $12-15

"gel3," white body, white container, *promotional*, 4c $10-13

"HR RAVION," red body, white container, *promotional*, 4c $10-13

"IBSI," white body, white container, *promotional*, 4c $10-13

"intencite," white body, white container, *promotional*, 4c $10-13

"JEV DERBEZ," white body, white container, white grille, base, and interior, *promotional*, 4c..............................$12-15

"JP SERVICE PALETTES," white body, white container, *promotional*, 4c..........$10-13

"JTR," red body, white container, *promotional*, 4c $10-13

"majorette pub," red body, white container, *promotional*, 4c $15-18

"montfort LA PUB QUI ROULE," white body, white container, *promotional*, 4c .$10-13

"PAREDES," white body, white container, *promotional*, 4c $10-13

"PROCIM," white body, white container, *promotional*, 4c $10-13

"PROGICIELS GRHISI," white body, white container, *promotional*, 4c...............$10-13

"SERNAM," white body, white container, *promotional*, 4c $12-15

"SPIDSAC," red body, white container, *promotional*, 4c $10-13

"Tedur," white body, white container, *promotional*, 4c $10-13

"TOUS LES PANNEAUX," red body, white container, *promotional*, 4c..........$10-13

"TRANSAXE," white body, white container, *promotional*, 4c $10-13

"VanDyck," white body, white container, *promotional*, 4c $10-13

"Kingsmill," white body, white container, *promotional*, 4c $10-13

"Gaspard," yellow body, yellow container, *promotional*, 4c $12-15

"AIR FRANCE," white body, white container, *promotional*, 4c $12-15

"Thames Barrier," red body, white container, black tampo on sides, "Made in France," bought in England at the Thames Barrier gift shop in 1991, *promotional*, 4c $12-15

"Klöckner MOELLER," white body, white container, *German promotional*, 4c ..$10-13

"MEDIAVEHICLES, A GE Capital Company," "mediavehicles.com," white body, white container, *US promotional*, 4c $5-7

"ATLAS," "Le choix, Le prix, La competence en plus!," red body, white container, *French promotional*, 4c $10-13

266-A Renault 18, 1:60, 1979–1985—It looks like this car was only available in its taxi form in the 200 series, while the variations with the roof spoiler are all from 300 series sets.

yellow, white interior, blue windows, passenger, no accents, white and red "TAXI" light on roof, brown driver and passenger, 3spb......................................$6-8

yellow, white interior, blue windows and headlights, white and red "Taxi" sign on roof, brown driver and passenger, 3kk.......................................$4-6

yellow, white interior, clear windows, "TAXI" sign on roof, yellow and blue labels on sides and hood, "radio taxi," blue graphics, brown driver and passenger, 3kk......................$4-6

yellow, "TAXI" sign on roof, blue and yellow labels on sides and hood, "radio taxi," brown driver and passenger, 3spb ...$4-6

yellow, "TAXI" sign on roof, blue and yellow tampos on sides and hood, "radio taxi," brown driver and passenger, 3spb $4-6

metallic blue, white interior, clear windows, yellow spoiler on roof, no driver or passenger, 3spb, part of 368-A.......$4-6

light metallic blue, white interior, clear windows, white spoiler on roof, 3kk, part of 368-A $6-8

light red, white interior, white spoiler on roof, clear windshield, 3kk, part of 368-A...$4-6

metallic silver.................................$6-8

266-B Landrover 4x4, opening plastic rear door, 1:60, 1987

beige, black roof rack and interior, clear windows, black rear door, large taillights, "Made in France," 5d.....................$3-5

beige, black roof rack and interior, clear windows, black rear door, yellow, red and black accents, "4x4 SAFARI" graphics on hood, small taillights, "Made in France," 5d $2-4

tan, black roof rack and interior, clear windows, black rear door, black and white zebra stripes, small taillights, "Made in France" deleted from base, "Made in Thailand," 5d $3-5

tan, black roof rack, red "Safari" on yellow background on hood, gray and brown mud splatters on body, small taillights, "Made in France" deleted from base, 5d $2-4

red, black roof rack and interior, clear windows, black rear door, large taillights, "Made in France," 8sp $3-5

red, black roof rack and interior, 5d........$3-5

red, black interior and rear door, no roof rack, transparent blue light bar, yellow and black tampo on sides and hood, "Fire Dept," small taillights, "Made in France" deleted from base, "Made in Thailand," 5d $3-5

white, black roof rack and interior, clear windows, black rear door, black and white zebra stripes, small taillights, "Made in France," 5d $3-5

white body with "4x4 Safari" tampo on hood, black roof rack and rear door..........$3-5

white, black interior and rear hatch, black light bar on roof, blue "NASA," red accents, 5d, part of 362-B.....................$2-4

white, black interior and rear door, transparent red light bar on roof, blue "NASA," red accents, large taillights, "Made in France," 8sp, part of 362-B $2-4

white, black interior, black rear door, red light bar on roof, blue "NASA," red accents, 6sp, in NASA set $2-4

white, black interior, white rear door, solid red light bar on roof, blue "NASA," red accents, large taillights, "Made in France," 5d, part of 362-B.........................$2-4

white, black roof rack, red "Safari" on yellow background on hood, gray and brown mud splatters on sides of body, small taillights, "Made in France" deleted from base, 5d.....................$2-4

white, black interior and rear door, no roof rack, red light bar, black "POLICE" tampo on sides, small taillights, "Made in France" deleted from base, "Made in Thailand," 5d $3-5

yellow, black roof rack and interior, clear windows, black rear door, white, blue, red and black tampo, "Telefunken," "249," and "Shell," large taillights, "Made in France," 8sp.....................$3-5

yellow, blue "CAMEL 4x4" label on hood, no roof rack, 8sp, found in Denmark......$6-8

yellow, black roof rack and interior, clear windows, black rear door, red and black tampo on hood, "Safari," small taillights, "Made in France" deleted from base, "Made in Thailand," 5d $3-5

yellow, red roof rack and rear door, "CIRCUS" graphics on sides, 5d, part of "CIRCUS" set towing lion in a red over yellow trailer. Special "CIRCUS" packaging $2-4

yellow, black interior and rear door, no roof rack, red light bar, blue and red tampo on sides, "FK enterprise," small taillights, "Made in France" deleted from base, "Made in Thailand," 5d $3-5

pale yellow, black roof rack and interior, clear windows, tropical scene with 'Safari,' 5st, 2000 part of 328-C set $2-4

orange, black roof rack and interior, clear windows, black rear door, small taillights, "Made in France," 5d....................$3-5

orange, black interior, no roof rack, clear windows, black rear door, "Made in France," 5d....................$2-4

orange, black interior, red light bar, clear windows, black rear door, "Made in France," 5d ..$2-4

bright fluorescent green, black interior, no roof rack, clear windows, black rear door, white, red and black accents, "4x4 SAFARI" graphics on hood, small taillights, "Made in France," 5d....................$2-4

black, brown interior and grille," clear windows, white and green tampo, "Stainless," "4," "Rallye," "Oil," and "Champion," brown luggage on roof, brown opening rear door, small taillights, "Made in Thailand," 5d, in set 328..$3-5

red, black interior and rear door, no roof rack, translucent red light bar, no accents, "Made in France" deleted from base, "Made in Thailand," 5d $3-5

267-A Excalibur, 1:56, 1979–1986

metallic light blue, black roof, white interior, light amber windshield, 8sp $5-7

metallic brown, 8sp $4-6

yellow with passenger, 8sp..................$6-8

silver, black roof, cream interior, amber windshield, 8sp $4-6

red, black roof, dark gray interior, blue windshield, 8sp $6-8

red, light gray roof, cream interior, amber windshield, 8sp $5-7

red, light gray roof, dark gray interior, 8sp ..$5-7

white, black top, dark gray interior, clear windshield, 8sp $5-7

white, black top, dark gray interior, green windshield, 8sp $5-7

267-B Crazy Car 4x4, raised chassis, 1:55, 1995, modified reissue of 223-B

black with white interior, red steering wheel and exhaust pipes, "FUNNY" on roof, "CRAZY CAR" on hood, ct4sp $3-5

gray blue with orange interior, ct4sp $4-6

blue with yellow interior, orange/yellow/red labels on hood and roof, ct4sp $4-6

red, white interior, "CRAZY CAR" accents on hood, "FUNNY" on rollbar, "Made in Thailand," ct4sp.............................$3-5

268-A Jeep CJ, with conventional, low chassis, with roll bar or roof, 1:54, 1980, compare to 244-B, 290-A

black, red interior, black roll bar, gold and red tampo on hood, "4x4," "Made in France," 5d $3-5

metallic light brown, white interior, yellow and black tampo on hood, 5d $4-6

yellow, bright green interior and roll bar, abstract green and black accents on hood $3-5

red, white interior,"Ewing Oil," 5d $3-5

fluorescent chartreuse, green interior and roll bars, green and black tampo on hood, "Made in France," 5d....................$3-5

beige, khaki camouflage tampo, black interior and roll bars, made Thailand, 5d $3-5

khaki, beige camouflage tampo, black interior and roll bars, made Thailand, 5d $3-5

268-B Chevrolet Corvette Turbo Racer, 1:57 (see 215-C)

268-C Pontiac Trans Sport SE Minivan, 1:55, 1993

black, white interior, clear roof and windows, gray bumpers, "Made in France," 8h ..$3-5

black, white interior, clear roof and windows, gray bumpers, "Made in France," 6sp.........$3-5

black, red interior, clear roof and windows, gray bumpers, "Made in France," 6sp $3-5

red, white interior, clear roof and windows, gray bumpers, "Made in Thailand," 8h $3-5

red, white interior, clear roof and windows, gray bumpers, "Made in Thailand," 8h red chrome..$3-5

red, white interior, clear roof and windows, gray bumpers, "Made in France," 6sp $3-5

red, white interior, clear roof and windows, gray bumpers, "Made in France," 6sp red chrome $3-5

red, white interior, clear roof and windows, gray bumpers, "Made in Thailand," 4c........$3-5

metallic blue, white interior, clear roof and windows, gray bumpers, "Made in Thailand," 4c........$3-5

metallic blue, white interior, clear roof and windows, gray bumpers, "Made in Thailand," 8h........$3-5

metallic blue, white interior, blue roof and windows, white bumpers, "Made in Thailand," 8h........$3-5

269-A Jeep Cherokee Ambulance, rear doors open, 1:64, 1980–1990

white, blue interior, blue windows and roof lights, blue accents, blue six-armed cross on hood, "AMBULANCE" on sides surrounded by a blue stripe, "Made in France," 5d........$3-5

white, blue interior, blue windows and roof lights, blue accents, looks same as 1 but lighter blue, blue six-armed cross on hood, "AMBULANCE" on sides, "Made in France" deleted from base, 5d........$3-5

white, white interior, blue windows and roof lights, red cross decal on hood, "Made in France," 5d........$3-5

white, white interior, blue windows and roof lights, no markings on sides, red cross on hood, "6" on front of raised roof, "Made in France," 5d $4-6

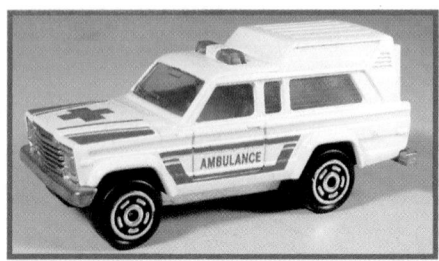

white, blue interior, blue windows and roof lights, red accents, red cross on hood, "AMBULANCE" on sides, 5d..................$3-5

This version may have the following labels from a Majokit applied: "EMERGENCY," "URGENZA," "NOTAUFNAHME," "URGENCES" as well as "AMBULANCE," "KRANKENWAGEN," OR "AMBULANZIA." A red cross label for the hood was also included. $5-7

white, blue interior, clear windows and roof lights, red accents, red cross on hood, "AMBULANCE" on sides, "Made in France," 5d........$3-5

white, blue interior, blue windows and roof lights, "Made in France," 5d........$3-5

269-B Ford Mondeo, 1994

red with tan interior, 8h, 1994 catalog ...$6-8

269-C Porsche Boxster, 1998

yellow with blue tampos, red "8" $3-5

pale gray with cream interior, no tampos, 6sp, 1999 ....$3-5

red with black interior, rally graphics, "11," 5st, 2000 ....$2-4

270-A Autobianchi A112, rear hatch opens, 1:53, 1984–1987

metallic gold, black interior, clear windows, black and red tampos, 3spn $6-8

metallic gold, black interior, clear windows, black and red tampos, 8h $6-8

orange, black interior, "A112," Abarth logo ..$6-8

red, black interior and bumpers, amber windows, white, green, red, and yellow labels on hood and sides, "A112," "Made in France," 3spb $6-8

red, black interior and bumpers, amber windows, white, green, red and yellow labels on hood and sides, "A112," "Made in France," 3spn $6-8

270-B Renault Clio, rear hatch opens, 1:53, 1991

red, black interior, black stripe on side with white "Clio," 8h $3-5

white, black interior, green stripes on sides, "apave," 8h, *promotional item for small company in France making safety certifications*, the phone number of the office of Lyon is on the trunk $6-8

metallic blue, dark gray interior, white "Clio" and black stripe on sides, 8h $3-5

270-C Ford Econoline Emergency Van / Ambulance, opening rear door, 1:63, 1998

white with red and gold Ambulance graphics, red interior and emergency lights, 6sp $3-5

blue with red emergency lights, white interior, "POLICE" on doors, Israeli Police insignia on hood and side, "Police" written in Hebrew on side of the truck, 6sp $8-10

yellow with red and blue graphics, "Enterprise," dark gray ladders on roof, 6sp ...$3-5

271-A Alfa 75, 1:55, 1988

red, black accents, black interior, no trim on grille $6-8

red, black accents, black interior, silver trim on grille $4-6

red, tan interior, 8h $3-5

red, white interior, clear windows, black bumpers, "FORZA ITALIA," green and white accents, "Made in France" deleted from baseplate, "Made in Thailand," 8h $3-5

red over black, black interior, white "Alfa Romeo" on sides, 8h $6-8

red, white interior, clear windows, black bumpers, "Made in France," 8h $3-5

271-B Alfa Romeo Giulietta, opening doors 1:55

blue, white base and interior, clear windows, "POLIZIA," "Made in France," 8h $4-6

blue, black base and interior, clear windows, "POLIZIA," "Made in France," 8h $4-6

red, black base and interior, clear windows black and silver accents, "Alfa Romeo," "Made in France," 3spb $3-5

red, black base and interior, clear windows, black and silver accents, "Alfa Romeo," 8h........$3-5

271-C Ford Econoline Van/Saloon Car, with raised roof, 1998

metallic teal blue with hot pink interior $3-5

white, "Diet Pepsi," 6sp $3-5

271-D Alfa Romeo Polizia, with roof light, front doors open, 1999

blue with white "POLIZIA" tampos, white interior, 8h $3-5

272-A Ford Tempo/Sierra, 1:58, 1984–1990

metallic blue, red interior, amber windows, silver accents, "SIERRA," 8h $2-4

metallic blue, yellow interior, amber windows, no tampos, 8h $2-4

silver, red interior, amber windows, red accents, 3spn $2-4

white, red interior, amber windows, blue tampos, "SIERRA" on sides, 8h $2-4

light yellow, red interior, amber windows, red tampos, "SIERRA," 8h $2-4

yellow, red interior, amber windows, red tampos, "SIERRA," 8h ....$2-4 yellow, red interior, amber windows, red tampos, "SIERRA," 3spn $3-5

272-B Renault Espace, 1997, adapted from Novacar series

white plastic body with orange trim, blue "AMBULANCE" and logo $3-5

273-A Toyota Tercel 4WD, 1:55, 1986–1990

blue, black interior, clear windows, silver "4WD" on doors, "Made in France," 6sp $4-6

blue, black interior, clear windows, black "4WD" on doors, "Made in France," 6sp.........$4-6

metallic periwinkle blue, black interior, clear windows, black "4WD" on doors, "Made in France," 6sp $4-6

metallic sea green, black interior and bumpers, clear windows, black "4WD" on doors, 6sp $4-6

metallic green, black interior and bumpers, clear windows, 6sp.....................$4-6

red, black interior, clear windows, black "4WD" on doors, 6sp $4-6

bright orange, no markings, 6sp...........$4-6

bright orange, black interior, clear windows, black "4WD" on doors, "Made in France," 6sp.........................$4-6

metallic gold, black "4WD" on doors, 6sp $4-6

273-B Roadster, loosely based on a Dodge Viper, 1:58, 1994

red with black interior $3-5

273-C Forklift, 1999

yellow with steel gray cage and lift $3-5

yellow with black cage and lift, 2000 Catalog $3-5

274-A Super Dump Truck *Benne carriere*, 1:100

yellow with chrome hubs, silver dumper, ct3c $3-5

yellow with black hubs, silver dumper, ct3c $3-5

yellow with chrome hubs, silver dumper, ct4s, 1999 ....$3-5

275-A Renault 11 Encore, sliding sunroof, 1:54, 1984–1988

red with black lower body, yellow interior, yellow graphics, 3spn.........................$3-5

red with black lower body, yellow interior, gold and black graphics, 3spn................$3-5

red with black lower body, yellow interior, 8h.............................$3-5

dark maroon with black lower body, yellow interior, black sunroof, yellow "11" and stripe, 3spn $4-6

metallic green with black, orange and silver rally accents....................................$5-7

white with black lower body, red interior, amber windshield, black/yellow/ red/light blue rally accents, "25," "MICHELIN" on rear doors, 8h $3-5

white with black lower body, red interior, amber windshield, black/yellow/red/ light blue rally accents, "25," "MICHELIN" removed from rear doors 8h $3-5

white with black lower body, red interior, amber windows, amber sunroof, 8h, in set 317-J with kayak trailer....................$2-4

275-B Ford Escort GT, doors open, 1:55, 1992

yellow with green interior, red and black rally tampos, "5," 4c....................$3-5

276-A Toyota 4x4 Runner / 4Runner, conventional low chassis, 1994

red with black interior, black stripe, silver "4X4 Runner" on sides, 5d.......................$2-4

metallic maroon, 5d..........................$2-4

pale yellow, black interior, "Moto Racing" and checkerboard graphics, 5d 1998 ....$2-4

pale yellow, black interior, "Moto Racing" and checkerboard graphics, 5st 2000 ....$2-4

276-B Toyota 4x4 Runner, 4Runner, modified, raised chassis, red with rally tampos, ct4sp ..$3-5

277-A Toyota Landcruiser 4x4, conventional low chassis, back window opens, 1:53, 1981–1982

beige, green accents "RAID 86" and map of Africa on roof, "African safari, Kenya" ...$4-6

red, yellow interior and accents, black lower body $3-5

white, black zebra stripes, black interior....$4-6

metallic green with black/orange/silver "Rallye" accents $5-7

white, red interior, "Jungle King" on roof...$4-6

green, red interior, amber windows, black, red and white accents on sides, "43," "Rally," ctsc .$3-5

silver, amber windows, no tampos, ctsc ...$4-6

golden brown, white interior, amber windows, white rear hatch, ctsc $3-5

red, yellow interior, amber windows, black, red and silver accents on sides, ctsc ..$3-5

green, amber windows, no accents, ctsc ..$4-6

277-B Toyota Landcruiser 4x4, modified, raised chassis, back window opens, 1:53, 1983–1987

beige, red interior and rear door, amber windows, red "AFRICAN SAFARI" with green lion face, ct4sp $6-8

black, red interior and rear door, amber windows, gold accents, "RAID 86" and map of Africa on roof, "African safari, Kenya," ct4sp $6-8

bright green, yellow interior and rear door, amber windows, blue "AFRICAN SAFARI" with black lion face, ct4sp $6-8

red, yellow interior and rear door, light amber windows, black and gold accents, "Rally 43," ct4sp $6-8

white, red and gold "Rallye" accents, green and black "STAR 80," ct4sp $6-8

red, black interior, black zebra stripes, ct4sp $6-8

white, black interior and rear door, clear windows, black zebra stripes, ct4sp.......$6-8

metallic brown, red, yellow and orange decals, ct4sp $6-8

white, red interior, green accents," RAID 86" and map of Africa on roof, "KENYA" and "african safari" on sides, ct4sp...$6-8

white, "POLICE," yellow interior and rear door, amber windows, blue and red accents, ct4sp.............................$6-8

yellow, "CAMEL 4x4" label on roof, ct4sp, found in Copenhagen....................$3-5

bright green, yellow interior and rear door, amber windows, ct4sp $6-8

white, red interior and rear door, clear windows, red "AFRICAN SAFARI" with green lion face, ct4sp ....$6-8 red, yellow interior and rear door, light amber windows, black stripe under side windows, ct4sp $6-8

277-C Harvester, 1999
light green with pale gray cab, 1999 Catalog $3-5
bright green with black cab, 2000 Catalog $3-5

278-A Western Locomotive, 1:87, 1981–1987
metallic blue with red cowcatcher $8-10
metallic green with red cowcatcher $8-10
steel gray with red cowcatcher $8-10
black with red cowcatcher, *Sonic Flashers* $8-10
black with yellow cowcatcher, *Sonic Flashers* $8-10

278-B Mobile Home Camping car, pickup truck camper, compare to 313-B, 1991–present
hot pink with beige camper, 8h $4-6

lime green, opaque windshield, white camper with blue windows, 8h $4-6

blue with white camper, 4c....................$4-6
blue with white camper, 8h $4-6
red, blue windshield, white camper, blue and white mountain scene on hood, doors and camper, 8h $3-5
hot pink with beige camper, blue tires, 6sp ...$4-6
hot pink with white camper, 8h $3-5
red, "Coca Cola," no camper on back, black air deflector on roof, part of set with 5th wheel trailer, 8h, see 313-B $1
red, blue windshield, white camper, blue and white mountain scene on camper only, 8h $3-5

279-A Fourgon (Van) Police Van, windows all around, 1:65, 1981–1989, compare to 234-C, 234-D, 234-E, 250-B

blue, white interior/grille/fenders, label on sides has red outer stripes, wide white stripe in the middle with blue "POLICE," clear light and windshield, 6sp.................$3-5

blue, white interior/grille/fenders, two blue and one thin red stripe on top of wide white stripe, blue "POLICE," clear light and windshield, 6sp $3-5
blue, white interior/grille/fenders, blue "POLICE" on white rectangle tampo on sides of van, blue light and windshield, 6spk..$3-5
white, blue interior/grille/fenders, blue and red "POLICE" accents, 6sp $3-5

279-B Stock Car, rw, 1:60, 1993
metallic blue with red and white tampos, pink interior, yellow roll cage $3-5
metallic blue with red and white tampos, yellow interior, pink roll cage $3-5
green with orange and white tampos, yellow interior, pink roll cage.....................$3-5
green with orange and white tampos, pink interior, yellow roll cage $3-5
bright blue with red and white racing tampos, yellow interior, hot pink roll cage.......$3-5

279-C '58 Corvette, 1:58 1999
light blue, white cove, white interior, clear window, 6sp.......................................$4-6
white, red "Coca Cola" on doors, "Radio Grill" on roof, 6sp, issued by Coke and Walmart for Walmart's Radio Grill restaurant.......$5-7
red, white coves, white "Coca Cola" on doors, "Radio Grill" on roof, 6sp, issued by Coke and Walmart for their Radio Grill restaurant at Walmart $5-7
blue, white cove, "Pepsi Cola" on doors and trunk, Pepsi cap on roof, 6sp............$4-6
light blue, white cove, red interior, clear window, 6sp.......................................$4-6

280-A Renault 5 LeCar, no rear view mirrors or antenna, front doors open, 1:51, 1983–1986, compare to 257-A
metallic light olive green with yellow interior, black/orange/yellow tampos..........$6-8
white, 4c, yellow windshield and interior, black/orange/yellow stripes on sides ...$6-8
white, 4c, yellow windshield and interior, yellow tampos + tennis racquet, "Tennis" $6-8
pink, red hearts all over body, yellow windows, white interior, 4c..............$6-8

280-B Ferrari F40, 1:58, 1989
red with no rear window glazing, rw $3-5

red with rear window glazing, rw $3-5

Kool Kromes red, rw red chrome...........$3-5
Kool Kromes yellow, rw yellow chrome ..$3-5
yellow, rw, 1999 Catalog $3-5

281-A Peugeot 205 GTI/CTI Hardtop Sedan, 1:53, 1985–present, also 210-D, compare to 210-C, 281-B, unpainted metal base
yellow, black interior, clear windows, red/black/blue accents, black "205" on roof, 6sp $2-4
yellow, black interior, clear windows, "205" with red and black stripes, 6sp.........$2-4
white, black interior, clear windows, "205" with red and black stripes, 6sp.........$2-4
white, black interior, clear windows, "205" with red faded and black stripes, 6sp $2-4
silver-gray, black interior, clear windows, 6sp, promo $5-8
white, black interior, clear windows, red "205 Peugeot" on hood, 6sp $2-4

yellow and red, black interior, clear windows, "FLASH TEAM, saphir lignes," "17," "205 Chrono," 6sp....................................$2-4

white, black interior, clear windows, "En Avant/La Region," 6sp, promo $5-8
red, black interior, clear windows, "Gti" with black lion on hood, 6sp $2-4
black, red interior, clear windows, "Gti" with gold lion on hood, 6sp $2-4
metallic blue, white interior, clear windows, "Gti" with lion on hood, 6sp $2-4
white, red interior, clear windows, "Police," 6sp $2-4
white, red interior, clear windows, "Police," 6sp red $2-4
white, black interior, clear windows, "Police," 6sp $2-4

281-B Peugeot 205 GTI/CTI Cabriolet, 1:53, see 210-C, compare to 210-D / 281-A Hardtop

281-C Mack Cement Truck, 1998
yellow cab, red base with blue barrel, 6sp $3-5
yellow cab, red base with orange barrel, 6sp, 1999 ....$3-5

282-A F1 Ferrari, 1:55, 1986 – present

red with yellow, black, silver, and blue accents, "Agip," "27," "FIAT," "F1 FERRARI" on base, "Made in France," rw.................$2-4

red with yellow, black and blue accents, "Agip," "27," "FIAT," "F1 FERRARI" deleted from base, "Made in France," rw $2-4

red with yellow, black and blue accents, "Agip," "28," "FIAT," "F1 FERRARI" on base, "Made in France," rw $2-4

red with yellow, black and blue accents, "Agip" tampo deleted, "28," "FIAT," "F1 FERRARI" on base, "Made in France," rw..........$2-4

red with white, black, blue and yellow accents, "1" on nose, "Agip," "FIAT," "TAG 1," "F1 FERRARI" on base, "Made in France" deleted from base, rw $2-4

red with silver, black, blue and yellow accents, silver replaces the white from 4, "1" on nose, "Agip," "FIAT," "TAG 1," "F1 FER-RARI" on base, "Made in France" deleted from base, rw $2-4

red with silver, black, blue and yellow accents, silver replaces the white from 4, "1" on nose, "Agip," "FIAT," "TAG 1," "F1 FERRARI," and "Made in France" deleted from base, rw $2-4

red with white, blue and yellow accents, "1" on nose, "Agip," "FIAT," "PIONEER" on sides, Shell logo on sides and front, rw........$2-4

283-A Crane Truck, 1:100, 1982–present, compare to 251-C

red with blue crane base, black boom, red hook, 3spn...................................$4-6

yellow with yellow crane, black boom, red hook, 4c $2-4

yellow with opaque windows, yellow crane, black boom, silver hook, "Made in France," 4c $2-4

red with blue crane base, black boom, black hook, 4c.....................................$2-4

yellow with clear windows, yellow crane, black boom, silver hook, "Made in France" deleted from base, 4c $2-4

283-B Utility Truck, 1:100, 1998, see 251-B

284-A Saab 900 Turbo, front doors open, 1:62, 1982–1988

black, red interior, amber windows, silver "TURBO" tampo on sides, 3kk $3-5

black, red interior, amber windows, silver "TURBO" tampo on sides, 4c $3-5

metallic blue, cream interior, pale yellow windows, white "TURBO" on sides, 4c..$3-5

metallic green, cream interior, pale yellow windows, silver "TURBO" on sides, 4c $3-5

silver, white interior, amber windows, no tampos 3kk $3-5

silver, white interior, amber windows, no tampos 4c $3-5

silver, white interior, amber windows, black "TURBO" tampos, 4c......................$3-5

284-B Snowmobile *Moto-Neige*, 1992, identified as #284 only on package, see 249-A, 259-C

285-A Lancia Monte Carlo, 1:50, 1982–1987

mustard yellow with amber windows, black interior, black "MONTE CARLO," 6sp.....................................$4-6

white, red accent, amber windows, black "68" on doors and hood, 6sp $3-5

white, black interior, clear windows, "Tour de Course," "guillaume," "6," blue and red accents, 6sp.................................$4-6

red, amber windows, black interior and bumpers, black tampo on the sides "MONTE CARLO," 6spk.................$4-6

yellow, amber windows, black interior and bumpers, black tampo on the sides "MONTE CARLO," 6spk $4-6

285-B Jeep Cherokee Sheriff, 1990, compare to 224-C

white, blue tampos on doors with white "SHERIFF" and a star, gray interior, "911" on hood, clear windows, opaque red roof light, "4x4" on base, 5d $2-4

white, blue tampos on doors with white "SHER-IFF" and a star, gray interior, "911" on hood, clear windows, with orange roof light, "4x4" on base, 5d.................$2-4

white roof and doors, blue front and rear, black "SHERIFF" on doors, tampo on hood, red roof light, 5d.................$2-4

white, blue tampos on doors with white "SHERIFF" and a star, gray interior, "911" on hood, clear windows, translucent red roof light, "JEEP CHERO-KEE" on base, 5d $2-4

286-A British Bus, 1:125, 1982–1986, see 259-G

286-B Fiat Tipo, 1:54, 1990

metallic blue, white tampos and interior, "TIPO" on sides, 8h...................................$3-5

red, white interior, white tampos, 8h $3-5

yellow with clear windows, red interior, racing tampos, "1," "Supertrapp Racing Team," etc., 8h...............................$3-5

287-A Toyota Hi-Lux Pickup, conventional chassis, 1:56, compare to 292-A

orange, ct4sp, silver, black, and yellow tampos, "4 x 4" $4-6

orange, ct4sp, black interior, dark green, yellow and dark orange tampos, "Toyota 4x4" $4-6

white, no tampos, 5d.........................$4-6

orange, black and yellow tampos, "GLADIATOR," 5d, part of set with farm and log trailers $4-6

blue, no tampos, black rollbar, 5d $4-6

blue, yellow and red tampo, "Night Hawk" on doors and hood, 5d, part of 323-D $4-6

green, yellow and red tampo, "Night Hawk" on doors and hood, 5d, part of 323-D $4-6

white, black interior and rear cargo bed, amber windows, black/orange/red tampo on sides and hood, conventional chassis, 5d............................$4-6

white, black interior and rear cargo bed, amber windows, black/orange/red tampo on sides and hood, raised chassis, ct4sp $4-6

287-B Toyota Hi-Lux Pickup 4x4, modified 4x4 chassis, see 292-A

287-C Bulldozer, 1989

yellow with black plastic cab, light gray plastic plow, "A" and "2228710" on base of blade ...$3-5

yellow with black plastic cab, dark gray plastic plow $2-4

yellow with black plastic cab, light gray plastic plow, "B" and "2228710" on base of blade $3-5

yellow with black plastic cab, light gray plastic plow, "B" and "2228710" on base of blade, smooth rectangle around "Majorette" on base $3-5

288-A Renault Kangoo Van/Saloon car, windows on sides, 1998

yellow with tampos, bright blue interior $4-6

blue with red interior, 4kk, 2000 Catalog..$4-6

289-A F1 MacLaren, 1986–1991

white, black interior, red tampo in front of cockpit extends to start of front wing, Honda symbol on nose, "HONDA" on sides with red and black tampos, "A SENNA" on right side of car, "A PROST" on left side of car, "Made in France" and "1984 McLaren International Ltd" on base, rw $3-5

white, black interior, red tampo in front of cockpit extends to start of front wing, Honda symbol on nose, "HONDA" on sides with red and black tampos, "A SENNA" on right side of car, "Made in France" deleted from base, "1984 McLaren International Ltd" on base, rw $3-5

white, black interior, same red and black accents as 1 and 2, no Honda accents, "1" on nose, "HERCULES" front wings, "BOSS" beside cockpit, "Made in France" and "1984 McLaren International Ltd" on base, rw $3-5

white, black interior, red in front of cockpit extends to nose, no Honda accents, "8" on nose, green "WARE" on sides, "TOP" on side pods, "T.WILMARK" on sides, "Made in France" and "1984 McLaren International Ltd" deleted from base, rw..............$3-5

289-B Renault Kangoo Panel Van, no windows on sides behind door, 1998

red with bright blue interior $4-6

290-A Jeep 4x4 Rallye CJ, 1984–1987, reissued in 1992, modified raised chassis, open, with roll bar, compare to 244-B, 268-A

black, red interior, black roll bar, gold accents and red "4x4" on hood, ct4sp.........$2-4

black, red interior rollbar, yellow, orange, and red label on hood, "Made in France," ct4sp...$2-4

black, red interior, black roll bar, red/orange/yellow accents......................................$2-4

yellow, green interior, black roll bar, black and green abstract design on hood.........$2-4

fluorescent lime green, bright green interior and roll bar, black and green abstract design.....$2-4

290-B '57 T-Bird, 1999

red with white flames on hood and front fenders, white roof................................$3-5

red, white "Coca Cola" on doors, "Drink Coca Cola" on trunk, "Radio Grill" on roof, 6sp; issued by Coke and Walmart for their Radio Grill restaurant at Walmart.......$4-6

291-A Chevrolet Blazer Pickup 4x4, 1:62, 1984–present, also 228-D, compare to 228-C, 228-E

blue with yellow interior, black and gold accents, "4WD" on doors and hood, ct4sp $3-5

red, amber windshield, black and white horses on sides, "WILD MUSTANG" on hood, black light bar, ribbed roof, "Made in France" $2-4

yellow, red interior, red and black accents, black rally lights behind cab.............$3-5

black, yellow interior, amber windshield, multicolor "INTERNATIONAL FOUNDATION" on hood, ct4sp $2-4

red, yellow interior, "Coca-Cola," black light bar, sun accent, ct4sp....................$3-5

black, yellow interior, amber windshield, yellow wheels, multicolor "INTERNATIONAL FOUNDATION" on hood, ct4sp......$2-4

red, yellow interior, amber windshield, "4WD" on doors and hood, black light bar, ribbed roof, "Made in France," ct4sp...........$2-4

yellow, amber windshield, black and red accents, "4WD" on hood and doors, black light bar, ribbed roof, "Made in France," ct4sp $2-4

yellow, amber windshield, black and red accents, "4WD" on hood and doors, black light bar, ribbed roof, "Made in France," black ct4spb $2-4

black, bovine skull on hood, red, white and yellow accents, "TEXAS" on doors, red lamps, no ridges on roof, ct4sp $2-4

yellow, amber windshield, black and red accents, "4WD" on hood and doors,

black light bar, no ridges on roof, "Made in France," ct4sp $2-4

yellow, black interior, amber windshield, orange, red and blue accents, "SODA" on hood and doors, ribbed roof, "Made in France," ct4sp $2-4

292-A Toyota Hi-Lux Pickup, with modified raised 4x4 chassis, rollbar, compare to 287-A

fluorescent lime green with red "WESTERN" on doors, black "RODEO" on roof, ct4sp ..$3-5

metallic gold with silver, black, and red "4X4 Toyota," ct4sp $3-5

metallic blue with red and yellow tampos "NIGHT HAWK," ct4sp..................$3-5

red with black interior, yellow, black, and silver tampos, ct4sp.............................$3-5

yellow with black interior, rally tampos, ct4sp...$4-6

black and red with red interior and wheels, "APPLE JAZZ," *Smelly Speeders*, **ct4sp......$3-5**

metallic pink with blue, black and silver tampos, "Toyota 4x4" white interior, ct4sp......$3-5

hot pink with yellow flames, "GLADIATOR," ct4sp...$3-5

metallic blue with no markings, black interior, chrome roll bar ct4sp $3-5

white, amber windows, orange, black and red accents, "Made in France," ct4sp.....$2-4

orange, red,black and yellow tampos, "4x4 Toyota," yellow ct4sp $2-4

293-A Pontiac Firebird Turbo, with oversized engine, see 258-C, compare to 248-B

white with red and blue stars and stripes ..$3-5

yellow with black and red tampos..........$3-5

293-B Jaguar XJ6, front doors open, 1:65, 1990

black, red interior, clear windows, 8h $2-4

silver with red interior..............................$2-4

metallic green, 4c, red interior $2-4

metallic green, 8h, red interior $2-4

metallic blue, red interior, 8h $2-4

black, red interior, amber windows, front license plate numbers removed, 4c ...$2-4

293-C Jaguar Police, with roof lights, opening front doors, 1999, also see 205-D

white, red and yellow side stripe, "Police" on hood and trunk, red interior, 8h, 1999 ....$2-4

white, red and yellow side stripe, "Police" on hood and trunk, red interior, 5pw, 2000 ....$3-5

294 Not issued

295-A Ford Transit TUG Custom Tow Truck, 1996, compare to 243-C

red, white interior and bumpers, amber windows, "JACK'S TOWING 24 HR SERVICE," 6sp $3-5

fluorescent orange, amber windows, white interior and bumpers, "RACING SERVICE," black bed, 6sp $3-5

fluorescent orange, amber windows, white interior and bumpers, "RACING," black bed, 6sp...$3-5

fluorescent orange, amber windows, white interior and bumpers, "RACING SERVICE," yellow, green and black label of motorcycle silhouette on roof, black bed, 6sp.......$3-5

white, amber windows, "Total" and grapgics on doors, black bed, 6sp $3-5

296-A Chevrolet El Camino SS Pickup, 1:59, 1988–present

red chrome body, white interior and truck bed, clear windows, white flame tampo on sides, "Made in France," *Kool Kromes*, 8h red chrome $3-5

red, white interior, clear windshield, white "EL CAMINO SS" on sides, "Made in France," 8h $2-4

metallic blue, white interior, clear windshield, white "EL CAMINO SS" on sides, "Made in France," 8h..................................$2-4

metallic blue, white interior and truck bed, clear windows, red and white tampo on sides, "EL CAMINO," "Made in France" deleted from baseplate, "Made in Thailand," 8h $3-5

metallic blue, white interior and truck bed, clear windshield, red "EL CAMINO SS" on sides, 4c $2-4

dark blue, blue interior and truck bed, clear windows white, pink, red, yellow, and black tampo, "DWEEBS," "Made in France" on baseplate, 8h $3-5

fluorescent green, red interior and truck bed, clear windows, white, pink, yellow, red and black tampo, "CRY BABY," "Made in France" on baseplate, 8h $3-5

flourescent green, white interior and truck bed., clear windows, red and white tampo on sides, "EL CAMINO," "Made in France" deleted from baseplate, "Made in Thailand," 8h $3-5

flourescent green, red interior and truck bed., clear windows, red and white tampo on sides, "EL CAMINO," "Made in France" deleted from baseplate, "Made in Thailand," 8h $3-5

flourescent green, white interior and truck bed, clear windows, no tampos, "Made in France" deleted from baseplate, "Made in Thailand," 8h.................................$3-5

white, red interior and truck bed, clear windows, red and blue tampo accents, "AMERICAN THUNDER," 8h $2-4

white, red interior and truck bed, clear windows, orange and green tampo, "INDY" and "CRASH," "Made in France," 8h $3-5

white, red interior and truck bed, clear windshield, red and blue accents, "American Off Road," "Made in France," 8hbl, blue wheels from Glider set, 320-G.........$3-5

white, red interior and truck bed, clear windows, blue and red tampo, "American Off Road," "Made in France," 8h $3-5

pink, white interior and truck bed, clear windows, white and blue tampo, "INDY" and "CRASH," "Made in France," 8h......$3-5

purple chrome body, white interior and truck bed, clear windows, white flame tampo on sides, "Made in France," 8h blue chrome $3-5

magenta chrome body, white interior and truck bed, clear windows, white flame tampo

on sides, "Made in France," 8h light blue chrome $3-5

blue chrome body, white interior and truck bed, clear windows, white flame tampo on sides, "Made in Thailand," 8h blue chrome $3-5

yellow, white interior and truck bed, clear windows, "EL CAMINO" in red on sides, 8h $3-5

white, dark blue interior and truck bed, clear windows, red and blue tampo, Coast Guard emblem on hood and doors, "COAST GUARD" on rear fenders, 8h..$3-5

297-A Mack Dump Truck, 1:100, 1988–1995, compare to 256-C

metallic blue, chrome exhaust and grill, clear windshield, metallic silver metal dumper, 6sp...$2-4

yellow, chrome exhaust and grill, opaque windshield, metallic silver metal dumper, 6sp...$2-4

yellow, black exhaust and grill, opaque windshield, gray plastic dumper, 6sp.......$2-4

royal blue, chrome exhaust and grill, clear windshield, metallic silver metal dumper, 6sp...$2-4

light blue, chrome exhaust and grill, clear windshield, metallic silver metal dumper, 6sp...$2-4

297-B Mack Wreck Truck, 1:100, see 256-C

297-C Ford Skip Truck, 1998

blue, black base, green skip, 4c.............$2-4

blue, white base, orange skip, 4c...........$2-4

298-A Ford Recycling Lorry, 1998

green, black base, red and blue recycling containers, 4c.....................................$2-4

green, black base, yellow and blue recycling containers, 4c.................................$2-4

Majorette Supers / Series 230, steerable versions of selected 200-Series cars

201.S Fiat Coupe, yellow $3-5

202.S Fiat Coupe Racing, silver $3-5

203.S Mustang Convertible, black $3-5

204.S Mustang Convertible, red $3-5

205.S Mustang Hardtop, yellow $3-5

206.S Mustang Hardtop Sport, black $3-5

207.S Renault Clio, turquoise $3-5

208.S Renault Clio Rallye, blue $3-5

209.S Ferrari 456 GT, red with Ferrari logo on hood, black interior, clear windows, 6sp..$3-5

210.S Ferrari 456 GT Racing, black with chocolate interior, white accents, double thin red on white stripe up hood and to back of roof, 6sp..$3-5

211.S Ford Mondeo, silver with chocolate brown
interior, clear windows, 8d $3-5

212.S Ford Mondeo Rallye
blue with charcoal interior, clear windows,
white rally markings, 8d $3-5

213.S Roadster, based on a Dodge Viper RT/10
red with black interior $3-5

214.S Roadster Sport, based on a Dodge Viper
RT/10
metallic teal with white double racing stripe,
black "8" in white circle on hood, 5d .$3-5

215.S Ferrari GTO
yellow with clear windows, black Ferrari logo
on hood, black interior, 6sp $3-5

216.S Ferrari GTO Racing
red with clear windows, black interior, gold
"23" on roof, hood and doors, 6sp ..$3-5

217.S Stock car
white with yellow interior, clear windows, red
and black racing accents, black "7" in red
circle on hood and roof, 6sp $3-5
red $3-5

218.S Stock car
light blue $3-5
black $3-5

219.S Porsche Boxster
silver, 1996 ....$3-5
metallic blue, 1998 ....$3-5

220.S Porsche Boxster Sport
metallic teal, 1996 ....$3-5
metallic silver with red tampos $3-5

221.S Mondeo Police, 1998
black with white trim, bumpers................$3-5
white, two lateral dark blue stripes, right side
has "POLIISI," Finnish, left "POLIS"
(Swedish), 8h $5-7

222.S Peugeot 406
red, 1997 ....$3-5

223.S Peugeot 406, 1998
1. orange with racing tampos $3-5

224.S Volkswagen Golf IV, 1999..............$3-5

225.S Dodge Concept car, "Copperhead,"
1999 ....$3-5

226.S BMW Z3 Coupe, 1999.................$3-5

Majorette Special Forces Series 220 / Squad Forces

Special Forces was introduced in 1995 as
a series of military versions derived from 200-
series models. 300 and 600 series models
were added in 2000, and the name was
changed to Squad Forces. Figures and playsets
were also added.

220.1 4x4 Chevrolet Pickup with Machine Gun
dark green, ct4sp, white star on hood, black
gun, blue windows........................$3-5

dark green, ct4sp, tan camouflage, black gun,
blue windows $3-5
tan, ct4sp, dark green camouflage, black gun,
blue windows $3-5

220.2 Missile Launcher Truck
dark green, 4c, dark gray missiles, black missile base, dark gray roof unit, white star on
doors $3-5
tan, 4c, dark green camouflage, black missiles,
dark gray missile base, tan roof unit $3-5

220.3 Tank with Cannon
dark green $3-5
dark green, tan camouflage $3-5
tan, dark green camouflage $3-5

220.4 Military Ambulance
dark green, 4c, blue windows and roof lights,
"AMBULANCE" on hood, dark green
cross on white background $3-5
dark green, 8h, blue windows and roof lights,
"AMBULANCE" on hood, dark green
cross on white background $3-5
dark green, 8h, blue windows and roof lights, tan
camouflage, "AMBULANCE" on hood, dark
green cross on white background; the tan
camouflage can be either light or dark...$3-5
tan, 8h, dark green camouflage, light blue
windows and roof lights, "AMBU-
LANCE" on hood, tan cross on white
background..$3-5
tan, 8h, light blue windows and roof lights,
"AMBULANCE" on hood, tan cross on
white background $3-5

220.5 Impala Military Police
dark green, 4c, "Military Police" on doors and
hood, blue windshield and emergency
light $3-5
dark green, 8h, "Military Police" on doors and
hood, blue windshield and emergency
light..$3-5
dark green, 8h, tan camouflage, "Military
Police" on doors and hood, blue windshield and emergency light $3-5
tan, 8h, dark green n camouflage, "Military
Police" on doors and hood, blue windshield and emergency light $3-5

220.6 Tank Rocket Launcher
dark green $3-5
tan, dark green camouflage, black missile
launcher......................................$3-5
dark green, tan camouflage, black missile
launcher...$3-5

220.7 Military Jeep
dark green, CT4s, black roof, white star on
hood $3-5
dark green, 5d, tan camouflage, black interior
and roll bar, no roof $3-5

tan, 5d, dark green camouflage, black interior
and roll bar, no roof $3-5

220.8 Anti-Aircraft Truck
dark green, 4c, tan camouflage, black cannon, white star on door $3-5
dark green, 4c, tan camouflage, black cannon, light gray roof unit....................$3-5
dark green, 4c, tan camouflage, black cannon, dark gray roof unit $3-5
tan, 4c, dark green camouflage, black can-
non $3-5

220.9 6x6 Armored car with Cannon
dark green, 4sc, green cannon, white star on
front...$3-5
dark green, 4cs, green cannon, tan camou-
flage $3-5

220.10 6x6 Armored car Missile Launcher
dark green, 4sc, black missile launcher....$3-5
tan, 4sc, black missile launcher...............$3-5
tan, 4sc, dark green camouflage, black missile
launcher $3-5

220.11 Unimog
dark green, 5d, tan camouflage, blue windshield and roof lights $3-5

220.12 Unimog
tan, 5d, dark green camouflage, blue windshield and roof lights $3-5

220.13 4x4 Command car Jeep, 1998
khaki $3-5

220.14 Ford Econoline Military Police Van, 1999
tan, 6sp, dark green camouflage, "MILITARY
POLICE," black interior, star on door $3-5
dark green, 6sp, tan camouflage, "MILITARY
POLICE," black interior, star on door $3-5

Chevrolet Blazer 4x4 Missile Launcher, 2000
dark green with tan and blue-gray camou-
flage, ct4s $3-5

Chevrolet El Camino with Missile Launcher Trailer,
2000
dark green with tan and blue-gray camouflage, 5pw, green trailer, 5d...........$6-8

Ford Econoline Van with Cannon Trailer, 2000
dark green with tan and blue-gray camouflage, 6sp, green trailer, 5d............$6-8

Ford Econoline Van with Rocket Launcher Trailer,
2000
khaki with light brown and blue-gray camouflage, 6sp, khaki trailer, 5d.............$6-8

Jeep CJ with Missile Launcher Trailer, 2000
khaki with light brown and blue-gray camouflage, ct4s, khaki trailer, 5d $6-8

Jeep Grand Cherokee with Cannon Trailer, 2000
khaki with light brown and blue-gray camouflage, 5d, khaki trailer, 5d $6-8

Jeep Grand Cherokee with Missile Launcher Trailer,
2000

khaki with light brown and blue-gray camouflage, 5d, khaki trailer, 5d $6-8

Long Rocket Launcher Truck, 2000
dark green with tan and blue-gray camouflage, ct4s.................................$6-8

Range Rover, 2000
tan, dark green camouflage, "SPECIAL FORCE" on sides, white star on doors, 5st.........$3-5

Unimog with Cannon Trailer, 2000
dark green with tan and blue-gray camouflage, 5d $6-8

Volvo Explorateur with Missile Launcher Trailer, 2000
dark green with tan and blue-gray camouflage, 5d $6-8

Volvo Explorateur with Rocket Launcher Trailer, 2000
khaki with light brown and blue-gray camouflage, ct3c, khaki trailer, 5d $6-8

900.5 50 piece Special Forces set, 1999 ....$50-60

Majorette 300 Series

While the 300 Series consists mostly of 200 Series vehicles with trailers, it also features buses, stretch limos, and semi-tractor/trailers. Many early sets were called Super Tandems. Since it is possible to mix and match some vehicles and trailers, the values indicated represent models sealed in their original package. Many of the trailers are only available in 300 Series sets and are indicated as such by an asterisk*. Many models were issued in various color combinations and with different markings.

310-A Autobus Saviem Paris Bus, open deck on the back, "CONCORDE," "CHAMPS ELY-SEES," 1:87, 1979–1987
white upper, light green lower, medium amber windows, white interior, decal has dark blue "Salon de Paris" and yellow Arch de Triomphe on a light blue background, 3spb $8-10
white upper, green lower, light amber windows, white interior, decal has dark blue "Salon de Paris" and lemon Arch de Triomphe on a light blue background, 3spb.........$8-10
white upper, green lower, light amber windows, white interior, decal has light blue "Salon de Paris" and orange-yellow Arch de Triomphe on a white background, 3spb $8-10
white upper, green lower, dark amber windows, pale yellow interior, decal has dark blue "Salon de Paris" and yellow Arch de Triomphe on a dark blue background, 4c...$8-10

white upper, light green lower, medium amber windows, white interior, decal has dark blue "Salon de Paris" and yellow Arch de Triomphe on a white background, 3spb $8-10
white upper, light green lower, medium amber windows, white interior, decal has black "Salon de Paris" and yellow Arch de Triomphe on a white background, 3spb...$8-10

310-B Scraper Earth Mover, 1:100, 1993

yellow, black wheels with yellow hubs..$5-7

311-A Snow Top Truck, 242-A and Horse Trailer, 1979–1980
red, yellow canopy, 2 headlights, blue windshield and roof lights, "RODEO" tampo, yellow over red trailer with picture of horse's head on side, 3spb $10-13
red, yellow canopy, 2 headlights, blue windshield and roof lights, "RODEO" tampo, yellow over red trailer with picture of horse's head on side, 3kk............$10-13

311-B Volvo 245 DL Station Wagon, 220-A and Horse Trailer*, 1981 ....$9-12

311-C Simca 1308, 240-A and Horse Trailer*, 1982–1983
metallic bright blue, gray interior, 3spb, 240-A-9; trailer: blue with white canopy, red ramp, horse head on canopy.........$8-10

311-D BMW 733, 256-B and Horse Trailer*, 1984–1986
white; white trailer with khaki trailer cover ..$7-9
burgundy, beige interior, amber windows, no sunroof, "Ligue Rhone Alpes" tampo on hood, 3spb; burgundy trailer with khaki trailer cover, picture of horse's head, 4spn $7-9
white, amber windows, green/orange/yellow horse and horseshoe label on hood, light brown interior, no sunroof, 3spb; green trailer with khaki trailer cover, picture of horse's head, 4spn $7-9

311-E Volvo 760 GLE, 230-B and Horse Trailer*, 1987–1991
metallic dark green, red interior, 8h; metallic dark green trailer with white trailer cover, 1988 ....$5-7
metallic silver car with black and red tampos, red interior, metallic silver trailer with red canopy, horse sticker $5-7

311-F Peugeot 205 GTI Hardtop, 281-A and Horse Trailer*, 1992–1995

red with black trim and interior, black insignia on hood, red horse trailer with white canopy..............................$3-5

311-G Chevrolet Blazer 4x4 Pickup and Horse Trailer*, 1996–1999
red with black and white horse graphics, ct4s, black trailer with white canopy, 1996 catalog $6-8
metallic blue $4-6
black with red "TEXAS" banner on doors, red interior, ct4s, with black trailer, yellow canopy, 1999 catalog $4-6

312-A Fighter Plane Transporter, generic cab with dual exhausts, with or without roof light, 1:100, 1989
blue cab, blue tint windows, black base, 4c; silver trailer, blue and white airplane with red wings, blue tint canopy, 4c $4-6
blue cab, blue tint windows, black base, 4c; silver trailer, white and blue airplane with red wings, blue tint canopy, 4c $4-6
olive drab cab, blue tint windows, black base, 4c; silver trailer, black and white airplane with black wings, blue tint canopy, from *Special Forces* 3-pack, 4c..............$5-7
olive drab cab, blue tint windows, black base, 4c; silver trailer, white and black airplane with black wings, blue tint canopy, from *Special Forces* 3-pack, 4c..............$5-7
blue tractor, silver trailer, blue and white airplane with red wings $4-6

313-A Wrecker and Sedan, 1973–1978
no details available $14-17

313-B Pickup Camper, 209-A, and Sterckeman Caravan, 259-B, 1979–1980
orange pickup camper, white camper with green, yellow and red stripe stickers on sides, 3spb, white trailer with matching green, yellow and red stripe stickers with orange below stripes, 1980 catalog $25-30

313-C Citroën CX, 265-A, and Sterkeman Caravan, 259-B, 1981..........................$20-25

313-D Peugeot 604, 238-A, and Sterkeman Caravan, 259-B, 1982......................$16-20

313-E Camping car Pickup Truck with Fifth Wheel Trailer, pickup is a variation of 278-B, 1992–present
hot pink pick-up with "4x4 Country" on hood, mountain print on sides, white air deflector, 8h; white trailer with pink awning, 8h ..$5-7

247

hot pink with no markings, white trailer.....$5-7

red pick-up, mountain print on hood and sides of cab, black air deflector, 8h; white trailer, rust awning, 8h $5-7

red pick-up, mountain print on hood only, black air deflector, 8h; white trailer, rust awning, 8h $5-7

red pick-up, mountain print on sides only, black air deflector, 8h; white trailer, rust awning, 8h...$5-7

red pick-up, "4x4 COUNTRY" on hood, white mountain and green tree print on sides, black air deflector, 8h; white trailer, rust awning, 8h $5-7

red pick-up, "4x4 COUNTRY" on hood, white mountain and green tree print on sides, black air deflector, 8h; white trailer, green awning, 8h $6-8

lime pick-up, "4x4 COUNTRY" on hood, white mountain and pink tree print on sides, black air deflector, 8h; white trailer, pink awning, 8h...............................$5-7

flourescent pink pick-up, "4x4 COUNTRY" on hood, white mountain and green tree print on sides, black air deflector,8h; white trailer, rust awning, 8h $6-8

red pick-up, dull yellow sun drinking Coke on hood, white "Coca Cola" on sides, black air deflector, 8h; white trailer, dull yellow sun drinking a Coke on sides, rust awning, 8h...$8-10

red pick-up, bright yellow sun drinking Coke on hood, white "Coca Cola" on sides, black air deflector, 8h; white trailer, bright sun drinking a Coke on sides, rust awning, 8h..$8-10

red pick-up, white "Coca Cola" on soccer ball on hood, white "Coca Cola" and white "FOOT-BALL" on sides, black air deflector, 8h; turquoise trailer, white "Coca Cola" on soccer ball on sides, rust awning, 8h $8-10

red pick-up, clown face on hood, yellow "CIRCUS" and stars on sides, black air deflector, 8h; yellow trailer, clown face and "CIRCUS" on sides, rust awning, 8h..$5-7

red pick-up, clown face on hood, yellow "PINDER" and stars on sides, black air deflector, 8h; yellow trailer, clown face and "PINDER" on sides, rust awning, 8h $8-10

314-A Citroën DS21, 213-A, with Boat and Trailer*, 1969–1971

no details available $30-35

314-B Peugeot 204C, 230-A, with Boat and Trailer*, 1972–1973

metallic light blue, white interior, thc, unpainted trailer, bw1, white over red boat with red motor $20-25

314-C Volkswagen 1302, 202-B, with Boat and Trailer, *Hors-Bord*, 1974–1978

red with lightning bolt on trunk with orange and white boat on blue trailer $16-20

red with lightning bolt on trunk with orange and white boat on red trailer........$16-20

314-D Simca 1100 T1, 234-B, with Boat and Trailer*, 1979–1980

black with white "POLICE" decals, 3spb, white boat with white "POLICE" decals....................................$12-15

red, white interior, 3spb; green trailer with white over red boat $10-13

red, white interior, 3spb; silver trailer with white over orange boat $10-13

314-E BMW 733, 256-B, and Boat Trailer, 1981

green, 3spb, with red over yellow boat $8-10

314-F Citroën CX, 265-A, and Boat Trailer, 1982

metallic bright blue, gray interior, 3spb, 265-A 4; trailer: unpainted, red over white boat, 4sp...................................$8-10

314-G Saab 900 Turbo Sedan, 284-A, with Boat and Trailer*, 1983–1988

metallic blue, boat has blue hull and white deck...$8-10

black, yellow windshield, silver "TURBO," 4c; boat has white hull and red deck ...$8-10

black, yellow windshield, silver "TURBO," 4c; unpainted trailer, boat has red hull and white deck...................................$8-10

314-H Honda Accord, 219-D, with Boat and Trailer, 1989–1992

metallic mint green with red interior, boat has red hull, white deck, silver trailer $6-8

314-I Dump Truck, generic cab with dual exhausts, compare to 377-C, 1:100, 1993–1998

olive drab cab, blue tint windows, black base, chrome exhausts, 4c; silver trailer, Special Forces 3-pack, 4c $5-7

red cab, blue tint windows, black base, chrome exhausts, 4c; silver trailer, 4c.............$5-7

yellow cab, blue tint windows, black base, chrome exhausts, 4c; silver trailer, 4c ..$5-7

red cab, blue tint windows, black base, chrome exhausts, 4c; silver trailer, 8h.............$5-7

red cab, blue tint windows, black base, chrome exhausts, 4c; silver trailer, 3kk $5-7

dark blue cab, chrome exhausts; silver trailer, 4c..$5-7

metallic blue cab, blue tint windows, black base, chrome exhausts, 4c; silver trailer, 4c....$5-7

yellow cab, blue tint windows, black base, gray exhausts, 4c; silver trailer, 4c $5-7

314-J Volvo Dump Truck, 1999–present

red cab, opaque windows, black base, 4c; silver trailer, 3kk $4-6

yellow cab, opaque windows, black base, 4c; silver trailer, 4c, ...$4-6

315-A Citroën DS21, 213-A, and Sterckeman Lovely 400 Travel Trailer, 236-A, 1969–1971

no details available $30-35

315-B Mercedes 280SE, 237-A, and Sterckeman Lovely 400 Travel Trailer, 236-A, 1972–1973

no details available $12-15

315-C Volkswagen K70, 210-A, and Sterckeman Lovely 400 Travel Trailer, 236-A, 1974–1976

pink car $20-25

blue car, 3kk $20-25

yellow car, 3kk $20-25

red car, 3kk .....$20-25fluorescent orange car, 3kk $20-25

metallic blue-green car, 3spb; trailer: white, 3spb $20-25

315-D Chrysler 180, 208-B, and Sterckeman Lovely 400 Travel Trailer, 236-A, 1977–1978

no details available $12-15

315-E Volkswagen Golf, 210-B, with Sterckeman Lovely 400 Travel Trailer, 236-A, 1979–1980, no details available $15-18

315-F Western Train, 278-A, and Passenger Coach*, 1:87, 1981

green with red cowcatcher, black wheels; red coach with white roof, black wheels, 1981.......................................$10-13 blue with red cowcatcher, black wheels; red coach with white roof, black wheels, 1986. $10-13,

black with red cowcatcher, blue wheels; red coach with white roof, black wheels, *Sonic Flashers*, 1992 ....$12-15

black with red cowcatcher, blue wheels; red coach with white roof, black wheels, *Sonic Flashers* $12-15

black with red cowcatcher, black wheels; red coach with white roof, blue wheels, *Sonic Flashers* $12-15

black with yellow cowcatcher, black wheels; yellow coach with black roof, black wheels, *Sonic Flashers*, 1992 ....$12-15

315-G Ford Transit Wrecker, 245-E, and Utility Trailer, 1:100, 1997

yellow, "BCR Enterprise," blue and red accents, black bed, yellow interior, white bumpers, 6sp; trailer is yellow with white top $4-6

316-A Farm Tractor, 208-C and Dump Trailer*

dark green tractor with yellow fenders, ft2, yellow trailer with green tailgate, 5d $6-8

dark green tractor with black fenders, ft2, yellow trailer with green tailgate, 5d $6-8

green tractor with black fenders, ft2, yellow trailer, 5d $4-6

light green tractor with black fenders, ft2, green trailer with black tailgate, 5d $4-6

light yellow tractor with bright green fenders, ft2, yellow trailer with unpainted frame, green tailgate, 5d.........................$4-6

light green tractor with black fenders ft2, yellow trailer with green tailgate, 8sp $6-8

red tractor with black fenders, ft2, red trailer with black tailgate, 5d $5-7

red tractor with black fenders, ft2, yellow trailer with black tailgate, 5d $4-6

red tractor with black fenders, ft2, red trailer with green tailgate, 5d $5-7

red tractor with black fenders, ft2, yellow trailer with green tailgate, 5d....................$5-7

317-A Renault R17 TS, 260-A with Alpine F3 Racer, 227-A, and Trailer* 1969–1971

hot pink, 3kk, with aqua racer, metallic yellow-green trailer $15-18

lime green, 3kk, with aqua racer, yellow trailer..................................$15-18

317-B Renault R16, 221-A with Alpine F3 Racer, 227-A, 1969–1972

317-C Volkswagen 1302, 202-E with Alpine F3 Racer* and Trailer*, 1972–1974

red, 3spb with blue racer $12-15

317-D Mercedes-Benz 350SL Convertible, and Race car Trailer, 1:60, 1975–1978

white, red interior, 3spb; blue race car, 4sp; red trailer, 4sp $12-15

317-E Fiat 127, 203-A with Alpine F3 Racer* and Trailer*, 1979–1981

hot pink, 3kk, with aqua racer, "5" on nose, and metallic yellow-green trailer....$12-15

hot pink, 3kk, with aqua racer, "3" on nose, and red trailer..........................$12-15

blue, 3kk, with aqua racer, "3" on nose, and red trailer $12-15

metallic blue, 3kk, with aqua racer, "3" on nose, and yellow trailer...............$12-15

lime green, 3kk, with aqua racer, "4" on nose, and yellow trailer $12-15

red, 3kk with blue racer, red trailer, 4sp...$12-15

orange, white interior, amber windows, 3kk with blue racer, red trailer, 4sp.....$12-15

317-F Volkswagen Golf GTI 16S, 235-E and Kayak Trailer, 1982 ....$12-15

lime green, blue and white accents, 6sp; unpainted trailer, 4spn; red over yellow and yellow over red kayaks $8-10

317-G Fiat Ritmo / Strada, 239-C, and Kayak Trailer, 1983–1985

red with black accents, "ABARTH 2000," 3spb; white over red and red over white kayaks..$6-8

317-H Ford Thunderbird, 217-A and Kayak Trailer*, 1986

red, black trim, 8h, 2 kayaks, yellow and red $5-7

yellow, black interior, clear windshield, 8h, unpainted trailer, 2 kayaks, yellow and red $5-7

317-I Renault 11 Encore, 275-A and Kayak Trailer, 1987–1988

white, red interior, yellow windshield, yellow and black stripes on sides, "25," blue "180 Ch" on hood with yellow and black stripe, 8h; unpainted trailer, 4spn; 2 kayaks, yellow and red $8-10

white, black lower body, red interior, amber windows, amber sunroof, 8h; unknown kayak trailer $8-10

317-J Renault Super Cinq GT Turbo, 205-C and Kayak Trailer*, 1989–1990

blue, pink trim and interior, 6sp, unpainted trailer, 2 kayaks, white and red $5-7

317-K Ford Econoline Van with Covered Trailer, 1999

yellow with "ENTERPRISE" and diagonal red stripes along side, ladder and pipe on

roof, 6sp, orange trailer with yellow canopy, 1999 catalog $4-6

318-A Jeep 4x4, 290-A and F1 Racer, 238-B, 1986

green, yellow roof, red interior, red/yellow/ orange tampo on hood, 5d, white race car, yellow driver $8-10

black, no roof, red interior, 5d, green race car, "Benetton"...............................$4-6

black, no roof, red interior, 5d, yellow race car, "Tictel," "12," rw $4-6

black, no roof, red interior, 5d, blue race car, "Rallye," "12," rw......................$4-6

black, beige roof, yellow racer, 1995 ....$4-6

yellow, no roof, green racer, 1993 ....$4-6

319-A Mercedes Car Transporter, 1:100, 1980–1986

red cab, clear windows, black base, 3kk; red lower trailer, yellow upper trailer, 2 silver plastic cars, 3kk $8-10

red cab, 3spb; red lower trailer, yellow upper trailer, 2 silver plastic cars, 3kk $8-10

orange cab, clear windows, black base, 3kk, orange lower trailer, yellow upper trailer, 2 silver plastic cars, 3kk $8-10

yellow cab, 3kk; red lower trailer, yellow upper trailer, 2 silver plastic cars, 3kk...$8-10

light blue cab, clear windows, black base, 3kk; light blue lower trailer, yellow upper trailer, 2 red plastic cars, 3spb.......$8-10

light blue cab, clear windows, black base, 3kk; light blue lower trailer, yellow upper trailer, 2 red plastic cars, 3kk $8-10

light blue cab, 3kk, light blue lower trailer, yellow upper trailer, 2 red plastic cars, 3kk....$8-10

light blue cab, clear windows, black base, 3kk/3spb; light blue lower trailer, yellow upper trailer, 2 red plastic cars, 3spb $8-10

white cab, clear windows, black base, 3kk; red lower trailer, yellow upper trailer, 2 silver plastic cars, 3kk $8-10

319-B Magirus Car Transporter, 1:100, 1981–1982

red cab, amber windows, black base, 3kk; red lower trailer, yellow upper trailer, 2 silver plastic cars, 3kk $8-10

red cab, amber windows, black base, 3spb; blue lower trailer, yellow upper trailer, 2 silver plastic cars, 3kk ....$8-10 orange cab, amber windows, black base, 3kk; orange lower trailer, yellow upper trailer, 2 silver plastic cars, 3kk $8-10

319-C car Transporter, generic cab with dual exhausts, 1:100, 1983–1986

orange cab, amber windows, black base, chrome exhausts, 4c; orange lower trailer, yellow upper trailer, 2 silver plastic cars, 3kk $8-10

319-D Scania car Transporter, 1:100, early 1980s

white cab, clear windows, black base, 3spb; light blue lower trailer, yellow upper trailer, 2 red plastic cars, 3kk, not confirmed that this was originally packaged this way............................$8-10

319-E Extending Ladder Fire Engine, 1:86, 1990

red body, blue windows, black base, "F.D.N.Y. 55," label, chrome trim and grille, light gray ladder, 6sp $6-8

red body, blue windows, black base, "F.D.N.Y. 55," label, chrome trim and grille, white ladder, 6sp $6-8

red body, blue windows, black base, "F.D.N.Y. 55," tampo, chrome trim and grille, dark gray ladder, 6sp $4-6

red body, blue windows, black base, "F.D.N.Y. 55," tampo, white plastic trim and grille, dark gray ladder, 6sp $4-6

320-A Bernard Semi Log Trailer *Fardier*, with 3 logs, 1:100, 1969–1973—These models have the early Bernard cab with a wraparound bumper that is cast as part of the base.

red cab, chrome grille, clear windows, silver-gray base, bw3/bw1; red trailer, "bark" logs, metal chain link ties, bw1 ....$16-20

orange cab, chrome grille, clear windows, silver-gray base, bw3 /bw1; red trailer, "bark" logs, metal chain link ties, bw1.......$16-20

pale blue cab, chrome grille, clear windows, silver-gray base, bw3 /bw1; light blue trailer, "bark" logs, metal chain link ties, bw1...$16-20

320-B Bernard Semi Log Trailer *Fardier*, with 3 logs, 1:100, 1973–1976—These models have the current Bernard cab with the bumper cast as part of the cab

red cab, chrome grille, clear windows, gray base, bw5; green trailer, natural color logs, yellow plastic ties, bw5 ....$8-10

red cab, chrome grille, clear windows, gray base, bw5; blue trailer, natural color logs, yellow plastic ties, bw5 ....$8-10

lime cab, chrome grille, clear windows, gray base, bw5; red trailer, natural color logs, yellow plastic ties, bw5 ....$8-10

bright green cab, chrome grille, clear windows, gray base, bw5; blue trailer, natural color logs, yellow plastic ties, bw5...$8-10

yellow cab with silver painted trim on chassis, chrome grille, clear windows, black base, bw5; yellow trailer, natural color logs, yellow plastic ties, bw5...................$15-18

lime cab, chrome grille, clear windows, gray base, bw5; blue trailer, natural color logs, yellow plastic ties, bw5 ....$8-10

yellow cab, chrome grille, clear windows, gray base, 3kk/5sp; unpainted trailer, natural color logs, yellow plastic ties, 3kk.....$8-10

yellow cab, chrome grille, clear windows, gray base, 3kk; unpainted trailer, natural color logs, yellow plastic ties, 3kk............$8-10

320-C Scania Semi Log Trailer, with 3 logs, 1:100, 1976–1979

dark green cab, clear windows, black base, unpainted trailer, natural color logs, red and white striped paper ties, 3kk $10-13

metallic blue cab, clear windows, white base, 3kk; unpainted trailer, natural color logs, yellow plastic ties, 5sp $8-10

blue cab, clear windows, white base, 3kk; unpainted trailer, natural color logs, yellow plastic ties, 3kk $8-10

yellow cab, clear windows, black base, 3kk; unpainted trailer, natural color logs, yellow plastic ties, bw1 ....$8-10

red cab, clear windows, white base, 3kk; unpainted trailer, natural color logs, yellow plastic ties, 3kk $8-10

yellow cab, clear windows, black base, 3kk; unpainted trailer, natural color logs, yellow plastic ties, 3spb $8-10

320-D Fiat 127, 203-B and Glider Trailer, 1973–1976

green, white interior, clear windshield, 3spb; unpainted trailer, orange glider, no cover...................................$10-13

320-E Volkswagen Rabbit 210-B and Glider Trailer*, 1982–1985

210-B 1, red with yellow "GOLF," 3spb and glider trailer, white glider, yellow trailer.........$6-8

210-B 1, red with yellow "GOLF," 3spb and glider trailer, white glider, blue wings, red trailer $6-8

210-B 5, silver, 3spb and glider trailer $6-8

320-F Alfa Romeo, 271-A and Glider Trailer*, 1986

no details available...............................$6-8

320-G Toyota Tercel, 273-A and Glider Trailer*, 1987–1990

metallic blue car, black interior, clear windshield, silver "4WD" and stripe, 6sp; blue trailer, red glider with white wings, yellow cover..$6-8

red car..$6-8

orange car, black interior, clear windshield, black "4WD" and stripe, 6sp; blue trailer, red glider with white wings, yellow cover..$6-8

orange car, black interior, clear windshield, black "4WD" and stripe, 6sp; black trailer, red glider with white wings, yellow cover..$6-8

320-H Renault 25, 222-B and Glider Trailer, 1987–1991

pale metallic green, dark gray interior, 8h; black trailer, red glider with white wings, yellow cover $6-8

pearl blue, black interior, clear windows, 8h; black trailer, red glider with yellow wings, amber cover $6-8

320-I Mercedes 300 TE, 250-C and Glider Trailer*, 1991, no details available....................$4-6

320-J El Camino and Glider Trailer*, 1991–1993

hot pink pickup $3-5

bright green pickup................................$3-5

white, red interior, clear windshield, red and blue accents, "American Off Road," 8hbl, blue wheels $3-5

320-K GMC Jimmy and Glider Trailer*, 1995

blue, 5d, 1995 catalog........................$5-7

321-A Mercedes Covered Utility Truck and Utility Trailer, 1:100, 1981–1986, see 233-A

metallic light blue, blue windows, white canopy with road works signs on sides, 3kk; matching blue trailer with 3 small windows and white top, 4spn...............$4-6

metallic dark blue, blue windows, white canopy with road works signs on sides, 3kk; matching blue trailer with 3 small windows and white top, 4spn.......$4-6

light green, light blue windows, white canopy, 3spb; matching light green trailer with 3 small windows and white top, 4spn...$4-6

orange with white tow bar, yellow canopy with "works" stickers, blue windows, 3kk; matching orange trailer with 3 small windows and yellow top, 4spn $4-6

321-B Semi Power Boat Transporter, generic cab with dual exhausts, 1:100, 1989–present

red cab, chrome exhausts, blue tint windows, black base, 4c; silver trailer, 8p; boat – white cabin, red hull, opaque windows.........$4-6

red cab, chrome exhausts, blue tint windows, black base, 4c; silver trailer, 8p; boat – white cabin, red hull, blue tint windows.........$4-6

red cab, chrome exhausts, blue tint windows, black base, 4c; silver trailer, 8p; boat – yellow cabin, black hull, blue tint windows $4-6

red cab, chrome exhausts, blue tint windows, black base, 4c; silver trailer, 8p; boat – black cabin, yellow hull, blue tint windows $4-6

red cab, chrome exhausts, blue tint windows, black base, 4c; silver trailer, 8p; boat—red cabin, white hull, opaque windows $4-6

red cab, chrome exhausts, blue tint windows, black base, 4c; silver trailer, 8p; boat—red cabin, white hull, blue tint windows $4-6

red cab, gray exhausts, blue tint windows, black base, 4c; silver trailer, 8p; boat—red cabin, red hull, blue tint windows $4-6

red cab, chrome exhausts, blue tint windows, black base, 4c; silver trailer, 8p; boat – purple cabin, yellow hull, blue tint windows.............$7-9

red cab, gray exhausts, blue tint windows, black base, 4c; silver trailer, 8p; boat—red cabin, yellow hull, blue tint windows, 2000 ....$4-6

red cab, chrome exhausts, blue tint windows, black base, 4c; silver trailer, 8p; boat – white cabin with "Coca Cola" and sun design, light blue hull, blue tint windows $8-10

yellow cab, chrome exhausts, dark blue windows, black base, 4c; silver trailer, 4spn; boat – red cabin, white hull, opaque windows...............................$6-8

light blue cab, gray exhausts, blue tint windows, black base, 4c; silver trailer, 8p; boat—black cabin, yellow hull, blue tint windows......................................$4-6

olive drab cab, gray exhausts, blue tint windows, black base, 4c; silver trailer, 8p; boat—black cabin, yellow hull, blue tint windows, *Special Forces 3-pack* $5-7

olive drab cab, gray exhausts, blue tint windows, black base, 4c; silver trailer, 8p; boat—yellow cabin, black hull, blue tint windows, *Special Forces 3-pack* $5-7

olive drab cab, gray exhausts, blue tint windows, black base, 4c; silver trailer, 8p; boat—black cabin, olive drab hull, blue tint windows $6-8

hot pink generic cab, chrome exhausts, blue tint windows, black base, 4c; silver trailer, 8p; boat – black cabin, yellow hull, blue tint windows, ...$7-9

blue cab, gray exhausts, blue tint windows, black base, 4c; silver trailer, 8p; boat—red cabin, red hull, blue tint windows, 2000...................................$4-6

321-C Magirus Semi Sloop Transporter, 1:100

red cab, silver trailer, 4kk, boat: white deck, yellow hull, yellow mast, 4kk $6-8

322-A Bernard Semi Low Loader Trailer, 1:100, 1968–1972—These models have the early Bernard cab with a wrap-around bumper that is cast as part of the base.

yellow cab, chrome grille, clear windows, silver-gray base, bw3/ bw4; yellow trailer, light gray tailgate, 2 axles each with 3 sets of 2 thin black wheels $18

red cab, chrome grille, clear windows, silver-gray base, bw3/bw1; red trailer, dark gray tailgate, 2 axles each with 3 sets of 2 thin black wheels $18

light blue cab, chrome grille, clear windows, silver-gray base, bw3/bw1; light blue trailer, dark gray tailgate, 2 axles each with 3 sets of 2 thin black wheels $18

322-B Bernard Semi Low Loader with Crane *Surbaisse*, 1:100, 1973–1976—These models have the current Bernard cab with the bumper cast as part of the cab.

orange cab, chrome grille, clear windows, gray base, bw1; red trailer, black crane with chrome hook, light gray tailgate, 2 axles each with 2 sets of 2 thin black wheels.....................................$16-20

yellow cab, chrome grille, clear windows, gray base, bw1; yellow trailer, black crane with chrome hook, light gray tailgate, 2 axles each with 2 sets of 2 thin black wheels $16-20

yellow cab, chrome grille, clear windows, gray base, bw1; red trailer, black crane with chrome hook, light gray tailgate, 2 axles each with 2 sets of 2 thin black wheels.....................................$16-20

blue cab, chrome grille, clear windows, gray base, 3kk/ 3spb; blue trailer, black crane with chrome hook, no tailgate, 2 axles each with 3kk wheels $16-20

blue cab, chrome grille, clear windows, gray base, 3kk; red trailer, black crane with chrome hook, no tailgate, 2 axles each with 3kk wheels $16-20

metallic aqua cab, chrome grille, clear windows, gray base, bw1; yellow trailer, black crane with chrome hook, light gray tailgate, 2 axles each with 3 sets of 2 thin black wheels $16-20

blue cab, chrome grille, clear windows, gray base, bw1; red trailer, black crane with chrome hook, no tailgate, 2 axles each with 2 wide black wheels.............$16-20

yellow cab, gray base, 3kk; red trailer, black crane, 3kk, no other information available..$16-20

blue cab, chrome grille, clear windows, gray base, 3kk; red trailer, black crane with chrome hook, no tailgate, 2 axles each with 3kk wheels $16-20

orange cab, chrome grille, clear windows, gray base, bw1; metallic red trailer, black crane with chrome hook, light gray tailgate, 2 axles each with 2 sets of 2 thin black wheels – This metallic red trailer is noticeably different from the trailer in 322-B–1. ....$16-20

322-C Dauphin 2SA365 Helicopter, 1:87, 1988

Coast Guard, label, white body, red undercarriage, blue canopy, black interior and rotor blades, red rear stabilizers $6-8

Police, tampo, white body, blue undercarriage, blue canopy, black interior and rotor blades, blue rear stabilizers.......$4-6

323-A Renault R16 and Glider Trailer*, 1969–1972

red, red interior, unpainted hubs, unpainted trailer, black wheels, red glider with white wings $15-18

323-B *Planeur* Fiat 127, 203-B, and Glider Trailer*, with orange and white "Wasmer 26 Squale" glider, 1973–1976

metallic yellow-green with orange trailer.......................................$12-15

metallic yellow-green with yellow trailer ...$12-15

red with orange trailer.......................$12-15

lime green with metallic yellow-green trailer $12-15

blue with metallic yellow-green trailer.....$12-15

323-C Tractor, 208-C and Livestock Trailer*, 1982–1985

red tractor with black fenders, light gray seat and steering wheel, red trailer with black bull...$6-8

light yellow tractor with green fenders, black interior, green trailer with yellow tailgate, white bull, 8sp $4-6

light yellow tractor with green fenders, black interior, brown trailer with yellow tailgate, white bull, 8sp $4-6

323-D Toyota Hi-Lux Pickup, 287-A, and Livestock Trailer*, 1986

red truck with "Gladiator" tampos, yellow trailer..$3-5

orange truck, black interior, silver and black stripe on side, yellow, black and silver tampo on hood, 5d, orange trailer, white bull.......................................$6-8

pink truck with "Gladiator" tampos, yellow trailer.......................$3-5

yellow truck with "Western" tampos, red trailer.......................$3-5

green, yellow, and red tampo, "Night Hawk" on doors and hood, 5d, blue trailer, white bull, ct4sp.......................$3-5

blue truck, yellow and red tampo, "Night Hawk" on doors and hood, 5d, blue trailer, white bull, ct4sp.......................$3-5

blue truck with no markings, 5d, yellow trailer, ctsc.......................$3-5

blue, 5d, 287-A 5 with yellow trailer.......$3-5

blue truck, yellow and red tampo, "Night Hawk" on doors and hood, 5d, orange trailer, white bull, ct4sp.......................$3-5

324-A Bernard Semi Open Trailer Gondola Truck *Maraicher*, 1:100, 1968–1971—These models have the early Bernard cab with a wrap-around bumper that is cast as part of the base.

orange cab, clear windows, silver-gray base, bw3/bw1; orange open trailer, silver-gray insert, silver-gray base, bw1 .$15-18

gray cab, clear windows, silver-gray base, bw3/bw1; orange open trailer, silver-gray insert, silver-gray base, bw1 .$15-18

blue cab, clear windows, silver-gray base, bw3/bw1; orange open trailer, silver-gray insert, silver-gray base, bw1 .$15-18

red cab, clear windows, silver-gray base, bw3/bw1; orange open trailer, gray insert, blue base, bw1 ....$15-18

red cab, clear windows, gray base, bw5; blue open trailer, yellow base, bw5 .....$15-18

324-B Bernard Semi Open Trailer, Gondola Truck *Maraicher*, 1:100, 1972–1976—These models have the current Bernard cab with the bumper cast as part of the cab.

red cab, clear windows, gray base, bw5; blue open trailer, unpainted base, bw5 ....$12-15

red cab, clear windows, gray base, bw5; blue open trailer, red base, bw5.........$12-15

red cab, clear windows, gray base, red open trailer, red base, bw1? $12-15

yellow cab, clear windows, gray base, bw5; red open trailer, orange base, bw5 ......$12-15

metallic green cab, clear windows, bw5; gray base, blue open trailer, neon green base, bw5..........................$12-15

red cab, clear windows, gray base, 3kk; red open trailer, red base, 3kk $12-15

red cab, clear windows, gray base, 3kk; red open trailer, unpainted base, 3kk ...$12-15

metallic blue cab, clear windows, gray base, 3kk; red open trailer, unpainted base, 3kk $12-15

yellow cab, clear windows, gray base, 3kk; red open trailer, unpainted base, 3kk..........................$12-15

red cab, clear windows, gray base, 3kk; blue open trailer, unpainted base, 3kk....$12-15

metallic blue cab, clear windows, gray base, 3kk/3spb; blue open trailer, red base, 5sp..........................$12-15

324-C Magirus Semi Open Trailer, Gondola Truck *Maraicher*, 1:100, 1977–1978

red cab, amber windows, gray base, 3kk; blue open trailer, unpainted base, 3kk...$12-15

metallic blue cab, amber windows, gray base, 3kk; red open trailer, unpainted base, 3kk..........................$12-15

324-D Scania Semi Open Trailer, Gondola Truck *Maraicher*, 1:100, 1977–1978

metallic blue cab, clear windows, white base, 3kk; blue open trailer, orange base, 3kk..........................$12-15

metallic blue cab, white base, 3kk, red open trailer, unpainted base, 3spb $12-15

metallic blue cab, white base, 3kk; red open trailer, unpainted base, 3kk $12-15

324-E Mercedes Semi Open Trailer Gondola Truck *Maraicher*, 1:100, 1979

red cab, clear windows, black base, 3kk; red open trailer with silver trim, unpainted base, 3kk $12-15

324-F Magirus Pressurized Tanker *Citerne*, 1:100, 1983

blue cab, black base, white upper tank body, blue tank cover, blue tank base, "L'AIR LIQUIDE," 3kk, 4c.......................$6-8

324-G Pressurized Tanker *Citerne*, generic cab with dual exhausts, 1:100, 1983–1988

medium blue cab, clear windows, black base, 3spn; white upper tank body, blue tank cover, blue tank base, "L'AIR LIQUIDE," 4c......$6-8

light blue cab, clear windows, black base, 4c; white upper tank body, blue tank cover, blue tank base, "L'AIR LIQUIDE," 4c ..$6-8

324-H Volvo Pressurized Tanker *Citerne*, 1:100, 1989–1998

white cab, opaque windows, yellow tank trailer with white upper, "SHELL," 4c ...$5-7

324-I Renault Kangoo with Boat and Trailer, 1999

blue, 6sp, boat has white hull, red deck and motor, 4sp $4-6

325-A Peugeot 404, 206-A and Horse Trailer*, 1969–1971, no details available $25-30

325-B Simca 1100 T1, 234-B with Travel Trailer, 1976–1978

blue, white interior, 3spb; white trailer with surf graphics $10-13

325-C Peugeot 604, 238-A with Travel Trailer, 1983 ....$8-10

325-D Mercedes-Benz 450SE, 249-A and Travel Trailer*, 1984–1985

bronze, yellow interior, clear windshield, 3kk; beige over bronze trailer with yellow interior, amber windows, 4c..................$6-9

325-E Ford Sierra, 272-A and Travel Trailer*, 1986–1990

blue, white interior, amber windshield, silver tampos, "SIERRA," 8h; white over blue trailer, red interior, amber windows, cream door, 4c $4-6

white, red interior, amber windshield, blue tampos, "SIERRA," 8h; white over blue trailer, red interior, amber windows, cream door, 4c....................$4-6

325-F Ford Mustang GT Convertible, 227-C and Travel Trailer*, 1991–1994

yellow lower, white upper on trailer, yellow Mustang $4-6

red lower, white upper on trailer, metallic blue Mustang $4-6

325-G Volkswagen Golf and Travel Trailer*, 1996

blue Golf, 4c, with matching blue and white trailer $4-6

325-H Chevrolet El Camino Pickup, 296-A and Travel Trailer*

red lower, white upper on trailer, red pickup with white interior $4-6

325-I Alfa 75, 271-A with Travel Trailer

red, white interior, clear windshield, 8h; white

over dark blue trailer, red interior, amber windows, cream door, 4c $8-10

325-J Volkswagen Golf, 264-C with Travel Trailer
blue, green base and bumpers, yellow interior, clear windows, "25," "RACING," rally tampos, 8h; white over dark blue trailer, 4c $6-8

326-A Western Stagecoach drawn by three horses, 1:80, 1983–1986

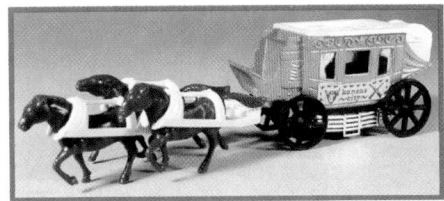

metallic gold-brown with cream plastic top and harness, yellow "Kansas City" label, brown plastic horses $16-20

green with red plastic top and harness, yellow "kansas city" label, black plastic horses $16-20

326-B Mercedes-Benz Stretch Limo, 1:58, 1991
metallic teal, amber windows, chrome grille, steering wheel and dual rear antennae, black base, 6sp $3-5
metallic teal, amber windows, chrome grille, steering wheel and dual rear antennae, gray base, 6sp $3-5
metallic silver, amber windows, chrome grille, steering wheel and dual rear antennae, gray base, 6sp $3-5
blue, light amber tint windows, chrome grille, steering wheel and dual rear antennae, gray base, 6sp $3-5
white, opaque black windows, gray plastic grille, steering wheel and dual rear antennae, gray base, 6sp $5-7
red, clear windows, gray plastic grille, steering wheel and dual rear antennae, gray base, "Coca Cola," 6sp $6-8
red, light blue tint windows, gray plastic grille, steering wheel and dual rear antennae, gray base, "Wild Cherry PEPSI," 6sp $5-7

327-A Ford Double Tanker, 245-C with Tanker Trailer*, narrow side windows 1:100, 1985–The same printing appears on the canopy of both the cab and the trailer.
"Milky the good milk," pale blue cab and bed, amber windows, gray interior, black + gray base, white tank, 3spn; trailer: white tank; pale blue bed, 4c $8-10
"Milky the good milk," pale blue cab and bed, clear windows, gray interior, black + gray base, white tank, 3spn; trailer: white tank; pale blue bed, 4c $8-10

"Milky the good milk," pale blue cab and bed, clear windows, gray interior, black + gray base, white tank, 4c; trailer: white tank; pale blue bed, 4c $8-10
"Milky the good milk," pale blue cab and bed, clear windows, black base, white tank, 4c; trailer: white tank; pale blue bed, 4c $8-10
"Shell," yellow cab and bed, clear windows, black base, white tank, 4c; trailer: white tank, yellow bed, 4c $6-8

327-B Ford Tanker with Tanker Trailer*, 1:100, 1992, 245-D, no long narrow side windows on cab—The same printing appears on the canopy of both the cab and the trailer.
"Esso," tampo, white cab, bed, and tank, clear windows, black base, 4c; trailer: white tank and bed, 4c $6-8
"PETROL COMPANY," tampo, yellow cab and bed, clear windows, black base, white tank, 4c; trailer: white tank; yellow bed, 4c $4-6
"Shell," tampo, yellow cab and bed, clear windows, black base, white tank, 4c; trailer: white tank, yellow bed, 4c $4-6
"GT Gas Tanker," tampo, orange cab and bed, clear windows, black base, gray tank, 4c; trailer: gray tank, orange bed, 4c $4-6
Star "20420653," tampo, sand cab, bed, and tank, clear windows, black base, 4c; trailer: sand tank and bed, 4c $8-10
Cartoon cow, milk, and grass, tampo, pale blue cab and bed, white tank, clear windows, black base, 4c; trailer: white tank and bed, 4c, 2000 .... $3-5
"GT Gas Tanker," tampo, red cab and bed, clear windows, black base, gray tank, 4c; trailer: gray tank, red bed, 4c, 2000 .... $4-6

328-A Chrysler 180, 208-A and Sailboat Trailer* $12-15

328-B Toyota Safari Landcruiser, 277-A and Lion Cage Trailer*, 1987–1993
green, amber windows, blue "AFRICAN SAFARI" and black lion face on roof and sides, yellow hatch, ctsc; trailer: dark green cage on green trailer, 4spn, brown lion $8-10
green, amber windows, blue "AFRICAN SAFARI" and black lion face on roof and sides, yellow hatch, ctsc; trailer: black cage on green trailer, 4spn, brown lion $8-10
cream, amber windows, blue "AFRICAN SAFARI" and black lion face on roof and sides, yellow hatch, ctsc; trailer: dark

green cage on cream trailer, 4spn, brown lion $8-10
cream, amber windows, blue "AFRICAN SAFARI" and black lion face on roof and sides, yellow hatch, ctsc; trailer: medium green cage on cream trailer, 4spn, brown lion $8-10
cream, amber windows, red "AFRICAN SAFARI" and green lion face on roof and sides, yellow hatch, ctsc; trailer: medium green cage on cream trailer, 4spn, brown lion $8-10

328-C Land Rover, 266-B with Lion Cage Trailer*, 1994 to present
black with white and green accents, dark butterscotch interior and roof rack, 8d, bright green trailer with yellow cage, dark butterscotch lion $6-8
yellow, "CIRCUS" graphics on sides, red roof rack and rear door, 5d, yellow trailer with red cage, brown lion, 4spn, Special "CIRCUS" packaging $5-7
white, "Safari" and "4x4" on hood, 5d, green trailer with yellow cage, brown lion, 4spn $4-6
pale yellow, black roof rack and interior, clear windows, tropical scene with 'Safari,' 5st; pale yellow trailer with gray cage, brown lion, 8p, 2000 .... $4-6

white with black and white zebra stripes, 8d, white trailer with black cage, brown lion $6-8

329-A Space Craft Shuttle Transporter, 1:100, 1987–1994
white transporter and shuttle, "space 3000" label on cab, "space shuttle 3000" label on shuttle, cab has clear windows, 6sp $7-9
white transporter and shuttle, "space 3000" label on cab, "space shuttle 3000" label on shuttle, cab has opaque windows, 5d $6-8
white transporter and shuttle, "space 3000" tampo on cab, "3000" tampo on sides of transporter, "space shuttle 3000" label on shuttle, cab has opaque windows, 5d $5-7
silver-gray transporter and white shuttle, red "ESPACE 2000" and planets tampo on

cab, red "050370" tampo on sides of transporter, "ESPACE 2000" and planets label on shuttle, cab has opaque windows, 5st, 2000 ....$4-6

330 not issued

331-A Peugeot 204, 230-A, and Kayak Trailer*, 1969–1973

turquoise, black interior, gray hub with black tire; trailer: 2 kayaks, orange over white and white over orange, gray hub, black tire $12-15

red, black interior, thc5; trailer: 2 kayaks, red over white and white over red, gray hub, black tire..$12-15

331-B Fiat 127, 203-B and Kayak Trailer*, 1974–1978?

yellow, white interior, amber windows, 3spb; trailer: 2 kayaks, white over red and red over white, unpainted trailer, 4sp..$12-15

331-C Volkswagen 1302, 202-A, and Kayak Trailer*, 1974–1978?

pink, lightning bolt on hood, 3kk; trailer: blue, bw1, 2 kayaks, white over red and red over white $25-30

331-D Volkswagen 1302, 202-B, and Kayak Trailer*

red with lighting bolt on trunk, 3kk, orange and white kayaks on metallic yellow-green trailer $16-20

red with flower on trunk, 3kk, orange and white kayaks on red trailer $16-20

metallic blue, 3kk, orange and white kayaks on unpainted metal trailer $16-20

red with lighting bolt on trunk, 3kk, orange and white kayaks on red trailer.....$16-20

red with flower on trunk, 3kk, orange and white kayaks on metallic yellow-green trailer...................................$16-20

331-E Road Grader Leveling Scraper, 1:100, 1994

yellow body, gray plastic blades, large 3kk..$8-10

sand body, gray plastic blades, large 3kk...$10-13

332 not issued

333-A Simca, 240-A and Motorcycle Trailer*

metallic blue car, 3spb, with white trailer, red and yellow motorcycles $4-6

333-B Ford Transit TUG, 295-A, and Motorcycle Trailer*

fluorescent orange with "RACING SERVICE," 6sp; black trailer, yellow and green motorcycles.............................$4-6

fluorescent orange, yellow windshield, white interior and bumpers, "RACING,"

black bed, 6sp; black trailer, yellow and green motorcycles................$4-6

fluorescent orange, yellow windshield, white interior and bumpers, "RACING SERVICE," yellow, green, and black label of motorcycle silhouette on roof, black bed, 6sp; black trailer, yellow and green motorcycles.................$4-6

333-C GMC Jimmy, 249-D and Motorcycle Trailer* $4-6

334-A Ford 5000 Farm Tractor, 253-A and Log Trailer, carrying a real "log," 1970s

blue tractor with white fenders, ft4 white hubs, red trailer $16-20

blue tractor with white fenders, ft4 white hubs, blue trailer................................$16-20

metallic bright blue tractor with white fenders, black ft3 wheels, metallic bright blue trailer $16-20

334-B Tractor and Log Trailer, 1994

green tractor with black and yellow trailer....$8-10

335-A Toyota 4-Runner, 276-A, and Moto Trailer with motorcycle, 1995

red with black stripe on sides, gray interior, no graphics, 5d; unpainted trailer, red plastic motorcycle, 8p........................$4-6

pale yellow, black interior, "Moto Racing" graphics, 5d; unpainted trailer, blue plastic motorcycle, 8p..........................$4-6

same as 2., 5st, 2000 ....$4-6

metallic red with black stripe on sides, black interior, 5d; black trailer, blue plastic motorcycle, 8p, 1995 catalog.........$6-8

336-A El Camino and Bicycle Trailer with two bicycles, 1995

blue with white interior, "EL CAMINO" on sides, 8d; black trailer, pink and blue plastic bikes, 8p, 1995 catalog $8-10

336-B Mercedes 300 TE and Bicycle Trailer with two bicycles, 1997

green with dark gray interior and lower body, 6sp; unpainted trailer, 2 red bicycles, 8p, 1999 catalog................................$6-8

337 not issued

338-A DAF 2600 Crane Truck with Sloop Trailer, 1971

metallic yellow, black crane, bw1; trailer: blue, bw1; boat: white hull, green deck $15-18

metallic yellow, black crane, bw1; trailer: metallic yellow, bw1; boat: white hull, blue deck.......................................$15-18

red, black crane; trailer: red, bw1; boat: red hull, white deck.........................$15-18

338-B Mercedes 280SE and Sloop Trailer*, 1970–1972

pink, amber windows, white interior, thc; red trailer, black wheels, white over blue boat, blue mast $12-15

338-C Chrysler 180, #208-B and Sloop Trailer*, 1972–1977

metallic green car, white interior, amber windows, 3spb; unpainted trailer, bw1, blue and white boat.........$10-13

338-D Volkswagen Golf GTI, 235-E and Sloop Trailer*, 1979–1981

green with blue and white graphics, Volkswagen logo, 6sp, boat has orange hull, white deck, silver trailer $4-6

green with orange and white rally graphics, 6sp, boat has orange hull, white deck, silver trailer $4-6

green with blue and white graphics, Volkswagen logo, 6sp, silver trailer, boat has white hull, orange deck...........$4-6

blue, 3spb; silver trailer, 4sp, boat with blue hull, yellow deck $4-6

338-E BMW 733, 256-B and Sloop Trailer, 1982

silver, 3kk, 8; trailer: unpainted, boat is blue over yellow $8-10

338-F Oldsmobile Omega, 253-B and Sloop Trailer, 1983–1984

metallic blue, white interior, amber windows, 3spn, boat is yellow over blue..$8-10

338-G Honda Accord, 219-B and Sloop Trailer*, 1985–1988

yellow with blue accents, red interior, boat has yellow hull, light blue deck, silver trailer $6-8

338-H Volkswagen Golf GTI, 264-C and Sloop Trailer*, 1989–1994
   metalflake blue, 8h $4-6
   metallic silver, 8h, orange over white sailboat, 8p $4-6
338-I Ford Mustang GT Convertible, 227-C and Sloop Trailer
   yellow, black interior, "Official Pace Car," 6sp, trailer: unpainted, boat is orange over white $4-6
338-J Blazer and Sloop Trailer*, 1995–present
   blue, 5d; unpainted trailer, 8p; boat has orange hull, white deck $4-6
339-A Cadillac Stretch Limo, 1:58, 1987–1995
   black, amber windows, unpainted metal grille and base, white plastic interior and boomerang rear antenna, "Made in France," 5d $3-5
   white, amber windows, unpainted metal grille and base, white plastic interior and boomerang rear antenna, "Made in France," 5d $3-5
   white, amber windows, unpainted metal grille and base, white plastic interior and boomerang rear antenna, "Made in France" deleted from baseplate, "Made in Thailand," 5d $3-5
   metallic gray, amber windows, unpainted metal grille and base, white plastic interior and boomerang rear antenna, "Made in France," 8sp $10-13
   metallic gray, amber windows, unpainted metal grille and base, white plastic interior and boomerang rear antenna, "Made in France," 5d $3-5
   metallic blue, amber windows, unpainted metal grille and base, white plastic interior and boomerang rear antenna, "Made in France" deleted from baseplate, "Made in Thailand," 5d $3-5
   purple, amber windows, unpainted metal grille and base, white plastic interior and boomerang rear antenna, 5d $6-8
   two-tone white/steel blue, amber windows, unpainted metal grille and base, white plastic interior and boomerang rear antenna, 5d $6-8

340-A Peugeot 504, 239-A and House Trailer, 236-A, 1970–1972 ....$15-18
340-B Chrysler 180, 208-A and House Trailer, 236-A, 1974–1977 ....$16-20
340-C BMW 3.0 CSI and Digue Baronette GT Travel Trailer, 1974–1977
   metallic red car, yellow windshield, 3kk; white trailer with light blue windows, 5sp $16-20
   metallic red car, clear windshield, 3spb; white trailer with light blue windows, 3spb $16-20
   metallic green, white interior, 3spb; white trailer with light blue windows, 3kk $16-20

yellow, white interior, 3kk; white trailer with light blue windows, 3kk.......................$16-20

340-D Volvo Semi Container Truck, 1:100, 1990—Trailer roof and rear door colors are specified only if they are different from that of the trailer's main body color.
   red cab, opaque windows, black base, 4c; red trailer, "CHALLENGE COMPANY," label, 4c.....................................$4-6
   red cab, opaque windows, black base, 4c; yellow trailer with red rear doors, "HOLLY-WOOD," label, 4c.......................$4-6
   red cab, white "Coca Cola," tampo, opaque windows, black base, 4c; white trailer, "Coca Cola" polar bear scene, label, 4c.............................$8-10
   purple cab, opaque windows, black base, 4c; purple trailer, "Cadbury"s DAIRY MILK Buttons," label, 4c......................$10-13
   yellow cab, opaque windows, black base, 4c; red trailer, "Cadbury's Creme Eggs," label, 4c..................................$10-13
   red cab, opaque windows, black base, 4c; red trailer, "majorette Mini TRANSPORT," label, 4c....................................$5-7
   purple cab, opaque windows, black base, 4c; purple trailer, "Cadbury"s DAIRY MILK," label, 4c.........................$10-13
   red cab, opaque windows, black base, 4c; red trailer, "Coca Cola" soccer, label, 4c $8-10
   white cab with red "Coca Cola" tampo, opaque windows, black base, 4c; red trailer, "Coca Cola" soccer, label, 4c...................................$8-10

white cab, sea green "Ames," tampo, opaque windows, black base, 4c; white trailer, "Ames 40th Anniversary," label, 4c ..$3-5
   white cab opaque windows, black base, 4c; white trailer, no tampo or label, 4c ...$4-6
   red cab, opaque windows, black base, 4c; yellow trailer with white rear doors, "HOLLYWOOD," label, 4c............$4-6
   red cab, opaque windows, black base, 4c; orange trailer with orange rear doors, "HOLLYWOOD," label, 4c.............$6-8
   white cab, opaque windows, black base, 4c; white trailer, "HOLLYWOOD," label, 4c..$6-8
   yellow cab, black "calberson," tampo, opaque windows, black base, 4c; yellow trailer, black "calberson," tampo, French promotional, 4c $10-13
   sand cab, white star and green camouflage, tampo, opaque windows, black base, 4c; sand trailer, white star/white SPECIAL FORCE"/green camouflage, label, 4c...$8-10
   yellow cab with "CIRCUS" tampo, opaque windows, black base, 4c; red trailer with yellow rear doors, "CIRCUS," label, 4c $4-6
   yellow cab with "PINDER" tampo, opaque windows, black base, 4c; red trailer with yellow rear doors, "PINDER," label, 4c........$8-10
   red cab, opaque windows, black base, 4c; gray trailer, "diet PEPSI" label, 4c $6-8
   red cab, opaque windows, black base, 4c; red trailer, white, blue and black "TRANSPORTS ALLOIN" label, "Made in France," 4c...$4-6
341 not issued
342-A DAF 2600 Covered Platform Truck, 241-A and Covered Trailer, 243-A, 1:100, 1970–1972
   blue cab, clear windows, gray base, chrome grille, no interior, green canopy, gray platform, "SERVICES RAPIDE LEMPEREUR and DUPARC," decal, bw3/bw1; trailer: green canopy, gray plastic platform, base, and hitch, "SERVICES RAPIDE LEMPEREUR and DUPARC," decal, bw6.........$20-25
   light green cab, clear windows, gray base, chrome grille, no interior, orange canopy, gray platform, "SERVICES RAPIDE LEMPEREUR and DUPARC," decal, bw5; trailer: orange canopy, gray plastic platform, base, and hitch, no decal on trailer, bw5 ....$20-25
343-A Safari Truck, 225-A, with Dinghy and Raft Trailer*, 1973–1978

red with paint streaks, dark gray canopy, gray inflatable raft on orange trailer ..$16-20

orange with paint streaks, dark gray canopy, gray inflatable raft on orange trailer............................$16-20

yellow with paint streaks, dark gray canopy, gray inflatable raft on orange trailer.........$16-20

yellow with paint streaks, dark gray canopy, gray inflatable raft on metallic yellow-green trailer $16-20

yellow with paint streaks, gray inflatable raft on yellow trailer $16-20

black with green, brown and white paint streaks off hood and down sides, 3kk, dark green canopy, black brush bar, gray inflatable raft on green trailer........$16-20

yellow with paint streaks, olive drab canopy, black brush bar, 3kk, gray inflatable raft on blue trailer..........................$16-20

yellow with paint streaks, olive drab canopy, black brush bar, 3spb, gray inflatable raft on silver trailer............................$16-20

olive drab, no accents, 3spb, with olive drab raft $30-35

343-B Mercedes 450, 249-B with Dinghy and Raft Trailer*, 1979–1981

silver, 3spb; yellow over red dinghy

343-C Volvo 245 DL Station Wagon, 220-A and Raft Trailer*, 1982–1983

343-D JP 4, 252-B with Dinghy and Raft Trailer*, 1984–1987

red with white plastic trim, black roll cage, blue surfboard, 6sp; red over white dinghy, 4spn $4-6

blue with pink plastic trim, yellow roll cage, blue surfboard, 6sp; red over yellow dinghy, 4spn $4-6

343-E Alfa 75, 271-A with Dinghy and Raft Trailer*, 1988–1991

red, white interior, 8h; unpainted trailer, dark blue over white dinghy, 4spn $4-6

343-F Renault 25, 222-A with Dinghy and Raft Trailer*, 1988–1991

metallic burgundy, clear windshield, 8h; unpainted trailer, white over dark blue dinghy...$4-6

343-G El Camino, 296-A with Dinghy and Raft Trailer*, 1996

green, white interior, red 'EL CAMINO' on sides, 8h; white over orange raft with gray trailer, 8p $4-6

blue, white interior, red "EL CAMINO" on sides, 8h ; blue over white raft with gray trailer, 8p $4-6

white, dark blue interior and truck bed, clear windows, red and blue tampo, Coast Guard emblem on hood and doors, "COAST GUARD" on rear fenders, 8h, white over orange raft, black motor, unpainted metal trailer, 8p $5-7

white, dark blue interior and truck bed, clear windows, red and blue tampo, Coast Guard emblem on hood and doors, "COAST GUARD" on rear fenders, 8h, red raft, black motor, unpainted metal trailer, 8p...$5-7

343-H Peugeot 205, 281-A with Dinghy and Raft Trailer*

white with red and black graphics, red and white raft on silver metal trailer $4-6

343-I Toyota RAV-4, 230-E with Dinghy and Raft Trailer*

metallic green with silver lower body, tan interior, 5st; unpainted trailer, red dinghy, 8p $3-5

344-A DAF 2600 Tanker, 245-A, and Tanker Trailer*, 1970–1972

no details available $16-20

344-B Circus Caravan Fourgon (Van), 234-A, and Animal Trailer*

yellow with red interior and fenders, "ELEPHANT RESERVE" and graphics tampos, 6sp, red trailer with yellow cage, light gray elephant $4-6

yellow with red interior and fenders, "Magic Circus" and graphics tampos, 6sp, red trailer with yellow cage, light gray elephant.......$4-6

345-A Ford Skip Truck and Trailer, 1998

blue with green and yellow skips $4-6

blue with orange and red skips...............$4-6

346-A Recycling Lorry and Trailer, 1998

green with yellow, white, blue and red recycling containers $4-6

347 thru 349 not issued

350-A Cabin Cruiser Transporter, 1:100, 1988–1995

red, opaque windows, "RACING TEAM," label on cab, white over blue boat with "RACING TEAM 3," tampo on top, clear windshield, 5d...............................$6-8

red, clear windows, "RACING TEAM," label on cab, blue over white boat with "RACING TEAM," label on top, clear windshield, 5d......................................$6-8

navy blue, opaque windows, "RACING TEAM," tampo on cab, "COMPETITION," tampo on sides, neon pink boat with "RACING TEAM," tampo on top, blue tint windshield, 6sp $6-8

metallic blue, opaque windows, "RACING TEAM," tampo on cab, "COMPETITION," tampo on sides, pink boat with "RACING TEAM," tampo on top, blue tint windshield, 5d...............................$4-6

red, opaque windows, "RACING TEAM," tampo on cab, "COMPETITION," tampo on sides, white/blue boat with "RACING TEAM," tampo on top, blue tint windshield, 5d..................................$4-6

red, opaque windows, "RACING TEAM," tampo on cab, "COMPETITION," tampo on sides, blue/white boat with "RACING TEAM," tampo on top, blue tint windshield, 5d..................................$4-6

metallic blue, blue tint windows, "RACING TEAM," tampo on cab, "COMPETITION," tampo on sides, black/chartreuse boat with "RACING TEAM 3," tampo on top, blue tint windshield, 5d...$4-6

red, blue tint windows, "HOT ENGINE 3," tampo on cab, "RACING TEAM," tampo on sides, black/yellow boat with "RACING TEAM 3," tampo on top, blue tint windshield, 5d...............................$4-6

red, blue tint windows, "HOT ENGINE 3," tampo on cab, "RACING TEAM," tampo on sides, black/chartreuse boat with "RACING TEAM 3" on top, blue tint windshield, 5d.................................$4-6

red, blue tint windows, "HOT ENGINE 3," tampo on cab, "RACING TEAM," tampo on sides, neon chartreuse/black boat with "RACING TEAM 3" on top, blue tint windshield, 5d.................................$6-8

red, clear windows, "RACING TEAM," label on cab, blue over white boat with "RACING TEAM" tampo on top, clear windshield, 5d.................................$6-8

red, clear windows, "RACING TEAM," label on cab, white over blue boat with "RACING TEAM" tampo on top, clear windshield, 8sp.................................$15-18

350-B Long Rocket Launcher Truck, 1:100, 2000

olive, opaque windows, white logo—parachute and airplane and "GN 270257," tampo on cab; gray and brown camouflage on cab and sides, tampo, Squad Forces, 5stol $5-7

sand, opaque windows, black logo—crossed swords and shield with eagle's head and "B.CO 210966," tampo on cab; gray and brown camouflage on cab and sides, tampo, Squad Forces, 5stgy $5-7

351-A Citroën Maserati SM, 250-A, and Road Signs, 1:80, 1971–1973

no details available $15-18

351-B Volkswagen Van, 226-B, and Road Signs, 1:80, 1974

yellow, white interior, service tampos...$12-15

orange, white interior, blue red and white tampos, "SERVICE AUTOROUTE"......$12-15

351-C Wrecker, 212-B and Road Signs, *Signaux*, 1:80, 1973–1975

orange, amber windows and roof light, "SERVICE" label with red and white diagonal stripes on doors, unpainted boom, 3kk.................................$12-15

352-A Ski-Doo Snowmobile, 249-A and Sled*, *Moto-Neige*, 1971–1976

yellow with light green sled, clear windshield, chrome skis $20-25

yellow with light green sled, amber windshield, chrome skis............................$20-25

yellow with red sled, amber windshield...$20-25

red with red sled, clear windshield, "Shell" decal on right side, tiger's head on left side...$20-25

orange, amber window, black seat, chrome handlebars and skis, "CALTEX" label, blue sled, chrome skis.......................$20-25

352-B Farm Tractor, #253, with Log Trailer

no details available $20-25

353 not issued

354-A Ford 5000 Tractor, 253-A and Log Trailer

blue tractor, white fenders, ft3, red trailer $16-20

blue tractor, white fenders, ft3, blue trailer $16-20

red tractor, white fenders, ft3, unpainted trailer with ft3 wheels $16-20

355-A Volvo Semi Oil Tanker, 1:100, 1990

yellow cab, opaque windows, black base, 4c; white tank, yellow bed, "Shell," label, 4c.................................$5-7

white cab, opaque windows, black base, 4c; white tank, yellow bed, "Shell," label, 4c.................................$5-7

white cab, opaque windows, black base, 4c; white tank, white bed, "elf," label, 4c.................................$5-7

yellow cab, opaque windows, black base, 4c; white tank, yellow bed, "Shell," tampo, 4c.................................$4-6

white cab, opaque windows, black base, 4c; white tank, white bed, "Total" with blue, red, and orange broken vertical stripes, tampo, 4c.................................$4-6

red cab, opaque windows, black base, 4c; white tank, white bed, "Total" with blue, red, and orange broken vertical stripes, tampo, 4c.................................$4-6

white cab, opaque windows, black base, 4c; white tank, white bed, "Total" with only the red broken vertical stripe, tampo, 4c.................................$8-10

yellow cab, opaque windows, black base, 4c; white tank, yellow bed, "PETROL COMPANY," tampo, 4c $3-5

red cab, opaque windows, black base, 4c; white tank, yellow bed, "PETROL COMPANY," tampo, 4c $3-5

white cab, opaque windows, black base, 4c; white tank, yellow bed, "PETROL COMPANY," tampo, 4c $3-5

white cab, opaque windows, black base, 4c; white tank, white bed, ice cube design and red "Coca Cola," tampo, 4c.................................$8-10

white cab, red "Coca Cola," tampo, opaque windows, black base, 4c; white tank, white bed, ice cube design and red "Coca Cola," tampo, 4c.................................$8-10

olive drab cab, white star and tan camouflage, tampo, opaque windows, black base, 4c; olive drab tank and bed, "PETROL," tampo, 4c.................$8-10

blue cab with Pepsi logo and "PEPSI," tampo, opaque windows, black base, 4c; blue tank, red bed, Pepsi logo and "PEPSI," tampo, 4c.................................$6-8

356 thru 360 not issued

361-A Bernard Semi Container, ribbed Truck, 1:100, 1974–1978—Trailer roof and rear door colors are specified only if they are different from that of the trailer's main body color.

red cab, clear windows, gray base, 3kk; white trailer, unpainted base, "A&P Weeeeeo!," tampo, 3kk.............$10-13

red cab, clear windows, gray base, 3kk/5sp; white trailer, unpainted base, "A&P Weeeeeo!," tampo, 3spb...........$10-13

yellow cab, clear windows, gray base, 3kk/5sp; white trailer, unpainted base, "A&P Weeeeeo!," tampo, 5sp $10-13

yellow cab, clear windows, gray base, 3kk/3spb; white trailer, unpainted base, "A&P Weeeeeo!," tampo, 3kk.....$10-13

dark green cab, clear windows, gray base, 3kk; white trailer, unpainted base, "A&P Weeeeeo!," tampo, 5sp.............$10-13

metallic blue cab, clear windows, gray base, 3kk; white trailer, unpainted base, "A&P Weeeeeo!," tampo, 3kk.............$10-13

red cab, clear windows, gray base, 3kk; white trailer, red base, white "Kronenbourg," tampo, 3spb...................$12-15

red cab, clear windows, gray base, 3kk/3spb; white trailer, red base, white "Kronenbourg," tampo, 3spb.......$12-15

yellow cab, clear windows, gray base, 3kk; red trailer, unpainted base, white "Kronenbourg," tampo, 3spb...................$12-15

red cab, clear windows, gray base, bw5; white trailer with tan roof and rear doors, unpainted base, "SHOP-RITE," tampo, bw5.................................$12-15

red cab, clear windows, tan base, 3kk; white trailer with tan roof and rear doors, unpainted base, "SHOP-RITE," tampo, 3kk......$12-15

blue cab, clear windows, gray base, 3kk; white trailer, red base, red "ITC," tampo, 5sp.................................$10-13.

red cab, clear windows, brown base, 3kk/5sp; white trailer, red base, red "ITC," tampo, 5sp.....................$10-13

yellow cab, clear windows, gray base, 3kk; white trailer, unpainted base, red "ITC," tampo, 3kk ....$10-13 orange cab, clear windows, gray base, 3kk/3spb; white trailer, unpainted base, red "ITC," tampo, 5sp $10-13

yellow cab, clear windows, gray base, 3kk/3spb; white trailer unpainted base, red "MAJORETTE CONTAINER," tampo, 3kk $10-13

yellow cab, clear windows, gray base, 3kk; white trailer, red base, red "MAJORETTE CONTAINER," tampo, 3kk $10-13

yellow cab, clear windows, gray base, bw5; white trailer with blue roof and rear doors, unpainted base, red "MAJORETTE CONTAINER," tampo, bw5 ....$11-14

dark green cab, clear windows, gray base, 3kk/3spb; white trailer, yellow base, red "MAJORETTE CONTAINER," tampo, 3kk $10-13

light green cab, clear windows, gray base, 3kk/3spb; white trailer, yellow base, red "MAJORETTE CONTAINER," tampo, 3kk $10-13

light green cab, clear windows, gray base, 3kk; white trailer, red base, red "MAJORETTE CONTAINER," tampo, 3kk $10-13

light green cab, clear windows, gray base, 3kk/3spb; white trailer, unpainted base, red "MAJORETTE CONTAINER," tampo, 3kk $10-13

red cab, clear windows, gray base, 3kk; white trailer, unpainted base, red "MAJORETTE CONTAINER," tampo, 3kk $10-13

red cab, clear windows, gray base, 3kk; white trailer, unpainted base, red "MAJORETTE CONTAINER," tampo, 3spb $10-13

red cab, clear windows, gray base, 3kk/5sp; white trailer, unpainted base, plum "MAJORETTE CONTAINER," tampo, 3kk $10-13

red cab, clear windows, charcoal base, bw5; blue trailer, unpainted base, white "MAJORETTE CONTAINER," tampo, bw5 ....$12-15

orange cab, clear windows, tan base, 3kk/3spb; tan trailer with white roof and rear doors, unpainted base, red "MAJORETTE CONTAINER," tampo, 3spb $11-14

orange cab, clear windows, gray base, bw5; white trailer with blue roof and rear doors, unpainted base, red "MAJORETTE CONTAINER," tampo, bw5 ....$11-14

metallic blue cab, clear windows, gray base, 3kk; white trailer, unpainted base, red "MAJORETTE CONTAINER," tampo, 3spb $10-13

blue cab, clear windows, gray base, bw5; white trailer, unpainted base, red "MAJORETTE CONTAINER," tampo, bw5 ....$10-13

blue cab, clear windows, medium gray base, bw1; blue trailer, unpainted base, white "MAJORETTE CONTAINER," tampo, bw1 ....$16-20

dark blue cab, clear windows, gray base, 3kk; white trailer with blue roof and rear doors, red base, red "MAJORETTE CONTAINER," tampo, 3kk $10-13

red cab, clear windows, gray base, bw5; gray trailer, unpainted base, no tampo, bw5 ....$12-15

metallic red cab, clear windows, gray base, bw5; white trailer, unpainted base, red "MAJORETTE CONTAINER," tampo, bw5 ....$10-13

dark orange cab, clear windows, gray base, bw5; white trailer, orange base, red "MAJORETTE CONTAINER," tampo, bw5 ....$10-13

orange cab, clear windows, gray base, bw5/3kk; blue trailer with tan roof and rear doors, unpainted base, white "MAJORETTE CONTAINER," tampo, bw5 ....$12-15

metallic blue cab, clear windows, gray base, 3kk/5sp; white trailer, unpainted base, red "MAJORETTE CONTAINER," tampo, 3kk $10-13

dark red cab, clear windows, gray base, bw5; white trailer, unpainted base, red "MAJORETTE CONTAINER," tampo, bw5 ....$12-15

yellow cab, clear windows, gray base, 3kk/3spb; white trailer, unpainted base, "A&P Weeeeeo!," tampo, 3spb ..$10-13

orange cab, clear windows, gray base, 3kk/3spb; white trailer, red base, "A&P Weeeeeo!," tampo, 3kk $10-13

pale green cab, clear windows, gray base, 3kk; white trailer, red base, red "ITC," tampo, 3kk $10-13

yellow cab, clear windows, gray base, 3kk; white trailer, red base, red "ITC," tampo, 3kk $10-13

361-B Magirus Semi Container, ribbed truck, 1:100, 1977–1978

red cab, amber windows, gray base, 3kk/3spb; white trailer, unpainted base, "A&P Weeeeeo!," 3spb $10-13

red cab, amber windows, black base, 3kk; white trailer, red base, red "MAJORETTE CONTAINER," 5sp $10-13

olive drab cab, amber windows, gray base, 3kk; olive drab trailer with khaki roof, olive drab rear doors, khaki base, model comes with a selection of labels to be applied by purchaser, 3kk $20-25

361-C Bernard Semi Container, smooth Truck, 1:100, 1973–1978

yellow cab, clear windows, gray base, 3kk; gray trailer, white "MAJORETTE CONTAINER," tampo, 3kk $15-18

metallic blue cab, clear windows, gray base, 3kk; white trailer, unpainted base, red "MAJORETTE CONTAINER," tampo, 3spb $10-13

red cab, clear windows, gray base, 3kk/5sp; white trailer, unpainted base, "Two Guys" in center with small credit card in upper front corner on sides, "Two Guys" on front end of trailer, tampo, 3spb $12-15

blue cab, clear windows, brown base, 3kk; white trailer, unpainted base, "Two Guys" in center with small credit card in upper front corner on sides, "Two Guys" on front end of trailer, tampo, 5sp $12-15

blue cab, clear windows, gray base, bw1; white trailer, unpainted base, "Two Guys" with large credit card taller than "Two Guys" towards front on sides, "Two Guys" on front end of trailer, tampo, bw1 .$12-15

blue cab, clear windows, gray base, 3kk; white trailer, unpainted base, "Two Guys" in center with small credit card in upper front corner on sides, tampo, 3kk $10-13

blue cab, clear windows, gray base, 3kk; off-white trailer, unpainted base, "Two Guys" in center with small credit card in upper front corner on sides, "Two Guys" on front end of trailer, tampo, 5sp $10-13

cream cab, clear windows, gray base, "chambourcy" decal on roof of cab, bw1; white trailer, red base, "chambourcy YOGHOURTS-DESSERTS-FROMAGES FRAIS," decal, bw1 ....$12-15

aqua cab, clear windows, gray base, bw1; white trailer, red base, "chambourcy YOGHOURTS–DESSERTS-FROMAGES FRAIS," decal, bw1 ....$12-15

red cab, clear windows, tan base, 3kk; white trailer, unpainter base, red "WESTERN AUTO" outlined in black above "Over 4,700 Stores to Serve You," label, 3kk $12-15

red cab, clear windows, gray base, 3kk; white trailer, unpainted base, red "WESTERN AUTO" outlined in black above "Over 4,700 Stores to Serve You," label, 3kk $12-15

blue cab, clear windows, gray base, 3kk/3spb; white trailer, unpainted base, "WESTERN AUTO" on upper front and "Over 4,700 Stores to Serve You" on lower rear, tampo, 3kk $10-13

red cab, clear windows, gray base, 3kk/3spb; white trailer, unpainted base, "WESTERN AUTO" on upper front and "Over 4,700 Stores to Serve You" on lower rear, tampo, 3spb $10-13

red cab, clear windows, gray base, 3kk/3spb; white trailer, unpainted base, "WESTERN AUTO" sign with crown logo towards front and "Over 4,700 Stores to Serve You" on lower rear, tampo, 3kk $10-13

red cab, clear windows, gray base, 3kk; white trailer, unpainted base, "WESTERN AUTO" sign with crown logo towards front and "Over 4,700 Stores to Serve You" on lower rear, tampo, 3kk $10-13

yellow cab, clear windows, gray base, 3kk/5sp; white trailer, unpainted base, "MAJORETTE CONTAINER" with boat on one side of trailer and plane on other side, tampo, 5sp $10-13

yellow cab, clear windows, gray base, 3kk/5sp; white trailer, unpainted base, "MAJORETTE CONTAINER" with boat on one side of trailer and plane on other side, tampo, 3spb $10-13

yellow cab, clear windows, gray base, 3kk; white trailer, unpainted base, white "MAJORETTE CONTAINER" with boat on one side of trailer and plane on other side, tampo, 3spb $10-13

dark green cab, clear windows, gray base, 3kk/3spb; white trailer, unpainted base, "MAJORETTE CONTAINER" with boat on one side of trailer and plane on other side, tampo, 3spb $10-13

dark green cab, clear windows, gray base, 3kk; white trailer, unpainted base, "MAJORETTE CONTAINER" with boat on one side of trailer and plane on other side, tampo, 3spb $10-13

blue cab, clear windows, gray base, 3kk; white trailer, unpainted base, "MAJORETTE CONTAINER" with boat on one side of trailer and plane on other side, tampo, 3spb $10-13

red cab, clear windows, gray base, 3kk; white trailer, unpainted base, "MAJORETTE CONTAINER" with boat on one side of trailer and plane on other side, tampo, 3spb $10-13

yellow cab, clear windows, gray base, 3kk; yellow trailer, unpainted base, "SHOP-RITE Supermarkets," tampo, 3kk $12-15

orange cab, clear windows, gray base, 3kk; white trailer, unpainted base, "KIDDIE CITY," tampo, 3kk....................$10-13

orange cab, clear windows, gray base, 3kk/5sp; white trailer, unpainted base, "KIDDIE CITY," tampo, 3kk..........$10-13

red cab, clear windows, gray base, 3kk; white trailer, unpainted base, "child world," tampo, 3kk $10-13

white cab, clear windows, gray base, 3kk; white trailer, unpainted base, "TOYS R US," tampo, 3kk $10-13

white cab, clear windows, gray base, 3kk; white trailer, unpainted base, "TOYS R US," tampo, 3spb......................$10-13

white cab, clear windows, gray base, 3kk/3spb; white trailer, unpainted base, "TOYS R US," tampo, 3kk $10-13

metallic blue cab, clear windows, gray base, 3kk; white trailer, unpainted base, "TOYS R US," tampo, 5sp $10-13

red cab, clear windows, gray base, 3kk; white trailer, unpainted base, "KAY BEE Toy and Hobby Shop," tampo, 3kk...............................$10-13

red cab, clear windows, gray base, 3kk/3spb; white trailer, unpainted base, "KAY BEE Toy and Hobby Shop," tampo, 3kk.......$10-13

blue cab, clear windows, gray base, 3kk/3spb; white trailer, unpainted base, "A&P Weeeeeo!," tampo, 3spb ..$10-13

orange cab, clear windows, gray base, 3kk/3spb; white trailer, unpainted base, "A&P Weeeeeo!," tampo, 3kk.....$10-13

orange cab, clear windows, gray base, 3kk; white trailer, unpainted base, "ROAD-WAY," tampo, 3kk $12-15

tan cab, clear windows, gray base, bw1; tan trailer with white roof and tan rear doors, unpainted base, "GRANTS," tampo, 3kk....$10-13

metallic blue cab, clear windows, gray base, 3kk; gray trailer, unpainted base, "WAL-MART," tampo, 3spb..................$12-15

metallic blue cab, clear windows, gray base, 3kk; white trailer, unpainted base, "CAL-DOR," decal, 3spb $12-15

red cab, clear windows, gray base, 3kk/3spb; white trailer, unpainted base, "CALDOR," decal, 5sp/3spb......$12-15

yellow cab, clear windows, gray base, 3kk; white trailer, unpainted base, "Mirafi 140 CELANESE," tampo, *promotional*, 3spb.....................................$12-15

red cab, clear windows, gray base, 3kk; white trailer, red base, "CARDINAL'S TOY and VARIETY SHOP," label, *private issue*, 3kk $10-13

blue cab, clear windows, gray base, 3kk/3spb; white trailer, unpainted base, "THOMAS McAULIFFE THE MIXED-UP COLLECTOR," label, *private issue*, 3kk $10-13

yellow cab, clear windows, gray base, 3kk/5sp; white trailer, unpainted base, "MAJORETTE CONTAINER" with boat on one side of trailer and plane on other side, tampo, 3kk $10-13

dark green cab, clear windows, gray base, 3kk/3spb; white trailer, unpainted base, "MAJORETTE CONTAINER" with boat on one side of trailer and plane on other side, tampo, 5sp $10-13

dark blue cab, clear windows, gray base, 3kk; gray trailer, unpainted base, "WAL-MART," tampo, 3kk....................$10-13

red cab, clear windows, tan base, 3kk; tan trailer with white roof, unpainted base, red "MAJORETTE CONTAINER," tampo, 5sp..$10-13

yellow cab, clear windows, gray base, 3kk; tan trailer with white roof, unpainted base, red "MAJORETTE CONTAINER," tampo, 3kk $10-13

red cab, clear windows, gray base, 3kk/3spb; white trailer, unpainted base, "MAJORETTE CONTAINER" with boat on one side of trailer and plane on other side, tampo, 3spb $10-13

metallic blue cab, clear windows, gray base, 3kk/3spb; white trailer, red base, "KIDDIE CITY," tampo, 3kk.....................$10-13

yellow cab, clear windows, gray base, 3kk/3spb; white trailer, unpainted base, "KIDDIE CITY," tampo, 3kk..........$10-13

yellow cab, clear windows, gray base, 3kk/5sp; white trailer, unpainted base, "A&P Weeeeeo!," tampo, 3spb ..$10-13

red cab, clear windows, gray base, 3kk; white trailer, unpainted base, "A&P Weeeeeo!," tampo, 3kk.............$10-13 pale green cab, clear windows, tan base, 3kk/3spb; white trailer, unpainted base, "A&P," in a brown square Weeeeeo!," tampo, 3spb $12-15

cream cab, clear windows, gray base, bw5; white trailer, red base, red "MAJORETTE" above green "MA VOITURE MINIATURE PREFEREE" on a yellow label, bw5 ....$20-25

361-D Magirus Semi Container, smooth truck, 1:100, 1977–1978

metallic blue cab, amber windows, gray base, 3kk/3spb; white trailer, "majorette CONTAINER" with plane on one side of trailer and boat on the other side, tampo, 3spb $10-13

red cab, amber windows, gray base, 3kk; white trailer, unpainted base, "Jumbofret," tampo, 3spb $10-13

red cab, amber windows, gray base, 3kk; white trailer, unpainted base, "PEPSI," label, 3kk $12-15

red cab, amber windows, gray base, 3kk; white trailer, unpainted base, "child world," tampo, 3kk $10-13

red cab, amber windows, gray base, 3kk; white trailer, unpainted base, "child world," tampo, 3spb $10-13

red cab, amber windows, gray base, 3kk; white trailer, unpainted base, "Children's Palace," tampo, 3spb $10-13

red cab, amber windows, gray base, 3kk/3spb; white trailer, unpainted base, "Children's Palace," tampo, 3kk...$10-13

red cab, amber windows, black base, 3kk; yellow trailer, unpainted base, "TRANSFRI-GO," tampo, 3kk $10-13

red cab, amber windows, black base, 3kk/3spb; white trailer, unpainted base, "TRANSFRIGO," tampo, 3kk $10-13

metallic blue cab, amber windows, gray base, 3kk; white trailer, unpainted base, "A&P Weeeeeo!," tampo, 3kk..............$10-13

red cab, amber windows, gray base, 3kk; white trailer, unpainted base, "A&P Weeeeeo!," "Weeeeeo!" on light green background, tampo, 3spb..........$10-13.

red cab, amber windows, tan base, 3kk; white trailer, unpainted base, "Stop Shop Great Beef!," tampo, 3kk $10-13

red cab, amber windows, gray base, 3kk; white trailer, unpainted base, "Stop Shop Great Beef!," tampo, 3kk $10-13

yellow cab, amber windows, black base, 3kk; yellow trailer, unpainted base, "CHAL-LENGE COMPANY," label, 3kk...$12-15

red cab, amber windows, black base, 3kk; red trailer, unpainted base, "CHALLENGE COMPANY," label, 3kk $12-15

orange cab, amber windows, black base, 3kk; white trailer, unpainted base, "ROAD-WAY," tampo, 3kk $12-15

red cab, amber windows, gray base, 3kk; white trailer, unpainted base, "SIMBA," tampo, English promotional, 3kk .$12-15

metallic blue cab, amber windows, gray base, 3kk/3spb; white trailer with blue tampo sides, unpainted base, "BLACK-POOL," tampo, English promotional, 3kk $12-15

metallic blue cab, amber windows, gray base, 3kk; white trailer, unpainted base, "child world," tampo, 3kk $10-13

red cab, amber windows, black base, 3kk; white trailer, unpainted base, "A&P Weeeeeo!," "Weeeeeo!" on sea green background, tampo, 3spb..........$10-13

361-E Semi Container, smooth truck, generic cab with dual exhausts, 1:100, 1982

red cab, amber windows, black base, 3spn; white trailer, unpainted base, "TRANS CONTINENT" tampo, 3kk..........$10-13

light blue cab, clear windows, black base, 4c; white trailer, unpainted base, "point S FRANCE," label, 3kk.................$10-13

light blue cab, clear windows, black base, 4c; white trailer, unpainted base, "EXPRESS LINES," label, 3kk $10-13

royal blue cab, clear windows, black base, 4c; white trailer, unpainted base, "EXPRESS LINES," label, 3kk........$10-13

light blue cab, amber windows, black base, 3spb; white trailer, unpainted base, "ALLOIN," label, 4c $10-13

royal blue cab, clear windows, black base, 4c; white trailer, unpainted base, "ALLOIN," label, 4c $10-13

royal blue cab, opaque windows, black base, 4c; white trailer, unpainted base, "ALLOIN," label, 4c $10-13

red cab, clear windows, black base, 3spb; white trailer, unpainted base, "PEPSI," label, 3kk $12-15

red cab, clear windows, black base, 4c; white trailer, unpainted base, "PEPSI," label, 3kk $12-15

orange cab, amber windows, black base, 4c; white trailer, unpainted base, "ROAD-WAY," tampo, 3kk $12-15

red cab, amber windows, black base, 4c; white trailer, unpainted base, "ROAD-WAY," tampo, 3kk $12-15

red cab, amber windows, black base, 3spn; white trailer, unpainted base, "demeco," tampo, 3kk $10-13

blue cab, opaque blue windows, black base, 4c; white trailer, unpainted base, "deme-co," tampo, 3kk...........................$10-13

red cab, amber windows, black base, 4c; white trailer, unpainted base, "demeco," tampo, 3kk $10-13

red cab, amber windows, black base, 3spn; white trailer, unpainted base, "TEXAS HOMECARE The Big One," tampo, English promotional, 3kk $12-15

red cab, amber windows, black base, 3spb; white trailer, unpainted base, "CATS WHISKERS," tampo, English promotional, 3kk $12-15

white cab, clear windows, black base, 4c; white trailer, unpainted base, "RANK XEROX," tampo, French promotional, 4c $14-17

red cab, amber windows, black base, 3spn; white trailer, unpainted base, "CORNWALL," tampo, English promo-tional, 3kk $12-15

red cab, clear windows, black base, 3spn; white trailer, unpainted base, "DEVON," tampo, English promotional, 3kk .$12-15

red cab, amber windows, black base, 3spn; white trailer, unpainted base, "Jersey," tampo, English promotional, 3kk.$12-15

red cab, amber windows, black base, 3spn; white trailer, unpainted base, "CHANNEL ISLANDS," tampo, English promotional, 3kk $12-15

red cab, amber windows, black base, 3spn; white trailer with red tampo sides, unpaint-ed base, "ISLE OF MAN," tampo, English promotional, 3kk $12-15

red cab, amber windows, black base, 4c; white trailer, unpainted base, "WALES," tampo, English promotional, 3kk.$12-15

red cab, amber windows, black base, 4c; white trailer, unpainted base, "I LOVE Wroxham," tampo, English promotional, 3kk $12-15

red cab, amber windows, black base, 3spn; white trailer, unpainted base, "LONDON," tampo, English promotional, 3kk ...$12-15

light blue cab, amber windows, black base, 3spn; white trailer, unpainted base, "ENGLISH LAKES," tampo, English pro-motional, 3kk...........................$12-15

red cab, amber windows, black base, 3spn; white trailer, unpainted base, "Guernsey," tampo, English promotional, 3kk .$12-15 red cab, amber windows, black base, 3spn; white trailer, unpainted base, "ISLE OF WIGHT," tampo, *English promotional*, 3kk $12-15

light blue cab, opaque windows, black base, 4c; white trailer, unpainted base, "SOPREMA," tampo, *Dutch promotional*, ...$14-17

red cab, amber windows, black base, 4spn; white trailer, unpainted base, "ROAD-WAY," tampo, 3kk $12-15

361-F Mercedes Semi Container, smooth truck, 1:100, 1979–1981

green cab, amber windows, black base, 3kk; white trailer, red base, "Jumbofret," tampo, 3kk $10-13

green cab, amber windows, black base, 3kk; white trailer, unpainted base, "Jumbofret," tampo, 3kk $10-13

green cab, clear windows, black base, 3kk; white trailer, unpainted base, "Jumbofret," tampo, 3kk $10-13

white cab, clear windows, black base, 3spb; white trailer, unpainted base, "Atlas Van Lines," tampo, 3kk...................$10-13

white cab, clear windows, black base, 3kk; white trailer, unpainted base, "Atlas Van Lines," tampo, 3kk...................$10-13

white cab, clear windows, black base, 3kk/3spn; white trailer, unpainted base, "Atlas Van Lines," tampo, 3kk......$10-13

light blue cab, clear windows, black base, 3kk; white trailer, unpainted base, "Atlas Van Lines," tampo, 3kk $10-13

white cab, clear windows, black base, 3kk; white trailer, unpainted base, "TRANSFRI-GO," tampo, 3kk $10-13

yellow cab, clear windows, black base, 3kk/3spb; yellow trailer, unpainted base, "TRANSFRIGO," tampo, 3kk $10-13

yellow cab, clear windows, black base, 3kk; yellow trailer, unpainted base, "TRANSFRI-GO," tampo, 3kk $10-13

yellow cab, clear windows, black base, 3kk; yellow trailer, unpainted base, "TRANSFRI-GO," tampo, 3spb $10-13

light blue cab, clear windows, black base, 3spb/3kk; white trailer, unpainted base, "TRANSFRIGO," tampo, 3kk $10-13

light blue cab, clear windows, black base, 3kk; white trailer, unpainted base, "TRANSFRIGO," tampo, 3kk $10-13

light blue cab, clear windows, black base, 3spb; white trailer, unpaint-ed base, "TRANSFRIGO," tampo, 3kk $10-13

red cab, clear windows, black base, 3kk; white trailer, unpainted base, "TRANS CONTINENT," tampo, 3kk.........$10-13

green cab, clear windows, black base, 3kk; white trailer, unpainted base, "TRANS CONTINENT," tampo, 3kk.........$10-13

light blue cab, clear windows, black base, 3spb; white trailer, unpainted base, "ROADWAY," tampo, 3kk..........$12-15

white cab, clear windows, black base, 3kk; white trailer, unpainted base, "GOOD YEAR," tampo, *English promotional*, 3kk.....$12-15

white cab, clear windows, black base, 3kk; white trailer, unpainted base, "All the best from BIRDS EYE Wall's," tampo, *English promotional*, 3kk $14-17

white cab, clear windows, black base, 3kk; white trailer, unpainted base, "JACK-SONS Long Loaf," tampo, *English pro-motional*, 3kk $12-15

red cab, clear windows, black base, 3kk; white trailer, unpainted base, "trailerent INTERNATIONAL TRAILER RENTALS," tampo, *English promotional*, 3kk .$12-15

white cab, clear windows, black base, 4c; white trailer, unpainted base, "Curty Payen," tampo, *French promotional*, 4k.....$14-17

yellow cab, clear windows, black base, 3kk; green trailer, unpainted base, "GTW transport," tampo, *Dutch promotional*, 3kk $14-17

red cab, clear windows, black base, 3kk; yel-low trailer, unpainted base, "nationale vereniging de zonnebloem breda aan-dacht voor zieken is gezond!," tampo, *Dutch promotional*, 3kk $14-17

white cab, clear windows, black base, 3kk; white trailer with blue tampo sides, unpainted base, "SCARBOROUGH," tampo, *English promotional*, 3kk.$12-15

white cab, clear windows, black base, 3kk; white trailer, unpainted base, "Somerset," tampo, *English promotional*, 3kk.$12-15

white cab, clear windows, black base, 3kk; white trailer, unpainted base, "NOR-FOLK," tampo, *English promotional*, 3kk $12-15

white cab, clear windows, black base,3kk; white trailer with yellow tampo sides, unpainted base, "TORBAY," tampo, *Eng-lish promotional*, 3kk $12-15

white cab, clear windows, black base, 3kk; white trailer, unpainted base, "Ireland," tampo, *English promotional*, 3kk .$12-15

white cab, clear windows, black base, 3kk; white trailer, unpainted base, "SCOTLAND," tampo, *English promotional*, 3kk.....$12-15

red cab, clear windows, black base, 3kk; white trailer, unpainted base, "SUPER SKEGNESS," tampo, *English promotion-al*, 3kk $12-15

white cab, clear windows, black base, 3kk; white trailer, unpainted base, "Wincanton," tampo, *English promotional*, 3kk ..$12-15

white cab, clear windows, black base, 3kk; white trailer, unpainted base, "BRS Trail-er Rental," tampo, *English promotional*, 3kk $12-15

white cab, clear windows, black base, 3kk; white trailer, unpainted base, "CARRY-MASTER," tampo, *English promotional*, 3kk $12-15

white cab, clear windows, black base, 3kk/3spb; white trailer, unpainted base, "NORFOLK," tampo, *English promotional*, 3kk $12-15

yellow cab, clear windows, black base, 3kk; yellow trailer, red base, "TRANSFRIGO," tampo, 3spb $10-13

green cab, clear windows, black base, 3kk/3spb; white trailer, unpainted base, "Jumbofret," tampo, 3kk $10-13

dark blue cab, clear windows, black base, 3kk; white trailer, unpainted base, "Atlas Van Lines," tampo, 3kk $10-13

white cab, clear windows, black base, 3spb; white trailer, unpainted base, "TRANSFRI-GO," tampo, 3kk $10-13

white cab, clear windows, black base, 3kk; white trailer, unpainted base, "mikihouse," tampo, *promotional*, 3kk $15-18

361-G Scania Semi Container, smooth Truck, 1:100, 1977–1978

red cab, clear windows, white base, 3kk; white trailer, unpainted base, "child world," tampo, 3kk $10-13

361-H Semi Container, smooth Truck, 1:100, 1982—Generic cabover cab with white air deflector unless specified otherwise.

red cab, amber windows, black base, 4c; white trailer, unpainted base, "stoc SUPERMARCH-ES," label, *French promotional*, 3kk.$14-17

red cab, amber windows, black base, 4c; white trailer, unpainted base, "Grandways," tampo, *English promotional*, 3kk....$12-15

red cab, amber windows, black base, 4c; white trailer, unpainted base, "If they drive...its Glucophage," tampo, *English promotional*, 3kk $12-15

red cab, amber windows, black base, 4c; white trailer, unpainted base, "The London Toy and Model Museum," tampo, *English promotional*, 3kk ....$12-15 red cab, amber windows, black base, 4c; white trailer, unpainted base, red "Transflash," tampo, *English promotional*, 3kk..............................$12-15

blue cab, amber windows, black base, 4c; white trailer, unpainted base, blue "Transflash," tampo, *English promotional*, 3kk..............................$12-15

blue cab, amber windows, black base, 4c; white trailer, unpainted base, "Genty," tampo, *English promotional*, 3kk..$12-15

blue cab, amber windows, black base, 4c; white trailer with blue tampo sides, unpainted base, "MIDLANDS STORAGE LTD.," tampo, *English promotional*, 3kk.....................$12-15

metallic blue cab, amber windows, black base, 4c; yellow trailer with blue tampo sides, unpainted base, "SWANAGE," tampo, *English promotional*, 3kk.$12-15

metallic blue cab, amber windows, black base, 4c; white trailer with blue tampo sides, unpainted base, GT. YARMOUTH," tampo, *English promotional*, 3kk.$12-15

red cab, amber windows, black base, 4c; white trailer, unpainted base, green "PORTSWOOD Toy and Card CENTRE," tampo, *English promotional*, 3kk.$12-15

blue cab, amber windows, black base, 4c; white and blue trailer, unpainted base, "roadexpress" and "Meadows," tampo, *English promotional*, 3kk.............$12-15

362-A Fire Rescue, 204-A with Barge and Trailer*
red, 3spb...........................$16-20

362-B Land Rover 4x4, 266-B with NASA Radar Trailer*
white with blue tampos, red light bar, circle-dash-circle wheels, white trailer with black radar.........................$12-15

white with blue tampos, red light bar, 8-spoked wheels, white trailer with black radar.........................$12-15

363-A BMW 2800 CS Coupe, 235-A with Racer and Trailer* $12-15

364-A Bernard Tanker, 1:100

"Esso," red cab with white tank trailer....$12-15

"Shell," red cab, 5sp on cab and trailer....$12-15

364-B Magirus Tanker, 1:100
"Shell" $4-6

"Texaco".........................$16-20
"Agip" $6-8
white cab, white tank, "Petro Canada" $6-8

364-C Scania Tanker, 1:100
"Esso," small, red cab, clear windows, black base, 3kk, white tank, red base, 3kk $15-18

"Esso," larger standard size, white cab, clear windows, black base, 3kk, white tank, red base, 3kk $8-10

"Mobil," white cab, clear windows, black base, 3kk, white tank, red base, 3kk.......$15-18

"Agip," white cab, clear windows, black base, 3kk, white tank, black base, 3kk...$10-13

"Agip," white cab, clear windows, black base, 3spb, white tank, black base, 3kk...$10-13

"Agip," white cab, clear windows, black base, 3spb, white tank, black base, 3spb $10-13

"Shell," yellow cab, clear windows, black base, 3spb, white tank, red base, 3spb.......$8-10

"TEXACO," red cab, clear windows, black base, 3kk, white tank, red base, 3kk $10-13

"TEXACO," red cab, clear windows, black base, 3kk, white tank, red base, 3spb.......$10-13

"EWING OIL CO.," red-orange cab, clear windows, black base, 3kk, white tank, red base, 3kk...........................$20-25

364-D Mercedes Tanker, 1:100
"Esso," white cab, clear windows, black base, 3kk, white tank, red base, 3kk $8-10

"Esso," white cab, amber windows, black base, 3kk, white tank, unpainted base, 3kk...............................$8-10

"Mobil," red cab, amber windows, black base, 3kk, white tank, red base, 3kk........$15-18

"Mobil," metallic blue cab, clear windows, black base, 3kk, white tank, red base, 3kk...............................$15-18

"Agip," label, yellow cab, clear windows, black base, 3kk, white tank, black base, 3kk $15-18

"Agip," white cab, clear windows, black base, 3kk, white tank, black base, 3kk.....$10-13

"Shell," yellow cab, clear windows, black base, 3kk, front/ 3kk, rear 1/ 3spb, rear 2, white tank, red base, 3kk $8-10

"Shell," yellow cab, clear windows, black base, 3kk, white tank, red base, 5sp.........$8-10

"TEXACO," red cab, clear windows, black base, 3kk, white tank, red base, 3kk......$10-13

"PETRO-CANADA," white cab, clear windows, black base, 3kk, white tank, black base, 3kk $15-18

364-E Tanker, generic cab with white, unless specified otherwise air deflector, 1:100

"TEXACO," red cab, amber windows, black base, 4c, white tank, black base, 3kk..........$12-15

365-A Bernard Semi Sailboat Carrier/Sloop Hauler, 1:100

lime cab, clear windows, gray base, 3kk, red trailer, 3kk, boat has yellow hull and mast, white deck......................................$8-10

365-B Magirus Semi Sailboat Carrier/Sloop Hauler, 1:100

red cab, amber windows, black base, 3kk, yellow trailer, boat has red hull and mast, white deck $8-10

red cab, silver trailer, boat has red hull and mast, white deck $8-10

red cab, silver trailer, boat has white hull and mast, yellow deck $8-10

pink cab, silver trailer, boat has lime hull and mast, pink deck............................$8-10

red cab, silver trailer, boat has blue hull and mast, white deck $8-10

red cab, silver trailer, boat has yellow hull and mast, white deck $8-10

light blue cab, 3kk, silver trailer, boat has red hull and mast, white deck, ...$8-10

red cab, amber windows, black base, 3kk, yellow trailer, boat has white hull and mast, peach deck, 3kk................$8-10

red cab, amber windows, black base, 3spb, yellow trailer, boat has red hull and mast, white deck, 3kk $8-10

red cab, clear windows, black base, 3kk, yellow trailer, boat has white hull and mast, red deck, 3kk $8-10

red cab, amber windows, black base, 3kk, red trailer, boat has white hull and mast, red deck, 3kk $8-10

orange cab, amber windows, black base, 3kk, yellow trailer, boat has red hull and mast, white deck, 3kk $8-10

orange cab, amber windows, black base, 3kk, yellow trailer, boat has white hull and mast, red deck, 3kk $8-10

365-C Scania Semi Sailboat Carrier/Sloop Hauler, cab has cast roof light, 1:100

red cab, clear windows, black base, 3kk, yellow trailer, boat has white hull and mast, red deck, decal of scuba diver on bow, 3kk....$15-18

red cab, clear windows, white base, 3kk, red trailer, boat has yellow hull and mast, white deck, 3kk $8-10

metallic aqua cab, clear windows, white base, 3kk, red trailer, boat has white hull and mast, yellow deck, 3kk $8-10

metallic blue cab, clear windows, white base, 3kk, red trailer, boat has white hull and mast, yellow deck, 5sp $8-10

365-D Semi Sailboat Carrier/Sloop Hauler, generic cab with dual exhausts, 1:100

red cab, blue tint windows, black base, 4c, silver trailer, boat has blue hull and mast, white deck, 4c......................:.....$8-10

blue cab, blue tint windows, black base, 4c, silver trailer, boat has blue hull, mast, and deck, 4c.........................$10-13

blue cab, blue tint windows, black base, 4c, silver trailer, boat has blue hull and mast, fuchsia deck, 4c $8-10

blue cab, blue tint windows, black base, 4c, silver trailer, boat has fuchsia hull and mast, blue deck, 4c.....................$8-10

blue cab, blue tint windows, black base, 4c, silver trailer, boat has lime hull and mast, fuchsia deck, 4c $8-10

blue cab, blue tint windows, black base, 4c, silver trailer, boat has fuchsia hull and mast, lime deck, 4c $8-10

red cab, opaque blue windows, black base, 4c, silver trailer, boat has yellow hull and mast, white deck, 3kk $8-10

red cab, opaque blue windows, black base, 4c, silver trailer, boat has white hull and mast, yellow deck, 4c....................$8-10

lime cab, blue tint windows, black base, 4c, silver trailer, boat has green hull and mast, pink deck, 4c $8-10

lime cab, blue tint windows, black base, 4c, silver trailer, boat has pink hull and mast, green deck, 4c $8-10

hot pink cab, blue tint windows, black base, 4c, silver trailer, boat has pink hull and mast, green deck, 4c.....................$8-10

orange cab, amber windows, black base, 3spn, silver trailer, boat has yellow hull and mast, white deck, 3kk.............$8-10

366-A Saviem Canvas Back Truck, 241-B and Trailer*, 1976–1984—The same printing appears on the canopy of both the cab and the trailer.

red cab, clear windows, gray base, cream canopy, "MAJORETTE metal," tampo, 3kk; trailer: red body, cream canopy, 3spb $10-13

red cab, clear windows, gray base, cream canopy, "MAJORETTE metal," tampo, 3kk/5sp; trailer: red body, cream canopy, 3spb..................$10-13

green cab, clear windows, gray base, cream canopy, "MAJORETTE metal," tampo, 3kk; trailer: green body, cream canopy, 3spb.............................$10-13

olive drab cab, clear windows, gray base, khaki canopy, 3kk; trailer: olive drab body, kahaki canopy, 3spb, comes with various labels to be applied by purchaser......................$20-25

red cab, clear windows, black base, white canopy, "SERNAM," tampo, 3kk/5sp; trailer: red body, white canopy, 3kk $10-13

metallic blue cab, clear windows, black base, white canopy, "SERNAM," tampo, 3kk; trailer: metallic blue body, white canopy, 3spb $10-13

metallic blue cab, clear windows, black base, white canopy, "SERNAM," tampo, 3spb; trailer: metallic blue body, white canopy, 3spb $10-13

metallic blue cab, clear windows, black base, white canopy, "SERNAM," tampo, 3kk; trailer: metallic blue body, white canopy, 3kk $10-13

white cab, clear windows, black base, blue canopy, "adidas," tampo, 3kk; trailer: white body, blue canopy, 3spb ...$10-13

white cab, clear windows, black base, blue canopy, "adidas," tampo, 3kk; trailer: white body, blue canopy, 3kk $10-13

metallic blue cab, clear windows, black base, yellow canopy, "SAVIEM," tampo, 3kk; trailer: metallic blue bed, yellow canopy, 3kk $10-13

metallic blue cab, clear windows, black base, yellow canopy, "MICHELIN," tampo, 3spb; trailer: metallic blue body, yellow canopy, 3spb.........................$10-13

red cab, clear windows, gray base, cream canopy, orange "COPERTONE SINTETI-CO"/red "SYNTHETIC TARPAULINS," tampo, 3kk; trailer: red body, cream canopy, 3kk.............................$10-13

green cab, clear windows, gray base, cream canopy, orange "COPERTONE SINTETI-CO"/red "SYNTHETIC TARPAULINS," tampo, 3kk/5sp; trailer: green body, cream canopy, 3spb $10-13

green cab, clear windows, gray base, cream canopy, orange "COPERTONE SINTETI-CO"/red "SYNTHETIC TARPAULINS," tampo, 3kk; trailer: green body, cream canopy, 3kk.............................$10-13

red cab, clear windows, gray base, cream canopy, green "BACHES SYNTHEI-TIQUES"/blue "BESCHICHTETE PLA-

NEN," tampo, 3kk; trailer: red body, cream canopy, 3kk $10-13

green cab, clear windows, gray base, cream canopy, green "BACHES SYNTHEI-TIQUES"/blue "BESCHICHTETE PLA-NEN," tampo, 3kk/5sp; trailer: green body, cream canopy, 3kk..........$10-13

366-B Ford Covered Truck with long narrow windows on sides of cab, 241-C and Trailer*

green with yellow cargo covers, "majorette" $4-6

green with yellow cargo covers, "super cargo" $4-6

white with blue cargo covers, "majorette"...$4-6

white with white cargo covers, "majorette" $4-6

white with white cargo covers, "elf" $4-6

red with white cargo covers, "Coca-Cola" ice cubes, 1995.............................$6-8

blue, "Cadbury Roses Chocolates" $8-10

366-C Ford Covered Truck, without long narrow windows on sides of cab, 241-D and Trail-er*, 1:100, 1992–present—The same printing appears on the canopy of both the truck and the trailer.

white body, clear windows, black base, blue canopy, "MOVING STUDIO," tampo, 4c; trailer: white body, blue canopy, 4c.....$4-6

white body, clear windows, black base, white canopy, "elf Competition," label, 4c .$4-6

red with white cargo covers, "Coca-Cola" ice cubes, 4c, shown in 1995 catalog, but not reported $5-7

367-A Bernard Canvas Back Covered Truck, 1:100, 1976–1977

red cab, clear windows, gray base, 3kk; cream canopy top, yellow-orange bed, blue "ma voiture miniature preferee," red "MAJORETTE," blue "Metal," unpainted base, 5sp $8-10

red cab, clear windows, gray base, 3kk; cream canopy top, yellow-orange bed, black "ma voiture miniature preferee," red "MAJORETTE," black "Metal," unpainted base, 3kk.............................$8-10

red cab, clear windows, gray base, 3kk; cream canopy top, yellow-orange bed, black "ma voiture miniature preferee," red "MAJORETTE," black "Metal," red base, 3kk $8-10

red cab, clear windows, gray base, 3kk/3spb; pale orange canopy top, cream bed, black "ma voiture miniature preferee," red "MAJORETTE," black "Metal," unpainted base, 3kk $8-10

red cab, clear windows, gray base, 3kk; pale orange canopy top, cream bed, black "ma voiture miniature preferee," red "MAJORETTE," black "Metal," red base, 3kk $8-10

red cab, clear windows, tan base, 3kk; pale orange canopy top, cream bed, black "ma voiture miniature preferee," red "MAJORETTE," black "Metal," red base, 3kk $8-10

lime cab, clear windows, gray base, 3kk/3spn; cream canopy top, yellow-orange bed, black "ma voiture miniature preferee," red MAJORETTE," black "Metal," red base, 3kk..................$8-10

yellow cab, clear windows, gray base, 3kk/3spn; cream canopy top, yellow-orange bed, blue "ma voiture miniature preferee," red "MAJORETTE," blue "Metal," unpainted base, 5sp $8-10

blue cab, clear windows, gray base, 3kk/3spn; cream canopy top, yellow-orange bed, black "ma voiture miniature preferee," red "MAJORETTE," black "Metal," unpainted base, 3kk..............$8-10

orange cab, clear windows, gray base, 3kk/3spn; cream canopy top, pale yellow bed, blue "ma voiture miniature preferee," red "MAJORETTE," blue "Metal," unpainted base, 3kk....................$8-10

red cab, clear windows, gray base, 3kk; green canopy top, pale orange bed, black "ma voiture miniature preferee," red "MAJORETTE," black "Metal," red base, 3kk $10-13

red cab, clear windows, gray base, 3kk/5sp; pale orange canopy top, green bed, black "ma voiture miniature preferee," red "MAJORETTE," black "Metal," red base, 5sp............................$10-13

red cab, clear windows, gray base, 3kk; green canopy top, cream bed, black "ma voiture miniature preferee," red "MAJORETTE," black "Metal," red base, 3kk............................$10-13

red cab, clear windows, gray base, 3kk/5sp; cream canopy top, green bed, black "ma voiture miniature preferee," red "MAJORETTE," black "Metal," unpainted base, 5sp $10-13

red cab, clear windows, gray base, 3kk/3spb; cream canopy top, pale orange bed, blue "ma voiture miniature preferee," orange "MAJORETTE," blue "Metal," unpainted base, 3kk $8-10

red cab, clear windows, gray base, 3kk; cream canopy top, pale orange bed, black "ma voiture miniature preferee," brown "MAJORETTE," black "Metal," unpainted base, 3kk....................$8-10

red cab, clear windows, gray base, 3kk; cream canopy top, pale orange bed, black "ma voiture miniature preferee," red "MAJORETTE," black "Metal," unpainted base, 5sp $8-10

green cab, clear windows, gray base, 3kk/5sp; cream canopy top, pale orange bed, blue "ma voiture miniature preferee," red "MAJORETTE," blue "Metal," unpainted base, 3kk................................$8-10

green cab, clear windows, gray base, 3kk; pale orange canopy top, cream bed, blue "ma voiture miniature preferee," red "MAJORETTE," blue "Metal," unpainted base, 3kk.............................$8-10

yellow cab, clear windows, tan base, 3kk; pale orange canopy top, pale orange bed, black "ma voiture miniature preferee," red "MAJORETTE," black "Metal," unpainted base, 5sp....................$8-10

367-B Magirus Canvas Back Covered Truck, 1:100, 1979–1980

yellow cab, amber windows, black base, 3kk; gray canopy top, brown bed, "TRANSWORLD," unpainted base, 3kk $10-13

yellow cab, amber windows, black base, 3kk; blue canopy top, yellow bed, "DANZAS," unpainted base, 3kk....................$8-10

metallic blue cab, amber windows, black base, 3kk; yellow canopy top, blue bed, "MICHELIN," unpainted base, 3kk..$8-10

blue cab, amber windows, black base, 3kk; pale orange canopy top, dark blue bed, blue "ma voiture miniature preferee," red "MAJORETTE," blue "Metal," unpainted base, 3kk..............................$8-10

367-C Scania Canvas Back, Covered Truck, 1:100, 1980

lemon cab, clear windows, black base, 3kk; cream canopy top, yellow-orange bed, black "ma voiture miniature preferee," red "MAJORETTE," black "Metal," unpainted base, 3kk $8-10

yellow cab, clear windows, black base, 3spb/3kk; blue canopy top, yellow bed, "DANZAS," unpainted base, 3kk ...$8-10

yellow cab, clear windows, black base, 3kk; blue canopy top, yellow bed, "DANZAS," unpainted base, 3kk.....................$8-10

yellow cab, clear windows, black base, 3spb; blue canopy top, yellow bed, "DANZAS," unpainted base, 3kk.....................$8-10

dark blue cab, clear windows, black base, 3kk; yellow canopy top, blue bed, "MICHELIN," unpainted base, 3kk.....................$8-10

dark blue cab, clear windows, black base, 3spb; yellow canopy top, blue bed, "MICHELIN," unpainted base, 3kk...$8-10

metallic blue cab, clear windows, white base, 3kk; pale orange top, cream bed, black "ma voiture miniature preferee," red "MAJORETTE," black "Metal," unpainted base, 3kk.................................$8-10

367-D Mercedes Canvas Back Covered Truck, 1:100

light blue cab, clear windows, black base, 3kk/3spn; blue canopy top, pale yellow bed, "DANZAS," unpainted base, 3kk $8-10

367-E, F, G, and H are a new casting that has no undercarriage attached to the trailer bed.

367-E Scania Canvas Back Covered Truck, 1:100

dark blue cab, clear windows, black base, 3kk; yellow canopy top, blue bed, "DANZAS," 4spn $8-10

367-F Mercedes Canvas Back Covered Truck, 1:100, 1981

dark blue cab, clear windows, black base, 3spb/3kk; yellow canopy top, dark blue bed, "MICHELIN," 4spn $8-10

367-G Canvas Back Covered Truck, generic cab with white air deflector unless specified otherwise, 1:100, 1981

red cab, clear windows, black base, 4c; white canopy top, "RENAULT," 4spn $8-10

red cab, amber windows, black base, 4c; white canopy top, "RENAULT," 4spn.......................................$8-10

red cab, amber windows, black base, 4c; white canopy top, "RENAULT" with black stripe underneath, 4spn $8-10

white cab, amber windows, black base, 4c; white canopy top, "RENAULT" with black stripe underneath, 4spn $8-10

367-H Canvas Back Covered Truck, generic cab with dual exhausts, 1:100, 1999

red cab, gray plastic exhausts, blue tint windows, black base, 4c; trailer: red body; yellow canopy top, "majorette" and 4 cars, label, 8p $4-6

368-A Ford Capri, 251-A, and St. Tropez Travel Trailer, 201-A, 1979–1981

red, white roof, white interior, green windows, 3spb, white trailer, red interior, clear windows, "Music Pop" with guitar on door, 3spb......................................$16-20

368-B Renault 18i, 266-A, and St. Tropez Travel Trailer, 201-A, 1982–1985

blue car, white interior, clear windows, yellow spoiler on roof, 3spb; trailer: yellow, blue label with dolphin, 3spb..............$12-15

light red, 3kk, 266-A 9; trailer: white with "Music Pop," guitar on door, 3spb..........$12-15

369-A Farm Tractor, 208-A, and Hay Trailer*, 1980–1987

red cab with gray interior, black stack and chassis; red plastic trailer with unpainted metal hitch/base, black rear gate, knobby large black wheels $6-8

blue tractor, white fenders, black steering wheel, ft3; red plastic trailer, yellow stakes, 8sp black wheels $6-8

370-A House Trailer Caravane *Residentielle*, 1:100, 1976–1979

white body with picture of red fence and evergreens on sides, 3spb.................$25-30

cream body, yellow floor, red interior, clear side windows with red curtains, small clear roof window, large green roof and front windows that open, red flowers on 3 sides of side windows, unpainted base, 3spb..............................$14-17

cream body, yellow floor, red interior, clear side windows with red curtains, small clear roof window, large green roof and front windows that open, red flowers on 2 sides of side windows, unpainted base, 3spb.......................................$14-17

yellow body, yellow floor, red interior, clear side windows with red curtains, small clear roof window, large green roof and front windows that open, "JOE CIRCUS," clown with 2 red and 2 blue stripes on white hat, stars, elephant, 3spb....$14-17

yellow body, yellow floor, red interior, clear side windows with red curtains, small clear roof window, large green roof and front windows that open, "JOE CIRCUS," clown with 1 red and 1 blue stripe on white hat, stars, elephant, 3spb....$14-17

yellow body, red floor, red interior, clear side windows with red curtains, small clear roof window, large blue roof and front windows that open, "CLOWNS," "PINDER," 3 clown faces, stars, 4c $8-10

white body, red floor, red interior, clear side windows with red curtains, small clear roof window, large green tint roof and front windows that open, "COCA COLA," soccer balls, 4c $8-10

370-B Deep Sea Explorer Transporter, 1:100, 1987–1994

blue, opaque windows, "sea explorer," label on cab, 6sp; yellow-orange submarine, dark blue canopy, "001 submarine," label ..$5-7

light blue, clear windows, "sea explorer," label on cab, 6sp; yellow-orange submarine, light blue tint canopy, "001 submarine," label...$5-7

blue, opaque windows, "sea explorer," tampo on cab, "001 submarine," tampo on sides, 5d; yellow-orange submarine, medium blue tint canopy, "001 submarine," label..........$5-7

blue, opaque windows, "sea explorer," tampo on cab, "001 submarine," label on sides, 5d; yellow submarine, medium blue tint canopy, "001 submarine," label $5-7

blue, opaque windows, "sea explorer," tampo on cab, "001 submarine," tampo on sides, 5d; bright orange submarine, medium blue tint canopy, stylized sun label $5-7

purple, opaque windows, stylized sun, tampo on cab, "Submarine 001," tampo on sides, 5d; bright orange submarine, medium blue tint canopy, stylized sun label $7-9

dark blue, opaque windows, "RACING TEAM," tampo on cab, "COMPETITION," tampo on sides, 5d; bright orange submarine, medium blue tint canopy, stylized sun label $5-7

dark blue, opaque windows, "RACING TEAM," tampo on cab, "COMPETITION," tampo on sides, 6sp; bright orange submarine, medium blue tint canopy, stylized sun label................$5-7

371-A Gazelle Helicopter, 1:70, 1976

red upper, white base, light green tint canopy, white interior, black blades and skids, yellow "SECURITE CIVILE," label, white tail assembly with red, white, and blue roundel, label $15-18

red upper, white base, green tint canopy, white interior, black blades and skids, white "SECURITE CIVILE," label, white tail assembly with red, white, and blue roundel, label $15-18

blue upper, white base, amber tint canopy, white interior, black blades and skids, white "GENDARMERIE," label, white tail assembly with red, white, and greenish-blue roundel, label $15-18

green upper, white base, amber tint canopy, white interior, black blades and skids, green "TELEVISION," label, white tail assembly with blue "SA 341," label.....................................$15-18

red upper, red base, amber tint canopy, white interior, black blades and skids, black "SOS POMPIER SOS," label, red tail assembly with black "SOS" and red flames $15-18

yellow upper, yellow base, green tint canopy, white interior, black blades and skids, black "ADAC," red cross in a white circle, and black "Katastrophen Schutz," labels on body, *German issue* $15-18

white upper, white base, blue tint canopy, white interior, red blades and skids, red cross and black "CROIX ROUGE," label, white tail assembly with a red cross, label $15-18

red and blue, amber tint canopy, no design (no further information available) $18

white upper, blue base, blue tint canopy, white interior, red blades and skids, black "PRESIDENT," label, blue tail assembly with red, white, and blue roundel $15-18

red upper, red base, amber tint canopy, white interior, black blades and skids, black "SOS AMBULANCE," label, red tail assembly, part of 601-A-3 set $15-18

olive drab upper, khaki base, amber tint canopy, white interior, black blades and skids, khaki tail assembly, no design, model comes with a selection of labels to be applied by purchaser $20-25

white upper, blue base, amber tint canopy, red interior, blue blades and skids, red "POLICE," label blue tail assembly $12-15

white upper, blue base, amber tint canopy, red interior, blue blades and skids, blue "POLICE" with red and blue design, label, blue tail assembly.......................$12-15

white upper, red base, amber tint canopy, black interior, black blades and skids, blue "RESCUE" with red and blue design, label, red tail assembly $12-15

white upper, red base, light amber tint canopy, white interior, red blades and skids, black "EWING OIL CO. DALLAS," label, red tail assembly with small yellow bar, label.................................$16-20

blue upper, white base, amber tint canopy, black interior, black blades and skids, white "RESCUE," tampo, white tail assembly........$5-7

red upper, red base, amber tint canopy, black interior, black blades and skids, white "RESCUE," tampo, red tail assembly ..$5-7

red upper, red base, amber tint canopy, black interior, black blades and skids, black "TURBO," tampo, red tail assembly...$5-7

sand upper body, sand base, amber tint canopy, black interior, black blades and skids, black "AIR FORCE" and star surrounded by green camouflage, tampo, sand tail assembly, part of 601-A Special Forces set......................................$8-10

red upper, white base, dark green canopy, white interior, black blades and skids, yellow "SECURITE CIVILE," label, white tail assembly with red, white, and blue roundel, label $15-18

blue upper, white base, amber tint canopy, white interior, black blades and skids, white "GENDARMERIE," label, white tail assembly with red, white, and dark blue roundel, label $15-18

orange upper, white base, amber tint canopy, white interior, black blades and skids, orange "TELEVISION," label, white tail assembly with blue "SA 341," label $15-18

red upper, red base, amber tint canopy, white interior, black blades and skids, thick dark black "SOS POMPIER SOS," label, red tail assembly with dark black "SOS" and red flames, the printing on this model is much darker and thicker than that on variation 5 ....$15-18

white upper, white base, dark blue tint canopy, white interior, silver blades and red skids, red cross and black "CROIX ROUGE," label, white tail assembly with a red cross, label $15-18

372-A Chrysler Simca 1308, 240-A, and Kayak Camper Trailer, 1977–1978

metallic silver, blue tinted windows, cream interior, "CHRYSLER SIMCA" decal with Chrysler logo, 3kk; trailer blue over white, red kayak, 4sp $8-10

372-B Citroen CX, 265-A, and and Kayak Camper Trailer, 1979–1980................$6-8

372-C Peugeot 604, 238-A, and and Kayak Camper Trailer, 1981 ....$5-7

372-D Ford Capri, 251-A, and and Kayak Camper Trailer, 1983–1984

blue, red roof, white interior, amber windows, 3spb; trailer blue over white, white over red kayak, 4sp $8-10

blue, white roof, white interior, amber windows, 3spb; trailer blue over white, red over white kayak, 4sp...................$8-10

372-E Renault 11 Encore, 275-A, and Kayak Camper Trailer*, 1985–1986

red with black plastic lower body, amber windows, 3spn, trailer has red lower, black upper, 4sp, kayak has black hull, yellow deck $8-10

372-F Peugeot 205 GTI Hardtop, 281-A, and Kayak Camper Trailer*, 1987–1988

black, red plastic trim and interior, gold insignia on hood, red and black trailer, yellow and red kayak $4-6

372-G Peugeot 205 GTI/CTI Cabriolet, 210-C, and Kayak Camper Trailer*, 1989–1992

silver with pink interior and midline, blue, orange and yellow splatter tampos, black and white trailer with red hull and white upper on kayak.............................$4-6

blue, white trim and interior, red and white tampos, white and light blue trailer, white and red kayak $4-6

373-A Neoplan, Autocar Airport Bus, 1:87, 1977–present

white upper, yellow lower, pale amber windows, pale green interior, "LONDON <<< PARIS <<< MADRID," tampo, 3kk $6-8

white upper, red lower, pale amber windows, pale green interior, "LONDON <<< PARIS <<< MADRID," tampo, 3spn ..$6-8

white upper, red lower, pale amber windows, pale green interior, "LONDON <<< PARIS <<< MADRID," tampo, 3kk $6-8

white upper, yellow lower, pale amber windows, pale green interior, "FRANKFURT <<< BERN <<< ROMA," tampo, 3kk...................$6-8

white upper, green lower, pale amber windows, pale green interior, "FRANKFURT <<< BERN <<< ROMA," tampo, 3kk.......$6-8

white upper, red lower, pale amber windows, pale green interior, "FRANKFURT <<< BERN <<< ROMA," tampo, 3kk......$6-8

white upper, blue lower, medium blue windows, ivory interior, "NEOPLAN Jetliner," decal, 3spb $8-10

orange-yellow upper, mustard orange lower, pale amber windows, pale green interior, "School Bus," decal, 3spb, 1978 ..$8-10

red upper, white lower, medium blue windows, ivory interior, eight coats of arms, decal, 3kk, 1979 ....$8-10

white upper, cream lower, dark amber windows, cream interior, medium blue/small size "AIR FRANCE," tampo, 3spb, 1980–1984 ....$6-8

white upper, cream lower, dark amber windows, cream interior, medium blue/small size "AIR FRANCE," tampo, 3kk, 1980–1984 ....$6-8

white upper, cream lower, medium blue windows, ivory interior, dark blue/small size "AIR FRANCE," tampo, 3spb, 1980–1984..$6-8

white upper, white lower, pale blue windows, cream interior, light blue/small size "AIR FRANCE," tampo, 3spb, 1980–1984 ..$6-8

white upper, cream lower, clear windows, cream interior, medium blue/small size "AIR FRANCE," tampo, 3kk, 1980–1984 ..$6-8

white upper, white lower, pale blue windows, cream interior, medium blue/small size "AIR FRANCE," tampo, 3spb front, 3kk rear, 1980–1984 ....$6-8

white upper, cream lower, medium blue windows, ivory interior, dark blue/medium size "AIR FRANCE," decal, 3kk, 1980–1984 ....$6-8

white upper, dark blue lower, medium blue windows, ivory interior, dark blue/large size "AIR FRANCE," decal, 3kk, 1980–1984 ....$6-8

white upper, medium blue lower, dark blue windows, ivory interior, dark blue/large size "AIR FRANCE," decal, 3kk, 1980–1984 ....$6-8

beige "AIR FRANCE," 3spb, 1980–1984 ....$6-8

beige upper, white lower, pale amber windows, ivory interior, "IBERIA," tampo, 3spn, 1983 ....$6-8

cream upper, white lower, medium amber windows, cream interior, "IBERIA," tampo, 3kk, 1983 ....$6-8

white upper, white lower, medium amber windows, ivory interior, "IBERIA," tampo, 3spn, 1983 ....$6-8 white upper, yellow lower, amber windows, "Happy Holidays," label, 1987–88 catalog $6-8

dark red upper, white lower, dark amber windows, pale yellow interior, "Happy Holidays," parrot towards front on both sides, dark blue sky, label, 4c, 1987–88...$6-8

red upper, white lower, dark amber windows, pale yellow interior, "Happy Holidays," parrot towards rear on driver's side, pale blue sky, label, 3spn, 1987–88 ......$6-8

red upper, white lower, dark amber windows, pale yellow interior, "Happy Holidays," parrot towards rear on driver's side, pale blue sky, label, 3kk, 1987–88 ....$6-8

red upper, white lower, dark amber windows, pale yellow interior, "croisiere," label, 4c, 1989 ....$6-8

white upper, red lower, pale blue windows, cream interior, "croisiere," label, 4c, 1989 ....$6-8

white upper, red lower, dark blue windows, pale yellow interior, "croisiere," label, 4c., 1989 ....$6-8

white upper, yellow lower, pale blue windows, "croisiere," label $6-8

white upper, red lower, medium blue windows, cream interior, no printing, 4c $5-7

pale yellow upper, mustard orange lower, clear windows, light blue interior, "PTT," label, 4c...................................$12-15

white upper, red lower, medium amber windows, ivory interior, "British Airways," decal, 3spb $12-15

green upper, white lower, pale amber windows, ivory interior, "VARIG," decal, 3spb $12-15

red upper, red lower, pale amber windows, ivory interior, "QANTAS," decal, 3kk.............................$12-15

orange-yellow upper, mustard orange lower, pale amber windows, ivory interior, "Lufthansa," decal, 3kk................$12-15

white upper, white lower, pale amber windows, ivory interior, "TWA," label, 3kk $12-15

white upper, blue lower, pale amber windows, ivory interior, "SWISSAIR," label, 3kk $12-15

red upper, white lower, pale amber windows, ivory interior, "JAPAN AIR LINES," decal, 3kk $12-15

white upper, white lower, pale blue windows, cream interior, "3 running feet" logo, "ISLE OF MAN," tampo, red stripe, *English promotional*, 3kk.......................$10-13

white upper, white lower, dark amber windows, pale yellow interior, "Holiday Express," "LAKELAND," tampo, orange accents, *English promotional*, 4c.$10-13

white upper, white lower, medium blue windows, pale yellow interior, "Holiday Express," "JERSEY," tampo, red accents, *English promotional*, 3spb..........$10-13

white upper, white lower, medium blue windows, pale yellow interior, "Holiday Express," "LOOE Cornwall," tampo, red accents, *English promotional*, 3spb $10-13

44. white upper, white lower, pale blue windows, pale yellow interior, "Holiday Express," "GUERNSEY," tampo, red accents, *English promotional*, 3spb $10-13

white upper, white lower, dark blue windows, pale yellow interior, "Holiday Express," "Porthcawl," tampo, red accents, *English promotional*, 3spb.....................$10-13

white upper, white lower, medium blue windows, pale yellow interior, "Holiday Express," "DEVON," tampo, red accents, *English promotional*, 3spb..........$10-13

white upper, white lower, pale blue windows, pale yellow interior, "Holiday Express," "BLACKPOOL," tampo, red accents, *English promotional*, 3spb $10-13

white upper, white lower, medium blue windows, pale yellow interior, "Holiday Express," "LAND'S END," tampo, red accents, *English promotional*, 3spb $10-13

white upper, white lower, pale blue windows, pale yellow interior, "Holiday Express," "BOURNEMOUTH," tampo, red accents, *English promotional*, 3kk............$10-13

white upper, white lower, pale blue windows, pale yellow interior, "Holiday Express," "ISLE OF WIGHT," tampo, red accents, *English promotional*, 3kk............$10-13

white upper, white lower, pale blue windows, pale yellow interior, "Holiday Express," "MARGATE," tampo, red accents, *English promotional*, 3kk......................$10-13

white upper, white lower, pale amber windows, ivory interior, "Holiday Express," "Brighton," tampo, *English promotional*, 3spb $10-13

white upper, white lower, pale amber windows, ivory interior, "Holiday Express," "London," tampo, *English promotional*, 3spb $10-13

white upper, white lower, pale amber windows, ivory interior, "Holiday Express," "Torbay," tampo, *English promotional*, 3spb $10-13

white upper, cream lower, pale blue windows, pale yellow interior, "Holiday Express," "Somerset," tampo, *English promotional*, 3kk $10-13

white upper, white lower, pale blue windows, cream interior, black "K. H. NORTON GROUP" on a green stripe on sides, tampo, 3 business addresses on roof, tampo, *English promotional*, 4c..$10-13

white upper, blue lower, pale blue windows, hot pink interior, "MIAMI BEACH," label, without dots in the palm leaves, 4c, 1990–1992.................................$5-7

white upper, metallic blue lower, pale blue windows, cream interior, "MIAMI BEACH," label, with dots in the palm leaves, 4c, 1990–1992 ....$5-7

white upper, blue lower, medium blue windows, cream interior, "MIAMI BEACH," label, without dots in the palm leaves, 4c, 1990–1992.................................$5-7

white upper, white lower, medium blue windows, cream interior, "MIAMI BEACH," label, with dots in the palm leaves, 4c, 1990–1992.................................$6-8

white upper, black lower, red/yellow/blue abstract accents, 1993 ....$6-8

white upper, black lower, pale blue windows, hot fuschia interior, orange stars and balls on sides, stars, balls and fish caricatures on roof, tampo, 4c, 1993.............$8-10

white upper, black lower, pale blue windows, hot pink interior, orange stars and blue balls, tampo, 4c blue wheels, 1994 ....$5-7

white upper, black lower, medium blue windows, hot pink interior, orange stars and blue balls, tampo, 4c blue wheels, 1994..$5-7

white upper, blue lower, pale blue windows, hot pink interior, orange stars and blue balls, tampo, 4c, 1994 ....$5-7

yellow upper, blue lower, pale blue windows, dull red interior, "TRAVEL" with sunset horizon logo, label, 4c, 1995 ....$5-7

yellow upper, mustard yellow bottom, pale blue windows, blue interior, black stripe and "SCHOOL BUS," tampo, three ovals cover up "Made in France," 4c, 1996–1997 ....$4-6

yellow upper, mustard yellow bottom, pale blue windows, dark blue interior, black stripe and "SCHOOL BUS," tampo, the three ovals that covered up "Made in France" are now removed, 4c, 1996–1997 ....$4-6

yellow upper, mustard yellow bottom, pale blue windows, purple interior, school supplies and black "SCHOOL BUS," tampo, 4c, 1998 ....$4-6

lemon upper, mustard yellow bottom, clear windows, purple interior, school supplies and black "SCHOOL BUS," tampo, 4c, 1999 ....$4-6

red upper, red lower, pale blue windows, white interior, yellow sun holding coke bottle, towards frontand white "Coca Cola," towards rear, label, 4c, 1996 ....$8-10

red upper, red lower, pale blue windows, white interior, white "Coca Cola," towards front and yellow sun holding coke bottle, towards rear, tampo, 4c, 1997 ....$8-10

white upper, red lower, pale blue windows, white interior, "EAT FOOTBALL SLEEP FOOTBALL DRINK Coca Cola, over soccer ball," tampo, 4c, 1998 ....$8-10

blue upper, blue lower, medium blue windows,dull red interior, "PEPSI," Pepsi logo, and bubbles, tampo, 4c, 2000 .....$8-10

red upper, black lower, pale blue windows, yellow interior, "Racing Team" accents, tampo, "CHAMPION," "SPORT," 4c, 2000 ....$8-10

red upper, white lower, dark amber windows, pale yellow interior, "Happy Holidays," parrot towards front on both sides, dark blue sky, label, 4c, 1987–88 ....$6-8

red upper, white lower, amber windows, pale yellow interior, "Happy Holidays," parrot towards front on both sides, dark blue sky, label, 4c, 1987–88 ....$6-8

light blue upper, white lower, pale amber windows, ivory interior, "SABENA belgian world airlines," decal, 3kk $12-15

orange-yellow upper, mustard orange lower, "Lufthansa," decal, 3spb $12-15

white upper, red lower, pale amber windows, pale green interior, "LONDON <<< PARIS <<< MADRID," tampo, 3spn ..$6-8

374-A Safari Truck, 225-A and Covered Trailer*, 1978–1982

truck: zebra stripes, green canopy with "AFRICAN SAFARI" label, red tires on roof, black brush bar, green tinted windows, 3spb; trailer: zebra stripes with green canopy with "AFRICAN SAFARI" label $8-10

truck: zebra stripes, green canopy with "AFRICAN SAFARI" label, red tires on roof, black brush bar, green tinted windows, 3kk; trailer: zebra stripes with green canopy with "AFRICAN SAFARI label" $8-10

truck: white with black zebra stripes, tiger head label on hood, green canopy with "AFRICAN SAFARI" label, red tires on roof, black brush bar, green tinted windows, 3spb; trailer: zebra stripes with green canopy with "AFRICAN SAFARI" label $8-10

374-B Toyota Landcruiser, 277-A, and Covered Trailer*, 1983–1986

metallic light green with cream interior, amber windows, ctsc, trailer matches color of vehicle with yellow canopy, ctsc, 1984 catalog $8-10

yellow, "RAID 86," map of Africa on roof, ctsc, khaki trailer with red canopy, ctsc, 1986 catalog $8-10

375-A Ford Transit TUG, 295-A, and F1 Racer, 1993–1999

red with white interior, amber windows, "24," "EMERGENCY ROAD SERVICE," 6sp, red F1 racer, "FIAT," "Pioneer," rw, 1999 catalog $4-6

red with white interior, amber windows, "Jack's 24 Hr. Service," 6sp, red racer, "FIAT," "Agip," rw, 1993–1996 ....$4-6

blue with red interior, clear windows, 6sp, blue F1 racer, rw, 2000 catalog $4-6

376-Aa Range Rover Rescue Team, 246-B open back, and Tank Trailer*, 1978–1987

red, white interior and ladder, clear windows, blue riders in back, 8sp; trailer is red with white hoses and it has a French Fire shield tampo on the sides.....................$8-10

red, white interior and ladder, blue windshield, blue riders in back, 5d; trailer is red with white hoses and it has a French Fire shield tampo on the sides $8-10

red, white interior, clear windows, white ladder. "Rescue Team 3" label on hood, 8sp; red trailer, "Rescue Team 3" label on sides, 4spn $8-10

376-Ab Range Rover Rescue Team, 246-C closed back, and Tank Trailer*, 1988–?

red, black interior, clear windows, gray ladder, "District 3 Fire Dept." on sides, 5d, red trailer, "District 3 Fire Dept." label on sides, 8p ..$6-8

red, black interior, blue windows, white ladder, "Rescue Unit," 5d, red trailer, "Rescue Unit" label on sides, 4spn $6-8

red, black interior, clear windows, gray ladder, "District 3 Fire Dept." on sides, 5st, red trailer, "District 3 Fire Dept." on sides, 8p........$6-8

377-A Magirus Heavy Duty Dump Truck Semi-Benne carriere, 1:100, 1978–1982

blue cab, silver trailer, 3spn $6-8

red cab, silver trailer, 3spn....................$6-8

blue cab, amber windows, black base, 3kk; silver trailer, 3kk $5-7

blue cab, amber windows, gray base, 3kk; silver trailer, 3kk $6-8

red cab,amber windows, black base, 3spb; silver trailer, 3spb $5-7

red cab, amber windows, black base, 3spb; silver trailer, 3kk $5-7

blue cab, 3spn; silver trailer, 3kk $5-7

red cab, amber windows, black base, 3kk; silver trailer, 3spb......................$5-7

377-B Scania Heavy Duty Dump Truck Semi-Benne carriere, 1:100, 1983, red with silver trailer, 3spn..............................$7-9

377-C Mercedes Heavy Duty Dump Truck Semi-Benne carriere, 1:100, green cab, clear windows, black base, 3kk; silver trailer, 3spb ..$6-8

377-D Heavy Duty Dump Truck, generic cab with dual exhausts, 1:100

orange cab, clear windows, black base, 4c; silver trailer, 3kk, ...$5-7

orange cab, amber windows, black base, 3spn; silver trailer, 3kk....................$5-7

light blue cab, amber windows, black base, 3spn; silver trailer, 3kk....................$5-7

378-A Mercedes 450SE and Motorcycle Trailer, 1978–1979

bronze, red interior, light amber windows, 3spb; black trailer, 4spn, red and yellow motorcycles $9-12

378-B Volvo 245 DL Station Wagon, 220-A and Motorcycle Trailer, 1980 ....$8-10

378-C Simca 1308 and Motorcycle Trailer, 1981

blue, white interior, light amber windows, 3spb; white trailer, 4spn, red and yellow motorcycles $6-8

378-D Racing Team Van, 234-A and Motorcycle Trailer*

yellow van with red interior, red and black "racing team" stickers......................$4-6

378-E Ford US Van, 250-B and Motorcycle Trailer*, 1982

black van with red/orange/yellow flame accents, 6sp; black trailer with green and yellow motorcycles $6-8

black van with red/orange/yellow flame accents, 6spk; black trailer with red and yellow motorcycles $6-8

379-A Hopper Tank Truck, 1:100 ....$6-8

379-B Magirus Powder Transporter, 1:100, 1979–1985

orange cab, amber windows, black base, 3spb; silver-gray tank, yellow trim, orange base with hole at top rear, 3kk.........$5-7

orange cab, amber windows, black base, 3kk; silver-gray tank, yellow trim, orange base without hole at top rear, 3kk $5-7

red cab, amber windows, black base, 3spb; silver-gray tank, yellow trim, red base with hole at top rear, 3spb $5-7

red cab, amber windows, black base, 3kk; silver-gray tank, yellow trim, red base without hole at top rear, 3kk, rear 1/3spb, rear 2 ....$5-7

red cab, amber windows, black base, 3kk; silver-gray tank, yellow trim, red base without hole at top rear, 3kk $5-7

379-C Powder Transporter, generic cab with dual exhausts, 1:100, 1997

red cab, chrome exhausts, amber windows, black base, 4c; silver-gray tank, yellow trim, red base with hole at top rear, 4c........$4-6

red cab, chrome exhausts, blue windows, black base, 4c; gray tank, yellow trim, red base without hole at top rear, 4c $4-6

yellow cab, gray exhausts, blue windows, black base, 4c; gray tank, yellow trim, red base without hole at top rear, 4c $4-6

olive drab cab, gray exhausts, blue windows, black base, 4c; olive drab tank, white trim, olive drab base without hole at top rear, 4c $8-10

olive drab cab, amber windows, black base, red tank with gray tank base, 4c, from Special Forces 2-pack $4-6

yellow cab, gray exhausts, blue windows, black base, 4c; red tank, yellow trim, yellow base without hole at top rear, 4c, 2000 ....$4-6

380 and 381 not issued

382-A Land Rover with Compressor, yellow...$4-6

382-B Mercedes Utility Truck with Compressor, 1979–1983

orange, blue canopy, white interior, blue windshield, 3kk; trailer, blue over orange, 4spn $15-18

orange, white interior, blue windshield, yellow canopy with blue/red/yellow/black roadsign accents on the sides, 3kk; trailer, yellow over orange, 4spn............$15-18

382-C Toyota Hi-Lux Pickup, 292-A, with Compressor, 1984–1987

white with orange and black stripe tampos on sides and hood, black interior, amber windows, orange, black and red accents, 5d, orange compressor trailer with white upper half, 4spn $12-15

orange with silver and black side stripe tampos, yellow and black tampo on hood, black interior, clear windows, 5d, orange compressor trailer with white upper half, 4spn..$10-13

Majorette 600 Series, 1:87 Scale, HO Gauge Semi-Tractor/Trailers

601-A Helicopter Transporter with 371-A Gazelle Helicopter—Cab is a C.O.E. Sleeper with dual chrome exhausts, triple roof horns cast separately from the roof, and a plastic airfoil.

blue cab, orange and yellow graphics, yellow airfoil, gray trailer, red and white helicopter $7-9

red cab, "Engine #45 District 2 Fire Dept.," no airfoil, gray trailer, red helicopter.......$4-6

red cab, amber windows, yellow/orange/black tampo, black air foil, rd/6lr; silver trailer, red ramp, cable housing, and base, yellow cable reel, 6lr; 371-A-10 helicopter, "SOS AMBULANCE" $10-13

red cab, amber windows, yellow/orange/black tampo, black air foil, rd/6lr; silver trailer, red ramp, cable housing, and base, yellow cable reel, 6lr; 371-A-13 helicopter, blue "POLICE"....................$10-13

red cab, amber windows, gold/white/black tampo, white air foil, rd/6lr; silver trailer, yellow ramp and cable reel, black cable housing and base, 6lr; 371-A-12 helicopter, red "POLICE" $10-13

blue cab, amber windows, white/light blue/dark blue tampo, white air foil, rd/6lr; silver trailer, yellow ramp and cable reel, black cable housing and base, 6lr; 371-A-14 helicopter, "RESCUE" $10-13

red cab, amber windows, "ENGINE #45 DISTRICT 2 FIRE DEPT.," white air foil, rd/6lr;

gray trailer, red ramp and cable reel, black cable housing and base, 6lr; 371-A-17 helicopter, "RESCUE" $8-10

black cab, amber windows, white stars, pink and blue landscape tampo, white air foil, rd/6lr; silver trailer, red ramp and cable reel, black cable housing and base, 6lr; 371-A-18 helicopter, "TURBO" $8-10

black cab, amber windows, white stars, pink and blue landscape tampo, white air foil, rd/6lr; silver trailer, red ramp and cable reel, black cable housing and base, 6lr; 371-A-17 helicopter, "RESCUE" $8-10

black cab, amber windows, white stars, pink and blue landscape tampo, white air foil, rd/6lr; silver trailer, red ramp and cable reel, black cable housing and base, 6sp; 371-A-17 helicopter, "RESCUE" $8-10

red cab, amber windows, gold/white/black tampo, black air foil, rd/6lr; silver trailer, red ramp, yellow cable reel, black cable housing and base, 6lr; 371-A-12 helicopter, red "POLICE" $10-13

blue cab, amber windows, white/light blue/dark blue tampo, white air foil, rd/6lr; silver trailer, yellow ramp and cable reel, black cable housing and base, 6lr; 371-A-16 helicopter, "RESCUE" $10-13

red cab, amber windows, gold/white/black tampo, yellow air foil, rd/6lr; silver trailer, yellow ramp and cable reel, black cable housing and base, 6lr; 371-A-12 helicopter, red "POLICE" $10-13

601-B Helicopter Transporter with 371-A Gazelle Helicopter, 1999—Cab is a C.O.E. Sleeper with dual exhausts, but no roof horns or airfoil.

olive cab with gray and brown camouflage, clear windows, gray dual exhausts, 6spol; olive trailer, olive ramp, black cable reel, cable housing and base, 6spol; 371-A-19 sand helicopter, "AIR FORCE," *Special Forces*...............................$10-13

602-A Semi Front End Loader Transporter with 263-A Front End Loader, cab is a C.O.E. Sleeper with dual chrome exhausts, amber windows, chrome interior, triple roof horns cast separately from the roof, and a plastic air foil 1:87, 1983

metallic blue cab, amber windows, orange and yellow graphics, white airfoil, gray trailer with orange 263-A Front End Loader, rd/6lr $7-9

metallic blue cab, amber windows, orange and yellow graphics, yellow air foil, rd/6lr; gray trailer, yellow ramp and cable reel, black cable housing and base, 6lr; 263-A orange front end loader, light gray engine and stack, ct3c $10-13

red cab, amber windows, gold/silver/black tampo, yellow air foil, rd/6lr; gray trailer, yellow ramp and cable reel, black cable housing and base, 6lr; 263-A orange front end loader, light gray engine and stack, ct3cb..............$10-13

lime cab, amber windows, orange/yellow/green tampo, yellow air foil, rd/6lr; tan trailer, yellow ramp, cable housing and base, red cable reel, 6lr; 263-A orange front end loader, light gray engine and stack, ct3cb..............$10-13

yellow cab, amber windows, black/orange tampo, white air foil, rd/6lr; gray trailer, yellow ramp and cable reel, black cable housing and base, 6lr; 263-A orange front end loader, light gray engine and stack, ct3cb..............$10-13

yellow cab, amber windows, orange/black tampo, white air foil, rd/6lr; gray trailer, yellow ramp and cable reel, black cable housing and base, 6lr; 263-A yellow front end loader, black bucket, light gray engine and stack, ct3c...............$10-13

dark green cab, amber windows, red/yellow/black desert scene tampo, white air foil, rd/6lr; silver trailer, yellow ramp and cable reel, black cable housing and base, 6lr; 263-A yellow front end loader, black bucket, dark gray engine and stack, ct3c...................$8-10

orange cab, amber windows, red/yellow/black desert scene tampo, white air foil, rd/6lr; silver trailer, yellow ramp and cable reel, black cable housing and base, 6lr; 263-A yellow front end loader, black bucket, dark gray engine and stack, ct3c...........................$8-10

603-A Kenworth Ribbed Semi Container Truck, 1983—Cab is a KW Conventional Sleeper with dual chrome exhausts, opening hood, and 2 horns cast into roof.

metallic blue cab, clear windows, red, white, and blue tampo with 2 blue stars on hood and 4 blue stars on sleeper roof, rd/6lr; white container, metallic blue base, blue "TRANS" and 4 white stars on red label and blue "USA" and 2 white stars on red label, 6lr $10-13

metallic blue cab, amber windows, red, white, and blue tampo with 2 blue stars on hood and 4 blue stars on sleeper roof, rd/6lr; white container, metallic blue base, blue "TRANS" and 4 white stars on red label and blue "USA" and 2 white stars on red label, 6lr $10-13

metallic blue cab, amber windows, red, white, and blue tampo with 2 blue stars on hood and 4 blue stars on sleeper roof, rd/6lr; red container, metallic blue base, blue "TRANS" and 4 white stars on red label and blue "USA" and 2 white stars on red label, 6lr $10-13

604-A Kenworth Semi Freight Truck, 1983—Cab is a KW Conventional Sleeper with dual chrome exhausts, opening hood, and 2 horns cast as part of the roof.

dark blue cab, amber windows, rd/6lr; dark blue container, black base, "BorgWarner," label, 6lr...$12-15

black cab, amber windows, gold filigree on hood and sleeper roof, rd/6lr; black trailer, red base, "King of the Road" and lion, label, 6lr...................................$10-13

black cab, amber windows, gold stylized hawk on hood, gold "Night hawk" on sleeper roof, rd/6lr; black trailer, red base, "Night Hawk" and stylized hawk on gold label, 6lr, 1986 ....$10-13

black cab, amber windows, red eagle on hood, gold cactus on cab roof, white "CANYON" on sleeper roof, rd/6lr; black trailer, red base, western sunset scene with red-orange tint, label, 6lr $10-13

black cab, amber windows, gold stylized hawk on hood, gold "Night Hawk" on sleeper roof, rd/6lr; black trailer, red base, western sunset scene with yellow-brown tint, label, 6lr $10-13

blue cab, clear windows, eagle head on hood, 3 white stars on red bar on sleeper roof, rd/6lr; red trailer, blue base, eagle head and "EAGLE TRUCK," label, 6lr $10-13

black cab, amber windows, red eagle on hood, gold cactus on cab roof, white "CANYON" on sleeper roof, rd/6lr; black trailer, blue base, eagle head and "EAGLE TRUCK," label, 6lr..........$10-13

blue cab, amber windows, eagle head on hood, 3 white stars on red bar on sleeper roof, rd/6lr; red trailer, blue base, eagle head and "EAGLE TRUCK," label, 6sp $10-13

light blue cab, clear windows, rd/6lr; white trailer, black base, "CP Express and Transport," label, 6lr $20-25

metallic blue cab, amber windows, red, white, and blue tampo with 2 blue stars on hood and 4 blue stars on sleeper roof, rd/6lr; white trailer, black base, "CP Express and Transport," label, 6lr $15-18

yellow cab, clear windows, rd/6lr; yellow trailer, black base, "Home Hardware," label, *Canadian promotional*, 6lr $25-30

orange-yellow cab, amber windows, girl in snowsuit on hood, "Diplom-Is" on sleeper roof, rd/6lr; white trailer, black base, "Diplom-Is Hele Norges iskrem!," label, *Norwegian promotional*, 6lr..........$4-60

red cab, clear windows, rd/6lr; white trailer, "HiWay Market," label, *Canadian promotional*, 6lr $4-60

white cab, amber windows, rd/6lr; white trailer, red base, "CGM," tampo, 6lr ..$15-18

orange cab, amber windows, rd/6lr; gray trailer, black base, "DAY and ROSS," orange label, 6lr $25-30

red cab, amber windows, rd/6lr; white trailer, "HiWay Market," label, *Canadian promotional*, 6lr $4-60

white cab, amber windows, rd/6lr; white trailer, "WILD TURKEY," label, 6sp $4-60

604-B Semi Freight Truck, 1993–Cab is a C.O.E. Sleeper with dual chrome exhausts, triple roof horns cast separately from roof, and plastic air foil.

white cab, white air foil, amber windows, chrome interior, "Peter Pan EXTRA CRUNCHY," rd/6lr; white trailer, red base, "Peter Pan EXTRA CRUNCHY," *Road Eaters*, 6lr $4-6

red cab, white air foil, amber windows, chrome interior, "Willy Wonka's NERDS," rd/6lr; white trailer, red base, "Willy Wonka's NERDS," *Road Eaters*, 6lr $4-6

red cab, white air foil, amber windows, chrome interior, "Campbell's Dinosaur VEGETABLE SOUP," rd/6lr; red trailer, red base, "Campbell's Dinosaur VEGETABLE SOUP," *Road Eaters*, 6lr...................................$4-6

blue tractor with red trailer, red/white/blue "EAGLE TRUCK" stars and stripes, 1995...$4-6

white tractor with blue trailer, "Shark Monster" $4-6

604-C Kenworth Semi Freight Truck, 1993—Cab is a KW Conventional Sleeper with a single chrome exhaust, dual roof horns cast as part of the roof, and a narrow window in the sleeper.

red cab, clear windows, gray interior, "Campbell's Teddy Bear," rd/6lr; red trailer, red base, "Campbell's Teddy Bear," *Road Eaters*, 6lr $4-6

bright green cab, clear windows, gray interior, "CRY BABY," rd/6lr; bright green trailer, red base, "CRY BABY," *Road Eaters*, 6lr ..$4-6

black cab, clear windows, gray interior, "CHESTER CHEETAH," rd/6lr; black trailer, red base, "CHESTER CHEETAH," *Road Eaters*, 6lr $4-6

604-D Kenworth Semi Freight Truck, 1995?—Cab is a KW Conventional Sleeper with a cast air deflector and roof window, no exhausts.

blue cab, amber windows, chrome interior, eagle on hood and "EAGLE TRUCK" on air deflector, rd/6lr; red trailer, blue base, eagle and "EAGLE TRUCK," label, 6lr $6-8

blue cab, amber windows, chrome interior, eagle on hood and "EAGLE TRUCK" on air deflector, rd/6lr; red trailer, blue base, eagle and "EAGLE TRUCK," label, 6sp...............$6-8

white cab, amber windows, chrome interior, shark on side and "SHARK monster" on air deflector, 6sp; blue trailer, black base, shark and "SHARK monster," label, 6sp........$6-8

white cab, amber windows, chrome interior, "Coca Cola" on air deflector, 6sp; red trailer, black base, yellow sun, bottle of Coca Cola, and "Coca Cola," label, 6sp...$12-15

red cab, amber windows, chrome interior, "Coca Cola" on air deflector, 6sp; red trailer, black base, yellow sun, bottle of Coca Cola, and "Coca Cola," label, 6sp.......................................$12-15

red cab, amber windows, chrome interior, "PINDER" on sides and on air deflector, 6sp; yellow trailer, black base, "Le Cirque PINDER" and 4 elephants, label, 6sp..$12-15

white cab, amber windows, chrome interior, red and yellow "majorette" on air deflector, 6sp; white trailer, black base, red and yellow stripe with "majorette," "WE'RE ON THE MOVE!!," both are tampos, 6lr.......$10-13

605-A Semi Oil Tanker and Trailer, 1983—Cab is a C.O.E. Sleeper with dual chrome exhausts, triple roof horns cast separately from roof, and plastic air foil.

yellow cab, red air foil, amber windows, chrome interior, "Shell," rd/6lr; 2 white trailers, yellow base, red trim, "Shell," 6lr...$10-13

yellow cab, white air foil, amber windows, chrome interior, "Shell," rd/6lr; 2 white trailers, yellow base, red trim, "Shell," 6lr $10-13

605-B Mercedes Semi Double Oil Tanker and Trailer, 1994—Cab is a Mercedes-Benz C.O.E. Sleeper with no exhausts, dual roof horns and air foil cast on roof, and plastic sun visor.

yellow cab, black sun visor, clear windows, red interior, "Shell," rd/6lr; 2 white trailers, black base, red trim, "Shell," 6lr $8-10

yellow cab, black sun visor, clear windows, red interior, "Shell," rd/6lr; 2 white trailers, black base, red trim, "Shell," 6sp $8-10

606-A Kenworth Semi Tanker, 1983—Cab is a KW Conventional Sleeper with dual chrome exhausts, opening hood, and 2 horns cast as part of the roof.

orange cab, amber windows, chrome interior, "GULF" on hood, rd; gray tank with orange ends, black base, "GULF" on wide orange stripe, label, 6lr.......$12-15

metallic silver cab, amber windows, chrome interior, Texaco star-T logo upright, rd/6lr; gray tank with black ends, black base, "TEXACO" in front of star-T logo, label, 6lr $10-13

metallic silver cab, amber windows, chrome interior, Texaco star-T logo upside down, rd/6lr; gray tank with black ends, black base, "TEXACO" in front of star-T logo, label, 6lr, error...........................$25-30

silver-gray cab, amber windows, chrome interior, Texaco star-T logo upright, rd/6lr; gray tank with black ends, black base, "TEXACO" in front of star-T logo, label, 6lr $10-13

metallic silver cab, amber windows, chrome interior, Texaco star-T logo upright, rd/6lr; gray tank with orange ends, black base, "GULF" on wide orange stripe, label, 6lr, packaging error $12-15

metallic silver cab, amber windows, chrome interior, Texaco star-T logo upright, rd/6lr; gray tank with black ends, black base, "TEXACO" in front of star-T logo, label, 6lr..................................$10-13

606-B Kenworth Semi Tanker—Cab is a KW Conventional Sleeper with dual chrome exhausts and 2 horns cast as part of the roof, hood does not open.

metallic silver cab, amber windows, chrome interior, Texaco star-T logo upright, rd/6lr; chrome tank, black base, "TEXACO" in front of star-T logo, label, 6lr.........$15-18

silver-gray cab, amber windows, chrome interior, Texaco star-T logo upright, rd/6lr; gray tank, black base, "TEXACO" in front of star-T logo, label, 6lr $8-10

silver-gray cab, amber windows, chrome interior, Texaco star-T logo upright, rd/6lr; gray tank, black base, "TEXACO" in front of star-T logo, label, 6sp $8-10

606-C Kenworth Semi Tanker, 1995—Cab is a KW Conventional Sleeper with a cast air deflector and roof window, no exhausts.

silver-gray cab, amber windows, chrome interior, Texaco star-T logo upright, rd/6lr; gray tank, black base, "TEXACO" behind star-T logo, label, 6lr.............................$6-8

silver-gray cab, amber windows, chrome interior, Texaco star-T logo upright, rd/6lr; gray tank, black base, "TEXACO" in front of star-T logo, label, 6sp $6-8

silver-gray cab, amber windows, chrome interior, Texaco star-T logo upright, rd/6lr; dull gray tank, silver-gray base, "TEXACO" in front of star-T logo, label, 6sp.............$6-8

white cab, amber windows, chrome interior, red "Coca Cola" on air foil, 6sp; white tank, silver-gray base, Coke bottle, "Coca Cola," and bear faces, label, 6sp $10-13

red cab, amber windows, chrome interior, red "Coca Cola" on air foil, 6sp; white tank, silver-gray base, Coke bottle, "Coca Cola," and bear faces, label, 6sp $10-13

orange cab, amber windows, chrome interior, 6sp; gray tank, black base, "GT GAS TANKER," label, 6sp, 1999 ....$7-9

607-A Double Semi Freight Truck, 1984—Cab is a C.O.E. Sleeper with dual chrome exhausts, triple roof horns cast separately from roof, and plastic air foil.

metallic pink cab, yellow air foil, amber windows, chrome interior, yellow/orange graphic, rd/6lr; yellow trailers, unpainted base, "Pink Trucks" with yellow, purple, and orange graphics, label, 6lr....$15-18

dark blue cab, yellow air foil, amber windows, chrome interior, yellow/orange graphic, rd/6lr; dark blue trailers, unpainted base, "Road Dragon" and green dragon, label, 6lr....$15-18

light blue cab, white air foil, amber windows, chrome interior, rd/6lr; white trailers, unpainted base, "CP Express and Transport," label, 6lr $15-18

607-B Kenworth Double Semi Freight Truck, 1998—Cab is a KW Conventional Sleeper with a single chrome exhaust, dual horns cast as part of the roof, and a narrow window in the sleeper.

red cab, opaque windows, no interior, "PINDER," 6sp; yellow trailers, unpainted base, "Le Cirque PINDER," label, 6sp....$12-15

red cab, opaque windows, no interior, globe and "Transport COMPANY," 6sp; gray trailers, unpainted base, "Transport COMPANY," label, 6sp, 1999 ....$8-10

red cab, opaque windows, no interior, "PINDER," 6sp; yellow trailers, unpainted base, clown's face, label on front trailer, "Le Cirque PINDER," label on rear trailer, 6sp, 1999....$12-15

608-A Double Semi Freight Truck, 1984—Cab is a C.O.E. Sleeper with dual chrome exhausts, triple roof horns cast separately from roof, and plastic air foil.

dark blue cab, yellow air foil, amber windows, chrome interior, yellow/orange graphic, rd/6lr; dark blue trailers, unpainted base, blue, yellow, and orange stripes with "rainbow" and "r" on the yellow stripe at bottom of trailers, label, 6lr....$15-18

609-A Kenworth Auto Transporter, 1984—Cab is a KW Conventional Sleeper with dual chrome exhausts, opening hood, and 2 horns cast as part of the roof.

purple cab, amber windows, green and yellow accents, rd/6lr; purple trailer with

neon lime upper deck and loading ramp, "AL 5 " at rear of trailer and "auto line 5" on bottom sides, labels, 6lr.........$12-15

yellow cab, amber windows, green and black accents, rd/6lr; black trailer with yellow upper deck and loading ramp, "AL 5" at rear of trailer and "auto line 5" on bottom sides, labels, 6lr, 1986....$12-15

610-A Kenworth Rocket Transporter, 1985?—Cab is a KW Conventional Sleeper with a single exhaust, dual roof horns cast as part of the roof, and a narrow window in the sleeper.

white cab, clear windows, black interior, chrome exhaust, "space 3000," rd/6lr; white trailer, black cradle, white rocket, "space 3000," labels, rw $10-13

white cab, clear windows, gray interior, chrome exhaust, US flag and "NASA," rd/6lr; white trailer, black cradle, white rocket, red "NASA" on trailer, black "United States NASA" and flag on rocket, labels, rw, 1987....$8-10

white cab, clear windows, neon lime interior, chrome exhaust, US flag and "NASA," rd/6lr; white trailer, black cradle, white rocket, red "NASA" on trailer, black "United States NASA" and flag on rocket, labels, rw....$8-10

white cab, opaque windows, no interior, chrome exhaust, US flag and "NASA," 6sp; white trailer, black cradle, white rocket, red "NASA" on trailer, black "United States NASA" and flag on rocket, labels, rw....$8-10

black cab, clear windows, yellow interior, chrome exhaust, satellite dish and "TELESTAR," rd/6lr; white trailer, black cradle, yellow rocket, red "TELESTAR" on rocket, tampo, rw, 1996 ....$8-10

olive cab, clear windows, no interior, silver-gray exhaust, gray and brown camouflage, plane/parachute logo, "RD 50370," 6spol; olive trailer, black cradle,

gray rocket, white star and "AIR FORCE" on trailer, black star and "AIR FORCE" on rocket, tampos, *Special Forces*, rwol, 1999....$10-13

611-A Kenworth Semi Circus Trailer, with two cages, animals inside, 1985?—Cab is a KW Conventional Sleeper with a single chrome exhaust, dual roof horns cast as part of the roof, and a narrow window in the sleeper. One or both cages may contain plastic bears or big cats.

red cab, clear windows, black interior, black base, yellow, black, and gold "Magic Circus" graphics with 2 stars on sleeper, rd/6lr; black trailer, 2 yellow cages with red roofs, clown and "Magic Circus," label, 6lr....$10-13

red cab, clear windows, white interior, black base, yellow, black, and gold "Magic Circus" graphics with 2 stars on sleeper, rd/6lr; black trailer, 2 yellow cages with red roofs, clown and "Magic Circus," label, 6lr....$10-13

red cab, clear windows, gray interior, black base, yellow, black, and gold "Magic Circus" graphics with no stars on sleeper, rd/6lr; black trailer, 2 yellow cages with red roofs, clown and "Magic Circus," label, 6lr, 1990 ....$10-13

red cab, clear windows, gray interior, black base, yellow, black, and gold "Magic Circus" graphics with 2 stars on sleeper, rd/6lr; blue trailer, 2 white cages with red roofs, red, white, and blue clown and "CIRCUS" graphics, label, 6lr....$8-10

red cab, clear windows, gray interior, black base, yellow, black, and gold "Magic Circus" graphics with no stars on sleeper, rd/6lr; blue trailer, 2 white cages with red roofs, red, white, and blue clown and "CIRCUS" graphics, label, 6lr....$8-10

red cab, clear windows, gray interior, black base, red, white, and blue clown and "CIRCUS" graphics, rd/6lr; blue trailer, 2 white cages with red roofs, red, white, and blue clown and "CIRCUS" graphics, label, 6lr, 1992....$8-10

yellow cab, clear windows, gray interior, black base, gradient "Magic CIRCUS," rd/6lr; blue trailer, 2 cream cages with red roofs, "Magic CIRCUS Magic" and white stars on blue background, label, 6lr..$8-10

yellow cab, clear windows, red interior, black base, gradient "Magic CIRCUS," rd/6lr; blue trailer, 2 cream cages with red roofs, blue clown and "MAGIC CIRCUS," .... tampo, 6lr.............................$8-10

yellow cab, clear windows, gray interior, black base, gradient "Magic CIRCUS," rd/6lr; blue trailer, 2 cream cages with red roofs, blue clown and "MAGIC CIR-CUS," tampo, 6sp $8-10

yellow cab, opaque windows, no interior, silver-gray base, gradient "Magic CIRCUS," 6sp; blue trailer, 2 cream cages with red roofs, blue clown and "MAGIC CIRCUS," tampo, 6sp $8-10

yellow cab, clear windows, red interior, black base, gradient "Magic CIRCUS," rd/6lr; blue trailer, 2 cream cages with black roofs, blue clown and "MAGIC CIRCUS," tampo, 6lr...........................$8-10

yellow cab, clear windows, red interior, black base, gradient "Magic CIRCUS," rd/6lr; blue trailer, 2 cream cages with black roofs, blue clown and "MAGIC CIRCUS," tampo, 6sp............................$8-10

yellow cab, clear windows, gray interior, black base, gradient "Magic CIRCUS," rd/6lr; blue trailer, 2 yellow cages with red roofs, red, white, blue. and yellow clown and "MAGIC CIRCUS," tampo, 6sp...$8-10

yellow cab, opaque windows, no interior, black base, gradient "Magic CIRCUS," 6sp; blue trailer, 2 yellow cages with red roofs, red, white, blue. and yellow clown and "MAGIC CIRCUS," tampo, 6sp $8-10

yellow cab, opaque windows, no interior, black base, clown face and 2 stars, 6sp; blue trailer, 2 yellow cages with red roofs, red, white, blue. and yellow clown and "MAGIC CIRCUS," tampo, 6sp, 1996...$8-10

red cab, opaque windows, no interior, silver-gray base, yellow "PINDER," 6sp; yellow trailer, 2 red cages with yellow roofs, wild animals and "Le Cirque PINDER," label, 6sp, 1998 ....$12-15

red cab, opaque windows, no interior, silver-gray base, yellow "PINDER," 6sp; green trailer, 2 red cages with yellow roofs, wild animals and "Le Cirque PINDER," label, 6sp..$14-17

612-A Hook and Ladder Fire Engine, 1986—

Cab is a C.O.E. Sleeper with dual chrome exhausts, triple roof horns cast separately from roof, and plastic air foil.

red cab, white air foil, amber windows, chrome interior, yellow "55 F.D.N.Y" with black shadow, rd/6lr; red trailer, white ladder, gray frame, "FIRE DEPT," label, rd...................................$10-13

red cab, white air foil, amber windows, chrome interior, black "55 F.D.N.Y" with yellow shadow, rd/6lr; red trailer, gray ladder, white frame, "FIRE DEPT," label, rd $10-13

red cab, white air foil, amber windows, chrome interior, black "55 F.D.N.Y" with yellow shadow, rd/6lr; red trailer, gray ladder, gray frame, "FIRE DEPT," label, rd $10-13

red cab, white air foil, amber windows, chrome interior, black "55 F.D.N.Y" with yellow shadow, rd/6lr; red trailer, white ladder, gray frame, "FIRE DEPT," label, rd $10-13

red cab, white air foil, amber windows, chrome interior, gold "ENGINE NO.45 DISTRICT 2 FIRE DEPT.," rd/6lr; red trailer, gray ladder, white frame, "DISTRICT NO.2," label, rd $8-10

"Engine No. 45 DISTRICT 2 FIRE DEPT.," silver ladder $6-8
"55 F.D.N.Y.," white ladder..................$6-8

612-B Hook and Ladder Fire Engine, 1999—Cab is a C.O.E. Sleeper with dual chrome exhausts, no roof horns or air foil

red cab, amber windows, chrome interior, gold "ENGINE NO.45 DISTRICT 2 FIRE DEPT.," rd/6lr; red trailer, gray ladder, white frame, "DISTRICT NO.2", label, rd...$6-8

613-A Kenworth Semi Speed Boat Transporter, 1987—Cab is a KW Conventional Sleeper with a single chrome exhaust, dual roof horns cast as part of the roof, and a narrow window in the sleeper.

blue cab, clear windows, gray interior, pink, blue, and white "MIAMI" graphics, pink and blue stripes on sleeper, rd/6lr; white trailer with white cradle, 6lr; boat has light blue deck, dark blue hull, and white interior, "MIAMI," label $10-13

blue cab, clear windows, gray interior, pink,

blue, and white "MIAMI" graphics, pink and blue stripes on sleeper, rd/6lr; white trailer with white cradle, 6lr; boat has dark blue deck, light blue hull, and white interior, "MIAMI," label $10-13

blue cab, clear windows, gray interior, pink, blue, and white "MIAMI" graphics, no stripes on sleeper, rd/6lr; white trailer with gray cradle, 6lr; boat has light blue deck, dark blue hull, and white interior, "MIAMI," label $10-13

blue cab, clear windows, gray interior, pink, blue, and white "MIAMI" graphics, no stripes on sleeper, rd/6lr; white trailer with gray cradle, 6lr; boat has dark blue deck, light blue hull, and white interior, "MIAMI," label $10-13

blue cab, clear windows, gray interior, pink, blue, and white "MIAMI" graphics, no stripes on sleeper, rd/6lr; white trailer with gray cradle, 6lr; boat has black deck and hull, hot pink interior, "MIAMI," label $10-13

black cab, clear windows, yellow interior, pink, blue, and yellow globe and filigree graphics, rd/6lr; blue trailer with yellow cradle, 6lr; boat has black deck and hull, hot pink interior, "MIAMI," label $10-13

black cab, clear windows, neon lime interior, pink and yellow globe and filigree graphics, rd/6lr; hot pink trailer with yellow cradle, 6lr; boat has black deck and hull, hot pink interior, "EXTREME," label $8-10

black cab, clear windows, neon lime interior, pink and yellow globe and filigree graphics, rd/6lr; silver trailer with yellow cradle, 6lr; boat has black deck and hull, hot pink interior, "EXTREME," label..............$8-10

black cab, clear windows, neon lime interior, pink and yellow globe and filigree graphics, rd/6lr; silver trailer with black cradle, 6lr; boat has black deck and hull, hot pink interior, blue/black "RACING TEAM" on white background on red, label $8-10

red cab, clear windows, neon lime interior, black "RACING TEAM" on white, rd/6lr; silver trailer with black cradle, 6lr; boat has white deck, red hull, hot pink interior, blue/black "RACING TEAM" on white background on red, label.............$8-10

red cab, clear windows, neon lime interior, black "RACING TEAM" on white, rd/6lr; silver trailer with black cradle, 6lr; boat has red deck, white hull, hot pink interior, blue/black "RACING TEAM" on white background on red, label.............$8-10

red cab, clear windows, gray interior, black "RACING TEAM" on white, rd/6lr; silver trailer with black cradle, 6lr; boat has red deck, white hull, hot pink interior, blue/black "RACING TEAM" on white background on red, label.............$8-10

red cab, clear windows, neon lime interior, black "RACING TEAM" on white, rd/6lr; silver trailer with black cradle, 6lr; boat has red deck, white hull, black interior, red and white "RACING TEAM," tampo $6-8

red cab, clear windows, yellow interior, black "RACING TEAM" on white, rd/6lr; silver trailer with black cradle, 6lr; boat has red deck, white hull, black interior, red and white "RACING TEAM," tampo $6-8

red cab, clear windows, neon lime interior, black "RACING TEAM" on white, rd/6lr; silver trailer with black cradle, 6lr; boat has white deck, red hull, black interior, red and white "RACING TEAM," tampo $6-8

red cab, opaque windows, no interior, black "RACING TEAM" on white, 6sp; silver trailer with black cradle, 6sp; boat has red deck, white hull, black interior, red and white "RACING TEAM," tampo $6-8

red cab, opaque windows, no interior, black "RACING TEAM" on white, 6sp; silver trailer with black cradle, 6sp; boat has white deck, red hull, black interior, red and white "RACING TEAM," tampo.................$6-8

red cab, opaque windows, no interior, sun holding coke bottle, 6sp; silver trailer with black cradle, 6sp; boat has red deck, white hull, black interior, red "Coca Cola," tampo $10-13

red cab, opaque windows, no interior, sun holding coke bottle, 6sp; silver trailer with black cradle, 6sp; boat has white deck, red hull, black interior, white "Coca Cola," tampo $10-13

613-B Kenworth Semi Speed Boat Transporter—Cab is a KW Conventional Sleeper with a cast air deflector and roof window, no exhausts.

red cab, amber windows, chrome interior, white "Coca Cola" on air deflector, 6sp; silver trailer, black cradle, 6sp; boat has red deck, white hull, black interior, red "Coca Cola," tampo $12-15

red cab, amber windows, chrome interior, white "Coca Cola" on air deflector, 6sp; silver trailer, black cradle, 6sp; boat has

white deck, red hull, black interior, white "Coca Cola," tampo $12-15

613-C Kenworth Semi Speed Boat Transporter, 1999—Cab is a C.O.E. Sleeper with dual chrome exhausts, no roof horns or air foil.

blue cab, amber windows, chrome interior, white fish and red "PONTOON LAGON," 6sp; silver trailer with black cradle, 6sp; boat has white deck, red hull, black interior, red and white "RACING TEAM," tampo $6-8

614-A Kenworth Cattle Transporter, 1988—Cab is a KW Conventional Sleeper with dual chrome exhausts, opening hood, and 2 horns cast as part of the roof.

light metallic green cab, amber windows, chrome interior, lime and silver design, rd/6lr; yellow trailer, dark green side and rear doors, unpainted base, 6lr $10-13

dark metallic green cab, amber windows, yellow and silver design, rd/6lr; yellow trailer, green side and dark rear doors, unpainted base, 6lr..$10-13

614-B Kenworth Cattle Transporter—Cab is a KW Conventional Sleeper with dual chrome exhausts, hood does not open, and 2 horns cast as part of the roof.

light green cab, amber windows, chrome interior, black "KANSAS," black filigree, and red stars on hood, rd/6lr; brown trailer, light green side and rear doors, unpainted base, 6lr..................................$10-13

614-C Kenworth Cattle Transporter, 1996—Cab is a KW Conventional Sleeper with a cast air deflector and roof window, no exhausts.

light green cab, amber windows, chrome interior, black filigree and red stars on hood, rd/6lr; brown trailer, light green side and rear doors, unpainted base, 6sp.....$8-10

light green cab, amber windows, chrome interior, black filigree and red stars on hood, rd/6lr; cream trailer, light green side and rear doors, unpainted base, 6lr $6-8

light green cab, amber windows, chrome interior, black filigree and red stars on hood, rd/6lr; cream trailer, light green side and rear doors, unpainted base, 6sp.......$6-8

light green cab, amber windows, chrome interior, black filigree and red stars on hood, 6sp; cream trailer, light green side and rear doors, unpainted base, 6sp.......$6-8

red cab, amber windows, chrome interior, seal with ball, stars, and "PINDER," 6sp; yellow trailer, red side and rear doors, unpainted base, 6sp..................$12-15

615-A Semi Pro-Stock Firebird Transporter, 1993—Cab is a C.O.E. Sleeper with dual chrome exhausts, triple roof horns cast separately from roof, and plastic air foil.

white cab, white air foil, amber windows, chrome interior, stars and stripes, rd/6lr; red trailer, red plastic cover, white loading ramp, red, white, and blue flag, stars, and "Number One," label, 6lr; car is a No. 258-C white Pontiac Firebird, stars and stripes and red "Number One," tampo, 6sp $12-15

white cab, white air foil, amber windows, chrome interior, stars and stripes, rd/6lr; black trailer, white plastic cover, white loading ramp, racing flags, "AL" on shield, and "Grand Prix," label, 6lr; car is a No. 258-C-1 white Pontiac Firebird, stars and stripes and red "Number One," tampo, 6sp $12-15

hot pink cab, white air foil, amber windows, chrome interior, black and gold graphic, "motor ROK," rd/6lr; black trailer, white plastic cover, white loading ramp, racing flags, "AL" on shield, and "Grand Prix," label, 6sp; car is a No. 258-C yellow Pontiac Firebird, red splash, various ads, and "8," tampo, 6sp $8-10

hot pink cab, white air foil, amber windows, chrome interior, black and gold graphic, "motor ROK," rd/6lr; black trailer, white plastic cover, white loading ramp, racing flags, "AL" on shield, and "Grand Prix," label, 6lr; car is a No. 258-C chartreuse Pontiac Firebird, red splash, various ads, and "8," tampo, 6sp $8-10

616-A Semi Bulldozer Transporter with 287-C Bulldozer, 1992—Cab is a C.O.E. Sleeper with dual chrome exhausts, amber windows, chrome interior, triple roof horns cast separately from the roof, and a plastic air foil.

dark blue cab, silver/light blue/dark blue tampo, white air foil, rd/6lr; silver trailer, yellow loading ramp and cable reel, black cable housing and base, 6lr; 287-C-1 Bulldozer $10-13

sea green cab, "302 BLUE'S TRUCKING CO.," white air foil, rd/6lr; silver trailer, yellow loading ramp and cable reel, black cable housing and base, 6lr; 287-C-1 Bulldozer ....$9-12 pale blue cab, "302 BLUE'S TRUCKING CO.," white air foil, rd/6lr; silver trailer, yellow loading ramp and cable reel, black cable housing and base, 6lr; 287-C-1 Bulldozer $9-12

yellow cab, "302 BLUE'S TRUCKING CO.," white air foil, rd/6lr; silver trailer, yellow loading ramp and cable reel, black cable housing and base, 6lr; 287-C-1 Bulldozer $9-12

white cab, "302 BLUE'S TRUCKING CO.," white air foil, rd/6lr; silver trailer, yellow loading ramp and cable reel, black cable housing and base, 6lr; 287-C-1 Bulldozer $9-12

yellow cab, "302 BLUE'S TRUCKING CO.," white air foil, rd/6lr; gray trailer, red loading ramp and cable reel, black cable housing and base, 6lr; 287-C-2 Bulldozer $9-12

616-B Mercedes Semi Bulldozer Transporter with 287-C Bulldozer, 1994—Cab is a C.O.E. Sleeper with no exhausts, dual roof horns and air foil cast on roof, and plastic sun visor.

pale blue cab, black sun visor, clear windows, red interior, black, purple, and yellow desert scene, "EVASION" on red banner on air foil, rd/6lr; silver trailer, yellow loading ramp and cable reel, black cable housing and base, 6lr; 287-C-2 Bulldozer..................................$8-10

pale blue cab, black sun visor, clear windows, red interior, black, purple, and yellow desert scene, "EVASION" on red banner on air foil, rd/6lr; gray trailer, red loading ramp and cable reel, black cable housing and base, 6sp; 287-C-2 Bulldozer $8-10

royal blue cab, black sun visor, clear windows, red interior, black, light blue, and yellow desert scene, "EVASION" on yellow banner on air foil, rd/6lr; gray trailer, red loading ramp and cable reel, black cable housing and base, 6sp; 287-C-2 Bulldozer.....$8-10

616-C Mercedes Semi Bulldozer Transporter with 287-C Bulldozer, 1996—Cab is a C.O.E. Sleeper with no exhausts or sun visor, dual roof horns and air foil cast on roof.

yellow cab, opaque windows, no interior, bulldog and "BULLDOG CONSTRUCTION," 6sp; silver trailer, red loading ramp, black cable reel, housing and base, 6sp; 287-C-1 Bulldozer $6-8

617-A Kenworth Semi Crane Truck, 1991—Cab is a KW Conventional Sleeper with a single chrome exhaust, dual roof horns cast as part of the roof, and a narrow window in the sleeper.

yellow cab, clear windows, gray interior, diagonal black stripes and "ENTERPRISE," rd/6lr; yellow trailer, black crane and undercarriage, 6lr $7-9

yellow cab, clear windows, gray interior, diagonal black stripes and "ENTERPRISE," rd/6lr; yellow trailer, black crane and undercarriage, 6sp.........................$7-9

yellow cab, clear windows, red interior, diagonal black stripes and "ENTERPRISE," rd/6lr; yellow trailer, black crane and undercarriage, 6lr..........................$7-9

yellow cab, opaque windows, no interior, diagonal black stripes and "ENTERPRISE," rd/6lr; yellow trailer, black crane and undercarriage, 6lr..........................$6-8

618-A Seaplane Transporter, 1993—Cab is a C.O.E. Sleeper with dual chrome exhausts, triple roof horns cast separately from the roof, and a plastic airfoil.

neon chartreuse cab, white air foil, amber windows, chrome interior, "F.VZTN," rd/6lr; black trailer, 6lr; plane has red body, neon chartreuse propeller and skids, black cowling and wings, "F.VZTN"........$8-10

neon chartreuse cab, white air foil, amber windows, chrome interior, "F.VZTN," rd/6lr; black trailer, 6lr; plane has red body, black propeller and skids, neon chartreuse cowling and wings, "F.VZTN".......................$8-10

neon chartreuse cab, white air foil, amber windows, chrome interior, "F.VZTN," 6sp; black trailer, 6lr; plane has red body, neon chartreuse propeller and skids, black cowling and wings, "F.VZTN"........$8-10

neon chartreuse cab, white air foil, amber windows, chrome interior, "F.VZTN," 6sp; black trailer, 6lr; plane has red body, black propeller and skids, neon chartreuse cowling and wings, "F.VZTN" $8-10

orange cab, white air foil, amber windows, chrome interior, red/yellow/black desert scene, rd/6lr; black trailer, 6lr; plane has red body, neon chartreuse propeller and skids, black cowling and wings, "F.VZTN" $7-9

orange cab, white air foil, amber windows, chrome interior, red/yellow/black desert scene, rd/6lr; black trailer, 6lr; plane has red body, black propeller and skids, neon chartreuse cowling and wings, "F.VZTN" $7-9

orange cab, white air foil, amber windows, chrome interior, red/yellow/black desert scene, rd/6lr; black trailer, 6lr; plane has red body, blue propeller and skids, red cowling and wings, "PONTOON LAGON" $7-9

orange cab, white air foil, amber windows, chrome interior, red/yellow/black desert scene, rd/6lr; black trailer, 6lr; plane has red body, red propeller and skids, blue cowling and wings "PONTOON LAGON" $7-9

metallic blue cab, white air foil, amber windows, chrome interior, fish and "PONTOON LAGON," rd/6lr; black trailer, 6sp; plane has yellow body, blue propeller and skids, red cowling and wings, "PONTOON LAGON" $6-8

metallic blue cab, white air foil, amber windows, chrome interior, fish and "PONTOON LAGON," rd/6lr; black trailer, 6sp; plane has yellow body, red propeller and skids, blue cowling and wings, "PONTOON LAGON" $6-8

618-B Seaplane Transporter, 1999—Cab is a C.O.E. Sleeper with dual chrome exhausts, no roof horns or air foil.

blue cab, white air foil, amber windows, chrome interior, fish and "PONTOON LAGON," 6sp; black trailer, 6sp; plane has yellow body, blue propeller and skids, red cowling and wings, "PONTOON LAGON" $6-8

blue cab, white air foil, amber windows, chrome interior, fish and "PONTOON LAGON," 6sp; black trailer, 6sp; plane has yellow body, red propeller and skids, blue cowling and wings, "PONTOON LAGON" $6-8

619-A Mercedes car carrier, 1996—Cab is a C.O.E. Sleeper with no exhausts, dual roof horns and air foil cast on roof, and black plastic sun visor.

metallic teal cab, black sun visor, clear windows, red interior, "TRUCK FORCE" on cab doors and air foil, rd/6lr; black trailer with gray upper ramp, red loading ramp, 6lr; car is a yellow No. 248-C-2 Pontiac Firebird, red splash, various ads, and "8," tampo, 6sp $7-9

metallic teal cab, black sun visor, clear windows, red interior, "TRUCK FORCE" on cab doors and air foil, rd/6lr; black trailer with gray upper ramp, red loading ramp, 6lr; car is a purple No. 221-E Renault Safrane, gray interior, 6sp $7-9

metallic teal cab, black sun visor, clear windows, red interior, "TRUCK FORCE" on cab doors and air foil, rd/6lr; black trailer with gray upper ramp, red loading ramp, 6sp; car is a metal flake silver No. 254-C-2 Citroen XM, black interior, 8h $7-9

Special Forces olive cab with gray and brown camouflage, clear windows, no interior, 6spol; olive trailer, no upper ramp, olive loading ramp, black cable reel, housing, and base, 6spol; 220.3 Special Forces tank, olive with tan camouflage, 1999 ....$10-13

619-B Mercedes car carrier—Cab is a C.O.E. Sleeper with no exhausts or sun visor, dual roof horns and air foil cast on roof.

royal blue cab, opaque windows, no interior, red splash and "EVASION" on cab doors and air foil, 6sp; black trailer with gray upper ramp, red loading ramp, 6sp; car is a black 260-C-9 Mercedes-Benz 500SL Roadster, dark gray interior, 6sp $6-8

white cab, opaque windows, no interior, green and white recycling logo, 6sp; black trailer with gray upper ramp, red loading ramp, 6sp; car is a black 260-C-9 Mercedes-Benz 500SL Roadster, dark gray interior, 6sp..............................$6-8

619-C Mercedes car carrier—Cab is a C.O.E. Sleeper with dual chrome exhausts, triple roof horns cast separately from the roof, and a plastic airfoil.

hot pink cab, white air foil, amber windows, chrome interior, black and gold graphic, "motor ROK," rd/6lr; black trailer, gray upper ramp, 6sp; car is a black 260-C-9 Mercedes-Benz 500SL, dark gray interior, 6sp $6-8

hot pink cab, white air foil, amber windows, chrome interior, black and gold graphic, "motor ROK," rd/6lr; black trailer, gray upper ramp, 6sp; car is a red 220-C-2 Honda NSX, tan interior, 8h $6-8

620-A Construction Truck with Crane, 1998—Cab is a KW Conventional Sleeper with a single chrome exhaust, dual roof horns cast as part of the roof, and a narrow window in the sleeper.

yellow cab, opaque windows, no interior, construction symbol and 8 red chevrons, 6sp orange trailer with dark gray plastic bed, yellow site hut with orange roof, yellow crane, orange compressor and cement mixer, 6sp.............................$8-10

621-A Recycling Lorry with Crane, 1998—Cab is a C.O.E. Sleeper with no exhausts or sun visor, dual roof horns and air foil cast on roof.

white cab, opaque windows, no interior, green and white recycling logo, 6sp; lime trailer with white plastic bed, and crane, red, yellow, green, orange, and blue containers, 6sp $8-10

Majorette 800 Series–Airport, 1995

801-A Boeing 747/400
  Cathay Pacific $4-6
  Air France $4-6
  Thai Airways.......................$4-6
802-A Airbus
  Singapore Airlines $4-6
  Air France $4-6
  Alitalia $4-6
  Swissair $4-6
803-A Boeing 767
  KLM $4-6
  Delta Airlines $4-6
  Air Canada $4-6
  Japan Air Lines, JAL $4-6
  SAS $4-6
804-A Douglas MD 80
  Alitalia $4-6
  Iberia................................$4-6
  SAS $4-6
805-A Douglas DC 10
  Iberia................................$4-6
  Japan Air Lines, JAL $4-6

Majorette 1000 Series–Deluxe Collection, approximately 1:60 Scale

1001 Jaguar XJ-SC
  blue $8-10
  green $8-10
1002 Ferrari F40
  red $8-10
  yellow $8-10
1003 Porsche 911
  white $8-10
  silver $8-10
1004 Lamborghini Countach
  black................................$8-10
  red $8-10
1005 Ferrari Testarossa
  white $8-10
  red $8-10

1006 Rolls Royce Corniche II
  metallic red........................$8-10
  metallic bronze $8-10
1007 Mercedes 500 SL
  metallic silver $8-10
  metallic bronze $8-10

Majorette 2400 Series, Legends, 1988–present, approximately 1:32 Scale

2401-A 1957 Chevrolet Bel Air, 1988
  black, red interior, red and yellow flames ..$5-7
  light blue, white interior.....................$5-7
  yellow, white roof and side panels, white interior, 2000 ....$5-7
  copper, white roof and side panels, white interior, 2000........................$5-7
2402-A 1956 T-Bird, 1988
  red, red roof, white interior.................$5-7
  yellow, yellow roof, yellow interior $5-7
  white, white roof, red interior.................$5-7
  green, white roof, green interior, 2000 ...$5-7
2403-A 1963 Corvette Stingray Split Window, 1988
  yellow, brown interior..........................$5-7
  red, white interior, 2 white and gold stripes $5-7
  red, white interior.................................$5-7
  black, red interior, 2000 ....$5-7
  red, tan interior, 2000 ....$5-7
2404-A 1965 Mustang, 1988
  red, red roof, white interior.................$5-7
  blue, white roof, black interior $5-7
  white, black interior, 2 blue stripes, "GT 350" $6-8
  blue, blue roof, white interior.................$5-7
2405-A 1957 Corvette, 1990
  red, white coves, white interior $5-7
  white, silver coves, red interior, 2000......$5-7
  turquoise, white coves, white interior, 2000 ....$5-7
2406-A Mercedes 300SL Gullwing, 1991
  silver, red interior $5-7
  black, gray interior, 2000 ....$5-7

Majorette 2500 Series–Grand Sport, approximately 1:38 scale, Made in Hong Kong, 1983

2501 Porsche 959 ....$8-10
2502 Ferrari 328 GTB, red, chrome wheels with star on them $8-10
2503 Pontiac Trans Am $8-10
2504 Lamborghini Countach $8-10

Majorette Hot Rods, 1990–present

2601 '32 Ford Coupe with removable engine cowl

orange with blue, black, and white
tampos $6-8
red with blue, black, and white tampos ...$6-8
green with black, yellow, and white
tampos $6-8
red, orange, and yellow flames $6-8
2602 '41 Willys Coupe with removable engine
cowl
yellow, red flames on side $6-8
yellow, black and white checkered flag on
side $6-8
red, yellow flames $6-8
black, red flames on side, Hot Rod
3 pack $6-8
2603 '34 Ford Sedan with removable engine
cowl
black with red, and yellow flames $6-8
black with white, red, and gold stripe
tampos $6-8
blue with light blue flames on side $6-8
red with red and yellow flames $6-8
2604 '57 Chevrolet with 2 interchangeable turbo
engines
red, yellow flames $6-8
white, flames on side, black interior $6-8
2605 Pickup Hot Rod with removable engine
cowl, 1991
orange, black fenders, "HOT ROD" on
doors...$6-8
blue, blue fenders, white tampos, "HOT
TRUCK" on doors $6-8
black, red and yellow tampos $6-8

Majorette Dragsters 2700 Series

"Pullback Motorized," "Racing Start Button," "High-
Speed"
Red, "Red Target" $7-9
Orange, "Big Bullitt" $7-9
yellow, checkered flags on sides, "SUPER
CAMS" $7-9
white, red flames on sides, "HOT ENGINE" $7-9

Majorette 3000 Series

30xx Scania Super 140 Texaco Tanker
Information from collector Ron Gold indicates this
Texaco tanker was produced in the 3000 series, but
he is unable to identify which one. Several model
numbers have been applied to what has only been
described as a generic tanker in researched text,
including #s 3040, 3041, and 3044. The speculative value immediately below reflects the collectability
and undocumented rarity of this model.
Texaco $30-35

3006-A Kenworth Semi Tractor, 1995 ....$6-8
3007-A Dune Buggy, 1986

red, white roof, black interior, "bab buggy"
label on roof, "26" label on rear, red,
blue and white accents, 5 spoke wheels,
1986...$8-10
3008-A Impala Police, 1:41, 1986
white, black panels, blue interior, blue windows, gold "HIGHWAY PATROL" and
star on doors and hood, "911" and
"HIGHWAY PATROL" on trunk, spoked
wheels...$8-10
light blue, "Police NYPD" $6-8
3009-A Impala Taxi, 1:41, 1986
yellow, blue interior, clear windows, "BRONX
ZOO" sign on roof, "870," "444-4444,"
fares on rear fender, spoked wheels ...$8-10
3010-A Magirus Dump Truck, 6 point star rims,
1980–1986
red cab, red base, front and rear bumpers, silver dump, amber windows and emer-
gency lights on the roof, yellow interior,
chrome front grille and chrome mirrors and
exhaust pipes, tampo on the rear bumper,
6st $8-10
green cab, gray base, front and rear bumpers,
yellow dump, amber windows and emergency lights on the roof, yellow interior,
chrome front grille and chrome mirrors and
exhaust pipes, tampo on the rear bumper,
6st $8-10
3011-A Magirus Towing Truck, 1980–1985,
reissued as 3026-A
yellow cab and bed, red crane, unpainted
metal hook, amber windows and emergency lights on the roof, red interior, rear
tampo on the bumper, ct3c, 1980 ...$8-10
blue cab and bed, yellow crane, unpainted
metal hook, amber windows and emergency lights on the roof, red interior,
rear tampo on the bumper, 6 star
wheels $8-10
yellow cab and bed, red crane, unpainted metal
hook, amber windows and emergency lights
on the roof, red interior, rear tampo on the
bumper, 6 star wheels $8-10
red cab, gray bed, red crane, yellow crane
base, unpainted metal hook, amber windows and emergency lights on the roof,
red interior, no rear tampo on the bumper,
6 star wheels, 1986, #3026 ....$8-10
3011-B 4x4 Chevrolet Blazer Hawaii, 1999
blue with yellow trim and topper $6-8
3012-A Farm Tractor, with side mower, 1980–present
green, white cage, black roof, silver motor and
wheat cutting blade, black front and rear
bumpers and exhaust pipe with a brown
man $8-10

red, white cage, black roof, silver motor and
wheat cutting blade, black front and rear
bumpers and exhaust pipe with a brown
man, 8 lug front wheels.................$8-10
3012-B Farm Tractor, no side mower
lime green $6-8
3013-A Safari Land Rover $12-15
3013-B Toyota Safari Landcruiser Raid, with luggage rack on roof, grille guard on front,
1980–1987, reissued 1996
brown, yellow roof rack, black luggage, yellow bumpers, 8 lug wheels..........$12-15
blue, brown interior and roof luggage, black
roof and rear hatch, clear windows, 5
spoke wheels....................................$12-15
beige, red interior, black roof luggage, green roof
and rear hatch, amber windows, "TRANS
AFRICA," "MONROE," "12," "Mampe,"
"KYOSHO," shell logo, red elephant symbol,
5 spoke wheels, 1986 ....$12-15
white, red interior, clear windows, black roof
rack, red luggage, red bumpers, black
grille guard, red, blue and black accents,
"TOYOTA" and "205" on doors, red 5
spoke wheels............................$12-15
3014-A Toyota Landcruiser FJ40, no luggage
rack, winch on front, 1980–1981—A version
of this can be found with a grille guard on
front and was used only in sets.
brown, white roof, yellow bumpers, 8 lug
wheels......................................$12-15
brown, white roof, amber windows, white
interior, gray bumpers, grille guard on
front, 8 lug wheels......................$12-15
yellow, white roof, amber windows, red
interior, grille guard on front, 8 lug
wheels......................................$12-15
3014-B Peugeot 806 Van, 1996
red, spoked wheels, 1996 catalog $8-10
3014-C Mercedes E 280 Wagon, 1997
No details available $8-10
3015-A Chevrolet Blazer 4x4 Pickup, 1981–1987
dark red with orange lower body color and
cap, clear windows, orange/red/yellow
and green tampo on the hood, "4x4,"
8kk $8-10
pale green, black lower body and cap, black
interior, clear windows, "FRUIT OF THE
LOOM," "T-Shirts," 5 spoke wheels ..$8-10
3015-B Mercedes M-Class, 1999
light maroon $6-8
3015.1-A Mercedes M Class Fire Van, 1999
red with white bumpers and trim $6-8
3016-A CJ7 Jeep, 1983
blue with shark graphics, white roof, red
seats...$6-8

red, black roof, yellow interior, gold, red, and orange foil labels on sides and hood, "RENEGADE," 6t wheels...............$8-10

black, red roof, red interior, red and gold accents, "night hawk," "4x4," 5 spoke wheels.....................$8-10

3017-A Mercedes Garbage Truck, 1:55, 1982–1983

silver cab, orange box with silver rear, blue windows, black front bumper and front grill, black base, 6 star wheels.......$8-10

3017-B Mercedes 230GE 4x4 Police, 1:53, 1988

white, red interior, clear windows, blue and red accents, "POLICE" on hood and doors, red light bar and two blue lights on roof, has rear seats, back door cast into body, clear plastic turn signals protrude from front of hood, 5 spoke wheels ...$6-8

black, blue interior, clear windows, white and gold accents, "HIGHWAY PATROL," "POLICE," "911," gold accents on hood, "911" on roof, red light bar and two blue lights on roof, no rear seat, spoked wheels...........................$8-10

black, blue interior, clear windows, white and gold accents, "HIGHWAY PATROL," "POLICE," "911," gold accents on hood, "911" on roof, red light bar and two blue lights on roof, 5 spoke wheels........$8-10

red, yellow interior, clear windows, yellow scribble tampos, cartoon lion's head on hood and doors, "The King" on the roof, red light bar with two blue lights on rear of roof, black plastic base, opening black plastic back door, protruding turn signal lights are cast into hood, has rear seat, 5 spoke wheels..................................$6-8

3018-A Mercedes Covered Truck, 1982–1983

red cab with yellow bed, red canopy, white/light blue/blue/black "Fret Express" labels, clear windows, black front grille and bumper, opening green rear door, 6st wheels..................................$12-15

red cab with yellow bed, red canopy, white/brown/black/yellow "Service International" label, clear windows with a black front grille and bumper, opening green rear door, 6st wheels.........$12-15

red cab with yellow bed, red canopy, white/light blue/blue/black "Fret Express" labels, blue windows, black front grille and bumper, opening yellow rear door, 6st wheels..................................$12-15

3018-B Range Rover, 1989

white with "Free Way" tampos, red interior,

amber windows, 5 spoke wheels, 1989 catalog...$8-10

bright blue with fluorescent splash graphics, 5 spoke wheels................................$8-10

blue with rally graphics, 5 spoke wheels...$8-10

blue, red interior, no accents, 5 spoke wheels $8-10

yellow, black interior, clear windows, "General Contractor Road Crew," 5 spoke wheels in set 954 ....$8-10

3019-A Renault Master T35 Road Repair Truck, 1:45, 1991

orange, black interior, blue windows and roof light, gray bed, "JS and CO," black and white accents, 6st, 4 road signs and 6 pylons on rear.............................$8-10

yellow, black interior, amber windows and roof light, gray bed, "RD0370," "Construction" on the sides of the cab and hood, black accents, 6st, 4 road signs and 6 pylons on rear, in set 954....$8-10

3020-A Excalibur, 1981–1989

red, burgundy fenders, silver accents, white roof, white interior, spoked wheels ..$8-10

blue, dark blue fenders, white roof, cream interior, spoked wheels $8-10

green, black fenders, white roof and interior, spoked wheels..............................$8-10

3021-A Ambulance, 1982–1992

white, red roof, fenders and head light rims, red "Ambulance," red cross and two red stripes tampo on the sides, blue windows, blue emergency lights on top and sides of roof, 5 spoke wheels $8-10

white, blue roof, fenders and head light rims, blue windows, blue emergency lights on top and sides of roof, orange and blue accents, "AMBULANCE," "24H/24," blue 6 pointed cross, 5 spoke wheels with white walls $8-10

3022-A Holiday Van, 1982–1984, reissued as 3030.2, 1995

silver with red roof and fenders, amber windows, tropical sunset sticker on sides, spoiler on roof, 1984 catalog......$12-15

3023-A Armored Security Truck, 1984 but shown in 1983 catalog

red with white roof, orange/red/yellow with gold tampo on the sides and roof, amber windows, yellow interior, chrome front grille and head lights, white base and front bumper, 6t wheels, acts as a coin bank..............$8-10

gold with red roof, "Bank Security" shield stickers on sides, 1984 catalog $12-15

3023-B Mercedes E280 Van, 1997

no details available $8-10

3023.1-A Mercedes E280 Bicycle Racing Team Assistance Van, with 2 bicycles on back, 1999

yellow with checkered flag tampos, 1999 catalog $6-8

3024-A Service Van, 1985-1987

yellow, red roof and fenders, amber windows, red, blue and green graphics, "TV service," stylized TV on sides, spoked wheels $8-10

gray, blue roof and fenders, blue windows, "BELL," Bell Canada," "12B34567" on sides, spoked wheels..................$30-35

gray, blue roof and fenders, blue windows, "BELL," Bell Canada," "12B34567" on sides, 5 spoke wheels with white walls...........$30-35

3025-A Renault Master T35 Breakdown Truck, 1:45, 1986, reissued 1996

red, gray bed, light blue windows, "2424 Service," blue and white decals, 6 star wheels, green Jeep on bed..........$10-13

fluorescent yellow cab, "24/24 Service," 6 star wheels, black Land Rover on bed, 1996 catalog $10-13

yellow with red diagonal stripes, "ENTERPRISE CB," blue windows, 6 star wheels, yellow Land Rover on bed, 1999 catalog....$8-10

3026-A Crane Truck, 1986 reissue of 3011

red with red boom, yellow pulley and crane platform, 6 star wheels, 1986 catalog...$12-15

3026-B Ford Mustang, 1995

yellow, 1995 catalog.........................$8-10

3027-A Toyota 4x4 Rallye, 1987 only

white cab, black cage over cab, red interior, clear windows, unpainted base, black bed, white cover, white, red and black "FACOM" labels on cover, 5 spoke wheels........$8-10

3027-B Camaro Convertible, 1995

blue with brown interior, 1995 catalog..$8-10

3028 Racing Semi-Tractor, 1:60.................$6-8

3029 Ford Model A Van $6-8

3030-A Front End Loader, 1984, reissued as 4501, 1995

yellow, orange cab, red interior, dark red/orange/white tampo on the sides, "8," orange wheel rims...............$10-13

yellow, black cab, red interior, dark red/orange/white label on the sides, "8," gray wheel rims $10-13

3030.1-A Winnebago Minnie Winnie Camping car, 1994, white.............................$10-13

3030.2-A Holiday Van, 1995

silver, red roof and fenders, red interior, amber windows, pastel tropical scene labels on sides, "Holiday," spoked wheels.......$7-9 blue, yellow roof and fenders, yellow interior, amber windows, pastel surf scene labels on sides, "Holidays," spoked wheels with whitewalls $7-9

3030.3-A Ambulance Van, 1995
white with orange hood and side stripe tampos, "NYC EMS" on sides, "AMBU-LANCE" on sides and hood, 1995 catalog $7-9

3030.4-A Fire Truck *Pompier*, 1995
red, "NEW YORK #1 FIRE DEPT." on doors, chrome plastic snorkel and horns.......$7-9

3031-A Cement Truck, 1983–1987, reissued 1992–1994, 2000
green cab, gray base, red motor, yellow mixer with a red/white stripe, yellow and red "E&B" label on the doors, amber windows, yellow interior, green rear cement shute, 6st wheels, 1984 ....$16-20
yellow cab, orange mixer with a orange/white stripe, black chassis, clear windows, no tampo on the doors, yellow rear cement shute, 6st wheels.......$12-15
orange cab, yellow mixer with a orange/white stripe, gray chassis, yellow interior, amber windows, "E&B" label on doors, yellow rear cement shute, 6st wheels, 1986 ....$12-15
orange cab, yellow mixer with a orange/white stripe, gray chassis, yellow interior, amber windows, black and yellow "TP" tampo on doors, yellow rear cement shute, 6st wheels.....................................$12-15

3031-B Peugeot 806 Van, 1997
no details available $9-12

3031.1-A Peugeot 806 Taxi Van, 1999
yellow with checkerboard design along sides, 1999 catalog..................................$6-8

3031.2-A Peugeot 806 Police Van, 1999
white with red and blue stripes on sides, 1999 catalog...$6-8

3032-A Heavy Duty Transporter, with 226-A Road Roller and 263-A Front End Loader, 1984
blue, yellow interior, yellow with red "EandB" label on the doors, light gray carrier, blue ramp, 6st wheels; 226: Road Roller, yellow and a 263:Front End Loader, orange on back......................................$12-15
metallic blue, yellow interior, black and yellow "TP" tampo on the doors, light gray carrier, metallic blue ramp, 6st wheels; 226: Road Roller, yellow and a 263: Front End Loader, yellow on back..............$12-15
orange, yellow interior, black and yellow "TP" tampo on the doors, light gray carrier, orange ramp, 6st wheels; 226: Road

Roller, yellow and a 263: Front End Loader on back.........................$12-15

3032.1-A Ford F350 Wrecker, 1999
red, "Rainbow Heavy Duty Towing" $6-8

3032.2-A Ford F350 Pickup, 1999
metallic blue (US only) $6-8

3033-A Fire Engine, 1984
U.S. Fire Engine, red, white roof and tool doors, that open, metallic silver base, red, yellow and black "SOS" and "590.00.00" tampo on the sides, amber windows and emergency light on the roof with yellow interior, chrome colored front grill, head lights and air horns, 8kk wheels....................$12-15
U.S. Fire Engine, red, white roof and tool doors, that open, metallic silver base, red, yellow and black "SOS" and "590.00.00" tampo on the sides, amber windows and emergency light on the roof with yellow interior, chrome colored front grill, head lights and air horns, 6t wheels $12-15
U.S. Fire Engine, red, white roof and tool doors, that open, gray base, "FIRE DEPT ENGINE NO 2" labels, amber windows and emergency light on the roof with yellow interior, chrome colored front grill, head lights and air horns, 6t wheels....................................$12-15
U.S. Fire Engine, red, white roof and tool doors, that open, black base, "FIRE DEPT NEW YORK" labels, "ENGINE 5 FDNY," amber windows and emergency light on the roof with yellow interior, chrome colored front grill, head lights and air horns, 6t wheels $12-15

3034-A Shovel Engine, 1984, reissued as 4506
red, silver engine cover, black interior, "Poclain" on the shovel and rear of machine, orange wheel rims $10-13
yellow, silver-gray engine cover, black lower body, black interior, black boom, yellow shovel, gray wheel rims $10-13

3034-B Renault Premium Container Truck
red cab, "Majorette" logo on white container with red roof..............................$10-13

3035-A Kenworth Wrecker, 1985
black cab, white bed, "Highway Patrol," "POLICE," "911," 5 spoke wheels ..$10-13
blue cab and bed, gray and black boom, "24 hr EXPRESS TOWING," "HEAVY DUTY," "8735469," red, yellow, white and black labels, 5 spoke wheels $10-13

3036-A Kenworth Dump Truck, 1986
orange, gray dump, black chassis, gray interior,

clear windows, yellow and black accents, "RandG" on hood and doors, "ICC MC 1410," 5 spoke wheels................$12-15
black, gray dump, black chassis, gray interior, clear windows, yellow and orange accents, 5 spoke wheels $12-15
blue, gray dump, black chassis, US flag on hood, "EAGLE TRUCK" on doors, 5 spoke wheels, in set 954 ....$12-15

3037-A Toyota Garbage Truck, 1:35, 1987
green cab, white box, red interior, clear windows, black grill, green and white label with hippo, 5 spoke wheels.........$12-15

3037.1-A Scania Garbage Truck, 1999
blue with "CLEAN PLANET" and graphics on sides of container, 1999 catalog ..$10-13

3038 Road Roller, 1992, reissued as 4504
yellow, black cab, red interior, black stack, gray hubs and roller....................$10-13
yellow, black cab, red interior, black stack, yellow hubs and roller, red, blue and black accents, "82 Performant"............$10-13

3038-B Bank Security, 1999
grayish white with red roof, blue front bumper, 1999 catalog $10-13

3039 Bulldozer, 1989, reissued as 4505
yellow, black roof, treads and hydraulics, red and black stripe accents with "ENTER-PRISE" $10-13

3040-A Scania 140 Super Tanker, elliptical tank 1:60, 1979
"elf antar," white cab, amber windows, red grille and interior, silver-gray chassis, black base, ct3c; white tank with red trim, silver-gray bed, red base, "elf antar," decal on sides, "elf," decal on rear, taillight label, ct3c-3045, 1980......................$15-18
"Shell," yellow cab, amber windows, red grille and interior, silver-gray chassis, black base, ct3c; white tank with red trim, yellow bed, gray base, "Shell" and logo, tampo on sides, Shell logo, decal on rear, taillight label, ct3c-3040, 1982? $15-18
"Shell," lemon cab, amber windows, white, may have faded to cream grille and interior, silver-gray chassis, gray base, Shell logo, decal, ct3c; white tank with chrome trim, lemon bed, gray base, "Shell" and logo, label on sides, Shell logo, decal on rear, taillight label, ct3c-3040, 1979 ....$15-18
"BP," green cab, amber windows, red grille and interior, black chassis, red base, ct3c; white tank with chrome trim, black bed, gray base, "BP" and wide red stripe, decal on sides, "BP," decal on rear, taillight label, ct3c-3041 ....$30-35

"Esso," white cab, amber windows, red grille and interior, silver-gray chassis, black base, ct3c; white tank with blue trim, silver-gray bed, gray base, "Esso" in blue-outlined oval between 2 wide broken red stripes, tampo on sides, "Esso" in blue-outlined oval, decal on rear, taillight label, ct3c-3041, 1983 ....$15-18

"Esso," white cab, amber windows, yellow grille and interior, gray chassis, gray base, "Esso" in blue-outlined oval, decal, taillight label, ct3c; white tank with chrome trim, gray bed, gray base, "Esso" in blue-outlined oval between 2 wide red stripes, decal on sides, "Esso" in blue-outlined oval, decal on rear, ct3c-3041, 1979 ....$15-18

"Esso," red cab, amber windows, yellow grille and interior, black chassis, red base, ct3c; silver-gray tank with silver-gray trim, black bed, red base, white "Esso" on wide red stripe, decal on sides, red "Esso" in white rectangle, decal on rear, taillight label, ct3c-3041 ....$15-18

"EWING OIL CO.," red-orange cab, amber windows, yellow grille and interior, silver-gray chassis, black base, ct3c; white tank with red trim, red-orange bed, gray base, "EWING OIL CO. DALLAS," decal on sides and rear, taillight label, ct3c-3041, 1982...$40-60

"FINA," light blue cab, amber windows, yellow grille and interior, silver-gray chassis, black base, ct3c; white tank with blue trim, silver-gray bed, red base, "FINA" with short red and blue stripes, decal on sides, blue "FINA" in white circle on red triangle on rear, taillight label, ct3c-3044 and 3045, 1980......................$30-35

"Gulf," orange cab, amber windows, red grille and interior, black chassis and base, ct3c; silver-gray tank with orange trim, black bed, gray base, "Gulf" on wide orange stripe, decal on sides, "Gulf" on rear, taillight label, ct3c-3040 ....$16-20

"Mobil," greenish-tan cab, amber windows, red grille and interior, silver-gray chassis, black base, ct3c; greenish-tan tank with red trim, silver-gray bed, gray base, "Mobil" and Flying Horse logo, decal on sides, "Mobil" on rear, taillight label, ct3c-3040 and 3045, 1982 ....$30-35

"TEXACO," red cab, amber windows, yellow grille and interior, silver-gray chassis, black base, ct3c; red tank with red trim, gray bed, red base, "TEXACO," decal on sides, "TEXACO," decal on rear, taillight label, ct3c-3040, 3044, and 3046, 1981..$15-18

"TEXACO," gray-brown cab, amber windows, red grille and interior, silver-gray chassis, black base, ct3c; silver-gray tank with silver-gray trim, black bed, red base, "TEXACO," label on sides and rear, no taillight label, ct3c-304X $15-18

"TEXACO," silver cab, amber windows, red grille and interior, black chassis, red base, ct3c; silver-gray tank with silver-gray trim, black bed, red base, "TEXACO," label on sides and rear, no taillight label, ct3c-304X $15-18

"PETRO-CANADA," white cab, amber windows, red grille and interior, silver-gray chassis, black base, ct3c; white tank with blue trim, silver-gray bed, red base, "PETRO-CANADA," decal preceeds maple leaf logo on both sides, "PETRO-CANADA" beneath maple leaf logo, decal on rear, taillight label, ct3c-304X.......$15-18

"PETRO-CANADA," cream cab, amber windows, red grille and interior, brown chassis, black base, ct3c; cream tank with white trim, brown bed and base, "PETRO-CANADA," decal follows maple leaf logo on driver's side and preceeds maple leaf logo on passenger side, "PETRO-CANADA" beneath maple leaf logo, decal on rear, taillight label, ct3c-304X $20-25

"SUNOCO," dark blue cab, amber windows, yellow grille and interior, yellow chassis, black base, ct3c; dark blue tank with yellow trim, gray bed, gray base, "SUNOCO" and logo, decal on sides, logo, decal on rear, taillight label, ct3c-304X.........$16-20

"SERGAZ," white cab, amber windows, red grille and interior, silver-gray cab chassis, black base, ct3c; white tank with white trim, silver bed, silver-gray base, "SERGAZ" with green and black stripe, decal on sides, logo, decal on rear, taillight label, ct3c-304X $25-30

"Olieselskabet Danmark," white cab, amber windows, red grille and interior, red chassis, black base, "OK," decal, ct3c; white tank with red trim, red bed, gray base, "Olieselskabet Danmark," decal on sides; "OK," decal on rear, taillight label, ct3c-304X $25-30

"ARAL," light blue cab, amber windows, yellow grille and interior, silver-gray cab chassis, red base, ct3c; white tank with light blue trim, silver-gray bed, red base, white "ARAL" in a dark blue, decal on sides,

white "ARAL" in a dark blue diamond, decal on rear, taillight label, ct3c-3047, 1981 ....$30-35

3040-B White Tanker, "WHITE" cast above cab grille, elliptical tank, 1:60, 1984

"Shell," yellow cab, clear windows, chrome grille and interior, silver-gray chassis, black base, 6st; white tank with red trim, yellow bed, gray base, logo and "Shell," tampo on sides, logo, decal on rear, ct3c-3040 ....$12-15

"SUNOCO," dark blue cab, clear windows, chrome grille and interior, silver-gray chassis, black base, 6st; dark blue tank with yellow trim; gray bed, gray base, logo and SUNOCO, decal on sides; logo, decal on rear, ct3c-304X $12-15

"Esso," red cab, clear windows, chrome grille and interior, silver-gray chasis, black trim, 6st; silver-gray tank with silver-gray trim, black bed, red base, white "Esso" on red stripe, decal on sides, red "Esso" in white rectangle, decal on rear, ct3c-304X $12-15

"Ultramar," light blue cab, clear windows, chrome grille and interior, silver-gray chassis, black base, 6st; silver-gray tank with silver-gray trim, black bed, gray base, "Ultramar," decal on sides, "Ultramar" and bird logo, decal on rear, ct3c-304X $20-25

3040-C Renault Tanker, elliptical tank 1:60, 1998

"Total," white cab, amber windows, black grille and yellow interior, red chassis, black base, ct3c; white tank with blue trim, red bed, gray base, "Total," tampo on sides and rear, ct3c-304X.......$25-30

3041-A Tanker Truck—see 3040-A, B, or C for details.

Scania Super 140, "Ewing Oil Co. Dallas," based on the "Dallas" TV show........$35-45

Scania Super 140, green cab, tank has BP logo and red stripe.....................$30-35

3041-B Jeep 4x4 with Bass Boat

red with yellow roof, boat has blue hull, white deck..$10-13

3042-A Saviem Semi Covered Trailer, 1979 – 19-87

"Saviem" was taken off front grille for 1983.

blue cab, red chassis, yellow interior, amber windows, black front grill, chrome "SAVIEM" on front grill; trailer: red base, blue bed with a red cover, that removes, blue /white/black "Lasser International" tampo on the sides $12-15

blue cab, red chassis, white interior, light amber windows, ct3c; trailer has red base, blue bed, orange cover, "Bourgey Montreuil," ct3c $12-15

green cab, orange chassis, white interior, light amber windows, red "bm" on white label on doors, ct3c; trailer has yellow base, green bed, orange cover, "Bourgey Montreuil," ct3c.............................$12-15

blue cab, yellow interior and front bumper, ct3c; trailer: blue bed, yellow cover, "MICHELIN," ct3c......................$12-15

3042-B Mercedes 4x4 and Racing Boat, 1988
red, white interior, clear windows, black roof rack and luggage, black rear door, light blue, dark blue and white accents, "RACING team," 5 spoke wheels; trailer: blue, black base, ctsc; boat: red, white interior and motor, red, white and blue labels, "RACING team," "1" $12-15

white, red interior, clear windows, 2 blue lights and a red light bar on roof, black rear door, red, yellow and blue accents, "Indy Crash," "First Lap," "Club 110" on sides and hood, 5 spoke wheels; trailer: white, black base, ctsc; boat: blue over pink, black interior and motor, black, white, pink and blue labels, "RACING team," "1" $12-15

red, white interior, clear windows, black roof rack and luggage, black rear door, light blue, dark blue and white accents, "RACING team," 5 spoke wheels; trailer: white, black base, ctsc; boat: red, white interior and motor, red, white and blue labels, "RACING team," "1" $12-15

3042-C Jeep 4x4 and Racing Boat Trailer
blue Jeep with white roof, red interior, red racing boat, white trailer..................$12-15

3043-A Helicopter "Agusta," 1979
white, red rotor blades, blue windows, white interior, chrome motor, yellow and black "Ewing Oil Co. Dallas" tampo on the sides $16-20

white, red rotor blades, blue windows, white interior, chrome motor, red/black "Ambulance G.O." tampo on the sides...$10-13

white upper, red middle, blue lower bode, red rotors, white interior, blue windows, chrome motor, "POLICE" and "57483" tampos, red, white, and blue label on tail, comes with orange plastic accessory kit with pylons and skis....................$10-13

3044 Tanker–See 3040-A, B, or C for details.
3044-A Scania Super 140 Tanker Truck
yellow cab, white tank with yellow chassis, "Shell" $12-15

grayish brown cab and tank with silver-gray chassis, "Mobil".........................$12-15

red cab and tank with silver-gray chassis, "Texaco"....................................$12-15

blue cab, tank has FINA name with red and blue stripes.....................................$18

light tan cab and tank with silver-gray chassis, "Petro-Canada"...........................$12-15

3044-B Renault Premium Covered Trailer Semi, 1999
"Michelin," blue and yellow...............$10-13

3045 Tanker–See 3040-A, B, or C for details.
3045-B Lincoln Super Stretch Limo, 1989
white with white landau roof, gray interior, tinted windows, spoked white walls $15-18

silver-gray with black landau roof, gray interior, tinted windows, spoked white walls $12-15

black with black landau roof, gray interior, tinted windows, spoked white walls ..$15-18

metallic blue with blue landau roof, gray interior, tinted windows, spoked white walls......$12-15

white with tan landau roof, gray interior, tinted windows, spoked white walls $15-18

metallic blue with gray landau roof, gray interior, tinted windows, spoked white walls..$15-18

metallic blue with black landau roof, gray interior, tinted windows, spoked white walls ..$15-18

3046-A Tanker–See 3040-A, B, or C for details
3046-B Neoplan Bus, 1992
black with abstract tampos...................$8-10

blue with abstract tampos $8-10

white, "PARIS," red base,blue tint windows, "PARIS," 6 star wheels...................$8-10

white, red base, blue tint windows, famous cities and landmarks, "NEW YORK," "PARIS," "SAN FRANCISCO," "LONDON," "ATHINA," "PISA," etc., 6 star wheels...$8-10

3047-A Tanker–See 3040-A, B, or C for details
3048 not issued
3049-A Toyota Truck and Tandem Trailer, 1988–1989
black, red interior, clear windows, unpainted base, red frame and rear fenders, black bed, white cover, red, blue, and black "EXPRESS" label, 5 spoke wheels; trailer has white cover on black bed, unpainted base, red, blue, and black "SERVICES" label, 5 spoke wheels.................$12-15

blue, blue interior, clear windows, unpainted base, red frame and rear fenders, black bed, red cover, yellow, blue, and black "EXPRESS" label, 5 spoke wheels; trailer has red cover on black bed, unpainted base, yellow, blue, and black "SERVICES" label, 5 spoke wheels.................$12-15

3049-B Tractor and Tank Trailer, 1994
lime green tractor with gray side cutter,

white cab with black roof, orange tank on trailer..............................$10-13

3050-A Toyota Landcruiser and Racing Boat, 1981–1987
metallic blue with yellow roof, black boat on yellow trailer, 1986 catalog $12-15

3050-B Mercedes 4x4 and Racing Boat
no details available $10-13

3050-C Unimog and Trailer, 1999
orange with white canopy, 1999 catalog.......................................$10-13

3051-A Tractor and Hay Trailer, 1981–1988
red, white cab, black roof, red wheel rims, gray motor, gray side mower, brown man, 8 lug front wheels, red rear wheels; trailer: red with a yellow base and slatted rails on top, 8 lug wheels $12-15

red, white cab, black roof, red wheel rims, gray motor, gray side mower, brown man, 8 lug front wheels; trailer: red with a black base and slatted rails on top, 6t $12-15

orange, white cab, black roof, red wheel rims, gray motor, gray side mower, brown man; trailer: orange with a black base and slatted rails on top, 6t $12-15

3051-B Tractor and Hay Trailer, new streamlined tractor, haybales in trailer, 1999
bright green tractor with red trailer, yellow bales $12-15

3052-A Toyota Landcruiser and Horse Trailer, 1982–1988 reissued 1996
black, red interior, amber windows, white roof, no roof rack, white rear door, white, red and blue accents, "olympic jumping," black base, 5 spoke; trailer: white over black, white rear ramp, white side door, black base, ctsc......................$12-15

blue, brown interior and roof luggage, black roof and rear hatch, clear windows, 5 spoke wheels; trailer: white over black, white rear ramp, white side door, black base, ctsc $12-15

3052-B Jeep and Horse Trailer, 1989
green, white roof, red interior, clear windshield, "Racing Club" tampos on sides and hood, black base, 5 spoke; trailer: white over green, white doors, ctsc $12-15

3052-C Mercedes M Class and Horse Trailer, 1999
metallic dark green, 1999 catalog $12-15

3053-A Blazer 4x4 and Camping Trailer, 1982–1988, reissued as 3065
green, white lower body and cap, white interior, clear windows, 8kk wheels; trailer white over pale green, amber windows, ct3c $12-15

pale green, black lower body and cap, black interior, clear windows, "FRUIT OF THE LOOM," "T-Shirts" 5 spoke wheels; trailer white over pale green, amber windows, ct3c, 1986.............................$12-15

gold-brown, cream lower body and cap, white interior, clear windows, 8kk; trailer cream over gold-brown, amber windows, ct3c.............................$12-15

green, beige lower body and cap, white interior, "4x4" label on hood, 8kk; trailer beige over burgundy, amber windows, ct3c.............................$12-15

3053-B Range Rover and Camping Trailer, 1989

metallic red, trailer has metallic red lower, white upper.............................$12-15

bright blue with fluorescent splash graphics, 5 spoke; trailer: white over blue, amber windows ctsc.............................$12-15

baby blue, red interior, purple, green and yellow graphics, 5 spoke; trailer; cream over baby blue, ctsc.............................$12-15

cream, red interior, amber windows, gold and black accents, "Freeway" on sides and hood, black base, 5 spoke; trailer: cream over red, amber windows, ctsc $12-15

hunter green, red interior, 5 spoke; trailer; cream over hunter green, amber windows, ctsc.............................$12-15

3054-A Tractor and Tanker Trailer, 1982–1984

green with white cab, black roof, white tank on green trailer, 1984 catalog.....$12-15

3054-B Tractor and Dumping Trailer, new streamlined tractor, 1999

green, white cage, black roof, green wheel rims, gray motor, gray side mower, brown man; trailer: green, white tank $12-15

3055-A GM Semi Container, 1986 only, reissue of 3068

white cab, amber windows, metallic silver chassis, red deflector, ct3c; trailer: white, red white and blue "PEPSI" label, ct3c, 1986 catalog.............................$12-15

3055-B Volvo Semi Container, 1987

red cab, black interior, clear windows, unpainted chassis, black base, white, blue and black tampo, "EAGLE TRUCKS," 6st; trailer: white, gray base, white, blue, silver, red and black labels, "EAGLE TRUCKS," ctsc.............................$12-15

blue cab, black interior, clear windows, unpainted chassis, black base, silver, red and black tampo, "EAGLE TRUCKS," 6st; trailer: white, gray base, white, blue, silver, red and black labels, "EAGLE TRUCKS," ctsc.............................$12-15

red cab, 6st; trailer: white, ctsc, "Coca Cola" label $12-15

3056 not issued

3057-A Camaro and Racing Boat, 1995

blue with brown interior, white trailer with red boat, 1995 catalog $10-13

3058 and 3059 not issued

3060-A Scania Sailboat Transporter, 1979–1985

orange cab, blue chassis, amber windows, yellow interior and front grill, ct3c; trailer: orange, " KERIAN NICE" tampo on the sides, ct3c; sail boat: white over light blue, blue masts, orange interior, amber windows, orange "716" tampo on the sides $16-20

red cab, metallic silver chassis, amber windows, yellow interior and front grill, gray base, "KERIAN TOULON" tampo on doors, ct3c; trailer: red, yellow fenders, brown boat cradle and base, red decal with "KERIAN NICE" on sides, decal on back bumper with "LONG VEHICLE," ct3c; sail boat: white over yellow, blue masts, orange interior, amber windows, picture of Dolphin on front sides, red "FRANCE" tampo at back sides.............................$16-20

3060-B White Sailboat Transporter, 1986

blue cab, chrome interior, clear windows, silver-gray chassis, 6st; trailer: yellow, red base, "BOATransporter" on red and blue label, ct3c; sailboat: white over blue, yellow interior, amber windows, blue mast, red and blue label, "seabird".......$16-20

3061-A Saviem car carrier without cars, cab hinges forward, 1979–1988, compare to 3092, the "Saviem" was taken off the front grille for 1983

yellow cab, red base, amber windows, yellow interior, black front grill; trailer: yellow base and rear ramp, red bed, red upper carrier, that removes, white "Mondial Assistance" tampo on the sides, ct3c ...$12-15

light blue cab, dark yellow base, amber windows, yellow interior, black front; trailer: yellow base and light blue bed, dark yellow upper carrier, that removes, black/red/white/yellow "Majorette" and "trans auto" tampo on the sides, ct3c.............................$12-15

yellow cab, blue base, amber windows, black front grill; trailer: blue rear ramp, blue bed, blue upper carrier, that removes, yellow " TRANSPORTS GEFCO" tampo on the sides, ct3c $12-15

blue cab, orange base, amber windows; trailer: orange base and blue bed, orange upper carrier, that removes, black/red/white/orange "Majorette" and "trans auto" tampo on the sides $12-15

red cab, "Majo Transport" on doors, orange bumper and chassis, orange over red trailer, ct3c wheels $12-15

3061-B Renault Saviem car carrier, without cars, cab tilts, issued as 3092 with cars

yellow cab, black trailer with yellow upper section $12-15

metallic blue with yellow lower body, metallic blue trailer with yellow upper section, 1984 catalog $15-18

3062-A Saviem Double Container, 1979–1981

blue, white interior, light amber windows, orange chassis, ct3c; trailer has red bed, white containers, orange tops, yellow, red, white and black "SuperTrans" labels, brown rear door, red and yellow bumper decal, ct3c $12-15

light blue, white interior, light amber windows, red chassis, ct3c; trailer has red bed, white containers, orange tops, pale blue, dark blue red and white "SuperTrans" labels, brown rear door, red and yellow bumper decal, ct3c $12-15

3062-B GM Double Container, 1:60, 1982–1985

orange, white interior, light amber windows, white air deflector, metallic silver chassis, ct3c; trailer has metallic silver bed, white containers, orange tops, pale blue, dark blue red and white "SuperTrans" labels, brown rear door, red and yellow bumper decal, ct3c $12-15

red, yellow interior, clear windows, orange air deflector, gray chassis, ct3c; trailer has red bed and orange containers with red tops, red/black/yellow tampo on the sides "Fast truckKing," bumper decal, ct3c $12-15

3062-C Double Container Trailer Semi, new "Euro" style cab

pale blue cab, "Trans World," 1999 catalog.............................$10-13

3063-A Scania Semi Dump Truck, 1979–1985

red cab, silver chassis, amber windows, yellow interior and front grill; trailer: red base, silver dump, ct3c.........................$12-15

3063-B White Semi Dump Truck, 1986 only

red cab, chrome interior, clear windows, silver-gray chassis, 6st; trailer: gray, red chassis, ctsc...$16-20

3064-A Autocar Mercedes Bus, 1981

white over blue, blue interior, clear windows, blue base, label of tropical scene and "sun tours," two pale blue stripes running between wheels, 6 star wheels $12-15

white over blue, amber windows, no accents, 6 star wheels $12-15

white over blue, off-white interior, clear windows, yellow/orange/white stripe tampos on the sides, 6 star wheels.....$12-15

3065-A Blazer 4x4 and Camping Trailer, 1981, renumbered as 3053 for 1982 – see 3053 ....$12-15,

3065-B GM Racing car Transporter, 1:60, 1986-1992, continued in set 3098 after 1992

white cab, amber windows, red air deflector, metallic silver chassis, ct3c; trailer: white, red roof, "HONDA," "F-1," "WORLD Champion 1986, 1987, 1988" label, other side has "HONDA RACING TEAM," "ALAIN PROST," "AYRTON SENNA," #289 race car, ct3c ...$15-18

white cab, amber windows, red air deflector, metallic silver chassis, ct3c; trailer: white, red roof, black labels, "GOODYEAR," "F1 RACING TEAM," Shell logo, other side has graphic of a race car, "F1 RACING TEAM TURBO," #289.3 race car, ct3c $15-18

red cab, amber windows, red air deflector, metallic silver chassis, ct3c; trailer: red, red roof, red labels, "Ferrari," "Agip," other side has "CHAMPION," "Agip," "SKF," "arexons," "LONGINES," "WEBER," "FIAT," "MAGNETI MARELLI," "Ferrari," #282 race car, ct3c $15-18

yellow cab, amber windows, blue air deflector, metallic silver chassis, ct3c; trailer: yellow, blue roof, white "RACING F1 TEAM SERVICE" label and yellow "F1 TEAM SERVICE" on one side, other side has yellow "RACING F1 TEAM SERVICE" label and graphic of a race car with "elf," "12," and "RACING," no race car?, ct3c $15-18

3066-A Blazer 4x4 and Motorcycle Trailer, 1981 only, no details available $16-20

3066-B Van and Motorcycle Trailer, 1982–1989

silver, red roof, fenders, head light rims and base, amber windows,"Holiday" tampo on the sides, spoked wheels; trailer: black; motorcycles: blue with white saddlebag, red with black saddlebag...........$16-20

black, red roof, fenders, head light rims and base, red interior, amber windows, yellow, white and red label "SuperFast" and picture of motorcycle, other side has picture of motorcycle racer, "SuperFast," spoked wheels; trailer: black, ctsc; motor-

cycles: blue with white saddlebag, yellow with black saddlebag $16-20

blue, yellow roof, fenders, head light rims and base, yellow interior, amber windows, yellow, red and blue label "WINNER'S team," other side has yellow, red and blue picture of motorcycle racer, spoked wheels; trailer: black, ctsc; motorcycles: blue with white saddlebag, yellow with black saddlebag.......................$16-20

3067-A GM Semi Horse Trailer, 1:60, 1983

forest green cab, metallic silver chassis, white air deflector, amber windows, white over forest green trailer windows, label with picture of rider jumping a horse over 2 bars on one side, picture of 4 brown horses running in a green field on the other, ct3c $16-20

red cab, metallic silver chassis, white air deflector, white interior, amber windows, label of horseshoe with horse's head on deflector; trailer: white over red, brown doors, amber windows, label with picture of rider jumping a horse over 2 bars on one side, picture of 4 brown horses running in a green field on the other, ct3c $16-20

red cab, metallic silver chassis, white wind deflector; trailer: white with red base, brown side doors, one on each side that open, horses inside, labels of rearing horse with rider tipping hat on both sides with red on black "RODEO," ct3c $16-20

red cab, metallic silver chassis, yellow air deflector, yellow interior, amber windows, yellow, black, red, and blue label on deflector, "RODEO TEXAS," trailer: yellow over red, brown doors, amber windows, label with picture of cowboy with lasso and "RODEO TEXAS" on both sides, ct3c $16-20

red cab, metallic silver chassis, yellow air deflector, brown interior, amber windows, yellow, black, red and blue label on deflector, "RODEO TEXAS," trailer: yellow over red, brown doors, amber windows, label with picture of cowboy with lasso and "RODEO TEXAS" on both sides, ct3c $16-20

3068-A GM Semi Container, 1984–1985 renumbered 3055 in 1986

Pepsi $16-20

3069-A Dune Buggy Set, interchangeable bodies, 1984

blue body with roll bar and red body with white roof, 1984 catalog.........................$16-20

3070-A Jeep and Dune Buggy Trailer, 1986–1990

white with "kleber racing cross," "elf," blue and red accents, black roof, yellow trailer, white dune buggy with red and blue accents, yellow interior, 1986 catalog $16-20

3070-B Range Rover and Buggy, 1991

blue, red interior, amber windows, white, red and gold accents, "RACING All Roads 4x4" on sides and hood, 5 spoke; trailer: blue, black buggy holder, ctsc; buggy: blue, red interior, black roll bar, white label with red stripes and blue stars, 5 spoke $12-15

3071-A Volvo car carrier, without cars, 1:60, 1989–present

yellow cab, black interior, clear windows, unpainted chassis, two red stripes and "C10" on sides, "Globetrotter" on front of roof, 6st; trailer: red upper deck and ramp, gray lower deck, black base, 6st...$12-15

blue cab with silver trailer black upper deck, 1993–96 catalogs $12-15

yellow cab with silver trailer, red upper deck, 1989 catalog $12-15

red cab, silver trailer, black upper deck, 1999 catalog....................................$12-15

3072-A Mercedes 230 GE and Lamborghini Trailer, 1989

white, red interior, clear windows, 2 blue lights and a red light bar on roof, black rear door, yellow, blue and red accents, "ASSISTANCE," "Le Mans," "Shell," "SPORT," "SERVICE," Shell logo, spoked white wall wheels; trailer: red, black base, red and yellow label with "Le Mans ASSISTANCE," ctsc; car: black, red interior, gold wheels, #2504 ....$16-20

cream, red interior, clear windows, 2 blue lights and a red light bar on roof, black rear door, yellow, blue and red accents, "ASSISTANCE," "Le Mans," "Shell," "SPORT," "SERVICE," Shell logo, 5 spoke wheels; trailer: red, black base, red and yellow label with "Le Mans ASSISTANCE," ctsc; car: black, red interior, gold wheels, #2504 ....$16-20

3073-A Volvo Racing Boat Transporter, 1:60, 1990

pink cab, black interior, clear windows, unpainted chassis, black and yellow accents, "3 Fatal OCEAN," 6st; trailer: black, black base, pink "Fatal OCEAN," gray lower deck, black base, pink boat cradle, 6st; boat: green over pink, blue and yellow accents, "Fatal OCEAN 3" $16-20

pink cab, black interior, clear windows, unpainted chassis, black and yellow accents, "3

Fatal OCEAN," 6st; trailer: black, black base, pink "Fatal OCEAN," gray lower deck, black base, pink boat cradle, ct3c; boat: green over pink, blue and yellow accents, "Fatal OCEAN 3" $16-20

red cab, black interior, clear windows, unpainted chassis, 6st; trailer: white, black base, red boat cradle, ct3c; boat: red, red, blue, white and black labels, "MAGNUM," "1," "MAGNUM" on wing $16-20

red cab, black interior, clear windows, unpainted chassis, blue and white "MAGNUM" tampo on sides of cab, 6st; trailer: white, black base, red boat cradle, blue "MAGNUM" on side, ct3c; boat: red, red, blue, white and black labels, "MAGNUM," "1," "MAGNUM" on wing $16-20

red cab, 6st; trailer: white; boat: red over white, "Coca Cola" $16-20

3074-A White Semi Airplane Transporter, 1:60, 1990

dark blue, navy cab, chrome interior, clear windows, silver-gray chassis, red and white tampos with eagle head on door, 6st; trailer: gray, white plane holder, red, white and blue labels, "F.148," and eagle's head on sides, ctsc; plane: blue over white, blue canopy, red, white and blue labels, "F.148" and eagle's head on tail $16-20

blue cab, chrome interior, clear windows, silver-gray chassis, red and white tampos with eagle head on door, 6st; trailer: gray, white plane holder, red, white and blue labels, "F.148," and eagle's head on sides, ctsc; plane: navy blue over white, blue canopy, red, white and blue labels, "F.148" and eagle's head on tail $16-20

3075 Volvo Semi Dragster Transport, 1993

red cab, yellow trailer, 6 star wheels, blue "Big Bullit" dragster $10-13

3076-A Semi Oil Tanker, "WHITE" cab with no "WHITE" cast above grille, circular tank 1:60, 1994

"Shell," white cab, clear windows, chrome grille and interior, silver-gray chassis, black base, 6st; white tank with red trim, "Shell" and logo, tampo on sides, black base, 6st, 1994 .... $8-10

"PETROL COMPANY," yellow cab, clear windows, chrome grille and interior, silver-gray chassis, black base, 6st; white tank with red trim, black base, "PETROL COMPANY," tampo on sides, 6st, 1997 .... $8-10

"Coca Cola," white cab, clear windows, chrome grille and interior, silver-gray chassis, black base, red "Coca Cola" on hood and ice cube on doors, tampo, 6st; red tank with white trim, black base, white "Coca Cola" on red background, label on sides, 6st, 1997 .... $12-15

"GT GAS TANKER," orange cab, clear windows, chrome grille and interior, silver-gray chassis, black base, 6st; gray tank with red trim, black base, "GT GAS TANKER," tampo on sides. 6st, 1999 .... $8-10

"SPECIAL FORCES," olive cab with camouflage design and white Special Forces logo, tampo on hood and doors, smoke windows, silver-gray plastic grille and interior, olive chassis, black base, 6stol; olive camouflage tank with olive trim, olive base, white "SPECIAL FORCES," tampo on sides, 6stol, 1999–grille, interior, side mirrors, engine, exhaust pipe, and gas tanks are silver-gray plastic........... $12-15

3076-B Semi Oil Tanker, No "WHITE" cast above cab grille, elliptical tank 1:60, 1998

"WYNN'S," white cab, clear windows, chrome grille and interior, silver-gray chassis, black base, "WYNN's," tampo on hood, 6st; white tank with red trim, metallic silver bed, red base, "Wynn's," tampo on sides, promotional, ct3c-304X....... $25-30

3077-A Jeep 4x4 with Motorcycle Trailer, 1996

white with red roof, rally graphics $12-15

black, red interior, brown roof, 5 spoke wheels; trailer unpainted and black, red motorcycle with blue and white accents $12-15

3078 through 3089 not issued

3090-A Renault Saviem car carrier with 5 cars, 1979–1983, has "Saviem" on grill

red with white base, red trailer with yellow upper deck, 1980 catalog.......... $20-25

3090.1-A Kenworth Log Transporter and Land Rover, 266-B

green cab with "FOREST SERVICE" stickers with graphics, 6 star wheels, gray trailer, red crane boom, brown plastic logs, 6 star wheels, Land Rover is red with red roof light bar, 5d, 1999 catalog $20-25

3090.2-A Boat Transporter

Coast Guard, red, white and blue $12-15

Beach Patrol, red, yellow and blue $12-15

3091 Snorkel Fire Engine, 1984–1987

red, yellow roof and rear fenders, yellow interior, amber windows, gray base and bumpers, red boom base, red boom, silver gray boom rest and extra hoses, white steering levers, light blue, dark blue and yellow labels with a blue bird and "RESCUE UNITY," 6t wheels $12-15

red, yellow roof and rear fenders, yellow interior, amber windows, gray base and bumpers, red boom base, red boom, silver-gray boom rest and extra hoses, black steering levers, light blue, dark blue and yellow labels with a blue bird and "RESCUE UNITY," 6t wheels $12-15

3091-B Fiat Monospace with Motorcycle and Sea-Doo Trailer, 1997

metallic teal blue with silver trailer, 1996 catalog... $12-15

3092-A Saviem car Transporter with five cars, no "Saviem" on grill, 1984–1988

red cab, yellow base, amber windows, yellow interior, black front grill; trailer: yellow base and red rear ramp, yellow bed, yellow upper carrier, that removes, black "Majorette" tampo on the sides $16-20

3092-B Holidays Van with Hot Rod and Trailer, 1994–1995

blue with yellow roof and trim, red trailer with yellow Hot Rod, 1994–95 catalogs... $12-15

3092-C Holidays Van with Dune Buggy and Trailer, 1996

blue with yellow roof and trim, white flame stickers with red border, yellow trailer with red dune buggy, 1996 catalog ... $12-15

3093-A White Building Transporter, 1985–1986

red cab, chrome interior, clear windows, silver-gray chassis, orange, yellow and black tampo, "SH," "sweet home," 6st; trailer: red, black base, yellow holder, black ties, white, red and yellow Majokit house with green shutters, rw $18

3093-B Racing Truck Transporter, 1993–1998

white, blue air deflector, silver and black chassis; trailer is black, red ramp; racing truck has white cab, blue spoiler.......... $12-15

3094-A Volvo Super Helicopter Transporter and Landrover, 1987

white cab, black interior, clear windows, unpainted chassis, black and red tampo, "TURBO COPTER," 6st; trailer: red, unpainted base, black helicopter holder, ctsc; helicopter: black, white interior, blue windows, red rotors, white accents, "TURBO COPTER," Landrover: orange, black interior, clear windows, black rear door, no roof rack or light, 5d $16-20

white cab, black interior, clear windows, unpainted chassis, black and red tampo, "TURBO COPTER," 6st; trailer: red, unpainted base, black helicopter holder, ctsc; helicopter:

black, white interior, blue windows, red rotors, white accents, "TURBO COPTER," Landrover: orange, black interior, clear windows, black rear door, translucent red light bar on roof, 5d $16-20

white cab, black interior, clear windows, unpainted chassis, black and red tampo, "TURBO COPTER," 6st; trailer: white fenders and pink helicopter holder; Landrover: orange, black interior, clear windows, black rear door, translucent red light bar on roof, 5d $16-20

3094-B Kenworth Helicopter Transporter and Land Rover, 1995

black and white, Police.....................$16-20

3095-A White car carrier with 5 cars, 1:60, 1989

blue cab, chrome interior, clear windows, silver-gray chassis, tampo on doors of yellow car with orange stripe and arrow, 6st; trailer: silver-gray with red upper deck and ramp, black base, 6st; 5 cars: #209 Porsche 911, #240 Impala Police car, #215 Corvette, #223 '57 Chevrolet, and #291 Chevrolet Blazer $20-25

blue cab, chrome interior, clear windows, metallic silver chassis, tampo on doors of yellow car with orange stripe and arrow, 6st; trailer: silver-gray with red upper deck and ramp, black base, 6st; 5 cars: #249 Celica, #231 Mercedes 190, #217 Thunderbird, #235 Golf, and #230 Volvo.....................................$20-25

3095-B Kenworth car carrier with four cars, 1995–present

blue with yellow flame stickers, "Hot Truck" in red with white outline, gray trailer with black upper deck, 1999 catalog..........$16-20

teal with yellow lower body, yellow flames with red tips, "Hot Truck" in white, gray trailer with black upper deck, 1996 catalog...$16-20

3096-A Fire Engine with Extension Ladder, 1988

red, white roof and rear fenders, yellow interior, amber windows, gray base and bumpers, red boom base, white ladder, black steering levers, "FIRE DEPT ENGINE NO. 2" labels, 6t wheels............$14-17

3096-B Snorkel Fire Engine *Incendie Nacelle*, 1997

red with white cab upper, "FIRE DEPT.NEW YORK" sticker on sides of cab, silver metal horn and light array on cab roof, amber windows...................................$12-15

3097-A White Semi Bulldozer Transporter, 1:60, 1989

yellow, chrome interior, clear windows, gray chassis, red and black thin stripe tampo, 6st; trailer: gray, black base, yellow ramp,

black box under bulldozer blade, rw; bulldozer: yellow, black roof, treads and hydraulics, red and black stripe accents with "ENTERPRISE" $16-20

yellow, chrome interior, clear windows, metallic silver chassis, red and black thin stripe tampo, 6st; trailer: gray, black base, yellow ramp, black box under bulldozer blade, rw; bulldozer: yellow, black roof, treads and hydraulics, red and black stripe accents with "ENTERPRISE" $16-20

yellow, chrome interior, clear windows, unpainted chassis, red and black thin stripe tampo, 6st; trailer: gray, black base, yellow ramp, no box on trailer, rw; bulldozer: yellow, black roof, treads and hydraulics, red and black stripe accents with "ENTERPRISE," in set 954 .....$16-20

3098-A GM Racing Transporter Set, 1:60, 1990

yellow cab, amber windows, blue air deflector, metallic silver chassis, ct3c; trailer: yellow, blue roof, white "RACING F1 TEAM SERVICE" label and yellow "F1 TEAM SERVICE" on one side, other side has yellow "RACING F1 TEAM SERVICE" label and graphic of a race car with "elf," "12," and "RACING," #289 McLaren race car in trailer, 2 #238 F1 Racers and a #282 Ferrari, ct3c...........................$16-20

3099-A White Semi Transporter with Cable car, 1:60, 1991 ....$14-17

3099-B Chevrolet Custom Pickup with Beach Buggy and Trailer, 1995

white upper, red lower, "Chevrolet Sport Side," white trailer with red dune buggy ...$12-15

Ref: 3010-3020 Majorette Range Rover, 1:36

metallic turquoise, orange tinted windows, tow hook $12-15

Majorette 4X4 Super Movers, 1986, 4x4 vehicles with oversized tires and modified raised chassis

3101 Jeep Night Hawk

black with red roof, "night hawk" tampos ..$8-10

3102 Blazer Sheriff

blue with white topper, "N845 Sheriff" ...$8-10

3103 Blazer Demon Killer

red with silver roll bar, white "Demon Killer" tampos, "12" $8-10

3104 Toyota Desert Fox

white with black roof, orange and black "Desert Fox" tampos $8-10

Majorette All-American Road Kings, 1:32 scale models, 1995

3201 .95 Mustang GT, yellow..................$4-6

3202 '95 Camaro Convertible, bright blue $4-6

3203 Chevrolet Sportside Extended Cab, white with black lower body $4-6

3204 Chevrolet Sportside and Camper Top, red with black lower body and camper top ...$4-6

3205 Chevrolet Dooley Custom Pickup $4-6

3206 Chevrolet Dooley Custom Pickup with Camper Top.....................................$4-6

3231 Mustang and Motorcycle Trailer $8-10

3232 Camaro and Sea-Doo Trailer $8-10

3233 Chevrolet Pickup and Motorcycle Trailer..$8-10

3234 Chevrolet Dooley Custom Pickup and Sea-Doo Trailer $6-8

Majorette Ultra Custom, 1:32 custom vehicles, 1995

3221 '95 Mustang $4-6

3222 '95 Camaro.................................$4-6

3223 Custom Chevrolet Dually $4-6

3224 Custom Chevrolet Dually and Camper Top..$4-6

Majorette Traffic Jammers

3403 Range Rover 4x4 Roarin' Monster, green...$10-13

Majorette Club / Super Club 1/24

With the purchase of Solido in 1993, Majorette gained access to the superb large-scale models to incorporate at will into the Majorette collectibles assortment. Some Club 1/24 and Club 1/18 models are representatives of this merger.

4101 Bugatti 55 de la Chapelle

red, brown interior, brown fenders, no frame on windshield $12-15

brown with red scallops, light brown interior, brown fenders, windshield has chrome frame and mirrors $12-15

4102 Jaguar E Type

British racing green, light brown interior ..$12-15

4103 Ferrari 365 GT Daytona

red, black interior $12-15

yellow $12-15

4104 AC Cobra 427, top down, compare to 4212

dark blue, white seats, "5," double white stripe down middle of car.....................$10-13

white, "5," double blue stripe down middle of car...$10-13

red, white seats, "5," double white stripe down middle of car $10-13

4107 Chevrolet Silverado Pickup, 1995

yellow, white, red, blue, and black accents, "MOTOR," "256," "Speed" ....$8-10 red, silver, and red accents, "4x4" on sides, "Chevrolet" on tailgate $8-10

4108 Jeep Grand Cherokee Limited, 1995
black, red interior $8-10

4110 Jeep Grand Cherokee Sheriff, 1996
white, blue "Sheriff" on doors...............$8-10

4111 Chevrolet Silverado
red, white accents with a black shadow, "John's Towing, Emergency Road service" on doors, "24 hr. service" on hood, black roll bar and grille guard.................$8-10

4112 Chevrolet Silverado Rallye, 1996
yellow, blue, and red accents, "MOTOR 256" on doors $8-10

4113 Jeep Grand Cherokee Rallye, 1997 ..$8-10

4114 Jeep Grand Cherokee Fire Chief, 1997 ....$8-10

4151 Ferrari Daytona, red, 1997 ....$8-10

4152 Ferrari Daytona, yellow, 1997.........$8-10

4153 Porsche 944 Coupe, yellow, 1997
green, racing tampos, First Lap, Champion, Super BBL Racing, STAR 1997 ......$8-10

4154 Porsche 944 Coupe, red, 1997 ......$8-10

4155 Ford GT 40, white, 1997 ....$8-10

4156 Ford GT 40, light blue, 1997 ....$8-10

4157 Formula 1, red, 1997 ....$8-10

4158 Formula 1, white, 1997 ....$8-10

4159 Formula Indy, black, 1997..............$8-10

4160 Bugatti Roadster, red, 1997 ....$8-10

4161 Lamborghini Countach, orange, 1997 ....$8-10

4162 Proto "Baja," white, 1997 ....$8-10

4201 Porsche 944 Turbo
charcoal gray, white 'PORSCHE" on door sills...$8-10

white, black seats, light gray interior, black"PORSCHE" on door sills $8-10

silver...$8-10

white, black seats, brown interior, "10", "turbo cup," "DUNLOP," "FORMULE SHELL," "FACOM," red, black and yellow accents $8-10

4202 Chevrolet Corvette Coupe
metallic red, light gray seats, dark gray rest of interior, light red "CORVETTE" on doors, chrome rims...................................$8-10

red, '"ZR-1" on doors, light gray interior ...$8-10

metallic blue, dark gray seats, light gray rest of interior, chrome rims.....................$8-10

red, white seats, pale yellow rest of interior, "CORVETTE" on doors, gold rims ...$8-10

4203 Lamborghini Countach 5000 Quattrovalvole
red, white interior, blue windows, chrome rims...$8-10

white, brown interior, blue windows, chrome rims...$8-10

black, white interior, clear windows, gold $8-10

4204 Chevrolet Corvette Roadster
yellow, dark gray seats, light gray rest of interior, "Official Pace car, 70th Indianapolis 500—May 25, 1986"..................$8-10

white, light gray seats, dark gray rest of interior, "Official Pace car, 70th Indianapolis 500—May 25, 1986"...........$12-15

pink, black interior $8-10

black, light gray interior $8-10

4205 Porsche 944 Turbo Coupe
white $8-10

silver $8-10

4206 Peugeot 405 Turbo 16
yellow, blue seats, U shaped black wing, white hubs, "203," "RACING SERVICE," "PIONEER," red, white and blue decals, "Esso" on front, "203" on roof, small black crash bar on front $8-10

white, blue seats, large black wing, large black air dam on front, mainly blue decals,"2," "Pikes Peak," "Shell" on front, "PIONEER SETTON" on hood and roof...........$8-10

4208 Porsche 944 S2 Cabriolet
red, black seats, gray interior, black convertible top cover, white "PORSCHE" on door sills..$8-10

4209 Peugeot 405 T16 "Pikes Peak" $8-10

4210 Mercedes-Benz 500 SL Roadster
dark gray/black over gray $8-10

red over maroon, light red interior $8-10

beige over brown, brown interior..........$8-10

4211 Lamborghini Diablo
red $8-10

yellow $8-10

4212 AC Cobra 427, top up, compare to 4104
metallic red...$8-10

metallic teal $8-10

4213 Mercedes 500 SL Coupe
gray $8-10

4214 Ford GT 40
light blue, orange stripe, black "6" on white roundel, black interior, chrome and red wheels, LeMans $8-10

red $8-10

white, blue stripe on doors, "1" on white roundel outlined in black...............$8-10

4215 1993 Porsche 911, silver-gray $8-10

4217 Ford Mustang Convertible, 1995.....$8-10

4218 Ferrari 550 Maranello, red,1997 ...$10-13

4219 Ferrari 550 Maranello, yellow,1997 ..$10-13

Majorette Club 1/24 Metal Kit Easy-to-assemble metal kits

4301 Porsche 944 Turbo........................$8-10

4302 Jaguar Type E $8-10

4303 Ferrari 365 GT Daytona $8-10

4304 AC Cobra 427..............................$8-10

4305 Chevrolet Corvette Coupe $8-10

4306 1993 Porsche 911, 1995 ....$8-10

4311 Lamborghini Diablo $8-10

4312 Ferrari 365 GTB Daytona, 1997 .....$8-10

4313 Porsche 944 Coupe, 1997 ....$8-10

4314 Ford GT 40, 1997 ....$8-10

4315 Formula 1, 1997 ....$8-10

4316 Bugatti Roadster, 1997 ....$8-10

4317 Lamborghini Countach, 1997..........$8-10

4318 Proto "Baja," 1997 ....$8-10

Majorette Club 1/18 Majorette/Solido Models–1994

4401 Peugeot 605, 1994
Racing #52, yellow..............................$25-30

Racing, #18, blue.................................$25-30

Racing, #52, green...............................$25-30

Racing, #52, white/blue $25-30

no stickers, white $25-30

no stickers, green $25-30

4402 1964 Mini Cooper, 1994
green $25-30

black $25-30

Racing, #10 yellow...............................$25-30

4403 Ferrari 365 GTS Convertible, 1994
yellow $25-30

4404 1936 Ford Pickup Truck, 1994
green $25-30

yellow/red..$25-30

"Hot Truck," blue/black $25-30

4405 1955 Cadillac Eldorado, 1994
white $25-30

4406 1958 Volkswagen Beetle, 1994
orange $25-30

blue $25-30

4407 Citroën ZX Rallye Raid, 1994
red, "34," rally tampos, yellow rims and rear wing $25-30

4408 BMW 850i, 1994
silver...$25-30

4409 Lexus LS 400, 1994
red $25-30

green $25-30

4410 Mercedes 500 SL Convertible, 1994
gray and black $25-30

red $25-30

4411 1964 AC Cobra 427 Convertible, 1994
blue, white stripe across hood, "16," white seats $25-30

red $25-30

4412 1957 Chevrolet Corvette Convertible, 1994
black..$25-30

4413 1955 Ford Thunderbird, 1995
    red, black and white interior $25-30
    light blue, black, and white interior......$25-30
4414 Jeep Grand Cherokee Laredo, 1995
    red $25-30
4415 Jeep Grand Cherokee Limited, 1995
    black, brown interior, gold pin stripe ...$25-30
4416 1957 Chevrolet Nomad, 1995
    red $25-30
4417 Toyota Land Cruiser, 1995
    red $25-30
4418 Mercedes 600 S Coupe, 1995
    metallic teal $25-30
    Racing, #22, black $25-30
4419 Ferrari F355
    red $25-30
4420 Ferrari F355
    Racing, #6, yellow..............................$25-30
4421 Jeep Wrangler California, with surfboard,
    1997, green $25-30
4422 Jeep Wrangler, 1997
    red $25-30
4423 Jeep Wrangler Rallye, 1997
    white..$25-30
4424 Jeep Grand Cherokee Rallye, 1997
    Rally, #441, white $25-30

Majorette Platinum 1/18
4451 Lotus / Caterham Super Seven
    green/yellow $25-30
4452 Ferrari Dino 246 GT
    red $25-30
4453 Lamborghini Miura, 1997
    red $25-30
4454 Bugatti EB 110, 1997
    blue $25-30
4455 Porsche 911 Carrera 4 Cabriolet, 1997
    red $25-30
4456 Ferrari 328 GTS, 1997
    red $25-30
4457 Porsche 911 Turbo, 1997
    yellow $25-30
4459 Ferrari 550 Maranello
    red $25-30

Majorette Construction / Super Construction, 4500 series
This series was released in 1990 with a single model, 4501 Dump Truck.
4501-A Dump Truck, 1990, later renumbered
    4514 and packaged with a #266 Landrover..$12-15
4501-B Front End Loader $10-13
4502 Cement Mixer $10-13
4503 Heavy Duty Transporter with Wheel
    Loader..$10-13

4504 Roller..$10-13

4505 Bulldozer with Payloader and Rear Drag Claw..$10-13

4506 Wheeled Excavator $10-13

4507 Dump Truck, 1997 ....$10-13

4508 Truck with Crane, 1997...............$10-13

4509 Unimog Road Maintenance Sand Truck,
    1999 ....$10-13
4510 Earth Mover, 1991
    yellow, black cab, stack and hydraulics, gray
        scoop, gray rims $10-12
    yellow, black cab, stack and hydraulics, gray
        scoop, yellow rims $10-12
4511 Telescoping Mobile Crane, 1991
    yellow, black boom with "Enterprise," clear
        windows, yellow rims, black cable reel,
        black engine cover and stacks, black levelers $14-17
4512 Leveling Scraper, Road Grader,
    1993 ....$14-17
4513 Crawler Shovel............................$14-17
4514 Dump Truck and Land Rover $14-17
4515 Caterpillar Tracked Crane $14-17
4517 Earth Mover Scraper....................$14-17
4518 Maxi Dump Truck, 1997 ....$14-17
4519 Excavator Loader Tractor, 1999.....$14-17
4550 Construction Set, Earth Mover, Construction
    Mover and Float, 1992 ....$25-30

941 Construction Set: Dump Truck, Road Grader,
    Telescoping Crane, and Semi-Bulldozer Transporter, 1992 ....$40-65

6000 Series Motorcycles, 1:18, 1999
6001 Ducati 916
    red $12-15
6003 Yamaha 650 XVS Drag-Star
    orange and brown $12-15
6004 BMW K1200R
    red $12-15
    yellow, 2000 catalog $12-15
6005 KTM 400ZX
    orange $12-15
6006 Ducati 748
    yellow $12-15
6007 Suzuki TL 1000S
    red $12-15
6008 Yamaha 650 XVS Drag-Star
    blue and white....................................$12-15
    orange, 2000 catalog $12-15
6009 Yamaha BWS Spy
    blue $12-15
6010 KTM 540 SXC
    orange $12-15
6011 BMW K1200 RS
    yellow $12-15
6012 Suzuki 1000 Street-Bike
    yellow $12-15
6015 Kawasaki 1500 Classic Tourer
    green $12-15
6016 MV August
    red and silver......................................$12-15
6017 Kawasaki VN 1500
    black and red......................................$12-15
6018 Voxan Roadster
    yellow $12-15
6019 Voxan Cafe Racer
    silver..$12-15

2000 Models – Majorette did not assign model numbers in 2000 catalog. The 6000 series is listed alphabetically below.

BMW K1200 RS
    red $12-15
Ducati 748
    yellow $12-15
Ducati 996
    red $12-15
Husqvarna 610 Cross
    yellow, #111 ....$12-15
Husqvarna 610 enduro
    yellow, #4 ....$12-15
Husqvarna Super Motard
    yellow, #1 ....$12-15

Kawasaki VN 1500
  red and black..................$12-15
KTM 400 SX
  orange $12-15
MV Agusta 750 F4
  red and silver..................$12-15
Suzuki GSX-R750
  blue $12-15
Suzuki GSX-R Racing
  yellow $12-15
Yamaha 650 XVS Drag Star
  blue $12-15
Yamaha TL 1000 S
  red $12-15

Majorette Collector Cruisers, reissues of 1:43 scale Solido castings, 1999
1957 Cadillac Eldorado Convertible, red with
  white interior......................$6-8
1961 Ford Thunderbird Convertible, powder blue
  with white interior $6-8
1964? Ford Mustang Convertible, red with black
  interior $6-8
1984 Chevrolet Corvette Convertible Coupe,
  black with red interior $6-8
1965 Ford Mustang GT Hardtop, dark blue with
  white roof $6-8
1969 Chevrolet Corvette Hardtop Coupe,
  yellow $6-8

Malibu International Ltd. (also see Motorworks)

The first year that these 1:32 and 1:64 scale import tuners showed up in Wal-Mart stores packaged as Motorworks models was 2004. The name Malibu International is imprinted only on the base of each car. They are nicely trimmed and detailed with opening doors and rear hatch, and they retail for $5–7 each. Quality is exceptional for a relativley low-priced toy but they are somewhat lacking in accurate proporation. Only a brief sampling is provided below. Value for others in the assortment is the same. More recently, larger models have shown up from Malibu International under the Lexani brand.

Acura RSX Type-S, 1:32

metallic blue and silver with blue chrome hubs, yellow seats, opening doors and rear hatch, packaged as Wal-Mart Motorworks model.$6-8

Toyota MR2 Spyder, 1:64

yellow **$4-5**

Mandarin

Mandarin toys are 1:64 scale models made in Singapore, except for two character models. Some are Playart reissues.

Chevrolet Camaro 1967 Coupe, #101.....$5-10
Datsun 280Z, #104..................$5-10
Datsun Skyline, #103 ....$5-10
Disney Uncle Scrooge, 7"...........$14-19
Hanna Barberra Yogi Bear, 4" $14-19
Honda 9 Coupe, #107...............$5-10
Leyland Double Decker Bus
  green, #108 ....$5-10
  "London Express," #109 ....$5-10
  "Singapore Air," #110 ....$5-10
  "World Travels," #111 ....$5-10
Mitsubishi Colt, #112 ....$5-10
Mercedes-Benz 230SL Coupe, #113 ....$5-10
Toyota Celica
  Mk 1, #114.......................$5-10
  Mk 2, #115.......................$5-10
Toyota 2000GT, #116 ....$5-10
Volkswagen Van
  "Mandarin Toy," #119...........$5-10
  Police, #120.....................$5-10
  Ambulance, #117 ....$5-10

Mangalick

Mangalick models are offered as cast iron toys of unknown vintage and heritage, but are apparently newer models based on prices and description.

1900 "Coca-Cola" Truck, 12"................$30-35
1930 Allis Tractor, 8" $20-25
1930 Ford Farm Tractor, 5" $20-25
1930 Ford Model A "Coke," 5" $20-25
1930 Ford Model AA "Coke," 9" $20-25
1930 John Deere Tractor, 8" $20-25
1930 John Deere Tractor, 12" $20-25
1930 Mack Dump Truck, 8" $20-25
8-Horse Beer Wagon, 24" $30-35
Horse Drawn Fire Wagon, 7" $20-25
Horse Drawn Van, "Bond Tea," 12".........$20-25

Horse Drawn Wagon, "Coke," 7"..........$20-25
Horse Drawn Wagon, "US Mail," 7".......$20-25

Manoil

Jack and Maurice Manoil started the Manoil legacy from Manhattan, New York, in 1934. Sculptor Walter Baetz is the source of the wonderful classic streamlined Art Deco styling of these attractive models. The company later moved to Brooklyn, then Waverly, New York, where it continued until 1955.

Now, authentic reproductions of these classics are being manufactured from the original molds by Pride Lines of Lindenhurst, New York.

Below is a listing of the original models and current values.

Manoil Pre-War Models, 1935 – 1941
Coupe, #702 ....$90-105
Roadster, #704 ....$90-105
Rocket Bus, #706 ....$120-135
Sedan, #700 ....$90-105
Sedan, #701 ....$90-105
Sedan, #705 ....$90-105
Wrecker, #703 ....$90-105

Manoil Military Vehicles, 1941 – 1945
Armored Car with Anti-Aircraft Gun, #74..$55-60
Armored Car with Siren, #71
  siren cast separately................$50-55
  siren cast into vehicle $65-70
Chemical Truck, #104 ....$25-30
Five Barrel Gun on Wheels, #105 ....$20-25
Gasoline Truck, #103..............$20-25
Large Shell on Truck, #96 ....$20-25
Pontoon on Wheels, #97 ....$35-40
Shell Carrier with Soldier on Shell Box,
  #71 ....$20-25
Soup Kitchen, #70 ....$20-25
Tank, #95 ....$20-25
Torpedo on Wheels, #98 ....$20-25
Tractor, #73 ....$25-30
Water Wagon, #72 ....$20-25

Manoil Post-War Models, 1945 – 1955
Aerial Ladder Fire Truck, #711............$375-425
Bus, #713 ....$25-30
Commercial Truck, #715 ....$20-25
Convertible, #718 ....$20-25
Fire Engine, #709 ....$30-40
Hard Top Convertible, #717 ....$25-30
Oil Tanker, #710..................$25-30
Pumper, #712 ....$375-425
Ranch Wagon, #720 ....$20-25
Roadster, #708
  horizontal radiator $45-60

vertical radiator $90-120
Sedan, #707 ....$50-55
Sedan, #716 ....$20-25
Sport Car, #719 ....$20-25
Towing Truck, #714 ....$20-25

Märklin

Märklin has long been one of the most prominent German toy makers of the twentieth century. While better known for toy trains, in the 1930s Märklin produced a beautiful assortment of construction kits that, when assembled, resulted in a stylish period vehicle. Chassis, body, electric light set, and motor were each sold separately.

New Märklin commemorative models, pre-assembled, are being offered for hundreds of dollars. The original Märklin construction kit models are currently worth $200 to $900.

Armored Car
    Body, #1108G $225-275
    Camouflaged, 14½" $2,000-2,500
Basic Chassis, #1101C $50-75
Clockwork Motor, #1109M $75-90
Driver (composition), #99R $25-40
Electric Lighting Set, #1110B $45-60
F1 Racer, #308, 12" $475-525
Kubelwagen, diecast, 3½" $625-675
Lorry (Pickup) Body, #1105L $225-275
Mercedes Racing Car
    complete with chassis and motor,
      #1133R $175-225
    aluminum, complete with chassis and motor,
      #1133AL $200
    wind-up, 12" $750-900
Mercedes 1936 Truck, new model, 1994,
    #L1500 ....$450
Pullman Limousine Body, #1104 ....$225-275
Racing (Sports Car) Body, #1107R $175-225
Road Working Machine, 3⅝" $175-225
Streamlined Coupe Body, #1103St $225-275
Tanker Body, #1106T $375-425
Troop Carrier
    6-Wheel, diecast, 4½" $625-675
    10-Wheel, diecast, 5" $850-1,000
Water Truck, with working faucet,
    15" $3,250-3,750

Märklin 1:43

Beginning in the 1950s, Märklin produced an assortment of excellent 1:43 scale diecast, a few of which are listed below.
Mercedes-Benz 350 SL $80-95
Porsche 356
    red, no interior $80-95
    cream, no interior $80-95

Porsche 907
    Car #19, orange, #1815 ....$80-95
    Car #19, yellow, #1815 ....$80-95
Porsche 910
    Car #16, red, #1810 ....$80-95
    Car #17, white, #1810 ....$80-95
    Car #19, brown and mustard,
    #1810 ....$80-95
Porsche 911T Targa
    gold, #1800 ....$80-95
    red, #1800 ....$80-95
Porsche 914
    silver, #1826 ....$80-95
    orange, #1826 ....$80-95

Märklin Limited Edition Commemorative Models, 1990 – 1995

Fire Engine, #1990, red, 1990
    issue.....................................$450-600
Gold Transporter (Armored Truck), #1993, blue
    and black, 1993 issue................$450-600
Lorry, #1992, red and green, 1992
    issue $450-600
Racing Car, #1995, red and white, 1995
    issue $450-600
Reichspost (Postal Van), #1990, yellow and black,
    1990 issue.............................$450-600
Standard Tanker, #1993, red and blue,
    1993 issue.............................$450-600

Marque

Stephen Demosthenes reports of these 1:43 white metal models and kits of unknown origin.

Porsche 1948 Prototype 1, white metal kit,
    #1....................................$65-80
Porsche 1949 Gmund Coupe, Le Mans 1951,
    white metal kit, #2 ....$65-80
Porsche 917/30, red, yellow w/black stripes,
    car #6, "Cam 2" decals..................$65-80

Mars, Inc.

A few promotional race car toys have been made for Mars, Inc., the candy company. Models were made in China by an unnamed manufacturer and distributed by KMS, 1445 N. Rock Rd., Wichita, KS 67206.

Buick Regal Stock Car Racer, 1:48, white with
    brown and red accents, "SNICKERS" #8 ..$4-5
Ford Thunderbird Stock Car Racer, 1:48, white
    with red accents, "BABY RUTH" #1 ....$4-5

Marsh

Marsh models are 1:43 scale replicas from England that feature full photo-etched

metal cockpits, dashboards, engines, and wheels.

1962 Cobra 260, Billy Krause #98 ...$200-225
1963 Cobra 289 Sebring, Gurney #15.$200-225
1964 Cobra 289 Road America, Miles/Bucknum/Johnson $200-225
1964 Cobra 289 Sebring, Gurney
    #11 ....$200-225
1964 Cobra "Flip Top," Miles Nassau....$200-225
1963 Corvette GS Sportster $200-225
1964 Corvette GS Sebring $200-225
1966 Corvette GS Roadster $200-225
1966 Ford Mk II LeMans $200-225
1967 McLaren $200-225
1970 McLaren $200-225
1971 McLaren $200-225
1968 McLeagle $200-225

Martino Models

Marty Martino produced resin hand-built models made in the United States.

1954 Buick Skylark Convertible, 1:43 .....$65-70
1986 Chevrolet Corvette Indy, silver-gray,
    1:25 ....$65-70
1957 Oldsmobile $50-55

Martoys (also see Bburago)

Martoys of Spain began in 1974, later becoming Bburago of Italy in 1977.

Alpine Renault
    1:24 ....$35-40
    Rally, 1:24 ....$35-40
Audi 80 GT, 1:24 ....$35-40
BMW 3.0 CS 1:24 ....$35-40
Fiat 127
    1:24 ....$35-40
    Vigili Urbani, 1:24 ....$35-40
Lancia Beta, 1:24 ....$35-40
Lancia Stratos, 1:24 ....$35-40
Porsche 911
    S, #0102, 1:24, red with black interior ..$45-50
    Police, #0111, white with green hood, Police
    decals $45-50
Porsche Carrera RS, #0114
    yellow with Martini decals, car #8......$45-50
    silver with Martini decals, car #8........$45-50
Range Rover, 1:24 ....$45-50
Renault 5 Le car, 1:24 ....$40-45

Marusan

Marusan Shoten Ltd. of Japan, better known for superb tin toys in the 1950s which are now highly valued, produced a few diecast toys for the British market in 1960 and 1961. Models are identified by the name "San" on the base. Their resemblance to Dinky toys may not be a coincidence. The Avenue Bus and Morris J Van appeared the year after the Dinky versions went out of production.

Marusan Diecast Toys

Avenue Bus, #8505 ....$100-125
Austin Van, #8507 ....$100-125
Euclid Dump Truck, #8506 ....$100-125
Ford Milk Truck, #8504 ....$100-125
Daimler Ambulance, #8503 ....$100-125
Morris J Mail Van, #8502 ....$100-125
Panhard Semi Truck, #8501 ....$100-125
Toyota Truck $100-125

Marushin

Marushin models are made in Japan. The only automotive models currently known to have been produced by Marushin are a 1:43 scale Lancia Stratos and a 1:8 scale Porsche engine kit. In addition, several Japanese fighter planes were at one time also produced in diecast.

Lancia Stratos, white, red and green,
    1:43 ....$15-20

Marx

Since its inception in 1921, Louis Marx has made a lot of toys, but it was only in the mid-to late 1960s that the company produced a small line of diecast toys. They are crude and heavy, with very little detail, but they are rare. A few are listed below. Marx went bankrupt in 1980, and most of its assets went to American Plastics. The Linemar brand is reportedly the result of a marketing/manufacturing agreement between Marx and the Line Brothers of Tri-Ang fame. Linemar toys were produced in Japan. Lumar is a similar cooperative effort between Marx and an unknown partner. Below is a small sampling of their enormous assortment.

Marx Diecast Toys

1967 Cadillac Eldorado $15-20
1969 Chevrolet Camaro $15-20
1967 Mercury Cougar $15-20
1967 Mustang Convertible $15-20
Oldsmobile, #38, 2" $15-20
Volkswagen Beetle $15-20

Marx Pressed Steel, Tin Lithographed, and Plastic Toys

A&P Box Truck, 28," early 1960s $200-250

Acme Markets Tractor/Trailer Truck, late
    1950s $300-350
Aero Oil Company Truck, Circa 1930,
    5½" $475-525
Airflow, 4" $90-120
Allied Van Lines, tin friction, Linemar,
    1950s $175-225
Ambulance, #8500, 1930s, 14" $450-500
Ambulance, "M.D. War Dept.,"
    1930s $600-850
Cloverdale Farms Milk Truck, 11½".......$175-225
Cadillac Roadster, tin wind-up, luggage carrier
    has trunk with tools, 1930s $450-600
Corvette Coupe, plastic, friction, 8" $85-100
Dick Tracy Squad Car, #1, friction, 6¾".$275-300
Dick Tracy Squad Car, #1, friction,
    11" $375-450
Ford Convertible, 1951, 11" $100-125
Ford Model T, plastic $75-90
Lumar Utility truck with tools $375-425
Mayflower Van, 13" $200-250
Old Jalopy, tin wind-up with graffiti,
    1950s $225-275
Pepsi-Cola Truck, plastic, 7," 1950s ...$250-300
Toy Town Express Van Lines Deluxe Service, tin
    litho $225-275
Tricky Taxi, friction, 4½" $100-125
UPS Truck, plastic, 10" $175-200
Walgreen's Ice Cream Trailer Truck,
    21" $375-450
Woolworth's Trailer Truck, 1960s.......$375-450
Yellow Cab, "LMN 52," tin wind-up, 1940s,
    6½" $300-350

Mascot

Whether the one documented model from this unknown manufacturer is diecast zinc alloy or white metal is unknown.

1950 Chrysler Town & Country, 1:43 .....$80-95

Master Models

Master Models are 1:43 scale white metal miniatures made in England.

1960 Autocar Rolloff Flatbed, 1:43.....$125-140
1960 Chevrolet Ambulance, 1:43 ....$85-100
1960 Chevrolet C80 Fire Ambulance,
    1:43 ....$85-100

Masterpieces in Miniature

Masterpieces in Miniature are HO gauge (1:87 scale) diecast models made in England.

American Motors Jeep Gladiator Pickup Truck, yel-
    low...$10-15

Master Toy Company (see Maisto)

Masudaya

What else this Japanese company makes aside from one distinctive miniature of Robby the Robot from the classic movie *The Forbidden Planet* is a mystery. But this massive little replica weighs in at well over a pound, pretty heavy for its size—just 5½" tall. This hard-to-find diecast collectible may still be available from just a few sources for $30 retail. Value below reflects sec-ond-market value.

Robby the Robot, 5½" $40-55

Matchbox

Lesney's Matchbox toys have been the world's most popular diecast toys since 1947. Only Hot Wheels has overshadowed Matchbox in U.S. brand name recognition. Today, the Matchbox name lives on despite the transfer of the venerable brand from Lesney to Universal of Hong Kong in 1982, then to Tyco Toys in 1992. When Tyco was purchased by Mattel in 1995, Matchbox became part of the Mattel empire. The complete story of Matchbox toys can be found in Dana Johnson's book *Matchbox Toys 1947 to 2003* from Collector Books ($24.95 retail).

Mark One Collectibles (see Dimension 4)

Mattel (see Fisher-Price, Hot Wheels, Matchbox)

Max Models (see Paul's Model Art/ Minichamps)

Maxwell Mini Auto Toys (Matchbox of India)

Maxwell Mini Auto Toys of Calcutta, India, was a subsidiary of Matchbox of London, Eng-land, produced in the 1970s. Notably odd wheels and somewhat boxy shapes typify these toys intended for the local market in India. Several models are recognizable as Matchbox castings, although comparatively more crude.

007 James Bond Lotus Esprit, #589 ....$12-15
Aircraft Carrier, #529 ....$12-15
Ambassador Mark II 4-door Sedan,
    #510 ....$10-12
Ambassador Mark II Fire Service, #520 ...$10-12
Ambassador Mark II State Patrol, #521 ....$10-12

Ambassador Mark II Yellow Cab Taxi, #522 ....$10-12
Animal Carrier, #548 ....$15-18
Big Jeep Highway Patrol, #605 ....$12-15
Big Jeep Fire Ladder Truck, #606 ....$12-15
Big Jeep Police, #607 ....$12-15
Big Jeep Armoured Car, #608 ....$12-15
Boeing Passenger Jet "Air-India," #557 .....$12-15
Boeing Passenger Jet "B.O.A.C.," #543 ..$10-12
Boeing Passenger Jet "B.O.A.C.," #545 ..$12-15
Boeing Passenger Jet "Lufthansa," #539 ...$10-12
Boeing Passenger Jet "Swissair," #546 .....$12-15
Chevrolet Impala 1959, #558 ....$12-15
Chevrolet Impala 1959 Highway Patrol, black and white, #559.....................$12-15
Chevrolet Impala 1959 Fire Chief, red and white, #560 ....$12-15
Chevrolet Impala 1959 Police, red and white, #561 ....$12-15
Chevrolet Impala 1959 Taxi, yellow and black, #562 ....$12-15
Double Decker Bus, #517 ....$10-12
Douglas Skyhawk Navy Jet, #573...........$10-12
Eicher Tractor, #599 ....$15-18
Escort 335 Tractor, #572 ....$15-18
Fiat 1100 Premier President 4-door Sedan, #507 ....$10-12
Fiat 1100 Premier President Taxi, #523 ...$10-12
Field Gun and plastic base, #587...........$10-12
Field Gun, #588...............................$10-12
Ford 3600 Tractor, #569 ....$15-18
Ford Mustang with opening doors, #590 ..$12-15
Ford Tractor, #549.............................$12-15
Formula One Racing Car, #504 ....$10-12
Freeman Intercity Commuter Coach (Matchbox copy), #525 ....$10-12
Freight Carrier, #535 ....$10-12
Greyhound Luxury Coach, #503 ....$10-12
Helicopter, #576................................$10-12
Hindusthan Mini Tractor, #579 ....$12-15
H.M.T. Zetor Tractor, #570....................$15-18
Honda Motorcycle, #544 ....$10-12
Hovercraft SRN6, #516 ....$10-12
Jeep Ambulance, #519 ....$10-12
Jeep Ambulance, #551 ....$10-12
Jeep Armoured Car, #571 ....$10-12
Jeep Carrier, #554................................$5-7
Jeep CJ3, #550.................................$10-12
Jeep FC150 Pickup, #610 ....$10-12
Jeep Fire Service with ladder, #531........$10-12
Jeep with Canopy, #518 ....$10-12
Jeep with Exposed Engine, #508 ....$10-12
Lincoln Ambulance Car, yellow, #515 .....$10-12
Lincoln Continental, #505 ....$10-12
Lincoln Fire Chief, #514.........................$10-12
Lincoln Police Car, red, #513 ....$10-12

MG 1100 (marketed as Mercedes 1100), #506 ....$10-12
MIG Jet, #541 ....$10-12
Military Tank, #501 ....$10-12
Mini Jeep, #543 ....$5-7
Mirage Jet, #542 ....$10-12
Pipe Carrier, #534...............................$10-12
Racing Car, #552.................................$5-7
Racing Min, #511i $10-12
Rescue Helicopter, #580 ....$10-12
Riley MPH 1934 Vintage Car (Matchbox Models of Yesteryear copy), #574 ....$10-12
Road Roller, #502 ....$10-12
Setra Coach (Matchbox copy), #528 ......$10-12
Small Petrol Tanker "HP," #581 ....$10-12
Small Petrol Tanker "IBP," #582............$10-12
Small Petrol Tanker "Indian Oil," #583 .....$10-12
Small Petrol Tanker "Esso," #584...........$10-12
Small Petrol Tanker "Caltex," #585 ....$10-12
Small Petrol Tanker "Burmah–Shell," #586 ....$10-12
Swaraj Tractor, #601 ....$15-18
Tata "Campa Cola," #577 ....$10-12
Tata "Coca-Cola" Truck, #547 ....$12-15
Tata "Cold Spot Cola" Truck, #537 ....$10-12
Tata "Thums Up Cola," #578 ....$10-12
Tata Ambulance Bus, #533 ....$10-12
Tata Big Petrol Tanker "Bharat Petroleum," #603 ....$20-25
Tata Big Petrol Tanker "Assam Oil," #604 ..$20-25
Tata Brake Van Service Tow Truck, #538 ..$10-12
Tata Circus Van, #536 ....$10-12
Tata Dump Truck, #575 ....$10-12
Tata Fruit Carrier Stake Truck, #540.........$10-12
Tata Medium Petrol Tanker "Assam Oil," #598 ....$20-25
Tata Medium Petrol Tanker "Bharat Petroleum," #597 ....$20-25
Tata Medium Petrol Tanker "Burmah–Shell," #596 ....$20-25
Tata Medium Petrol Tanker "Caltex," #595 ....$20-25
Tata Medium Petrol Tanker "Esso," #594..$20-25
Tata Medium Petrol Tanker "HP," #591....$20-25
Tata Medium Petrol Tanker "IBP," #592...$20-25
Tata Medium Petrol Tanker "Indian Oil," #593 ....$20-25
Tata Mini Bus, #524 ....$10-12
Tata Passenger Coach "B.O.A.C.," #532 ..$10-12
Tata Passenger Coach "Indian Airlines," #530 ....$10-12
Tata Petrol Tanker "HP Oil," #563 ....$15-18
Tata Petrol Tanker "IBP Oil," #564 ....$15-18
Tata Petrol Tanker "Indian Oil," #565 ......$20-25
Tata Petrol Tanker "Esso," #566 ....$20-25
Tata Petrol Tanker "Caltex," #567 ....$20-25

Tata Petrol Tanker "Burmah–Shell," #568 ....$10-12
Tata School Bus, #527 ....$10-12
Tata Van, #526..................................$10-12
Two Seater Coupe, #555 ....$5-7
Vauxhall Guildsman (Matchbox copy), #509 ....$12-15
Volkswagen Beetle, #553 ....$5-7
Volvo P 1800, #512 ....$10-12
World War I Bi-Plane, #602 ....$15-18

May Cheong (see Maisto)

May Tat (also see Maisto)

May Tat is the bottom-of-the-line budget division of Maisto, producing unidentifiable unmarked toys in the so-called 1:60 scale. Since they bear no markings except on the package, they are considered generic, and are therefore valueless to the collector for anything other than a curiosity.

One example of May Tat toys is a series called Fun Wheels, two each of six different vehicles sold in a twelve-car display box—no individual packages. The models are barely recognizable due to drastically shortened bodies and exaggerated styling. More recognizable as real cars are the 1:43 scale pullback-action toys by May Tat, with brand names embossed on the chassis.

BMW Cabriolet, white, 1:43 ....$1-2

Mercedes-Benz, metallic blue, 1:43.......$1-2

McGregor (also see Politoys/Polistil)

McGregor is the Mexican subsidiary of Politoys, later known as Polistil, of Italy. Here is just a small sampling of models produced. Models are distinguished by the McGregor name on the base, the unusual 1:45 scale in which they are produced, and the words "Hecho en Mexico" (Made in Mexico).

Bentley, British green with black fenders and black top $15-20
Berliet, light yellow with black roof $15-20
BRM F1, purple, 1:41, #200 ....$11-16
De Sanctio F3, green, 1:41, #201 ....$11-16
Fiat, 1899, dark blue with red top, white interior $15-20
Fiat, 1911, sky blue with black fenders and black top-nice car $15-20
Fiat 501 S. Sport, 1910, green with black fenders and black top..................$15-20
Fiat 525 S. Reale, 1929, silver with black fenders and black top..................$15-20
Fiat Balilla, black with off-white fenders $15-20
Honda F1, brown & white, 1:41, #203 ..$11-16
Isotta Fraschini, 1902, dark blue with off-white fenders, white interior....................$15-20
Isotta Fraschini, kind of a dark mustard yellow, black top $15-20
Itala Palombella, cream-colored body, black roof, yellow fenders $15-20
Lancia Landa, yellow with black fenders and black top $15-20

Mebetoys (also see Hot Wheels Gran Toros)

Now a subsidiary of Mattel, Mebetoys of Italy were originally an independent toy manufacturer based in Italy. They arrived on the scene in 1966. Mebetoys were purchased by Mattel around 1970 and have been referred to as "overgrown Hot Wheels."

Models continued to be produced under the Mebetoys brand name even as recently as 1985.

The 6600 series in particular echoes a number of Hot Wheels trademark names, although their resemblance to their namesake is minimal. Nevertheless, they bore the Hot Wheels name on the base and were produced between 1970 and 1972. The series was dubbed Gran Toros, a name now owned by Playing Mantis and issued under the Johnny Lightning brand.

Abarth
  695 SS, 1:43, #6608, 1971 ....$65-75
  3000 SP, 1:43, #6624, 1971 ....$80-90
Alfa Romeo
  158-159 Grand Prix, 1:24, #1, 1977 ....$30-40
  33 Rally "Agip," 1:43, #6425, 1985..................................$30-40
  33 Turbo, 1:43, #6103, 1985 ....$30-40
  33/3, 1:43, #6612, 1971 ....$65-75
  2600, 1:43, A-4, 1966 ....$30-40
  Alfasud, 1:43, A-57, 1972 ....$30-40

Alfasud, 1:43, #8555, 1973............$30-40
Alfasud Sprint, 1:25, #8616............$30-40
Alfasud Sprint, 1:43, A-105 ....$30-40
Alfasud TI Rally, 1:43, A-90, 1975....$30-40
Alfasud Trofeo, 1:43, A-97, 1976.....$30-40
Alfasud Vacation Car, 1:43, A-117, 1980..................................$30-40
Alfetta, 1:43, A-76, 1974 ....$30-40
Alfetta Carabinieri, 1:25, #8567 ......$30-40
Alfetta Carabinieri, 1:43, A-82, 1974..$30-40
Alfetta Fire Chief, 1:43, A-92, 1975..$40-50
Alfetta Polizia, 1:43, A-83, 1974 .....$30-40
Duetto Spyder, 1:43, A-18, 1967 .....$30-40
Duetto with Bicycles, 1:43, A-65, 1972 ....$30-40
Giulia TI, 1:42, A-3, 1966 ....$30-40
Giulia TI Carabinieri, 1:42, A-7, 1966 ....$30-40
Giulia TI Policia, 1:42, A-8, 1966 .....$30-40
Giulietta, 1:25, #6722, 1981 ....$30-40
Giulietta, 1:43, A-111 ....$30-40
Giulietta Carabinieri, 1:25, #6761, 1981 ....$30-40
Giulietta Carabinieri, 1:43, A-135, 1981 ....$30-40
Giulietta Polizia, 1:25, #6762, 1981..................................$30-40
Giulietta Polizia, 1:43, A-136, 1981...$30-40
Giulietta Rally, 1:25, #6870, 1983 ..$30-40
Giulietta Special, 1:25, #6758, 1981 ....$30-40
Giulietta Special, 1:43, A-138, 1981 ....$30-40
Iguana, 1:43, A-45, 1970 ....$30-40
Junior Zagato, 1:43, A-46, 1971 ......$30-40
P2 Grand Prix, 1:24, #2, 1977........$30-40
Giulietta, 1:25, #8623 ....$30-40
Arrows MP4 Formula 1, 1:25, #6862, 1983 ....$30-40
Audi
  100 ADAC, 1:43, A-141, 1984......$30-40
  100 GLS, 1:43, A-118, 1980 ....$30-40
  100 GLS, 1:25, #6740, 1980........$30-40
  100 NASA, 1:25, #6830, 1983 ....$30-40
  100 Polizei, 1:43, A-140, 1984 ....$30-40
  100 with Rubber Boat, 1:25, #6882, 1983..................................$30-40
  Quattro Rally, 1:25, #6116, 1984 ...$40-50
  Quattro Rally, 1:25, #6867, 1983 ...$40-50
  Quattro Rally, 1:43, #6091, 1985 ...$30-40
  Quattro Rally, 1:43, #6906, 1983 ...$30-40
Autobianchi
  A112, 1:43, A-48, 1971 ....$30-40
  A112 Abarth, 1:43, A-58, 1972 ......$30-40
  A112 Abarth, 1:43, A-112 ....$30-40
  Primula, 1:43, A-5, 1966................$30-40

Primula with Oil Drums, 1:43, A-66, 1972..................................$30-40
Bertone Runabout, 1:43, A-44, 1970.....$30-40
BMC Mini 90, 1:43, A-86, 1976..........$30-40
BMW
  316, 1:25, #8619 ....$30-40
  320, 1:25, #6719, 1981 ....$30-40
  320, 1:43, A-103 ....$30-40
  320 Alpina, 1:25, #6765, 1980.....$30-40
  320 Alpina, 1:25, #8638 ....$30-40
  320 Rally, 1:25, #6731, 1980 ....$30-40
  320 Rally, 1:43, A-113 ....$30-40
  320 Wind Surfer, 1:25, #6804, 1981..................................$30-40
  635 Rally, 1:43, #6904, 1983 ....$30-40
  730 Sedan, 1:25, #6739, 1980.....$30-40
  730, 1:43, A-120, 1980 ....$30-40
  735 Rally, 1:25, #6874, 1983 ....$30-40
  2000 CS, 1:43, A-17, 1967 ....$30-40
BRM P160, 1:28, #6672, 1972........$65-75
Brabham
  BT 34, 1:28, #6675, 1973 ....$65-75
  Formula 1, 1:25, #6861, 1983 ....$30-40
Chaparral
  2F, 1:43, A-23, 1968 ....$40-50
  2F, 1:43, #6606, 1971 ....$80-90
  2J, 1:43, #6628, 1972 ....$80-90
Chevrolet
  Astro II, 1:43, #6602, 1970...........$65-75
  Corvette 1983, 1:43, #6908, 1983 ....$30-40
  Corvette 1984, 1:43, #6073, 1985..................................$30-40
  Corvette Rondine, 1:43, A-22, 1967 ....$40-50
Citroën
  Dyane, 1:25, #6711, 1981 ....$40-50
  Dyane, 1:25, #6878, 1983 ....$30-40
  Dyane, 1:43, A-84, 1974 ....$30-40
  Dyane 6, 1:25, #8599 ....$30-40
  Dyane Rally, A-109, 1:43 ....$30-40
  Dyane Special, 1:25, #6792, 1981..................................$30-40
  Dyane Vacation Car, 1:43, A-99, 1976..................................$30-40
  Visa, 1:43, A-134, 1981...............$30-40
  Visa, 1:25, #6767, 1981...............$30-40
  Visa Rally, 1:25, #6872, 1983........$30-40
DeTomaso Ford Pantera
  1:43, A-102 ....$30-40
  1:43, #6627, 1972.......................$65-75
Ferrari
  250 GT, 1:25, #6846, 1983 ....$30-40
  312 BB, 1:28, #6671, 1972 ....$65-75
  312 BB, 1:43, A-56, 1972 ....$40-50
  312 BB, #8558, 1:32 ....$30-40

312 PB, 1:25, #8568 ....$30-40

365 GTC-4, 1:43, A-50, 1972........$40-50

512 S Pininfarina, 1:43, A-100,
1976...$40-50

512 S Pininfarina, 1:43, #6621,
1971...$80-90

Boxer, 1:43, #8565, 1973 ....$30-40

Can-Am, 1:43, #6601, 1970.........$80-90

Formula 1, 1:25, #6858, 1983 ....$30-40

P4, 1:43, A-27, 1968 ....$40-50

P4, 1:43, #6614, 1971 ....$65-75

PB, 1:43, #6121, 1984 ....$30-40

PB Prototype, 1:43, #6910, 1983....$30-40

PB Prototype, 1:43, #8553, 1973....$40-50

Fiat

124, 1:43, A-16, 1967 ....$30-40

124 Raid, 1:43, A-75, 1974 ....$30-40

124 Safari, 1:43, A-41, 1970 ....$30-40

124/128 Taxi, 1:43, A-43, 1970...$30-40

126, 1:28, #8564 ....$30-40

126, 1:43, #8556, 1973...............$30-40

126, 1:43, A-62, 1972 ....$30-40

127, 1:43, A-54, 1972 ....$30-40

127 Rally, 1:43, A-68, 1972 ....$30-40

128, 1:43, A-59, 1972 ....$30-40

128 Coupe, 1:43, A-77, 1974........$30-40

128 Rally, 1:43, A-60, 1972 ....$30-40

131, 1:43, A-85, 1975 ....$30-40

131 Abarth, 1:25, #6728, 1981 ....$30-40

131 Abarth Parmalat, 1:25, #6743,
1981...$30-40

131 Rally, 1:43, A-98, 1976 ....$30-40

131 Rally, 1:43, A-152, 1981 ....$30-40

170 Garbage Truck, 1:43, #2510........$12

170 Container Truck, 1:43, #2512 ......$12

170 Semi-Trailer Truck, 1:43, #2514 .....$12

170 Lumber Semi, 1:43, #2517 ....$12

170 Container Semi, 1:43, #2519 ....$12

240 Flat Truck with Kart, #6802,
1:25 ....$30-40

242 Pickup with Kart, 1:25, #6881,
1983...$30-40

242 Safari, 1:25, #6726, 1980......$30-40

850, 1:42, A-1, 1966 ....$30-40

1100R, 1:43, A-9, 1967 ....$30-40

1500, 1:42, A-2, 1966 ....$30-40

1500 Fire Chief, 1:42, A-21, 1967...$30-40

1500 Policia, 1:42, A-15, 1967 ......$30-40

Abarth 131, A-110, 1:43 ....$30-40

Abarth 131 Rally, 1:43, A-131,
1981...$30-40

Abarth Ritmo Rally, 1:25, #6800,
1981...$30-40

Dino with Boat, 1:43, A-52, 1972 ....$30-40

Farm Tractor, 1:43, #2501 ....$12

Nuova 500, 1:43, A-36, 1969 ....$30-40

Panda, 1:25, #6785, 1981 ....$30-40

Panda 30, 1:43, A-125, 1980 ....$30-40

Panda Rally, 1:25, #6869, 1983.....$30-40

Ritmo, 1:25, #6748, 1981..............$30-40

Ritmo 65, 1:43, A-119, 1980..........$30-40

Ritmo Alitalia, 1:25, #6784, 1981 ...$30-40

Ritmo Rally, 1:25, #6871, 1983 ......$30-40

Ritmo Special, 1:25, #6757, 1981 ..$30-40

Ritmo Special, 1:43, A-139, 1981....$30-40

Uno, 1:25, #6850, 1985................$30-40

Uno, 1:43, #6420, 1985 ....$30-40

Uno, 1:43, #6849, 1983 ....$30-40

Uno "Wrangler Jeans," 1:43, #6050,
1985...$30-40

Ford

Boss Mustang 302, 1:43, #6611,
1971..$100-120

Escort, 1:43, A-53, 1972................$30-40

Escort, 1:43, #8551, 1973 ....$30-40

Escort Mexico, 1:43, A-55, 1972 .....$30-40

Escort Mexico, 1:43, #8552, 1973 ...$30-40

Fiesta, 1:25, #8620......................$40-50

Fiesta, 1:43, A-106 ....$30-40

Fiesta Special, 1:43, A-127, 1980 ...$30-40

Fiesta Rally, 1:25, #6742, 1980......$30-40

Fiesta with Skiers, 1:25, #6883,
1983...$30-40

Granada, 1:43, A-121...................$30-40

Granada 1978, 1:25, #6733,
1980...$40-50

Granada Giro D'Italia, 1:25, #6885,
1983...$40-50

Granada Special, 1:43, A-145,
1981...$30-40

GT Mark II, 1:43, A-24, 1968 ....$40-50

GT Mark II, 1:43, #6607, 1971 ......$80-90

Mirage, 1:28, #8563, 1973...........$40-50

Sierra XR4, 1:43, #6099, 1985 ....$30-40

Sierra XR4 Rally, 1:43, #6430,
1985...$30-40

Innocenti Mini

DeTomaso, A-108, 1:43 ....$30-40

Mini Minor, 1:43, A-28, 1968 ....$30-40

Mini Minor Hippy, 1:43, A-71,
1974...$40-50

Mini Minor Rally, 1:43, A-31,
1969...$30-40

Iso Rivolta S4, 1:43, A-30, 1968 ....$30-40

Jeep

CJ7 Renegade, 1:43, #6097, 1985..$30-40

Desert Jeep, 1:43, A-122, 1980......$30-40

Laredo, 1:43, #6911, 1983............$30-40

Rally Service Car, 1:43, A-149,
1981...$30-40

Renegade with Motocross Cycle, 1:25,
#6886, 1983 ....$30-40

Kenworth

Container Semi, 1:43, #6188, 1985...$30-40

Dumper Semi, 1:43, #6191, 1985 ..$30-40

Tanker Semi, 1:43, #6186, 1985 ....$30-40

Lamborghini

Miura, 1:43, #6605, 1971.............$65-75

Miura P400, 1:43, A-20, 1967 ....$30-40

Urraco, 1:43, A-47, 1971 ....$30-40

Lancia

037 Turbo, 1:25, #6845, 1983......$30-40

037 Turbo Martini, 1:43, #6905,
1983...$30-40

Beta Coupe, 1:25, #8582..............$30-40

Beta Fire Squad, 1:25, #6805,
1981...$30-40

Beta Giro D'Italia, 1:25, #6715,
1981...$30-40

Delta, 1:25, #6877, 1983 ....$30-40

Flavia, 1:43, A-6, 1966 ....$30-40

Fulvia Alitalia, 1:43, A-91, 1975 .....$30-40

Fulvia Coupe, 1:43, A-11, 1967 ......$30-40

Fulvia Marlboro, 1:43, A-73, 1974...$30-40

Fulvia Rally, 1:43, A-32, 1969 ....$30-40

Squadra SK, 1:24, #6807, 1981 ....$30-40

Stratos HF Bertone, 1:43, A-49,
1971...$30-40

Land Rover

1:25, #6702, 1980.....................$30-40

Ambulance, 1:43, A-42, 1970 ....$40-50

Fire Truck, 1:43, A-74, 1974 ....$45

Trans American, 1:43, A-40, 1969 ...$30-40

U. S. Army, 1:43, A-67, 1972 ....$30-40

Ligier Formula 1, 1:25, #6860, 1983 ....$30-40

Lola T-212 Can-Am, 1:43, #6629,
1972 ....$65-75

Lotus

Climax Formula 1, Jolly Series, 1:66........$12

Europa, 1:43, A-39, 1969...............$40-50

Europa, 1:43, #6618, 1971 ....$80-90

Ford 72, 1:28, #6673, 1972..........$65-75

Formula 1, 1:25, #6864, 1983 ....$30-40

JPS, 1:28, #6677, 1973................$65-75

Mantis, 1:43, #6625, 1971 ....$65-75

March-Ford, 1:28, #6676, 1973 .....$65-75

Maserati

Biturbo, 1:25, #6844, 1983 ....$30-40

Biturbo Racing, 1:43, #6051, 1985...$30-40

Biturbo Rally, 1:43, #6901, 1983 ....$30-40

Bora, 1:43, A-72, 1973.................$40-50

Bora, 1:43, #8554, 1973 ....$40-50

Mistral, 1:43, A-10, 1967 ....$40-50

McLaren Can-Am, 1:43, #6626,
1972 ....$65-75

Mercedes-Benz

250 SE, 1:43, A-19, 1967.............$30-40

280 SE, 1:28, #6700, 1981 ....$30-40

280 SE, 1:28, #6708, 1982 ....$30-40
280 SE, 1:28, #8595 ....$30-40
280 SE Rally, 1:28, #6745, 1981...$30-40
500 SEC Rally, 1:43, #6423,
    1985.......................................$30-40
500 SEC Rally, 1:43, #6900,
    1983.......................................$30-40
Auto Carrier Semi, 1:43, #9610,
    1985.......................................$30-40
C-111, 1:43, #6622, 1971 ....$65-75
Container Semi "Hapag-Lloyd," 1:43,
    #9607, 1985 ....$30-40
Livestock Semi, 1:43, #9606,
    1985.......................................$30-40
Tanker Semi "Shell," 1:43, #9609,
    1985.......................................$30-40
Morris Mini-Minor, 1:43, A-61, 1973 .....$30-40
NSU Ro 80 Wankel, 1:43, A-37,
    1969 ....$30-40
Opel
    Kadett Fastback, 1:43, A-13, 1967...$30-40
    Kadett Rally, 1:25, #6117, 1984.....$30-40
    Kadett Rally, 1:25, #6868, 1983.....$30-40
    Kadett Rally, 1:43, A-34, 1969 ....$30-40
    Monza, 1:25, #6734, 1981 ....$30-40
    Monza Coupe, 1:43, A-124,
        1980..................................$30-40
    Monza Special, 1:25, #6787,
        1981..................................$30-40
    Monza Special, 1:43, A-143,
        1981..................................$30-40
    Monza with Surfboard, 1:25, #6884,
        1983..................................$30-40
Peterbilt
    Box Semi "Goodyear," 1:43, #9554,
        1985..................................$30-40
    Dumper Semi, 1:4, #95583, 1985 ..$30-40
    Livestock Semi, 1:43, #9557, 1985 .$30-40
    Tanker Semi "BP," 1:43, #9553,
        1985..................................$30-40
Peugeot
    305, 1:25, #6766, 1981...............$30-40
    305, 1:25, #6880, 1983...............$30-40
    305, 1:43, A-133, 1981 ....$30-40
Pontiac Firebird
    1:43, #6427, 1985 ....$30-40
    1:43, #6903, 1983 ....$30-40
Porsche
    911 Targa, 1:25, #6808, 1981 .....$30-40
    911 Targa, 1:25, #6879, 1983 .....$30-40
    911 Targa, 1:25, #8573 ....$30-40
    911 Turbo "Coca-Cola," 1:43, #6065,
        1985..................................$30-40
    911 Turbo "Gitanes," 1:43, #6067,
        1985..................................$30-40
    911 Turbo Rally, 1:43, #6907, 1983....$30-40

912, 1:43, A-12, 1967 ....$40-50
912 Rally, 1:43, A-33, 1969 ....$40-50
912 Rally, 1:43, A-78, 1974 ....$40-50
912 with Skis, 1:43, A-64, 1973 .....$40-50
917, 1:43, #6623, 1971...............$80-90
917 Gulf, 1:43, A-101, 1976 ....$40-50
924, 1:25, #6713, 1981...............$30-40
924, 1:25, #8612.......................$30-40
924, 1:43, A-93, 1976 ....$40-50
924, orange with brown interior, 1:43,
    A-98....................................$40-50
924 Martini, 1:25, #8640, 1979....$40-50
924 Rally, 1:25, #6732, 1980 ....$40-50
924 Turbo, 1:25, #6764, 1980......$40-50
928 Pirelli, 1:25, #6875, 1983.......$40-50
928 Rally, 1:25, #6737, 1980 ....$40-50
928 Rally, 1:25, #6823, 1983 ....$40-50
956 Canon, 1:25, #6119, 1984....$40-50
Carrera 10, 1:43, A-25, 1968 ....$40-50
Carrera 10, 1:43, #6613, 1971 .....$80-90
London-Sydney Rally, 1:43, A-51,
    1972....................................$40-50
Renault
    5TL, 1:43, A-69, 1974...................$30-40
    5TL Rally, 1:43, A-94, 1975 ....$30-40
    Formula 1, 1:25, #6866, 1983.......$40-50
Rolls-Royce Silver Shadow, 1:43, A-26,
    1968 ....$40-50
Silhouette, 1:43, #6616, 1971 ....$65-75
Simca
    1307, 1:25, #8618 ....$30-40
    1308, A-107, 1:43 ....$30-40
    1308 GT, 1:43, A-128, 1980........$30-40
Talbot
    Horizon Rally, 1:25, #6873, 1983...$30-40
    Horizon Special, 1:25, #6788,
        1981..................................$30-40
    Horizon Special, 1:43, A-142,
        1981..................................$30-40
    Matra 530 Vignale, 1:43, A-38,
        1969..................................$30-40
    Matra MS 120, 1:28, #6670,
        1972..................................$65-75
    Matra Murena Rally, 1:43, #6069,
        1985..................................$30-40
    Matra Murena Rally, 1:43, #6071,
        1985..................................$30-40
    Matra Mureno Rally, 1:43, #6899,
        1983..................................$30-40
    Matra Rancho, 1:25, #6747, 1980..$30-40
    Matra Rancho, 1:43, A-123, 1980...$30-40
    Matra Rancho Rally, 1:25, #6810 ....$30-40
    Simca Horizon, 1:43, A-129, 1981...$30-40
Toyota
    2000GT, 1:43, A-29, 1968...........$30-40
    2000GT, 1:43, #6617, 1971 ....$65-75

Torpedo Dragster, 1:43, #6604,
    1971.......................................$65-75
T'rantula Dragster, 1:43, #6603, 1971....$65-75
Twin Mill, 1:43, #6615, 1971.............$65-75
Tyrrell-Ford, 1:28, #6674, 1972..........$65-75
Volkswagen
    1302, 1:25, #8574 ....$30-40
    1303, 1:43, A-70, 1974 ....$30-40
    1303 Jeans, 1:43, A-88, 1975........$30-40
    Golf, 1:43, A-87, 1976 ....$30-40
    Golf 4-door, 1:24, #6709, 1981.....$40-50
    Golf 4-door, 1:25, #8596 ....$40-50
    Golf ADAC, 1:43, A-114 ....$30-40
    Golf Cabriolet, 1:25, #6803 ....$30-40
    Golf Cabriolet, 1:43, #6909,
        1983..................................$30-40
    Golf Cabriolet Rally, 1:43, #6082,
        1985..................................$30-40
    Golf Polizei, 1:25, #8637 ....$30-40
    Golf Polizei, 1:43, A-115...............$30-40
    Golf Rally, 1:43, A-126, 1980 ....$30-40
    Golf Rally, 1:25, #6741, 1980.......$30-40
Volvo
    343, 1:25, #6755, 1981...............$30-40
    343, 1:25, #6756, 1981...............$30-40
    343, 1:25, #6876, 1983...............$30-40
    343, 1:43, A-130, 1981 ....$30-40
    Auto Transporter Semi, 1:43, #6196,
        1985..................................$30-40
    Auto Transporter Semi, 1:43, #9562,
        1985..................................$30-40
    Box Semi "Martini," 1:43, #9560,
        1985..................................$30-40
    Container Semi, 1:43, #6192,
        1985..................................$30-40
    Container Semi "Sea-Land," 1:43, #9561,
        1985..................................$30-40
    Dumper Semi, 1:43, #9564,
        1985..................................$30-40
    Livestock Semi, 1:43, #6194,
        1985..................................$30-40
Williams Formula 1, 1:25, #6863,
    1983 ....$30-40
Willys Jeep
    1:25, #6797, 1981 ....$30-40
    Baja Jeep, 1:43, A-80, 1974 ....$30-40
    Carabinieri, 1:43, A-95, 1976........$30-40
    Fire Jeep, 1:43, A-81, 1974.............$30-40
    Military Jeep, 1:43, A-79, 1974 ....$30-40
    Police, 1:43, A-89, 1975 ....$30-40
    United Nations, 1:43, A-96,
        1976..................................$30-40
Yogi Bear & Boo Boo Character Car, A-35,
    1969 ....$60-70

Meboto (see Moboto)

Meccano (also see Dinky)

In 1901, Frank Hornby patented construction kits, dubbed "Meccanics Made Easy," that would become Meccano Constructor Sets. Prior to the introduction of Dinky Toys, Meccano produced a number of constructor sets. The problem with providing a price guide for Meccano Constructor sets is that they are rarely offered on the market whether unassembled in original box or as completed models. Meccano went into receivership in 1979, but the French subsidiary remained in business and still operates today.

Now, new Meccano Erector sets are being produced, the rights to the "Erector" name having been purchased in 1990 by the still-functioning French Meccano subsidiary. Prior to that time, Erector was a trademark of A. C. Gilbert.

MegaMovers

MegaMovers, distributed by Megatoys of Los Angeles, California, produced a great assortment of five 1:55 scale pickup trucks and six 1:24 scale models called Luxury Classics. Evidence of the care put into producing these larger toys is seen in remnants of car wax found on one model purchased, the BMW 850i from the Luxury Classics series. The latest MegaMovers to be marketed were repackaged Maistos.

They also made a series of smaller models that are basically scrap metal and plastic, lacking detail and accuracy but low priced.

3½" Trucks, approximately 1:55 Scale
Chevrolet
1955 Stepside Pickup, yellow.................$1-2
S-10 Pickup, bright pink.......................$1-2
C-150 Sportside Pickup, metallic silver.....$1-2
C-1500 454SS Pickup, metallic charcoal
 gray $1-2
1953 Ford Pickup Street Machine, red.........$1-2

Luxury Classics, approximately 1:24 Scale
BMW 850i, metallic red $6-8
Ferrari F40, red $6-8
Lamborghini Diablo, yellow.........................$6-8
Mercedes-Benz 500SL
 Convertible, white $6-8
 Coupe, metallic gray $6-8
Porsche 959, black $6-8

Two-and Three-Piece Vehicle Sets
Cheaply made models that are essentially inexpensive generic models.

Action Team includes car with boat and trailer, Van and horse trailer $1-2
Army Set includes Van, tank, utility vehicle, and pickup truck..................................$1-2
Police Set includes police car, police van, and police helicopter $1-2
Construction Set includes car, fork lift, cement truck and signs.................................$1-2
Construction Set includes car, fork lift, soft drink truck and signs.............................$1-2
Emergency Set includes utility vehicle, pickup, and ladder truck................................$1-2
Motorcycle Set includes silver motorcycle, yellow motorcycle and two signs......................$1-2
Motorcycle Set includes green Army motorcycle, blue motorcycle, and two signs $1-2

Classy Chassies
A series of 12 pull-back action 1:38 scale cars called Classy Chassies have been especially manufactured in China for Kmart by a company called Road Runners. These toys are relatively accurate renderings of actual cars, considering they sell for around $3. The 1995 versions of these cars have been repackaged as MegaMovers 4¾" cars.
Chevrolet
 Camaro, white.....................................$3-5
 '57 Chevy, red....................................$3-5
 '56 Corvette, red $3-5
 Corvette Sting Ray, silver.......................$3-5
Ferrari
 F-40, black.......................................$3-5
 Testarossa, metallic blue $3-5
 250GTO, red $3-5
 318S, metallic gold..............................$3-5
Ford
 Mustang, metallic green $3-5
 Thunderbird Convertible, white $3-5
 Thunderbird Hardtop, black $3-5
Lamborghini Diablo, yellow.........................$3-5

Megatoys (see MegaMovers)

Mego

Mego at one time produced 1:64 scale diecast cars called Jet Wheels, made in Hong Kong, and another series called Speed Burners, fast little cars powered by rechargeable NiCad batteries and designed to compete with Hot Wheels Sizzlers. No model list is available for Speed Burners. Jet Wheels are not to be confused with Jet models from Buby of Argentina.

Mego Jet Wheels
1968 AMC AMX, 1:64 ....$8-10

1968 Buick Riviera, 1:64.....................$8-10
1967 Chevrolet Camaro, 1:64 ....$8-10
1967 Chevrolet Corvair, 1:64.................$8-10
1968 Chevrolet Corvette, 1:64................$8-10
1968 Ford Mustang GT, 1:64...................$8-10
1968 Ford Torino, 1:64.......................$8-10
1967 Mercury Cougar, 1:64....................$8-10
1968 Pontiac Bonneville Convertible, 1:64 ..$8-10
Eagle F1, 1:64...............................$8-10
Ferrari F1, 1:64.............................$8-10
Lotus F1, 1:64 ....$8-10

Mercury

Torino, Italy, has been the home of Mercury since 1932. Once the premier manufacturer of diecast miniature vehicles, Mercury suffered in the face of increasing competition from Politoys, Mebetoys, and others. By 1980, the last Mercury models were made and the company folded.

Mercury Models
Aero
 1:40, 1945, #1 ....$90-120
 1:80, 1950, #41 ....$20-30
Alfa Romeo
 33, 1:43, 1968, #64........................$30-40
 33, 1:43, 1970, #53........................$30-40
 33, 1:66, 1969, #808.......................$50-60
 1900, 1:48, 1955, #16......................$50-60
 1951, 1:80, #44B...........................$20-30
 Alfasud 1200, 1:32, 1972,
  #653 ....$30-40
 Alfetta Carabinieri, 1:43, 1966,
  #58 ....$20-30
 Alfetta GT and Caravan, 1977,
  #404 ....$30-40
 Alfetta GT and Trailer, 1:43, 1977,
  #415 ....$30-40
 Alfetta GT and Trailer, 1:43, 1977,
  #419 ....$30-40
 Alfetta GT Rally, 1:43, 1976, #53 ....$20-30
 Alfetta GT, 1:43, 1975, #306 ....$30-40
 Alfetta Kenya Safari Car, 1:43, 1976,
  #211 ....$30-40
 Alfetta with Roof Rack, 1:43, 1976,
  #55 ....$20-30
 Giulia Canguro, 1:43, 1965, #29 ...$35-45
 Giulia GT, 1:43, 1965, #40 ....$30-40
 Giulia Ti, 1:43, 1966, #4...............$25-35
 Giulietta Sprint, 1:48, 1956, #3 ....$40-50
 Giulietta Ti, 1:43, 1975, #20 ....$35-45
 Giulietta, 1:48, 1956, #17...........$45-55
 Grand Prix, 1:40, 1951, #35 ....$85-95
 Montreal Bertone, 1:43, 1969,
  #67 ....$25-35

Montreal, 1:43, 1970, #304..........$30-40
Montreal, 1:66, 1969, #809..........$50-60
Allis-Chalmers Bulldozer, 1961, #517.....$50-60
Americana
    1:40, 1946, #4 ....$90-120
    1:80, 1950, #41C $20-30
    with Steering, 1:40, 1950, #90 ....$80-90
Ape Triporteur, 1952, #215 ....$30-40
Ariete Field Gun, 1951, #214 ....$20-30
Army Tank, 1952, #231 ....$30-40
Austin-Western
    Road Grader, 1961, #522..............$50-60
    Road Roller, 1961, #518.................$50-60
Autobianchi Bianchina, 1:48, 1958, #6 ..$20-30
Autocar
    Single Axle Dump Truck, 1959,
        #508..$50-60
    Twin Axle Dump Truck, 1959,
        #508 ....$50-60
Auto-Union
    1950, 1:80, #42B $20-30
    Grand Prix, 1947, 1:40, #32 ....$90-120
Bentley S Series, 1:48, 1957, #30 .....$85-95
Bertone Panther, 1:43, 1969, #68 ....$25-35
Bianchina Panoramica, 1:48, 1962,
    #11 ....$20-30
Bisonte Crane Truck, 1945, #121 ....$80-90
Blaw-Knox Cement Mixer, 1960,
    #515 ....$50-60
BMW 320
    and Caravan, 1:43, 1977, #420 ....$30-40
    and Trailer, 1:43, 1977, #416 ....$30-40
    Monte Carlo Rally, 1:43, 1966,
        #56 ....$20-30
    Police Car, 1:43, 1976, #59...........$20-30
    Rally, 1:43, 1977, #217 ....$30-40
    with Boat, 1:43, 1976, #219 ....$30-40
    with Luggage Rack, 1:43, 1976,
        #218 ....$30-40
    1:43, 1976, #6 ....$20-30
Cable Conveyor, #135 ....$80-90
Cadillac
    62 Sedan, 1:40, 1949, #9.........$140-155
    Eldorado, 1:48, 1956, #28 ....$140-155
    1:80, 1950, #48A.......................$20-30
Cannon, 1952, #232 ....$30-40
Car Transporter Trailer, 1:50, 1957,#100 ..$40-50
Carabo Bertone, 1:43, 1969, #303 ......$30-40
Caravan Trailer
    1:40, 1946, #7 ....$45-55
    1:66, #804 ....$50-60
Caterpillar
    12 Road Grader, 1958, #504.........$50-60
    Giant Road Grader, 1959, #506 .....$50-60
Chapparal
    2F, 1:43, 1968, #30 ....$55-65

2F, 1:66, 1969, #802 ....$30-40
2J, 1:43, 1971, #310 ....$30-40
Ciclope
    Crane Truck, 1:40, 1948, #94 ......$90-120
    Dump Truck, 1:40, 1948, #94.......$90-120
    Flat Truck, 1:40, 1948, #94 ....$90-120
    Ladder Truck, 1:40, 1948, #94......$90-120
Cisitalia
    1100, 1:40, 1951, #37.................$85-95
    1100, 1:80, 1951, #44D $20-30
    Grand Prix, 1:40, 1951, #38 ....$85-95
    Grand Prix, 1:80, 1951, #44E $20-30
Covered Truck, 1:80, 1951, #47A $20-30
Covered Wagon, 1:66, 1969, #850 ....$70-80
Crane Truck
    1:40, 1947, #23 ....$85-95
    1:80, 1951, #47B $20-30
Dino Pininfarina, 1:66, 1969, #810.......$50-60
Drott Tractor Shovel, 1960, #514 ....$50-60
Dump Truck, 1:40, 1947, #22 ....$90-120
Ercole
    Flatbed Semi-Trailer Truck, 1:80, 1951,
        #49C $20-30
    Semi-Trailer Tanker, 1:80, 1951,
        #49B $20-30
    Semi-Trailer Truck, 1:80, 1951,
        #49A......................................$20-30
Euclid
    C-6 Bulldozer, 1961, #519 ....$50-60
    L-30 Tractor Shovel, 1961, #520 ......$50-60
    TS-24 Road Scraper, 1960, #513 ....$50-60
    Twin Axle Dump Truck, 1959,
        #505......................................$50-60
Farina
    1:40, 1946, #2 ....$90-120
    1:80, 1950, #41A $20-30
Ferrari
    250 Le Mans, 1:66, 1969, #806 ....$50-60
    250 Le Mans, 1:43, 1964, #39 ......$35-45
    312P, 1:43, 1970, #306 ....$30-40
    330 P2, 1:43, 1967, #28 ....$30-40
    330 P4, 1:43, 1969, #65 ....$30-40
    330 P4, 1:66, 1969, #803 ....$30-40
    330P Nurburgring, 1:43, 1966, #60...$45-55
    330P Sebring, 1:43, 1966, #57......$70-80
    330P Sebring, 1:43, 1966, #59......$70-80
    512S Pininfarina, 1:43, 1971,
        #66 ....$30-40
    750, 1:50, 1960, #21 ....$55-65
    Dino Sport, 1:43, 1966, #45 ....$30-40
    Grand Prix, 1:40, 1951, #36 ......$120-130
    Modulo Pininfarina, 1:32, 1971,
        #651 ....$30-40
    P5, 1:66, 1969, #815 ....$50-60
    Supersqualo, 1:43, 1956, #53 ....$80-90
    1:80, 1951, #44C........................$20-30

Fiat 124
    1:43, 1976, #46 ....$30-40
    Coupe, 1:43, 1969, #300 ....$30-40
Fiat 125
    Rally, 1:43, 1957, #25 ....$20-30
    1:43, 1969, #25 ....$25-35
Fiat 127 Rally
    1:43, 1971, #311 ....$30-40
    1:43, 1972, #318 ....$30-40
Fiat 128
    1:43, 1969, #22 ....$25-35
    Carabinieri, 1:48, 1974, #10.........$20-30
    Fire Chief, 1:43, 1974, #9 ....$20-30
    Polizia, 1:43, 1974, #8 ....$20-30
Fiat 130
    1:43, 1971, #26 ....$20-30
    and Caravan, 1:43, 1977, #401 ....$30-40
    and Caravan, 1:43, 1977, #402 ....$30-40
    Ambulance, 1:43, 1976, #7............$20-30
    Carabinieri, 1:43, 1975, #5............$30-40
    Familiare Carabinieri, 1:43, 1976,
        #63...$20-30
    Familiare, 1:43, 1976, #304...........$30-40
    Fire Chief, 1:43, 1971, #4 ....$20-30
    Mirafiori, 1:43, 1974, #1 ....$20-30
    Polizia, 1:43, 1975, #3 ....$20-30
    Polizia, 1:43, 1976, #210 ....$20-30
    Rally, 1:43, 1974, #2 ....$20-30
    Rally, 1:66, #807 ....$50-60
    Taxi, 1:43, 1975, #11 ....$20-30
    Wagon and Caravan, 1:43, 1977,
        #406.......................................$30-40
    Wagon and Trailer, 1:43, 1977,
        #418.......................................$30-40
    Wagon and Trailer, 1:43, 1977,
        #431.......................................$30-40
    Wagon with Boat, 1:43, 1976,
    #212..$30-40
    Wagon with Luggage Rack, 1:43, 1976,
        #205.......................................$20-30
    Wagon with Skis and Caravan, 1:43, 1977,
        #405.......................................$30-40
    Wagon with Skis, 1:43, 1976,
        #204.......................................$20-30
    with Boat, 1:43, 1976, #208 ....$20-30
    with Roof Rack, 1:43, 1976, #209...$20-30
    with Skis and Caravan, 1:43,
        1977, #408 ....$30-40
    with Skis, 1:43, 1976, #12 ....$20-30
Fiat 132 GLS, 1:43, 1973, #313 ....$30-40
    Police Car, 1:43, 1975, #320.........$30-40
    Rally, 1:43, 1973, #317.................$30-40
Fiat 214
    Rally, 1:43, 1972, #312.................$30-40
    Sport Coupe, 1:43, 1969, #302 .....$30-40
Fiat 217, 1:66, #806........................$50-60

Fiat 1300
- 1:48, 1961, #9 ....$30-40
- Polizia, 1:43, 1964, #35 ....$25-35

Fiat 1400
- 1:80, 1950, #48C........................$20-30
- 1950, #11 ....$85-95
- Spider, 1:48, 1960, #7 ....$35-45

Fiat 1800, 1:48, 1959, #2 ....$30-40

Fiat 2300 S, 1:43, 1962, #23 ....$35-45

Fiat 238
- High-Roof Van, 1:66, 1969, #873 ...$50-60
- School Bus, 1:66, 1969, #872........$50-60
- Truck, 1:43 1970, #90 ....$70-80
- Truck, 1:43, 1970, #91 ....$70-80
- Truck, 1:43, 1970, #92 ....$70-80
- Truck, 1:43, 1970, #93 ....$70-80
- Van, 1:66, 1969, #870..................$50-60

Fiat 242
- Camper with Luggage Rack, 1:43, 1977, #508 ....$50-60
- Camper, 1:43, 1977, #503...........$50-60
- Crane Truck, 1:43, 1977, #506 ......$50-60
- Fire Truck, 1:43, 1977, #507 ....$50-60

Fiat 500C
- 1:40, 1950, #10 ....$45-55
- 1:80, 1950, #48B........................$20-30

Fiat 500L, 1:43, 1967, #17 ....$25-35

Fiat 600
- 1:48, 1955, #18 ....$35-45
- Multipla, 1:48, 1957, #19 ....$35-45

Fiat 607
- Container Truck, 1:43, 1977, #502..................................$50-60
- Tank Truck, 1:43, 1977, #510........$50-60

Fiat 682N
- Bus, 1958, #98...........................$70-80
- Car Transporter, 1:50, 1957, #99....$70-80
- Covered Truck, 1:50, 1956, #97 .....$70-80
- Dump Truck, 1:50, 1956, #97........$70-80
- Truck with Controls, 1:50, 1957, #134...$80-90

Fiat 692
- Car Transporter Semi, 1:43, 1977, #534...$50-60
- Container Semi, 1:43, 1977, #531...$50-60
- Tanker Semi, 1:43, 1977, #532 .....$50-60

Fiat 697
- Cement Mixer, 1:43, 1977, #509 ...$50-60
- Cement Truck, 1:50, 1977, #101 ....$40-50
- Dump Truck, 1:43, 1977, #501.......$50-60
- Dump Truck, 1:50, 1977, #102.......$40-50
- Dump Truck, 1:50, 1977, #103.......$40-50
- Tank Truck, 1:50, 1977, #100........$40-50

Fiat 850
- 1:43, 1965, #38 ....$20-30

Bertone, 1:43, 1965, #12..............$25-35
Coupe, 1:43, 1967, #44 ....$30-40

Fiat SL
- 1:43, 1972, #314 ....$30-40
- 1:43, 1972, #315 ....$30-40
- Rally, 1:43, 1973, #316 ....$30-40

Fiat Abarth 1000
- 1:43, 1965, #42 ....$30-40
- Bialbero, 1:43, 1966, #41..............$30-40

Fiat Abarth SS595, 1:43, 1970, #14 ....$25-35

Fiat Balilla, 1:43, 1967, #70 ....$30-40

Fiat Campagnola
- 1:35, 1977, #80 ....$20-30
- 1:43, 1975, #305 ....$30-40
- 1:66, #801 ....$30-40
- and Boat Trailer, 1:43, 1977, #423...$30-40
- ACI Service Car, 1:43, 1975, #28 ..$20-30
- African Tour and Caravan, 1:43, 1977, #403...$30-40
- African Tour Car, 1:43, 1976, #206.$20-30
- Ambulance, 1:35, 1977, #82 ....$20-30
- Ambulance, 1:43, 1975, #32 ....$20-30
- Army Ambulance and Trailer, 1:43, 1977, #413...$30-40
- Carabinieri, 1:43, 1975, #31..........$20-30
- Fire and Trailer, 1:43, 1977, #414 ..$30-40
- Fire Car, 1:43, 1975, #30 ....$20-30
- Fire Truck, 1:35, 1977, #84 ....$20-30
- Mexico, 1:35, 1977, #81 ....$20-30
- Police Car, 1:35, 1977, #83 ....$20-30
- Polizia, 1:43, 1975, #29 ....$20-30
- Safari, 1:43, 1975, #33 ....$20-30
- Safari, 1:43, 1976, #202 ....$20-30
- with A-Gun, 1:43, 1977, #213........$40-50
- with Lance-Rockets, 1:43, 1977, #214...$30-40
- with Radio, 1:43, 1977, #215 ....$30-40
- with Searchlight, 1:43, 1977, #216...$30-40
- with Snowplow, 1:43, 1975, #34....$20-30
- Wrecker, 1:43, 1976, #201 ....$20-30

Fiat Cement Truck, 1:66, #809 ....$50-60

Fiat Dino
- Bertone, 1:43, 1967, #63...............$35-45
- Pininfarina, 1:43, 1967, #48 ....$30-40

Fiat Farm Tractor, 1:66, #810 ....$50-60

Fiat Nuova
- 500, 1:48, 1958, #1 ....$25-35
- 1100, 1:48, 1954, #13..................$45-55

Fiat Open Truck, 1:66, #803 ....$30-40

Fiat Ritmo, 1:43, 1978, #50 ....$20-30

Fiat Tank Truck, 1:66, #802 ....$30-40

Fiorenti Power Shovel, 1:20, 1957, #132...$80-90

Fiorentini Excavator, 1955, #221 ....$30-40

Ford GT 40, 1:66, 1969, #804............$50-60
Ford Mustang, 1:66, 1969, #813 ....$50-60
Fred Flintstone's Car, 1971, #751 ......$140-155

Golia-Ercole
- Cattle Truck, 1948, #92 ....$115-125
- Cattle Truck, 1948, #93 ....$115-125
- Open Truck, 1948, #92 ....$115-125
- Open Truck, 1948, #93 ....$115-125

Grand Prix Car
- Hockenheim, 1:66, #1204 ....$50-60
- Jarama, 1:66, #1201 ....$50-60
- Monte Carlo, 1:66, #1202 ....$50-60
- Zandvoort, 1:66, #1205 ....$50-60
- Zeltweg, 1:66, #1203 ....$50-60

Heavy Tractor, 1952, #64 ....$70-80

Horse Drawn
- Covered Wagon, 1950, #302 ....$70-80
- Flat Wagon, 1950, #301 ....$70-80
- Log Cart, 1950, #306 ....$70-80
- Open Cart, 1950, #312 ....$70-80
- Tank Cart, 1950, #313 ....$30-40

Innocenti
- 90-120 Rally, 1:43, 1975, #23.......$35-45
- 90-120 with Skis, 1:43, 1976, #24....$20-30
- 950, 1:48, 1961, #10 ....$20-30

International Bulldozer, 1960, #514 ......$50-60

Ital Design Manta, 1:43, 1970, #305....$30-40

Jack's Demon Dragster, 1:43, 1969, #69 ....$20-30

Lamborghini
- 1:66, 1969, #811 ....$50-60
- Marzal, 1:66, 1969, #805 ....$50-60

Lambretta
- 125 LC Moped, 1952, #214..........$30-40
- 125 LC, 1952, #217 ....$30-40
- 125 C Moped, 1952, #213 ....$30-40
- Triporteur, 1952, #216.................$30-40

Lancia
- Appia 3, 1:48, 1959, #5 ....$30-40
- Appia I, 1:48, 1955, #14 ....$45-55
- Aprilia, 1:25, 1946, #60 ....$70-80
- Aprilia, 1:40, 1946, #3 ....$30-40
- Aprilia, 1:80, 1950, #41B $20-30
- Aurelia, 1:25, 1950, #61 ....$70-80
- Aurelia, 1:80, 1950, #48D $20-30
- Aurelia, 1950, #12 ....$55-65
- Beta Coupe Rally, 1:43, 1974, #52...$25-35
- Beta Coupe, 1:43, 1974, #303 ......$30-40
- Beta Rally, 1:43, 1976, #203..........$20-30
- Beta with Skis and Caravan, 1:43, 1977, #409...$30-40
- Beta with Skis, 1:43, 1976, #54 ....$20-30
- D-24, 1:48, 1957, #26 ....$85-95
- D-50, 1:43, 1956, #54 ....$80-90
- Flaminia, 1:48, 1957, #8...............$40-50

Honda

750 Police Motorcycle, #615	$35-45
CB750, 1972, #608	$35-45
US90 Army 3-Wheeler, 1972, #609	$35-45
Kawasaki 750cc Mach IV H2, 1972, #610	$35-45
Laverda 750 SF, 1972, #605	$35-45
MV 350CC, 1971, #602	$35-45
Yamaha Scrambler, 1972, #606	$35-45

Mercury Industries USA (see Lit'l Toy)

Merit

Merit toys were introduced in 1940 by J. Randall, J. Ltd. The brand name was derived from the company's address: Merit House, 67 Bunhill Row, London, England. J. Randall manufactured toys and games, and is particularly well known for its 1:32 scale plastic Grand Prix race car kits. In addition, there was one built model offered by Merit:

1949 AEC Mammoth Flatbed Lorry, "Bowaters" Newsprint Lorry, plastic, 1:50 scale	$60-75

Merlin

Just two Merlin models have been documented from this British toy manufacturer, a Jeep and a race car. Both are single-cast zinc alloy with metal wheels. The race car had a rubber band gear-drive motor. Merlin toys are identified by the name, description, and model number inside the casting.

1947 Maserati-style Racing car, A200	$30-45
1944 Willys Civilian Jeep Willys, A100	$30-45

Message Models (see Fun Ho!)

John Robinson
The Trans-Sport Shop
Message Models and Books
P O Box 239 Northbridge
New South Wales, 2063, Australia

In the 1990s, Message Books and Models (also known as Message Models and Books) became the new owner of old Fun Ho! castings and tooling.

Metalcar

Metalcar (or Metal Car) is a brand of models from Hungary.

Alpine A310 Police, 1:64, #31	$5-7

Audi

2000 4-door Sedan, 1:64, #15	$5-7
Quattro Coupe, 1:43, #13	$20-30
Batmobile, 1:64, #28	$25-40

BMW

3.0 Turbo, 1:43, #1	$20-30
525 Ambulance, 1:43, #10	$20-30
525 Polizei, 1:43, #11	$20-30

Cessna Plane

Military, 1:64, #36	$5-7
Police, 1:64, #35	$5-7
Citroën SM Coupe, 1:64, #26	$5-7
Datsun 126X, 1:64, #1	$4-6
Dodge Van Police, 1:43, #12	$20-30
Ferrari 275 Coupe, 1:64, #32	$5-7

Futura

Container Dump Truck, 1:64, #3	$4-6
Dump Truck, 1:64, #21	$5-7
Garbage Truck, 1:64, #20	$5-7
Oil Truck "Mobil," 1:64, #19	$5-7
Oil Truck "SHELL," 1:64, #18	$5-7
Tow Truck, 1:64, #4	$4-6
Tow Truck, 1:64, #22	$5-7
Hanomag Truck, 1:64, #33	$5-7
Helicopter, USA, 1:64, #11	$5-7
Honda 750 Motorcycle, 1:64, #5	$4-6

Jeep CJ5

4x4, 1:64, #25	$5-7
Hardtop, 1:64, #23	$5-7
Open, 1:64, #24	$5-7
Lamborghini Espada Coupe, 1:64, #17	$5-7

Mercedes-Benz

190 4-door Sedan, 1:64, #27	$5-7
406 Bank Police, 1:64, #7	$4-6
406 Police, 1:64, #6	$4-6
406 Service, 1:64, #8	$4-6
Fire Ladder Truck, 1:43, #5	$20-30
Garbage Truck, 1:43, #4	$20-30
SeaLand Truck, 1:04, #23	$20-30
Tow Truck, 1:43, #6	$20-30
Truck, 1:43, #3	$20-30

Mercury 406

Ambulance, 1:64, #14	$5-7
Police, 1:64, #13	$5-7
Metchy F1 Racer, 1:64, #34	$5-7
Motorboat, 1:64, #30	$5-7
Mustang Police, 1:25, #15	$25-35
Opel Kadett Police, 1:43, #14	$20-30
Opel Senator 4-door Sedan, 1:64, #12	$5-7

Porsche 928

Coupe, 1:64, #9	$4-6
Police, 1:64, #29	$5-7
Scania Bus, 1:64, #38	$5-7
Steam Train Engine, 1:64, #16	$5-7
Surtees F1 FIRESTONE, 1:43, #7	$20-30
Unimog 406 Truck, 1:64, #37	$5-7

Volkswagen

Dune Duggy, 1:64, #10	$4-6
Golf JPS, 1:43, #8	$20-30
Golf Police, 1:43, #9	$20-30

Metal Cast Products Company

From 1929 to 1940, Metal Cast Products Company produced slush-mold toy vehicles as an outgrowth of the S. Sachs company, producer of toy soldiers.

Manufacture of these models were franchised to various other smaller firms, while Metal Cast handled the marketing and distribution. Models are well made and nicely painted. Values are currently low for their vintage, but could rise somewhat as more collectors become aware of them. The problem sometimes is in identifying models, since franchisers didn't always put a manufacturer name on the models. Fred Green Toys is one of the franchisers whose name is most often found on the base.

Cadillac 2-door Sedan, #40, 5¼"	$45-60
Convertible Coupe, #63	$15-20
Dump Truck, #42, 5¼"	$15-20
Fire Engine Ladder Truck, #61, 4½"	$20-25
Fire Engine Steam Pumper with water cannon, #65, 4"	$20-25
Fire Engine Steam Pumper with no water cannon, no number, 3⅞"	$20-25
Packard 2-door Convertible, top down, #41, 5¼"	$30-35
Racer, #62, Bluebird-style Record Car, 4½"	$30-35
Streamline airflow-style Sedan, #60, 4"	$25-30
Stake Truck, #64, 4¼"	$20-25
Truck and Moving Van Trailer, #01-02, 6"	$15-20
Truck and Tank Trailer, #01-03, 6"	$15-20
Truck and Open Rack Stake Trailer, #01-04, 6"	$15-20
War Tank, #08, 4"	$65-80

Metalcraft

From 1931 to 1937, Metalcraft produced exceptional pressed steel trucks from their factory in St. Louis, Missouri. The Great Depression of the 1930s was a bad time to start a toy company, and the company folded under the economic pressure, but not before producing some of the most stylish, streamlined toy trucks ever made.

BFG Wrecker	$500-650
Bunte Candies Truck, 12"	$425-500
Buster Brown Shoes Truck	$500-650
Clover Farm Stores Truck	$850-1,000

Coca-Cola Truck
    rubber tires, ten glass bottles in a rack, 11",
        circa 1931 ....$850-1,000
    steel tires, ten glass bottles in a rack, 10½",
        circa 1931 ....$600-750
    stamped metal, 12", circa
        1936 ....$850-1,000
CW Brand Coffee
    Delivery Van, 11" $450-550
    Dump Truck, 10" $450-550
    Wrecker.....................................$600-750
Deckers Iowana Truck....................$950-1,100
Delivery Van, pressed steel, 11" $425-500
Dump Truck with electric headlights,
    24" $375-500
Esso Stake Truck with barrels, 12" $1,050-1,200
Goodrich Silvertown Tires Wrecker with three
    spare tires................................$425-500
Hardy's Salt Truck..............................$425-500
Heinz Truck, "Baked Beans," "Bottled Vinegar,"
    "Rice Flakes," "Spaghetti," "Tomato Ketchup,"
    12" $375-450
Ice Truck $425-500
Kroger Food Express Truck, 11" $500-650
Krug Bakery Truck..............................$800-950
Leslie Vacuum Packed Coffee Truck......$750-900
Machinery Hauling Truck.................$850-1,000
Meadow Gold Butter Truck with battery powered
    lights, 13" $500-650
Plee-Zing Quality Products Delivery Van,
    11" $475-550
Pure Oil Tanker with electric lights,
    14¾" $950-1,100
Sand-Gravel Dump Truck....................$325-400
Shell Motor Oil Stake Truck with eight oil
    drums $850-1,000
St. Louis Truck, 11" $375-450
Steam Shovel....................................$175-250
Sunshine Biscuits Truck.......................$475-550
Towing & Repairs Truck.....................$475-550
Toy Town Grocery Truck $500-600
Waldorf Lager Truck..........................$850-1,000
Weatherbird Shoes Truck....................$425-500
Werks Tag Soap Truck........................$550-650
Weston's English Biscuits Truck $475-550
White King Express Truck, 12" $475-550

Metal Masters

Metal Masters were a prolific toy manufacturer east of the Mississippi from the late 1930s to the 1950s. It originated in Pottstown, Pennsylvania. Identifying them is easy since every model is imprinted on the underside with "Metal Masters Co." and "Made In U.S.A." Although cast from a single mold, similar to Tootsietoys and Midgetoys, Metal Masters differentiate themselves by sleek, angular contours and classic lines that typify the Art Deco period in which they were made.

Metal Masters are prototypical toys, which means that, while hinting at real cars from the 1930s, the toys make no attempt at replicating real vehicles. They instead reflect the styling of such great marques as Bugatti, Packard, Stutz, LaSalle, Duesenberg, Cord, and Auburn, combining elements from each to create a unique look all their own.

Since Metal Masters are stylized and represent no particular automobile, it is impossible to list them by make and model. So they are listed below by vehicle type, however nondescript. Identification is made simpler by the fact that there were only eight basic castings, with some of them modified to create different models. The Station Wagon was produced with and without a wind-up motor, and was also adapted into an Ambulance by applying a different paint scheme. The Pick Up Truck was also modified to serve as a Tow Truck and a Fire Truck.

Like many toys made in the first half of the twentieth century, distribution of Metal Masters was limited to the general region from which the toys are produced. While they are apparently still easy to find in some parts of the Eastern U.S., you'll rarely find them anywhere in the west, particularly in the Pacific Northwest. While visiting my family in Michigan and Wisconsin, I went to an antique shop where I was able to find Metal Masters toys by the dozen, although I couldn't afford to buy any at $35–60 a pop. Back here in Oregon, I've never seen a single one.

Values below represent models in new condition with little or no visible wear.

Bus, 7¼", circa 1938 ....$45-60
Fire Truck, 10" long, circa 1940
    with removable ladders $75-90
    with wind-up motor and ladders $120-150
Jeep, 5½", circa 1947.........................$50-65
Roadster, 7", circa 1938.......................$45-60
Station Wagon, 8½", circa 1940
    without wind-up motor $60-75
    with wind-up motor $65-80
    Ambulance...................................$65-80
Pickup Truck, 7 inches, circa 1938
    Pickup Truck $45-60
    Tow Truck $45-60
    Fire Truck $65-80
Tow Truck
    "ABC Towing Service," 10", circa
    1940..$95-110
    with wind-up motor, 10", circa
    1940...$105-120
Tractor with driver, 5", vintage not
    reported $105-120

Metal Miniatures

These are unpainted one-piece highly detailed cast metal vehicles in 1:87 scale (HO gauge), of which one is listed as available from Walthers.

Caterpillar Tractor, 340-44 ....$2-4

Metosul

Metosul is a Portuguese brand of toys resembling Corgi and Dinky Toys, possibly some older castings purchased from another producer, according to Dr. Craig S. Campbell, an avid collector of less common diecast cars. Metosul cars are typically 1:43–1:45 scale, while their trucks are 1:50 and buses 1:72.

Peter Foss adds that the Osul company of Portugal produced plastic toy cars starting in 1932. In 1964, they started a line of diecast metal Osul toys and dubbed them "Metosul." The company continued producing Metosul cars until around 1980. Foss says that Metosul castings are of lesser quality than Dinky or Corgi, and that there aren't many unique models offered in the assortment.

The reason for the variance in quality is due to several models that are recastings of old Matchbox Models of Yesteryear dies, and at least one former CIJ casting, a Notin Rulote Camping Caravan.

Metosul 1:43 Scale

Alfa Romeo Giulietta Roadster
    #3, 1:43.......................................$30-35
    Policia, #3, 1:43.............................$30-35
    GNR, #3, 1:43 ....$30-35
    GNR BT, #3, 1:43...........................$30-35
Citroën DS19
    #2, 1:43...$40
    Aluguer, #22, 1:43 ....$30-35
    Bombieros, #48, 1:43 ....$30-35
    Feuerwehr, #82, 1:43 ....$30-35
    GNR, #61, 1:43 ....$30-35
    Policia, #22, 1:43 ....$30-35
    Taxi Lisbon, turquoise & black, #20,
        1:43.....................................$35-40
    Taxi Portugal, #120, 1:43...............$30-35
    and Caravan, #43, 1:43.................$60-70
Mercedes-Benz 190D
    #9, 1:43......................................$45-50
    Policia, #9, 1:43.............................$45-50

Taxi, #9, 1:43 ....$45-50
Mercedes-Benz 200
  #10, 1:45.....................................$25-30
  Aluguer, #16, 1:45 ....$25-30
  Army, #27, 1:45 ....$30-35
  Bombeiros, #52, 1:45 ....$25-30
  Emergencia, #51, 1:45 ....$25-30
  Policia, #25, 1:45 ....$25-30
  Polizie, #30, 1:45 ....$25-30
  Taxi, #10, 1:45 ....$25-30
  Taxi Amsterdam, #110, 1:45 ....$25-30
Mini Cooper, #108, 1:43 ....$30-35
Morris Mini Minor, #7, 1:43 ....$30-35
Notin Rulote Camping Caravan, #19,
  1:43 (former CIJ casting)......................$25-30
Peugeot 204
  4-door Sedan, #24, 1:43 ....$25-30
  Aluguer, #32, 1:43 ....$25-30
  Taxi, #31, 1:43 ....$25-30
Peugeot 304 Estate Wagon
  #49, 1:43.....................................$25-30
  Bombeiros, #60, 1:43 ....$25-30
  JAE Municipal, #58, 1:43 ....$25-30
  Policia, #55, 1:43 ....$25-30
  Police, #59, 1:43 ....$25-30
Renault
  Floride, #1, 1:43 ....$25-30
  R16, #14, 1:43 ....$25-30
  R16 GNR, #14, 1:43 ....$25-30
  R16 Taxi, #15, 1:43 ....$25-30
  R16 Aluguer, #16, 1:43 ....$25-30
Rolls-Royce Silver Ghost, #12, 1:43........$20-25
Volkswagen 1200
  #4, 1:43 ....$35-40
  Army, #4, 1:43.................................$60-70
  Bombeiros, #57, 1:43 ....$30-35
  GNR, #8, 1:43 ....$30-60
  GNR BT, #6, 1:43 ....$35-40
  Policia, #5, 1:43 ....$35-40
  Polis, #56, 1:43 ....$30-35
Volkswagen Transporter, #42, 1:43 ....$20-25
Volvo P1800 Coupe
  #11, 1:43.....................................$25-30
  GNR BT, #18, 1:43 ....$25-30
  Policia, #17, 1:43 ....$25-30
  Polis, #117, 1:43 ....$25-30

Metosul 1:50 Scale
Mercedes-Benz 1113
  Army cargo Transport Truck, light green &
    olive, #38, 1:50 ....$35-40
  Bombeiros, #53, 1:50 ....$25-30
  Correios, #50, 1:50.........................$30-35
  Dump Truck, #26, 1:50 ....$30-35
  EGT Truck, #37, 1:50 ....$30-35
  GNR Truck, #39, 1:50 ....$30-35

JAE Truck, #41, 1:50 ....$30-35
Policia Truck, #40, 1:50.......................$30-35
Tanker, "GALP," #46, 1:50 ....$25-30
Tanker, "SACOR," #28, 1:50 ....$35-40
Tanker, "SONAP," #29, 1:50 ....$35-40
Tanker Bombeiros, #54, 1:50 ....$35-40

Metosul 1:72 Scale
Leyland Atlantean Double Decker Bus
  "Carris," #23, 1:72 ....$30-35
  "Carris," #45, 1:72 ....$25-30
  "Gazcidla," #36, 1:72 ....$30-35
  "SMC," #34, 1:72 ....$30-35
  "STCP," #33, 1:72 ....$30-35
  "STCP," #44, 1:72 ....$25-30
  "Transul," #35, 1:72 ....$30-35
  maroon & gray, 1:72 ....$30-35

Metropolitain

Metal model kits in 1:8 scale were offered by this company based in Italy. A short list of Metropolitain models was found in a 1986 Danhausen catalog.

1907 Itala 35/45 CV
  unassembled $1,000-1,500
  correctly assembled $2,000-2,500
1907 Mercedes Grand Prix, produced in 1986
  unassembled $1,000-1,500
  correctly assembled $2,000-2,500
1912 Mercer 35T 55CV, produced in 1987
  unassembled $1,000-1,500
  correctly assembled $2,000-2,500

Mettoy (also see Corgi)

Phillipp Ullman founded Mettoy in Northampton, England, in 1933. Ullmann owned Tipp & Co. of Germany, a manufacturer of tinplate toys. He partnered with Arthur Katz. The name "Mettoy" was the contraction of the phrase "Metal Toys." Production during the 1930s concentrated on lithographed tinplate toy cars and airplanes with clockwork motors. By 1946, Mettoy began replacing their tinplate toys with diecast and plastic ones.

In 1948, under the encouragement of Marks & Spencer retail stores, Mettoy contracted with Birmingham Aluminium Casting Co. of Smethwick, England, to produce a series of six diecast toys dubbed "Heavy Cast Mechanical Toys" measuring 6½ to 7½ inches long. They were also marketed as Castoys. In 1949, Mettoy moved to their new facility in Swansea, South Wales, under the direction of Phillipp Ullman's son Henry who had just returned from the U. S. with new insights into the diecast toy indus-

try. In 1954, Mettoy purchased Playcraft Toys Ltd. and changed their name to Mettoy-Playcraft. A year later, in 1955, Mettoy changed its focus in an effort to become the best manufacturer of diecast toys. It was in this year that they introduced the Corgi range, and Mettoy was afterwards eclipsed by its own new brand.

Mettoys/Castoys
Breakdown Lorry, 1954, plastic, #632, 4⅛",
  1:50 ....$75-90
Citroën Sedan, 11" $325-400
Coupe..$700-850
Fire Engine, 1954, plastic, #633, 4⅞",
  1:50 ....$75-90
Ford Consul Saloon, diecast 1952, plastic
  1954, #890, 1:43........................$75-90
Karrier Bantam "C.W.S. Soft Drink," diecast,
  red, 1:50 ....$75-90
Open Lorry, plastic, 1954, #631, 4⅞",
  1:50 ....$75-90
Racer #7, 5"......................$1,500-2,000
Rolls Royce Saloon
  diecast, 1950, with motor, #605, 4½",
    1:48..$75-90
  diecast, 1950, with retractable bumpers and
    motor, #606, 4½" $75-90
  Wraith Saloon, diecast, with motor, 1950;
    3", 1:60, #505 ....$75-90
  stamped steel, 14" $1,000-1,250
Sedan, stamped steel, 14" $575-650
Standard Vanguard
  Police Car, with motor, 1951; 2⅞",
    #510..$75-90
  Taxi, with motor, 1951, 2⅞", #511....$75-90
  Fire Chief, 1951, with ladder and motor,
    #512, ⅞"..................................$75-90
  Saloon, 1950, diecast, with motor, ⅞", 1:60,
    #502..$75-90
  Saloon, 1950, diecast, with motor, 4", 1:43,
    #602..$75-90
  Saloon, 1950, diecast, with retractable
    bumpers & motor, 4½", #603 ......$75-90
  Saloon, 1953, plastic, with motor, #604/1,
    4" $75-90
  Saloon, 1953, plastic, without motor, #604,
    4" $75-90
Steam Roller, clockwork......................$200-250
Streamlined Express Bus, wind-up, 7¼", 1:43.$75-90
Tipping Lorry, plastic, 1954, #630, 4⅛",
  1:50 ....$75-90
Tractor, tin wind-up, 8" $100-125

Miber

Miber models are plastic 1:87 scale models, often plain with stickers included for detailing, reportedly made in Nuremberg, Germany. According to Pantera model collector Markus R. Karalash, this company has produced HO scale (1:87) DeTomaso Panteras along with some other models. In addition, Mazda model collector Werner Legrand of Brecht, Belgium, offered this additional information: "Miber definitely had produced more than only the Pantera.

"I have a few (of course) Mazda models in my small collection, but I also know somebody with some Miber Toyotas. The finishing of those items is very poor in comparison to some other 1:87 scale manufacturers as Herpa, Wiking, etc.

"The interesting part is that they produced models that no others did, and the price wasn't bad either. They even promised (in 1992) a model of the NSX, too.

"I also found an extract of a Dutch article, dated 1985, on Miber models made by LH Industries. Briefly, it says that Miber often has announced items but, unfortunately, didn't always keep their promises."

DeTomaso Pantera, 1:87
    #1152 ....$6-8
    #2152 ....$6-8
    #9152 ....$6-8
Mazda 323, 1:87, #1271
    white $6-8
    cream $6-8
Toyota Celica 2000 GTR, 1:87
    white, "Monte Carlo '89" stickers,
        #2042 ....$6-8
    teal, "BP," "Leyton House Formula One Racing
        Team" tampos, #2043 ....$6-8
    red $6-8

Micro Champs (see Paul's Model Art)

Micro Machines

Galoob was the pre-eminent toy company to produce the world's smallest series of toy vehicles, numbering in the thousands of models.

Up until the re-release of the Star Wars motion picture in 1997, Micro Machines had produced only plastic models in very small scale. As the enhanced version of the movie returned to theaters with new scenes added and an audio upgrade to THX Dolby surround sound, Galoob introduced its first series of diminutive diecast models to commemorate the event, as listed below. Models were made in China for Lewis Galoob Toys, Inc. based in south San Francisco, California. With the

release of *Star Wars Episode 1: The Phantom Menace*, Micro Machines offered more quality diecast models along with their vinyl and plastic assortment.

While rarely involving any diecast components other than the base, Galoob's Micro Machines are nevertheless an intriguing assortment of tiny plastic toys. For 1999, Micro Machines offered a new collector edition series of very accurate scale models in approximately 1:87 scale. The first to show up in stores is the Corvette Series 1, an exceptional assortment of high quality replicas with opening hoods or removable roofs.

Galoob has since been purchased by Hasbro. Hasbro Micro Machines first began making their appearance in full force in retail stores in 2002.

Galoob Micro Machines Collector Edition Corvette Series 1
Manta Ray Experimental with opening hood,
    blue with silver accents $3-4
1963 Grand Sport Racer with opening hood,
    white and blue with red accents $3-5
1968 Convertible with removable Convertible
    top, white $3-5
1968 Convertible with removable Convertible
    top, red $3-5
1978 T-Top Coupe with removable T-Top,
    black with silver and red accents $3-5
1996 Grand Sport with removable top, royal
    blue with white racing stripe $3-5
1997 Coupe with opening hood, red $3-5

Galoob Micro Machines Star Wars Diecast Models
Millenium Falcon $6-8
Imperial Star Destroyer $6-8
Imperial Tie Fighter $6-8
Jawa Sandcrawler $6-8
X-wing Starfighter $6-8
Y-wing Starfighter $6-8
Royal Starship of the Naboo Princess $6-8
Trade Federation Battleship $6-8
Trade Federation Droid Starfighter $6-8
Gian Landspeeder $6-8

Galoob The Real Adventures of Jonny Quest 4-piece sets in original package
#1 Safari Adventure Set $8-10
#2 Deep Dive Adventure Set $8-10
#3 Climbing Adventure Set $8-10
#4 Arctic Adventure Set $8-10
#5 High Seas Adventure Set $8-10
#6 Western Adventure Set $8-10

Galoob Micro Machines standard 4-piece set
    in original package $5-7
Galoob Micro Machines, individual models out
    of package ....$1 or less each
Hasbro Micro Machines standard 4-piece set in
    original package $4-5
Hasbro Micro Machines, individual models out
    of package ....$1 or less each

Hasbro Micro Machines standard 5-pack, 2004 Chemical Containment Set depicted..$5-6

Micro Models

History: Six attempts in 42 years

Micro Models, The First Range

The first successful producer of quality diecast toy cars in Australia was Micro Models, a company whose success was strongly connected with the successful introduction of the Holden automobile to Australia, New Zealand, and surrounding island nations. From 1952 to 1960, Micro Models produced beautifully rendered, distinctively down-under cars in roughly 1:43 scale and trucks in approximately 1:72 scale.

But they weren't all Holdens. In fact, the first toy produced by Micro Models was a Vauxhall Velox, a British car, designated GB-1. It was followed by a Holden Utility, more popularly known as a Ute, the Australian version of the pickup truck and designated GB-2. This was followed by yet another British replica, a Jaguar XK-120, marked GB-3. Two British Bedford trucks followed, both using the same chassis. GB-4 was a flatbed, or tray, truck, and GB-5 was a dump truck. GB-6, a 4-wheel trailer, rounded out the first offering from Micro Models.

Many popular models followed, until 1958 when import barriers to Australia were lifted, and toys from around the world began seeping into the previously isolated continent. Because of increasing competition from foreign producers, Micro Models ceased operation in Australia in 1958.

The Second Range

Meanwhile in 1956, a second range of Micro Models had begun in New Zealand by Lincoln Industries, originally under an arrangement with the Australian company. The New Zealand series continued through 1960 and is strongly connected with the most recent series of Micro Models reissued from New Zealand. Lincoln Industries is believed to have had a connection with the British firm of D.C.M.T. (Die Casting Machine Tools Ltd.)

The Third Range

Kevin F. Meates of New Zealand purchased the brand in 1962 but didn't resume producing models until 1970. The Micro Models brand was finally resurrected in 1970 by the Meates family of New Zealand under the company names of Matai and Torro, and celebrated limited success in the manufacturing and marketing of new models through 1976.

The Fourth Range

In 1982, a company based in Western Australia obtained the rights to use the Micro Models brand to launch a series of plastic versions of the Holden FJ Panel Van in five different colors. The series was met with only meager interest and the company ceased production shortly afterward.

The Fifth Range

Weico Models Australia took the first stab at reproducing early Micro Models in white metal, in both kit and built form. On their bases were marked the words "Micro Reproductions." When properly assembled and painted, they were indistinguishable from the originals until inspected more closely. Their greater weight and distinguishing inscription then became the obvious give-away of a reproduction.

The Sixth Range

In 1994, after two years of preparation, Micro Models Ltd of Christchurch, New Zealand, unveiled authentic replicas of the original series offered between 1952 and 1958. The reason they could so faithfully reproduce the originals is that the company retained much of the original component dies and tooling, most in good condition, from the first company. These most current Micro Models commemorate those first quality offerings from the Australian manufacturer with new castings from original molds.

The First Range, Australia 1952–1961

Bedford SB Suburban Bus, G-31 ....$95-120

Bedford Tipper Truck, GB-5 ....$140-165
Bedford Tray (Flatbed) Truck, GB-4 ......$140-165
Chrysler Royal Sedan, G-40 ....$160-185
Commer 7-Ton Dump Truck, GB-11 .....$145-165
Commer Articulated Tanker
    Mobilgas, G-27 ....$160-185
    Peters Ice Cream, G-27 ....$160-185
    Shell, G-27 ....$160-185
    Commer Tanker, GB-22 ....$120-145
Ferguson Tractor
    G-26 ....$120-145
    Front End Loader, G-28 ....$120-145
    Ford Customline Sedan 1956, G-34 ..$125-145
Ford Mainline Utility, G-35 ....$125-150
Ford O.H.V. V-8
    Dump Truck, G-37 ....$125-150
    Tray (Flatbed) Truck, G-39 ....$125-150
    Truck, G-29 ....$125-150
    Ford Zephyr Sedan, GB-7 ....$105-130
Holden FC Station Wagon, G-42 ....$125-150
Holden FE
    Coupe Utility with tow hook, G-38...$125-150
    Sedan, G-33 ....$125-150
    Holden FJ
    Police, GB-17 ....$120-145
    Sedan, GB-17 ....$120-145
    Taxi, GB-17 ....$120-145
Holden FJ Panel Van
    PMG (Post Master General), GB-21...$120-145
    Royal Mail, GB-21 ....$120-145
    Taxi Trucks, GB-21 ....$120-145
Holden FX
    Police, GB-9 ....$145-170
    Sedan, GB-9...............................$145-170
    Taxi, GB-9 ....$145-170
    Utility (Pickup) with tow hook, GB-2 ..$125-150
Humber Super Snipe, GB-10 ....$130-155
International
    Ambulance, GB-20 ....$120-145
    Delivery Van, Micro Models,
    GB-8...$145-170
    Delivery Van, Peters Ice Cream,
    GB-8 ....$145-170
    Drink Truck, GB-16 ....$140-165
    Tow Truck, GB-23 ....$120-145
    Jaguar Sports XK120, GB-3 ....$120-145
Large Trailer, GB-19 ....$120-145
MGA Sports Car, G-32 ....$140-165
Mobilgas Petrol Pump, G-30..................$65-80
Morris Fire Engine, GB-13 ....$120-145
Repair Hoist, GB-14 ....$65-80
Semi-Trailer, GB-18 ....$120-145
Small Trailer, GB-6 ....$80-95
Talbot-Lago Racing Car, GB-12 ....$145-170
Vanguard Estate Car, GB-15 ....$120-145
Vauxhall Cresta Sedan 1958, G-41....$125-150

Vauxhall Velox Sedan, GB-1.............$175-200
Vickers Viscount 700 Passenger Airliner, Trans-
    Australia Airlines, GB-24 ....$160-185
Volkswagen Bus, G-36 ....$125-150
Volkswagen Sedan, GB-25 ....$120-145

The Second Range, New Zealand 1956–1960

Bedford S
    Tip Truck, #4307 ....$125-150
    Tray (Flatbed) Truck, #4304 ....$125-150
    Bedford SB Bus, #4336 ....$125-140
Caterpillar Bulldozer, #4354 ....$125-140
Caterpillar Tractor.............................$125-140
Chrysler Royal Sedan, #4353 ....$125-140
Commer 7 Ton Dump Truck, #4314 ...$125-140
Commer Articulated
    Logging Truck, #4342 ....$125-140
    Low Loader, #4341.....................$125-140
    Semi-Trailer, #4316 ....$125-140
    Tanker, Milk Tanker, #4332 ....$125-140
    Tanker, Shell, #4317 ....$125-140
    Commer Tanker, Shell, #4315 ......$125-140
Ferguson Tractor, #4337 ....$125-140
Ford Customline Sedan, #4338..........$125-140
Ford Mainline Utility, #4343 ....$125-140
Ford O.H.V. V8
    Dump Truck, Micro Models,
    #4346 ....$125-140
    Truck, #4347 ....$125-140
    Truck with tilt, #4350 ....$125-140
    Truck, Military with tilt, #4349 ....$125-140
    Ford Zephyr Six Sedan, #4305.....$125-140
Ford Zephyr Zodiak Sedan, #4323 ....$125-140
Garage Repair Hoist, #4313 ....$45-60
Holden FC Station Wagon, #4352 ....$125-140
Holden FE
    Coupe Utility (Matai/Torro product
    only)................................$125-140
    Sedan, #4339 ....$125-140
    Holden FJ Panel Van
    #4320 ....$125-140
    Royal Mail NZPO, #4345 ....$125-140
Holden FX
    Coupe (Utility), #4302 ....$125-140
    Sedan, #4311 ....$125-140
    Sedan Police, #4309 ....$125-140
    Sedan Taxi, #4312 ....$125-140
Humber Super Snipe Sedan
    #4306 ....$125-140
    Traffic, #4331 ....$125-140
International
    Ambulance, #4327......................$125-140
    Ambulance, Military, #4348.........$125-140
    Drink Truck, Coca-Cola, #4351 ....$125-140
    Tow Truck, #4328 ....$125-140

Van, Micro Models, #4333 ....$125-140
Jaguar XK-120, #4303 ....$125-140
Large Trailer, #4321 ....$125-140
Massey Harris Front End Loader,
    #4340 ....$125-140
Massey Harris Tractor, #4322...........$125-140
MGA Sports Car, #4334 ....$125-140
Morris Fire Engine, #4318 ....$125-140
Petrol Pump Set, Mobilgas, #4335 .....$125-140
Small Trailer, #4308 ....$125-140
Standard Vanguard Estate Car, #4319 .$125-140
Talbot-Lago Racing Car, #4310 ....$125-140
Vauxhall Velox Sedan, #4301 ....$125-140
Vicker Viscount Passenger Aircraft, TAA,
    #4329 ....$125-140
Volkswagen Microbus, #4344 ....$125-140
Volkswagen Sedan, #4330 ....$125-140

The Third Range, Matai and Torro, New Zealand, 1970s

Chrysler Royal, G-40 ....$125-140
Ford Customline Sedan, G-34 ....$125-140
Ford Mainline Utility, G-35 ....$125-140
Holden FC Station Wagon, G-42 ....$125-140
Holden FE
    Special Sedan, G-33 ....$125-140
    Utility, G-38 ....$125-140
    International
    Delivery Van, Micro Models logo without
        micrometer, GB-8 ....$125-140
    Drink Truck, GB-16.......................$125-140
    Tow Truck, GB-23 ....$125-140
    MGA Sports Car, G-32...................$125-140
Morris Fire Engine, beacon replaces bell,
    GB-13 ....$125-140
Vanguard Estate Car, GB-15 ....$125-140
Vauxhall Cresta, G-41 ....$125-140
Volkswagen Sedan, GB-25 ....$125-140

The Fourth Range, Micromodels in Plastic, 1982–1983

Holden FJ Panel Van
    Corlett Brothers "Sunglow" Bread Products,
        gray.................................$45-60
    Corlett Brothers Belmont Bakers, blue...$45-60
    Corlett Brothers Bakers, green.............$45-60
    Kodak, yellow $60-70
    Watsonia, red $40-55

The Fifth Range, Micro Reproductions in White Metal, 1980s

Bedford SB Suburban Bus (G-31)...........$90-110
Chrysler Royal Sedan (G-40), #8 ....$90-110
Ford Customline Sedan 1956 (G-34),
    #4....................................$90-110
Ford Mainline Utility (G-35), #7.............$90-110

Holden FC
    Panel Van (never issued in the original
        Micro Models range), #11 ....$90-110
    Station Wagon (G-42), #6 ....$90-110
Holden FE
    Coupe Utility with tow hook (G-38),
        #14................................$90-110
    Sedan (G-33), #9 ....$90-110
Holden FJ
    Panel Van (GB-21), #5 ....$90-110
    Sedan (GB-17), #2 ....$90-110
Holden FX
    Sedan (GB-9), #1 ....$90-110
    Utility (Pickup) with tow hook (GB-2),
        #3 ....$90-110
    Humber Super Snipe (GB-10),
        #10................................$90-110
Vanguard Estate Car (GB-15), #19 ....$90-110
Vauxhall Cresta Sedan 1958 (G-41),
    #12....................................$90-110
Vauxhall Velox Sedan (GB-1), #18 ....$90-110
Volkswagen Bus (G-36), #13 ....$90-110
Volkswagen Sedan (GB-25), #20 ....$90-110

The Sixth & Present Range, 1994–Present

Bedford SB Bus, 1:55
    English Bus, 2,000 produced,
        MM523................................$35-50
    Micro Bus Lines, 2,000 produced,
        MM411................................$35-50
    Micro Bus Lines, red, 900 produced,
        MM508................................$35-50
    Micro Bus Lines, blue, 900 produced,
        MM508................................$35-50

Micro Bus Lines, green, 900 produced, MM508 ....$35-50

    no production #s, MM025 ....$35-50
    no production #s, MM025 ....$35-50
    NZ Road Services MM608 ....$35-50
Brentware Petrol Tanker, 1:43, no prod #s,
    MM802 ....$35-50
Chrysler Royal Sedan, 1:43, Australia Police,
    2,000 produced, MM522 ....$30-45
Ford Bottle Truck, 1:64, Coca Cola,
    MC005 ....$45-60
Ford Customline Sedan, 1:43

two-tone green with window glazing, 950
    produced, MM605 ....$45-60

pale blue and white, Victoria Police, 950 produced, MM514......................$40-55

black with window glazing, 1956 Springbok Tour of New Zealand, 1250 produced, MM701 ....$35-50
1956 All Black Springbok, MP701 ....$30-45
Ford Mainline Ute, 1:43
    1953 All Blacks, no prod #s, MP804 ..$45-60
    1953 English Tour, no prod #s,
        MM804................................$30-45

Dept of Civil Aviation, pale mustard, 395 produced, MM011......................$30-45

Micro Models, maroon, 2,000 produced, MM408 ....$30-45
Micro Models, no production #s,
    MM024 ....$30-45
    Newspaper Delivery, 2,000 produced,
        MM520................................$30-45
Ford OHV F6 Truck, 1:43
    NZ Kiwi Team, no prod #s,
        MP805 ....$35-50

HZ Army, 950 produced, MM509........$30-45
Micro Models "bigger and better," out of prod, MM601 ....$30-45
Ford Zephyr Mark 1 Sedan, 1:43
  1950 All Blacks, no prod #s, MP803 ..$35-50
  Australia Police SA, 395 produced,
    MM022 ....$30-45
  New Zealand MOT, 2,000 produced,
    MM521 ....$30-45

NZ Transport Department, black, 850 produced, MM515 ....$30-45

NZPO Regional Engineer, gray, 395 produced MM013 ....$30-45

Queensland Police, 2,000 produced, MM409 ....$30-45
Holden FC

Special Wagon, 1:43, red and white, 950 produced, MM607 ....$40-55

Station Sedan, 1:43, gray, 850 produced, MM516 ....$30-45

  Adelaide Mega Swap Meet `98,
    MP801 ....$35-50
Holden FE

Sedan, 1:43, SA Police Traffic Division Highway Patrol, light blue, 875 produced, MM506 ....$30-45

Sedan, red & white, 950 produced, MM604 ....$45-60
  Utility, 1:43, New South Wales Dept. of Works,
    395 produced, MM020 ....$50-65

Utility, 1:43, New South Wales Public Works, yellow, 2,000 produced, MM403 ....$30-45

Utility, 1:43, Tasmania Police Force, 875 produced, MM511 ....$45-60

Utility, 1:43, "Mega" Toy Swapmeet `97, 400 produced, MP702 ....$45-60
Holden FJ Panel Van, 1:43
  Australia Mail, 350 produced, MM005 ..$30-45

New Zealand Royal Mail, gold ensignia, 2,000 produced, MM404 ....$30-45

New Zealand Royal Mail, black and white ensignia, 2,000 produced, MM410 .....$30-45
  plastic, 1:43 MM804 ....$35-50

"Mega" Toy Swapmeet Adelaide `96, 400 produced, MP601 ....$45-60

  Briggs & Stratton, no prod #s, MP802 ....$35-50
  Coca Cola, MC503 ....$45-60
  Coca Cola, plastic, red, no prod #s, MC004 ..$30

Lea & Perrin Worcestershire Sauce, 850 produced, MP602 ....$50-65

NZ Royal Mail, red, MP502 ....$30-45
Sydney Model Auto Club, 250
produced, MP703 ....$30-45
New Zealand Mail, 395 produced,
MM017..................................$45-60

New Zealand Model Vehicle Club, Inc., 25th Jubilee, Dunedin, January 1994, light blue, 279 produced, MM003 ....$50-65

New Zealand Transport Department, white "Traffic" sign on roof, 375 produced, MM008..................................$30-45

Holden FJ Special Sedan, 1:43
Australia Fire Control NSW, 395
produced, MM014 ....$30-45
Australia Police NT, 395 produced,
MM018..................................$30-45

Forrestville Toy Fair Aug '97, pale green, no prod #, MP703..............................$35-50

Gray Cabs, light brown, 2,000 produced,
MM605 ....$30-45

Grey Cabs, Sahara tan, 950 produced, MM601 ....$30-45

New South Wales Fire Control, 2,000 produced, MM402..................................$30-45

NZ Police, 375 produced, MM004 ..$30-45
Taxi, 395 produced, MM029 ....$30-45
twotone gray, 395 produced, MM02 ...$30-45

Wellington Taxis, black, 2000 produced, MM505 ....$30-45

Holden FX Sedan, 1:43

Australia Police Victoria, 395 produced, MM026 ....$30-45

cream, 395 produced, MM016 ....$30-45
gold plated, no prod #s, MM805 .....$55-70

light green, 950 produced, MM512 ....$40-55

light green, 2,000 produced, MM517...$30-45
Taxi, 1:43, 350 produced, MM006 ....$50-65
Traffic Patrol, white, 2000 produced,
MM405..................................$30-45
Victoria Police, 375 produced, MM012....$30-45
Holden FX Utility, 1:43

Security, MP401....................$35-50

MSS Security, cream, no prod #s, MP501 ....$35-50

NZAA, yellow with black cargo cover, 950 produced, MM606..................................$40-55

The Press, blue, 2,000 produced, MM503 ..$30-45
International, 1:64
Bottle Truck, Coca Cola, MC003 ....$30

Breakdown Truck, New Zealand AA, yellow, 600 produced, MM702............$30-45

Breakdown Truck, Parks 24 Hr. Towing, red, 600 produced, MM703................$35-50

Delivery Van, Anchor Icy Cold Milk, cream, no prod #s, MM510 ....$30-45

Delivery Van, Micro Models "better than ever," 2,000 produced, MM501 ....$30-45

Delivery Van, Micro Models "better than ever," no prod #s, MM027 ....$50-65

Delivery Van, Micro Models "we're back," maroon, no prod #s, MM001 ....$30-45

Delivery Van, "New Zealand Model Vehicle Club, Inc. 25th Jubilee, January 1994, Dunedin," dark blue, 120 produced, MM002 ....$50-65

Delivery Van, Peter's Ice Cream, 385 produced, MM009 ....$50-65

Truck, Coca Cola, MC001 ....$45-60
Jaguar XK120, 1:43

dark green, 2,000 produced, MM407..$30-45
silver, 2,000 produced, MM519 ......$30-45

silver, 950 produced, MM602 ....$45-60
white, no production #s, MM015 ......$30-45
gold plated, no prod #s, MM806 .....$55-70
MGA Roadster, 1:43

yellow, Canterbury University Christchurch 1995, 600 produced, MP503 ....$40-55

dark blue, 2,000 produced, MM602 .$30-45

light blue, 850 produced, MM513 ....$40-55
no prod #s, MM028 ....$30-45
red, 2,000 produced, MM502 ....$30-45

Morris Fire Engine, 1:43, 1450 produced, MM507 ....$30-45

Petrol Bowser, 1:43, no prod #s, MM803 ....$35-50

Vanguard Estate Van, 1:43

cream, 950 produced, MM603 ....$30-45

Lea & Perrin Worcestershire Sauce, MP603 ....$30-45

Vauxhall Cresta PA, 1:43, mountain rose, 1500 produced, MM701 ....$30-45

Vauxhall Velox, 1:43, magenta, no prod #s, MM701 ....$30-45

Vauxhall Wyvern Sedan, 1:43, black with silver trim, 1,500 produced, MM609 ....$30-45

Vickers Viscount Passenger Jet, TAA, 2,000 produced, MM603 ....$30-45
Volkswagen Beetle, 1:43
  green, no prod #s, MM704 ....$30-45
  maroon, no prod #s, MM801 ....$30-45
Volkswagen Coca Cola Van, 1:43, MC002 ....$40-55
Volkswagen Microbus, 1:43
  Ambulance, cream, 1,250 produced, MM504 ....$30-45
  Ambulance, 395 produced, MM023 ....$30-45
  Australia Police New Zealand, 2,000 produced, MM604 ....$30-45
  Fire Communications,, 2,000 produced, MM518 ....$30-45
  light blue, 950 produced, MM406 ....$30-45
  pale blue, no production #s, MM019 ..$30-45

Micromodels (see Deoma)

Micro Pet

These Japanese models were manufactured by Taiseiya of Tokyo primarily for the Asian market in the 1960s. They are rare in the US since they are long obsolete, relatively unknown, and never marketed in the US. Of all the models offered, only a few were American cars; the large majority were Japanese models.

Chevrolet Impala, #9
    blue and white $140-165
    chrome-plated.............................$190-215
Chevrolet Impala Police car, #10
    black and white............................$140-165
Datsun Bluebird, #2
    red and gray................................$115-140
    chrome-plated.............................$165-190
Datsun Bluebird Station Wagon, #17
    blue and white $115-140
    yellow and brown.........................$115-140
    chrome-plated.............................$140-165
Delahaye, 1901 ....$115-140
Ford Falcon, #12
    red and black................................$140-165
    two-tone green $140-165
Ford Falcon Police car, #16
    black and white............................$140-165
Hillman Minx, #15
    red $115-140
    blue and white $115-140
    blue and cream $115-140
Isuzu Bellel 2000 Saloon, #19
    green and white $115-140
Mazda Coupe R 360, #7
    white and red, or orange and gray ..$115-140
    chrome-plated.............................$165-190
Nissan Cedric, #5
    blue, pink, or copper and gray $115-140
    chrome-plated.............................$165-190
Nissan Light Truck, #18
    brown and green.........................$115-140
    blue and gray $115-140
Peugeot
    top down, 1896 ....$115-140
    top up, 1896 ....$115-140
Prince Bus, #14
    pink, white and blue
    red and white...............................$165-190
    chrome-plated.............................$190-215
Prince Skyline, #6
    copper and gray or blue and gray...$115-140
    chrome-plated.............................$165-190
Prince Skyway Station Wagon, #11
    pink and gray...............................$115-140
    red, yellow and white..................$115-140
Subaru 360, #1

    blue and copper $115-140
Toyota Corona Station Wagon, #8
    green and gray, or orange and
    cream $115-140
    chrome-plated.............................$165-190

Microtoys (see Deoma Micromodels)

Midgetoy

Midgetoy Incorporated
Attn: Jeff Lee
7219 Pioneers Blvd. #809
Lincoln, Nebraska 68506
e-mail: MidgetoyInc@onebox.com
phone: 312-777-4000 ext.
3296–voicemail/fax

The post-war goal of brothers Alvin and Earl Herdklotz was "to produce low-cost diecast vehicles both sturdy and precisely detailed." Their goals mirrored those of the Tootsietoy firm after World War II, and their Midgetoy models are of similar construction, that being generally a single cast pot metal body with no chassis. From 1946 to 1984, Midgetoys were produced in various sizes and available at many discount retail outlets. Thousands, or at least hundreds, of different models were issued. It would be interesting to see a book devoted especially to these proliferous toys. Typical values are from $10 to $15 each.

Around 1985, the Herdklotz brothers sold the business to a group of investors who did nothing with the factory for several years. Ultimately they bought it back and have been selling off existing stock for the last fifteen years. The machinery has gone into disrepair and current inventory is dwindling as they patiently seek just the right buyer for the company. They don't seem to be in much of a hurry.

In 2003, Jeff Lee, nephew of the Herdklotz brothers, assumed the role of sales agent for the remaining inventory. Contact information is listed above.

A website has been created at www.midgetoy.com to chronicle the company and its distinctive toys.

American LaFrance
    Fire Truck, 2" Pee-Wee Series, 1969 ......$2-4
    Pumper, open cab, 2½" to 3½" Junior Series,
      late 1950s..................................$11-14
    Pumper, closed cab, 2½" to 3½" Junior
      Series, early 1950s...................$13-16
    Pumper, rubber tires, 4" King-Size Series,
      early 1950s..............................$21-24

    Pumper, rubber tires, 6" Jumbo Series ..$26-29
Army
    Ambulance, circa 1950s, 3⅞" $12-16
    Amphibious Vehicle, rubber tires, 2½" to
      3½" Junior Series, 1949 ....$21-24
    Halftrack, rubber tires, 4" King-Size Series,
      late 1950s..................................$18-21
    Howitzer, rubber tires, 2½" to 3½" Junior
      Series, 1949.........................$9-11
    Howitzer, plastic tires, 2½" to 3½" Junior
      Series, 1950s..........................$6-8
    Jeep, rubber tires, 2½" to 3½" Junior Series,
      late 1950s.................................$9-11
    Personnel carrier, rubber tires, 4"
      King-Size Series, late 1950s........$18-21
    Tank, rubber tires, 4" King-Size Series....$18-21
    Truck, circa 1950s, 4½" $12-16
    Truck & Cannon, circa 1950s, 4½" &
      3¼" $27-32
Cadillac
    2-door Coupe, rubber tires, 4" King-Size
      Series, early 1950s....................$22-25
    4-door Convertible, rubber tires, 6" Jumbo
      Series $24-27
    4-door Sedan, Military, 4" King-Size
      Series $16-19
    4-door Sedan, rubber tires, 4" King-Size
      Series $18-21
    Ambulance, 2½" to 3" New Junior Series,
      1971 ....$10-12
    Convertible, rubber tires, 2½" to 3½" Junior
      Series, 1949.............................$16-19
Camping Trailer, purple, circa 1950s, 2⅜"....$4-6
Convertible, blue, circa 1950s, 5⅜".........$19-24
Chevrolet
    Chevy-style Dragster, 2" Pee-Wee Series,
      1969 ....$2-4
    Corvette 1968 L88 Stingray, 2½" to 3" New
      Junior Series, 1971 ....$3-5
    Corvette Convertible, rubber tires, 2⅞", Junior
      Series, late 1950s $11-14
    Corvette Convertible Dragster, green, 2" Pee-
      Wee Series, 1969.......................$2-4
    Dump Truck, 2½" to 3½" Junior Series,
      1946...................................$22-26
    El Camino, red, circa 1970s, 3" $2-4
    Oil Truck, 2½" to 3½" Junior Series,
      1946...................................$22-26
    Stake Truck, 2½" to 3½" Junior Series,
      1946...................................$22-26
Chrysler-style Convertible Roadster, rubber tires,
    4" King-Size Series $21-24
Drag Racer, 2" Pee-Wee Series, 1969.........$2-4
Ford
    C600 Oil Truck, 1956, 4"...............$15-20
    Dragster, 2" Pee-Wee Series, 1969........$2-4

GT, 2" Pee-Wee Series, 1969..............$2-4
Hot Rod, rubber tires, 2½", Junior Series, 1950s $11-14
Mark IV, 2½" to 3" New Junior Series, 1971 ....$4-6
Mustang, 2½" to 3" New Junior Series, 1971 ....$2-4
Oil Tanker, "Midgetoy Oil Co.," rubber tires, 6" Jumbo Series, 1957 ....$24-27
Pickup Truck, 2½" to 3" New Junior Series, 1971 ....$2-4
Pickup Truck, rubber tires, 4" King-Size Series, early 1950s.............................$21-24
Torino, 2½" to 3" New Junior Series, 1971 ....$2-4
Torino Fire Chief, 2½" to 3" New Junior Series, 1971 ....$2-4
Torino Police, 2½" to 3" New Junior Series, 1971 ....$2-4
V-8 Hot Rod, rubber tires, 3", Junior Series, 1948.......................................$21-24
V-8 Hot Rod, plastic tires, 2½" to 3½" Junior Series, 1950s $11-14
Wrecker, rubber tires, 2½" to 3½" Junior Series, late 1950s...............................$11-14
Wrecker, 2½" to 3" New Junior Series, 1971 ....$2-4
Indy-Style Race car, silver, circa 1950s, 3"....$17-20
Jaguar XKE, 2½" to 3" New Junior Series, 1971 ....$2-4
Jeep, red, 2" Pee-Wee Series, 1969............$1-3
MG Roadster
green, 2" Pee-Wee Series, 1969 ....$2-4
rubber tires, 2½" to 3½" Junior Series, 1958.......................................$12-15

Midget Racer, 1½" $6-10

Military Jeep, circa 1950s, 1¾"...................$5-7
Mobile Artillery, rubber tires, 6" Jumbo Series, 1957 ....$24-27
Oil Tanker
Military, rubber tires, 4" King-Size Series, late 1950s $19-22
rubber tires, 4" King-Size Series, late 1950s $22-25
Open Cockpit Curtis Craft Racer, 2½" to 3½" Junior Series, 1950.........................$21-24
Open Cockpit Roadster, 2" Pee-Wee Series, 1969...$2-4
Pickup Jeep, blue, circa 1950s, 5¾".........$19-24
Porsche Convertible Dragster, 2" Pee-Wee Series, 1969..$2-4
Rear-Engine car
no rear window, rubber tires, 2½" to 3½" Junior Series, 1948 ....$11-14
outlined rear window, plastic tires, 2½" to 3½" Junior Series, 1950s $32-36
Scenicruiser Bus
"Midgetoy Bus Line," rubber tires, 6" Jumbo Series.......................................$24-27
rubber tires, 2½" to 3½" Junior Series, 1955......................................$13-16
Spaceship
open front window, two plastic tires, 2½" to 3½" Junior Series, 1950s $21-24
open front window, two rubber tires, 2½" to 3½" Junior Series, 1950s $45-55
no front window, two rubber tires, 2½" to 3½" Junior Series, 1950s $40-50
no front window, three rubber tires, 2½" to 3½" Junior Series, 1950s $55-65
Sunbeam Racer
plastic tires, 2½" to 3½" Junior Series, 1950s $17-20
rubber tires, 2½" to 3½" Junior Series, 1950.....................................$21-24
Utility Truck, rubber tires, 6" Jumbo Series...$24-27
Van
Ambulance, rubber tires,, 4" King-Size Series, late 1950s...............................$13-16
Red Cross Ambulance, rubber tires, 4" King-Size Series, late 1950s........$17-20
with open side windows, rubber tires, 4" King-Size Series, late 1950s........$17-20
Volkswagen Beetle, plastic tires, 2½" to 3½" Junior Series, 1960..........................$13-16

Midget Toys

Midget Toys, produced in France for just one year in 1959, are not to be confused with Midgetoys of the United States.

3-Axle Semi-Trailer, 1:86........................$45-50
Citroën DS19, 1:86..............................$45-50
Crane Truck, #14, 1:86..........................$45-50
Farm Tractor, #4, 1:86..........................$45-50
Flat Truck, #1, 1:86 ....$45-50
Jaguar D-Type, 1:86.............................$45-50
Lumber Semi-Trailer Truck, #2, 1:86.........$45-50
Open Semi-Trailer Truck, #5, 1:86 ....$45-50
Panhard Dyna Convertible, #6, 1:86 ......$45-50
Quarry Dump Truck, #3, 1:86.................$45-50
Transformer Semi-Trailer, 1:86................$45-50
Vanwall Formula 1, 1:86 ....$45-50
Vespa 400 Mini-Car
1:43...$75-90
1:86...$45-50

Midwestern Home Products, Inc.

Midwestern Home Products, Inc.
Wilmington, DE 19803

"Generic, crude, yet charming" best describes models marketed by Midwestern Home Products, Inc., of Wilmington, Delaware, not a manufacturer, but a marketer of repackaged toys.

A set of three 4" fire engines made in China, while poorly cast, possess that ineffable charm that makes them attractive novelty items, although relatively worthless as collectibles. At $1 apiece, their crude castings with sharp edges make them unsuitable for children and are better left in their original blisterpack. Once removed, they are no longer distinguishable as Midwestern brand toys.

Two of the three fire engines were found to have a logo embossed into the base that resembles a cluster of pine trees with a leaping deer, the whole of which is surrounded by a double circle, with the cryptic letters "SM" at the bottom of the circle. It was later determined that the symbol is the trademark for Summer Manufacturing, a brand of inexpensive, generic toys from Asia.

Ladder truck, #8114.................................$1-2
Closed-cab pumper/turret, #8115 ....$1-2
Open-cab pumper truck, #8116 ....$1-2

Mid-West Metal Novelty Manufacturing Company

In 1923, C. E. Stevenson started making slush mold toys in his home. Within two years, he connected with Western Diecasting of Clay Center, Kansas. Soon after he arranged to make molds for the other two toy makers in the area, C. A. W. Novelty Company and Kansas Toy and Novelty Company. By 1931, Stevenson moved on to begin Lincoln White Metal Works from Lincoln, Nebraska. The problem in identifying many of these models is a lack of a maker's mark. Many Mid-West models looked just like their Tootsietoy counterparts. The distinction is in the wheel design, a sleek metal disk, often painted, often with detailed lugnut design.

Buick Coupe, 3"...................................$45-60
Buick Roadster, 3⅝"...............................$60-85
Buick Sedan, 3$^{1}/_{16}$" $60-85
Bus, Overland, 3½"................................$40-65
Bus, Yellow Coach, 3¾"...........................$35-55
Coupe, 3½" $60-85

Ford Model A Sedan 2-door, 2¾" $60-85
Ford Model T Touring car $35-55
Mack AC Roadster, 3⅜" $60-85
Mack AC Truck, 3¼" $60-85
Midget Racer with driver, 2¾" $40-65
Packard Roadster, 3⅜" $60-85
Racer with driver, 3⅜" $60-85
Touring car, top up, 3⅛" $40-55
Town car with chauffeur, 3⅜" $85-110
Yellow Taxi Cab, 2¾" $60-85

Mignon

Mignon is a series of 1:24 scale diecast motorcycles and two go-karts manufactured in Italy for a few years in the early 1960s. Their downfall was unfortunately due to the lack of interest in collecting motorcycle miniatures at the time. Interest is now on the increase, due in part to the rising popularity and number of Harley-Davidson collectibles hitting the market nowadays.

Aermacchi a la Verde 350cc, #112 ....$30-45
Aermacchi Chimera 250, #19, 3¼" $30-45
BMW R-26 250cc, #104, 3¾" $30-45
Gilera Extra Rosso 175, #15, 3¼" $30-45
Gilera G.T. 175, #17, 3¼" $30-45
Go Kart "900," 2¾" $30-45
Go Kart Baby, 3" $30-45
Guzzi Falcone 500, #110, 4⅜" $30-45
Guzzi Lodola 175, #11, 3¼" $30-45
Guzzi Zigolo 110, #13, 3¼" $30-45
Harley-Davidson 1200, #102, 3⅜" $30-45
Honda CS-92 Sport, #108, 3½" $30-45
Viberti 3-Wheel Vivi, #21, 3⅜" $30-45

Mignot, C.B.G.

Lilliput Motor Company, Ltd., offers this informative history of the obscure C.B.G. Mignot brand of quality toys: "Since the company's founding in 1785 by Mr. Lucotte, considered to be the inventor of the "ronde bosse" (three dimensional) technique of casting toy soldiers and figures, C.B.G. Mignot's manufacturing methods have remained unchanged. They continue to employ the same bronze molds, later sculptured in tempered steel, some of which are more than a century old. The artisans fill the molds with a proprietary alloy consisting of lead, tin, antimony, and other alloys. After air-cooling, the molds are carefully removed, the castings are individually de-burred. Then, the separate parts are soldered together. Then, the fully assembled figure gets hand painted and finished. Finally, the groups of figures are put together into the matching diorama boxes,

which are wonderful works of art in their own right!"

As pictured in Lilliput's Catalog #16 from September 1997, several sets are available. The Bugatti set depicts a Bugatti Type 35 in the pits at Le Mans, and features a gas pump, driver, and milestone. The Tour de France set features an old Peugeot 203 Convertible with driver and cameraman leading four bicyclists across the finish line.

The Citroën In Jungle set is a fabulous two-tier scene with two Citroën vehicles, explorers, natives, flora, and fauna. The Madagascar Expedition set is even more spectacular, with three tiers. The top tier features a mighty steamer ship with smaller vessels surrounding it. The middle tier features a landing party disembarking from a dinghy to meet some sophisticated-looking natives. The bottom tier features several British sailors encountering more natives. (The sailors don't look very friendly.) All three levels are enhanced by scenic backgrounds of sea and jungle.

Bugatti, LPCBG3, 10" x 5¾" x 5½" $165-200
Citroën in Jungle, LPCBG1, 12" x 2" x 9" .$425-460
Madagascar Expedition, LPCBG8, 18½" x
     14½" x 3½" $1,000-1,050
Tour de France, LPCBG9, 10" x 5¾" x 5½" ..$200-235

Mikansue

Mikansue models are 1:43 scale white metal kits produced and marketed by Mike and Sue Richardson of England. By the numbers, it would appear that their product line represented nearly a hundred different models. Besides these European cars, Mikansue also represents a line of US automobiles in their Americana series.

Thanks to the contributions of Dario "Dino" Vidovic via e-mail, this list is now much more complete.

Mikansue Series

AC 16/70 Supercharged 1936, #16 ...$110-125
Austin Healey Sprite 1958, #2 ....$110-125
Austin Ruby 7 1935, #14 ....$110-125
Ford 100E Anglia Popular 1954/1961,
     #25 ....$110-125
Ford Cortina 1600E Saloon 1967-68,
     #34 ....$110-125
H.R.G 1500 1948, #8 ....$110-125
Healey Elliott Saloon 1950, #18 ....$110-125
Jowett R4 Jupiter Sports 1954, #24 .....$110-125
Morris 8 Series E Saloon 1948, #27 ...$110-125
Morris Minor 1000 Traveller Break 1965,
     #35 ....$110-125

Morris Minor 1000 Pickup 1965, #37 ...$110-125
Morris Minor 1000 van 1965, #38 ...$110-125
Morris Mosquito Saloon 1943, #29 ...$110-125
Riley 1.5 l Saloon 1964, #28 ....$110-125
Riley 1,5 l RME Saloon 1954-55, #33 ...$110-125
Riley Monaco Saloon 1934, #31 ....$110-125
Rover 100 P4 Saloon 1960, #32 ......$110-125
Squire 1.5 l supercharged 1935, #13 ...$110-125
Triumph Dolomite roadster 1938, #30 ...$110-125
Triumph Mayflower Saloon 1952,
     #26 ....$110-125
Triumph TR 2 TR3 Sports 1954-57,
     #39 ....$110-125
Triumph Vitesse 1969, #36 ....$110-125
TVR 3 l Coupe 1978, #22 ....$110-125
Wolseley Hornet Swallow 1933, #12 ..$110-125

Mikansue Competition Series

Adler Le Mans 1936, #22 ....$110-125
Aero Minor LM 1949/50, #41 ....$110-125
Allard J2R Le Mans 1953, #15 ....$110-125
Aston Martin Spa 1948, #19 ....$110-125
Arnolt-Climax 1957, #31 ....$110-125
Austin Healey Record Car 1954, #26 ....$110-125
Austin Healey Sprite Mk 2 Rallye, #24 .....$110-125
Austin Healey Sprite Record Car 1959,
     #51 ....$110-125
ATS F1 1978, #20 ....$110-125
Brabham BT37 F1 1972, #17 ....$110-125
BRM V16 F1 Mark 1 1950, #67 ......$110-125
Climax Sport LM 1955, #65 ....$110-125
Connaught L-Type Sports 1949, #60 ..$110-125
Cooper Bristol 1953, #40 ....$110-125
Cooper Jaguar Sports P. Whitehead 1954,
     #58 ....$110-125
Cosworth 4WD F1 Prototype 1969,
     #49 ....$110-125
Cunningham Ferrari 375 LM 1954,
     #68 ....$110-125
Dellow 2-Seater 1951, #4 ....$110-125
ERA G-Type F2 1952 Stirling Moss,
     #66 ....$110-125
Fiat 128 Imola 1976, #12 ....$110-125
Frazer Nash Le Mans Coupe 1953,
     #18 ....$110-125
Healey Westland tourer Mille Miglia 1948,
     #64 ....$110-125
Jaguar Alta 1952, #1 ....$110-125
Jaguar Lister Coupe Le Mans 1963,
     #63 ....$110-125
Lancia Ferrari 1956 French Grand Prix,
     #30 ....$110-125
Lotus XI Coupe 1957, #47 ....$110-125
Lotus XV Sports LM 1959, #62 ....$110-125
March 751 F1 Lavazza, #102 ....$110-125
Martini F1 1978, #23 ....$110-125

MG EX-181 Record Car, #38 ....$110-125
MG TC Special LM 1949, #69 ....$110-125
MGA LM1960 Special Coupe, #61 ..$110-125
MGB Le Mans 1964, #33 ....$110-125
Morgan Le Mans 1939, #14 ....$110-125
OSCA 750 Spyder LM 1958, #57 ....$110-125
Shadow DN 3 F1 1974, #25 ....$110-125
Sigma Le Mans 1975, #9 ....$110-125
Simca 570 ccm Sports LM 1939,
   #56 ....$110-125
Tojeiro Climax LM 1962, #35 ....$110-125
Vanwall F1 1961, #50 ....$110-125
Vanwall F1 Special 2l 1954, #48 ......$110-125
Vanwall Lightweight F1 Front Engine 1960,
   #59 ....$110-125

Mikansue Americana Series

American Bantam Roadster 1938,
   #15 ....$110-125
Austin Nash Metropolitan 1954, #10 ..$110-125
Chevrolet Styleline 1950, #13 ....$110-125
Kaiser Henry J Sedan 1952, #16 ....$110-125
Kaiser Manhattan Sedan 1953, #19 ...$110-125
Kurtis 500 Roadster 1953, #9 ....$110-125
La Salle Saloon 1940, #5 ....$110-125
Muntz Jet Roadster 1954, #11 ....$110-125
Nash Healey Le Mans Coupe 1953,
   #18 ....$110-125
Plymouth PA4 Coupe 1931, #7 ....$110-125
Studebaker Starlight Coupe 1950,
   #12 ....$110-125
Studebaker Starlight Coupe 1953,
   #17 ....$110-125
Willys 77 Sedan 1938, #14 ....$110-125

Milano

Italy is the assumed home of Milano models, apparently a different manufacturer than Milano 43.

1897 Gauthier Wehrle $24-29

Milano 43

Harvey Goranson reports, "These are resin hand built Ferrari racing cars, typically obscure ones from little known races or also-rans. Very nice. Last list I saw was in a May, 1992 issue of TSSK [?], where the numbers went up to 43. (Coincidence?)" No model list has yet been provided.

Milestone Development Corporation

Milestone Development Corporation has produced a few NHRA models under the Milestones brand, sold exclusively through Promotorsports Collectibles (PMC). No other information is known about the brand or the company. In November 2003, PMC's website at www.promotorsports.com listed four models:

Milestones item #DSR360 Gary Scelzi NHRA Dodge Dealers Nitro Funny car — a special production by Schumacher Racing made by Milestones and sold exclusively through PMC Collectibles and the Gary Scelzi Racing Teams and sponsors.
Scale: 1:16
Release date: Nov/Dec 2003
Production: 2,600
Price: $190

Milestones # DSR361 Whit Bazemore Team Mopar Nitro Funny car — a special production by Schumacher Racing made by Milestones and sold exclusively by PMC Collectibles and the Whit Bazemore Racing Team and sponsors.
Scale: 1:16
Release date: Nov/Dec 2003
Production: 2,600
Price: $190

Milestones item #DSR362 Tony Schumacher ARMY Top Fuel Dragster—a special production by Schumacher Racing made by Milestones sold exclusively through PMC Collectibles and the Tony Schumacher Racing Teams and sponsors.
Scale: 1:16
Release date: Nov/Dec 2003
Price: $190

Milestones #DSR363 Tony Schumacher Camelflouge Special paint scheme top fuel dragster—a special production by Schumacher Racing made by Milestones and sold exclusively through PMC Collectibles and the Tony Schumacher Racing Teams and sponsors.
Scale: 1:16
Release date: Nov/Dec 2003
Price: $190

Milestone Miniatures

Milestone Miniatures Limited
25 West End
Redruth
Cornwall
TR15 2SA
England
telephone: +044 01209 218356
fax: (+044) 01209 217983
e-mail: info@modelcars.co.uk
web: www.modelcars.co.uk

Milestone Miniatures of Cornwall, England, manufactures a variety of precision 1:43 scale models.

Milestone Miniatures – The Milestone Series

1966 Alvis TF21 Coupe $70-85
1946 Scammell Show Tracs...............$260-275
1954 Riley Pathfinder $80-95
1952 Ford Zephyr Convertible................$80-95
1935 Ford Model Y Fordor Saloon $90-105
1935 Ford Model Y Tudor Saloon $90-105
1963 Austin A60 Van $70-85
1960 Austin A60 Pickup $75-90
1927 Austin SS Swallow Saloon...........$90-105
1927 Austin SS Swallow 2 Seat $90-105
1930 Austin Ulster................................$75-90
1964 Humber Super Snipe Series 5 ....$80-95

Milestone Miniatures – The Jaguar Collection

1927 Austin Swallow $90-105
1955 Jaguar Mk 1, maroon or British racing
   green $80-95
1959 Jaguar Mk 2 Staffordshire Police.....$80-95
1948 Jaguar Mk 5..............................$80-95
1956 Jaguar Mk 7M $75-90
1957 Jaguar Mk 8 ....$85-100
1959 Jaguar Mk 9 Saloon....................$85-100
1958 Jaguar Mk IX Hearse $80-95
1961 Jaguar Mk 10 ....$75-90
1972 Jaguar V12 E Type, white or silver ..$80-95
1961 Jaguar E Type Coupe, red, blue, white
   or silver $80-95
1966 Jaguar 420G, two-tone brown and
   cream $85-100
1969 Jaguar XJ6 ....$75-90
1972 Jaguar XJ12 ....$75-90
1972 Jaguar XJ12 Silverstone Fire car,
   bright red $85-100
1948 Jaguar XK120 ....$80-95
1958 Jaguar XK150 ....$80-95
1967 Jaguar S Type.............................$80-95
1935 Jaguar SS Airline $85-100
1936 Jaguar SS1 ....$80-95
1936 Jaguar SS100 Coupe $80-95
1936 Jaguar SS100 Tourer....................$80-95
1984 Jaguar XJR5 Quaker State
   (Le Mans Series) $90-105
1984 Jaguar XJS $85-100
1996 Jaguar XJR Silverstone Fire car......$85-100
1996 Jaguar XK8 ....$80-95
1998 Jaguar XKR $90-105
MILESTONE Chequered Flag Series
1936 Jaguar SS 100 Alpine Cup Winner...$90-105
1939 Jaguar SS 100 Shelsley Walsh Twin
   Rear.......................................$85-100

1950 Jaguar XK 120 Tourist Trophy Winner $85-100
1953 Jaguar C Type Winner Le Mans ...$85-100
1955 Jaguar MK VII M Silverstone Hawthorn $85-100
1957 Jaguar D Type Winner Le Mans ...$90-105

Milestone Jaguar Jubilee Series
1972 Jaguar V12 E Type H/Top $75-90
1957 Jaguar XK 150S Roadster $80-95
1967 Jaguar XJ 13 ....$80-95
1994 Jaguar XJR $80-95
1960 Jaguar Mk 2 Monza Record Car $80-95
1951 Jaguar C Type Le Mans Winner $80-95
1968 Jaguar XJ6 Launch car $75-90
1947 Jaguar XK120 Jabbeke Record Car .$75-90
1938 Jaguar SS 100 "Old No 8" $80-95
1938 Jaguar 2.5 Litre $75-90
1937 Jaguar 2.5 Litre Lady Lyons car $80-95

Milestone Jaguar World Series
1957 Jaguar Mk 8 Saloon $85-100
1956 Jaguar Mk 7 Monte Carlo Rally Win $85-100
1927 Austin Swallow Saloon 1927 ......$90-105
1927 Austin Swallow 2 Seat 1927 ......$90-105

Milestone Miniatures – The Spirit of Brooklands
1930 Austin Ulster $75-90
1932 Birkin Bentley $90-105
1925 Fiat Mephistopheles $90-105
1934 MG K3 Magnette $75-90
1935 Napier-Railton $95-110
1936 MG NA Bellevue Special $75-90
1934 Morgan Jap Relay car $75-90
1935 Frazer Nash £48 ....$75-90
1930 Brooklands Riley $75-90
1919 Sunbeam V12 ....$90-105
1926 Thomas Leyland Special $90-105
1921 Chitty Chitty Bang Bang $90-105

Milestone Miniaturs – The 43rd Avenue Collection
1965 Plymouth Sport Fury $85-100
1951 Studebaker Champion Business Coupe $75-90
1951 Studebaker Commander Business Coupe $75-90
1947 Cadillac Series 62 Sedan $90-105
1936 Ford 3 Window Coupe $80-95
1956 Oldsmobile Super 88 Convertible ...$85-100
1959 Chevrolet Nomad Impala Station Wagon..................................$85-100
1951 Studebaker Panorama Commander ..$75-90
1936 Ford Convertible with Dickie (Rumble) Seat $80-95
1968 Ford Torino Coupe GT.................$80-95

1966 Mercury Comet Cyclone $85-100
1959 Dodge Royal Saloon $90-105

Milestone Miniatures Gold Seal Presentation Sets

Milestone Connoisseur Limited Editions
1930 Austin Ulster $125-150
1932 Birkin Bentley $150-175
1925 Fiat Mephistopheles $150-175
1934 MG K3 Magnette $150-175
1935 Napier-Railton $150-175
1936 MG NA Bellevue Special $125-150
1934 Morgan Jap Relay car $125-150
1935 Frazer Nash $125-150
1930 Brooklands Riley $125-150
1919 Sunbeam V12 ....$150-175
1926 Thomas Leyland Special $150-175
1921 Chitty Chitty Bang Bang $150-175

Milestone Jaguar Legends Collection Gift Sets
1927 Austin Swallow Saloon, Green-Green; 1936 SS1 Coupe, Blue/Black, GS1 ....$250-275
1938 SS 100 Open Sports, White; 1939 SS100 Coupe, Silver, GS2 ....$250-275
1934 SS1 Open Drop Head, Dark Blue; 1935 SS Airline Saloon, Maroon, GS3 ....$250-275
1949 Mk 5 Saloon, Silver/Black; 1950 Mk 7 Saloon, Metallic Blue, GS4 ....$250-275
1955 Mk 1 Saloon, British Racing Green; 1962 Mk 2 Wire Wheel, Metallic Dark Blue, GS5 ....$250-275
1956 Mk 8 Saloon, gray/gray; 1961 Mk 10 Saloon, Metallic Blue, GS6 ....$250-275
1972 XJC Coupe, Maroon; XJ12 Saloon, Pale Green, GS7 ....$250-275
1947 XK 120 Jabbeke Record Car, Cream; 1953 XK120 Bubble Record Car, British Racing Green, GS8 ....$250-275
1953 C Type Le Mans Winner, British Racing Green; 1957 D Type Ecurie Ecosse, Flag Blue, GS9 ....$250-275
1965 XJ 13 Experimental car, British Racing Green; 1984 XJR 5 Quaker State Le Mans, White, GS10..............$250-275
1950 XK 120 Drop Head Open, White; 1958 XK150 Coupe, Gold, GS11 ....$250-275
1961 XKE Coupe, White; 1996 XK8 Roadster Open, British Racing Green, GS12.......................$250-275
1972 XKE V12 Roadster, Black; 1984 XJS Coupe, Metallic Blue, GS13 ....$250-275

Milestone Models (also see Big River Models)

Milestone Models of South Africa made just two models. More recently, Milestone Models moved to Sydney, Australia, and is responsible for a cooperative effort with Big River Models to produce an exquisite 1937 Chevrolet Ute (Pickup) in 1997.

1961 Ford Falcon, 1:43 ....$70
1960 Plymouth Valiant, 1:43 ....$70

Milestones (see Milestone Development Corporation)

Milton

Milton toys are made in Calcutta, India, from old Corgi, Dinky, Corgi Jr., and other manufacturers' dies. Milton Morgan produced a number of toys under the brand name of Mini Auto Cars, not to be confused with Miniautotoys from Dugu. The quality is noticeably inferior to the original Corgi Jrs.

Articulated Lumber Transporter, 1:50,#317 ..$35-40
Army Ambulance, 1:70, #312 ....$10-15
Articulated Refrigeration Truck, 1:50, #315 ....$35-40
Articulated Tank Truck, "BURMAH-SHELL," 1:50, #314 ....$40-45
Articulated Tank Truck, "CALTEX," 1:50, #314 ....$35-40
Articulated Tank Truck, "Esso," 1:50, #314 ....$40-45
Articulated Tank Truck, "Indian Oil," 1:50, #314 ....$40-45
Articulated Tank Truck, "Mobilgas," 1:50, #314 ....$40-45
Austin-Healey, 1:90, #205 ....$15-20
BMW 507, 1:90, #204 ....$15-20
Chevrolet Impala, #303.......................$30-35
Chevrolet Impala Fire Chief, #309 ....$30-35
Chevrolet Impala Police car, #308 ....$35-40
Chevrolet Impala State Patrol, #305 ....$35-40
Chevrolet Impala Taxi, #306 ....$35-40
Commer "Coca-Cola" Truck, #334 ....$60-65
Commer Ambulance, #320 ....$40-45
Commer Army Ambulance, #321 ....$40-45
Commer Fruit Carrier, #332 ....$40-50
Commer Milk Van, #325 ....$40-45
Commer Open Truck, #324 ....$40-45
Commer Pickup, #323 ....$40-45
Commer School Bus, #322 ....$40-45
Commer Van "Milton," #319 ....$40-45
D. D. Bus, "Insist on Milton Mini Cars," 1:50, #337 ....$50-55
Flat Truck, 1:70, #301 ....$10-15

Foden Tank Truck "urmah-Shell," 1:50,
#331 ....$5-10
Foden Tank Truck "Caltex," 1:50, #330 ....$5-10
Ford Model T, #336 ....$20-25
Ford Mustang, #329 ....$35-40
Jaguar 3.8 Saloon, #327 ....$40-45
Ladder Truck, 1:70, #344 ....$10-15
Lumber Truck, 1:70, #311 ....$10-15
Luxury Coach, 1:50, #316 ....$50-55
Mercedes Fire Ladder Truck, 1:64 ....$5-10
Mercedes-Benz 220 Coupe, 1:90, #202...$15-20
Mini Bus, #349 ....$20-25
Morris Mini Minor, #333 ....$45-50
Open Truck, 1:70, #302 ....$10-15
Plymouth Suburban, #304 ....$35-40
Plymouth Suburban Ambulance, #307 .....$35-40
Pontiac Firebird, 1:90, #203.................$20-25
Racing car, #341 ....$20-25
Roadster, #342 ....$20-25
Royal Mail Van, 1:70, #313 ....$15-20
Studebaker Golden Hawk, #310...........$40-45
Tipping Truck, 1:50, #338 ....$25-30
Tractor and Trailer, #335 ....$40-45
Volkswagen 1200, 1:90, #201 ....$20-25

Mimick Toys (see Charbens)

Minialuxe

Minialuxe is a series of plastic car models begun in France between 1954 and 1959. Here is just a small sampling.

1909 Ford Model T Roadster, top up,
1:43 ....$15-18
1911 Ford Model T Roadster, top down,
1:43 ....$15-18
1908 Lanchester, 1:43.........................$15-18
1913 Muller Sedan, 1:64 ....$8-11
1912 Park Royal Landau, 1:43 ....$15-18
1906 Peugeot, 1:43 ....$15-18
Peugeot 204 4-door Sedan, 1:43..........$15-18
Peugeot 504 4-door Sedan, 1:43..........$15-18
Peugeot 604 4-door Sedan, 1:43..........$15-18
Renault 17 Coupe, 1:43......................$15-18
Renault 30, 1:43 ....$15-18
Simca 1000 Police, 1:43 ....$15-18

Miniature Auto Emporium

These are 1:43 scale models of exacting detail.

1939 Buick Limo $185-200
1959 Cadillac Convertible, top up..........$65-80
1959 Cadillac Fire car $65-80
1965 Chevrolet Corvette Convertible, top up.....$65-80
1965 Chevrolet Corvette Convertible,
top down $65-80

1961 Chrysler Convertible, top up $115-130
1961 Chrysler Convertible, top down..$115-130

Miniature Pet

Miniature Pet is a short-lived brand from Japan that produced just one model before vanishing from the market. The distinguishing mark on the base is an oval with an "N" inside of it.

1958 Opel Kapitan 4-door Sedan, #1,
1962 ....$30-35

Miniature Vehicle Castings Inc. (also known as MVC)

Robert E. Wagner started Miniature Vehicle Castings Inc. in New Jersey in 1985, producing an exquisite series of 1930s and 1940s vehicles in 1:43 scale. Models are made of diecast lead from silicone molds, and represent some of the most beautiful renderings of vintage models on the market.

1941 Divco Milk Truck "Sunrise Dairy,"
1985 ....$30-40
1934 Dodge 2-door Sedan, 1993 ....$30-40
1937 Dodge 2-door Humpback, 1985...$30-40
1938 Dodge Step Van, 1985 ....$30-40
1939 Dodge 2-door Sedan, 1985 ....$30-40
1940 Dodge 2-door Sedan, 1985 ....$30-40
1937 Ford 2-door Sedan, 1985 ....$40-45
1937 Ford 2-door Sedan, "New York
Fire," 1985 ....$55-65
1938 Ford Standard Sedan Deluxe,
1985 ....$30-40
1940 Ford Logging Semi, 1985............$45-55
1941 Ford C.O.E. Flatbed Truck, 1985 ..$30-40
1941 Ford C.O.E. Dump Truck, 1985 ....$30-40
Ford P600 "Coca-Cola" Van $24-36
Ford P600 "UPS" Van...........................$24-36
1935 Hudson 2-door Sedan, 1985........$30-40
1937 Hudson Terraplane 2-door, 1985....$30-40
1938 Hudson Coupe, 1993 ....$30-40
1934 Oldsmobile 2-door Humpback,
1985 ....$30-40
1936 Oldsmobile 4-door Humpback,
1985 ....$30-40
1936 Plymouth 4-door Sedan, 1985 ......$30-40
1936 Plymouth 4-door Taxi, 1985.........$30-40
1936 Plymouth Pickup, 1993 ....$30-40
1937 Plymouth 5-window Coupe, 1985...$30-40
1938 Plymouth 2-door Sedan, 1985 ......$30-40
1935 Pontiac 2-door Sedan, 1993 ....$30-40
1935 Pontiac 3-window Coupe..............$30-40
1937 Studebaker 3-window Coupe, 1985...$30-40

Miniautotoys (see Dugu)

Minic (see Tri-Ang)

Minichamps (see Paul's Model Art)

Minicraft (see Academy Minicraft)

Minimac

Below is a list of known Minimac models from Brazil.

Case 580H Tractor with Backhoe, 1:43 ..$75-90
Cat D4E Bulldozer, 1:50 ....$25-35
Dresser A450E Motorgrader, 1:50 ....$45-60
Ford Jeep
Coca-Cola, 1:43..............................$16-24
Fire Brigade Chief, red, 1:43 ....$16-24
Red Cross Ambulance, white and red,
1:43...$16-24
U.N., white and black, 1:43............$16-24
Military Jeep, Army, green, 1:43........$16-24
Galion Road Grader, 1:50 ....$45-60
Huber Road Grader, yellow, 1:87 ....$16-24
Hyster H-150F Forklift, 1:43 ....$20-25
Komatsu Motorgrader. 1:50 ....$45-60
March 762 F.2
"Camel" #12, yellow, 1:25 ....$24-32
"Esso" #1, white/red/blue, 1:25 ......$24-32
"Hollywood" #9, red/white/blue,
1:25 ....$24-32
"Marlboro," Senna, 1:25..................$45-60
Massey Ferguson
275 Farm Tractor with canopy, red,
1:43 ....$28-36
3366 Dozer, yellow, 1:43 ....$28-36
Scania 4x2 Truck
1:50 ....$22-28
"Coca-Cola," 1:50 ....$28-36
Scania Refrigerator Semi "Coca-Cola,"
1:50 ....$48-56
Scania Semi Van, 1:50 ....$28-36

Mini Marque 43

Mini Marque 43 models are 1:43 scale white metal models hand built in England in very limited quantities.

Auburn
1934 Auburn 652Y Convertible Sedan,
top down, #18B $160-170
1935 Auburn 851 Boattail Speedster,
#28C $215-225
Cadillac
1954 Eldorado Convertible, top down,
#24A.................................$200-210
1954 Eldorado Convertible, top up,
#24B.................................$200-210

Chevrolet
  1955 Bel Air Sports Coupe, #12A ..$170-180
  1955 Bel Air Nomad, #12B $160-170
  1957 Corvette, top off, #38B $150-160
  1958 Corvette, top off, baby blue,
    #27B..........................$150-160
  1961 Corvette, top off, #31B $150-160
  1962 Corvette, top on, #37A.......$150-160
  1962 Corvette, top off, tan, #37B...$150-160
  1962 Corvette, top off, white,
    #37B..........................$150-160
  1962 Corvette, top on, #37C $150-160
  1958 Impala Convertible with Continental
    kit, top down, #30B...............$200-210
  1958 Sports Coupe with Continental
    kit, #30A $200-210
Cord
  1937 Cord 812 Sportsman Convertible
    Coupe, top up, #34D $170-180
Duesenberg
  1929 Model J, top down, #25C ..$215-225
Ford
  1957 Fairlane Convertible, top down,
    #2B $180-190
Lincoln
  1959 Continental Convertible, top down,
    #36A $190-200
  1964 Continental Convertible, top down,
    #26A $180-190
Packard
  1932 Dual Cowl Phaeton.............$130-140
  Clark Gable's 1934 LeBaron Boattail
    Speedster......................$200-210
  1953 Caribbean Convertible........$200-210

Mini Metals (see Simba)

Mini Power (see Shinsei Mini Power)

Mini Racing

According to avid collector Harvey Goranson, Mini Racing began in 1976 by Frenchmen Jean-Yves Puillet and Bernard Hue of 65 Rue Tolbiac, 75013 Paris, France. (This address info is nearly 20 years old.) Their first two models, a Porsche "Pink Pig" from Le Mans '71 and a Simca CG Coupe, were eventually available both as kits or built, but began as kits only. The kits number well over 200 today and they are still going. Around 1981 or so, they began offering resin kits, and that may be the medium they are all made in today. My opinion—if there's another kit of the same car available, buy it.

"Those Mini Racing kits I have," says Goranson, "are with me only because no one else

makes, or is likely to make, the vehicle represented. Poor mold line placement, bad proportions, bad decal fit, etc.... Sort of a French John Day. Maybe they've improved—I haven't bought one in 15 years or so. By the way, I own the 1981 Decadenet Belga, but never built it because the decals just aren't proportioned right. It did not finish LeMans in the 9th hour."

Decadenet Belga, 1:43 ....$24-28
Porsche "Pink Pig," 1:43 ....$24-28
Simca CG Coupe, 1:43 ....$24-28

Miniroute

Miniroute models are 1:43 scale hand builts made in France.

Citroën Jumpy Ambulance.......................$25-40
Peugeot 304 Fire Van Allier $25-40

Minix

According to uk.geocities.com/minixcars website, "Minix plastic model cars and other Minix vehicles and accessories were manufactured by Tri-Ang Rovex at their Margate, Kent, UK, factory from 1964 onwards.

"All of the vehicles," states the website, "were made to OO scale (1:76) with the sole exception of the AEC-Strachans bus which was approximately 1:135. The reason for this exception was to enable this model to fit the standard size 'sparking plug' box in which the individual models were sold." Although only seventeen different models were produced, each model was issued in a wide variety of colors, wheel styles and bases over the years. An example is given of the many color variations of the Ford Anglia. Since no values have ever been documented, the values listed below are based on an educated guess.

4/5 Berth Caravan, 1:87, #16 ....$30-45
AEC-Strachans inter-state bus, 1:135, #14 ..$30-45
Austin 1800, 1:87, #12 ....$30-45
Austin A60, 1:87, #5 ....$30-45
Ford Anglia, 1:87, #1
  pale yellow with silver wheels, chrome
    base, 1964–1972....................$30-45
  red with silver wheels, chrome base,
    1964–1972............................$30-45
  white with silver wheels, chrome base,
    1964–1972............................$30-45
  yellow with silver wheels, chrome base,
    1964–1972............................$30-45
  blue with silver wheels, chrome base,
    1964–1972............................$30-45

  dark green with silver wheels, chrome base,
    1964–1972............................$30-45
  light green with silver wheels, chrome base,
    1964–1972............................$30-45
  emerald green with silver wheels, chrome
    base, 1964–1972....................$30-45
  orange with silver wheels, chrome base,
    1964–1972............................$30-45
  black with silver wheels, chrome base,
    1964–1972............................$30-45
  emerald green with black wheels, white base,
    1972 or later $30-45
  red with black wheels, white base, 1972 or
    later $30-45
  dark green with black wheels, white base,
    1972 or later $30-45
  dark green with black wheels, chrome base,
    1972 or later $30-45
  bright blue with black wheels, white base,
    1972 or later $30-45
  white with black wheels, white base, 1972 or
    later $30-45
Ford 15 CWT Van, 1:87, #13 ....$30-45
Ford Corsair, 1:87, #6 ....$30-45
Hillman Imp, 1:87, #10 ....$30-45
Hillman Minx, 1:87, #8.........................$30-45
Morris 1100, 1:87, #2..........................$30-45
Rambler 770 Classic, 1:87, #17 ....$30-45
Simca 1300, 1:87, #9 ....$30-45
Sunbeam Alpine, 1:87, #7 ....$30-45
Triumph 2000, 1:87, #4 ....$30-45
Vauxhall Cresta estate / station wagon, 1:87,
  #15 ....$30-45
Vauxhall Victor 101, 1:87, #11 ....$30-45
Vauxhall Viva, 1:87, #3 ....$30-45

Mira

Until recently, Mira of Spain offered detailed scale models in 1:18, 1:25, 1:43 and 1:64 scales. Of late, Mira's 1:18 scale models have dominated their product line, but they were more prominently known in the 1970s for their 1:43 scale models. As of September 2000, Mira became a part of the Solido line, purchased by Ideal Loisirs of France, owner of the Majorette brand as well as Verem and Norev of France and Novacar of Portugal.

1955 Buick Century
  Convertible, top down, red, #6134 ...$30-35
  Convertible, top down, Belfast green,
    #6185....................................$30-35
  Coupe, red, #6131 ....$30-35
  Coupe, Belfast green, #6186 ....$30-35
  Coupe, metallic green with beige roof,
    #6283...................................$30-35

Coupe, metallic red with beige roof,
#6284 ....$30-35
Coupe, metallic red with black roof,
6285 ....$30-35
Coupe, beige with black roof, #6286 ...$30-35
Coupe, black with beige roof, #6287 ..$30-35
Fire Chief, red, #6119 ....$30-35
Sun State Police, black and white,
#6118 ....$30-35
Taxi, yellow, #6116 ....$30-35
1950 Chevrolet Panel Truck
maroon, #6231 ....$30-35
forester green, #6232 ....$30-35
cream medium, #6233 ....$30-35
mariner blue, #6234 ....$30-35
Military Ambulance, olive drab,
#6241 ....$30-35
1950 Chevrolet Suburban carryall
forester green, #6238 ....$30-35
cream medium, #6239 ....$30-35
mariner blue, #6240 ....$30-35
Military Police, olive drab, #6244 ......$30-35
Boston Fire Department Panel Truck, red,
#6242 ....$30-35
Police Panel Truck, black with white side
doors, #6243 ....$30-35
School Bus, orange-yellow, #6245 ....$30-35
1950 Chevrolet Military Pickup, olive drab,
#6246 ....$30-35
1953 Chevrolet Corvette Convertible, top down
cream, #6153 ....$30-35
black, #6281 ....$30-35
1953 Chevrolet Pickup
metallic green, #6190 ....$30-35
burgundy, #6191 ....$30-35
black, #6202 ....$30-35
red, #6203 ....$30-35
white, #6204 ....$30-35
Tanker, red with white tank, #6221 ....$30-35
Tanker, red with white closed topper,
#6223 ....$30-35
Tanker, blue with white tank, #6270 ..$30-35
Tanker, blue with white closed topper,
#6271 ....$30-35
1954 Chevrolet Corvette Convertible
top down, metallic pennant blue,
#6195 ....$30-35
top down, sportsman red, #6198 ......$30-35
top up, cream with black roof, #6189 ...$30-35
top up, metallic pennant blue with cream roof,
#6197 ....$30-35
top up, sportsman red with tan roof,
#6200 ....$30-35
top up, black with beige roof, #6282 ...$30-35
top up, harvest gold with black roof,
#6299 ....$30-35

1954 Chevrolet Corvette Coupe
cream, #6188 ....$30-35
pennant blue #6196 ....$30-35
sportsman red, #6199 ....$30-35
black, #6280 ....$30-35
1955 Chevrolet Bel Air
Convertible..............................$30-35
Hardtop..............................$30-35
1989 Ferrari 348 TB
red, #6101 ....$30-35
metallic silver, #6227 ....$30-35
pennant blue, #6230 ....$30-35
1989 Ferrari 348 TS
pennant blue, #6231 ....$30-35
red, #6105 ....$30-35
1991 Ferrari Testarossa 512 TR
Cabriolet, red, #6145 ....$30-35
Cabriolet, metallic silver, #6175 ......$30-35
Cabriolet, pennant blue, #6178 ......$30-35
Coupe, red, #6144..............................$30-35
Coupe, metallic silver, #6174 ....$30-35
Coupe, pennant blue, #6177 ....$30-35
1992 Ferrari 348 Spider
Cabriolet, pennant blue, #6179 ......$30-35
Cabriolet, red, #6181 ....$30-35
Cabriolet, top down, metallic silver,
#6228 ....$30-35
Coupe, red, #6180..............................$30-35
1995 Ferrari F-50
Cabriolet, red, #6205 ....$30-35
Cabriolet, metallic blue, #6209 ......$30-35
Cabriolet, metallic silver, #6226 ......$30-35
Coupe, red, #6201..............................$30-35
Coupe, pennant blue, #6208 ....$30-35
Coupe, metallic silver, #6229 ....$30-35
1949 Ford Convertible
top down, blue, #6248 ....$30-35
top down, red, #6249..............................$30-35
top up, blue with tan roof, #6252 ......$30-35
top up, red with tan roof, #6253 ......$30-35
1949 Ford Coupe
blue, #6250 ....$30-35
red, #6251 ....$30-35
Fire Department, #6255 ....$30-35
Police, #6254 ....$30-35
1956 Ford F-100 Pickup
metallic burgundy, #6156 ....$30-35
red, #6158 ....$30-35
metallic blue, #6159 ....$30-35
metallic dark green, #6183 ....$30-35
1964½ Ford Mustang Convertible
top down, cream, #6114..............................$30-35
top down, red, #6127 ....$30-35
top up, red with white roof, #6142 ....$30-35
top down, burgundy, #6288 ....$30-35
top down, Caspian blue, #6289 ......$30-35

top down, champagne beige,
#6290..............................$30-35
top up, metallic burgundy with tan roof,
#6294..............................$30-35
top up, Caspian blue with tan roof,
#6295..............................$30-35
top up, champagne beige with tan roof,
#6296..............................$30-35
1964½ Ford Mustang Coupe
cream, #6113 ....$30-35
red, #6126 ....$30-35
burgundy, #6291 ....$30-35
Caspian blue, #6292 ....$30-35
champagne beige, #6293 ....$30-35
champagne beige, #6149 ....$30-35
1965 Ford Mustang Fastback
red, #6150 ....$30-35
Caspian blue, #6170 ....$30-35
1966 Ford Mustang Convertible, top up, black
with white roof, red interior, #6023 ...$30-35
1998 Ford F-150 Shortbox Flareside
Supercab Pick-Up 4x4 XLT
metallic red brighten, #6217 ....$30-35
red, #6218 ....$30-35
Pacific green, #6219 ....$30-35
1950 GMC Panel Truck
permanent red, #6212..............................$30-35
oakwood brown, #6213 ....$30-35
Narva green, #6214 ....$30-35
1950 GMC Suburban Carryall
permanent red, #6235 ....$30-35
oakwood brown, #6236 ....$30-35
Narva green, #6237 ....$30-35
Lamborghini Diablo Super Deportivo
red, #6106 ....$30-35
pennant blue, #6107 ....$30-35
metallic silver, #6108 ....$30-35

Mira 1:25 Scale
Audi 200 4-door Sedan.......................$16-20
Benetton Ford.............................$18-22
BMW Brabham "Olivetti" $18-22
BMW 323i
2-door Sedan $16-20
Coupe.............................$16-20
Ferrari 348 TB $16-20
Ferrari Spa "Goodyear" $18-22
1956 Ford Thunderbird.......................$16-20
Lancia 037 "Martini" $16-20
Lotus Ford.............................$18-22
Mercedes-Benz 190E 2.3 Sedan $18-22
Mercedes-Benz 500 4-door Sedan..........$16-20
Mercedes-Benz 540K $16-20
Nissan Jeep.............................$16-20
Porsche 911 "Rothman's Paris-Dakar" ...$24-28
Porsche 928.............................$16-20

Renault Espace
Ambulance $16-20
Fire $16-20
Williams Honda $18-22
Williams Renault $18-22

Mira 1:43 Scale
Citroën CX Sedan $15-19
Mercedes-Benz 450 SE $15-19
Pegaso Fire $18-22

Mira 1:64 Scale
Caravan Ambulance $4-6
Chrysler 150 4-door Sedan $4-6
Ford Fiesta 2-door Sedan $4-6
Land Rover Ambulance $4-6
Mercedes 450 4-door Sedan $4-6
Seat 1200 Coupe $4-6
Seat 131E 4-door Sedan $4
Seat 128 Coupe $4-6

Mitrecraft
Only one model has been documented from Mitrecraft of Great Britain.

Austin A35 4-door Sedan, 1:43 ....$35-45

MK Models
Only one example of MK Models is known of this brand presumed to originate from somewhere in the former Eastern Bloc (Russian republics).

Tatra Semi Oil Tanker, 1:120 ....$5-7

Moboto (or Meboto)
Like so many other obscure brands, only a few models by Moboto (possibly spelled Meboto) of Turkey have been documented.

Lamborghini Marzal, 1:43 ....$11-15
Lancia Fulvia Coupe, 1:43 ....$11-15
Mercedes-Benz 250 Sedan, 1:43 ....$11-15

Modelauto/Sun Motor Company, Bugattiana, Rapide, Bijou
Modelauto produces models under the brands of Sun Motor Company, Bugattiana, Rapide, and Bijou. Sun Motor Company is known, among other things, for replica firefighting equipment, as so richly illustrated in Toys for Collectors' catalog. Modelauto of Leeds, England, was started in 1974 by Rod and Val Ward. They also produce Model Auto Review 10 times a year and host the Somerville Society for collectors of that prestigious brand of scale

models. In addition, they are exclusive UK distributors for a few other exceptional brands—Paradise Garage, Doorkey, Oto, and Scottoy.

All models are offered in kit form as well as finished models. The first price range represents the kit price. The second price range is for factory built, finished models.

Modelauto / Sun Motor Company, 1:43 Scale Commercial Vehicles
AOMA Caravan 1920s-30s,
#202 ....$35-50 ....$60-75
Autocar U70
2 axle open truck,
#224 ....$50-65 ......$110-125
articulated tractor unit NYC,
#225 ....$40-55 ......$100-115
Avgas tanker, #223 ...$75-90 ......$150-165
civilian tanker B-A or Skelly,
#220 ....$75-90 ......$150-165
Fire Dept. tanker, #222 .$75-90 ......$150-165
fire pumper, #226 .....$85-100 ......$130-145
US Navy tanker, #221 .$75-90 ......$150-165
Bedford O
sided lorry, LEP, #185 $50-65 ......$110-125
tipper, Ahearn, #186 .$50-65 ......$110-125
Bedford OS
with generator, fairground,
#178 ....$50-65 ......$110-125
Breakdown lorry,
#156 ....$50-65 ......$100-115
Refuse lorry, #176 .....$50-65 ......$110-125
tipper, Marples, #157 .$40-55 ......$100-115
Bedford OX
with Queen Mary articulated trailer,
#201 ....n/a $170-185
articulated tanker, Pickford's,
#210+213 ....$95-110 ....$190-205
articulated tanker, Pool,
#210+213 ....$95-110 ....$190-205
articulated tractor unit,
#210 ....$40-55 ....$90-105
Queen Mary Helicopter Services,
#201 ....$85-100 ....$170-185
Bedford OY
cab, transkit for Corgi,
#158 ....$12-16 ....n/a
GS lorry (livery varies),
#155 ....$40-55 ......$100-115
plank-side, Charringtons,
#179 ....$50-65 ......$110-125
plank-side, Cirkus Arena,
#179 ....$50-65 ......$110-125
tackle wagon, livery varies,
#177 ....$55-70 ......$110-125
Tanker, Pool, #154 ....$40-55 ......$100-115

Tanker, Esso, #154 ....$40-55 ......$100-115
Tanker, Caltex, #154 .$40-55 ......$100-115
Van, BRS, #175 ....$50-65 ......$110-125
Van, GWR, #175 .....$50-65 ......$110-125
Van, LMS, #175 ....$50-65 ......$110-125
Bogie bolster trailer 2+2 axle,
#209 ....$40-55 ....$90-105
Commer Superpoise Van
McVities, #191 ....$75-90 ......$150-165
Cadbury, #191 ....$75-90 ......$150-165
Daimler CVD6 Bus 1949, Exeter,
#150 ....$90-105 ....$185-200
Diamond T
articulated tractor, Crook & Will,
#127 ....$60-75 ......$170-185
articulated tractor, Stoof Breda,
#145 ....$60-75 ......$145-160
articulated tractor, Pickford's,
#144 ....$60-75 ......$145-160
ballast, Crook & Willington,
#126 ....$75-85 ......$170-185
British Army canvas cab artic,
#143 ....$60-75 ......$145-160
British Army canvas cab closed,
#139 ....$75-85 ......$170-185
British Army articulated tractor,
#140 ....$60-75 ......$145-160
Heavy Haulage, Pickford's,
#128 ....$75-85 ......$170-185
Heavy Haulage, Stoof/Mamut,
#129 ....$75-85 ......$170-185
Heavy Haulage, Sunters,
#130 ....$75-85 ......$170-185
Heavy Haulage, Wynns,
#131 ....$70-85 ......$170-185
M20 British Army Hercules engine,
#133 ....$75-85 ......$170-185
M20 British Army, #124 .$75-85 ......$170-185
M20 US Army, #125 $75-85 ......$170-185
Recovery (TFL) Avon,
#136 ....$75-85 ......$170-185
Recovery (TFL), Hudson,
#135 ....$75-85 ......$170-185
Recovery (TFL), J&H,
#137 ....$75-85 ......$185-200
Thurston's Fair,
#132 ....$100-115 ..$170-185
tractor, STAG (France),
#134 ....$75-85 ......$170-185
US Army articulated tractor,
#141 ....$60-75 ......$145-160
Dyson 85-ton well trailer,
#205 ....$90-105 ....$185-200
ERF KV
4 axle flat, Gardner 1950s,
#245 ....$85-100 ...$160-175

4 axle tanker, Shell-BP,
#246 ....$85-100 ....$160-175
6x4 tipper, Pointer,
#242 ....$85-100 ....$160-175
Fairground TRANSKIT for bus or Van,
#149 ....$20-25 ....n/a
Ford 7V
1930s box van, Ford,
#167 ....$50-65 ......$110-125
1930s Breakdown lorry,
#163 ....$50-65 ......$110-125
1930s Open, Imperial Airways,
#165 ....$50-65 ......$110-125
1930s tanker, Pratts,
#166 ....$50-65 ......$110-125
1940s articulated tractor,
#161 ....$40-55 ......$145-160
1940s box Van, LNER,
#162 ....$50-65 ......$145-160
1940s Shell airfield tanker,
#160 ....$65-80 ......$145-160
articulated flat, Pickford's,
#161+211 ....$95-110 ....$190-205
wartime tanker, Pool,
#164 ....$50-65 ......$110-125
Ford ET6 Coachbuilt Van
Jays, #192 ....$75-90 ......$150-165
BOAC, #192 ....$75-90 ......$150-165
Ford Thames Trader
flat lorry, #250 ....$50-65 ......$110-125
Lubricants tanker, #251 $55-70 ......$120-135
Guy Invincible
4 axle tanker, Regent,
#236 ....$85-100 ....$160-175
6x4 tipper, Wimpey,
#232 ....$85-100 ....$160-175
6x4 tractor unit, #23 ..$75-90 ......$150-165
8 wheel flat, Wynns,
#235 ....$85-100 ....$160-175
Guy Warrior 4x2 articulated tractor unit,
#230 ....$40-55 ......$100-115
King 150 ton 6 axle well trailer,
#206 ....$130-145 ..$215-240
King 3 ax articulated low load trailer,
#207 ....$105-120 ..$185-200
Leyland Comet bus
Laing, #195 ....$75-90 ......$150-165
BOAC, #195 ....$75-90 ......$150-165
Leyland E, Yorks service vehicle,
148 ....$75-90 ......$150-165
Leyland Hippo 6x4 tipper, Willment,
#261 ....$85-100 ....$160-175
Leyland Octopus flat, BRS,
#260 ....$85-100 ....$160-175
Mann Egerton Breakdown crane, transkit,
#159 ....$12-16 ....n/a

Queen Mary articulated trailer, various decals,
#200 ....$85-100 ....n/a
Rex Caravan 1930s-40s,
#203 ....$35-50 ....$60-75
Rotinoff Atlantic
large cab Sunters,
#170 ....$75-90 ......$185-200
small cab Parnaby,
#171 ....$75-90 ......$185-200
small cab Smith,
#173 ....$75-90 ......$185-200
small cab Sunter,
#172 ....$75-90 ......$185-200
Sales Trailer Circus, Refreshments, RN, etc,
#204 ....$40-55 ....$75-90
Scammell Super Constructor
Marples, #183 ....$75-90 ......$185-200
Pickford's, #180 ....$75-90 ......$185-200
Sunters, #181 ....$75-90 ......$185-200
Wynns, #182 ....$75-90 ......$185-200
Single axle articulated trailer
oval tanker, #213 $55-70 ....$110-125
European style, #212. $45-60 ......$105-120
US style, #211 ....$45-60 ......$105-120
Super Pacific Prime Mover, Wynn's,
#190 ....$90-105 ....$185-200

Modelauto Bugattiana 1:43 Models from UK

Bugatti
T252 Cabriolet,
BU006 ....$55-70 ......$110-125
T35B Sports 2 seat aero,
BU005 ....$55-70 ......$110-125
T40 Grand Sport 1930,
BU001 ....$45-60 ......$105-120
T40 Sahara, Loiseau 1930,
BU002 ....$55-70 ......$110-125
T45 16 Cylinder,
BU004 ....$55-70 ......$110-125
T57C Shah of Iran,
BU012 ....$55-70 ......$110-125
T57SC Colonel Giles,
BU010 ....$55-70 ......$110-125
T57SC Colonel Giles Rally,
BU011 ....$55-70 ......$110-125

Modelauto Rapide 1:43 Models from UK

Austin Healey 100S sports,
RA005 ....$40-55 ....$90-105
Bantam (American Austin)
Sports 38, RA009 .....$45-60 ......$105-120
Sports two tone,
RA009 ....$105-120 ..$105-120
pickup civil 1939,
RA011 ....$105-120 ..$105-120

pickup stakeside 39,
RA012 ....$50-65 ......$115-130
pickup US Army 1939,
RA013 ....$45-60 ......$105-120
pickup Fire dept 1939,
RA014 ....$50-65 ......$115-130
avgas tanker 1939,
RA015 ....$45-60 ......$105-120
BSA Scout
Open sports 1930s,
RA008 ....$40-55 ......$105-120
Open sports, two tone,
RA008 ....$50-65 ......$115-130
Coupe, RA010 ....$45-60 ......$105-120
Jaguar Mark VII red, blue, gray, green,
RA002 ....$40-55 ....$90-105

Modelauto Bijou Models, from various countries

Vespa parascooter, French Army with bazooka,
#1, 1:30 ....$20-30 ....$25-40
Bugatti T52 Baby (by Auto Replicas), #2,
1:43 ....$20-30 ....$30-45
Austin Pathfinder pedal car (ex Rapide 100), #3,
1:43 ....$15-20 ....$25-40
London E1 tram, Model Auto Show '95,
#6 ....n/a $9-12
Inflatable boat with outboard motor, #7,
1:43 plastic ....n/a $6-8

ModelCast (also see Chrono)

ModelCast is a newly emerging company based in San Jose, California. They offer quality diecast models of civilian and military models. Their website at www.isaacnet.commodelcast/ describes the various models they offer. Here is their product line as listed on their website. The models they offer are so similar to those offered by Chrono A that I suspect a connection, likely that Chrono A manufactures them for ModelCast.

ModelCast 1:18 Scale

Aston Martin DB5 1963
Aqua Verda Green, #1001 ....$15-20
Peony Red, #1002 ....$15-20
Light Ice Blue, #1003 ....$15-20
Lotus Elise Open Convertible
Yellow, #1020 ....$15-20
Blue, #1021 ....$15-20
Black, #1022 ....$15-20

ModelCast 1:43 Scale

Dodge Command car
US Army, closed, RO53 ....$7-9
US Army, open, RO54 ....$7-9
D-Day, RO55 ....$7-9

Dodge Weapons carriers
US Army, open, R046 ....$7-9
US Army, closed, R047 ....$7-9
Liberation de Paris, R048 ....$7-9
Hummer
Ambulance with camouflage, R038 ....$7-9
Ambulance Desert Storm, R039 ....$7-9
Willys Jeep
D-Day 1944, closed, R001 ....$7-9
Liberation de Paris 1944, open, R002 ....$7-9
Military Police 1945, open, R003 ....$7-9

Model Pet (see Asahi)

Model Plan (also see Toyo Kogyo)

www.modelplanning.co.jp/

Based in Japan, Model Planning Co., Ltd., is the source for 1:87 scale Toyo Kogyo models and 1:130–1:150 scale Model Plan vehicles of solid diecast metal. Unfortunately, their website is all in Japanese text and indecipherable (at least by me). No complete model list has been found.

Alfa Romeo GTA, 1:150 ....$20-25
Fiat 500, 1:150 ....$20-25

Model Planning Co. (see Model Plan, Toyo Kogyo)

Model Power

Model Power, based in Farmingdale, New York, produces over 2,400 O, HO, and N gauge items intended for model railroad layouts, although most are buildings, street lights, layout accessories, and rolling stock. Their series of O scale fire trucks are similar in detail to Ertl's recently introduced models, but are priced somewhat higher ($13 to $15) because of their limited availability, and possess no livery, which leaves the model crying out for customizing.

Perhaps the most interesting part of the Model Power story for diecast toy collectors is that they obtain their diecast models from other manufacturers and repackage them as their own. The fire trucks listed below are all Gaia brand models. The Scania Bus is by Playart. Eidai is also a brand repackaged as Model Power. The package is all that identifies these models as Model Power.

American LaFrance Fire Pumper, 1:87
(Gaia) $13-16
American LaFrance Ladder Truck, 1:87
(Gaia) $15-18
American LaFrance Snorkel Truck, 1:87
(Gaia) $15-18

Scania Bus, "AVIS Courtesy Bus," 1:87
(Playart) $10-13

Model Products Corporation (MPC)

Model Products Corporation (MPC) is best known for producing 1:25 scale plastic dealer promotional models. A recent find by collector Tom Brown indicates MPC also applied their molds to a series of gravity racers called Dyno-Racers.

1980 Chevrolet Corvette, 1:25 ....$9-12
1980 Chevrolet El Camino, 1:25 ....$45-55
1980 Chevrolet Monte Carlo $65-70
1980 Chevrolet Monza $45-55

Model Toys (see Doepke)

Models of Yesteryear (see Matchbox)

Moko (also see Matchbox)

Moses Kohnstam established Moko around the turn of the century. Although he died in 1912, his legacy lives on in the British office of Moko, a company renowned for representing toy manufacturers the world over. He contracted such toy companies as Gunthermann, Distler, and Fischer, and others to produce made-to-order toys to bear the Moko label.

Early Matchbox toys are marked as "A Moko Lesney Product." Other toy companies relied on Moko for distribution, such as Gama, Tippco, Levy, and carette.

Most Moko toys are tin wind-up toys dating around the late 1920s, currently valued $1,000 to $1,500. At least one diecast toy tractor, probably an early Lesney, was packaged only as "A Moko Toy" in an off-white box with red and blue graphics on it.

Massey Harris Tractor and Trailer..........$95-110

Montego

The Montego brand is represented by one miniature cruise ship, the Rotterdam, 12 inches long, originally offered for $38.

The Rotterdam Cruise Ship, 12" $45-60

Moose Mountain Toymakers Limited

Parsippany, New Jersey, is headquarters for Moose Mountain Toymakers Limited, manufacturer of two particular playsets first discovered in August 1998 at a local Wal-Mart store. Sets are in the rough form of a bucket, with a strap handle for carrying. Inside are various diecast

toys that fit the theme of the set. Each "bucket" sells for just under $10, and the diecast toys inside are exceptionally well made even though rendered indistinguishably generic when removed from the sets in which they are contained.

Car Wash–Gas–Oil Set..........................$9-12
includes: Ten lightweight diecast cars with opaque black windows, plastic bases, and no interiors, car wash / gas station with ramps and accessories, peel & stick labels for signs, etc.
Dump N' Load Set..................................$9-12
includes: quarry truck, dump truck, crane truck, scoop loader, and bulldozer, conveyor belt, power shovel, with ramps, "rocks," human figures and accessories, peel & stick labels for signs, etc.

Morestone

Morris & Stone of Great Britain started marketing a line of toys in 1946 from their shop at 95 Church Street, Stoke Newington, London, England. Morestone models are more than vaguely similar to Dinky Toys. Most collectors know Morestone by their more familiar "Budgie Miniatures," a name adopted in 1959.

0-6-0 Tank Locomotive $45-60
Austin A95 Westminster Countryman, #15...$25-40
Austin FX3 Taxi, #13 ....$30-45
Austin-Healey 100, #16 ....$30-45
Aveling-Barford Road Roller $45-60
Bedford car Transporter $120-150
Bedford Dormobile $160-185
Bedford Van, AA, #4 ....$20-35
Compressor......................................$50-65
Cooper-Bristol Racing car, #6 ....$20-35
Daimler Ambulance $100-125
Fire Engine, clockwork motor with bell $90-120
Fire Escape
large $90-120
small $75-90
Ford Thames 5 cwt. Van, #17 ....$45-60
Foden 8-wheel Truck
Dumper, #18 ....$40-55
Flat Lorry $120-150
Flat Lorry with chains....................$120-150
Open Lorry...................................$120-150
Petrol Tanker.................................$120
Horse Drawn Covered Wagon
with 4 Horses................................$80-95
with 6 Horses...............................$100-125
Horse Drawn Gypsy Caravan............$150-175
Horse Drawn Hansom Cab $60-75

Horse Drawn Snack Bar.....................$100-125
International Articulated Refrigeration Truck....$60-75
Karrier "GPO Telephones" Van, #10 ....$35-50
Klückner Side Tipping Truck.....................$75-90
Land Rover
 AA, #3, 3" $100-125
 AA, 4¼" $145-170
 Breakdown Service $100-125
 Military Police...........................$180-200
Leyland Double Deck Bus $120-150
Maudslay Horse Box, #9 ....$40-55
Mercedes-Benz Racing Car, #7 ....$25-40
Morris Commercial Van, #11 ....$25-40
Motorcycle and Sidecar
 AA, #1 ....$120-150
 RAC, #2 ....$120-150
Packard Convertible, #14 ....$40-55
Plymouth Belvedere Convertible, #20 ....$45-60
Prime Mover with Trailer $50-65
Racing Car...$45-60
Road Sweeper.................................$120-150
Rover 105R, #19 ....$25-40
Scammell Articulated Tank Truck $60-75
Sleigh with Father Xmas.....................$100-125
Solo Motorcycle $75-90
Stage Coach
 with 2 horses.............................$100-125
 with 4 horses.............................$100-125
State Landau with 6 horses $50-65
Volkswagen 1200 Sedan, #8 ....$35-50
Volkswagen Microbus, #12 ....$40-55
Wells Fargo Stage Coach
 with 2 Galloping Horses...............$100-125
 with 4 horses.............................$100-125
Wolseley 6180 Police car, #5 ....$75-90

Morestone Noddy Character Toys

Big Ears on Bicycle
 approx. 2½".................................$75-90
 approx. 1¾".................................$60-75
Clown on Bicycle, approx. 2½"...............$75-90
Noddy and His car
 approx. 4"...................................$75-90
 approx. 2"...................................$50-65
Noddy on Bicycle With Trailer $65-80
Noddy's Garage Set.........................$160-180

Moskovich

Moskovich is a 1:43 scale brand from Moscow, Russia. The quality is excellent for the price. Doors, hood, and trunk generally open, and detailing is extensive. This list was provided by a dealer in Siberia known only by his e-mail address: prol@algonet.se. Moskovich is also the brand name of an automotive manufacturer based in Moscow, Russia, based on information provided by collector Werner Legrand of Belgium, so the 1:43 scale models are apparently miniatures of the full-scale Moskovich vehicles.

Moskovich
 1500 standard, #IZH.....................$8-10
 Ambulance, #408 ....$8-10
 Book van, #433 ....$9-11
 Estate, #426 ....$8-10
 Estate, #427 ....$8-10
 Estate airport service car, #426..........$8-10
 Estate airport service car, #427..........$8-10
 Estate rally support, #426................$8-10
 Estate with luggage rack, #426..........$8-10
 Estate with luggage rack, #427..........$8-10
 Fastback standard, #2141.................$9-11
 Fastback, ALEKO, #2141 ....$10-12
 Fastback with symbols, #2141 ....$10-12
 Fastback traffic police with beacon,
  #2141...............................$13-15
 Pickup $8-10
 Saloon, #403 ....$12-14
 Saloon, #408 ....$8-10
 Saloon, #412 ....$8-10
 Saloon ambulance, #412 ....$8-10
 Saloon rally car, #408 ....$8-10
 Saloon rally car, #412 ....$8-10
 Saloon with luggage rack, #408 ....$8-10
 Saloon with luggage rack, #412 ....$8-10
 Saloon taxi, #408 ....$8-10
 Saloon taxi, #412 ....$8-10
 Saloon traffic police, #408.............$8-10
 Saloon traffic police, #412.............$8-10

Motor City Classics

1:18 scale classics from the 1930s to the 1960s comprise this collection of diecast models from the Florida-based company started in 1998, the dreamchild of Maurice Oujevolk of Intermarket USA. His nitpicking and constant tweaking resulted in some spectacular models, but his striving for perfection was his ultimate demise as cost overruns and retooling for the tiniest details put the line in jeopardy. As deadlines passed, the manufacturing process was repeatedly delayed until production at the China manufacturing facility finally halted altogether in 2001. The product line has since started up again and new models have again begun to appear.

Airstream Travel Trailer
 Stainless Steel $55-70
1939 Chevrolet Woody Station Wagon
 Italian Cream..............................$45-60
 Yosemite Green $45-60

Granville Gray..................................$45-60
1939 Chevrolet Woody Wagon Trailer
 Italian Cream..............................$30-45
 Yosemite Green $30-45
1948 Chrysler Town & Country Convertible,
 top down
 Catalina Tan, #5001 ....$45-60
 Yellow Lustre, #5003 ....$45-60
 Gunmetal Gray, #5004 ....$45-60
 Heather Green, #5007 ....$45-60
 Military Blue $45-60
1931 Ford Model A Deluxe Roadster
 Stone Brown, #20001 ....$45-60
 Washington Blue, #20002...............$45-60
 Brewster Green, #20003 ....$45-60
 Bronson Yellow, #20005 ....$45-60
 Riviera Blue $45-60
1931 Ford Model A Pickup Truck
 Lombard Blue $45-60

Valley Green................................$45-60

 Rubelite Red $45-60
 Backyard Junker, Rust and Primer $45-60
 Black.......................................$45-60
 Firemen Red $45-60
 Handyman's Truck with tools,
  stepladder.............................$45-60
1931 Ford Model A Tow Truck
 Blue-Gray.................................$45-60
1931 Ford Model A Tudor Coupe

Kewanee Green.............................$45-60

 Police, Black...............................$45-60
1949 Ford Custom 2-door Woody
 Station Wagon
 Sea Mist Green, #30001 ....$45-60
 Fez Red, #30002 ....$45-60

Miami Cream, #30003 ....$45-60
Light Blue, #30004 ....$45-60
"Surf Shop," Sea Mist Green $45-60
"Surf Shop," Bayview Blue..................$45-60
"Lifeguard," Blazing Red....................$45-60
Horse Trailer
   Blue $45-60
1954 Polaris Snowmobile
   Snowy White $45-60
   Red $45-60
1957 Studebaker Golden Hawk

Tiara Gold (April 2000) $45-60

Arctic White (April 2000)..................$45-60
Woodsmoke Gray (April 2000).........$45-60
Apache Red (April 2000)...................$45-60
Project Car, Rust and Primer.................$45-60

Motor City USA, Design Studio & USA Models

13400 Saticoy St., No. 12
North Hollywood, CA 91605
phone: 818-503-4835
fax: 818-503-4580

Motor City USA 1:43 scale (except where noted) hand-built models have been produced, along with Design Studio and USA Models in the United States by partners Alan Novak and Gene Parrill since 1986. USA Models are somewhat less detailed and less expensive models than their Motor City and Design Studio counterparts, also listed below.

Motor City USA

1955 Cadillac 4-door Sedan, MC-2.....$75-100
1954 Buick Skylark, MC-40...............$260-285
1953 Chevrolet
   2-door Hardtop, MC-7 ....$225-250
   Ambulette, body by National,
     MC-9....................................$200-225
   Convertible, MC-8 ....$260-285
   Sedan Delivery, MC-9 ....$225-250
1955 Chevrolet
   Convertible, top down, MC-6..........$75-100
   Nomad Wagon, MC-5....................$75-100
1956 Chevrolet Convertible, MC-31...$260-285
1948 Chrysler Town & Country Convertible,
   MC-22....................................$260-285
1949 DeSoto 4-door Sedan, MC-1 ......$75-100

1950 Ford
   2-door Sedan, MC-12 ....$160-185
   4-door Sedan Police, MC-14 ....$160-185
   Convertible, MC-10 ....$260-285
   Coupe, MC-11 ....$225-250
   Crestliner, MC-15 ....$260-285
   Wagon, MC-13 ....$260-285
1951 Lincoln Cosmopolitan Convertible,
   mint green, MC-34.......................$175-200
1949 Nash
   Police car, MC-3 ....$170-195
   Yellow Cab, MC-3 ....$160-185
1959 Nash Metropolitan, MC-41 ......$225-250
1950 Oldsmobile 88
   Convertible, top down, burgundy,
     MC-69 ....$175-200
   Hardtop, black, MC-70...................$175-200
1956 Oldsmobile 98
   2-door Hardtop, MC-68 ....$135-160
   Convertible, top down, MC-67......$135-160
Pickup, MC-58 ....$135-160
1955 Studebaker President Speedster, MC-71
   yellow and olive $175-200
   pink and black $175-200

Design Studio

1956 Airstream Trailer, DS-10 ....$120-145
1948 Buick Coupe, DS-5 ....$120-145
Cadillac Custom Coupe, DS-132........$135-160
1953 Chevrolet Ambulette, DS-9AMB...$215-240
1956 Chevrolet Convertible
   DS-7 ....$135-160
   2-door, top down, DS-6...............$175-200
1934 Ford 3-Window Coupe, DS-105
   yellow $75-100
   black with flames "California Kid".....$85-110
   red $75-100
1936 Ford 3-Window Custom Coupe, DS-111
   yellow $75-100
   black..$75-100
   wine $75-100
1937 Ford Convertible, DS-113
   red $75-100
   purple..$75-100
   yellow $75-100
1937 Ford "Flat Back" 2-door Sedan, DS-114
   yellow $75-100
   red $75-100
   turquoise $75-100
1940 Ford 2-door Coupe, DS-118 .....$135-160
1940 Ford 2-door Street Rod, DS-117
   red $75-100
   black..$75-100
1940 Ford Convertible, top up, DS-9 ..$215-240
1940 Ford Custom Street Rod
   yellow, DS-129 ....$135-160

red, DS-129 ....$135-160
1950 Ford Custom Convertible
   top down, yellow, DS-109 ....$135-160
   top up, red, DS-109 ....$135-160
1950 Ford Custom Coupe, DS-108....$135-160
1951 Ford Custom Woody Wagon,
   DS-131................................$135-160
1949 Hudson Commodore, DS-3.......$135-160
1952 Hudson Hornet Stock car,
   DS-200.................................$160-185
K.S.Pittman Custom Street Rod, red,
   DS-122KS.............................$135-160
1949 Mercury Custom Coupe, DS-115
   orange-red with white accent........$135-160
   wine red with white accent...........$135-160
1958 Oldsmobile Convertible, DS-4 ...$120-145
   purple with white accent $135-160
   black..$135-160
   metallic orange with white accent...$135-160
1933 Willys Pro Street Rod, 1:24 scale,
   DS-116
   purple with yellow flames $200-225
   red..$200-225
1941 Willys Coupe, Pro Street, DS-110
   blue $75-100
   yellow $75-100
   red $75-100

U.S.A. Models

1955 Cadillac 62
   Convertible, top down, black, USA-6....$65-90
   Coupe De Ville, turquoise with white roof,
     USA-7 ....$65-90
1958 Cadillac Series 75 Limousine, introduced in
   1997, USA-1
   dark metallic blue finish $65-90
   silver with black roof $65-90
1955 Chrysler Imperial Hardtop, pink with white
   roof, USA-2.............................$65-90
1949 Nash
   Los Angeles Fire Chief's car, red,
     USA-3F $65-90
   Los Angeles Police car, black with white doors,
     USA-3P.................................$65-90
   Yellow Cab, USA-3T $65-90
1951 Chevrolet Bel Air 2-door Hardtop,
   slate green with dark green roof,
     USA-4 ....$65-90
1954 Chevrolet Bel Air 4-door Sedan, USA-5
   brown with cream roof.....................$65-90
   blue with white roof $65-90
1940 Ford 2-door Sedan, tan, USA-11 ...$65-90
1940 Ford 4-door
   Sedan, USA-8, burgundy $65-90
   Sedan, dark green $65-90
   Yellow Cab, USA-9.........................$65-90

Los Angeles Police car, black with white
doors, USA-10 ....$65-90
Fire Chief's car, red, USA-13 ....$65-90
1940 Ford Pickup, USA-14 ....
1951 Ford Crestliner, USA-17
two-tone brown and caramel $65-90
black with cream roof $65-90
two-tone black and green $65-90
Hudson Convertible, USA-18
1951 Chevrolet Bel Air 2-door
Convertible, black, USA-21 ....$65-90
1955 Chevrolet 210 2-door
Sedan, light blue, USA-22 ....$65-90
Convertible, USA-25 ....$65-90
Chrysler Town & Country Convertible,
USA—34 ....$65-90

Motormax (also see Redbox, Zee Toys/Zylmex)

www.motormaxtoys.com
Motormax Toy Factory Ltd.
Hong Kong Office & Showroom
7/F, Tower 1, South Seas Centre
75 Mody Road, Tsimshatsui East
Kowloon, Hong Kong
phone: 852-2722-8080
fax: 852-2722-8999
e-mail: hk@motormaxtoy.com (FOB Hong Kong)
RBI Toys Inc.
Los Angeles Office, Showroom & Warehouse
1460 Archibald Avenue
Ontario, California 91761 USA
phone: 909-930-2788
fax: 909-930-2382
e-mail: sales@rbitoys.com (FOB California, U.S.A.)
RBI Distributors Ltd.
UK Office & Showroom
The Hithercroft Industrial Estate
Lesterway, Oxon, OX10 9TH, UK
Phone: 1491-833-477
Fax: 1491-832-547
e-mail: uk@motormaxtoy.com (FOB Wallingford, UK)

Motormax Superwheels Box

Motormax is the latest brand name applied to toys issued by Red Box Inc. (RBI), based in New York City. Older 3" Motormax castings are based largely on reissues of Zee Toys Dynawheels models and a few of their older Zylmex castings.

These days, the Motormax line covers automobile models in 1:18, 1:24, 1:43, and 1:64 scales, 1:6 scale motorcycle models, and an assortment of aircraft models. Their product line is immense. It is important to remember that many of these models are still available at or below retail. Below is a brief listing of selected Motormax models.

Acura Integra Type R
yellow, Road & Track, 1:24 ....$9-12
orange, Road & Track, 1:24 ....$9-12
2003 Acura NSX
metallic blue, 1:18, #73140 ....$15-20
metallic yellow, 1:18, #73140 ....$15-20
Audi A4 Cabriolet, 1:18, #73148 ....$15-20
Audi A8, 1:18, #73149.....................$15-20
2002 BMW 7-Series
metallic dark silver, 1:18, #73132 ....$15-20
black, 1:18, #73132 ....$15-20
BMW M1

yellow, 3"................................$2-3
BMW X5
blue, 1:18 ....$15-20

metallic silver, 3", #6025.............$2-3
BMW Z3

metallic silver blue, 3", #6001 ....$2-3

1949 Buick Convertible
beige, 1:18..............................$15-20
red, 1:18 ....$15-20
1953 Buick Skylark
metallic red, 1:18, #73129 ....$15-20
light patriot blue, 1:18, #73129 ....$15-20
Chevrolet Bel Air Concept
red, 1:18, #73142.......................$15-20
light patriot blue, 1:18, #73142 ....$15-20
Chevrolet Camaro

metallic dark green, 3" $2-3
1958 Chevrolet Corvette
red, 1:18 ....$15-20
blue, 1:18 ....$15-20
1961 Chevrolet Corvette Mako Shark Experimental
gradient dark blue upper to white lower body
with bubble roof, 1:24 ....$15-20

black, 3", Super Wheels #6048...............$2-3
1998 Chevrolet Corvette Convertible

black, 3", #6002 ....$2-3

red, 3", Super Wheels #6002...............$2-3
Chevrolet Corvette Stingray III

maroon, 3", Super Wheels #6007 ....$2-3

Chevrolet Corvette Indy

metallic silver gray, 3", Super Wheels
#6008 ....$2-3

Chrysler Panel Cruiser

purple, 3", Super Wheels #6031 ....$2-3

Chrysler PT Cruiser

metallic red, 3", #6016 ....$2-3

metallic yellow, 3", #6016, Novelty Inc. Col-
lector's Edition $2-3

metallic silver, 3", Super Wheels #6016 ...$2-3

Dodge Charger

metallic blue, 3", Zee Toys Dynawheels
D122 reissue......................................$2-3

2003 Dodge Viper RT/10
    metallic blue, 1:24, #73290 ....$9-12
    red, 1:18, #73137........................$15-20
    red, 1:24, #73290.........................$9-12
    silver, 1:18, #73137.....................$15-20

1940 Ford Deluxe Coupe

burgundy, 1:24 (at one time offered by Fairfield Mint but retracted from their catalog
for gross inaccuracies of detail and propor-
tion)..$12-16

Ford Expedition

metallic blue, 3", Super Wheels #6021 ....$2-3

Ford Explorer

metallic dark green with metallic silver trim,
blue tinted windows, 3", #6061 ....$2-3

Ford F-650 Super Crewzer

black, 1:18 ....$20-25

2002 Ford Focus ZX3
    sonic blue, 1:18, #73127 ....$15-20
    infra-red, 1:18, #73127 ....$15-20

1964½ Ford Mustang Convertible
    metallic green, 1:18, #73142 ....$15-20
    light blue, 1:18, #73142 ....$15-20

1998 Ford Mustang Convertible

metallic dark green, 3", #6006..................$2-3

red, Super Wheels #6006, 3".....................$2-3

2004 Ford Mustang GT Concept Convertible
    light yellow, 1:24, #73256 ....$9-12
    black, 1:24, #73256.........................$9-12

Mustang Mach III

bright red, 3", #6009.................................$2-3

metallic dark green, Super Wheels #6009,
3" $2-3

Honda Accord
    Tuner version, 1:18, #73146 ....$15-20

Humvee
camouflage, 1:24 Scale, #73252 ......$9-12

Jaguar XKE

metallic blue, 3", Zee Toys Dyna Wheels D110 reissue......$2-3

2004 Land Rover Discovery
Bonatti gray, 1:18, #73139 ....$15-20
green, 1:18, #73139 ....$15-20

Kawasaki Mojave 250
1:6, #76254 ....$9-12

Lamborghini Diablo

metallic orange, 3" $2-3

Lexus SC430 Convertible
off white, 1:18 ....$15-20

Lincoln Navicross Concept
burgundy, 1:18, #73143 ....$15-20
black, 1:18, #73143......................$15-20
burgundy, 1:24, #73276 ....$9-12
black, 1:24, #73276..........................$9-12

Lincoln Navigator

black, 3", # 6044..........................$2-3

Mazda MX-5 Miata

metallic dark blue, #6024 ....$2-3

2000 Mercedes-Benz S-Class
black, 1:24, #73291 ....$9-12

champagne, 1:24, #73291..............$9-12
Nissan Skyline GT-R, 1:24
Road & Track, purple $15-20
Pagani Zonda C12
red, 1:18, #73147..........................$15-20
metallic blue, 1:18, #73147 ....$15-20
blue, 1:24, #73272 ....$9-12
black, 1:24, #73272........................$9-12
2003 Peugeot 307CC
red, 1:24, #73286..........................$9-12
light blue, 1:24, #73286 ....$9-12
Peugeot RC
Red, 1:24, #73287..........................$8-10
Black, 1:24, #73287........................$8-10
Plymouth Prowler

purple, 3", #6045 ....$2-3

1999 Pontiac Firebird

red with black roof, 3", #6005..........................$2-3

black, Super Wheels #6005, 3" $2-3

1969 Pontiac GTO Judge, 1:18, #73133
orange..........................$15-20
metallic blue $15-20
Pontiac Rageous

metallic red, 3", Super Wheels #6047 ....$2-3
metallic blue, Super Wheels #6047, 3" ..$2-3
Porsche 911
black, 1:18 ....$15-20

metallic silver, 3" $2-3
Porsche Boxster

metallic silver, 3", #6018..........................$2-3
Roadster

red, 3" $2-3

Saleen SR
white, 1:24, #73246 ....$9-12
blue, 1:24, #73246 ....$9-12
Site Supervisor Car

yellow, 3"..........................$2-3
Toyota Camry

white, 3" $2-3

2003 Toyota Celica

yellow, 3", #6011..........................$2-3

Toyota Hiace

ezVan, blue with yellow graphics, 3", #6022, promotional (ezVan was a Hong Kong courier service that ceased operation in December, 2000) $6-8

Toyota Land Cruiser

metallic blue-green, 3", #6010.................$2-3

Volkswagen Beetle

yellow, 3"...$2-3

Volkswagen Nardo W12 Show Car
   metallic orange, 1:24, #73241 ....$9-12
   black, 1:24, #73241 ....$9-12

Volvo 760 GLE

**metallic graphite gray, 3", Zee Toys D84
Dynawheels reissue..................................$2-3**

Motorworks (see Maisto, Malibu International and others)

"Motorworks" is a Wal-Mart proprietary brand name, as is "kid connection." Diecast toy cars are made by various manufacturers and packaged as Motorworks models. Manufacturers include Maisto, Malibu International, and several others. Refer to the brand on the base of the model for cross-reference in this book. Some Motorworks models are generic, meaning that they have no identifying marks on the model, only on the proprietary box. A sampling is listed below.

1955 Chevrolet Nomad, pale yellow with white roof, 1:24 ....$9-12

1940 Ford Panel Van, metallic dark blue, 1:24 ....$9-12

Mini Cooper, metallic maroon with white roof, 1:18...$12-15

Mountain Service International, Inc. (See Pole Position Collectibles)

MPC (See Model Products Corporation)

MR

MR Collection Models
Via San Gabriele del carso 9/A
21047 Saronna (Va)–Italy
tel: 02 9626748
fax: 02 9600787

MR's website at http://mrc.lrcser.it/mr/default.html reports that "...M.R. Collection Models s.n.c. is a small firm specialized and producing special models of collection cars. Established in 1988, our firm depends upon a staff of nine highly specialized people.

"In 1993, after several years of experience, we began introducing some sets of models. Every stage of the productive process is made rigorously by hand: The execution of the prototype, the assembling, the painting is carried out in the store; everything is done to ensure high quality products. Our series constituted of only 499 pieces, are numbered, equipped with warranty of quality, and assembled by only a highly specialized modelist. All products are manufactured in a modern factory with the most up-to-date technology."

What it doesn't say is whether the models are diecast, white metal, resin or other material.

Alfa Romeo 1900C Sprint
   1951 Cabriolet, red $200-225
   1951 Cabriolet, dark green..........$200-225
   1951 Cabriolet, metallic gray $200-225
   1954 Coupe, cream $200-225
   1954 Coupe, dark gray..............$200-225
   1954 Coupe, black....................$200-225
Ferrari 365 1971 GTC/4
   red $200-225
   metallic blue...............................$200-225
   yellow $200-225
Ferrari 400 1961 S.A. Convertible
   red $200-225
Ferrari Dino 206GT, 1967
   red $200-225
   metallic gray $200-225
   yellow $200-225
Ferrari F40
   1987 Street with Engine $200-225
   1994 Camp Italiano GT, red........$200-225
Porsche 356 Speedster, 1948
   silver $200-225
   yellow.......................................$200-225
Porsche 911, 1996
   Carrera 4S, Polar Silver $200-225
   Carrera 4S, Midnight Blue $200-225
   Carrera 4S, Guards Red...............$200-225
   Carrera Turbo, Speed Yellow $200-225
   Carrera Turbo, Forest Green $200-225
   Carrera Turbo, Arena Red.............$200-225
   GT2, Speed Yellow $200-225
   GT2, Guards Red $200-225
   GT2, Polar Silver $200-225

GT2 Evo II, Polar Silver $200-225
GT2 Evo II, White $200-225
RS, Speed Yellow $200-225
RS, Midnight Blue $200-225
RS, Polar Silver $200-225

MRE

Harvey Goranson reports: "MRE–Again, the info comes from Ma Collection. Begun by Michel El Koubi in Paris, the first dozen or so models were conversions of Solido diecasts (MS series — "Modification Solido"). In 1976, he brought out a range of white metal models — mostly Porsche racing cars at first. By 1979, he had stopped making kits, as he had gotten the racing bug in 1977, driving a Lola T296. Some of the built models from 1977 bear the signature of Dominique Esparcieux (ESDO). They also sold transkits — I had their 1977 Mirage Renault TK for Solido 38."

Simca CG Prototype, 1:43 ....$18-23
Porsche 936 Le Mans 1977, white with
    Martini decals, car # 4 ....$18-23

MTC

Of the many generic diecast toys on the market, MTC is just another one. These inexpensive toys are made in China and marketed by MTC, Inc., of south San Francisco, California. The line includes airplanes, cars, and other vehicles. Their collector value will likely not exceed their original purchase price of usually less than $2.

MTECH

Epoch Co., Ltd.
12-3, 1-Chome, Komagata, Taito-Ku
Tokyo 111, Japan
tel: 81-3-3843-8144
fax: 81-3-3841-8150

MTECH is a brand from Japan introduced in the mid-1990s that offers some fairly nice specimens of popular Japanese cars. Produced in 1:43 scale, MTECH models represent mostly late model cars, both in street and race/rally versions.

A Japanese-language book just published in Asia provides detailed photos of some two or three dozen examples. Determining make and manufacturer of specific models is difficult, but several models can be identified among the mix and are listed below. Other models are not as easy to identify but appear to be representatives of Lexus, Honda, Mitsubishi, Toyota, Nissan, and Mazda. A departure from the usual is the representation of the BMW Z3 with right hand steering and driver. While MTECH models are available in England, they have not yet been spotted in the U. S. A phone number to the manufacturer is provided in the book: 03 (3843) 9177.

Upon finally obtaining an MTECH model, I discovered that Epoch Company Limited, Japan, is in fact the producer of MTECH models. Thanks to Hiromitsu Higuchi, international sales & marketing manager for Epoch and Diecast Toy Collectors Association member, I've been able to make the connection between the company and the brand.

BMW Z3 Road Star
    red, top up with right hand drive and
        driver, MC-01-A $10-12
    silver, top down with right hand drive and
        driver, MC-01-B........................$10-12
City Bus "Pepsi" $10-15
Crane Truck, MC-02, 1997 ....$20-24
Daihatsu Midget II
    blue, MM-04-A $10-12
    yellow, MM-04-B $10-12
Isuzu Freight Van
    "Art Corporation The 0123", MT-07-D.....$17-20
    "McDonald's," MT-07-E $17-20
    blue and cream cab, silver cargo box,
        MT-07 ....$15-18
Isuzu Supermedic, MP-07 ....$17-20
Hino Liesse
    Limousine Bus, MB-02, 1997 ....$15-18
    Route Bus, MB-02-A, "Doraemon" $16-19
    Route Bus, MB-02-C, red, "McDonald's" ...$19-22
    Route Bus, MB-03, 1997 ....$15-18
Hino Ranger
    Auto carrier Truck, MT-05 ....$20-24
    Beverage Truck, MT-01, "Hino" $15-18
    Beverage Truck, MT-01-C, "Asahi Super
        Dry" $17-20
    Beverage Truck, MT-01-D, "Art
        Corporation The 0123" $19-22
    Camion, MR-06 ....$20-24
    Car carrier, "Doraemon carrier car,"
        MT-09 ....$15-18
    Cement Mixer Truck, MT-04 ....$20-24
    Dump Truck, MT-02.........................$20-24
    Fire Engine, MP-05 ....$20-24
    Garbage Truck, MT-03......................$20-24
    Snorkel Fire Truck, "Doraemon Ladder Truck,"
        MP-09 ....$15-18
    Wrecker Truck, MT-06 ....$20-24
Honda Minivan....................................$8-12
Honda CR-V
    silver, MS-16-A $8-12

green, MS-16-B $8-12
Hydraulic Power Shoveler, MC-01, 1997....$20-24
Mazda Efini RX-7
    red, MS-03 ....$8-12
    silver, MS-04 ....$8-12
Mazda Miata, gold, MC-03 ....$8-12
Mazda Miata, green, MC-03.................$8-12
Mitsubishi Delica Space Gear
    Ambulance, MP-01 ....$16-20
    black, MS-10 ....$8-12
    green, MS-09 ....$8-12
    Patrol car, MP-02 ....$10-12
Mitsubishi Lancer GSR EvoIII
    yellow-orange, MS-11 ....$8-12
    red, MS-12 ....$8-12
Mitsubishi Lancer WRC, MR-05.............$12-15
Nissan Altima Falken GT-R, MR-04 ....$10-12
Nissan Cedric
    white, MS-13 ....$8-12
    dark blue, MS-14............................$8-12
    Patrol car, MP-03 ....$15-18
    Patrol car, MP-10 ....$15-18
    Taxi, MP-04 ....$10-12
Nissan Endless Advan GT-R, MR-03.........$10-12
Nissan March Cabriolet with 2 figures
    green, MC-02-A $10-12
    red, MC-02-B $10-12
Nissan Prince Chiba GT-R, blue, MR-07 .....$8-12
Nissan Skyline GT-R
    purple, MS-07 ....$8-12
    silver, MS-08 ....$8-12
    Patrol car, MP-06 ....$10-12
Subaru Legacy Touring Wagon GT............$8-12
Suzuki Wagon R
    silver, MM-01-A $9-12
    "Doraemon Pizza Delivery," MM-01-C....$11-14
Toyota Blistz Supra, MR-01 ....$10-12
Toyota High Ace
    silver, MS-15 ....$8-12
    light blue, "Doraemon," MB-01 ....$9-11
    Kindergarten Bus, fluorescent yellow,
        MB-01 ....$15-18
Toyota RAV4
    red, MS-05 ....$8-12
    blue, MS-06 ....$8-12
Toyota Supra
    black, MS-01 ....$8-12
    silver, MS-02 ....$8-12
Wheel Loader, MC-03 ....$18-22

Muky

Muky toys have been called the Hot Wheels of Argentina even though they have no direct connection with the Mattel brand, although some castings may be recasts from the original, albeit worn-out, Hot Wheels dies.

Models in the Muky Collection are made in Gualeguay, Argentina, which is in Entre Rios province about 100 miles north of Buenos Aires, but across the Parana River. Thanks to Dr. Craig Campbell, associate professor of geography at Youngstown State University, for the geography lesson, and Kimmo Sahakangas for the list.

Ford GT 40
    #20 ....$4-6
    Turbo, with spoiler, #10 ....$4-6
Ford Mark IV
    #18 ....$4-6
    Turbo with spoiler (also called MK IV
      Turbo), #9 ....$4-6
Cadillac Eldorado, #21 ....$4-6
Chapparal 2 G, #28 ....$4-6
"Chevelle SS" (based on Hot Wheels
    Custom AMX), #11 ....$4-6
Custom pickup based on Hot Wheels Deora
    Arenero MUKY, #13 ....$4-6
    Camion Jaula (Stake Truck), #25 ....$4-6
    Casa Rodante MUKY (Camper), #17 .....$4-6
    Cisterna MUKY (Tanker), #23 ....$4-6
    Furgon MUKY (Van), #27 ....$4-6
    Rapit Urbano, #33 ....$4-6
    Skoda Baby (Pipe Truck), #29 ....$4-6
    Volcador MUKY (Dump Truck), #31 ....$4-6
Corvette Special, #16 ....$4-6
Dodge Charger, #15 ....$4-6
Ferrari 308 ....$4-6
'36 Ford Coupe (with hinged rumble seat),
    #30 ....$4-6
'41 Ford Coupe $4-6
Lincoln Continental, #12 ....$4-6
Lamborghini Special (based on Hot
    Wheels Torero), #22 ....$4-6
Lancia 3000 (Super Turbo with spoiler), #32 .....$4-6
Lola GT 40
    #14 ....$4-6
    with spoiler, #8 ....$4-6
"Mac Laren" MGA
    #34 ....$4-6
    Turbo with spoiler, #19 ....$4-6
1968 Plymouth Fury
    Policia (Police), #24 ....$4-6
    Bomberos (Fire Chief), #35 ....$4-6
    Servicio Medico (Paramedic), #36 ....$4-6
    Taximetro (Taxi), #37 ....$4-6
Super Turbo, #26 ....$4-6
Volkswagen Beetle $4-6

Muscle Machines

From the Muscle Machines website at www.musclemachines.com:

Funline Merchandising Company was incorporated in 1993. The first products were 4x4 diecast trucks. In 1994 friction power was added to the trucks. From 1994 to 1998 various toys were added to the product line.

In 1998 licenses were obtained from Chrysler, Ford, and General Motors to cover a brand new issue of classic muscle cars. Muscle Machines was formed as a division of Funline. Development began in 1999 and in the fall of 2000 the 1969 Camaro, 1970 Barracuda and the 1966 Mustang diecasts were introduced in 1:18 scale followed shortly by 1:64 scale diecasts of the 1969 Camaro, 1970 Barracuda, 1966 Mustang, 1969 Chevelle, 1966 GTO, and the 1962 Corvette. The models were immediately a huge success. Demand grew for all makes, body styles and years of cars and trucks.

The prototype models are designed and developed in the United States then sent to China for tooling, casting, painting, assembly, and packaging. Muscle Machines are distributed worldwide with the U.S. being the main market. They are available in a wide variety of retail stores and through mail order houses.

The Muscle Machine lineup has recently expanded to include all categories of cars, monster trucks, motorcycles, and military vehicles. Many innovative all new products are in the design stages now. The success of Muscle Machines is due to the company's commitment to quality, value, and exciting products.

In September 2003 Funline Merchandising Co., Inc. was acquired by Action Performance Company of Phoenix, Arizona. Funline will continue to operate as an independent company.

The Muscle Machine model list is immense, encompassing a broad assortment of models in 1:18, 1:24, and 1:64 scales. Only a few models are considered worth more than retail price to collectors who specialize in these toys. For the large majority though, values remain at or just slightly above retail price.

2002 Acura RSX Type S, Muscle Tuners, 1:64 ....$4-6

Datsun Bluebird 510, Muscle Tuners, 1:64 ....$4-6

2001 Ford FR200, Muscle Tuners, 1:64 ..$4-6

Jeep $4-6

MVC (see Miniature Vehicle Castings)

MZKT

Alex Litovskiy reports of the MZKT brand from Belarus but doesn't provide any details.

N

Nacoral Intercars

Nacoral is a brand of models from Spain that are of lesser quality than Pilen/Auto Pilen models. While most Nacoral models are 1:43 scale, a few 1:25 scale models were also produced, according to collector John Dean. In addition, Nacoral produced at least one racing motorcycle measuring 14 cm, or about 5½ inches long, according to Werner Legrand of Belgium, making it roughly a 1:12 or 1:10 scale model.

Nacoral 1:43 Scale

1968 AMC Javelin AMX, 1:43 ....$20-25
1969 Chevrolet Corvette
    blue, 1:43 ....$20-25
    red, 1:43 ....$20-25
1968 Chevrolet Camaro Europa, 1:43 ...$20-25
Ferrari Dino, 1:43 ....$20-25

Ford Fiesta, 1:43 ....$20-25
1968 Ford Thunderbird, 1:43
    dark blue $20-25
    orange $20-25
    red $20-25
Matra Bagheera, 1:43 ....$20-25
Matra Sport, 1:43 ....$20-25
Mercedes-Benz 280 Sedan, 1:43 ....$20-25
Porsche 911S
    orange, Bosch, Shell, Monte Carlo,
       Martini, #3517 ....$20-25
    red, white interior, Bosch, Shell, Monte
       Carlo, Martini, #3517 ....$20-25
    Rally with driving lights and skis, white
       #18, Bosch, Shell, Monte Carlo,
       Martini, 1:43, #3556 ....$20-25
Porsche 917, metallic blue-green, white
    interior, 1:43, #3515M..................$20-25
Scania 10 x 8 Covered Truck, blue &
    yellow, 1:43..............................$20-25

Nacoral 1:25 Scale
1968 Chevrolet Corvette, red, 1:25........$25-30
Citroën Maserati, 1:25 ....$25-30
Fiat 600, 1:25 ....$25-30
Mercedes-Benz C111, 1:25 ....$25-30
Mini, 1:25 ....$25-30
Renault 5, 1:25 ....$25-30
Rolls Royce Silver Cloud III, 1:25 ....$25-30

Other Nacoral Models
Suzuki 750 Vallelunga GT Racing Motorcycle,
    5½"...$15-20

National Motor Museum Mint (also see Fairfield Mint)

Fairfield Mint and National Motor Museum Mint appear to be synonymous. Both are located in Norwalk, Connecticut, and both produce similar catalogs that feature vehicles from Corgi, SunStar, Signature Models, and others, without actually mentioning the manufacturer's brand name. It is understood that both businesses have made agreements with major diecast model manufacturers to produce models especially for them. See Fairfield Mint for model listing.

National Products (also see Banthrico)

National Products started at the Chicago World's Fair in 1934 and continued producing promotional models through the 1940s and 1950s. Around 1948, Banthrico purchased the company and issued subsequent models under the National Products Division Banthrico.

Buick Super
    1939 4-door $850-1,000
    1940 4-door $1,000-1,250
    1946 4-door $500-650
    1947-48 4-door $350-425
    1949 4-door $300-350
    1950 4-door $350-400
Buick Century 1941 4-door..........$1,000-1,250
Chevrolet Fleetline 2-door Aero Sedan
    1947 ....$325-375
    1948..$350-400
Chrysler Airflow 1934 4-door.............$825-875
Chrysler New Yorker
    1946 4-door $150-175
    1947-48 4-door.........................$150-175
    1949 4-door $300-325
DeSoto Custom
    1946-48 4-door $375-400
    1949 4-door $300-325
Diamond T 1935 Stake Truck.......$4,000-4,500
Dodge Custom 1946-48 4-door........$150-175
Dodge Model B
    1948-50 Pickup Truck $375-400
    1948-50 Stake Truck $375-400
Dodge Coronet 1949 4-door............$300-325
Fargo
    1948-50 Pickup Truck $450-500
    1948-50 Stake Truck $450-500
Federal 1936 Tanker $850-1,000
Ford F-1
    1948-50 Panel Truck $350-375
    1948-50 Pickup Truck $325-375
    1951 Panel Truck $425-475
    1951 Pickup Truck......................$400-450
    1952 Panel Truck $350-375
    1952 Pickup Truck $325-350
Ford F-2
    1948-50 Stake Truck $500-550
    1951 Stake Truck $425-475
    1952 Stake Truck $350-375
Ford F-100 1953 Pickup Truck............$325-350
Graham 1934 4-door.................$1,000-1,250
GMC
    1948-50 FC Pickup Truck $200-225
    1948-50 FF Dump Truck...............$250-275
    1954 100 Pickup Truck $275-300
    1958 350 Dump Truck $325-350
Hudson Terraplane 1934 ....$750-1,000
International
    1934-36 C Panel Truck..........$2,750-3,000
    1937-40 D Panel Truck.........$2,750-3,000
    1947 KB Phone Truck with boom and
       pole $500-550
Lincoln Cosmopolitan
    1949 4-door $375-400
    1950 4-door $525-600

Mack 1940-53 L Tanker...................$350-375
Mercury
    1949 4-door $375-400
    1950 4-door $450-500
    1950 4-door Pace car $500-575
Nash 600 1949 4-door
    single color $175-200
    two-tone $225-250
Nash Statesman 1950 4-door
    single color $175-200
    two-tone $225-250
Nash Rambler 1950-52 Convertible....$475-500
Plymouth Special Deluxe 1946-48
    4-door $300-325
Pontiac Streamliner 1948 4-door........$175-200
Pontiac Chieftain 1949 4-door $275-300
REO
    1936 4-door $900-1200
    1937 Tanker $900-1200
Studebaker
    1934 "Replica of Giant World's Fair
       Studebaker" on trunk $350-425
    1934 President 4-door $375-425
    1934 T Stake Truck $1,000-1,250
    1935 President 4-door, smaller
       scale...................................$900-1,200
    1935 President 4-door, larger
       scale................................$3,250-3,750
    1936 President 4-door, approx.
       4½"....................................$475-500
    1936 President 4-door, approx.
       6½"....................................$750-800
    1938 Commander 4-door.........$750-1,000
    1947-48 Commander 2-door $250-275
    1949 Commander 2-door...........$250-275
    1949-53 2R Pickup Truck $350-375
    1949-53 2R Stake Truck $450-475
White
    1936-40 Stake Truck $525-550
    1939-40 Horse Delivery Van with
       pop-out engine $550-575
    1941 Stake Truck $550-575
    1941-42 Horse Delivery Van with
       pop-out engine $575-600
    1949-65 3000 Stake Truck Cabover
       with engine $350-400

National Toys

The nation in this case is Italy. The year is 1961. Four 1:45 scale plastic models were produced by this company.

Alfa Romeo Giulietta Sprint $45-60
Fiat 1500 Roadster..............................$45-60
Fiat 1800 Sedan $45-60
Vanwall Formula 1 ....$45-60

Neff-Moon

Charles Neff and William Moon founded Neff-Moon in Sandusky, Ohio, in 1923, to produce pressed steel toys with interchangeable parts. The beginning of the Great Depression in 1929 spelled the end for Neff-Moon toys.

Coupe	$300-500
Dump Truck	$300-500
Emergency Truck	$350-500
Grocery Van	$300-500
Sedan	$300-500
Sedan, 12"	$900-1,200
Sedan Delivery Truck	$500-750
Taxi, 12"	$500-750
Tow Truck, 16"	300-500
Truck with interchangeable parts	$1,250-1,500

Neuhierl

It was in Fürth, Bavaria, in 1920 that Josef Neuhierl first starting manufacturing tin toys, but it wasn't until 1963 that Josef, with his son's assistance, stepped into toy history by introducing the first 1:32 scale Carrera Racing Track.

Moving to Nürnberg, then experiencing internal restructuring during the 1990s, the Neuhierl company was purchased by the Stadlbauer Group in 1999. The Carrera tradition still survives through the new owners. The newest addition to the line is the 1:43 scale Carrera GO!!! series and videogame interfaces. Unfortunately, no product list has been found.

Nevco

Nevco
Box 2355
Atascadero, CA 93423 USA
phone: 805-466-8685

One of the newest companies to appear on the market is Nevco. Their first model is a replica of a classic 1930s streamlined toy car with Art Deco box silkscreened by hand. Their second is a sleek transporter for the first model.

"The Special," burgundy and gold, limited edition of 4,000	$175-200
"The Transporter"	$275-300

Nevins International, Ltd.

A pair of 1:43 scale models made by Nevins International, Ltd. were recently offered on specially marked boxes of Kellogg's Corn Flakes. The two-car set is of the Brooks & Dunn Metal Rodeo Legends Racing cars representing 5:8 scale replicas of early NASCAR racers. In 1998 or thereabouts, this mail-away promo cost just a dollar.

Brooks & Dunn Metal Rodeo Legends Racing two-car set	$16-24

New Clover (also see Clover)

New Clover models are made in Asia by New Clover International Ltd of Hong Kong.

Bobcat X225 Skid Loader, 1:25	$35-40
Bobcat 743B Skid Loader, 1:19	$25-30
Bobcat 753 Skid Loader, 1:50	$10-15
Bobcat 753 Skid Loader, 1:25	$25-30
Bobcat 7753 Skid Loader, 1:25	$25-30
Melroe (Bobcat) M-200 1959-1962 Loader, 1:25 (replica of 1st machine built by Melroe Company)	$18-23
Semi Flatbed with three Bobcat 753 Skid Loaders, 1:50	$55-60
Kiamaster Ambulance, 1:43	$18-23
Kiamaster Kombi, 1:43	$18-23
Pontiac Firebird Coupe, 1:59	$5-8

New-Ray (or New Ray)

New Ray Toys USA
14317 East Don Julian Rd
City of Industry, CA 91746 USA
tel: 626-330-1711
fax: 626-330-1722
toll-free: 877-8NEWRAY (877-863-9729)

New Ray Toys Company Ltd.
Unit 4, 9-11, 12/F.,
Houston Centre, 63 Mody Road,
Tsimshatsui East, Hong Kong
e-mail to:info@new-ray.com
tel: (852) 2721 4693
fax: (852) 2721 3553
www.new-ray.com

Previously distributed by
Midwestern Home Products, Inc.
1105 Orange St.
Wilmington, DE 19801 USA

New-Ray toys are manufactured in China by New-Ray Toys Co., Ltd. The first examples of New-Ray toys found are approximately 1:43 scale farm tractors with driver and flywheel drive. Tractors are sold separately or with trailers that include detachable containers. Sold in either yellow or orange, the tractors sell for $4 each, while the tractor/trailer combinations sell for $6.

The most popular model found from New-Ray is a neat little Hummer faithfully reproduced in 1:32 scale. The doors open on this top-down version which is labeled on the box as being distributed by Midwestern Home Products, Inc. of Wilmington, Delaware.

Since finding the Hummer, the author has noticed a lot more New-Ray toys, mostly pickup trucks and jeeps of similar construction and quality, showing up at Wal-Mart and other stores.

Also offered by New-Ray are small (1¼ to 1½ inch long), inexpensive diecast toy cars and motorcycles with pull-back action. Their lack of detail, accuracy, and markings result in little or no collectible value.

In 1998, New-Ray issued an assortment of 1:43 scale models dubbed the "Open Top Collections," convertible sports cars in acrylic flip-top display boxes. Mercedes, Mustangs, and Golfs comprise most of the models in the series. Besides being sold individually in fliptop display boxes, they have also been found in window box 4-packs. Since then, the line has been renamed the "City Cruisers Collection."

A more recent find is of a Volkswagen New Beetle in various colors. Marked with the name Boley, a toy and novelty distributor, and Speedy Wheels on the box, the bottom of the model reveals that it is made by New Ray. Speedy Power and Speedy Wheels were at one time produced by ToyMark.

Alfa Romeo

1938 8C 2900, yellow with black fenders, 1:43 ....$5-6

1962 Giulietta Spider 1600CC, black with cream interior, 1:43	$5-6
1989 Spider, white with gray interior, 1:43	$4
1996 Spider, red with black interior, 1:43	$5-6

BMW
1988 M3 Convertible, metallic maroon with butterscotch interior, 1:43	$5-6
1995 M3 Convertible, metallic slate blue-green with butterscotch interior, 1:43	$5-6

2000 Z8, metallic silver, 1:43 ....$5-6

Buick

1949 Roadmaster Dynaflow, light green with blue interior, 1:43 ....$5-6

1955 Century Convertible, metallic light pine green, 1:43 ....$5-6

1958 Century Convertible, pink, 1:43 .....$5-6

Cadillac
  1955 Eldorado, red with cream and red
    interior, 1:43 ....$4-5

1959 Series 62 convertible, bright metallic sky blue with off-white and red interior, 1:43 .....$4-5

1976 Coupe De Ville convertible, white with red interior, 1:43 ....$4-5

Chevrolet Corvette Convertible

1957, silver and red with red interior, 1:43 ....$4-5

1967, metallic light blue, 1:43 ....$5-6
1969, bright orange-pink, 1:43 ....$5-6
Chrysler C-300 convertible, 1955 (actual car
  was never produced as a convertible)

black with white and red interior, 1:43...$4-5
  pale blue with dark blue and white
    interior, 1:43 ....$4-5
Chrysler Turbine Car Convertible, 1967
  (actual car was never produced as a
  convertible)
    yellow $5-6
    copper..$5-6
Ford Mustang
  1964? Convertible, black with white interior,
    1:43 ....$5-6

1964? Convertible, gold with red and black interior, 1:43..$5-6

  1988 GT Convertible, green with gray
    interior, 1:43 ....$5-6
  1994 GT Convertible, yellow, tan
    interior, 1:43 ....$5-6

Fastback, black with gold racing stripes, 1:32..$7-8

Mach III Concept car, red, 1:43 ....$5-6

1956 Ford Thunderbird, yellow with black and white interior, 1:43 ....$4-5

Hummer, #45323, 1:32
  red with light gray interior $5-6
  blue with white interior..........................$6-7
Jaguar
  1961 E-Type Cabriolet, green with cream
    interior, 1:43 ....$5-6
  1988 XJ-S V12 Convertible, silver, 1:43 ....$6-7
  XKE, green, 1:43 ....$6-7
Jeep
  CJ7, 1:32, red with black roll bar and
    interior $6-7
  Dakar, 1:32, pale bronze, #54203 ......$6-7
  Icon, 1:32, dark gray with silver roll bar,
    black interior, #54083 ....$6-7
  Willys, 1:32, Army green......................$5-6
Lamborghini 4 x 4, silver with black interior,
  1:32...$6-7
Land Rover Station Wagon, #44323, 1:32
green with white roof and interior $5-6
  yellow with black roof and interior..........$6-7
Mercedes-Benz M-Class, 1:32
  dark blue...$6-7
  300 SL Roadster, 1957, black with
    butterscotch interior, 1:43 ....$5-6
  280 SL, 1968, red, gray interior, 1:43...$5-6

300 GD, maroon, 4-wheel drive friction motor, 1:32..$7-8

  350 SL, 1971, greenish silver with gray interi-
    or, 1:43 ....$5-6
  600 SL, 1992, metallic brass with cream and
    charcoal interior, 1:43 ....$5-6
MGB, 1967, blue with cream interior,
  1:43..$5-6
MGF, 1996, red with red and black interior,
  1:43..$5-6

Shelby Series 1, metallic blue with white racing stripes, 1:43................................$5-6

Volkswagen
1200 Cabriolet, baby blue, 1:43 ....$5-6
Concept One Convertible, yellow with
yellow and black interior, 1:43 ....$5-6
1988 Golf Cabriolet, green, 1:43 ....$5-6
1993 Golf Cabriolet, white, red interior,
1:43 ....$5-6

Willys Jeep, 1:32 ....$6-8

New Trax (see Top Gear Trax)

Nicky Toys (also see Dinky)

Nicky Toys began in Calcutta, India, by S. Kumar & Company, also known as Atamco Private Ltd., in 1968 when some older Dinky tooling was obtained from Meccano. Nicky Toys' noticeably poorer castings are the result of old dies that were already worn out by extensive use. The company continued to produce such toys until the 1970s.

Bentley S Coupe $30-35
Daimler Jaguar 3.4 ....$25-30
   Police $45-50
Dump Truck $50-55
Howitzer $25-30
Jaguar D-Type $25-30
Jaguar E-Type...................................$25-30
Jaguar Mark Ten $25-30
Lincoln Continental............................$45-50
Mercedes-Benz 220 SE $35-40
   Taxi $40-45
MGB..$25-30
Mighty Antar Tank Transporter $75-80
Military Ambulance...................................$35-40
Plymouth Fury
   Convertible.....................................$45-50
   Hardtop..$45-50
Standard 20 Mini Atlas Kenebrake
   Ambulance......................................$25-30
   Bus $25-30
Triumph Vitesse..................................$25-30
Universal Army Jeep $45-50
Universal Jeep....................................$45-50
Vanwall...$30-35

Volkswagen 1500 ....$45-50
   Police $45-50

Niedermeier

All but the name remains a mystery regarding this obscure German toy manufacturer.

Nigam

Resembling crude versions of Mercury models, Nigam models were produced in Italy in 1948.

Alfa Romeo Grand Prix, #1 ....$100-125
Auto-Union Grand Prix, #2 ....$100-125
E.R.A. Grand Prix, #6.......................$100-125
Gardner's MG Record Car, #3 ....$100-125
Maserati Grand Prix, #4 ....$100-125
Mercedes-Benz Grand Prix, #5 ....$100-125

N.J. International

N. J. International is represented by 1:87 scale (HO gauge) unpainted cast metal kits.

Aerial Ladder Fire Truck
   kit $39-44
1964 Chevrolet Corvette Sting Ray
   kit $6-8
   assembled & painted..........................$9-12
1965 Ford Shelby GT-350 Mustang
   kit $6-8
   assembled & painted..........................$9-12
Jeep Gladiator Pickup Truck
   kit $6-8
   assembled $9-12
Mack C Ladder Truck........................$69-74 kit
Mack C, tractor only ....$29-34 kit
Mack MB Tractor Tilt Cab..................$25-30 kit
Pierce Mid-Ship Pumper....................$35-40 kit
Pumper Kit with 4-door Closed Cab .....$37-44 kit
Snorkel Fire Truck..............................$39-44 kit
UPS Delivery ....$19-24 kit

Norev

M. Veron started the firm called Norev (Veron spelled backwards) in a suburb of Lyon, France, in 1953. His brother Emile Veron later founded the company that produced Majorettes.

The first Norev models were plastic in 1:43 scale. Later models were made of diecast metal with tinplate or plastic chassis. Norev's product line included 1:72 scale "Mini-Jet" series, the larger "Maxi-Jet," and "Jet-Car" series.

Mini-Jet models are currently valued around $5-8 each. Maxi-Jets are a series of trucks for $12-16, and Jet-Cars are valued between $5

and $30. Norev is now believed to be out of business, and it is reported that Eligor of France has acquired many of Norev's dies.

It has been recently reported that Majorette F of France now owns Norev, which wouldn't be a surprise since M. Veron of Lyon, France, is likely a close relative of Emile Veron, founder of Majorette F, also of Lyon, France.

Norev Plastic Series, 1:43
Citroën 15CV 6, #3, 1954-1959 ....$12-15
Citroën Ami 6 Break, #2, 1965-1980 ....$12-15
Ford Vedette 54, #2, 1953-1959 ....$30-40
Opel Rekord L-1700, #1, 1965-1969 ....$12-15
Panhard Dyna, #4, 1954-1960 ....$36-48
Panhard PL17 Break, #4, 1965-1971.....$24-36
Peugeot 201, 1930, #6, 1966-1971 ...$16-24
Peugeot 203, #8, 1955-1958 ....$36-48
Peugeot 204, #5, 1965-1980.................$6-12
Peugeot J7 Van, #7, 1967-1973...........$24-32
Renault 16/16TX, #3, 1965-1980 ....$8-12
Renault 4CV, #5, 1955-1957..............$36-48
Simca Aronde 9, #1, 1953-1956 ....$45-55
Simca Aronde 9 Elysee, #5,
   1956-1962 ....$32-40
Simca Trianon, #7, 1955-1958 ....$32-40
Simca Versailles, #6, 1955-1959..........$36-48

Norev Mini-Jet series, 1:72
Bertone Trapeze, #412.........................$5-8
Chevrolet Camper Pickup, #460 ....$5-8
Ford Mustang, #424 ....$5-8
Matra Bagheera, #402 ....$5-8
Peugeot 504, #405 ....$5-8

Norev Maxi-Jet Series
Caravan $12-16
DAF Circus Truck $12-16
Volvo Breakdown Truck $12-16
Saviem Drinks Truck $12-16

Norev Jet-Cars
Ford Taunus 12M................................$20-24
Lancia Stratos.....................................$8-12
Matra F1 ....$20-24
Mercedes C-111 ....$12-16
Peugeot 404 Coupe............................$30-36
Renault 4L $28-32
Volkswagen 1500 ....$28-32

Norscot
Norscot Group, Inc.
10510 North Port Washington Rd.
Mequon, WI 53092 USA

Norscot is a recently discovered brand of 1:50 to 1:64 scale Caterpillar construction equipment. The copyright date of 1998 on the package indicates the relatively new company has been around at least a couple of years. Their resemblance to Ertl models, including the package which features a stamped serial number, may not be a coincidence. Typical prices range from $15 to $46 US.

Cat D6H Track-Type Tractor, 1:64 ....$15-20
Cat Challenger 85D Agricultural Tractor,
    1:64 ....$15-20

Nostalgic

Some Nostalgic models are copies of older Tootsietoys. Further information is unknown.

Ahrens-Fox 1931 Fire Truck, #685, 1:43....$65-70
Allard 1951 J2 Roadster, #675, 1:43.....$65-70
Buick 1953 Skylark Convertible
    top down, green, #273, 1:43 ....$60-65
    top up, #290, 1:43........................$65-70
Chevrolet
    1935 Van "7-Up," #703, 1:43 ....$65-70
    1935 Van "Cities Service," #696,
        1:43..................................$65-70
    1935 Van "Coke," #688, 1:43 ....$65-70
    1935 Van "Conoco," #700, 1:43....$65-70
    1935 Van "Evening Standard," #669,
        1:43..................................$60-65
    1935 Van "Exide," #699, 1:43 ....$65-70
    1935 Van "Goodyear," #704,
        1:43..................................$65-70
    1935 Van "Shamrock Oil, #698,"
        1:43..................................$65-70
    1935 Van "Standard Oil," #697,
        1:43..................................$65-70
    1935 Van "Sunoco," #702, 1:43.....$65-70
    1935 Van "Tri-Star," #701, 1:43 ......$65-70
    1935 Van "UPS," #705, 1:43 ....$65-70
    1960 Van "UPS," brown & gold,
        #681, 1:43 ....$60-65
Chevrolet Corvette
    1956 Roadster, red, #660, 1:43......$65-70
    1964 Coupe, #243, 1:43 ....$60-65
    1975, #230, 1:43 ....$60-65
    1982, #227, 1:43 ....$60-65
Cord 1937 Coupe, #220, 1:43 ....$60-65
Divco 1950 Van
    "Borden's," #687, 1:43 ....$65-70
    "Coca-Cola," #806, 1:43 ....$65-70
    "Fire," #803, 1:43 ....$65-70
    "Police," #809, 1:43 ....$65-70
    "Sealtest," #802, 1:43.................$65-70
Ford
    1915 Model T Fire Ladder Truck, red,

#667, 1:43 ....$65-70
1915 Model T Police Van, black &
    white, #668, 1:43 ....$60-65
1930 Model A 5-window Coupe, green
    & black, #223, 1:43.................$60-65
1930 Model A Pickup, #677,
    1:43.....................................$60-65
1930 Model A 4-door Sedan, #205,
    1:43.....................................$60-65
1930 Model A Canopy Pickup, #202,
    1:43.....................................$60-65
1930 Model A Roadster, "Spearmint,"
    white & green, #204, 1:43 ....$60-65
1930 Model A Roadster, "Toledo
    Show," #204, 1:43 ....$60-65
1930 Model A Roadster, top down,
    #203, 1:43 ....$60-65
1931 Model AA Dump Truck, #219,
    1:43.....................................$60-65
1931 Model AA Chemical Fire Truck,
    #683, 1:43 ....$65-70
1932 Coupe Fire Chief, red & black,
    #229, 1:55 ....$60-65
1936 Army Ambulance, green, #248,
    1:43.....................................$65-70
1936 Roadster, #234, 1:43 ....$65-70
1936 UPS Van, brown & gold, #611,
    1:43.....................................$60-65
1936 UPS Van, brown & gold, #662,
    1:43.....................................$65-70
1936 Van, maroon, #692, 1:43......$65-70
1939 Wagon, metallic light blue,
    #279, 1:43 ....$65-70
1965 Mustang 2+2, black, #270,
    1:43.....................................$60-65
Graham 1932 Van "REA," #680, 1:43....$60-65
International 1954 Soda Truck
    "Pepsi," white, blue and red, #652,
        1:55.................................$60-65
    "Coca-Cola," #657, 1:55 ....$60-65
LaSalle
    1934 Coupe, #673, 1:43 ....$65-70
    1934 Roadster, #682, 1:43 ....$65-70
Lincoln 1941 Continental, #281, 1:43....$65-70
Mack
    1931 Mack AC Fire Hose Truck, #690,
        1:43.................................$65-70
    1954 Mack B Fire Pumper, #689,
        1:43.................................$65-70
Porsche 356
    Coupe, #222, 1:43 ....$65-70
    Roadster, #678, 1:43..................$65-70
Seagrave 1932 Fire Truck, #686, 1:43 ..$65-70
Willys Jeepster
    1950 #684, 1:43 ....$65-70
    1950 "Coke," #691, 1:43 ....$65-70

Novacar (also see Majorette)

Originally produced by the Portuguese company Minia Portos Juguetes E Brinquedos Lda., Novacar became a division of Majorette of France in 1993. Novacar is a series of small-scale toy vehicles with plastic bodies and metal chassis, except for number 112 F1 Racer, which has a diecast metal body and plastic chassis. Models were most recently available as the new Majorette 100 Series and usually sold in sets of four cars. Some models from the plastic Novacar series are now being offered in diecast metal as part of the Majorette assortment.

Chevrolet Corvette, #103
    white with black "23", green & red
        accents $2-3
    white with red "23," green & red accents ..$2-3

black with white "Corvette" and Chevrolet logo $2-3

    black with silver "Corvette" and Chevrolet
        logo $2-3
    clear with red flecks, dark red & white
        interior $2-3
    clear with silver flecks, purple & pink interior ..$2-3
Chevrolet Extended Cab Pickup, #116

black with white accents $2-3

    black with skyroof..............................$2-3
    clear with red flecks, dark red & white
        interior $2-3
    clear with yellow flecks, lime green & pink
        interior $2-3
Chevrolet Impala Police car, #109
    white with blue & gold markings.............$2-3

black with white & gold markings $2-3

F1 Racer, #112
   yellow with red & black accents, red plastic base $2-3

black with gold & red accents, white plastic base $2-3

Ferrari 308, #101

light yellow with red interior $2-3
   darker yellow with red interior................$2-3

Ferrari F40, #120
   red $2-3

Ferrari Testarossa, #104

red with "Ferrari" & logo on hood...........$2-3
   red with "S RACING" on hood $2-3

Ford Escort GT, #114

yellow $2-3

Ford Van, #121
   purple with flame accents $2-3

Honda Acura NSX, #117

red with black interior...........................$2-3
   red with white interior $2-3

Jeep, #119
   blue with black top, yellow accents (1995) ...$2-3

Kenworth Semi Tractor, #108

blue with red & white stars & stripes $2-3

Mercedes-Benz 500SL, #105

silver-gray with black interior, "500SL" on doors $2-3
   silver-gray with red interior, no markings ...$2-3

Nissan 300 ZX, #102
   light blue with red interior, black & gold accents $2-3

darker blue with black interior, black & gold accents...$2-3
   clear with silver flecks, blue-gray & yellow interior $2-3
   clear with silver flecks, purple & white interior $2-3

Nissan Pathfinder/Terrano, #107
   red with "FIRE DEPT." markings $2-3
   red with black & white Rally markings $2-3

green with black & white Rally markings....$2-3

white with black & gold "SHERIFF" markings $2-3

Peugeot 605, #106

white with black interior.............................$2-3
   white with red interior $2-3

Porsche LeMans GT Racer, #111

black with white accents, "TOP DRIVERS" on nose $2-3
   clear with yellow flecks, lime green interior $2-3
   clear with silver flecks, blue-gray interior $2-3

Renault Espace Van, #110

red with "Espace" on sides in script lettering $2-3
   white with blue "Ambulance" markings, orange accents $2-3
   yellow with blue & red Rally accents........$2-3

Volkswagen Caravelle Van, #113
   red with black & gold accents $2-3

red with "Surf" graphics (Majorette #248 version)...$2-3

NSG Marketing Corp. (also see Traffic Stoppers and Summer)

There seems to be a connection between NSG and Summer models. NSG Marketing Corporation currently produces a variety of inexpensive toys and sets of crudely cast vehicles in roughly 1:64 scale called Traffic Stoppers. Summer models appear to be larger models of slightly more accurate scale and detail, though still crude compared to other 1:43 scale models.

Traffic Stoppers are virtually unidentifiable out of their package as anything but generic. Even in the package, they are currently worthless to collectors.

Nutmeg Collectibles

In 1990, Mark Dadio founded Nutmeg Collectibles, a company that established a symbiotic relationship with Matchbox by arranging to produce custom variations of Matchbox number 32 Modified Racer and number 34 Sprint Racer.

Nutmeg Modified Racer (Matchbox #32,
production version introduced in 1988)
red body, black interior, chrome
exhausts, "Mike 15".....................$6-9
yellow body, green interior, chrome
exhausts, "44 Reggie/Magnum
Oils"....................................$6-9
white body, red interior, chrome exhausts,
"U2 Jamie".............................$6-9
white body, black interior, chrome exhausts,
"1 Tony/Universal Joint Sales"..........$6-9
red body, red interior, black exhausts,
"36" & stripes.........................$6-9
red body, orange-yellow interior,
black exhausts, "12" & stripes...........$6-9
white & blue body, blue interior,
black exhausts, "ADAP 15"............$6-9
white body, translucent blue interior,
black exhausts, "41" & stripes..........$6-9
red body, red interior, chrome exhausts,
"38 Jerry Cook".......................$6-9
white body, orange interior, chrome
exhausts, "Maynard Troyer"...........$6-9
dark blue body, black interior,
chrome exhausts, "3 Ron Bouchard"...$6-9
orange-yellow body, green interior,
chrome exhausts, "4 Bugs".............$6-9
red body, red interior, chrome exhausts,
"42 Jamie Tomaino"...................$6-9
orange-yellow body, red interior,
chrome exhausts, "4 Satch Wirley"...$6-9
dark blue body, blue interior, chrome
exhausts, "3 Doug Heveron".........$6-9

black body, black interior, chrome exhausts,
"21 George Kent".....................$6-9
dark blue body, black interior, black exhausts,
"12"...................................$6-9
blue body, black interior, chrome exhausts, "3
Mike McLaughlin".....................$8-10
Nutmeg Sprint Racer (Matchbox #34,
production version introduced in 1990)
red body, white driver, blue "Williams
5M"...................................$6-9
red body, white driver, white "Williams
5M"...................................$8-10
black body, white driver, "TMC 1".........$6-9
white body, red driver, "Schnee 8D".......$6-9
yellow body, white driver, "Ben Cook &
Sons 33x"..............................$6-9
blue body, white driver, "Ben Allen 1a"...$6-9
red body, white driver, "7 Joe Gaerte"....$6-9
red body, white driver, "4 Gambler".......$6-9
yellow body, white driver, "17 F&G
Classics East"..........................$6-9
yellow body, white driver, "7c Vivarin-D.
Blaney"................................$6-9
powder blue body, white driver, "69
Schnee-D. Krietz".....................$6-9
black body, white driver, "49 Doug
Wolfgang".............................$6-9

NuToyz

A division of Parkway International (HK) Ltd.
9/FL., New East Ocean Centre
9 Science Museum Rd.
T.S.T. East, Hong Kong, China

NuToyz Just Truckin' Metal Trucks appear to be Hong Kong knock-offs of Remco Tuff Ones. Similarities in packaging and style of manufacturing is so similar that one might conclude that one is manufactured by the other. Construction is a combination of pressed steel and molded plastic. Value remains around retail price of $3–4 each.

Ny-Lint

David Nyberg and Bernard C. Klint formed Ny-Lint Tool and Manufacturing Company of Rockford, Illinois, in 1937. They started producing pressed steel toys in 1946. The brand survives today as a subsidiary of Funrise Toy Corporation and is still based in Rockford, Illinois. Below is just a small sampling, most of which I had as a child in the 1960s.

Ford Econoline Ambulance with stretcher, #6700,
12".......................................$200-250

Ford Pickup and U-Haul Box Trailer,
1960s $200-250

Jalopy, 9⅝", #6800, 1960s $60-75
Army Jeep, 12" $150-175
Ranch Truck, Chase & Sanborn, 14"....$150-175
Vacationer Bronco and Travel Trailer,
20" $200-250
Bronco and Zoo Trailer and Cage with zoo animals, 20" $200-250

NZG

NZG Modelle GmbH
Sigmundstr. 147
90431 Nürnberg
Germany
phone: 0911/65965-0
fax: 0911/611776
e-mail: info@nzg.de
www.nzg.de/

Nürnberger Zinkdruckguß, otherwise known as NZG, began in Nürnburg, Germany, in 1968, by producing an assortment of construction vehicles. The company stuck with the heavy equipment theme until 1984, when a series of 1:43 scale Porsches and 1:35 scale Mercedes-Benz models were introduced, along with a few trucks and buses. A large assortment of current models is available from fine toy and model dealers. According to an undated but recent NZG catalog, NZG was for some time distributed by Schuco Toy Co., Inc., New York, a division of Schuco of Germany. NZG is still in business, with new models currently being produced.

B&T High Rise Forklift, #316, 1:25..........$30-45
Blaw-Knox Paver, #245, 1:50...............$60-75
Case
1845 Uni-loader, 1:35 ....$40-55
850B Angle/tilt dozer, 1:35............$40-55
Caterpillar
16G Grader, #387, 1:50 ....$75-90
245 Excavator, #160, 1:50...........$45-60
245 with hydraulic hammer, #377,
1:50......................................$55-70
325L Excavator, #367, 1:50..........$40-55
416 Backhoe with Hammer, #378,
1:50......................................$35-45
416B Backhoe Loader, #285.2,
1:50......................................$30-45
428 Backhoe, silver anniversary Edition,
#285.1L, 1:50 ....$30-45

428 Backhoe with Hammer, #378.1,
1:50..$35-45
627 Scraper, #126, 1:50 ....$45-60
966F Wheel Loader, #237, 1:50.....$35-50
966F Wheel Loader, Silver Anniversary
Edition, #237.06, 1:50 ....$45-60
966F Wood Loader, #376, 1:50.....$45-60
988B Wheel Loader, #167, 1:50 ....$55-70
994 Wheel Loader, #366, 1:50.........$159
D4E Track Dozer, #205, 1:50.........$25-40
D7 Dozer WW II, #386, 1:50.....$125-140
D9N Track Dozer, #298, 1:50.........$45-60
PR450 Pavement Profilier, #299,
1:50..$45-60
Demag
Automatic Remote Control Lift, #370,
1:50.......................................$25-30
H 485 S Loader, #357, 1:50 ......$160-175
Paver, #231, 1:50............................$30-45
Fiat Ducato Fire Dept. Van, #310F, 1:43...$20-30
Grove
RT 760 Rough Terrain Crane, #149,
1:50.......................................$45-60
Scissor Lift, 1:50, #374 ....$25-30
TM9120 Truck Crane, #380,
1:50....................................$115-130
Kaelble Wheel Loader SJ14B, #389,
1:50 ....$45-60
Kramer Tremo Utility Truck, #300,
1:35 ....$20-25
Krupp S400 Mining Excavator, #194,
1:50 ....$75-90
Lift Truck "Bulli," #321.2.................$20-25
Mercedes
0404 Touring Bus, #361, 1:43 ....$45-60
Unimog, #371, 1:43.......................$25-30
Unimog, #371.1, 1:50....................$25-30
Unimog UN, #371.3, 1:50 ....$30-40
Michigan L150 Wheel Loader, #359,
1:50 ....$45-60
O&K Grader F 156A, #332, 1:50 ....$40-55
Porsche
911, #390, 1:43 ....$20-30
911 C2/4 Turbo, #393, 1:43 ....$20-30
911 Speedster, #327, 1:43.............$20-30
911 Targa, #267, 1:43, 1986.......$30-45
968 Cabriolet, #364, 1:43 ....$20-30
968 Coupe, #363 ....$20-30
Saris Trailer, #373 ....$15-20
Scania City Bus CN112, #293, 1:50 ....$40-55
Sennebogen 613M Telecrane, #392,
1:50 ....$40-55
Vogele 1800 Pave, #385r, 1:50...........$45-60
Volvo
Articulated Bus, #311, 1:50 ....$45-60
VME BM A25 Dumper, #365, 1:50....$35-45

VME L150 Wheel Loader with
attachments, #359, 1:50 ....$45-60
Wirtgen Pavement Profiler, #379, 1:50 ...$45-60
Zeppelin
206 Track Loader, #257, 1:50 ....$40-55
908 Wheel Loader, #235, 1:50 ......$20-25

O

OddzOn

OddzOn is an offshoot of the Russ Berrie plush toy company that reportedly produced a few diecast toys, along with an eclectic offering of other unusual toys. The Vortex Mach 110 football, Koosh ball, and associated Koosh spin-offs are their most visible products. The company also owns Tinkertoys and Rubik's Cube, but no model list is known for their diecast vehicles.

Off 43

This unusual brand showed up in a detailed ad in *Model Auto Review* magazine out of Great Britain. They produce 1:43 scale diecast models made in Italy.

Romeo Van
Abarth Spark Plugs $50-55
Alitalia $40-45
Ambulance, Milan, white and green ...$40-45
Ambulance, Milan, white and blue $40-45
Ambulance, military, olive..................$40-45
Fire Vigil del Fuoco $40-45
Hi Roof Ambulance, Italian Red Cross....$40-45
Michelin, M Bibendum on roof...........$40-45
Ola (Italian detergent) $40-45
plain red...$40-45
Police, Guardia di Finanza, gray........$40-45
Fiat Campagnola
open roof, gray................................$40-45
open roof, stone...............................$40-45
closed roof, Malpensa Airport............$45-50

OGDI Toys of Yesterday

John Hodges
Toys of Yesterday
50 Chiswick Village
London W4 3BY, England

When *Collecting Toys* (Kalmbach Publishing, Waukesha, Wisconsin,) was still being published, the magazine featured an article in its August 1995 issue on John Hodges's Toys of Yesterday, toy cars modelled after Meccano Dinky toys but representative of vehicles Meccano planned to produce but didn't.

Hodges felt a loss when Dinky's British-based Meccano Ltd. went out of business in

1979. So in his spare time, Hodges's attempted to fill the void. His first model, produced in 1980, was so authentic of the Dinky styling that European model journals praised his work, and the London Toy Museum purchased one for its collection.

Since then, Hodges has produced a few other models, all reasonably priced and neatly boxed.

Bugatti 1930s Roadster.........................$35-40
Daimler Conquest 1950s Sports car, metallic
burgundy, #907 ....$35-40
Ford Consul MKII Saloon, #834
metallic red $35-40
green $35-40
Ford Prefect, 1948, light green, #856 .....$35-40
Jaguar XK150 Coupe, metallic blue,
#823 ....$35-40
Jouett Bradford Van, #812
Lyons Tea, green..............................$35-40
Unigate, white.................................$35-40
Esso, red...$35-40
Hovis Bread, yellow $35-40
Walls' Ice Cream, light blue $35-40
Ovaltine, orange..............................$35-40
Jouett Javelin 1950 Saloon, red, #845.....$35-40
Triumph Dolomite, red, 1980, #801 ....$35-40

Old Cars

Old Cars brand of Turin, Italy, is so named for its first models of antique cars introduced in 1978. Their current line represents anything but old cars, consisting of modern buses, racing transporters, vans, fire trucks, and heavy equipment. Still the name remains, and the company keeps producing so many variations of its basic models that not even the owner of the company could list them all.

Brown-Moxy Articulated Dump Truck, #85021,
1:50 ....$50-65
Fiat
360hp Dump Truck, #702................$45-60
EU 175 Forklift, #252, 1:28.............$20-25
Military Command car, #311 ....$20-25
Fiat-Allis
Compactor, #609, 1:50..................$45-60
Dozer, closed cab, #601, 1:50........$45-60
Dozer, open cab, #606, 1:50..........$45-60
FE45 Excavator with rubber treads, #610,
1:50...$50-65
Truck and Trailer with Wheel Loader,
#900..$90-105
Wheel Loader, #608, 1:50..............$50-65
Wood Loader, #605, 1:50..............$45-60

Fiat-Ferrari Racing car Transporter
1959, #560 ....$65-80
with three Brumm Ferrari models,
1959, #560-3 ....$115-130

Iveco
Ferrari F-1 Maintenance Van, #550 ...$20-30
Ferrari Transporter, 1980, #770-2 ....$79
with two F-1 Ferrari models $110-125
Orlandi Euroclass Touring Bus, #730 ....$50-65
Orlandi Touring Bus, #690 ....$45-60
Padane Touring Bus, #710 ....$50-65
Padane Two-Tone Touring Bus,
#720 ....$55-70
Truck with Flat Bed Trailer, #704,
1:43 ....$45-60
Turbo City Bus, #700 ....$50-65
Turbodaily Van, #520 ....$20-35
Komatsu Articulated Dump Truck, #85022,
1:50 ....$55-70
Rossi Wheel Loader, #603, 1:50 ....$40-55
Scania Benneton F-1 Race car Transporter,
#1200 ....$85-100

Old Kingston Product Corporation

Previously documented in *O'Brien's Toy Cars & Trucks* as Kingston Producers of Kokomo, Indiana, a recent e-mail inquiry indicates that the name of the company is the Old Kingston Product Corporation.

Their products included large scale toy car kits that, once assembled, would run on their own electrified steel track. On the original box was declared "Electricar, The Auto Builder, the fastest and most fascinating electric floor toy." They were produced in the 1930s, and the company likely went out of business prior to World War II.

The Electricar Stake Body Builder is a 1920s era truck chassis and cab with interchangeable beds that apparently produced a wrecker, a stake truck, a dump truck, or an ice truck.

Duesenberg, with transformer and steel track,
12" $3,500-4,000
Electricar Auto Builder, The Red Arrow Racer, 15",
1930s $450-550
Electricar Stake Body Builder, truck with extra beds
and rail track $325-375
Electricar Set with Red Arrow Racer and
Truck $900-1,200

Omega

One model is known of this otherwise unknown brand, thanks to Russell Alameda of San Jose, California.

Opel 4-door Sedan, red with pull-back action,
1:43 ....$10-12

One43

A single model has been seen by this company in the form of a 1:43 scale 1910 Brooke Swan Car. This most unusual car, designed to resemble a swan, was commissioned and used by Pratap Singh, the last Maharajah of Nabha. The state of Nabha, India, was founded in 1755 and continued to exist until 1948 when it was absorbed into the Indian Union.

In late 2003, One43 offered this unusual car for $285 US as the first in a series of 1:43 scale models of distinction.

1910 Brooke Swan Car $300-325

1936 Mercedes-Benz 540K Cabriolet ...$275-300

Onyx (also see Vitesse)

Although Onyx models were produced in association with the Vitesse Group of Portugal, the line represents a distinct brand by itself and is listed below for that reason.

Alfa Romeo 156
"Selenia" F. Giovinardi, BTCC 1998,
#XT124 ....$25-35
"Selenia" N. Larini, BTCC 1998,
#XT123 ....$25-35
"TV Spielfilm" N. Larini STW Cup
1998, #XT110 ....$25-35
"TV Spielfilm" S. Modena STW Cup
1998, #XT109 ....$25-35
Chevrolet Vectra "Ini" A. Guerra, South American
Touring Cars Championship 1998,
#XT130 ....$25-35
Dallara F398 F3
"Arohipel" Leinders, German F3
Champion 1998, #XFC99004 ...$25-35
"Fina" D. Saelens, French F3
Champion 1999, #XFC99001 ...$25-35
"Kwik Fit" Haberfeld, British F3

Champion 1998, #XFC99003 ...$25-35
"Manitou" O. Terrien 1998,
#XFC99006 ....$25-35
"Pink" Crevels Italian F3 Champion
1998, #XFC99005 ....$25-35
"Tobi" P. Dumbreck, winner Macau
Grand Prix 98, #XFC99002 ....$25-35
Holden Vectra Murphy-Ingall Bathurst
1000 1998, #XTC99014 ....$25-35
Honda Accord
"Castrol Grundig" R. Moen, BTCC
1998, #XT126 ....$25-35
"Christy's" M. Pigolo Italian
1998, #XTC99003 ....$25-35
"DHL" H. Heger, STW Cup 1997,
#XT055 ....$25-35
"Haribo" R. Colciago Italia 1997,
#XT107 ....$25-35
"Hart" P. Cunningham, North American
Touring car Championship 1997,
#XT043 ....$25-35
"Jas" G. Tarquini, STW Cup 1998,
#XT105 ....$25-35
"Jas" T. Kristensen, STW Cup 1998,
#XT106 ....$25-35
"Kaliber" J. Thompson, BTCC 1998,
#XT103 ....$25-35
"Kaliber" P. Kox, BTCC 1998,
#XT104 ....$25-35
"Labatt Blue" N. Crompton, North
American Touring car Championship 1997, #XT044 ....$25-35
"Rock-It Cargo" R. Gravett, BTCC
1998, #XT127 ....$25-35
"Stella Artois" T. Tassin, Belgian Procar
1997, #XT045 ....$25-35
D. Leslie, BTCC 1996, #XT041 ....$25-35
G. Tarquini, BTCC 1997, #XT054 ....$25-35
J. Kaye, BTCC 1996, #XT042 ....$25-35
J. Thompson, BTCC 1997, #XT053 ....$25-35
Nissan R390 GT1
"Calsonic" #32, 3rd Le Mans
1998, #XLM99003 ....$25-35
"Clarion" #30, 5th Le Mans
1998, #XLM99001 ....$25-35
"Jomo Number," 10th Le Mans
1998, #XLM99004 ....$25-35
"Zexel" #31, 6th Le Mans
1998, #XLM99002 ....$25-35
Roadcar, metallic blue, #XLM99014 ..$25-35
Nissan Primera
"100+Alloy Wheels" M. Neal, BTCC
1998, #XT122 ....$25-35
"Castrol-Kager-RTL," STW Cup
1997, #XT059 ....$25-35
"Nismo" Kasikam Asian Championship

1998, #XTC99002 ....$25-35

"Rosberg Team" M. Krumm, STW
1998, #XT101 ....$25-35

"Rosberg Team" R. Asch STW 1998,
#XT102 ....$25-35

"Vodaphone" A. Reid, BTCC 1997,
#XT058 ....$25-35

"Vodaphone" A. Reid, BTCC 1998,
#XT100 ....$25-35

"Vodaphone" D. Leslie, BTCC 1997,
#XT057 ....$25-35

"Vodaphone" D. Leslie, BTCC 1998,
#XT099 ....$25-35

D. Leslie, BTCC 1999,
#XTC99011 ....$25-35

L. Aiello, BTCC 1999, #XTC99010 ..$25-35

Opel Vectra

"Emma" Bathurst Australia 1997,
#XT085 ....$25-35

"Paulaner" A. Burgstaller, STW Cup
1997, #XT064 ....$25-35

"Paulaner" M. Reuter, STW Cup
1997, #XT063 ....$25-35

"Promarkt" K. Thiim, STW Cup
1997, #XT065 ....$25-35

"Promarkt" U. Alzen, STW Cup
1997, #XT066 ....$25-35

"Qantas" P. Brooks, Bathurst Australia
1997, #XT086 ....$25-35

Peugeot 406

"Efsa" C. Bueno, South American Touring
cars Championship 1998,
#XT129 ....$25-35

"Esso Ultron" J. Watts, BTCC 1997,
#XT049 ....$25-35

"Esso Ultron" P. Radish, BTCC 1998,
#XT090 ....$25-35

"Esso Ultron" T. Harvey, BTCC
1997, #XT048 ....$25-35

"Esso Ultron" T. Harvey, BTCC
1998, #XT089 ....$25-35

"Hasseroder" H. Heger, STW Cup
1996, #XT036 ....$25-35

"Hasseroder" J. Van Ommen, STW
Cup 1997, #XT051 ....$25-35

"Hasseroder" J. Van Ommen, STW
Cup 1998, #XT092 ....$25-35

"Hasseroder" L. Aiello, STW Cup
1996, #XT035 ....$25-35

"Hasseroder" L. Aiello, STW Cup
1998, #XT091 ....$25-35

"Hasseroder" L. Aiello, STW Cup
Champion 1997, #XT050 ....$25-35

"Total" P. Watts, BTCC 1996,
#XT033 ....$25-35

"Total" T. Harvey, BTCC 1996,

#XT034 ....$25-35

"Total" L. Brookes, BTCC 1997,
#XT070 ....$25-35

E. Bachelart Belgian Procar 1996,
#XT037 ....$25-35

Factory Test Car 1996, #XT038 ....$25-35

V. Radermacker Belgian Procar
1997, #XT052 ....$25-35

Porsche 911 GT2

"Fina Bastos," 24h. Zolder 98,
#XCL99002 ....$25-35

"French Flag" Jarrier French Champion
1998, #XCL99001 ....$25-35

Porsche 996 Pirelli Supercup

"UPS" M. Basseng 1998,
#XCL99013 ....$25-35

"Voss" S. Ortelli 1998, #XCL99012 ....$25-35

"Walker Monroe," Huisman, 1st
1998, #XCL99011 ....$25-35

Porsche GT1 1998

"Mobil" #25, 2nd Le Mans 1998,
#XLM99008 ....$25-35

"Mobil" Test Versions, carbon
brown, #XLM99012 ....$25-35

"Mobil" #26, winner Le Mans
1998, #XLM99009 ....$25-35

Roadcar, white, #XLM99013 ....$25-35

Zakspeed "Jever," white, Silverstone
1998, #XLM99011 ....$25-35

Zakspeed "Jever" green Silverstone
1998, #XLM99010 ....$25-35

Renault Clio Sport 24v

Cup Presentation, yellow,
#XCL99010 ....$25-35

Roadcar Salon De Paris 1998,
#XCL99009 ....$25-35

Renault Laguna

"ANZ" Bathurst Australia 1997,
#XT084 ....$25-35

"D. C. Cook" T. Rustad, BTCC
1998, #XT121 ....$25-35

"Nescafe" A. Menu, BTCC 1997,
#XT087 ....$25-35

"Nescafe" Fujitsu Bouillon, BTCC
1999, #XTC99006 ....$25-35

"Nescafe" Fujitsu Plato, BTCC
1999, #XTC99005 ....$25-35

"Nescafe" J. Plato, BTCC 1997,
#XT088 ....$25-35

Williams A. MENU BTCC Champion
1997, #XT046 ....$25-35

Williams J. PLATO BTCC 1997,
#XT047 ....$25-35

Renault Megane

Coupe Breitex Ickx 24 Hr. Spa
1998, #XCL99014 ....$25-35

Cup "Magic" Kanber French Champion
1998, #XCL99008 ....$25-35

Cup Campani Italian Champion
1998, #XCL99006 ....$25-35

Cup Magalhaes Portugal Champion
1998, #XCL99007 ....$25-35

Renault Spider

"Gauloises" Servia Spider Eurocup
1998, #XCL99003 ....$25-35

"Swan" J. Plato, winner British Spider
1997, #XCL99004 ....$25-35

"Tessitura" A.Belicchi Eurocup Champion
1998, #XCL99005 ....$25-35

Toyota GT1

"Esso" #27, 9th Le Mans 1998,
#XLM99005 ....$25-35

"Venture Safenet," Le Mans 1998,
#XLM99007 ....$25-35

"Zent" # 28, Le Mans 1998,
#XLM99006 ....$25-35

Roadcar, red, #XLM99015 ....$25-35

Vauxhall Vectra

"Controlled" M. LEMMER BTCC
1998, #XT125 ....$25-35

"Masterfit" D. Warwick, BTCC
1998, #XT093 ....$25-35

"Masterfit" J. Cleland BTCC 1998,
#XT094 ....$25-35

"Masterfit," Bathurst 1998,
#XTC99004 ....$25-35

D. Warwick, BTCC 1997, #XT062 ....$25-35

D. Warwick, BTCC 1997, #XT083 ....$25-35

J. Cleland, BTCC 1999,
#XTC99013 ....$25-35

J. Cleland, BTCC 1997, #XT061 ....$25-35

J. Cleland, BTCC 1997, #XT082 ....$25-35

Y. Muller, BTCC 1999, #XTC99012 ....$25-35

Volvo S40

"Volvo Sweden" J. Nilson, Swedish
Touring car Champ. 1998,
#XT128 ....$25-35

G. Morbidelli, BTCC 1998, #XT114 .$25-35

K. Burt 1997, #XT068 ....$25-35

R. Rydell, BTCC 1997, #XT067 ....$25-35

R. Rydell, BTCC 1998, #XT113 ....$25-35

R. Rydell, BTCC 1999,
#XTC99007 ....$25-35

Rydell-Richards, winner Bathurst 1000
1998, #XTC99001 ....$25-35

V. Radermacker, BTCC 1999,
#XTC99008 ....$25-35

Oriental Omnibus Company (also see Corgi)

In 1997, Corgi introduced a series of buses based on those seen in the streets of Hong

Kong. The series coincides with their Original Omnibus Co. offerings

Original Omnibus Co. (also see Corgi)

Original Omnibus Co. is a new line from Corgi Collectibles. The series consists of new versions and new models in Corgi's popular line of 1:76 scale diecast buses.

AEC Breakdown Lorry–MacBraynes,
   #41501 . . . . $45-60
Bedford OB Coach
   Hants & Dorset with roof quarterlights,
     3,800 made $45-60
   Loch Tay Trundler/Vista Coachways,
     #42506 . . . . $45-60
   with quarterlights,Malta, #42505 . . . $45-60
   with quarterlights, Crosville, #42504 . $45-60
Burlingham Seagull Coach
   N & C, #40307 . . . . $45-60
   Seagull Coaches, #40309 . . . . . . $45-60
   Happiways Tours Ltd, #40306 . . . . . $45-60
   Ribble, #40308 . . . . $45-60
Bus Garage Kit, #95400 . . . . $45-60
Bus Station Kit, #44901 . . . . $45-60
Dennis Dart
   Citybus (Standard), #42803 . . . . . $45-60
   Eastern National Bus $45-60
   London Bus Lines, #42806 . . . . . . $45-60
   Orpington Buses, #42810 . . . . . . $45-60
   Plymouth Citybus, #42805 . . . . . . $45-60
   Stevensons of Uttoxeter, #42804 . . . $45-60
   The Bee Line, #42807 . . . . $45-60
   VFM Buses, #42809 . . . . $45-60
Guy Tower Wagon, Birmingham City
   Transport, #42201 . . . . $45-60
Leyland Breakdown, Ribble, #41801 . . . $45-60
Leyland Leopard, Ballykissangel,
   #40205 . . . . $45-60
Leyland Lynx Mk I
   Beeline, #43108 . . . . $45-60
   City Line, #43101 . . . . $45-60
   London United, #43106 . . . . $45-60
   Wycombe Bus, #43102 . . . . $45-60
   Yorkshire Traction (McDonald's),
     #43105 . . . . $45-60
Leyland Lynx Mk II
   Nottingham City Transport, #43104 . $45-60
   Stagecoach Transit, #43107 . . . . . $45-60
Leyland Olympean
   North Western Bee Line, #43006 . . $45-60
   Stagecoach Scotland, #43005 . . . . $45-60
   Wear Buses, #43001 . . . . $45-60
Leyland Olympean 3-Axle
   China Motor Bus (Standard), #43206 . $45-60

Kowloon & Canton Railway Co.,
   #43202 . . . . $45-60
   Citybus (Handover), #43204 . . . . . $45-60
   Citybus (Standard), #43205 . . . . . $45-60
   Kowloon Motor Bus (Handover),
     #43203 . . . . $45-60
Optare Delta
   Crosville, #42906 . . . . $45-60
   Edinburgh Transport, #42907 . . . . $45-60
   Gateshead Supershuttle, #42901 . . . $45-60
   P.M.T., #42905 . . . . $45-60
   of Trent Bus, 4000 made $45-60
Plaxton Beaver 2, Stagecoach
   Manchester, #43402 . . . . $45-60
Plaxton Premiere
   Express Shuttle, #43302 . . . . . . $45-60
   Oxford Citylink, #43301 . . . . . . $45-60
Van Hool Alizee
   Bakers Dolphin, #42706 . . . . . . $45-60
   Bluebird (Bus Company of the Year
     1996), #42708 . . . . $45-60
   Citybus (Standard), #42707 . . . . . $45-60
   Clarkes of London, #42713 . . . . . $45-60
   Eavesway Travel (with football club
     decals), #42709 . . . . $45-60
   Eurolines, #42714 . . . . $45-60
   OK Travel, #42705 . . . . $45-60
   Railair, #42710 . . . . $45-60
   Shearings 500th, #42715 . . . . . . $45-60
   Speedlink, #42711 . . . . $45-60
Weymann Trolleybus–Bradford
   Corporation, #40104 . . . . $45-60

Orobr

Orobr of Germany produced tinplate lithographed toy cars with driver, opening rear doors, and wind-up motor, in the early 1900s.

Bus $1,000-1,250
Double Decker Bus
   6" $500-650
   9½" $1,000-1,250
Express Wagon, 6" $600-750
Ford Model T Sedan
   6", black $500-650
   6", other colors $700-850
   7¾" $850-1,100
Ford Model T Touring car, 8" $850-1,100
Limousine
   5⅞", with luggage rack $650-900
   6", cream with red trim $300-500
   8¼", red with gray trim $300-500
Mercedes Pullman Limousine, electric lights, four
   opening doors, driver,
   9½" $2,000-2,500
Taxi, 6" $650-800

Oto

Oto models are 1:43 diecast reissues of Pilen models from Spain produced for the Netherlands market. The unrelated Holland-Oto brand was previously known as Efsi Toys, a brand still sold in Germany. Thanks to Jan Scholten for the update.

Adams Brothers Probe Show car, #014 . $10-14
Chevrolet Astro Show car, #007 . . . . . $12-16
Citroën SM, 2 colours, #005 . . . . $12-16
Ferrari
   512 Show car, #008 . . . . $10-14
   P5 Show car, #012 . . . . $10-14
Intermeccanica Indra Show car, #018 . . . $7-9
Mercedes-Benz 250C Coupe, #001 . . . $12-16
Mini Cooper
   #003 . . . . $12-16
   MC Rally, #003M $12-16
Opel Manta A, 5 colours, #004 . . . . . . $12-16
Porsche
   917, #009 . . . . $12-16
   Carrera 6, #010 . . . . $12-16
Seat-Fiat
   127, 4 colours #017 . . . . $7-9
   600 Saloon, #002 . . . . $9-12
   850 Spyder, #016 . . . . $12-16
Stratos Bertone Show car, #013 . . . . $10-14
Vauxhall SRV Show car, #011 . . . . . . $10-14
Volkswagen Buggy, #015 . . . . $9-12

Oxford Die-Cast Limited

Oxford Die-Cast U.K.
P O Box 195
Tring, Herts HP23 4JF
United Kingdom
phone: 01442 828422
www.oxforddiecast.co.uk/
Oxford Die-Cast U.S.A.
P O Box 2085
Woodstock, GA 30188 USA
phone: 770-924-5443

Started in 1993, Oxford has a rich history of the diecast market with many of its employees originally employed by Corgi and Mettoy. Its first product rolled off the production lines in 1993, and since then it has manufactured in excess of 5,000,000 products. Many of its products can be found as promotional items on a whole variety of retail items. It also has its own club, the Oxford Die-Cast Club, which has grown to 15,000 members.

Chevrolet Open Bed Truck
   "Tesco Quality Provisions" $10-12

with tilt "Radio Times"............ $10-12
Ford Model T Delivery Truck
  "Georgia Farm" $10-12
  "Pasco's Dog Food" $10-12
  "Radio Times".................. $10-12
  "Tesco Gold The Perfect Cup of Tea" . $10-12
  "Pasco's Dog Food" $10-12
  "Zeb's Country Store" on sides . $15-18
Morris Cowley Bullnose
  "Radio Times"................. $10-12
  "Pasco's Dog Food" $10-12
  "St. Dalfour" high fruit content spread . $10-12
  "Tesco" $10-12
Thornycroft Bus
  "Pasco's Dog Food" $10-12
  "Tesco Every Little Helps" $10-12
  "Radio Times"................. $10-12

P

Palitoy

Palitoy was founded in Leicester, England, in 1919 by A. E. Pallet under the name Cascelloid Ltd. The company made celluloid toys. The name Palitoy was first used in 1936 when the company switched from the highly flammable celluloid to the newly developed and safer modern plastic then known as Bexoid.

In the 1930s, Palitoy specialized in dolls and Walt Disney Mickey Mouse character toys. After WWII, Palitoy produced the Tressy doll and Action Man, along with trains, construction sets, plastic toys for small children, and a few cars. Palitoy purchased Chad Valley in 1978, then ceased production in 1985.

The distinction of Palitoy cars is that the cardboard container was decorated as a building, adding to the collector value as well as the play value.

1940 American Coupe
  with Motor, 1:40 .... $45-60
  without Motor, 1:40 .... $40-55
1948 Bedford Van
  "Fish," 1:43 .... $40-55
  "Baker," 1:43 .... $40-55
  "Milk," 1:43 .... $40-55
  "Electricity," 1:43 .... $40-55
1947 Coach, 1:45 .... $40-55
1948 Jaguar Saloon, 1:41 .... $40-55
1952 Triumph Mayflower Saloon, 1:45 . $40-55

Pan Toys

While marketed from Duesseldorf, Germany, Pan Toys are essentially generic toys made in China. Remove them from their package and they are unrecognizable as any partic-ular brand. Of particular note is the Pan Toys ambulance, spelled "AMBURANCE" on the package. A chrome plastic base declares only that the model is "Made in China." Its only value is in the distinctive package. By itself, the model is relatively worthless. Thanks to Karl Schnelle for the information.

Ambulance, "Feuerwehr" (Fire Truck), red with white ladder on roof
  in pkg $4-6
  out of pkg. $1-2

Papillon Toys (also see Richmond Toys)

87 High Street
Whitton, Twickenham
Middlesex, TW2 7LD, United Kingdom
phone: (+44) 0208 755 3637
fax: (+44) 0208 893 8077
e-mail: papillontoys@ukgateway.net
www.papillontoys.co.uk/

Papillon Toys of Great Britain is owned by Robert Charrington and encompasses a variety of toys and toy brands, including Wooden Train World (www.woodentrainworld.co.uk), Play-MoreGames (www.playmoregames.co.uk), and Richmond Toys (www.richmondtoys.com). In particular, Richmond Toys offers a selection of toys from British classic TV shows like *The Sweeney, Minder, and Sooty.* In addition is an assortment of fire engines, police cars, and ambulances from "London's Burning" and "The Bill." Other categories include milk floats, London Fire Brigade, and Crime Stopper vehicles. See Richmond Toys for a list of applicable models. The Richmond Toys subsidiary was started in 1998 with the introduction of the diecast three-wheel milk float.

Milk Float, three-wheeler, "E Express,"
  1998 .... $24-32

Paradise Garage

Paradise Garage represents contemporary 1:43 diecast models made in China for the Australian market. The brand, introduced in 1996 by Zimbler Pty Ltd. of Melbourne, is offered outside of Australia almost exclusively by Modelauto of Leeds, England.

1996 Ford Falcon EF Futura, Reef Green or Cardinal Red, introduced in 1998 . . $42-48
1998 Ford Falcon XR8, white or red, introduced in 1999............. $42-48

1994 Holden Commodore VS Acclaim, Stratos Blue or Kira Aqua, introduced in 1996 .... $42-48
1996 Holden Commodore VS Berlina, Velvet Blue or Masai Red, introduced in 1997 .... $42-48

Paragon Models & Art

1431B S.E. 10th St.
Cape Coral, FL 33990
941-458-0024

Paragon Models & Art is yet another new arrival in the diecast scale model field. Produced in Spain for the Florida-based company, the first Paragon model appears to be a 1950 Chevrolet Panel Truck in 1:18 scale.

1950 Chevrolet Panel Truck, 1:18
  cream medium $25-40
  forester green $25-40
  mariner blue $25-40

Parker White Metal (see Erie)

Past-Time Hobbies (see PTH Models)

Pathfinder Models

Pathfinder is a series of excellent white metal models from England. Typical subjects are British cars of the 1950s. Production of each casting is reportedly limited, so there is a base of avid collectors who snap up most of the new issues.

Armstrong Siddeley, #12 .... $75-90
Austin Devon, #19 .... $75-90
Austin Hereford, #16 .... $75-90
Bristol 401, #3 .... $75-90
Daimler Conquest 1957, #24........ $75-90
Daimler Dart SP250, open, #9 ...... $75-90
Ford Consul Capri GT, #8 .... $75-90
Hillman Super Minx, #17 .... $75-90
Humber Hawk 1952, #21 .... $75-90
Jensen 541, #1 .... $75-90
Jensen CV8, #10............. $75-90
Jowett Javelin, #4 .... $75-90
Jowett Jupiter, #18
  open.................... $75-90
  closed $75-90
Morris Eight Series E, #25 .... $75-90
Morris Minor, open, #22 .... $75-90
Morris Oxford
  #13 .... $75-90
  1954 Series II, #20 .... $75-90
Reliant Scimitar, #5............. $75-90
Riley 1.5, #14 .... $75-90

Rover 90, #2 . . . . $75-90
Standard 10, #11 . . . . $75-90
Sunbeam Rapier, #15 . . . . $75-90
Triumph 2000 Mk I, #27 . . . . $75-90
Vauxhall Cresta PA, #6 . . . . $75-90
Vauxhall Victor FB, #23 . . . . $75-90
Vauxhall Wyvern, #26 . . . . $75-90
Wolseley 6/80, #7 . . . . $75-90

Paul's Model Art/Minichamps

Paul's Model Art (PMA) was founded by Paul Gunter Lang in Aachen, Germany, where they are currently based. In 1998, Action Performance purchased a controlling interest in Paul's Model Art.

PMA/Minichamps designs and markets diecast scale replicas of motor vehicles, including models of Formula 1 and GT race cars as well as factory production cars. Its products are marketed pursuant to license agreements with some of the world's most popular race car drivers, team owners, and car manufacturers, including exclusive licenses with Michael Schumacher, Jacques Villeneueve, Ferrari, McLaren, and others. Their product line is massive. The extensive list below includes only their street models. Their assortment of race cars would make the list twice as long.

The Max Models name is applied to a large number of Minichamps, but upon examination of one specimen and its box, there is no mention of Paul's Model Art or Minichamps anywhere. What is found on the box is the name Danhausen Modelcar of Aachen, Germany. There has been great confusion as to just what models are legitimate Minichamps and which ones aren't. For simplicity's sake, Max Models are listed below as they were listed in a recent Minichamps catalog.

1:18 Scale Minichamps

Benetton B194, Schumacher '94 . . . . . . $40-45
Benetton Ford B193, 1:18 . . . . $50-55
BMW R 1200 C Motorbike, canyon red,
    #182 026200 . . . . $45-50
BMW Z-3 1996 Roadster
    Bond blue $30-40
    red $30-35
McLaren MP4/8
    Senna '93, 1:18 . . . . $40-45
    Hakkinen '93, 1:18 . . . . $30-35

1:24 Scale Minichamps

Volkswagen Karmann Ghia 1970 Coupe
    red, #241 245000 . . . . $50-55
    silver, #241 245001 . . . . $50-55

    cream, #241 245003 . . . . $50-55

1:43 Scale Minichamps/Max Models

Alfa Romeo
    156, silver, #430 120700 . . . . $40-45
    German Championship, #8, Larini . . $35-40
    German Championship, #14,
        Danner $35-40
Audi
    A3, 1996, metallic dark blue,
        #430 015100 . . . . $40-45
    A4, 1995, blue, #430 015000 . . . $40-45
    A4, 1995, silver, #430 015001 . . . $40-45
    A4, 1995, red, #430 015002 . . . . $40-45
    A4, 1995, red, #430 015009 . . . . $40-45
    A4 Avant, 1995, metallic gray,
        #430 015010 . . . . $40-45
    A4 Avant, 1995, metallic green,
        #430 015011 . . . . $40-45
    A6, 1997, metallic blue,
        #430 017100 . . . . $40-45
    A6 Avant, 1998, laser red,
        #430 017110 . . . . $40-45
    A8, 1994, black, #430 013000 . . $40-45
    A8, 1994, metallic cashmere,
        #430 013001 . . . . $40-45
    A8, 1994, metallic ruby red,
        #430 013002 . . . . $40-45
    A8, 1994, Isis red, #430 013005 . $40-45
    TT, 1998, yellow, #430 017220 . . $40-45
    V8, 1991, metallic titanium,
        #430 T01000 . . . . $45-50
BMW
    1600 Saloon, 1966–1975, orange,
        #430 022100 . . . . $40-45
    1600 Saloon, 1966–1975, yellow,
        #430 022101 . . . . $40-45
    1600 Saloon, 1966–1975, light
        green, #430 022102 . . . . $40-45
    1600 Saloon, 1966–1975, white,
        #430 022104 . . . . $40-45
    2002 Turbo, white, #430 022200 . $40-45
    3-Series, 1975–1983, orange,
        #430 025400 . . . . $40-45
    3-Series Cabriolet, 1993, metallic
        green, #430 023330 . . . . $40-45
    3-Series Cabriolet, 1993, metallic
        black, #430 023331 . . . . $40-45
    3-Series Cabriolet, 1993, metallic red,
        #430 023332 . . . . $40-45
    3-Series Coupe, 1992, blue, #430
        023320 . . . . $40-45
    3-Series Coupe, 1992, yellow,
        #430 023321 . . . . $40-45
    3-Series Coupe, 1992, red, #430
        023322 . . . . $40-45

3-Series Saloon, 1992, silver,
    #430 023300 . . . . $40-45
3-Series Saloon, 1992, black,
    #430 023301 . . . . $40-45
3-Series Saloon, 1992, red,
    #430 023302 . . . . $40-45
501-502 Sedan, 1954–1961 . . . . $40-45
502 V8 Saloon, 1954–1961, white,
    #430 022400 . . . . $40-45
502 V8 Saloon, 1954–1961, black,
    #430 022401 . . . . $40-45
502 V8 Saloon, 1954–1961, dark
    red, #430 022402 . . . . $40-45
507 Cabriolet, 1956–1959 . . . . . . $40-45
507 Cabriolet, 1956–1959, top
    up. $40-45
507 Hardtop, 1956–1959. . . . . . . $40-45
507 Hardtop, 1956–1959, red,
    #430 022530 . . . . $40-45
507 Hardtop, 1956–1959, silver,
    #430 022531 . . . . $40-45
507 Hardtop, 1956–1959, cream,
    #430 022532 . . . . $40-45
507 Cabriolet, top down, 1956–1959,
    red, #430 022507 . . . . $40-45
507 Cabriolet, top down, 1956–1959,
    silver, #430 022508 . . . . $40-45
507 Cabriolet, top down, 1956–
    1959, cream, #430 022509 . . $40-45
507 Cabriolet, top up, 1956–1959,
    red, #430 022520 . . . . $40-45
507 Cabriolet, top up, 1956–1959,
    black, #430 022521. . . . . $40-45
507 Cabriolet, top up, 1956–1959,
    green, #430 022522 . . . . $40-45
635 CSi, 1982–1987, black,
    #430 025121 . . . . $40-45
700 LS Saloon, 1960–1961,
    metallic anthracite, #430
    023700 . . . . $40-45
700 LS Saloon, 1960–1961, cream,
    #430 023701 . . . . $40-45
700 LS Saloon, 1960–1961, silver,
    #430 023702 . . . . $40-45
700 Sedan, 1960–1961 . . . . $40-45
E 1, 1993, yellow, #430 023000 . $40-45
E 1, 1993, metallic blue,
    #430 023001 . . . . $40-45
E 1, 1993, red, #430 023002 . . . $40-45
M3 GTR Street, 1993, white,
    #430 023380 . . . . $40-45
M3 GTR Street, 1993, black, #430
    023381 . . . . $40-45
M3 GTR Street, 1993, red, #430
    023382 . . . . $40-45
E-1 Electromobile, 1993 . . . . $40-45

E-1 Electromobile 1994 Concept car . $40-45
M-3 Coupe, 1992 . . . . $40-45
M Roadster, 1996, orange, #430
024360 . . . . $40-45
Z3 2.8, 1997, black, #430
024331 . . . . $40-45
Z3 1.9, silver, #430 024341 . . . . . $40-45

Bugatti EB 110
1991, blue, #430 102110 . . . . . . $40-45
1991, red, #430 102111 . . . . $40-45
1991, black, #430 102112 . . . . . $40-45
Supersport, 1993, #430 102115 . . $40-45

Chevrolet Corvette, 1997, metallic blue,
#430 142621 . . . . $40-45

Dodge Viper
GTS, 1993, black, #430 144020 . $40-45
GTS, 1993, blue, #430 144021 . . $40-45
GTS, 1993, red, #430 144022 . . . $40-45
RT/10,1993, yellow, #430
144030 . . . . $40-45
RT/10, 1993, blue, #430
144031 . . . . $40-45
RT/10, 1993, red, #430 144032 . $40-45

Ferrari
250 GTO, 1962, red, #430
072000 . . . . $40-45
456 GT 2+2, 1992, red, #430
072400 . . . . $40-45
456 GT 2+2, 1992, yellow, #430
072401 . . . . $40-45
456 GT 2+2, 1992, dark blue,
#430 072402 . . . . $40-45
512 M, 1994, silver, #430
074120 . . . . $40-45
512 M, 1994, yellow, #430
074121 . . . . $40-45
512 M, 1994, red, #430
074122 . . . . $40-45
512 TR, 1992, red, #430
072500 . . . . $40-45
512 TR, 1992, yellow, #430
072501 . . . . $40-45
512 TR, 1992, black, #430
072502 . . . . $40-45
550 Maranello, 1996, yellow,
#430 076022 . . . . $40-45
F130, 1995, silver, #430 075150 . $40-45
F130, 1995, yellow, #430
075151 . . . . $40-45
F130, 1995, red, #430 075152 . . $40-45
F355 GTB, 1994, yellow, #430
074020 . . . . $40-45
F355 GTB, 1994, black, #430
074021 . . . . $40-45
F355 GTB, 1994, red, #430
074022 . . . . $40-45

F355 GTS, 1994, red, #430
074052 #37 . . . . $40-45
F355 Spider, 1995, top down, red,
#430 074032 . . . . $40-45
F355 Spider Softtop, 1995, top up,
red, #430 074042 . . . . $40-45
F50, 1995, red, #430 075152 . . . $40-45
F50 Spider, 1995, yellow, #430
075161 . . . . $40-45

Ford
Capri, 1969, silver, #430
085500 . . . . $40-45
Capri RS, 1970, yellow with black hood,
#430 085801 . . . . $40-45
Escort RS Cosworth, 1992, red, #430
082104 . . . . $40-45
Fiesta, 1995, blue, #430 085000 . $40-45
Focus Wagon, metallic blue, #430
087010 . . . . $40-45
Indy, 1993, Newman/Haas/Andretti,
1:43 . . . . $40-45
Ka, 1996, red, #430 086400 . . . . $40-45
Mondeo Wagon, 1993, red,
#430 082010 . . . . $40-45
Mondeo Wagon, 1993, metallic
green, #430 082011 . . . . $40-45
Mondeo Wagon, 1993, black,
#430 082012 . . . . $40-45
Mondeo 4-door Police, white and
green "Polizei," #430 082090 . $40-45
Mondeo 4-door Saloon, 1993, red,
#430 082000 . . . . $40-45
Mondeo 4-door Saloon, 1993, yellow,
#430 082001 . . . . $40-45
Mondeo 4-door Saloon, 1993, blue,
#430 082002 . . . . $40-45
Mondeo 5-Door Saloon, 1993, red,
#430 082070 . . . . $40-45
Mondeo 5-Door Saloon, 1993, yellow,
#430 082071 . . . . $40-45
Mondeo 5-Door Saloon, 1993, blue,
#430 082072 . . . . $40-45
Mondeo Wagon, 1997, red,
#430 086310 . . . . $40-45
Mondeo Sedan, 1997, silver,
#430 086300 . . . . $40-45
Mustang Cabriolet, 1994, metallic
blue, #430 085631 . . . . $40-45
Puma, metallic black, 1997, #430
086520 . . . . $40-45
Scorpio 4-door Saloon, 1995, blue,
#430 084000 . . . . $40-45
Scorpio 4-door Saloon, 1995, black,
#430 084001 . . . . $40-45
Scorpio 4-door Saloon, 1995, red,
#430 084002 . . . . $40-45

Scorpio Wagon, 1995, dark gray,
1:43, #430 084010 . . . . $40-45
Scorpio Wagon, 1995, green, 1:43,
#430 084012 . . . . $40-45
Taunus, 1960, white with red roof,
#430 085100 . . . . $40-45

Honda CR-X, 1989 . . . . $40-45

Jaguar
Mk II, 1959–1967, British racing
green, #430 130600 . . . . $40-45
Mk II, 1959–1967, dark red, #430
130602 . . . . $40-45
XJ12 Saloon, 1995, #430
130502 . . . . $40-45
XJ220, 1992, metallic blue, #430
102220 . . . . $40-45
XJ220, 1992, yellow, #430
102221 . . . . $40-45
XJ220, 1992, silver, #430
102222 . . . . $40-45
XJ6 Saloon, 1995, #430 130500 . $40-45
Sovereign Saloon, 1995, #430
130501 . . . . $40-45

Jeep Grand Cherokee
1993, black, #430 149660 . . . . . $45-50
1993, metallic green, #430
149661 . . . . $45-50

Lamborghini Miura
1966–1971, yellow, #430
103000 . . . . $40-45
1966–1971, gold, #430
103001 . . . . $40-45
1966–1971, red, #430 103002 . . $40-45

Lancia Stratos Street
1972–1978, yellow, #430
125020 . . . . $40-45
1972–1978, red, #430 125022 . . $40-45

Lotus Super 7, 1968, red, #430
135632 . . . . $40-45

Mercedes-Benz
180 Saloon, 1953–1957, gray,
#430 033100 . . . . $40-45
180 Saloon, 1953–1957, black,
#430 033101 . . . . $40-45
180 Saloon, 1953–1957, red,
#430 033102 . . . . $40-45
190 E 2.3-16, 1984–1988, metallic
blue black, #430 035600 . . . . $40-45
190 E Evolution 1, 1990, metallic blue
black, #430 B03000 . . . . $40-45
190 E Evolution 1, 1990, signal red,
#430 R03000 . . . . $40-45
190 E Evolution 1, 1990, metallic pearl
gray, #430 G03000 . . . . $40-45
190 E Evolution 2, metallic blue black,
#430 B03100 . . . . $40-45

190 E Evolution 2, metallic pearl gray,
#430 G03100 . . . . $40-45

190 E Evolution 2, red, #430
R03100 . . . . $40-45

190 SL Cabriolet, 1955–1962, white,
#430 033130 . . . . $40-45

190 SL Cabriolet, 1955–1962, silver,
#430 033131 . . . . $40-45

190 SL Cabriolet, 1955–1962, red,
#430 033132 . . . . $40-45

200 T Wagon, 1980–1985, red,
#430 032210 . . . . $40-45

220 S, 1956–1959, black, #430
033000 . . . . $40-45

220 SE Saloon, 1956–1965, #430
034000, #430 034001, #430
034002 . . . . $40-45

230 CE Coupe, 1977–1985, gold,
#430 032220 . . . . $40-45

230 CE Coupe, 1992, crystal green,
#430 003403 . . . . $40-45

230 E, 1992, zircon silver, #430
003203 . . . . $40-45

280 CE Coupe, 1977–1985, silver,
#430 032221 . . . . $40-45

280 SL Cabriolet, 1968–1971, silver,
#430 032230 . . . . $40-45

280 SL Cabriolet, 1968–1971, red,
#430 032231 . . . . $40-45

280 SL Cabriolet, 1968–1971, dark
blue, #430 032232 . . . . $40-45

280SL Cabriolet, 1968–1971, top
down, light blue, #430
032234 . . . . $40-45

280SL Cabriolet, 1968–1971, top up,
white with black top, #430
032240 . . . . $40-45

280SL Cabriolet, 1968–1971, top up, red
with white top, #430 032241 . . $40-45

280SL Cabriolet, 1968–1971, top up,
black with white top, #430
032242 . . . . $40-45

280SL Pagode, 1968–1971, gold,
#430 032250 . . . . $40-45

280SL Pagode, 1968–1971, white,
#430 032251 . . . . $40-45

280SL Pagode, 1968–1971, red,
#430 032252 . . . . $40-45

280 TE Wagon, 1980–1985, metallic
blue, #430 032212 . . . . $40-45

300 CE Coupe, 1992, almadin red,
#430 003408 . . . . $40-45

300 CE-24 Cabriolet, 1992, dark
blue, #430 003514 . . . . $40-45

300 CE-24 Cabriolet, 1992, signal red,
#430 003550 . . . . $40-45

300 CE-24 Cabriolet, 1992, smoke
silver, #430 003551 . . . . $40-45

300 CE-24 Coupe, 1992, bornite,
#430 003414 . . . . $40-45

300 D, 1992, almadin red, #430
003209 . . . . $40-45

300S Cabriolet, 1951–1958, top
down $40-45

300S Cabriolet, 1951–1958, top up,
black, #430 032320 . . . . $40-45

300S Cabriolet, 1951–1958, top up,
dark blue, #430 032321 . . . . . $40-45

300S Cabriolet, 1951–1958, top up,
white, #430 032322 . . . . $40-45

300S Cabriolet, 1951–1958, top
down, black, #430 032330 . . . $40-45

300S Cabriolet, 1951–1958, top
down, blue, #430 032331 . . . $40-45

300S Cabriolet, 1951–1958, top
down, dark red, #430
032332 . . . . $40-45

300S Coupe, 1951–1958, silver,
#430 032324 . . . . $40-45

300SL "Caracciola" $40-45

300SL Spyder $40-45

300TD Wagon, 1992 metallic blue
black, #430 003310 . . . . $40-45

350SL Cabriolet, 1971–1980, top down,
silver, #430 033430 . . . . $40-45

350SL Cabriolet, 1971–1980, top down,
dark blue, #430 033431 . . . . . $40-45

350SL Cabriolet, 1971–1980, top down,
red, #430 033432 . . . . $40-45

350SL Cabriolet, 1971–1980, top down,
white, #430 033440 . . . . $40-45

350SL Cabriolet Hardtop, 1971–1980,
silver, #430 033450 . . . . $40-45

400E Sedan, 1992 . . . . $40-45

450SLC, 1972–1980, silver,
#430 033420 . . . . $40-45

450SLC, 1972–1980, metallic green,
#430 033421 . . . . $40-45

450SLC, 1972–1980, gold, #430
033422 . . . . $40-45

500E V8 Saloon, 1992, black, #430
003240 . . . . $40-45

500E V8 Saloon, 1992, metallic anthracite,
#430 003241 . . . . $40-45

600SEC Coupe, 1992, black, #430
032600 . . . . $40-45

600SEC Coupe, 1992, malachite green,
#430 032601 . . . . $40-45

600SEC Coupe, 1992, smoke silver, #430
032602 . . . . $40-45

C180, 1993, Esprit red, #430
032101 . . . . $40-45

C220, 1993, metallic Classic green, #430
032100 . . . . $40-45

C280, 1993, Sport, silver, #430
032102 . . . . $40-45

C36 AMG, 1993, metallic blue black,
#430 032160 . . . . $40-45

C36 AMG, 1993, yellow, #430
032161 . . . . $40-45

C36 AMG, 1993, silver, #430
032162 . . . . $40-45

C-Class Sedan, 1993 (180, 220, 280) . . $40-45

C-Class Taxi, 1994, white, #430
032195 . . . . $40-45

C-Class 1AAF World Championship, #430
032105 . . . . $45-50

E-Class 4-door Sedan, 1994, metallic blue
black, #430 033500 . . . . $40-45

E-Class 4-door Sedan, 1994, metallic blue,
#430 033501 . . . . $40-45

E-Class 4-door Sedan, 1994, red, #430
033502 . . . . $40-45

E-Class 2-door Coupe, 1994, metallic
blue-black, #430 033520 . . . . $40-45

E-Class 2-door Coupe, 1994, metallic
blue, #430 033521 . . . . $40-45

E-Class 2-door Coupe, 1994, Bornite
metallic dark gray, #430
033522 . . . . $40-45

E-Class Cabriolet, 1994, metallic blue
black, #430 033530 . . . . $40-45

E-Class Cabriolet, 1994, metallic blue, #430
033531 . . . . $40-45

E-Class Cabriolet, 1994, metallic
rosewood, #430 033532 . . . . $40-45

E-Class Taxi Saloon, 1994, white,
#430 033595 . . . . $40-45

E-Class Taxi Wagon, 1994, white,
#430 033596 . . . . $40-45

E-Class Wagon, 1994, metallic blue
black, #430 033540 . . . . $40-45

E-Class Wagon, 1994, metallic blue,
#430 033541 . . . . $40-45

E-Class Wagon, 1994, green, #430
033542 . . . . $40-45

W123 Taxi Saloon, off white, #430
032295 . . . . $40-45

W123 Taxi Wagon, off white, #430
032296 . . . . $40-45

W123 4-door Saloon 200D, 1975–1985,
yellow, #430 032200 . . . . $40-45

W123 4-door Saloon 230E, 1975–1985,
white, #430 032201 . . . . $40-45

W123 4-door Saloon 280E, 1975–1985,
silver, #430 032202 . . . . $40-45

W123 2-door Coupe 230CE, 1977–1985,
gold, #430 032220 . . . . $40-45

W123 2-door Coupe 230CE, 1977–1985, silver, #430 032221 . . . . $40-45

W123 2-door Coupe 230CE, 1977–1985, metallic blue, #430 032222 . . . $40-45

W123 Wagon 200T, 1980–1985, red, #430 032210 . . . . $40-45

W123 Wagon 230TE, 1980–1985, silver, #430 032211 . . . . $40-45

W123 Wagon 280TE, 1980–1985, metallic blue, #430 032212 . . . . . . $40-45

W123 Police Saloon, white and green, #430 032290 . . . . $40-45

W123 Police Wagon, white and green, #430 032291 . . . . $40-45

W124 Sedan, 1992 (250D, 300E, 300D) . . $40-45

W124 Coupe (230CE, 300CE, 300CE-24) $40-45

W124 Convertible (300CE-24) $40-45

MGB

Cabriolet, 1962–1969, black, #430 131030 . . . . $40-45

Cabriolet, 1962–1969, red, #430 131032 . . . . $40-45

Softtop, 1962–1969, cream, #430 131040 . . . . $40-45

Softtop, 1962–1969, British racing green, #430 131041 . . . . $40-45

Mitsubishi Pajero

Long, 1997, red, #430 163770 . . . $45-50

Long, 1991, black, #430 163471 . $45-50

Short, 1991, metallic blue, #430 163370 . . . . $45-50

NSU

1000 L, 1964–1972, light blue, #430 015200 . . . . $40-45

TT, 1967–1972, Targa orange, #430 015300 . . . . $40-45

Opel

Kadett A Saloon, 1962–1965, yellow, #430 043000 . . . . $40-45

Kadett A Saloon, 1962–1965, blue gray, #430 043001 . . . . $40-45

Kadett A Saloon, 1962–1965, red, #430 043002 . . . . $40-45

Kadett A Caravan, 1962–1965, gray, #430 043010 . . . . $40-45

Kadett A Caravan, 1962–1965, blue, #430 043011 . . . . $40-45

Kadett A Caravan, 1962–1965, white, #430 043012 . . . . $40-45

Kadett C, 1973–1977, red, #430 045601 . . . . $40-45

Kadett C Coupe, 1973–1977, signal green, #430 045620 . . . . $40-45

Kadett C Caravan, 1973–1977, red, #430 045611 . . . . $40-45

Kadett 4-door Saloon, 1951–1953, dark red, #430 043300 . . . . $40-45

Kadett 4-door Saloon, 1951–1953, black, #430 043301 . . . . $40-45

Kadett 4-door Saloon, 1951–1953, gray, #430 043302 . . . . $40-45

Omega 3000 Evolution 4-door Sedan, metallic black, #430 004001 . . $40-45

Rekord P1 2-door Saloon, 1958–1960, green with white roof, #430 043200 . . . . $40-45

Rekord P1 2-door Saloon, 1958–1960, red with white roof, #430 043204 . . . . $40-45

Rekord P1 2-door Saloon, 1958–1960, blue with white roof, #430 043206 . . . . $40-45

Rekord P1 Caravan Wagon, 1958–1960, yellow with white roof, #430 043210 . . . . $40-45

Rekord P1 Caravan Wagon, 1958–1960, blue with white roof, #430 043211 . . . . $40-45

Rekord P1 Caravan Wagon, 1958–1960, red with white roof, #430 043212 . . . . $40-45

Rekord P1 Caravan, 1958–1960, gray with white roof, #430 043215 . $40-45

Peugeot

306 2-door, 1995, red, #430 112502 . . . . $40-45

306 Cabriolet, 1995, red, #430 112532 . . . . $40-45

306 Cabriolet, 1995, metallic black, #430 112531 . . . . $40-45

306 4-door, 1995, metallic blue, #430 112571 . . . . $40-45

306 4-door, 1995, metallic gray, #430 112570 . . . . $40-45

Porsche

356 C Cabriolet, 1963–1965, silver, #430 062330 . . . . $40-45

356 C Cabriolet, 1963–1965, cream, #430 062331 . . . . $40-45

356 C Cabriolet, 1963–1965, red, #430 062332 . . . . $40-45

356 C Carrera, 1963–1964, black, #430 062361 . . . . $40-45

356 C Carrera, 1963–1964, red, #430 062362 . . . . $40-45

356 C Coupe, 1963–1965, dark blue, #430 062320 . . . . $40-45

356 C Coupe, 1963–1965, silver, #430 062321 . . . . $40-45

356 C Coupe, 1963–1965, red, #430 062322 . . . . $40-45

356 Speedster, ivory with red interior, #430 065531 . . . . $40-45

406 Coupe, 1997, metallic red, #430 112620 . . . . $40-45

911, 1964, red, #430 067121 . . . $40-45

911 Cabriolet, 1994, silver, #430 063030 . . . . $40-45

911 Cabriolet, 1994, black, #430 063031 . . . . $40-45

911 Cabriolet, 1994, red, #430 063032 . . . . $40-45

911 Carrera 2/4, 1992, anthracite, #430 062121 . . . . $40-45

911 Carrera 2/4, 1992, metallic violet, #430 062122 . . . . $40-45

911 Coupe, 1978–1988, red, #430 062020 . . . . $40-45

911 Coupe, 1978–1988, white, #430 062021 . . . . $40-45

911 Coupe, 1978–1988, black, #430 062022 . . . . $40-45

911 Coupe, 1993, red, #430 063007 . . . . $40-45

911 Coupe, 1993, blue, #430 063008 . . . . $40-45

911 GT 3 Street Version, black, #430 986990 . . . . $40-45

911 RS, 1995, yellow, #430 065100 . . . . $40-45

911 Speedster, 1988, red, #430 066130 . . . . $40-45

914, 1969–1973, green, #430 065662 . . . . $40-45

993 Coupe $40-45

993 Cabriolet $40-45

Boxster, 1993, silver, #430 063130 . . . . $40-45

Cup "Cald." $34

Cup, "Land" $34

Cup, #9, 1993 . . . . $34

Dauer 962 GT Street, yellow, #430 064001 . . . . $40-45

Renault

8 Gordini, 1964–1968, blue, #430 113550 . . . . $40-45

Alpine A 110, 1963–1976, metallic blue, #430 113600 . . . . $40-45

Saab

9-5 Saloon, 1997, metallic green, #430 170640 . . . . $40-45

900 4-door, 1995, black, #430 170500 . . . . $40-45

900 4-door, 1995, aubergine, #430 170501 . . . . $40-45

900 Cabriolet, 1995, red, #430 170532 . . . . $40-45

Sauber Mercedes

    C-9, #61 . . . . $40-45

    C-11, #1 . . . . $40-45

Seat Arosa, 1997, red, #430

    057100 . . . . $40-45

Toyota Celica SS II Coupe

    1994, black, #430 166620 . . . . . $40-45

    1994, red, #430 166622 . . . . $40-45

Triumph TR 6, 1968–1976, British racing

    green, #430 132751 . . . . $40-45

Volkswagen

    1200 Beetle "Split Window," 1949, black with

      open sunroof, #430 052000 . . . $40-45

    1200 Beetle "Split Window," 1949, gray

      with solid roof, #430 052001 . . $40-45

    1200 Beetle "Split Window," 1949, blue with

      closed sunroof, #430 052002 . . $40-45

    1200 Cabriolet, 1951–1952, top down,

      green, #430 052030 . . . . $40-45

    1200 Cabriolet, 1951–1952, top down,

      gray, #430 052031 . . . . $40-45

    1200 Cabriolet, 1951–1952, top down,

      red, #430 052032 . . . . $40-45

    1200 Cabriolet, 1951–1952, top down,

      two-tone anthracite and cream, #430

      052034 . . . . $40-45

    1200 Cabriolet, 1951–1952, top up, green

      with brown roof, #430 052042 . $40-45

    1200 Beetle, 1953–1957, oval window,

      green gray, #430 052100 . . . . $40-45

    1200 Beetle, 1953–1957, oval window,

      pale blue, #430 052101 . . . . . $40-45

    1200 Beetle, 1953–1957, oval window,

      red, #430 052102 . . . . $40-45

    1302 Cabriolet, 1970–1972, top down,

      yellow, #430 055030 . . . . $40-45

    1302 Saloon, 1970–1972, orange, #430

      055000 . . . . $40-45

    1303 Cabriolet, 1972–1980, top down,

      black, #430 055130 . . . . $40-45

    1303 Saloon, 1972–1974, metallic blue,

      #430 055100 . . . . $40-45

    Beetle, 1 Millionth, limited edition of 9,999

      pieces, gold, #430 052103 . . . . . $75

    Concept Car Cabriolet, 1994,various colors,

      #430 054030, #430 054031, #430

      054032 . . . . $40-45

    Concept Car Saloon, 1994, various colors,

      #430 054000, #430 054001, #430

      054002 . . . . $40-45

    Golf, 1997, jazz blue, #430

      056001 . . . . $40-45

    Golf, 1997, red, #430 056000 . . . $40-45

    Hebmueller Cabriolet, 1949–1950, top

      down, two-tone black and red, #430

      052130 . . . . $40-45

Hebmueller Cabriolet, 1949–1950, top

    down, black, #430 052132 . . . $40-45

Hebmueller Cabriolet, 1949–1950, top

    down, two-tone red and cream, #430

    052134 . . . . $40-45

Hebmueller Cabriolet, 1949–1950, top up,

    two-tone red and cream,

    #430 052142 . . . . $40-45

Karmann Ghia Cabriolet, 1957, top down,

    light blue, #430 005031 . . . . . $40-45

Karmann Ghia Cabriolet, 1957, top down,

    metallic blue-gray, #430 051033 . $40-45

Karmann Ghia Cabriolet, 1957, top up,

    white with black top, cream,

    #430 005061 . . . . $40-45

Karmann Ghia Coupe, 1955, red with

    white roof, #430 005003 . . . . $40-45

Karmann Ghia Coupe, 1955, yellow with

    black roof, #430 005004 . . . . $40-45

Karmann Ghia Coupe, 1955, blue with

    cream roof, #430 005005 . . . . $40-45

Kastenwagen (Delivery Van), 1963, blue,

    #430 052200 . . . . $40-45

Kastenwagen (Delivery Van), 1963, light

    gray, #430 052201 . . . . $40-45

Kastenwagen (Delivery Van), 1963, light

    green, #430 052202 . . . . $40-45

Lupo, 1998, jazz blue, #430 058100 . $40-45

New Beetle, 1998, red, #430 058001 . $40-45

Samba Bus, 1958–1960, 25 windows, two-tone

    gray and blue, #430 052200 . . . $45-50

Samba Bus, 1958–1960, 25 windows,

    two-tone green and light green, #430

    052201 . . . . $45-50

Samba Bus, 1958–1960, 25 windows,

    two-tone red and cream, #430

    052202 . . . . $45-50

Volvo

    850 Wagon, 1994 . . . . $40-45

    850 Saloon, 1994, smoke silver, #430

      171401 . . . . $40-45

    850 Wagon, 1996, red, #430

      171411 . . . . $40-45

    V40 Wagon, 1996, black, #430

      171511 . . . . $40-45

Wartburg A312 Saloon

    1958, two-tone blue and white, #430

      015900 . . . . $40-45

    1958, two-tone red and white, #430

      015901 . . . . $40-45

1:64 Scale Models From Paul's Model Art / Microchamps

1993, Ford Indy, Newman/Haas/Andretti,

    1:64 . . . . $8-12

Paya

Rafael Paya, a tinsmith by trade, started Paya of Spain in 1902. In 1906, his sons Emilio, Pascual, and Vincente established Spain's first toy factory. The quality of Paya's toys surpassed those of other European toy manufacturers in their boldness of colors and precision of their graphics. In the 1930s, Raimundo Paya contributed to the further growth of the company.

As with most toy manufacturers, the Second World War put a stop to toy production. The company resumed in 1946 and continued for several years after that.

In 1985, Lino reissued all of the old Paya tinplate toys as limited editions of 5,000 units per model. They were last seen offered by Liliput of Yerington, Nevada.

It has been reported that Paya made diecast toys, but no documentation has been found to support that claim. Below is a sampling of Paya tin lithographed vehicles, all of which featured clockwork motors.

Auto Convertible Sedan 1925, 19¾" . $275-300

Chrysler Airflow Sedan, 13" $500-650

Coupe, with opening doors, hand painted

    and stenciled, 13" $2,250-2,500

Limousine, hand painted and stenciled,

    electric lights, 19" $1,500-1,750

Packard Futura Cabriolet 1949, 13¾" . $150-175

Sedan, steel, opening doors, electric lights,

    19" $1,000-1,250

Peachstate Muscle Car Collectibles Club

P O Box 1537

Winder GA 30680

1-800-536-1637 or

1-770-307-1042

fax 1-770-867-0786

A recent magazine ad states, "Peachstate Muscle Car Collectibles Club offers limited edition production quantities of only 2,500 cars per production run of quality diecast 1960s and 1970s-era muscle car replicas. These 1:18 scale beauties are produced exclusively for Peachstate by The Ertl Company and will not be available elsewhere. In addition, each car includes a serialized certificate." Their assortment also includes 1950s models.

1971 Buick GSX, Stratomist blue $38-42

1955 Chevrolet Bel Air, gold $38-42

1970 Chevrolet Chelvelle 454 SS $38-42

1963 Chevrolet Corvette, saddle tan . . . $38-42

1970 Chevrolet El Camino, forest green . $38-42
Dodge Daytona, blue $38-42
Ford Boss 429 Mustang, candy apple red . $38-42
1969 Ford Mustang Shelby GT-500 . . . $38-42
1969 Plymouth Road Runner, red $38-42
1969 Pontiac GTO, black $38-42
Pontiac Trans Am, black $38-42
1965 Shelby Cobra, silver $38-42

P.E.M. (see Precision Engineered Models, also see Hartoy)

Penguin (also see Tri-Ang)

From 1947 to 1952, the Penguin brand of plastic toy cars powered by a rubber band was produced by International Model Aircraft Ltd. of Merton, England, itself a part of the Lines Brothers' toy empire that included the more popular Tri-Ang Minic toys.

Armstrong Siddeley Hurricane Coupe, 1946, 1:40, #455 . . . . $45-60
Buick Super 8 Sedan, 1947, 1:38 . . . . $60-75
Ford Tudor Sedan, 1946, 1:38 . . . . . . $45-60
Jaguar XK 120, 1950, 1:38 . . . . $45-60
Jowett Javelin Saloon, 1947, 1:40, #457 . $45-60
Maserati Racing car, 1947, 1:40, #451 . $45-60
Riley Saloon, 1946, 1:40, #453 . . . . . $45-60
Riley Police car, 1946, 1:40 . . . . $45-60
Willys Military Jeep, 1945, 1:40 . . . . . $45-60

Penjoy/PenJoy Company

56 Newcomer Road
Mount Joy PA 17552-9344 USA
phone: (717)653-7330
fax: (717)653-2662
contact: Phil Wallauer
e-mail: penjoywm@webcom.com
website: www.penjoy.com

Penjoy is one of only two US-based manufacturers of diecast collectibles. In addition, there is also a Penjoy Collectors Club which offers a quarterly newsletter. Below is a sampling of retail issues of Penjoy model trucks with detailed description and price:

ADM Trucking Inc., fleet replica of Decatur, IL, based hauler, white sleeper with brown, red, and orange stripes $35-50
Admiral Transportation, fleet replica of Bellmawr, NJ, based carrier, green sleeper with green logo on white trailer, limited edition of 500 . . . . $30-45
Alling & Cory, fleet replica of major paper distribution company, blue day cab with large air foil and ferring $35-50

ANR Advance, fleet replica of Milwaukee-based ANR Advance Transportation Company rigs hauling general freight throughout North America, nose of trailer and back doors bear the ANR Advance logo $35-50
Bestway Trucking Inc., fleet replica of Indiana based common carrier. All white sleeper with Bestway two-color diamond logo on cab doors, rear doors, and trailer nose. limited edition of 300. Retail . . . $39.00; Club Member price. $29.00
Diecast Toy Collectors Association 5th Anniversary, commemorates the November 1998 Fifth Anniversary, 250 planned, only 94 produced $40-55
Emcea Transfer, fleet replica of Canadian based carrier, white sleeper with red stripes and lettering, limited edition of 300 . . . . $35-50
Fox River Foods refrigerated van, fleet replica of food service distributor based in Illinois, Indiana, and Wisconsin features 4-color graphics on side panels and logos on cab doors and rear doors of trailer, limited edition, trailer floors imprinted, 400 produced. $30-45
GE Appliance, sleek replica from major manufacturer, white sleeper with GE logo in gray, red accent stripe, and GE slogan "We bring good things to life," limited edition of 500 . . $35-50
Kane Freight Lines Inc., replica of PA-based carrier serving the northeast US and all of Canada. "Kane is able" slogan printed on white trailer sides and rear doors in green to match green sleeper, limited edition of 400 . . . . . $35-50
KAT, INC. refrigerated sleeper rig, fleet replica of Indiana-based food hauler covering 25 states, tractor is equipped with chrome front wheels just like the real thing, limited edition, 1,000 produced $35-50
Kinard Trucking Co., fleet replica of York, PA-based carrier, blue sleeper cab and white trailer panels with unique chrome finished roof, floor, and rear doors, limited edition of 500. . . . $45-60
Landstar Ranger, five scale Mack sleeper boxes painted in black primer are the load on this red flatbed pulled by a white sleeper . $40-55
Lions Delivery Service Ltd., fleet replica of Ontario, Canada-based carrier, steel blue cab and large air foil with fairing, white trailer, orange lion head logo with dark blue printing, limited edition of 400 . . . . $35-50
Lukens Steel, flatbed manufactured for Coatesville, PA-based specialty steel manufacturer, trailer features a unique load of a scaled steel billet and stainless steel coil as produced by Lukens, limited edition of 3000 . . . . $40-55
Maine's Paper & Food Service Inc., fleet replica of

refrigerated sleeper of Conklin, NY, wholesale distributor, white truck with red and black graphics, limited edition of 500 . . . . $35-50
Malone Freight Lines, from Birmingham, AL, a silver spread-axle flatbed with red sleeper tractor, ideal for attaching your own loads . . $35-50
Martin's Chips, replica of Thomasville, PA, snack producer, white day cab, small airfoil, and trailer with colorful graphics. limited edition of 500 . . . . $35-50
NCR Systems Media, black sleeper cab and white trailer with black and blue graphics produced for NCR Systems with new logo, limited edition of 300 . . . . $40-55
Nestlés Quik, fleet replica of company trucks found operating out of Nestle regional terminals, duplication of award-winning graphics features four-color process printing on rear doors, and results in one of most colorful trucks produced in 1:64 scale $45-60
NM Transfer Co. Inc., white trailer and day cab with large air foil and fairing duplicates this Wisconsin-based carrier, red and blue logo and graphics $35-50
Pitt-Ohio Express Inc., fleet duplicate of Pittsburgh-based carrier, red day cab with airfoil and white trailer, limited edition of 5,000 . $30-45
Plymouth Rock, fleet duplicate of MA-based carrier, striking black and yellow graphics on white trailer and yellow day cab with large airfoil and fairings, first truck produced with detailed printing of all safety placards on trailer nose and rear doors $35-50
R.E.D. Industries, the first Penjoy dump truck with a factory-produced simulated load, unusual features include printed clearance lights and warning beacon light, limited edition of 1,000 . $40-55
Richfield Youth Park, white sleeper truck produced as fundraiser for Richfield Youth Park Association, shows full-color baseball field on one side of trailer and soccer field on other side, very colorful truck, limited edition of 500 . . $45-60
Simpson Motor Truck, Inc., promotional truck commissioned by a PA Mack dealer, cream sleeper cab with brown graphics on cream refrigerator trailer, limited edition of 400 . . . . . . $35-50
Spangler's Flour Mill, white day cab with small airfoil and blue trailer commemorates historic Mount Joy, PA, flour mill built in 1855, graphics include near photo quality renditions of old mill, flour bags, etc. limited edition of 268 . $45-60
Star of the West Milling Co., fleet replica of Michigan-based mid-western hauler, yellow day cab and trailer with white and green graphics, limited edition of 400 . . . . $35-50
Tex-Pack Truck Lines, fleet duplication of Texas-

based carrier, white day cab with small airfoil, white trailer with red and blue graphics, limited edition of 250 . . . . $35-50

Truck Air Transfer, fleet duplication produced for 10th Anniversary of southern California contract carrier, all white sleeper with blue logo graphics, limited edition of 400 . . . . $35-50

Wegman's, fleet replica of Rochester, NY-based chain of food markets operating in New York and Pennsylvania featuring Wegman's current "pile of vegetables" theme on side panels $40-55

Weis Markets (#1), fleet replica of Weis Markets based in Sunbury, PA, brown day cab with large airfoil and fairing, white trailer with brown and yellow logo graphics. . . . $35-50

Weis Markets (#2), fleet duplication with new corporate graphics released in 1997, white trailer and day cab with small airfoil and red and blue graphics, limited edition of 4,000 . . . . $35-50

Weis Markets 85th Anniversary Special Edition truck to commemorate anniversary, special logo on side panels plus trailer converted to refrigerator trailer, limited edition of 7,500 . . . . . . $40-55

Yellow Freight, fleet replica of carrier recognized throughout North America, distinctive orange cab with white airfoil and trailer, and orange logo $35-50

Yellow Freight Calendar, fleet replica except trailer side panels are 1998 calendar with 1999 calendar inside, new year calendar panels available from factory, great desktop item . . $35-50

Yuengling Brewery, fleet duplicate of America's oldest operating brewery located in Pottsville, PA, since 1829, striking four-color process graphics on side panels and rear doors depict Yuengling eagle logo and lager beer bottles, limited edition of 5000 . . . . $45-60

Penny (also see Politoys/Polistil)

Penny is a brand of very detailed 1:66 scale toys from Politoys/Polistil of Italy. They were produced from 1967 and continued through the early 1970s. Models feature opening hoods, narrow "wire" wheels and hard rubber tires. Thanks to Don Heine for the information.

Politoys Penny Series

Alfa Romeo 2600 Sprint Bertone
  metallic blue, 1967, #25 . . . . $8-12
  olive green, 1967, #35 . . . . $8-12
Alfa Romeo Giulia
  1300 Junior GT, white, 1968, #28 . . $8-12
  1300 Police, olive green with blue light on top, 1968, #46 . . . . $8-12
  Canguro, silver, 1967, #22 . . . . . . $8-12
  SS, metallic dark gray, 1967, #26 . . $8-12

Brabham-Climax Formula 1, silver, 1967, #5 . . . . $8-12
Brabham-Repco Formula 1, dark green, 1968, #11 . . . . $8-12
BRM Formula 1
  blue, 1967, #1 . . . . $8-12
  H-16, metallic lime gold, 1967, #8 . . $8-12
Cooper-Maserati Formula 1, blue, 1967, #6 . . . . $8-12
Eagle-Climax Formula 1, metallic green, 1967, #7 . . . . $8-12
Eagle-Weslake Formula 1, metallic blue, 1968, #14 . . . . $8-12
Ferrari 250 GT, dark yellow, 1967, #21 . . . . $8-12
Ferrari Formula 1
  V6, red, 1967, #4 . . . . $8-12
  V12, red, 1967, #9 . . . . $8-12
Fiat 850 Coupe, silver, 1967, #30 . . . . $8-12
Honda V12 Formula 1, white, 1967, #10 . . . . $8-12
Iso Rivolta
  metallic burgundy, 1969, #32 . . . . . $8-12
  and Boat Trailer, metallic dark blue with yellow trailer, 1969, #53 . . . . $15-18
Lancia Flavia Zagato Sport, metallic green, 1967, #27 . . . . $8-12
Lotus-BRM H-16 Formula 1, dark green, 1968, #15 . . . . $8-12
Lotus-Climax Formula 1
  dark green, 1967, #3 . . . . $8-12
  yellow, 1967, #2 . . . . $8-12
Maserati 3500 GT, silver, 1967, #29 . . . $8-12
McLaren-Ford Formula 1, white, 1968, #12 . . . . $8-12
McLaren-Serenissima Formula 1, red, 1968, #13 . . . . $8-12
Mercedes-Benz 230 SL, metallic dark green, 1969, #34 . . . . $8-12
Porsche 912, tan, 1968, #24 . . . . $8-12
Romeo Minibus, red, 1970, #54 . . . . . $12-15

Pepe

Pepe has produced miniature models of Opels, Volkswagens, Renaults, Fiats, and others, in 1:25 and 1:43 scale.

Austin Mini Ambulance, #37, 1:25 . . . . $16-20
Cooper F1 Racer, #45, 1:25 . . . . $16-20
Fiat 692 Truck
  Mixer, #48, 1:25 . . . . $16-20
  Refrigerator Van, #50, 1:25 . . . . . . $16-20
  Stake Truck, #51, 1:25 . . . . $16-20
Jeep CJ2 Army, #52, 1:25 . . . . $16-20
Lotus F1 Racer, #46, 1:25 . . . . $16-20
Opel 1957 Wagon, #43, 1:43 . . . . $16-20

Opel Fire Truck
  Ladder Truck, #17, 1:25 . . . . $16-20
  Pumper Truck, #15, 1:25 . . . . $16-20
Opel Rekord Ambulance, #41, 1:43 . . . $16-20
Opel Tow Truck, #16, 1:25 . . . . $16-20
Renault 5
  Ambulance, #33, 1:25 . . . . $16-20
  Fire, #34, 1:25 . . . . $16-20
  Police, #32, 1:25 . . . . $16-20
  Taxi, #35, 1:25 . . . . $16-20
Saviem Dump Truck, #42, 1:43 . . . . . . $16-20
Volkswagen Beetle Fire Chief, #26, 1:25 . $16-20
Volkswagen Pickup Split Window, #18, 1:25 . . . . $16-20

Phat Boyz

Produced by Simple Wishes, Inc., of La Quinta, California, Phat Boyz distinguish themselves by their dimensions—they are designed after real cars and trucks except that they have been flattened and widened to give them a surreal appearance. Starting out with assorted two-packs, the line has expanded since its inception to include three-packs, a car carrier, interlocking play sets with streets and buildings, remote control cars, launchers and more. Phat Boyz are manufactured in China.

Phat Boyz models from 2003 Two-Packs

1957 Chevrolet Bel Air
  red with white roof, #4 . . . . $2-3

turquoise with cream roof, #12 . . . . . . $2-3
1963 Chevrolet Corvette

metallic blue, #12 . . . . $2-3
  orange, #3 . . . . $2-3
1969 Chevrolet Camaro SS
  maroon, #4 . . . . $2-3
  white with red flames, #5 . . . . $2-3

2002 Chevrolet Corvette Z06, red, #2 . . . . $2-3

City Bus, from City Bus Stop play set . . $4-5
1964 Ford Galaxie 500

lime green, #7 . . . . $2-3

metallic lavender, #9 . . . . $3-4
1966 Ford Mustang

blue, #9 . . . . $3-4

cream, #11 . . . . $2-3
1990 Ford Mustang

(color unknown), #8 . . . . $3-4

dark blue with white accents, #11 . . . . . $2-3

yellow, #10 . . . . $2-3
1998 Ford Mustang

red with white roof, #1 . . . . $2-3

yellow with white roof, #2 . . . . $2-3

1956 Ford Pick-up, bright blue, #6. . . . . $2-3
1957 Ford T-Bird, purple with cream roof, #10. . $2-3
1949 Mercury

beige, #7 . . . . $2-3

orange, #6 . . . . $2-3

1968 Pontiac GTO

bright blue, #5 . . . . $2-3

red with yellow flames, #3 . . . . $2-3

yellow, #1 . . . . $2-3
1956 Ford Pick-up (color unknown), #8 . . . . $3-4

Piccolino

Piccolino models are not to be confused with Schuco Piccolo models. The Piccolino range is an assortment of delicate 1:76 scale white metal models and kits made in Britain by Bellini starting in 1985. According to Crister Skoglund of Sweden, one leaflet distributed at the introduction of the new brand states that the models are going to be produced by Master Models Ltd., Guernsey, C.I., UK.

Their original address was Bellini Models, Ltd., Charwell House, Wilsom Road, Alton, Hants, GU34 TJ, Great Britain.

Upon digging through some old literature, Skoglund found a letter dated February 1992 that says that from now on all orders should be sent to Rae Models, Corrie Road, Addlerstone, Surrey, KT15 2LP, UK. So it would appear that Rae Models bought the company around January 1992 according to Skoglund's research.

Below is an alphabetical list provided by Skoglund, who writes "....I have listed all Piccolino models in the OO scale I know of. The first column is their catalog number.... As you can see, the models are divided into different categories. 'WLS' stands for 'World Land Speed' record cars, 'Grand Prix' for 'Grand Prix' Formula One models etc. The 'slash K' (/K) was added to the number to indicate that it is in kit form. The second column doesn't need any explanation."

Most prices are retail for unbuilt kits. Ready built models are about double the price. £1 UK is equal to about $1.60 US. Current value is estimated at far right.

Piccolino also produced some 1:24 scale extremely detailed models, according to Bill Cross, another avid collector. No list of those is currently known.

Alfa Romeo

1931 (Monza), Grand Prix 48/K . . . $45-60

512 prototyp 1942, Grand Prix 75/K . $45-60

6c 1931, HSC 92/K $45-60

Bimotore 1934, Grand Prix 36/K . . $45-60

Disco Volante 1953, HSC065/K . . . $45-60

159 1951, Grand Prix 10/K $45-60

P3–1934, Grand Prix 33/K $45-60
Allard J2X 1950, HSC 99/K $45-60
Alvis FWD 1929, SLC 140 . . . . $45-60
Aquila Italiana 1913, SLC 125/K . . . $45-60

Aston Martin

DB3 S Coupe 1957, HSC 10/K . . . $45-60

Ulster 1935, HSC 53/K $45-60
Austin Healy 100 1954, HSC 14/K . . . $45-60
Austin Taxi 1934, SLC 88 . . . . $45-60
Auto Union 1936, Grand Prix 1/K $45-60
Bentley

3 Litre 1927, HSC 58/K $45-60

4½-Litre 1929, HSC 54/K $45-60
Birkin Bentley 1929, Grand Prix 46/K . . $45-60
Bluebird

(Arrol Aster) 1929, WLS 10/K $45-60

1925, WLS 4/K $45-60

1933, WLS 15/K $45-60

1935, WLS 9/F $45-60

1964, WLS 19/K $45-60
BMW M3 1991, HSC 69/K $45-60
Brabham BT 19 1966, Grand Prix

66/K $45-60
BRM

(Original) 1949, Grand Prix 80/K . . $45-60

P25 1959, Grand Prix 3/K $45-60

P261 High Exhaust 1965, Grand Prix

30/K $45-60

P48 1960, Grand Prix 8/K $45-60

P56 1962, Grand Prix 56/K $45-60
Budweiser 1979 rocketcar, WLS 28/K . $45-60
Bugatti

251 1955, GP082/K $45-60

Type 35 1924, Grand Prix 29/K . . . $45-60
Buick Tourer 1924, SLC 141 . . . . $45-60
Caterham Lotus 7 1981, HSC 34/K . . . $45-60
Connaught A 1952, Grand Prix 14/K . . $45-60
Cooper

Bobtail 1955, HSC 45 . . . . $45-60

Bristol 1953, Grand Prix 55/K $45-60
De Dion Buton 1904, SLC 123 . . . . . . $45-60
Delage 1.5 Litre 1927, Grand Prix 40/K . $45-60
ERA B Type 1936, Grand Prix 2/K $45-60
Ferrari

156 Shark Nose 1961, Grand Prix

51/K $45-60

250 Berlinetta 1960, HSC 37/K . . . $45-60

250 GTO 1962, HSC 22/K $45-60

250 Testa Rossa 1959, HSC 24/K . . $45-60

330 LMB 1963, HSC 51/K $45-60

330 P4 1967, GT 6/K $45-60

330 TR 1962, HSC 25/K $45-60

365 (Daytona) 1973, HSC 35/K . . . $45-60

375 MM Le Mans 1954, HSC 9/K . $45-60

375 Thinwall 1953, Grand Prix 39/K . $45-60

500 1952, Grand Prix 11/K $45-60

512S 1970, GT 15/K $45-60

Dino 206S 1967, GT 4/K $45-60

Dino 246 1959, Grand Prix 22/K . . $45-60

F40–1987, HSC 104/K $45-60

Ford
GT 40 1968, GT 11/K $45-60
RS200 1987, HRC 3/K $45-60
Frazer Nash
1935, HSC 66/K $45-60
1952, HSC 100/K $45-60
Golden Arrow 1929, WLS 12/K $45-60
Golden Rod 1965, WLS 020/K. $45-60
Gordini 2 Litre–1952, Grand Prix 42/K . $45-60
Grand Prix Sunbeam 1923, Grand Prix
90/K $45-60
Healy Silverstone 1960, HSC 18/K . . . $45-60
Jaguaar
C Type 1953, HSC 2/K $45-60
SS 100 1939, HSC 55/K $45-60
XJR5 1983, GT 25/K. $45-60
XJR8 1987, GT 1:K $45-60
XJR 9–1988 LM winner, GT 8/K . . . $45-60
XK 120 1950, HSC 56/K $45-60
Lagonda M45R 1935, HSC 109/K . . . $45-60
Lancia D50 1955, Grand Prix 18/K . . . $45-60
Lister Jaguar (Costin) 1959, HSC 13/K.. $45-60
London Taxi 1958, RV 10. . . . . $45-60
Lotus
16 1958, Grand Prix 21/K $45-60
18 1960, Grand Prix 52/K $45-60
25 1962, Grand Prix 59/K $45-60
33 1965, Grand Prix 64/K $45-60
Elan 1970, HSC 44/K. $45-60
Maserati
(Bird Cage) 1961, HSC 73/K. . . . $45-60
2.9 1934, Grand Prix 49/K $45-60
250 F 1957, Grand Prix 17/K $45-60
48/CTL 1948, GP058/K $45-60
McLaren
M1C 1965, GT 3/K $45-60
M8C 1970, GT 2/K $45-60
Mercedes-Benz
W196 1954, Grand Prix 15/K . . . $45-60
300 SL 1952, HSC 50/K $45-60
300SLR 1955, HSC 33/K $45-60
SSK 1928, HSC 60/K. $45-60
W154 1938, Grand Prix 32/K . . . $45-60
MG
EX 120 1931, WLS 33/K $45-60
EX 127 1933, WLS 35/K $45-60
EX 135 1939, WLS 29/K $45-60
EX 181 1957, WLS 30/K $45-60
K3 (Pointed Tail) 1933, HSC 101/K . $45-60
K3 Magnette 1933, HSC 76/K . . . $45-60
M Type (Racing) 1930, HSC 102/K. $45-60
M Type 1930, HSC 90/K $45-60
No. 1 Kimber Special 1925, HSC
67/K $45-60
SA 2 Litre 1937, SLC 130. . . . . . . $45-60
TD 1952, HSC 15/K. $45-60

TF 1954, HSC 109/K $45-60
Napier Bluebird 1927, WLS 7/K $45-60
Peugeot 205 Turbo 1984, HRC 1:K . . . $45-60
Porsche
917 K 1970, GT 16/K $45-60
956 1983, GT 24/K. $45-60
F1-804 1962, Grand Prix 12/K . . . $45-60
Railton 1938, WLS 16/K. $45-60
Renault AX 1908, SLC 124. . . . . $45-60
Rover 6HP 1906, SLC 120. . . . . $45-60
Salmson 1926, HSC 38/K $45-60
Spice
Pontiac (IMSA) 1986, GT 62/K. . . . $45-60
SE89 1989, GT 48/K. $45-60
Tiga Lamborghini 1986, GT 65/K.. $45-60
Sunbeam 1000HP 1927, WLS 8/K . . . $45-60
Talbot
105 1931, HSC091/K. $45-60
Lago 1949, Grand Prix 9/K $45-60
Thrust II 1983, WLS 26/K $45-60
Thunderbolt 1938, WLS 17/K $45-60
Triplex (Stutz Black Hawk) 1928, WLS
11/K $45-60
Trojan Achilles 1928, SLC 68 . . . . . . $45-60
Vanwall 1958, Grand Prix 5/K. $45-60
Vauxhall 30-98–1913, HSC 1:K. $45-60

Piccolo (see Schuco)

Pilen (see Auto Pilen)

Pioneer

A brand that would likely fall into the generic category is Pioneer. The brand was recently discovered by collector Robert Speerbrecher while stationed in Jakarta, Indonesia. Pioneer toys are made in China, and as Mr. Speerbrecher reports, "They have a line of cars that come with a bunch of accessories in them like a small play set on a blister pack. Most sets have one vehicle and a trailer, or two vehicles and some other accessories like picnic tables, trees, ramps in the Off-Road Set, etc. There is a real neat Military Set with a Jeep and a tank. Both sets are diecast, plus some army guys and a way-out-of-scale hand grenade.

"The sets come on a large blister pack with printing only on the front. The card and blister pack plastic are pretty thin. The one I bought is a pink Mercedes 500SL Convertible pulling an all plastic trailer with two wind-surfing boards on it. It comes with a table, four chairs, and an umbrella for the table. Pretty neat set really for $1.50.

"The Mercedes is diecast with a plastic base. Really not a bad casting, better than many of the real cheap Chinese ones. As good as the Majorette 500SL but not as good as the

Hot Wheels one. The other vehicles were army jeeps, cars, trucks, etc. All are not too bad quality. The military set is real neat."

Later, Speerbrecher added, "Here's some more info. They have at least 4 sets. One is a Military Set with a green Jeep, a green 4X4 ute [utility, or pickup] type vehicle, a couple of army guys, and a hand grenade. The second is the Dive Set with a minivan pulling a trailer, a diver, and a few fish. The third is a Holiday Set with a minivan pulling a boat on a trailer, a few people, and a picnic table. The fourth is a Holiday Set with a Mercedes 500SL pulling a trailer with a windsurf board, a few people, and a table. Really the vehicles are not bad, and the set is a real value at about $1.50, a lot for the money. Especially the Military set with the two diecast vehicles. The cars are all about 1:64 scale. Funny thing is that the people are way out of scale and the hand grenade with the military set is bigger than the vehicles."

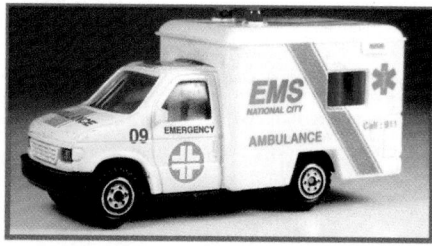

Ambulance, Pioneer Pro Engine Street Machine, 3", 1:64 . . . . $1-2

Cement Mixer, Pioneer Pro Engine Heavy Truck, 3," 1:55 . . . . $1-2

Chevrolet Blazer 4x4, Pioneer Pro Engine Street Machine, 3," 1:64 . . . . $1-2

Fire Engine, Pioneer, 3".............$1-2

Hovercraft, Pioneer Pro Engine Street Machine, 3".........................$1-2

Hummer, red with white roof, Pioneer, 3". $1-2

Jeep Grand Cherokee, Pioneer Pro Engine Street Machine, 3", 1:64 ....$1-2

Mercedes A Class, blue, Pioneer Pro Engine, 4", 1:32......................$2-3

Mercedes C Class, silver, Pioneer Pro Engine, 4", 1:36....................$2-3

Mitsubishi Pajero Jr., white, Pioneer Pro Engine, 4", 1:36....................$2-3

Police, Pioneer Pro Engine Street Machine, 3", 1:64............................$1-2

Power Shovel, Pioneer Pro Engine Heavy Truck, 3", 1:55.....................$1-2

Rally Racer, Pioneer Pro Engine Street Machine, 3", 1:64 ....$1-2

RV, Pioneer Pro Engine Street Machine, 3",1:64............................$1-2

Suzuki SUV, Pioneer Pro Engine Street Machine, 3", 1:64 ....$1-2

Tour Van, Pioneer Pro Engine Street Machine, 3", 1:64 ....$1-2

Toyota RAV4, Pioneer Pro Engine, 3".. $1-2

Toyota RAV4 Police, Pioneer Pro Engine, 3"..................................$1-2

Piranha

Piranha white metal models are produced under the auspices of ABC Brianza.

1969 Dodge Daytona Hardtop, 1:43,
   #PH003 ....$80-90
1961 Ferrari GTO Prototype, 1:43,
   #PH004 ....$80-90

Platypus

Platypus Industrie produces hand-built models of incredible detail. Its recent release of a 1:50 scale Euclid R260 Mining Truck is an exquisitely detailed rendering that accurately portrays the massive size of this huge vehicle. More information can be obtained by phoning (in England) +44 1548 844114.

Euclid R260 Mining Truck, 1:50 . . . . . . $30-45
Tamrock DHA 1000S crawler drill rig,
   1:50 . . . . $30-45
Unit Rig Lectra Haul MT-3700 Mining Truck,
   1:50 . . . . $30-45

Playart (also sold as Sears Roadmates, Woolworth's Peelers, Charmerz, Model Power)

For about 15 years, from about 1975 to 1990, Playart of Hong Kong produced a wonderful array of toy vehicles. It is a wonder they are not more popular, but it is likely due to the heavy competition in the U.S. market.

Playart toys have been marketed and packaged under many other names, most notably Sears Roadmates and Model Power, but the models themselves prominently display the Playart logo on the base, making identification easy and unmistakable.

The charm and quality of Playart toys make them worth keeping as collectibles. Their current value is still low, since most collectors are unaware of them. It is uncommon to find very many of them at toy shows or other second-market sources.

According to Dave Weber of Warrington, Pennsylvania, Playart at one time produced a series of models called Charmerz for New York distributor Charles Merzbach, who also packaged and marketed Majorettes in the US in the late 1960s. Alex Lakhtman reports that Playart models also were sold in Woolworth's and under the name "Peelers." Fastwheels is another name associated with Playart.

Alfa carabo Bertone, green, Playart
   Fastwheels #7113 . . . . $8-10
Alfa Romeo P33, red, Playart Fastwheels
   #7112 . . . . $8-10
Alfa Romeo Alfetta GT, Playart Fastwheels
   #7198 . . . . $6-8
Alpine Renault A310 V6, Playart Fastwheels
   #7265 . . . . $6-8
AMC AMX 390, red, Playart Fastwheels
   #7110 . . . . $8-10

AMC Javelin SST
   1:64, Playart Fastwheels #7107 . . . . . . $6-8
   green, Playart Fastwheels #7157 . . . . $8-10
American LaFrance
   Fire Ladder Truck, 1:87 . . . . $10-12
   Fire Snorkel Truck, 1:87 . . . . $8-10
Audi Quattro, Playart Fastwheels #7241 . . . $6-8
Austin Mini Cooper S Mk II, red or
   ochre $10-12
Batmobile, Playart Fastwheels #7100 . . . $12-16
Beach Buggy (Dune Buggy), Playart
   Fastwheels #7180 . . . . $6-8
BMW 2002, purple, Playart Fastwheels
   #7135 . . . . $8-10
BMW 633, Playart Fastwheels #7274 . . . . $6-8
BMW Spicup, Playart Fastwheels #7174 . . $6-8
Brabham Racer, Playart Fastwheels
   #7190 . . . . $6-8
BRM Racer, Playart Fastwheels #7195 . . . . $6-8
Bulldozer
   Playart Fastwheels #7161 . . . . $6-8
   red with yellow blade, green cab . . . $10-12
Cadillac Eldorado, brown, Playart Fastwheels
   #7115 . . . . $8-10
Cement Mixer (Ford?)
   orange, red and gray $10-12
   blue, red and gray $10-12
   blue, red barrel, Playart Fastwheels
     #7126 . . . . $8-10
Chevrolet Astro-1, Playart Fastwheels
   #7121 . . . . $8-10
Chevrolet Blazer, 1:72
   Highway Patrol, black & white, 1:72, Sears
     Roadmates #7242H $4-6
   Highway Patrol, Playart Fastwheels
     #7242A $6-8
   Police, Playart Fastwheels #7242a $6-8
   silver, Playart Fastwheels #7242 . . . . . $6-8

silver, Sears Roadmates #7242 . . . . $6-8
Chevrolet Camaro
   Convertible, top up, 1:18 . . . . $24-30
   1967 1:64 . . . . $5-7
   1977 Z28, 1:64 . . . . $4-6
   SS, blue, Playart Fastwheels #7109 . . $8-10
   SS, yellow, Playart Fastwheels #7109 . $8-10
   Z-28, Playart Fastwheels #7207 . . . . . $6-8
   Z-28, Playart Fastwheels #7245 . . . . . $6-8

Chevrolet Caprice Classic

metallic purple, 1:72, Sears Roadmates
#7214 . . . . $5-7
   Fire Chief, 1:72 . . . . $4-6

Police car, black & white, 1:72, Sears Roadmates #7232 . . . . $5-7

Yellow Cab Taxi, 1:72, Sears Roadmates
#7217 . . . . $5-7

   Playart Fastwheels #7214 . . . . $6-8
   Fire Chief, Playart Fastwheels #7218 . . . $6-8
   Police, Playart Fastwheels #7232 . . . . . $6-8
   Taxi, Playart Fastwheels #7217 . . . . . . $6-8
Chevrolet Corvette Stingray
   Mako Shark, Playart Fastwheels #7106,
     purple $8-10
   Mako Shark, Playart Fastwheels #7106, teal
     blue $8-10
   Playart Fastwheels #7136 . . . . $6-8

sea green, Sears Roadmates $7-9
   Street Machine, Playart Fastwheels
     #7236 . . . . $6-8
Citreon CX 2200, Playart Fastwheels #7197 . $6-8
Combine Harvester
   Playart Fastwheels #7166 . . . . $6-8
   blue, Sears Roadmates #7166 . . . . . . $7-9
Container Truck, SeaLand (Ford?), green
   and white $10-12

Container Wagon (Open Container Truck),
Playart Fastwheels #7164 . . . . $6-8

Custom Van

Pirates, Playart Fastwheels #7247A $6-8

Sea Gulls, Playart Fastwheels #7247B . . $6-8

Stars & Stripes, Playart Fastwheels
#7247C $6-8

Swirls, Playart Fastwheels #7247D $6-8

U.S. Mail, Playart Fastwheels #7247E . . $6-8

Datsun 240Z, Playart Fastwheels #7137 . . . $6-8

DeTomaso Pantera, 1:64, Playart
Fastwheels #7248 . . . . $6-8

Diesel Road Roller, Playart Fastwheels #7165 . $6-8

Dodge Challenger

red with black roof, 1:72, Sears Roadmates
#7178 . . . . $4-6

Rallye, Playart Fastwheels #7178 . . . . . $6-8

Dodge Omni 024, 1:67

metallic green, Sears Roadmates #7202 . $4-6

Playart Fastwheels #7202 . . . . $6-8

Dodge Paramedic, 1:64 . . . . $4-6

Double Decker London Bus, Playart Fastwheels
#7162 . . . . $6-8

Douglas DC-10 "American Airlines" $4-6

Dump Truck

(Ford?), apple green cab, metallic g
reen-gold dumper $10-12

(Volvo?), yellow with orange dumper,
#7185 . . . . $10-12

(Volvo?), yellow with green and
yellow-orange dumper, #7186 . . $10-12

brown-purple cab, orange tipper, Playart
Fastwheels #7128 . . . . $8-10

Estate Wagon, Playart Fastwheels #7172 . . $6-8

Farm Tractor with Plow, 1:72 . . . . $5-7

Ferrari BB 512, Playart Fastwheels #7219 . . $6-8

Fiat 124 Sport, Playart Fastwheels #7158 . . $6-8

Fiat Dino, Playart Fastwheels #7134 . . . . . . $6-8

Fiat X1/9, 1:64, Playart Fastwheels
#7196 . . . . $6-8

Fire Engine

With Ladder, Playart Fastwheels #7183 . . $6-8

With Snorkel, Playart Fastwheels
#7184 . . . . $6-8

Fire Tender, Playart Fastwheels #7168 . . . . $6-8

Fire Truck, Playart Fastwheels #7130 . . . . . . $6-8

Ford Box Truck

"Pepsi-Cola," 1:120, Sears Roadmates
#7260P $6-8

"7-Up," 1:120, Sears Roadmates
#7260U $6-8

Ford Cab With Sleeping Cabin, Playart
Fastwheels #7253 . . . . $6-8

Ford Capri 1600 GT, 1:64, Playart
Fastwheels #7150 . . . . $6-8

Ford Cement Truck, Playart Fastwheels
#7226 . . . . $6-8

Ford Cortina GXL, light green, Playart
Fastwheels #7155 . . . . $8-10

Ford Dump Truck, Playart Fastwheels
#7228 . . . . $6-8

Ford Fire Chief Station Wagon, red, Playart
Fastwheels #7118 . . . . $8-10

Ford Freight Truck, Playart Fastwheels
#7260 . . . . $6-8

Ford Freight Truck–7-Up, Playart Fastwheels
#7260u $6-8

Ford Freight Truck–Pepsi Cola, Playart Fastwheels
#7260p $6-8

Ford Mustang

1966 Convertible, lime green or red . . . $6-8

1969 Hardtop Coupe $6-8

GT, Playart Fastwheels #7120 . . . . . . $8-10

Hardtop, Playart Fastwheels #7116 . . $8-10

Ford Paramedic Van, Playart Fastwheels
#7209 . . . . $6-8

Ford Petrol Tanker, Shell, Playart Fastwheels
#7231 . . . . $6-8

Ford Police car, white, Playart Fastwheels
#7132 . . . . $8-10

Ford Police Tactical Force Van, Playart Fastwheels
#7213 . . . . $6-8

Ford Thunderbird, Playart Fastwheels #7103

purple $8-10

beige $8-10

Ford Turbo Mustang, Playart Fastwheels
#7271 . . . . $6-8

Forklift Truck, Playart Fastwheels #7177 . . . . $6-8

Freight Truck (20' Truck), Playart Fastwheels
#7160 . . . . $6-8

Garbage Collector Truck, Playart Fastwheels
#7163 . . . . $6-8

Gasoline Truck, Playart Fastwheels #7131 . . $6-8

Greyhound City Bus, 1:156, Playart Fastwheels #7234
(exact copy of Tomica grayhound Bus) . . $12-15

Helicopter

"Air Sea Rescue" $6-8

"Coke" $6-8

"Fire" $6-8

Honda 2GS, yellow-green, Playart Fastwheels
#7152 . . . . $8-10

Honda Accord, Playart Fastwheels #7256 . . $6-8

Honda N360, Playart Fastwheels #7139 . . $6-8

Honda S800 Convertible, yellow with robin's egg blue
tonneau cover, Playart Fastwheels #7140 . . $6-8

Honda Z GS, turquoise $10-12

Hyster 70 Forklift, 1:64 . . . . $8-10

Isuzu 117 Coupe, Playart Fastwheels #7145 . . $6-8

Jaguar E Type 2+2, green, Playart Fastwheels
#7123 . . . . $8-10

Jeep, Playart Fastwheels #7222 . . . . $6-8

Jensen FF, pink-beige, Playart Fastwheels
#7111 . . . . $8-10

Jeep CJ U.S. Mail, 1:64 . . . . $6-8

Lamborghini 3000 Silhouette, 1:64, Playart
Fastwheels #7210 . . . . $6-8

Lamborghini Countach LP500S, 1:67

red, Sears Roadmates #7246 . . . $8-10

Playart Fastwheels #7246 . . . . $6-8

Lamborghini Miura, dark green, Playart Fastwheels #7108 . . . . $8-10

Lancia Fulvia 1600 HF, Playart Fastwheels
#7239 . . . . $6-8

Lancia Stratos, 1:64

Playart Fastwheels #7259 . . . . $6-8

Sears Roadmates #7259 . . . . $8-10

Lola Racer, Playart Fastwheels #7192 . . . . . $6-8

Lotus Elite, Playart Fastwheels #7199 . . . . . $6-8

Lotus Esprit, 1:64, Playart Fastwheels #7243 . $6-8

Lotus Racer, Playart Fastwheels #7194 . . . . $6-8

London Bus, 1:100 . . . . $6-8

Man From U.N.C.L.E. Thrushbuster car,
Playart Fastwheels #7119 . . . . $15-18

Mangusta 5000 Ghia, Playart Fastwheels
#7105 . . . . $6-8

Maserati Marzal, Playart Fastwheels
#7125 . . . . $8-10

Matra Simca Bagheera, Playart Fastwheels
#7203 . . . . $6-8

Mazda Cosmo, Playart Fastwheels #7249 . $6-8

Mazda Truck, 1:64

Pickup, Playart Fastwheels #7251 . . . . . $6-8

Wrecker Truck, orange $8-10

Mazda RX-7, Playart Fastwheels #7205 . . . $6-8

Mazda Wrecker Truck, Playart Fastwheels
#7229 . . . . $6-8

Mclaren Racer, Playart Fastwheels #7193 . . $6-8

Mercedes Ambulance, Playart Fastwheels
#7167 . . . . $6-8

Mercedes-Benz 350 SL, Playart Fastwheels
#7154 . . . . $6-8

Mercedes-Benz C111, dark metallic maroon, Playart Fastwheels #7114 . . . . $8-10

Mitsubishi Hi-Pup Coupe Galant GTO MR, Playart
Fastwheels #7156 . . . . $6-8

Nissan Sunny 1200 Coupe GX, Playart Fastwheels #7147 . . . . $6-8

Opel GT, 1:64

light metallic brown, Playart Fastwheels
#7104 . . . . $8-10

white, Playart Fastwheels #7104 . . . . . $8-10

Opel Senator, Playart Fastwheels #7275 . . . $6-8
Pickup Truck, Playart Fastwheels #7127. . . . $6-8
Plymouth Barracuda, Playart Fastwheels
 #7101 . . . .$8-10
Police Van, Playart Fastwheels #7173 . . . . . $6-8
Pontiac Firebird
 Playart Fastwheels #7206 . . . . $6-8
 Trans Am, Playart Fastwheels #7220 . . . $6-8
Porsche 914, Playart Fastwheels #7138 . . $6-8
Porsche 928, Playart Fastwheels #7201 . . $6-8
Porsche Carrera 910, Playart Fastwheels
 #7102 . . . .$8-10
Porsche Targa 911S, Playart Fastwheels
 #7144 . . . . $6-8
Range Rover, Playart Fastwheels #7182 . . . $6-8
Renault A110, Playart Fastwheels #7211 . . $6-8
Rolls Royce Silver Cloud, 1:64, Playart
 Fastwheels #7133 . . . . $6-8
Rover 2000 TC, Playart Fastwheels #7151 . $6-8
Scania Bus "AVIS Courtesy Bus," 1:87 . . $10-12
Scania Dump Truck, Playart Fastwheels
 #7186 . . . . $6-8
Scania Freight Truck with Canvas Top, Playart
 Fastwheels #7187 . . . . $6-8
Scania Open Platform Freight Truck
 With Girders, Playart Fastwheels #7189. $6-8
 With Pipes, Playart Fastwheels #7188 . . $6-8
Scania Tipper Truck, Playart Fastwheels
 #7185 . . . . $6-8
Shadow Racer, Playart Fastwheels #7191 . . $6-8
Shovel Tractor (Road Tractor With Shovel),
 Playart Fastwheels #7171 . . . . $6-8
Skip Dumper (Earth Dumper), Playart
 Fastwheels #7181 . . . . $6-8
Tanker, Shell (Ford?) $10-12
Toyota, brown, Playart Fastwheels #7117 . $8-10
Toyota 2000 GT, blue, Playart Fastwheels
 #7122 . . . .$8-10
Toyota Celica, 1:64, 1600 GT, Playart Fast-
 wheels #7142 . . . . $6-8
Toyota Corolla Sprinter SL, Playart Fastwheels
 #7146 . . . . $6-8
Toyota Corona Mark II 1900 Hardtop SL,
 Playart Fastwheels #7141 . . . . $6-8
Toyota Crown Hardtop SL, Playart Fastwheels
 #7143 . . . . $6-8
Tractor, Playart Fastwheels #7176 . . . . $6-8
Tractor With Angledozer (Bulldozer Tractor),
 Playart Fastwheels #7169 . . . . $6-8
U.S. Jeep, Army #7852 on sides $10-12
U.S. Jeep, Civilian, yellow $10-12
U.S. Mail Jeep, Playart Fastwheels #7244a . $6-8
Volvo 164E Station Wagon, lime green,
 Playart Fastwheels #7175 . . . . $6-8
Volvo 166, 1:64 . . . . $4-6
Volvo 244, Playart Fastwheels #7258 . . . . $6-8

Volvo 343, Playart Fastwheels #7255 . . . . $6-8
Volkswagen Bug, red, Playart Fastwheels
 #7124 . . . .$8-10

**Volkswagen Microbus, metallic lime
green** **$8-10**

Volkswagen Porsche 914, Playart
 Fastwheels #7138 . . . . $6-8
Volkswagen Station Wagon, Playart
 Fastwheels #7179 . . . . $6-8
Wrecker Truck, Playart Fastwheels #7129 . $8-10
Yamaha Super Discmatic Rotary Coupe,
 Playart Fastwheels #7148 . . . . $6-8
Zetor Tractor, Playart Fastwheels #7170 . . . $6-8

Playing Mantis (see Johnny Lightning)

Play Power

Play Power models are most likely made in Japan.

Play Power Airplanes

E/T Mk.2 "Patrol of France," red/white/blue,
 2¾" $2-4
McDonnell-Douglas F-16 "USAF Thunderbirds,"
 red/white/blue, 2¾" $2-4
McDonnell-Douglas F-15 "USAF Bicentennial,"
 red/white/blue, 2¾" $2-4
McDonnell-Douglas AV-8A "Red Arrows,"
 red/white/blue, 2¾" $2-4
McDonnell-Douglas F-18 "USAF Blue Angels,"
 blue/yellow, 2¾" $2-4

Play Power Vehicles

BMW 2-door Sedan Police car,
 white/yellow/black, 2¾" $2-4
Chevrolet Pickup Truck "Western Forest
 Service," bright pink, 3" $2-4
Chevrolet Forest Service Tow Truck, bright
 green/yellow, 3⅓" $2-4
Chevrolet Van Ambulance, white/red/black,
 2⅝" $2-4
Hino Snorkel Fire Engine, red/white, 3¼" . . . $3-5

Playskool (also see Fisher-Price, Matchbox)

Playskool has produced many types of preschool toys for decades, but only for a short time in the early 1980s did the company market diecast toys in a series of heavy one-piece vehicles driven by Sesame Street characters. The most common one is Oscar the Grouch driving his garbage truck. Each model is larger than the average diecast toy vehicle, about 2 to 2½" tall and 3" long. Popular at the time but rare now, each model is worth about $6-8.

More recently, Tyco has acquired the Sesame Street license and has issued new models under the Tyco Preschool, Matchbox, and Fisher-Price brands, all of which have since been swallowed up by the Mattel toy giant.

Playskool preschool diecast models listed below feature Barney the Dinosaur and his friends. Twelve models have been so far documented.

Baby Bop Airplane $2-3
Baby Bop Convertible $2-3
Baby Bop Drum Car $2-3
Baby Bop School Bus $2-3
Barney Cement Mixer $2-3
Barney Convertible $2-3
Barney Dump Truck $2-3
Barney Fire Truck $2-3
Barney Race car $2-3
BJ Bulldozer $2-3
BJ Dump Truck $2-3
BJ Fire Truck $2-3

Playtoy

According to avid collector John Dean of Federal Heights, Colorado, Belgium is home to this short-lived brand that produced just three models in kit form. Carlo Brianza is known to have assembled such models and sold them under his own ABC Brianza brand. They are presumed to be 1:43 scale models, but might in fact be larger. Values below are highly speculative and arbitrary guesses.

1953 Buick Skylark $100-150
1957 Cadillac Eldorado $100-150
Chrysler Town and Country
 Convertible $100-150

Playtrucks

Playtrucks are from Greece. Further information is unknown.

Caterpillar Traxcavator, #22, 1:43 . . . . $16-20
Scania 6x4 Cement Truck, #20, 1:43 . . $16-20

PM

Pressomeccanica, or PM, models of Milan, Italy, were produced in the post-war 1940s. Nine models are known to exist. The actual name of the company is even longer: Pressofusione Meccanica.

O.M. Taurus
Covered Truck, 1:43............$75-125
Dump Truck, 1:43...............$75-125
Fire Truck, 1:43................$75-125
Open Truck, 1:43...............$75-125
Street Sweeper, 1:43..........$75-125
Tank Truck with Trailer, 1:43.....$175-200
Wrecker, 1:43..................$75-125

Lancia Ardea
Ambulance, white with red cross decals,
    1:40....................$75-125
Fire Van, 1:40................$75-125
Loudspeaker Van, 1:40.........$75-125
Van, 1:40....................$75-125

Streamlined Race Car............$600-750

Pocher

Pocher (pronounced Po-share) Prestige series 1:8 scale diecast metal car kits are unexcelled in accuracy and detail for their price... if you can afford one. Italian-made Pochers are top of the line in price, scale, quality, and detail. The reason for the high price becomes obvious when you realize these models measure 19 inches long and contain over 2,000 parts! Each of these sleek statements of status is a streamlined rolling work of art, representing the ultimate automotive icon of its era. Pocher also produces precision scale automotive engines.

Alfa Romeo
    assembled..............$1,000-1,250
    unassembled $350-400
Alfa Romeo 8C 2300
    Monza 1931
        assembled..........$1,000-1,250
        unassembled $300-400
    Monza 1932 Grand Prix Monaco
        assembled..........$1,000-1,250
        unassembled $300-400
    Coupe Elegant
        assembled..........$1,250-1,500
        unassembled $350-400
Alfa Romeo Spider 1932 Touring Gran Sport
    assembled..............$1,000-1,250
    unassembled $300-400
Bugatti 50T
    1932 Suprafile, black & red
        assembled $900

        unassembled $200-300
    1933, black & yellow
        assembled..........$1,250-1,500
        unassembled $350-400
    1933, blue & silver
        assembled $800-1,000
        unassembled $200-300
Ferrari F-40, red
    assembled $800-1,000
    unassembled $200-300
Ferrari Testarossa, yellow
    assembled $800-1,000
    unassembled $200-300
Fiat F2 1907 Grand Prix
    assembled $1,000-1,250
    unassembled $350-400
Mercedes-Benz 500K/AK 1935 Cabriolet, black
    assembled $800-1,000
    unassembled $200-300
Mercedes-Benz 540K
    1936 30T Sport Roadster
        assembled..........$1,000-1,250
        unassembled $350-400
    1936 Cabriolet Special
        assembled..........$1,000-1,250
        unassembled $350-400
    Cabriolet Special, white
        assembled $800-1,000
        unassembled $200-300
    Roadster
        assembled..........$1,000-1,250
        unassembled $350-400
Porsche 911
    black
        assembled $800-900
        unassembled $200-250
    silver
        assembled..........$1,000-1,250
        unassembled $350-400
Rolls-Royce Ambassador, 1933, green
    assembled..........$1,250-1,500
    unassembled $350-400
Rolls Royce Phantom II, 1932
    assembled $1,250-1,500
    unassembled $350-400
1934 Torpedo Cabriolet
    assembled $1,250-1,500
    unassembled....................$450
Volvo F12 Intercooler Truck
    assembled $1,250-1,500
    unassembled $350-400

Pocher 1:43 Scale Models

While the 1:8 scale models may be too expensive, the smaller 1:43 scale Pocher models listed below, while rare, may be had for

somewhat less.
Fiat 124.....................$125-150
Fiat 850.....................$125-150

Pocher Scale Model Engines
Ferrari Testarossa 12-cylinder engine...$90-100
Volvo F16 engine.................$90-100

Pocket Cars (see Tomica)

Pocketoy (see Brimtoy)

Poclain

Poclain is best known as the French heavy equipment manufacturer. Poclain plastic miniatures were made mainly by Bourbon of France around 1973 and sold as promotional models. Current estimates put their value around $25 to $35 each.

Pole Position Collectibles

Mountain Service International, Inc.
4710 Lee Highway
Bristol, VA 24201
703-669-4700

Pole Position Collectibles are a recent entry into the diecast racing collectibles arena. Resembling Racing Champions, they are made in China for Mountain Service International of Bristol, Virginia. These approximately 1:64 scale models authentically re-create the markings of actual stock cars. The colorful, distinctive blisterpack is designed by Gibson & Lane Graphic Designs, as indicated on the package. Models sell for $1 to $2 each.

Polistil (see Politoys)

Politoys/Polistil (also see Penny)

Politoys M of Italy began in 1960 as a manufacturer of plastic 1:41 scale models. In 1965, Politoys produced their first series of higher quality diecast vehicles. Because of the similarity of names between Politoys of Italy and Palitoys of Great Britain, the Politoys name was changed to Polistil around 1970.

The Politoys/Polistil product line covers hundreds of models in a variety of scales, from 1:16 scale to 1:64. Reissues and new Polistil models have most recently been produced by McGregor of Mexico.

The Jensen models are particularly interesting, in their rarity and in the their use of the letters "FF" which stands for "Ferguson Formula," an advanced four-wheel-drive system.

Bertone Ford Mustang 2+2, #549, 1:43,
1969 ....$30-45
Bertone Corvair, #551, 1:43, 1968.......$30-45
DeTomaso Pantera, 1:43, c. 1972 ....$30-45
Ferrari 308, 1983, 1:16 ....$45-60

Ferrari P4, #574, 1:43, 1968 ....$30-45

Ford Escort, 1:64 ....$10-15
Ford Lola GT, c. 1972, 1:43 ....$30-45
Jensen FF Coupe Vignale, #573, 1:43
   maroon, with rubber tires $45-60
   silver, with speed-type wheels.............$45-60
Oldsmobile Toronado, #567, 1:43,
1970 ....$60-75
Opel Diplomat, #521, c. 1972 ....$40-55
Osi 1200 Coupe, #533, 1:43, c. 1972 ..$35-50
Samurai, #580, 1:43, 1970 ....$25-40

Poll

One Poll model, made of tin, is known.

Gravel Loader, 24" $65-80

PP Models

PP models are 1:43 scale miniatures from
England.

Jaguar SS100 Roadster $40-55
Morris 1000 4-door Sedan $40-55
Morris 1000 Convertible.........................$40-55
Triumph Spitfire....................................$40-55
Daimler SP250 Roadster $40-55
Jensen 541 Coupe.................................$40-55
1939 Studebaker Coupe $40-55

Praliné (see Busch/Praliné)

Prämeta

Five Prämeta models were produced in Germany in 1951. Sporting clockwork motors and
a transmission with three forward gears, neutral,
and reverse, they were made within a 1:30 –
1:40 scale range, except for the Volkswagen,
which was made to a slightly larger scale and
reportedly didn't have a wind-up mechanism.
Prämetas are solid cast in several color variations with silver-painted windows, or silver metal
with green painted windows.

1947-48 Buick 405 Sedan, 5¾",
1:40 ....$325-375
Jaguar XK120 Coupe, 6", 1:30.........$325-375
Mercedes-Benz 300 Sedan, 5¾", 1:37 ...$325-375
Opel Kapitän Sedan, 5¾", 1:33.........$325-375
Volkswagen....................................$400-500

Precision Accucast (see Accucast)

Precision Autos (also see John Day Models)

Precision Autos are reportedly the result of a
frustrated Englishman named John Day, who
could not find replicas of the models he wanted,
so he started making his own. John Day is credit-
ed with bringing expensive handcrafting techniques on models costing thousands of dollars
down to merely hundreds of dollars.

Inaltera, 1:43 scale $200-400

Precision Engineered Models (also see Hartoy)

Hartoy's success with American Highway
Legends prompted the introduction of Precision
Engineered Models, 1:64 scale trucks with trailers. The series has reportedly proven even more
successful than the AHL line.

Kenworth T600
   Stanley, M70505............................$45-60
   Wiley Sanders Truck Lines, M70506 ....$45-60
   Auto Palace, M70510 ....$45-60
   Weyerhaeuser, M70511 ....$45-60
   Benton Express, M70513 ....$45-60
   Bekins Van Lines, M70515 ....$45-60
   Summerford Truck Lines, M70517......$45-60
   Landstar Ligon, M70519 ....$45-60
   Danny Herman Trucking, M70520 .....$45-60
   Edward Brothers with refrigerator
     unit, M70522 ....$45-60
   Super Service, M70529 ....$45-60
Mack CH600
   Hershey's American Dream, M71500 ..$45-60
   Georgia-Pacific, M71507 ....$45-60
   Pitt-Ohio Express, M71508 ....$45-60
   Sweeney Transportation, M71509.....$45-60
   Carroll Fulmer, M71511...................$45-60
   Sweeney Transportation II, M71513 ..$45-60
   Coastal Transport flatbed, M71704 ...$45-60
   Schwerman tank trailer, M71802 ......$45-60
   CTL Distribution chemical tank trailer,
     M71803 ....$45-60
   Kenan fuel tank trailer, M71903 ....$45-60
International 9800
   Schneider National II, M72507 ....$45-60

   tractor trailer, M72508 ....$45-60
Freightliner FLD 120
   Auto Works, M73505 ....$45-60
   Landstar Ranger, M73523................$45-60
   Burlington Motor carriers, M73524 ....$45-60
   Transport Systems, M73526 ....$45-60
   Landstar Inway van, M73527 ....$45-60
   Transport America, M73528...............$45-60
   Dart with red tractor, M73531 ....$45-60
   Fleetline, M73532 ....$45-60
   DeBoer, M73533 ....$45-60
   National carriers with refrigerator unit,
     M73534 ....$45-60
   Dart with blue tractor, M73535 ....$45-60

Precision Miniatures

Harvey Goranson reports that Precision
Miniatures, like Precision Autos, are white metal
kits, a built-up range begun by Gene Parrill
when he owned Marque Products in the Los
Angeles, California, area. The first models were
Porsches, then Indy cars, Ferraris, and a Duesenberg were added. Harvey says, "I suspect the
Indy cars were planned as IMRA kits, since
these were 1:40 scale. I have a '57 Ferrari
Testa Rossa (pontoon fender) from the Targa Florio race, and a '48 Novi Indy racer, plus a kit
of an Indy McLaren. The '70s Indy kits were
extremely well cast and detailed—not for begin-
ners."

"In 1982 or '83," Harvey continues, "I went
to LA for a weekend because I got a crazy deal
on a plane ticket. I visited Marque Products on a
day when Gene was doing trial runs casting
Hudson Hornets. It was fascinating watching the
white metal castings being made. Gene later
introduced other '50s American cars in the Precision range, plus the Laser and Mustang you list,
then found his niche with the Motor City, Design
Studio, and (lately) USA Models ranges."

1984 Chrysler Laser $75-90
1964½ Ford Mustang Convertible, red.....$75-90
1951 or 1952 Hudson Convertible $125-140
1951 or 1952 Hudson Coupe $125-140

Pride Lines (also see Manoil)

Pride Lines Ltd. (Manoil remakes)
651 West Hoffman Ave.
Lindenhurst, NY 11757
phone: 516-225-0033
fax: 516-225-0099

Pride Lines Ltd. vehicles are diecast in the
USA using original sixty-year-old Manoil molds.
(See Manoil.) Each highly-stylized model is cast
from the finest pewter and hand painted to per-

fection. All vehicles have rubber tires, two-piece metal construction and baked enamel finish. Each model is approximately 4½ inches long.

Pride Lines Manoil Reproductions
City Police $50-65
Coupé $50-65
Fire Chief $50-65
Fire Truck $50-65
Phaeton Convertible $50-65
Roadster $50-65
Sedan $50-65
Sheriff $50-65
Speedster Sedan $50-65
Taxi Sedan $50-65
Taxi Toy Truck $50-65

Pride Lines Manoil Disney Character Cars
Daisy Duck Roadster, baby blue and
　　yellow $85-100
Donald Duck Roadster, red and blue $85-100
Goofy Wrecker, red $85-100
Goofy Roadster, orange and black $85-100
Mickey Mouse Roadster, yellow and
　　purple $85-100
Minnie Mouse Roadster, pink and baby
　　blue $85-100
Scrooge McDuck, green and cream with
　　24 karat gold-plate trim $100-125

Process
Process models are made in the United States.

1961 Jaguar XKE Roadster, 1:43 .... $15-20

Pro Engine (see Pioneer)

Progetto K
Progetto K of Italy offers a huge range of currently available 1:43 scale models. The largest selection is offered by Exoto Inc., 1040-F Hamilton Rd., Duarte, CA 91010, for $22 each, in its quarterly publication/catalog Exoto Tifosi, available for $5 from Exoto Inc.

To list this exhaustive selection would consume many pages. Suffice it to say that many models are produced in various liveries, which makes the selection broader. I will attempt to provide a reasonable representation of the product line. You will have to rely on Exoto for specific color and marking variations.

Abarth 1000 1968 Group 5 .... $20-30
Alfa Romeo Giulia
　　1963 GT $20-30
　　1965 GTA $20-30

1967 GTA $20-30
1968 GTA $20-30
Austin Healey Mk 1 "Frogeye" 1958 Convertible
　　top down $20-30
　　top up $20-30
Ferrari 166 MM 1952 .... $20-30
Ferrari 225
　　Coupe 1952 .... $20-30
　　S 1952 .... $20-30
Ferrari 250 MM 1952 .... $20-30
Ferrari TR 1958 .... $20-30
Fiat 124 Spyder $20-30
Lancia Fulvia
　　1965 Coupe $20-30
　　HF 1966 Coupe $20-30
Maserati T60/61 1959 "Birdcage" $20-30

Protar
Protar of Italy is best known for its exquisite 1:9 scale motorcycle models in plastic and metal. They also produced a number of plastic Formula 1 and Grand Prix race cars in 1:12 and 1:24 scale.

Protar Motorcycles
Ducati
　　1991 red street version, 1:9 .... $55-60
　　1991 racing version, 1:9 .... $55-60
　　1995 916SP5, 1:9 .... $55-60
　　1995 Senna, 1:9 .... $50-55
　　1996 Senna, 1:9 .... $60-65
　　Superbike Chili, 1:9 .... $60-65
Kawasaki ZX-7R 1996 Street, 1:9 .... $55-60
Moto Guzzi
　　1971 V7, 1:9 .... $50-55
　　V-850 California, 1:6 .... $250-275
　　Carabinieri, 1:9 .... $50-55
　　Polizia, 1:9 .... $50-55

Protar Race Cars
Alfa Romeo 179 F1, 1:12 .... $175-225
Ferrari 312
　　B F1, 1:12 .... $175-225
　　T, 1:12 .... $175-225
Fiat Mephistophelle Grand Prix, 1923,
　　1:12 .... $175-225
Renault Turbo RE23, 1:12 .... $175-225

Provénce Mouláge
Provénce Mouláge models are precision 1:43 scale resin kits of which a certain number are shipped to dealers as pre-assembled demo models. The majority are sold as kits, unassembled and unpainted. Finishing the model includes sanding and trimming to smooth the surface and remove excess material from windows,

wheel wells and other openings and edges. Prices below are for unfinished models in the original box.

1950 Buick 2-door Hardtop $115-130
1950 Buick Station Wagon $115-130
1949 Delahaye 173 4.5L LeMans $50-65
1982 Camaro $50-65
Facel 2-door Coupe $65-80
Facel Facellia Coupe $65-80
1975 Ferrari Daytona Luchard $50-65
1981 Ferrari Pininfarina $50-65
1946 Ford 2-door Sedan $115-130
1946 Ford Station Wagon $115-130
1957 Jaguar D-Type LeMans $50-65
1960 Jaguar 3.8L Sedan $50-65
1963 Jaguar 3.8L Sedan $50-65
1985 Jaguar XJR6 .... $50-65
Volkswagen 1303 "Beetle"
　　Convertible $90-105

PTH Models
Past-Time Hobbies, Inc.
9311 Ogden Ave.
Brookfield, IL 60513
708-485-4544
PTH (Past-Time Hobbies) Models of England produces a stunning assortment of 1:43 scale models new and old. The Dodge Viper GTS models were created in 1997 for their US division.

Chevrolet Camaro Z28 Coupe, 1972, metallic
　　orange-yellow or white, #3 .... $130-155
Chevrolet Corvette, 1982, metallic brown-silver,
　　"Collectors Edition," #5 .... $140-165
Chevrolet Impala
　　SS, 1995, black, #6 .... $130-145
　　Sports Coupe, 1960, metallic orange-brown,
　　　#7 .... $130-155
Chevrolet Monte Carlo SS 454, 1970, red,
　　#4 .... $130-155
Dodge Viper GTS Coupe
　　orange with black stripes, 1:43, 1997,
　　　50 made $145-170
　　blue with white stripes, 1:43, 1997, 50
　　　made $150-175
Ford 1958 "Chicago Police," #17C ... $130-155
Packard 1934
　　Model 1106 Coupe, deep blue,
　　　#8 .... $150-175
　　with vinyl roof, metallic green, #9 ... $150-175

Pyro
Some of the most memorable and highly cherished toys of the fifties are Pyro plastic toys. From the 1950s until 1969, Pyro operated out

of Pyro Park, Union City, New Jersey. In the 1950s, Woolworth's retail price for Pyro Toys was generally 39 cents (slightly higher in the south and the west to account for additional shipping costs).

Regarding the Pyro X-400 Space Explorer, it still had its 79 cent price tag attached from the G. C. Murphy Company, a department store from the early 1940s. In April 2004, its owner Ron Allyn Swartley sold this fanciful toy from his childhood for $637 on eBay!

Army Tank, P-1020	$50-65
Balloon Racer, 3½"	$25-30
Bulldozer Front Loader	$90-120
Canteen Truck	$50-65
City Bottling Truck, 4"	$20-25
City Builders Truck, 5½"	$20-25
Coca-Cola Truck, 5½"	$125-175
Express Truck, 1950s	$25-30
Ford, 1932, C-295	$10-12
Ice & Coal Truck, 5½"	$20-25
Lumber Loader	$40-55
Lunch Wagon Truck, 5½"	$30-40
Mobile Anti-Aircraft Truck, P-1015	$75-100
Mobile Radar Truck, P-957	$75-100
Mobile Searchlight Truck, P-958	$75-100
Mobile Sound Truck, P-956	$75-100
Motorcycle	$50-65
Planter's Mr. Peanut's Peanut Wagon, 5½"	$90-120
Planter's Peanuts Semi with trailer, 5½"	$90-120
Planter's Peanuts Semi Stake Truck, 5½"	$90-120
Race Car, 3½"	$20-25
Race Car, 4"	$30-45
Ranch Horse Transport, 5½"	$30-45
Range Patrol Truck, 5"	$25-30
Road Roller	$20-25
Soap Box Supersonic Racer, 4¾"	$125-175
Soldier Transport, P-955	$30-45
Steam Roller	$20-25
Bandwagon Truck, 5½"	
"Elect Marvin Griffin Governor"	$100-125
"Get On The Bandwagon"	$100-125
Twin 40mm Mobile Gun, P-1097	$75-100
US Army Ambulance	$20-25
US Army Mobile Units Set	$25-40
US Army Set, 21 pieces	$30-45
US Army Stake Trailer Truck, 5½"	$15-20
US Army Truck	$15-20
US Navy Truck	$15-20
US Marine Corps Truck	$15-20
X-400 Space Explorer, early 1940s	$600-650

Q

Q-Models

Q-Models are especially nice 1:24 scale plastic and metal kits made in Japan.

1959 Ferrari 250 Testa Rossa	$225-300
1960 Ferrari 250 Testa Rossa Le Mans	$225-300

Qualitoys (See Benbros)

Quarter Mile (see Great American Dreamcars)

Quartzo (also see Vitesse)

Minibri Ltd.
P O Box 283
4471 Maia Codex
Portugal
fax: 351-2-9017464

Quartzo is a brand produced in cooperation with the Vitesse Group of Portugal and marketed by Minibri, which focuses on NASCAR models in 1:43 scale. As with most diecast models, Quartzo models are made in China.

Brabham Repco BT24
J. Brabham, 1st Canadian Grand Prix 1967, #Q4042	$25-35
J. Brabham, Belgian Grand Prix 1967, #QFC99002	$25-35
Dennis Hulme, World Champion 67, #QWC99009	$25-35
Dennis Hulme, 1st German Grand Prix 1967, #Q4043	$25-35
J. Rindt, Monaco Grand Prix 1968, #QFC99001	$25-35

Chevrolet Lumina
#14 Terry Labonte "Kelloggs"	$25-35
#41 Joe Nemechek, "Meineke"	$25-35

Cooper Climax T51
J. Brabham, winner British Grand Prix 1959, #Q4099	$25-35
T. Brooks, Monaco Grand Prix 1960, #QFC99008	$25-35
O. Gendebien, Belgian Grand Prix 1960, #QFC99007	$25-35
B. McLaren, winner USA Grand Prix 1959, #Q4101	$25-35
"Walker Team" Stirling Moss, 1st Italian Grand Prix 1959, #Q4100	$25-35
M. Trintignant Monaco Grand Prix 1959, #Q4130	$25-35
R. Salvadori, German Grand Prix 1959, #Q4131	$25-35

Cooper Ferrari T51
G. Cabianca, Italian Grand Prix 1960, #QFC99026	$25-35
G. Munaron, British Grand Prix 1960, #QFC99025	$25-35

Ferrari 126CK
D. Pironi Monaco Grand Prix 1981, #Q4160	$25-35
G. Villeneuve, 1st Spanish Grand Prix 1981, #Q4159	$25-35

Ferrari 156
G. Bagheti, Italian Grand Prix 1961, #Q4155	$25-35
R. Ginther, Italian Grand Prix 1961, #Q4156	$25-35
Phil Hill, Italian Grand Prix 1961, #Q4153	$25-35
Phil Hill, Monaco Grand Prix 1962, #Q4165	$25-35
Phil Hill, winner Belgian Grand Prix 1961, #QFC99004	$25-35
Phil Hill, World Champion 1961, #QWC99011	$25-35
W. Mairesse, Monaco Grand Prix 1962, #Q4166	$25-35
W. Von Trips, Italian Grand Prix 1961, #Q4154	$25-35
W. Von Trips, winner British Grand Prix 1961, #QFC99003	$25-35

Ferrari 312 T
C. Regazzoni, winner Italian Grand Prix 1975, #Q4032	$25-35

Ferrari 312 T2
N. Lauda, 1st Dutch Grand Prix 1977, #Q4083	$25-35
C. Regazzoni, Belgian Grand Prix 1976 #Q4068	$25-35
C. Reutemann, 1st Brazilian Grand Prix 1977, #Q4084	$25-35
C. Reutemann, 1st Brazilian Grand Prix 1978, #Q4085	$25-35
G. Villeneuve, Canadian Grand Prix 1979, #Q4086	$25-35

Ferrari 312 T3
C. Reutemann, 1st British Grand Prix 1978, #Q4095	$25-35
C. Reutemann, 1st USA (East) Grand Prix 1978, #Q4168	$25-35
C. Reutemann, Monaco Grand Prix 1978, #Q4098	$25-35
G. Villeneuve, 1st Canadian Grand Prix 1978, #Q4096	$25-35
G. Villeneuve, Italian Grand Prix 1978, #Q4167	$25-35
G. Villeneuve, USA-West Grand Prix 1978, #Q4097	$25-35

Ferrari 375
Alberto Ascari 1st Italian Grand Prix 1951, #Q4117	$25-35
Alberto Ascari 1st Spanish Grand Prix 1950, #Q4115	$25-35

F. Gonzales, Italian Grand Prix 1951,
#Q4169......................................$25-35

D. Serafini, Italian Grand Prix 1950,
#Q4116......................................$25-35

P. Taruffi, Swiss Grand Prix 1951,
#Q4119......................................$25-35

L. Villoresi, Italian Grand Prix 1951,
#Q4118......................................$25-35

Ferrari 500 F2

Alberto Ascari, winner Europe Grand Prix
1952, #Q4125 ....$25-35

Alberto Ascari, World Champion
1952, #QWC99008................$25-35

G. Farina, winner German Grand Prix
1953, #Q4128 ....$25-35

R. Fisher, Swiss Grand Prix 1952,
#Q4163......................................$25-35

M. Hawthorn, winner French Grand Prix
1953, #Q4129 ....$25-35

L. Rosier, British Grand Prix 1953,
#Q4164......................................$25-35

J. Swaters, 1st Avus Grand Prix 1953,
#Q4170......................................$25-35

P. Taruffi, winner Swiss Grand Prix
1952, #Q4124 ....$25-35

Ferrari 625

Alberto Ascari, Italian Grand Prix 1954,
#Q4157......................................$25-35

M. Trintignant, winner Monaco Grand
Prix 1955, #Q4158..................$25-35

Ferrari 246 Dino

P. Collins, winner British Grand Prix 1958,
#QFC99036.............................$25-35

L. Musso, Argentina Grand Prix 1958,
#QFC99035.............................$25-35

Ferrari 312

M. Parkes, French Grand Prix 1966,
#QFC99018.............................$25-35

John Surtees, winner Belgian Grand
Prix 1966, #QFC99017...........$25-35

Ferrari 312 T2

N. Lauda, winner Dutch Grand Prix 1977,
#QFC99027.............................$25-35

G. Villeneuve, Canadian Grand Prix 1977,
#QFC99028.............................$25-35

Ferrari 312 T3

J. Scheckter, Brazilian Grand Prix
1979, #QFC99031 ....$25-35

G. Villeneuve, Brazilian Grand Prix
1979, #QFC99032 ....$25-35

Ferrari 375

Alberto Ascari, winner German
Grand Prix 1951,
#QFC99019.............................$25-35

L. Rosier, winner ALBI Grand Prix 1951,
#QFC99020.............................$25-35

Ferrari 625

G. Farina, Argentina Grand Prix 1950,
#QFC99014.............................$25-35

M. Hawthorn, Italian Grand Prix 1954,
#QFC99013.............................$25-35

Ford, #27

Bill Elliott, "McDonald's" $25-35

Ford Fairlane 1956

NY Police Radar Unit.....................$45-60

Honda RA272

R. Bucknum, French Grand Prix 1965,
#QFC99010.............................$25-35

R. Bucknum, Mexican Grand Prix 1965,
#Q4094......................................$25-35

R. Ginther, French Grand Prix 1965,
#QFC99009.............................$25-35

R. Ginther, winner Mexican Grand Prix 1965,
#Q4093......................................$25-35

Lotus 25

Jim Clark, winner British Grand Prix 1963,
#QFC99011.............................$25-35

T. Taylor, Monaco Grand Prix 1963,
#QFC99012.............................$25-35

Lotus 25

Jim Clark, 1st British Grand Prix 1963,
#Q4139......................................$25-35

T. Taylor, Monaco Grand Prix 1963,
#Q4140......................................$25-35

Lotus 33

Jim Clark, 1st British Grand Prix 1965,
#Q4151......................................$25-35

M. Spence, British Grand Prix 1965,
#Q4152......................................$25-35

Lotus 49

Graham Hill, Dutch Grand Prix 1967,
#Q4002......................................$25-35

Jim Clark, 1st Dutch Grand Prix 1967,
#Q4001......................................$25-35

Lotus 49B

"Gold Leaf" Mario Andretti, USA Grand Prix
1968, #Q4009 ....$25-35

D. Atwood, Monaco Grand Prix 1969,
#QFC99029.............................$25-35

"Gold Leaf" J. Rindt, South Africa Grand Prix
1969, #Q4011 ....$25-35

"Rob Walker" Jo Siffert, S. Africa Grand Prix
1969, #Q4013 ....$25-35

Lotus 72

"Brook Bond OXO" G. Hill, Canadian Grand
Prix 1970, #Q4021...................$25-35

"Gold Leaf" E. Fittipaldi, British Grand Prix
1971, #Q4044 ....$25-35

"Gold Leaf" J. Miles, German Grand Prix
1970, #Q4020 ....$25-35

"Gold Leaf" J. Rindt, winner German Grand
Prix 1970, #Q4019..................$25-35

"Gold Leaf" R. Wisell, German Grand Prix
1971, #Q4045 ....$25-35

Lotus 72D

"JPS," E. Fittipaldi, British Grand Prix 1972,
#Q4022......................................$25-35

"JPS," E. Fittipaldi, Italian Grand Prix 1972,
#Q4026 ....$25-35

"JPS," R. Peterson, winner Italian Grand Prix
1972, #Q4025 ....$25-35

"Lucky Strike," D. Charlton, British Grand
Prix 1972, #Q4024..................$25-35

Lotus 72E

J. Ickx, Belgian Grand Prix 1975,
#QFC99006.............................$25-35

J. Ickx, German Grand Prix 1974,
#Q4070......................................$25-35

R. Peterson, Monaco Grand Prix 1974,
#Q4069......................................$25-35

R. Peterson, Swedish Grand Prix 1975,
#QFC99005.............................$25-35

Lotus 78

Mario Andretti, winner USA Grand Prix 1977,
#Q4087......................................$25-35

G. Nilsson, Japanese Grand Prix 1977,
#Q4091......................................$25-35

G. Nilsson, winner Belgium Grand Prix 1977,
#Q4088......................................$25-35

R. Peterson, USA West Grand Prix 1978,
#QFC99021.............................$25-35

H. Rebaque, German Grand Prix 1978,
#Q4092......................................$25-35

Lotus Ford 72C+B145

Jochen Rindt, World Champion 1970,
#QWC99010 ....$25-35

March 701

H. Hahne, German Grand Prix 1970,
#QFC99016.............................$25-35

H. Pescarolo, South Africa Grand Prix 1971,
#QFC99015.............................$25-35

"ELF" J. Servoz-Gavin, Spanish Grand Prix
1970, #Q4106 ....$25-35

"ELF" Jackie Stewart, winner Spanish Grand
Prix 1970, #Q4105...................$25-35

"STP" C. Amon, French Grand Prix 1970
#Q4102......................................$25-35

"STP" J. Siffert, German Grand Prix 1970,
#Q4103......................................$25-35

"STP" Mario Andretti, Spanish Grand Prix
1970, #Q4104 ....$25-35

R. Peterson, Spanish Grand Prix 1970,
#Q4107......................................$25-35

March 711

"Motul" H. Pescarolo British Grand Prix 1971,
#QFC99033.............................$25-35

"STP" R. Peterson Italian Grand Prix 1971,
#QFC99034.............................$25-35

A. Soler Roig, French Grand Prix 1971, #Q4121.................................$25-35

N. Lauda, Austrian Grand Prix 1971 (first N. Lauda F1 race), #Q4122...........$25-35

R. Peterson, South African Grand Prix 1951, #Q4120.................................$25-35

Matra MS80

Jackie Stewart, Monaco Grand Prix 1969, #QFC99022............................$25-35

Jackie Stewart, Monaco Grand Prix 1969, #Q4017.................................$25-35

Pontiac Grand Prix

#40 Frankie Kerr, "Dirt Devil" $25-35

Peugeot 905

#1 winner Le Mans 1992, #QLM99009..$25-35

#2 Baldi-Alliot-Jabouille, 3rd Le Mans 1992, #QLM99010 ....$25-35

#5 Baldi-Alliot-Jabouille, Le Mans 1991, #QLM99003 ....$25-35

#6 Rosberg-Dalmas-Raphanel, Le Mans 1991, #QLM99004 ....$25-35

Porsche 804

Bonnier, French Grand Prix 1962, #Q4109.................................$25-35

Dan Gurney, winner French Grand Prix 1962, #Q4108.................................$25-35

Porsche 956

Short, "Danone," 4th Le Mans 1985, #QLM99005 ....$25-35

Porsche 962C

Long, "Fortuna," 2nd Le Mans 86, #QLM99002 ....$25-35

Long, "Primagaz," 2nd Le Mans 1987, #QLM99008 ....$25-35

Long, "Rothmans," winner Le Mans 86, #QLM99001 ....$25-35

Long, "Rothmans," winner Le Mans 1987, #QLM99007 ....$25-35

Short, "Alpha," 3rd Le Mans 1990, #QLM99006 ....$25-35

Short, "Fuji Golf" Le Mans 1990, #QLM99012 ....$25-35

Short, "Rizla" Le Mans 1990, #QLM99011 ....$25-35

Renault RE20/22

J.-P. Jabouille, Argentina Grand Prix 1980, #Q4162.................................$25-35

Renault RE20/24

R. Arnoux, Monaco Grand Prix 1980, #Q4161.................................$25-35

Renault RE30B

Alain Prost, winner Brazilian Grand Prix 1982, #Q4033.................................$25-35

Renault RS01

J.-P. Jabouille, Monaco Grand Prix 1978, #QFC99030..........................$25-35

RS01/01 J.-P. Jabouille, British Grand Prix 1977, #Q4048 ....$25-35

RS01/01 J.-P. Jabouille, Dutch Grand Prix 1977, #Q4049 ....$25-35

RS01/02 J.-P. Jabouille, USA Grand Prix 1978, #Q4050 ....$25-35

RS01/02 R. Arnoux, Argentina Grand Prix 1979, #Q4051 ....$25-35

Renault RS11

J.-P. Jabouille, 1st French Grand Prix 1979, #Q4061.................................$25-35

Renault RS12

R. Arnoux USA Grand Prix 1979, #Q4062.................................$25-35

Tyrrell 001

P. Revson, USA Watkins Glen Grand Prix 1971, #QFC99023 ....$25-35

"Blade Nose" Jackie Stewart, winner Monaco Grand Prix 1971, #Q4036 ....$25-35

"Blade Nose" Jackie Stewart, USA Grand Prix 1970, #Q4035 ....$25-35

Tyrrell 002

"Blade Nose" F. Cevert, Monaco Grand Prix 1971, #Q4037 ....$25-35

"Buff Nose" F. Cevert, USA Grand Prix 1971 winner, #Q4047 ....$25-35

Tyrrell 003

"Buff Nose" Jackie Stewart, British Grand Prix 1971 winner, #Q4046 ....$25-35

Tyrrell 004

"Buff Nose" French Grand Prix 72 P. Depailler, #Q4065 ....$25-35

"Lucky Strike" E. Keizan, South African Grand Prix 1973, #Q4066..................$25-35

Tyrrell P34 Six-Wheels

R. Peterson, Belgian Grand Prix 1977, #QFC99024............................$25-35

"City Bank" P. Depailler, Monaco Grand Prix 1977, #Q4041 ....$25-35

"City Bank" R. Peterson, Monaco Grand Prix 1977, #Q4040 ....$25-35

P. Depailler, Spanish Grand Prix 1976, #Q4027.................................$25-35

Williams Renault FW14B

N. Mansell, World Champion 92, #QWC99012 ....$25-35

Quiralu

Now one of the most popular brands on the collector market, Quiralu was at one time a totally obscure French brand of sandcast toys. Their current popularity is due in part to the re-issue of many of the original models as faithful reproductions. That alone wouldn't necessarily make them sell, but the real reason is the recognition by collectors of the charm and quality of these fine toys. Reproductions can be purchased for a reasonable price, while original models are quickly rising in value.

The original Quiralu brand was introduced in 1933 by a Mr. Quirin of Luxeuil, France. The combination of his name and the primary metal, aluminum, used in the production of these models provides the name derivation.

It wasn't until 1955 that the firm started producing 1:43 scale models. The latest of the original models were introduced in 1959, with production ceasing soon afterward.

Quiralu Originals

Simca Trianon, 1955, #1 ....$70-95

Simca Versailles, 1955, #2 ....$70-95

Simca Regence, 1955, #3 ....$70-95

Peugeot 403, single color with no plastic windows, 1956, #4............................$70-95

Peugeot 403, two-tone, no plastic windows, 1956, #5............................$70-95

Peugeot 403, single color with plastic windows, 1956, #6............................$80-105

Peugeot 403, two-tone with plastic windows, 1956, #7............................$80-105

Mercedes-Benz 300SL, single color, 1956, #8 ....$115-130

Mercedes-Benz 300SL, two-tone, 1956, #9 ....$115-130

Simca Marly Break Station Wagon, single color, 1957, #10 ....$70-95

Simca Marly Break Station Wagon, two-tone, 1957, #11............................$70-95

Simca Marly Ambulance, 1957, #12..$110-135

Porsche Carrera, single color, 1957, #13 ....$300-350

Porsche Carrera, two-tone, 1957, #14 ..$300-350

Jaguar XK140, 1957, #15...............$110-135

Messerschmitt Auto-Scooter, 1958, #16 ..$90-120

Rolls-Royce Silver Cloud, 1958, #17...$110-135

Vespa 400 2CV, 1958, #18 ....$70-95

BMW Velam Isetta Bubble car, #19......$90-120

Renault Etoile Filante, with decals, 1958, #20 ....$90-120

Renault Etoile Filante, no decals, 1958, #21 ....$80-105

Peugeot D4A Van, red, 1958, #22 ....$325-375

Peugeot D4A Van, yellow or green, 1958, #23 ....$325-375

Peugeot D4A Army Ambulance, 1958, #24 ....$350-400

Berliet GBO Covered Truck, 1959, #25 ....$275-325

Berliet GBO Dump Truck, 1959, #26 ....$275-325

Berliet GBO Covered Trailer, 1959,
#27 ....$115-130

Quiralu Reproductions
1958 BMW Isetta Velam Bubble car, #812...$35-50
1960 Citroën ID19 Ambulance $35-50
1960 Citroën ID19 Station Wagon, #815...$35-50
1957 Jaguar XK140 Roadster, #827 ......$35-50
Mercedes-Benz 300 SL, #814 ....$35-50
1956 Messerschmitt Tiger Auto-Scooter,
#810 ....$35-50
Peugeot 403 Sedan, #816....................$35-50
Peugeot D4A Military Ambulance $35-50
Peugeot D4A Van, red, #818................$35-50
Peugeot D4A Van, white, #818.............$35-50
Peugeot D4A Van, yellow, #818............$35-50
Porsche 356 Coupe, #813....................$35-50
1956 Renault World Speed Record,
#835 ....$35-50
1957 Rolls-Royce Silver Cloud, #826 ......$35-50
Simca Marly Station Wagon, #830 ....$35-50
1958 Vespa 400 Sedan, #811.............$35-50

R

R&M
Virtually nothing is known of this obscure brand. More information would be greatly appreciated.

Berta Racer, 2" $4-5
Cheboom Racer, 4" $4-5

R. W. (see Ziss)

Race Image Collection (also see Corgi, Dimension 4,)
Race Image Collection is a series of 1:43 scale diecast NASCAR models manufactured by Lucky Plan Industries. (See Speedway Collection.)

The distinction, if any, is that the Race Image Collection is an assortment of high quality, low priced racing models offered in mass market retail stores such as Wal-Mart. Models sell for about $5 each. The Race Image brand is also connected with Corgi.

Raceway Replicars
Information provided by Russell Alameda indicates that at least two models were made under this brand.

Ford
#6 Mark Martin, "Valvoline," 1:24, limited
edition of 5,000.....................$300-325
#28 Davy Allison, "Valvoline," 1:24, limited
edition of 5,000.....................$300-325

Racing Champions
Founded in 1989 by Bob Dods and Boyd Meyer in Glenn Ellyn, Illinois, Racing Champions has been a leading producer and marketer of collectibles, available at over 20,000 retail outlets throughout North America, including Wal-Mart, K-Mart, Toys `R' Us, and Target. The company is best known for its extensive line of officially licensed diecast replicas from the five most popular racing series, including NASCAR. Racing Champions also markets several lines of non-racing diecast vehicle replicas and, in 1997, launched a new category of adult collectible pewter figures. Additional Racing Champions product information can be found on the Internet at www.RacingChamps.com.

Racing Champions offers an assortment of models that specialize in race car and transporter replicas. Like most modern diecast toys, Racing Champions are manufactured in China and other Asian manufacturing centers. Miniature race car replicas are a collecting specialty in themselves, attracting a specialized group numbering in the thousands of collectors. Racing Champions offers race cars of all types, including NASCAR, NASCAR Craftsman Truck, NHRA, CART, World of Outlaws, and Indy Racing League, in 1:24, 1:64, and 1:144 scale. Thousands of models are offered representing every race driver in each category. The product line-up could fill a book. So this book will focus on Racing Champions' offerings with a somewhat broader appeal.

The freshest series of diecast models to hit the market in years was Racing Champions Mint Editions. Introduced in 1996, this series is comprised of classic cars past and present in 1:56 to 1:61 scale. The first models included a display stand with an enameled "license plate" representing the hood or fender ornament. Later models were issued with a window display box.

In 1999, Racing Champions purchased the venerable Ertl Company of Dyersville, Iowa, and became RC2.

Acura (see Honda / Acura)

AMC

1977 Pacer, yellow, Street Machines.....$2-3

Buick
1949 Buick Riviera
Dade County (Florida) Police, Police USA
1998, #67..$5-7
blue, Mint Editions 1997, #113 ....$5-7
dark green, Mint Editions 1997, #122...$5-7
Glen Allen #99 Luxaire, Stock Rods 1997,
#26..$4-6
Hank Williams Jr. Hot Country Steel, #2 ..$6-8
light green, Mint Motor Trend 1998,
#159...$4-6

silver chrome, Mint Editions Chrome $4-6
yellow, Mint Editions 1997, #117 ....$5-7
1957 Buick Century
red, Mint Motor Trend 1998, #198.......$4-6
St. Louis County (Missouri) Police, Police
USA 1998, #91 ....$5-7
1970 Buick GSX
white, Mint Motor Trend 1998, #186 ....$4-6
yellow, Mint Motor Trend 1998, #180...$4-6
Lorain County (Ohio) Sheriff, Police USA
1998, #74......................................$5-7
1971 Buick GSX
black, Mint Motor Trend 1998, #199 ....$4-6
1987 Buick Grand National
Bernalillo County (New Mexico) Police,
Police USA 1998, #63 ....$5-7
black, Mint Motor Trend 1998, #168 ....$4-6
D.A.R.E. car, Police USA 1998, #50 .....$5-7
silver, Mint Motor Trend 1998, #181 .....$4-6

Cadillac
1959 Cadillac Eldorado Convertible
Hank Williams Jr. Hot Country Steel, #10..$6-8
blue, Mint Editions 1997, #92 ....$5-7
pink, Mint Editions 1997, #84 ....$5-7
red, Mint Editions 1997, #88................$5-7

Chevrolet
1955 Chevrolet Bel Air
beige, Mint Motor Trend 1998, #140 ...$4-6
black, Mint Editions 1997, #119..........$5-7
black and white, Hot Rod Magazine #18,
October 1998 ....$9-12
black with flames, Hot Rod Magazine #14,
October 1998 ....$9-12
blue, Hot Rod Magazine #16, October
1998...$9-12

dark purple, Hot Rod Magazine #10, September 1998 ....$9-12
Idaho State Police, Police USA 1998, #16 ....$5-7
Indiana State Police, Police USA 1998, #39 ....$5-7
Indianapolis (Indiana) Police, Police USA 1998, #79 ....$5-7
light green and white, Mint Motor Trend 1998, #135 ....$4-6
metallic gray and tan, Hot Rod Magazine #19, November 1998.................$9-12
metallic green and pearl, Hot Rod Magazine #28, December 1998 ....$9-12
metallic pink and silver, Hot Rod Magazine #21, November 1998..................$9-12
purple and white, Hot Rod Magazine #25, December 1998..................$9-12
red, orange, blue and silver, Hot Rod Magazine #12, September 1998 ..$9-12
red and white, Hot Rod Magazine #8, September 1998 ....$9-12
Toronto (Ontario) Metro Police, Police USA 1998, #22..........................$5-7
white and gray, Mint Motor Trend 1998, #169 ....$4-6
Wyoming Highway Patrol, Police USA 1998, #29..............................$5-7

1955 Chevrolet Bel Air Convertible
two-tone blue, Mint Editions 1997, #72..$5-7
two-tone green, Mint Editions 1997, #76.....$5-7

baby blue with white roof, Street Machines $2-3

1956 Chevrolet Nomad
Albuquerque (New Mexico) Police, Police USA 1998, #87 ....$5-7
brown, Mint Motor Trend 1998, #144...$4-6
Chicago (Illinois) Fire Dept. Fire Rescue USA, 1999, #11 ....$5-7
light green, Mint Editions 1997, #126....$5-7
Ocean County (New Jersey) Sheriff, Police USA 1998, #65 ....$5-7
red, Mint Editions 1997, #129 ....$5-7
Riverside (Illinois) Fire Dept., Fire Rescue USA, 1999, #1 ....$5-7

1957 Chevrolet Bel Air
black, Mint Editions 1996, #25 ....$5-7
black, Mint Editions 1997, #93.............$5-7

black with orange and yellow flames, Mint Edition Hot Rods 1996, #2 ....$4-6
black with flames, Mint Edition Hot Rods 1996, #13 ....$4-6

black with white roof, Street Machines...$2-3
blue, Mint Editions 1997, #89 ....$5-7
bright teal, Mint Editions 1996, #31.......$5-7
Chicago (Illinois) Police, Police USA 1998, #70 ....$5-7
Colma (California) Fire Department, Police USA 1998, #43 ....$5-7
Darrell Waltrip #17 Western Auto, Stock Rods 1997, #9 ....$4-6
green, Mint Editions 1997, #103 ....$5-7
Jeff Green #29 Cartoon Network, Stock Rods 1997, #31 ....$4-6
magenta with hood scoop and silver trim, 1:61 scale, Hot Rod Magazine 1997, #7 ....$4-6
Military Police, Police USA 1998, #9 .....$5-7
red, Mint Editions 1996, #4.................$5-7
red with hood scoop and silver trim, 1:61 scale, Hot Rod Magazine 1997, #1 ....$4-6
Ricky Craven #25 Hendrick, Stock Rods 1997, #14..............................$4-6
Shelton (Connecticut) Police Department, Police USA 1998, #25 ....$5-7
St. Paul (Minnesota) Police, Police USA 1998, #33..............................$5-7
tan, Mint Editions 1996, #15 ....$5-7
Terry Labonte #5 Kellogg's, Stock Rods 1997, #1 ....$4-6
Texas Highway Patrol, Police USA 1998, #27 ....$5-7
turquoise, Mint Editions 1996, #9 ....$5-7
Washington State Police, Police USA 1998, #4...............................$5-7
White Settlement (Texas) Police, Police USA 1998, #56 ....$5-7
yellow, Mint Editions 1996, #21 ....$5-7

1957 Chevrolet Bel Air Convertible
Dennis Setzer #43 Lance Snacks, Stock Rods 1997, #27...........................$4-6

1958 Chevrolet Impala
Benton County (Indiana) Sheriff, Police USA 1998, #71 ....$5-7
black, Mint Editions 1997, #104...........$5-7
brown, Mint Editions 1997, #118 ....$5-7

Darrell Waltrip #17 Western Auto, Stock Rods 1997, #21 ....$4-6
Grinnell (Iowa) Police, Police USA 1998, #53 ....$5-7
Los Angeles County (California) Sheriff, Police USA 1998, #10 ....$5-7
Michigan State Police, Police USA 1998, #7 ....$5-7
red, Mint Editions 1997, #77...............$5-7
Ricky Craven #2 Raybestos, Stock Rods 1997, #29...........................$4-6
Ricky Craven #25 Hendrick, Stock Rods 1997, #8.............................$4-6
yellow and white, Mint Motor Trend 1998, #151...............................$4-6

1960 Chevrolet Camaro
Washington DC Metro Police, Police USA 1998, #51.............................$5-7

1960 Chevrolet Corvair Monza
blue, Mint Motor Trend 1998, #209......$4-6
dark red, Mint Motor Trend 1998, #189 ...$4-6
gray-green, Mint Motor Trend 1998, #204 ....$4-6
New Orleans (Louisiana)Police, Police USA 1998, #49.............................$5-7
Portland (Maine) Fire Dept. Fire Rescue USA, 1999, #6...........................$5-7
white, Mint Motor Trend 1998, #197 ...$4-6

1960 Chevrolet Impala
Arkansas State Police, Police USA 1998, #15 ....$5-7
black, Mint Motor Trend 1998, #146 ....$4-6
light blue, Mint Editions 1997, #128......$5-7
North Dakota State Patrol, Police USA 1998, #48..............................$5-7
Ohio Highway Patrol, Police USA 1998, #18..............................$5-7
Pennsylvania State Police, Police USA 1998, #34..............................$5-7
red, Mint Motor Trend 1998, #187.......$4-6
white, Mint Editions 1997, #125...........$5-7

1962 Chevrolet
black with flames, Hot Rod Magazine #5, August 1998 ....$9-12
magenta and yellow, Hot Rod Magazine #7, September 1998 ....$9-12
metallic blue with white scallops, Hot Rod Magazine #9, September 1998 ...$9-12
purple and metallic orange, Hot Rod Magazine #1, August 1998 ....$9-12
purple, Hot Rod Magazine #11, September 1998 ....$9-12
red, Hot Rod Magazine #3, August 1998 ....$9-12
red with flames, Hot Rod Magazine #13, October 1998 ....$9-12

turquoise and magenta, Hot Rod Magazine #27, December 1998 ....$9-12

white with pink flames, Hot Rod Magazine #30, December 1998 ....$9-12

1964 Chevrolet Impala SS

Ankeny (Iowa) Police, Police USA 1998, #32 ....$5-7

blue, Mint Editions 1996, #18 ....$5-7

Frohna (Missouri) Police, Police USA 1998, #84 ....$5-7

Iowa Highway Patrol, Police USA 1998, #12 ....$5-7

Jeff Green #29 Tom & Jerry, Stock Rods 1997, #15................$4-6

plum red with silver flames, Mint Edition Hot Rods 1996, #4 ....$4-6

plum, Mint Editions 1996, #28................$5-7

metallic gray, Mint Editions 1996, #23...$5-7

metallic light blue, Mint Editions............$4-6

Vermilion County (Illinois) Sheriff, Police USA 1998, #54 ....$5-7

white, Mint Editions 1996, #38 ....$5-7

1966 Chevrolet Nova

Berkeley (California) Police, Police USA 1998, #81 ....$5-7

Billy Dean, Hot Country Steel, #11 ....$6-8

black, Mint Motor Trend 1998, #179 ....$4-6

Kansas City (Missouri) Police, Police USA 1998, #46 ....$5-7

red, Mint Motor Trend 1998, #185.......$4-6

red with white accents, Hot Rod Magazine 1999, #135 ....$4-6

St. Louis (Missouri) Metro Police, Police USA 1998, #42 ....$5-7

1968 Chevrolet Camaro

black, Mint Editions 1997, #101...........$5-7

blue, Mint Editions 1997, #116 ....$5-7

blue, Mint Motor Trend 1998, #191......$4-6

D.A.R.E. Car, Police USA 1998, #24 ....$5-7

Joe Nemechek #42 Bell South, Stock Rods 1997, #32................$4-6

red, Mint Editions 1997, #112 ....$5-7

1969 Chevrolet Camaro

black with white stripes, Mint Motor Trend 1998, #141 ....$4-6

orange with white stripes, Mint Motor Trend 1998, #163 ....$4-6

Tim McGraw, Hot Country Steel, #7 ......$6-8

Tim McGraw, Hot Country Steel, #17 ....$6-8

yellow with black stripes, Mint Motor Trend 1998, #136 ....$4-6

1970 Chevrolet Chevelle SS

black, Mint Editions 1997, #124..........$5-7

Dallas (Texas) Police, Police USA 1998, #44 ....$5-7

dark blue, Mint Editions 1996, #60 ......$5-7

maroon and silver, Hot Rod Magazine 1997, #12 ....$4-6

red, Mint Editions 1997, #67 ....$5-7

silver, Mint Editions 1997, #82 ....$5-7

white with black stripes, Mint Motor Trend 1998, #158 ....$4-6

1975 Chevrolet Van

Appleton (Wisconsin) Fire Dept., Fire Rescue USA, 1999, #13 ....$5-7

1978 Chevrolet Chevelle

orange, Street Machines..........................$2-3

1986 Chevrolet El Camino SS

Steve Grissom #41 Hedrick, Stock Rods 1997, #24................$4-6

St. Louis (Missouri) Fire Dept. Fire Rescue USA, 1999, #2 ....$5-7

black, Mint Editions 1997, #105...........$5-7

silver, Mint Editions 1997, #99 ....$5-7

white, Mint Editions 1997, #96 ....$5-7

Reno (Nevada) Police, Police USA 1998, #72 ....$5-7

Salt Lake City (Utah) Police, Police USA 1998, #97 ....$5-7

1992 Chevrolet Caprice

Elmwood Park (Illinois) Fire Dept. Fire Rescue USA, 1999, #7 ....$5-7

D.A.R.E. car, Police USA 1998, #90 .....$5-7

Dallas (Texas) Police, Police USA 1998, #96 ....$5-7

West Virginia State Police, Police USA 1998, #89 ....$5-7

1996 Chevrolet Camaro

black, Mint Editions 1996, #34.............$5-7

blue, Mint Editions 1996, #24 ....$5-7

Chevrolet Special Service, Police USA 1998, #92 ....$5-7

Kansas Highway Patrol, Police USA 1998, #59 ....$5-7

metallic green, Mint Editions 1996, #39 ....$5-7

New York State Police, Police USA 1998, #41 ....$5-7

Royal Canadian Mounted Police, Police USA 1998, #23 ....$5-7

two-tone blue and yellow, Hot Rod Magazine 1997, #11 ....$4-6

Utah Highway Patrol, Police USA 1998, #73................$5-7

white, Mint Editions 1996, #29.............$5-7

Wisconsin State Police, Police USA 1998, #83 ....$5-7

Chevrolet Corvette

1953 Chevrolet Corvette

Sterling Marlin #4 Kodak, Stock Rods 1997, #30................$4-6

1954 Chevrolet Corvette

blue and green, Mint Motor Trend 1998, #155 ....$4-6

1957 Chevrolet Corvette

black, Mint Motor Trend 1998, #176 ....$4-6

red, Mint Motor Trend 1998, #173.......$4-6

white, Mint Motor Trend 1998, #184 ....$4-6

1963 Chevrolet Corvette

dark beige, Mint Editions 1996, #51 .....$5-7

fluorescent orange-red with yellow accents, "blown" engine, 1:53 scale, Hot Rod Magazine, 1997, #2........$4-6

LeAnn Rimes, Hot Country Steel, #20......$6-8

metallic dark blue, Mint Editions 1996, #46 ....$5-7

red, Mint Editions 1996, #36................$5-7

Robert Pressley #29 Cartoon Network (Scooby), Stock Rods 1997, #4.......$4-6

silver, Mint Editions 1996, #56 ....$5-7

white, Mint Editions 1996, #41 ....$5-7

1997 Chevrolet Corvette

black, Mint Editions 1997, #87............$5-7

Florida Highway Patrol, Police USA 1998, #80 ....$5-7

red, Mint Editions 1997, #107............$5-7

white, Mint Editions 1997, #83............$5-7

yellow, Mint Editions 1997, #78 ....$5-7

1998 Chevrolet Corvette

D.A.R.E. Car, Police USA 1998, #68 ....$5-7

Chevy Pickup Truck

1950 Chevrolet 1500 Pickup

lime green with yellow flames, Mint Edition Hot Rods 1996, #1 ....$4-6

1950 Chevrolet 3100 Pickup

brown, Mint Editions 1996, #19 ....$5-7

dark blue, Mint Editions 1996, #7 ....$5-7

dark green, Mint Editions 1996, #2 ....$5-7

red, Mint Editions 1996, #13...............$5-7

green, Mint Editions 1997, #100 ....$5-7

Chrysler

Chrysler Crossfire $4-6

Dodge

1970 Dodge Superbee

metallic copper with black roof, Mint Motor Trend 1998, #210 .... $4-6

purple, Mint Motor Trend 1998, #167 ... $4-6

two-tone gray, Mint Motor Trend 1998, #203 .... $4-6

white, Mint Motor Trend 1998, #162 .... $4-6

yellow, Mint Motor Trend 1998, #196 ... $4-6

1996 Dodge Ram Pickup

black, Mint Editions 1996, #22 .... $5-7

black with yellow, green, and pink slash, oversized tires, Mint Edition Hot Rods 1996, #6 .... $4-6

blue, Mint Editions 1996, #12 .... $5-7

Honolulu Harbor (Hawaii) Police, Police USA 1998, #66 .... $5-7

Maine State Police, Police USA 1998, #95 ... $5-7

purple and silver, Hot Rod Magazine 1997, #8 .... $4-6

red, Mint Editions 1996, #17 .... $5-7

silver, Mint Editions 1996, #33 .... $5-7

white, Mint Editions 1996, #27 .... $5-7

white with gold accents, Hot Rod Magazine 1997, #3 .... $4-6

1996 Dodge Viper GTS

blue with white racing stripe, Mint Editions 1996, #1 .... $5-7

LeAnn Rimes, Hot Country Steel, #1 ... $10-12,

silver with white stripes, Mint Motor Trend 1998, #171 .... $4-6

Washtenaw County (Michigan) Sheriff, Police USA 1998, #64 .... $5-7

Dodge M80 Concept Truck

yellow with gray fenders $4-6

Edsel

1958 Edsel

with top, yellow, Mint Motor Trend 1998, #166 .... $4-6

light blue, Mint Editions 1997, #106 ...... $5-7

light blue, Mint Editions 1997, #110 ...... $5-7

Milwaukee (Wisconsin) Fire Department, Police USA 1998, #30 .... $5-7

pink, Mint Editions 1997, #102 .... $5-7

Ford

1932 Ford Coupe

Arizona Highway Patrol, Police USA 1998, #11 .... $5-7

black, Mint Editions 1997, #64 .... $5-7

blue, Mint Editions 1997, #69 .... $5-7

California Highway Patrol, Police USA 1998, #61 .... $5-7

cream, Mint Editions 1997, #127 .... $5-7

gray, Mint Editions 1997, #123 .... $5-7

Mark Martin #6 Valvoline, Stock Rods 1997, #17 .... $4-6

New Jersey State Police, Police USA 1998, #17 .... $5-7

Ricky Rudd #10 Tide, Stock Rods 1997, #22 .... $4-6

Ted Musgrave #16 Primestar, Stock Rods 1997, #5 .... $4-6

1937 Ford Convertible

black, Mint Motor Trend 1998, #137 .... $4-6

royal blue, Mint Motor Trend 1998, #142 ... $4-6

tan, Mint Motor Trend 1998, #175 .... $4-6

1937 Ford Coupe

Alan Jackson, Hot Country Steel, #4 ...... $6-8

1940 Ford Coupe

black with flames, Hot Rod Magazine #20, November 1998 .... $9-12

dark red, Hot Rod Magazine #29, December 1998 .... $9-12

metallic orange and silver, Hot Rod Magazine #23, November 1998 .... $9-12

red with flames, Hot Rod Magazine #26, December 1998 .... $9-12

red, Hot Rod Magazine #22, November 1998 .... $9-12

yellow and orange, Hot Rod Magazine #24, November 1998 .... $9-12

1940 Ford Sedan Delivery

Chicago (Illinois) Police, Police USA 1998, #93 .... $5-7

Rescue Service, Fire Rescue USA #13 .. $5-7

1956 Ford Thunderbird

Alan Jackson, Hot Country Steel, #9 .... $6-8

blue with black roof, Mint Editions 1996, #26 .... $5-7

gray, Mint Editions 1996, #16 .... $5-7

pale lavender, Mint Editions 1996, #11 .. $5-7

pink, Mint Editions 1996, #32 .... $5-7

red, Mint Editions 1996, #37 .... $5-7

yellow with white roof, Mint Editions 1996, #6 .... $5-7

1950 Ford Coupe

Bill Elliott #94 Mac Tonight, Stock Rods 1997, #25 .... $4-6

blue, Mint Editions 1997, #80 .... $5-7

Georgia State Patrol, Police USA 1998, #28 .... $5-7

gray, Mint Editions 1997, #95 .... $5-7

Jeff Burton #99 Exide, Stock Rods 1997, #6 .... $4-6

Illinois State Police, Police USA 1998, #78 .... $5-7

Iron Mountain (Michigan) Fire Dept., Fire Rescue USA, 1999, #5 .... $5-7

maroon, Mint Editions 1997, #61 .... $5-7

Maryland State Police, Police USA 1998, #88 .... $5-7

Michigan State Police, Police USA 1998, #38 .... $5-7

Nevada Highway Patrol, Police USA 1998, #14 .... $5-7

New York City Police Department, Police USA 1998, #8 .... $5-7

Ricky Rudd #10 Tide, Stock Rods 1997, #12 .... $4-6

silver, Mint Editions 1997, #98 .... $5-7

Tennessee Highway Patrol, Police USA 1998, #69 .... $5-7

yellow, Street Machines $2-3

1956 Ford Crown Victoria

Alaska State Troopers, Police USA 1998, #5 .... $5-7

Bill Elliott #94 Mac Tonight, Stock Rods 1997, #16 .... $4-6

black, Mint Editions 1996, #58 .... $5-7

black and red, Mint Editions 1997, #86 .. $5-7

Colorado State Police, Police USA 1998, #1 .... $5-7

Harwood Heights (Illinois) Police, Police USA 1998, #58 .... $5-7

light blue, Mint Editions 1996, #48.........$5-7

mint green, Mint Editions 1996, #53......$5-7

New Brunswick (New Jersey) Safety Patrol, Police USA 1998, #21 ....$5-7

Rick Mast #75 Remington, Stock Rods 1997, #23.........................$4-6

Sacramento (California) Police, Police USA 1998, #31 ....$5-7

1957 Ford Ranchero

Billy Dean, Hot Country Steel, #6 ....$6-8

black and white, Mint Editions 1997, #130..$5-7

Ernie Irvan #28 Texaco–Havoline, Stock Rods 1997, #33.........................$4-6

light blue, Mint Editions 1997, #114......$5-7

red and white, Mint Motor Trend 1998, #145 ....$4-6

1980 Ford Bronco

Chicago (Illinois) Police, Police USA 1998, #86.........................$5-7

Grand Chute (Wisconsin) Fire Rescue, Fire Rescue USA, 1999, #9.....................$5-7

Ford Mustang

1964? Ford Mustang

Billy Dean, Hot Country Steel, #8 ....$6-8

black, Mint Editions 1997, #87.............$5-7

gradient metallic fuchsia upper to purple middle to silver lower, 1:56 scale, Hot Rod Magazine 1997, #5.....................$4-6

Hank Williams Jr., Hot Country Steel, #5 ...$6-8

maroon, Mint Edition Hot Rods 1996, #7..$4-6

red, Mint Editions 1997, #81 ....$5-7

Rusty Wallace #2 Penske, Stock Rods 1997, #18.........................$4-6

Ted Musgrave #16 Primestar, Stock Rods 1997, #19 ....$4-6

1965 Ford Mustang

red with white top, Mint Motor Trend 1998, #207 ....$4-6

1968 Ford Mustang

Bill Elliott #94 McDonald's, Stock Rods 1997, #2.........................$4-6

black, Mint Editions 1996, #55.............$5-7

Jeff Burton #99 Exide, Stock Rods 1997, #20.........................$4-6

metallic gold, Mint Editions 1996, #10....$5-7

metallic green, Mint Editions 1996, #44..$5-7

mint green, Mint Editions 1996, #50......$5-7

red, Mint Editions 1996, #5 ....$5-7

Rick Mast #75 Remington, Stock Rods 1997, #13.........................$4-6

1968 Ford Mustang Fastback GT

yellow with green flames, Mint Edition Hot Rods 1996, #3 ....$4-6

1997 Ford Mustang

D.A.R.E. Car, Police USA 1998, #19 ....$5-7

green, Mint Editions 1997, #73 ....$5-7

Mark Martin #6 Valvoline, Stock Rods 1997, #3.........................$4-6

orange, Mint Editions 1997, #121 ....$5-7

red, Mint Editions 1997, #62...............$5-7

yellow, Mint Motor Trend 1998, #201...$4-6

Ford Pickup

1935 Ford Pickup

black, Mint Editions 1997, #66.............$5-7

gray, Mint Editions 1997, #75 ....$5-7

red, Mint Editions 1997, #71 ....$5-7

1940 Ford Pickup

Alan Jackson, Hot Country Steel, #12 .....$6-8

Alan Jackson, Hot Country Steel, #22 ....$6-8

black, Mint Motor Trend 1998, #157 ....$4-6

Hank Williams, Hot Country Steel, #13 ..$6-8

Randy Travis, Hot Country Steel, #19 ....$6-8

red, Mint Editions 1997, #120 ....$5-7

tan, Mint Motor Trend 1998, #148 ....$4-6

1948 Ford F-1 Pickup

black, Mint Motor Trend 1998, #164 ....$4-6

dark green, Mint Motor Trend 1998, #133 ....$4-6

red, Mint Motor Trend 1998, #139.......$4-6

Illinois State Police, Police USA 1998, #36 ....$5-7

1953 Ford F-100 Pickup

black, Mint Motor Trend 1998, #188 ....$4-6

black, Mint Motor Trend 1998, #202 ....$4-6

blue, Mint Motor Trend 1998, #177......$4-6

red, Mint Motor Trend 1998, #161 ....$4-6

Santa Clara County (California) Central Fire Dist., Fire Rescue USA, 1999, #12 ..$5-7

1965 Ford F-100 Pickup

light blue, Mint Motor Trend 1998, #149....$4-6

red, Mint Motor Trend 1998, #134.......$4-6

yellow, Mint Motor Trend 1998, #192...$4-6

1959 Ford F-250 Pickup

New Mexico State Police, Police USA 1998, #82 ....$5-7

black, Mint Motor Trend 1998, #174....$4-6

green, Mint Motor Trend 1998, #178....$4-6

1996 Ford F-150

black, Mint Editions 1996, #40.............$5-7

1997 Ford F-150 Pickup

Alan Jackson, Hot Country Steel, #3 ....$6-8

blue back, black front, Mint Edition Hot Rods 1996, #5.........................$4-6

Huntington Beach (California) Lifeguard, Fire Rescue USA, 1999, #8 ....$5-7

red, Mint Editions 1996, #30...............$5-7

US Border Patrol, Police USA 1998, #75 ....$5-7

white, Mint Editions 1996, #35.............$5-7

white, Mint Editions 1996, #45.............$5-7

1997 Ford F-150 Tow Truck

Boston (Massachusetts) Fire Dept. Fire Rescue USA, 1999, #4 ....$5-7

1999 Ford F-350 Pickup

Westchester (Illinois) Fire Dept., Fire Rescue USA, 1999, #3 ....$5-7

Delaware State Police, Police USA 1998, #94 ....$5-7

black, Mint Motor Trend 1998, #172 ....$4-6

red, Mint Motor Trend 1998, #165 ....$4-6

tan, Mint Motor Trend 1998, #156 ....$4-6

Tuscaloosa County (Alabama) Sheriff, Police USA 1998, #52 ....$5-7

Causeway Police Department, Police USA 1998, #26.........................$5-7

New York City Fire Dept., Fire Rescue USA, 1999, #10 ....$5-7

silver, Mint Motor Trend 1998, #195.....$4-6

Honda/Acura

1994 Acura Integra, "The Fast and the Furious" $4-6

Honda / Acura NSX (Tomy Japan) "The Fast and the Furious," 1:59 ....$4-6

1995 Honda Civic, "The Fast and the Furious" $4-6

Hudson

1951 Hudson Hornet, green, Mint Editions $6-8

Jeep

Jeep Compass Concept Car...................$4-6

Mercury

1949 Mercury
Bill Elliott #94 McDonald's, Stock Rods 1997,
#28 ....$4-6
black, Mint Editions 1997, #74.............$5-7

black, Street Machines...............................$2-3
blue, Mint Editions 1997, #65 ....$5-7
California Highway Patrol, Police USA
1998, #60................................$5-7
Florida Highway Patrol, Police USA
1998, #2..................................$5-7
gray, Mint Editions 1997, #70............$5-7
green, Mint Editions 1997, #85 ....$5-7
Hank Williams, Jr. Hot Country Steel,
#18 ....$6-8
Homewood (Illinois) Fire Dept., Fire Rescue
USA, 1999, #14 ....$5-7
Missouri Highway Patrol, Police USA
1998, #6..................................$5-7
Oklahoma Highway Patrol, Police USA
1998, #45...............................$5-7
1969 Mercury Cougar Eliminator

yellow, Mint Editions...............................$4-6

yellow, Street Machines $2-3

Oldsmobile

1969 Oldsmobile 442
blue, Mint Motor Trend 1998, #154......$4-6
crimson, Mint Editions 1997, #63..........$5-7
gold, Mint Editions 1997, #79.............$5-7
metallic deep blue with silver and fuchsia
accents, 1:58 scale, Hot Rod Magazine
1997, #4.................................$4-6
metallic deep blue with silver and fuchsia
accents, 1:58 scale, Hot Rod Magazine
1997, #4.................................$4-6
San Francisco (California) Police, Police USA
1998, #35................................$5-7
two-tone orange and black, Hot Rod
Magazine 1997, #9.....................$4-6
two-tone orange and black, Hot Rod
Magazine 1997, #9.....................$4-6
white, Mint Editions 1997, #68.............$5-7

Packard

1953 Packard, Mint Editions....................$6-8

Plymouth

1960 Plymouth
Suffolk County (New York) Police, Police
USA 1998, #55 ....$5-7
Chicago (Illinois) Police, Police USA
1998, #20................................$5-7
1964 Plymouth
Sparta (Mississippi) Police, Police USA
1998, #47................................$5-7
1968 Plymouth
Detroit (Michigan) Police, Police USA
1998, #40................................$5-7
Kansas Highway Patrol, Police USA
1998, #13................................$5-7
Los Angeles (California) Police Department,
Police USA 1998, #3 ....$5-7
Nassau County (New York) Police, Police
USA 1998, #62 ....$5-7
New York City Police, Police USA 1998, #57..$5-7
Virginia State Police, Police USA 1998, #77..$5-7
1968 Plymouth Superbird
blue, Mint Editions 1997, #97 ....$5-7
gold, Mint Editions 1997, #109...........$5-7
orange, Mint Editions 1997, #90 ....$5-7
red, Mint Editions 1997, #94..............$5-7
1970 Plymouth Barracuda
D.A.R.E. Car, Police USA 1998, #37 ....$5-7
lime green, Mint Motor Trend 1998, #183..$4-6

orange, Mint Motor Trend 1998, #143..$4-6
purple, Mint Motor Trend 1998, #138...$4-6
1970 Plymouth Superbird
blue, Mint Editions 1996, #59 ....$5-7
blue, Mint Motor Trend 1998, #160......$4-6
mustard yellow with black top, Mint Edition
Hot Rods 1996, #8 ....$4-6
red, Mint Editions 1996, #54.............$5-7
1996 Plymouth Prowler
Billy Dean, Hot Country Steel, #16 ....$6-8
1997 Plymouth Prowler
purple, Mint Editions 1997, #108 ....$5-7
red, Mint Editions 1997, #131 ....$5-7
silver, Mint Editions 1997, #115 ....$5-7
yellow, Mint Editions 1997, #111 ....$5-7

Pontiac

1966 Pontiac GTO
maroon with gold and silver accents, Hot
Rod Magazine 1999, #136...........$4-6
Philadelphia (Pennsylvania) Police, Police
USA 1998, #76 ....$5-7
black with gold stripe, Mint Motor Trend
1998, #208 ....$4-6
teal, Mint Motor Trend 1998, #200.......$4-6
1968 Pontiac Firebird
black, Mint Motor Trend 1998, #190 ....$4-6
maroon, Mint Motor Trend 1998, #206 ..$4-6
1969 Pontiac GTO "The Judge," 1:62 scale
Bobby Labonte #18 Interstate Batteries,
Stock Rods 1997, #7 ....$4-6
black, Mint Editions 1996, #52............$5-7
orange, Mint Editions 1996, #42 ....$5-7
red, Mint Editions 1996, #57..............$5-7
red, Mint Editions 1997, #91 ....$5-7
red with gold accents, Hot Rod Magazine
1999, #133 ....$4-6
metallic red with orange and white accents,
Hot Rod Magazine 1997, #6.........$4-6
school bus yellow, Mint Editions 1996, #47...$5-7
two-tone yellow and blue, Hot Rod Magazine
1997, #10...............................$4-6
white, Mint Motor Trend 1998, #170 ....$4-6
1978 Pontiac Firebird Trans Am
black, Mint Editions 1997, #132..........$5-7
gold, Mint Motor Trend 1998, #152 .....$4-6

red, Street Machines $2-3
silver, Mint Motor Trend 1998, #194.....$4-6
Travis Tritt, Hot Country Steel, #21 ....$6-8

yellow, Mint Motor Trend 1998, #147...$4-6

1996 Pontiac Firebird

    black, Mint Editions 1996, #3 ....$5-7

    dark teal, Mint Editions 1996, #49 ....$5-7

    Derrike Cope #36 Skittles, Stock Rods

        1997, #11.............................$4-6

    metallic bright blue, Mint Editions 1996, #43...$5-7

    purple, Mint Editions 1996, #8..............$5-7

    red, Mint Editions 1996, #20................$5-7

    white, Mint Editions 1996, #14............$5-7

1996 Pontiac Hurst Firebird

    red with black top, Mint Motor Trend

        1998, #205 ....$4-6

Pontiac Pro Street Firebird

    metallic pink and silver, Hot Rod

        Magazine #17, October 1998 ....$9-12

    two tone with flames, Hot Rod

        Magazine #15, October 1998 ....$9-12

Pro Stock

    black w/orange stripes, Hot Rod

        Magazine #2, August 1998.........$9-12

    metallic red, Hot Rod Magazine #4,

        August 1998..............................$9-12

    silver and purple with pink stripe, Hot Rod

        Magazine #6, August 1998.........$9-12

Studebaker

1951 Studebaker

    black, Mint Motor Trend 1998, #193 ....$4-6

    green, Mint Motor Trend 1998, #150....$4-6

    light green, Mint Motor Trend 1998, #182 ..$4-6

    maroon, Mint Motor Trend 1998, #153.$4-6

silver chrome, Mint Editions Chrome $4-6

South Bend (Indiana) Police, Police USA 1998,

    #85..$5-7

Toyota

1995 Toyota Supra, "The Fast and the Furious"..$4-6

Willys

1941 Willys Gasser

    Hank Williams, Jr., Hot Country Steel,

        #15 ....$6-8

    LeAnn Rimes, Hot Country Steel, #14......$6-8

Racing Champions Fantasy Cars–Found in Stackers display systems

Dragon, metallic purple...........................$2-4

Tuner, yellow...$2-4

Racing Champions Mint Edition Gift Sets

Five car sets with a special Racing Champions diecast emblem have been issued starting in September 1996.

Gift Set #1 (September 1996) $25-30

    includes:

        1996 Dodge Viper GTS, red

        1950 Chevrolet 3100 Pickup, black

        1968 Ford Mustang, blue

        1964 Chevrolet Impala, red

        1953 Chevrolet Corvette, white

Gift Set #2 (October 1996)....................$25-30

    includes:

        1996 Dodge Viper GTS, white

        1956 Ford Thunderbird, black

        1996 Dodge Ram, green

        1997 Ford F-150, bright teal blue

        1953 Chevrolet Corvette, red

Gift Set #3 (November 1996) $25-30

    includes:

        1963 Chevrolet Corvette, black

        1969 Pontiac GTO "Judge," blue

        1956 Ford Crown Victoria, pink

        1970 Plymouth Superbird, yellow

        1953 Chevrolet Corvette, black

Gift Set #4 (December 1996) $25-30

    includes:

        1950 Ford Coupe, black

        1956 Ford Crown Victoria, red

    1969 Olds 442 W-30, silver

    1964½ Ford Mustang, white

    1970 Plymouth Superbird, orange

Racing Champions Hot Rods 1:144 Scale

1957 Chevrolet $2-3

1950 Chevrolet Pick Up...........................$2-3

1950 Ford Coupe....................................$2-3

1958 Chevrolet Impala $2-3

1964.5 Ford Mustang $2-3

1970 Plymouth Superbird $2-3

1996 Dodge Viper..................................$2-3

1996 Dodge Ram...................................$2-3

1963 Chevrolet Corvette $2-3

1932 Ford $2-3

1969 Pontiac GTO $2-3

Other Racing Champions

HOT COUNTRY STEEL, 1:64 scale .....$6-8 each

HOT ROCKIN' STEEL, 1:64 scale ....$6-8 each

TRANSPORTERS, 1:64 scale, many

    liveries ....$10-12 each

LIMITED EDITION TRANSPORTERS, 1:64 scale, many liveries....................$20-24 each

NASCAR STOCK CARS, 1:64 scale, many

    liveries ....$4-6 each

WORLD OF OUTLAWS, 1:24 scale sprint

    racers, many liveries ....$10-12 each

WORLD OF OUTLAWS, 1:64 scale sprint

    racers, many liveries ....$4-6 each

STREET WHEELS, 1998-1999, inexpensive castings of popular cars accented in wild trim and colors and flashy chrome wheels ..$1-2 each

Racing Collectables Club of America, Inc. (RCCA) (see Action Performance)

Racing Collectables Club of America, Inc.

6600 Highlands Parkway, Suite B

Smyrna, GA 30082

phone: 404-333-0305

fax: 404-333-0265

    Racing Collectibles, Inc. (RCI) models are issued by the Racing Collectables Club of America, a division of Action Performance. Their first issues were made by Revell in 1:64 scale. Eventually RCCA was able to begin producing their own models. Revell has continued producing the 1:64 scale NASCAR models under their own name and Action Performance. Revell was ultimately purchased by Action Performance circa 1999.

Racing Collectables, Inc. (RCI) (see Action Performance)

Radar

Radar info comes from Ma Collection, according to Harvey Goranson. He reports that Radar in Portugal made plastic 1:43–1:45 toys of varying quality and made from 1960 to 1970.

BMW Isetta $12-15
Citroën 2CV $12-15
Double-Deck Bus $12-12
Mercedes 300SL Gullwing, 1:43 .... $12-12
OSCA racer $12-15
Porsche 550 Spyder, 1:43 .... $12-15
Tramcar with trailer, 1951 .... $12-15

Radon (also see Agat)

These are 1:43 scale diecast made in Russia and converted by G+A Models of the Ukraine for Henri Orange of Paris. Most recently, Radon has been reorganized to create the new company of Agat.

Lada Niva Police, Ukraine $25-40

R.A.E.

R.A.E. Models
Unit 2
Service Road Off Corrie Road
Addlestone, Surrey
KT15 2LP Great Britain
tel: 01932 846298
fax: 01932 853292

Established in 1975 primarily to offer a general model-making service for industrial product development, R.A.E Models is located South of London, close to Junction 11 on the M25 Motorway.

Bentley Corniche Convertible $140-165
Bentley T Series $140-165
Jaguar XK120 .... $75-90
Jaguar XK150 .... $95-110
Lea France Tourer $100-115
MG 179 Record Car $80-95
MG A $80-95
MG B Roadster, 1:20 .... $125-140
MG C Tourer, open, 1:43 .... $125-140
MG Midget $90
MG RV8 Convertible, top down, 1:43 ... $125-140
MG SA Convertible $140-155
MG SA Saloon $140-155
MG TVR 3000M, 1:43 .... $115-130
Rolls-Royce Corniche Convertible $140-155
Rolls-Royce Silver Shadow $150-165
Rolls-Royce Silver Shadow II $150-165
Triumph TR6, 1:43 .... $45-60

Raf

Raf represents 1:43 scale models from Russia.

2203 Minibus
Standard $11-16
Taxi $11-16
Traffic Police $11-16
Ambulance $11-13
Fire $11-16
Post Office $11-16
Books $11-16
wth symbols $11-16

Ralstoy

The Ralston Toy and Novelty Company, or Ralstoy, was founded in Ralston, Nebraska, in 1939. Combining surviving molds and dies from Best Toy Co. of Manhattan, Kansas, and Kansas Toy Co. of Clifton, Kansas, the former mayor of Ralston, Dr. Felix Despecher, started producing inexpensive slush-mold toys. When Dr. Despecher died and World War II dominated the need for lead and other metals, successor Paul Massey turned to making wooden toys.

When the war was over, the first Ralstoy diecast models were produced. Some, but not all, Ralstoys have the Ralstoy name on them, due to the inheritance of dies from the other companies. Most recent models have been produced as promotional items for moving companies and others.

Aircraft, #32 .... $15-20
Army Tank, 2¼", "US Army," #74 .... $25-30
Army Tank, 3⅛," #107 .... $25-30
Chevrolet 1982 Step Van, #1 .... $18-24
Dump Truck, 3⅜", #42 .... $35-45
Large Transporter with #74 Tank & #32
Aircraft, #101 .... $65-80
Muzzle Loading Cannon on Wheeled
Platform, #23 .... $25-30
Oldsmobile Sedan $150-175
Phillips 66 Tanker $75-100
Railway Gun, 3¼", #108 .... $25-35
Safety-Kleen Van $30-45
Tanker Truck, 3⅜", #102 .... $30-40
Tanker Truck and Trailer, 7¾", #3 .... $45-60
Tractor, 3," #48 .... $25-35

Ralstoy Moving Vans, 1:64, 8½"

Allied Van Lines $30-40
Atlas Van Lines $30-40
Bekins Van Lines $30-40
Global Van Lines $30-40
Greyhound Van Lines $30-40
Lyon Van Lines $30-40
Mayflower Moving Van $30-40
Neptune Van Lines $30-40
North American Van Lines, #20 .... $30-40
Red Ball Van Lines $30-40
Republic Van Lines $30-40
Stevens Van Lines $30-40
United Van Lines $30-40
Wheaton Van Lines $30-40

Rami

Les Retrospectives Automobiles Miniature, known variously as R.A.M.I., RAMI, or Rami, are model miniatures representative of actual cars on display at the Musee Francais de l' Automobile (French Automobile Museum) near Lyons, and other museums.

Since 1958, Rami has produced an exceptional assortment of vintage and antique car replicas. Production continued until 1980. No additional models have been offered since.

Amedee Bollee 1878 La Mancelle, 3⅜",
1966, #30 .... $50
Audibert & Lavirotte 1898, 2¾", 1966, #27 .. $50
Berliet 1910 Limousine, 3¾", 1968, #33 ...... $50
Brasier 1908 Landaulet, 3¼", 1967, #32 ..... $50
Bugatti 1928 Type 35, 3⅜", 1959, #6 .... $50
Citroën 1924 5CV Roadster, 2⅞", 1958, #4 .... $50
Citroën 1925 B2 Limousine, 3½", 1959, #7 .. $50
De Dion 1900 Cab, 2⅛", 1958, #5 .... $50
De Dion-Bouton 1900 Vis-A-Vis, 2⅛",
1958–1970, #2 .... $50
De Dion-Bouton 1902 Racing car, 3¼",
1968, #35 .... $50
Delage 1932 Torpedo, 4⅝", 1968, #37 ...... $50
Delahaye 1904 Phaeton, 2⅞", 1965, #26 ... $50
Delauney-Belleville 1904, 3⅜", 1964, #20 ... $50
Ford 1907 Model R Tourer, 3¼", 1963, #16 .. $50
Ford 1908 Model T, 3¼", 1963, #15 .... $50
Gauthier-Wehrle 1897 Cab, 2⅜", 1961, #12 .... $50
Georges Richard 1902 Tonneau, 2⅝", 1964,
#21 .... $50
Gobron-Brillie 1899 Double Phaeton, 2½", 1961,
#11 .... $50
Hautier 1898 Electric Taxi, 3½", 1964, #19 ..... $55
Hispano-Suiza 1934 Town car, 3¾", 1960,
#10 .... $50
Lacroix De La Ville 1898, 3¼", 1968, #36 .... $50
Leon bollee 1911 Double Sedan, 3¾",
1966, #28 .... $50
Lion-Peugeot 1907 Double Phaeton, 2¾",
1958, #3 .... $50
Lorraine-Dietrich 1911, 3⅜", 1965, #24 .... $50
Luc Court 1901 Racing car, 2¾", 1967, #31 .... $50
Mercedes 1927 SSK, 3⅞", 1969, #38 .... $55
Mieusset 1903 Runabout, 2⅝", 1968, #34 ... $50

Motobloc 1902 Tonneau, 2⅝", 1971, #2 ....$50
Packard 1912 Landaulet, 3½", 1962, #13 ...$55
Panhard & Levassor 1895 Tonneau, 2½",
   1965, #25 ....$50
Panhard & Levassor 1899 Tonneau Ballon,
   3⅛", 1964, #18 ....$50
Panhard & Levassor 1908 La Marquise, 3⅞",
   1964, #17 ....$50
Peugeot 1898 Coupe, 3," 1962, #14 ....$50
Renault 1900 Tonneau, 2¾", 1965, #23 ......$50
Renault 1907 Taxi De La Marne, 3½", 1958,
   #1 ....$50
Rochet-Schneider 1895 Vis-A-Vis, 2¾", 1960,
   #9 ....$50
S.P.A. 1912 Sports Sar, 4," 1966, #29 .....$50
Scotte 1892 Steam car, 2¾", 1965, #22 .....$55
Sizaire & Naudin 1906 Racing car, 2⅞", 1959,
   #8 ....$50

Rapide (see Modelauto)

Rapitoy

The most interesting model listed in the Rapitoy of Argentina assortment is a Mercedes van with "Matchbox" livery. It is uncommon for one toymaker to promote another, but this seems to be a rare exception...unless Rapitoy put the Matchbox name on the model to convince the buyer it was a Matchbox toy.

Dodge Charger Show car, 1:64 ....$4-6
Ford F-100 Pickup, 1:64 ....$4-6
Mercedes-Benz 350SL, top up, 1:64 ....$4-6
Mercedes Van "Matchbox," 1:43 ....$17-22
Mercedes Van "Ferrari," 1:43 ....$17-22
Mercedes Van "Fargopan," 1:43 ....$17-22
Siva Spyder, 1:64 ....$4-6

Ra-Ro

Of these 1:43 scale models, produced in 1948 from Milan, Italy, four are known. Such models are also identified as Cisitalia, Osca, and Stanguellini models. Obviously, easy identification requires more data.

Alfa Romeo, 3¾" $75-90
Ferrari, 3⅞" $75-90
Maserati, 3¾" $75-90
Veritas, 3¾" $75-90

Rasant

Frank Wagner first inquired about Rasant of Germany in an e-mail inquiry. The model he found is of a Ford Taunus that looks similar to a 1961 Ford Thunderbird. The base of the model reads "Ford Taunus 17M, RASANT, Made in Germany." The vintage and style of the car raises the question of why the base is not imprinted with "East Germany" or "West Germany" since it was apparently produced in the midst of the Cold War and a divided Germany.

Mr. Wagner later wrote that at the beginning of the 1960s, the German toy company Rasant was founded in Gunzenhausen. They wanted to produce slot car models like the Faller AMS system. In 1964 they presented their system with models in near HO scale. The system was not accepted by the market. They changed the system in the way that the cars could be driven on any slot car system with 16mm contacts. But that failed again, so they produced their cars as non-slot cars. In 1969, Rasant had to stop production. Mr. Wagner's Ford Taunus represents one of those last non-slot car models produced.

The wheels are spun metal. The black tires appear to be hard rubber. Several versions of some models include German Fire Chief (feuerwehr), Street Works (strassenwacht), Police (polizei), Post, and Ambulance (Ambulanz). Much of the information on these models was extracted from a German-language website by Frank Wagner.

BMW 2000 ....$15-35
Cadillac Fleetwood $15-35
Ford Taunus 17M, red, 2½" (65mm)...$15-35
Mercedes-Benz 220 SE $15-35
Mercedes-Benz 250 SE $15-35
Opel Diplomat $15-35
Opel Kapitan.....................................$15-35

RBI (see Redbox, Motormax)

RCCA (see Racing Collectables, Inc.)

RCI (see Racing Collectables, Inc.)

Reader's Digest (also see High Speed)

Along with various offers from *Reader's Digest* come special promotional gifts. Several of these gifts are miniature vintage cars, trucks, and airplanes. These are not generally available anywhere else, but Toy Liquidators has obtained a few of these sets for resale. The manufacturer is not indicated, but they are made in China.

Collector's Set of Classic Car Miniatures $3 per set

Each package includes six boxed vintage 1:87 scale cars, numbered on base. Outer box has full-color photos of each model around the four sides. Inside is a 5" x 7½" descriptive sheet that provides details of each model. While these models are inexpensively made and lacking in accuracy and detail, they are a charming set nonetheless. Made in Macau, copyright 1989, The Readers Digest Association Inc., Pleasantville NY 10570.

1901 Fiat Modello 8 CV, No. 301 ....$1-2
1910 Ford Model T, No. 304 ....$1-2
1907 Peugeot, No. 303 ....$1-2
1906 Rolls-Royce, No. 302 ....$1-2
1912 Simplex, No. 305 ....$1-2
1914 Vauxhall, No. 306.........................$1-2

Collector's Set of Classic Trucks $5 per set

This is a set of four mostly plastic vintage trucks about the size of Matchbox Models of Yesteryear (1:43 scale) packaged in two boxes inside of a larger box, with note included that says "Your FREE Gift... along with our thanks for ordering from *Reader's Digest*. Made in China.

1912 Ford Model T Ambulance $1-2
1912 Ford Model T Tanker $1-2
1918 Delivery Van $1-2
1910 Water Wagon $1-2

Collector's Set of Miniature Biplanes $5 per set

This is a set of four diecast miniature biplanes, each with 3" wingspan, individually boxed and packaged in a larger box describing each model. A note inside the box says "Your Free Gift...along with our thanks for ordering *Reader's Digest* music." Made in China.

1928 Boeing PT-17 Kaydet $1-2
1928 Boeing P-12E $1-2
1918 British S.E. 5A.............................$1-2
1918 Curtiss JN-4D Jenny $1-2

Reader's Digest Toy Cars by High Speed

Among the offerings from *Reader's Digest* are some particularly realistic toy cars in roughly 1:55 scale (about 3 inches long).

Real Cars (see Esci)

Real Wheels (see Ja-Ru)

Realistic

Realistic toys are cast aluminum vehicles manufactured in Freeport, Illinois, during the late 1940s and early 1950s. Some models used the original molds from Arcade cast-iron toys.

1939 Studebaker President Yellow Cab,
8¼"..$100-115
Greyhound Bus, Silversides, 8¾"..........$100-115
Trailways Bus, 8¾"............................$100-115

Realtoy

In just the past few years, Realtoy has made a dramatic appearance in the form of some exceptional playsets. Sets feature from 25 to 75 pieces which include trees, outdoor furniture, human and animal figures as well as a great assortment of attractively decorated vehicles and a big playmat. Interestingly, many models bear a striking resemblance to Matchbox, Hot Wheels, and Majorettes, some even appearing to be outright knockoffs. Realtoy International Limited, Wah Fung Industrial Centre, Kwai Fung Rd., N.T. Hong Kong. Sets were available from Wal-Mart, Toys "R" Us, and other retailers.

Record

Record models are 1:43 scale vehicles made in France.

1952 Chevrolet 2-door Hardtop, #1.......$55-65
1952 Chevrolet 4-door Sedan, #3..........$55-65
1952 Chevrolet Convertible, #4.............$55-65
1952 Chevrolet Fastback Coupe, #2.....$55-65
1984 Ferrari GTO, #102.....................$55-65
Ferrari Testarossa, #103.......................$55-65
Ferrari 365 GTB, #111........................$55-65
Opel Ascona "Bastos," #99.................$55-65

Redbox (also see Motormax, Zee Toys/Zylmex)

200 Fifth Avenue
New York, NY 10010
or
Hithercroft Ind Estate, Lesterway
Wallingford, Oxon OX10 9TH U.K.

In 1997, Zyll Enterprise, known for Zylmex and Zee Toys, was purchased by Redbox. Selected Zylmex and Zee Toys were then being reissued with the new Redbox brand on the base and on the box. In July 1997, Redbox started selling the former Zyll 1:24 scale diecast vehicles formerly sold as Z-Wheels. Since then, more Zee Toys have been showing up in multipack and single-pack sets. More recently, Redbox has issued their models under the Motormax brand.

GMC Pick-up, 3"...................................$1-2
Chevrolet 454 SS Pick-up, 3"................$1-2
Chevrolet Blazer, 3"..............................$1-2
GMC Jimmy, 3"....................................$1-2
Ford Explorer, 3"...................................$1-2

Reen Replica

One of the previously unknown brands from Japan, Reen Replica models are likely produced in the early to mid-1960s, according to collector Robert Speerbrecher (see Silver Pet). Models are of moderate detail and of unknown scale but are probably around 1:43 scale.

1937 Nissan 70 Sedan.........................$20-25
1957 4-door Sedan, Japanese car..........$20-25

Rei

Rei 1:43 scale models are Schuco models of Germany made in Brazil. Models of other scales are produced for Rei by Matsuda.

Collector Brian Willoughby of Murray, Kentucky, reports that in addition to the 1:43 scale models, Rei also produced several of the former 1:66 scale Schuco models. Willoughby says, "If you are familiar with the original Schuco castings, the [Rei models] were packaged in the same little plastic boxes with the same piece of foam in the bottom to secure the model. All traces of the Schuco name and the wording 'Made in Germany' were removed from the models and the boxes (which had the Schuco name molded into the top and 'Made in Germany' molded into the bottom). I actually have a small catalog that came with one of the 1:66 REIs I have that lists some of the models. I say 'some' due to the fact that I have other REI/Schuco castings that are not illustrated in the brochure."

"Furthermore," continues Willoughby, "Rei also recycled several Siku dies during the 1970s. I don't know what all they re-issued from the former Siku line, though they definitely produced their own rendition of Siku's Ford Capri. There are others, though I don't know exactly which ones."

Alfa Romeo F1 "Parmalat," 1:43.............$18-24
Audi 100 Coupe, 1:66 (REI/Schuco).........$6-8
Lamborghini Cheetah Fire Chief, 1:43.....$18-24
Lotus F1 "JPS," 1:43............................$18-24
Mercedes-Benz C-111, 1:43..................$8-12
Peterbilt Semi Van "Coca-Cola," 1:43......$18-24
Peterbilt Semi Van "Transbras," 1:43........$18-24
Peterbilt Semi Van "Esso," 1:43...............$18-24
Peterbilt Semi Van "Petrobras," 1:43........$18-24

Peterbilt Semi Van "Mobil," 1:43............$18-24
Peterbilt Semi Van "Shell," 1:43.............$18-24
Peterbilt Semi Van "Alfa Romeo," 1:43.....$18-24
Peterbilt Semi Van "Ferrari," 1:43............$18-24
Peterbilt Semi Van "JPS," 1:43...............$18-24
Peterbilt Semi Van "Marlboro," 1:43........$18-24
Peterbilt Semi Van "Renault," 1:43..........$18-24
Toyota Celica LB2000 GT, 1:64
(REI/Matsuda)...................................$6-8
Volvo Bus, 1:43.................................$18-24

Remco

Since about 1955, Remco has represented a major force in the toy market. Remco Tuff Ones are durable diecast and plastic toys most recently associated with Road Champs, Inc. and Jakks Pacific, Inc., according to packaging on models issued with a 1998 copyright. Value remains at or near retail on all but the oldest Remco issues generally made of pressed metal and plastic, often with battery-operated working parts.

Renaissance

Renaissance models are 1:24 scale hand-made masterpieces assembled from 195 white metal, resin, plated, photoetched, and machine parts, and produced in genuine Ferrari colors, with production limited to 500 pieces of each model worldwide.

1958 Ferrari 250 Testarossa Le Mans 58,
red #14, R3..............................$675-725
Ferrari 250 California Spyder, available in red,
blue, dark red, silver, or brown, R1B..$675-725
Ferrari 275 GTB/4 Spyder NART, available in
red, yellow, black, metallic red, or silver,
R2...$675-725

Renwal

Usually associated with plastic toys, Renwal produced a few diecast models that featured crude paint jobs and rough castings. Nevertheless, the rarity of these toys establishes their high value.

Chevrolet Sedan, #8005...................$120-140
City Bus, 4"....................................$72-80
Convertible, 3," #147........................$24-28
Convertible, #8015...........................$72-90
Convertible, 4"................................$96-108
Coupe, 3," #144..............................$32-36
Coupe, 4".......................................$72-80
Delivery Truck, #8010........................$72-90
Ferrari Racer, #8001........................$160-200
Fire Truck, 3," #145..........................$24-28

Fire Truck, #8014 ....$72-90
Ford Sedan, #8006..........................$120-140
Ford Sunliner Convertible, #8023 ....$36-40
Ford Victoria Hardtop, #8028 ....$36-40
Futuristic Two-door Coupe, #8020 ....$24-30
Gasoline Truck, 3," #148 ....$24-28
Gasoline Truck, #8008 ....$72-90
Gasoline Truck, #8021 ....$24-30
Gasoline Truck, 4" $72-80
Hook & Ladder, 3," #146.....................$24-28
Hot Rod, #8012....................................$72-90
Jeep, #8013 ....$72-90
Ladder Fire Truck, #8022 ....$24-30
Maserati Racer, #8002 ....$160-200
Pick-Up Truck, 3," #149 ....$24-28
Pick-up Truck, #8011 ....$72-90
Pick-Up Truck, #8039 ....$24-30
Plymouth Convertible, #8004 ....$120-140
Pontiac Convertible, #8003 ....$120-140
Pumper Fire Truck, #8040 ....$24-30
Racer, 3," #150.................................$48-52
Racer, #8009 ....$96-108
Sedan, 3," #143 ....$32-36
Sedan, #8007 ....$72-90
Speed King Racer, #8041 ....$48-64

Replex

Replex Maquettes de Collection en Metal
Sapois 88120
Vagney–France

Replex of France produces scale models of
military vehicles, commercial trucks, emergency
vehicles, and heavy equipment.

ACMAT 6x6 Flatbed Sand, 1:50, 178 ....$88
ACMAT 6x6 Flatbed, olive drab, 1:43, 200...$108
ACMAT 6x6 Semi Tractor/Trailer, 1:43, 179 ..$128
ACMAT 6x6 Semi Tractor/Trailer, 1:50, 167 ..$128
ACMAT 6x6 Troop Transport, 1:50, 202...$118
ACMAT FFM Fire Pumper, 1:50, 201 ....$108
ACMAT TPK 4x4 Troop Transport, 1:50,
    203 ....$118
AMX 30 Euromissile Tank, 1:50, 102 ....$38
DAF FA 1300 Commercial Transport with
    deflector, "TNT/IPEC," 1:43, 159 ....$44
DAF FA 1300 Tractor and Chassis, 1:43, 129 ..$44
Fenwick Forklift, 1:25, 107 ....$28
International Harvester 844 Farm Tractor,
    1:43, 109 ....$14
International Harvester Combine, 1:43, 106 ...$48
Iveco 80-13 AV Dump Truck, 1:43, 166 ....$42
Iveco 90.13 Commercial Transport, 1:43, 127...$44
Iveco Magirus TRM 2000 Military Transport,
    1:43, 206 ....$44
Liebherr 981 Shovel, 1:53, 104.................$54
Mack 200 American Stake Truck, 1:43, 120 ..$42

Mack 200 Commercial Transport
    "Michelin," 1:43, 150....................$44
Mack 200 Commercial Transport "MIKO,"
    1:43, 124 ....$44
Mack 200 Commercial Transport, "Ryder,"
    1:43, 212 ....$44
Mack 200 Fire Pumper, 1:43, 244 ....$44
Mack 200 USA Double Cabin Fire Truck,
    1:43, 151 ....$48
Magirus Deutz 1919 Bus, 1:43, 114 ....$44
Magirus Deutz 1925 Ladder Fire Truck, 1:43,
    119 ....$44
Magirus Deutz 90/13 cargo Transport
    "Panzani," 1:43, 118 ....$44
Magirus Tractor and Chassis, 1:43, 135 ......$44
Manitou MLT626RT Bucket Lift, 1:43, 269 ....$48
Mercedes 1928AS38 Tar Spreader Semi,
    1:50, 207 ....$68
Poclain 1000 Track Excavator, 1:50, 111...$64
Poclain 1000 Track Shovel, 1:50, 113........$64
PPM Crane, 1:50, 112........................$58
Renault 1000 Transport, camouflage, 1:43,
    284 ....$84
Renault Fire Equipment Truck, 1:43, 172.......$44
Renault Fire Equipment Truck, 1:43, 195.......$44
Renault R340 Tar Spreader Semi, 1:50, 208 ...$68
Renault RVI 75-130 Forest Fire Truck,
    1:43, 141 ....$44
Renault RVI 85-150 Civil Protection Truck,
    1:43, 198 ....$44
Renault RVI 85-150 Forest Fire Truck, 1:43,
    142 ....$44
Renault RVI 95-130 Forest Fire Truck, 1:43,
    140 ....$44
Renault RVI Commercial Transport "Danza," 1:43,
    130 ....$44
Renault RVI Dump Truck, 1:43, 204..............$44
Renault RVI Emergency Medical Treatment
    Vehicle, 1:43, 164 ....$44
Renault RVI Fire Auxiliary Truck, 1:43, 163 ....$44
Renault RVI Fire Auxiliary Truck, 1:43, 165 ....$44
Renault RVI Fire Equipment Truck, 1:43, 162...$44
Renault RVI JK90 Fire Service, 1:43, 136 ......$44
Renault RVI JN 90 Fire Equipment Truck, 1:43,
    147 ....$44
Renault RVI JN 90 Fire Pumper, 1:43, 146....$48
Renault RVI JN-90 Ladder Fire Truck, 1:43,
    143 ....$44
Renault RVI JP 13 Fire Ladder Truck, 1:43, 145 ...$48
Renault RVI S 170 Commercial Transport,
    "Vittel," 1:43, 197 ....$44
Renault RVI S 170 Commercial Transport,
    1:43, 123 ....$44
Renault RVI S 170 Tractor and Chassis,
    1:43, 122 ....$44
Renault RVI SIDES Fire Pumper, 1:43, 144.....$48

Renault RVI TRM 2000 Military Transport,
    1:43, 101 ....$44
Renault RVI TRM 2000 Water Cannon Fire
    Truck, 1:43, 148 ....$44
RVI Carniva Fire Ladder Truck, 1:48, 169 .....$58
RVI Military Water Cannon, 1:43, 187 ....$44
RVI Premier Security Truck Type 85-200,
    1:43, 186 ....$44
RVI-TRM 2000 Covered Transport, green
    camouflage, 1:43, 210......................$44
Shelter 650 SH Load to 200, 1:50, 205 .....$28
Shelter Euromissile, olive drab, 1:50, 100.....$38
Shelter Generator Load, 1:50, 176.............$78
Shelter Rita SH30 Load to 17, 1:50, 177.....$34
Sides 2000 Doubai Airport, yellow, 1:43, 110 ..$44
Sides 2000 Geneva Airport, red, 1:43, 116...$44
Sides 2000 Paris Airport, red, 1:43, 108.....$44
SPZ Euromissile, 1:50, 103 ....$38
TechnoCar/BalkanCar Forklift, 1:25, 105 ....$28
VAB 4x4 Ambulance, 1:43, 240 ....$44
VAB 4x4 Ambulance, tan with red crescent,
    1:43, 243 ....$44
VAB 4x4 Armored Assault Vehicle, 1:43, 259...$44
VAB 4x4 Armored Assault Vehicle, 1:43, 261...$44
VAB 4x4 Armored Assault Vehicle, 1:43, 262...$44
VAB 4x4 Armored Assault Vehicle, khaki,
    1:43, 260 ....$44
VAB 4x4 Armored Troop Transport, 1:43, 209...$58
VAB 4x4 Armored Troop Transport, 1:43, 233 ..$44
VAB 4x4 Armored Troop Transport, khaki
    camouflage, 1:43, 216......................$44
VAB 4x4 Armored Turret T25, green
    camouflage, 1:43, 245......................$44
VAB 4x4 Armored Turret T25, khaki
    camouflage, 1:43, 247......................$44
VAB 4x4 Turret T25, 1:43, 239................$44
VAB 6x6 Armored Ambulance, 1:43, 241 ...$44
VAB 6x6 Armored Assault Vehicle, 1:43, 155 ..$58
VAB 6x6 Armored Assault Vehicle, green
    camouflage, 1:43, 265......................$44
VAB 6x6 Armored Assault Vehicle, sable
    camouflage, 1:43, 266......................$44
VAB 6x6 Armored Troop Transport, 1:43, 156...$58
VAB 6x6 Armored Troop Transport, 1:43, 263 ..$44
VAB 6x6 Armored Turret T25, green
    camouflage, 1:43, 246......................$44
VAB 6x6 Armored Turret, 1:43, 154............$58
VAB 6x6 F.I.N.U.L., white, 1:43, 190 ....$58
VAB 6x6 SATCP Mistral, 1:43, 242 ....$44
VAB 6x6 Troop Transport, sable
    camouflage, 1:43, 264......................$44
VAB 6x6 Turret T25, 1:43, 248 ....$84
VAB Armored Police Assault Vehicle, blue,
    1:43, 191 ....$44
VAB Panhard Armored Troop Transport, 1:43,
    174 ....$44

VBL Police Armored Personnel Transport, white,
    1:43, 192 ....$44
VBL-Panhard Armored Troop Transport, green
    camouflage, 1:43, 211 ....$44
Volvo F 614 Cab & Chassis, 1:43, 115 ......$44
Yanmar B27 Mini Excavator, 1:30, 274 ......$38

Repli-Cars (see Bayshore Repli-Cars)

Replicars

Replicars are 1:43 scale models made in England, currently offered for around $60 each.

1932 Alfa 8C Roadster, #29 ....$60-75
1932 Alfa Castagna, top up, #35 ....$60-75
1925 Austin Van "Lucas," #101 ....$60-75
1921 Bugatti Brescia, #4 ....$60-75
1934 ERA, #1 ....$60-75
1951 Ferrari 166M, #13 ....$60-75
1951 Jaguar C Type, #32 ....$60-75
1958 Jaguar XK150, #36 ....$60-75
1975 Lotus Super 7, #18 ....$60-75
1934 MG K3, #6 ....$60-75
1936 Morgan 2-Seater, #44 ....$60-75
1968 Morgan Plus 8, #7 ....$60-75
1937 Packard 4-door Sedan, #24 ....$60-75
1937 Packard Roadster, #16 ....$60-75
1937 Packard Tourer, #24 ....$60-75
1937 Packard Town car, #24 ....$60-75
1954 Sunbeam Alpine Roadster, #28 .....$60-75
1974 Triumph TR6, #14 ....$60-75

Replicast

Replicast Record Models
132 Linaker Street
Southport
Merseyside PR8 5DF
England
phone: 00 44 (0)1704 542233
fax: 00 44 (0)1704 500164
e-mail: info@linaker.u-net.com
www.merseyworld.comreplicast/

Since 1984, Replicast Record Models has been operated from Merseyside, England, by founder Frank C. Harris. The company offers models of speed record cars and boats in various scales and materials. Most but not all models are available in both kit and built form. The most prolific series is of 1:43 scale white metal land speed record cars. Also available are fiberglass boat kits that can be adapted for radio control. Values have been converted from British pounds. List is based on information off the Replicast website as of January 7, 2000.

Replicast Land Speed Record Cars, 1:43 Scale

1899 Jeantaud Electric, 94 mm, resin,
    white metal, photo-etched, J.S.05
    kit $61
    built $218
1902 Electric Torpedo, Baker, 125 mm,
    resin, G.B.10, not available as kit
    built $172
1910 Steam Rocket, Stanley, 113 mm,
    resin, white metal, photo-etched, J.S.07
    kit $64
    built $221
1914 Benz, L. Hornstead, 110 mm, resin,
    photo-etched, G.B.11, built $246
1919 Packard, De Palma, 118 mm, resin
    kit, D.S.1 ....$66
    built $221
1920 Double Duesenberg, T. Milton,
    117 mm, resin, G.B.12, built..............$228
1922 Sunbeam KLG, M. Campbell,
    110 mm, white metal, LSR.3
    kit $99
    built $213
1924 Sunbeam Bluebird, M. Campbell,
    135 mm, white metal, LSR.5
    kit $99
    built $213
1925 Sunbeam Bluebird, M. Campbell,
    135 mm, white metal, LSR.2
    kit $99
    built $213
1926 BABS, Parry Thomas, 120 mm,
    white metal, Pand.21a
    kit $100
    built $303
1927 BABS, Parry Thomas, 135 mm,
    white metal, Pand.21b
    kit $87
    built $288
1927 Sunbeam 1000 hp, H. Segrave,
    170 mm, white metal, W.M.2
    kit $80
    built $153
1927 Sunbeam Bluebird, M. Campbell,
    142 mm, white metal, Pand.2
    kit $80
    built $216
1929 Arrol Aster Bluebird, M. Campbell,
    155 mm, white metal, photo-etched, Pand.3
    kit $75
    built $201
1929 Golden Arrow, H. Segrave, 195 mm,
    white metal, W.M.1
    kit $80
    built $153

1930 Silver Bullet, Kaye Don, 220 mm,
    white metal, Pand.1
    kit $75
    built $201
1931 Stutz Black Hawk, F. Lockhart,
    118 mm, white metal, Pand.17
    kit $49
    built $159
1931 Napier Bluebird, M. Campbell,
    160 mm, white metal, Pand.4
    kit $100
    built $403
1932 Napier Bluebird, M. Campbell,
    160 mm, white metal, Pand.5
    kit $100
    built $403
1935 Bluebird, Sir M. Campbell, 193 mm,
    resin, white metal, MOM.7
    kit $61
    built $128
1937 Thunderbolt, G. Eyston, 216 mm,
    resin, white metal, MOM.3
    kit $72
    built $180
1936 Mercedes Benz Class B., R. caracciola,
    140 mm, resin, white metal, G.B.6
    kit $44
    built $133
1937 Auto Union "AVUS," B. Rosemeyer,
    140 mm, resin, white metal, G.B.4
    kit $44
    built $133
1937 Mercedes Benz "AVUS," H. Lang,
    140 mm, resin, white metal, G.B.5
    kit $44
    built $133
1937 Auto Union Class B., B. Rosemeyer,
    140 mm, resin, white metal, G.B.1
    kit $41
    built $128
1938 Mercedes Benz Class B., R. caracciola,
    144 mm, resin, white metal, G.B.2
    kit $47
    built $138
1938 Auto Union Class B., B. Rosemeyer,
    142 mm, resin, white metal, G.B.3
    kit $47
    built $138
1938 Railton Special, J. Cobb, 200 mm,
    resin, J.S.05a
    kit $61
    built $242
1938 Thunderbolt, G. Eyston, 250 mm,
    resin, white metal, MOM.4
    kit $72
    built $180

1939 Daimler Benz T.80, H. Stuck,
190 mm, resin, Pand.18
kit...$75
built.......................................$216

1947 Railton Mobil Special, J. Cobb,
200 mm, resin, J.S.05b
kit...$61
built.......................................$242

1959 Challenger, M. Thompson, 140 mm,
resin, M.S.1
kit...$55
built.......................................$131

1960 Challenger, M. Thompson, 140 mm,
resin, M.S.2
kit...$55
built.......................................$131

1960 Spirit of Salt Lake, Athol Graham,
150 mm, white metal, LSR.6
kit...$99
built.......................................$205

1960 Anteater, Art Arfons, 120 mm, resin,
Fad.5, built.................................$221

1960 Bluebird CN7, D.M. Campbell,
210 mm, resin, white metal, MOM.5
kit...$72
built.......................................$174

1960 Flying Caduseus, Dr. N. Ostich,
200 mm, resin, white metal, MOM.8
kit...$80
built.......................................$242

1963 Flying Caduseus, Dr. N. Ostich,
200 mm, resin, white metal, MOM.9
kit...$80
built.......................................$270

1963 Wingfoot Express 1, T. Green,
170 mm, resin, J.S.06
kit...$61
built.......................................$259

1964 Bluebird CN7, D.M. Campbell,
210 mm, resin, MOM.6
kit...$72
built.......................................$174

1964 Wingfoot Express 1, T. Green,
170 mm, resin, J.S.02
kit...$61
built.......................................$259

1964 Autolite Special, M. Thompson,
218 mm, resin, J.S.04
kit...$61
built.......................................$274

1965 Wingfoot Express II, R. Tahoe,
200 mm, white metal, Pand.20
kit...$100
built.......................................$318

1965 Bluebird CMN8, D. Campbell,
178 mm, resin, J.S.03
kit...$54
built.......................................$201

1965 Goldenrod, Summers Bros.,
225 mm, white metal, LSR.4
kit...$82
built.......................................$205

1965 Spirit of America "Sonic 1,"
C. Breedlove, 237 mm, resin, J.S.01
kit...$61
built.......................................$242

1965 Green Monster, A. Arfons, 160 mm,
white metal, photo-etched, MOM.11
kit...$99
built.......................................$401

1970 Blue Flame, G. Gabelich, 270 mm,
resin, white metal, MOM.10
kit...$97
built.......................................$405

1979 Budwieser Rocket, S. Barrett,
247 mm, resin, white metal, MOM.1
kit...$80
built.......................................$288

1983 Thrust II, R. Noble, 195 mm, white
metal, LSR.1
kit...$99
built.......................................$262

1985 Minnesota Special, R. Palm,
168 mm, resin, Pand.19
kit...$57
built.......................................$174

1991 Speed-O-Motive, Al Teague,
200 mm, resin, Fad.6
built.......................................$238

1997 Thrust SSC, R. Noble, 380 mm,
resin, white metal, photo-etched, R.S.1
built.......................................$572

Replicast 1:43 Scale Speed Record Boats

1930 Miss England II, H. Segrave,
267 mm, resin, white metal, Rep.1
kit...$79
built.......................................$241

1937 Bluebird K3, M. Campbell, 193 mm,
resin, white metal, Rep.2
kit...$66
built.......................................$203

1938 Bluebird K3, M. Campbell, 180 mm,
resin, white metal, Rep.3
kit...$66
built.......................................$203

1939 Bluebird K4, M. Campbell, 185 mm,
white metal, photo etched, Rep.4
kit...$98
built.......................................$287

1952 Crusader K6, J. Cobb, 220 mm,
resin, Rep.5

kit...$71
built.......................................$211

1955 Bluebird K7, D. Campbell, 190 mm,
resin, white metal, Rep.6
kit...$69
built.......................................$201

1955 Bluebird K7, D. Campbell (Lake
Mead), 190 mm, resin, white metal, Rep.7
kit...$69
built.......................................$2001

1964 Bluebird K7, D. Campbell, 190 mm,
resin, white metal, Rep.8
kit...$69
built.......................................$201

1967 Bluebird K7, D. Campbell, 190 mm,
resin, white metal, Rep.9
kit...$69
built.......................................$201

1967 Hustler, Lee Taylor, 220 mm, resin,
white metal, Rep.10
kit...$74
built.......................................$206

1980 US Discovery, Lee Taylor, 290 mm,
resin, Rep.11
kit...$79
built.......................................$209

1953 Laura 3a, Mario Verga, 175 mm,
resin, white metal, Rep.12
kit...$79
built.......................................$209

Reuhl Products, Inc.

Reuhl Products, Inc.
4505 Belt Line Hwy, R3
Madison, Wisconsin USA

What made Reuhl toys of Madison, Wisconsin, unique was that they were sold as diecast construction kits, with the emphasis on developing a child's manual dexterity. They were promoted in 1950 as educational "put-together" toys, requiring no glue or tools. Reuhl models were also available fully assembled, and some models were made of plastic, wood, fiberglas, or even Bakelite.

Reuhl's main source of revenue was through contracts with Caterpillar and Massey-Harris. When those contracts ended in 1958, so did the company.

Caterpillar D-7, T-4000.....................$450-500
Caterpillar Grader No. 12...........$1,800-2,000
Caterpillar Ripper $375-425
Caterpillar Scraper No. 70, 16" plastic,
S-4500....................................$650-750
Cedar Rapids Rock Crusher..........$1,100-1,250
Cedar Rapids Paver....................$150-200

DW-10 ....$700-800
Farmall Cub, T-3000, 6¼" $150-200
Lorain TL-25 Shovel.....................$1,425-1,675
Massey Harris Combine....................$375-425

Revell

Revell is best known for its 1:25 scale plastic model kits. But in 1960, Revell's British factory produced a number of diecast models for the British market.

In November 1997, Action Performance Companies Inc. announced that it had reached an agreement in principle to purchase the motorsports diecast collectibles business of Revell-Monogram Inc., by then a unit of Binney & Smith Inc. of Easton, Pennsylvania, for $15 million in cash, and also to form a broad-ranging and long-term strategic alliance with Revell-Monogram. The acquisition includes a 10-year licensing agreement that will provide Action with exclusive use of the trademarked brand names of Revell-Monogram's U.S. motorsports diecast product lines, "Revell Racing" and "Revell Collection," and existing U.S. distribution channels.

Action will exclusively market and distribute Revell-Monogram's plastic model kits into its trackside distribution channel and assist Revell-Monogram in obtaining motorsports merchandise licenses with drivers and racing teams for plastic model products.

Revell-Monogram, the world leader in plastic model kits, is a business unit of Binney & Smith, maker of Crayola and Liquitex brand products and a subsidiary of Hallmark cards Inc. of Kansas City, Missouri. Action Performance is the leader in the design, marketing, and distribution of licensed motorsports merchandise. Its products include a broad range of motorsports-related apparel, souvenirs, diecast car replica collectibles, and other memorabilia.

While Revell is best known for its plastic model kits, the company started a few years ago producing large scale car replicas that have established a loyal following for their accuracy, detail, and affordability. In addition, it seems that Revell produced a series of diecast Chryslers in approximately 1:64 scale some time in the late 1960s or early 1970s.

Revell-Monogram was purchased in 2001 by Alpha International, the low-key parent company to GearBox Collectibles.

British Revell Diecast Models
Ford Consul Deluxe Saloon, 1960,
    H-903-959..................................$75-90
Jaguar 2.4L. Saloon, 1960, H-902-958 ..$75-90

Morris 1000 Traveller, 1960,
    H-907-953................................$75-90
Rover 3L Saloon, 1960, H-900-956 ......$75-90
Triumph TR3 Roadster, 1960, H-905-951 ...$75-90
Vauxhall Cresta Saloon, 1960,
    H-904-950..................................$75-90
Volkswagen 1200 Saloon, 1960,
    H-906-952..................................$75-90
Volkswagen Coupe Karmann-Ghia, 1960,
    H-901-957..................................$75-90

US Revell Diecast Models
1961 Chrysler Imperial Sedan, #714......$25-30
1961 Chrysler Windsor Convertible, #713 ...$25-30

Revell Lowrider Magazine, 1:64 scale
For 1999, Revell introduces a new series of 1:64 scale diecast models, this time representing low rider custom cars.
1971 Buick Riviera, "Green's Dragg'n," #3 ..$4-6
1939 Chevrolet Sedan Delivery, "Cherry
    Bomb," #4 ....$4-6

1947 Chevrolet Sedan, metallic red, #147 ..$4-6
1961 Chevrolet Impala, "Purple Rose," #1 ...$4-6
1964 Chevrolet Impala, "Castillo de Oro," #2..$4-6

1996 Chevrolet Impala, metallic greenish yellow $2-4

Revell 1:20 Scale Creative Masters
At least six Creative Masters models were produced around 1987 to 1988, according to Jon Pierce of Winder, Georgia. The only one he specifically mentions is the 427 Cobra as indicated below, which he says is no longer being produced.
427 Cobra $30-40

Revell 1:18 Scale
1965 Mustang Convertible, aqua with top
    down, #8753 ....$25-30
1969 Corvette Convertible, metallic blue
    with open top, #8691 ....$25-30
1969 Corvette Convertible, red with open

top, #8755 ....$25-30
1969 Mustang Convertible, red with top
    up, #8757 ....$25-30

Acura NSX, red with black roof, #8692...$25-30
BMW 850i Coupe, #8690 ....$25-30
Bugatti EB110, #8501 ....$25-30
Bugatti EB110S Sport, #8503.............$25-30
Ferrari Mythos, #8659 ....$25-30
Ferrari Mythos by Pininfarina, #8500.......$25-30

Goggomobil T250................................$25-30
Mercedes-Benz 500 SL Convertible, #8671 ..$25-30
Mercedes-Benz 500 SL Coupe, #8654...$25-30
Porsche 911 Turbo, top down, #8660 ....$25-30
Porsche 911 Turbo, top up, #8670 ....$25-30
Volkswagen Beetle Convertible, baby blue with
    black roof $25-30

Revell 1:12 Scale
1954 Mercedes-Benz 300 SLR, #8851.....$120
1962 Ferrari 250 GTO, #8853 ....$120

Revival

While Brumm of Italy produces a series called "Revival," it is not to be confused with Revival models, incidentally also from Italy. They are 1:20 scale models of incredible detail and accuracy. Most of the details are hidden beneath the cowlings.

1931-32 Alfa Romeo P3 Muletto $360-375
1932-35 Alfa Romeo P3 TF $400-425
1946-51 Alfa Romeo 159................$360-375
1936 Auto Union Tipo C $440-465
1936-37 Auto Union Tipo C Hillclimb ...$450-475
1937 Auto Union Tipo C Streamliner...$460-485
Auto Union Tipo C Avus $625-650
1924 Bugatti Type 35 TF..................$400-425

1952 Ferrari 500 F2 ....$360-375
1961 Ferrari 156 120 Degree $360-375
1907 Fiat F-2 130HP.................$350-365
1956 Lancia Ferrari D50 ....$390-415
1957 Maserati 250 ....$360-375
1938 Mercedes-Benz M163 ....$425-450

Rex/Rextoys

33, Avenue du Rumine
Lausanne, Switzerland

Around 1960, Rex produced a small assortment of diecast models from its original home in Germany. The company eventually moved to its most recent home in Lausanne, Switzerland. In the meantime, the company had apparently been out of business for some time before the rights were purchased to resume production. Latest reports indicate that Rex is again out of business.

Rex 1:43 Scale Models

1939 Cadillac Coupe de Ville, #2 ....$35-50
1939 Cadillac Coupe de Ville, #3 ....$35-50
1939 Cadillac 4-door Sedan, #4 ....$35-50
1939 Cadillac Roadster, #6 ....$35-50
1939 Cadillac 4-door Convertible, #12 ..$35-50
1938-40 Cadillac V-16 2-door Coupe $30-45
1938-40 Cadillac V-16 Cabriolet, top down.....$30-45
1938-40 Cadillac V-16 Formal Sedan.....$30-45
Chrysler Airflow 4-door Sedan,, #21 ....$35-50
1935 Ford T48 Fordor Sedan, olive & black,
    #42 ....$25-40
1935 Ford Van Army Ambulance, #45 ...$35-50
Ford Delivery "Bell Telephone," #45 ....$35-50
1935 Ford Woody Wagon, #46 ....$35-50
1935 Ford Woody Wagon, #47 ....$35-50
1935 Ford 4-door Sedan U.S.Army, #48....$35-50
1935 Ford 4-door Sedan Taxi, #50.......$35-50
1935 Ford 4-door Sedan Police, #51 .....$35-50
1935 Ford Coupe, #52 ....$25-40
1935 Ford Coupe, #53 ....$35-50
1935 Ford Coupe Fire, #54 ....$35-50
1935 Ford Coupe Police, #55 ....$35-50
1935 Ford Coupe, Ghost Patrol, #56 .....$35-50
1961 Ford Thunderbird, 4⅝".................$75-90
Mercedes-Benz 300SL Roadster, 4",1959..$65-80
Opel Kapitän Sedan, 4½", 1959.............$65-80
1940 Packard Super 8 Sedan, #61 ....$35-50
Rolls-Royce Phantom, #33......................$35-50

Rex 1:87 Scale (Ho Gauge) Models

Ford Taunus Sedan, 2⅛", 1:87...............$15-25
Volkswagen Transporter, 1¾", 1:87.........$15-25

RHI

Particularly crude little toys seem to be typical of the RHI brand made in Japan.

Camper $1-2
Wrecker............................$1-2

Rhino

Rhino Toys Manufacturing Ltd.
Unit 11, 4/F,. Harbour Centre, Tower 1, Hunghom, Kowloon, Hong Kong

Rhino toys generally fall into the category of generic toys. The definition of "generic" in this case is any toy that, once taken out of its package, becomes an unmarked and unidentifiable toy.

While they are lightweight with lots of plastic components, Rhino does however present a few twists that set them apart from other generic toys. Their various farm sets that include tractors, milk tankers, fences, buildings, and farmhands are a good value as a toy. Collectibly speaking, these sets are attractive enough to maintain their original value but not likely to increase past retail price in terms of rising collector value for several decades.

Richmond

The previously unheard-of Richmond firm apparently produced an all-metal wrecker, color blue, with a seal on top saying "another fine Richmond scale model." More information is needed.

Richmond Toys (also see Papillon Toys)

87 High Street
Whitton, Twickenham
Middlesex, TW2 7LD, United Kingdom
phone: (+44) 0208 755 3637
fax: (+44) 0208 893 8077
email: papillontoys@ukgateway.net
www.papillontoys.co.uk/

Richmond Toys, the diecast division of Papillon Toys, offers a selection of licensed toys from British classic TV shows like *The Sweeney, Minder* and *Sooty*. In addition is an assortment of fire engines, police cars and ambulances from *London's Burning* and *The Bill*. Other categories include milk floats, London Fire Brigade and Crime Stopper vehicles. Richmond Toys are a subsidiary of Papillon Toys of Great Britain.

Fire Engine, 5⅛"
    Blackwall livery, from the TV series
        London's Burning, 5" $15-18
    Oxfordshire $15-18
    Bow $15-18
    Bromley $15-18
    Chelsea $15-18
    Euston $15-18

Hampshire $15-18
Hayes $15-18
Heston $15-18
Hornsey $15-18
Ilford $15-18
Leyton $15-18
Somerset $15-18
Southwark $15-18
Strathclyde $15-18
Sutton $15-18
Tooting $15-18
Land Rover Discovery 4x4, from the British
    TV series *The Bill*, 4-¾".........$9-11
Ambulance, 4½"
    London Ambulance Service...............$10-12
    Diana, Princess of Wales Children's
        Hospital, Birmingham Ambulance
        (Limited Edition)........................$16-20
    Great Ormond Street Hospital Ambulance
        (Limited Edition) $16-20
    St Johns Ambulance (Limited Edition) $16-20
Milk Float, 3-wheel, 2¹⁵⁄₁₆"
    Dairy Dairy, blue $8-10
    Express Dairy, white $12-15
Ford Granada Consul, from the TV series
    The Sweeney, 4¾"........................$20-24
Ford Model A Delivery Van, 2¹⁵⁄₁₆"
    Dairy Dairy, cream $8-10
    NDBI Home & Life, white $8-10
Minder car, from the British TV series
    Minder $20-24
Scampi's Emergency Services, from the British
    TV series *The Sooty Show* $8-10
Sooty's Coach, from the British TV series
    The Sooty Show $8-10
Sooty's Police car, from the British TV series
    The Sooty Show $8-10
Sue's Ambulance, from the British TV series
    The Sooty Show $8-10
Summer Holiday Bus.....................$12-14
Sweep's Fire Engine, from the British TV series
    The Sooty Show $8-10
Vauxhall Omega police car
    with Sunhill markings, from the British TV
        series *The Bill*, 4½".................$8-10
    with Crimestoppers markings, from the
        British TV series *Crimestoppers*,
        4½" $9-11

Rich Toys

One model, the Bluebird record car, is known to have been produced by Richtoys in the latter half of the 1930s. The 1:50 scale model is made of plaster and flour, a material rarely used in England but more frequently used in France.

Bluebird V12 Rolls Royce Land Speed Record
Car (301.1 mph in 1935)...............$40-50

Ricko

Ricko Limited
4/F., Ming Sang Industrial Building
19 Hing Yip Street, Kwun Tong,
Kowloon, Hong Kong, China
tel: (852)2951-0873
fax: (852)2793-2277

Ricko US Wholesale Distributor:
M & D International Distributors, Inc
DBA Ricko America
PO Box 292946
Davie, Florida 33329-2946
phone: (954) 792-2025
fax: (954) 792-2026
e-mail: sales@rickoamerica.com
website: www.rickoamerica.com

The Ricko America website describes the Ricko product line as "a great new line of 1:18 diecast cars for your collection. Our subject matter is uncommon and distinctly continental! We feature modern and vintage BMW, Mercedes, Alfa, Lancia, and more. For the Euro Auto enthusiast there are models here you simply will not find anywhere else in the market. In addition to stock versions we have great Rally cars that are packed with the kind of subtle details that really turn collectors on!

"Ricko is brand new in the US market, and we are happy to say that the initial reaction to our line has been overwhelmingly positive. Because of the immediate loyalty of the US die cast customer, Ricko will focus on US subject matter this year and next, offering great new models of modern and vintage US cars including Lincoln, Cadillac, and Vector. Releases will begin in October 2003 and continue through 2004."

1968 Alfa Romeo 33.2
    Daytona, red, #32132R, February 2004..$40-45
    #23 Andretti/Bianchi, #32145,
        February 2004 ....$40-45
    #22 Casoni/Biscaldi, #32144,
        February 2004 ....$40-45
    Museo, #32143, February 2004......$40-45
    Imola #2 Casoni Dini, #32146,
        February 2004 ....$40-45
    Mugello #7 Facetti/Biscaldi,
        #32147, 2004 ....$40-45
    Targa Florio #182 Baghetti/
        Biscaldi, #32148, 2004 ....$40-45
    Targa Florio #262 De Adamich,
        #32149, 2004 ....$40-45

Alfa 147
    Cup version, red, #32136R..............$40-45
    red, #32111R........................$40-45
    silver, #32111S $40-45

Alfa 156 GTA
    red, #32139, end of August 2004....$40-45
    black, #32139, end of August 2004 ...$40-45
    Racing, red, #32139, end of
        August 2004 ....$40-45
    Racing, 2004, #32140 ....$40-45

2000 Alfa Romeo Spider Veloce
    black, #32107B, February 2004......$40-45
    red, #32107R, February 2004 ....$40-45

1936 BMW 328 Roadster
    blue, #32133R.........................$40-45
    dark brown, #32105B.................$40-45
    silver, #32105S $40-45

1956 BMW 507
    blue, #32106B........................$40-45
    red, #32106R $40-45

BMW DIXI
    #32138, 2004 ....$40-45

BMW Z4
    metallic blue, #32117B, February 2004 ..$40-45
    metallic gray, #32117G, February
        2004..$40-45
    red, #32117R $40-45

1934 Cadillac V16
    #32131, 2004 ....$40-45

2003 Cadillac Escalade ESV
    black, #32129, mid-June 2004 ....$40-45
    white, #32129, mid-June 2004 ....$40-45

2003 Cadillac Sixteen
    black, #32126, early July 2004........$40-45

2004 Cadillac CTS V Series
    black, #32134, mid-June 2004 ....$40-45
    silver, #32134, mid-June 2004 ....$40-45

1986 Ford RS 200
    white, #32137, early June 2004.......$40-45
    Rally, blue, #32121, early June 2004...$40-45

1935 Horch 851 Pullman
    black, #32109B, February 2004......$40-45
    moss green, #32109G $40-45

1937 Horch 930V Limousine
    black, #32152, mid-June 2004 ....$40-45
    yellow, #32152Y, 2004 ....$40-45

Lancia Delta HF
    Astra, #32125, 2004 ....$40-45
    Esso, #32112 ....$40-45
    Martini Monte Carlo, #32123, 2004..$40-45
    Oikos, #32118, 2004 ....$40-45
    Repsol, #32110, February 2004 ......$40-45
    Sitma, #32116, 2004 ....$40-45
    Totip, #32124, 2004 ....$40-45
    Integrale Evo 2, black, #32113B,
        February 2004 ....$40-45

Integrale Evo 2 Rally, #32114R........$40-45
Integrale Evo 2, red, #32113R.........$40-45
Integrale Evo 2, yellow, #32113Y $40-45

1934 Lincoln Model K
    black, #32120B, 2004...................$40-45

1963 Lincoln Continental Convertible
    yellow, #32122, end of June 2004...$40-45

1927 Mercedes Benz 630K
    red, #32101R, February 2004........$40-45

1952 Mercedes Benz 300SL W194
    #32115R, February 2004 ....$40-45

1955 Mercedes Benz Type 300c
    Cabriolet, black, #32127B $40-45
    Cabriolet, cream, #32127C.............$40-45
    Coupe, black, #32102B, February 2004 ...$40-45
    Coupe black and silver, #32102S.....$40-45
    Coupe, cream, #32102C...............$40-45

1981 Mercedes Benz 500SLC
    Champagne, #32103C $40-45
    Rally, #32104R.........................$40-45
    red, #32103R, February 2004 ....$40-45
    yellow, #32101Y.......................$40-45

Vector W8 Twin Turbo
    black, #32119B, February 2004......$40-45
    red, #32119R, February 2004 ....$40-45

1936 Wanderer W25K Roadster
green, #32108G $40-45
ivory, #32108V $40-45

Rio

One of the most popular brands of high-quality 1:43 scale model vehicles is Rio of Italy. Begun in 1961 by Reno Tattarletti and continued by his son Massimo, Rio is still in business producing excellent models in various scales. Dr. Force's book *Classic Miniature Vehicles Made in Italy* devotes nine pages to detailing the Rio line. This book presents just a brief summary of Rio models.

Alfa Ricotti 1914
    1973, #55 ....$25-30
    1981, #81 ....$25-30

Alfa Romeo
    1932 6C 1750, 1965, #19..........$25-30
    1932 B-Type, 1962, #5.................$25-30
    1934 B-Type Targa Florio, 1980, #70 .....$25-30
    1935 B-Type Hill Climb car, 1980, #71 ..$25-30

Bianchi
    1905 Landaulet, 1967, #28 ....$25-30
    1906 Coupe De Ville, 1965, #18....$25-30
    1909 Closed Landaulet, 1963, #10...$25-30
    1909 Open Landaulet, 1963, #11...$25-30

Bugatti
    1927 Royale, top up, 1968, #36.....$25-30
    1927 Royale, top down, 1968, #37..$25-30

1927 Royale Double Sedan, 1976, #66 ..$25-30
1927 Type 41 Royale, 1972, #54 ...$25-30
1929 Royale Coupe, 1981, #74 .....$25-30
1931 Type 50 Le Mans, 1985,
    #1002.......................................$25-30
1932 Type 50 Sport Coupe, 1970,
    #48..$25-30
1933 Type 501983, #1001 ....$25-30
1938 57C Atlantic Coupe, 1981,
    #78 ....$25-30
1938 57C Atlantic Coupe,
    1982, #1000..............................$25-30
Royale Torpedo, top up, 1990, #94 ...$25-30
Royale Torpedo, top down, 1990, #95 ....$25-30
Royale Weymann, 1990, #96 ....$25-30

Cadillac 1931 V16
    top up, 1981, #76........................$25-30
    top down, 1981, #77 ....$25-30
Chalmers-Detroit 1909, 1964, #16 ....$25-30
Citroën
    1956 Cabriolet, open top, #98 ....$25-30
    1956 DS19 Sedan, #97 ....$25-30,
    1958 ID19 Station Wagon, #99 .....$25-30,
    1959 DS19 Monte Carlo, #109 .....$25-30,
    1962 Fire Ambulance, #117 ....$25-30,
    ID19 Ambulance, #116 ....$25-30,
    ID19 Sedan, #111..........................$25-30,
    De Dion-Bouton 1894 Steam Victoria,
    1967, #30..................................$25-30
Delahaye 1935 135M, 1976, #63.......$25-30
Deusenberg
    1933 SJ Spider, 1987, #86 ....$25-30
    1934 SJ Phaeton, closed top, 1969,
    #45...$25-30
    1934 SJ Phaeton, open top, 1969, #46 ...$25-30
Ferrari
    1967 365 GTB Daytona, red, 1986,
    #200..$25-30
    1967 365 GTB Daytona, same as 200,
    #R1..$25-30
    1967 365 GTB Daytona Spider, black,
    1986, #201 ....$25-30
    1967 365 GTB Daytona Spider, same as
    201, #R2 ....$25-30
    1967 365 GTB4 Daytona, red, 1989,
    #110..$25-30
    1967 365 GTB4 Daytona Spider, 1989,
    #120..$25-30
    1967 365 GTB4 Daytona Spider, 1990,
    #121..$25-30
    1973 365 GTB Daytona Spider, same as
    202, #R3 ....$25-30
    1973 365 GTB Le Mans, 1989, #202..$25-30
    1973 365 GTB4 Le Mans, 1989, #130 ..$25-30
Fiat
    1901 8 HP, 1967, #31 ....$25-30

1902 12 HP Tourer, 1966, #26 ......$25-30
1903 16-24 HP Tourer, 1967, #32 ...$25-30
1905 24 HP Limousine, 1967, #27 ..$25-30
1905 60 HP Tourer, top up, 1966,
    #23 ....$25-30
1905 60 HP Tourer, top down, 1966,
    #24 ....$25-30
1905 PS Limousine, 1981, #75........$25-30
1906 24 HP Double Phaeton, 1966,
    #25 ....$25-30
1908 18-24 HP Landaulet, 1969,
    #38 ....$25-30
1910 Type 2 Limousine, 1964, #14...$25-30
1912 Model O Open Spyder, 1963,
    #12 ....$25-30
1912 Model O Spyder, 1962, #7 ...$25-30
1912 Model O Tourer, 1962, #6.....$25-30
1914 18BKL Army Truck, 1982, #A1 ...$25-30
1914 18BKL Covered Truck, gray,
    1982, #A3 ....$25-30
1914 18BKL Open Truck, maroon,
    1982, #A4 ....$25-30
1914 18BKL Stake Truck, 1982, #A2 ..$25-30
1914 18BKL with Santa & present, limited
    edition, 1993, #CH93 ....$35-40
1915 18BL Bus, yellow, 1965, #20...$25-30
1915 18BL Bus, blue, 1986, #87 ....$25-30
1919 501 Sport, 1961, #3.............$25-30
1919 501 Tourer, 1961, #4............$25-30
1921 V12 Dorsay De Ville, 1971,
    #49...$25-30
1923 519 S Limousine, 1974, #59 ...$25-30
1923 519S Tourer, top up, 1974, #57 ..$25-30
1923 519 S Tourer, top down, 1974,
    #58 ....$25-30
1932 Balilla 2-door, 1964, #13.......$25-30
Ford
    1902 999, 1980, #69..................$25-30
    1956 Thunderbird Convertible, pale
    green, 1990, #R4 ....$25-30
    1956 Thunderbird Hardtop, lavender,
    1990, #R5 ....$25-30
General 1902 Grand Prix, 1973, #56 ...$25-30
Hispano-Suiza
    1932 Limousine, 1976, #65..........$25-30
    1932 Town car, 1975, #61 ....$25-30
    1936, top up, 1985, #83 ....$25-30
    1936, top down, 1985, #84..........$25-30
Isotta-Fraschini
    1924 Type 8A, no cab roof, 1962,
    #9...$30-35
    1924 Type 8A Spyder, 1964, #15 ...$25-30
    1924 Type 8A with cab roof, 1962,
    #8...$30-35
    1929, top up, 1976, #67 ....$25-30
    1929, top down, 1976, #68...........$25-30

1930 Castagna Torpedo, 1988, #89 ..$25-30
Itala
    1906 Peking-Paris, 1961, #2 ....$25-30
    1906 Targa Florio, 1961, #1...........$25-30
Lamborghini
    1968 Miura Roadster, top down, #R9 ..$35-40
    1968 Miura S Coupe, #R8 ....$35-40
Lancia 1929 Dilambda Torpedo
    green, 1969, #41.........................$25-30
    red, 1969, #42...........................$25-30
Le Jamais Contente 1899, 1975, #60 ....$25-30
Leyat 1923, 1976, #62 ....$25-30
Lincoln
    1928 Sport Phaeton, top up, 1971,
    #50..$25-30
    1928 Sport Phaeton, top down, 1971,
    #51..$25-30
    1941 Continental, top up, 1969,
    #43..$25-30
    191 top down, 1969, #44..............$25-30
    1941 Continental Coupe, 1985,
    #82..$25-30
Mercedes
    1908 70 HP Limousine, 1968, #33...$25-30
    1909 Open Tourer, 1964, #17........$25-30
Mercedes Simplex 1902, 1967, #29.....$25-30
Mercedes-Benz
    1927 SSK, 1981, #80 ....$25-30
    1931 SSKL, 1981, #79 ....$25-30
    1937 770K Pullman, 1985, #85 .....$25-30
    1937 Cabriolet, 1966, #21 ....$25-30
    1937 Cabriolet, 1966, #22 ....$25-30
    1955 190SL Convertible, white,
    1990, #R6 ....$25-30
    1955 190SL Convertible, cream,
    1990, #R7 ....$25-30
    1957 3001988, #90......................$25-30
    1960 300D, top up, #101 ....$25-30
    1960 300D, top down, #102 ....$25-30
    1960 300D Landau, #100 ....$30-35
    1960 300D Landau with Pope, #100P ..$35-40
    Hitler's 1942 770, 1976, #64........$45-50
Renault
    1907 Type X Double Sedan, 1968,
    #34..$25-30
    1910 Taxi De La Marne, 1968, #35 ..$25-30
    1923 40 HP Torpedo, top up, 1971,
    #52..$25-30
    1923 40 HP Torpedo, top down,
    1971, #53 ....$25-30
Rolls-Royce
    1923 20 top up, 1981, #72...........$25-30
    1923 20 top down, 1981, #73........$25-30
    1931 Phantom II, top up, 1969, #39...$25-30
    1931 Phantom II, top down, 1969,
    #40..$25-30

Thomas Flyer 1908 New York-Paris, 1970,
#47 ....$25-30

Volkswagen

1939 Beetle Cabriolet, top down,
#105 ....$25-30

1939 Beetle Sedan with Sunroof, #104.$25-30

1939 Beetle Split Window, #106.....$25-30

1939 Beetle Standard Hardtop, #103 ..$25-30

1949, 1988 (see 189-194), #88.....$25-30

1949 Beetle, black, 1988, #189 .....$25-30

1949 Beetle, gray, 1988, #190 ......$25-30

1949 Beetle, red, 1988, #191 ....$25-30

1949 Beetle, green, 1988, #192.....$25-30

1949 Beetle, cream, 1988, #193 ....$25-30

1949 Beetle, blue, 1988, #194.......$25-30

1949 Beetle Cabriolet, top down,
1990, #92 ....$25-30

1949 Beetle Cabriolet, top up,1990,
#93 ....$25-30

1950 Beetle, top down, #107.........$25-30

1953 Beetle, ivory, 1990, #91 ....$25-30

1953 Beetle, charcoal gray, 1989,
#10200 ....$25-30

1953 Beetle, maroon,1989, #10201 ..$25-30

1953 Beetle, cream, 1989, #10202 ..$25-30

1955 One Millionth Beetle, #108 .....$25-30

Rivarossi

Rivarossi of Italy produced some interesting plastic Fiat and Mercedes models in 1:43 and 1:87 scales, specifically designed for railroad layouts. Their automotive replicas are now obsolete and out of production, and no model list is available.

In addition, Rivarossi has produced exquisite ship models and detail components.

River Series

Identifiable only by the name "River Series" and "J.L." on the key that winds their clockwork motors, River Series toys were produced by Jordan & Lewden, 52A Brooksby's Walk, Homerton, London E9, England, during the 1950s. Just prior to 1960, the dies were sent to Lincoln Industries Ltd. in New Zealand where they were produced as Lincoln Toys.

In the early 1960s, the dies went back to England and then to Israel for Gamda, at which time plastic windows were added, wheels were improved and two-tone paint jobs were applied. Due to their lack of markings, River Series cars have often been mistaken for DCMT Impy Lone Star Roadmaster models.

At least one model, the 1952 Standard Vanguard Phase II Estate, was reissued by Micro Models of Australia.

Three primary series were produced in the River Series line:

1. 1:40–1:45 scale cars with or without friction motors

2. Two types of lorries (flatbed trucks), a forward control lorry and an articulated lorry, in 1:55–1:60 scale and offered in civilian and military versions

3. A series of railway locomotives

River Series Cars

Austin A40 Somerset, 98mm $60-75
with original box...........................$85-100

Buick 1953 Coupe. 108mm.............$60-75
with original box...........................$85-100

Daimler Conquest, 100mm.................$60-75
with original box...........................$85-100

Ford Prefect 100E, 97mm................$60-75
with original box...........................$85-100

Standard Vanguard 2-door Estate car,
98mm..$60-75
with original box...........................$85-100

Standard Vanguard Phase II Saloon,101mm...$60-75
with original box...........................$85-100

River Series Trucks

Articulated Flat Lorry, 145mm.................$75-90
with original box...........................$90-120

Articulated Tanker, 151mm.....................$75-90
with original box...........................$90-120

Cable Layer...................................$75-90
with original box...........................$90-12

Car carrier with four miniature cars, 94mm...$75-90
with original box...........................$90-120

Excavator,114mm..............................$75-90
with original box...........................$90-120

Gully Emptier with movable boom extending
over the cab................................$75-90
with original box...........................$90-120

Horse Transporter.............................$75-90
with original box...........................$90-120

River Transport Lorry with two miniature
cars, 101mm $75-90
with original box...........................$90-120

Tipper Lorry, 94mm $75-90
with original box...........................$90-120

Tower Wagon, 94mm...........................$75-90
with original box...........................$90-120

River "Here Comes the Army" Series

Armoured car, 97mm $75-90
with original box $90-120

Army Covered Wagon $75-90
with original box...........................$90-120

Army Crane, 94mm $75-90
with original box $90-120

Army Open Wagon, Limber and Field
Gun..$75-90

with original box...........................$90-120

Army Tanker, 101mm $75-90
with original box...........................$90-120

Army Articulated Low Loader, 163mm......$75-90
with original box...........................$90-120

Field Gun, 101mm............................$45-60
with original box...........................$85-100

Limber, 63mm $35-45
with original box...........................$55-65

River Series Railway Locomotives

Furness Railway "Old Copperknob,"
90mm..$45-60
in original box.............................$85-100

GNR Stirling No. 1, 110mm................$45-60
with original box...........................$85-100

LNWR 2-4-0 Locomotive, 105mm...........$45-60
with original box...........................$85-100

Stephenson's Rocket, 48mm................$45-60
with original box...........................$85-100

Roach Industries

E. R. Roach Industries of Mount Vernon, Ohio, is known to have produced one large diecast toy race car made in 1945.

Old Racer, 10¼", red, hard black rubber tires,
spare tire on rear $60-85

Road Champs

Road Champs, Inc.
a subsidiary of JAKKS Pacific, Inc
22761 Pacific Coast Highway, Suite 226
Malibu, CA 90265 USA

As early as 1980, Road Champs produced various 1:64 scale toy cars with opening doors under the auspices of JRI (Jack Robbins Inc.), founded by Jack Robbins and originally based in a suburb of Philadelphia. One of many new arrivals on the diecast market, Road Champs moved to Harrison, West Caldwell, then Union, New Jersey.

Road Champs made its mark in 1993 with its introduction of a nine-car series of 1993 Chevrolet Caprice State Police cars. The ever-expanding series features relatively faithful 1:43 scale reproductions of U.S. and Canadian police cruisers with more Caprice variations, the addition of 1994 Ford Crown Victoria, a 1996 Chevrolet Suburban, and a 1998 Ford Crown Victoria multiply the number of police cars added every year.

Now owned by Jakks Pacific, Road Champs are making an even bigger mark on the diecast toy industry with new models and packaging more focused toward the adult collector.

Before the highly popular state police series, the 1:87 scale "Anteaters" series, named after those curved-nose semi tractors, was the primary item marketed by Road Champs. They remain a popular segment of the Road Champs line-up, now marketed simply as Die Cast Cabs & Trailers.

1:64 scale offerings include Country Tour Buses, a now discontinued series that featured graphics and names of several country music stars; their Fire Rescue Series is still a popular line of models of firefighting equipment, including International and Boardman trucks, and most recently Chevrolet Suburbans; the Deluxe series continues to offer the unusual items such as a Zamboni, International Ramp Wreck Truck, garbage and recycling trucks, an International school bus, and Mercedes stretch limousines.

1:87 scale buses are another currently popular but hard to find assortment that includes a classic grayhound bus and several liveries of city and municipal buses.

The popularity of Road Champs has grown with the expanding police car series, and Road Champs has catered to collectors by producing a great assortment of vintage automobiles in 1:43 scale.

Unfortunately, the direction of Road Champs has changed since 2002, and the focus has shifted away from 1:43 scale diecast and toward plastic Motocross toys and electronic interactive toys.

Road Champs State, U.S. Territory & Canada Provincial Police Vehicles, 1:43 Scale

A perennial favorite with collectors, the Pennsylvania police car issued in 1993 was reportedly worth $250 according to the back of 1999 Road Champs Police car packages.

Alabama, 1957 Ford Crown Victoria, 1998 issue..$6-8
Alabama, 1993 Chevrolet Caprice, no license plate, closed wheel wells........$20-25
Alabama, 1993 Chevrolet Caprice, 1996 license plate, closed wheel wells........$10-12
Alabama, 1998 Ford Crown Victoria, 1998 license plate................................$6-8
Alaska, 1955 Chevrolet Bel Air, 1998 issue..$6-8
Alaska, 1993 Chevrolet Caprice, 1996 license plate, closed wheel wells........$10-12
Alaska, 1998 Ford Crown Victoria, 1998 license plate (never produced)
Arizona, 1957 Ford Crown Victoria, 1998 issue..$6-8
Arizona, 1993 Chevrolet Caprice, no license plate....................................$20-25
Arizona, 1993 Chevrolet Caprice, 1996 license plate....................................$10-12

Arizona, 1993 Chevrolet Caprice, 1997 license plate, open wheel wells.............$7-9
Arkansas, 1957 Ford Crown Victoria, 1998 issue..................................$6-8
Arkansas, 1993 Chevrolet Caprice, no license plate, closed wheel wells..................$20-25
Arkansas, 1993 Chevrolet Caprice, 1995 license plate, closed wheel wells........$12-15
Arkansas, 1993 Chevrolet Caprice, 1996 license plate, closed wheel wells........$10-12
Arkansas, 1998 Ford Crown Victoria, 1998 license plate....................................$7-9
Arkansas, 1998 Ford Crown Victoria, 1999 license plate....................................$6-8
California, 1957 Ford Crown Victoria, 1998 issue..................................$6-8
California, 1993 Chevrolet Caprice, no license plate, closed wheel wells........$20-25
California, 1993 Chevrolet Caprice, 1995 license plate, closed wheel wells........$12-15
California, 1993 Chevrolet Caprice, 1996 license plate, closed wheel wells........$10-12
California, 1993 Chevrolet Caprice, 1996 license plate, open wheel wells..........$10-12
California, 1998 Ford Crown Victoria, 1998 ..$6-8
Colorado, 1957 Ford Crown Victoria, 1998 issue..................................$6-8
Colorado, 1993 Chevrolet Caprice, 1996, closed wheel wells..........................$10-12
Colorado, 1993 Chevrolet Caprice, 1997, open wheel wells..............................$8-10
Colorado, 1998 Ford Crown Victoria, 1998 license plate....................................$6-8
Florida, 1957 Ford Crown Victoria, 1998 issue...$6-8
Florida, 1994 Ford Crown Victoria, no license plate................................$16-20
Florida, 1994 Ford Crown Victoria, 1996 license plate................................$10-12
Florida, 1998 Ford Crown Victoria, 1998 license plate................................$6-8
Georgia, 1957 Ford Crown Victoria, 1998 issue..................................$6-8
Georgia, 1993 Chevrolet Caprice, no license plate, closed wheel wells..................$20-25
Georgia, 1994 Ford Crown Victoria, 1996 license plate, open wheel wells..........$10-12
Georgia, 1998 Ford Crown Victoria, 1998 license plate....................................$6-8
Georgia, 1999 Ford Crown Victoria with matching pin, 1999 license plate...........$7-9
Idaho, 1957 Ford Crown Victoria, 1998 issue..................................$6-8
Idaho, 1993 Chevrolet Caprice, 1996 license plate, closed wheel wells.................$10-12
Idaho, 1993 Chevrolet Caprice, 1996 license plate, open wheel wells....................$10-12

Idaho, 1998 Ford Crown Victoria, 1998 license plate..................................$6-8
Illinois, 1957 Ford Crown Victoria, 1998 issue..................................$6-8
Illinois, 1993 Chevrolet Caprice, no license plate, closed wheel wells..................$20-25
Illinois, 1993 Chevrolet Caprice, 1995 license plate, closed wheel wells........$12-15
Illinois, 1993 Chevrolet Caprice, 1996 license plate, closed wheel wells........$10-12
Illinois, 1998 Ford Crown Victoria, 1998 license plate....................................$6-8
Indiana, 1957 Ford Crown Victoria, 1998 issue..................................$6-8
Indiana, 1994 Ford Crown Victoria, 1996 license plate....................................$10-12
Indiana, 1998 Ford Crown Victoria, 1998 license plate....................................$6-8
Iowa, 1957 Ford Crown Victoria, 1998 issue..................................$6-8
Iowa, 1994 Ford Crown Victoria, 1997 license plate....................................$8-10
Iowa, 1998 Ford Crown Victoria, 1998 license plate....................................$6-8
Kansas, 1957 Ford Crown Victoria, 1998 issue...$6-8
Kansas, 1994 Ford Crown Victoria, 1996 license plate....................................$10-12
Kansas, 1998 Ford Crown Victoria, 1998 license plate....................................$6-8
Kentucky, 1957 Ford Crown Victoria, 1998 issue..................................$6-8
Kentucky, 1994 Ford Crown Victoria, 1996 license plate $10-12
Kentucky, 1994 Ford Crown Victoria, 1997 license plate $8-10
Louisiana, 1955 Chevrolet Bel Air, 1998 issue..$6-8
Lousiana, 1994 Ford Crown Victoria, no license plate.................................$15-20
Lousiana, 1994 Ford Crown Victoria, 1995 license plate $12-15
Lousiana, 1994 Ford Crown Victoria, 1996 license plate $10-12
Louisiana, 1998 Ford Crown Victoria, 1998 license plate.............................$6-8
Maine, 1993 Chevrolet Caprice, 1996 license plate, open wheel wells..........$10-12
Maine, 1998 Ford Crown Victoria, 1998 license plate....................................$6-8
Maryland, 1957 Ford Crown Victoria, 1998 issue..................................$6-8
Maryland, 1993 Chevrolet Caprice, no license plate, closed wheel wells........$20-25
Maryland, 1993 Chevrolet Caprice, 1996 license plate, closed wheel wells........$10-12
Maryland, 1993 Chevrolet Caprice, 1997 license plate, open wheel wells...........$8-10

Maryland, 1998 Ford Crown Victoria, 1998 license plate $6-8

Massachusetts, 1994 Ford Crown Victoria, 1997 license plate $8-10

Massachusetts, 1998 Ford Crown Victoria, 1998 license plate..........$6-8

Massachusetts, 1999 Ford Crown Victoria with matching pin, 1999 license plate..........$7-9

Michigan, 1957 Ford Crown Victoria, 1998 issue $6-8

Michigan, 1993 Chevrolet Caprice, no license plate, closed wheel wells $20-25

Michigan, 1993 Chevrolet Caprice, 1995 license plate, closed wheel wells........$12-15

Michigan, 1993 Chevrolet Caprice, 1996 license plate, closed wheel wells, Dare Logo $10-12

Michigan, 1998 Ford Crown Victoria, 1998 license plate..........$6-8

Michigan, 1999 Ford Crown Victoria, 1999 license plate, 10,000 Limited Edition with Brass Lapel Pin..........$8-10

Minnesota, 1993 Chevrolet Caprice, no license plate, closed wheel wells $20-25

Minnesota, 1993 Chevrolet Caprice, 1996 license plate, closed wheel wells........$10-12

Minnesota, 1998 Ford Crown Victoria, 1998 license plate $6-8

Mississippi, 1994 Ford Crown Victoria, 1996 license plate..........$10-12

Mississippi, 1994 Ford Crown Victoria, 1997 license plate $8-10

Mississippi, 1998 Ford Crown Victoria, 1998 license plate $6-8

Missouri,1957 Ford Crown Victoria,1998 issue ..$6-8

Missouri, 1994 Ford Crown Victoria, no license plate $15-20

Missouri, 1994 Ford Crown Victoria, 1996 license plate..........$10-12

Missouri (red), 1998 Ford Crown Victoria, 1998 license plate $6-8

Missouri (blue), 1998 Ford Crown Victoria, 1998 license plate $6-8

Montana,1955 Chevrolet Bel Air,1998 issue ..$6-8

Montana, 1994 Ford Crown Victoria, 1997 license plate $8-10

Nebraska, 1957 Ford Fairlane, 1998 issue ..$8-10

Nebraska, 1994 Ford Crown Victoria, 1996 license plate..........$10-12

Nebraska, 1998 Ford Crown Victoria, 1998 license plate $6-8

Nevada, 1993 Chevrolet Caprice, no license plate, closed wheel wells $20-25

Nevada, 1993 Chevrolet Caprice, 1996 license plate, closed wheel wells........$10-12

Nevada, 1998 Ford Crown Victoria, 1998 license plate $6-8

New Jersey, 1957 Ford Crown Victoria, 1998 issue $6-8

New Jersey, 1993 Chevrolet Caprice, no license plate, closed wheel wells $20-25

New Jersey, 1993 Chevrolet Caprice, 1996 license plate, closed wheel wells........$10-12

New Jersey, 1998 Ford Crown Victoria, 1998 license plate $6-8

New Mexico,1957 Ford Fairlane,1998 issue ..$8-10

New Mexico, 1993 Chevrolet Caprice, 1995 license plate, closed wheel wells........$12-15

New Mexico, 1993 Chevrolet Caprice, 1996 license plate, open wheel wells..........$10-12

New Mexico, 1998 Ford Crown Victoria, 1998 license plate $6-8

New York, 1957 Ford Crown Victoria, 1998 issue ..$6-8

New York, 1993 Chevrolet Caprice, no license plate, closed wheel wells, light blue ..$150-175

New York, 1993 Chevrolet Caprice, no license plate, open wheel wells, light blue......$10-12

New York, 1993 Chevrolet Caprice, no license plate, open wheel wells, dark blue $10-12

New York, 1993 Chevrolet Caprice, 1996 license plate, closed wheel wells, dark blue......$10-12

New York, 1998 Ford Crown Victoria, 1998 license plate $6-8

New York, 1998 Chevrolet Camaro, 1999 license plate, 10,000 Limited Edition with Brass Lapel Pin..........$9-11

North Carolina, 1955 Chevrolet Bel Air, 1998 issue..........$6-8

North Carolina, 1993 Chevrolet Caprice, 1997 license plate $8-10

North Carolina, 1998 Ford Crown Victoria, 1998 license plate..........$6-8

North Dakota, 1994 Ford Crown Victoria, 1996 license plate $10-12

North Dakota, 1998 Ford Crown Victoria, 1998 license plate (never produced)

Ohio, 1955 Chevrolet Bel Air, 1998 issue ...$6-8

Ohio, 1993 Chevrolet Caprice, no license plate, closed wheel wells, Anniversary $70-100

Ohio, 1993 Chevrolet Caprice, 1996 license plate, closed wheel wells, Normal......$10-12

Ohio, 1998 Ford Crown Victoria, 1998 license plate $6-8

Oklahoma, 1993 Chevrolet Caprice, no license plate, closed wheel wells $20-25

Oklahoma, 1993 Chevrolet Caprice, 1996 license plate, closed wheel wells........$10-12

Oklahoma, 1993 Chevrolet Caprice, 1997 license plate, open wheel wells..........$7-9

Oklahoma, 1998 Ford Crown Victoria, 1998 license plate (never produced)

Ontario Provincial Police, 1994 Ford Crown Victoria, 1996 license plate $10-12

Oregon, 1993 Chevrolet Caprice, no license plate, closed wheel wells $20-25

Oregon, 1994 Ford Crown Victoria, 1996 license plate, open wheel wells..........$10-12

Oregon, 1998 Ford Crown Victoria, 1998 license plate (never produced)

Pennsylvania, 1993 Chevrolet Caprice...$250-300

Puerto Rico, 1994 Ford Crown Victoria, 1997 license plate $8-10

Quebec Provincial Police, 1993 Chevrolet Caprice, no license plate, closed wheel wells $20-25

Quebec Provincial Police, 1993 Chevrolet Caprice, 1996 license plate, closed wheel wells $10-12

Royal Canadian Mounted Police, 1993 Caprice, no license plate, closed wheel wells ...$20-25

Royal Canadian Mounted Police, 1993 Caprice, 1995 license plate, closed wheel wells $12-15

Rhode Island, 1994 Ford Crown Victoria, no license plate..........$16-20

Rhode Island, 1994 Ford Crown Victoria, 1996 license plate $10-12

Rhode Island, 1998 Ford Crown Victoria, 1998 license plate $6-8

South Carolina, 1993 Chevrolet Caprice, no license plate..........$20-25

South Carolina, 1993 Chevrolet Caprice, 1996 license plate $10-12

South Carolina, 1998 Ford Crown Victoria, 1998 license plate (never produced)

South Dakota, 1994 Ford Crown Victoria, 1996 license plate $10-12

South Dakota, 1998 Ford Crown Victoria, 1998 license plate..........$6-8

Tennessee, 1957 Ford Fairlane, 1998 issue ..$8-10

Tennessee, 1993 Chevrolet Caprice, 1996 license plate $10-12

Tennessee, 1998 Ford Crown Victoria, 1998 license plate $6-8

Texas,1957 Ford Crown Victoria,1998 issue...$6-8

Texas, 1993 Chevrolet Caprice, 1996 license plate, closed wheel wells........$10-12

Texas, 1993 Chevrolet Caprice, 1996 license plate, open wheel wells..........$10-12

Texas, 1998 Ford Crown Victoria, 1998 license plate $6-8

Utah, 1993 Chevrolet Caprice, 1995 license plate, closed wheel wells $12-15

Utah, 1993 Chevrolet Caprice, 1996 license plate, closed wheel wells $10-12

Utah, 1998 Ford Crown Victoria, 1998 license plate (never produced)

Vermont, 1993 Chevrolet Caprice, 1996 license plate, closed wheel wells $10-12

Vermont, 1993 Chevrolet Caprice, 1997 license plate, open wheel wells $7-9

Vermont, 1998 Ford Crown Victoria, 1998 license plate $6-8

Virginia, 1993 Chevrolet Caprice, no license plate $20-25

Virginia, 1993 Chevrolet Caprice, 1996 license plate, closed wheel wells $10-12

Virginia, 1998 Ford Crown Victoria, 1998 license plate $6-8

Washington, 1994 Ford Crown Victoria, 1996 license plate $10-12

Washington, 1994 Ford Crown Victoria, 1997 license plate $8-10

Washington, 1998 Ford Crown Victoria, 1998 license plate.........................$6-8

Washington D.C., 1994 Ford Crown Victoria, 1995 license plate $12-15

Washington D.C., 1994 Ford Crown Victoria, 1996 license plate $10-12

Washington, DC, 1998 Ford Crown Victoria, 1998 license plate.........................$6-8

West Virginia, 1955 Chevrolet Bel Air, 1998 issue $6-8

West Virginia, 1993 Chevrolet Caprice, 1996 license plate $10-12

West Virginia, 1993 Chevrolet Caprice, 1997 license plate, open wheel wells ..$8-10

West Virginia, 1998 Ford Crown Victoria, 1998 license plate.........................$6-8

Wisconsin,1955 Chevrolet Bel Air,1998 issue...$6-8

Wisconsin, 1993 Chevrolet Caprice, no license plate, closed wheel wells $20-25

Wisconsin, 1993 Chevrolet Caprice, 1996 license plate, closed wheel wells $10-12

Wisconsin, 1998 Ford Crown Victoria, 1998 license plate (never produced)

Wyoming, 1994 Ford Crown Victoria, 1996 license plate.........................$10-12

Wyoming, 1994 Ford Crown Victoria, 1997 license plate.........................$8-10

Wyoming, 1998 Ford Crown Victoria, 1998 license plate (never produced)

Road Champs Captial City and Municipal Police and Taxis, 1:43 Scale

1997 Anaheim, CA $8-10
1997 Annapolis, MD $8-10
1996 Atlanta, GA $10-12
1999 Atlanta, GA,1999 Ford Crown Victoria, 10,000 Limited Edition with Brass Lapel Pin.........................$8-10
1997 Augusta, ME $8-10
1998 Austin, TX $6-8
1997 Baton Rouge, LA $8-10
1998 Bentonville, AR $6-8

1998 Bismarck, ND $6-8
1997 Boise, ID.........................$8-10
1999 Boston, MA (1999 Ford Crown Victoria) 10,000 Limited Edition with Brass Lapel Pin.........................$6-8
1996 Branson, MO $10-12
1997 Charleston, WV $8-10
1996 Chicago, IL $10-12
1997 Chicago, IL $8-10
1999 Chicago, IL, 1998 Ford Crown Victoria, 10,000 Limited Edition with Brass Lapel Pin.........................$8-10
1995 Chicago, IL Checker Taxi, 1993 Chevrolet Caprice.........................$15-20
1997 Columbia, SC $8-10
1997 Columbus, OH $8-10
1997 Denver, CO $8-10
1997 Des Moines, IA $8-10
1996 Dyersville, IA $10-12
1997 Gettysburg, PA $8-10
1998 Green Bay, WI $6-8
1997 Hartford, CT $8-10
1997 Helena, MT $8-10
1997 Indianapolis, IN $8-10
1997 Jackson, MS $8-10
1998 Jefferson City, MS $6-8
1999 Kansas City, MO, 1999 Ford Crown Victoria, 10,000 Limited Edition with Brass Lapel Pin.........................$9-11
1996 Lancaster, PA.........................$10-12
1996 Las Vegas, NV, 1994 Ford Crown Victoria.........................$8-10
1997 Las Vegas, NV.........................$8-10
1997 Little Rock, AR $8-10
1997 Lincoln, NE $8-10
1997 Louisville, KY $8-10
1998 Miami Beach, FL $6-8
1998 Montgomery, AL $6-8
1998 Montpelier, VT $6-8
1997 Montreal, Quebec $8-10
1997 Nashville, TN $8-10
1997 New Orleans, LA.........................$8-10
1995 New York City Taxi, 1993 Chevrolet Caprice, boxed $9-11
1996 Niagara Falls Regional PD, Ontario ..$10-12
1997 Niagara Regional Police, 1994 Ford Crown Victoria $8-10
1997 North Pole, AK $8-10
1998 Oklahoma City, OK $6-8
1998 Olympia, WA $6-8
1996 Orlando, FL $10-12
1997 Phoenix, AZ $8-10
1997 Port Authority, NY/NJ $8-10
199? Portland, OR $15-
1997 Providence, RI $8-10
1997 Richmond, VA.........................$8-10

1997 Sacramento, CA.........................$8-10
1998 St. Paul, MN $8-10
1997 Salt Lake City, UT $8-10
1997 Savannah, GA $8-10
1997 Springfield, IL $8-10
1997 Tallahassee, FL $8-10
1997 Topeka, KS $8
1997 Trenton, NJ $8-10
1996 U.S. Park Service $8-10
1996 Vancouver, BC $8-10

Other Road Champs Police and Fire Vehices, 1:43 Scale

Bowling Green, KY Fire Chief, Chevrolet Suburban.........................$6-8
Hartford, CT Fire Chief, Chevrolet Suburban ..$6-8
Lancaster, PA, Dodge Ram with Horse Trailer.........................$8-10
Nassau County, NY PD, Chevrolet Suburban with Horse Trailer $8-10
Nevada K-9, Chevrolet Suburban $6-8
New Jersey, Chevrolet Suburban $6-8
Philadelphia, PA Fire Chief, Chevrolet Suburban ...$6-8
Rhode Island, Chevrolet Suburban $6-8
St. Louis, MO Fire Chief, Chevrolet Suburban .$6-8
Washington, D.C., Chevrolet Blazer $8-10
West Virginia, Jeep Grand Cherokee $6-8

Road Champs Vintage Trucks, 1:43k Scale with matching billboard (65400 series) or without billboards (64500 series), introduced in 1998

#64500 Series without matching billboard
1953 Chevrolet Service Tow Truck, #64502.........................$7-9
1954 Chevrolet Pepsi Panel Van, #64505.........................$7-9
1956 Ford Texaco with Oil Drums, #64503.........................$7-9

1959 Chevrolet El Camino, #64504.........$7-9
1961 Chevrolet Apache, #64501 ....$7-9
#65400 Series with matching billboard
1961 Chevrolet Apache, #65401 ......$9-11
1953 Chevrolet Service Tow Truck, #65402.........................$9-11
1956 Ford Texaco with Oil Drums, #65403.........................$9-11
1959 Chevrolet El Camino, #65404...$9-11
1954 Chevrolet Pepsi Panel Van, #65405.........................$9-11

Road Champs Ford Truck Series–1:43 Scale, officially licensed by the Ford Motor Company

Ford Explorer
 red and beige, 1994 ....$4-6
 green and beige, 1994........................$4-6
Ford F100 1956 Pickup
 red, 1994 ....$4-6
 green, 1994 ....$4-6
Ford F150 Flareside Pickup
 metallic aqua, 1994 ....$4-6
 dark blue, 1994 ....$4-6

Road Champs Chevrolet Truck Series, 1:43 Scale

1953 Chevrolet C3100 Pickup
 orange, 1995 ....$4-6
 green, 1995 ....$4-6
 primer brown, 1995............................$5-7
1994 Chevrolet Suburban
 silver and black, 1994........................$4-6
 red/silver, 1994..................................$4-6
1994 Chevrolet Big Dooley Extended Cab
 Pickup, dual rear wheels
 black, 1994..$4-6
 burgundy, 1994 ....$4-6
1995 Chevrolet S-10 ZR2 with tool box
 black with silver trim, 1995....................$4-6
 red with black trim, 1995 ....$4-6
 Garden State Parkway Maintenance,
  yellow body with a silver tool box $7-9
1995 Chevrolet Blazer
 blue with silver trim...............................$4-6
 black with silver trim $4-6
 teal, 1995 ....$4-6

Road Champs Jeep Series, 1:43 Scale

1995 Jeep Grand Cherokee Limited
 black $4-6
 white $4-6
 silver $4-6
1995 Jeep YJ
 blue $4-6
 orange $4-6
 Sahara green $4-6

Road Chams Fabulous '50s, 1:43 Scale models with accompanying billboard, introduced in 1998

1955 Chevrolet Bel Air
 two-tone gray and tan $9-11
 two-tone white and red........................$9-11
1959 Chevrolet Impala
 Convertible, burnt orange $9-11
 Soft Top $9-11
 Hardtop $9-11

1957 Ford Fairlane
 Convertible..$9-11
 Convertible with Continental Kit $9-11
 Hardtop...$9-11
1955 Oldsmobile 98 Starfire Convertible
 two-tone blue and white $9-11
 two-tone orange-red and white $9-11
1958 Pontiac Bonneville Convertible
 pace car $9-11
 black $9-11
1958 Pontiac Bonneville Hardtop..............$9-11
1955 Pontiac Safari Station Wagon
 brown and white....................................$9-11
 blue and white $9-11

Road Champs Corvette Classics

Chevrolet Corvettes in 1:43 scale with commemorative metal license plate. According to Robert Jacaszek, probably only seven were produced. Others were, as described in Road Champs bulletins, either not produced or have been discontinued.
1953 Corvette Convertible, white, #61501...$9-11
1954 Corvette, #61505 ....$9-11
1955 Corvette Soft Top, #61504 if ever
 produced $18-23

1955 Corvette Hard Top V-8, red, #61506 ..$9-11
1957 Corvette (actually a 1955 with coves
 painted on) $9-11
1963 Corvette Split Window $9-11
1966 Corvette Stingray Hard Top (C-5),
 61511, if ever produced.................$18-23
1967 Corvette L88 Stingray Convertible (C2),
 61510, if ever produced.................$18-23
1975 Corvette, never produced
1978 25th Anniversary Corvette, silver,
 #61502 ....$9-11
1978 Corvette Indy Pace Car, black, 61507 $9-11
1982 Corvette Collector Edition (C-2) (never produced)
1983 Corvette Collector Edition, discontinued
 05/98, #61509, if ever produced ...$18-23
1984 Corvette Targa Top (C-4), discontinued
 05/98, #61513, if ever produced ...$18-23
1986 Corvette Indy Pace car discontinued
 05/98, #61514, if ever produced ...$18-23
1988 35th Anniversary Corvette, white, discontinued
 05/98, #61515, if ever produced $18-23
1993 40th Anniversary Corvette discontinued
 05/98, #61516, if ever produced ...$18-23
1997 Corvette (C-5), red, #61503 ....$9-11

1998 Corvette (C-5) Convertible, white,
 #61508 ....$9-11
1998 Corvette (C-5) Indy Pace Car, #61517 ..$9-11

Road Champs Muscle Cars, 1:43 Scale

1959 Chevrolet Camaro Hardtop Z-28 .....$9-11
1967 Chevrolet Camaro Hardtop Z-28 .....$9-11
1967 Chevrolet Camaro Convertible Pace
 Car...$9-11
1969 Chevrolet Camaro Convertible Pace
 Car...$9-11
1969 Dodge Charger Daytona $9-11
1969 Dodge Charger Standard $9-11
1968 Ford Mustang Boss 302 Louver Back..$9-11
1969 Pontiac GTO "The Judge" $9-11

Road Champions Collectibles Classic Scenes, 1999–1:43 scale–packaged in a clear display box with accessories

1953 Chevrolet 3100 Pickup
 Chevrolet, green with 6 oil drums in back and
  accessory engine $9-11

Texaco, red with gas pump, no pay load...$9-11
 Texaco, red with gas pump, six oil drums in
  back $9-11
 Goodyear, silver with 4 accessory tires..$9-11
1954 Chevrolet Panel Van, Pepsi-Cola, blue with
 matching handtruck $9-11

1959 Chevrolet El Camino, Pepsi-Cola, blue and white with matching vending machine $9-11

1956 Ford F-100 Pickup

Hershey's, chocolate brown with bottles of Hershey syrup in crate $9-11

Hershey's, chocolate brown with matching vending machine..........................$9-11
Ford, blue with six oil drums in back and accessory engine $9-11

Mobilgas, black with gas pump, no payload **$9-11**

Mobilgas, black with gas pump, six oil drums in back $9-11
Mobilgas, black with gas pump $9-11

Texaco, red with gas pump...................**$9-11**

Road Champions Collectibles Then & Now Sets, 1:43 Scale

1953 Chevrolet 3100 Pickup, turquoise, & 1995 Chevrolet S-10 Pickup, navy blue.......$12-15
1953 Chevrolet 3100 Pickup, orange with purple trim & 1995 Chevrolet S-10 Dually Pickup, red and black with silver and white accents $9-11
1953 Chevrolet Corvette, burgundy & 1998 Chevrolet Corvette, yellow.......$12-15
1955 Chevrolet Bel Air, Alaska Territorial Police & 1995 Chevrolet Caprice, Alaska State Trooper $12-15
1955 Chevrolet Bel Air, two-tone metallic light blue and white & 1997 Chevrolet Blazer, metallic olive green $12-15
1956 Ford F-100, black & 1993 Ford Explorer, metallic green gray with white, orange and pink trim $9-11
1957 Ford Fairlane, New York State Police & 1998 Ford Crown Victoria, New York State Police......................................$12-15
1961 Chevrolet Apache 10 Pickup, red & 1996 Chevrolet S-10 Pickup, blue with white & yellow trim..................................$12-15
1961 Chevrolet Apache 10 Pickup, gold with purple flames & 1996 Chevrolet S-10 Pickup, white with purple trim.........................$9-11
1969 Dodge Daytona, white with red tail stripe and spoiler & 1996 Dodge Ram Pickup, black with red and yellow flame accents.............$12-15

1969 Dodge Daytona, red with white tail stripe and spoiler & 1996 Dodge Ram Pickup, metallic light blue with bright pink accents ..$9-11

Road Champions Collectibles Cover Cars, 1:43 Scale, packaged in a clear display box with miniature magazine cover depicting the car

1955 Chevrolet Bel Air
  "Rod & Custom" magazine, red $8-10
  "Car Craft" magazine, yellow $8-10
1955 Chevrolet Corvette, "Corvette Fever" magazine, red $8-10
1969 Chevrolet Camaro, "Chevrolet High Performance" magazine, silver $8-10

1970 Chevrolet Chevelle, "Chevrolet High Performance" magazine, orange **$8-10**

Road Champions Collectibles Limited Edition Anniversary Cars, 1:43 Scale, packaged in clear plastic display box

30th Anniversary

1969 Chevrolet Camaro SS **$8-10**

1969 Dodge Daytona **$8-10**
1969 Hurst Oldsmobile 442.............$12-15

1969 Pontiac GTO **$8-10**
1969 Ford Mustang Boss $8-10
40th Anniversary:
  1959 El Camino $8-10

1959 Impala **$8-10**
50th Anniversary:
  1949 Mercury..................................$8-10
  1949 Oldsmobile $12-15
  1949 Ford Woody $15-

Road Champs Car & Driver Famous Highway Series

Porsche 959 ....$6-8
Plymouth Prowler.....................................$6-8
Dodge Viper..$6-8

Other Road Champs 1:43 Scale Vintage Cars

1932 Ford Coupe, several variations $6-8

1955 Chevrolet Bel Air, red **$6-8**

1949 Mercury, several variations including two stock and two custom $6-8
1955 Chevrolet Nomad, purple, Peterson Series I.............................$10-12

Road Champs Flip Tops–cars with lever on bottom that retracts the convertible top

Capri $5-7
Corvette $5-7
Mercedes...$5-7
Miata $5-7
Saab 900 ....$5-7
Volkswagen $5-7

Road Champs Boardman Emergency Vehicles, 1:64 Scale, introduced in 1995

Boardman Tower Unit
  Boston Fire Department........................$5-7
  St. Louis Fire Department $5-7
Washington, D. C. Fire Department $5-7
Boardman/International Fire Pumper
  Boston Fire Department........................$5-7
  St. Louis Fire Department $5-7
  Washington, D. C. Fire Department $5-7
Boardman/International JB-Res-Q
  Boston Fire Department........................$5-7

St. Louis Fire Department $5-7
Washington, D. C. Fire Department $5-7

Road Champs Deluxe Series, 1:64 Scale Commercial, Municipal, and Emergency Vehicles

American LaFrance Fire Engine with
   Movable Boom Crane $4-6
Delivery Van
   Cheetos $4-6
   Pepsi $4-6
   United States Postal Service $6-8
Elgin Pelican Street Sweeper $6-8
International
   Beverage Delivery Truck, Pepsi $4-6
   Beverage Delivery Truck, Snapple $4-
   Recycling Truck $4-6
   School Bus, Golden Rule $4-6
   School Bus $4-6
   Snow Plow Dump Truck, red with
      black accents, 1999 issue $4-6
   Wrecker, blue and white, 1999 issue $4-6

Jerr-Dan Auto Salvage Transporter, red, white & blue $4-6

Jerr-Dan Auto Salvage Transporter, burgundy
   & white $4-6
Mercedes-Benz Airport Stretch Limousine
   metallic silver $4-6
   white $4-6
Peterbilt Refuse/Recycling Truck
   burgundy $4-6
   gray $4-6
   white $4-6
Winnebago Chieftain Motor Home
   beige $5-7

white $4-6
   "Bug" theme $4-6
Zamboni
   blue and white $6-8
   with flames $4-6

Road Champs Anteaters / Cabs & Trailers, 1:87 Scale Semi-Trucks and Trailers

"Allied Van Lines" $6-8

"Bekins Van Lines" $6-8

"Cotter & Company True Value Hardware Stores" $10-12

"Dole" $5-7
"Exxon" Tanker $4-6

"Frito Lay" $4-6

"Goodyear" $4-6

"Hershey's Kisses" $4-6

"Horseless Carriage Automobile Transportion" $7-9

Livestock Truck $4-6
Low Loader Transporter "Tri State Haulers" $6-8
"Mayflower" Moving Van, C.O.E. $6-8
"Mayflower" Moving Van, conventional $6-8
NASA Rocket Transporter $4-6
"Pepsi" $4-6
"Pilot" Tanker Truck $4-6
Pipe Truck $6-8

"Reese's Pieces" $4-6
Sand Hopper Truck $4-6
"Snapple" $4-6

Road Champs Eagle Coach Country Tour Bus Series, 1:64 Scale

Alabama $10-12
Clint Black $10-12
Billy Ray Cyrus $10-12
Diamond Rio $10-12
Vince Gill $10-12
George Jones $10-12
Lorrie Morgan $10-12
Ricky Skaggs $10-12
Marty Stuart $10-12
Randy Travis $10-12
Travis Tritt $10-12
Tanya Tucker $10-12
Hank Williams Jr. $10-12

Road Champs City and Tour Buses, 1:87 Scale Municipal Transit Buses and One Greyhound

CTA (Chicago Transit Authority) Bus $5-7
NJT (New Jersey Transit) Bus $5-7
MCTO (Metropolitan Council) $5-7
MTA (Metropolitan Transit Authority) $5-7
1997 Metro, Houston TX $5-7
1997 A.C. Transit, Oakland CA $5-7
Sun Tours Bus $5-7
DBM Gad About Tour Bus $5-7
1997 Metro-Houston TX $5-7
1997 A.C. Transit, Oakland CA $5-7
Eagle Coach Greyhound $5-7

Road Champs Flyers–Historic military aircraft, approx. 4" long

AH-64 Apache Helicopter $4-6
B-17 "Sally Ann" Bomber painted in colors of
   the 91st Bomb Group, Bassingbourne, Eng-
   land $4-6
B-25 Mitchell "Panchito" with markings of B-25
   owned by National War Plane Museum ... $4-6
B-29 Super Fortress $4-6
B-747 Air Force One Presidential Airplane Limited
   Edition $6-8
Douglas C-47, D-Day markings $4-6
Douglas DC-3 Commercial Jet, 1:200 scale
   Pan Am Airlines $4-6
   Eastern Airlines $4-6

Alaska Airlines $4-6
F-4U Corsair flown by "Pappy" Boyington,
    legendary Congressional Medal of Honor
    winner $4-6
F-111
    Aardvark Two-Seat Tactical Fighter-Bomber of
        the U. S. Air Force $4-6
    Leopard, flesh color with black leopard
        spots, 2000 variation $4-6
F-117A Blackhawk Stealth $4-6
F-14 Tomcat "Jolly Roger" $4-6
F-16 Falcon Fighter of the U. S. Air Force
    "Thunderbirds" $4-6
F-18
    Hornet High-Tech Navy Super Fighter......$4-6
    Wildcat, blue with yellow accents, Blue
        Angels, U.S. Navy, 2000 variation ...$4-6
Orbiter Space Shuttle $4-6
P-38J Lightning........................$4-6
P-47 Thunderbolt "Lil Friend" 56th Fighter
    Group, Halesworth, England $4-6
P-51D Mustang $4-6
SR71 Blackbird $4-6

Road Champs Sports Series Trucks
Tennis, white truck with tennis graphics, tennis
    court on roof, 1:64 ....$4-6
Touchdown, white truck with football
    graphics, football field on roof, 1:64 ......$4-6

Other Road Champs Models
Ford 1998 Crown Victoria, Toys 'R' Us
    Geoffrey, 1998 license plate $8-10
Chevrolet 1955 Taxi, Old Navy,
    blue and white $8-10
Airport Shuttle Van, 1:64 ....$2-3
Caterpillar D10N bulldozer, mustard yellow,
    all plastic, new for 2000, 1:43 ....$4-6
Chevrolet Big Dooley Pickup, black with
    orange flames bordered in yellow,
    2000 variation, 1:43 ....$4-6
Chevrolet Caprice U.S.C.G. Ocean
    Guard, 2000 variation, 1:43 ....$4-6
Chevrolet S10 ZR2 Pickup
    U.S.C.G. Ocean Guard, 2000
        variation, 1:43 ....$4-6
    County Works Road Crew, red, 2000
        variation, 1:43 ....$4-6
Chevrolet Step Van, "Mooring's Dairy," white
    with black cow spots, 2000 variation,
    1:64 ....$4-6
Chevrolet '57 Bel Air, red with opening
    doors, 1:64 ....$4-6
Chevrolet Corvette
    '57, white, opening doors, NJ07029
        on bottom.....................$4-6

'68, silver with blue accents, "24 fury" on
    top, opening doors, NJ07028 on
    bottom $4-6
'82, white with flames and "Vette" on
    top, opening doors, NJ07029 on
    bottom $4-6
'85, black with red & white "Vette" on
    hood, opening doors, NJ07029 on
    bottom $4-6
Dodge Ram Pickup, fuchsia with yellow, orange
    and red-orange flames, 2000 variation,
    1:43 ....$4-6
Dodge Viper GTS, red with black interior,
    2000 variation, 1:43.................$4-6
Dump Truck, yellow, Hard Hats series...........$1-2
Eagle Coach, "HALLOWEEN" graphics,
    silver lower, black upper, 2000 variation,
    1:64 ....$4-6
Ferrari, brown with black & gold accents,
    opening doors and rear engine cover $1-2
Fiero, two-tone green with "Sp" & spoiler on top,
    opening doors and rear engine cover $1-2
Firebird, pink, opening doors, "Star cruiser
    #50" on hood & top, JRI inc. 1982
    NJ07029 on bottom $1-2
Ford Aeromax 120, red cab, white trailer
    with "HAPPY BIRTHDAY" graphics, 2000
    variation, 1:64 ....$4-6
Ford Crown Victoria Fire Chief, red, "052"
    on roof, white shield, 2000 variation,
    1:43................................$4-6
Ford Econoline Van, white "U-HAUL" with
    Nevada graphics, new for 2000, 1:43...$4-6
Ford Explorer, white with bright blue zigzag
    bordered in black, white interior, 2000
    variation, 1:43 ....$4-6
Ford F150 Pickup, white, "U-HAUL," Idaho
    graphics on hood, 2000 variation, 1:43 ...$4-6
Ford Model A, red, doors and rumble seat
    open, 1:64........................$6-8
Jaguar, green with "Slice #51" on top,
    opening doors, NJ07029 on bottom $1-2
Kenworth T600A U-HAUL semi, white with
    Kansas graphics, 2000 variation, 1:87 ..$4-6
Plymouth Prowler 1998, purple with black
    roof, gray bumpers, 2000 variation,
    1:43................................$4-6
Porsche 911, purple, opening doors, 928
    on hood, NJ07C23 on bottom..............$1-2
Porsche 959, silver with black interior, 2000
    variation, 1:43 ....$4-6
Stake Truck, Farmer Brown, 3" $1-2
Toyota Pickup, 1:64
    with Camper Topper, black $1-2
    with Camper Topper, red, 1:64............$1-2
    Wrecker, 1:64 ....$1-2

U-Haul Truck, white with Mississippi graphics,
    2000...............................$4-6
Volvo Cement Truck, white with green base,
    2000, 1:64 ....$4-6

Road Chaps 2004 Plastic Toys

**Chevrolet Avalanche 4x4 with motorcycle
trailer and two motorcycles $9-12**

Power Crawlers Baja X-Treme $9-12

Power Crawlers Rock Buggy................$9-12

Power Crawlers Sand Racer................$9-12

Turbo Chargers Sports Car..................$9-12

Road Legends (see Yat Ming)

Road Machine

Road Machine is an obscure import from Hong Kong.

Porsche 928, 1:64....................................$4-5

Roadmaster (also see D.C.M.T., Impy, and Lone Star)

Roadmaster, also spelled Road-Master, is part of the brand name given to a line of toy cars made by D.C.M.T. of London, England. The more common name is Impy, short for Lone Star Road-Master Impy Super Cars. For more information, see D.C.M.T. and Lone Star.

Roadmates

Over the years, Sears has offered an assortment of toy vehicles called Roadmates. Individual models in blisterpacks were usually repackaged Playart models, while sets were most often Zee Toys Pacesetters. Since the models themselves are recognized by their brand names, and the Roadmates name was only on the package, they are listed in their respective headings.

Road Rovers (also see Hallmark, LJN)

Hallmark offered several crude but charming diecast toy cars in the 1970s called Road Rovers. A connection with LJN has also been reported. Go to Hallmark for list and values.

Road Runners (see MegaMovers)

Road Tough (see Yat Ming)

Rob Eddie (see Brooklins)

Roberts

One model, a six-wheeler with a bucket loader on the front, has been found with Roberts stamped on the front of the grill. More information is needed.

Six-Wheeler with Bucket Loader..............$10-20

Robin Hood

Robin Hood toys are roughly 1:38–1:40 scale inaccurate toys made from 1946 to 1950 by Toy Products Ltd., of Argent Works, Bolt Lane, Walsall, England. Their specialty was diecast zinc alloy toy cars and animals on wheels. In 1948, clockwork motors were added to a few models.

1946 Allard Roadster.............................$40-55
American Station Wagon......................$45-60
Fire Engine..$40-55
Flat Truck...$40-55
Furniture Van..$40-55
1946 Lea Francis Coupe, clockwork motor ..$50-65
1942 Mercury Sedan, clockwork motor ...$55-70
Open Truck..$40-55
1946 Rolls Royce Saloon, "Thrupp & Mabery"..$45-60
Roadster "Baby car"..............................$40-55
Streamlined Coupe...............................$40-55
Tanker Truck...$40-55

Roco

Roco models are ready-to-run pre-colored 1:87 scale vehicles made in Austria. Walthers HO catalog lists a huge assortment. While it may be that some Roco models are diecast, they are more likely plastic. The detail and accuracy is, nevertheless, noteworthy of inclusion in this book. When applicable, Walthers catalog number is included with model description. Here is a sample listing. Many other models are currently available.

Covered Trailer, 625-1309 ....$4-6
Dodge
   Red Cross Jeep, Truck & Field Kitchen
      Trailer, 625-1388.....................$11-13
   Swiss Emergency Truck, 625-1348 ....$10-12
   Tow Truck, 625-1712 ....$9-11
Land Rover
   625-1381 ....$11-13
   KLFA Fire Truck, 625-1359 ....$11-13
   Red Cross, 625-1380.......................$11-13
Magirus
   2312 Fire Ladder Truck, 625-1349 ...$20-24
   3-Axle Dump Truck with Trailer, 625-
      1543.......................................$23-28
   D Tipping Semi Trailer, 625-1546 .....$20-24
   DLF 16 Fire Truck, 625-1396............$16-21
   DLK 23-12 with Turn Ladder, 625-
      1346 ....$21.49
   Dump Truck, 625-1527....................$15-20
   Highway Maintenance, 625-1655....$17-20
   M5 "Schenker," 625-1569...............$12-15
   TLF Fire Truck, 625-1386.................$15-20

TLF 16 Fire Pumper, 625-1366..........$15-20
Tractor & Trailer "DB/TFG,"
   625-1524 ....$17-22
Tractor & Trailer "Danzas," 625-1538....$15-20
MAN
   THW 5-Ton with Canvas Hood,
      625-1302 ....$9-11
   THW 5-Ton Equipment Truck, 625-1308 ..$6-8
   THW 5-Ton with Trailer, Red Cross,
      625-1339 ....$9-11
   630 L2A Red Cross Bus & Trailer,
      625-1387 ....$11-14
   630 L2A Technical Rescue Service,
      625-1372 ....$8-10
   630 with Repair Shop, 625-1410.....$12-15
Mercedes-Benz
   4500 Tanker, 625-1526..........$25-30
   DL Ladder, 625-1398 ....$20-24
   LF 8 Fire Truck, 265-1351 ....$11-14
   LF 8 Fire Truck with Trailer & DKW
      Portable Motor Pump, 625-1375 ...$15-20
   LF 25, 625-1374 ....$18-23
   L4500 D122 Ladder Truck, 625-1361 ..$20-24
   SRF Repair Truck with Hiab Crane &
      removable Container, 625-1369 ...$19-24
   TLFA 4000 Rosenbauer, 625-1379...$16.49
   1017 Police Truck with Canvas,
      625-1383 ....$11-14
Mercedes 1838
   "Schenker," 625-1576 ....$28-33
   with "Kieserling" Double Trailers,
      625-1571 ....$28-33
   with "Kohne & Nagel" Double Trailers,
      625-1577 ....$27-32
   with "Sixt" Trailer, 625-1579.............$28-32
Mercedes Unimog
   Road Building Vehicle Set Add-On,
      625-1547 ....$50-55
   1300 & Sauer Komet Bus Construction
      Site Set, 625-1561....................$19-24
   1300 Utility, 625-1503 ....$30-35
   S with Canvas Hood, Red Cross,
      625-1338 ....$8-10
   1300L Fire Ambulance, 625-1364......$9-12
   4-Wheel Drive Fire Engine, 625-1304 ...$9-12
Munga
   DKW Red Cross, 625-1301 ....$5-7
   Fire Dept. Radio car, 625-1300 ....$5-7
   Jeep Red Cross, 625-1329 ....$4-6
Opel Blitz
   TLF 15, 625-1398..........................$12-15
   with Fire Extinguisher Trailer, 625-1337...$14-19
Pinzgauer 6x6 Command car, 625-1386 ..$15-20
Renault
   "Kolner Flitzer," 625-1584 no price provided
   3-Axle Tractor Trailer "Beck," 625-1567....$17-20

DLK 23-12 Fire Ladder Truck, 625-1371 ..$20-24
G Service, 625-1656 ....$15-20
Tractor Trailer "Rouch," 625-1528 .....$15-20
Saurer Bus
    "Komet" tour Bus, 625-1602..............$15-20
    Austrian Postal, 625-1600 ....$15-20
Steyr
    91 Semi with "Gondrand" 3-Axle Trailer,
       625-1557 ....$17-22
    91 Semi with "Ischler Saltz" Trailer,
       625-1520 ....$15-20
    91 Semi with "SpEdition Gartner" Trailer,
       625-1514 ....$15-20
    91 Tractor with Flatbed and Power
       Shovel, 625-1516 ....$37-42
    680 TLF Fire Truck, 265-1342..........$14-19
    Construction Vehicle with Accessories,
       625-1533 ....$25-30
THW Field Kitchen Trailer, 625-1320 ....$4-6
Volkswagen
    Ambulance, 625-1355.................$7-9
    Ambulance Van, 625-1377 ....$7-9
    Bus and Field Kitchen Unit Truck, 625-
       1376 ....$18-22
    Double Cab Fire Fighting Unit, 625-1362...$6-8
    Minibus with Horse Trailer, 625-1384....$18-23
    THW, 625-1323 ....$5-7
    Type 2 Ambulance, 625-1372............$8-10
    Type 2 Command car, 625-1370.......$8-10
    Type 2 DB Railway Police, 625-1382 ....$7-9
    2-Unit Mini Bus Set, 625-1385..........$18-22
Volvo FL10
    "Laurie Ashley" Freight Truck, 625-1583.$12-15
    Truck & Trailer, unmarked, 625-1575 ..$25-29
    "Kuhlzug" Refrigerator Truck & Trailer,
       625-1581 ....$28-32
    with "La Maxilaterale" Trailer, 625-1430..$24-28
    with "Kuhne & Nagel" Double Trailers, 625-
       1570 ....$25-30
    with Double Trailers, unmarked, 625-1430 ...$24-28
    with Silo Moving Equipment, 625-1561 ..$24-29
Willys Jeep Fire Dept., 625-1365................$7-9
Construction Set with Site Truck and Two Site
    Office Trailers, 625-1545.................$26-31

Roco Emergency Helicopters
MBB BO 105
    Police, 625-1391 ....$9-12
    Rescue, 625-1392 ....$9-12
    Rescue, ADAC, 625-1390 ....$9-12

Rolux
Rolux models are lead alloy miniatures made in France in the early 1940s.

Limousine, lead body, aluminum chassis....$45-60

Army Staff car, same as limousine with military markings...$45-60

ROS (see Agritec)
ROS is reportedly a brand of Agritec of Spain, makers of diecast construction and farm equipment. See Agritec for model list.

Roskopf
Roskopf models are 1:87 scale plastic vehicles made for the German market. The brand is associated with Wiking and Siku of Germany. While not perfect, the online universal translator at www.systranbox.com/systran/box was used to fairly successfully translate these model descriptions from German to English.

Berliet Feuerwehr (Fire Department)—TLF,
    #509 00 ....$10-20
Bundesgrenzschutz Sonderwagen 2
    (Alliance Boundary Protection Special
    Vehicle 2) #554 00 ....$10-20
Büssing BS 16 L
    Pritschen-Hängerzug (Plank Bed Tractor/
       Trailer), #485 02 ....$10-20
    Pritschen-Hängerzug (Plank Bed Tractor/
       Trailer), #486 00 ....$10-20
    Pritschen-Sattelzug (Plank Bed "Cot-Saddle"
       Tractor/Trailer), #441 00 ....$10-20
    Tanksattelzug (Tanker Tractor/Trailer) #411
       02 ....$10-20
Hanomag WD
    Schlepper (Tractor), #290 00 ....$10-20
    Schlepper mit Möbelanhänger (Tractor
       with Furniture Trailer), #382 01 ....$10-20
    Schlepper mit zwei Kohlenanhängern (Tractor
       with Two Coal Trailers), #381 01 ..$10-20
Junkers (Squire) F 13
    #982 00.....................................$15-25
    #983 00.....................................$15-25
Man (ONE)
    Möbel-Hängerzug (Moving Van Tractor/
       Trailer), #373 02 ....$10-20
    Pritschen-Hängerzug (Plank Bed Tractor/
       Trailer), #378 01 ....$10-20
Mercedes-Benz
    Ziegler Feuerwehr (Ziegler Fire Department)
       LF 8, #508 01 ....$10-20
    Ausflugsbus (Excursion Bus), #392 01 ...$10-20
    Cabriolet, geschleppen (Convertible,
       top up), #214 02 ....$10-20
    Cabriolet, offen (Convertible, top
       down), #212 01 ....$10-20
    Feuerwehr (Fire Truck), #221 00 ....$10-20
    L 1000 Kastenwagen (Box Truck),
       #260 02 ....$10-20

    L 1000 Lieferwagen (Van), #253 02 ..$10-20
    L 2 Würtheim Post Kastenwagen (Postal
       Service Box Truck), #264 01.......$10-20
    L 5 Coal Truck / Trailer, #369 01 .....$10-20
    L 5 Möbelwagen (Moving Van Tractor/
       Trailer), #342 00 ....$10-20
    L 5 Pritschen-Hängerzug (Plank
       Bed Tractor/Trailer), #376 01.....$10-20
    L 5 Pritschenwagen (Plank Bed Tractor/
       Trailer), #314 00 ....$10-20
    L 5 Tankwagen (Tanker Tractor/Trailer),
       #362 01 ....$10-20
    Möbelwagen (Moving Van), #352 00....$10-20
    N 56 Feuerwehr–Rüstwagen (Fire
       Department Ambulance), #341 00..$10-20
    N 56 Pritschenwagen (Plank Bed Tractor/
       Trailer), #302 02 ....$10-20
    Polizei (Police), #220 00 ....$10-20
    Stuttgart Taxi (closed), #201 00 ....$10-20
    Stuttgart Taxi (open), #200 00..........$10-20
    Stuttgart Landaulet, #211 00 ....$10-20
    Stuttgart Limousine, #210 01 ....$10-20
Renault Camiva Feuerwehr (Carniva Fire
    Department)–TLF, #505 00 ....$10-20
Udet Flamingo Kunst-und Schulflugzeug (Art
    and Training Airplane), #981 00 ......$15-25

Ross (see Agritec)
Ross, reportedly a division of Agritech of Spain according to collector / dealer Bill Molyneaux, represents a set of high-quality heavy equipment models from Italy. Production of models listed below has been discontinued, and limited quantities are offered through Toys for Collectors while supplies last. A larger assortment is offered by Diecast Miniatures, who chose to spell Ross with one "s." See Agritec for model list.

Rosso
Exoticar once offered one Rosso model, presumed, but not known, to be 1:12 scale.

Ferrari Formula One...........................$375-425

Rovex
Rovex Scale Model Co. was founded in London, England, in 1951, and purchased the same year by the Lines Brothers, owners of Tri-Ang branded toys. Rovex was merged into the Tri-Ang line in 1970, and the company name was changed to Rovex Tri-Ang Ltd., which now included Scalextric and Hornby.

In 1972, Rovex was sold to Dunbee-Combex Ltd. and the whole conglomerated product line was liquidated. The Rovex product line was represented by clockwork plastic toy cars.

Austin A40 Van, 1949, 1:48 ....$35-45
Austin A40 Somerset Saloon, 1952, 1:50 ...$35-45
Bentley Limousine, 1:50 ....$35-45
Commer Coach, 1:50 ....$35-45

Rozkvet Mini Models

Collector Neil Edwards reports of an unusual model Skoda 120 made in Czechoslovakia by a company called Rozkvet VDI Mini Models. He paid $1 for it at a flea market. As with most Eastern European models, this one is assumed to be produced in 1:43 scale.

Skoda 120, white body, black interior, unpainted
base $15-20

RS Toys

As reported by collector Staffan Kjellin of Sweden, RS Toys were made in Sweden. The company manufactured only three different cars in 1936 and maybe early 1937. They were a 1935 De Soto, 1935 Chevrolet, and 1935 Volvo Carioca. Only a few each of these are known to have survived. Replicas have recently been made from the original mold found some years ago by Kaj Wicklander. They are all signed and numbered.

1935 Chevrolet, 103mm $750-1,000
 reproduction $125-200
1935 De Soto, 98mm original $750-1,000
 reproduction $125-200
1935 Volvo carioca, 105mm $750-1,000
 reproduction $125-200

Ruehl (see Reuhl)

Ruestes

Ruestes models are made in Argentina.

Renault 17 Coupe, 1:43 ....$12-15
Renault 12 Wagon, 1:43 ....$12-15

Rullero

Rullero models, like Ruestes, are made in Argentina.

Ike Torino Rally, 10" $22

Russ

Best guess is that these toys were produced by the same Russ Toy Company that is best known for plush toys.

Austin Mini, Bump & Go, 2¾" $10-12
Volkswagen Beetle, Bump & Go, 2¾" $10-12

Russian models (also see Agat, Govroski, Lada, Litan, Lomo, Moskovich, Radon, Saratov, Uaz, Volga)

Since the collapse of communism and the beginning of "glasnost," Russian exports have started appearing in growing quantities in the US. A wide variety of toys are included in the assortment of goods coming from former Soviet Republics. Among them are a large selection of diecast models. Since private corporations have not been widely established, most Russian products are generic. However, most recently, several Russian brand names have emerged such as Radon, Agat, Litan, Saratov, and Lomo, as reported by Alexander Yurcenko in the June 1997 issue of *Model Auto Review*.

Below is a sampling of Russian models that have recently become a lot more popular.

Alfa Romeo, #66 ....$14-19
Amo Type 4 Fire Truck, #81 ....$51-56
Chaika
 GAZ 13 Limousine, #35 ....$22-27
 GAZ14 Limousine, #56 ....$22-27

Limousine, 1:43 ....$15-20
GAZ Ford AAA 1934 Fire Truck, #101 ...$25-30
IZ Jupiter Police Motorbike & Side car, 1:24,
 #78 ....$24-29
Kamaz 4310 Postal Truck, #117 ....$29-34
Krupp KMK 4070
 4-axle Crane, 1:50, #115 ....$125-140
 5-axle Crane, 1:50, #116 ....$135-150
Lada Niva 4WD, #38 ....$24-29
Moskvitch
 402 Sedan, #2 ....$14-19
 Patrol car $15-20
 Pickup, #40 ....$14-19
Russian Armored Vehicle, crude cast,
 plastic wheels, thick steel axles $15-20
Russobalt
 Landau, #50 ....$19-24
 Sedan, #49 ....$19
 Tourer, #37 ....$19-24
UAZ
 452 Military Bus Van, #125 ....$29-34
 469 4WD Road Police Jeep, #108 ...$24-29
Volga GAZ 24 Sedan, #26 ....$14-19
Volkswagen RAF 977 Van, #64 ....$27-32

Zil
 Dump Truck, #59 ....$24-29
 Limousine $15-20
Zis
 5-Ton Truck, #83 ....$24-29
 Type 2 Fire Truck, #71 ....$37-42
 Type 5 Fire Pumper, #77 ....$37-42
 Type 6 3-axle Pumper Fire Truck, #127 ..$42-47
 Type 8 St. Petersburg City Bus, wood & metal,
 very limited quantities, #506 ...$135-150

RW (see Ziss)

S

Sablon

Sablon toys are 1:43 scale cars made in Belgium from 1968 to 1970. They are fairly accurate representations with opening doors and hoods. After 1970, Nacoral took over the tooling and reissued some of the models under the Nacoral InterCar brand.

BMW
 1600 GT, white, #5 ....$50-65
 1600 GT, orange-red, #8 ....$50-65
 2000 CS, red, #4 ....$45-60
 Glas 3000 V8, red, #12 ....$45-60
Lamborghini Marzal, white, #6 ....$50-65
Mercedes-Benz
 200, white, #13 ....$250-300
 250 SE, metallic bronze, #2 ....$45-60
 250 SE Polizei, white, #10 ....$45-60
 Covered Truck, orange-red with yellow
 truck bed, #157 ....$35-50
 Dropside Truck, blue cab, orange-red
 truck bed, #158 ....$35-50
 Dump Truck, yellow, #152 ....$45-60
 Livestock Truck, yellow cab, green truck
 bed $35-50
 Open Truck, #151 ....$35-50
 Van, blue, #153 ....$35-50
 Tank Truck, orange-red, #154 ....$40-55
 Wrecker, white cab, orange-red truck
 bed, #155 ....$50-65
NSU Ro 80, light gray, #7 ....$45-60
Porsche 911
 Targa Convertible, metallic green, #1 ...$45-60
 Targa Hardtop, orange-red, #9 ....$45-60
 Polizei, white, #11 ....$45-60
Renault 16
 ivory, #3 ....$45-60
 Police, dark blue, #14 ....$45-60

Sabra (also see Cragstan, Gamda/ Gamda-Koor)

1:43 scale models comprise this intriguing

series from Sabra of Israel produced in the early 1970s first by Cragstan, then by Gamda-Koor, under the Detroit Seniors name.

Cadillac Coupe de Ville	$48-52
1964 Chevrolet Chevelle Wagon	
Fire Chief	$24-28
Israeli Ambulance	$24-28
U.S. Ambulance	$24-28
Chevrolet Corvair	$24-28
Plymouth Barracuda	$36-40
Pontiac GTO	$36-40

Safar

A single model is known to have been produced in 1947 under the Safar brand of Italy.

Fastback Coupe, 4"	$45-60

Safir

From 1961 to 1978, Safir of France produced a wide variety of 1:43 scale miniature models. Though not very successful, many of their models were copied by Hong Kong firms known for producing cheap unlicensed knock-offs of other manufacturers' products. Safir models are typically valued at $10 to $25 each.

1923 Citroën	
Ambulance, #12	$20-25
Fire Truck, #11	$20-25
1924 Citroën Taxi	
10 H.P., #9	$20-25
Landau, #21	$20-25
top up, #22	$20-25
top down, #23	$20-25
Ferrari 312 T2, #80	$20-25
1901 Fiat 8 H.P., #14	$20-25
1911 Ford Model T Roadster "Tin Lizzie"	
20 H.P., #8	$20-25
1910 Gregoire Triple Sedan, #101	$20-25
Ligier-Matra JS5, #81	$20-25
Lola T70	
Austrian Grand Prix, #31	$20-25
Daytona, #33	$20-25
Monza, #35	$20-25
Nurbhring, #34	$20-25
Paris 1000 KM, #32	$20-25
Temorada, #30	$20-25
1901 Mercedes	
#15	$20-25
9 H.P., #20	$20-25
1898 Panhard, #17	$20-25
1892 Peugeot	
Toit Bois, #19	$20-25
Vis-A-Vis, #1	$20-25

1895 Peugeot, #1	$20-25
1896 Peugeot, top down, #4	$20-25
1898 Peugeot Victoria, #2	$20-25
1899 Peugeot Victoria, #3	$20-25
1900 Peugeot Coupe, #18	$20-25
Porsche 911 Kyalami, #55	$20-25
Porsche 917	
Brands Hatch #12, blue with white stripes, #44	$20-25
David Piper, #54	$20-25
Daytona #3, white with red stripes, #41	$20-25
Daytona, #72	$20-25
Ecurie Hollandaise #18, yellow, #45	$20-25
Gulf Porsche-Wyer, #74	$20-25
Hockenheim, #53	$20-25
John Wyer, #71	$20-25
Le Mans #23, white with stripe, #43	$20-25
Le Mans, #70	$20-25
Martini, #75	$20-25
Monza #7, blue with Gulf stripes, #42	$20-25
Nurbhring, #73	$20-25
Temorada, Buenos Aires #28, white, #40	$20-25
Porsche 917K	
12 Hour Sebring #3, Silver with red and blue stripes, #62	$20-25
Ecurie Gulf-John Wyer #19, blue with orange, #61	$20-25
Essais Le Mans #3, blue with white stripe, #51	$20-25
Le Mans 1971 #22, white with red stripe, #60	$20-25
Martini Racing, #21, Silver with blue and red stripes, #65	$20-25
Nurburgring, yellow with green stripes, #55, #63	$20-25
Porsche 917L Le Mans	
#3, blue with green stripes, #50	$20-25
'70 #25, white with red stripes, #52	$20-25
Ecuri Gulf, John Wyler, blue with orange, #18, #64	$20-25
1899 Renault, #16	$20-25
1900 Renault Coupe 35 H.P., #10	$20-25
1902 Renault Paris to Vienna, #7	$20-25
1906 Renault Town car	
top up, #24	$20-25
top down, #25	$20-25
Tyrell P34	
#4, #82	$20-25
#33, #83	$20-25
1908 Unic Taxi	
open cab, #26	$20-25
closed cab, #27	$20-25
1901 Vis-A-Vis Decauville	
4½ H.P., #6	$20-25
5 H.P., #5	$20-25

Saico

D & P International Enterprises Limited
12/F, Kyoei Commercial Building,
3 Hillwood Road, Tsimshatsui, Kowloon,
Hong Kong
tel: (852) 2992 0085
fax: (852) 2992 0640
e-mail: dapint@netvigator.com
website: www.mbmags.comdapint
Key executive for contacts:
Ms Zuie Lo, Marketing Manager

Saico is a brand of D & P International Enterprises Limited, a specialist in the manufacture and exporting of diecast model cars and remote-controlled model cars since the early 1990s. In addition to producing under its own brands of "Saico" and "Saicon," the company accepts OEM and ODM orders.

1982 Chevrolet Camaro, 1:24	$6-7
1965 Chevrolet Chevelle Malibu	
SS, 1:24	$5-6
Convertible Lowrider, gold, 1:24	$7-8
Convertible Lowrider, silver, 1:24	$7-8
Convertible, 1:24	$6-7
Gasser, 1:24	$6-7
Hardtop Lowrider, gold, 1:24	$7-8
Hardtop Lowrider, silver, 1:24	$7-8
Hardtop, 1:24	$6-7
1958 Chevrolet Impala	
Convertible, 1:24	$6-7
Convertible Lowrider, gold, 1:24	$6-7
Convertible Lowrider, silver, 1:24	$6-7
Hardtop, 1:24	$5-6
Hardtop Lowrider, gold, 1:24	$6-7
Hardtop, 1:24	$7-8
Hardtop Lowrider, gold wheels, 1:24	$6-7
Hardtop Lowrider, silver, 1:24	$7-8
Hardtop Lowrider, silver, 1:24	$6-7
1970 Chevrolet Monte Carlo SS454	
white 1:24	$5-6
gold, 1:24	$6-7
silver, 1:24	$6-7
1987 Chevrolet Monte Carlo Gasser, 1:24	$6-7
1956 Chevrolet Pick Up, 1:24	$7-8
1966 Chevrolet Pick Up	
1:24	$7-8
two-tone, 1:24	$7-8
Lowrider, 1:24	$6-7
with design, 1:24	$7-8
1998 Chevrolet S10 Pick Up, 1:43	$2-3
1999 Chevrolet S10 Pick Up, 1:43	$2-3
1999 Chevrolet Silverado, 1:43	$2-3
Chrysler PT Cruiser	
1:24	$6-7
2000, 1:34	$3-4

1957 Dodge Sweptside, 1:40 ....$2-3
1999 Mitsubishi Pajero, 1:34 ....$3-4
City Coach Mini, 5" $2-3

St. Louis

Six diecast models were produced in 1981 under the St. Louis brand. They are 1:43 scale versions of American cars of the 1940s and 1950s, valued at $5–8 each.

Sako

Sako models of Argentina are 1:25 scale tin models made in the late 1960s.

Chevrolet
1966 Taxi $22-25
1966 Police Ambulance $22-25
1967 Camaro 2-door Hardtop Rally ..$22-25
Porsche 906 Rally $22-25

Sakura

Sakura models are typical of Japanese diecast manufacturer, offering a mix of 1:43 scale and 5 to 5½" long models for around $20 each.

Chevrolet Corvette Coupe, 1:43, #3 ....$20-24
Hino Bus
Airport Bus, #5 ....$20-24
red, 5", #1 ....$20-24
1:43, #3 ....$20-24
1:43, #6 ....$20-24
Honda 360 Pickup, 1:43 #1 ....$20-24
Honda Life Police, 1:36, #602 ....$20-24
Isuzu Fire Pumper, 5½", #2 ....$20-24
Lancia Stratos, 1:43, #13 ....$20-24
Maserati Bora, 1:43, #11 ....$20-24
Neoplan Double Decker Bus, 5½", #2 ......$20-24
Nissan Cedric 4-door Sedan, Fire, 1:43,
#4071 ....$20-24
Nissan Kombi, 1:43, #4086 ....$20-24
Nissan Police, 1:43, #4088 ....$20-24
Nissan R382, 1:64 #105 ....$20-24
Nissan School Bus, 5", #4085 ....$20-24
Nissan Skyline
4-door Sedan Fire, 1:43, #111 ....$20-24
Van, Police, 1:43, #609 ....$20-24
Van, Fire, 1:43, #610 ....$20-24
Van, Ambulance, 1:43, #611 ....$20-24
Suzuki Jeep, 1:36, #3 ....$20-24
Toyota Celica Mk 2 Coupe, 1:43 ....$20-24
Toyota Land Cruiser, 1:36, #8152 .....$20-24
Toyota Mk 2 4-door Sedan, 1:43, #8549 ...$20-24

Salza

Salza models of France have been confused with Cofalu models, except that Salzas are cast aluminum, while Cofalus are plastic. All models are representative of Tour de France support vehicles.

Aspro Ambulance, 4½" $40-50
Jeep with Bicycles, 3½" $40-50
Gendarmerie Jeep, 3½" $40-50
Press Jeep, 3½" $40-50
Peugeot 203 Convertible, 5¼" $40-50
Peugeot 404 Sedan, 5¼" $40-50
Peugeot D4A
Van, 4" $40-50
Loudspeaker Van, 4" $40-50

Sam Toys

Although in business since 1911, Sam Toys of Italy didn't start producing miniature cars until 1958. All Sam Toys are plastic and currently sell for $10 to $15 each.

Saratov

According to the June 1997 issue of *Model Auto Review*, Saratov remains one of the largest manufacturers of scale models in Russia. A large portion of their current offerings is dominated by Ural motorcycle models. No list is available.

Savoye Pewter Toy Company

Back in the 1930s, "pewter" and "slush mold" were alternate descriptions applied to lead alloy toys, since banned after the discovery that lead was poisonous when taken internally. Savoye produced a wide assortment of "pewter" toys in North Bergen, New Jersey, from 1930 until 1936.

Ambulance $35-40
Army Gun Truck, 3¼" $40-45
Beer Truck, 4⅜" $80-90
Bus, 5th Avenue, 4¾" $125-140
Bus, Cross-Country, 3⅜" $40-45
Bus with Mack Cab, 7½" $45-50
Convertible $35-40
Coupe, 3⅜" $40-45
Coupe, 3⅜" $30-35
Fire Engine, 3¾" $35-40
Fire Truck, 4¼" $45-50
Fire Truck, 3¾" $35-40
Milk Van $40-45
Moving Van $55-60
Pickup Truck $40-45
Police Patrol Van $50-55
Racer, 4¼" $30-35
Roadster, 3½" $40-45
Roadster, 3⅜" $40-45
Stake Truck, 4½" $25-30

Stake Truck, 5¾" $35-30
Tank car Set, 10¼" $80-90
Tow Truck, 4" $40-45
Tractor, 2¾" $30-35
Tractor, 3" $20-25

Scale Models (also see Ertl, Scamold)

Ertl is the parent company to the Scale Models brand, some of which are produced in unpainted pewter-like finish. Asheville DieCast of Asheville, North Carolina, is arguably the largest supplier of Ertl, Scale Models, Spec-Cast, Liberty Classics, and others. But Diecast Miniatures offers a considerable selection as well. Below is just a sampling. Like Liberty Classics, Ertl Promotionals, Spec-Cast, and others, Scale Models specialize in producing models with various advertising livery.

Another company, Scale Models, Ltd., is from England and produced accurate replica race cars under the Scamold brand. (See Scamold.)

American Eagle WWII Airplane, 10" $18-24
Hedge Hopper Helicopter, 10" $18-24
Allis WC Tractor, 1:64 ....$5-7
Case Steam Engine, 1:64 ....$7-9
Dain Commercial Car $15-18
Deutz 6275 Tractor, 1:64 ....$5-7
Ford 4WD 946 Tractor, 1:64 ....$7-9
Hart Parr Tractor, 1:64 ....$7-9
1931 International Harvester Tanker "Gilmore
Oil Company" $31-36
1932 International Harvester Tractor, 1:64 ...$5-7
Massey Ferguson 44 Tractor, 1:64 ....$5-7
MM Comfort Tractor, 1:64 ....$5-7
Oliver 70 Tractor, 1:64 ....$5-7
Oliver 770 Tractor, 1:64 ....$5-7
Oliver 880 Tractor, 1:64 ....$5-7
Rumely Tractor, 1:64 ....$7-9
White 185 Tractor, 1:64 ....$5-7
White 4270 4WD Tractor, 1:64 ....$7-9

Scaleworks

It was in the early months of the year 2000 that this model started appearing in ads and articles in various magazines. Scaleworks is apparently a new diecast model company of which only one model is known, a precision scale model of Craig Breedlove's Spirit of America record car. A removable body panel on the model exposes fully detailed J-79 General Electric jet turbine engine and tube frame, rolling wheels and tampo printing.

Craig Breedlove's Spirit of America Land
   Speed Record Jet car, DPS-SPA99-C,
   1:43 ....$50-65

Scamold

Scale Models Ltd. of Great Britain was founded in 1939 by D.Tilley, owner of a shop at the Brooklands raceway. The company manufactured Scamold diecast racing cars from until 1950. They are relatively accurate scale models based on cars that raced at Brooklands. Pre-war boxes are marked "Manufactured by Scale Models Ltd, Brooklands Track, Weybridge, Eng." Post-war boxes dropped that designation. Models were produced in 1:50 scale lead alloy (slush mold), and 1:35 scale zinc alloy (diecast) models and kits.

1937 Alta 4 cylinder 1500 Race car,
   #105, diecast, 1:35 ....$90-120
Austin Seven Race car, #202, diecast kit,
   1:35 ....$60-75
1924 Bentley 3 Litre Sports car, #208,
   diecast kit, 1:35 ....$60-75
1931 Bugatti 51 Race car, #206,
   diecast kit, 1:35 ....$60-75
1937 ERA 1500 Racing car, slush mold,
   1:50 ....$75-90
1937 ERA 6-cylinder 1500 Race car,
   diecast, 1:35, #101 ....$90-120
1934 ERA E Type Race car, #207,
   diecast kit, 1:35 ....$60-75
1937 Maserati 8 CTF Race car, #103,
   diecast, 1:35 ....$90-120
MG TC Sports car, #204, diecast kit,
   1:35 ....$60-75
1938 Midget Racer, slush mold, 1:50 .....$75-90
1937 Riley T.T. Sports car, #209,
   diecast kit, 1:35 ....$60-75

Schabak

Schabak models are from Nurnburg, Germany. Started in 1966, Schabak started producing diecast cars after Schuco went out of business. The company has since become associated with Gama, the current owner of the Schuco name. Except where noted all models are produced in 1:43 scale.

Audi
   1989 Coupe, #1050.................$15-20
   1989 V8, #1024 ....$20-25
Audi 80
   1986, #1025 ....$20-25
   1992 Sedan, #1031-B..............$15-20
   1987 Quattro, #1035..............$20-25

1987 Quattro Police car, #1036 ......$20-25
Audi 90 Quattro
   1984, #1030 ....$20-25
   1987, #1031-A $20-25
   1988, #1037 ....$20-25
   1988 Rally, #1038 ....$20-25
Audi 100 Avant
   1984, #1020 ....$20-25
   1984 Quattro, #1021 ....$20-25
   1987 DSK car, #1022 ....$20-25
BMW 535i 1988
   #1150 ....$20-25
   Doctor's car, #1156 ....$20-25
   Fire Department car, white &
      orange-red, #1155..............$20-25
   Fire Department car, red with white
      fenders, #1154.................$20-25
   Police car, white and green, #1153...$20-25
   Police car, white with green stripes,
      #1152 ....$20-25
   Taxi, #1151 ....$20-25
BMW M5 1989, #1158 ....$20-25
BMW Z1 1989
   #1160 ....$20-25
   Convertible, 1:25, #1600.........$35-40
Ford Fiesta 1989, #1086..............$20-25
Ford Granada 1985, 1:25, #1501 .....$35-40
Ford Scorpio D 1985, 1:25,
   #1500 ....$35-40
Ford Sierra
   1987 Notchback, 1:25, #1510 .....$35-40
   1987 Notchback, 1:25, #1511 .....$35-40
   1987 Notchback, 1:25, #1080 .....$20-25
   1988 Cosworth, 1:25, #1512 ......$35-40
   1988 Cosworth, 1:25, #1513........$35-40
   Polizei, 1:25, #1514 ....$35-40
   Police car, 1:25, #1081 ....$20-25
Ford Transit 1986
   Bus, 1:35, #1300 ....$30-35
   Van, 1:35, #1301 ....$30-35
Porsche 1993 Carrera 2
   Convertible, #1110 ....$25-30
Volkswagen Caravelle
   1986 Ambulance, #1041............$20-25
   1986 Bus, #1040 ....$20-25
   1986 CONDOR, #1046 ....$20-25
   1988 Police Bus, green, #1047 ....$20-25
   1988 Police Bus, white and green,
      #1048 ....$20-25
Volkswagen Corrado 1988, #1018.......$20-25
Volkswagen Golf
   1983, #1002 ....$20-25
   1984 ADAC car, #1003.............$20-25
   1987 GTI, #1008 ....$20-25
   1984 PTT car, #1002/3............$20-25
   1984 Tuning, #1004 ....$20-25

Volkswagen Jetta
   1979, #1001 ....$20-25
   1984, #1010 ....$20-25
   Police car, #1011 ....$20-25
   1984 Tuning, #1012 ....$20-25
Volkswagen Passat
   1988, #1015 ....$20-25
   1988 Van, #1016 ....$20-25
Volkswagen Transporter
   1986, #1042 ....$20-25
   1986 Fire Van, #1043 ....$20-25
   1986 LUFTHANSA, #1045 ....$20-25

Schuco (also see Spiel-Nutz)

Schuco GmbH & Co.
Werkstr. 1
90765 Fürth, Germany
tel: ++49 911 97 65 04
fax: ++49 911 97 65 415
www.schuco.de/

Schuco has been around for a long time, beginning in 1912 as a distinctive brand of clockwork tin toys. Now that the original Schuco company has gone out of business, Gama has purchased the company and is now producing remakes of many of the original models as well as new models, now marketed in the U.S. by Lilliput Motor Company of Yerington, Nevada.

The Piccolo series in particular, never having attracted much attention when they were introduced in 1957, are now rising in value. These small 1:90 scale models, usually about an inch long, are described by Dr. Edward Force as "rather uninspiring little blobs." Despite his negative review, the charisma of these tiny models is what still attracts collectors today.

Schuco's main entry into the diecast market happened in the late 1950s with the introduction of precision scale models in 1:43 and 1:66 scale. Now, the Schuco brand celebrates a revival with new 1:18 scale models added to the growing assortment.

Regarding Schuco Piccolo models, collector Crister Skoglund of Sweden at one time offered several original Piccolo models for sale at $90 without the box $150 in original box. This indicates that values are rising considerably on these tiny metal blobs. Reissues from the 1990s are now available and listed below along with the originals.

Schuco toys are sold in various markets under different names. Lilliput, Nutz, Oldtimer, Paya (from Spain), and Rei are all trademark brands from Schuco. Rei in particular is a brand name of Schuco models sold in Brazil.

Presented below is an extensive list of Schucos, both diecast and otherwise. Replicas are now being made from the original machining and are listed just below the original version.

Akustico 2002, 5½", 1:43, 1940s, #2002 ....$150-165
Alfa Romeo 1048, 4", Micro Racer, 1950s, #1048 ....$175-190
Anno 2000, 5½", 1:43, 1940s, #2000 ...$150-165
Audi 100, 1:43, 1976, #639..............$25-30
Audi 100 Coupe, 2¾", 1971, #821 ....$10-15
Audi 100 GL, 2¾", 1972, #852 ....$10-15
Audi 100 LS, 2¾", 1971, #817 ....$10-15
Audi 50, 1:43, 1974, #622................$25-30
Audi 80 Fire Chief, 2½", 1974, #876 .....$10-15
Audi 80 GL, 1:43, 1972, #611............$25-30
Audi 80 GL, 2½", 1973, #862..............$10-15
Audi 80 LS, 1:43, 1972, #610.............$25-30
Audi 80 LS, 2½", 1973, #855................$10-15
Audi 80 Police car, 1:43, 1974, #634 ...$25-30
Austin Mini, Piccolo, 1:90, 1996, #331 ...$25-30
Austin-Healey 100 Six, 2", Piccolo, 1:90, 1958, #709-A $75-90
BMW 1600, 2¾", 1971, #808.............$10-15
BMW 200 tii, 2½", 1972, #845............$10-15
BMW 2000, blue, 1:43, 1995, #2161 ...$45-60
BMW 2000, maroon, 1:43, 1995, #2162 ..$45-60
BMW 2000, white, 1:43, 1995, #2163 ....$45-60
BMW 2000 Police, 1:43, 1996, #2165....$45-60
BMW 2000 Taxi, 1:43, 1995, #2164...$45-60
BMW 2002, 2½", 1971, #809.............$10-15
BMW 2002, blue, 1:43, 1996, #2221 .$45-60
BMW 2002, silver, 1:43, 1996, #2223.......$45-60
BMW 2002, yellow, 1:43, 1996, #2222...$45-60
BMW 2500, 2¾", 1972, #829............$10-15
BMW 2800, 2¾", 1972, #830.............$10-15
BMW 2800 CS, 2¾", 1971, #815 ....$10
BMW 3.0, blue, 1:43, 1996, #2191 ...$45-60
BMW 3.0, red, 1:43, 1996, #2192.....$45-60
BMW 3.0 CSL, 2¾", 1974, #875..........$10-15
BMW 316, 1:43, 1975, #626............$25-30
BMW 316i, metallic black, 1:43, 1996, #4003 ....$50-65
BMW 316i, metallic green, 1:43, 1996, #4002 ....$50-65
BMW 318ti, metallic blue, 1:43, 1996, #4013 ....$50-65
BMW 318ti, metallic red, 1:43, 1996, #4012 ....$50-65
BMW 318ti, yellow, 1:43, 1996, #4011 ...$50-65
BMW 320, 1:43, 1975, #627............$25-30
BMW 320 Rally car, 1:43, 1976, #636...$25-30
BMW 327 Cabriolet, 1:18, 1996, #0012.....................................$270-295
BMW 327 Coupé, 1:18, 1996, #0021 ....$290-315
BMW 328, black, 1:43, 1996, #2181 ..$45-60
BMW 328, silver, 1:43, 1996, #2182...$45-60
BMW 328 Soft Top, green, 1:43, 1996, #2423...............................$45-60
BMW 328 Soft Top, red, 1:43, 1996, #2421 ....$45-60
BMW 328 Soft Top, white, 1:43, 1996, #2422 ....$45-60
BMW 328i Touring, metallic green, 1:43, 1996, #4083...............................$50-65
BMW 328i Touring, red, 1:43, 1996, #4081 ....$50-65
BMW 328i Touring, silver, 1:43, 1996, #4082 ....$50-65
BMW 335 Limo, ivory and brown, 1:43, 1996, #2232..............................$45-60
BMW 335 Limo, light green and green, 1:43, 1996, #2233..............................$45-60
BMW 335 Limo, maroon and black, 1:43, 1996, #2231 ....$45-60
BMW 501, 1:43, 1950s, #2014 ....$180-210
BMW 501 Fire Chief, 1:43, 1995, #2040 ....$60-75
BMW 502, gray, 1:43, 1996, #2015 ...$45-60
BMW 502, ivory, 1:43, 1996, #2016...$45-60
BMW 502, maroon, 1:43, 1996, #2017 ....$45-60
BMW 502 Fire Chief, 1:43, 1996, #2043 ....$45-60
BMW 502 Police, 1:43, 1996, #2042 ..$45-60
BMW 502 Taxi, 1:43, 1996, #2041 ...$45-60
BMW 503 V-8, gray, 1:43, 1996, #2242 ....$45-60
BMW 503 V-8, ivory, 1:43, 1996, #2241 ....$45-60
BMW 503 V-8, red, 1:43, 1996, #2243 ....$45-60
BMW 507, green, 1:43, 1995, #2171 ..$45-60
BMW 507, silver, 1:43, 1995, #2173...$45-60
BMW 507, black, 1:43, 1995, #2172...$45-60
BMW 507 Convertible, 2", Piccolo, 1:90, 1958, #707........................$75-90
BMW 520, 1:43, 1973, #617............$25-30
BMW 520 Police car, 1:43, 1976, #635 ....$25-30
BMW 525, 1:43, 1973, #625............$25-30
BMW 535 Doctor's car, 1:43, 1976, #637 ....$25-30
BMW 630 CS, 1:43, 1976, #629.......$25-30
BMW Dixi Cabriolet, black, 1:43, 1996, #2291 ....$45-60
BMW Dixi Cabriolet, red and white, 1:43, 1996, #2292 ....$45-60
BMW Dixi Cabriolet, yellow and black, 1:43, 1996, #2293 ....$45-60
BMW Dixi Sedan, green, 1:43, 1995, #2152 ....$45-60
BMW Dixi Sedan, ivory, 1:43, 1995, #2153 ....$45-60
BMW Dixi Sedan, maroon, 1:43, 1995, #2151 ....$45-60
BMW Formula Two, 2½", 1972, #841....$10-15
BMW Isetta (open top), green, 1:43, 1995, #2091 ....$45-60
BMW Isetta (open top), red, 1:43, 1995, #2093...............................$45-60
BMW Isetta (open top), yellow, 1:43, 1995, #2092...............................$45-60
BMW Turbo, 1:43, 1973, #613..........$25-30
BMW Turbo, 2½", 1973, #865.............$10-15
BMW Turbo Turbo, 2½", 1973, #864.....$10-15
BMW Z3, black, 1:43, 1996, #4142...$50-65
BMW Z3, green, 1:43, 1996, #4143 ..$50-65
BMW Z3, red, 1:43, 1996, #4141......$50-65
BMW Z3 Soft Top, blue, 1:43, 1996, #4253 ....$50-65
BMW Z3 Soft Top, silver, 1:43, 1996, #4251 ....$50-65
BMW Z3 Soft Top, yellow, 1:43, 1996, #4252 ....$50-65
Boat and Trailer, 2", Piccolo, 1:90, 1962, #764 ....$85-100
Brabham Ford Formula One, 2½", 1972, #847 ....$10-15
Buick, 9", #5311 ....$375-425
Bussing Cement Carrier, 5⅜", 1972, #906 ..$20-25
Bussing Covered Semi-Trailer Truck, 4½", 1972, #905.................................$20-25
Bussing Dump Truck, 3", 1972, #902 .....$20-25
Bussing Flat Truck, 3-7/8", 1972, #903..$20-25
Bussing Open Truck, 3¾", 1972, #901....$20-25
Bussing Quarry Dump Truck, 2¾", 1972, #904 ....$20-25
Cadillac DeVille Convertible, 11", 1960s plastic, #5505 ....$150-165
Camping Trailer, 2", Piccolo, 1:90, 1958, #722 ....$75-90
Citroën DS 19, 2", Piccolo, 1:90, 1958, #719 ....$75-90
Coles Crane Truck and Trailer, Piccolo, 1:90, #775 ....$85-100
Coles Hydraulic Crane, Piccolo, 1:90, #799..$75-90
Conveyor belt, 4½", Piccolo, 1:90, 1962, #759 ....$85-100
Dalli, 6½", 1950s, tin car, plastic driver, Micro Racer, #1011 ....$150-165
Demag Power Shovel, 3⅛", Piccolo, 1:90, 1962, #760................................$75-90
Demag Power Shovel, 3⅜", 1972, #907...$20-25
Deutz Bulldozer, 2¼", Piccolo, 1:90, 1962, #754 ....$85-100
Deutz Caterpillar Tractor, 2", Piccolo, 1:90, 1962, #753 ....$85-100

Deutz Farm Tractor, 1¾, Piccolo, 1:90,
1962, #752 ....$85-100

Dingler Road Roller, 1½", Piccolo, 1:90,
#771 ....$85-100

DKW 3=6, black, 1:43, 1996,
#2271 ....$45-60

DKW 3=6, green, 1:43, 1996,
#2272 ....$45-60

DKW 3=6, ivory, 1:43, 1996, #2273 ....$45-60

DKW 3=6, Piccolo, 1:90, 1997, #351 ..$25-30

DKW 3=6 Cabriolet, dark blue, 1:43,
1996, #2373 ....$45-60

DKW 3=6 Cabriolet, gray, 1:43, 1996,
#2372 ....$45-60

DKW 3=6 Cabriolet, maroon, 1:43,
1996, #2371 ....$45-60

Elektro Ingenico, 8½, remote control,
1950s, #5311 ....$400-415

Examico 4001, 6", 1950s, #4001 ....$225-240

Faun Quarry Dump Truck, 3⅜", 1972,
#908 ....$20-25

Faun Quarry Dump Truck, 3⅜", Piccolo,
1:90, #774 ....$85-100

Faun Street Sweeper, 2¼", Piccolo, 1:90,
1962, #758 ....$85-100

Ferrari Formula Two, 2½", 1972, #840 ....$10-15

Ferrari Grand Prix Car, 2", Piccolo, 1:90,
1958, #701 ....$75-90

Fex, 6", Micro Racer, 1950s, #1111 ..$100-115

Firebird II Experimental car, Piccolo, 1:90,
2", 1958, #710 ....$75-90

Ford Capri 1700 GT, 2½", 1971, #816 ...$10-15

Ford Capri 1700 GT Rally, 2⅜", 1972,
#834 ....$10-15

Ford Capri II, 2½", 1974, #874 ....$10-15

Ford Capri RS, 2½", 1974, #877 ....$10-15

Ford Consul, 2¾", 1973, #858 ....$10-15

Ford Custom 300 1957, 4", Micro
Racer, 1950s, #1045 ....$180-210

Ford Escort, 2⅜, 1975, #881 ....$10-15

Ford Escort 1300 GT, 2⅜", 1971, #810 ...$10-15

Ford Escort Rally, 2⅜", 1972, #851 ....$10-15

Ford Escort Rally, 2⅜", 1975, #888 ....$10-15

Ford Granada, 2¾", 1973, #859 ....$10-15

Ford Hot Rod, 1¾", Piccolo, 1:90, 1964,
#725 ....$75-90

Ford Model T 1917, Oldtimers 1990s
reproduction, #1237 ....$180-210

Ford Taunus 20M, 2¾", 1971, #807 ......$10-15

Ford Taunus GT Coupe, 2⅜", 1972, #837 .....$10-15

Ford Taunus GXL Coupe, 2⅜", 1972, #838 ....$10-15

Ford Transit Bus, 2⅜", 1974, #913 ....$20-25

Ford Transit Fire Van, 2⅜", 1975, #890 ....$10-15

Ford Transit Van, 2⅜", 1974, #912 ....$20-25

Fork Lift truck, 2¾", Piccolo, 1:90,
1962, #765 ....$85-100

**FX Atmos Experimental car, Piccolo, 1:90,
2", 1958, #711 ....$75-90**

Gas Station, 8", 1950s, #3054 ....$100-115

Girato Mercedes, plastic body with diecast grille
and bumpers, 9.44" 1960, #4000 ...$400-450

Go Kart 1035, 4",, Micro Racer 1950s,
#1035 ....$180-195

Goggomobil, red, 1:43, 1996, #2072 ...$40-55

Goggomobil, yellow, 1:43, 1996, #2070 ......$40-55

Goggomobil, green, 1:43, 1996, #2071 ....$40-55

Goggomobil Fire Chief, 1:43, 1996, #2075 ...$45-60

Goggomobil Tu-Tone green and white,
1:43, 1996, #2073 ....$45-60

Goggomobil Tu-Tone red and white,
1:43, 1996, #2074 ....$45-60

Goliath Tempo Pritsche, gray, 1:43,
1995, #2052 ....$60-75

Goliath Tempo Pritsche, red and gray,
1:43, 1995, #2053 ....$60-75

Goliath Tempo Van, 1:43, 1995, #2063 ..$60-75

Grand Prix Racer, 6", Micro Racer,
1950s, #1070 ....$150-165

Grand Prix Racing Edition, 1024S, 1997
Replica of 1075 with replica of #1070
Ferrari Racer, 1912 produced worldwide,
Micro Racer, #1075 ....$275-325

Henschel Covered Semi, 4½", Piccolo,
1:90, #773 ....$75-90

Hopper Trailer, 2¾", Piccolo, 1:90,
1962, #768 ....$85-100

Hot Rod 1036, 4½", Micro Racer
1950s, #1036 ....$180

Isetta "Der Stern," 1:43, 1997, #2107 ...$40-50

Isetta "Lufthansa," 1:43, 1996, #2102 ...$40-50

Isetta (closed roof), black, 1:43, 1996, #2303 ....$45-60

Isetta (closed roof), light blue, 1:43,
1996, #2302 ....$45-60

Isetta (closed roof), maroon, 1:43,
1996, #2301 ....$45-60

Isetta Delivery, beige, 1:43, 1997, #2411 ....$45-60

Isetta Delivery, green, 1:43, 1997, #2412 ....$45-60

Isetta Police, 1:43, 1996, #2100 ....$40-50

Isetta Racer #13, 1:43, 1996, #2105 ...$40-50

Jaguar, 5½", 1940s, Micro Racer, #1250 ...$300-350

Krupp Bucket Truck, 3⅛", Piccolo, 1:90,
1962, #767 ....$85-100

Krupp car Transporter, 8", Piccolo, 1:90,
1962, #761 ....$75-90

Krupp Cement carrier, 5½", Piccolo,
1:90, #778 ....$85-100

Krupp Cement Mixer, 3⅜", Piccolo,
1:90, #772 ....$85-100

Krupp Cherry Picker, 3½", Piccolo, 1:90,
#770 ....$85-100

Krupp Crane Truck, 4", Piccolo, 1:90,
#769 ....$85-100

Krupp Dump Truck, 3¼", Piccolo, 1:90,
1960, #748 ....$85-100

Krupp Flat Truck, 4", Piccolo, 1:90, 1960,
#749 ....$85-100

Krupp Lumber Truck, 6", Piccolo, 1:90,
1962, #751 ....$85-100

Krupp Open Truck, 3¾", Piccolo, 1:90,
1960, #746 ....$85-100

Krupp Quarry Dump Truck, 3¼", Piccolo,
1:90, 1960, #750 ....$85-100

Krupp Tank Truck, 3¼", Piccolo, 1:90,
1962, #763 ....$85-100

Lasto, 4½", 1950s, #3042 ....$100-125

Liebherr Tower Crane, 6¼" high, Piccolo,
1:90, 1962, #762 ....$90-115

Linhoff Road Paver, 5", Piccolo, 1:90,
#777 ....$85-100

Lloyd 600, blue, 1:43, 1995, #2081 ....$45-60

Lloyd 600, green, 1:43, 1996, #2084 ..$40-50

Lloyd 600, red, 1:43, 1995, #2080 .....$45-60

Lloyd 600 Race Car, 1:43, 1996, #2083 ..$45-60

Lloyd Alex TS, blue and white, 1:43,
1996, #2201 ....$45-60

Lloyd Alex TS, gray and white, 1:43,
1996, #2202 ....$45-60

Lloyd Alex TS, green and white, 1:43,
1996, #2203 ....$45-60

Lotus Ford 72 Formula One, 2½",
1974, #870 ....$10-15

Lotus Formula One Racer, Micro
Racer, #1071 ....$100-125

Magico Car and Garage, 6", 1950s ..$225-250

Magico, 5½", 1:43, 1950s, #2008 ...$100-115

Magirus Ladder Truck, 4", Piccolo, 1:90,
1960, #745 ....$85-100

Magirus Tow Truck, Piccolo, 1:90, 1996,
#301 ....$35-45

Magirus Wrecker, 3", Piccolo, 1:90,
1960, #747 ....$85-100

Magirus-Deutz 232D Dump Truck, 3⅜",
1973, #909 ....$20-25

Magirus-Deutz 232D Quarry Dumper, 4",
1975, #917 ....$20-25

Man Doubledeck Bus, 3", Piccolo,
1:90, #776 ....$85-100

Maserati Grand Prix, 2", Piccolo, 1:90,
1958, #706 ....$75-90

Matra Ford Formula One, 2½", 1972,
#842 ....$10-15

Matra Simca Bagheera, 2½", #878 ....$10-15

Mercedes 170 V Box "Deutsche Bundespost," 1:43, 1996 limited edition of 2,000, #2255 ....$60-75

Mercedes 170 V Box "Maggi," 1:43, 1996 limited edition of 2000, #2254 ....$60-75

Mercedes 170 V Pickup, blue, 1:43, 1996, #2261 ....$45-60

Mercedes 170 V Pickup, ivory, 1:43, 1996, #2262 ....$45-60

Mercedes 170 V Van "Deutsche Reichspost," 1:43, 1996, #2253 ....$50-65

Mercedes 170 V Van, black, 1:43, 1996, #2252 ....$45-60

Mercedes 170 V Van, maroon and black, 1:43, 1996, #2251 ....$45-60

Mercedes 190SL, 8", 1:43, 1950s, #2095 ....$275-290

Mercedes 2.5L F1 single seater in silver with red no 4, Piccolo, 1:90, 1958, #703 ....$90-105

Mercedes Formula Racer 2.5L, 4", Micro Racer, 1950s, #1043 ....$180-205

Mercedes Simplex 1902, Oldtimers 1990s reproduction, #1239 ....$160-175

Mercedes-Benz 0303 Bus, 7", 1975, #916 ....$45-60

Mercedes-Benz 170V Delivery Van, 1:18, 1996, #0032 ....$280-305

Mercedes-Benz 170V Mail Van, 1:18, 1996, #0034 ....$300-325,

Mercedes-Benz 170V Truck with Tarp, 1:18, 1997, #0041 ....$290-315

Mercedes-Benz 190 SL, 2", Piccolo, 1:90, 1958, #713 ....$75-90

Mercedes-Benz 190SL, 4", Micro Racer, 1950s, #1044 ....$200-215

Mercedes-Benz 1928 SSK, 8", 1950s...$175-190

Mercedes-Benz 1936 Grand Prix, 2", Piccolo, 1:90, 1958, #704 ....$75-90

Mercedes-Benz 200 Police car, 2¾", 1971, #806 ....$10-15

Mercedes-benz 200 Taxi, 2¾", 1971, #823 ....$10-15

Mercedes-Benz 200, 2¾", 1971, #805 ....$10-15

Mercedes-Benz 220 Coupe, 2", Piccolo, 1:90, 1958, #717 ....$75-90

Mercedes-Benz 220 S, 2¼", Piccolo, 1:90, 1960, #724 ....$75-90

Mercedes-Benz 220S, Micro Racer, #1038 ....$180-205

Mercedes-Benz 250 CE, 2¾", 1971, #820 ..$10-15

Mercedes-Benz 300 SL, Piccolo, 1:90, 2", 1958, #709-B $75-90

Mercedes-Benz 300SL, Piccolo, 1:90, 1997, #391 ....$25-30

Mercedes-Benz 350 SE Doctor's Car, 1:43, 1976, #633-B $25-30

Mercedes-Benz 350 SE Police Car, 1:43, 1973, #616 ....$25-30

Mercedes-Benz 350 SE Taxi, 1:43, 1975, #633-A $25-30

Mercedes-Benz 350 SE, 1:43, 1972, #612 ....$25-30

Mercedes-Benz 350 SE, 3", 1973, #866..$10-15

Mercedes-Benz 350 SL Convertible, 3", 1972, #844 ....$10-15

Mercedes-Benz 450 SE Police Car, 3", 1974, #868 ....$10-15

MercedesBenz 450 SE, 1:43, 1973, #618 ..$25-30

Mercedes-Benz 450 SE, 3", 1974, #873...$10-15

Mercedes-Benz Bus, 3", 1972, #900......$20-25

Mercedes-Benz Bus, 3", Piccolo, 1:90, 1960, #740 ....$75-90

MercedesBenz C-111, 2¾", 1971, #828.......$10-15

Mercedes-Benz Delivery Van, 2", Piccolo, 1:90, 1960, #741 ....$75-90

Mercedes-Benz Fire Van, 1⅞", Piccolo, 1:90, 1962, #756 ....$85-100

Mercedes-Benz Grand Prix F1, 2", streamlined, Piccolo, 1:90, 1958, #702 ....$75-90

Mercedes-Benz Grand Prix, 2", Piccolo, 1:90, 1958, #703 ....$75-90

Mercedes-Benz Low Loader, 4", Piccolo, 1:90, 1960, #742 ....$85-100

Mercedes-Benz Refrigerator Van, 5½", Piccolo, 1:90, 1960, #743 ....$85-100

Mercedes-Benz Searchlight Truck, 1¾", Piccolo, 1:90, 1962, #755 ....$85-100

Mercedes-Benz Tanker Semi, 4", Piccolo, 1:90, 1960, #744 ....$85-100

Mercedes-Benz V 230, metallic black, 1:43, 1996, #4282 ....$45-60

Mercedes-Benz V 230, red, 1:43, 1996, #4283 ....$45-60

Mercedes-Benz V 230, silver, 1:43, 1996, #4281 ....$45-60

Mercer 1913 Type 35J, Oldtimers 1990s reproduction, #1235 ....$180-205

Mercer Auto, 7½", Micro Racer, 1950s, #1225 ....$175-190

Mercer, 1036/1, 4", Micro Racer, 1950s, #1036/1 ....$180-205

MGA Coupe, 2", Piccolo, 1:90, 1958, #714 ....$75-90

Micro Racer 101, 3½", 1950s Porsche style, #101 ....$175-190

Micro Racer 102, 3½", 1950s Indy style, #102...........................$175-190

Micro Racer 104, 3½", 1950s Indy style, #104 ....$175-190

Micro Racer, 4", Micro Racer, 1950s, #1040 ....$180-205

Midget Racer, 2", Piccolo, 1:90, 1958, #705 ..$75-90

MirakoCar Polizei, Micro Racer, 4¾", #1001/1 ....$150-165

MirakoCar, 4½", Micro Racer, 1950s, #1001 ....$150-165

Monkey Car, 6", 1930s, orange/black, smiling monkey $2,500-2,750

Motodrill Clown, 5", composition head, Micro Racer, 1950s, #1007 ....$750-800

Mystery Car, 5½", 1950s, non-fall action, Micro Racer, #1010 ....$175-190

NSU 1000TTS, red, 1:43, 1996, #2283 ...$45-60

NSU 1000TTS, silve, 1:43, 1996, #2281 ..$45-60

NSU 1000TTS, white, 1:43, 1996, #2282 ..$45-60

NSU-Fiat Spyder, 2", Piccolo, 1:90, 1958, #716 ....$75-90

Opel 1901 Doctor-Wagen with opening top, Oldtimers 1990s reproduction, #1228..............................$180-205

Opel 1901 Doctor-Wagen, Oldtimers 1990s reproduction, #1238 ....$160-175

Opel Admiral 2800 E, 3", 1971, #819...$10-15

Opel Ascona Voyage, 2½", 1972, #846..$10-15

Opel Commodore GS Rally, 2¾", 1971, #822 ....$10-15

Opel Commodore GS, 2¾", 1971, #811 ....$10-15

Opel Commodore, 2¾", 1973, #857 .....$10-15

Opel GT 1900, 2⅜", 1971, #814.........$10-15

Opel GT-J, 2½", 1972, #848 ....$10-15

Opel Manta SR, 2½", 1972, #849 ....$10-15

Opel Manta SR, 2⅜", 1972, #839 ....$10-15

Opel Rekord II, 2¾", 1973, #856 ....$10-15

Porsche 356, 4", Micro Racer, 1950s, #1047 ....$200-215

Porsche 911 S Racing Car, 2⅜", 1972, #835 ....$10-15

Porsche 911S Police Car, 2⅜", 1971, #825 ..$10-15

Porsche 911S, 2½", 1971, #813 ....$10-15

Porsche 917, 2½", 1972, #843 ....$15-20

Porsche 917, 2½", 1972, #854 ....$15-20

Porsche 924, 1:43, 1975, #628 ....$25-30

Porsche Boxter Hard Top, metallic gray, 1:43, 1996, #4233 ....$50-65

Porsche Boxter Hard Top, metallic green, 1:43, 1996, #4231 ....$50-65

Porsche Boxter Open, blue, 1:43, 1996, #4221 ....$50-65

Porsche Boxter Open, red, 1:43, 1996, #4223 ....$50-65

Porsche Boxter Open, yellow, 1:43, 1996, #4222 ....$50-65

Porsche Boxter Soft Top, metallic black, 1:43, 1996, #4243 ....$50-65

Porsche Boxter Soft Top, orange, 1:43, 1996, #4242 ....$50-65

Porsche Boxter Soft Top, white, 1:43, 1996, #4241 ....$50-65

Porsche Carrera S, dark metallic blue,
1:43, 1996, #4322 ....$50-65

Porsche Carrera S, red, 1:43, 1996,
#4321 ....$50-65

Porsche Carrera, light blue, 1:43, 1996,
#4151 ....$55-80

Porsche Carrera, metallic blue, 1:43,
1996, #4152 ....$55-80

Porsche Carrera, silver, 1:43, 1996,
#4153 ....$55-80

**Porsche Spyder, 2", Piccolo, 1:90, 1958,
#708 ....$75-90**

Porsche Turbo, metallic black, 1:43, 1996,
#4112 ....$55-80

Porschee Turbo, red,1:43,1996, #4111 ..$55-80

Porsche Turbo, yellow, 1:43, 1996,
#4113 ....$55-80

Radio 4012, 6", musical car, 1950s,
#4012 ....$375-425

Radio car with Garage Set, new limited edition,
lithographed garage with #5000 Radio car,
Micro Racer, #1072 ....$350-365

Rally 1034, 4", Micro Racer, 1950s,
#1034 ....$100-115

Renault 16 TS, 2½", 1973, #860 ....$10-15

Renault 16, 2½", 1972, #850 ....$10-15

Renault 17 TS, 2½", 1973, #861 ....$10-15

Renault 17, 2½", 1972, #853 ....$10-15

Renault 5, 2⅛", 1974, #871 ....$10-15

Renault 6CV Voiturette 1911, Oldtimers
1990s reproduction, #1230 ....$180-205

Replica `57 Ford Custom 300 Police Car,
Micro Racer, #1045 ....$55-80

Replica `57 Ford Custom 300, Micro
Racer, #1045..........................$50-65

Replica 1958 Volkswagen, Micro Racer,
#1046 ....$50-65

Replica Akustico Tutone, special limited
edition, 1:43, #2002 ....$180-205

Replica Akustico with opening hood and
Fritz, 1:43, #2002 ....$260-275

Replica Akustico with working horn, 1:43,
#2002 ....$150-165

Replica Auto Union Studio II Kit, Micro
Racer, #1222 ....$130-145

Replica BMW 501, dark blue, 1:43,
1996, #2014 ....$55-80

Replica BMW 501, white, 1:43, 1996,
#2012 ....$55-80

Replica Chrome Examico, #4001 ....$175-190

Replica Chrome Ferrari Grand Prix Racer,
Micro Racer, #1070 ....$125-140

Replica Examico with opening hood,
#4001 ....$195-210

Replica Examico, #4001 ....$165-180

Replica Ferrari Classic Grand Prix Racer,
red, Micro Racer, #1070............$100-115

Replica Girato Mercedes, plastic body
with diecast grille and bumpers, 9.44"
1996, #4000 ....$250-265

Replica Magirus Deutz Fire Truck, 1996,
#745 ....$40-50

Replica Mercedes `36 Grand Prix, Piccolo,
1:90, 1995, #704 ....$25-30

Replica Mercedes 2.5L F1, Piccolo, 1:90, 1995,
#703 ....$25-30

Replica Mercedes Formula Racer 2.5L, Micro
Racer, #1043.........................$50-65

Replica Mercedes Streamliner, Piccolo, 1:90,
1995, #702 ....$25-30

Replica Mercedes Tractor with Lowboy, Piccolo,
1:90, 1996, #742 ....$40-50

Replica Mercedes-Benz 190 SL, Piccolo, 1:90,
2", 1996, #713 ....$25-30

Replica Mercedes-Benz 190SL, Micro Racer,
#1044 ....$50-65

Replica Mercedes-Benz 220 S, Piccolo, 1:90,
1996, #724 ....$25-30

Replica Mercedes-Benz 220S, Micro Racer,
#1038 ....$50-65

Replica Porsche 356, Micro Racer, #1047 ...$50-65

Replica Porsche Spyder, Piccolo, 1:90,
1996, #708 ....$25-30

Replica Radio Auto with music box,
#5000 ....$300-315

Replica Studio II Auto Union Typ C, Micro
Racer, #1220 ....$90-105

Replica Studio Racer 1050 1936 Grand
Prix Mercedes, #1050..................$80-95

Replica USA Midget, Micro Racer, #1041 .....$50-65

Replica USA Midget, Micro Racer, #1042 ....$50-65

Replica Volkswagen Fire Chief, Micro
Racer, #1039.........................$55-80

Replica Volkswagen, Piccolo, 1:90, 1996,
#712 ....$25-30

Replica Wonder Auto Mystery Car, Micro
Racer, #1010 ....$100-115

Replica Wonder Auto Mystery Car, Tu-Tone
Blue, Micro Racer, #1010 ....$120-135

Scientific Forklift $125-140

Stake Truck 1049, 4", Micro Racer,
1950s, #1049 ....$175-190

Station car 3118, 4½", 1950s, #3118......$100-115

Studio Racer 1050 with tools, 5½", Micro
Racer, 1950s, #1050 ....$225-230

Synchromatic 5700, resembles Packard
Hawk, 11", 1950s, #5700...$1,000-1,150

Telesteering 3000 Limo, 4", 1950s, #3000...$80-95

Tempo "Deutsche Bundespost," 1:43, 1996
limited edition of 2,000, #2135 ....$60-75

Tempo "Dunlop," 1:43, 1996 limited edition
of 2,000, #2210 ....$60-75

Tempo "Persil," 1:43, 1996 limited edition
of 2,000, #2211 ....$60-75

Tempo "Shell," 1:43, 1996 limited edition
of 2,000, #2136 ....$60-75

Tempo "Trix-Express," 1:43, 1996 limited
edition of 2,000, #2140 ....$60-75

Tempo Fire Truck, 1:43, 1996 limited
edition of 2,000, #2212 ....$60-75

Tempo Tarp, green, 1:43, 1996, #2120 ...$55-80

Tempo Tarp, red, 1:43, 1996, #2121 ...$55-80

Tempo Van, gray, 1:43, 1996, #2062 ..$55-80

Tempo Van, ivory and green, 1:43,
1996, #2064 ....$55-80

Tipping Trailer, 3", Piccolo, 1:90,
1962, #757 ....$85-100

Tyrell Ford Formula One, 2½", 1973, #863 ...$10-15

USA Midget, 4", Micro Racer,
1950s, #1041 ....$180-205

USA Midget, 4", Micro Racer,
1950s, #1042 ....$180-205

Varianto 3010 Super, service station with two
4½" tin cars, 1950s, #3010.........$325-340

Varianto 3010, playset with two 4½" tin cars,
1950s, #3010 ....$180-205

Varianto 3041 Limo, 4", 1950s, #3041 ...$150-165

Varianto 3064, 8" plastic, 1950s, #3064 .....$50-65

Varianto Box 3010/30, tin garage and 3041
Limo, 4½", #3010/30, 1950s.....$200-215

Varianto Bus 3044, 4", 1950s, #3044......$100-115

Varianto Electro 3112, 4" truck,
1950s, #3112 ....$100-115

Varianto Electro 3112U, 4½" truck,
1950s, #3112U $100-115

Volkswagen 1300, 2½", 1971, #818.....$10-15

Volkswagen 1302 S, 2½", 1972, #832....$10-15

Volkswagen 1958, 4", Micro Racer,
1950s, #1046 ....$175-190

Volkswagen 411 Fire Chief, 2¾", 1971,
#824 ....$10-15

Volkswagen 411, 2¾", 1971, #812.......$10-15

Volkswagen ADAC Service car, 2½",
1972, #833 ....$10-15

Volkswagen Ambulance, 2⅝", 1974, #914..........$20-25

Volkswagen Beetle Herbie, Piccolo, 1:90,
1997 Limited Edition, #265 ....$35-40

Volkswagen Bully Van, "Shell," Piccolo,
1:90, 1996 Limited Edition, #322 ....$35-40

Volkswagen Bully Van, Piccolo, 1:90,
1996, #321 ....$25-30

Volkswagen Cabriolet, Piccolo, 1:90, 1997, #401 .... $25-30
Volkswagen Fire, Piccolo, 1:90, 1996 Limited Edition, #712 .... $35-40
Volkswagen Golf Mail car, 1:43, 1976, #638 .... $25-30
Volkswagen Golf Mail car, 2¼", 1975, #882 .... $10-15
Volkswagen Golf Rally, 1:43, 1975, #624 .... $25-30
Volkswagen Golf, 1:43, 1974, #621 .... $25-30
Volkswagen Golf, 2¼", 1974, #880 .... $10-15
Volkswagen K70, 2¾", 1972, #831 .... $10-15
Volkswagen Karmann-Ghia and Boat Trailer, 3½", Piccolo, 1:90, 1962, #766 .... $85-100
Volkswagen Karmann-Ghia and Trailer, 3½", Piccolo, 1:90, 1958, #723 .... $65-80
Volkswagen Karmann-Ghia, 2", Piccolo, 1:90, 1958, #715 .... $75-90
Volkswagen Kombi, 2⅝", 1973, #910 .... $20-25
Volkswagen LT35 Pickup, 3¼", 1976, #919 .... $20-25
Volkswagen Mail truck, 2⅝", 1974, #915 .... $20-25
Volkswagen Passat TS, 1:43, silver, 1973, #614 .... $25-30
Volkswagen Passat TS, 2½", 1974, #872 .... $10-15
Volkswagen Passat TS, red, orange-red or yellow-green, 1:43, 1973, #615 .... $25-30
Volkswagen Passat Variant ADAC car, 1:43, 1975, #630 .... $25-30
Volkswagen Passat Variant Fire Chief, 1:43, 1975, #631 .... $25-30
Volkswagen Passat Variant, 1:43, 1974, #619 .... $25-30
Volkswagen Passat, 2½", 1973, #867 .... $10-15
Volkswagen Police Bus, 2⅝", 1975, #889 .... $10-15
Volkswagen Police/Fire Chief, 2", Piccolo, 1:90, 1958, #720 .... $75-90
Volkswagen Polizei, 4", Micro Racer, 1950s, #1039 .... $180-205
Volkswagen Polizei, Piccolo, 1:90, 1996 Limited Edition, #712 .... $35-40
Volkswagen Polo, 1:43, 1975, #623 .... $25-30
Volkswagen Porsche 914 Race Control Car, 2⅜", 1974, #869 .... $10-15
Volkswagen Porsche 914 S, 2⅜", 1971, #826 .... $10-15
Volkswagen Porsche 914-6 Racing car, 2⅜", 1972, #836 .... $10-15
Volkswagen Porsche 914-6, 2⅜", 1971, #827 .... $10-15
Volkswagen Scirocco Racing Service car, 1:43, 1975, #632 .... $25-30
Volkswagen Scirocco, 1:43, 1974, #620 .... $25-30
Volkswagen Scirocco, 2⅜", 1974, #879 .... $10-15
Volkswagen Transporter, 2⅝", 1973, #911 .... $20-25
Volkswagen, 2", Piccolo, 1:90, 1958, #712 .... $75-90
Volkwagen Beetle ADAC, Piccolo, 1:90, 1997 Limited Edition, #266 .... $35-40
Volvo PV 544, 2", Piccolo, 1:90, 1958, #718 .... $75-90

Schwung

Schwung is a brand name of 1:32 scale tin toys made in Germany.

Opel Rekord 4-door Sedan $16-20
Opel Fire Chief $24-28
Opel Police $24-28
Opel Ambulance $24-28
Skoda Dump Truck $24-28
Tatra 815 Van $16-20

Schylling

P O Box 667
Ipswich, MA 01938
toll free: 800-541-2929
fax: 978-356-5959

Schylling once produced only tin toys. Now they have expanded into being a wholesale toy distributor. Besides their own assortment of tin-plate toys and ornaments, they now offer an array of intriguing toys from other manufacturers, including diecast toys from Kintoy/Kinsmart, Superior/Sunnyside, and others.

SCM

Colin Jesmer wrote via e-mail that he has an SCM model diecast car, and he wondered how old it is and if it is worth any money. "The car is not built," he wrote. "The car is a 1:64 scale put-together model with a marking on the top of the inside that says 'E1 SCM.' It may be a Ford Thunderbird. There is an address on one of the pieces which is 'P.O. Box 74 R.S. PA. 16673'."

Based on the zip code, the complete address is "P O Box 74, Roaring Spring, Pennsylvania 16673." The closest match I could find for such a business is SCM Metal Products Incorporated, Johnstown, Pennsylvania.

Upon calling them, I found that SCM is now OMG Americas. On recommendation from OMG's receptionist, I contacted Russ Kelly in purchasing. Mr. Kelly has been with SCM since 1973, but he knows of no diecast toys of any kind ever produced by the company, adding that their manufacturing is in "powder castings," and that they don't do, and have never done, any diecasting. The mystery continues.

Scorchers (Hot Wheels)

Hot Wheels Scorchers were introduced in 1979 and consist of plastic bodies and spring activated motors. They are mentioned here separately because they are so distinctively different from Hot Wheels, and are highly collectible. Prices listed are highly speculative since I've found no reputable source for values in any of the fourteen collector reference books published on Hot Wheels. Twelve original Scorchers were issued in 1979. Six more models were added in 1981.

Blackbird, #2589, 1979 .... $45-60
Blue Fever, #1597, 1981 .... $45-60
Britework, #1596, 1981 .... $45-60
Capri Turbo, #2896, 1979 .... $45-60
Chevrolet Light, #2894, 1979 .... $45-60
Cookin' Camaro, #2895, 1979 .... $45-60
Cool Capri, #2645, 1979 .... $45-60
El Camino Real, #2643, 1979 .... $45-60
Firebrand, #1594, 1981 .... $45-60
Good Looker, #2642, 1979 .... $45-60
Magnum Fever, #2892, 1979 .... $45-60
Magnum XE, #2641, 1979 .... $45-60
Sundrifter, #1595, 1981 .... $45-60
Time Bender, #1505, 1981 .... $45-60
Turbo 928, #1593, 1981 .... $45-60
Vandemonium, #2893, 1979 .... $45-60
White Thunder, #2640 .... $45-60
Zappin' Z-28, #2544, 1979 .... $45-60

Scottoys

Scottoys are white metal reproductions of obsolete Mercury models of Italy. Each 1:48 to 1:66 scale model was offered in two to three colour choices.

Alfa Romeo
- 1900 Saloon, SC04 .... $50-55
- Giulietta SC03 .... $50-55
- Giulietta Sprint, SC08 .... $50-55

Autobianchi Bianchina, SC11 .... $50-55
Cadillac Eldorado, SC06 .... $60-70
Fiat
- 600 Multipla two-tone, SC02 .... $50-55
- 600 Saloon, SC01 .... $45-55
- 1100 Saloon, SC05 .... $50-55
- Nuova 500, SC09 .... $50-55

Innocenti 950, SC07 .... $50-55
Lambretta scooter, 1:30, SC17 .... $30-40
Lancia Appia
- 1a, SC19 .... $50-55
- 1a Taxi, SC19 .... $50-55
- 3a, SC10 .... $50-55
- 3a Taxi, SC10T $50-55

Vespa scooter
- gold, SC17G, limited edition of 250 .... $35-45
- 1:30, SC18 .... $35-45

1:30, SC18 kit $30-40

Septoy

Gasquy brand models were first issued as Septoys, produced in Belgium. See the complete listing under Gasquy.

Shackleton

Collector Bill Cross reports regarding Shackleton, "I believe these are Foden truck (lorry, in my native language!) models made by Abbey-Corinthian Games of London in the 1950s. I have an advertisement in front of me, in a 1958 issue of *Meccano Magazine*. These were magnificent diecast and pressed steel models of 1950s Foden trucks. Actually, there were three models in the range: a 3-axle Foden Flatbed, a matching 4-wheel Dyson flatbed trailer, and a 3-axle dump. The trucks were powered by a wind-up motor in the cab, driving the rear wheels through a driveshaft and scale differential....Operating Ackerman steering as well. Some parts, I remember from ownership as a (very lucky) child, were very fragile — springs broke very easily. The models came completely apart with nuts and bolts. The cab and bed were diecast. Frame parts, fenders, etc. were pressed steel. Weak parts were 'Chinese Cheese Metal.' I remember that the flatbeds came in yellow, the dump truck I think in red and green. In good condition, these now bring several hundred pounds. Original price in 1958 was 65 shillings, about $22 I think, at the 1958 exchange rate."

Foden 3-Axle Flatbed Lorry (Truck) $850-1,000
Dyson 4-wheel Flatbed Trailer $450-600
3-Axle Dump $450-600

Shinsei Mini Power

Shinsei Mini Power models of Japan are highly accurate scale models produced from the mid 1970s through the early 1990s. Listed below are known models and current values. Shinsei also made tin litho battery-operated toy cars and other items.

Aerial Ladder Fire Engine, 1:64, #4101 ..$30-40
Amphibious Bulldozer, 1:64, #4136.......$20-30
Asphalt Finisher, 1:64, #4121 ....$25-35
BMW 3.5 CSL Coupe, 1:43, #407.......$15-20
Bucket Crawler Crane, 1:64, #4107 .....$25-35
Bucket Wheel Excavator, 1:64, #4103...$30-40
Bulldozer, 1:64, #4113 ....$15-20
CAT
   325 Hydraulic Excavator, 1:50, #950 ..$8-10
   922C Wheel Loader, 1:75, #601 ....$45-60

Chemical Fire Engine, 1:64, #4108 ....$15-25
Chevrolet Corvette Stingray, 1:56, #452 ...$8-10
Crane Truck, 1:64, #4124 ....$35-45
Dozer Shovel, 1:64, #4114 ....$15-25
Dump Truck, 1:64, #4110 ....$15-25
Earth Drill, 1:64, #4131 ....$20-30
Fuso TOKYO OSAKA, 1:43, #625 ....$25-35
GMC
   Cement Mixer, 1:43, #4216............$20-30
   Conrete Pump Truck, 1:43, #4234....$20-30
   Crane Auger, 1:43, #4235...............$20-30
   Dump Truck, 1:43, #4215 ....$20-30
   Garbage Collector, 1:43, #4220.....$20-30
   Oil Tanker SHELL, 1:43, #4217 ....$20-30
   Refrigerator Van, 1:43, #4218 ....$20-30
   Street Sweeper, 1:43, #4233...........$20-30
   U. S. Trucking, 1:43, #4219............$20-30
Gulf Mirage, 1:43, #402.......................$20-25
Heavy Vehicle carrier, 1:64, #4137 ....$25-35
Hitachi
   EX 1800 Mining Excavator, 1:60, #620..$90-105
   EX 200 Excavator, 1:48, #618 ....$50-60
   LX 70 Wheel Loader, #619 ....$45-55
Hydraulic
   Crawler Crane, 1:64, #4130............$30-40
   Excavator, 1:64, #4112 ....$20-30
   Motor Grader, 1:64, #4126 ....$15-25
   Motor Scraper, 1:64, #4125 ....$25-35
K201 Aerial Work Vehicle, 1:64, #4106..$35-45
KATO NK 800 Hydraulic Crane, 1:61, #605...$75-90
Kenworth
   Car Transporter, 1:99, #62 ....$12-15
   SKYWAY, 1:99, #61 ....$12-15
Komatsu
   D 475 Dozer with Ripper, 1:48, #617...$75-90
   HD 785 Heavy Dump Truck, 1:45, #658 ..$8-10
   PC 200 Shovel, #921 ....$75-90
   PC 650 Excavator, 1:50, #614.......$75-90
   WA 350 Wheel Loader, 1:50, #615...$50-65
Lamborghini
   Countach, 1:50, #421 ....$8-10
   Jota, 1:64, #4422 ....$6-8
Lancia Stratos, 1:43, #4412 ....$20-25
Lift Truck
   1:64, #4122 ....$20-30
   with Roll Clamp, 1:64, #4123..........$20-30
Loader Shovel, 1:64, #4129 ....$25-35
Macadam Roller, 1:64, #4128...............$25-35
Mechanical Truck Crane, 1:64, #4102 ..$30-40
Mercedes-Benz
   Cement Mixer, 1:43, #4316 ....$20-30
   Concrete Pump Truck, 1:43, #4334 ..$20-30
   Crane Auger, 1:43, #4335 ....$20-30
   Dump Truck, 1:43, #4315 ....$20-30
   Garbage Collector, 1:43, #4320.....$20-30
   Oil Tanker, 1:43, #4317 ....$20-30

   Refrigerator Van, 1:43, #4318 ....$20-30
   Street Sweeper, 1:43, #4333...........$20-30
   Van Truck, 1:43, #4319 ....$20-30
Pile Driver, 1:64, #4127 ....$20-30
Snorkel
   Chemical Fire Engine, 1:64, #4109 ..$15-25
   Fire Engine, 1:64, #4104 ....$15-25
T911 Aerial Work Vehicle, 1:64, #4105.....$35
TMC 860 Wheel Loader, 1:50, #675 ....$45
Tractor
   Multi Ripper, 1:64, #4132 ....$20-30
   Shovel, 1:64, #4111 ....$15-25

Sibur

These are older hand-built diecast models from France.

GMC
   6X6 Army Open Truck, 1:43.............$35-45
   6X6 Army Closed Truck, 1:43 ....$35-45
   Army Bookmobile, 1:43 ....$35-45
   Truck Paris-Dakar, 1:50....................$35-45

Sieperwerke (see Siku)

Signature Models

Signature Models were introduced in 2002 and represent exceptional 1:18 and 1:32 scale diecast cars from China. They have been simultaneously marketed as National Motor Mint and Fairfield Mint issues. Some are reported to be Anson reissues.

1936 Chrysler Airflow
   1:18..$30-40

1:32 ....$10-1

1955 Chrysler Imperial
   1:18..$30-40
   1:32..$10-15

1932 Chrysler LeBaron, 1:32 ....$10-15
1936 Cord
   1:18..$30-40
   1:32..$10-15

1937 Cord Supercharged
   1:18 ....$30-40
   1:32 ....$10-15
1934 Duesenberg
   1:18 ....$30-40
   1:32 ....$10-15
1930 Hudson
   1:18 ....$30-40
   1:32 ....$10-15
1953 Nash
   1:18 ....$30-40
   1:32 ....$10-15
1930 Packard
   1:18 ....$30-40

1:32 ....$10-15

1930 Packard LeBaron, 1:18 ....$30-40
1941 Plymouth
   1:18 ....$30-40
   1:32 ....$10-12
1954 Plymouth Concept, 1:32 ....$10-15
1917 Reo Touring
   1:18 ....$30-40

1:32 ....$10-15

1963 Studebaker Avanti, 1:18 ....$30-40

1:32 ....$10-15

Siku (also see Roskopf)

Siku is a division of Sieperwerke, a venerable German company established in 1921 by Richard Sieper. The name "Siku" is an acronym formed from the first two letters of the Sieper name combined with the first two letters of "kunststoff," the German word describing synthetic material or plastic.

From 1949 to 1963, Siku toys were made of plastic, but in 1963, as Matchbox started marketing their products in Germany, the first Siku diecast models were produced in an attempt to keep up with the increasing competition. 1:55 scale models marketed in the US are packaged as Siku "Super Series" models. While the predominant scale for Siku is 1:55, they are also produced in 1:64 scale and in the 1:32 scale "Farm Series."

Models listed below include the model year (when known), description, production years and current value range.

5x2 Containers for 2920, #7016, ...$5-10
ADAC Automobile Club Testing Service,
   #3430, 1993– $45-48
ADAC Breakdown Service, #1323, 1997–...$6-8
ADAC Breakdown Truck with car,
   #2520, 1993– $24-27
ADAC Car Club Motorbike, #1324, 1997–..$4-6
ADAC Helicopter, #831, 1992– $5-10
ADAC Helicopter, #2228, 1993– $21-24
ADAC Pick-Up-Service, #1313, 1994– $5-8
ADAC Recovery Van, #2534, 1996–....$24-27
Airbus 320, #1021, 1993– $5-10
Airbus A340-200, #1927, 1993– $15-25
Aircraft Tractor, #162, 1961–1963.......$30-45
Airport Fire Engine, #826, 1992–.......$5-10
Airport Luggage Tractor (133) and Trailer
   (134), #135, 1960–1963 ....$45-75
Airport Luggage Tractor, #133, 1960–1963...$25-40
Airport Luggage Trailer with luggage,
   #134, 1960–1963 ....$20-35
Alfa Romeo Montreal, #321, 1971–1974..$20-35
Alfa Romeo Montreal, #1025, 1975–1981 ..$9-12
Amazone Seed Drill, #1952, 1993– $15-25
Ambulance "NOTARZT," #1911,
   1975–1984 ....$18-20
Ambulance "UNFALL-NOTFALL," #1911,
   1985–1986 ....$15-25
Animal Wagon, #69, 1957–1962.......$65-80
Army Jeep, #92, 1958–1964 ....$50-65
Army Jeep, #197, 1962–1965 ...$30-45-50
Army Trailer, #196, 1962–1965 ....$45-60
Army Unimog, #131, 1960–1965 ....$40-55
Articulated Bus, #3517, 1996–.............$45-48
Audi 100 "Arzt-Notfall-Einsatz," #353,
   1973–1974 ....$20-30
Audi 100 Arzt-Notfall-Einsatzwagen,
   #1313, 1975 ....$8-10
Audi 100 AVant, #1057, 1984–1988 ....$6-10
Audi 100 LS, #1019, 1975–1982.........$9-12
Audi 100LS, #308, 1970–1974 ....$20-35

Audi 200 5T, #1041, 1982–1988 ....$5-10
Audi 80 Convertible, #841, 1992–..........$5-10
Audi A 4, #1086, 1997– $4-6
Audi A 6, #1092, 1998– $4-6
Audi A6 AVant, #1079, 1994– $4-6
1958 Auto Union 1000, #145, 1960–1965..$50-65
Beet Trailer, #2859, 1993– $30-32
Bergmann Manure Spreader, #2964, 1998–..$33-36
Berliet Quarry Dumper, #200, 1963–1966...$65-80
Binz Ambulance, #1931, 1998– $15-25
1955 BMW Isetta 250, #51, 1957–1958..$65-80
1957 BMW Isetta 250/300, #51,
   1959–1963 ....$65-80
1959 BMW 700 Coupe, #139,
   1960–1965 ....$60-85
BMW 1500, #202, 1962–1968 ....$30-45
BMW 2000CS Polizei Loudspeaker Car, #1321,
   1975–1977 ....$6-10
BMW 2000CS, #266, 1967–1974.....$20-30
BMW 2000CS, #1011, 1975–1981.....$9-12
BMW 320i, #1028, 1994–...............$5-10
BMW 501, #36, 1956–1963 ....$75-90
BMW 600, #86, 1958–1963 ....$65-80
BMW 633 CSi, #1035, 1978–1989 ....$5-10

BMW 730iL, #1052, 1996–..........................$4-6
BMW 735iL, #1070, 1988– $4-10
BMW Police Patrol car 5-10, #1352, 1994–..$12-15
BMW Polizei (Police) Loudspeaker car,
   #341, 1997–1974 ....$20-35
BMW R1100RS Motorbike, #1047, 1996–..$4-6
BMW Z3 Hardtop, #850, 1998– $4-6
BMW Z-3, #846, 1997– $4-6
Boeing 737, #1020, 1994–...............$5-10
Boeing 747-400, #1926, 1993– $15-25
Boeing 767-200, #1719, 1993– $12-14
1952 Borgward Diesel 4-Ton Dump Truck,
   #32, 1955–1962 ....$65-80
1954 Borgward Hansa 1500 Isabella,
   #35, 1956–1963 ....$85-100
Borgward 1800 Sedan with skis,
   #66, 1957–1959 ....$90-105
Borgward 1800, #28, 1955–1959 ....$85-100
Borgward 2400 Pullman, #29,
   1955–1959 ....$115-130
Borgward 2400, #27, 1955–1960 ....$85-100
Borgward Grocer's Truck, #102, 1959–1961.$125-150
Borgward Isabella Sedan with skis,
   #66, 1960 ....$95-110
Borgward Kubelwagen, #94, 1958–1968..$50-65

Borgward Log Truck, #61, 1957–1965 ..$50-65
Borgward Snowplow Truck,
   #89, 1958–1961 ....$85-100
Borgward Troop carrier, #195, 1962–1967 ...$45-60
1956 Buick Riviera, #74, 1957–1963 ...$65-80
Buick Wildcat Sport Coupe, #255,
   1965–1971 ....$25-40
Bulldozer, #823, 1992– $5-10
Bulldozer, #3435, 1998– $45-48
Bus, "EuropaBus," #3121, 1993– $30-45
Bus, Red upper, white lower, scenery on
   sides, "erdgas," #3121, 1993– $30-45
Büssing 1½ Deck Aerobus,
   #72, 1957–1964 ....$120-150
Büssing Trambus 6.5 Ton,
   #39, 1956–1969 ....$110-125
Cable Trailer, #207, 1963–1964 ....$30-45
Cadillac Fleetwood 75, #265, 1966–1971 ..$30-45
Cadillac Fleetwood, #209, 1963–1968 ..$60-75
Camaro Z28, #1051, 1983– $4-10
Cambridge Roller, #2263, 1997– $21-24

Camping Car, #2536, 1:55, 1996– $24-27

Canoe Trailer, #121, 1959–1965 ....$20-30
Car Trailer, #53, 1957–1964 ....$20-35
Cargo Trailer, #259, 1966–1972 ....$15-25
Case CS150 Tractor, #2963, 1998– .. $33-36
Caterpillar Shovel, #3518, 1996– $45-48
Cement Mixer, #813, 1992– $5-10
Cement Mixer, #3431, 1994– $45-48
Champion Rotary Cropper, #2264, 1997– ..$21-24
Chevrolet Corvette Sting Ray, #282,
   1968–1974 ....$20-35
Chevrolet Corvette, #1055, 1984– $4-10
1961 Chrysler Windsor, #186, 1962–1965 ..$65-80
Circus Train (48, 68 & 69),
   #117, 1957–1961 ....$170-215
Circus Wagon, #68, 1957–1962 ....$65-80
Citroën 2 CV, #75, 1957–1961 ....$65-80
Citroën 2 CV, #1089, 1998– $4-6
Citroën 2CV, #1032, 1985– $12-15
Citroën DS 19, #76, 1957–1964 ....$75-90
Citroën DS21, #290, 1968–1974 ....$35-50
Citroën DS21, #1014, 1975–1980 ......$15-25
Citroën SM, #322, 1971–1974 ....$20-35
Citroën SM, #1026, 1975–1981 ....$15-25
Citroën Xantia, #1087, 1997– $4-6

Claas Automatic Hay Loader, #3454,
   1993– $45-48
Claas Baler, #2262, 1996– $21-24
Claas Jaguar 695 Combine, #3854, 1993– ..$55-60
Claas Jaguar 695 Forage Harvester,
   #3855, 1994– $55-60
Claas Lexion 480, #4150, 1997– $70-75
Claas Teleskoplader Ranger 911 T,
   #3455, 1994– $45-48
Claas Tipping Trailer, #2866, 1993– $30-32
Claas Whirl Rake, #2560, 1994– $24-27
Coach, #806, 1992– $5-10
Container Grabber with Container,
   #3725, 1998– $45-48
Container Transporter Truck, "Sea Land,"
   #1016, 1993– $4-10
Conveyor Belt, #125, 1959–1963 ....$30-45
Corn Seed Drill, #2260, 1994– $21-24
Covered Trailer, #44, 1957–1965 ....$25-35
Covered Trailer, #1325, 1976–1979 ....$10-12
Covered Truck Trailer, #37, 1956–1963 ..$20-35
Crane Bridge, #214, 1963–1965 ....$85-100
Credé Forklift, #132, 1960–1965 ....$30-45
Crop Sprayer, #1955, 1993– $15-25
Cultivator, #107, 1959–1961 ....$20-35
DAF Garage Transporter, #3425, 1993– ..$45-48
DAF Loader Truck and Trailer with Beams,
   #3812, 1989– $55-60
DAF Low Loader with Gas Station,
   #4018, 1994– $70-75
DAF Hentocar Tour Bus, #129, 1959–1968 ..$90-120
Deutz AgroXtra Tractor with Twin Rear Wheels,
   #2956, 1993– $33-36
Deutz Baler, #2862, 1993– $30-32
Deutz Combine, #1024, 1993– $5-10
Deutz DX 85 Tractor with Trailer,
   #1513, 1996– $8-10
Deutz DX 85 Tractor with Vacuum
   Tanker, #1515, 1996– $8-10
Deutz DX 85 Tractor, #843, 1995– $4-6
Deutz Fahr Agrostar with Rear Digger,
   #3756, 1997– $45-48
Deutz Fahr Agrostar with Scraper and
   Toolbox, #3457, 1997– $45-48
Deutz Hay Rake, #2254, 1993– $21-24
Deutz Rotary Mower, #1953, 1993– $15-25
Deutz-Fahr Agrostar 6.61 Turbo Tractor,
   #2850, 1993– $30-32
Deutz-Fahr Agrostar DX6.61 Turbo Tractor with
   Tandem-Axle Trailer, #3751, 1993– ..$45-48
Deutz-Fahr Agrotron 6.05 tt, #2958, 1994– .$33-36
Deutz-Fahr Agroxtra Tractor with Front
   Mower, #3156, 1994– $30-45
Deutz-Fahr AgroXtra Tractor, #2863, 1993– ..$30-32
Deutz-Fahr DX6.31 Turbo Forestry Tractor, #3550,
   1993– $45-48

Deutz-Fahr Fun-Trac Tractor, #2865, 1993– ...$30-32
Deutz-Fahr M36.10 Corn Combine
   Harvester, #4052, 1993– $70-75
Deutz-Fahr Round Baler, #2556, 1993– ..$24-27
Deutz-Fahr Top Liner Combine Harvester,
   #4051, 1993– $70-75
Deutz-Fahr Tractor with Vacuum Tanker,
   #3752, 1993– $45-48
Diesel Tractor with Dump Trailer,
   #254, 1966–1973 ....$30-45
Disc Harrow, #1950, 1993– $15-25
1952 DKW Covered Truck, #24,
   1955–1962 ....$75-90
1952 DKW Kombi Van, #23, 1955–1959 .$75-90
1952 DKW Pickup Truck, #25,
   1955–1961 ....$75-90
1953 DKW Sonderklasse Sedan, #26,
   1955–1959 ....$85-100
DKW F12, #224, 1964–1966 ....$30-45
DKW Junior, #141, 1960–1964 ....$35-50
DKW-Auto Union 4x4 F 91 / 6, #189,
   1962–1965 ....$50-65
Doubledecker Coach, #1353, 1994– ..$5-10
Dropside Trailer, #128, 1959–1963 ......$20-35
Duck Amphibian, #183, 1962–1966 ....$75-90
Dump Truck, #848, 1997– $4-6
Dumper Truck, #814, 1992– $5-10
1958 Edsel, #98, 1959–1963 ....$65-80
Emergency Doctor, #1339, 1995– $5-7
Euclid S-7/E 915R "ATHEY" Earth Mover,
   #280, 1968–1972 ....$30-45
Excavator, #801, 1992– $5-10
Fahr Diesel Tractor, #48, 1957–1965 ....$30-45
Farm Animals, 1 horse, 1 cow, 1 pig, 1 sheep,
   1 goat, #2558, 1993– $24-27
Farm Dump Trailer, #2552, 1993– $24-27
Farm Trailer, #60, 1957–1965 ....$20-35
Farm Trailer, #225, 1964–1968 ....$15-25-30
Farm Trailer, #2551, 1993– $24-27
Faun 3-Axle Ladder Truck, #2924,
   1993– $33-36
Faun Airport Foam Tender, #3411,
   1975–1985 ....$45-48
Faun Crane Truck, #2914, 1979– $33-36
Faun Gully Emptier, #2932, 1997– $33-36
Faun Hydraulic Crane, #4010, 1975– ...$70-75
Faun K10/26AP Dump Truck,
   #249, 1965–1973 ....$20-30
Faun Refuse Truck, #2931, 1997– $33-36
Faun Snow Plow Sand Truck,
   #337, 1972–1974 ....$30-45
Faun Snow Plow Truck, #2212, 1975–1981 ....$21-24
Faun Telescoping Crane Truck, #3723, 1994– ..$45-48
Faun UK 10 Side Tipper, #198, 1962–1965 ..$65-80
Fendt Farmer 308 LS Tractor with Front
   Loader, #3450, 1993– $45-48

Hanomag Henschel ADAC Vehicle Safety Check Truck, #343, 1973–1974.....$30-45

Hanomag Henschel ADAC Vehicle Safety Test Veh., #3710, 1975–1978 ....$50-55

Hanomag Henschel ARAL Gas Station Transporter, #3712, 1975–1977....$45-48

Hanomag Henschel ARAL Service Station Transporter, #355, 1974 ....$30-45

Hanomag Henschel ARAL Tanker, #3110, 1975–1977 ....$30-45

Hanomag Henschel Container Transporter, #3111, 1975–1977 ....$30-45

Hanomag Henschel Covered Truck and Trailer, #354, 1973–1974 ....$20-30

Hanomag Henschel Covered Truck, #338, 1972–1974 ....$10-15

Hanomag Henschel Covered Truck, #1616, 1975–1982 ....$10-12

Hanomag Henschel Garage Transporter, #307, 1971–1974 ....$30-45

Hanomag Henschel Garage Transporter, #3410, 1975–1977 ....$45-48

Hanomag Henschel Pipe Laying Truck, #350, 1973–1974 ....$30-45

Hanomag Henschel Pipe Loader Truck, #3711, 1975–1978 ....$45-48

Hanomag Henschel Tank Truck, #360, 1974 ..$30-45

Hanomag Henschel Truck, #1916, 1975–1981 ....$20-35

Hanomag Henschel with Horse Trailer, #1917, 1975 ....$15-25

Hanomag Henschel Wrecker, #257, 1974...$30-45

Hanomag Henschel Wrecker, #1910, 1975–1978 ....$15-25

Hanomag K 60 E Dozer, #99, 1959–1965..........................$65-80

Hanomag K 65 Bulldozer (99) and Two Trailers (154), #158, 1961–1969 ....$105-150

Hanomag Markant 3-Ton Covered Truck, #175, 1961–1967 ....$45-60

Hanomag Poultry Truck with four cages, #106, 1959–1965 ....$55-70

Hanomag Robust 900 Farm Tractor with Trailer, #303, 1969–1973 ....$20-30

Hanomag Robust 900 Farm Tractor, #287, 1969–1974 ....$15-25

Hanomag Robust 900 with Trailer, #329, 1972–1973 ....$40-55

Hanomag Tanker, "Esso," #210, 1963–1965 ....$85-100

Hanomag Tractor and Tipping Trailer, #165, 1961–1965 ....$60-75

Hanomag Tractor with Winch, #182, 1962–1966 ....$45-60

Hanomag, #1611, 1975–..................$10-12

Hanomag-Henschel Container Transporter, #318, 1971–1974 ....$20-35

Harrow, #1957, 1993–..........................$15-25

Hatra Front Loader, #103, 1959–1967 ..$55-70

Hay Elevator with hay bales, #2555, 1993–..$24-27

Hay Rake with driver, #64, 1957–1962..$20-35

Hay Rake, #242, 1964–1965 ....$25-40

Helicopter with Floats, orange with blue pontoons, "Katastrophenschutz," #2614, 1993–..........................$27-30

Henschel Auto Transporter with five cars, #101, 1959–1963.................$250-300

Henschel Auto Transporter, #100, 1959–1967 ....$85-100

Henschel Cable carrier, #152, 1960–1963 ....$85-100

Henschel Cement Truck, #164, 1961–1967 ....$85-100

Henschel Covered Semi, #124, 1959–1964 ....$70-95

Henschel Crane Truck, #42, 1956–1961..$65-80

Henschel Flatbed Trailer Semi, #43, 1956–1964 ....$65-80

Henschel Rocket carrier with U. S. Air Force Atlas Rocket, #179, 1961–1965 ....$150-175

Henschel Scraper, #177, 1961–1964 ...$65-80

Henschel Tanker Semi, "Struver–Tankwagen," #41, 1956–1959 ....$95-110

Henschel Tanker Semi, 21 Kiloliter, "BV–ARAL," #45, 1957–1962 ....$95-110

Henschel Tanker Semi, 21 Kiloliter, "Esso EXTRA MOTOR OIL," #47, 1957–1967 ....$95-110

Henschel Tanker Semi, 21 Kiloliter, "SHELL," #46, 1957–1967 ....$85-100

Henschel-Sattelzug F201S-2A "ARAL" Semi Tanker, #288, 1968–1974 ....$35-50

Horse Box Trailer with horse, #2559, 1993–..........................$24-27

Horse Trailer, #149, 1960–1964 ....$30-45

Hose Drum Irrigator, #2258, 1994–......$21-24

House Trailer, #54, 1957–1965............$30-45

Hydraulic Crane, #1326, 1997–..............$4-6

Hydraulic Excavator, #3510, 1993– $45-48

Iveco Camping Car, #1022, 1993– $5-10

Iveco Double Container Truck, #3424, 1993–..........................$45-48

Iveco Double Freighter, #3421, 1989–...$45-48

Iveco Pickup, #840, 1992–.....................$5-10

Iveco Racing Truck, #1018, 1994–..........$4-10

Iveco Recycling Truck with Trailer, #3813, 1993–..........................$55-60

Jaguar E 2+2, #294, 1968–1974 ......$20-30

Jaguar E 2+2, #1015, 1975–1982 ...$12-15

Jaguar XJ6, #1069, 1988–..................$4-10

Jeep (92) and Field Kitchen Trailer (136), #137, 1960–1963 ....$90-120

Jeep (92) and Trailer (93), #119, 1958–1963 ....$70-90

Jeep CJ-5 with Sport Boat, #2525, 1988–1989 ....$24-27

Jeep CJ-5, #1053, 1983–.....................$4-10

Jeep CJ-7 with Travel Trailer, #2518, 1990–...$24-27

Jeep CJ-7, #1058, 1985–.....................$4-10

Jeep Trailer, #93, 1958–1964 ....$20-35

Jeep with Trailer, #228, 1964–1972......$30-45

Kässbohrer Track Groomer, #2528, 1989– $24-27

Kemna Roller, #79, 1958–1966...........$50-65

Kenworth "BP" Tanker Semi, #3418, 1986–1989 ....$45-48

Kenworth Sand Transporter, #3420, 1987–1988 ....$45-48

Klaus Autodumper, #260, 1966–1973 ..$20-30

Klaus Shovel Truck, #185, 1962–1965 ..$45-60

Krupp 15 C 5 Dump Truck, #105, 1959–1965 ....$30-45

Krupp 15-Ton Crane, #193, 1962–1966 ....$65-80

Krupp DK 801 Dumper, #208, 1963–1965 ..$65-80

Krupp Meiller Bucket Truck, #163, 1961–1965 ....$75-90

Ladder Trailer, #176, 1961–1963.........$20-35

Ladder Truck with flashing lights and siren, #3780, 1992–..........................$45-48

Lamborghini 400GT Espada with Building Transporter Trailer, #333, 1972–1974.....$30-45

Lamborghini Espada 400 GT, #1024, 1975–1981 ....$9-12

Lamborghini Espada 400GT, #317, 1971–1974 ....$20-35

Lamborghini Fire car, #1618, 1975–1977.....$10-12

Lamborghini Fire Hunter, #344, 1973–1974 ..$25-40

Lamborghini Fire Truck, #1336, 1978 ....$8-10

Land Rover Defender Pickup, #2561, 1998–...$24-27

Land Rover Defender Softtop, #2562, 1998–..$24-27

Large Volume Lorry "M. Schneider Hamburg–Paris–Amsterdam," #3815, 1996–.........................$55-60

Lattice Mast Crane, #4310, 1997–........$70-75

Latticed Mast Crane, #4810, 1998–.....$70-75

Liebherr Bulldozer, #2529, 1989–.........$24-27

Liebherr Fast Erecting Tower Crane, #3913, 1992–.........................$62-66

Liebherr Mobile Crane, #258, 1965–1972 ..$15-25

Liebherr Power Shovel, #188, 1962–1968...$70-85

Liebherr Tower Crane, #159, 1961–1969...$105-120

Lincoln Continental Mark III, #298, 1969–1972 ....$25-40

Linde Forklift Truck, #1717, 1993– $12-14

Linde Forklift, #1629, 1986– $10-12

Livestock Trailer, #2257, 1993–..........$21-24

Livestock Transporter, #815, 1992–.........$5-10

Lloyd Arabella, #142, 1960–1963.......$60-85

Lloyd LP 400 S, #5, 1955–1959........$80-100

Loader, #2225, 1990–...................$21-24

Lockheed Tristar L-1011, #1720, 1993–..$12-14

Log Trailer, #62, 1957–1965................$20-35

Log Trailer, #263, 1966–1968..............$20-30

Lorry with Awning, #2618, 1994–.........$27-30

Lorry with Trailer, Lufthansa cargo, #3816, 1998– $55-60

Low Loader Trailer, #120, 1959–1964 ..$30-45

Low Loader with Boat, #1613, 1996–....$10-12

Low Loader with Excavator, #1611, 1996–...$10-12

Low Loader with Helicopter, #1610, 1996–...$10-12

Low Loader with Payloader, #4012, 1980–....$70-75

Low Loader with Rocket, #1614, 1998–..$10-12

Low Loader with Space Shuttle, #1612, 1996– $10-12

Low Loarder with Garage, #3724, 1997–..$45-48

Mack Heavy Wrecker and Man Truck, #3717, 1982–1984 ....$45-48

Mack Heavy Wrecker, #2917, 1981–1989 ..$33-36

Mack Low Loader with Power Shovel, #4013, 1981–1988 ....$70-75

Mack Semi-Freighter, #3117, 1982–1986 ..$30-45

Magirus Auto Transporter, #275, 1967–1973.........................$30-45

Magirus Cement Truck, #291, 1969–1974 ..$30-45

Magirus Concrete Truck, #2512, 1975–1977 ....$24-27

Magirus Deutz M250 D22 FK 6x4 Dump Truck, #281, 1968–1979.........................$30-45

Magirus Dump Truck, #2514, 1975 ....$24-27

Magirus Garbage Truck, #126, 1959–1966 ..$60-85

Magirus Garbage Truck, #274, 1967–1974 ..$45-60

Magirus Sand Truck, #347, 1973–1974 ..$20-30

Magirus Skip Truck, #362, 1974 ....$25-40

Magirus Skip Truck, #2813, 1975 ....$30-32

Magirus Street Sweeper, #157, 1960–1964 ....$85-100

Magirus Transporter with Tractors, #352, 1973–1974 ....$85-100

Magirus Transporter, #289, 1968–1972...$35-50

Magirus, #2511, 1975–1977 ....$24-27

Mail Trailer, #217, 1963–1965............$50-65

Man "AIR FRANCE" Bus, #3417, 1982–1987 ....$45-48

Man ARAL Tanker, #2810, 1975–1977 ..$30-32

Man Building Transporter and Trailer, #3715, 1980–1986 ....$45-48

Man Bus, #3720, 1987–1992 ....$45-48

Man Circus Transporter with two Cage Trailers, #3722, 1987– $45-48

Man Container Truck, #348, 1973–1974 ..$25-40

Man Container Truck, #2811, 1975 ....$30-32

Man Loader Truck with Loader Crane, #3415, 1980–1985 ....$50-55

Man Low Loader with Car Wash Station, #4019, 1994– $70-75

Man Lumber Truck with Crane, #349, 1973–1974 ....$20-35

Man Lumber Truck, #2812, 1975–1978 ..$30-32

Man Racing Fuel Tanker "Renndienst," #331, 1971–1974 ....$30-45

Man Road Maintenance Lorry with traffic signs, #2610, 1993– $27-30

Man Semi-Tanker, #3119, 1989–..........$30-45

Man Transporter with Wheel Loader, #3716, 1982–1986 ....$45-48

Man Tree Transporter, #2915, 1980–1982 ..$45-48

Manure Spreader, #2553, 1993– $24-27

Man-Volkswagen Covered Truck with Trailer, #1919, 1982– $15-25

Man-Volkswagen Express Truck, #1625, 1983– $10-12

Maserati Boomerang, #351, 1974 ......$15-25

Maserati Boomerang, #1034, 1978–1983...$9-12

Maserati Boomerang, #1330, 1975–1977 ..$6-10

Maserati Mistral, #295, 1968–1974 .....$20-30

Massey Ferguson 4270 Tractor, #2654, 1998– $27-30

Massey Ferguson 9240 with Twin Rear Wheels, #2960, 1997– $33-36

Massey Ferguson 9400 Tractor, #2868, 1996– $30-32

Massey Ferguson Front End Loader, #3453, 1993– $45-48

Massey Ferguson MF 284 Tractor with Farm Trailer, #3750, 1993– $45-48

Massey Ferguson MF284 with Transporter Box, #2853, 1993– $30-32

Massey Ferguson Tractor with Hay Trailer, #2227, 1990– $21-24

Massey-Ferguson Tractor, #847, 1997– $4-6

Matra Simca Rancho, #1340, 1979–1988...$4-10

McLaren, #1046, 1976–1986.........$7-10

McLaren, #1328, 1976–1981.........$6-10

Meili Agromobil, #173, 1961–1964 .....$45-60

Menck Loader, #3114, 1975–1977.....$34-38

Menck M 60 Excavator, #130, 1959–1969..$60-85

Menck Power Crane Shovel, #325, 1971–1974 ....$20-30

Menck Power Shovel, #213, 1963–1969 ..$65-80

1949 Mercedes-Benz 170 S, #4, 1955–1959.........................$85-100

1949 Mercedes-Benz 170 S Taxi, #78, 1957–1961 ....$115-130

1953 Mercedes-Benz 180, #2, 1955–1961 ....$75-90

1953 Mercedes-Benz 180 (2) and Horse Trailer (149), #150, 1960–1961 ....$85-100

1953 Mercedes-Benz 180 Taxi, #78, 1957–1961 ....$95-110

Mercedes-Benz 180 Ambulance with two stretchers, #71, 1957–1960 ....$75-90

Mercedes-Benz 180 Police, #52, 1957–1961 ....$30-45

1961 Mercedes-Benz 190, #190, 1962–1965.........................$35-50

Mercedes-Benz 190, #250, 1965–1969..$20-30

Mercedes-Benz 190 Police, #52, 1962–1965.........................$30-45

Mercedes-Benz 190 Polizei, #1311, 1985–1988 ....$8-10

Mercedes-Benz 190 SL Convertible, #59, 1957–1964 ....$30-45

Mercedes-Benz 190 Taxi, #192, 1962–1964 ....$35-50

Mercedes-Benz 190E, #1054, 1984–1988....$4-10

Mercedes-Benz 190E Fire Command car, #1349, 1993– $4-10

Mercedes-Benz 200 Ambulance, #1613, 1981–1988 ....$10-12

Mercedes-Benz 208 Schulbus, #1628, 1983–1988 ....$10-12

1951 Mercedes-Benz 220, #3, 1955–1961 ..$75-90

Mercedes-Benz 220 A Sedan, #33, 1956–1960 ....$85-100

1951 Mercedes-Benz 220 Taxi, #78, 1957–1961 ....$100-125

1960 Mercedes-Benz 220 S, #146, 1960–1965 ....$45-60

Mercedes-Benz 230 SL, #229, 1964–1968...$25-40

Mercedes-Benz 250 SE Taxi, #244, 1968–1971 ....$25-40

Mercedes-Benz 250, #250, 1970–1974 ..$15-25

Mercedes-Benz 250, #309, 1970–1974 ..$20-35

Mercedes-Benz 250, #1020, 1975–1984 ..$9-12

Mercedes-Benz 250 Polizei, #1318, 1975–1984 ....$15-25

Mercedes-Benz 250 Taxi, #1317, 1975–1984 ....$15-25

Mercedes-Benz 250/8 Taxi, #244, 1972–1974 ....$20-35

Mercedes-Benz 250 SE, #256, 1966–1969 ..$30-45

Mercedes-Benz 260 E Binz Ambulance, #1630, 1989– $10-12

Mercedes-Benz 280 GE, #1044, 1982– ..$4-10

Mercedes-Benz 280 GE with Fire Boat and Trailer, #1923, 1989– $15-25

Mercedes-Benz 280 GE with Horse Trailer, #1917, 1989– $15-25

Mercedes-Benz 280 SL, #302, 1969–1974 ..$20-35

Mercedes-Benz 280 SL, #1017, 1975–1984 ....$12-15

1953 Mercedes-Benz 300, #1, 1955–1961 ....$75-90

Mercedes-Benz 300, #1311, 1989– $4-10

Mercedes-Benz 300 E, #1063, 1986– $4-10

Mercedes-Benz 300 SE, #191, 1962–1965 ..$35-50

Mercedes-Benz 300 SL, #221, 1963–1969 ..$25-40

Mercedes-Benz 300 SL, #1073, 1988– ..$4-10

Mercedes-Benz 300 TE Station Wagon, #1064, 1986– $4-10

Mercedes-Benz 300 TE Taxi, #1310, 1993 ..$5-10

Mercedes-Benz 315 Truck and Trailer, #91, 1958–1963 ....$85-100

Mercedes-Benz 500 SE, #1042, 1982– ..$4-10

Mercedes-Benz 500 SEC, #1052, 1983– ..$4-10

Mercedes-Benz 500 SEL Convertible, #1011, 1993– $4-10

Mercedes-Benz 500 SEL Hardtop, #1012, 1993– $4-10

Mercedes-Benz 500 SEL, blue, doors open, 1:43, limited edition, #3426, 1993– ..$45-48

Mercedes-Benz 500 SEL, gold, doors open, 1:43, limited edition, #3427, 1993– $45-48

Mercedes-Benz 600 Pullman Limousine, #253, 1965–1972 ....$30-45

Mercedes-Benz 809 Binz Ambulance, #1920, 1987– $15-25

Mercedes-Benz 809 Police Bus, #1921, 1987– $15-25

Mercedes-Benz 809 Postwagen, #1922, 1987– $15-25

Mercedes-Benz 2232, #2511, 1978– 1982 ....$24-27

Mercedes-Benz ADAC Vehicle Safety Test Vehicle, #3710, 1979–1981 ....$45-48

Mercedes-Benz ADAC with Auto Transport Trailer and car, #2221, 1983– $21-24

Mercedes-Benz ADAC, #2211, 1975–1981 ....$21-24

Mercedes-Benz ARAL Tanker, #3110, 1978–1979 ....$30-45

Mercedes-Benz Auto Transporter with five cars, #4017, 1993– $70-75

Mercedes-Benz Auto Transporter, #3112, 1975– $30-45

Mercedes-Benz Auto Transporter, #3419, 1986– $45-48

Mercedes-Benz Binz Ambulance Van, #292, 1969–1974 ....$20-35

Mercedes-Benz Binz Ambulance, #233, 1964–1970 ....$25-40

Mercedes-Benz Binz Ambulance, #1928, 1993– $15-25

Mercedes-Benz Binz Red Cross Recovery Van, #2015, 1993– $18-20

Mercedes-Benz Binz Rescue Van, #2011, 1993– $18-20

Mercedes-Benz BP Double Tanker, #3718, 1983–1985 ....$45-48

Mercedes-Benz Bucket Truck, #2219, 1978–1982 ....$30-32

Mercedes-Benz Bus "TOURIST BUS," #1624, 1980–1986 ....$10-12

Mercedes-Benz Bus with Trailer "AIRPORT SER-VICE," #1918, 1981–1983 ....$15-25

Mercedes-Benz Bus with Trailer "HOLIDAY INN," #1918, 1986–1988 ....$15-25

Mercedes-Benz Bus with Trailer, #1918, 1983–1985 ....$15-25

Mercedes-Benz C-Class, #1029, 1994– ...$5-10

Mercedes-Benz Cement Mixer, #2922, 1989– $33-36

Mercedes-Benz Cement Mixer, #0813 ..$8-10

Mercedes-Benz Covered Cargo Truck, #2517, 1986–1988 ....$24-27

Mercedes-Benz Covered Lorry with Twin Axle Trailer, Container Service, #3515, 1998 ....$45-48

Mercedes-Benz Covered Lorry with Twin Axle Trailer, Eurotrans, #3515, 1994– $45-48

Mercedes-Benz Covered Lorry with Twin Axle Trailer, JumboCargo, #3515, 1994– $45-48

Mercedes-Benz Covered Transport, #3412, 1975–1983 ....$45-48

Mercedes-Benz Crane Truck, #293, 1969–1974 ....$25-40

Mercedes-Benz Crane Truck, #2816, 1975–1978 ....$30-32

Mercedes-Benz Double Decker Touring Coach, #3814, 1993– $55-60

Mercedes-Benz Double Freighter, #3421, 1987–1988 ....$45-48

Mercedes-Benz Double Freighter, #3714, 1984–1985 ....$50-55

Mercedes-Benz Dump Trailer Truck, #2919, 1984– $33-36

Mercedes-Benz Dump Truck, #2923, 1989– $33-36

Mercedes-Benz E 230, #1048, 1996– $4-6

Mercedes-Benz E 290 T Station Wagon, #1088, 1997– $4-6

Mercedes-Benz Esso Tanker, #3110, 1980–1983 ....$30-45

Mercedes-Benz Europ 1200 Binz Ambulance, #1613, 1975–1980 ....$15-25

Mercedes-Benz Europ 1200L Binz Ambulance, #306, 1970–1974 ....$20-35

Mercedes-Benz Extending Ladder Fire Truck, #2819, 1978– $30-32

Mercedes-Benz Fire Command Truck, #357, 1974 ....$20-35

Mercedes-Benz Fire Equipment Truck with hydraulic boom & small boat, #3512, 1993– $45-48

Mercedes-Benz Fire Truck, #2815, 1975–1977 ....$30-32

Mercedes-Benz Freight Truck with hand truck and pallets, #2523, 1986–1989 ....$24-27

Mercedes-Benz G Fire Command Wagon, #1344, 1983– $4-10

Mercedes-Benz G Police Command Wagon, #1346, 1986– $4-10

Mercedes-Benz G-Wagon Ambulance, #805, 1992– $5-10

Mercedes-Benz G-Wagon Police Van, #804, 1992 ....$5-10

Mercedes-Benz GE with Sport Boat, #2525, 1990– $24-27

Mercedes-Benz Garage Transporter, #3410, 1978–1981 ....$45-48

Mercedes-Benz Garbage Truck, #2820, 1984– $30-32

Mercedes-Benz Glass Transporter, #63, 1957–1962 ....$65-80

Mercedes-Benz Hazardous Waste Truck, #2617, 1994– $27-30

Mercedes-Benz Highway Sand Truck with Snow Plow, #2527, 1989– $24-27

1950 Mercedes-Benz L 3500 Dump Truck, #31, 1955–1963 ....$50-60

Mercedes-Benz Ladder Fire Engine,
#3433, 1996– $45-48

Mercedes-Benz Lorry with Low Loader Trailer
and Excavator, #4111, 1993– $70-75

Mercedes-Benz LP 315 Open Back Truck,
#88, 1958–1968 ....$65-80

Mercedes-Benz LP 315 Truck (88) and
Trailer (128), #153, 1960–1963 ...$85-105

Mercedes-Benz LP608 ADAC Auto Salvage
Truck, #319, 1971–1974...............$20-35

Mercedes-Benz LP608D Silo Transporter, #336,
1972–1974 ....$30-45

Mercedes-Benz LP608D Street Maintenance
Truck, #335, 1972–1974...............$30-45

Mercedes-Benz Mail Truck, #216,
1963–1965 ....$125-150

Mercedes-Benz MB Trac 800 Tractor w/Tipping
Hopper, #2951, 1993– $33-36

Mercedes-Benz MB Trac 800 Tractor with
Snow Plow, #3451, 1993–.............$45-48

Mercedes-Benz Metz DL 30H Fire Ladder Truck,
#261, 1966–1974 ....$50-60

Mercedes-Benz Metz DL 22 Fire Ladder Truck,
#56, 1957–1966.......................$115-130

Mercedes-Benz Metz LF 15 Fire Truck, #55,
1957–1964 ....$115-130

Mercedes-Benz Moving Van, #97,
1958–1963 ....$115-130

Mercedes-Benz Parking Lot Transporter, #3713,
1977–1984 ....$50-55

Mercedes-Benz Polizei Wagon, #1627, 1983–.$10-12

Mercedes-Benz Postal Truck "Deutsche Bundespost," #305, 1970–1974...............$20-35

Mercedes-Benz Postwagen, #1912,
1975–1987......................................$15-25

Mercedes-Benz Racing Truck, #1017, 1993–..$4-10

Mercedes-Benz Recycling Lorry with Trailer,
#1511, 1994– $9-12

Mercedes-Benz Recycling Transporter, #2920,
1986–..$33-36

Mercedes-Benz Refrigerated Van, #96,
1958–1961 ....$125-150

Mercedes-Benz Refuse Truck, #2926, 1992–..$33-36

**Mercedes-Benz Refuse Truck, #2931,
1:55 ....$15-20**

Mercedes-Benz Roll-Off Skip Loader,
#3125, 1993–....................$30-45

**Mercedes-Benz S500, chrome, #1035,
1:55..$5-8**

Mercedes-Benz Shell Tanker, #3511,
1993–..$45-48

Mercedes-Benz Silo Transporter, #155,
1960–1965 ....$85-100

Mercedes-Benz Silo Transporter, #2516, 1975–..$24-27

Mercedes-Benz SkipTruck, #2826, 1989–.$30-32

Mercedes-Benz SLK, #851, 1998–.............$4-6

Mercedes-Benz Snorkel Fire Truck with Snorkel
Trailer, #2921, 1986–1989 ....$33-36

Mercedes-Benz Snorkel Truck with working
water pump, #3720, 1992–...........$45-48

Mercedes-Benz Sprinter Bus, #1930, 1997–..$15-25

Mercedes-Benz Sprinter Post, #1929, 1997–.$15-25

Mercedes-Benz SSK, #1074, 1988–........$4-10

Mercedes-Benz Street Cleaning Truck, #2824,
1988–..$30-32

Mercedes-Benz Street Sign Truck, #2513,
1975–1980 ....$24-27

Mercedes-Benz Street Sign Truck, #2513,
1989–..$24-27

Mercedes-Benz Tanker, #2524, 1986–..$24-27

Mercedes-Benz Tipper Lorry, #2616, 1993–..$27-30

Mercedes-Benz Tower Truck, #156,
1960–1964 ....$85-100

Mercedes-Benz Tractor, 12 Meter Trailer,
SIKU-TRANSPORT, #3721, 1993–...$45-48

Mercedes-Benz Truck with hydraulic boom
platform, #3428, 1993–.................$45-48

Mercedes-Benz Truck, #2214, 1975–1978...$21-24

Mercedes-Benz Unimog, #1620,
1975–1983 ....$10-12

Mercedes-Benz Unimog, #1620, 1984–..$10-12

Mercedes-Benz Unimog Hydraulic DBP
Truck, #361, 1974 ....$30-45

Mercedes-Benz Unimog with driver, no
roof, #104, 1959–1965 ....$30-45

Mercedes-Benz Water Service Van,
#339, 1972–1974......................$20-30

Mercedes-Benz Water Truck,
#2213, 1975–1980......................$21-24

Mercedes-Benz with Refuse Containers,
#2017, 1997–.................................$18-20

Mercedes-Benz Wrecker with Auto Salvage
Trailer, #2220, 1979–1988 ....$21-24

Mercedes-Benz Wrecker, #1622,
1978–1989 ....$10-12

Mercedes-Benz Ziegler Water Cannon
w/working pump, #3429, 1993– ...$45-48

1960 Mercury Voyager Station Wagon,
#170, 1961–1965......................$70-85

1953 Messerschmitt Kabinenroller,
#30, 1955–1963.......................$90-105

Metz Airport Fire Tender, #332, 1972–1974...$20-30

Michigan 180 Wheel Dozer with Plow, #326,
1971–1974 ....$30-45

Michigan Grader-Tractor, #2210,
1975–1977 ....$21-24

Military Pontoon Bridge Transporter, #108,
1959–1964 ....$100-125

Milk Cans for 2853, #7050 ....$5-10

Mini Cooper, #1031, 1977–.....................$4-6

Mini Cooper Pizza Delivery, #1367, 1977–..$4-6

Mobile Tower Construction Crane,
#4210, 1992– $70-75

Morgan Plus 8, #836, 1992–..............$5-10

Morgan Plus 8, #1062, 1986– $4-10

Motor Home with Accessories,
#3129, 1998 ....$30-45

New Holland 5635 Tractor, #2652, 1997–..$27-30

New Holland L 75, #2653, 1997– $27-30

Nissan 300ZX, #1061, 1985– $4-10

1953 NSU Fiat 1100, #34, 1956–1964 ..$85-100

1956 NSU Fiat 600, #49, 1957–1962 ..$65-80

NSU Prinz, #84, 1958–1963 ....$55-70

O&K Heavy Duty Tipper Truck, #2934,
1997–...$33-36

Oldsmobile 98 Holiday Sports Coupe,
1964–1969, #245, 1964–1968 ......$25-40

Oldsmobile Toronado and Caravan,
#1915, 1975–1979....................$30-33

Oldsmobile Toronado with Boat and
Trailer, #297, 1969–1974.............$30-45

Oldsmobile Toronado, #267, 1967–1974 ..$25-40

1952 Opel Blitz 1¾ Ton Truck, #10, 1955–1961 ....$60-75

1953 Opel Caravan Station Wagon, #9, 1955–1959 ....$75-90

1953 Opel Caravan with luggage, #67, 1957–1959 ....$95-110

1953 Opel Rekord Sedan, #7, 1955–1959 .$75-90

1954 Opel Kapitän Sedan, #8, 1955–1959 ....$75-90

1958 Opel Rekord Sedan, #83, 1958–1961 ....$85-100

1960 Opel Blitz Covered Truck, #168, 1961–1967 ....$30-45

1960 Opel Caravan with luggage, #67, 1960 ....$110-125

1960 Opel Caravan, #147, 1960–1964 ..$45-60

1960 Opel Kapitän, #148, 1960–1965 ....$45-60

1960 Opel Rekord, #171, 1961–1964 .$35-50

1963 Opel Rekord, #223, 1964–1966 .$25-40

Opel 1200, #143, 1960–1961 ....$85-100

Opel Astra Caravan Estate car, #1036, 1995– $5-8

Opel Blitz Mail Truck, #70, 1957–1966 .$50-65

Opel Blitz Truck (10) and Trailer (44), #109, 1957–1961 ....$85-110

Opel Capitan (8) and Travel Trailer (54), #111, 1957–1961 ....$115-135

Opel Caravan 1500 (1963), #226, 1964–1966 ....$20-35

Opel Frontera Sport, #1027, 1994– $5-10

Opel Frontera with Boat and Caravan, #2532, 1996– $24-27

Opel Frontera with Boat, #1354, 1996– $5-8

Opel Frontera with Horse Box, #2010, 1996– $18-20

Opel Frontera with Motor Bike Trailer, #2531, 1996– $24-27

Opel Frontera with Motorcycle and Trailer, #2231, 1997– $21-24

Opel GT 1900, #1018, 1975–1978 ...$20-35

Opel GT1900, #304, 1970–1974 ......$20-30

Opel Kadett SR, #1047, 1982–1989 ..$5-10

Opel Kadett, #204, 1963–1966 ....$25-40

Opel Kapitän (#252) with Westfalia Travel Trailer, #279, 1968–1971 ....$45-60

Opel Kapitän (1964), #252, 1965–1970 ..$25-40

Opel Olympia, #286, 1968–1969 ....$50-65

Opel Omega ADAC Road Patrol car, #1320, 1997– $4-6

Opel Omega Caravan Estate car, #1054, 1996– $4-6

Opel Rekord Caravan with skis and louge, #272, 1967–1972 ....$45-60

Opel Rekord Coupe, #271, 1967–1974 .$30-45

Opel Senator, #1040, 1981–1988 ....$4-10

Overhead Maintenance Lorry, #2930, 1993– $33-36

Pallets for 1717, #7015, ...$5-10

Pam Tanker Semi 21 Kiloliter, #58, 1957–1959 ....$20-35

Panzer Gepard, #2911, 1976–1979 ....$33-36

Panzer Leopard A1, #2912, 1977–1979 ....$33-36

Panzer Leopard A3 Tank, #2910, 1976–1979 ....$33-36

Peterbilt Sloop Transporter with Boat, #4014, 1983–1988 ....$70-75

Peterbilt Space Shuttle Transporter, #4016, 1988– $70-75

Peterbilt with Grove Low Loader Trailer, #2408, 1992– $21-24

Peugeot 205 Cabriolet, #1071, 1988– .$4-10

Peugeot 205 Convertible, #838, 1992– ...$5-10

Peugeot 505 STI, #1043, 1982–1988 ....$5-10

Piggy Back Forklift, #1721, 1997– $12-14

Pipe Transporter with Trailer, #1512, 1996– .$8-10

Police Boat Transporter, #2823, 1989– ..$30-32

Police Car with Loudspeaker, #1356, 1996– ..$5-7

Police Helicopter, #807, 1992– $5-10

Police Helicopter, #2222, 1986 ....$21-24

Police Information Bus, #2928, 1994– $33-36

Police Mini Bus, #2016, 1996– $18-20

Police Motorbike, #1325, 1997– $4-6

Polizei Helicopter, #2531, 1993–1995 ...$24-27

Pontiac Bonneville Convertible, #262, 1966–1971 ....$60-75

Pontiac GTO "The Judge," #328, 1972–1974 ....$30-45

Pontiac GTO Convertible, #277, 1967–1972 ....$45-60

Porsche 1.5 L Racer, #181, 1962–1965 ....$35-50

Porsche 356 Coupe, #18, 1955–1964 ..$90-105

Porsche 901 Polizei, #235, 1964–1970 ....$25-40

Porsche 901, #234, 1964–1969 ....$25-40

Porsche 911 Cabriolet, #1067, 1987– $4-10

Porsche 911 Convertible, #837, 1992– $5-10

Porsche 911 Rallye, #1345, 1986– $4-10

Porsche 911 Targa Highway Emergency car, #1316, 1978–1988 ....$6-10

Porsche 911 Targa, #234, 1970–1974 ..$25-40

Porsche 911 Targa, #1010, 1975–1987 ..$8-12

Porsche 911 Turbo Highway Emergency car, #1316, 1989– $4-10

Porsche 911 Turbo, #1059, 1985– $4-10

Porsche 928 Emergency Doctor, #1339, 1979–1994 ....$4-10

Porsche 928, #1037, 1979– $6-10

Porsche 959, #1068, 1987– $6-10

Porsche Boxster, #849, 1998– $4-6

Porsche Carrera 906, #285, 1968–1974 ..$20-35

Porsche Carrera 906, #1013, 1975–1982 ...$6-10

Porsche Police car, #160, 1961–1964 ..$65-80

Porsche Racing Team, #2217, 1985–1986 ..$21-24

Porsche Spyder, #87, 1958–1965 ....$75-90

Porsche Standard T Diesel Tractor, #218, 1963–1972 ....$35-50

Porsche Turbo 917/10, #1045, 1976– ...$6-10

Porsche Turbo 917/10, #1329, 1976–1981 ..$6-10

Post Van, #1085, 1997– $4-6

Potato Digger, #90, 1958–1962 ....$30-35

Potato Digger, #3856, 1994– $55-60

Power Shovel, #3413, 1978– $45-48

Pumper with working water pump and flashing lights, #3880, 1992– $55-60

Range Rover Emergency Vehicle, #1338, 1979–1989 ....$5-10

Range Rover with Horse Box, #2010, 1993– .$18-20

Range Rover with Horse Trailer, #1917, 1980–1988 ....$15-25

Range Rover with Sailboard, #1626, 1982–1987 ....$18-20

Range Rover with Travel Trailer, #2532, 1993– $24-27

Range Rover, #1036, 1978–1986 ....$5-8

Range Rover, #1341, 1979–1986 ....$4-10

Rear Digger Tractor with Front End Loader, #2818, 1977–1985 ....$30-32

Rectangular Hay Bales for 2862, #7062 ...$5-10

Recycle Containers for 3813, #7017, ...$5-10

Recycling Skip Truck with Skip Trailer, #3516, 1994– $45-48

Recycling Transporter, #828, 1992– $5-10

Red Cross Helicopter, #2535, 1993– $24-27

Refuse Truck, #811, 1992– $5-10

Renault 4CV, #50, 1957–1961 ....$85-100

Renault 5, #1038, 1979–1988 ....$5-10

Renault Ceres 95X Tractor, #2867, 1994– ..$30-32

Renault Dauphine, #140, 1960–1965 ...$50-65

Renault Floride Convertible, #161, 1961–1963 ..$50-65

Renault Tractor with Front End Loader, #1925, 1993– $15-25

Renault Tractor with Rear Digger, #3755, 1993– $45-48

Renault Tractor with Trailer, #2226, 1990– $21-24

Renault Turbo BMX Transport and Trailer, #3115, 1989– $30-45

Renault Turbo Hollis Transport and Trailer, #3115, 1987–1988 ....$39-42

Renault Turbo Semi-Freighter, #3117, 1986–1988 ....$30-45

Renault TX145-14 Tractor, #2856, 1993– $30-32

Rescue Van Ambulance, #835, 1992– $5-10

Rethmann Recycling Transporter, #3723, 1988–1992 ....$45-48

Reversible Farm Plow, #1956, 1993–.....$15-25
Robuster III/48 Dumper, #151, 1960–1964..$45-60
Roller Harrow, #1958, 1994–.............$15-25
Roller Trailer, #174, 1961–1964..........$30-45
Roller Trailer, #241, 1964–1968..........$15-25
Roller, #2935, 1998–.....................$33-36
Roll-Off Skip Loader, #3128, 1994–.......$30-45
Rosenbauer Airport Crash Truck w/working
    water pump, #3722, 1993–............$45-48
Rosenbauer Airport Crash Truck, limited
    edition, #3513, 1993–................$45-48
Rotary Mowers, #2265, 1998–..............$21-24
Round Bale Trailer, #2860, 1993–.........$30-32
Round Baler, #2266, 1998–................$21-24
Round Bales for 2556, #7056,.............$5-10
Saab 9000, #1066, 1987–..................$4-10
Scania Low Loader with Wheel Loader and
    Power Shovel, #3911, 1990–ﾠ.........$62-66
Scania Wreck Truck, #1014, 1994–.......$4-10
Scraper, #803, 1992–.....................$5-10
Seed Drill, #2261, 1996–.................$21-24
Seed Drill, #2651, 1997–.................$27-30
Shell Gas Station Transporter,
    #3910, 1987–1989.....................$62-66
Side Dumping Trailer, #278, 1967–1969..$20-30
Sign Pack, #1050, 1976–..................$5-10
Siku Racing Team, #2217, 1978–...........$21-24
Silage Block Cutter, #1960, 1996–.......$15-25
Silage Blocks for 1960, #7051............$5-10
Simon Snorkel, #1019, 1994–..............$5-10
Skip Lorry with Trailer, #1518, 1998–.........$4-6
Skip Truck, #1013, 1994–.................$4-10
Slurry Tanker, #2869, 1998–..............$30-32
Space Shuttle, #817, 1992–...............$5-10
Steyr 9094 Tractor, #2864, 1993–.........$30-32
Steyr 9145 Tractor, #2962, 1998–.........$33-36
Steyr Tractor with Twin Wheels Front and
    Rear, #2959, 1997–...................$33-36
Streetcar (40) and Trailer (57),
    #113, 1957–1961.....................$120-150
Streetcar Trailer, #57, 1957–1963.......$55-70
Streetcar, #40, 1956–1969...............$65-80
Suzuki SJ413, #1072, 1988–...............$4-10
Tank Trailer, #169, 1961–1963...........$20-35
Tanker Citerne, #1030, 1994–.............$5-10
Taxi, #1355, 1996–.......................$5-7
Tempo Matador Bus, #220, 1963–
    1969.................................$30-45
Tempo Matador Camping Van with Kayak,
    #264, 1966–1971......................$45-60
Tempo-Matador Overhead Truck, #184,
    1962–1964............................$75-90
Tempo-Matador with Container, #166,
    1961–1964............................$60-75
Tipper Truck and Trailer, #1516, 1997–....$8-10
Tipper Truck, #808, 1992–................$5-10

Tipper Truck, #822, 1992–................$5-10
Tipper Truck, #1091, 1998–...............$4-6
Tipper Truck, #1514, 1996–...............$8-10
Tipping Hopper Trailer, #154,
    1960–1965............................$20-35
Tipping Loader Trailer, #2650, 1994–....$27-30
Tipping Trailer, #178, 1961–1963.......$20-35
TOPAS Tanker, #3118, 1989................$30-45
TOPAS Tanker, #3422, 1989–...............$45-48
Tower Construction Crane, #4112,
    1993–................................$70-75
Toyota 2000GT, #316, 1971–1973 ....$20-35
Track Type Lattice Boom Clamshell
    Excavator, #3514, 1993–.............$45-48
Tractor (48) and Cultivator (107),
    #122, 1959–1961.....................$60-80
Tractor (48) and Hayrake (64),
    #116, 1957–1961.....................$65-90
Tractor (48) and Lumber Trailer (62), #114,
    1957–1961............................$65-90
Tractor (48) and Open Trailer (60), #115,
    1957–1961............................$60-85
Tractor (48) and Potato Digger (90), #118,
    1957–1961............................$65-90
Tractor with Front End Loader, #1038, 1996–....$4-7
Tractor with Front Mower, #3156,
    1994–................................$30-45
Tractor with Silage Block Cutter, #3157,
    1996–................................$30-45
Tractor with Trailer, #1913, 1975–.........$15-25
Trailer with Awning, #1959, 1994– $15-25
Trailer with Farm Produce, #2259, 1994–...$21-24

Tram, #1615, 1983– $8-10
Truck Road Maintenance Lorry, #1322,
    1997–................................$6-8
Truck Truck with Piggy Back Forklift, #2933,
    1997–................................$33-36
Unimog BP, #2515, 1975–1977 ....$24-27
Unimog Excavator, #2615, 1993–...........$27-30
Unimog Red Cross Truck, #2218,
    1978–1985............................$21-24
Unimog Side-Mount Scoop with Pipe
    Trailer, #2820, 1978–1981 ....$34-36
Unimog Snow Plow, #821, 1992–...........$5-10
Unimog Snow Plow, #2212,
    1982–1983............................$21-24
Unimog Snow Plow, #2212, 1984–.........$21-24
Unimog U1500 with Linde Forklift Truck, #2522,
    1985–................................$24-27

Unimog Winter Service with Snowblower, Snowplow & Hopper/Spreader, #2827, 1993–................................$30-32

Unimog with Awning, #1026, 1994–.......$5-10
Unimog with Builder's Hut, #1510, 1994–..$9-12
Unimog with Builder's Hut, #2533,
    1993–................................$24-27
Unimog with Crane, #1023, 1993–...........$5-10
Unimog with Dumper Truck, #2232, 1997–..$21-24
Unimog with Grass Cutter, #2929, 1994– ..$33-36
Unimog with Hydraulic Loader, #2537,
    1996–................................$24-27
Unimog with Motor Boat, #1517, 1997–....$8-10
Unimog with Road Work Signs,
    #2230, 1996–.........................$21-24
Unimog with Sign Trailer,
    #2215, 1975–1983 ....$21-24
Unimog with Sign Trailer,
    #2215, 1984–1989 ....$21-24
Unimog with Site Office Trailer,
    #2822, 1987–1988.....................$30-32
Unimog with Site Trailer "HEITKAMP,"
    #2519, 1984–1989.....................$24-27
Unimog with Site Trailer, #2519, 1980–
    1983.................................$23-28
Unimog with Tandem Trailer, #2223,
    1988–................................$21-24
Unimog, #1716, 1993–.....................$12-14
Unimog, green, #3153, 1993–..............$30-45
Vacuum Tanker Trailer, #2252, 1993– ...$21-24

Vespa ET4 Scooter, #852, 1998.............$4-6

1950 Volkswagen Ambulance, #14,
    1955–1959............................$60-75
1950 Volkswagen Kastenwagen Van, #17,
    1955–1959............................$50-65

1950 Volkswagen Kombi Bus, #16, 1955–1963 ....$50-65

1952 Volkswagen Covered Truck, #15, 1955–1961 ....$50-65

1953 Volkswagen 1200, #13, 1 955–1959..................................$90-105

1957 Volkswagen 1200, #13, 1960–1964 ....$105-120

Volkswagen 411, #300, 1969 .....$50-65

Volkswagen 1200 "Beetle," #230, 1964–1969 ....$25-40

Volkswagen 1200 (13) and Car Trailer (53), #112, 1957–1961..................$125-155

Volkswagen 1200 Mail Car, #199, 1963–1965 ....$85-100

Volkswagen 1200 with antenna on roof, #231, 1964–1968 ....$30-45

Volkswagen 1300 ADAC, #1324, 1975–1984 ....$18-24

Volkswagen 1300 Beetle, #311, 1970–1974..................................$20-35

Volkswagen 1300 Beetle, #1022, 1975–1986..................................$15-25

Volkswagen 1303 cabriolet, blue, opening doors, 1:43, limited edition, #2612, 1993– ..$27-30

Volkswagen 1303 cabriolet, white, opening doors, 1:43, limited edition, #2613, 1993– $27-30

Volkswagen 1500 Driving School car, #219, 1963–1964 ....$85-100

Volkswagen 1500 Station Wagon, #187, 1962–1964 ....$45-60

Volkswagen 1500 Variant, #247, 1965–1968..................................$25-40

Volkswagen 1500, #180, 1962–1965...$35-50

Volkswagen 181 "Thing," #1032, 1976–1984 ....$8-10

Volkswagen 181 Fire Command Vehicle, #1335, 1977–1982 ....$20-30

Volkswagen 181 Military, #1332, 1976–1979 ....$20-35

Volkswagen 181 with Raft, #1333, 1977–1982 ....$20-35

Volkswagen Beetle 1303 LS Convertible, #1077, 1989– $4-10

Volkswagen Beetle 1303 LS, #1078, 1990– $4-10

Volkswagen Beetle Convertible, #839, 1992– $5-10

Volkswagen Bus, #211, 1963–1964........$35-50

Volkswagen Bus, #1031, 1975–1976.....$7-10

Volkswagen Bus, #1331, 1976–1980.....$6-10

Volkswagen Bus Ambulance, #1619, 1975–1978 ....$10-12

Volkswagen Bus Bundespost-Peilwagen, #1314, 1975–1980..................$7-10

Volkswagen Bus Highway Service Truck, #1315, 1975–1988 ....$5-10

Volkswagen Bus Military Ambulance, #1621, 1976–1979 ....$18-20

Volkswagen Bus Polizei (Police) Loudspeaker Van, #212, 1963–1970 ....$30-45

Volkswagen Bus Postal Van, DEUTSCHE BUNDESPOST, #320, 1970–1972 ..$20-35

Volkswagen Bus with radar, #1312, 1975...$4-10

Volkswagen Caravelle, #825, 1992– $5-10

Volkswagen Covered Pickup Van, #1347, 1990– $4-10

Volkswagen Delivery Van, #820, 1992– ...$5-10

Volkswagen Eurovan, sky blue, #0820/0824/0825, 1:55 ....$6-8

Volkswagen Eurovan Police Team Van, white & green, #1350, 1994–............$5-10

Volkswagen Eurovan Police, green, #1351, 1994–..............................$4-10

Volkswagen Fire Rescue Bus, #834, 1992–...$5-10

Volkswagen Golf ADAC with antenna, #1312, 1985–1986 ....$7-10

Volkswagen Golf ADAC withno antenna, #1312, 1987– $4-10

Volkswagen Golf Cabriolet, #1039, 1980–..$4-10

Volkswagen Golf Convertible, #842, 1994–..$5-10

Volkswagen Golf DBP, #1337, 1979–1984 ..$6-10

Volkswagen Golf Driving School, #1025, 1994– $5-10

Volkswagen Golf IV, #1090, 1998–...........$4-6

Volkswagen Golf Pick Up, #1049, 1983–...$4-12

Volkswagen Golf, #1010, 1993–.............$4-8

Volkswagen Golf, #1033, 1977–.........$7-10

Volkswagen Karmann Ghia 1500, #248, 1965–1969 ....$25-40

Volkswagen Karmann Ghia Convertible, #81, 1958–1961 ....$85-100

Volkswagen Karmann Ghia Coupe, #80, 1958–1965 ....$75-90

Volkswagen LT 28, #1334, 1977– $4-10

Volkswagen LT 28 Camper with Travel Trailer, #2518, 1980–1989 ....$24-27

Volkswagen Medi-Mobil, #1623, 1979–1989 ....$10-12

Volkswagen Passat ADAC, #1614, 1976–1981 ....$10-12

Volkswagen Passat ADAC, #1342, 1979–1986 ....$20-35

Volkswagen Passat Polizei Loudspeaker car, #1321, 1990 ....$4-10

Volkswagen Passat Variant Polizei Loudspeaker, #1321, 1978–1989 ....$5-10

Volkswagen Passat Variant Station Wagon, #1061, 1996– $4-6

Volkswagen Passat Variant, #1029, 1975–1984 ....$8-12

Volkswagen Passat Variant, #1076, 1989– $4-10

Volkswagen Pickup Van, #1030, 1975–1989 ....$4-10

Volkswagen Police Bus, #194, 1962–1963.$45-60

Volkswagen Police Van, #833, 1992–......$5-10

Volkswagen Porsche 914/6, #1023, 1975–1980 ....$12-16

Volkswagen Porsche Rennpolizei, #1323, 1975–1978 ....$6-10

Volkswagen School Bus, white, #824, 1992–...$5-10

Volkswagen Sharan, #1046, 1996– $4-6

Volkswagen Transporter Service Van, #1343, 1982– $6-10

Volkswagen Transporter, #1314, 1981–...$4-10

Volkswagen Transporter, many variations, #1331, 1981– $4-20

Volkswagen Vanagon Ambulance "Malteser Hilfsdienst," #356, 1974 ....$20-30

Volkswagen Vanagon Bus with Radar in front compartment, #345, 1973–1974 ....$20-30

Volkswagen Vanagon Postal Van, DBP PEILWAGEN, #320, 1973-74.........$20-35

Volkswagen-Porsche 914/6 "Rennpolizei," #346, 1973–1974 ....$20-30

Volkswagen-Porsche 914/6, #312, 1970–1974 ....$20-35

Volvo 7 Covered Transport, #3116, 1982–1984 ....$30-45

Volvo 760 GLE, #1065, 1986–1989......$4-10

Volvo ARAL Gas Station Transporter, #3712, 1978–1985 ....$45-48

Volvo Cargo Truck and Trailer, #3115, 1978–1985 ....$39-43

Volvo Cement Truck, #2817, 1977–1984..$30-32

Volvo Container Transporter, #3111, 1978–1985 ....$30-45

Volvo Covered cargo Truck, #2517, 1976–1983 ....$24-27

Volvo Crane Truck with Boat, #2814, 1975–1983 ....$30-32

Volvo Double Freighter, #3714, 1979–1983 ....$50-55

Volvo F7 Double Freighter, #3414, 1979–1980 ....$45-48

Volvo F7 Street Sign Truck, #2513, 1981–1985 ....$24-27

Volvo Fire Watch Tower Transporter, #4015, 1985–1989 ....$70-75

Volvo FL10 Hollis Transport and Trailer, #3115, 1986 ....$30-45

Volvo FL6 Loader Truck with Loader Crane, #3415, 1986 ....$45-48

Volvo FL6 Street Sign Truck, #2513, 1986–1988 ....$24-27

Volvo Payload Hauler, #2825, 1989– $30-32

Volvo Pipe Loader Truck, #3711, 1979–1982 ....$45-48

Volvo Refrigerated Truck, #2916, 1981–1984 ....$33-36

Volvo Tanker Semi, #3416, 1982–1986 ..$45-48

Volvo V 40, #1084, 1997– $4-6

Volvo, #2514, 1976–1986 ....$24-27

Water Cannon, #1034, 1994– $5-7

Wheel Loader with Accessory Plow, #3123, 1993– $30-45

Wheel Loader, #1924, 1990 ....$15-25

White Horse Transporter, #3721, 1987–1988 ....$50-55

White Loader Truck with Loader Crane, #3415, 1987 ....$45-48

White Old Timer "Coca-Cola" Truck, #2821, 1986–1987 ....$30-32

White Old Timer "Sinalco" Truck, #2821, 1987 ....$30-32

White Old Timer Truck, #2521, 1985–1987 ....$24-27

White Old-Timer Beverage Delivery Truck, #2860, 1988– $30-32

Wood Transporter with Colored Pencils, #3915, 1996– $62-66

Wrecker Truck, #844, 1996– $4-6

Wrecker Truck, #3432, 1994– $45-48

Wrecker with Trailer, #2526, 1988– $24-27

Zettelmeyer Europ L2000 Front End Loader, #270, 1967–1974 ....$20-35

Zettelmeyer Europ S12 Road Roller, #299, 1969–1974 ....$15-25

Zettelmeyer Europ S12, #1612, 1975–1983 ....$10-12

Zettelmeyer Loader, #2510, 1975– $24-27

Zettelmeyer Wheel Loader, #3120, 1990–..$30-45

Zundapp Janus 250, #73, 1957–1963 .$65-80

Siku Junior Plastic Toys

Claas Tipping Trailer, #2882 ....$28-30
Fendt Farmer Favorit 926, #2982 ....$32-35
Massey-Ferguson 6150, #2881 ....$28-30
Side Tipping Trailer, #2583 ....$24-27
Tractor with Claas Tipping Trailer, #3881 ..$54-60
Tractor with Side Tipping Trailer, #3781 ..$48-50

Silhouette

Silhouette models of France are 1:43 scale kits.

1982 Dumont Fuji, #1014 ....$14-19
1982 Rondeau M382, #1011 ....$14-19

Silver Pet

Silver Pet is likely a company that existed for a short time in the 1960s. Models feature crude castings with a stamped tin or thin pressed steel base. All the models are silver. "Pet" is a common Japanese word meaning "small." The term is used in toy car brands such as Micropet, Diapet, and Miniature Pet, and real Japanese car brands such as Toyopet. Silver Pet models are stylized toy cars based on real cars of the late 1950s.

Simba

Simba Toys GmbH & Co
Werkstraße 1
90765 Fürth-Stadeln, Germany
telefon: 0911/976501
fax: 0911/9765120
e-mail: simbatoys@simbatoys.de
www.simbatoys.de/
Simba España
S. A. Edificio Euro 3
Frederic Mompou
No. 5 6º 1a
08960 Sant Just Desvern
C.I.F. A-59.129.551
Barcelona, Spain
Simba Toys Hungaria Kft
H-1033 Budapest, Hungary
Dovzce Simba Toys Praha
Simba Toys Polska Sp. z o.o.
00-975 Warszawa ul. Pulawska 14
Warsaw, Poland

The Germany-based Simba produces, among other toys, a line of quality diecast models manufactured in China and dubbed "Mini Metalls" (with two L's). One package identifies one of their models only as a "Concept Car." A local toy store reported that the model was recalled when Volkswagen protested the US marketing of the toy that is an obvious unlicensed knockoff model of their New Beetle.

Similarly, their Jeep Grand Cherokee is marked only as a "Family Car." I wonder if Daimler/Chrysler will catch up with that one and demand it also be recalled.

The "spinning top" logo and accompanying text on the base reveals that the toy is produced in China by Tins Toys.

In addition, R. C. Johnston of White Rock, British Columbia, reports of a pair of diecast miniatures produced by Comet Miniatures of England in 1988, also dubbed "Mini Metals" (with one "L"), to commemorate the popular TV series *Voyage to the Bottom of the Sea.*

Ford Ka $4-6
Jeep Grand Cherokee "Family Car" $4-6
Mercedes-Benz
  CLK GTR, 1:43.................$4-6
  A-Class $4-6
1998 Volkswagen Beetle "Concept Car"
  Convertible, baby blue with silver fenders, 1:36 ....$4-6
  Convertible, lime green with white fenders, 1:36 ....$4-6
  Hardtop, red with black roof, 1:36.........$4-6
  Hardtop, yellow with black roof, 1:36 ....$4-6

Singfund

On November 1, 1998, Collector Robert Speerbrecher reported, "Found a new diecast brand... maybe. It's a company out of China called Singfund Industries Ltd. They make several single-carded and sets of fire trucks and emergency vehicles. I've seen two different 1:64 scale hook and ladder fire trucks on individual blisterpacks and two different sets with several fire and rescue vehicles of mixed scale. Thing is, they tend to be only 30 to 40% diecast. Usually just the cab of the vehicle and, on some, part of the trailer. They are cheap stuff like many China toys. Maybe better than the really crude ones but not as good as Yat Ming for example."

Sizzlers (also see Hot Wheels, Johnny Lightning)

The distinction of these rechargeable battery-powered race cars is that they represent the first commercial application of nickel-cadmium rechargeable batteries, back in the early 1970s. Originally produced by Mattel, Sizzlers became a brand owned, but never used, by the Estes Model Rocket Company.

In 1996, Playing Mantis obtained licensing from Estes to produce a new line of Sizzlers under the Johnny Lightning brand. New models retail for around $10. Original Sizzlers are valued from $30 to 120. After losing the license to produce Sizzlers, Mattel attempted to compensate by producing X-V Racers, a line which remained available until just the past year or two, and touting "From the original makers of Sizzlers" on the package, demonstrating an attempt to capitalize on the name they regrettably gave up.

Mike Grove is the undisputed Sizzlers expert and has written and published a small booklet on them. Contact him at the address below.

Mike Grove
Sizzlers Hotline
1047 E 5th St
Fremont, NE 68025
402-727-9505
e-mail: Sizzler@aol.com

Skoglund & Olson

AB Skoglund & Olson i Gefle is a brand name of cast iron and other toys made in Sweden in the late 1920s and early 1930s. Very little else is known about them, but values are quite high for these rare toys.

Bugatti Racer, cast iron, 7½",
    1929–1930 ....$4,000-6,000
Bus, 10½"..................................$1,500-2,500
Tank Truck, 10½"......................$2,000-3,000
Wrecker, "Central Garage," 11¼"..$1,250-2,250

Sky

Sky is an obscure brand of 1:43 scale models the origin of which remains unknown.

1961 Ford Thunderbird Indy Pace Car,
    #5089 ....$165–190
1950 Mercury
    Coupe, #501 ....$145-170
    Indy Pace Car, #5041 ....$165–190
1937 Packard 4-door Sedan
    #509 ....$145-170
    Fire Chief, #510 ....$175-200

Skybirds

In 1932, A.J.Holliday first produced the Skybirds line of accurate wooden kits in his shop at Aldermanbury Avenue 3, London, England. The first models were of World War I airplanes, with accessories such as a hangar, control tower, and buildings made of wood, and figures and soldiers made of lead.

Lead cast airplanes were introduced in 1933, along with military trucks and guns. Around the same time model cars in 1:65 – 1:72 scale were introduced. The accuracy of airplane models such as the Hawker Hart, D.H.Comet, Fairey Gordon, Comper Swift, Blackburn Seagrave made Skybirds a leader in collectible toys of the era. A few Taylor & Barrett toy vehicles were sold in conjunction with their airplane models.

Skybirds Lead Cast Vehicles

A. A. Gun, #12 ....$45-60
Aircraft Refuelling Tender "Thompson,"
    #35A, 1936, with or without "TB
    Aircraft Refuelling Tender" on
    sides $45-60
Air Mail Van, #34 (Taylor & Barrett) .$45-60
Ambulance, #33A (Taylor & Barrett) .$45-60
Armored Car, #36A, 1940 ....$45-60
Army Lorry, #36B, 1936 ....$45-60
Army Motorcycle Set, #9, 1935 .....$45-60
Fire Tender, #31 (Taylor & Barrett) ...$45-60
Royal Mail Service car, #34B (Taylor &
    Barrett) $45-60
Petrol Tender, #35B (Taylor & Barrett)..$45-60
Petrol Tender, Military, #36 ....$45-60
Petrol Tender, Civilian "Essolube,"
    #36 ....$45-60
Saloon car (Taylor & Barrett) $45-60
Scammell Military Gun Tractor (diecast)...$45-60
Tank (Johillco) $45-60

Skybirds Figures Sets

Royal Air Force Figures Set #1, 1933 ......$45-60
Royal Flying Corps Set #2, 1933............$45-60

Skyline

Tin Wizard Modelcars and Skyline Models
c/o Thomas Wolter Modelltechnik
Talstrasse 170
D-69198 Schriesheim, Germany
phone: 06203/68680
fax: 06203/68329
e-mail: THWOLTER@aol.com
website: www.tinwizard.de
or www.toynet.de/tinwizard

Handmade 1:43 and 1:24 scale white metal models with plated parts comprise this series from Schriesheim, Germany. Also see Tin Wizard Models.

Skyline Models, 1:43 Scale White Metal

Cadillac Convertible Series 62 (1955),
    ready made, #6201 ....$125-140
Cadillac Eldorado
    Convertible, top down (1960), ready
      made, #6212 ....$150-175
    Convertible, top up (1960), ready
      made, #6213 ....$150-175

Convertible, top up (1960), ready
    made, #6214 ....$150-175
Indianapolis Pace car (1960), ready
    made, #6211 ....$150-175
Chevrolet Corvette Indianapolis Pace car
    (1978), ready made, #6221 ....$175-200
Ford Thunderbird
    Hardtop (1963), kit, #5050 ....$50-65
    Hardtop (1963), white, ready made,
      #5051 ....$125-140
    Hardtop (1963), red, ready made,
      #5053 ....$125-140
    Hardtop (1963), pink, ready made,
      #5054 ....$125-140
    Indianapolis Pace car (1961), kit,
      #5080...................................$50-65
    Indianapolis Pace car (1961), metallic gold,
      ready made, #5089 ....$125-150
Mercury
    "N.Y. Fire Chief" (1950), kit, #5020...$50-65
    "N.Y. Fire Chief" (1950), red, ready made,
      #5021 ....$125-150
    Convertible (1950), kit, #5030 ....$50-65
    Convertible (1950), white, ready made,
      #5031 ....$125-140
    Convertible (1950), red, ready made,
      #5032 ....$125-140
    Convertible (1950), black, ready made,
      #5033 ....$125-140
    Coupe (1950), kit, #5010 ....$50-65
    Coupe (1950), beige white, ready made,
      #5012 ....$125-140
    Coupe (1950), blue, ready made,
      #5014 ....$125-140
    Coupe (1950), green, ready made,
      #5015 ....$125-140
    Indianapolis Pace Car (1961), kit,
      #5040 ....$50-65
    Indianapolis Pace Car (1961), yellow, ready
      made, #5041 ....$125-150
Nash Statesman 1950
    kit, #5150 ....$50-65
    blue, ready made, #5151...........$125-140
    blue, ready made, #5153...........$125-140
    red, ready made, #5152...........$125-140
    Taxi, kit, #5160 ....$50-65
    Taxi, yellow, ready made, #5161 ..$125-150
Packard 4-door Sedan 1937
    kit, #5090...............................$50-65
    white, ready made, #5091 ....$125-140
    bordeaux red, ready made, #5093 ..$125-140
    blue, ready made, #5094...........$125-140
    Feuerwehr (Fire Department) CH
      (1937), ready made, #5100......$50-65
    Feuerwehr (Fire Department) CH (1937),
      red, ready made, #5103 ....$125-150

Slik Toys

Lansing, Iowa, is home to Slik Toys, originally called Lansing Slik-Toys. They are mostly one-piece cast aluminum toys, with a few plastic models. Kipp is another name often found imprinted on the toys. Several very realistic 1:16 scale Oliver farm tractors were produced by the company.

During the 1940s and 1950s, The Lansing Company made Slik-Toys which were simple wooden cars and trucks. During World War II, they made 30,000 toys daily from scraps of wood only 10 to 12 inches long. When the war ended and metal became available again, The Lansing Company switched to aluminum because it was sturdier than wood. While Slik-Toys can be found in stores across the country, manufacturing has never left Iowa.

In 1959, Norbert Spinner purchased the Slik-Toy name and dies from the Lansing Company. His company, Armor Industries, continued to sell the Slik-Toy line throughout the United States until December 31, 2002.

In March 2003, Norbert Spinner's grandson Nicholas Spinner reopened the Slik Toy line business and created Grandpa's Farm Toys. In March 2004, he introduced his online store for retail customers at www.grandpasfarmtoys.com. This site was developed for their strong farm toy line. Most of the old car dies and other toys dies were destroyed in 1960–1970s. Nicholas is still debating on whether to make new dies for the old car toys unless he sees a strong demand for the toys which even to this today are still made in Iowa, even though Nicholas lives in Minneapolis–St. Paul, Minnesota.

Original Lansing Slik-Toys

Bulldozer	$130-145
Combine	$300-325
Fastback Sedan	
#9600, 7"	$40-55
Taxi, #9600, 7"	$40-55
Firetruck	
#9606, 6"	$35-50
#9700, 3½"	$35-50
Grader, 9½"	$100-125
Metro Van, #9618, 5"	$40-55
Oliver	
70 Tractor, #9804, red with rubber wheels	$70-85
77 Tractor, 7¾"	$450-500
880 Tractor	$800-900
Open Stake Truck, #9602, 7"	$40-55
Pickup Truck	
#9601, 7"	$40-55
#9605, 6"	$35-50
#9703, 4"	$35-50
Roadster, #9701, 3½"	$35-50
Sedan 4-door, #9604, 6"	$35-50
Semi Tractor Trailer	
Flatbed Truck, #9613, 8"	$40-55
Grain Truck, #9611, 8"	$40-55
Log Truck, 8"	$40-55
Milk Truck, #9610, 8"	$45-60
Stake Truck, #9500, 11"	$60-75
Station Wagon, #9704, 4"	$30-45
Tank Truck	
#9603, 7"	$35-50
#9705, 4"	$30-45
Wrecker, #9617, 5"	$30-45

Currently Available Slik Toys

Massey Harris Tractor Model 44	$50-60
Minneapolis Moline Tractor Model U	$100-120
Oliver	
60 Tractor with Man	$40-50
70 Tractor	$50-60
880 Tractor Model	$75-85
10" Wagon, stamped steel	$7-9
3" Planter, cast aluminum	$3-5
4" Disc, cast aluminum with plastic discs	$3-5
4" Wide Drag, cast aluminum with wire hitch	$3-5
5" 3-Bottom Plow, cast aluminum	$3-5
5" Mower, cast aluminum	$3-5
5" Tractor, cast aluminum	$5-7
5" Trailer, cast aluminum	$4-6
5" Wide Front Tractor, cast aluminum	$7-9
5" Plow, cast aluminum	$3-5
5" Side Delivery Rake, cast aluminum body with stamped steel teeth	$7-9
5" Spreader, cast aluminum body with revolving beaters	$4-6
5" Tractor with man	$5-7
5" Wide Double Disc, cast aluminum body with plastic discs	$3-5
6" Grader, cast aluminum	$3-5
6" Long Mini Tractor and Trailer Set, cast aluminum bodies fastened together permanently	$4-6
7" Baler, cast aluminum body with rotating beater	$7-9
7" Bulldozer, cast aluminum body with stamped steel blade	$7-9
7" Tractor, cast aluminum	$6-8
7" Wagon, stamped steel wagon with movable holster	$4-6
7" Wide Mechanical Mower, cast aluminum with stamped steel blade	$7-9
8" Wide Double Drag, cast aluminum body with wire hitch	$3-5
9" Grader, cast aluminum body with adjustable scraper blade	$6-8
4-Piece Man Tractor Set, includes: 1 #9816 Tractor, 1 #9821 Plow, 1 #9825 Mower, 1 #9827 Disc	$12-15
4-Piece Tractor Set, includes: 1 #9876 Tractor, 1 #9821 Plow, 1 #9822 Drag, 1 #9827 Disc	$12-15
4-Piece Tractor Set With Spreader, includes: 1 #9876 Tractor, 1 #9825 Mower, 1 #9826 Planter, 1 #9832 Spreader	$13-16
Bulldozer & Trailer Set, includes: 1 #9864 Bulldozer, 1 #9803 Trailer	$13-16
Tractor & Disc Set, includes: 1 #9828 Tractor, 1 #9872 Disc	$11-14
Tractor & Plow Set, includes: 1 #9828 Tractor, 1 #9874 Plow	$11-14
Tractor & Trailer Set, includes: 1 #9828 Tractor, 1 #9803 Trailer	$12-15
Tractor & Wagon Set, includes: 1 #9828 Tractor, 1 #9817 Wagon	$12-15

SM

An obscure Hong Kong-based company known only as SM produces inexpensive but nevertheless attractive miniature cars and trucks usually sold in budget sets. The distinguishing mark is a logo of a pine tree with a leaping deer in front of it, embossed on the base of each toy. Value of vehicles is between 25 and 50 cents each when purchased in a set. Otherwise they are worth 10–20 cents each.

Small Wheels and Western Models

As EWA & Miniature cars USA puts it, "Western Models were one of the first companies in the world to make high quality hand-built metal models. The company was founded in the early 1970s just southeast of London, England and moved in the mid '80s to Taunton in the southwest of England. They now have a range of about 70 quality 1:43rd scale models of European and American race and street cars, old and new, plus some interesting record cars. A few new models are introduced annually and some withdrawn, which makes the models very collectible.

"Small Wheels is another name used by Western for some of their models. All are made in the Western factory to the same high standards."

Small Wheels 1:24 Scale

Ferrari Lusso	$310-335
Jaguar	
Mark 2 Vicarage	$350-375
XJ13, kit	$150-175
XK150	$330-355

Small Wheels 1:43 Scale

1952 Bentley R Continental, #5..........$100-125
1953 Chevrolet Corvette Roadster,
    #13 kit.....................................$50-75
1958 Chrysler Windsor 2-door Hardtop,
    #14 ....$100-125
1957 DeSoto
    Firesweep 4-door Sedan, #12.......$100-125
    Firesweep Sedan, #12 kit.................$50-75
    4-door Sedan Taxi, #12T $100-125
Ferrari 275 GTB, #2 ....$110-135
1958 Ford Custom Taxi, #17 ....$124
1967 Ford Mustang GT, #10 ....$100-125
1948 Hudson Commodore
    4-door Sedan, #15..........................$98-109
    Police, #15P $109-119
Jaguar Mk 2
    blue with disc hubs, #4...................$90-115
    red with wire wheels, #4 ....$110-135
Jaguar XK140, #1 ....$100-125
    Rolls Royce SC2 Convertible
    top up, #3 ....$110-135
    top down, #3 ....$110-135
Saab 96
    #8 ....$100-125
    Rally, #9 ....$100-125

Smart Toys

Smart Toys Ltd.
Rm. 822, Peninsular Ctr.
67 Mody Rd.
Kowloon, Hong Kong, China

Collector Robert Speerbrecher first discovered Smart Toys on a trip to Bangkok in December 1998. Smart Toys are China-produced commercial and construction vehicles. Sold in multipacks in Bangkok and labeled as "for display–not a toy," they showed up in March 1999 at a liquidator store in Redmond, Oregon, in individual flip-top display boxes for $1 each. They are labeled as HO gauge 1:87 scale and are barely discernable as Smart Toys except for an embossed brand name on the base of the box. Speerbrecher questions whether the quality is good enough to be called a collectible, but they do possess charm and operating parts that make them excellent little toys, and great additions to HO gauge dioramas and train layouts.

More recently found is a set of eight HO gauge semi-tractor trailers. If it weren't for the diecast upper cab portion of the tractor, these couldn't be called diecast at all since the rest of the model is plastic. Quality is still excellent for their $2 price tag. Two types of tractors are used for these models, a cab-over-engine (COE) and a conventional. Each is packaged in a stur-

dy, clear fliptop box similar to the construction toys but with a longer package to accommodate the 7 inch trucks.

Smart Toys HO Gauge Construction

Bulldozer, yellow, with Stop sign and
    man with shovel $3-4
Cement Mixer, yellow, with Do Not
    Enter sign $3-4
Power Shovel, orange, with sign $3-4
Road Roller, burgundy, with "Stop" sign
    and flag man $3-4
Tractor, burgundy, with two signs and woman
    carrying a milk can...................................$3-4
Tractor with Grabber, green, with One
    Way sign and construction worker
    holding a rake $3-4
Unimog
    burgundy cab, with One Way sign and
        construction worker carrying a
        bucket..$3-4
    yellow cab, with One Way sign and
        construction worker carrying a
        bucket..$3-4
Wheel Loader with dumping cargo
    platform, green, with One Way sign $3-4

Smart Toy HO Gauge Trucks

Hanjin, bright blue box trailer with white COE
    tractor..$3-4
Hapag-Lloyd, orange box trailer with yellow
    conventional tractor $3-4
Hyundai, bright orange box trailer with white
    conventional tractor $3-4
K-Line, red box trailer with white COE tractor ..$3-4
Kuhne & Nagel, dark blue box trailer with
    light blue accent stripe and matching
    dark blue COE tractor.............................$3-4
Maersk, silver-gray box trailer with dark gray
    COE tractor $3-4
Mitsui O.S.K. Lines, pale gray box trailer with
    dark gray COE tractor $3-4
OOCL, pale gray box trailer with yellow
    conventional tractor $3-4

Smer

Smer models are made in Czechoslovakia.

Ford Model T Roadster, kit, 1:32............$14-19

Smith Family Toys

Collector Henri Mueller discovered this unusual brand of semi-tractors of unknown scale. The package offers the brand name "John Smith" as well as "Smith Family Toys" accompanying an illustration of four models as listed below.

California Hauler Conventional Sleeper Cab, yellow with red and black trim $4-6
Highway Express Conventional Sleeper Cab,
    black with red, blue and white accents....$4-6
Long Haul Conventional Sleeper Cab, red with
    yellow and black trim............................$4-6
Pacer Cabover, red with yellow accents $4-6

Smith-Miller

Smith-Miller toys are sturdy cast metal and aluminum replicas of trucks of the era around 1945 when they were introduced in Santa Monica, California. The Smith-Miller firm later became Miller-Ironson before fading into oblivion in 1954. So popular were these "Smitty" trucks to collector/enthusiast Fred Thompson that he purchased the defunct company lock, stock, and barrel in 1979.

Under Thompson's vision, Smith-Miller still produces quality reproductions of these classic toys, along with new models and replacement parts for older ones.

Smitty toys remain a testament to the quality of the era, even though Smitty Toys were considered expensive for their time, from $7 to $28 each. What's perhaps most intriguing about the new models produced since 1979 is that they retail for around the same price as the old ones are currently worth on the second market. All models listed below have been issued in the last 20 years.

Aerial Ladder Semi, 6-wheel Tractor and
    4-wheel Trailer, SMFD, 36",
    #410 ....$800-900
Arden Milk Truck with 12 Milk Cans,
    4-wheel, 14", #204-A $325-375
Bekins
    Van, 6-wheel Tractor and 4-wheel
        Trailer, #406 ....$650-800
    Vanliner, 14-wheel, 2½", #208-B ...$325-375
Blue Diamond Dump Truck, 10-wheel,
    18½", #408 ....$1,700-2,000
Chevrolet
    Bekins Van, plain tires, hubcaps,
        14-wheel $525-575
    Coca-Cola, plain tires, 4-wheel......$850-950
    Flatbed Tractor-Trailer, unpainted
        wood trailer, plain tires, hubcaps,
        14-wheel $350-450
    Milk Truck, 1945–46, plain tires, hubcaps,
        4-wheel $400-500
Coca-Cola Truck with 16 Coca-Cola Cases,
    4-wheel, 14", #206-C $900-1,000
Dump Truck, 11½", #402 ....$350-450
Ford
    Bekins Van, 1944, plain tires, hubs ..$400-500

Coca-Cola with Wood Soda Cases,
1944, 4-wheel $900-1,000
GMC
Bank of America with Lock and Key,
4-wheel, #404-B $400-500
Coca-Cola, 16 Coca-Cola Cases,
4-wheel, #306-C $900-1000
Hi-Way Freighter Tractor-Trailer, 14-wheel,
#310-H $300-400
Kraft Foods, 4-wheel, #304-K........$600-700
Lumber Tractor-Trailer with 8 Timbers,
14-wheel, #406-L..................$425-475
Lyon Van Lines Tractor-Trailer, 14-wheel,
#308-V $650-750
Lyon Van Tractor-Trailer, 10-wheel,
#407-V $650-750
Machinery Hauler, 13-wheel,
#408-H $1,700-2,000
Material Truck with 4 barrels, 2 timbers,
#402-M.........................$400-500
Materials Truck with 4 Barrels, 3 Timbers,
#302-M.........................$400-500
Mobilgas Tanker with 2 Hoses, 14-wheel,
#409-G $500-600
P.I.E., 14-wheel, #412-P $625-725
Pacific Intermountain Express "P.I.E."
Tractor-Trailer, #312-P $600-700
Rack Truck, 6-wheel, #303-R........$350-450
Rack Truck, 6-wheel, #403-R........$250-300
Redwood Logger Tractor-Trailer with
3 Logs, #307-L $1,100-1,250
Silver Streak Express Tractor-Trailer,
14-wheel, #311-E $550-650
Silver Streak Tractor-Trailer, 14-wheel,
#411-E $475-575
Super cargo Tractor-Trailer with 10 Barrels,
14-wheel, #309-S $400-500
Transcontinental Tractor-Trailer,
14-wheel, #410-F $375-475
Triton Oil with 3 Drums, #305-T.....$350-450
Triton Oil with 3 Drums, 6-wheel ,
#405-T $375-475
Wrecker, 4-wheel, #301-W $250-300
Wrecker, 6-wheel, #401-W $450-550
Heinz Grocery Truck, 6-wheel, 14",
#203-H $475-575
Lumber
Trailer, 17", #404-T $300-400
Truck, 19", #404 ....$750-850
Truck with 60 Boards, 6-wheel, 14",
#201-L $700-800
Mack "B"
Associated Truck Lines, 14-wheel....$500-600
Jr. Fire Truck with Warning Light, Battery-Oper-
ated, 4-wheel $950-1,100
Orange Dump, 10-wheel $1,800-2,100

P.I.E., 18-wheel $850-950
Material Truck with 3 Barrels, 3 cases, 18
boards, 4-wheel, 14", #202-M...$900-1,000
Oil Truck with 4 drums, 6-wheel, 14",
#205-P $450-550
Pacific Intermountain Express "P.I.E." 6-wheel
Tractor and 8-wheel Cast Aluminum
Trailer, 29", #409 ....$900-1,000
Red Ball, 14-wheel, 23½", #212-R $375-475
Scoop Dump, 14", #403 ....$250-300
Searchlight Truck Hollywood Film ad, 18½",
#407 ....$300-400
Silver Streak Tractor, 6-wheel, 28",
#405 ....$350-450
Stake Truck, 14-wheel, 23½", #210-S..$500-600
Sunkist Special, 14-wheel, 23½", #211-L..$375-475
Timber Giant with 3 Logs, 14-wheel,
23½", #209-T $325-425
Tow Truck, 4-wheel, 15", #401 ....$250-300

SMTS (Scale Model Technical Services)

SMTS is an English company, making white metal models for US Model Mint (at one time), Conquest and Madison, as well as their own ranges. Voiturette is a related brand from SMTS. Latest addition to the SMTS line is Goldvarg of Argentina. (See Goldvarg.)

Arrows A6
Barclay, #1, 1:43 ....$100-115
GPI, #1, 1:43 ....$80-95
Aston Martin
DB4 GT Zagato, #5, 1:43...........$100-115
P214 Racer 1963, #44, 1:43 .....$100-115
Project 215 1963, #33, 1:43......$100-115
Bentley Speed 6 LeMans 1930, #7, 1:43...$120-135
Brabham BT26 Racer 1967, #22, 1:43 .....$140-155
BRM P56, #26, 1:43 ....$110-125
Bugatti 35 Racer, #25, 1:43 ....$110-125
Don Garlits Swamp Rat 1 Dragster, 1:43 ..$100-120
Eagle Weslake Racer, #9, 1:43.........$120-135
Ferrari
216C3, #2, 1:43 ....$80-95
312B 1970, #13, 1:43.....$140-155
Lola T90 Racer, #41, 1:43 ....$120-135
Lotus
30 Racer, #34, 1:43 ....$100-115
33 Grand Prix 1965, #6, 1:43....$120-135
38 Indy Racer 1965, #10, 1:43 ..$100-115
40 Racer, #35, 1:43 ....$100-115
56 Indy 1968, #11, 1:43 ....$100-115
56B F1 1968, #12, 1:43 ....$85-100
Elite 1957, #4, 1:43 ....$100-115
Europa, #8, 1:43 ....$100-115
Europa GLTL, #8, 1:43 ....$90-105

Europa Special Twincam, #15,
1:43 ....$120-135
Seven, #16, 1:43 ....$110-125
Seven 1957, #18, 1:43 ....$110-125
March 701, #17, 1:43 ....$135-150
STP Paxton Turbine Indy 1967, #14,
1:43 ....$120-135
Toleman TG184, #3, 1:43 ....$120-135
Watson Roadster
1959, #2059, 1:43 ....$120-135
1960, #2060, 1:43 ....$120-135
1961, #2061, 1:43 ....$120-135
1962, #2062, 1:43 ....$130-145
1963, #2063, 1:43 ....$120-135
1964, #2064, 1:43.........$130-145

Solido

Oulins 28260
Anet, France
phone: +33 (0) 2 37 65 81 00
fax: +33 (0) 2 37 64 51 31
www.solido.fr/

Solido of Nanterre, France, was formed in 1932 by Ferdinand de Vazeilles. While this book presents just a survey of the wide range of high-quality models produced by Solido, a more detailed study is presented by Dr. Edward Force, renowned author and collector of a wide variety of diecast toys, in his book titled *Solido Toys* by Schiffer Publishing.

In 1980, Majorette purchased the Solido company and continues the tradition of producing quality miniature replica vehicles. The brand survives today under the auspices of Groupe Ideal Loisirs, the French toy conglomerate.

From 1980 to 1982, an assortment of Solido models was sold as 1300 series Cougar models and packaged in a simple bubble card. If not for the partially visible Solido logo at the bottom of the card, it would be easy to think this was a distinct brand of diecast toys.

Dr. Force's book indicates that Cougar models were also marketed as Dinky Toys. After April 1982, when Dinky was purchased by Universal and incorporated into The Dinky Collection from Matchbox, the Cougar series was renamed the Solido 1300 Series.

Models in the Portugal-produced Solido 1200 series are 1988–89 reissues of the 1300 Cougar series. Each model is produced in at least two color variations.

Solido L'Age D'Or (The Age of Gold, or Golden Age) Series represents vintage cars, while the Yesterday series represents recent classics and HiFi / ToDay represents modern cars.

AC Cobra 1965
Solido 1960s Series #4533 ....$20-25
427, Solido Racing Series #1909 .....$20-25

Acmat VLRA
Forest Fire Tender, Solido Tonergam Series 2 #3125, 1994 ....$20-25
Tanker, Solido Tonergam Series 2 #3126, 1994 ....$20-25

Alfa Romeo
1939 2500 Sport Convertible, top down, Solido L'Age D'Or Series #4160, 1:43 ....$20-25
1939 2500 Sport Convertible, top up, Solido L'Age D'Or Series #4161, 1:43 ....$20-25
1968 carabo, Yesterday Series #1816, 1994 reissue................................$20-25

Alfasud, 1:43, Cougar series #1310, 1981–1982 ....$20-25
Alfasud, 1:43, #1310, 1982–1987.......$20-25
Alfetta GTV, 1:43, Cougar series #1305, 1980–1982 ....$20-25
Alfetta GTV, 1:43, #1305, 1982–1986.......$20-25
Alfetta GTV, 1:43, #1354, 1987 ....$20-25

Alpine
1965 F3, #1110, 1:43, 1996 Nostalgia reissue $20-25
1968 3 L, Solido Racing Series #1929, 1996 reissue................................$20-25
1970 A110, Yesterday Series #1803.$15-20
1972 A310, Yesterday Series #1814, 1994 ....$15-20
1973 A 110 Monte-Carlo, Solido Racing Series #1904 ....$20-25
1973 A110 Monte-Carlo, Yesterday Series #1804 ....$15-20
Renault A 310, Hi-Fi/ToDay Series #1503 ....$15-20
Renault A442B, 1:43, #1333, 1984–1986 ....$20-25

AMX
10 Tank, Solido Military #6076 ....$20-25
13/105 Tank, Solido Military #6058 ..$20-25
30 B2 Tank, Solido Military #6079 ...$20-25
30 Tank, Solido Military #6060 ....$20-25

Audi
1983 Quattro, 1994 reissue, Solido Racing Series #1916 ....$20-25
Quattro, 1:43, #1328, 1983–1987 ..$20-25
Quattro, 1:43, #1215, reissue of Cougar #1328 ....$15-25

Bentley
1961 S2, Prestige Series #8007, 1:18, 10½" $30-35
1987 Continental, Hi-Fi/ToDay Series #1512................................$15-20

Berliet
Hoist, Solido Tonergam Series 2 #3112....................................$20-25
Jet Spray Truck, Solido Tonergam Series 2 #3107 ....$20-25

BMW
1979 M1, Yesterday Series #1812 ....$20-25
1990 Series 3, Hi-Fi/ToDay Series #1521 ....$20-25
1993 3 Series Convertible, Hi-Fi/ToDay Series #1529, 1994 ....$20-25
530, 1:43, Cougar series #1304, 1980–1982..........................$20-25
530, 1:43, #1304, 1982–1986 ....$20-25
530, 1:43, #1217, reissue of Cougar #1304 ....$15-25
M1, 1:43, #1329, 1983–1986.....$20-25
M1, 1:43, #1209, reissue of Cougar #1329 ....$15-25
M1, 1:43, #1355, 1987 ....$20-25

Bugatti
1930 Royale, 1:43, Solido L'Age D'Or Series #4036 ....$20-25
1930 Royale Type 41, Prestige Series #8001, 1:18, 11" $35-40
1939 Atalante, Solido L'Age D'Or Series #4088, 1:43 ....$20-25
1939 Atalante Convertible, Solido L'Age D'Or Series #4109, 1:43 ....$20-25

Buick Super 1950
top down, #4512 ....$20-25
black, James Dean, 1994 Signature Series #9901, 1:43 ....$25-30
pink, Marilyn Monroe, 1994 Signature Series #9904, 1:43 ....$25-30
Convertible, top up, #4511 ....$20-25
Hard Top, #4523 ....$20-25

Cadillac
1931 452A, Solido L'Age D'Or Series #4085, 1:43 ....$20-25
1931 Delivery Van, Coca-Cola, #9601, 1:43 ....$20-25
1931 Fire Chief Van, 1:43, Solido L'Age D'Or Series #4070 ....$20-25
1931 V16 452.A Police car, 1:43, Solido L'Age D'Or Series #4057 ....$20-25
1931 Van, 1:43, Solido L'Age D'Or Series #4065 ....$20-25
1955 Eldorado, red, James Dean, 1994 Signature Series #9801, 1:18 ..$50-60
1955 Eldorado, white, Marilyn Monroe, 1994 Signature Series #9804, 1:18 ....$50-60
1955 Eldorado Convertible, top down, Prestige Series #8011, 1:18 ....$30-35
1955 Eldorado Convertible, top up, Prestige Series #8012, 1:18 ....$30-35

1955 Eldorado Convertible, Coca-Cola, top down, #9507, 1:18 : $35-35
1957 Eldorado, Coca-Cola, #9610, 1:43 ....$20-25
1957 Eldorado Biarritz Convertible, Solido 1960s Series #4500....................$20-25
1957 Eldorado Seville, #4520 ....$20-25
HQ, Solido Military #6003 ....$20-25

Car Transporter, #7006.........................$20-25

Chevrolet
1946 Pick-Up Truck, Pepsi-Cola #99022, 9⅝" $15-25
1950, #4508 ....$20-25
1950, Coca-Cola, #9607, 1:43......$20-25
1950 Checker Cab Taxi, #4529 .....$20-25
1950 Fire car, #4518 ....$20-25
1957 Bel Air Convertible with Continental Kit, baby blue, Prestige Series #8045, 1:18, 11", 1996.....................$30-35
1958 Corvette Convertible, red, #1201, 1:12, 1994 ....$120-150
1958 Corvette Hardtop, turquoise, #1202, 1:12, 1995 ....$120-150
1968 Corvette, Yesterday Series #1813, 1994................................$15-20
1968 Corvette, Solido Racing Series #1910................................$20-25
1983 Camaro Z 28, Hi-Fi/ToDay Series #1507 ....$15-20
1984 Corvette Convertible, Hi-Fi/ToDay Series #1514 ....$15-20
1984 Corvette Hardtop, Hi-Fi/ToDay Series #1513 ....$15-20
Camaro, 1:43, #1338, 1984, 1987 ...$20-25
Camaro Racing, 1:43, Hi-Fi/ToDay Series #1509, 1988–1989 ....$20-25
H, Solido Military #6033 Q $20-25

Chrysler Windsor 1946
#4513 ....$20-25
Coca-Cola, #9608, 1:43 ....$20-25
Police, #4530...............................$20-25
Taxi, #4514 ....$20-25
HQ, Solido Military #6042 ....$20-25

Citroën
1930 C4F Delivery Van, Coca-Cola, #9606, 1:43 ....$20-25
1930 C4F Tanker, #4422 ....$20-25
1930 C4F Truck, Pepsi-Cola #99058, 1:43 ....$15-25
1930 C4F Van, #4429...................$20-25
1939 15 CV, 1:43, Solido L'Age D'Or Series #4032 ....$20-25
1939 15 CV, Solido L'Age D'Or Series #4115, 1:43 ....$20-25
1939 Traction Fire Brigade, Solido L'Age D'Or Series #4166, 1:43 ....$20-25

1952 15 CV, #4519......................$20-25

1952 15 CV Monte Carlo, #4526...$20-25

1952 15 CV Monte-Carlo, Solido
   Racing Series #1903 ....$20-25

1952 15 CV Taxi, Solido 1960s
   Series #4536 ....$20-25

1963 DS 19 Sedan, white with black
   roof, Prestige Series #8033,
   1995, 1:18, 10⅜".....................$30-35

1963 DS 19 Presidentielle, black, Prestige
   Series #8035, 1:18, 10⅜", 1996...$30-35

1963 DS 19 Rallye, blue with white roof,
   233" on doors, Prestige Series
   #8034, 1996, 1:18, 10⅜".........$30-35

1966 2CV, Prestige Series #8028,
   closed roof, 1994, 1:18 ....$30-35

1966 2CV, open roof, red, Prestige
   Series #8029, 1994, 1:18........$30-35

1966 2CV, open roof, gray, Prestige
   Series #8029, 1:18 ....$30-35

1966 2CV, open roof, red & white, Prestige
   Series #8030, 1994, 1:18........$30-35

1966 2CV, Coca-Cola, red, top open,
   #9509, 8⅞", 1:43 ....$20-25

1966 2CV Charleston, Prestige Series
   #8040, 8⅞",............................$30-35

1966 2CV Raid, gray with map on sides, spare
   on hood, Prestige Series #8036.......$30-35

1970 SM, Yesterday Series #1807...$15-20

1979 2CV open roof, Yesterday Series
   #1819, 1995 reissue $20-25

1989 XM, Actua Series #8501, 1:18....$30-35

1991 ZX Aura, Hi-Fi/ToDay Series
   #1523 ....$15-20

1991 ZX Rallye Raid, Actua Series
   #8503, 1:18 ....$30-35

1991 ZX Volcane, Hi-Fi/ToDay
   Series #1524...........................$15-20

2 CV, 1:43, Cougar series #1301,
   1980–1982..............................$20-25

2CV, 1:43, #1210, reissue of Cougar
   #1301......................................$15-25

2CV 1979, Yesterday Series #1820,
   1995 reissue............................$20-25

2CV6, 1:43, #1359, 1987 ....$20-25

2VC6, 1:43, #1301, 1982–1987 ..$20-25

C35 with Ladder, Solido Tonergam
   Series 1 #2118 ....$20-25

CX 2400 Ambulance, 1:43, #1365,
   1987..$20-25

Traction FF1, 50th Anniversary of the
   Liberation of France and Northwestern
   Europe 1944–1994,
   4494/39 ....$35-45

Visa, 1:43, #1201, reissue of Cougar
   #1302.....................................$15-25

Visa, 1:43, Cougar series #1302,
   1980–1982.............................$20-25

Visa, 1:43, #1302, 1982–1987.....$20-25

Combat car M20, Solido Military #6104,
   1995 reissue $20-25

Cooper 1959 F2, #1102, 1:43, 1994
   Nostalgia reissue......................$20-25

Cord 1930 L 29
   1:43, Solido L'Age D'Or Series #4055 .$20-25
   Spider, 1:43, Solido L'Age D'Or Series
      #4080....................................$20-25

Crane, Fire Department, Solido Tonergam
   Series 2 #3102 ....$20-25

DAF
   Covered Truck "DANZA," Solido Tonergam
      Series 3 #3501 ....$25-30
   Double Covered Truck, IPONE, Solido Ton-
      ergam Series 3 #3507 ....$25-30

Delage 1938 Coupe De Ville, Solido L'Age
   D'Or Series #4051 ....$20-25

Delahaye 1937 135 M, 1:43, Solido L'Age
   D'Or Series #4048 ....$20-25

Desert Jeep with Trailer, Solido Military
   #6108 ....$20-25

Destroyer M10 Tank
   50th Anniversary of the Liberation of France
      and Northwestern Europe 1944–1994,
      4494/43 ....$35-45
   Solido Military #6068......................$20-25
   Solido Military #6202, 1995 reissue .$20-25

Dodge
   1940 Covered Pickup, Coca-Cola, yellow with
      blue cover, #9603, 1:43, 1996....$20-25
   1940 Fire Department Recovery Truck,
      #4428..................................$20-25
   1940 Pickup "Sunlight," #4430 ....$20-25
   1940 Platform Truck, Coca-Cola, yellow with blue
      platform, #9605, 1:43, 1996 ....$20-25
   1940 Platform Truck, Coca-Cola, #9609,
      1:43 ....$20-25
   1940 Stake Truck "Pepsi," #4427 .....$20-25
   4x4, Solido Military #6111 ....$20-25
   4X4 WC 51, 50th Anniversary of the Libera-
      tion of France and Northwestern Europe
      1944–1994, 4494/34 ....$35-45
   4X4 WC 54, 50th Anniversary of the Libera-
      tion of France and Northwestern Europe
      1944–1994, 4494/12 ....$35-45
   4X4 WC 56 Command Car, 50th Anniversary
      of the Liberation of France and Northwestern
      Europe 1944–1994, 4494/13 ....$35-45
   4X4 WC 56 Command Car, 50th Anniversary of
      the Liberation of France and Northwestern
      Europe 1944–1994, 4494/35 .....$35-45
   4x4 with Protective Cover, Solido Tonergam
      Series 1 #2147, 1996 variation $20

6x6, Solido Military #6107 ....$20-25

6X6 WC 63, 50th Anniversary of the Liberation of France and Northwestern Europe
   1944–1994, 4494/22............$35-45

6X6 WC 63, 50th Anniversary of the Liberation of France and Northwestern Europe
   1944–1994, 4494/36............$35-45

Command car, Solido Military
   #6110......................................$20-25

Command car, Solido Military
   #6117......................................$20-25

Pickup, 50th Anniversary of the Liberation of
   France and Northwestern Europe
   1944–1994, 4494/37............$35-45

Signal Corp, Solido Military #6114...$20-25

Tanker, Solido Tonergam Series 1
   #2123......................................$20-25

Tow Truck, Solido Tonergam Series 1 #2143,
   1996 variation $20-25

WC 51, Solido Tonergam Series 1 #2136,
   1994.......................................$20-25

WC 51 4X4, Solido Military #6103, 1995
   reissue....................................$20-25

WC 51 Tanker, Solido Tonergam Series 1
   #2140, 1995 variation $20-25

WC 51 with Trailer, Solido Tonergam Series
   2 #3128, 1995 variation $20-25

WC 54, Solido Tonergam Series 1
   #2128......................................$20-25

WC 54 Ambulance, Solido Military
   #6043......................................$20-25

WC 56 Hose and Ladder, Solido Tonergam
   Series 1 #2139, 1995 variation...$20-25

WC 56 with Inflatable Raft and Trailer,
   Solido Tonergam Series 2 #3127,
   1995 variation $20-25

WC54 "Signal Corps," Solido
   Military #6004........................$20-25

Duesenberg
   1931 J Spider, Solido L'Age D'Or
      Series #4035 ....$20-25
   1935 Model J, Solido L'Age D'Or
      Series #4156, 1:43 ....$20-25

English Bus
   Coca-Cola, #9701, 1:50 ....$20-25
   Country English Bus, Solido Bus
      Series #4404........................$20-25

Facel Vega 1962
   Hard Top, Solido 1960s Series #4515 ..$20-25
   Convertible, top down, Solido 1960s
      Series #4516 ....$20-25

Ferrari
   1956 500 TRC, #1101, 1:43, 1994
      Nostalgia reissue $20-25
   1962 2.5 L, #1108, 1:43, 1995
      Nostalgia reissue $20-25

1963 250 GTO, Solido 1960s Series #4506 ....$20-25

1969 365 GTS Convertible, top down, Prestige Series #8017, 1:18.......$30-35

1969 365 GTS Convertible, top up, Prestige Series #8018, 1:18.......$30-35

1972 365 GTB4, Yesterday Series #1810..................................$15-20

1972 365 GTB4, Yesterday Series #1811..................................$15-20

1976 BB, Yesterday Series #1802....$15-20

Berlinetta Boxer, Hi-Fi/ToDay Series #1515..................................$15-20

Fiat

1960 500, white, Prestige Series #8042, 7½", 1:18, 1996 ....$30-35

1960 500 (open), red, Prestige Series #8043, 7½", 1:18, 1996..........$30-35

1961 Abarth, #1109, 1:43, 1996 Nostalgia reissue $20-25

1965 500 Racing, red with "29" and white racing stripe, Prestige Series #8044, 1:18, 7½", 1996 ....$30-35

1977 131 Racing, 1994 reissue, Solido Racing Series #1913 ....$20-25

Ritmo, 1:43, #1303, 1982–1987 ...$20-25

Ritmo/Strada, 1:43, #1202, reissue of Cougar #1303 ....$15-25

Ritmo-Strada, 1:43, Cougar series #1303, 1980–1982.......................$20-25

Fire Engine, Solido Tonergam Series 1 #2106 ....$20-25

Fire Jeep, 1:43, #1322, 1982–1985 ....$20-25

Ford

1934 Panel Truck "Ford Parts," Prestige Series #8067, 1:18, 9½" $25-30

1934 Pickup Covered Delivery "Perrier," Prestige Series #8010, 1:18, 9½" ..$30-35

1934 Roadster, Coca-Cola, #9504, 1:18..................................$35-40

1934 Roadster, black, Humphrey Bogart, 1994 Signature Series #9802, 1:18..................................$50-60

1934 Roadster, Pepsi-Cola #99054, 9½"..................................$15-25

1934 Roadster Convertible, top down, Prestige Series #8008, 1:18, 9½"..................................$30-35

1934 Roadster Convertible, top up, Prestige Series #8009, 1:18, 9½" $30-35

1934 Sedan "Checker Cab," Pepsi-Cola #99020, 9½"..........................$15-25

1936 Custom Roadster, Prestige Series #8039, 1:18, 9½"....................$30-35

1936 Delivery Truck, Pepsi-Cola #99055, 9½"..................................$15-25

1936 Fire Department Tanker, Prestige Series #8005, 1:18, 9½"....................$30-35

1936 Fire Department Tow Truck, #4432..................................$20-25

1936 Panel Truck, Pepsi-Cola #99057, 1:43..................................$15-25

1936 Pickup, Prestige Series #8002, 1:18, 9½"..................................$30-35

1936 Pickup, Custom Series #8303, 1:18..................................$30-35

1936 Pickup, Coca-Cola, #9503, 1:18..$35-40

1936 Pickup "MICHELIN," Prestige Series #8024, 1:18 ....$30-35

1936 Pickup Fire Truck, Prestige Series #8026, 1994, 1:18 ....$30-35

1936 Pick-Up Truck, Pepsi-Cola #99021, 9½"..................................$15-25

1936 Pick-Up Truck, Pepsi-Cola #99053, 9½"..................................$15-25

1936 Pick-Up Truck, Pepsi-Cola #99056, 1:43..................................$15-25

1936 Pickup with Cover, Coca-Cola, black, #9617, 1:43, 1996.................$20-25

1936 Platform Truck, Pepsi-Cola #99052, 9½"..................................$15-25

1936 Roadster, Coca-Cola, red with navy fenders, #9510, 9½," 1:18, 1996..$35-40

1936 Tanker, Prestige Series #8027, 1994, 1:18..................................$30-35

1936 V8, Coca-Cola, #9611, 1:43.$20-25

1936 V8 Sedan, Solido L'Age D'Or Series #4159, 1:43 ....$20-25

1936 V8 Coal Truck, #4435, 1995 variation $20-25

1936 V8 Fire Department Tanker, #4434..................................$20-25

1936 V8 Pickup "Kodak," #4433.....$20-25

1936 V8 Pickup "MIKO," #4436, 1995 variation $20-25

1936 V8 Platform Truck, Coca-Cola, red with brown platform, #9612, 1:43 ....$20-25

1936 V8 Platform Truck, Pepsi-Cola #99059, 1:43 ....$15-25

1936 V8 Taxi, Solido L'Age D'Or Series #4163, 1:43 ....$20-25

1936 Van "New York Times," #4431 ..$20-25

1936 Wreck Truck, Prestige Series #8037, 1:18, 9½"..........................$30-35

1955 Pickup, Prestige Series #8046, 9½," 1:18, 1996..........................$30-35

1961 Thunderbird, Solido 1960s Series #4505..................................$20-25

1963 Thunderbird Grand Sport, Solido 1960s Series #4517....................$20-25

1964 GT40, Solido 1960s Series #4531..................................$20-25

1964 GT40 Le Mans, Solido 1960s Series #4532 ....$20-25

1964½ Mustang, 1994, Solido 1960s Series #4540 ....$20-25

1964½ Mustang, Coca-Cola, #9615, 1:43, 1995 ....$20-25

1965 Mustang, Solido Racing Series #1922, 1994 ....$20-25

1967 Mk IV, Solido Racing Series #1928, 1996..................................$20-25

Escort GL, 1:43, #1315, 1982–1986..$20-25

Escort RS Turbo, 1:43, #1207, reissue of Cougar #1315 ....$15-25

Escort RS Turbo, 1:43, #1350, 1986–1987..........................$20-25

Fiesta, 1:43, Cougar series #1313, 1981–1982..........................$20-25

Fiesta, 1:43, #1313, 1982–1985 ...$20-25

Panel Truck "Milk Delivery," Pepsi-Cola #99019 1934, 9½"..................$15-25

Sierra XR4, 1:43, #1206, reissue of Cougar #1340 ....$15-25

Sierra XR4i, 1:43, #1340, 1985–1987 ..$20-25

General Grant Tank

Solido Military #6211 ....$20-25

Solido Military #6071 ....$20-25

General Lee Tank

Solido Military #6067 ....$20-25

GMC

50th Anniversary of the Liberation of France and Northwestern Europe 1944–1994, 4494/23 ....$35-45

Solido Military #6032 ....$20-25

"Le Roi," 50th Anniversary of the Liberation of France and Northwestern Europe 1944–1994, 4494/32 ....$35-45

"Tourelle," 50th Anniversary of the Liberation of France and Northwestern Europe 1944–1994, 4494/33............$35-45

1944 Troop Transporter, Solido Military #9423..................................$20-25

Compressor, Solido Military #6115 ...$20-25

Compressor Truck, Solido Military #6001..................................$20-25

Covered Truck, Solido Tonergam Series 2 #3121..................................$20-25

Covered Truck, Solido Military #6036..$20-25

Covered Truck, Solido Military #6101, 1995 reissue $20-25

Fire Engine Recovery Truck, Solido Tonergam Series 2 #3110 ....$20-25

Lot 7, Solido Military #6118 ....$20-25

Lot 7 Recovery Truck, Solido Military #6002..................................$20-25

Road Maintenance Truck, Solido Tonergam Series 2 #3113 ....$20-25

Tanker, Solido Tonergam Series 2
#3115..$20-25

Tanker, Solido Tonergam Series 2
#3116..$20-25

Tow Truck, Solido Tonergam Series 2
#3117..$20-25

Truck with accessories, Solido Military #6106,
1995 variation $20-25

Turret Truck, Solido Military #6047.....$20-25

with accessories, Solido Military #6109...$20-25

with Protective Cover, Solido Tonergam Series
2 #3132, 1996 reissue $20-25

Half Track

Hanomag, Solido Military #6208......$20-25

Recovery Vehicle, Solido Military
#6069..$20-25

US M3, 50th Anniversary of the Liberation of
France and Northwestern Europe
1944–1994, 4494/41............$35-45

Hispano Suiza 1926 Torpedo Convertible,
top down, Solido L'Age D'Or Series
#4162..$20-25

Iveco

1980 TransAfrica, Solido Racing Series
#1911..$20-25

Covered Truck, Solido Tonergam Series 1
#2129..$20-25

Tanker, Solido Tonergam Series 2
#3118..$20-25

Jagdpanther Tank

Solido Military #6064......................$20-25

Solido Military #6206, 1995
reissue...$20-25

Jaguar

1938 SS 100, 1:43, Solido L'Age D'Or
Series #4002 ....$20-25

1978 XJ 12, Yesterday Series
#1806...$15-20

XJ 12, Hi-Fi/ToDay Series #1501......$15-20

Jeep

Ambulance, Solido Military
#6112...$20-25

and Trailer, Solido Military #6034 .....$20-25

and Trailer, Solido Military #6113 .....$20-25

and Zodiac Inflatable Raft with Trailer, Solido
Military #6041 ....$20-25

Auto-Union and Trailer, Solido Military #6037
$20-25

Rally, 1:43, #1331, 1984–1987 ....$20-25

with Hose Reel, Solido Tonergam Series 1
#2117..$20-25

with Ladder and Trailer, Solido Tonergam
Series 2 #3133, 1996 variation .$20-25

Kaiser Jeep

Crane Truck, Solido Military #6070 ...$20-25

M 34, Solido Military #6005 ....$20-25

Kassböhrer

Expedition Track Rammer, Solido Tonergam
Series 4 #3602 ....$20-25

Track Rammer and Sand Spreader, Solido Tonergam Series 4 #3603 ....$20-25

Track Rammer, Solido Tonergam Series 4
#3601 ....$20-25

Track Rammer, Fire Department, Solido Tonergam
Series 4 #3607 ....$20-25

Lamborghini 1990 Diablo, Hi-Fi/ToDay Series
#1527 ....$15-20

Lancia

1978 Stratos, Yesterday Series #1809...$15-20

1978 Stratos, Solido Racing Series
#1906..$20-25

1983 Rally, Solido Racing Series #1923,
1995 variation $20-25

Rally, 1:43, #1205, reissue of Cougar
#1327 ....$15-25

Rally, 1:43, #1327, 1983–1987 ....$20-25

Land Rover

1980, 1994 reissue, Solido Racing Series
#1914..$20-25

and Trailer, Solido Tonergam Series 2
#3134, 1996 variation $20-25

and Trailer, Solido Military #6039 .....$20-25

Leopard Tank, Solido Military #6055 ......$20-25

Lola 1962 Climax V8 F1, #1103, 1:43, 1994
Nostalgia reissue $20-25

London Bus, Solido Bus Series #4402......$20-25

Lotus 1960 F1, #1105, 1:43, 1994 Nostalgia
reissue $20-25

Mack

Fire Engine, Solido Tonergam Series 2
#3106..$20-25

Freighter "TEAM HUSQVARNA," Solido Tonergam Series 3 #3508 ....$25-30

R 600 Fire Engine, Solido Tonergam Series 3
#3511 ....$25-30

R600 Fire Brigade Tanker, Solido Tonergam
Series 3 #3513 ....$25-30

R600 Fire Truck Semi, Solido Tonergam Series
3 #3514 ....$25-30

Marmon

Recovery Truck, Solido Tonergam Series 1
#2124...$20-25

Tanker, Solido Tonergam Series 1
#2121...$20-25

Maserati

1956 250, #1104, 1:43, 1994 Nostalgia
reissue $20-25

1970 Indy, Yesterday Series #1801..$15-20

Matra Rancho, #1326, 1983-1987.......$20-25

Mercedes-Benz

1930 SSKL, 1:43, Solido L'Age D'Or Series
#4004..$20-25

1938 540K Convertible, Solido L'Age D'Or
Series #4086, 1:43 ....$20-25

1954 300 SL, Solido 1960s Series
#4502..$20-25

1986 Unimog Rallye, Solido Racing Series
#1912..$20-25

Ambulance, Solido Tonergam Series 1
#2133..$20-25

Express Emergency Van and Trailer, Solido
Tonergam Series 1 #2130 ....$20-25

Fire Brigade Tanker, Solido Tonergam Series 3
#3512 ....$25-30

Jet Spray Truck, Solido Tonergam Series 2
#3114..$20-25

Ladder Truck, Solido Tonergam Series 2
#3111..$20-25

Semi Trailer "ANDROS Fruits," Solido Tonergam Series 3 #3510 ....$25-30

Semi Trailer "BRIDGESTONE," Solido Tonergam Series 3 #3510 ....$25-30

Snow Plow, Solido Tonergam Series 4
#3606 ....$20-25

Tender, Solido Tonergam Series 1 #2132.$20-25

Training Simulator, Solido Tonergam Series 3
#3516..$25-30

Unimog, Solido Tonergam Series 1
#2125...$20-25

Unimog, Solido Military #6038.........$20-25

Unimog Ambulance, Solido Tonergam Series
1 #2131 ....$20-25

Unimog Ambulance, Solido Military
#6046 ....$20-25

Unimog Breakdown Tow Truck, Solido Tonergam Series 1 #2134 ....$20-25

Unimog Forest Fire, Solido Tonergam Series 1
#2127...$20-25

Unimog Forest Fire Tender, Solido Tonergam
Series 1 #2146, 1996 variation ..$20-25

Van with Zodiac Raft, Solido Tonergam Series
2 #3122 ....$20-25

with Foam Cannon, Solido Tonergam Series 2
#3131, 1996 reissue $20-25

190, 1:43, #1337, 1984–1987 ....$20-25

190, 1:43, #1352, 1986–1987 ....$20-25

190, Hi-Fi/ToDay Series #1506.......$15-20

1986 190 2.3/16S, Hi-Fi/ToDay Series
#1510..$15-20

1989 SL Convertible, Hi-Fi/ToDay Series
#1517..$15-20

1989 SL Coupe Hard Top, Hi-Fi/ToDay
Series #1518 ....$15-20

1993 500 SEL, Hi-Fi/ToDay Series #1535,
1996..$15-20

Mini Cooper

1968, Solido Racing Series #1930,
1996..$20-25

1969, green, Yesterday Series #1821,
1996..$20-25

1969, red, Yesterday Series #1822,
1996..$20-25

1995 British Open, Hi-Fi/ToDay
Series #1536, 1996.................$15-20

1995 Cabriolet, Hi-Fi/ToDay Series
#1537, 1996.........................$15-20

S 1964, blue with white fenders,
Prestige Series #8021, 1:18.......$30-35

S 1964, Prestige Series #8022, 1:18..$30-35

S 1964, Custom Series #8305, 1:18..$30-35

S 1964 Rallye, Prestige Series #8023,
1:18....................................$30-35

Nissan Prairie
1:43, #1341, 1985–1987.............$20-25

1:43, #1216, reissue of Cougar
#1341................................$15-25

Opel GT 1900, 1968, Yesterday Series
#1805.................................$15-20

Open Top Bus, Solido Bus Series #4417...$20-25

Packard
1937 Convertible, Solido L'Age D'Or
Series #4099, 1:43..................$20-25

1937 Sedan, 1:43, Solido L'Age D'Or
Series #4047........................$20-25

1937 Sedan, silver with black fenders,
Humphrey Bogart, 1994 Signature
Series #9902, 1:43.................$25-30

HQ, Solido Military #6006...........$20-25

HQ, Solido Military #6116...........$20-25

Sedan HQ, 50th Anniversary of the Liberation
of France and Northwestern Europe
1944–1994, 4494/38.............$35-45

Panhard
1959 DB, #1107, 1:43, 1995
Nostalgia reissue.......................$20-25

AML 9, Solido Military #6025 0.......$20-25

Patton M47 Tank, Solido Military
#6065..................................$20-25

Peugeot
104 ZS, 1:43, Cougar series #1316,
1981–1982...........................$20-25

104 ZS, 1:43, #1316, 1982–1985..$20-25

19 Express and Trailer, Solido Tonergam
Series 2 #3130, 1995 variation .$20-25

1975 Safari, 1994 reissue, Solido Racing
Series #1917........................$20-25

1978 504 Coupe, Yesterday Series #1818,
1995 reissue.........................$20-25

1978 504 Coupe Rallye, Solido Racing
Series #1924, 1995 reissue.......$20-25

1984 205 GTI, Hi-Fi/ToDay Series
#1508.................................$15-20

1989 605, Hi-Fi/ToDay Series #1516...$15-20

1989 605, Actua Series #8502, 1:18..$30-35

205 GTI, 1:43, #1349, 1986–1987..$20-25

205 GTI, 1:43, #1351, 1986–1987..$20-25

305, 1:43, #1320, 1982–1985....$20-25

504, 1:43, #1306, 1982–1985....$20-25

504, 1:43, #1311, 1981 toy show prototype (pre-production only)........$150-200

504 Sedan, 1:43, Cougar series #1306,
1980–1982...........................$20-25

504 V6, 1:43, #1335, 1984–1985..$20-25

505, 1:43, #1312, 1982–1987....$20-25

604, #40, 1:43.......................$15-20

J9 Ambulance, red, Solido Tonergam
Series 1 #2126......................$20-25

J9 Ambulance, yellow, Solido Tonergam
Series 1 #2135......................$20-25

Porsche
Spyder, 1955, #1106, 1:43, 1994
Nostalgia reissue.......................$20-25

Carrera, 1973, Yesterday Series
#1808.................................$15-20

Carrera, 1973, Solido Racing Series
#1920.................................$20-25

924, 1:43, #1324, 1983–1985....$20-25

928 GT, 1989, Hi-Fi/ToDay Series
#1525.................................$15-20

928, 1:43, #1336, 1984–1987....$20-25

928S, Hi-Fi/ToDay Series #1505.....$15-20

934, 1:43, #1204, reissue of Cougar
#1323................................$15-25

934 Turbo, 1:43, #1323, 1983–1987..$20-25

935, 1979 Solido Racing Series #1925,
1995 reissue........................$20-25

935, 1:43, #1214, reissue of Cougar
#1332................................$15-25

935 Turbo, 1:43, #1332, 1984–1987..$20-25

936, 1:43, #1334, 1984–1986....$20-25

944, 1984, Hi-Fi/ToDay Series #1502..$15-20

944, 1:43, #1348, 1986–1987....$20-25

Priest M7 B1, Solido Military #6209.......$20-25

PT 76 Tank, Solido Military #6075.........$20-25

PZ IV, Solido Military #6207.................$20-25

Range Rover
1978, Yesterday Series #1817,
1995..................................$20-25

1984 Rallye, Solido Racing Series #1927,
1995..................................$20-25

Renault
14, 1:43, Cougar series #1309,
1981–1982...........................$20-25

14, 1:43, #1309, 1982–1985......$20-25

18, 1:43, #1318, 1982–1987......$20-25

1923 40 CV Presidentielle, top down,
Solido L'Age D'Or Series #4165,
1:43..................................$20-25

1925 40 CV Sedan, 1:43, Solido L'Age
D'Or Series #4059....................$20-25

1926 40 CV Landaulet, Solido L'Age D'Or
Series #4149, 1:43..................$20-25

1934 Reinastella, Solido L'Age D'Or
Series #4097, 1:43..................$20-25

1954 4 CV, 1994, Solido 1960s Series
#4537.................................$20-25

1954 4 CV Open Top, 1994, Solido
1960s Series #4538..................$20-25

1954 4CV Rallye, Solido Racing Series
#1919, 1994........................$20-25

1961 Dauphine Sedan, Solido 1960s
Series #4541, 1995..................$20-25

1961 Dauphine Open Roof, Solido
1960s Series #4542, 1995......$20-25

1962 Dauphine "1093," Solido Racing
Series #1926, 1995.................$20-25

1964 4 L Sedan, Solido 1960s Series
#4544, 1996........................$20-25

1985 5 Maxi Turbo, Solido Racing
Series #1908........................$20-25

1990 Clio, Hi-Fi/ToDay Series #1519..$15-20

1991 Clio 16 S, Hi-Fi/ToDay Series
#1520.................................$15-20

1991 Clio 16S "Coupe," Hi-Fi/ToDay
Series #1526........................$15-20

1991 Espace, Hi-Fi/ToDay Series #1522...$15-20

1991 Espace, Coca-Cola, red,
#9614, 1:43.........................$20-25

1991 Espace Fire Van, Hi-Fi/ToDay
Series #1534, 1996.................$15-20

1992, Actua Series #8504, 1:18.....$30-35

1992 Twingo, 1994, Hi-Fi/ToDay
Series #1528........................$15-20

1992 Twingo, Hi-Fi/ToDay Series
#1530, 1994........................$15-20

1993 Clio "Williams," Hi-Fi/ToDay
Series #1531, 1994.................$15-20

1993 Clio Rallye, Solido Racing
Series #1918........................$20-25

1993 Twingo Open Top, Hi-Fi/ToDay
Series #1532, 1994.................$15-20

1994 Trafic, Coca-Cola, red, #9616,
1:50, 1995..........................$20-25

1995 19 Convertible, Hi-Fi/ToDay
Series #1533, 1995.................$15-20

25, 1:43, #1339, 1985–1987......$20-25

25, 1:43, Hi-Fi/ToDay Series
#1504, 1988–1989..................$15-20

4 Van, 1:43, #1213, reissue of
Cougar #1325.......................$15-25

4L (open), Solido 1960s Series #4545,
1996..................................$20-25

4L Van, 1:43, #1325, 1983–1987...$20-25

4L Van, 1:43, #1330, 1983–1986...$20-25

5, 1:43, Cougar series #1317,
1981–1982...........................$20-25

5 Maxi Turbo, 1:43, #1208, reissue of
Cougar #1321 ....$15-25

5 TL, 1:43, #1317, 1982–1983 .....$20-25

5 Turbo, 1:43, 1982–1985 ....$20-25

Express Van, 1:43 ....$12-16

Express with Trailer, Solido Tonergam
Series 1 #2122 ....$20-25

Express with Trailer, Solido Tonergam
Series 1 #2142, 1996 variation...$20-25

Field Casualty Vehicle, Solido Tonergam
Series 3 #3515 ....$25-30

Fire Tanker Semi, red, Solido Tonergam
Series 3 #3509 ....$25-30

Fuego, 1:43, #1203, reissue of
Cougar #1308 ....$15-25

Fuego, 1:43, Cougar series #1308...$20-25

Fuego, 1:43, #1308, 1982–1987 ..$20-25

Maxi 5 Turbo, 1:43, #1353,
1986–1987...............................$20-25

Paris Bus, Solido Bus Series #4401 ....$20-25

R35 Tank, Solido Military #6205,
1995 reissue.............................$20-25

Super 5, 1:43, #1211, reissue of Cougar
#1353 ....$15-25

Super 5, 1:43, #1357, 1987.........$20-25

Traction Gaz FFI, Solido Military #6102,
1995 reissue.............................$20-25

Trafic, Solido Tonergam Series 1 #2137,
1994 ....$20-25

Trafic Ambulance, Solido Tonergam
Series 1 #2138, 1994 ....$20-25

Trafic Bus, Solido Tonergam Series 1
#2141, 1995 variation $20-25

Trafic Civil Security, Solido Tonergam
Series 1 #2145, 1996 variation...$20-25

Trafic with Inflatable Raft and Trailer, Solido
Tonergam Series 2 #3129, 1995
variation $20-25

Trafic with Ladder, Solido Tonergam Series 1
#2144, 1996 variation $20-25

Rolls Royce

1939, pale yellow with black fenders,
Orson Welles, 1994 Signature Series
#9903, 1:43 ....$25-30

1939 Convertible, Solido L'Age D'Or
Series #4077 ....$20-25

1939 Coupe, 1:43, Solido L'Age D'Or
Series #4071 ....$20-25

1961, silver with black hood, Orson Welles,
1994 Signature Series #9803, 1:18 ..$50-60

1961 Silver Cloud II, Prestige Series
#8006, 1:18, 10"".....................$30-35

1987 Corniche, Hi-Fi/ToDay Series
#1511 ....$15-20

Saviem First Aid, Solido Tonergam Series 1
#2101 ....$20-25

Sherman

Bulldozer Tank, Solido Military #6077..$20-25

Egyptian Tank, Solido Military #6078..$20-25

M4 A3, Solido Military #6210 ....$20-25

M4A3, 50th Anniversary of the Liberation of
France and Northwestern Europe
1944–1994, 4494/42............$35-45

M4A3 Tank, Solido Military #6201,
1995 reissue.............................$20-25

Tank, Solido Military #6053 ....$20-25

Sides 2000

Mark 3 Paris, Solido Tonergam
Series 2 #3119 ....$20-25

Mark 3 Strasbourg, Solido Tonergam
Series 2 #3123 ....$20-25

Somua S35 Tank, Solido Military #6074..$20-25

Special Convoy Transport, #7013 ....$20-25

Studebaker Silver Hawk 1957, 4521 ...$20-25

Hard Top, #4522 ....$20-25

Talbot

1937 T, 1:43, Solido L'Age D'Or Series
#4003......................................$20-25

Horizon, 1:43#1321#1319,
1982–1985...............................$20-25

Tagora, 1:43, Cougar series #1307,
1980–1982...............................$20-25

Tagora, 1:43, #1307, 1982–1985.$20-25

Tigre Tank

Solido Military #6212......................$20-25

Solido Military #6063......................$20-25

Solido Military #6204, 1995 reissue...$20-25

Toyota 1977 Celica, 1994 reissue, Solido
Racing Series #1915......................$20-25

Triumph Spitfire Mk 1 1962

Solido Racing Series #1921, 1994...$20-25

Solido 1960s Series #4539, 1994...$20-25

Tucker Torpedo 1948, #4524 ....$20-25

US Half-Track Radio M3, Solido Military #6203,
1995 reissue $20-25

US Jeep

50th Anniversary of the Liberation of France
and Northwestern Europe 1944–1994,
4494/11..................................$35-45

and Trailer, 50th Anniversary of the Liberation
of France and Northwestern Europe
1944–1994, 4494/21............$35-45

and Trailer, Solido Military #6105,
1995 reissue.............................$20-25

SAS & Trailer, 50th Anniversary of the Liberation of France and Northwestern Europe
1944–1994, 4494/31............$35-45

with accessories, Solido Military #6049...$20-25

with Trailer, Solido Military #6048 .....$20-25

V.A.B. 4X4

Solido Military #6027......................$20-25

Solido Military #6007......................$20-25

Visa 4x4 Tele-Union

A2, 1:43, #1342, 1982–1987 ......$20-25

RTL, 1:43, #1343, 1982–1987.......$20-25

Monte Carlo, 1:43, #1344,
1982–1987................................$20-25

SSR, 1:43, #1345, 1982–1987 .....$20-25

Canada, 1:43, #1346, 1982–1987..$20-25

Volkswagen

1949 Beetle Coca-Cola, #9505,
1:18...$35-40

1949 Beetle Sedan, Coca-Cola, #9506,
1:18...$35-40

1949 Beetle Sedan Hardtop, Prestige Series
#8016, 1:18 ....$30-35

1949 Beetle Sedan hardtop, Custom Series
#8304, 1:18 ....$30-35

1949 Beetle Convertible, top down, Prestige
Series #8014, 1:18 ....$30-35

1949 Beetle Convertible, top up, Prestige
Series #8015, 1:18 ....$30-35

1949 Beetle Convertible, top down, Custom
Series #8302, 1:18 ....$30-35

1958 Beetle, Coca-Cola, white with blue
top, red fenders, #9511, 9½", 1:18,
1996 ....$35-35

1958 Beetle Sedan, Custom Series
#8306, 1:18 ....$30-35

1958 Beetle Rallye, Prestige Series #8038,
1:18, 9½", 1996 ....$30-35

1966 Van, Solido 1960s Series
#4534.......................................$20-25

1966 Van, Michelin, Solido 1960s Series
#4543, 1996 ....$20-25

1966 Van, red & white, Prestige Series
#8031, 1994, 1:18 ....$30-35

1966 Van, purple, PEACE AND LOVE,
FLOWER POWERED, Prestige Series
#8032, 1994, 1:18 ....$30-35

1966 Van, yellow and blue, Michelin,
Prestige Series #8041, 1:18, 8⅞",
1996 ....$30-35

1966 Van, Coca-Cola, red upper, white
lower body, #9508, 8⅞", 1:18 ....$35-35

1966 Van, Coca-Cola, #9613, 1:43...$20-25

1966 Van, Coca-Cola, red upper, white lower
body, #9618, 1:43, 1996 ....$20-25

1966 Van Fire Brigade, Solido 1960s Series
#4535.......................................$20-25

Golf, 1:43, Cougar series
#1314, 1981–1982 ....$20-25

Golf, 1:43, #1314, 1982–1984.....$20-25

Golf GTI, 1:43, #1212, reissue of
Cougar #1314 ....$15-25

Golf GTI, 1:43, #1358, 1987.........$20-25

Volvo Front End Loader, Solido Tonergam
Series 2 #3124, 1994 reissue $20-25

Somerville

The Somerville Society
c/o Rod Ward
Modelauto
120 Gledhow Valley Road
Leeds LS17 6LX England
tel: +44 (0)113 268 6685
fax: +44 (0)1977 681991
e-mail: hotline@modelauto.co.uk
website: www.modelauto.co.uk

Somerville 1:43 scale high quality hand-built models are made in Great Britain. Most models are issued in more than one color variation. The Somerville Society is a now-defunct organization devoted to the appreciation of these fine models.

Austin Allegro, #143 ....$100-115
Ford
    Anglia 1949 A494CV, top up or down,
        #117..................................$90-105
    Popular E190 1937 Sedan, #103 ..$90-105
Fordson Van
    with fish design, #112....................$90-105
    with tractor design, #118.................$70-85
    "Castrol," #109 ....$90-105
    "India Tyres," #107 ....$90-105
    "L...East," #113...........................$90-105
    "Somerville," #111 ....$90-105
    "Turf," #110 ....$90-105
    Butcher, #114..............................$90-105
Hillman Minx Convertible, top down, #133 ..$119
Mercedes-Benz
    260D, #102 ....$90-105
    300 SL, #105 ....$90-105
1937 Riley Kestrel, #129 ....$100-115
Rover P2 14 Sports, #134 ....$110-125
Saab
    900 Cabriolet, #130......................$90-105
    9000 Turbo 1985, #122 ....$90-105
    9000 CD 1987, #127 ....$90-105
    9000 CS 1992, #132.....................$100-115
    9000 CS Police, #139....................$110-125
    92, #119 ....$90-105
    93A, #144 ....$100-115
    95 Estate, #123 ....$100-115
    97 Sonett, #125 ....$90-105
Standard Flying 12 Sedan, #106 ....$100-115
Sunbeam
    Alpine 1953, #137 ....$110-125
    Talbot, #120 ....$90-105
    Talbot 90 Drophead, #141 ....$100-115
Taxi, #100 ....$90-105
Volvo
    210 Van, #140...........................$100-115
    544 Station Wagon, #128 ....$90-105
    Amazon, #124...........................$110-125

Amazon 123 GT, #136 ....$90-105
Jakob, #126...........................$100-115
PV444 1947, #121 ....$90-105
Valbo 445 1953 Cabriolet, #138 ..$110-125

South Eastern Finecast

Dave Ellis
South Eastern Finecast
Glenn House, Hartfield Road, Forest Row
Sussex RH18 5DZ Great Britain
tel: 01342 824711
fax: 01342 822270

South Eastern Finecast produces white metal 1:24 and 1:43 scale model kits, according to various Internet sources. Until Paul Carpenter e-mailed me in March 2000 asking me why I didn't list them, I had never heard of them before. The company apparently also makes etched brass locomotive kits for hobbyists. Thanks to Fred Emig for the list of models.

South Eastern Finecast 1:24 Scale Car Kits

Austin Mk 1
    Morris Mini, #A209.....................$35-50
    Mini Cooper, #A210....................$35-50
Bentley 4.5 Litre, #A201 ....$35-50
Bugatti Type 59, #A202.................$35-50
Car Transporter Trailer, #A230 ....$20-25
Jaguar SS100, #A204 ....$35-50
MG TC, #A205 ....$35-50
MGA
    1500/1600, #A211 ....$35-50
    1600 Coupe, #A212....................$35-50
MGB
    GT, #A208 ....$35-50
    GT, (Rubber Bumper), #A214...........$35-50
    GT, V8, #A215 ....$35-50
    Roadster (Rubber Bumper), #A213 .....$35-50
    Roadster, #A207 ....$35-50
Morgan Plus 8, #A216 ....$35-50
Rolls Royce Silver Ghost, #A206 ....$35-50
Vauxhall 30/98E, #A203 ....$35-50

South Eastern Finecast 1:24 Scale Autokits

1932 Alfa Romeo, #A008 ....$35-50
1925 Austin 7, #A014 ....$35-50
Brabham BT24, #A022...................$35-50
BRM 1962/1963, #A001 ....$35-50
1927 Bugatti 35B, #A005 ....$35-50
Delage, #A015 ....$35-50
1934 ERA 1.5 Litre, #A006 ....$35-50
1961 Ferrari 1.5 Litre, #A003 ....$35-50
1963 Lotus 25, #A002 ....$35-50
1965 Lotus 33, #A012 ....$35-50
Lotus
    38 Indianapolis, #A011 ....$35-50

Super Seven, #A007 ....$35-50
Mercedes SSKL, #A013 ....$35-50
1933 MG K3, #A017 ....$35-50
MG M, #A010 ....$35-50
1950 MG TD, #A018......................$35-50
MG TF, #A021 ....$35-50
1928 Miller 91, #A019...................$35-50
1934 Morgan 3-Wheeler, #A020 ....$35-50
Porsche 904, #A009 ....$35-50

South Eastern Finecast 1:43 Scale Car Kits

Austin 7
    Open Tourer, #A033 ....$20-30
    Ulster 2-Seat, #A034 ....$20-30
Austin "C" Cab Van, #A041 ....$20-30
Austin Box Saloon, #A040 ....$20-30
Car Trailer, #A050.......................$15-25
1922 Citroen 5CV, #A030 ....$20-30
Daimler Dart SP250, #A031 ....$20-30
Frazer Nash TT, #A038..................$20-30
MG K3, #A035 ....$20-30
Morgan 3-Wheeler, #A036...............$20-30
Morris Bull Nose, #A037.................$20-30
Riley Imp/MPH, #A032 ....$20-30

Spa Croft Models

98 High Street, Tibshelf
Derbyshire DE55 5NU
England
tel. & fax: +01773 872780
Contact Mike Coupe
e-mail: SpaCroft@aol.com
website: www.spacroftmodels.bizland.com

As reported by company representative Mike Coupe, Spa Croft Models is a small but growing manufacturer of fine quality white metal models of British cars. Models are of a quality similar to Crossway, Kenna, and Somerville. Spa Croft Models was established in 1995.

Spa Croft Models does not have any distributors in the US although their products have been sold in the States. They are sold in the UK mainly through Modelauto, Wheels, JM Toys, Crossway, B&L Models, and Peregrine Models, as well as on Spa Croft's own website.

Austin A70 Hampshire, SPC3
    gray green................................$145-155
    dark blue $145-155
Austin A70 Hampshire Countryman (Woody Wagon)
    elfin green...............................$145-155
    cream $145-155
Hillman Minx Californian.................$145-155
Morris Isis Series II, SPC1
    Damask red and gray..................$115-125

gray & turquoise $115-125
Morris Oxford Series III......................$145-155
Standard Vanguard Phase I, SPC4
    pale metallic green.......................$115-125
    pale bronze $115-125
Standard Vanguard Phase III $145-155
FC Vauxhall VX 4/90, SPC2
    White with red side flash..............$115-125
    Fawn with black side flash.............$115-125

Spark/Spark Model

Collector J. J. Lasne reports that Sparkmodel is based in France with production in China. The brand is represented by a very thorough 1:43 scale collection of modern "24 Hours of Le Mans" race cars as well as other exotic sports and racing cars. Bizarre is an offshoot brand of Sparkmodel. A long list of current models can be found on the worldwide web at www.sparkmodel.com.

Morgan Aero 8
    metalllic orange, SPNM 01 ....$35-40
    British metallic green, SPNM 02.........$35-40
    metallic blue, SPMN03 ....$35-40
    silver, SPMN04 ....$35-40
Pagani Zonda GR
    No 61, Le Mans 2003, SCZP 04 .....$35-40
TVR Tuscan R
    No 91, Le Mans 2003, SCTR01 ......$35-40
    No 92, Le Mans 2003, SCTR02 ......$35-40

Spec-Cast

428 6th Avenue NW
P. O. Box 368
Dyersville, IA 52040-0368

Spec-Cast is a spin-off of the J. L. Ertl company. Spec-Cast models of Dyersville, Iowa, are generally diecast banks in the form of scale model cars, trucks, and airplanes. Liberty Classics is in turn a division of Spec-Cast made in Libertyville, Illinois. Both brands focus on mostly 1:38 scale models. The difference is that Spec-Cast focuses more on producing unmarked models, whereas Liberty Classics specializes in advertising collectibles, sporting logos, and livery from various companies, to be used as a promotional model.

1932 Ford Hot Rod, 1:24......................$15-20

Collectors may subscribe to Spec-tacular News for $8 for 1 year ($11 outside of U.S.) $14 for 2 years ($16 outside of U.S.) You may also obtain the latest Spec Cast catalog for $2.

Specialty Diecast (see Dimension 4)

Speed Burners (see Mego)

Speed Burners are an obscure series of diecast cars produced by Mego around the late 1960s to early 1970s.

Speed Classics (see Etzel's Speed Classics)

Speed Wheels

Speed Wheels are of a quality almost comparable to Hot Wheels, at least the Series V models that sold for about 70 cents each. Lesser quality cars are available for 40 cents but are not worth collecting, according to Russell Alameda. The parent company and accompanying information is still under research.

Speedway Collection (see Dimension 4)

Speedy Power (also see ToyMark)

Speedy Power is a recently discovered brand of 1:32 scale diecast toys from Toymark Co., Ltd. They retail for $3.99 each. Features include opening doors and pullback motor. Recent evidence indicates the brand has been purchased and is now marketed by New-Ray.

1997 BMW Z-3 Convertible
    metallic teal $5-7
    red $5-7
Jeep...$5-7
Land Rover...$5-7

Speedy Racer (see Speedy Power and ToyMark)

Spiel-Nutz

Collector Bob Yates reports, "After the decline of the original Schuco Micro Racers series and before they became the 'Micro Racers' (Lilliput) of today, there were some released under this name. I have a 'Spiel-Nutz' Micro Racer 1043 as marked on the key and the rubber nose piece (where Schuco used to put their name). My understanding is that the die maker for Schuco received the Micro Racer series dies from Schuco as severance when they folded in 1975. His name was Nutz and he made some of these under his

name. It looks exactly like the the original Schuco Mercedes Micro Racer 1043."

Spiel-Nutz Micro Racer 1043 ....$60-75

Spot-On (also see Tri-Ang)

Spot-On is a brand of 1:42 scale models from Belfast, Northern Ireland, according to collector Brian Willoughby. Introduced in 1959, Spot-On was a division of Great Britain's Tri-Ang brand, established by the Line Brothers in 1935. Quality is excellent, and popularity of these models in Europe and rarity in the U.S. keeps values high.

AEC Mammoth Major 8
    flat float with sides and oil drum
      load, #110/3D.......................$300
    Shell BP Tanker, #110/4 ....$750
    with flat float, #110/2 ....$300
    with flat float and brick load "London
      Brick Co.," #110/2B $300
    with flat float and sides "British Road
      Services," #110/3 ....$325
AEC Routemaster Bus, #145 ....$725
Armstrong Siddeley Sapphire 236,
    #101 ....$150
Aston Martin DB3, #113 ....$200
Austin 1800, #286 ....$100
    with row boat, #410 ....$125
Austin A40, #154 ....$125
Austin A60 with roof rack and skis, #184 ...$125
Austin FX4 Taxi Cab, #155.....................$125
Austin Healey
    100-Six Sports car, #105 ....$200
    Sprite, #219 ....$175
Austin Prime Mover
    and flat float with sides, #106A/1 ....$300
    and flat float with sides and crate
      load, #106A/1C........................$375
    with flat float, no sides, #106A/0 ....$125
    with MGA Sports car in Crate
      "BMC," #106A/0C $400
Austin Seven Mini, #211 ....$175
Bedford
    "Tonibell" Ice CreamVan, #265 ....$175
    10-ton tanker, "Shell BP," #158A/2 .....$775
    Military Field Kitchen, #417 ....$150
Bentley
    4-door Sports Saloon, #102 ....$200
    Supercharged 4.5 Liter, #263............$125
BMW Isetta Bubble car, #118 ....$125
Bristol 406, #115...................................$175
Bullnose Morris Cowley, #266 ....$100
Caterpillar D9 Bulldozer, #116 ....$675
Commer
    Security Van, #273 ....$250

Window Cleaners Van, #315 ....$200
Crash Service Land Rover, #402 ....$125
Daimler Dart SP250, #215 ....$225
ERF 68G
    flat float with sides, #109/3 ....$250
    flat floatwith sides and barrel load,
    #109/3B $300
    with brick load, #109/2B $275
    with flat float, #109/2 ....$225
    with flat float and wood planks,
    #109/2P $300
Express Dairies Milk Float, #271 ....$150
Fiat 500, #185 ....$150
Fiat Multipla, #120 ....$125
Fire Dept, Land Rover, #316 ....$175
Ford Anglia, #213 ....$125
Ford Consul Classic, #259 ....$150
Ford Thames Trader
    with garage load, #111A/0G $375
    with log load, #111A/0T $275
    with sides "British Railways," #111A/1 ....$275
    with sides and sack load, #111A/1S $275
Ford Zephyr 6, #270 ....$150
Ford Zodiac, #100 ....$125
    with lights, #100SL $150
Goggomobil Super, #131 ....$125
Hillman Minx, #287 ....$100
    and dinghy, #403 ....$125
Humber Super Snipe
    Estate, #183 ....$200
    with luggage rack, #306 ....$200
Jaguar 3.4 Mk I, #114 ....$175
    Police car, white and black, #256 ....$250
Jaguar E Type, #217 ....$225
Jaguar Mk 10, #218 ....$175
Jaguar S Type, #276 ....$200
Jaguar XK-SS, #107 ....$200
Jensen 541, #112 ....$225
Jones Mobile Crane, #117 ....$325
Lambretta Scooter, #229 ....$175
Land Rover
    and Missile carrier, #419 ....$300
    and Trailer, #308 ....$175
    RAC, #258 ....$200
    Long wheelbase, #161 ....$125
Massey Harris Tractor, #137 ....$600
Meadows Friskysport, #119 ....$125
Mercedes-Benz 230SL
    #278 ....$125
    #407 ....$125
MG 1100, #267 ....$125
MG Midget Mk II, #281 ....$175
MG PB Midget 1935 , #279 ....$125
MGA Sports car, #104 ....$200
Morris 1100, #262 ....$125
    with canoe, #274 ....$100

Morris Mini Van, #404 ....$425
    "Post Office Telephones," #210/2 ....$175
    "Royal Mail," #210/1 ....$175
Morris Minor 1000, #289 ....$200
Mulliner Luxury Coach, #156 ....$400
NSU Prinz, #193 ....$150
Police "Z" Car, #309 ....$175
RAF Land Rover, #415 ....$150
Renault Floride Convertible, #166 ....$125
Rolls-Royce
    Phantom V, Royal, #260 ....$425
    Silver Wraith, #103 ....$275
Rover 3-Litre, #157 ....$200
    with lights, #157SL $225
Sailing Dinghy, #136 ....$30
    and Trailer, #135 ....$60
Sunbeam Alpine
    Convertible, #191/1 ....$200
    Hard top, #191/2 ....$200
Tourist Caravan, #264 ....$75
Triumph TR3A, #108 ....$200
United Dairies Milk Float, #122 ....$150
Vauxhall Cresta
    PA, #165 ....$225
    PB, #280 ....$125
    PB "BEA," #405 ....$125
Volkswagen
    1200 Rally, #195 ....$125
    Beetle 1200, #307 ....$275
    Variant with skis, #401 ....$500
Volvo
    122S, #216 ....$175
    P1800, #261 ....$125
Wadham Ambulance, #207 ....$500

Stahlberg (or Stallberg)

Several plastic models from Stahlberg of Finland have been produced to be sold as dealer promotional models.

Mercedes 300 Wagon, 1:25 ....$25-30
Saab Lancia 600 4-door Sedan, 1:25 ....$25-30
Volvo 245 GL Wagon, 1:25 ....$25-30

Starter

Starter is the brand name of 1:43 scale resin-cast kits and hand-built models produced in France.

Alfa Romeo
    1st Le Mans 1931 ....$110-125
    1st Le Mans 1932 ....$110-125
    1st Le Mans 1933 ....$110-125
    1st Le Mans 1934 ....$110-125
Alpine A442B 1st Le Mans 1978 ....$90-105
Aston Martin
    DB2 ....$100-115

DB7 Zagato Salon de Paris $115-130
DBR1 1st Le Mans 1959 ....$90-105
Audi Quattro
    HB M Carlo $80-95
    n°6 rallye Monte Carlo 1986 ....$80-95
    S1 Pikes Peak 87 ....$80-95
Audi R8
    1st Le Mans 2000 ....$90-105
    1st Le Mans 2001 ....$90-105
    1st Le Mans 2002 ....$90-105
Austin Healey 100 4 n°33 Le Mans 1
953 ....$95-110
Bentley
    1st Le Mans 1924 ....$110-125
    1st Le Mans 1927 ....$110-125
    1st Le Mans 1928 ....$110-125
    1st Le Mans 1929 ....$110-125
    1st Le Mans 1930 ....$110-125
    EXP Speed 8 n°7 1st Le Mans 2003 ...$90-105
BMW 3.0 CSL
    Calder Le Mans 1975 ....$115-130
    Millimetree n°41 Le Mans 197- $115-130
    UFO n°71 Le Mans 1977 ....$115-130
BMW V12 LMR 1st Le Mans 1999 ......$90-105
BMW X5 n°207 Paris-Dakar 2004 .....$115-130
Bugatti
    1st Le Mans 1937 ....$110-125
    1st Le Mans 1939 ....$110-125
Chenard & Walker 1st Le Mans 1923 ...$110-125
Citroen BX 4TC Monte Carlo 1986 ....$80-95
Citroen Saxo VTS $60-75
Citroen XM V6 1990 ....$60-75
Citroen Xsara
    berline $60-75
    coupe or $60-75
    WRC n°3 Winner Monte Carlo
    2004 ....$115-130
Courage C60
    JPX n°13 Le Mans 2003 ....$115-130
    Pescarolo Sport n°17 Le Mans 2003 ...$115-130
    Peugeot Pescarolo n°18 Le Mans
    2003 ....$115-130
Courage C65 JPX n°31 Le Mans 2003 ..$115-130
Dallara Oreca n°14 Le Mans 2002 ......$90-105
De Tomaso Pantera n°32 Le Mans 1972 ...$95-110
Delahaye 1st Le Mans 1938 ....$110-125
Ferrari 166 1st Le Mans 1949 ....$110-125
Ferrari 250 1st Le Mans 1965 ....$90-105
Ferrari 250P 1st Le Mans 1963 ....$90-105
Ferrari 275P 1st Le Mans 1964 ....$90-105
Ferrari 288 GTO Evoluzione $115-130
Ferrari 330 TRI 1st Le Mans 1962 ....$90-105
Ferrari 360 Modena
    GTC $115-130
    JMB Racing n°70 Le Mans 2003 ....$115-130
    Red Bull Daytona 2004 ....$115-130

Ferrari 375 MM
   1st Le Mans 1954 promotion $90-105
   Cunningham n°6 Le Mans 1954 ...$115-130
Ferrari 408 ....$115-130
Ferrari 512 BBLM Pozzi 3M n°63 Le Mans
   1979 ....$115-130
Ferrari 550
   Luc Alphand Aventures n°72 Le Mans
     2003 ....$115-130
   Prodrive n°88 winner LM-GTS Le Mans
     2003 ....$115-130
Ferrari 575 GTC, presentation $115-130
   Winner Estoril 2003 FIA-GT $115-130
Ferrari 612 Scaglietti
   metallic gray $115-130
   metallic red $115-130
Ferrari P3 P4 n°21 Le Mans 1967 ....$75-90
Ferrari TR58 1st Le Mans 1958 ....$90-105
Ferrari TR60 1st Le Mans 1960 ....$90-105
Ferrari TR61 1st Le Mans 1961 ....$90-105
Ford Capri 1st Race Walter Rhörl Olympia
   Rallye 1972 ....$80-95
Ford GT40
   1st Le Mans 1968 ....$90-105
   1st Le Mans 1969 ....$90-105
Ford Mirage Gulf 1st Le Mans 1975 ....$90-105
Ford MK II 1st Le Mans 1966 ....$90-105
Ford MK IV 1st Le Mans 1967 ....$90-105
Ford RS 200 Usine rallye Acropole 1986 ...$80-95
Honda S800 fast back blanche promotion ...$60-75
Jaguar C 1st Le Mans 1953 ....$110-125
Jaguar D
   1st Le Mans 1955 ....$90-105
   1st Le Mans 1956 ....$90-105
   1st Le Mans 1957 ....$90-105
Jaguar Proto RD6 ....$115-130
Jaguar SILK CUT 1st Le Mans 1988 ....$90-105
Jaguar XJR12
   1st Le Mans 1990 ....$90-105
   N°34 Le Mans 1991 ....$75-90
   N°35 Le Mans 1991 ....$75-90
Jaguar XJS JPS Macao 1984 ....$65-80
Jaguar XK120 Ghia Supersonic $100-115
Jaguar XK120C 1st Le Mans 1951 .....$110-125
Jaguar XK140
   Cabriolet PROMOTION $95-110
   Coupe $100-115
   Roadster $100-115
Jaguar XKR8 Daytona 2002 ....$95-110
Joest Porsche 1st Le Mans 1997 ....$90-105
Lagonda 1st Le Mans 1935 ....$110-125
Lamborghini Marzal Salon de Geneve
   1967 ....$115-130
Leader Panoz N°22 Le Mans 2002 .....$95-110
Lister Storm n°20 Esaais Le Mans
2003 ....$115-130

Lorraine
   1st Le Mans 1926 ....$110-125
   1st Le Mans 1925 ....$110-125
MacLaren F1 GTR 1st Le Mans 1995 ....$90-105
Matra 670 1st Le Mans 1972 ....$90-105
Matra 670 B
   1st Le Mans 1973 ....$90-105
   1st Le Mans 1974 ....$90-105
Mazda 767B Mazdaspeed Le Mans
   1989 ....$95-110
Mazda 787 1st Le Mans 1991 ....$90-105
Mercedes 300 SL 1st Le Mans 1952 ..$110-125
Mitsubishi Lancer WRC n°9 Monte Carlo
   2004 ....$115-130
Mitsubishi Pajero n°203 winner Paris-Dakar
   2004 ....$115-130
Morgan Aero Dewalt n°73 Le Mans
   2002 ....$95-110
Norma Ford M2000 n°21 LM 03 ......$115-130
Pagani Zonda
   C12S street version $115-130
   C12S Cabriolet...........................$115-130
   GR carsport America n°61 Le Mans
     2003 ....$115-130
Peugeot 106 n°25 rallye Tour de Corse
   1997 ....$80-95
Peugeot 205 Turbo 16 1st M Carlo 85 ...$80-95
Peugeot 307 WRC n° 5 6 Monte Carlo
   2004 ....$115-130
Peugeot 406 Taxi
   1 film $75-90
   2 film $75-90
Peugeot 905
   1st Le Mans 1992 ....$90-105
   1st Le Mans 1993 ....$90-105
Peugeot Pompier H2O concept car Mondial
   2002 boite vitrine luxe $110-125
Peugeot Taxi 3 avec chenilles $90-105
Porsche 1st Le Mans 1996 ....$90-105
Porsche 911 GTI 1st Le Mans 1998 .....$90-105
Porsche 917K
   1st Le Mans 1970 ....$90-105
   1st Le Mans 1971 ....$90-105
Porsche 936
   JULES 1st Le Mans 1981 ....$90-105
   MARTINI 1st Le Mans 1976 ....$90-105
   MARTINI 1st Le Mans 1977 promotion ..$90-105
   New Man 1st Le Mans 1984 ....$90-105
   New Man 1st Le Mans 1985 ....$90-105
Porsche 956
   ROTHMANS 1st Le Mans 1982 .....$90-105
   ROTHMANS 1st Le Mans 1983 .....$90-105
Porsche 962 FAT 1st Le Mans 1994 .....$90-105
Porsche 962C
   n°33 Le Mans 1988 promotion $85-100
   ROTHMANS 1st Le Mans 1986 .....$90-105

ROTHMANS 1st Le Mans 1987 .....$90-105
Porsche K3 NR 1st Le Mans 1979 ....$90-105
Rondeau M379 1st Le Mans 1980......$90-105
Sauber C9 N°63 1st Le Mans 1989 ...$90-105
Saxo 14 I Vert Polynesien Light Green $60-75
Spyker C8 Double 12
   n°85 Le Mans 2002 ....$95-110
   n°85 Le Mans 2003 ....$115-130
Talbot Lago 1st Le Mans 1950 ....$110-125
Toyota Safari rallye 1985.................$80-95
TVR Dewalt Racesports Salisbury
   n°91 Le Mans 2003....................$115-130
   n°92 Le Mans 2003....................$115-130
Vaillante Lola N°10 Le Mans 2002......$95-110

Stjerne

A connection is likely between Stjerne of Denmark and Vilmer, also of Denmark, since Stjerne's Lambretta Scooter and Sidecar is identical to Vilmer's except in color.

Lambretta Motor Scooter and Sidecar, cream,
   2⅞" $125-150
Field Gun, Army green, 4¼".................$35-50

Streamlux

Streamlux toys are a short-lived series of small (approximately 1:80) scale diecast models from Streamlux Pty Ltd. of Australia that began in the 1950s and had disappeared by 1960 only to reappear in 1977 in kit form. In addition to the smaller models, one larger model—a Holden FE Sedan in 1:36 scale—was produced in 1957. Streamlux dies were purchased by Underwood Engineering in 1964, the castings improved and sold as Fun Ho! Midgets. Streamlux models are marked with the Streamlux brand on the base.

Airport Bus, One-and-a-Half Deck............$50-60
Austin
   Open Back Truck, 2" $65-70
   Petrol Tanker, 2"..........................$65-70
   Tip Truck, 2"...............................$80-90
Commer Coach, 2⅛".........................$65-70
Holden FE Special Sedan, 2⅛"
   coppered body, chrome base............$65-70
   coppered body, red painted base $65-70
Massey Ferguson 35 Tractor, unpainted, 1⅜" $65-70
Mercedes-Benz W196 Racer, 2" $65-70
Volkswagen
   Combi Bus, 2⅛"..........................$65-70
   Sedan, 1⅜"................................$65-70

Strombecker (see Tootsietoys)

Stylish Cars

Stylish cars are superb hand-built models, of which one is available from Diecast Miniatures.

1933 Duesenberg SJ Speedster, 1:43 ....$345-370

Summer

Summer models of Hong Kong are reported to be approximately 1:60 scale issues from NSG Marketing. Other NSG toys are offered as Traffic Stoppers. Both brands represent somewhat crude versions of popular car models. Both brands fall under the category of generic toys for the lack of identifying marks. Most Summer models are relatively unremarkable, cheaply made and considered fairly worthless. The company is a recent (circa 1990s) outgrowth of the explosion of crude diecast toys coming out of Hong Kong.

Coal Truck, 3" $1-2

Jaguar XJ, 3" $1-2
Mercedes-Benz 500K, 3" $1-2

Sun Motor Company (see Modelauto)

Sunnyside

21/F, Blk K
Shield Industrial Centre
84-92 Chai Wan Kok Street
Tsuen Wan
N. T. Hong Kong, SAR
website: www.sunnyside.com.hk
phone: + 852 2492 0276 (7 lines)
+ 852 2493 2366 (8 lines)
fax: + 852 2416 7401
e-mail: sunny@sunnyside.com.hk

Sunnyside models have been produced in Hong Kong by Sunnyside Ltd. since 1979. Most Sunnyside models are identified on the base by the distinctive "flying S" logo and a number preceded by "SS-." The majority of Sunnyside models feature pull-back action. The mistake of calling them "Superior" models is due to such description imprinted on most of their packages. According to company officials, it is a statement of quality, not brand. Maisto similarly uses the term "Superior" on their packaging

to describe their roughly 1:43 scale models.

BMW 325 M3 2-door Sedan $6-8
BMW 325i Convertible $6-8
BMW 635 CSi $6-8
BMW 728 4-door Sedan $6-8
BMW Z1 Roadster $6-8
Bugatti T44 Coupe $6-8
Bugatti T57 Coupe $6-8
1950 Buick Super Convertible, top down $6-8
1951 Cadillac Roadster............................$6-8
1953 Cadillac Convertible, top up $6-8
1955 Chevrolet 3100 Stepside Pickup Truck,
     1:24 ....$8-10
Chevrolet Astro Van $6-8
Chevrolet Astro "Fire Van" $6-8
Chevrolet Astro Van "Superman" $6-8
1955 Chevrolet Bel Air Nomad, 1:24.......$8-10
1995 Chevrolet C/K Pickup Truck, 1:24 ...$8-10
Chevrolet Suburban, 1:24 ....$8-10
1970 Chevrolet El Camino SS 454, 1:24 ...$8-10
1964 Chevrolet Impala Hardtop, 1:24......$8-10
1955 Chevrolet Nomad, 1:25 ....$6-8
1957 Chevrolet Bel Air 2-door Hardtop, 1:25 ..$9-11
Chevrolet Blazer Tow Truck Fire $6-8
Chevrolet Blazer Tow Truck Police $6-8
Chevrolet Blazer Ambulance $6-8
Chevrolet Blazer Police $6-8
1957 Chevrolet Corvette Hardtop $6-8
1957 Chevrolet Corvette Roadster $6-8
Hayashi Dome-O Exotic car $6-8
Excalibur Roadster...................................$6-8
Ferrari F40, 1:24 ....$6-8
Ferrari 288 GTO Coupe $6-8
Ferrari Testarossa, 1:40...........................$6-8
Ferrari Testarossa, 1:25...........................$9-11
Ford 3100 4WD Tractor............................$6-8

1932 Ford Coupe, #SS740........................$6-8

1955 Ford Crown Victoria, convertible, top down, 1:24 ....$6-8

1955 Ford Crown Victoria, hardtop, 1:24...$6-8

Ford Escort Convertible $6-8
Ford E100 Ambulance Van........................$6-8
Ford E100 Police Van $6-8
1998 Ford F-150 4x4 Offroad Pickup Truck...$8-10
1964½ Ford Mustang Convertible, 1:24 ......$6-8
Ford Shelby Cobra 427 S/C Convertible, 1:24 ..$6-8
1955 Ford Thunderbird Hardtop, 1:24 ....$6-8
1955 Ford Thunderbird Convertible, 1:24 ....$6-8
1959 Ford Galaxie Convertible $6-8
1952 GMC Wrecker, 1:34, issued 1999,
     opening doors and tool compartments
     red $13-15
     maroon...$13-15
     black $13-15
Jeep CJ5 ....$6-8
Jeep CJ5 Ambulance $6-8
Jeep CJ2 Army Jeep with top $6-8
Jeep Army Rocket Launcher......................$6-8
Jeep Army Machine Gun $6-8
Jeep Army Radar $6-8
John Deere 3130 Tractor..........................$6-8
International Harvester 4WD Tractor $6-8
Lamborghini Diablo, 1:24 ....$6-8
Lincoln Town Car Stretch Limousine, 1:34
     black..$15-20
     white $15-20
     silver...$15-20

gold...$15-20
gray $15-20
London Bus, dark green with cream upper
     window section, "Country Matches,"
     "24 Berkshire" $6-8
Mercedes-Benz 190E "Fire Dept." $6-8
Mercedes-Benz 500SEL Convertible, top
     down $6-8
Mercedes-Benz 500SEL Convertible, top up ...$6-8
1991 Mercedes-Benz 500SL Convertible,
     top down $6-8
Mercedes-Benz 540K Roadster $6-8
Mercedes-Benz 540K Coupe $6-8
1984 Mercedes-Benz 500SL Roadster $6-8
Mercedes-Benz 560SEC Coupe $6-8

Mercedes-Benz 207 Police $6-8
Mercedes-Benz 207 Fire $6-8
Michelotti Laser...$6-8
Nissan HD Fire Pumper Truck $6-8
Nissan HD Fire Ladder Truck $6-8
Nissan HD Fire Snorkel Truck......................$6-8
Nissan HD Fire Aerial Ladder Truck $6-8
Opel Omega 4-door Sedan $6-8
Pontiac Firebird Trans Am T-Top "Sunbeam
    Bread" #42 Race Car, yellow..........$15-20

1961 Porsche 356B, 1:24 ....$6-8
1986 Porsche 911 Roadster.........................$6-8
1989 Porsche 911 Roadster.........................$6-8
Porsche 959 Coupe $6-8
1931 Rolls Royce Phantom II $6-8

School Bus, #SS9853, 1:43 ....$6-8
1947 Talbot Convertible, top up $6-8
Volkswagen 1303 Beetle $6-8
Volkswagen Beetle.....................................$6-8
Volkswagen Beetle Convertible $6-8
Volkswagen Golf Cabriolet $6-8
Volkswagen LT Police Van $6-8
Volkswagen LT Fire Van $6-8

Sunshine Toys

Many Sunshine models were previously assumed to be Sunnyside models. Both feature a large assortment of pull-back action toys, but Sunshine models lack the "Flying S" logo and are designated by a single "S-" in front of the model number rather than the double "SS-" that marks them as Sunnyside models. Sunshine Toys are generally considered inexpensive generic toys.

Sun Star

Sun Star America Inc.
2415 Radley Court #2
Hayward, CA 94545 USA
phone: 510-670-0882
fax: 510-670-0883
e-mail: uscic@aol.com

Sun Star America Inc., based in Hayward, California, is a producer of exceptional 1:18 scale diecast cars manufactured in China. A likely connection with Chrono and the now-defunct Vitesse has been deduced from various sources. Most models are issued in more than one color.

1998 Austin London Taxi Cab $30-35
DeLorean $30-35
1957 Facel Vega HK500......................$35-40
1965 Ford F-100 Pickup........................$30-35

1957 Ford Fairlane Skyliner with retractable hardtop $30-35

1964 Ford Galaxie 500 ....$30-35
1999 Lincoln Stretch Limousine $40-45
1998 London Taxi Cab (see Austin London Taxi Cab)
Mercedes-Benz 350 SL...........................$30-35
1966 Mercedes-Benz 600
    Landaulet Limousine $40-45
Pullman Limousine $40-45
Mercedes-Benz E320 ....$30-35

1967 Mercury Cougar XR7 ....$30-35
1956 Porsche 356A Coupe $30-35
1970 Triumph Spitfire $30-35

Volkswagen Open Convertible $30-35

Suntoys

Suntoys International Co., Ltd.
ChinaChem Golden Plaza
77 Mody Road
TST East, Kowloon, Hong Kong
e-mail: sunyip@snotoyshk.com

A Suntoys car carrier in roughly 1:87 scale was discovered at a liquidator store with a copyright date of 2002. The front of the blister pack provided all the address and descriptive information. The back of the package is plain gray cardboard with no printing. The toy itself is mostly plastic with no markings except "Made in China" on the base of the tractor. The only diecast part is the cab shell.

Suntoys Express Wheels Big Rig Car Carrier, blue diecast cab with red and metallic gray accents, blue plastic airfoil, black plastic base, orange plastic trailer with metallic gray upper ramp and opening tailgate, 1:87, 9", 2002
    in original package $2-4
    out of package......................................$1

Super Champion (see Champion)

Supercar Collectibles

Supercar Collectibles, Ltd.
Jim Thoren
7311 75th Circle North
Minneapolis, MN 55428 USA
phone: 612-425-6020
fax: 612-425-3357

Supercar Collectibles represent an offering of 1:18 scale diecast models most likely made in China.

Bill Jenkins' 1969 Camaro SS/C drag car ..$40-50
1969 Baldwin-Motion 427 Camaro $40-50

Superior (see Sunnyside, Maisto)

SVP

In 1948, the S. V. Paraboni company of Italy (SVP), produced just one model, reportedly a 1:43 scale model with clockwork motor and steering.

Fiat-Farina Coupe, 4½" $60-75

Swan Hill

Pleasanton, California, was home to the Swan Hill toy company, manufacturer of a heavy cast aluminum replica of a lumber hauler that stands about 8 inches high and measures about 8 inches long.

Cari-Car Lumber Hauler $60-90

T

Tai Cheong Toys

Tai Cheong Toys are classic examples of what diecast collectors usually refer to as "generic junk." The only distinguishing mark on these toys is the designation "TC" on the base followed by a number. Value will likely remain near the retail price of 3 for 99 cents. The package is also nondistinct except for a circular logo formed by a curved "T" and a sideways "C" in the lower left corner of the three-pack blister card. Some logos are imprinted with "Tai Cheong," others are not.

Taiseiya

Japan is home to Taiseiya, manufacturer of 1:43 scale models.

1912 Chevrolet Phaeton, pewter-like $24

Takara

Takara is a Japanese company of which little is known. Among their products are some toys made for Tonka called Turbo Tricksters. See Tonka for more information.

Tak-A-Toy (also see Welly)

Tak-A-Toy is an inexpensive brand of toys that, like so many other inexpensive toys, is usually rendered an unmarked generic toy once removed from package. Interestingly, at least one particular model is found to be an exception to this rule. One Audi Quattro in white with red, light blue, and black rally markings was found to be made by Welly and holds the distinctive Welly name on the base along with the number 8368. It was purchased for 89 cents from a local grocery store in November 1996. Welly toys are slightly better made than most in the budget genre of diecast toys and are usually marked with the brand name on the bottom. Tak-A-Toy is a division of Larami Corp., Philadelphia, PA 19107.

Tamiya

Tamiya is best known for quality plastic car kits and radio-controlled models. Recently Tamiya has begun producing a few large scale diecast models.

Tantal

Alex Litovskiy reports of the Tantal brand from Russia but doesn't provide any details.

Taylor, F. G.

F. G. Taylor & Sons was started in 1945 at 22 Hampden Road, Upper Halloway, London, England, by F. G. Taylor Sr. (founder of Taylor & Barrett), his son Fred Taylor and his son-in-law Fred Squires. The first models were simplified reissues of pre-WWII one-piece slush mold models. The designation "FGT" was applied to the toys, with the phrase "For Good Toys" as the marketing slogan. In 1962, long after toy car production had ceased, the company was sold to Barton & Co, a company specializing in doll house furnishings.

Ambulance (simplified variation of Dinky Toys
   #30) Electric Pumps, #146 ....$12-16
Fire Engine and Ladder, #16 ....$25-40
Fire Engine and men, #17 ....$25-40
Fire Escape and team of firemen, #42 .....$25-40
Fireplace and Fittings, #41 ....$15-20
Gents, #148 ....$15-20
HM Letterbox, #157 ....$15-20
HM Letterbox, Air Mail, #158 ....$15-20
Leyland Streamlined Coach $45-60
MG Magnette Racer $45-60
Mobile Animal Health Trust Van with doctor
   and monkey (post-WWII) $45-60
Oil Pump Cabinet, #156 ....$15-20
Traffic Beacon, #140 ....$10-15
Traffic Signs, #145 ....$12-16
Trailer Pump in action with firemen, #311 ...$25-40
Wagon Lorry $25-40

Taylor & Barrett

Fred G. Taylor and his brother-in-law Alfred R. Barrett founded Taylor & Barrett in London, England, in 1920. A. R. Barrett was previously employed as a lead caster at William S. Britains Ltd. Also joining the company in 1920 was A. R.'s brother S. Barrett, with A. R.'s oldest son Alfred Barrett Jr. joining in 1928, and A.R.'s second son Bert in 1934. Taylor & Barrett's factory was bombed during an air raid in 1940. The resulting resurrected companies after the war were F.G. Taylor & Sons (1945–1980) and A. Barrett & Sons Ltd. (1945–1982).

Air and Land Postal Service Set, #43 ...$120-150
Air and Water Tower, #200 ....$145-160
Air Mail Streamline, #138 ....$145-160
Air Pilot, #160 ....$50-65
Airplane Set, #306 ....$190-220
Atlanta Training Airplane, #123 ....$145-160
Baker and Barrow, #23 ....$120-130
Chauffeur, #162 ....$50-65
Children Hand-in-Hand, #149 ....$120-150
Citroën Air Mail Van, #124 ....$145-160
Citroën Ambulance Van, gray, #114 ...$145-160
Citroën Breakdown Lorry, #129 ....$145-160
Citroën Coupé, #116 ....$145-160
Citroën Covered Wagon, #302 ....$145-160
Citroën Military Ambulance Van, khaki,
   #114 ....$145-160
Citroën Milk Supply Van, white and red,
   #118 ....$145-160
Citroën Royal Mail Van, #113 ....$145-160
Citroën Saloon, #111 ....$145-160
Citroën Small Ambulance "Street" white,
   #117 ....$145-160
Citroën Small Fire Engine, #120 ....$145-160
Citroën Sports Roadster, #115 ....$145-160
Citroën Tanker, #128 ....$145-160
Citroën Transport van, #112 ....$145-160
Coster Set with Vegetables, #31 ....$60-75
DeHavilland Comet Airplane, #137 ...$120-150
Donkey Ride, Small Set, #47 ....$145-160
Donkey Ride, Large Set, #48 ....$160-175
Electric Pumps, #146 ....$60-75
Electric Service Station, #44 ....$60-75
Fire Brigade Set, Large #46 ....$175-190
Fire Brigade Set, Small, #307 ....$75-90
Fire Engine and Escape, #16 ....$145-160
Fire Engine and Firemen, #17 ....$145-160
Fire Escape, #136 ....$75-95
Fire Escape and Team of Firemen, #42 ....$65-75
Firemen, #135 ....$50-60
Fireplace and Curb, #131 ....$50-60
Fireplace and Fittings, #41 ....$50-60
Gents, #148 ....$60-75
Governess cart Set, #109 ....$145-160
HM Letterbox, #157 ....$75-85
HM Letterbox, Airmail, #158 ....$75-85
Ice Cream Cycle, "Ice Bricks," #29 ....$145-160
Ladies, #147 ....$60-75
Large Ambulance, Streamlined $145-160
Llama with cart Ride, #12 ....$145-160
Llama with cart, #92 ....$145-160
Mechanic, #161 ....$60-80
Motor Coach, Streamlined, #152 ......$150-175
Mounted Policeman, #143 ....$50-70
Oil Pump Cabinet, #156 ....$40-60
Pavement Straight Section, #150 ....$40-60

Pavement Corner Section, #151	$40-60
Petrol Pumps, #130	$40-60
Petrol Station, #40	$60-75
Pony with cart, #109	$145-160
Postman, #159	$60-80
Racer, #119	$145-160
Rickshaw set with Chinaman, #310	$150-175
Rickshaw set with Zulu, #310	$150-175
Road Cleaning Set, #49	$125-150
Rolls Royce Fire Engine, Streamline, #163	$145-160
Roman Chariot, #26	$150-175
Safety Island, #144	$50-75
Singer Saloon, #139	$145-160
Traffic Beacon, #140	$50-80
Traffic Set, #45	$65-80
Traffic Policeman, #142	$40-60
Traffic Signal, #141	$40-60
Traffic Signs, #145	$40-60
Trailer Pump in Action with Firemen, #311	$60-80
Trailer Pump with 3 Figures, #212	$60-80
Trolley Bus, Large, #204	$145-160
Trolley Bus, Small, #197	$140-150
Turntable Fire Escape, #15	$75-90
Water cart, #20	$150-175
Window Cleaner and Barrow, #22	$150-175

Taylor Made Trucks

c/o Toy Truck Collector
117 Cedar Lane
Englewood, NJ 07631
toll free: 1-800-685-0333 or
201-816-1166

Taylor Made Trucks is the brand name of a large assortment of plastic scale model trucks made by Toy Truck Collector of Englewood, New Jersey. Besides Hess Oil Company promo trucks, Toy Truck Collector has produced made-to-order plastic toy promotional trucks for Amoco, Citgo, Crown, Exxon, Getty, Lionel, Mobil, Phillips, Shell, Texaco, Unocal, Wilco, and others, all produced under the Taylor Made Trucks brand. Besides the oil companies, Taylor Made Trucks have also represented Sears, New Jersey Transit, Hershey's, Coca-Cola, and many other licenses.

Tbilisi

Collector Lemiere Bruno of France reports that Tbilisi is the alternate name of the town of Tiflis in the Russian province of Georgia. It is there that a small toy factory installed obsolete Norev casting equipment around 1980. In the USSR, no brand names were applied apart from those intended for export, hence the town name. "Poor finish for the domestic market as far as I remember," comments Bruno. "A couple of other Norevs were remanufactured there."

Robert Jacaszek adds: "Tbilisi is the name of Georgia capital. Up to the 1990s, Georgia was part of the Soviet Union. (The name Tifilis was used up to 1936.) Plastic models with this name were manufactured in the 1970s. In Poland, where I am living, in the late 1970s were available three models. These models were in 1:43 scale. These models were quite good (for the times). I had seen only photo of French Dinky Panhard 24 Coupe, but I think that these models were copies of French Dinky models. At the same time in Poland was available the first Soviet diecast model—Moskvitch in 1:43 scale. The name Tbilisi was only on plastic models. Only car name, scale, and 'Made in USSR' were on diecast models."

1927 Panhard, hard plastic body, black, 3½"	$8-10
Panhard 24 Coupe, white	$8-10
Renault Dauphine, white	$8-10

TD

One tinplate model is all that is known about this obscure US toy company.

1950 Caterpillar Bulldozer, tin, made in USA, 8"	$20-30

Team Caliber

Another recent arrival on the diecast scene is Team Caliber, a brand of 1:24 scale models largely comprised of race cars. The product line is constantly growing. Here is a list of their first issues.

Chevrolet Monte Carlo	
Bob Evans #1	$20-30
Terry Labonte #5 K-Sentials	$20-30
Terry and Justin Labonte #44 Slim Jim NASCAR Busch Series	$20-30
Dick Trickle #5 Schneider Busch	$20-30
Ford Taurus	
Mark Martin #6 Valvoline/Cummins Winston Cup	$20-30
Jeremy Mayfield #12 Mobil 1 25th Anniversary Winston Cup	$20-30
Pontiac Grand Prix	
John Andretti #43 STP Winston Cup	$20-30

Techno Giodi (see Giodi)

Technofix

Colorful tin lithographed windup toys, apparently produced in the late 1940s through the 1950s, are the specialty for Technofix of Germany. Play sets consist of wind-up cars, trolleys, trains, and cable cars on colorful lithographed tinplate dioramas. Typical value is $175–250.

Tekno (also see Dalia)

Tekno B. V.
Rotterdamseweg 370a
2629 HG Delft
Holland, The Netherlands
phone: +31 (0) 15 256 06 00
fax: +31 (0) 15 256 38 02
website: www.tekno.nl

Tekno toys are especially nice 1:43 scale models made in Denmark. Chico toys are the Colombia division of Tekno. Dalia of Spain established a working relationship with Tekno to produce a special line of models separate from the main Tekno line.

The Tekno line of tinplate toys was started in Denmark in 1920. The company survived through several economic and political crises, not least of which was World War II, until 1974 when the company finally folded and was purchased by Dutch importer Van Min. Thanks to Jan Scholten for the update. Tekno survives in Holland to this today and still offers an expanding line of diecast cars and trucks.

Alfa Romeo, #802	$45-60
Animal Truck, #773	$45-60
Army Truck Anti-Aircraft, #953	$75-90
Beer Trailer, "Carlsberg"	$30-35
Beer Truck, "Tuborg," with 20 cases, #736	$45-50
Chevrolet Monza GT	$35-40
Coal & Coke Truck	$30-35
Delivery Truck with barrels, 9 sacks and trolley	$30-35
Deutz Van Police	$30-35
Dodge Open Truck, #770	$45-50
1956 Ford Thunderbird Roadster, #809	$30-35
Ford Cable Truck	$20-25
1953 Ford Taunus Van	$35-40
Kul & Koks Truck (see Coal & Coke Truck)	
M.G., #804	$45-50
Mercedes-Benz Tow Truck	$20-25
Milling Machine, #709	$30-45
Motorcycle, #761	$75-90
Motorcycle and Sidecar, #762	$75-90
Motorcycle and Sidecar, #763	$75-90
Motorcycle and Sidecar, #764	$75-90

Scania CR-76 Bus, #851 | $35-40

Scooter Delivery, #444....$75-90
Scooter Solo, #442....$75-90
Trailer, 775....$30-45
Triumph Sports Car, #808....$45-60
Volkswagen 1500 Sedan....$100-125
Volkswagen Ladder Truck, #404, 1959..$150-175
Volkswagen Pickup, #406
no logo, two-tone....$150-175
Pre, turquoise....$175-200
Shell, yellow....$200-250
Shell Teepol, yellow and red....$175-200
VW Viser Varevogne, orange....$175-200
VW Viser Varevogne, gray....$175-200
Volkswagen Van, #405, 1959
Aage Hass, gray-blue....$200-250
Adam Arhus, dark red....$200-250
Adam Hobenhavn, dark red....$200-250
Albani, green, white and red....$200-250
Allers, white and blue....$200-250
Anders And, yellow....$200-250
Berlingske Tidende, green and yellow..$200-250
Blondal, dark green, red and silver (might be a customized version)....$200-250
Bosch, gray and light brown....$200-250
Bosch Elektrowerkzeuge, gray and light brown....$200-250
BP Service, green and white....$250-300
Buko Ost, white and yellow....$200-250
Caramba, orange and blue....$200-250
Cloetta, dark red....$200-250
Crome & Goldschmidt, light gray and red-brown....$200-250
Den Rode Lober, gray....$200-250
Den Rode Lober, gray and dark red..$200-250
E. Roed Sorensen, orange-red....$200-250
Fona, red and blue....$200-250
Familia Journalen, white and blue...$200-250
Franz Carl Weber, dark red....$200-250
Gillette, light blue and yellow....$250-300
Jerres Flygbus, white, black and orange....$200-250
Jolly Cola, white....$250-300
Jyllands-Posten, green with yellow roof....$200-250
K. Strmly Hansen, white....$200-250
Leeuwen Zegel, white and tan....$200-250
Lommeromanen, red, white and green....$200-250
Luklet, red....$200-250
Oma Margarine, tan....$200-250
Pre, turquoise....$200-250
Rode Kors (Red Cross), white ambulance....$250-300
Phonix, white blue and orange....$200-250
Phonix, red-orange and lavender....$200-250
Spies Heckler Lack, red and white..$200-250
Svensk Raddningstjanst, blue....$200-250
Tekno, dark blue and white....$300-350
Tekno Dansk Legetoj, dark blue and white....$300-350
Toms, orange, brown and gold....$200-250
VW Kolevogn, white....$200-250
VW Viser Varevogne, gray....$200-250
Volvo 2-Axle Truck....$10-15
Volvo 2-Axle Trailer....$8-10
Volvo Cement Truck....$15-20
Volvo F10 "SPETRA"....$30-35
Volvo Truck....$20-25
Volvo Timber Transporter, #439....$100-125
Wet Grinder, #713....$45-60

TfC (see Toys for Collectors)

Thomas Toys

Thomas Toys originated in 1944 in Newark, New Jersey, by founder Islyn Thomas, former general manager of Ideal Toy Company. Ben Shapiro of Acme Plastic was a partner in the company, so a close tie between Thomas and Acme Plastic toys results in a mixing of models between the two brands. Below is a sampling of Thomas Toys. Although some were sold individually, many models were only offered as part of a larger set.

Car and House Trailer, #131, 9½"....$30-35
Convertible Coupe with driver, #077, 1953-1954, 4½"....$12-16
Fire Chief Radio Car, #067, 4½"....$25-30
Jet Car, spring-action, #457....$45-60
Police Radio Car, #067, 4½"....$25-30
Streamlined Sedan, #077S, 4½"....$12-16
Taxi, #128, 1953, 4½"....$25-30

Timpo Toys

Timpo is a shortened version of Toy Importers Ltd. The brand was started in 1939 when World War II restricted imports to Great Britain, and the company began producing their own toys. While a few models were produced in 1940–1941, major production of the Timpo line was started in 1946. Timpo Toys ceased production in 1951–1952 due to war restrictions on the use of zinc. Some Timpo dies were eventually sold to Benbros. Timpo Toys are identified by the name cast somewhere on the toy.

AEC Monarch Brewery Lorry, 5⅛", 1950, reissued by Benbros....$80-100
Alvis 14 Police car, loudspeakers on roof, wire aerial, 4⅛", 1947....$35-45
Alvis 14 Saloon, 8⅛", 1947....$25-35
American Star Racer, 4", 1946....$20-25
Armstrong Siddeley Hurricane, 4⅛", 1947....$25-35
Articulated Box Van, 5⅞", 1947, reissued by Benbros
green, blue or red trailer with "Timpo Toys" decals....$40-50
black with "Pickfords" decals....$40-50
orange with "United Dairies" decals....$55-65
light blue and cream, "Wall's Ice Cream" decals....$55-65
dark blue and cream, "Lyons Tea" decals....$55-65
pale yellow, "Bishop & Sons" decals...$55-65
pale yellow, "John H. Lunn Ltd." decals..$55-65
Articulated Low Loader, 6⅞", 1947, reissued by Benbros....$15-25
Articulated Petrol Tanker, 5⅞", 1947, reissued by Benbros....$25-35
Austin 16 Saloon, black with Timpo toys underneath, (later reissued by Betal), 3⅝"....$50-70
Buick Saloon, composition wheels, 3⅞", 1947....$15-25
Forward Control Box Van, 3¾", 1949, reissued by Benbros....$55-65
Forward Control Luton Van, 3⅞", 1947
no decals....$25-35
"Smith's Crisps"....$55-65
"W.D. & H.O. Wills"....$55-65
Forward Control Tipper Lorry, 4", 1947....$25-35
Lincoln Convertible, 4½", 1947....$25-35
London Taxi, cast in two halves, 3¾", 1947....$35-45
MG Midget, composition wheels, 3¼", 1946....$25-35
MG Record Car, hollow cast lead, 3⅞", 1940....$35-45
MG Record Car, zinc diecast, 3¾", 1946....$20-25
Normal Control Box Van, with or without motor, 4⅛", 1949, reissued by Benbros
"Eveready"....$40-50
"Golden Shred"....$55-65
Normal Control Petrol Tanker, 4⅝", 1949, reissued by Benbros....$55-65
Packard Saloon with no base, 4½", 1946....$15-25
Packard Saloon with aluminum base and friction motor, 4½", 1948....$15-25
Pick-Up Truck, separate body and chassis, 3¾", 1940 (later reissued with name blocked out)....$50-60
Pick-Up Truck with 8 cast barrels, 4⅛", 1947....$25-35

Speed of the Wind Record Car, 3⅞", 1946 ....$25-35
Streamlined Fire Engine with aluminum ladders, no base, 4⅛", 1947 ....$40-50
Streamlined Fire Engine with aluminum ladders, aluminum base and friction motor, 4⅛", 1949 ....$40-50
Streamlined Saloon, separate body and chassis, 3⅞", 1940 ....$50-60
Timpo Saloon, similar to a Morris 8, 3⅝", 1946 ....$20-25
Utility Van, 4" (early casting) or 4⅛" (later casting) without motor 1947, with friction motor 1948
no decals, no motor $25-35
"Tyresoles Service," no motor $50-65
"His Master's Voice," with or without motor $50-65
green, with or without motor....................$50-65

Tin Wizard (also see Skyline and Zaugg)

Tin Wizard Modelcars and Skyline Models
c/o Thomas Wolter Modelltechnik
Talstrasse 170
D-69198 Schriesheim, Germany
phone: 06203/68680
fax: 06203/68329
e-mail: THWOLTER@aol.com
website: www.tinwizard.de
or www.toynet.de/tinwizard

Handmade 1:43, 1:24, and 1:18 scale white metal models and kits with plated parts comprise this series from Schriesheim, Germany. Also see Skyline Models. Some Tin Wizard models are reissues of Zaugg models of Switzerland.

Tin Wizard 1:43 Scale

DKW F12 Cabriolet (1965)
beige white, ready made, #1652 ....$75-90
green, ready made, #1651 ....$75-90
green, ready made, #1653 ....$75-90
kit, #1650 ....$40-50
Ferrari 340 Mexico (1953)
Racing car, yellow, ready made, #4014 ....$120-140
Road car, red, ready made, #4011 ....$120-140
Ferrari 410 Superamerica (1959)
blue, ready made, #1353 ....$140-160
kit, #1350 ....$55-75
red, ready made, #1351 ....$140-160
white, ready made, #1352 ....$140-160
Glas 1700 GT Coupe (1965)
blue, ready made, #1631 ....$85-105
gray, ready made, #1632 ....$85-105
green, ready made, #1633 ....$85-105
kit, #1630 ....$40-50
Jaguar E Kombi "Harold and Maude," black, ready made, #4061 ....$155-175
Maserati Mexico, ready made, #4053 ..$155-175
Opel Kapitän Cabriolet (1951)
bordeaux red, ready made, #3121 ..$120-140
gray, ready made, #3123 ....$120-140
kit, #3120 ....$50-70
white, ready made, #3122 ....$120-140
Opel Manta A (1970)
black, ready made, #1123 ....$85-105
kit, #1120 ....$40-50
red, ready made, #1121 ....$85-105
yellow, ready made, #1122 ....$85-105
Opel Super 6 Cabriolet
blue, ready made, #3102 ....$120-140
green, ready made, #3103 ....$120-140
kit, #3100 ....$50-70
red, ready made, #3101 ....$120-140
Porsche 550A 1500 RS "Le Mans " (1956), silver, ready made, #4021 ....$120-140
Saab Sonett I Roadster (1955)
blue, ready made, #1193 ....$115-135
kit, #1190 ....$50-70
red, ready made, #1191 ....$115-135
white, ready made, #1192 ....$115-135
Mille Miglia, ready made, #1199 ...$125-145
Saab Sonett III (1970)
emerald green, ready made, #1111 ....$120-140
kit, #1110 ....$50-70
red, ready made, #1112 ....$120-140
red, ready made, #1119 ....$120-140
yellow, ready made, #1118 ....$120-140
Saab Sonett III (1974), kit, #1113 ....$50-70
Volvo 242 GT (1978)
kit, #1160 ....$50-70
metallic silver, ready made, #1161 ....$125-145
Volvo 244 DL (1975)
green, ready made, #1171 ....$115-135
kit, #1170 ....$50-70
metallic gold, ready made, #1173 ..$115-135
yellow, ready made, #1172 ....$115-135
Volvo 244 GL "TAXI" (1975), ready made, #1179 ....$120-140
Volvo 245 DL Kombi (1975)
kit, #1180 ....$50-70
metallic blue, ready made, #1183 ..$120-140
red, ready made, #1181 ....$120-140
white, ready made, #1182 ....$120-140
Volvo ES 1800 Kombi (1971)
kit, #1200 ....$50-70
metallic blue, ready made, #1203 ...$120-140
metallic gold, ready made, #1202 ..$120-140
white, ready made, #1201 ....$120-140
Volvo PV 444A (1944)
Spezial black, ready made, #1131BS $95-115
Spezial gray, ready made, #1132AS $95-115
Spezial gray, ready made, #1132BS $95-115
Spezial black, ready made, #1131AS....$95-115
Standard black, ready made, #1131A ...$90-110
Standard black, ready made, #1131B....$90-110
Standard kit, #1130A $40-50
Standard kit, #1130B $40-50
Volvo PV 444D (1952)
Spezial "California," white, ready made, #1135KS....................$105-125
Spezial, red, ready made, #1133DS...$95-115
Spezial, blue, ready made, #1134KS.....$95-115
Spezial, gray, ready made, #1132HS....$95-115
Spezial, black, ready made, #1131H $90-110
Standard, black, ready made, #1131D..$90-110
Standard, black, ready made, #1131K ..$90-110
Standard, kit, #1130D $40-50
Volvo PV 444H (1954) Standard, kit, #1130H $40-50
Volvo PV 444K (1955) Standard, kit, #1130K $45-65
Volvo PV 444L (1957)
Spezial "California," white, ready made, #1135LS $105-125
Spezial, red, ready made, #1136LS ..$95-115
Standard, black, ready made, #1131L....................$90-110
Standard, kit, #1130L $45-65
Volvo PV 445 Cabriolet
"Valbo," black, ready made, #1141 ..$105-125
"Valbo," gold beige, ready made, #1142 ....$105-125
"Valbo," kit, #1140 ....$45-65
"Valbo," red, ready made, #1143...$105-125
Volvo PV 544 A (1958)
Spezial "California," white (1960), ready made, #1155BS....................$105-125
Spezial A, blue (1958), ready made, #1154AS $95-115
Spezial A, green (1958), ready made, #1157AS $95-115
Spezial B "Sport," red (1960), ready made, #1156BS....................$95-115
Spezial D "B18," gray (1961), ready made, #1152CS $95-115
Spezial D "B18," white (1962), ready made, #1155DS $95-115
Spezial D "Sport," red (1962), ready made, #1156DS $95-115
Spezial G "Sport," black (1965), ready made, #1151GS....................$95-115
Standard, black (1958), ready made, #1151A $90-110
Standard, kit, #1150A $45-65

Umrüstsatz PV 444 spezial, kit, #1130S....$15-20
Umrüstsatz PV 544 spezial, kit, #1150S....$15-20

Tin Wizard 1:24 Scale

Alfa Romeo Giulia Super 1, 3⅟₁₆ (1964-1971)
green, ready made, #8082..........$160-180
kit, #8080..................................$85-105
red, ready made, #8083............$160-180
white, ready made, #8081.........$160-180

Opel GT
"Aero," blue, ready made, #8061..$160-180
"Aero," kit, #8060.......................$85-105
"Aero," metallic blue, ready made, #8062..............................$160-180
"Aero," red, ready made, #8071..$160-180
"Cabriolet," kit, #8070.................$85-105
Coupe, black, ready made, #8051..............................$160-180
Coupe, kit, #8050.......................$85-105
Coupe, metallic blue, ready made, #8053..............................$160-180
Coupe, yellow, ready made, #8052..............................$160-180

Volkswagen "Hebmüller" Cabriolet (1949)
black and red, ready made, #8011..............................$200-220
brown-beige, ready made, #8012..$200-220
kit, #8010................................$120-140
red-beige, ready made, #8013....$200-220

Tin Wizard 1:18 Scale

Boom Trike
black, ready made, #Z1031........$195-215
kit, #Z1030..............................$100-120

Donkervoort
black, ready made, #Z1052........$200-220
green, ready made, #Z1054........$200-220
kit, #Z1050..............................$115-135
red, ready made, #Z1053.................$200
yellow, ready made, #Z1051.......$200-220

Heinkel Tourist 103A
black, ready made, #Z1011..........$90-110
blue, ready made, #Z1014...........$90-110
kit, #Z1010..................................$50-70
red, ready made, #Z1012............$90-110
turquoise, ready made, #Z1013......$90-110

Lomax
green, kit, #Z1061.....................$170-190
ready made, #Z1060.................$105-125

Norton Commando 750
green, ready made, #Z1021........$145-165
kit, #Z2020..................................$75-90

Rassler Trike
black, ready made, #Z1041........$195-215
kit, #Z1040..............................$100-120

Tins' Toys (also see Simba)

Simba offers an assortment of Volkswagen Concept 1 vehicles which bear a "spinning top" logo with the phrase "Tins Toys" across it. See Simba for details. Later Tins' Toys issues bear the name Tins' Toys. An example is provided below.

Lexus SC430 / Toyota Soarer, 1:36........$4-5

Tintoys

Tintoys are a punctuation mark in the novel of toy cars. Regardless, the few lightweight models produced under this brand name, while lacking in detail, are interestingly accurate 3" miniatures of the two cars discovered by the author. Their value won't likely soon rise, but are noteworthy nonetheless.

Cadillac Seville, 1:69...............................$1-2
Toyota Celica 2000GT Liftback, 1:63.........$1-2

Tipp & Company

Tipp & Company, also known as Tippco, produced tinplate toys in Germany starting in 1912. In 1933, owner Phillip Ullman fled Germany and settled in Great Britain where he started Mettoy. He returned to Germany after World War II and restarted Tippco.

Club Sedan, electric headlights, 17", 1933...................................$850-1,150
Eight Cylinder Sedan, 12"...........$1,250-1,500
Hitler's Car, #934......................$3,500-4,000
Provincial Omnibus Company Bus....$4,250-4,750

Tip Top Toy Co.

Slush mold (lead cast) vehicles dominate the Tip Top Toy Company's line of toys produced in San Francisco in the 1920s and 1930s.

Airflow, larger......................................$40-45
Airflow, smaller $30-35
Bus, 3⅜"..$40-45
Coupe, 2⅛"...$25-30
Coupe, 3⅜₁₆".......................................$35-40
1923 Dodge Coupe, 3⅛"......................$30-35
Gasoline Tanker, 3½"............................$35-40
1935 Hupmobile, 3¼"..........................$50-55
Parcel Delivery Panel Truck, 2⅛"..............$30-35
Pickup Truck with Tailgate, 3⁵⁄₁₆"..............$40-45
Stake Truck, 5⁵⁄₁₆"..................................$55-60
1935 Studebaker Sedan, 2⁹⁄₁₆"...............$45-50
Tanker, 2¹¹⁄₁₆"......................................$20-25
Tow Truck, 3⁵⁄₁₆"...................................$35-40

Toby Toys

Toby Toys was a trademark of Louis Marx & Co. Ltd., England, a British subsidiary of the US company. In 1932 Marx bought a factory in Dudley, Worcestershire, England, where they produced inexpensive tinplate toys. Beginning in 1947, they produced four diecast toys in zinc alloy (zamak) and plastic under the Toby Toys trademark. They are crude castings with plain paint jobs and no detailing.

In 1967, the English division of Louis Marx & Co. Ltd. was purchased by Dunbee-Combex. Mar Toys of Great Britain was another trademark of Louis Marx.

1947 Breakdown Lorry, Toby Toys #862, 1:55 scale $25-40
1947 Fire Engine, Toby Toys #863, 1:55 scale $25-40
1939 Jaguar SS100 Roadster, Toby Toys #861, 1:43 scale..........................$25-40
1947 Jaguar Saloon, Toby Toys #860, 1:43 scale $25-40

Togi

Collector Robert Speerbrecher comments, "Togi is one of my favorite makers. They are an Italian firm that makes diecast 1:23 scale Alfa Romeos. The company uses them to make factory promos, and I think they make some that are not promos. I have yet to see a Togi that's not an Alfa Romeo. They are generally very expensive compared to the Polistil from the same country."

Danhausen's 1986 catalog lists a few that aren't Alfa Romeos, as listed below.

Alfa Romeo 6C 1750
1930 Gran Sport, #237...............$75-100
1930 Gran Sport Mille Miglia, #238..$75-100
Alfa Romeo 2000 Berlina, #224.........$75-100
Alfa Romeo Alfasud
4-Tuerig, #235............................$75-100
T1, #236....................................$75-100
Alfa Romeo Alfetta, 1950 159 F1, #220...$75-100
Alfa Romeo Carabo 33, #233............$75-100
Alfa Romeo Giulietta
1955 Spyder 1300, #202............$75-100

1955 Spyder 1600, #203 ....$75-100
1960 Sprint Special, #242 ....$75-100
Alfa Romeo Grand Sport 1750 1933
  Carbone, #241 ....$75-100
Alfa Romeo GT 1300 Junior, #229 ....$75-100
Alfa Romeo GTA Route Special, #228 ...$75-100
Alfa Romeo GTV 2000, #230 ....$75-100
Alfa Romeo Montreal, #234 ....$75-100
Alfa Romeo Spider
  1300 Junior, #231 ....$75-100
  2000, #232 ....$75-100
Alfa Romeo Turbo Special, #200 ....$75-100
Lancia Lambda, 1925
  open, #239 ....$75-100
  closed, #240 ....$75-100

Tomica

Until around 1980, the Japanese gems known as Tomica Pocket Cars from Tomy were widely distributed in the US, even available in grocery stores. But because their high quality and accurate scale meant that they cost a little more than Hot Wheels and Matchbox, they were unable to compete with the lower-priced and better-known brands. The normal price for Pocket cars was around $1.25 to $1.75 each. Now they sell from private importers for $4–15 each. Their current value reflects the growing interest from collectors who discovered these terrific little toys too late to save them from disappearing from the U.S. market.

Another reason for a lack of popularity was their focus on Japanese vehicles such as Mazda, Hino, Mitsubishi, and Fuso. Now, models of Japanese vehicles are more desirable just because they are Japanese.

New models are still being produced but are not generally available in the U.S., as the Tomica series retreated to European and Asian markets where Pocket Cars still hold a better market share.

The numbering system for Pocket Cars is not particularly consistent, so the preferred method of listing them is alphabetically by description. Most models are well marked on the base, and are heavier than usual for their size, due to more metal and less plastic. It is known that the "F" represents a foreign vehicle, while lack of designation indicates Japanese vehicle.

Other companies, in an attempt to capture some of the Pocket Car market, produced cheap copies of many of these models. A major difference is that these generic knock-offs had plastic bases and other components, and lighter weight metal parts, and are generally unmarked. The generic versions are considered essentially worthless to collectors, except as an

oddity. After the 1980s, Tomicas were issued in Japan, Asia, and Europe under the Tomy brand.

Tomica Dandy models are 1:43 scale replicas whose detail, packaging, and accessories set them apart from most other models in their price range.

Models are listed below with model number, copyright date, and scale when available, and current value.

Tomica/Tomy Diecast Cars

Alpine Renault Sports Racer, #191-F48 ....$5-7
American LaFrance Ladder Chief,
  #160-F33/187-F33, c1978, 1:143 ..$8-10
Amusement Park Shuttle Bus, #49, 1:130 .....$5-7
Asahi Event Truck (similar to Coca Cola
  truck), #109, 1998 ....$4-6
Auto Transporter, #137-14 ....$12-15
Baja Jeep 4 Wheeler $6-8
BLMC Mini Cooper S Mark III, #F8, c1979,
  1:50 ....$8-10
BMW 3.5 CSL, #167-F30 ....$5-7

BMW 320i, #239-F43, 1:62 ....$5-7

Box Van, #35/36/37 ....$6-8

Bugatti Royale Coupe DeVille 1927, #186-F46, c1978, 1:80 ....$6-8

Bulldozer, #247-106 ....$8-10
Bus, #79, 1:130 ....$6-8
Cadillac Ambulance, #F-2 ....$12-15
Cadillac Seville 1981, #233-F45, 1:69 .....$6-8
Cadillac Superior Ambulance, #181-F60,
  c1976, 1:77 ....$10-12
Cadillac Fleetwood Brougham, #86-F2/211-F2,
  c1976, 1:77 ....$6-8
Camper Pickup, see Chevrolet Pickup
Canter Garbage Truck $4-6
Cargo Container, #100, 1:47 ....$8-10
Cargo Container Truck, Fuso, #7/67-90,91,
  1:127 ....$9-12
Cedric 280E $4-6
Celica LB 2000 GT, #33, 1:63 ....$5-7

Chemical Fire Engine, Datsun UD Condor, #145-94, 1:90 ....$12-15
Chevrolet Corvette, F21 ....$6-8

Chevrolet Pickup, #214-F44, 1:77 ....$6-8

Chevrolet Van

#F22, c1977, 1:78 ....$5-7

  Custom, #216-F23 ....$5-7
  Ambulance, #143-F22, c1977, 1:78 ....$6-8

Sheriff, #F22, c1977, 1:78 ....$6-8

Citroën "H" Truck, #97, 1:71 ....$5-10

Continental Mark IV, Ford Lincoln, #114-F4,
  c1976, 1:77 ....$5-7
Corvette, #144-F21 ....$5-7
Crane Picrover Mobile, #65-33, 1:96 ....$6-8
Custom Chevrolet Van, #216-F23 ....$5-7
Custom Stepside Pickup, #212-F44 ....$6-8
Daihatsu Midget, #62, 1:50 ....$5-7
Datsun 200SX, #235-6 ....$5-7
Datsun 260Z, #47-58 ....$5-7
Datsun 280Z Rally, #210-58 ....$5-7

Datsun UD Condor Chemical Fire Engine,
#145-94, 1:90 ....$12-15
Datsun R382 Racer, #25-22 ....$5-7
Datsun Silvia $4-6
Datsun Station Wagon, #138-47 ....$6-8
Datsun Tipper Truck, #136-56 ....$6-8

Datsun Touring Car 1932, #03-60, c1974, 1:49 ....$6-8

DeTomaso Pantera
#193-F55, silver $5-7
#F64, blue $5-7

Dodge Coronet Custom Police Car, #105/178-F8, c1976, 1:74 ....$7-9

Dodge Fire Chief, #163-F10 ....$6-8
Dodge Taxi, #139-F18 ....$6-8

Dynapac CC21 Road Roller, 1:62 ....$6-8

Dyna Vac, #18, 1:68 ....$5-7
Elf Backhoe, #152-64 ....$8-10
Elf Rally Renault, #238-F58 ....$6-8
Emergency Van, Chevy, #207-F22, c1977, 1:78 ....$6-8
Ferrari 308 GTB, #F35, 1:60 ....$5-7
Ferrari 312 Formula 1 Racer, #209-59 ....$5-7
Ferrari Dino 308 GTB, #155F35, c1977, 1:60 ...$5-7
Ferrari F1 ....$5-7

Fiat X1/9, #165-F28, 1:59 ....$5-7

Firebird Turbo, #243-F42 ....$5-7
Ford Livestock Truck, #F62, 1:95 ....$6-8
Ford Lotus Europa "John Player Special," #161-F36/164-F25 ....$6-8
Ford Model T

Convertible Coupe 1915, #112/248-F11, c1977, 1:60 ....$8-10

Delivery Van 1915, #134-F11/F13, c1977, 1:60 ....$8-10

Touring Car 1915, #125/246-F12/F11, c1977, 11:60 ....$8-10

Ford P-34 Tyrell Formula 1 Racer, #168-F32, c1977, 1:52 ....$6-8
Ford Fritos Truck, #236-F62, 1:95 ....$6-8

Formula 1, #117/120 ....$5-7

Fuji Subaru, #21, 1:50, depending on variations $4-20
Furukawa Wheel Loader, #36-63 ....$6-8

Fuso Truck Crane, #66 ....$5-7

Fuso Truck Series

Container Truck, #77-7/90/91, 1:127 ......$5-7

Freight Truck, #77-7/90/91, 1:127 ....$5-7

Pepsi Truck, #77-7/90/91, 1:127 ....$5-7

Tanker, #77-7/90/91, 1:127 ....$5-7
Gran Porsche, #197-F3 ....$5-7

Greyhound Bus "Americruiser," #222-F49, c1979, 1:156 ....$25-30

Hato School Bus $4-6
Hato City Bus $4-6
Heavy Crane, #141-66 ....$6-8
Hino Aerial Ladder Fire Truck, 1:125 ...$5-7

Hino Big Rig Semi-Trailer, #89-24 ......$10-12

Hino Cement Mixer, #29-52/-53/-54,
 1:102.................................$6-8
Hino Dozer carrier, #56, 1:102 ....$7-9
Hino Gasoline Truck, #29-52/-53/-54, 1:102...$6-8

**Hino Grandview Bus, #1, 1:154 ....$5-12
depending on variations**

Hino Truck, #29-52/-53/-54, 1:102 ..$6-8
Hitachi DH321 Dump Truck,
 #35-59, 1:117 ....$6-8
Holmes Wrecker, see Peterbilt Tow Truck
Honda Accord, #142-78 ....$5-7
Honda Acura NSX

black and red, #78, 1:59.....................$5-7

Patrol Car, black and white, #78, 1:59....$5-7
Honda Beat, #72, 1:50 ....$5-7

Honda City, #54, 1:57 ....$6-8
Honda Civic GL/CVCC, #241-83, c1974,
 1:57.................................$8-10

Honda Motorcycle, #42, 1:34 ....$8-10
Honda Stepwagon, #21 ....$8-10
Hovercraft, Mitsui Zosen, #93, 1:210$8-10
IMSA Turbo Toyota Celica, #217-65,
 c1979, 1:62 ....$5-7
Isuzu Bonnet Police Bus, #6, 1:110..$15-20
Isuzu Elf, 1:67 ....$8-10

Isuzu Hipac Van, #27, 1:70 ....$6-8

Isuzu Red Cross Van.........................$4-6
Isuzu Road Construction Truck, 1:78.............$5-7
Jaguar XJ-S, #199-F68, c1978, 1:67 ....$6-8
Jr. Hiway Bus, #101, 1:145 ....$8-10
Komatsu Bulldozer-Shovel, #66-106 ....$8-10

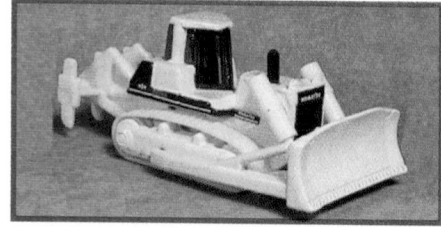

Komatsu D375A Bulldozer, #114, 1:135 ...$5-7

Komatsu D65A Bulldozer, #70, 1:87 ....$5-7

Komatsu Fork Lift, #34-48 ....$8-10
Komatsu Steam Shovel, #49-09 ....$12-15

Kubota Farm Tractor, #61-92, 1:42.......$8-10

LaFrance Ladder Chief, #160-F33/
 187-F33, c1978, 1:143 ....$8-10

Lamborghini Cheetah, #F65 ....$6-8
Lamborghini Countach, #162-F37/170-F50...$5-7
Lancia Stratos
 HF Racer, #153/159-F27 ....$5-7

Turbo Racer, #223-F66, c1987, 1:62.......$5-7

**Lincoln Continental Mark IV, #114-F4,
c1976, 1:77.....................................$8-10**
Lion Bus, #26 ....$5-7

London Bus, #F15, c1977, 1:130 ....$10-12

Lotus Elite, #F47, c1978, 1:63 ....$6-8

Lotus Esprit Special, #220-24.....................$5-7
Lotus Europa John Player Special, #161-F36/
 164-F25 ....$6-8

**Maserati Merak SS, #177-F45, c1978,
1:62..$6-8**

Mazda 787B, #34, 1:64 ....$7-9

Mazda Bongo Friendee Minivan
   Camper, 1:64 ....$7-9

Mazda Eunos / Miata Roadster, #111 ....$6-8

Mazda Familia 1500XG, #4, 1:59 ....$6-8

Mazda GT Racer, #158-80 ....$5-7
Mazda RX-500, #17-34 ....$5-7
Mazda Savannah

RX-7, #203/245-50, c1979, 1:60 ....$5-7

GT, #80, 1:59 ....$7-9

McLaren M26 Ford Formula 1, #224/
   169-F39 ....$5-7

Mechanical Sweeper, #113, 1:66 ....$6-8

Mercedes-Benz 300SL Gullwing, 1956,
   #221-F19 ....$6-8

**Mercedes-Benz 450SEL, #111/176-F7,
c1976, 1:67 ....$5-7**

**Mercedes Unimog, #184-F41, c1978,
1:70 ....$6-8**

Mini Cooper, F8 ....$6-8
Mitsubishi Big Rig Truck, Fuso, #62-07 ....$6-8

Mitsubishi Canter Garbage Truck, #47, 1:72 ...$6-8
Mitsubishi Car Transporter, #14, 1998 ....$4-6
Mitsubishi Condor Crane Truck with pipes,
   #80, 1:104 ....$5-7
Mitsubishi Airport Towing Tractor, #95, 1:110 ...$8-10
Mitsubishi Fuso Amusement Park Shuttle
   Bus, 1:130 ....$6-8
Mitsubishi Fuso Container Truck, #74, 1:102 ...$5-7
Mitsubishi Fuso Racing Transporter, #93, 1:102 ....$6-8
Mitsubishi Fuso Refrigerated Truck, 1:102 .....$5-7
Mitsubishi Jeep
   Bigfoot $6-8
   J58 ....$4-6
Mitsubishi Minica Toppo, #71, 1:56 ....$5-7
Mitsubishi McDonalds Truck, #65, 1998 .....$4-6

Mitsubishi Pajero Jr., #112, 1:56 ....$6-8

Mitsubishi Rosa School Bus, #60, 1:84 ....$5-7
Mitsui Zosen Hovercraft, #93, 1:210 ....$8-10
Mobile Picrover Crane, #65-33, 1:96 ....$6-8

Morgan Plus 6, #140-F26, c1977, 1:57 ...$6-8
Moving Van, #117-20 ....$8-10
Mustang II Ghia, #156/188-F38 ....$6-8
Newspaper Truck, #118-107 ....$15-20

Nissan 300ZX $6-8
Nissan Bluebird SSS Coupe, #1, depending
   on variations $7-20

**Nissan Caball Utility Truck, #54/87/88,
1:68 ....$6-8**

Nissan Caravan, #3, 1:66 ....$5-7

Nissan Cima, #31, 1:65 ....$6-8
Nissan Condor Crane Truck with pipes, #56/80,
   1:104 ....$5-7

Nissan Diesel

Aerial Ladder Fire Truck, #22, 1:120.......$5-7

Dump Truck, #16, 1:102.....................$8-10

Moving Van, #16, 1:102......................$6-8
Tanker, #16, 1:102...........................$6-8

Nissan Fairlady

280Z-T, #15, c1979, 1:61 ....$6-8

300ZX, 1:59 ....$6-8

Nissan Paramedic Ambulance, #51, 1:78....$5-7
Nissan Pulsar $4-6
Nissan Silvia.....................................$4-6

Nissan Skyline GT-R

33 Street, #20, 1:60 ....$6-8

Racing, #20, 1:60...............................$6-8

Off Road Cruiser, #226-2 ....$5-7
Off Road Dump Truck, 1:119 ....$7-9

Ohara Snow Tiger SM30, #84, 1:73 ....$12-15

Packard Coupe Roadster 1937, #179-F52, 1978, 1:72...................................$8-10

Pajero, #30, 1:62 ....$5-7
Panda Truck, #76, 1:102.....................$10-12
Pepsi Soft Drink Truck, #198-76 ....$8-10

Peterbilt Big Rig American

Cement Truck, #219-F63, c1978, 1:98....$5-7

Dump Truck, #205-F63, c1978, 1:98 ....$5-7

Holmes Tow Truck Wrecker, #171-F63, c1978, 1:98.....................................$5-7

Picrover Mobile Crane, #65-33, 1:96.........$6-8
Pizza Scooter, #82....................................$5-7
Police Bike, #4, 1:34 ....$5-7
Police Bus, Isuzu Bonnet Bus, #6, 1:110 ..$15-20
Police Car, Dodge Coronet Custom,
    #178-F8/9/10/18 ....$7-9
Police Van Special Weapons Team 2, Toyota Type
    HQ15V, #185-67, c1978, 1:81 ....$8-10

Pontiac Firebird Trans Am, #201-F42...$6-8
Porsche 356, #89, 1:59..................$5-7

Porsche 911S, #106-F3/F5/F17, c1976, 1:61..$6-8

Porsche 928, #204-F53 ....$5-7

Porsche, Gran Porsche, #197-F3 ....$5-7
Porsche Sports Racer, #237-F43 ....$5-7
Porsche Turbo 935, #183-F31 ....$5-7
Power Company Service Truck, Nissan
    Caball, #75-54/87/88, 1:68 ....$6-8
Propane Truck, #115-42 ....$6-8
Range Rover, 1:64 ....$7-9
Renault Elf Rally, #238-F58 ....$6-8

Rolls Royce Phantom VI, #110-F6, c1976, 1:78...$6-8

Rural School Bus, #109-F5, 1:108, c1976....$6-8
Sakai Tire Roller, #103-65, 1:90 ....$8-10
School Bus
    #91-01 ....$8-10

Rural, #109-F5, 1:108, c1976...................$6-8

Screamin' Sports Car, #180-71 ....$5-7
Sheriff's Van, Chevrolet Chevrolet Van,
    #242-F22, c1977, 1:78 ....$6-8
Sightseeing Bus, #130-41 ....$10-12
Silvia 240 SX, #6, 1:59, depending on
    variations $5-12

Snow Tiger, Ohara SM30, #147-84, 1:73...$12-15
Soarer Lexus Coupe, #5, 1:63 ....$5-7
Special Weapons Team Police Van, Toyota Type
   HQ15V, #185-67, c1978, 1:81.......$8-10
Squirt Fire Engine, #41-03 ....$6-8
Steam Shovel, Komatsu, #49/192-9.......$12-15
Street Sweeper, light yellow, #113, 1:66.....$5-7
Subaru Milk Truck, #96, 1:130 ....$5-7

Subaru Sambar Post Van, #31, 1:52.....$9-12

Subaru Post Van, #67, 1998.....................$4-6

Sakai Tire Roller, #65 ....$5-7

Super Bug Volkswagen, #195-F20, 1:60...$10-12
Suzuki Carry Stake Truck, #39, 1:55 ....$6-8
Suzuki Wagon R (Micro MPV), #71, 1998 ..$4-6
Swim School Bus, #83, 1:145 ....$5-7
Tadano Rough Terrain Crane, #218-2,
   c1979, 1:96 ....$5-7
Taxi, Toyota Crown, #4/27/32/110, 1:65....$8-10

Terex 72-81 Loader, #F38, 1:137 ....$5-7

Texaco Gas Truck, #234-F62 ....$6-8
Texaco Tanker, Fuso, #77-7/90/91, 1:127....$5-7
Telephone Truck, Nissan Caball,
   #244-54/87/88, 1:68 ....$6-8
Toyota 2000 GT, #22-05, c1974, 1:60...$10-12
Toyota Ambulance, #46-40.......................$6-8

Toyota Caribe (Tercel) $4-6
Toyota Celica Supra Racer, #65 ....$5-7

**Toyota Celica Supra LB 2000GT, #215-33,
c1978, 1:63......................................$6-8**

Toyota Corolla Levin, #78, 1:61 ....$6-8
Toyota Crown Taxi, #4/27/32/110, 1:65 ..$8-10

Toyota Dyna Vacuum Car, 1:68................$5-7

Toyota Estima, #99, 1:65 ....$6-8
Toyota Ex-7, #04-31 ....$6-8

Toyota Fork Lift FD200, #182-12............$8-10

Toyota Hiace
   Auto Wrecker, #38/50, 1:68 ....$8-10

Airport Stairway Truck, #38/50, 1:68...$10-12

Loudspeaker Vending Truck, #38/50,
   1:68 ....$15-20
Sushi Vendor, #38/50, 1:68 ....$15-20
Toyota Hilux
   Bigfoot, 1:65 ....$5-7
   Surf, #84, 1:65 ....$5-7

red with white design, #3, 1:65 ....$5-7
Toyota Hi-Ranger $5-7
Toyota Land Cruiser, #83-02 ....$8-10
Toyota MR2...$4-6

Toyota Quick Delivery Van, #93, 1:72.....$5-7

Toyota Previa, red & gray, #99, 1:64..........$5-7
Toyota Prius (Hybrid Vehicle), #86, 1998.....$4-6
Toyota RAV4, 1:57 ....$6-8
Toyota Spacio (Mini MPV), #16, 1998........$4-6

Toyota Street Maintenance Truck..........$5-7

Toyota Supra, 1:60 ....$6-8
Toyota Towing Tractor, #96, 1:50, with cargo
   container, #100, 1:47, & box van,
   #35/36/37 ....$25-30

**Toyota Type HQ15V Special Weapons
Team (SWAT) Police Van, #185-67, c1978,
1:81 ....$8-10**
Toyota Utility Truck, #128-38 ....$6-8
Toyota Wrecker, #129-39 ....$5-7
Turbo Firebird, #243-F42 ....$5-7
Turbo Porsche 935, #240-F31 ....$5-7
Tyrell P34 Formula 1 Ford, #168-F32,
   c1977, 1:52 ....$6-8
UD Condor Chemical Fire Engine, Datsun, #145-
   94, 1:90 ....$12-15

Unimog (see Mercedes-Benz Unimog)

Utility Truck Nissan Caball, #244-54/
87/88, 1:68 ....$6-8
Utility Truck Toyota, #1280-38 ....$6-8
Vette Racer, #175-F21 ....$5-7

Volkswagen Beetle, gold, #100, 1:60......$7-9

Volkswagen Convertible, #146/
225-F20, c1977, 1:60 ....$10-12

**Volkswagen Rabbit/Golf GLE, #232-F5,
1:56 ....$6-8**

Volkswagen Microbus, #166-F29 ....$18-24
Wheel Loader, #206-63 ....$8-10
Winnebago Chieftain Motor Home,
#92-F1, c1976, 1:97 ....$12-15

Tomica Dandy
Datsun Silvia Coupe $18-24
Fiat 131 Abarth $18-24
Hino Fire Ladder Truck, #2 ....$18-24
London Double Decker Bus $45-55
Mercedes 560 SEL, #G-8 ....$30-35
Mickey Mouse Fire Engine, red with yellow
plastic trim, gray wheels with gold
hubs, 2⅜" $8-12
Mini Cooper, #DJ015 ....$20-25
Nissan Caravan Police, #1 ....$18-24
Nissan Cedric 4-door Sedan Police Car ...$18-24
Nissan Condor Fire Truck $18-24
Nissan Skyline $18-24
Nissan Van Ambulance, #12 ....$18-24
Regent III RT London Transport Bus, #F19 ..$45-55
Toyota Landcruiser $18-24
1970 Toyota Mk2 2-door Hardtop,
#11 ....$20-25
Volkswagen Beetle, #DJ011 ....$20-25
Volkswagen Police, "METRO,"
#DE006 ....$20-25
Volkswagen Van, "NGK," #DT002 ....$24-28

Tomy (see Tomica)

Tonka

Most Tonka Toys are manufactured of stamped or pressed steel and do not qualify as diecast. But this brand from Mound, Minnesota, has a rich heritage that deserves mention. Vintage Tonka trucks of the 1950s are often selling for $100 to $400 each, and restored vehicles are also rising in value, to $50 and more. There is currently only one known book on Tonka trucks, covering 1947 to 1963.

Tonka Turbo Tricksters are produced for Tonka by Takara Co., Inc. of Macau. They are plastic toys with centrifugal flywheel motors that assist in making the cars do wild acrobatic tricks.

Tonka is now owned by Hasbro. Besides the usual large pressed steel toys, miniature Tonka toys have also shown up as kid's meal premiums at McDonald's.

An arrangement with Maisto in 1998 has resulted in four 3½ inch long diecast and plastic Maisto versions of several classic Tonka toys. The series was so popular that in 1999, Maisto expanded the assortment to 50 models. See Maisto for a list.

Tonka sets for 2000 include some mostly plastic but well-constructed sets of toy trucks and accessories originally manufactured by Kentoy of Hong Kong and marketed by Manley ToyQuest.

Tonkin

Tonkins are ready built 1:53 scale 1988 Ford twin trailer truck models last available from Jeff Bray Jr.'s Diecast Miniatures for just under $50 each.

Ford 1988 Twin Trailer Truck, various
versions $45-60

Tootsietoys

Tootsietoys were first introduced by Dowst Manufacturing after Charles Dowst saw a demonstration of the diecasting process at the 1893 Columbian Exposition (otherwise known as the Chicago World's Fair). He envisioned many applications of the process and started making the first diecast buttons. In 1914, he introduced the first Tootsie Toy, named after his brother's granddaughter Toots. (Later the name was changed to Tootsietoy.)

The Tootsietoy legacy can be divided into two eras—pre-war and post-war. The reason for this is that before World War II, Dowst concentrated on producing realistic replicas of popular vehicles of the era. The focus after the war shifted to producing less expensive toys that were

more affordable and therefore more accessible to children.

Serious collectors prefer pre-war Tootsietoys because of their greater detail and realism. Today's assortment of Tootsietoys runs the full gamut of styles, from crude generic toys to accurate miniature models, but the focus is still on affordability. While this book presents a survey of models, a more detailed study can be found in David Richter's *Collector's Guide to Tootsietoys* $24.95 from Collector Books.

In 1964, with the purchase of the Strombecker Corporation, one of the oldest companies in the US, Dowst's Tootsietoys became Strombecker's Tootsietoys.

Tootsietoys–A Survey
Bi-Wing Seaplane, #4650, 1926 ....$50
Bleriot Aeroplane
2", #4491, 1910 ....$105-120
2⅜", #4482, 1910 ....$200-225
Box Truck, 3", #234, 1942-1947 ....$20-25
Buick Series 50 Coupe 1924, 3",
#4636, 1924 ....$90-105
Buick Touring Car 1924, 3", #4641, 1925 ...$90-105
Cadillac Coupe, pre-WWII $30-40

Chevrolet Sedan 1950, 1951-1954 ......$30-45

Delivery Van, Special Issue
Adam, Meldrum & Anderson Co.,
#4630, 1924 ....$400
Bamberger, #4630, 1924 ....$400
Pomeroy's, #4630, 1924 ....$400
U. S. Mail, #4630, 1924 ....$600
Watt & Shand, #4630, 1924 ....$400
Fageol Bus 1926 Safety Coach, 3½",
#4651, 1927 ....$50
Federal 1924 Delivery Van
Delivery, #4630, 1924 ....$90-105
Grocery, #4630, 1924 ....$90-105
Laundry, #4630, 1924 ....$90-105
Milk, #4630, 1924 ....$90-105
Ford F6 1949 Oil Tanker
solid color, 4", 1950-1969 ....$20-25
two-tone with silver tank, 4", 1950-
1969 ....$15-20
Ford Model T 1914
Convertible, 3", #4570, 1914 ....$90-105
Pickup, 3", #4610, 1916 ....$90-105

Ford Oil Tanker, 6"
    Shell, 1949-1952 ....$55-65
    Texaco, 1949-1952 ....$45-55
Freight Train Set, #4627, 1925 ....$90-105
Graham Sedan, pre-WWII................$360-400
International KII Oil Tanker, 6"
    Shell, 1949–1955 ....$55-65
    Sinclair, 1949–1955 ....$45-55
    Standard, 1949–1955 ....$45-55
    Texaco, 1949–1955 ....$55-65
Limousine, 1⅞", #4528, 1911...............$45-60
Mack AC 1921, 3¼"
    Coal Truck, #4639, 1925 ....$90-105
    Stake Truck, #4638, 1925 ....$90-105
    Tank Truck, #4640, 1925 ....$90-105
Mack B-Line 1955 Oil Tanker
    "Mobil" decal, 1960–1965,
        1967–1969 ....$60-70
    "Tootsietoy" decal, 1960–1965,
        1967–1969 ....$75-85
Mack L-Line Oil Tanker with tank trailer, "Tootsi-
    etoy" decal, 1954–1959 ....$80-90
Oil Tanker, 3", #235, 1947–1954 ....$20-25
Passenger Train Set, #4626, 1925.......$90-105
RC 180 Oil Tanker, 1962 ....$45-55
Tractor, pre-WWII..................................$20
Wings Seaplane, 3¾", #4675, 1929 .....$65-75

**Yellow Cab, 1921–1933, 2¾", #4629,
1923** $90-105

Contemporary Tootsietoys

    Today's Tootsietoys represent a broad range of models, often with generous amounts of plastic incorporated into the design. The most popular line of Tootsietoys is their series called "Hard Body." Below is an assortment of models that fall under this category.

Tootsietoy Hard Body 1:32 Scale

1940 Ford Coupe.....................................$4-5
1997 Ford F-150, fuchsia $4-5
1959 Chevrolet El Camino
    Custom $4-5
    Lowrider $4-5
1996 Chevrolet Tahoe
    black $4-5

red $4-5

Tootsietoy Hard Body 1:43 Scale

Corvette $3-4
Ferrari F40..$3-4
Firebird $3-4
Mercedes-Benz Convertible.........................$3-4
Mercedes-Benz Coupe................................$3-4
Porsche Targa $3-4

Tootsietoy Hard Body 1:64 Scale

Corvette $1-2
Ferrari F40..$1-2
Flareside Pickup, Universal Air Lines $1-2
Jaguar XKE..$1-2

Top Gear Trax

Top Gear
Locked Bag 5300
Parramatta, New South Wales
2124 Australia

    It is truly remarkable that Top Gear models, begun in 1986, has remained so obscure outside of Australia until now. Their 1:43 scale renditions of Australia's own Holden automobiles are terrific. Holdens old and new, stock and street, station wagons and pickups... all are showcased by Top Gear in their latest brochure, provided by Bob Robinson of New South Wales, Australia.

Brabham XC Falcon GT, with Bathurst '77
    racing decals, TR10B $36-40
Chrysler Valiant Charger RT....................$45-50
Ford
    Bathurst Twin Set Ford Dealer Team
        Falcons, drivers Alan Moffat and
        Colin Bond, with video, TRS10 ....$60-75
    Falcon 1966 4-door Sedan...............$55-60
    Falcon XC Cobra, TR10 ....$32-36
    Falcon XC Cobra 1966 Coupe........$55-60
    Falcon GT 1974 (Mustang GT) $36-40
    XK Ford Falcon Van, 1961, wattle bark
        tan, TR27 ....$36-40
    XK Ford Falcon Utility, 1961, Merino
        white, TR29 ....$36-40
    XK Ford Falcon Utility, 1961, Botany
        green, TR29B $36-40
    XK Ford Falcon Wagon, 1960, torch
        red, TR30 ....$36-40
    XT Ford Falcon V8 GT, 1968, silver with
        burgundy stripes, TR24B $36-40
    XT Ford Falcon GT Sedan, 1968, cruise
        blue, TR24C $36-40
Holden
    48-215 (FX) Sedan, black, TR15........$36-40

48-215 (FX) Sedan, powder blue, TR15B ...$36-40
Charger, metallic green, TR11 ....$32-36
Charger Highway Patrol, white with roof-
    mounted lights and sirens, TR11B .$36-40
EH Holden 1960s Sedan, maroon and
    white $36-40
EH Holden 1960s Sedan, blue and
    white $36-40
EH Holden 1960s Wagon, gray and
    white, TR6 ....$36-40
EH Holden 1960s Wagon, Sorrel tan
    and white, TR6C $32-36
EH Holden Premier Sedan, valley mist,
    TR5D...$45-55
EK Holden 1960 Standard Sedan,
    Wedgewood blue, TR21 ....$36-40
EK Holden 1960 Standard Sedan,
    glade green, TR21B $36-40
FB Holden 1960 Standard Sedan,
    buckskin, TR20B $36-40
FB Holden 1960 Standard Sedan,
    pyramid coral, TR20C $36-40
Golden Holden 48-215 (FJ) commemorating
    Holden's 50th Anniversary (1948–
    1998), TRG15 ....$45-55
HK Monaro Racing, Palmer / West,
    TR3C $50-60
HQ Monaro Kingswood 1971 Sedan,
    mustard, TR17C.........................$36-40
HQ Monaro 80337 1971 Coupe, Purr
    Pull, TR18C $36-40
HT Monaro "Bathurst 69" Twin Set, Brock /
    Bond, TRS19..........................$80-100
HZ Holden 1977 Sandman Ute, Deauville
    blue, TR22 ....$36-40
HZ Holden 1977 Sandman Ute, Mandarin
    red, TR22B $36-40
HZ Holden 1977 Sandman Van, yellow,
    TR23 ....$36-40
HZ Holden 1977 Sandman Van, white,
    TR23B......................................$36-40
HZ Holden NRMA Road Service Van, blue
    and white, TR12 ....$36-40
LX Series Holden Torana SL/R 5000 and
    SS Hatchback, gift boxed twin pack,
    TRS14 ....$60-75
Monaco HK Coupe $45
Station Wagon 1963 ....$36-40
Torana GTR XU-1 white, TR8A $36-40
Torana GTR XU-1 lime green, TR8B $32-36
Torana GTR XU-1 "Strike Me Pink," TR8C ...$32-36
Torana SL/R 5000 Channel 7/Ron Hodgson
    with full racing decals, TR14B $36-40
Ute, 1951, Woodsman green...........$36-40
Ute, 1951, Navajo beige $36-40
Van 1953 ....$36-40

VL Holden Commodore, 1986, chardonnay,
   TR16.............................$36-40
VL Holden Commodore, 1986, Pacific blue,
   TR16B............................$36-40
Taxi
   Silvertop, TR13C....................$45-55
   Yellow Cab, TR13E...................$45-55
   B & W, TR13F........................$45-55
Australia's Hottest Ever Production cars!
   Limited Edition Gift Boxed Set TRG1,
   includes: Ford GTHO Phase 3 Falcon,
   wild violet Holden GTS Monaro Coupe,
   silver mink, Valiant R/T Charger, Hemi
   orange $95-120
Top Gear Trax display cabinet holds up to
   24 Top Gear Trax models, 15" high,
   12" wide, 3" deep, TD02.......$80-90

Top Marques

Unit 12 Durham Way
Heathpark Indust Est
Honiton, Devon EX14 1SQ
United Kingdom

   Top Marques are 1:43 scale models made
in Great Britain. The company was out of business by midyear 2002, according to an article
in the August 2002 issue of *Model Auto
Review*.

1951 Mercedes 170.....................$125-150
MG Ex181
   1957 Land Speed Record Car, Stirling
   Moss............................$125-150
   1959 Land Speed Record Car, Phil
   Hill, 254.91mph $125-150
1932 Rolls Royce Phantom II Brewster "Croydon"
   light yellow with light blue fenders,
   GS4 ....$125-150
   light green with dark green fenders,
   GS5 ....$125-150

Top Model Collection

Top Model Collection SRL
Via Cupa Terracina n. 33
80125 Naples, Italy
tel: 0039 81 2422508
fax: 0039 81 624947
e-mail: topmodel@iol.it
website: //members.tripod.comtopmodel
collection

   The Top Model Collection is an assortment
of 1:43 scale vintage European racing models
made in Naples, Italy. Models listed below
were issued in 1998–1999.

Alfa Romeo 412 Vignale

1951, red, street version, TMC147 ...$125-175
Mille Miglia 1951, silver, N.427, Bonetto,
   TMC146 ....$125-175
Aston Martin DBR1
   1960, metallic green street version,
   TMC170 ....$125-175
   3° Le Mans 1960, green, N.7, Border,
   Reivers, TMC169 ....$125-175
BMW 328
   1947, silver, street version,
   TMC155 ....$125-175
   Circuito Piacenza 1947, silver, N.132,
   Rovelli, TMC154 ....$125-175
Ferrari 121 LM
   red, street version, TMC138.........$125-175
   Le Mans 1955, red, N.3, Maglioli,
   Hill, TMC135 ....$125-175
   Le Mans 1955, red, N.4, Castellotti,
   Marzotto, TMC136 ....$125-175
   Le Mans 1955, red, N.5, Trintignan,
   Shell, TMC137 ....$125-175
   1955, yellow street version, TMC
   139 ....$125-175
Ferrari 166S Allemano
   Coupe' 1°Mille Miglia 1948, N.16,
   red, Biondetti, TMC142 ....$125-175
   Coupe' 1948, red street version,
   TMC145 ....$125-175
   Coupe' Intereurop Cup 1949, N.12,
   silver, Biondetti, TMC143 ....$125-175
   Supercortemaggiore 1949, N.6,
   red, Biondetti, TMC144 .$125-175
Ferrari 225S Grand Prix Monsanto 1953,
   black, N.28, TMC173................$125-175
Ferrari 315S
   1957, red, street version, TMC167 ...$125-175
   1957, yellow street version,
   TMC168 ....$125-175
   1° Mille Miglia 1957, red, N.535,
   Taruffi, TMC166 ....$125-175
   Le Mans 1957, red, N.8, Evans,
   Severi, TMC165 ....$125-175
Ferrari 335 MM
   Le Mans 1947, red, N.7, Hawthorn,
   Musso, TMC158 ....$125-175
   Le Mans 1957, red, N.6, Hill,
   Collins, TMC157 ....$125-175
   1947, red street version, TMC160 ..$125-175
   1957, yellow street version,
   TMC161 ....$125-175
   Mille Miglia 1947, red, N.531, De
   Portego, TMC159 ....$125-175
Ferrari 340 MM
   1953, red, street version,
   TMC141 ....$125-175
   Le Mans 1953, blue, N.16, Chinetti,

Cole, TMC140.....................$125-175
Vignale 1° Mille Miglia 1953, red,
   N.547, Marzotto, TMC156...$125-175
Ferrari 625 LM
   1956, red, street version, TMC152...$125-175
   3° Le Mans 1956, red, N.12, Trintignan,
   Gendebien, TMC149..........$125-175
   Le Mans 1956, red, N.10, Simon, Hill,
   TMC150 ....$125-175
   Le Mans 1956, red, N.11, De Portago,
   Hamilton, TMC151 ....$125-175
   1956, yellow street version,
   TMC153 ....$125-175
Maserati 6C Sport
   Grand Prix Piacenza 1947, red, N.146,
   Angiolini, TMC162 ....$125-175
   Grand Prix Piacenza 1947, silver, N.164,
   Barbieri, TMC171 ....$125-175
   Sassi Superga 1947, red, N.130, Angiolini,
   TMC163 ....$125-175
   1947, red, street version, TMC164...$125-175
   1947, red, street version, TMC172...$125-175
Talbot Lago T26GS Carrera Pan Am 1954
   blue, N.6, Rosier, TMC148.........$125-175
   blue, N.6, Rosier, TMC148/B......$125-175

Topper Toys (see Johnny Lightnings)

   Here is a brief chronology of the Topper Toy
company, original manufacturer of Johnny Lightnings. For more information, refer to the section
on Johnny Lightnings.

1953 Henry Orenstein begins marketing toys
   through supermarkets.
1966 De Luxe Topper Corp. incorporates
   (Delaware).
1966 Johnny Speed remote control car marketed.
1968 Name is changed to Topper Corp.
1969 Johnny Lightning line begins
   (February–March).
1970 Public stock offered.
1970 Federal Trade Commission (FTC) accuses
   Topper of false advertising. (Mattel is listed too.)
1971 Second public stock offered.
1972 Securities & Exchange Commission (SEC)
   suspends trading of Topper stock.
1972 Orenstein resigns as president.
1973 Topper files chapter 11 bankruptcy.
1973 Topper loses right to produce Sesame Street
   toys, goes out of business (December).
(Sources: Topper Fed from S-1 *Wall Street Journal*, FTC lawsuit copy courtesy of Donal
   Wells.)

Toy Collector Club of America
(see First Gear)

ToyMark (also see Speedy Power)

Recently discovered is Speedy Power brand diecast toys from Toymark Co., Ltd. Models found represent a 1:32 scale 1997 BMW Z-3 Convertible in two color schemes, purchased for $2.99 each ($3.99 suggested retail price). Features include opening doors and pullback motor. Model listing are under the Speedy Power section. Most recent evidence indicates, ToyMark, Speedy Power, Speedy Wheels, and Boley have all been purchased by New-Ray.

Toyo Kogyo

Produced by Model Planning Co., Ltd., the Histories Collection from Toyo Kogyo of Japan represents 1:87 scale diecast models. A partial list is provided thanks to Werner Legrand of Belgium.

Toyo Kogyo Histories Collection
1966 Mazda Carol
   white with blue roof, #20011 ....$12-18
   white with red roof, #20012 ....$12-18
   light blue with white roof, #20013 .....$12-18
   light gray with white roof, #20014 ....$12-18

Toys of Yesterday (see OGDI Toys of Yesterday)

Toys for Collectors

As if their incredible assortment of diecast models isn't enough, Toys for Collectors (TfC) introduced its own range of scale models in response to many requests from collectors. As stated in their Auto Miniatures catalog issue XVI, "Our objective is a small range of models with limited production runs to provide the serious collector with the alternatives not available elsewhere. The models are made of pewter, resin, or both, and production is shared in-house and overseas. Because of the effort and the time it takes to produce these miniatures, not all of them can be available at all times."

TfC began as a mail order source for diecast precision models from a large variety of manufacturers, and has become one of only a few premiere diecast mail order businesses in the U.S.

TfC's current catalog features beautiful full-color photos of models from Siku, Gama, Cursor, Conrad, and others, many of which are featured in this book.

Many of these TfC 1:43 scale models are already sold out and quickly rising in collector value.

TfC—The American Collection
1973 Cadillac Eldorado
   Indy Pace Car, #16 ....$150-175

Convertible, black with red interior,
   #17 ....$130-155
1984 Cadillac Seville
   #19 ....$130-155
   Elegante, #20 ....$140-165
1933 Chrysler Imperial
   Custom Eight Convertible, beige with red
     running board & fenders, #8 ...$145-170
   white "Indy Official Pace Car," #6....$150-175
1961 Ford Thunderbird, gold "Indy Official
   Pace Car," #5 ....$160-185
1958 Oldsmobile Super 88 Holiday Coupe
   white with red roof, #7 ....$145-170
   black with red roof, #7a $145-170
1970 Oldsmobile 4-4-2
   Hardtop Coupe, metallic mint green,
     #1 ....$120-145
   Hardtop Coupe, red with white roof,
     #1a $120-145
   W-30 Coupe, gold, #2 ....$145-170
   W-30 Coupe, yellow, #2a...........$145-170
   W-30 Convertible, yellow, #3 ....$145-170
   W-30 Convertible, white "Indy Official
     Pace Car," #4 ....$150-175
1970 Oldsmobile Cutlass S Holiday Coupe,
   metallic silver with black roof, #9 ...$125-140
1972 Oldsmobile Hurst Indy Pace Car,
   #15 ....$150-175
1939 Mack Service Truck, "NBC
   Engineering Department," #14 ......$130-155
1941 Mack Service Van, "Brewster Glass,"
   #21 ....$130-155
1944 Mack Delivery Van
   "Columbia Electric," #10..............$130-155
   "Fram Filters," #11 ....$130-155
1950 Mack L Type Oil Tanker "Riley,"
   #18 ....$120-145
1968 Mercury Cougar
   XR-7 Coupe, metallic red, #12 ......$130-155
   XR-7 Coupe, metallic blue, #12.....$130-155
   XR-7 Coupe, pale yellow, #12 ......$130-155
   7.0 Litre GT-E, bright orange-red,
     #13 ....$165–190
   7.0 Litre GT-E, metallic dark green,
     #13 ....$165–190

Toy Truck Collector (see Taylor Made Trucks)

Trademark Models

Diecast Promotions / Highway 61 Collectibles
P.O. Box 882
10478 St. Joseph Drive
Dubuque, IA 52004-0882
toll free: 877-874-5467
direct: 563-583-0636

www.wcinet.comdiecast/ag.cfm

While Diecast Promotions™ offers 1:64 scale trucks produced by F.F. Ertl III, Inc., and Highway 61™ offers an assortment of model cars, Trademark Models™ represents the company's line of agricultural and construction vehicles.

Traffic Stoppers

Originally, NSG Marketing Corporation of Passaic, New Jersey, marketed these cheaply made metal and plastic toys that retail for 50 cents to $1 a piece and offer generic representations of various trucks. Collectible value on such models is nonexistent, but they provide an interesting contrast to the accuracy and detail of other models. Once removed from the package, these models are rendered unidentifiable, as no markings exist as to make and manufacturer anywhere on the model, which defines it as a generic.

Most recently, these toys have been marketed by Rhino Toys Manufacturing Ltd., Hunghom, Kowloon, Hong Kong. See "generic" listing for photos of these and other such models.

Trax (see Top Gear Trax)

Tri-Ang

George Lines, founder in 1870 of the original Lines Company of England, was joined by brother Joseph, who later purchased George's share. In turn, three of Joseph's sons — Walter, William, and Arthur — formed a company called Lines Bros., Ltd. Tri-Ang is named for the company logo formed by three lines, representing the three Lines brothers.

Besides diecast toys, Tri-ang products included prams, bicycles, pedal cars, stamped steel truck, wooden toys, doll houses, and many other toys.

Tri-Ang Minic models are heavy steel clockwork toys introduced in 1935 with 14 models. The line quickly expanded, resulting in a large assortment of toys. A numbering system was established around 1938 or 1939. Many of the toys had working lights, presumably powered by a small battery.

Balloon Barrage Wagon and Trailer,
   Camouflage, 1940, #76M $200-225
Bentley Sunshine Saloon, 1938, #45M..$125-150
Bentley Sunshine Saloon, 1938, #57ME..$125-150
Bentley Tourer, 1938, #37M $125-150
Bentley Tourer, 1938, #55ME $125-150
Breakdown Lorry Wrecker, 1936, #48M...$200-225
Breakdown Lorry Wrecker, Camouflaged,
   1940, #48MCF.......................$150-175

Cabriolet, 1935, #6M......................$175-200
Canvas Tilt Lorry, 1939, #69M..........$150-175
Canvas Tilt Lorry, Camouflaged, 1940,
    #69MCF..............................$150-175
Caravan House Trailer, 1937, #16M...$200-225
Caravan Set Limousine and House Trailer,
    1937, #38M.........................$200-225
Caravan Set, tourer with passengers and
    caravan with electric light, 1937,
    #59ME $200-225
Caravan, 1937, #41ME $150-175
Carter Paterson Van, 1936, #22M.....$175-200
Construction Set, 1936, #65M $225-250
Daimler Sedanca, 1937, #43M $125-150
Daimler Sedanca, 1937, #51ME......$125-150
Daimler Sunshine Saloon, 1938,
    #46M.................................$125-150
Daimler Sunshine Saloon, 1938,
    #58ME $125-150
Daimler Tourer, 1937, #36M $125-150
Delivery Lorry with cases, 1936,
    #25M.................................$125-150
Delivery Lorry, 1935, #10M $175-200
Double Deck Bus, green, 1935,
    #61M.................................$225-250
Double Deck Bus, red, 1935, #60M ..$375-425
Dust Cart Refuse Truck, 1936, #32M..$125-150
Farm Lorry, 1939, #67M $175-200
Fire Engine, 1936, #62ME $225-250
Ford Light Van, 1936, #2M $125-150
Ford Royal Mail Van, 1936, #3M $125-150
Ford Saloon, 1936, #1M $125-150
Ford Saloon, Camouflaged, 1940,
    #1MCF $125-150
Learner's Car, 1936, #12M $125-150
Light Tank, 1935, #20M $125-150
Light Tank, 1940, #20MCF $125-150
Limousine, 1935, #5M $125-150
Log Lorry, 1939, #74M $150-175
Luton Transport Van, 1936, #24M......$175-200
Luton Transport Van, Camouflaged, 1940,
    #24MCF $150-175
Mechanical Horse and Fuel Oil Tanker, 1936,
    #31M.................................$175-200
Mechanical Horse and Lorry with Barrels, 1939,
    #72M.......................................$250
Mechanical Horse and Milk Trailer, 1939,
    #71M.................................$175-200
Mechanical Horse and Pantechnicon, 1935,
    #30M.................................$175-200
Mechanical Horse and Pool Tanker, 1940,
    #79M.................................$175-200
Mechanical Horse and Trailer, 1936,
    #40M.................................$150-175
No. 1 Presentation Set, 1937, #63M...$225-250
No. 2 Presentation Set, 1937, #64M...$225-250

Open Touring Car, 1935, #8M.........$125-150
Petrol Tank Lorry Oil Tanker, 1936,
    #15M.................................$150-175
Petrol Tank Lorry, Camouflaged, 1940,
    #15MCF $125-150
Pool Tanker, 1940, #78M $125-150
Racing Car, 1936, #13M.................$125-150
Rolls Royce Sedanca, 1936, #50ME ..$125-150
Rolls Royce Sedanca, 1937, #42M....$125-150
Rolls Royce Sunshine Saloon, #56ME ..$125-150
Rolls Royce Sunshine Saloon, 1938,
    #47M.................................$125-150
Rolls Royce Tourer, 1937, #35M........$125-150
Searchlight Lorry, 1936, #49ME $125-150
Searchlight Lorry, Camouflaged, 1940,
    #49MECF $125-150
Single Deck Bus, green, 1936, #53M..$125-150
Single Deck Bus, red, 1936, #52M....$125-150
Six Wheel Army Lorry, 1939, #66M ..$150-175
Six Wheel Army Lorry, Camouflaged, 1940,
    #66MCF $150-175
Sports Saloon, 1935, #4M $125-150
Steam Roller, 1935, #33M.................$90-120
Streamline Saloon, 1935, #9M..........$125-150
Streamline Sports, 1935, #14M.........$125-150
Taxi, 1937, #39M $125-150
Timber Lorry, 1939, #68M.................$175-200
Tip Lorry (Dump Truck), #23M...........$150-175
Tourer with Passengers, 1937, #34M...$125-150
Town Coupe, 1935, #7M $125-150
Traction Engine and Trailer, 1939,
    #54M.................................$150-175
Traction Engine, 1938, #44M...........$125-150
Tractor and Trailer with cases, 1936,
    #26M.................................$150-175
Tractor, 1935, #11M $50-75
Traffic Control Police Car, 1938,
    #29M.................................$125-150
Transport Van, 1935, #21M..............$125-150
Transport Van, 1940, #21MCF $125-150
Vauxhall Cabriolet, 1937, #19M.......$175-200
Vauxhall Cabriolet, Camouflaged, 1940,
    #19MCF $125-150
Vauxhall Tourer, 1937, #17M $150-175
Vauxhall Town Coupe, 1937, #18M..$125-150
S. S. United States luxury cruise ship,
    #M704 ....$40-60

Trident

Trident models of Austria are metal cast
1:87 scale modern military vehicles.

Trident Soviet Main Battle Tanks & Self-Propelled Guns

2S1 "Gvozdika" 122mm Howitzer $25-35
2S3 "Akatsiya" 152mm Howitzer............$30-40

T-62 with 115mm Gun $25-35
T-62A with 115mm Gun $25-35
T-64 with 125mm Gun $25-35
T-72 M1 with 125mm Gun $25-35
T-80 ERA with 125mm Gun & Reactive
    Armor.....................................$30-40

Trident Engineering Vehicles

DOK-L Engineering Tractor/End Loader $35-45

Trident Soviet Airborne Assault Weapons

ASU-57 with 57mm Gun........................$18-24
ASU-85 with 85mm Gun.........................$25-35
BMD-2 Airborne Combat Vehicle............$25-35

Trident Soviet Armored Personnel Carriers

BMP-1 Armored with 73mm Gun $25-35
BMP-2 with 30mm Gun $30-40
BRDM-2 Reconaissance Vehicle..............$25-35
BRDM-26 Armored Command Vehicle $25-35
BRM-1 Reconnaissance Vehicle with 73mm
    Gun..$25-35
BTR-60PA Armored $25-35
BTR-60PB Armored $25-35
BTR-70 Armored $25-35
BTR-80 Armored $30-40
MT-LBW Troop Transporter/Artillery
    Tractor....................................$25-35
PTS-M Amphibious Armored...................$40-50

Trident Light Trucks

Chevrolet Blazer..................................$10-15
1987 Chevrolet Suburban USAF Fire
    Truck......................................$10-15
Chevrolet Truck Ambulance....................$10-15
Chevrolet K-10 Blazer Sheriff.................$10-15
Chevrolet K-10 Blazer Park Police $10-15

Troféu

Troféu
c/o Replicar
P O Box 371
4501-912 Espinho, Portugal
fax: 351-22 734 4920

    Troféu of Portugal represents a collection of 1:43 scale diecast models mostly of European rally cars. Just a few models are decorated in numerous colors and markings to form a large assortment.

    I recently e-mailed Vitesse to ask about the connection with Troféu. Paulo Matinha of Vitesse Group wrote back to explain that, in the past, Vitesse shared their sales and distribution with Troféu along with their supply of know-how in diecast. With the change of factory plant to China, Vitesse was forced to stop their cooperation. Troféu remains today as one of the premiere European producers of quality 1:43 scale diecast models.

Alpine Renault A 110
- 1600S Monte Carlo 1972, #807 ....$30-45
- 1800S le Monte Carlo 1973, #810 ..$30-45
- 1800S le TAP Rally 1973, #811 ......$30-45
- 1800S Safari 1974, #812 ....$30-45
- 1800S Nicolas 1973, #813 ....$30-45
- Defense Monte Carlo 1973, #814....$30-45

Fiat 131 Abarth
- "Muleto" (Test car), red $30-45
- Le Mans..$30-45

Ford Sierra Cosworth
- Portugal Crash 1988, #116 ....$30-45
- Ireland McRae 1989, #118 ....$30-45

Ford Escort Mk I
- RS 1600 Broadspeed Fitzpatrick, 1974, #526 ....$30-45
- 1600 TC Silverstone Stewart 1970, #527.......................................$30-45

Ford Escort Mk II
- 1100 Popular 1978, #1001 ....$30-45
- 1300 Ghia 1978, #1002...............$30-45
- 1600 Sport 1978, #1003...............$30-45
- 1600 Harrier 1978, #1004 ....$30-45
- Mexico 1979, #1005.....................$30-45
- 1800RS 1979, #1006 ....$30-45

Porsche 936
- Martini Le Mans 5 Ickx/PesCarolo 1978, #1201 ....$30-45
- Martini Le Mans Wollek 1979, #1202.....................................$30-45
- Essex Le Mans Ickx/Redman 1979, #1203.....................................$30-45
- Essex Le Mans Wollek 1979, #1204...$30-45
- Jules Le Mans Ickx/Bell 1981, #1205 ..$30-45
- Jules Le Mans Mass/Schuppan 1981, #1206..........................$30-45

Porsche LMP1/98
- Carbon Paul Ricard 1998, #1301 ....$30-45
- Le Mans test Alboreto 1998, #1302 ...$30-45
- Le Mans Alboreto/Johanson 1998, #1303.....................................$30-45
- Le Mans Raphanel/Weaver 1998, #1304.....................................$30-45
- Le Mans Road Atlanta Alboreto 1998, #1305.....................................$30-45

Porsche WSC95
- Joest Donington Johansson 1997, #905.......................................$30-45

Saab 96
- Roadcar Standard 1960 ....$30-45
- 1st Monte Carlo 1962 ....$30-45
- 2nd East African Safari 1964 ....$30-45

Subaru Impreza 4x4 Turbo
- RAC Duckworth 1998, #623 ....$30-45
- Police 1997, #624 ....$30-45

Subaru Impreza WRC
- 555 Safari McRae 1997, #1103 .....$30-45
- Portugal C. McRae 1998, #1105.....$30-45
- Monte Carlo Kremer 1997, #1106...$30-45
- Russia Uspenskiy 1998, #1107 ....$30-45
- Q8 San Remo Dallavill 1998, #1108.$30-45
- RAC De Mevius 1998, #1109 ....$30-45

Toyota Celica GT4
- Castrol Safari Duncan 1996, #714 ...$30-45

Tron

Particularly classy are these 1:43 scale models reportedly produced by Angelo or Paolo Tron of Italy, both apparently designers of models for a variety of other companies as well.

1947 Cadillac Series 62 Convertible ..$185-210
1968 Chevrolet Corvette Tour de France Coupe $155-180
1949 Oldsmobile 88 Indy Pace Car...$175-200

Trophy Models

Trophy Models of Great Britain are selected Corgi models that have been gold plated and modified with diecast wire wheels, separate rubber tires and "Trophy Models" imprinted on their bases. They were produced in 1960.

1956 Austin Healey 100 Roadster..........$30-45
1958 BRM Racing Car.........................$30-45
1956 MGA Roadster $30-45
1955 Triumph TR2 Roadster $30-45
1958 Triumph TR3 Roadster $30-45
1957 Vanwall Racing car $30-45

True Dimensions

According to collector Dick Browne, True Dimensions was based in Minnesota. Browne reports, "I have a 1:43 white metal Kaiser-Darrin made by them. They made only 435, which was the exact production of the real car. They used only actual colors. Some of the models were top-up, some top-down, and some half-top. Mine is a pale green half-top. I wrote to them but didn't receive a reply. I imagine they are out of business."

Kaiser-Darrin, 1:43.............................$85-110

Tucker Box (also see Lincoln)

According to an article in *Diecast Collector* magazine by author Robert Newson, (Issue 18, April 1999), five models comprise the Tucker Box Series from Australia, an assortment consisting of fairly crude toys measuring about 2 inches long. Introduced in 1957 according to best information, Tucker Box toys were an Australian attempt to capitalize on the popularity of Matchbox toys from England.

A year later, the five original castings were incorporated into the Lincoln Matchbox Series of New Zealand. The name was changed to Motorway Mini Series under threat of trademark infringement by Lesney Products Company, the legitimate owner of the Matchbox brand until 1982.

The Tucker Box Series

Austin Petrol Tanker, 2¼"..........................$25-40
Fire Engine and ladder, 2" $25-40
Land Rover, 1¾"....................................$25-40
Massey Harris Tractor, 1-5/8"......................$25-40
Sand Truck / Pickup, 2¼"........................$25-40

The Lincoln Matchbox Series

Ambulance, 2⅞" $20-35
Breakdown Truck, 2⅛" $20-35
Dump Truck, 2" $20-35
Jaguar XK120 Roadster, 2⅛" $20-35
Land Liner Coach, 2¼"............................$20-35
Pantechnicon, 2-1/16" $20-35
Racing car, 2".......................................$20-35

Tuff Ones (see Remco)

Tuffy

Tuffy is a brand offered in the 1970s by Centsable Products, Inc., according to collector and writer Mark Rich. No model list is known.

Turner Toys

John C. Turner started independently producing Turner Toys of Ohio in 1915 after working with D. P. Clark and later with the Schieble Toy Company. Turner continued operating out of Dayton and Wapakoneta, Ohio, until the 1940s. Most Turner Toys are pressed steel trucks, but a few cars were made as well.

Ahrens-Fox Ladder Truck, 15", 1920..$1,000-1,200
Ahrens-Fox Pumper, 16"...............$1,500-1,700
Car Carrier $450-600
Crane Truck, 22" $550-650
Delivery Van, 12 1:2", 1920s......$2,000-2,500
Dodge Dump Truck, 28" $300-400
Fire Hook and Ladder Truck, 15".........$475-550
Fire Pumper Truck, 15"................$,1,500-1,750
Fire Pumper Truck, 26"................$1,000-1,250
Garage, 21" x 15" $450-600
Intercity Bus $1,000-1,250

Limousine $4,500-6,000
Lincoln Sedan, 26" $4,500-6,000
Mack Bulldog Dump Truck, 23" $900-1,050
Mack Ladder Truck $500-600
Overland Bus $2,000-3,000
Packard Racer, 26", 1924..........$2,000-2,250
Panel Truck, 13" $450-600
Roadster, 26" $2,000-2,500
Speedster, 17", 1920s...................$900-1,150
Yellow Taxi Cab, 9 ¾", 1927 ....$600-650

Turtle Creek Scale Models, Inc.

Just recently introduced to the 1:16 scale market are two late-model trucks from the new Turtle Creek Scale Models, Inc., of Beloit, Wisconsin. Seeing a niche for such a high-end model to accompany 1:16 scale tractor and farm equipment models, Gene Arner, who has worked for General Motors in their Kodiak/Topkick plant for 30 years, has reproduced this truck in two versions, a stake truck and a milk truck. The distinction of these new models is accuracy, detail, and workmanship. Made of spin-cast metal, trucks retail for $500 each, with a production limit of just 400 each, with a ratio of three Topkicks to one Kodiak, the same ratio in which the real ones are produced at GM.
Turtle Creek Models
2420 East Ridge Rd.
Beloit, WI 53511 USA
phone: 608-365-0579

GMC Topkick
    Milk Truck, 1:16, 300 produced ...$500-600
    Stake Bed Truck, 1:16, 300
        produced..........................$500-600
GMC Kodiak
    Milk Truck, 1:16, 100 produced ...$700-800
    Stake Bed Truck, 1:16, 100
        produced..........................$700-800

U

Uaz

Uaz of Russia at one produced a small series of metal cast 1:43 scale models.

Jeep, #469
    Baggy..................................$16-20
    Fire $16-20
    Military Covered $16-20
    Military Open.....................................$16-20
    Military Police $16-20
    Russian Traffic Police $16-20
    Traffic Police with horn $16-20
    UN $16-20
    with heavy-duty bumper.....................$16-20

Standard D Truck, #452 ....$12-16

Unique Industries, Inc.

Unique Industries, Inc.
Philadelphia, PA 19148 USA
Unique Party Favors
Etobicoke, Ontario
M9W 5T6 Canada
Unique Industries
Schrijnwererstraat 2
2984 BC Ridderkerk
Rotterdam Port Area
The Netherlands

Unique Industries produces a variety of inexpensive party favors. Among the assortment are some four-car sets of simple diecast vehicles. They are considered generic, and are rendered so once removed from the colorful blisterpack. Even though the cars are stylized "chubby" designs, the eight models are barely identifiable as a Porsche racer, Morris Mini, pickup truck, Volkswagen Beetle, Ferrari, sports car, compact car, and van. Value will likely remain low on these models made in China, but they are charming yet inexpensive additions to a collection of toys.

Compact Car $1-2
Morris Mini $1-2
Pickup Truck $1-2
Porsche Racer $1-2
Sports Car $1-2
Volkswagen Beetle..........................$1-2
Van $1-2

Universal (also see Matchbox)

David Yeh is, or at least in 1982 was, the C.E.O of Universal Holdings of Hong Kong. Among his 1980s acquisitions were such brands as Kidco, Champion of the Road, Kresge, Dinky Toys, and Matchbox which he held until selling the brand to Tyco in 1992. Kidco Lock-Ups and Burnin' Key Cars were briefly incorporated into the Matchbox line, as well as Dinky Toys, during that time.

Universal Hobbies Ltd., Inc. (also see Eagle Collectibles/Eagle's Race)

In 1999, Great Planes/Hobbico became the exclusive licensed distributor for Universal Hobbies and its Eagle's Race brand of diecast models in 1:43 and 1:18 scale. See Eagle's Race for a list of models and prices.

Uralskiy Sokol

Alex Litovskiy reports of the Uralskiy Sokol

brand from Russia but doesn't provide any details.

U.S.A. Models (also see Motor City, Design Studios)

USA Models are less detailed and much less expensive models than their Motor City and Design Studios counterparts, but still represent some fabulous models not commonly reproduced in miniature. The first release (USA-1) is a 1958 Cadillac Series 75 Limousine, in dark metallic blue finish, introduced in 1997, originally retailed for $79.

1958 Cadillac Series 75 Limousine
    dark metallic blue, USA 1 ....$80-95
    silver with black roof, USA 1A.........$85-100
1951 Chevrolet Bel Air 2-door, two-tone
    green, USA 4 ....$85-100
1954 Chevrolet Bel Air 4-door, brown and
    beige, USA 5 ....$85-100
1955 Chrysler Imperial, dark gray, USA
    2F..$85-100
1940 Ford 2-door Sedan, USA 11 ....$95-110
1950 Ford Custom Coupe, burgundy,
    USA 8 ....$85-100
1949 Mercury 2-door Custom, burgundy,
    USA 9 ....$85-100
1949 Nash Ambassador
    maroon, USA 3..............................$80-95
Los Angeles Police, black and white,
    USA 3P...$85-100
Yellow Cab, yellow, USA 3T..............$85-100
1941 Willys Coupe Street Rod, red,
    USA 10 ....$80-95

U.S. Model Mint (also see SMTS)

U.S. Model Mint
P O Box 505
Granger, IN 46530 USA

U.S. Model Mint models are white metal scale models in 1:43 scale similar to Brooklins, Durham, and others. They are distinguished by their beautifully represented cars of U.S. origin.

While the U.S. headquarters are in Granger, Indiana, U.S. Model Mint cars are made by SMTS of England.

1956 Chevrolet Bel Air
    Convertible, top down, two-tone turquoise
        and white, US-3 ....$100-125
    Convertible, top up, two-tone red and
        white, US-4 ....$100-125
    Hardtop, two-tone cream and black,
        US-1 ....$100-125

1950 Ford
    F-1 Pickup, red, US-2 ....$100-125
    Telephone Truck, dark green, "Bell
        Systems," US-10 ....$100-125
1969 Plymouth GTX, US-16 ....$100-125
1954 Studebaker Conestoga Station
    Wagon, baby blue, US-13 ....$100-125
1949 Willys
    Overland Jeepster, top down, cream
        with black interior, US-5 ....$100-125
    Overland Jeepster, top up, green with
        black top, US-6 ....$100-125
    Overland Jeepster Station Wagon, burgundy
        with wood paneling, US-7 ......$100-125
    Panel Delivery, red, "Drewry's Beer,"
        US-8 ....$100-125
    Panel Delivery, yellow, "Sterling Beer,"
        US-12 ....$100-125

UT

Gateway Global USA, Inc.
10485 NW 28th St
Miami, FL 33172-2152 USA
Gateway Global of Europe GmbH
Postfach 485
D-52005
Aachen, Germany
Gateway Global Limited
3/F, 8 Yip Cheong Street
On Lok Tsuen, Fanling
New Territories, Hong Kong

    Unique Toys (HK) Limited of China, otherwise known as UT, is the manufacturer of exceptional scale models. In 1999, UT was purchased by Gateway Global and incorporated into their product line along with their new Gate and AUTOart brands.

UT 1:18 Scale Models

Benetton B193, Patrese '93 ....$30-35
BMW E36 3-Series
    Cabriolet, black with cream interior,
        #20456 ....$30-35
    Coupe, yellow, #20451 ....$30-35
    Coupe, silver, #20452 ....$30-35
    318is Saloon, red, #20461 ....$30-35
    318is Saloon, white, #20462 ....$30-35
BMW E36 M3
    Convertible, violet, #20471 ....$30-35
    Convertible, blue, #20472 ....$30-35
    Convertible, yellow, #20473 ....$30-35
    Coupe, blue, 20467 ....$30-35
    Coupe, black, #20468 ....$30-35
    Coupe, yellow, #20466 ....$30-35
    GTR, black, #20481 ....$30-35
    GTR, white, #20482 ....$30-35

Saloon, white, #20476 ....$30-35
BMW E46 3-Series
    328i Saloon 6-cylinder, silver,
        #20512 ....$30-35
    4-door Sedan, #20511 ....$30-35
    Saloon, red, #20511 ....$30-35
    Saloon, silver, #20512 ....$30-35
BMW Z3
    1996 Roadster, James Bond metallic light
        blue with gray interior, #20400 ...$30-35
    1996 Roadster, red with gray/black
        interior, #20401 ....$30-35
    1996 Roadster 2.8, silver, #20402 ..$30-35
    1996 Roadster, baby blue, #20403 .$30-35
    Coupe, black with dark gray/black
        interior, #20422 ....$30-35
    Coupe 2.8, metallic silver, #20421 ...$30-35
    M Coupe, black with red/black
        interior, #20432 ....$30-35
    M Coupe, blue with black/gray
        interior, #20431 ....$30-35
    M Roadster, metallic blue with black/
        gray interior, #20412 ....$30-35
    M Roadster, red with red/gray interior ..$30-35
Chevrolet Caprice 1995
    Brea Police, black and white, #21022 ..$30-35
    Brossard, Quebec, Canada Police, white,
        #21023 ....$30-35
    Cheyenne Police, white, #21025 ......$30-35
    Chicago Police, white, #21020 ....$30-35
    Glendale Police, black and white,
        #21026 ....$30-35
    Miami Police, #21024 ....$30-35
    Metro–Dade Miami Police, white,
        #21025 ....$30-35
    New York Police, blue and white,
        #21021 ....$30-35
    New York City Taxi, yellow, #21011 .$30-35
    New York City Taxi, yellow, #21012 .$30-35
    Sebring Police, white, #21029 ....$30-35
    Watkins Glen Police, white, #21028 ..$30-35
Chevrolet Corvette
    1978 Coupe, black, #21071 ....$30-35
    1978 Pace car, black upper, gray lower
        body, #21070 ....$30-35
    1978 Coupe, red $30-35
    1978 Coupe, silver, #21072 ....$30-35
    1978 Coupe, yellow $30-35
    1998 Convertible, black, #21007 ....$30-35
    1998 Convertible, metallic lavender
        gray, #21010 ....$30-35
    1998 Convertible, red, #21006 ....$30-35
    1998 Convertible, silver, #21008 .....$30-35
    1998 Convertible, white, #21009 ....$30-35
    1998 Coupe, red, #21001 ....$30-35
    1998 Coupe, black, #21002 ....$30-35

    1998 Coupe, silver with black roof,
        21003 ....$30-35
    1998 Coupe, blue, #21004 ....$30-35
    1998 Coupe, silver, #21005 ....$30-35
    1999 Hardtop, black, #21042 ......$30-35
    1999 Hardtop, red, #21041 ....$30-35
    1999 Hardtop, silver, #21043 ....$30-35
    Mako Shark, blue upper to silver lower
        body, #21061 ....$30-35
Chevrolet Impala SS 1996
    black, #21031 ....$30-35
    metallic blue, #21032 ....$30-35
Ferrari 550 Maranello 1996
    red, #22121 ....$30-35
    silver, #22122 ....$30-35
Ferrari F355 Berlinetta 1994 Coupe
    red, #22101 ....$30-35
    yellow, #22102 ....$30-35
    black, #22103 ....$30-35
Ferrari F355 1994
    GTS, red, #22111 ....$30-35
    GTS, yellow, #22112 ....$30-35
    Spider, red, #22106 ....$30-35
Ford Escort RS Cosworth 1992
    black, #22704 ....$30-35
    red, #22701 ....$30-35
    Navy blue, #22702 ....$30-35
    white, #22703 ....$30-35
Ford Escort WRC 1997, silver, #22706 ...$30-35
Ford Expedition
    Eddie Bauer, black, #22710 ....$30-35
    Eddie Bauer, metallic red, #22711 ....$30-35
    Eddie Bauer, white, #22712 ....$30-35
    XLT, metallic teal blue, #22717 ....$30-35
    XLT, silver, #22716 ....$30-35
McLaren F1
    GTR 1996 Road car, pale orange,
        #26006 ....$30-35
    GTR 1997 Road car, black, #26011 ...$30-35
    Road car, silver, #26001 ....$30-35
Mercedes-Benz C 36 AMG
    black, #36102 ....$30-35
    silver, #26101 ....$30-35
    Safety car, silver, #26106 ....$30-35
Mercedes-Benz SLK AMG
    blue, #26153 ....$30-35
    red, #26154 ....$30-35
    silver, #26151 ....$30-35
    yellow, #26152 ....$30-35
Porsche 911 GT1 1996 Street
    metallic bright blue, #27842 ....$30-35
    silver, #27846 ....$30-35
    white, #27841 ....$30-35
Porsche 911 GT2
    red, #27833 ....$30-35
    silver, #27831 ....$30-35

yellow, #27832 ....$30-35
Porsche 911 Turbo
    black, #27812 ....$30-35
    light burgundy, #27811 ....$30-35
    silver, #27813 ....$30-35
    S, pale yellow, #27836 ....$30-35
Porsche 993
    Cabriolet, black, #27806 ....$30-35
    Cabriolet, burgundy, #27808 ....$30-35
    Cabriolet, silver, #27807 ....$30-35
    Carrera S, burgundy, #27827 ....$30-35
    Carrera S, metallic purple, #27828 ...$30-35
    Carrera S, silver, #27826 ....$30-35
    Coupe, light blue, #27801 ....$30-35
    Coupe, silver with black interior,
        #27802 ....$30-35
    Coupe, silver with tan interior,
        #27803 ....$30-35
    RS, bright blue, #27818................$30-35
    RS, red, #27816 ....$30-35
    RS, white, #27817 ....$30-35
    Targa, red, #27821 ....$30-35
Porsche 996
    Cabriolet, metallic dark blue, #27907 ...$30-35
    Cabriolet, yellow, #27906...............$30-35
    Coupe, black, #27902 ....$30-35
    Coupe, metallic green, #27901 ....$30-35
Porsche Boxster
    black, #27853 ....$30-35
    red, #27851 ....$30-35
    silver, #27852 ....$30-35
Sauber C12
    Wendinger '93 ....$30-35
    Frentzen '93 ....$30-35
    Lehto '93 ....$30-35
Volkswagen 1999 New Beetle...............$30-35
Williams FW15
    Hill '93.....................................$30-35
    Prost '93 ....$30-35

V

Vanguard (see Lledo)

Vanbo (also Vanke)

Manufacturers in China are realizing the growing popularity of quality diecast toys and models, and they are capitalizing on the trend. One of the newest such companies, begun in 1995, is ShenzhenVanke Fine Products Manufacture Company of Shenzhen, in the Peoples Republic of China. According to literature provided by Tom Hammel, editor of *Collecting Toys* magazine, Vanke produces a varied assortment of presentation pieces, model vehicles, and ornaments under the brand name Vanbo. Besides fine quality diecast cars and trucks, Vanke also pro-

duces fine award plaques, trophies, medals, sundials, desk sets, silver plates, clocks, globes, even presentation daggers, as well as other unusual items, all cast metal. Vanke even produced a model of Leonardo DaVinci's Flying Machine.

Vanbo car and truck models range from 1:12 to 1:87 scale. The RE series is designated exclusively for OEM and ODM sales (original manufacturer and dealerships only). The Mercedes-Benz 500K and Black Prince, model numbers 97002 and 97003 respectively, appear to be the two popular models that were recently issued by CMC of Germany. Both models won Vanke the "Best Model Medals of 1995 and 1996" by Mercedes GmbH.

No prices were included in the Vanke literature, so I've made an educated estimate for current values.

Benz First Automobile, 97001, 1:10, 1997
    issue $175-225
BMW Motorcycle, 96010, 1:12, 1996
    issue $35-45
Bugatti Royale Coupe Napoleon, RE003,
    1:18 ....$90-120
Cadillac circa 1910, RE005, 1:24........$75-90
Datong Tipping Lorry, 95050, 1:43, 1995
    issue $20-25
Fire Truck, 96046, 1:43, 1996 issue......$20-25
Jiefang (Liberation)
    Army Truck, 95030, 1:43, 1995
        issue................................$20-25
    Cannon Truck, 95035, 1:43, 1995
        issue................................$20-25
    Tip Truck, 95020, 1:43, 1995 issue...$20-25
    Tower Truck, 96088, 1:43, 1996 issue ...$20-25
Hispano-Suiza Open Boattail Roadster
    circa 1925, RE004, 1:24 ....$75-90
Hongqi (Red Flag) Car CA7220
    96121, 1:24, 1996 issue $20-25
    sterling silver on stand, 95010, 1:87,
        1995 issue $90-120
Mercedes-Benz 500K, 97002, 1:24,
    1997 issue...............................$125-150
Mercedes-Benz 770K circa 1920, RE002,
    1:24 ....$75-90
Mercedes-Benz Black Prince, 97003,
    1:24, 1997 issue $125-150
Rolls-Royce Silver Ghost circa 1915,
    RE001, 1:24 ....$75-90
Santana 2000, gold on stand, 95011,
    1:87, 1995 issue $250-300
Tanker Truck, 95045, 1:43, 1995 issue ...$20-25

Vanke (see Vanbo)

Vaz (see Lada)

Vector

Alex Litovskiy reports of the Vector brand from Ukraine but doesn't provide any details.

Verem

Verem of France is a producer of high quality low-cost models in 1:43 scale. Many models from Solido have been used to create Verem models. It is reported that Verems are higher quality than their Solido counterparts, comparable to the detailing done on Matchbox models by White Rose Collectibles. Cofradis is another company that uses modified Solido models. Verem is now part of the Ideal Loisirs toy empire of France, owner of Majorette, Novacar, Norev, Solido, and Mira brands.

4-Piece "Pinder Circus" Set, #950 ....$55-65
Alfa Romeo GTZ, green, #605 ....$20-25
Alpine A110, blue, #701 ....$20-25
Alpine A110, red, #650 ....$20-25
Cadillac Harlem 1931 Hearse, white,
    #307 ....$20-25
Chevrolet Camaro 1984, yellow, #506 ..$20-25
Citroën 11BL Circus, #91 ....$20-25
Citroën C4 Circus Truck, #93 ....$20-25
Citroën C4 Circus Van, #92.................$20-25
Citroën C4 Fire Ladder Truck, #102 ....$20-25
Citroën C4 Fire Van, #101 ....$20-25
Citroën C4 Fire Van, #104 ....$20-25
Citroën Fire Ambulance, #7 ....$20-25
Citroën Fire Ladder, #10 ....$20-25
Citroën Fire Van, #6 ....$20-25
Citroën SM, #402 ....$20-25
Delahaye Convertible, top down, #305 ...$20-25
Ferrari Berlinetta Boxer, red, #411 ....$20-25
Ferrari Daytona, red, #408 ....$20-25
Ferrari Daytona, yellow, #409 ....$20-25
Gulf Mirage 1974, blue, #611 ....$20-25
Lancia Stratos, black, #651 ....$20-25
Lancia Stratos, blue, #704 ....$20-25
Lola T280, yellow, #606 ....$20-25
Maserati Indy Coupe, #404 ....$20-25
Mercedes 1928 Convertible, top up, #301 ..$20-25
Oldsmobile Toronado 1966, #407 ....$20-25
Panhard 24BT, #312 ....$20-25
Peugeot 604, gold, #501 ....$20-25
Porsche 914, yellow, #413 ....$20-25
Porsche 928, black, #508 ....$20-25
Porsche Can Am 1973, white, #608 ......$20-25
Porsche Carrera, white, #412 ....$20-25
Porsche Carrera, white, #607 ....$20-25
Renault Reina Circus, #94 ....$20-25
Rolls Royce Silver Cloud, gold, #310.......$20-25

VF-Modelautomobile Germany

VF Modellautomobile
P O Box 100 618
D-52306 Düren, Germany

"VF" are the initials of Volker G. Feldkamp, proprietor of VF-Modelautomobile. The German company produces handmade white metal sedans, convertibles, stretch limousines, hearses, and ambulances. Cadillac, Lincoln, Rolls Royce, and Bentley, as well as DeLorean, Kaiser, Oldsmobile, Ford Thunderbird, Buick, Mercedes, all of the James Bond cars, and more, are all replicated in 1:43 scale and presented in wood-and-acrylic dustproof showcases, personalized for your collection or as an award. Each model is produced in quantities of no more than 100.

1959 Cadillac Hearse, Hess & Eisenhardt
    Coachwork, black with red interior,
    VF-CC0004 ....$260-285
1960 Cadillac Fleetwood 75 Limousine,
    black with red interior, or metallic dark red
    with black interior, VF-0005 ....$280-310
1971 Cadillac Eldorado Convertible, 5
    colors available, VF-AMC0001....$200-225
1996 Cadillac Catera Sedan $250-280

Victoria (also see Vitesse)

Although a brand of Vitesse, Victoria models hold their own in the collector market, so they are listed below as a separate and distinct line from Vitesse.

Chevy, 1944 8A Canvas Truck British Army
    Normandy, #R050...........................$22-26
Chevy, 1944 8A Canvas Truck Canadian
    Army D-Day 1944, #R051...............$22-26
Chevy, 1944 8A Troop Carrier Truck U.S.
    Army, #R052..................................$22-26
Citroën U23 FFI with Camouflage, #R043 ..$22-26
Citroën U23 French Army Troop Carrier,
    #R042...$22-26
Citroën U23 Troop Carrier Wehrmacht,
    #R044...$22-26
Dodge 1944 WC52 Weapons Carrier
    Liberation of Paris, #R048 ....$22-26
Dodge 1944 WC56 Command Car U.S.
    Army D-Day 1944, #R055...............$22-26
Dodge WC51 Weapons Carrier U.S. Army,
    Closed, #R047 ....$22-26
Dodge WC51 Weapons Carrier U.S. Army,
    open, #R046..................................$22-26
Dodge WC56 Command Car U.S. Army,
    Closed, #R053 ....$22-26
Dodge WC56 Command Car U.S. Army,
    open, #R054..................................$22-26

GMC CCKW353 6x6 Canvas Covered
    Truck U.S Army, #R058.................$22-26
GMC CCKW353 6x6 Canvas Covered
    Truck U.S. Army, #R056................$22-26
GMC CCKW353 6x6 Troop Carrier Truck
    D-Day 1944, #R057 ....$22-26
Hummer, #R00494 United Nations UN white
    2 door covered top.........................$24-28
Hummer Ambulance U.S. Army
    Camouflage, #R038 ....$22-26
Hummer Ambulance U.S. Army Desert Storm,
    #R039...$22-26
Hummer Command Car GulfWar Desert Storm
    MP, #R018 ....$22-26
Hummer open pick-up US NAVY, #R030...$22-26
Hummer Pickup US Camouflage, Desert Storm,
    #R024...$22-26
Hummer, 1994 U.S. Army Camouflage 4 door
    All Purpose, #R007........................$22-26
Hummer, 1994 U.S. Army Desert Storm
    Open All Purpose, brown, #R005......$32-36
Hummer, 1994 U.S. Army green 2 door
    open back All Purpose, #R006..........$22-26
Jeep GPA Amphibian, British, #R034......$22-26
Jeep GPA Amphibian, U.S. Army, #R032...$22-26
Jeep GPA Amphibian, U.S. Army, camouflage,
    #R033...$22-26
Jeep, 1944 Willys closed khaki, D-Day
    version, #R001 ....$22-26
Jeep, 1944 Willys open khaki Liberation of
    Paris, #R002 ....$22-26
Jeep, 1945 Willys open khaki, #R003
    Military Police $22-26
Jeep, 1978 Willys UN Lebanon, white with
    figures, #R023 ....$22-26
Jeep, US Army, Normandy 1944 Ambulance
    with figures, #R028 ....$22-26
Jeep, Willys Armoured car General LeClerc,
    #R017...$22-26
Mercedes 170V Afrika Korps, #R011......$22-26
Mercedes 170V cabrio limosine, #R012
    Wehrmacht parade $22-26
Mercedes 170V Wehrmacht with
    Camouflage, #R029 ....$22-26
Opel Blitz 3.5 Ton Ambulance Afrika
    Korps, #R026................................$22-26
Opel Blitz 3.5 Ton Canvas Covered
    Truck, #R021 ....$22-26
Opel Blitz 3.5 Ton Canvas Covered Truck
    Afrika Korps, #R020 ....$22-26
Opel Blitz 3.5 Ton Radio HQ
    Wehrmacht, #R025 ....$22-26
Opel Blitz 3.5 Ton Troop Carrier,
    #R019...$22-26
Renault Prairie Ambulance French
    Army, #R041 ....$22-26

Renault Prairie Command car French
    Army, #R040 ....$22-26
    unknown, #R027 ....$22-26
Volkswagen Beetle, #R01482E Afghan
    Beetle Army tan Coupe...................$22-26
Volkswagen Cabrio Hebmuller Military
    Police, doors, #R049 ....$22-26
Volkswagen Cabrio Hebmuller Military
    Police, no doors, #R045 ....$22-26
Volkswagen Kubelwagen Closed
    Normandy 1944 with Camouflage,
    #R031...$22-26
Volkswagen Kubelwagen Factory Test car,
    #R022...$22-26
Volkswagen Schwimmwagen, Afrika Korps,
    #R036...$22-26
Volkswagen Schwimmwagen, open, #R035
    gray $22-26
Volkswagen Schwimmwagen, Wehrmacht, top
    up, #R037 ....$22-26
VW, 1944 Beetle, #R015 Type 92 Wehrmacht
    charcoal burner $22-26
VW, 1944 Beetle, #R016 Type 92 2 door,
    black tire on roof...........................$22-26
VW, 1945 Beetle Kubelwagen Afrika Korps,
    Open, #R008.................................$22-26
VW, 1945 Beetle Kubelwagen, Wehrmacht,
    Open, #R009.................................$22-26
VW, 1945 Beetle Kubelwagen, closed, Hitler
    Yugend, #R010 ....$22-26
VW, 1945 Beetle Type 82e Wehrmacht,
    #R013...$22-26

Viking

There are actually two toy companies named Viking.

Viking Modell of Germany

Viking Modell, alternately marked Viking Model, was a German manufacturer of crude pot metal ships. Some are imprinted with "German Made," others "Made in Germany." Most are replicas of pre-WWII ships.

Viking of Ohio

One example is known from this company, a 27 inch long dump truck, presumably made of pressed steel. Vintage is unknown but presumed to be from the late 1940s or 1950s.

Dump Truck, 27 inches $1,200-1,450

Vilmer

Thanks to an article by Karl Schnelle dated February 10, 1995, titled "Vilmer Kvalitet," a short history of Vilmers is extracted below.

Production of Vilmer diecast model cars of Denmark started in 1955 or 1956 and lasted until 1966. The first models produced were Dodge trucks. These trucks were based on the same molds used for the Tekno Dodge series of the 1950s (Tekno of Denmark #948-958). Similar to the Tekno philosophy, the same cab and chassis were attached to every type body imaginable, all roughly 112 mm long.

There are three small differences between the Teknos and the Vilmers that help the collector easily tell which is which. The obvious difference is that the Tekno baseplate was changed to read Vilmer in the script style font used on all their models and boxes. Also, the Vilmer versions use a spare tire and wheel on top of the cab to control the steering; Tekno usually employs a spotlight for this purpose. The military Vilmer Dodges may use a tire, machine gun, or spotlight while the military Tekno use a machine gun. Finally, the Tekno versions appear to have an extra brace across the chassis under the rear wheels.

As companions to the 112 mm Dodges, a smaller range was also made. All the small Dodge trucks (military and civilian)are 98 mm and have a spare tire on the roof to control steering the front wheels. The spare wheel has a script "Vilmer" across the center while the four actual wheels have five cast lug nuts instead.

All the wheels are metal except for the military version which has olive drab plastic wheels of the same design. At least one version has no steering. These smaller Dodges are slightly bigger than the small Tekno Dodge trucks. The small Vilmer appear to be scaled-down versions of the larger Dodge, as opposed to a copy of the small Teknos. Both the small and large have "Vilmer Made in Denmark" on the baseplate under the cab. A tinplate grill is attached using three tabs to the front of both size Dodges. They also both use two white plastic headlights.

In 1957, Vilmer introduced a limited number of automobile models. The Vilmer W196R was said to be a copy of the Marklin version.

During 1957 to 1960, the series of Chevrolet 6400 trucks were produced which use many of the same bodies as the larger Dodge models and use a spare wheel or a machine gun for steering the front wheels.

After 1960, both Volvo and Mercedes-Benz trucks were made. Some of the best castings exist on these chassis. Not surprisingly the Vilmer versions were cruder than the Tekno castings but did include opening doors and hood on the Volvo and an opening hood on the Mercedes. Both the Volvo and Mercedes have the follow-ing components: plastic grill, clear plastic headlights, plastic wheels, plastic tail pipe and rear transmission, and front and rear suspension.

The Ford Thames Trader was introduced in 1964. Only four different models have been identified, which seems to make the Ford much rarer than the other models. The Ford had "Thames Trader" cast into the front of the cab above the grill. The grill was made up of a wide plastic insert with two clear headlights. All other models had only "Vilmer" and "Made in Denmark" somewhere on the base.

Because of the competition from Tekno, Vilmer ceased production in 1966. It appears that the Mercedes truck molds went to Metosul in Portugal and then on to Chico in Columbia. The baseplates were changed by both companies to update the manufacturer's name and country of origin. Chico also obtained the Volvo and Thames Trader molds at some point.

Mr. Schnelle cites the following as references and sources for the information he has compiled: Bertrand du Chambon, Frits Monsted, Bjorn Schultz, James Greenfield, and Richard Lay; Clive Chick (1989), *Made in Denmark, Part Three;* Horst Macalka (1990), *Catalog Corner;* Karl Schnelle (1990), *Vilmer & Airports;* anonymous (1957, 1964), *Legetojs-Tidende,* Danish toy wholesalers magazine, various pages.

While Mr. Schnelle's original article included many details not mentioned here, he did not offer values, current or otherwise. So an educated guess of $45–60 for each model is provided based on the quality and rarity of this series. Some models are likely worth as much as $90–100 or more, depending on collector interest, availability, quality, and condition.

Austin Champion (open)
blue, #580 .... $45-60
military, #580 .... $45-60
military with single gun in rear $45-60
Baggage cart, blue, yellow driver, suitcase, #339 .... $45-60
Bedford Truck
cattle transport, 1965, #620 .... $45-60
cattle truck (3-axle) and trailer, #621 ... $45-60
cement mixer, with chute, #677 .... $45-60
covered truck, #668 .... $45-60
dropside truck with MEJERIET milk tank, #624 .... $45-60
flat truck for milk, #624 .... $45-60
flat truck for milk with trailer, #625 ...... $45-60
gas tanker, Esso BENZIN SMOREOLIE (red), #672 .... $45-60

gas tanker, SHELL, #672 .... $45-60
military 4-cannon truck, #657 .... $45-60
military covered truck, #664 .... $45-60
military dropside truck, #663 .... $45-60
military dropside truck (3-axle)............ $45-60
military gas tanker, #654 .... $45-60
military searchlight, #658 .... $45-60
military tow truck (crane), #656.......... $45-60
military twin 40mm guns.................. $45-60
multi-rocket launcher (3 axle)............. $45-60
open truck, #671 .... $45-60
Red Cross covered truck, #665.......... $45-60
single canon truck, #661 .... $45-60
single-missile truck, #662 .... $45-60
spotlight truck, #670 .... $45-60
ten rocket launcher, #660 .... $45-60
tow truck, #669 .... $45-60
Chevrolet Truck
3-rocket truck, 1957-60, #455.......... $45-60
4-cannon truck, 1957-60, #457 .... $45-60
cement mixer with chute on back, #477 .... $45-60
cement truck, 2 round tanks, #476 ..... $45-60
covered truck, #468....................... $45-60
crane truck (wrecker), #469.............. $45-60
dropside truck, milk containers, #467 .. $45-60
dump truck with shovel, #474 .... $45-60
gas tanker, Esso, #472E.................. $45-60
gas tanker, SHELL, #472S................ $45-60
gas truck, military, #572 .... $45-60
military dropside truck, #463 .... $45-60
military spot light truck, with man, 1957, #458 .... $45-60
military tanker, #454 .... $45-60
open truck, #471........................... $45-60
Red Cross covered truck, #465.......... $45-60
single-cannon truck, 1957, #461 ..... $45-60
single-rocket truck, 1957, #462........ $45-60
spotlight truck, #470 .... $45-60
ten-rocket launcher, 1957-60, #460 ..$45-60
Dodge Truck
2-cannon truck, with man, 1955-6, #457.. $45-60
Carlsberg high-sided truck (with cover), 98 mm, #34x $45-60
cattle truck, 98 mm, #342 .... $45-60
cement truck, 1 round tank 1957, 98 mm, #350.......................... $45-60
crane truck (wrecker), #469.............. $45-60
dropside truck, 98 mm, #348 .... $45-60
flatbed with tailboard, 98 mm, #347...$45-60
flatbed, 98 mm, #341 .... $45-60
gas truck, 98 mm, #34x $45-60
ladder truck $45-60
military cattle truck, 98 mm, #542.....$45-60
military crane truck, 1955-56, #456 ..$45-60

military dropside truck, 1957, #463...$45-60
military dropside, 98 mm, #548........$45-60
military flatbed with tailboard, 98 mm,
   #547....................................$45-60
military flatbed, 98 mm, #541..........$45-60
military spot light truck, with man, #458...$45-60
military stake (timber) truck, 98 mm,
   #540....................................$45-60
military tarp covered truck, 1957, #464 ..$45-60
military towtruck, 98 mm, #546........$45-60
military wooden barrel truck, 98 mm,
   #545....................................$45-60
radar truck, with man, 1957, #459 ...$45-60
spotlight truck, with man $45-60
stake (timber) truck, 98 mm, #340......$45-60
tow truck, 98 mm, #346 ....$45-60
wooden barrel truck, 98 mm, #345 ...$45-60
Ford Thames Truck
   bucket truck, #720.....................$45-60
   cable truck, #730.......................$45-60
   crane FALCK, 1964, #725 ....$45-60
   truck with magnet, 1964, #725 .....$45-60
Ford Tractor, #578.............................$45-60
Lambretta Scooter, yellow $45-60
Massey Ferguson Tractor, 1965, #575 ...$45-60
Mercedes-Benz
   220, 1957 ....$45-60
   W196R, 1957 ....$45-60
Mercedes-Benz Truck
   cattle truck, 1965, #862 ....$45-60
   dump truck with front shovel, 1965,
      #856.................................$45-60
   FALCK tow truck...........................$45-60
   ladder truck, 1965, #857 ....$45-60
   military tarp covered, 1965, #854 ....$45-60
   milk truck, 1965, #851 ....$45-60
   Red Cross covered truck, 1965, #853 .$45-60
   refuse truck FODERBUS or plain, 1964,
      #855.................................$45-60
   SWISSAIR................................$45-60
   tarp covered truck, 1964, #852........$45-60
   tipping truck, 1965, #850 ....$45-60
   dump truck, #710 ....$45-60
Opel Record 1960
   sedan..................................$45-60
   station wagon, 1960 ....$45-60
Renault 4 CV, 1957, #475 ....$45-60
trailer for tractor, #576......................$45-60
Volvo (I) Truck
   covered truck, ASG $45-60
   covered truck, SABENA $45-60
   covered truck, plain $45-60
   flatbed and trailer, ramps, chocks $45-60
   flatbed with chains and trailer............$45-60
   flatbed, lowering sides, plain or DSB...$45-60
   tanker and trailer, SHELL, Esso, BP.......$45-60

Volvo 98 mm Truck
   covered truck, plain or KLM $45-60
   covered, Red Cross, white.................$45-60
   dropside, plain, BEA or Esso.............$45-60
   dump truck with shovel $45-60
   dumping cement truck, CRO BRETON ..$45-60
   ladder truck, FALCK, 1966, #2724 ...$45-60
   military....................................$45-60
   milk truck $45-60
   stake truck $45-60
Volvo Truck
   cattle truck, 1966, #2655 ....$45-60
   cement tipper, 1966, #2820............$45-60
   flatbed, small crane and tire bar, FALCK...$45-60
   milk truck, 1966, #2651 ....$45-60
   tarp covered truck (military), 1966,
      #2652................................$45-60
   tipping truck, 1966, #2723...............$45-60
   tow truck FALCK with crane,tow bar, 1966,
      #2722................................$45-60
Volvo PV 444, 1957, #444 ....$45-60

Vintage Casting

Located in New Jersey, Vintage Casting manufactures slushmold reproductions of Barclay and other toys from the 40s and 50s.

1940 Buick Special.............................$15-20

Vitesse (also see Onyx, Quartzo, Trofeu, Victoria)

Vitesse Group
Cinerius Ltd.
P O Box 106
4471 Maia Codex Portugal
fax: 351-2-9017464
e-mail: vitesse.group@mail.telepac.pt
website: www.vitessegroup.com

Vitesse (French for "Speed") is a popular brand of 1:43 scale models from Portugal. Victoria models are military models produced by Vitesse. See Victoria listing for more information. Other specialty offerings from Vitesse Group include Quartzo (NASCAR), Onyx (Formula One racers), Trofeu (rally and street), and Victoria (military).

Vitesse has since been purchased by Chrono, which in turn has been purchased by Sun Star, according to reliable sources. Quartzo, Onyx, Victoria, and Trofeu are reportedly still functioning separately.

Vitesse

Alfa Romeo 2000 Veloce 1971 Open Convertible, red, VCC99024 ....$25-35
Alfa Romeo Spider Duetto 1966
   Closed Cabriolet, yellow, VCC99007 ...$25-35

Hard top, ivory white, VCC99047 ....$25-35
Aston Martin DB4GT Zagato
   180L Kerguen Le Mans 1961,
      VCC99001 ....$25-35
   181L 1961, dark blue, VCC99026 ..$25-35
   182R Fiarman-Consten Le Mans 1961,
      VCC99043 ....$25-35
Aston Martin DB5
   "Paris-Peking" 1998VCC99012 ......$25-35
   1963, metallic silver gray, V98029 ...$25-35
   1963, peony red, V98079 ....$25-35
Austin Healey 3000
   1959 Open Convertible, black and
      Colorado red, VCC99019.........$25-35
   1963, open top, #15 ....$25-35
Austin Van Den Plas 1300 1963, dark
   metallic brown, VCC99034 ....$25-35
Buick Roadmaster 1958 2-door Coupe,
   #38 ....$25-35
Buick Special 1950 Convertible, #23......$25-35
   closed top, #451 ....$25-35
   open top, #450 ....$25-35
Cadillac 4 Carrera 1953 Panamerican,
   #40 ....$25-35
Cadillac Coupe, #282.........................$25-35
Cadillac Eisenhower, #286....................$25-35
Cadillac Eldorado
   open top, #280 ....$25-35
   1953 with Continental Kit, #50 ....$25-35
Cadillac Fire Department, #284..............$25-35
Chevrolet Bel Air 1955
   Open Convertible, coral red,
      VCC99017..........................$25-35
   Coupe, India ivory and black, V98072 ..$25-35
Chevrolet Corvette
   1969 Convertible, open top, #36 .....$25-35
   1971 Spyder "Daytona," #62 ....$25-35
   1997 Closed Coupe, light metallic
      pewter, V98037 ....$25-35
   1998 Open Convertible, red, V98086 ..$25-35
   Le Mans, #44 ....$25-35
   Le Mans, #111 ....$25-35
   "Pace Car Indianapolis" 1998,
      VMC99004 ....$25-35
   Coupe with Open Roof, red,
      VMC99018 ....$25-35
Chevrolet Impala
   1959 Convertible, closed top, #391 ...$25-35
   1959 Convertible, open top, #390 ...$25-35
   1959 Hardtop, #392 ....$25-35
   #7 Jim Reed, NASCAR, #394 ....$25-35
Chevrolet Jr. Johnson, #393 ....$25-35
Chevrolet Nomad 1957
   red and ivory, V98046 ....$25-35
   "Che Guevara," ivory and dusk
      plum, VCC99048 ....$25-35

Chrysler Fire Department, #373 ....$25-35
Chrysler Parks Department, #378 ....$25-35
Chrysler Town and Country 1947, #20 ...$25-35
Chrysler Windsor Sedan 1947, #370 ....$25-35
Citroën 2CV
  1948, silver gray (the first Citroën
    2CV), VCC99005 ....$25-35
  1960 with Snow Plough, V98002.....$25-35
  "Bamboo" 1982, green,
    VCC99030 ....$25-35
  "Marcatelo" 1976, V98056............$25-35
Citroën Berlingo
  5-Place, metallic calendula,
    VMC99006 ....$25-35
  Multispace 1997, Innsbruck green,
    V98048 ....$25-35
  Multispace Open Roof, Balmoral
    blue, VMC99024 ....$25-35
  Van "Citroën Assistance," V98084.....$25-35
Citroën DS 19
  Salon De Paris 1956, #690 ....$25-35
  1956, dark red (the first Citroën
    DS), VCC99021 ....$25-35
Citroën Traction
  11B 1953, black, VCC99029.........$25-35
  7A 1934, beige and black, V98068 ...$25-35
  7C 1934, Bordeaux red, VCC99045 ...$25-35
  7S 1934, pearl gray and black,
    VCC99014 ....$25-35
Citroën Xsara Rally P. Bugalski Catalunya
  Rally 1998, V98087.................$25-35
DeSoto Taxi, #421 ....$25-35
Ferrari 365 GT4 BB 1973, red,
  VCC99039 ....$25-35
Ferrari 508 GTB 1977, #600.............$25-35
Ferrari Dino, #17 ....$25-35
Ferrari Spyder California, #140 ....$25-35
Fiat 124 Spider 2000
  "50th Anniversary" 1981, champagne,
    VCC99032..........................$25-35
  Open Convertible 1979, metallic red,
    V98058 ....$25-35
Fiat Cinquecento
  1957 Open, celestial blue, the first Fiat 500,
    VCC99016..........................$25-35
  Rally "Target" A. Maselli Europa Cup
    1997, V98040 ....$25-35
Ford Escort
  "Belgacom" De Mevius Portugal Rally
    1997, V98076 ....$25-35
  WRC "Sainz" winner Acropolis Rally
    1997, V98041 ....$25-35
  WRC "Totta" F. Peres Rally de Portugal
    1997, V98054 ....$25-35
  WRC Kankkunen Finland Rally
    1997, V98065 ....$25-35

Ford Fairlane 1956
  Convertible, open top, #460............$25-35
  Purple Hog, NASCAR, #56 ....$25-35
  Victoria 1956, #10 ....$25-35
Honda S600
  1964 Closed Convertible, silver gray,
    VCC99040..........................$25-35
  Open Convertible 1966, red,
    VCC99009..........................$25-35
  Closed Convertible 1965, ivory, V98059 .$25-35
Jaguar Mk II
  3.4 1959, dove gray, VCC99042 ...$25-35
  British Saloon Car, Graham Hill
    1963, V98067 ....$25-35
Jaguar XK8
  Closed Convertible, carnival red,
    V98060 ....$25-35
  Open Convertible, titanium,
    VMC99015 ....$25-35
Lancia 037 Rally Pioneer Andruet Tour de France
  1984, V98071 ....$25-35
Lancia Stratos
  "Alitalia" Munari winner Rally Monte Carlo
    1976, V98045 ....$25-35
  "Marlboro" Munari winner Sanremo Rally
    1974, V98082 ....$25-35
  "Torino Car Show" 1971 red,
    VCC99025..........................$25-35
Lotus Elise
  1997 Open Convertible yellow,
    V98047 ....$25-35
Lotus Elise
  Closed Convertible 1997, Lotus racing green,
    V98083 ....$25-35
  Open Convertible, silver, VMC99001 .$25-35
Lotus Seven S2 1500
  1960 Open Convertible with doors, red and
    aluminum, V98055 ....$25-35
  1960 Open Convertible, British racing green,
    V98001 ....$25-35
Lotus Seven S3 1600
  1968 Convertible with doors,
    yellow, VCC99027...................$25-35
  1968 Open Convertible, aluminum
    and green, VCC99002 ....$25-35
Mack "Ryder" Truck, #433 ....$45-60
Mack Fire Pumper, white, #434...........$45-60
Mercedes-Benz 600
  Landaulet, #63 ....$25-35
  Pullman Limousine 1965, #33 ....$25-35
  with Pope, #81 ....$25-35
Mercedes-Benz ML320
  4x4, dark metallic blue, VMC99013 ..$25-35
  1998, imperial red, V98007 ....$25-35
Mercedes-Benz S600L
  brilliant silver, VMC99025 ....$25-35

Pullman Limousine 1997, dark metallic gray,
  V98050 ....$25-35
Messerschmitt KR 200 Kabinenroller
  (Cabrio-Limousine), #680 ....$25-35
  open top, #681 ....$25-35
  Tiger, closed top, #683 ....$25-35
  Tiger, open top, #684 ....$25-35
  1960, ivory and red, VCC99037.....$25-35
Mini "STUDIO 2" 1990, V98042 ....$25-35
Mini Beaubourg, VCC99003..............$25-35
Mini Cooper 1990, red and white,
  VCC99020 ....$25-35
Mini Moke
  "Australian" 1968, closed, blue,
    VCC99035..........................$25-35
  "Cagiva" 1997 Open Convertible,
    red, VCC99010 ....$25-35
Mini Neon 1991 Nordic blue,
  VCC99041 ....$25-35
Mitsubishi Carisma GT Burns Rally de
  Portugal 1997, V98064 ....$25-35
Mitsubishi Lancer
  Evolution G. Trelles Tap Rally de
    Portugal 1998, V98075 ....$25-35
  Evolution IV Roadcar 1997 Rallyart,
    V98036 ....$25-35
  Evolution IV Roadcar 1997, silver
    gray, V98035 ....$25-35
  Evolution IV Roadcar 1997, white,
    V98034 ....$25-35
  Evolution IV T. Makkinen winner Catalunya
    Rally 1997, V98053 ....$25-35
  Evolution IV Winfield T. Makinen Australia
    Rally 1997, V98089 ....$25-35
  Evolution VI 1999, white, VMC99019 ..$25-35
Mitsubishi Pajero
  Evolution Short, light metallic gray,
    VMC99014 ....$25-35
Mitsubishi Space Star 1998
  Firenze Gold, VMC99005 ....$25-35
  Scandinavia blue, VMC99026 ....$25-35
Morgan +8 1968
  Closed Convertible, Connaught green,
    VCC99011..........................$25-35
  Open Convertible, indigo blue,
    V98066 ....$25-35
Morris 1100 1962, ivory white,
  VCC99018 ....$25-35
Nash Metropolitan 1959
  Convertible, open top, #32............$25-35
  Hardtop Coupe, #25 ....$25-35
  Open Convertible, white and red,
    VCC99033..........................$25-35
Opel Ascona 400 "BASTOS" G. Colsoul-A.
  Lopes Rally Monte Carlo 1982,
    V98070 ....$25-35

Opel GT 1900 Coupe 1960, orange,
V98031 ....$25-35
Opel GT/J 1972, orange, VCC99046 ..$25-35
Opel Kadett "B"
1966 Coupe, dark blue, V98005 .....$25-35
1966 Coupe, dark red, V98006 ......$25-35
1966 Coupe, light blue, V98004 .....$25-35
1966 Coupe, light gray, V98003 .....$25-35
1966 Rally 1100, yellow and matte black,
V98081 ....$25-35
1967 Fastback Rally 1900, red and matte
black, V98044 ....$25-35
Coupe Rallye 1900 1967, metallic gray and
black, VCC99023 ....$25-35
Peugeot 306 Maxi
"Delecour" Tour de Corse 1997,
V98039 ....$25-35
"Panizzi" Tour de Corse 1997,
V98038 ....$25-35
"SG" A. Lopes Rally Tap-Portugal
1998, V98077 ....$25-35
Spain 1997 J. Azcona-J. Billmer,
V98028 ....$25-35
Peugeot 404 Injection 1972, metallic
silver, V98057 ....$25-35
Peugeot Partner
weekend red, V98049 ....$25-35
Combi Space, quartz gray,
VMC99016 ....$25-35
Porsche 904GTS
1964 silver gray, V98069 ......$25-35
#31 Schiller-Koch LeMans 1964,
VCC99031 ....$25-35
#34 Buchet-Ligier LeMans 1964,
VCC99006 ....$25-35
Porsche 911
Carrera RS 1992, Indian red,
VCC99038 ....$25-35
GT2 "Chereau" Le Mans 1997,
V98022 ....$25-35
GT2 "Fat Turbo" Le Mans 1997,
V98021 ....$25-35
GT2 "Jumbo" Le Mans 1997,
V98019 ....$25-35
GT2 "Konrad" Le Mans 1997,
V98024 ....$25-35
GT2 "Lloyd's" Le Mans 1997,
V98025 ....$25-35
GT2 "Navision" Le Mans 1997,
V98020 ....$25-35
GT2 "Philippe Charriol" Le Mans 1997,
V98023 ....$25-35
GT2 "Stadler" Le Mans 1997,
V98026 ....$25-35
GT2 "Taisan" Japan GT Championship
1997, V98027 ....$25-35

GT2 1998 Roadcar, Indian red,
VMC99003 ....$25-35
R 1967, #12 ....$25-35
Porsche 996
Carrera 3.4 1998, black, VMC99022...$25-35
Carrera 4 Coupe 1998, articulated silver
gray, VMC99008 ....$25-35
Open Convertible 1998, zenith metallic blue,
VMC99017 ....$25-35
Porsche Carrera Roadcar, #730 ....$25-35
Renault "Voiturette" 1898, red,
VCC99004 ....$25-35
Renault 4
"1960s" 1985, blue, VCC99022 ....$25-35
Jogging Open Convertible 1981,
V98043 ....$25-35
Renault 5
"Automatic" 1978, red, VCC99036..$25-35
Alpine 1976, metallic gray, VCC99013..$25-35
TL Sedan 1972, orange, V98030 .....$25-35
TS 1975 with Open Roof, red, V98080 ...$25-35
Turbo 1978, metallic blue, VCC99044 ..$25-35
Renault Clio 1998
metallic red, V98074 ....$25-35
Epicéa green, VMC99020 ....$25-35
Renault Espace
"F1 Staff Car," V98011 ....$25-35
white, VMC99012 ....$25-35
Renault Kangoo
"Pampa" 1998, metallic green,
VMC99011 ....$25-35
Express Van, red, V98062 ....$25-35
Saloon, Fiji green, V98061 ....$25-35
Renault Laguna
Break "F1 Medical Car," V98008 .....$25-35
Break with Mistral Surfboard, white,
VMC99021 ....$25-35
II Sedan 1998, nacré black,
VMC99007 ....$25-35
Renault Master 1998, glacier white,
V98073 ....$25-35
Renault Megane
Coupe "F1 Safety Car," V98009 ......$25-35
Maxi "Yacco" B. Rousselot Rally Lyon-Char-
boon 1998, V98078 ....$25-35
Open Convertible 1997, yellow,
V98032 ....$25-35
Renault Spider
"F1 Pace Car," V98010 ....$25-35
Renault Spider
"Tessitura Fabri" A. Belicchi Eurocup 1998,
V98085 ....$25-35
Pare Brise "Salon de Paris 1998," metallic
gray, VMC99002 ....$25-35
with front windscreen 1997, yellow,
V98033 ....$25-35

Steyr-Puch 650T 1960 Scooter, #31 ....$25-35
Toyota Corolla
Hatchback 1997, cool water,
V98052 ....$25-35
Liftback 1997, night shadow,
V98051 ....$25-35
WRC "Marlboro" F. Loix Portugal 1998,
V98088 ....$25-35
WRC D. Auriol Finland Rally 1997,
V98017 ....$25-35
WRC Grundholm Finland Rally 1997,
V98018 ....$25-35
WRC Sainz winner Rally Monte Carlo
1998, V98063 ....$25-35
Toyota Land Cruiser
long wheelbase, green and silver,
VMC99023 ....$25-35
short wheelbase, dark blue and silver,
VMC99010 ....$25-35
Toyota Picnic 1997
dark blue, V98012 ....$25-35
Toyota RAV4 1996
light metallic green, V98015 ....$25-35
light silver gray, V98016 ....$25-35
metallic blue, V98014 ....$25-35
metallic red, V98013 ....$25-35
Triumph TR3
1956 Open Convertible, #57 ....$25-35
Triumph TR3A
open top, #14 ....$25-35
1957 Open Convertible, British racing
green, VCC99028 ....$25-35
Volkswagen 1200
1959 with Sunroof, #2 ....$25-35
U. S. Dollar, #59 ....$25-35
Volkswagen Bulli
"Nestlés" Van, #555 ....$25-35
Van, #550 ....$25-35
Volkswagen Hebmeuller with Sunroof,
#405 ....$25-35
Volkswagen Karmann Convertible, top down,
#3 ....$25-35
Volkswagen KdF Saloon 1938, dull blue
(the first Volkswagen), VCC99015 .....$25-35
Volkswagen Kombi, #560 ....$25-35
Volkswagen Van Fire Department, #5 ....$25-35
White Tanker "Texaco," #250 ....$45-60

Vitesse City
Volkswagen 1955
Bulli, red and white, CV001C $25-35
Bulli, turquoise and white, CV001B $25-35
Combi, red and black, CV002A $25-35
Combi, yellow and white, CV002C $25-35
Chevrolet Nomad "State Highway Patrol,"
CPC99002 ....$25-35

Chrysler Windsor
    New York Police USA, CP004 ....$25-35
    "Dolmus" Taxi Istanbul, CT009...........$25-35
Citroën Berlingo, CMC99003 ....$25-35
Jaguar Mk II Police, CP003 ....$25-35
Jeep Amphibian Fire Brigade "Pompiers
    D' Angers," CS008 ....$25-35
Jeep Willys Fire Brigade
    "Pompiers De Rethel," CS001 ....$25-35
    "Pompiers Aeroport De Paris," CS002 ..$25-35
Mercedes-Benz 170V
    "Taxibal" Berlin 1952, CTW99001 ..$25-35
Mercedes-Benz 220SE
    "Dortmund Berufs Feuerwehr," CS005 ..$25-35
    Polizei, CP005 ....$25-35
    Taxi, CT007 ....$25-35
    Taxi Athens, CT018 ....$25-35
    Taxi Barcelona, CT011B $25-35
    Taxi Cairo, CT010 ....$25-35
    Taxi Copenhagen, CT015 ....$25-35
    Taxi Madrid, CT011A $25-35
    Taxi Singapore, CTW99002 ....$25-35
Morris LD150
    "McEwan's," CV028 ....$25-35
    "Whitbread," CV027 ....$25-35
    Evening Standard, CCC99002.........$25-35
    Metropolitan Police Control, CPC99005 ..$25-35
    Post Office Telephones, CV022 ....$25-35
    Royal Mail, CV021 ....$25-35
Opel Blitz 3½ Ton
    "Dusseldorf Feuerwehr," CS010.........$25-35
    Cargo High Canvas Covered Truck, blue,
        CL001A $25-35
    Cargo Low Canvas Covered Truck, dark
        green and black, CL001B...........$25-35
    Open Transport Truck, black, CL001C ...$25-35
Opel GT Polizei, CPC99004 ....$25-35
Peugeot 404
    French Police, CP006....................$25-35
    Taxi "G7" Paris, CT012A $25-35
    Taxi Buenos Aires, CT014...............$25-35
    Taxi Casablanca, CT013 ....$25-35
    Taxi Hong Kong, CT019 ....$25-35
    Taxi Nairobi, CT017 ....$25-35
    Taxi Paris, CT012B $25-35
    Taxi Saigon, CT016 ....$25-35
Peugeot Partner Electrique "La Poste,"
    CMC99001 ....$25-35
Renault 4 F4 Van
    "PTT" (French Post), CCC99001 ....$25-35
Renault 4L
    "Pompiers De Paris," CS007 ....$25-35
Renault 5
    Police De Paris, CPC99001 ....$25-35
Renault Colorale
    Taxi "Sahara Desert," CT008 ....$25-35

Renault Estafette
    "Aspro" Tour De France, CCC99003 ..$25-35
    "Gendarmerie," CP007 ....$25-35
    "Hoegaarden," CV026 ....$25-35
    "Kronenbourg," CV025 ....$25-35
    "Pompiers Sdis Doubs," CS003 ....$25-35
    Ambulance "Pompiers De Limoges,"
        CS004 ....$25-35
    Firestone, CV030........................$25-35
    French Police, CP002....................$25-35
    Michelin, CV029 ....$25-35
    Postes Belges, CV020 ....$25-35
    PTT (French Post), CV019 ....$25-35
Renault Kangoo
    DHL, CMC99002 ....$25-35
Renault Laguna
    Politie Amsterdam, CPC99003.........$25-35
Renault Master
    CMC99004 ....$25-35
Renault Prairie
    Pompier "Les Trois Epis," CS009 ....$25-35
Renault Scenic
    Taxi Paris, CTW99004 ....$25-35
Volkswagen 1200
    "Mexico City Taxi," CT001 ....$25-35
    "Rio De Janeiro Taxi, CT003 ....$25-35
Volkswagen Beetle
    "British Car Hire" Berlin 1947,
        CTW99005 ....$25-35
Volkswagen Bulli
    "Carlsberg," CV023 ....$25-35
    "Lufthansa," CCC99004 ....$25-35
    "Paulaner," CV024 ....$25-35
    Deutsche Bundespost, CV017 ....$25-35
    Polizei, CP001 ....$25-35
    Postes Suisses, CV018 ....$25-35
Volkswagen Kubelwagen "Frankfurt
    Feuerwehr," CS006........................$25-35

Vitesse Skid–Rally Cars
Citroën Xsara Kit Car
    "Primagaz" Trophee Andros 1999,
        #SKM99010.........................$25-35
    J. Puras Spain Rally 98, #SKM99022...$25-35
    P. Bugalski Tour de Corse
        1999, #SKM99038 ....$25-35
Fiat 124 Abarth
    "Mikkola-Todt" Monte Carlo 1975,
        #SKC99006 ....$25-35
Fiat Cinquecento Rallye
    "Nilo del Aquila" 93 J.ALESI, #SKC99001..$25-35
Ford Escort WRC
    "Gaz Prom" Nikonenko, Acropolis
        1998, #SKM99004 ....$25-35
    "Texaco" Papadimitrou, Acropolis
        1997, #SKM99017 ....$25-35

    "Toshiba" A. Schwarz, Great Britain
        Rally 1998, #SKM99029..........$25-35
    "Valvoline" Kirkos, Acropolis
        1998, #SKM99021 ....$25-35
Ford Focus WRC
    Martini C. McRae, Monte Carlo
        1999, #SKM99019 ....$25-35
    S. Jean-Joseph, Monte Carlo
        1999, #SKM99035 ....$25-35
Lancia Delta Integral 16v
    "Auriol-Occelli," winner 92,
        #SMC007 ....$25-35
Lancia Stratos
    "L'Automobile" Darniche, winner Tour
        de Corse 1981, #SKC99010....$25-35
    "Olio Fiat" F.Tabaton, Sanremo 1980,
        #SKC99002 ....$25-35
Mini Cooper
    "British Motor Heritage" Monte Carlo
        1997, #SKC99008 ....$25-35
Mitsubishi Carisma Evolution IV
    "Sony" Kuzas, Portugal 1998,
        #SKM99011.........................$25-35
Mitsubishi Lancer Evolution V
    T. Makkinen, World Champion 1998,
        #SKW99001 ....$25-35
    "Winfield" Makkinen Australian GP 1998,
        #SKM99009........................$25-35
    F. Loix Monte Carlo 1999,
        #SKM99037........................$25-35
    R. Burns, winner Rally Great Britain 1998,
        #SKM99003........................$25-35
    T. Makkinen, 1st Monte Carlo 1999,
        #SKM99028........................$25-35
Mitsubishi L200
    Galp Sousa, Granada-Dakar 1999,
        #SKM99015........................$25-35
    Smulevici, Granada-Dakar 1999,
        #SKM99016........................$25-35
Mitsubishi Pajero Evolution
    "ATAC" Strugo, Dakar 1999,
        #SKM99031........................$25-35
    "Geco Sport" Quandt, Dakar 1999,
        #SKM99032........................$25-35
    "Invesco" Cassegrain, Dakar 1999,
        #SKM99033........................$25-35
    "Mitsu Oil" Shinuzoka, Dakar 1999,
        #SKM99024........................$25-35
    "PIAA" Fontenay, Dakar 1999,
        #SKM99023........................$25-35
    "Picobello" Boxoeh, Dakar 1999,
        #SKM99040........................$25-35
    "Playstation" Kleinschmidt, 1999,
        #SKM99025........................$25-35
    "Fpee" Alphand, Dakar 1999,
        #SKM99039........................$25-35

Opel Ascona

"Denim" Arkentis-Javeris, San Marino 1982, #SKC99005 ....$25-35

Opel Ascona 400

Rothmans Rohrl winner 1982, #SMC009 ....$25-35

Opel Kadett Fastback 1900

M-C. Beaumont, Tour de Corse 1969, #SKC99007 ....$25-35

Peugeot 206 WRC

"Esso" Salon de Paris 1998, #SKM99012 ....$25-35

G. Panizzi Tour de Corse 1999, #SKM99026 ....$25-35

Presentation 1998, silver gray, #SKM99001 ....$25-35

Peugeot 306 Maxi "Switzerland" Rallye Du Valais 1998, #SKM99006 ....$25-35

Peugeot 404

"Nowicki-Cliff," winner Safari 1968, #SKC99004 ....$25-35

Porsche 911S

Waldegaard-Helmer, winner 1969, #SMC008 ....$25-35

Porsche 904GTS

"Buchet-Linge," Tour De France 1964, #SKC99003 ....$25-35

Renault 5 Turbo

"Gitanes" Saby-Tilber Tour de Corse 1980, #SKC99009 ....$25-35

Renault Megane Maxi

"Lebanon" J. Nasarallah 1998, #SKM99030 ....$25-35

"Renault Belgique" Princen 1998, #SKM99005 ....$25-35

"Turkey" N. Avci 1998, #SKM99014 ...$25-35

Seat Cordoba

P. LIATI Rallye Monte Carlo 1999, #SKM99034 ....$25-35

WRC M. Duez Rallye San Remo 1998, #SKM99018 ....$25-35

WRC Rovenpera, Finland Rally 1998, #SKM99007 ....$25-35

Toyota Corolla WRC

"ASG" M. Gronholm, Finland 1998, #SKM99008 ....$25-35

"Mobil 1" Zivas, Acropolis 1998, #SKM99013 ....$25-35

"Shell" Hagstrom DEFA Rally 1998, #SKM99020 ....$25-35

"Tein" Malaysia Rally 1998, #SKM99002 ....$25-35

C.Sainz Rallye Monte Carlo 99, #SKM99027 ....$25-35

D.Auriol Monte Carlo 1999, #SKM99036 ....$25-35

Toyota Land Cruiser Long

"JVC" Wambergue, Dakar 1998, #SKM99053 ....$25-35

Vitesse 2-Wheels—Motorcycles

Aprilia RSV 250 1998

"Aprilia Team" L. Capirossi, world champion, #TWR99023 ....$25-35

"Aprilia Team" M. Lucchi, #TWR99025 ...$25-35

"Aprilia Team" T. Harada, #TWR99024 ...$25-35

"Docshop Racing" J. Fuchs, #TWR99027 ...$25-35

"Nastro Azzuro" V. Rossi, #TWR99026 ...$25-35

Ducati 748SPS, 1999

yellow, #TWS99004 ....$25-35

Ducati 916

"Ducati ADVF" T. Corser, Superbike 1998, #TWR99043 ....$25-35

"Ducati" C. Fogarty, Superbike world champion 1998, #TWR99042 ....$25-35

"Remus Racing Team" Meklau, Superbike 1998, #TWR99044 ....$25-35

Ducati 996

Biposto, yellow, #TWS99002 ....$25-35

SPS, red, #TWS99003 ....$25-35

Honda NSR 500

"Gresino" 1998 A. Barros, #TWR99008 ....$25-35

"Kanemoto" 1998 M. Biaggi, #TWR99005 ....$25-35

"Movistar-Pons" 1998 C. Checa, #TWR99006 ....$25-35

"Movistar-Pons" 1998 J. Kocinski, #TWR99007 ....$25-35

"Repsol" 1998 A. Criville, #TWR99003 ....$25-35

"Repsol" 1998 M. Doohan, world champion 1998, #TWR99001 ....$25-35

"Repsol" 1998 T.Okada 1998, #TWR99002 ....$25-35

1998 "Movistar-Pons" Lavilla, German GP, #TWR99022 ....$25-35

Honda NSR/V2 500, 1998

"Dee Cee Jeans," J.V.D. Goorbergh, #TWR99011 ....$25-35

"Repsol," S. Gibernau, #TWR99004 ...$25-35

"Shell," G. McCoy, #TWR99010 ....$25-35

"Shell," J. Borja, #TWR99009 ....$25-35

"Team Millar," S. Smart, #TWR99013 ...$25-35

"Tecmas ELF," S. Gimbert,#TWR99012 ..$25-35

"Shell," F. Teixeira, Spanish GP, #TWR99020 ....$25-35

Racing Test Bike, #TWS99001 ....$25-35

Vespa

"98" 1946, green, #TWC99001 ....$25-35

125 1948, light metallic gray, #TWC99002 ....$25-35

125 1951, light green, #TWC99003 ....$25-35

125 1966, light beige, #TWC99006 ....$25-35

150GL 1963, off white, #TWC99005 ....$25-35

150GS 1955, silver gray, #TWC99004 ....$25-35

Yamaha YZR 500, 1998

"Red Bull" R. Laconi, #TWR99018 .....$25-35

"Red Bull" S. Crafar, #TWR99017 ....$25-35

"Team Rainey" Cadalora, French GP, #TWR99021 ....$25-35

"Team Rainey" J-M. Bayle, #TWR99015 ....$25-35

"Team Rainey" K. Nanba, #TWR99016 ....$25-35

"Team Rainey" N. Abe, #TWR99014 ..$25-35

"Yamaha Racing" Haga, Japanese GP, #TWR99019 ....$25-35

Vivid Imaginations (Tyco Canada)

The Vivid Imaginations brand from Tyco Canada surfaced recently with the introduction of an assortment of models based on Gerry Anderson's popular action adventure *Captain Scarlet and the Mysterons.* Several models have been produced based on this children's marionette-based TV series that debuted in 1966. The resurgence in popularity of Captain Scarlet has been bolstered by the reintroduction of another Gerry Anderson TV show called *Thunderbirds*, first broadcast in 1965. Models are available in sets or sold individually. Also offered by Vivid Imaginations are 12" tall action figures.

Vivid Imaginations Captain Scarlet and the Mysterons Models and Sets

Spectrum Command Team Set, complete ...$50-65 includes:

Spectrum Pursuit Vehicle, separate $20-25

Captain Scarlet's Spectrum Car, separate ...$8-10

Spectrum Jet Liner, separate $8-10

Angel Interceptor (2 each), separate $8-10

Spectrum Cloudbase H.Q. playset $90-110

Voiturette (see SMTS)

Volga (or V.Olga)

Besides being the name of Russia's most famous river, Volga is also a brand of Russian cars that also go by the name Gaz, to the best of my knowledge. These diecast replicas of this Russian standard automobile are exceptional quality for the price.

Volga 2401 Saloon Fire Chief $9-12
Volga 2401 Saloon Road Safety Service....$9-12
Volga 2402 Estate Standard.....................$9-12
Volga 2402 Estate Ambulance $12-15
Volga 2402 Estate Airport "Follow Me"....$12-15
Volga 2402 Estate, Closed Door..............$8-11
Volga 3102 Saloon Rally Car.................$12-15
Volga 3102 Saloon Fire Chief $12-15
Volga 3102 Saloon with Symbols $12-15
Volga 3102 Saloon Happy New Year....$12-15
Volga Gaz A Tourer, Open $12-15
Volga Gaz 66 Truck..........................$16–19
Volga Gaz 66 Tanker, United Nations $20-24
Volga Gaz 66 Airlines $20-24

W

Walker Model Service

Walthers HO Gauge Catalog features over three pages of 1:87 scale Walker Model Service kits consisting of unpainted cast white metal and styrene models with wire and wood details. Models represented are of vintage trucks for $15 to 56 each.

Walldorf

Walldorf is a manufacturer of 1:43 scale white metal kits from the town of Walldorf, Germany, not far from Frankfurt.

1949 Buick Roadmaster..........................$60-90
1977 Cadillac Sedan DeVille.................$60-90

Wannatoy (also see WT)

This Chinese brand encompasses some of the most inexpensive and inaccurate 3" toys on the market. They are generic in appearance and markings but might be connected with WT, another Chinese brand of similar toys.

Wedico

Wedico of Germany has offered a few 1:8 scale plastic kits and a large assortment of 1:16 scale metal truck kits and one car ferry.

Welly

Welly Diecast Factory Limited
Flat H.I.
18/F Shield Industrial Centre
84-92 Chai Wan Kok Street
Tsuen Wan, Hong Kong
tel: +852 2416 5487
fax: +852 2412 0042
e-mail: welly@wellydiecast.com
website: www.wellydiecast.com
Welly USA Inc.

23785 Cabot Blvd. Suite 320
Hayward, CA 94545 USA
Representative : Mr. Sherman Lin
tel: 510 782 8198 / 519 782 7731
mobile: 510 589 8866
fax: 510 782 8199
e-mail : wellyusainc@aol.com

Although Welly Die Casting Factory Ltd. started producing diecast toy vehicles in 1979, the company focus recently switched from the toy business to manufacturing collectible scale model replicas in 1:18, 1:24, 1:32, 1:36, 1:60, and 1:87 scale. Their catalog is extensive. Below is listed their 1:18 scale offerings for 2003. All Welly models are currently produced and available at or near retail price.

BMW
    328i, 1998, #9833, 1:18.............$20-30
    X5, #9842, 1:18.........................$20-30
    Z8, #9843, 1:18 ....$20-30
    745i, #2512, 1:18 ....$20-30
Cadillac

Escalade, 2002, 1:24 ....$12-16
Chevrolet

3100 Pick Up, 1953, #9836, 1:18..........$20-30
    Avalanche, 2001, #9852, 1:18 ......$20-30

Avalanche, 2001, 1:24 ....$12-16
    Borrego, #2513, 1:18 ....$20-30
    Camaro SS, 2002, #9861, 1:18.....$20-30

Chevelle SS 396, 1968, #9866, 1:24 ....$12-16

Chevelle SS 396, 1:64................................$2-4

Chevelle SS 454, 1970, #9855, 1:18 ....$20-30
    Corvette Convertible, 1999, #9840,
        1:18 ....$20-30
    Corvette Hardtop, 1999, #9839, 1:18...$20-30
    Fleetmaster, 1948, #9848, 1:18......$20-30
    Impala Convertible, 1960, #9864,
        1:18................................$20-30
    Impala Convertible, 1963, #9865,
        1:18................................$20-30
    Silverado Extended Cab Sportside Box,
        1999, blue, #9837, 1:18.........$20-30
    Silverado Extended Cab Sportside Box,
        1999, silver, #9844, 1:18........$20-30
    Special Deluxe, 1941, #9862, 1:18....$20-30

Suburban, 2001, #9854, 1:18................$20-30
Ford
    F-100 Pick Up, 1956, red, #9831,
        1:18..$20-30
    F-100 Tow Truck, 1956, green and cream,
        #9834, 1:18 ....$20-30
    F-150 Flareside Supercab Pick Up, 1999,
        #9835, 1:18 ....$20-30
    F-1 Pick Up, 1951, metallic teal, #9847,
        1:18.......................................$20-30
    Deluxe Cabriolet, 1936, #9867,
        1:18.......................................$20-30

Thunderbird Sports Roadster, 1962, #9868,
1:18 ....$20-30

Mustang, 1969, yellow with black accents,
#2516, 1:18 ....$20-30

GMC

Yukon Denali, #9863, 1:18 ....$20-30

Honda

S2000, Japanese version, red, #9845,
1:18 ....$20-30

Jaguar, S-Type, 1999, #9838, 1:18 ......$20-30

Lamborghini, Diablo SV, #9849, 1:18 ....$20-30

Mercedes-Benz

190SL, 1955, red, #9841, 1:18 .....$20-30

190SL, 1955, silver, #9841, 1:18...........$20-30

300S, 1955, #9859, 1:18 ....$20-30

C-Class, silver, #9853, 1:18 ....$20-30

C-Class Sports Coupe, #9860, 1:18 ...$20-30

Unimog U400, 1:24 ....$9-12

Mini Cooper

red with white roof, #9851, 1:18......$20-30

Oldsmobile

Super 88 Convertible, 1955, two-tone white
and red, #9869, 1:18 ....$20-30

Opel

Speedster, orange, #2511, 1:18......$20-30

Peugeot

406 Coupe, #9857, 1:18 ....$20-30

206 cc, #9858, 1:18 ....$20-30

Pontiac

GTO, 1966, dark green, #9856, 1:18 ...$20-30

Porsche

911 (996), 1997, yellow, #9832, 1:18 ..$20-30

911 Turbo, yellow, #9850, 1:18 .....$20-30

911, yellow, 1:24 ....$12-16

Volkswagen

Microbus, 1962, #9764, 1:32 ....$9-12

New Beetle, #9846, 1:18 ....$20-30

Western Models (also see Small Wheels and Western Models)

According to EWA & Model Miniatures
USA Inc., "Western Models were one of the first
companies in the world to make high quality
hand-built metal models. The company was
founded in the early 1970s just southeast of London, England, and moved in the mid '80s to
Taunton in the southwest of England. They now
have a range of about 70 quality 1:43 scale
models of European and American, race and
street cars, old and new, plus some interesting
record cars. A few new models are introduced
annually and some withdrawn, which makes the
models very collectible.

"Small Wheels is another name used by
Western for some of their models. All are made
in the Western factory to the same high standards."

Western Models

Alfa Romeo

8C 2900B Spyder 1938, WM35 ..$100-120

Frecia D'Oro 1947, open roof,
WMS62X $140-160

Villa D'Este 1949, WM54 ....$100-120

Bentley

6.5L Barnato 1930, WM32 ....$100-120

R Type Sedan 1953, lefthand drive,
WM58L..............................$120-140

R Type Sedan 1953, righthand drive,
WM58 ....$100-120

S III Saloon 1964, WMS49 ....$160-180

Bugatti

Royale 41 Esders 1931, WM29 ..$120-140

T57 Corsica TRR 1938, WM39 ...$100-120

Buick

Century 1941, California Highway Patrol,
WMS67P $200-220

Century Model 66S Sedanet 1941,
WMS67 ....$195-215

Electra Convertible 1959 Indy Pace Car,
WMS56P $195-215

Electra Convertible 1959, top down,
WMS56X $160-180

Electra Hardtop 1959, WMS56 ..$160-180

Invicta, top up 1959, WMS59 .....$160-180

Riviera 1972, WMS69 ....$160-180

Cadillac

Coupe DeVille 1949, WMS68 ....$175-195

Coupe DeVille Convertible 1949, top down,
WMS68X $175-195

Eldorado Biarritz 1960, top down,
WMS61X $160-180

Eldorado Seville 1960, WMS61 ..$160-180

V16 4-door Convertible 1933, top down,
WM28X $100-120

V16 4-door Convertible 1933, top up,
WM28.................................$120-140

Campbell

Bluebird 1933 Record Car, Rolls Royce
Powered, WM9 ....$120-140

1935 Record Car, Rolls Royce Powered,
WM42................................$140-160

Checker

New York Cab 1974, WM55 .....$185-205

Police Car 1974, white,
WMS55X $160-180

Chevrolet

Bel Air Convertible 1957, top down,
WMS44X $160-180

Bel Air Hardtop 1957, WMS44 ..$160-180

Camaro IROC-Z 1985, WP112 ...$140-160

Corvette 1953, WM13 ....$160-180

Chrysler

Imperial 1933, WM6.................$100-120

Imperial Lebaron Phaeton 1933, top down,
WMS37X $115-135

Imperial LeBaron 1933, top up,
WMS37 ....$135-155

Saratoga Hardtop 1959, WMS63 ......$160

Daimler
Straight 8 DE36 1948, WM40 ....$100-120

DeSoto
Adventurer Convertible 1959, top down,
WMS60X $160-180

Adventurer Hardtop 1959,
WMS60 ....$160-180

Police 1957, WM18 ....$185-205

Dodge
Custom Royal Lancer Convertible 1957, open
top, WMS64X $160-180

Custom Royal Lancer Hardtop 1957,
WMS64 ....$160-180

Polara 2-door Hardtop 1960,
WM70 ....$185-205

Viper 1992, WP125 ....$160-180

Viper 1992 Indy Pace Car, WP125P...$130-150

Duesenberg
SJ Special 1935, top down, WM24 ...$100-120

Ferrari
246 GT Dino 1957, open top,
WP107X $140-160

308 GTS 1982, WP110X...........$140-160

Testarossa 1984, WP113............$160-180

Ford
Fairlane 300 1958 Fire Chief,
WM17F $180-200

Galaxie Skyliner Convertible 1959, top
down with Continental Kit,
WMS46X $160-180

Galaxie Skyliner Convertible 1959, top
down without Continental Kit,
WMS46Z $160-180

Galaxie Skyliner Hardtop 1959, with
Continental Kit, WMS46 ....$160-180

Ranchero 1959, Mackechnie,
WM53 ....$100-120

Ranchero 1959, Mentone Co.,
WM53X $100-120

Golden Arrow
1929 Record Car, WM15 ....$120-140

Hudson
1942 Sedan, WM20 ....$180-200

1951 Police, WM15 ....$180-200

Jaguar
Mk V 2-door Convertible 1949,
WM41X $100-120

Mk V 4-door Sedan 1949,
WM41 ....$100-120

Mk V Sedan 1949 with landau roof,
WM41Z $100-120

SS1 Tourer 1936, WMS43 ....$160-180

XJRS Coupe 1990, WP120 ....$140-160

XJS V-12 Coupe 1987, WP115 ...$140-160

Jaguar XK120 FHC 1951, WM45...$100-120

Lincoln
Capri Convertible 1955,
WM74X $185-205

Capri Coupe 1955, WM74 ....$185-205

Lotus
WP104X $150-170

Esprit, WP104 ....$150-170

MG
EX 135 Gardner, WM38 ....$100-120

Napier Railton 1939 Record Car,
WM25 ....$120-140

Plymouth
Belvedere Convertible 1958, top down,
WMS51X $160-180

Belvedere Hardtop 1958 "Christine,"
WMS51 ....$160-180

Fury 1958, beige with gold trim,
WMS50 ....$160-180

Plaza Business Coupe 1958,
WMS65 ....$160-180

1958 Police, WM65P.................$185-205

Pontiac
Bonneville Convertible 1957, top down,
WMS66X $160-180

Bonneville Convertible 1957, top up,
WMS66 ....$160-180

Firebird TransAm 1978, WP118...$140-160

GTO 2-door Hardtop 1966, silver with a
black top, W1H...................$135-155

Rolls Royce
Silver Cloud III 1964, lefthand drive,
WM48C $100-120

Silver Cloud III 1964, righthand drive,
WM48 ....$75-95

Silver Dawn 1952, lefthand drive,
WM57L $120-140

Silver Dawn 1952, righthand drive,
WM57 ....$120-140

Sunbeam
1000HP 1927 Record Car,
WM23 ....$140-160

Thunderbolt
1938 Record Car, WM30 ....$140-160

Wheeler

Hong Kong is where these relatively
generic small-scale diecast toy cars are produced.

1975 AMC Pacer...................................$5-6

1968 Cadillac Eldorado $5-6

1963 Chevrolet Corvette Stingray...............$5-6

White Rose Collectibles

Fleer Collectibles
1120 Route 73
Suite 300
Mt Laurel, NJ 08054
phone: 800-343-6816
fax: 856-231-0383
For general company and product related
comments, suggestions, or questions...
info@fleer.com
For questions from dealers or for information
on becoming a dealer:
hobbyinfo@fleer.com
To report errors or send comments only
about this website:
webfeedback@fleer.com
website: www.fleercollectibles.com

Since 1989, White Rose Collectibles has
offered specialty limited edition collectibles. Hundreds of models and variations exist. White
Rose began by offering licensed promo versions
of Matchbox models.

One White Rose model marketed with hundreds of different markings is Matchbox's #38
Model A Van. Of the 400+ variations of this
Matchbox model, many such variations are due
to White Rose's marketing of a wide variety of
baseball and football team vans using the
Matchbox Model A.

More recent White Rose models don't indicate the original manufacturer, but state on the
box only that they are distributed by White Rose
Collectibles and made in China. White Rose
has since been purchased by Fleer, the bubble
gum company known for collector cards. The
new line is called Fleer diecast Collectibles.

For 1999, Fleer has expanded its promotional offerings to include the following:

Baseball Pick-Up Trucks, approx 2¾",
each includes a Fleer baseball
card ....$12 each

Baseball Transporters, 1:80 scale semi-
truck/trailers ....$12 each

TeamMates, double trailer
transporters ....$12 each

Miniature Zamboni, representing all 3
Hockey Leagues.................$12 each

NHL Motorcoaches with sound ....$12 each

Police Patrol Collection, 1949 Fords in
10 state trooper liveries ....$12 each

Matchbox Collector's Choice, 1994 From White Rose Collectibles

Twenty-four assorted models from the Matchbox 1–75 Series have been selected to form the
1994 Collector's Choice Series of models with

better-than-usual detailing and color variations. They originally retailed for $10 each. The 1995 series originally promised, but never delivered, 48 new variations.

#1 '57 Chevrolet $9-12
#2 Ambulance.......................................$9-12
#3 Flareside Pickup Truck $9-12
#4 Bulldozer..$9-12
#5 Model "A" Hot Rod $9-12
#6 '62 Corvette $9-12
#7 Corvette "T" Top $9-12
#8 Jaguar XK 120 ....$9-12
#9 Lamborghini Countach $9-12
#10 Ford LTD Police car........................$9-12
#11 Ford Bronco II $9-12
#12 GMC Wrecker.................................$9-12
#13 Grand Prix Racing Car.....................$9-12
#14 '87 Corvette $9-12
#15 Model Ford Model T $9-12
#16 Chevrolet Lumina $9-12
#17 Highway Maintenance Truck $9-12
#18 Jeep Eagle 4x4 ....$9-12
#19 Extending Ladder Fire Engine $9-12
#20 School Bus $9-12
#21 Camaro Z-28 ....$9-12
#22 Ferrari Testarossa............................$9-12
#23 Porsche 944 Turbo $9-12
#24 Ferrari F40 ....$9-12

White Rose International Hockey League (IHL) Zamboni, 1997

Originally priced at $15, these were available at Toy Liquidators in Troutdale, Oregon, at 2 for $5 in April 1998.

IHLW97-01 Chicago Wolves...................$3-15
IHLW97-02 Cincinnati Cyclones $3-15
IHLW97-03 Cleveland Lumberjacks $3-15
IHLW97-04 Utah Grizzlies $3-15
IHLW97-05 Detroit Vipers.......................$3-15
IHLW97-06 Fort Wayne Komets $3-15
IHLW97-07 Grand Rapids Griffins............$3-15
IHLW97-08 Houston Aeros $3-15
IHLW97-09 Indianapolis Ice $3-15
IHLW97-10 Michigan K-Wings $3-15
IHLW97-11 Kansas City Blades $3-15
IHLW97-12 Las Vegas Thunder................$3-15
IHLW97-13 Long Beach Ice Dogs $3-15
IHLW97-14 Manitoba Moose $3-15
IHLW97-15 Milwaukee Admirals $3-15
IHLW97-16 Orlando Solar Bears $3-15
IHLW97-17 Phoenix Roadrunners............$3-15
IHLW97-18 Quebec Les Rafales $3-15
IHLW97-19 San Antonio Dragons............$3-15
Volkswagen Delivery Truck.....................$11-13

Volkswagen Golf 4-door........................$8-10
Volkswagen Caravan Automobile Police...$12-14
Volkswagen Caravan Travel Trailer, Detleffs...$11-13
Volkswagen Caravelle Ambulance $8-10
Volkswagen Caravelle Fire Dept $7-9
Volkswagen Combi, black $8-10
Volkswagen Emergency Doctor $13-15
Volkswagen Golf A III Post Office $11-13
Volkswagen Golf ADAC.........................$6-8
Volkswagen Golf Cabriolet $7-9
Volkswagen Golf Convertible, red $10-12
Volkswagen Golf GTI $7-9
Volkswagen Kafer Convertible, top down,
    orange $5-7
Volkswagen Passat, turquoise $8-10
Volkswagen Passat Automobile Police.......$12-14
Volkswagen Passat Fire Brigade $12-14
Volkswagen Personnel Van $8-10
Volkswagen Police Van $14-16
Volkswagen Polo, blue $7-9
Volkswagen Polo, Deutsche Bundespost,
    yellow $8-10
Volkswagen Sharan Knirps......................$10-12
Volkswagen Station Wagon, black............$9-11
Volkswagen Telekom..............................$9-11
Volkswagen Variant, black $8-10
Volkswagen Variant, blue $8-10
Volkswagen Vento, black $3-5
Volkswagen Vento, maroon......................$7-9
Volvo 850, green $9-11
Volvo 850 Racing, with case $26-28
Volvo 850 Swedish Police $15-17
Volvo FL10 Truck with Gas Cylinders.......$13-15
Volvo Moving Van $17-19
Volvo Semi $16-18

Wiking (also see Siku, Roskopf)

Wiking is now owned by Sieper Werke GmbH, parent company to Siku toys. Wikings are highly accurate all-plastic 1:87 scale models made in Germany. Roskopf is a line of models issued under the Wiking brand.

Audi A6, black $10-12
Audi Font, burgundy...............................$7-9
Austin Healey 2000 Convertible, top down,
    green and cream...............................$11-13
Austin Healey 3000 Convertible, top down,
    red and yellow..................................$11-13
Berlin Double Decker D89 Bus $21-23
Berliner Double Decker D38 Bus $15-17
BMW Convertible $9-11
BMW 501 Christmas Model in Presentation
    Box $19-21
BMW Isetta, blue $10-12
BMW Isetta, red $10-12

BMW 3-Series Convertible, top down, violet $8-10
BMW 3-Series Touring Station Wagon $8-10
BMW 510i $6-8
Borgward Isabella, red...........................$5-7
Bulldozer Track Type Loader Traxcavator.......$7-9
Bulldozer Tractor with Blade...................$7-9
Bussing 8000 330 with trailer $12-14
Bussing 8000 Canvas Side Semi Trailer and
    Tractor..$12-14
Bussing 8000 Double Bottom "Kraft
    Ketchup"..$19-21
Bussing 8000 Tanker $12-14
Bussing 8000 Van with 2 trailers $17-19
Bussing 8000 Van with tri-axle trailer "German
    Federal Railways"...............................$20-22
Chevrolet 1957 Corvette Convertible, red .$11-13
Chevrolet 1957 Corvette Convertible,
    ivory $11-13
Citroën ID..$11-13
Citroën 15-Six, green $5-7
Citroën 2CV, closed $8-10
Citroën 2CV, open $8-10
Claas Dump Wagon...............................$13-15
Claas Front Mount Hay Cutter for Farm Tractor.....$7-9
DAF Double Bottom Truck $17-19
Deutz 1950s/1960s Farm Tractor, no cab,
    green $11-13
Deutz Farm Tractor, enclosed cab, green $6-8
Diamond T 1914 Dump Truck $8-10
Diamond T 1914 Grain Truck $7-9
Diamond T 1914 Service Truck, dry
    transfers included $7-9
Diamond T 1914 Tank Truck $8-10
Diamond T 1914 Tractor Trailer $8-10
Euro Wiking OAMTC Wrecker, yellow $16-18
Fendt Favorit 926 Farm Tractor $17-19
Fendt Xylon Mid-Mounted Engine Farm
    Tractor..$17-19
Fendt Xylon Mid-Mounted Engine Farm
    Tractor with Platform $17-19
Ferrari 348TS, red $8-10
Ferrari 348TS, yellow $8-10
Ford 17M $11-13
Ford 17M Polizei $12-14
Ford Galaxy Van $10-12
Ford Galaxy Polizei Van $15-17
Ford Taurus, 1940s English $5-7
Ford Taurus 12M, 1940s English, with
    case $18-20
Goli 3-Wheeler.....................................$10-12
Goli Stark $8-10
Grove 6-Axle Hydraulic Crane, "Thomen"....$40-42
Gypsy Motor Home Camper $15-17
Hanomag Delivery Truck $10-12
Hanomag Double Bottom Covered Flatbed
    Truck...$18-21

Hanomag ST100 Truck with two trailers ...$19-21
Horch 1937 Sedan $5-7
Hyster Logging Cruiser $10-12
Insley Model K Back Hoe Power Shovel ...$10-12
Iveco Container Truck........................$17-19
Iveco Delivery Euro Cargo Truck $15-17
Iveco Double Bottom Van....................$17-19
Iveco Euro cargo Truck "DB" $16-18
Iveco Euro DLK23-12 Ladder Truck.........$23-25
Iveco Euro Star Truck $23-25
Iveco Euro Van, Swiss Post Office $20-22
Iveco LF16 Pumper $17-19
Iveco LF16 Dutch Fire $17-19
Jaguar Sport Roadster, black.................$5-7
Jaguar E-Type Roadster, black................$11-13
John Deere Model A Farm Tractor,
    1938–1946, Styled, with Rubber Tires,
    Disc $6-8
John Deere Model A Farm Tractor, 1938-1946,
    Styled, with Rubber Tires, Planter.....$6-8
John Deere Model A Farm Tractor, 1938-1946,
    Unstyled, with Steel Wheels, pkg of 2.....$6-8
Krone Agricultural Trailer with Low Platform,
    green $7-9
Krone Agricultural Trailer with High Platform,
    green $7-9
Lanz 1938 Bulldog Farm Tractor.............$5-7
Magirus Equipment Truck.....................$10-12
Magirus Fire Wrecker, blue $13-15
Magirus S750 Van............................$21-23
Magirus S750 Van with 2-axle trailer $20-22
Man 1850 Cab $74-76
Man 36 Transport Truck, Stiebel Eltron......$28-30
Man Covered Flatbed $13-15
Man Double Bottom Post Office Truck ...$11-13
Man Double Bottom Van $15-17
Man Dump Truck, 1960s, brown $10-12
Man Dump Truck, 1990s, green $15-17
Man Dump Truck with Crane, 1990s,
    green $13-15
Man F90 Piggy Back Transport Truck $21-23
Man F90 Recycling Container Truck...........$9-11
Man F90 with Asphalt Boiler $20-22
Man F90 with Trailer $19-21
Man IAA94 Wiking LR Truck...................$19-21
Man L6600 Delivery Truck $11-13
Man L6600 Post Office Truck................$12-14
Man Steam Gut $26-28
Man Truck, MB Dehnhardt....................$29-31
Man Truck and Trailer, Double Bottom $27-29
Man NL 202 Town Bus, "Euro Wiking" ...$21-23
Man Post Office Truck.........................$19-21
Man Racing Truck, BP $29-31
Man Racing Truck, DEA $29-31
Man Racing Truck, Dehnhardt $29-31
Man Semi Refrigerated Van $19-21

Man Tractor, Service 24th $29-31
Man Tractor with van $13-15
Mazda MX-5 Convertible Coupe, top up, red ...$6-8
Mazda MX-5 Convertible Coupe, top down ...$6-8
Mercedes-Benz 1617 Fire Truck $9-11
Mercedes-Benz 1936 540K, brown..........$8-10
Mercedes-Benz 1939 Double Decker Bus...$15-17
Mercedes-Benz 220S $11-13
Mercedes-Benz 230GE Sport Utility, blue ...$9-11
Mercedes-Benz 230GE with Hors Trailer ..$13-15
Mercedes-Benz 230TE Ambulance $8-10
Mercedes-Benz 230TE Autobahn Police ...$10-12
Mercedes-Benz 300B, black...................$7-9
Mercedes-Benz 300SL Coupe, silver........$12-14
Mercedes-Benz 320 Sedan, blue $8-10
Mercedes-Benz 320SE, blue...................$7-9
Mercedes-Benz 500SL, gray and green......$7-9
Mercedes-Benz 500SL Convertible, black ...$8-10
Mercedes-Benz 570D Fire Dept $10-12
Mercedes-Benz Actros Container Lorry $31-33
Mercedes-Benz Ambulance....................$8-10
Mercedes-Benz Box Van with Trailer,
    Alpiners $29-31
Mercedes-Benz C200 Police $12-14
Mercedes-Benz C200 Sedan, black $11-13
Mercedes-Benz C240, silver $11-13
Mercedes-Benz Covered Van $8-10
Mercedes-Benz DLK 23-12 French Fire $17-19
Mercedes-Benz Double Bottom Trailer
    Truck $26-28
Mercedes-Benz E230 ....$9-11
Mercedes-Benz Fire Dept Sprinter Van $12-14
Mercedes-Benz Feuerwehr $10-12
Mercedes-Benz G230 Dutch Police with
    Horse Trailer $20-22
Mercedes-Benz G350 Police, green $8-10
Mercedes-Benz Garbage truck................$13-15
Mercedes-Benz Garbage truck, Paris........$20-22
Mercedes-Benz O 405 Transit Bus..........$27-29
Mercedes-Benz O 405 Post Bus.............$26-28
Mercedes-Benz O 395G Hinged Bus......$20-22
Mercedes-Benz O 404 Bus, right hand drive
    "FC Schalke 04" $37-39
Mercedes-Benz Pumper $11-13
Mercedes-Benz Roadster, black $10-12
Mercedes-Benz Semi Tanker, Shell $25-27
Mercedes-Benz Silo Transporter $20-22
Mercedes-Benz SK Hydrotherm with Trailer ...$37-39
Mercedes-Benz Sprinter Box Van, blue........$9-11
Mercedes-Benz Sprinter Van..................$8-10
Mercedes-Benz V230 Box Van, black......$10-12
Mercedes-Benz VRW Command car..........$8-10
Mitsubishi Pajero with Horse Trailer, black...$12-14
Mitsubishi Pajero, maroon....................$8-10
Motorcycle Set includes two motorcycles, one
    sidecar, one rider $4-6

Motor Grader $7-9
MUG Hinged Bus $21-23
O & K Shovel $12-14
Opel 1939 Blitz Covered Truck $10-12
Opel 1939 Ladder Truck.....................$7-9
Opel 1939 LF8 Blitz Fire Truck $8-10
Opel Senator $7-9
Opel Senator Police, Canton Zurich,
    Switzerland $16-18
Open Farm Wagon...........................$5-7
Peterbilt American Wrecker, Hank's $15-17
Peterbilt Double Bottom Covered Flatbed
    Truck $17-19
Peterbilt Old Time Moving Van with Trailer ...$20-22
Peterbilt Semi with Trailer $20-22
Porsche Automobile Police $11-13
Porsche Carrera 4, yellow $7-9
Renault AE500 Easy Tractor and Trailer $31-33
Renault AE500 Truck, Wandt.................$32-34
Renault with Trailer, Puma $20-22
Road Roller $8-10
Road Roller, Wimo-Bau $8-10
Rolls Royce Silver Shadow....................$5-7
Rolls Royce Silver Wraith, brown............$7-9
Scania Covered Flatbed.......................$26-28
Scania Early Model 411 Open Cab Truck...$9-11
Scania Refrigerated Semi.....................$28-30
Scania Semi Covered Flatbed Truck........$29-31
Scania Semi with tri-axle Canvas-Side
    Trailer.......................................$29-31
Site Office Trailer $8-10
Still R70-16 Forklift $6-8
Street Cleaner $10-12
Tractor with Low Loader Trailer, Wimo-Bau
    green and red $26-28
Trailer, 2-Axle Truck Trailer....................$8-10
Triumph TR4, blue $10-12
Triumph TR4 Convertible, top down, green ...$10-12
Unimog TLF 8/18 Fire Water Truck $10-12
Unimog with Loading Crane $15-17
Unimog with Snowplow $13-15
Unimog with Tar Kettle Trailer $9-11
Van with tri-axle trailer, "German Federal
    Railways" $20-22
Volkswagen A IV, dark green $8-10
Volkswagen ADAC...........................$11-13
Volkswagen Beetle 1961 ....$10-12
Volkswagen Beetle Deutsche Bundespost,
    yellow $5-7
Volkswagen Beetle Fire Brigade.............$10-12

Williams, A. C. (see A. C. Williams)

Wills Finecast

Great Britain served as home to this manufacturer of 1:24 and 1:32 scale metal kits. List-

ed in Danhausen's 1986 catalog, it is possible that the company later became South Eastern Finecast.

Winner's Circle (see Kenner, Action Performance)

Winross

PO Box 390
East Rochester, NY 14445
phone: 716-381-5638
fax: 716-381-5884

Since the 1960s, Winross of Palmyra and Rochester, New York, has offered quality 1:64 scale toy trucks manufactured exclusively in the U.S. Their literature states that their purpose is "to provide the private collector with the finest scale models hand crafted in the USA today, at factory direct prices. Each model featured on the Collector Series has been used in a unique promotion by the company it represents, and has been approved for private sale through this catalog. Winross by Mail is the catalog division of the Winross Company, Inc. These models are not available for retail nor intended for resale. Purchase is limited to six of any one model unless otherwise specified."

For collectors of Winross trucks, the Winross Collectors Club of America, Inc., publishes The Winross Model Collector, a monthly newsletter intended to "share and preserve the common interest of dedication to the collection and preservation of 1:64th scale Winross Trucks."

New variations are issued monthly, about six at a time. In 2001, Winross temporarily went out of business until being purchased by new owners operating from East Rochester, New York.

Reports indicate that, as of February 2004, Winross is again out of business, citing inability to compete with foreign (read Asian) competition.

Agway	$20-25
Air Products Pup '88	$38-43
Alliance Racing '92	$80-90
American Home Foods	$40-50
American Road Line	$45-55
ANR Double '91	$45-55
AP For the Long Haul	$45-55
Apache Transport	$65-75
Atlantic Tanker '91	$55-65
Auto Palace	$48-53
Batesville Casket Company Double Freighter, #120-8	$46-51
Burlington Northern	$45-50
Burlington Northern Double	$65-75
Campbell's Tanker V-8	$85-95

Campbell's Tomato Soup	$60-70
Carolina Double Freighter	$55-65
Carolina Mack	$60-70
Carrier Systems Container	$60-70
Central Freight, #119-3	$37-42
Chevron	$35-45
Crete '94	$50-60
Diamond Spring Water Van	$40-50
Dr. Pepper, #119-4	$39-44
Drydene Tanker	$60-70
Earnhardt Racing	$110-120
Eastman Chemical	$30-40
Ethyl Van, silver	$30-40
Exxon '86 Tanker	$65-75
Ford Historical #9	$26-31
Forex Halon Tanker	$35-45
General Chemical Corporation Freighter, #120-5	$35-40
Gerhart Racing	$265-285
Grand Prix Trucking	$65-75
Graves Double Freighter	$60-70
Gully Transportation	$55-65
HBI Service	$45-55
Hemway '75	$85-95
Hershey Tanker	$23-28
HTL '94	$45-55
International #7, #119-8	$46-53
Interstate '83	$185-205
JLG Crane	$40-50
John Zern	$35-45
Keebler	$55-65
KLM Nationwide	$60-70
Kodak 100 Years	$38-43
Kodak Gold Plus	$23-28
Kohl Bros., Inc.	$35-45
Leasway Aeromax	$45-55
Leasway White 7000	$45
Lebanon Valley Bank	$20-25
Lend Lease	$40-50
Lincoln Highway Garage	$150-170
May Trucking	$60-70
May Trucking Double	$125-140
Matlack Tanker	$240-260
McLean Double	$125-145
McLean 50th Anniversary	$100-120
MDR cartage	$48-53
MDR cartage White 7000	$45-55
MFX '83	$160-180
Midland Ross	$45-55
Mohawk carpet	$40-50
Molson Breweries, #119-1	$38-43
Morton Salt	$55-65
Mrs. Paul's	$60-70
Mrs. Paul's Tanker	$60-70
MS carriers	$50-60
Mt. Olive Pickle '91	$35-45

National Truck Driving Championships 1994 Tanker	$55-65
New Penn 50 Years	$85-95
North Penn	$215-230
Nussbaum Double Freighter	$65-75
Old Dominion	$41-46
Old Dominion Double Freighter	$60-70
Old Dominion Anniversary Double Freighter	$65-75
PIE '88	$65-75
PIE Nationwide	$55-65
PIE Nationwide Double Freighter	$65-75
Pitt-Ohio	$55-65
Penfield Trucking	$37-42
Polaroid	$38-43
Praxair, Inc., #119-6	$35-40
Preston 60th Anniversary	$50-60
Preston White 9000 Double Freighter	$70-80
Preston New Graphics Double Freighter	$55-65
Pyroil Tanker, #120-3	$37-42
Reeses Tanker	$120-140
Rite Aid	$26-31
Roadway '72	$85-95
Roadway '82	$65-95
Roadway White 9000	$65-75
Roadway	$55-65
Roadway Gray Trailers Double Freighter	$65-75
Roadway Double Freighter	$55-65
Rollins Rent Lease	$45-55
Seltzer Bologna Van	$38-43
Sharkey Transportation, #119-7	$36-41
Shell	$55-65
Sico Tanker '83	$95-105
Silver Eagle Company Double Freighter, #120-7	$42-47
Slice Delivery, #120-1	$35-40
Smith Transfer '72	$85-95
Smith Transfer ARA Double	$95-105
Snap-On Tools Freighter, #120-6	$37-42
Southeastern Express	$60-70
Spinnaker '90	$38-43
Spinnaker	$45-55
St. Johnsbury	$45-55
Stauffers of Kissel Hill	$35-45
Sunflower '94	$45-55
Super Bowl 25	$65-75
Super Bowl 26	$55-65
Super Bowl 27	$60-70
Terry Labonte Racing '92	$40-50
Tenn Ohio	$42-47
Terminal Freight	$50-60
Time DC '72	$130-150
TNT Reddaway Triple 75th	$55-65
TNT Redstar Express Double Freighter	$75-85
Trans America '74	$65-75
Travel Port	$38-43

Tyson Foods, #119-2 ....$37-42
Unisource Freighter, #120-4 ....$35-40
USA Eastern L/S Double........................$60-70
Valvoline, #119-5 ....$37-42
Walgreen's Freighter, #120-2 ....$36-41
Watkins 1994 Double Freighter $65-75
Weaver Chicken 50th Anniversary $55-65
Wheel Horse.......................................$55-65
White House Apples.............................$45-55
Wilbur Chocolate Tanker........................$60-70
Wilbur Chocolate Van $50-60
Wilson '72 ....$140-160
Winross, Rochester Chapter....................$60-70
Wisk $40-50
Wooster Motor Freight $55-65
Wyler's Soft Drink Mixes.........................$65-75
Yeager Supply $40-50
Yellow Freight '82 ....$48-53
Yellow Double Freighter..........................$45-55
Zembo Temple '92................................$30-40

Wolverine

B. F. Bain, a native of Wolverine, Michigan, founded Wolverine Supply & Mfg. Co. in Pittsburgh, Pennsylvania, in 1903. The company survived through the 1970s, in the process becoming a subsidiary of Spang Industries and moving to Boonville, Arkansas. Their brightly colored lithographed heavy tin toys are rare and have tremendous appeal for collectors.

The "Mystery Motor" drives some Wolverine toys when you push down on the rear part of the roof.

Bus, Wolverine Express, 14"...............$175-250
Mystery Car, 13" $250-300
Mystery Car and Trailer......................$375-450
Mystery Taxi, #33, 13"......................$350-425
Taxi, 13"...$325-375

World Zechin (see Grip Zechin)

WT (also see Wannatoy)

This Chinese brand encompasses some of the most inexpensive and inaccurate 3" toys on the market. They are generic in appearance and markings but might be connected with Wannatoy, another Chinese brand of similar toys. It is interesting to not that the WT model listed below is identical to Yat Ming's 3" Chevy Racer.

Chevy Racer (Corvette), WT #202..........$1-2

Wyandotte

William Schmidt and George Stallings started producing Wyandotte pressed steel toys in the fall of 1921. Arthur Edwards purchased a controlling share of the company and served as president and general manager until his death in 1932. Wyandotte continued producing distinctive pressed steel toys until going bankrupt in 1956.

This notable brand deserves a book of its own, as their product line is extensive and distinctive. Among their product offerings are lithographed buildings, cars, trucks, and construction equipment. A sample list of Wyandotte cars is provided below, but it is far from complete.

Air Speed Coupe, #309, 6", 1934–1937 ....$90-120

Ambulance
- #224, 6⅜", 1939.........................$85-115
- #340, 11¼", 1936-1939 ....$105-135
- #379, 6⅜", 1938.........................$85-115
- #817, 9½", 1952-1953................$95-125
  - 6½", 1952 ....$105-135

Auto Transport
- green cab, black trailer, four vehicles, electric lights, 21⅛", 1932................$285-310
- orange cab and trailer, four vehicles, 21⅛", 1932.........................$245-270
- orange cab and trailer, three vehicles, 19", 1932 ....$235-260
- red cab, four plastic cars, 9½", 1940s–1950s $70-95
- "Haul A Car" #482, plastic cab, metal trailer, four plastic cars, 8¾", 1950s $70-95
- "Auto Transport" #455, plastic cab, lithographed trailer, 10", 1952 ....$75-100
  - plastic cab, 10¼", 1952.........$125-150
- "Auto Transport" #1104, red and yellow lithographed cab and trailer, four Cadillacs, upper ramp, lowering tailgate, 22", 1953.................................$140-165
- "Transmobile Jr." "Transcontinental Auto Freight Lines," 12⅜", 1953 ....$125-150
- "Car-a-van" Auto Transport, lithographed cab, four cars, ramp, 23", 1954.....$110-135
- Auto Transport #611, four 5½" Cadillacs, 42", 1955 ....$110-135
- "Car-a-van" "Automotive Transport," three 5½" Cadillacs, loading ramp, 225½", 1956-57.....................................$100-125

Boattail Racer
- green and red with white rubber tires, electric lights, #333, 8⅝", 1934.........$150-175
- green and red with white rubber tires, no electric lights, #310, 5⅞", 1933–1934 ....$100-125
- red with yellow wooden wheels, electric lights, 8⅝", 1933 ....$175-200
- red with black wooden wheels, electric lights, 10¼", 1934 ....$200-250

Cadillac
- plastic with plastic wheels, 3", various colors, 1954...................................$85-100
- plastic with plastic wheels, 5⅝", 1952–1954, included on Wyandotte auto transports........................$85-100
- plastic with rubber tires, friction motor, various colors, #3100, 8¾", 1955 .....$145-160

Cord
- Convertible, wooden wheels, 13⅜", 1938–1939 ....$375-450
- Convertible, Fire Dept, brass bell on hood, wooden wheels, wind-up motor, 13⅜", 1937.........................$425-500
- Convertible, Fire Dept, brass bell on hood, black rubber tires, Zephyr motor, 13⅜", 1938.........................$375-450
- Convertible, Fire Dept, brass bell on hood, black rubber tires, wind-up motor, #384, 17⅜", 1939 ....$500-600
- Convertible, Fire Dept, brass bell on hood, black rubber tires, Zephyr motor, #601, 17¼", 1938–1939...............$500-600
- Zephyr Convertible, black rubber tires on wooden hubs, pull-back motor, #600, 13⅜", 1936–1937...............$500-600

La Salle Land Cruiser
- white rubber tires, #357, 15", 1936–1939 ....$175-200
- white rubber tires, electric lights, hood opens, #385, 15", 1939 ....$200-225
- black rubber tires, wind-up motor, #383, 15¾", 1938.........................$175-200

Sportsmans Convertible, plastic with black rubber tires, retractable top, #650, 12", 1947–1948 ....$145-160

X

Xonex

What distinguished this brand from Japan is a 1:24 scale model Mercedes Limousine designed after the one owned by Emperor Hirohito. Their most popular offerings were a series of scale model miniature bicycles and 1:3 scale pedal cars. Xonex has since gone out of business.

1935 Mercedes-Benz 770 Limousine, Emperor Hirohito, black & red $125-150

Xonex Miniature Replica Pedal Cars

Atomic Missile Jet, #162 ....$65-80
Blackhawk Plane, #415.........................$12-16

Boat with Figure, Coke, #530 ....$15-20
Bottle Truck, Coca-Cola, #220 ....$70-85
Champion
 Car, blue, #130 ....$50-65
 Car, blue, #430 ....$9-12
 Car, Campbell's, #315 ....$45-60
 Car, green, #132 ....$35-50,
 Dump Truck, yellow, #140 ....$60-75
 Fire Engine, red, #125 ....$40-55
 Taxi, yellow, #137 ....$50-65
 Taxi, yellow, #435 ....$9-12
Chief Car, white, Elite Series #2, #720 ...$12-16
Chrysler, #438 ....$10-15
Delivery Truck, Coca-Cola, #225 ....$70-85
Fire Chief
 red, #129 ....$45-60
 red, #425 ....$9-12
Fire Truck, red and white, #127 ....$50-65
Hot Rod
 blue, #134 ....$35-50
 with driver and car hop, Coke, #545 ...$15-20
Jolly Roger Boat, Elite Series #5, #750 .....$12-16
Kidillac
 Coke, #540 ....$12-16
 pink, Elite Series #3, #730 ....$12-16
Metro, Coke, #548 ....$20-30
Mustang
 red, #305 ....$40-55
 yellow, #307 ....$50-65
 white, #309 ....$35-50
Plane
 Coke "Fly Refreshed," #215 ....$55-70
 Coca-Cola, red, #510 ....$10-15
 Coke, "Fly Refreshed," #513 ....$12-16
 Campbell's, #616 ....$15-20
Police Car, black, #136 ....$45-60
Police Squad Car, black and white, #135 ...$45-60
Police Trike, #440 ....$9-12
Pursuit Plane
 Coca-Cola, red, #210 ....$50-65
 Ford, #610 ....$15-25
 Hershey, #612 ....$12-16
 Reese's, #614 ....$12-16
 silver, #410 ....$9-12
 silver, #110 ....$50-65
Rally Vespa, silver, #448 ....$12-16
Ranch Wagon, #143 ....$55-70
Rocket, Coca-Cola, #230 ....$30-45
Skipper Boat
 Campbells, #630 ....$15-20
 white, #160 ....$30-45
 Skippy Fire Truck, #420 ....$15-25
 Sky-King Trike, red, #165 ....$60-75
Snow Dome
 Young Mechanic, #810 ....$15-25
 First Ticket, #820 ....$15-25

Spitfire Pursuit Plane
 Elite Series #1, #710 ....$10-15
 #113 ....$55-70
Sprite Plane, Coca-Cola, silver, #213 ......$45-60
Squad Car, black and white, #437 ....$9-12
Stake Bed, Coca-Cola, #227 ....$40-55
Streak-O-Lite Wagon, #830 ....$15-25
Supersonic Jet, #445 ....$10-15
Tractor
 orange, #442 ....$10-15
 Campbell's, #640 ....$15-20
Trike
 Coca-Cola, #520 ....$10-15
 Good Humor, #620 ....$12-16
 Elite Series #4, #740 ....$12-16
Vespa Scooter
 blue, #153 ....$55-70
 blue, #449 ....$12-16
 Coca-Cola, red, #240 ....$50-65
 Coca-Cola, #550 ....$12-16
 red, #150 ....$35-50
 silver, #155 ....$45-60
Village Hook & Ladder Truck, #120 ....$65-80
Warhawk Pursuit Plane, #115 ....$45-60
Weapons Carrier, #167 ....$35-50

Y

Yat Ming

Yat Ming Industrial Factory Ltd.
3/F., William Enterprises Industrial Building
23-25 Ng Fong Street, San Po Kong
Kowloon, Hong Kong

Perhaps one of the most underrated toy companies, Yat Ming (also spelled Yatming), has produced some exceptional toys and precision models considering their original selling price is relatively low. Listed below is an assortment of models with current values. Older 1:64 scale models were released as "Fastwheel." New models are issued under the brand name of "Road Tough." Newer models are marketed under the "Road Legends" and "Road Signature" brands.

Yat Ming Road Signature/Road Legends/ Road Tough, 1:18 Scale

BMW
 1940 BMW 328 with removable top, #92288
  cream, 1999 ....$25-30
  red, 1999 ....$25-30
 1990 BMW 850i Sport Coupe,
  #92028 ....$25-30
Cadillac
 1949 Cadillac Coupe Deville
  Convertible 50th Anniversary Special Real
  Leather Edition, black, #92307,
  1999 ....$45-60

 Convertible, teal blue, #92308,
  1999 ....$25-30
 Hardtop, beige with bronze roof,
  #92309, 1999 ....$25-30
1958 Cadillac Eldorado Biarritz
 Police Chief, black and white, #92157,
  1999 ....$25-30
 Convertible, bronze, #92158, 1998 .$25-30

Convertible, blue, #92158, 1998 ....$25-30
Chevrolet
 1956 Chevrolet Bel Air
  Hardtop, #92129, red $25-30
  Hardtop, #92129, turquoise $25-30
  Convertible, top down, red, #92128,
   1999 ....$25-30
  Convertible, top down, turquoise,
   #92128, 1999 ....$25-30
  Convertible, top down, orange, #92128,
   1999 ....$25-30
  Convertible, top down, lime green,
   #92128, 1999 ....$25-30
 1957 Chevrolet Bel Air
  Convertible, top down, #92108, pastel
   green, 1999 ....$25-30
  Convertible, top down, #92108, light
   blue, 1999 ....$25-30

Convertible, top down, #92108, red, 1999 ....$25-30

 Fire Chief, red and white, #92106,
  1999 ....$25-30
 Police Chief, black and white, #92107,
  1999 ....$25-30
1957 Chevrolet Nomad Station Wagon
 metallic orange, #92088, 1999 .$25-30
 teal , #92088, 1999 ....$25-30
1957 Chevrolet Corvette
 black w/red trim, #92018, 1999 .$25-30
 Gasser, pink, #92019, 1998 .....$25-30
 Gasser, black, #92019, 1998 ...$25-30
 red with white trim, #92018,
  1999 ....$25-30

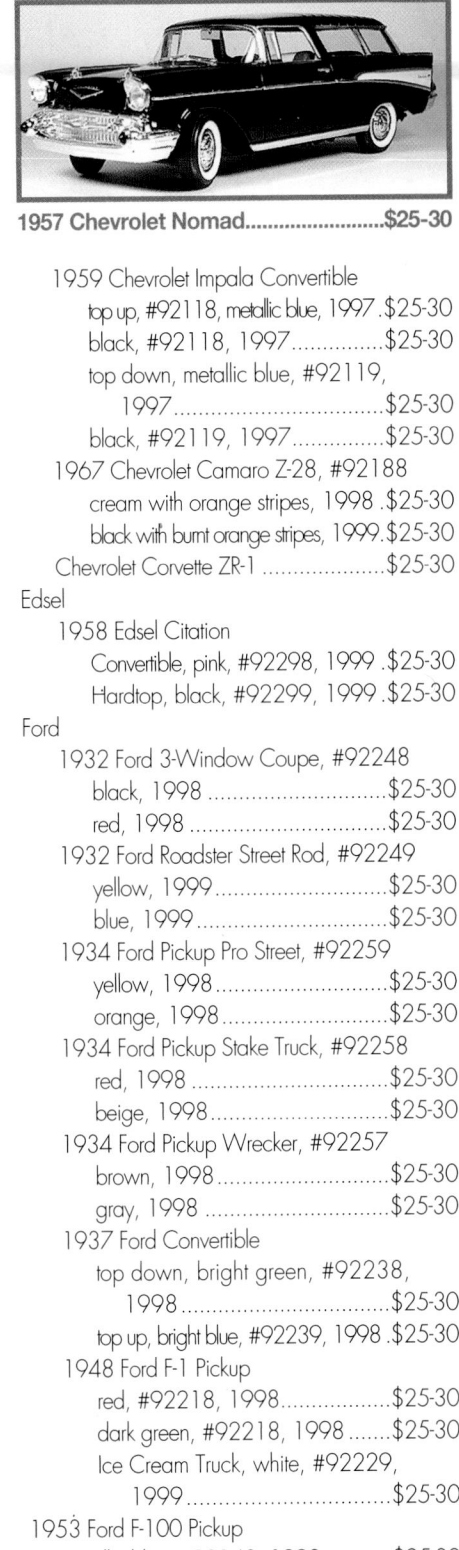

1957 Chevrolet Nomad.........................$25-30

1959 Chevrolet Impala Convertible
   top up, #92118, metallic blue, 1997 .$25-30
   black, #92118, 1997..............$25-30
   top down, metallic blue, #92119,
      1997.............................$25-30
   black, #92119, 1997...............$25-30
1967 Chevrolet Camaro Z-28, #92188
   cream with orange stripes, 1998 .$25-30
   black with burnt orange stripes, 1999.$25-30
Chevrolet Corvette ZR-1 ....$25-30

Edsel
  1958 Edsel Citation
   Convertible, pink, #92298, 1999 .$25-30
   Hardtop, black, #92299, 1999 .$25-30

Ford
  1932 Ford 3-Window Coupe, #92248
   black, 1998 ....$25-30
   red, 1998 ....$25-30
  1932 Ford Roadster Street Rod, #92249
   yellow, 1999..........................$25-30
   blue, 1999.............................$25-30
  1934 Ford Pickup Pro Street, #92259
   yellow, 1998 ....$25-30
   orange, 1998 ....$25-30
  1934 Ford Pickup Stake Truck, #92258
   red, 1998 ....$25-30
   beige, 1998............................$25-30
  1934 Ford Pickup Wrecker, #92257
   brown, 1998...........................$25-30
   gray, 1998.............................$25-30
  1937 Ford Convertible
   top down, bright green, #92238,
      1998 ....$25-30
   top up, bright blue, #92239, 1998 .$25-30
  1948 Ford F-1 Pickup
   red, #92218, 1998................$25-30
   dark green, #92218, 1998 ....$25-30
   Ice Cream Truck, white, #92229,
      1999 ....$25-30
  1953 Ford F-100 Pickup
   metallic blue, #92148, 1998 ....$25-30
   cream, #92148, 1998 ....$25-30
   burgundy, 1999.......................$25-30
   Mild Custom, #92149, bright yellow, 1998 .$25-30
   Mild Custom, #92149, starlight purple,
      1998 ....$25-30
   Wrecker, blue and white with red boom,
      #92228, 1998.................$25-30

1955 Ford Crown Victoria
   Hardtop, surf green and white, #92138,
      1997 ....$25-30
   Hardtop, pink and white, #92138,
      1998 ....$25-30
   Hardtop, yellow and black, #92138,
      1999 ....$25-30
   Mild Custom, burgundy, #92139, 1998 ..$25-30
   Mild Custom, black, #92139, 1998.$25-30
1955 Ford Thunderbird, #92068
   yellow, 1999...........................$25-30
   pink, 1999 ....$25-30
1957 Ford Courier Sedan Delivery, #92209
   dark green, 1998 ....$25-30
   burgundy with black roof, 1998 ..$25-30
1957 Ford Ranchero, #92208
   red and white, 1998 ....$25-30
   black and red, 1998 ....$25-30
1968 Ford Mustang Shelby GT-500KR, #92168
   copper green, 1998 ....$25-30
   cream, 1998 ....$25-30

Plymouth

1942 Plymouth Special Coupe............$25-30

1969 Plymouth Barracuda, #92178
   mango yellow, 1998 ....$25-30
   green, 1999...........................$25-30

Shelby
  1964 Shelby Cobra 427S/C
   blue with white racing stripe, #92058,
      1999 ....$25-30
   silver with black racing stripe, #92058,
      1999 ....$25-30

Toyota
  1992 Toyota Land Cruiser, #92098
   metallic green, 1998 ....$25-30
   metallic blue, 1999...................$25-30

Tucker
  1948 Tucker Torpedo, #92268
   blue, 1999 ....$25-30

cream, 1999.............................$25-30

Volkswagen
  1976 Volkswagen Beetle
   yellow, #92078, 1999 ....$25-30
   red, #92078, 1999.................$25-30
   Special Edition, #92079, orange with
      purple rear fenders, Flower Power
      decorations, 1998 ....$25-30
   Special Edition, #92079, white with pink
      rear fenders, Flower Power decorations,
      1999.............................$25-30
  1966 Volkswagen Karmann-Ghia, #92198
   green, 1998 ....$25-30
   orange, 1998 ....$25-30

Willys
  1941 Willys Coupe Hot Rod, #92278
   purple, 1999 ....$25-30
   black, 1999 ....$25-30

Yat Ming 1:24 Collection

1990 BMW 850i
   dark green, #93029.................$8-12
   burgundy, #93029...................$8-12
1957 Chevrolet Corvette
   red, #93019...........................$8-12
   baby blue, #93019..................$8-12
1957 Chevrolet Nomad
   teal, #93089..........................$8-12
   orange, #93089......................$8-12
1999 Land Rover Freelander
   purple, #93128, 1999...............$8-12
   #93129, 1999.........................$8-12
Range Rover
   dark green, #93099..................$8-12
   silver, #93099........................$8-12
1967 Volkswagen Beetle
   red, #93079...........................$8-12
   cream, #93079.......................$8-12

Yat Ming Road Tough 1:32 Scale

1952 Cadillac Convertible, top down, pale yellow $4-6

1952 Cadillac Convertible, top up, pale pink
   with cream top $4-6
1953 Cadillac Convertible, top down,
   light blue..............................$4-6
1953 Cadillac Convertible, top up, metallic
   red.......................................$4-6

Convertible, late 1940s, top down, metallic
green $4-6

Convertible, late 1940s, top up, yellow with
brown top $4-6

1959 Ford Convertible with Continental kit,
top down...$4-6

1959 Ford Convertible with Continental kit,
top up $4-6

Yat Ming 1:43 Collection

1949 Cadillac (packaged as K-Line).....$9-12
1957 Chevrolet Bel Air, #94201
   light blue $5-8
   yellow...$5-8
1957 Chevrolet Corvette, #94209
   red on white $5-8
   white on red $5-8
1957 Chevrolet Nomad, #94203
   teal $5-8
   orange $5-8

1967 Chevrolet Camaro Z-28, #94216
   cream $5-8
   red $5-8
Duesenberg Model J, 1:43, #8503 ....$5-7
1948 Ford F-1 Pickup, #94212
   blue $5-8
   dark green $5-8
1953 Ford F-100 Pickup, #94204
   red $5-8
   cream $5-8
1955 Ford Crown Victoria, #94202
   two-tone white and light blue.................$5-8
   yellow and black $5-8
1968 Ford Shelby Mustang GT 500-KR, #94214
   yellow..$5-8
   cream $5-8
1995 Ford F-150 Pickup, #94205
   light blue $5-8
   black $5-8
1998 Ford F-150 Pickup, #94217
   teal $5-8
   toreador red $5-8
1971 Plymouth GTX, #94218
   silver...$5-8
   fluorescent green $5-8
Rolls Royce Convertible, 1:43, #8504 ....$5-7
Volkswagen Karmann Ghia, #94206
   cream $5-8
   orange $5-8
1967 Volkswagen Beetle Convertible, #94210
   pink $5-8
   bright blue $5-8
1978 Volkswagen Rabbit Convertible, #94211
   red $5-8
   yellow..$5-8

Yat Ming 1:64 Scale 3 Inch Models
Adams Probe 16, #1005 ....$2-3
BMW, #1017 ....$2-3
BMW 635CSI, #1088 ....$1-2
1983 Chevrolet Camaro, MASK, #1086 ....$2-3
Chevrolet Concept Car, #1003 ....$2-3
Chevrolet Corvette

black with white, orange, and blue tampos,
Street Machine 2-pack..........................$1-2

Chevy Racer, white, #1002 ....$1-2
   yellow, #1040................................$1-2
Chevron, #1022 ....$2-3

Datsun 280 Z-T, #1062....................$1-2
Ford Boss Mustang, #1024..............$2-3
Ford Station Wagon, #1015.............$2-3
Ford Thunderbird, #1008.................$2-3
Hairy, (copy of Matchbox Hairy Hauler),
   #1021 ....$2-3
Jaguar E-Type 4.2, #1010 ....$2-3
Kenworth Truck with Trailer, 14", #1400 .....$3-4
   "Sea Land," #8201 ....$3-4
   "Exxon," #8202............................$3-4
   Gravel Dump Trailer, #8203 ....$3-4
   Auto Transporter Trailer, #8204 ....$3-4
Lamborghini Marzal, #1004 ....$2-3
Lamborghini Miura, #1001 ....$2-3
Maserati Bora, #1013 ....$2-3
Mercedes-Benz CLK

metallic blue, Street Machine 2-pack $1-2

yellow, Street Machine 2-pack $1-2

Mercedes-Benz 350 SL, #1011...................$2-3
Mercedes-Benz 450 SEL, #1012.................$2-3
Mercedes-Benz 500 SEC, #1087 ....$1-2
Nissan Laurel 200 SGX, #1007 ....$2-3
Opel Admiral, #1018 ....$2-3
Porsche 910, #1020 ....$2-3
Porsche 917, #1023 ....$2-3
Porsche Audi, #1019 ....$2-3
Porsche Targa, #1016.............................$2-3

Refuse Truck, lime green with white container, Save The Earth, Street Machine 2-
pack...$1-2

Saab Sonnet, #1014 ....$2-3
Toyota 2000 GT, #1006 ....$2-3

Toyota Supra, black with pink and yellow tampos, Street Machine 2-pack $1-2
Volkswagen, #1009 ....$2-3

Yat Ming 1:72 Scale Precision Series

Alfa Romeo 156 GTA, 1:72 ....$4-5

Audi RS4, 1:72 ....$4-5

BMW E46 M3, 1:72 ....$4-5

Jaguar X-Type, 1:72 ....$4-5

Lexus SC430, 1:72 ....$4-5

Mini Cooper S, 1:72...............................$4-5
Nissan 350Z, 1:72 ....$4-5

Yatming (see Yat Ming)

Yaxon

Yaxon of Italy inherited the Forma line of models in 1978. All models are currently being produced under the Giodi brand name.

Alfa Romeo 179 Formula 1, 1:43, 1980
    #710...$20-24
    #711...$20-24
Alfa Romeo 1980 Formula 1, 1:43, 1978,
    #701...$20-24
American Truck
    Covered Semi, #402 ....$40-48
    Freight Semi, #401 ....$40-48
    Tanker Semi, #403 ....$40-48
BMW M1
    BASF, 1:43, 1981, #808............$20-24
    Denim, 1:43, 1981, #801 ....$20-24
    Marlboro, 1:43, 1981, #800 ....$20-24
Brabham BT46 Formula 1, 1:43, 1979,
    #707 ....$20-24
Brabham-Alfa Romeo BT46, 1:43, #714 ...$20-24
Cable Drum Truck, 1:43, 1980, #313 ...$40-48
Circus Cage Truck
    1:43, 1980, #320 ....$40-48
    and Trailer, 1:43, #321 ....$40-48
Container Truck
    1:43, 1978, #317 ....$40-48
    with Semi-Trailer, 1:43, 1980, #306 ..$40-48
Conveyor Belt, 1:32, 1980, #002 ....$8-12
Covered Semi-Trailer Truck, 1:43, 1978,
    #305 ....$40-48
Fendt 308 LS Tractor, 1:43, 1982, #040 ..$20-24
Ferrari 312
    T2 Formula 1, 1:43, 1978, #700 ....$20-24
    T3 Formula 1, 1:43, 1979, #706 ....$20-24
    T4 Formula 1, 1:43, 1980, #709 ....$20-24
Ferrari 512 BB
    Jolly Club, 1:43, 1981, #807 ....$20-24
    Pozzi, 1:43, 1981, #806................$20-24
    Yaxon, 1:43, 1981, #811 ....$20-24
Fiat 780 tractor, 1:43, 1978, #055.......$20-24
Fiat 880 Tractor, 1:43, 1978, #056......$20-24
Fiat 880DT Tractor, 1:32, 1983, #090 ..$20-24
Fiat Laverda Combine, 1:43, 1984, #610 .....$20-24
Flat Semi-Trailer Truck with Lumber, 1:43,
    1978, #303 ....$40-48
Ford 8210 Tractor, 1:43, 1984, #045 ..$20-24
Ford Tractor, 1:43, 1980, #069............$20-24
Four-Wheel Trailer
    Open, 1:43, 1978, #081 ....$20-24
    Tipping, 1:32, #122 ....$20-24
Garbage Truck, 1:43, 1978, #302 ....$40-48
Hand Manure Spreader cart, 1:43, 1981,
    #010 ....$8-12

Hay Loader
    1:43, #017.....................................$8-12
    Trailer, 1:43, 1978, #082 ....$20-24
Hay Rake, 1:43, 1981, #012................$8-12
Hay Turner, 1:43, 1980, #004 ....$8-12
International 955 Tractor, 1:43, 1982,
    #030 ....$20-24
Irrigation Hose Reel Trailer, 1:43, 1980,
    #001 ....$8-12
Lamborghini Tractor, 1:43, 1982, #086...$20-24
Lancia Beta
    1:43, 1981, #804 ....$20-24
    1:43, 1981, #805 ....$20-24
    Martini, 1:43, 1982, #810 ....$20-24
Landini 12500 Tractor
    1:43, 1980, #060 ....$20-24
    with Front Loader, 1:43, 1981, #501 ..$20-24
    with Loader & Backhoe, 1:43, 1981,
      #502 ....$20-24
    with Plow and Backhoe, 1:43, 1981,
      #504 ....$20-24
    with Snowplow, 1:43, 1981, #503 ....$20-24
Leyland 802 tractor, 1:43, 1984, #035....$20-24
Ligier JS 11 Formula 1, 1:43, 1979,
    #708 ....$20-24
Livestock Trailer, 1:43, 1981, #006 ....$8-12
Lotus JPS3 Formula 1, 1:43, 1978, #704..$20-24
Manure Loader, 1:43, 1981, #008 ....$8-12
Manure Spreader Trailer, 1:43
    #014...$8-12
    1978, #071 ....$20-24
Massey-Ferguson 1134 Tractor, 1:43, 1980,
    #067 ....$20-24
Massey-Ferguson Six-Wheel Tractor, 1980, #138..$20-24
McLaren M26 Formula 1, 1:43, 1978, #703.......$20-24
Milk Can Rack, 1:43, 1981, #009..........$8-12
New Holland Combine, 1:32, 1982, #600.....$20-24
New Holland Hay Baler, 1:32, 1985,
    #120 ....$20-24
Open Truck
    with Shovel, 1:43, 1978, #311 ....$40-48
    with Trailer, 1:43, 1978, #304 ....$40-48
    with Trailer, 1:43, 1980, #312 ....$40-48
Overhead Service Truck, 1:43, 1978, #301 ..$40-48
Padane Z3 Bus, 1:43, 1980, #400 ......$40-48
Pig Cage, 1:43, 1981, #005 ....$8-12
Porsche 935
    Eminence, 1:43, 1981, #803..........$20-24
    Martini, 1:43, 1981, #802 ....$20-24
    Vaillant, 1:43, #812.....................$20-24
    Vaillant, 1981, #809 ....$20-24
Quarry Dump Truck, 1:43, 1980, #310 ...$40-48
Renault 4514 Tractor, 1:43, 1981, #050 .....$20-24
Renault RE20, 1:43, 1981, #712..........$20-24
Renault TX Tractor, 1:32, 1985, #100 ....$20-24
Roller Trailer, 1:43, 1980, #080...........$20-24

Rotary Hay Tender, 1:43, 1981, #011.....$8-12
Round Press, 1983, #091 ....$20-24
Same Galaxy Tractor
    1:43, 1982, #085.........................$20-24
    with Front Loader, 1:32, 1980, #106..$20-24
Semi-Trailer
    Tank Truck, 1:43, 1980, #308.........$40-48
    Truck, 1:43, 1978, #300 ....$40-48
Sheep Trailer, 1:43, 1981, #007 ....$8-12
Six-Bottom Plow, 1:43, 1980, #003.........$8-12
Steyr 8160 Tractor, 1:43, 1980, #059..$20-24
Steyr Six-Wheel Tractor, 1:32, 1980,
    #118 ....$20-24
Tank Trailer
    1:32, 1985, #121 ....$20-24
    1:43, #015 ....$8-12
    1:43, 1978, #072 ....$20-24
    1983, #092 ....$20-24
Tipping Four-Wheel Trailer, 1:43, #016 ....$8-12
Two-Wheel Farm Trailer, 1:43
    #013...$8-12
    1978, #070 ....$20-24
Volvo BM Tractor
    1:32, 1984, #110 ....$20-24
    1:43, 1984, #033 ....$20-24
Williams FW-07 Formula 1, 1:43, 1981,
    #713 ....$20-24
Wolf WR1 Formula 1, 1:43, 1978, #705 ..$20-24

Yidalux

Diecast Miniatures list just one 1:18 scale Yidalux model from Argentina.

Renault Trafic Fire Van, 1:18 ....$28-32

Yoder

Yoder models are accurate 1:16 scale tractor models made of ABS plastic by the Yoder family of New Paris, Indiana. The first Yoder models were produced in 1982. In 1996, the family sold their line of precision tractor molds to Spec-Cast, due to the increasing difficulty in obtaining licensing for the various brands of tractors produced and the rising cost of producing new molds. The original price for a Yoder tractor was $65 to $75. The first issues from 1982 have now been seen offered for $200. Presented below is the complete line of Yoder tractors produced from 1982 to 1996, including production quantity. Price in parentheses indicate the original retail price.

1982
#1 550 Oliver, square grill, 1,000 made
    ($55)...$150-200
#2 550 Oliver, slot grill, 1,000 made
    ($55)...$150-200

#3 550 Cockshutt, square grill, 1,000
    made ($55)................................$150-200

1985
#4 Super 55 Oliver, green wheels, 875
    made ($65)................................$175-225
#5 Super 55 Oliver, red wheels, 125
    made ($65)................................$250-300
#6 Case 800, original mold run, 175
    made ($250)..............................$375-400

1986
#7 Case 400, Lafayette show tractor,
    2,218 made ($44) $75-125
#8 Case 400, shelf-model, 1,000
    made ($57.50)...........................$100-125
#9 Case 700, Beaver Falls show, 1,008
    made ($44)................................$75-100
#10 Case 700, shelf model, 1,000
    made ($60)................................$100-125

1987
#11 John Deere 730 NF, Lafayette show
    tractor, 1,000 made ($44) $65-80

1988
#12 John Deere 730 NF, red, 225
    made ($200)..............................$275-300
#13 John Deere 730 WF, red, 225
    made ($200)..............................$225-275
#14 John Deere 730 WF, Lafayette show
    tractor, 4,800 made ($65) $70-80
#15 Allis Chalmers D-14, original mold run,
    225 made ($120) $150-175
#16 Allis Chalmers D-15, Beaver Falls
    show, 1,200 made ($54) $75-90
#17 John Deere 730 WF, industrial yellow,
    1,200 made ($65)...........................$80-95

1989
#18 Case 700, black, 225 made ($200).$260-275
#19 Case 400, black, 225 made ($200)...$260-275
#20 Case 400, orange, 300 made
    ($85)..$100-125
#21 John Deere 720 WF, electric start diesel,
    Beaver Falls show, 1,200 made ($65)...$75-90
#22 John Deere 720 WF, Gospel Echoes Team
    benefit sale, with emblem $260
#23 John Deere 720 NF, Gospel Echoes Team
    benefit sale, with emblem $260
#24 John Deere 720 NF, electric start diesel,
    3,010 made ($69).........................$70-75

1990
#25 International Harvester Super MTA NF,
    gas, 5,100 made ($69) $70-75

#26 International Harvester Super MTA NF,
    gas, Gospel Echoes benefit sale, with
    emblem ($65) $75-90
#27 John Deere 720 NF Pony Start, diesel,
    1,250 made ($69).........................$75-90
#28 John Deere 720 WF Pony Start, diesel,
    1,185 ($69)..................................$75-90

1991
#29 International Harvester Super MTA WF,
    gas, 1,954 made ($65) $70-75
#30 International Harvester Super MTA WF,
    gas, white, 225 made ($200)......$225-250
#31 International Harvester Super MTA NF,
    gas, white, 225 made ($200)......$225-250
#32 International Harvester Super MTA NF, gas
    with duals, Michiana Toy Club show tractor,
    630 made ($65)............................$70-75

1992
#33 International Harvester Super MTA NF,
    diesel, 670 made ($65)..................$70-75
#34 International Harvester Super MTN WF,
    diesel, 530 made ($65)..................$70-75
#35 International Harvester Super MTA NF,
    diesel with duals, Gospel Echoes benefit
    sale, with emblem................................$100
#36 International Harvester Super MTA WF,
    diesel with duals, Gospel Echoes benefit
    sale, with emblem................................$100
#37 John Deere 720 Standard, electric start,
    750 made ($69).........................$75-100
#38 John Deere 720 Standard, Pony Motor
    start, 1,110 made ($69) $70-90

1993
#39 John Deere 720 Standard, electric start,
    Gospel Echoes benefit sale, with
    emblem $100
#40 John Deere 720 Standard, Pony Motor
    start, Gospel Echoes benefit sale, with
    emblem...$100-125
#41 John Deere 730 Standard Moline, show
    tractor, 1,280 made ($69) $70-95
#42 John Deere 720 Standard, adjustable
    front axle, electric start $100-150
#43 John Deere 720 Standard, adjustable
    front axle, Pony Motor start............$100-150

1994
#44 John Deere 730 Standard, industrial,
    yellow, 1,000 made ($69)..............$70-95
#45 John Deere 730 Standard, adjustable
    front Axle, 3 point, no front weights,
    numbered signed, dated, 25 made
    ($85)...$125-150

#46 John Deere 730 Standard, Industrial, fixed axle, no 3 point or weights, regular hitch, numbered, signed, dated, 25 made ($85)........$125-150

#47 John Deere 730 Standard, Industrial, fixed axle, Nebraska Highway Dept., orange, 500 made ($125) $150-175

1995

#48 John Deere 730 Standard, Industrial, electric start.................................$100-125

1996

#49 John Deere 720 Standard, Industrial, electric start.................................$100-125

#50 John Deere 720 Standard, Industrial, Pony Motor start $100-125

Yorkshire

The Yorkshire Company
650 Roosevelt Road
Glen Ellyn, IL 60138
800-225-9319
312-790-0300

The Yorkshire Company is a relatively obscure brand from Glen Ellyn, Illinois, that around 1985–1989 produced several Bell System trucks. All of these models have the Bell System logo on the doors of the trucks and have 1984, 1985, or 1986 copyright dates on the boxes.

An advertisement from an October 1988 issue of *Antique Toy World* indicates that six different models were available directly from the manufacturer for $21.95 plus shipping and handling, $28.95 for model on marble base with pen. A name plate was available for $3.00 more.

Additional information indicates that another model was produced for the U. S. Postal Service in 1990. It was discontinued after the first issue, according to collector Lou Harmin, after the U. S. Congress told the U. S. Post Office that they were not in the business of selling toys and t-shirts. That policy has since changed, and new U.S.P.S. marketing has ensued in the form of stationery, keychains, and a host of other items but no more diecast models. Best information suggests the company is no longer in business.

Yorkshire Bell System Trucks

1st Edition 1931 Model A Ford Telephone Lineman / Installer Truck, issued 1984, 1:25...$80-100

2nd Edition 1950 Dodge Power Wagon Hydraulic Pole Digger / Derrick, issued 1985, 1:25...................................$80-100

3rd Edition 1931 Model A Ford Line Installation Utility Truck, issued 1985, 1:25 ......$80-100

4th Edition 1927 Model TT Ford Cherry Picker-Construction Truck, issued 1986, 1:25..$80-100

5th Edition 1927 Model TT Ford Pick Up Truck, issued 1987, 1:25.........$80-100

6th Edition 1917 Model TT Ford Wagon, black canvas roll-up side curtains, issued 1988, 1:25.........................$80-100

Other Yorkshire Trucks

8th Edition 1917 Model TT Ford Moving Van, white, 1989, 1:25 ....$80-100

1929 Model A Ford U.S. Postal Truck, 1990, 1:25 ....$100-120

Yot

Yot has produced generic toys made in Taiwan. EWA lists one Yot model in their worldwide website catalog.

Volkswagen Beetle 1200 Sedan, 1:60....$15-20

Z

Zaugg (also see Tin Wizard)

Zaugg miniatures are older high quality 1:43 scale hand-built models from Switzerland. They were occasionally sold as Empire models, according to collector Andreas Rutishauser. He reports that production was later taken over by Tin Wizard of Germany who reused the dies and made models under the Tin Wizard brand name. Many were issued as fire brigade, taxi, pace car, and other versions as well as the basic model.

1955 Cadillac Convertible $140-165
1951 Chevrolet Wagon....................$140-165
Citroën 2CV Sahara.........................$175-200
Commer Circus Van.............................$45-60
1970 Dodge Challenger $125-150
1959 Ford Edsel Pacer, resin with metal chassis $75-100
1963 Ford Thunderbird, resin with metal chassis $75-100
1950 Mercury $125-150
1968 Mercury Cyclone GT Coupe $150-175
1949 Nash Statesman $150-175
Volvo 122 Amazon...........................$100-125

Zax

In 1948, the Zax company of Bergamo, Italy, manufactured an assortment of 1:87 and 1:43 scale models.

Fastback Coupe, 1:43 ....$60-75
Fiat 1400 ....$24-32

Fiat 1400 Police Car.............................$24-32
Fiat 1400 Taxi......................................$24-32
Racing car, 1:43 ....$60-75
Racing car, 1:87 ....$24-32
Roadster, 1:43 ....$60-75
Roadster, 1:87 ....$24-32
Sedan, 1:87 ....$24-32
Speed Record Car, 1:43 ....$60-75
Speed Record Car, 1:87 ....$24-32

Zebra Toys (see Benbros)

Zee Toys / Zylmex (also see Motormax, Redbox)

Zylmex and Zee Toys are interchangeable brand names of Zyll Enterprise Ltd. Like most, these lightweight diecast and plastic toys are manufactured in China. Their quality varies and collector value remains comparatively low. However, some unusual models have been produced in past years. Besides a large array of models of different sizes and scales, two product lines stand out, both roughly 1:64 scale, dubbed "Pacesetters" and "Dynawheels." Pacesetters are the better quality of the two, usually sporting metal chassis, opening doors, and other parts, while Dynawheels are generally lighter, with plastic chassis and no opening parts.

Many other series exist, most notably Ridge Riders series of approximately 1:24 scale motorcycles, and Dyna-Flites military airplane toys. Other manufacturers that have carried the Zee Toys brand name include Edocar, a Dutch licensee, and Intex Recreation. Sets of Zee Toys Pacesetters were also issued through Sears as Roadmates.

Zyll Enterprise Ltd. went out of business in March 1996, and all the dies and trademarks were sold to the Hong Kong firm of Red Box International in 1997. The Zee Toys connection with Intex Corporation is that, up until 1993, Intex was the sole importer of Zee Toys to the U.S. Now, Zyll products were being sold under the Redbox, and more recently, Motormax brands.

Zee Toys Dynawheels

BMW M1, D85 ....$2-4
Camaro, D98 ....$2-4
Japanese Sports Coupe, D107 ....$2-4
Porsche 935, D69.....................................$2-4
Toyota 4-door sedan, D114....................$2-4

Zee Toys Pacesetters

Audi 100 ....$3-5
Audi 100 Sheriff..$3-5
Big Rig Tow Truck, P366 ....$3-5
Bulldozer, P307 ....$3-5

Cement Mixer, P309 ....$3-5
Chevrolet Ambulance Van, P346.................$3-5
Chevrolet Beretta Pro/Stock, P3205 ....$3-5
Chevrolet '35 Chevy, P361 ....$3-5
Chevrolet '57 Chevrolet Bel Air, P355.........$3-5
Chevrolet '57 Chevrolet Bel Air, doors
    open, Zylmex $4-6
Chevrolet '57 Chevrolet Hardtop $3-5
Chevrolet Chevrolet Blazer, P359 ....$3-5
Chevrolet '70s Camaro Z-28 Highway
    Patrol, P373 ....$3-5
Chevrolet '80s Camaro Pro/Stock, P399 .....$3-5
Chevrolet '80s Camaro Z28 Convertible,
    P381 ....$3-5
Chevrolet Camaro Z28 T-Top, P367............$3-5
Chevrolet '70s Chevelle Hardtop, P323 ....$3-5
Chevrolet Chevelle Malibu $3-5
Chevrolet Chevelle Sheriff $3-5
Chevrolet '63 Corvette, P364 ....$3-5
Chevrolet '57 Corvette, P365 ....$3-5
Chevrolet '69 'Vette, P3005 ....$3-5
Chevrolet '70s Corvette, P371 ....$3-5
Chevrolet '85 Corvette, P375 ....$3-5
Chevrolet Monza 2 + 2 ....$3-5
Chevrolet Monza Hatchback, P339...............$3-5
Chevrolet Early '70s Chevrolet Pick-up, P338 ..$3-5
Chevrolet Vega Hatchback $3-5
Citroën, P301 ....$4-6
Class 8 Wrecker, P3201 ....$3-5
Crane Truck, P311 ....$3-5
Crown School Bus, "32 VALLEY
    DISTRICT SCHOOLS," P322 ....$25
Datsun 280Z $3-5
Datsun Fairlady (240Z), P302 ....$3-5
Datsun KWIK-TV Wagon $4-6
Datsun '70s Pick-Up, P319 ....$3-5
Delorean, P374 ....$3-5
Dodge Charger Funny car, P393 ....$3-5
Dodge Custom Van
    Wheaties, P342.............................$12-15
    Van Killer, P343...............................$3-5
    Straight Arrow, P344 ....$3-5
    Kandy Van, P357 ....$3-5
Dodge '70s Pick-Up Camper, P360 ....$3-5
Dodge '70s Van, P320 ....$3-5
Double Decker Bus, P334 ....$3-5
Dump Truck, P310 ....$3-5
Farm Tractor, P349 ....$3-5
Ferrari 308 GTB..$3-5
Ferrari Testarossa $3-5
Fire Engine (Ladder Truck), P312 ....$3-5
Fire Engine (Pumper), P337 ....$3-5
Fire Engine (Snorkel), P316 ....$3-5
Flip Car I (Indy Champ/Max 2000),
    P3214 ....$3-5
Flip Car II (Manta Ray/Space Raycer), P3213 ..$3-5

Flip Car III (Bonneville Blaster/DD Coupe),
    P3215 ....$3-5
Flip Car IV (Retro Rod/Formula Fusion), P3216...$3-5
'70s Ford Country Squire Wagon,
    Zylmex P348 ....$5-8
Fork Lift Truck, P315 ....$3-5
Ford Bronco 4X4, P369 ....$3-5
Ford Country Squire $4-6
Ford Courier Pick-Up, "Fun Trucking," P353 ...$3-5
Ford Mark IV $3-5
Ford Mustang, Sears Roadmates $2-5
Ford Mustang Fastback Pro/Street, P392......$3-5
Ford Mustang II Cobra Street Racer, P351 ...$3-5
Ford '80s Mustang, P394 ....$3-5
Ford Pinto, P324 ....$3-5
Ford Pinto Mini Van, P358 ....$3-5
Ford '32 Roadster, P325 ....$3-5
Ford Sierra XR4i $3-5
Ford '56 Thunderbird, P356 ....$3-5
Ford '57 T-Bird $3-5
Ford '80s T-Bird Stock car, P390 ....$3-5
Ford Van (English), P335 ....$3-5
Front Loader, P308 ....$3-5
GMC Motor Home, P326 ....$5-7
Honda 600, P305 ....$3-5
Honda Coupe $3-5
Hydraulic Excavator, P314 ....$3-5
Hydraulic Excavator, P318 ....$3-5
Indy Racer $3-5
Jeep, P350 ....$3-5
Jeep, P368 ....$3-5
Lamborghini Marzal $3-5
Lancia Stratos $3-5
Lincoln Continental Mark IV, P363 ....$3-5
Loader, P379 ....$3-5
Lola Chevrolet T-70 ....$3-5
Lotus Europa..$3-5
Mangusta $3-5
Mazda GT, P304 ....$3-5
Mazda GT Police, P306 ....$3-5
Mazda Miata, P3212 ....$3-5
Mazda '70s RX-7, P372 ....$3-5
McLaren M8-A, P340...................................$3-5
McLaren M8-D CAN-AM $3-5
McLaren Indy car, P321 ....$3-5
Mercedes-Benz '30s Benz, P354 ....$3-5
Mercedes-Benz, P331 ....$3-5
Mercedes-Benz 300 SL Gullwing, red,
    P370, Sears Roadmates $4-10
Mercedes-Benz 450 SL, P352 ....$3-5
Mercedes-Benz 500 SEC $3-5
Mercedes-Benz 500 SL, #13 Edocar $3-5
Morris Mini Minor..$3-5
Nissan '80s Custom Pick-Up, P3206 ....$3-5
Nissan GTP, P3211 ....$3-5
Nissan Skyline 2000GT, P327.......................$3-5

Oil Tank Truck, P336 ....$3-5
Oldsmobile Aerotech, P3207 ....$3-5
Oldsmobile Funny car, P3208 ....$3-5
Plymouth '70 Hemi 'Cuda, P397 ....$3-5
Plymouth '70s Police, P345...........................$3-5
Plymouth Satellite Taxi, P345 ....$4-6
Pontiac Fiero, P396 ....$3-5
Pontiac Firebird Funny car, P383 ....$3-5
Pontiac Firebird Trans Am T-Top, P362 ....$3-5
Pontiac '80s Firebird, P382 ....$3-5
Pontiac '69 GTO, P391 ....$3-5
Porsche 928, P376 ....$3-5
Porsche 935 ....$3-5
Porsche 959 ....$3-5

Porsche Racer $2-4
Racing Rig, P385 ....$3-5
Rolls Royce $3-5
Sand Buggy, P3202.....................................$3-5
Scraper, P377 ....$3-5
Sprint car, P3204 ....$3-5
Super Van (from movie), P341 ....$3-5
Tipper Truck, P313 ....$3-5
Toyota Celica LB 2000GT, P330...................$3-5
Toyota Corolla 30 1400 GSL, P328 ....$3-5
Toyota Corona 2000GT, P329 ....$3-5
Toyota GT2000, P303 ....$3-5
Toyota Van, P333 ....$3-5
Track-Type Loader, P317 ....$3-5
U.S. Mail Truck, P347 ....$5-7
Volkswagen Beetle $3-5
Volkswagen Golf GTI $3-5
Volkswagen '70s Volkswagen Bus, P332 .....$3-5

Zee Toys Z Wheels Pacesetters Specials
This 1:24 scale model was discovered in
the clearance rack at Shopko. It is likely a product of test marketing, as only one specimen has
been found so far.
Chevrolet Corvette ZR-1 ....$10-15

Other Zee Toys
Bell 21 Racing Motorcycle............................$3-4
California Hauler Tractor Trailer,
    "Consolidated Freightways" $4-6
GT Bicycle $3-4
Honda Racing Motorcycle $3-4
Kawasaki 250 KDX Motorcycle....................$3-4
Kawasaki Mach 3 Motorcycle $3-4

Kawasaki Ninja $3-4
Mack Refrigerated Container Truck, "STP" $3-5
Mack Freighter, "Flying Tiger" $4-6
Maico 490 Motorcycle............................$3-5
Mercedes 540K Coupe $3-5
1989 Mercedes-Benz 500SL RDS, 1:18 ...$21-25
Mongoose Bicycle...................................$3-5
Peterbilt 2-Boom Wrecker $5-7
Porsche 911 Speedster, Intex, 1:18........$21-25
Sprint Racer $4-6
Suzuki RM125 Motorcycle $3-5

Zil

Zil models represent some of the best 1:43 models to come out of Russia. Price is low for these exceptional replicas.

Limousine, "Brezhnev," #115 ....$12-15
Limousine, "Wedding Car," #115 ....$16-20
Limousine, "Parade," #115 ....$16-20
Tank Truck, #MMZ-555 ....$21-25
Tipper, #MMZ-4502 ....$21-25
Truck, #4505 ....$21-25

Zinoki

There seem to be hundreds of inexpensive diecast and plastic toy brands coming out of China. Out of the package, the majority are rendered unidentifiable and hence generic. Zinoki is one of those. Two playsets have been found, a construction set and an emergency set. Each set sells for about $9–12 and contains over a dozen cheaply made mostly plastic toys consisting of just enough metal components to define them as diecast.

Ziss

Ziss models, also known as R.W. Ziss, were produced throughout the 1960s and early 1970s from Dusseldorf, Germany, until the death of Mr. Wittek, proprietor of the Mini-Auto company of Lintorf, on the outskirts of Dusseldorf.

1906 Adler Limousine, 1:43, 1964,
  #30 ....$25-30
1906 Adler Phaeton, 1:43, 1966, #39 ..$25-30
1913 Audi Alpensieger, 1:43, 1969,
  #60 ....$25-30
1913 Audi, top down, 1:43, #999 ....$20-25
Army Jeep, 1968, #300 ....$45-60

1910 Benz Landaulet, 1:43, 1966, #50..$25-30
1910 Benz Limousine, 1:43, 1964, #23..$25-30
1927 BMW Dixi, 1:40, 1968, #57 ......$25-30
1916 Chevrolet Phaeton, 1:43, 1969,
  #62 ....$25-30
Clark Fork Lift, 1:50, 1972, #292 ....$30-45
Deutz Farm Tractor, 1968, #297 ....$60-75
1932 Fiat Balilla, 1:43, 1972, #66......$25-30
Fiat 600 Farm Tractor, 1:43, 1971,
  #294 ....$60-75
Fiat Scraper, 1:24, 1972, #290............$30-45
1907 Ford Model T Roadster, 1:43, 1966,
  #16 ....$25-30
1908 Ford Model T, 1:43, #15............$25-30
1909 Ford Ranch Car, 1:43, 1966,
  #44 ....$25-30
1919 Ford Model T Torpedo, 1:43, 1966,
  #17 ....$25-30
Ford Transit Van with side windows, 1:43,
  1968, #401 ....$45-60
Ford Transit Van, 1:43, 1968, #400 ....$45-60
1924 Hanomag Coupe, 1:43, 1967,
  #53 ....$25-30
1924 Hanomag Kommissbrot, 1:43, 1967,
  #52 ....$25-30
Hanomag Cement Truck, 1:43, 1971,
  #415 ....$45-60
Hanomag Container Semi-Trailer Truck, 1:43,
  1970, #413 ....$45-60
Hanomag Dump Truck, 1:43, 1968,
  #410 ....$45-60
Hanomag Esso Tank Truck, 1:43, 1971,
  #414 ....$45-60
Hanomag Matador Open Truck, 1968,
  #298 ....$45-60
Hanomag Open Semi-Trailer Truck, 1:43,
  1968, #411 ....$30-45
Hanomag Open Truck, 1:43, 1970,
  #412 ....$45-60
1926 Henschel ARAL Tank Truck, 1:43,
  1967, #303 ....$45-60
1926 Henschel Open Truck, 1:43, 1967,
  #302 ....$45-60
Hyster 40 Fork Lift, 1:39, 1971, #293....$30-45
Krupp Hydraulic Hammer, 1:50, 1972,
  #289 ....$30-45
1925 Man BP Tank Truck, 1:43, 1968,
  #305 ....$45-60
1925 Man Bus, 1:43, 1969, #306 ....$60-75
1925 Man Open Truck, 1:43, 1967, #304..$45-60

1901 Mercedes Simplex, 1:43, 1963, #21 ..$25-30
1905 Mercedes Coupe, 1:43, 1966, #40 ...$25-30
1905 Mercedes Grand Prix, 1:43, 1972,
  #14..$25-30
1905 Mercedes Roadster, 1:43, 1966,
  #31 ....$25-30
Mercedes-Benz 1313 Dump Truck, 1:60,
  1971, #430 ....$45-60
Mercedes-Benz 600, 1:43, 1966, #301 ..$45-60
1904 N.A.G. Phaeton, 1:43, 1964, #27 ..$25-30
1904 N.A.G. Touren Sport, 1:43, 1966,
  #38 ....$25-30
1914 NSU Phaeton, 1:43, 1971, #65 ..$25-30
O & K Fork Lift, 1:50, 1972, #291 ....$30-45
O & K MH6 Excavator, 1971, #296 .....$60-75
O & K RH6 Excavator, 1971, #295 ....$60-75
1908 Opel Coupe, 1:43, #501 ....$20-25
1908 Opel Doktorwagen, 1:43, 1963,
  #20 ....$25-30
1908 Opel Stadt-Coupe, 1:43, 1963,
  #22 ....$25-30
1909 Opel Torpedo, 1:43, 1966, #43 ..$25-30
1971 Opel Commodore Coupe, 1:43,
  1971, #311 ....$30-45
1971 Opel Rekord Sedan, 1:43, 1971,
  #310 ....$30-45
1975 Opel Manta, 1:43, 1975, #312 ...$45-60
Three Musketeers Jeep, 1968, #299 ......$60-75
1969 Volkswagen Pickup Truck, 1:43,
  1970, #422 ....$45-60
1969 Volkswagen Transporter, 1:43,
  1970, #421 ....$45-60
1969 Volkswagen Van, 1:43, 1970,
  #420 ....$45-60

Zschopau

Zschopau models are plastic scale models, probably made in Germany circa 1960s to 1970s, based on the models offered.

Ferrari 275 Coupe, 1:30......................$18-24
Skoda S110R Coupe, 1:32 ....$14-18
Skoda 6X4 Dump Truck, 1:32 ....$18-24
Wartburg 1000 4-door Sedan, 1:32 ......$14-18
Wartburg 1000 Wagon, 1:32 ....$14-18

Zowees (see Hot Wheels)

Zylmex (see Zee Toys)

Resources

Toy Car Collectors Association

The Toy Car Collectors Association offers collectors a world of online resources at www.toynutz.com and through its official publication *Toy Car Collector Magazine.* Membership is $30 a year to the US, $40 to Canada, $50 to the rest of the world (US funds, please).

For further information or additions, corrections, questions, or suggestions, please write to...

Mr. Dana Johnson
Toy Car Collectors Association
c/o Dana Johnson Enterprises
PO Box 1824
Bend, OR 97709-1824
message phone: 541-318-7176
e-mail: toynutz@earthlink.net

Tales of Toy Cars

For a list of model cars by marque, visit www.breithaupts.com/minicars.htm. On his website, Doug Breithaupt offers an extensive listing of thousands of model cars, from Abarth to Zender.

Toy Car Collector's Guide Resources:

The private collection of Mr. Dana Johnson, Bend, Oregon

American Wheels, a Reference, by Jerry Rettig, published by ELC, copyright 2000

Brummillennium, published by Brumm s.n.c., Como, Italy, copyright 2002

Collecting Dinky Toys, by Mike Richardson, published by Francis Joseph (London, England), ISBN 1870703979, copyright 2001

Collecting The Tin Toy Car, 1950–1970, by Dale Kelley, Schiffer Publshing, ISBN0887400124, copyright 1984

The Collector's Guide to Bus Toys & Models, by Kurt M. Resch, Schiffer Publishing, ISBN 0764316311, copyright 2002

Copioni del mondo, published by Brumm s.n.c., Como, Italy, copyright 2002

Corgi Toys–The Ones With Windows, by Jim Wieland and Dr. Edward Force, Motorbooks International, ISBN 0879381123X, copyright 1981

Corgi Toys, 3rd Edition, by Dr. Edward Force, revised by Bill Manzke, Schiffer Publishing, ISBN 0764302531, copyright 1997

Diecast Cars of the 1960s, by Mac Ragan, MBI Publishing Company (Motor Books International), ISBN 0760307199, copyright 2000

Die Cast Price Guide, Post-War: 1946–Present, by Douglas R. Kelly, Antique Trader Books, ISBN 0930625277, copyright 1997

Dinky Toys, Revised 5th Edition, by Dr. Edward Force, Schiffer Publishing, ISBN 076431372X, copyright 1996, 1999, 2001

The Encyclopedia of Matchbox Toys, Revised & Expanded 3rd Edition, by Charlie Mack, Schiffer Publishing, ISBN 0764315714, copyright 2002

Fun Ho! Miniature Vehicles, A Collector's Guide, by E. D. Daw, published by the author, ISBN 0646292595, copyright 1997

The Golden Age of Automotive Toys 1925–1941, by Ken Hutchison and Greg Johnson, Collector Books, ISBN 0891457275, copyright 1997

Hot Cars, by the staff of Beckett Publications, ISBN 1887432698, copyright 1999

Tomart's Price Guide to Hot Wheels, 5th Edition, by Michael Thomas Strauss, Tomart Publications, ISBN 0914293524, copyright 2002

Tomart's Price Guide to Johnny Lightning Vehicles, by Mac Ragan, Tomart Publications, ISBN 0914293508, copyright 2001

Toy Cars of Japan and Hong Kong, by Andrew G. Ralston, Shiffer Publishing, ISBN 0764311964, copyright 2001

John Ramsay's British Diecast, Sixth Edition, by John Ramsay, Swapmeet Publications, Suffolk, England, ISBN 0950931993, copyright 1995

Les Jouet Anglais au 1/43ème (The British Toys in 1/43 Scale), Ma Collection CD-ROM by Michel Sordet, e-mail macosordet@bluewin.ch. website www.macosordet.com, copyright 2003

Kenton Toys, The Real Thing in Everything But Size, by Charles M. Jacobs, Schiffer Publishing, ISBN 0887409806, copyright 1996

Librumm 1972/2002, a Story of Models, by Danilo Castellarin, English translation by Jonathan Scott, published by Brumm s.n.c., Como, Italy, copyright 2002

Lledo Toys, by Dr. Edward Force, Schiffer Publishing, ISBN 076430013X, copyright 1996

Matchbox and Lledo Toys, by Dr. Edward Force, Schiffer Publishing, ISBN 0887401279, copyright 1988

Matchbox Cars, by Mac Ragan, MBI Publishing Company (Motor Books International), ISBN 0760309647, copyright 2002

Matchbox Toys, Revised 5th Edition, by Nancy Schiffer, Schiffer Publishing, ISBN 0764309919, copyright 2000

Miniature Emergency Vehicles, by Dr. Edward Force, Schiffer Publishing, ISBN 0887400310, copyright 1985

O'Brien's Collecting Toy Cars & Trucks, Identification & Value Guide, 3rd Edition, edited by Elizabeth Stephan, Krause Publications, copyright 2000

Promotional Cars & Trucks, 1934–1983, Dealership Vehicles in Miniature, by Steve Butler, Schiffer Publishing, ISBN0764312324, copyright 2001

Solido Toys, by Dr. Edward Force, Schiffer Publishing, ISBN 0887405320, copyright 1993

Standard Encyclopedia of Die Cast Vehicles, Identification and Values, edited by Dan Stearns, Krause Publications, ISBN 0873494199, copyright 2002

Today's Hottest diecast Vehicles, Edited by Elizabeth Stephan, Krause Publications, ISBN 0873419189, copyright 2000

Toy Car Collector's Guide, by Dana Johnson, Collector Books, ISBN 1574322478, copyright 2002

The Unauthorized Guide to Majorette Toys, by Dana Johnson, published by the author, copyright 2000

Walthers HO Model Railroad Reference Book 1999, published by Walthers, Milwaukee, Wisconsin, ISBN 0941952541, copyright 1998